THE OXFORD HANDBOOK OF

MEDIEVAL LATIN LITERATURE

Edited by

RALPH J. HEXTER
AND
DAVID TOWNSEND

UNIVERSITY PRESS

Oxford University Press is a department of the University of Oxford.
It furthers the University's objective of excellence in research, scholarship,
and education by publishing worldwide.

Oxford New York
Auckland Cape Town Dar es Salaam Hong Kong Karachi
Kuala Lumpur Madrid Melbourne Mexico City Nairobi
New Delhi Shanghai Taipei Toronto

With offices in
Argentina Austria Brazil Chile Czech Republic France Greece
Guatemala Hungary Italy Japan Poland Portugal Singapore
South Korea Switzerland Thailand Turkey Ukraine Vietnam

Oxford is a registered trade mark of Oxford University Press
in the UK and certain other countries.

Published in the United States of America by
Oxford University Press
198 Madison Avenue, New York, NY 10016

© Oxford University Press 2012

First issued as an Oxford University Press paperback, 2016

All rights reserved. No part of this publication may be reproduced, stored in a
retrieval system, or transmitted, in any form or by any means, without the prior
permission in writing of Oxford University Press, or as expressly permitted by law,
by license, or under terms agreed with the appropriate reproduction rights organization.
Inquiries concerning reproduction outside the scope of the above should be sent to the Rights
Department, Oxford University Press, at the address above.

You must not circulate this work in any other form
and you must impose this same condition on any acquirer.

Library of Congress Cataloging-in-Publication Data
The Oxford handbook of medieval Latin literature / edited by Ralph J. Hexter and David Townsend.
p. cm.
Includes bibliographical references and index.
ISBN 978-0-19-539401-6 (hardcover); 978-0-19-049709-5 (paperback)
1. Latin philology, Medieval and modern. 2. Latin literature, Medieval and modern—History and criticism.
3. Manuscripts, Latin (Medieval and modern) I. Hexter, Ralph J., 1952– II. Townsend, David, 1955–
PA2025.O94 2012
870.9'003—dc22   2011014667

Contents

Contributors ix

Preface xi
Ralph J. Hexter and David Townsend

Abbreviations xix

Part I. Framing the Field: Problematics and Provocations

1. The Current Questions and Future Prospects of Medieval Latin Studies 3
David Townsend

2. Canonicity 25
Ralph J. Hexter

Part II. Latinity as Cultural Capital

3. Latin as an Acquired Language 47
Carin Ruff

4. Latin as a Language of Authoritative Tradition 63
Ryan Szpiech

5. The Cultures and Dynamics of Translation into Medieval Latin 86
Thomas E. Burman

6. Regional Variation: The Case of Scandinavian Latin 106
Karsten Friis-Jensen

7. The Idea of Latinity 124
Nicholas Watson

Part III. Manuscript Culture and the Materiality of Latin Texts

8. Readers and Manuscripts   151
   Andrew Taylor

9. Gloss and Commentary   171
   Rita Copeland

10. Location, Location, Location: Geography, Knowledge, and the Creation of Medieval Latin Textual Communities   192
    Ralph J. Hexter

Part IV. Styles and Genre

11. Prose Style   217
    Gregory Hays

12. Verse Style   239
    Jean-Yves Tilliette [translated from French]

13. Crossing Generic Boundaries   265
    A. G. Rigg

14. Textual Fluidity and the Interaction of Latin and the Vernacular Languages   284
    Brian Murdoch

Part V. Systems of Knowledge

15. Martianus Capella and the Liberal Arts   307
    Andrew Hicks

16. Learned Mythography: Plato and Martianus Capella   335
    Winthrop Wetherbee

17. Biblical Thematics: The Story of Samson in Medieval Literary Discourse   356
    Greti Dinkova-Bruun

18. The Language, Form, and Performance of Monophonic Liturgical Chants   376
    Susan Boynton and Margot Fassler

Part VI. Medieval Latin and the Fashioning of the Self

19. Regimens of Schooling   403
    Mia Münster-Swendsen

20. Gender   423
    Sylvia Parsons and David Townsend

21. Sex and Sexuality   447
    Larry Scanlon

22. Medieval Latin Spirituality: Seeking Divine Presence   465
    Anne L. Clark

23. Modes of Self-Writing from Antiquity to the Later Middle Ages   485
    Gur Zak

Part VII. Periodizations

24. Late Antiquity, New Departures   509
    Marco Formisano

25. Renaissances and Revivals   535
    Monika Otter

26. Humanism and Continuities in the Transition to the Early Modern   553
    Ronald G. Witt

27. Medieval Latin Texts in the Age of Printing   573
    Paolo Chiesa [translated from Italian]

28. Medieval Latin in Modern English: Translations from the Nineteenth Century to the Present Day   593
    Jan M. Ziolkowski

Chronology of Medieval Authors   615

Index of Personal Names and Titles   625

Index of Selected Topics and Places   633

Contributors

Thomas E. Burman, University of Tennessee
Anne Clark, University of Vermont
Paolo Chiesa, Università degli studi di Milano
Rita Copeland, University of Pennsylvania
Susan Boynton, Columbia University
Greti Dinkova-Bruun, University of Toronto
Margot Fassler, University of Notre Dame
Marco Formisano, Humboldt Universität Berlin
Karsten Friis-Jensen, University of Copenhagen
Gregory Hays, University of Virginia
Ralph J. Hexter, University of California, Davis
Drew Hicks, Cornell University
Mia Münster-Swendsen, University of Copenhagen
Brian Murdoch, University of Stirling
Monika C. Otter, Dartmouth College
Sylvia Parsons, Independent Scholar
A.G. Rigg, University of Toronto
Carin Ruff, Independent Scholar
Larry Scanlon, Rutgers, The State University of New Jersey
Ryan Szpiech, University of Michigan
Andrew Taylor, University of Ottawa
David Townsend, University of Toronto
Jean-Yves Tilliette, Université de Genève
Nicholas Watson, Harvard University
Winthrop Wetherbee, Cornell University
Ronald G. Witt, Duke University
Gur Zak, The Hebrew University of Jerusalem
Jan Ziolkowski, Harvard University and Dumbarton Oaks
    Research Library and Collection

Preface

The Rationale of the *Handbook*

THE study of medieval Latin language and literature—Latin as it was used from roughly 500 to 1500 CE, as documented in a vast body of surviving texts—is a thriving enterprise. Over the nearly 125 years since medieval Latin was first conceived as a distinct discipline, scholars primarily in Europe and North America have made enormous contributions. Since the end of World War II centers for its study have grown in number and importance, and those same decades have seen a remarkable blooming of scholarship in the field. New generations of students bring new interests, leading to the exploration of hitherto underappreciated linkages, fresh perspectives on well-known texts, and first editions and studies of unpublished or hitherto only poorly edited texts. Small but industrious cadres of scholars currently work on medieval Latin language and literature with vigor and growing sophistication. Worldwide there are well-attended conferences. Publication flourishes. New journals join older, established periodicals, and websites and digital archives of texts proliferate. Meanwhile, the funding crises facing the humanities endanger the continuation of even some of the most established and illustrious institutions and enterprises in the field.

This *Oxford Handbook of Medieval Latin Literature* is intended to represent some of the discipline's best current thinking. It does so—and this intentionally—not as a comprehensive summation of recent work, although it certainly exemplifies such developments. Rather, we have conceived and structured the volume to open doors and pose questions, including vexed and difficult ones, rather than to offer settled answers. We have asked authors not to attempt comprehensive "coverage" but rather to present carefully selected examples in illustration of their argument and of the field's unresolved problematics, examples into which they can delve more deeply than is usually possible in handbook surveys. We hope that such an approach will suggest more vividly to readers the field's complexities and in so doing also illustrate directly its future potentials. Vast numbers of texts remain unedited and unpublished. One text is edited here for the first time as an appendix to an essay. (See Hicks, below.) Its inclusion here, perhaps against expectations of the "handbook" as a genre, further emphasizes the necessarily provisional and open-ended work essential to the pursuit of medieval Latin studies.

But while the *editio princeps* of a Latin text may seem to represent the acme of philological *akribeia*, we seek to engage an audience by no means restricted to specialists in medieval Latin. Certainly, we believe that scholars and advanced graduate students who have devoted many years to the study of medieval Latin will find much here to engage them, and at times to provoke them, in line with the practice of other handbooks and scholarly encyclopedias that present new information and advance new propositions. At the same time, we have asked our contributors to present their topics in terms accessible and engaging to nonspecialists, including those who do not read Latin (for all passages are translated into English). We particularly imagine that students of the ancient world will be interested to read of the *Nachleben* of the cultural complexes of the classical period over the arc of succeeding centuries. We hope the book will also serve students of medieval history and of the multiple linguistic and literary traditions—Greek, Hebrew, and Arabic as well as the European vernaculars—in dialogue with Latin in the Middle Ages.

We believe our collection also makes the case for the relevance of the Latin Middle Ages in contemporary contexts that have superseded the familiar national formations of more recent vintage. This might surprise some for whom medieval Latin literature seems obscure and esoteric, consisting of little-known texts of purely historical interest written in a debased form of a language already dead (to acknowledge the calumnies raised over many centuries by humanists and their classicist heirs). To mention just a few points—in summary form that begs expansion and careful nuancing—manuscript-based transmission, with marginal glossing, is more comparable to digital textual formations now in ascendance. The very fact that medieval Latin itself was increasingly a learned "second" language interrupts in instructive ways the assumptions we have about the alignment of spoken and written language (and ethnic and national polities). Without making too strong a claim, the way medieval Latin functioned might prove prophetic for international English—or perhaps for international Chinese—in ways that only time will tell. We believe that many of the essays presented below imply the possibility of such dialogue.

The editors and contributors to the *Handbook* generally take the view that the very features of medieval Latin language and literature that aroused the distaste of classicists—besides being historical phenomena worth study and analysis in their own right—are in fact surprisingly relevant and familiar to residents of post-modern global society. Medieval Latin was a living language, not a dead one, a language rooted in evolving praxis both written and oral, and, above all, a language used by a heterogeneous population. It was a language carried by soldiers and traders to new lands, changing in the mouths of those who still spoke it (in the earlier medieval centuries) as a first language and even more in the mouths of those who employed it as a second or third tongue. It was a language pressed to describe new things. It was, in short, a language of migration and displacement, of imperialists and subject peoples alike. It was supranational (or perhaps better, pre-national). In some ways and from some perspectives, as we have suggested, it looked like international English today, the second language of many people, a technical language for others. It became a medium for communication between people who had no other common language but for whom it was not a mother tongue. Eventually, the further development of Latin—one might better say "Latins"—led to the sundering of links between written and spoken forms. (Here one might better compare Chinese, the "same" as written throughout an enormous territory but in spoken forms vastly different and at times not mutually intelligible to speakers from distant regions.) Such historiolinguistic and sociolinguistic perspectives subtend many of the essays that follow.

Below we speak to the sequence and clustering of the twenty-eight essays that comprise the *Handbook*. Here let us highlight only the fact that we intend our organization of thematically interlocking essays, grouped conceptually, to maximize the volume's potential for dialogue with a broader scholarly community. This community, as we have noted, extends well beyond the core constituency of medieval Latin specialists (and those who aspire to that status) to embrace medievalists working in vernacular literatures and in collateral disciplines as well as non-medievalists who may be concerned to understand more fully the pre-modern dynamics that survive as a substrate of later European cultural formations. To encourage this kind of broader dialogue, we have sought to foreground those aspects of medieval Latinity that both distinguish it from the field of medieval languages and literatures in general and at the same time stand in illuminative relation to the dynamisms of other fields of medieval cultural expression. Such an approach contrasts with one organized principally according to more predictable primary categories of subject matter, periods, individual genres, or individual authors, approaches already well represented in existing scholarship (access to which is provided primarily in the "Suggestions for Further Reading" with which each essay concludes).

At the core of this agenda lies our conviction that medieval Latin was at once the vehicle of powerful ideologies and a capacious and uniquely charged space of cultural contestation, in which dialectics of (for example) control and resistance, homogenization and diversity, universal and local, learned and popular, played out powerfully and pervasively but in directions too complex to admit of reduction to easy generalization. While such a vision of the field's import has found some noteworthy voice particularly in the last fifteen to twenty years, we believe the field as a whole has still to realize the full potential of such an approach or to communicate it fully enough to the wider scholarly community. The result of such a lacuna in the available scholarship—particularly in the form of a fundamental handbook with such an orientation—has been the ongoing marginalization of medieval Latin, which is too often and too easily viewed as a monologic background to the putatively more dynamic creativity of emerging vernaculars and the cultural formations associated too often exclusively with those vernaculars. The study of medieval Latin literature too often remains, in the minds of scholars, consistently with their disciplinary formation, merely instrumental. At the same time, the status of the vernaculars in medieval culture is falsified to the extent that their interpenetration with Latinity is obscured if not ignored altogether. If the present volume corrects this lingering misprision of medieval cultural dynamics, it will have fulfilled one of our ambitions.

As noted, there are existing and excellent overviews of medieval Latin that approach the field in more conventional ways. We do not mean to be dismissive by using the word "conventional." Far from it. Such introductions are immensely valuable resources. To speak only of one essential and relatively recent handbook in English, there is *Medieval Latin. An Introduction and Bibliographical Guide,* edited by F. A. C. Mantello and A. G. Rigg.[1] Mantello-Rigg (as those in the field invariably call it) is particularly notable for its full coverage of genres and types of literature. There would seem to be particularly little reason to replicate such an organization. Many of our contributors (including the Rigg of Mantello-Rigg) refer to one or more of its eighty chapters in their bibliographies, and students, beginning and advanced, always have access to its even-handed and comprehensive embrace of the field. The present volume does not constitute a supplement to Mantello-Rigg. It offers rather a complementary introduction on very different principles. In other words, we strive for a balance between description and interpretation, a balance that we believe affords the best foundation we could offer readers.

The Organization of the *Handbook*

We have presented the twenty-eight essays in this *Handbook* in seven thematic clusters. In FRAMING THE FIELD: PROBLEMATICS AND PROVOCATIONS, we set out in two essays of our own the perspectives that inform our work on the volume as a whole. "The Current Questions and Future Prospects of Medieval Latin Studies" acknowledges the signal achievements of the field while advocating a critical engagement with interpretive methodologies that have energized other areas of medieval literary scholarship over the last twenty years. "Canonicity" interrogates the tenuous relevance of that concept to medieval Latin literature. The issue of "canon" is inseparable from the problematics of construing medieval Latin literary history, whose multiple imbrications seem to call for significant reconceptualization.

Next follow the five essays of LATINITY AS CULTURAL CAPITAL. Carin Ruff explores the implications of Latin's status as a learned language for all its users, arguing that as a language "differently alive" it offers a unique provocation to metalinguistic reflection and self-awareness. Ryan Szpiech points out the peculiar ambiguity of Latin's claim to linguistic authority, which always carries with it the inherent assumed superiority of Greek and Hebrew as sacred languages and of Arabic as a language of learning, points corroborated by Thomas Burman's essay on Latin as the target language of translation. Karsten Friis-Jensen considers one specific

---

1. Washington, DC: The Catholic University of America Press, 1996. This is a massive updating and expansion of the homespun—but pathbreaking and indispensable—handbook put out by Martin McGuire as the *Introduction to Medieval Latin Studies: A Syllabus and Bibliographical Guide* (1964) and distributed by Catholic University Press. Little of McGuire's original (or, for that matter, its 1977 revision by Hermigild Dressler) remains except the identity of the press.

instance of a regional Latinity in his study of Scandinavian authors, while Nicholas Watson probes the founding assumptions of the binary opposition of Latin and the vernacular languages. Each of these essays, in its own way, emphasizes Latinity as an agentive praxis rather than as an unproblematically transparent means of communication.

MANUSCRIPT CULTURE AND THE MATERIALITY OF LATIN TEXTS stresses the dependence of Latin textual culture on the concrete embodiment of the handwritten codex as artifact and material substrate. Andrew Taylor's essay opens this section of the *Handbook* with a consideration of manuscripts as objects subject to transformation by their successive users (and sometimes, in an all-too-literal sense, their consumers), whose interventions pass beyond accidents of textual transmission to impinge on the substance of the works themselves. Rita Copeland's account of glossing and commentary addresses sanctioned styles of readerly response as at once respectfully ancillary and potentially deconstructive of a text's authority—and indeed of its compositional integrity. Ralph Hexter's essay on the geography of knowledge reverses the common trope of writing as a means of universal dissemination. His treatment insists on the localization of knowledge and literary communities which exist only in the forms enabled by the physical presence of specific and unique manuscripts.

With essays on prose and verse style by Gregory Hays and Jean-Yves Tilliette, respectively, STYLES AND GENRE begins by establishing some of the basic parameters of Latinate readerly expectation. The clarity of such expectations—which to be sure, as both these essays make clear, is never absolute—is overturned by transgressions of generic boundaries, several specific varieties of which are examined in a third contribution by A. G. Rigg, including the ludic splicing of vernacular material into the Latin text. Brian Murdoch takes up at greater length the phenomenon of the Latin text's destabilization through the vagaries of interlinguistic exchange.

The essays in SYSTEMS OF KNOWLEDGE address four ubiquitous matrices of cultural capital in the Latin Middle Ages, namely the liberal arts (Andrew Hicks), mythography (Winthrop Wetherbee), the Bible and biblical allusion (Greti Dinkova-Bruun), and the liturgy (Susan Boynton and Margot Fassler). The first three essays of the cluster might recall the organization of Ernst Robert Curtius's *European Literature and the Latin Middle Ages* (1953, translated by Willard Trask, Princeton, NJ: Princeton University Press) in that they stress the centrality of these key topoi for the organization of encyclopedic knowledge across time, location, and a range of genres. Boynton and Fassler emphasize the performative aspects of a system, realized through repetition and voicing. All four essays illustrate how key bodies of knowledge, in their transmission across historical, geographical, and literary divides, function as "discourses" in a Foucaultian sense: that is, as repertories of intellectual possibility that enable and simultaneously circumscribe the parameters of intelligible cultural production.

Five essays gathered under the rubric MEDIEVAL LATIN AND THE FASHIONING OF THE SELF focus variously on the shaping of subjectivity by the circumstances of medieval Latin literary culture, beginning with Mia Münster-Swendsen's account of schooling in Latin as a technology of indoctrination. Three essays follow on the ways that Latin texts not only reflect but fundamentally inflect the production of central aspects of the interior self, namely, gender (Sylvia Parsons and David Townsend), sexuality (Larry Scanlon), and spirituality (Anne Clark). Gur Zak turns inside out the ostensible dearth of autobiography in a full-blown modern sense of that term through most of the Middle Ages. He instead frames the development of the genre up through and including Petrarch as a tradition of literary practices that themselves constituted the founding conditions of personal interiority.

The volume closes with five essays that survey and interrogate widely accepted assumptions about periods of continuity and moments of departure in Latin literary history (PERIODIZATIONS). Each author in his or her own way calls into question the presumed affinities and disjunctions that facilitate more or less standard narratives of influence and innovation while precluding alternative accounts. So, for example, Marco Formisano, in his survey of the late antique, urges that works of the fourth through seventh centuries by authors like Claudian, Ausonius, Ennodius, Venantius Fortunatus, and Isidore, among others, be viewed as already standing across a radical divide from the classical authors and texts which they ostensibly recall. Certainly the new modes of textuality these works explicitly and implicitly advance become the primary lens through which their successors in the Middle Ages look back at all earlier Latinity. Monika Otter cautions explicitly against an uncritical espousal of revival and renaissance as concepts of historical explanation, demonstrating how pervasively they function as instruments of ideology. Ronald Witt expounds substantial continuities between fourteenth-century humanism and its medieval antecedents in literary culture, continuities that belie representations of the humanist movement as a categorical break with the medieval past. Paolo Chiesa offers an account of the uneasy and sometimes belated passage of medieval Latin texts into the medium of print and their eventual transformed emergence in modern critical editions. Finally, Jan Ziolkowski considers the fortunes of Medieval Latin literature in Modern English translation.

*****

Alan of Lille depicted in *Anticlaudianus* the creation of a *novus homo*—a new human being. If, like Nature, we could fashion a new scholar of medieval Latin—and it is clear that they are coming into being already—she would control all registers of Latin, from Ciceronian to "vulgar," and with a skill that would let her read the most difficult of medieval Latin stylistic and linguistic experiments. She would also command Greek (and know Byzantine history and culture intimately), Hebrew, Arabic, and Germanic and Romance vernaculars at the very least. Some would have Scandinavian and Slavic languages as well. She would be conversant not only with secular literary texts but scripture, patristics, and liturgy, as well as scientific and philosophical texts. At the same time, and in complement to these prodigious attainments, she would possess the hermeneutic skills suited to understand each strand of these traditions as well as their intertwinings. She would be adept at the entire instrumentarium of critical theory—literary, social, and historical—that students of the vernaculars have been perhaps swifter to adapt and adopt. In sum, she—or he, of course—would be, to reference one of the foundational works of the Latin Middle Ages, Martianus Capella's *De nuptiis Philologiae et Mercurii*, the true child of Mercury and Philology.

*****

We would like to begin our acknowledgments by thanking Stefan Vranka and the editorial staff of Oxford University Press, New York, for their generous help and unflagging professionalism, and for their good advice and that of the press's anonymous readers. We also thank Hampshire College, the University of California, Davis, and the Center for Medieval Studies, University of Toronto, for various essential supports of this project. For their careful and sustained attention to detail and their dedicated, lively engagement, we thank our editorial assistants Jayna Brett in Toronto and Simon Pühler and Dr. Uwe Vagelpohl in Berlin. We are grateful as well to a number of our colleagues who helped us at various stages of the volume's genesis: Suzanne Akbari, Albert Ascoli, Isabelle Cochelin, Maura Lafferty, Maria Rosa Menocal, Danuta Shanzer, and Brian Stock. Finally, we wish to thank our friends for their forbearance as we worked on this project, and especially our husbands, Manfred Kollmeier and Jonathan Silin.

Abbreviations

AS	Acta Sanctorum
BAV	Bibliotheca Apostolica Vaticana
BL	British Library
BNF	Bibliothèque Nationale Française
CCCM	Corpus Christianorum, Continuatio Medievalis
CCSL	Corpus Christianorum, Series Latina
MGH	Monumenta Germaniae Historica
PG	Patrologia Graeca
PL	Patrologia Latina
RAC	*Reallexicon für Antike und Christentum*
TLL	*Thesaurus Linguae Latinae*

PART I

FRAMING THE FIELD: PROBLEMATICS AND PROVOCATIONS

CHAPTER 1

THE CURRENT QUESTIONS AND FUTURE PROSPECTS OF MEDIEVAL LATIN STUDIES

DAVID TOWNSEND

Philology as Achievement and Constraint

At the beginning of the twenty-first century, the study of medieval Latin literature stands heir to generations of rich philological accomplishment. Editorial projects of massively ambitious scope—some continuing from their inception in the nineteenth century or earlier—produced editions upon which scholars continue to rely, and, even when superseded, upon which subsequent efforts have often been founded. The establishment of reliable critical texts enabled wider-ranging studies—at the same time shaping such studies by providing the sense of a firm scientific foundation upon which further work could build. (Such reciprocities are palpably exemplified by the interactive relations between the Monumenta Germaniae Historica and the journal *Neues Archiv* and its antecedents; between the Acta Sanctorum and *Analecta Bollandiana*; between the Corpus Christianorum project and *Sacris Erudiri*.) The accumulated accomplishments of source study connected with these editorial efforts; the establishment of the provenance of individual manuscripts; studies of the transmission and availability of individual classical texts; and the reconstruction of the holdings of specific medieval libraries: all these afford the contemporary reader an unprecedentedly rich understanding of the context of medieval Latin literature. More recently, the creation of searchable digital textual databases has transformed our ability to trace lines of influence at a fine-grained and sophisticated level.

The most monumentally accomplished of these achievements have naturally claimed respect as the least easily replaceable and as least requiring duplication. The consequent bibliographic solidity has encouraged an operative assumption that editorial production at its best remains detached from the implication of editorial process in its own cultural moment; it has militated against the integration of more recent editorial theory, which has called into question the opposition of the text as a stable object of scrutiny in contradistinction to the task of interpretation. The fluidity of vernacular textual circumstances has by contrast had a more substantial impact on the theoretical deliberations of such works' editors, beginning with Bédier's early twentieth-century challenges to recensionist method, and continuing with models of textual *mouvance* introduced to medieval editorial theory by Paul Zumthor. A notable recent example of a more eclectic and self-consciously experimental Latinist editorial practice is the Ars Edendi project based at the University of Stockholm (http://www.arsedendi.org/), which views itself as a laboratory for discussion of the manifold problems encountered in presenting texts of anomalous and unruly transmission.

At the same time that a highly successful regimen of editorial work defined the limits of Latin literary studies, medieval Latinity's halting and incomplete disciplinary enfranchisement through most of the twentieth century within the broader field of North American medieval studies carried with it a risk of ossification. Despite intermittent attention to medieval Latin topics under the auspices of the American Philological Association, Departments of Classics, in their overriding preoccupation at the time with virtuosic command of the relatively narrow range of late Republican and early Imperial linguistic and literary norms, hardly offered medieval Latinists a ready affiliation. More focused attention was paid the field under the aegis of the Modern Language Association, beginning with a presidential address delivered in 1908 pleading for the importance of the subject's study (Coffman et al. 1924, 305). The formation of a Committee on Mediaeval Latin Studies, initially constituted under the auspices of the MLA in 1921 but soon reorganized independently in affiliation with the American Council of Learned societies, led in 1925 to the foundation of the Medieval Academy of America (Wenger 1982, 27). Such efforts were born of the best intentions to emphasize the natural and organic cross-fertilization of work on medieval vernacular texts in conjunction with the Latinate cultural matrix out of which they emerged, and on Latin texts in dynamic relation to the always interlinguistic circumstances of their production. But ironically, the hiving off of the field from more diachronically engaged conversation within traditional disciplines enabled the unchallenged subdivision of vernacular medievalism within the MLA along lines of national literatures, thus obscuring the pre-national continua of most medieval literary production. (It might, indeed, be observed that the transnational and metalinguistic character of medieval Latin literature [on which latter, see the essay by Carin Ruff in this volume] must have constituted something of an uncomfortable scandal to nationalistically inclined literary-historical narratives—narratives challenged, to be sure, by both Curtius and Auerbach, but powerful still even in the wake of World War II's demonstration of the bankruptcy of political and cultural nationalism.) The overriding emphasis upon cultural synthesis in much American medievalism of the early and mid-twentieth century encouraged the conception of medieval Latin not as a site of cultural contestation but as a tool for the preservation of stasis and the erasure of local difference.

Thus many North American medieval Latinists, in notable contrast to the institutional circumstances of German and most other European universities, came to pursue their research at the margins of departments (of English, modern languages, history, religion, or art as well as classics) in which the focus of their studies remained esoteric. Few would have described this situation as desirable. Yet the ensuing isolation encouraged a self-seriousness of mission that neither found itself required to make a case for relevance to the interests of colleagues within one's institution nor was easily deflected from its self-determined agenda by a wider range of competent interlocutors. In short, along with the disadvantages of an often arcane and hieratic status came a liberation from the demands of immediately engaged response to a larger academic community.

Such institutional circumstances explain in part the lag that developed between the concerns of medieval literary studies more broadly and those of medieval Latinists during the last third of the twentieth century. The virtually inexhaustible primary sources available to medieval Latinists afforded the field copious material with which it might have confronted the methodological shifts that revolutionized literary studies beginning in the 1970s, and which by the later 1980s were beginning to reshape the *lingua franca* of literary medievalism more specifically. The work of such scholars as Kevin Brownlee, Marina Brownlee, Jane Burns, Carolyn Dinshaw, Allen J. Frantzen, Jesse Gellrich, Sarah Kay, Alexandre Leupin, Stephen Nichols, and Lee Patterson, to name only a few, led the importation of a broad range of poststructuralist and materialist approaches into vernacular medieval studies. Such scholars brought to bear the concerns of Derridean deconstruction, Lacanian psychoanalysis, the responses of the new French feminisms to psychoanalytic thought, the broad, epistemologically based challenges to social, intellectual, and literary history posed by Michel Foucault, Mikhail Bakhtin's mapping of conflicting, dialectically charged generic expectations within a single work, and the debates over concepts of ideology and agency consequent on readings of Foucault and of Louis Althusser—these latter debates being particularly central within American New Historicism and the more Marxist-inflected movement of British cultural materialism. By the mid-1990s, such approaches transformed the intellectual profile of North American medievalism, and the ongoing work of these scholars, together with the initiatives of a subsequent cohort, began to build on these new foundations under less of an apologetic burden. By the end of the century, the theoretical wave had, for all its eclecticism, become something of an interpretive orthodoxy and the foil against which further work has begun to contest the dominance of these now-established approaches and their claims to general applicability.

Medieval Latin studies remained on the whole strikingly innocent of this trajectory. These years saw a few engagements with the new methodologies, for example Gerald Bond's study of the construction of subjectivity in the verse of Baudri of Bourgueil, articles by the author of the present essay on questions of gender in Walter of Châtillon's *Alexandreis* and in the hagiography of Goscelin of Canterbury, Bruce Holsinger's work on the sequences of Hildegard of Bingen and on the construction of racialized identity in the sermons of Bernard of Clairvaux, Ralph Hexter's work on the sexual heterodoxy of Ovidian reception, a collection of essays on ideologies of gender in twelfth-century Latin literature (Townsend and Taylor 1998), and the attention of scholars including Robert Bartlett, Nancy Partner, and Robert Stein to the ideologies of twelfth-century Latin historiography. Scholars brought theory to bear on the legacy of classical literature (for example, Christopher Baswell and Marilynn Desmond), but with a principal emphasis on vernacular adaptation rather than on the Latin texts, or else addressed to Latin texts questions whose multi-disciplinary dimensions framed their Latinity as incidental to their subject matter (as for example Alexandre Leupin's, Mark Jordan's, and Noah Guynn's approaches to Alan of Lille's diatribe against homoeroticism in the *De planctu Naturae*, Jordan's reading of Hrotsvit's life of the Cordovan martyr Pelagius, or Jeffrey Jerome Cohen's essays on several hagiographical and historical texts). The impact of current methodologies, with the exception of the reception studies of Hans Robert Jauss, has lagged even further in much Continental medieval Latin scholarship.

In short, medieval Latin studies remained for the most part resolutely grounded in the "old philology" of editorial practice, source study, codicological analysis, and traditional literary history. Such an approach bore rich fruit in, for example, a sustained, tirelessly inquisitive, and deeply erudite investigation of the literary milieu of tenth-century monastic Latinities in the work of Michael Lapidge; a signal account of the historiographical aims of early medieval historiography by Walter Goffart; a superb omnibus companion to medieval Latin studies edited by Frank Mantello and A. G. Rigg; the latter's magisterial history of Anglo-Latin literature; comprehensive accounts of simile and ecphrasis as devices of Latin epic in the work of Fritz Peter Knapp and Christina Ratkowistch, respectively; the proceedings of congresses held in 1988 (Heidelberg), 1993 (Florence), 1998 (Cambridge), 2002 (Santiago de Compostela), and 2006 (Toronto), organized under the auspices of the International Committee for Medieval Latin Studies. It is telling that a survey of the approaches represented by these five latter collections identifies fewer than half a dozen papers that could in any meaningful sense be said to engage hermeneutic methods articulated later than the 1960s.

The aversion to theory has led to a significant loss of opportunity in the field over the last thirty years. An engagement with contemporary debates over ideology and agency might have introjected a new vitality into the prosecution of source study and *Toposforschung*, had research more often substantively engaged transformations of a citation's illocutionary force in the concrete milieu of specific receptions. (A fine and venerable example of such engagements can in fact be found in the *Bedeutungsforschung* of Friedrich Ohly and his students.) The failure of the existing literature to recognize the full depth of the achievements of Hrotsvit of

Gandersheim dramatically exemplifies the desiderata left unfulfilled by the current state of the field. An overriding emphasis on the normative monastic context and the literary models for Hrotsvit's saints' lives and dramas as unproblematic documents of hagiographical edification has done little to convey her originality and the subversive, gender-critical potential of her texts (on which see Parsons and Townsend in this volume), precisely because Hrotsvit scholarship has made so little use of theories of the socially and culturally productive instability of the repetitive performance of sanctioned roles. Critics might have come to such a discussion through multiple channels: through deeper engagement with feminist models of mimetic performance derived from the work of Luce Irigaray; through Judith Butler's post-Lacanian description of the Law of gender's self-undermining reliance on endless performative iteration by those subject to it in order to remain in force; through Bourdieu's insistence that cultural capital is generated not for its own sake but in order to contest and remake agency within a concrete cultural formation. Instead, studies of Hrotsvit's Benedictine context have tended to impute an essential conservatism to her project, simultaneously reducing her choice of the dramatic form to a provincial bluestocking's adoption of an imperfectly understood literary convention (Sticca 1970, 1973, 1984). Even feminist studies of her work have tended to emphasize her self-legitimation within an essentially patriarchal literary tradition rather than reading her works as inhabiting a patriarchal tradition in order to subvert it (Wilson 1988; Newman, Stottlemyer, and Wiethaus in Brown et al. 2004). Such a situation contrasts with feminist work on the tradition of devotional literature, where, for example, Linda Georgianna and later Anne Clark Bartlett and Barbara Newman delineated the vividly contested wresting of agency from patriarchal discourses and social structures. The pursuit of *Toposforschung* and institutional contextualization through positive description, rather than in order to identify sites of discursive contestation, has sidelined the subversive agency of the most important woman writer between the end of antiquity and the twelfth century.

Inadequate theorization of cultural agency also contributes to a pervasive disregard for translation as a scholarly discipline in its own right. The academic marginalization of translation is hardly unique to medieval Latin studies: as Lawrence Venuti has variously observed, it is endemic across most areas of literary specialization and is rooted deeply in ideologies of intellectual property. But just as an undeconstructed binary between editorial practice on the one hand and a contextualized hermeneutic engagement with the text on the other has insulated the editing of medieval Latin texts from focused discussions of cultural negotiation, so also the notion of textual integrity as radically distinguished from reception history has deprivileged the work of making medieval Latin texts accessible to a wider scholarly audience (much less to a general reading public) for whom the original language remains inaccessible. (Concerted attempts at redress have included several series surveyed by Jan Ziolkowski elsewhere in this volume.)

To be sure, the abstention of medieval Latin studies from many of the theoretical engagements of the last thirty-five years might admit some partial justification. The more ludic aspects of deconstructive criticism of the 1980s now seem dated, the protest against the fiction of semiotic stability that they embodied at the time now something of a restatement of the obvious. More to the point, post-structuralist criticism presupposed from its outset linguistic conditions that hardly corresponded to the circumstances of medieval Latinity. As a protest against the orthodoxies of structuralism, the deconstructionist project aimed to expose the scientific certitudes of structuralist linguistics as chimerical, in the face of texts that embodied an illusory epistemological stability. Methods based in objection to an understanding of language as natural and stable within a community of native speakers merely belabored the obvious, in the eyes of many medieval Latinists, in relation to a language native to none of its users from the end of the eighth century on (to follow Roger Wright's and Michel Banniard's hypotheses on the definitive Carolingian split between Latin and Romance, as addressed elsewhere in this handbook by Carin Ruff). The founding premise of Derrida's grammatology—that the always already alienated semiotic slippage of writing is in fact prior in language to the illusory presence and solidity of speech—was arguably so self-evident to students of texts written in a language artificially acquired and self-consciously polished beyond the norms of any oral usage, that from some it elicited impatience rather than engagement. Analyses of epistemic and sociological shifts predicated on the work of Michel Foucault labor under the spectacular over-generalizations about the nature of medieval culture pervasive in his work. Post-structuralism's explosion of traditional philological rigor as an obscurantist myth was spectacularly ill-suited to analysis of a linguistic and literary culture that existed only by virtue of artificially internalized standards, in which the demonstration of semiotic slippage is arguably valid only *after* one has gotten the grammar right—in short, the culture of *grammatica* so extensively mapped by Martin Irvine. Ironically, the linguistic ambiguities of medieval vernaculars, particularly Old French, became more fertile ground for the application of post-structuralist method, in part because orthographic variation reflected and amplified the wider continuum of oral usage of a "natural" language—and more extrinsically, in part because scholars of these languages had more immediate institutional cause to engage colleagues in conversations across lines of periodization. The instability of the text as material object, in spite of its projection as a platonic ideal transcending its individual instantiations, is so obvious from the vantage of medieval book production that elaborate demonstrations of the point articulated in the context of post-Enlightenment culture were easily passed over as redundant by those whose work continuously engaged the fluidity of all but the most canonical medieval texts. (Medieval Latinists might have found more widely convincing critiques of editorial practice mounted with a view to the specific circumstances of medieval culture—like those of Paul Zumthor and later of Lee Patterson—had the vernacular focus of such treatments not limited the attention Latinists accorded them.)

And yet ironically, the grounding of pervasive resistance to contemporary theory in a deep respect for the circumstances of medieval Latin culture has itself further marginalized the field's study in the modern academy, precisely since those circumstances constituted the very elements of medieval Latinity's own powerful ideology of presence, continuity, and unifying authority—and so constitute today that ideology's recapitulation in secondary literature. By failing to push beyond the *prima facie* anachronism of contemporary theory, in order to adapt its insights to the objects of our study, we have risked abnegating analysis of the primary texts, instead merely replicating their conceptual frameworks. (Nancy Partner's appeal in 1996 to the "double discourse" advocated by Georges Devereux, in the course of her reply to objections against the anachronism of Freudian psychoanalysis, offered one trenchant critique of such a "surrender to ideology.") Instead of taking the foundational circumstances of medieval Latinity as a transparent given of the texts' semiotic condition, we might choose instead to interrogate them as parameters of the ideological formations that both enabled and circumscribed Latin as a discursive regime. Such an alternative approach might arguably equip us better to articulate the cohesion of our field as distinct, on the one hand, from the ancillary importance of reading competency in medieval Latin as a tool for anyone engaged in research in virtually any medievalist discipline, or on the other, from reliance upon an anachronistic concept of medieval Latin "literature" as a body of texts somehow unproblematically distinct from the vast preponderance of medieval Latin primary texts.

Medieval Latin studies cannot effectively resist further ghettoization by simple derivative adoption of methodologies framed as critiques of post-Enlightenment culture. Medieval Latinists must instead press the circumstances of medieval Latinity as a counterweight to the claims of received hermeneutic paradigms and, as a consequence of that counterweight, must assess and modify methodological orthodoxies. We can hardly afford to remain aloof from current conversations. We must instead inflect those conversations in terms better suited to the analysis of Latinate literary culture. (No better model for such interventions exists than the astute implicit responses of Brian Stock to the claims of postmodernist theory, beginning with his landmark study, *The Implications of Literacy*.) The field's ongoing vitality depends upon such engagements. Three areas are arguably of particular importance for its further development: sustained sociolinguistic attention to the fact of Latinity's status as an alienated mode of expression whose artificiality is itself the basis of its flexibility, throughout the period, as a tool of cultural agency; building on this, attention to the awareness specific texts demonstrate of their relation to a metropolitan centre of cultural authority from which the norms of this artificiality are disseminated—an approach obviously in dialogue with the interpretive resources of postcolonial theory; and a rigorous critique of the binary by which Latinity and vernacularity are articulated as a stable and mutually exclusive opposition—a critique that necessarily incorporates the legacy of deconstruction but which also must engage postmodern translation theory on issues of intertextual and interlinguistic exchange and the cultural work effected by the act of translation. The remainder of this essay offers a few brief sketches of the possibilities such approaches might offer for the study of specific texts.

The Sociolinguistics of a Universally Acquired Language

A sociolinguistic focus on artificial acquisition as the foundational circumstance of Latinity would allow us to attend to deliberately abstruse texts not as anomalous excrescences consigned to the periphery of our attention, but as works that more properly raise questions of how their linguistic and stylistic markers function in a specific literary milieu—of the cultural work that their specific difficulties perform. The rhetorical pragmatics of their lexical, syntactical, and stylistic choices must necessarily imply a particular relation to a fictive audience suited to their reception. Whether we read such choices as matters of self-consciously articulated intention or not, they embody an agency that both reflects and inflects the culture from which they emerge. By begging with particular intensity an enquiry into these dynamics, such texts invite us to attend to the opacity of Latin not as an accident of eccentrically misplaced erudition or a misprision of readerly competency, but as a central fact—indeed *the* necessarily central fact—of Latinity's function in medieval European culture, and the grounding condition that explains its tenacity in the face of the rising possibilities of vernacular alternatives.

By attending to the fictionality of these implied intratextual audiences as prior to the historical audiences the texts eventually reached, or failed to reach, questions of agency can be more fully addressed precisely because the alienation of the speaking subject from the language s/he deploys is the condition upon which all access to Latinate culture explicitly depends. Thus "arcane" texts stand not in opposition to a serviceably accessible Latinity, but as especially palpable reminders of conditions that subtend all medieval Latinity, an apogee of dynamics that govern the nature of medieval culture more generally—including (as Nicholas Watson's essay in this volume argues at greater length) the self-representation of the vernaculars as "natural" modes of expression.

Few texts invite such enquiries more readily than the cluster of monastic Latinities associated with a revived Benedictinism in tenth-century northern France and England. Such works include Frithegod's *Breviloquium Vitae Beati Wilfredi* (a verse paraphrase in just under 1400 hexameters of its more widely known eighth-century prose source), Abbo of St-Germain's *De bello Parisiacae urbis*, Lantfred of Winchester's life of St. Swithun, Wulfstan the Cantor's verse adaptation of the latter work, and the varied and eccentrically innovative output of Byrhtferth of Ramsey around the turn of the eleventh century. Scholars of the last twenty-five years, above all Michael Lapidge, have vividly delineated the historical circumstances of the Anglo-Latin literary monuments associated with this movement, which revolved around the careers of a triumvirate of energetic bishops (Oswald, Aethelwold, and Dunstan) closely associated with the West Saxon royal house. Studies have focused especially on the connections between the surviving texts and the monastic foundations created and fostered by these men and their royal patrons and have provided as well meticulous treatments of lexical and syntactic aspects of the texts' Latinity. But our understanding would be advanced further still by a more finely grained analysis of these texts' considerable stylistic peculiarities: their irrepressible delight in abstruse vocabulary, their self-conscious participation in a newly revived admiration for the early eighth-century works of Aldhelm, their sometimes excruciatingly elaborate periodic sentence structure, particularly in their showpiece prologues—in relation to the milieux of their immediately intended audience and subsequent receptions down to the twelfth century. The gratuitously elaborate artifice of these texts might suggest an indifference to their dissemination beyond a very narrow readership, and yet they emerged from centers of cultural and political capital to whose aspirations they can hardly be seen as indifferent. The cultural work they originally performed must necessarily have been prosecuted in and through precisely the eccentricities that seem to militate against their easy reception.

If such questions have yet to be adequately addressed, they might be taken up to particularly good advantage in a detailed study of these texts' reception by later generations of Anglo-Latin writers, especially the hagiographers and historiographers of the late eleventh and early twelfth centuries, and above all by William of Malmesbury, whose evaluations of his predecessors' style and reliability make him, in addition to being the most brilliantly original and self-consciously polished stylist of his generation, in some sense the first literary historian of England. William himself has been very well served by superb textual and historical scholarship (William of Malmesbury 1998, 2002; Thomson 1987), and his prime importance as an historical source assures energetic attention to the content of his work. But questions of style in relation to the author's political investments and his transmission and production of cultural capital can be at least as profitably posed in William's case as in that of the monastic writers of the late tenth century. William wrote his *magnum opus*, the *Gesta regum Angliae*, on the commission of the wife of Henry I and finished it as a presentation to the Empress Matilda; he produced his surviving hagiographical works for two of the most prominent monastic foundations of his day, each of them deeply concerned to enhance its prestige amidst rapidly shifting dynamics of ecclesiastical influence (William of Malmesbury 2002). Neither William's own stylistic choices nor his assessments of his predecessors remain innocent of the politico-cultural exigencies of his moment. His assessments of his predecessors prosecute shrewd rhetorical strategies for the positioning of his own texts. At no point in William's oeuvre is this more evident than in his account of literary antecedents in the prologues to his lives of Sts. Dunstan and Wulfstan, respectively.

Asser's celebrated and deeply peculiar biography of Alfred of Wessex, a work dating from 893, offers a further example of the always alienated and artificial nature of Latinity as itself contributing powerfully and essentially to an author's prosecution of cultural work. Despite its tenuous survival into modern times, Asser's text was clearly known to several later writers into the twelfth century (Asser 1983, 57). The tactical pragmatics of Asser's Latinity coincide with the moment that the alternative of a "natural" vernacular emerges in Alfred's translation program as an instrument of West Saxon hegemony (Discenza 2001). As a Welshman imported into this milieu, Asser's decision to write in Latin rather than in the aggressively promoted West Saxon of the day anchors a continued space of linguistic and political diversity in the face of an imperial project. It is in some of the most eccentric, "awkward," and artificial aspects of his text that he most effectively supports the preservation of difference and of resistance to Alfredian claims of unproblematically unitive and unifying authority (Townsend 2008).

Metropolitan Centres and their Peripheries

If Asser offers a third illustration of linguistic alienation as itself the foundational mechanism of Latinity's ongoing efficacy as cultural instrument, he also exemplifies the negotiation of a text's discursive position in relation to a perceived centre of metropolitan cultural authority. Latin serves to relativize the centralizing claims of the Alfredian project precisely because, by locating the text's vantage point "elsewhere," it defamiliarizes West Saxon specificities: the text positions itself as interpreting these for an implied reader to whom they are potentially foreign. For Asser, this metropolitan centre is itself problematically diffuse: his *Latinitas* is centered, if anywhere, in an already fragmented Carolingian empire, rather than in Rome. Yet however vaguely that "elsewhere" is located, in relation to it Asser's insular readers—Welsh, West Saxon, and speakers of other English dialects alike—are equally made aware of their peripheral status. Such a strategic location of Latinity bears comparison with other texts, among them one of the earliest surviving Latin works produced in England, the anonymous life of Gregory the Great from Whitby; the works of Hrotsvit; and the hagiography of one of William of Malmesbury's most heavily exploited sources, Osbern of Canterbury.

The anonymous Whitby life of Gregory from near the turn of the eighth century stands prominently in any account as among the earliest substantial monuments of Northumbrian Latin literature, but such attention as it generates usually remains confined to summary descriptions that impute a primitivist status to its anomalous structure and language. Its eccentric narrative structure is generally understood to attest a naive and imperfect acquaintance with hagiographic models the emulation of which already exerted a canonical influence on the form, as amply witnessed by most other surviving Northumbrian saints' lives. The text's anomalous grammar, especially judged against the syntactical clarity of Bede's *Historia ecclesiastica*, can easily be dismissed as evidence of the author's tenuous education—or else of vicissitudes of textual transmission in the century prior to the one surviving manuscript (Colgrave in *Earliest Life* 1968, 63–69). An alternative approach might instead read the text's stylistics (including questions of syntax) as negotiating its relation to a metropolitan centre that places the fictive audience in alienated relation to purely local, vernacular culture; and in relation, furthermore, to the gaze of an originary and authoritative metropolitan figure—Gregory himself— encountering the English in Rome for the first time. The close resonances of such an approach with postcolonial analyses of usage have been sketched out (Mehan and Townsend 2001); but a fuller analysis in such a key has yet to be pursued.

In addition to issues of feminist agency in the works of Hrotsvit already touched on above, scholarship would benefit from further historicized attention to her position in a powerful women's community that defined Gandersheim's own geographical specificity in relation to Latinity's metropolitan status, as now embodied in the Ottonian court. Such dynamics figure centrally in the epistles to the *sapientes* of the Ottonian court that preface the dramas of Book 2, where they emerge as explicitly articulated questions of Latin style as a marker of urbanity:

> Plures inveniuntur catholici cuius nos penitus expurgare nequimus facti . qui pro cultioris facundia sermonis . gentilium vanitatem librorum utilitati praeferunt sacrarum scripturarum . Sunt etiam alii sacris inherentes paginis . qui licet alia gentilium spernant . Terentii tamen figmenta frequentius lectitant . et dum dulcedine sermonis delectantur . nefandarum notitia rerum maculantur . . .

> [One finds many catholics (nor can we entirely exonerate ourselves from the charge) who prefer the vanity of pagan books, for the facility of their more refined speech, over the utility of Holy Scripture. Some others, though they cling to the Sacred Page and scorn other productions of the pagans, nevertheless pour constantly over the fictions of Terence; amidst their delight in the sweetness of his speech, they are sullied by the knowledge of his unspeakable subject matter . . .] (Hrotsvit 2001, 132)

> Quia enim attactu vestri favoris atque petitionis harundineo more inclinata . libellum quem tali intentione disposui . sed usque huc pro sui vilitate occultare . quam in palam proferre malui . vobis perscrutandum tradidi . decet ut non minoris diligentia sollicitudinis eum emendando investigetis quam proprii seriem laboris. Et sic tandem ad normam rectitudinis reformatum mihi remittite . quo vestri magisterio premonstrante . in quibus maxime peccassem possim agnoscere.

> [For since I have handed over to your scrutiny the book that I composed with such an intention— being bent like a reed at the touch of your favor and request, though I would have preferred to keep it hidden in its worthlessness rather than to publish it openly—it is fitting that you should examine and correct it with a diligence no less zealous than the process of my own labor. And so send it back to me eventually revised according to the correct norm, that being instructed by your expertise I may understand in what details I have most offended.] (Hrotsvit 2001, 135)

In the historical poems of Book 3, issues of the location of culture are articulated more obliquely, yet unmistakably, as a transmission of spiritual authority to Gandersheim both directly from Rome and from an imperial authority that has now devolved upon Saxony. Both the *Gesta Ottonis* and the *Primordia coenobii Gandeshemensis* negotiate the implicit tensions between Saxony's rise to imperial authority and its still-recent status as the rebellious edge of Carolingian Christendom. Most strikingly perhaps, an episode in the *Primordia* that narrates the revelation of the house's site (lines 185–232) echoes the prophecy of the foundation of Alba Longa in *Aeneid* 8.36–65, but embodying a nexus of further details that recall other tropes on the narrative pattern found in insular saints' lives, especially in texts with strong Celtic associations, between the tenth and twelfth centuries (Jankulak 2005). The *Primordia*'s concentration on the house's imperial foundation focuses the metropolitan status transferred within living memory to the Ottonian court more specifically on Gandersheim as a semi-autonomous regional power governed by aristocratic women. Oppositions of centrality to periphery (and of sacrality to profanity) subtend Hrotsvit's account in this episode and pervade her narrative verse more generally.

Latinity as a tool for the focalization of culture is crucial as well to English hagiography of the decades just after the Norman Conquest and the installation of Lanfranc of Bec as Archbishop. A discursive community's urgently problematic negotiation of internal cultural difference is nowhere more palpable than in the *vitae* of Dunstan and Aelfheah by Osbern, precentor of Christ Church, Canterbury. Despite the centrality of Dunstan's cult to the prestige of the cathedral community and the already well-established hagiographical tradition of the saint—two Latin versions of his biography were already extant—the strong associations of Dunstan's career with the history of the West Saxon royal house must necessarily have underlined the cultural divide between English and Norman monks. At the same time, the eccentric and now-dated Latinity of the earliest biography must have grated on readers accustomed to eleventh-century Continental developments of Latin style toward more classicizing norms. Osbern's second hagiographic subject was Aelfheah, who enjoyed a very tenuous claim to martyrdom on the grounds of his murder in 1012 by Danish invaders when he refused to collude with his captors in securing a ransom. His cult must have seemed shakily grounded indeed to Norman newcomers, and Eadmer narrates a conversation in which the young Anselm resolved Lanfranc's doubts over its legitimacy (Eadmer 1962, 50–54). Osbern in both these hagiographies variously elides pressing questions of English versus Norman usage, oral versus written transmission of tradition, and vernacular English versus Latin into questions of style couched in explicitly Ciceronian rhetorical categories: thus, most palpably, at the end of his prologue to the life of Dunstan, having reviewed the sources available to him (the two previous Latin lives and a now-lost vernacular life), a review of the faults and strengths of each of these sources is finally adjudicated through categories of style, and Lanfranc is addressed not as an ecclesiastical superior but as "totius Latinitatis magistro"—a master of all Latinity:

> Alii etsi satis eleganter non tamen satis diligenter, sed quantum ad nocturnum festivitatis officium satis esse judicavere, sermocinandi ad populum modo scripsere. Alii autem dum nimis diligenter, quemadmodum quaeque res acta sit explicare conarentur, elegantiam perdiderunt, atque in illud dicendi genus quod suffultum Romanae princeps eloquentiae vocat, inciderunt, quod facilius taedium legentibus quam aliquod audientibus emolumentum gignere consuevit.
>
> [Some wrote in a popular homiletic mode—though elegantly enough, yet not with enough industry, but only insofar as they judged sufficient for the night office of the feast. Others, while they wrote with excessive industry, to the extent that they attempted to expound everything that took place, lost all elegance and fell into the style called "propped up" by the prince of Roman eloquence—a style that more easily begets boredom in one's readers than it offers any profit to the listening audience.] (Osbern 1874, 69–70)

A full study of Osbern's classicizing stylistics as a *captatio benevolentiae* to counteract the fragmentation of his audience would not only enhance our understanding of the place of classical learning in English culture of the late eleventh century, it would also contribute to our understanding of the evolving relation of Latin, French, and English in Anglo-Norman culture, a field currently undergoing sweeping reassessment (e.g., Tyler 2009). A focus on the Latin text's active negotiation with the alternative possibilities of the vernacular, so central to the pragmatics of Osbern's response to his linguistic and cultural moment, is essential to a fuller understanding of other Latin texts as well that purport to translate or adapt vernacular materials, whether that claim is plausible despite the loss of the original (as in the case of both Osbern's and William of Malmesbury's lives of Dunstan as well as the latter's biography of Wulfstan), purely fictive (as in the case of Geoffrey of Monmouth's *Historia regum Britanniae*), or immediately evident in the survival of the vernacular source text—as in the case of Aethelweard's Chronicle, a Latin adaptation of the Anglo-Saxon Chronicle in a form very close to the surviving A-version that bears as well the marks of a close engagement with Bede and an admiration for the works of Aldhelm.

Aethelweard, ealdorman of Wessex and a principal patron of Aelfric of Eynsham's massive program of vernacular translation and homiletic adaptation, wrote his text at the request of a distant cousin, Matilda, abbess of Quedlinburg, sometime soon after 982 (Van Houts 1997). His work's clear dependence on its vernacular source has militated against sustained attention to its own aims and to the mannered, eccentric rhetoric by which it pursues them. Important studies have rehabilitated the peculiarities of Aethelweard's Latinity as the deliberate cultivation of a distinctive prose style (Winterbottom 1967) and established that his reorganization of the paratactic annalistic structure of the vernacular source positions the text in relation to antecedent and contemporary works, most notably Bede's *Historia ecclesiastica* and Widukind of Corvey's *Res gestae Saxonicae* (Van Houts 1997). But we would still benefit from a thoroughgoing analysis of Aethelweard's multiple shifts in registers of diction, and of how his departures of form and content might have been received by his Continental narratee or by English readers likely to know the sources themselves, and so to form their own judgments about the implications of such divergences.

Latinity and Vernacularity as a Continuum of Linguistic Register

In contrast to Aethelweard's clear but unacknowledged dependence on a vernacular source, the web of vexed relations between multiple versions, some of them Latin, some vernacular, of widely current texts, throws down a powerful challenge not only to widespread assumptions about how closely Latinity and canonicity map over one another, but also about any putative impermeability of the boundary between Latin and vernacular culture—a topic addressed at length elsewhere in this volume by Brian Murdoch. The complex relations between the multiple Latin versions of the romance of Apollonius of Tyre and their affiliations in turn with proliferating vernacular versions offer a case in point. Of the Latin romance, which may or may not have derived from a lost Greek original, multiple versions survive (Archibald 1991, 182–216). Of the vernacular versions, the earliest is a fragmentary Old English translation extant in a single manuscript of the eleventh century (*Apollonius of Tyre* 1958). Strikingly, in this version the incest riddle upon which the opening episode of the romance turns is given untranslated and then glossed—yet the gloss does not correspond exactly with the Latin it translates. Such a disjunction raises the question whether a translated text in a broadly Latinate milieu presupposes the opacity of the source language to the target audience (as we often assume of modern translation), or whether translation from but also to medieval Latin functions rather as a change of register within an interlinguistic competence that embraces, for the translator and readers alike, both source and target language. Such a practice would imply a more active intertextual awareness of the source text as a residue behind the translation, and with that more active awareness, the negotiation of a dialogic relationship between alternative versions of a text whose fullness is consequently at any given moment only partially present to the reader. We find in the explicit citation of Latin scripture in the Middle English texts of the *Ancrene Wisse* another example of a glossing practice where disjunctions between quoted Latin source and incorporated translation heighten the reader's awareness of interpretive gaps that invite a process of active comparative evaluation. The *Ancrene Wisse* incorporates excerpts from the Vulgate which are then in some cases translated literally, sometimes glossed with exegetical embellishment, and sometimes left entirely untranslated. The variation in practice hardly suggests a reductively functional translation practice as an accommodation of the reader's inadequate Latinity. (Sian Echard's analysis [1998] of the Latin apparatus of Gower's still later *Confessio Amantis* offers a third example of such dialogization from the vernacular side, suggesting that translation remained a mode of a broader multilingual habitus well beyond the putative eclipse of Latin as a literary language in England.)

Such texts, by importing Latinity into the vernacular, do more than simply gesture toward linguistic diversity; they undermine the self-sufficient authority of either the Latin or the vernacular version. The ghost of Latinity—and of the hermeneutic competencies that are seen as concomitant with Latinity—pervades texts like the Old English *Apollonius of Tyre* and the equally fluid multilingual textual tradition of the *Ancrene Wisse*. With the proliferation of new work on the multilingual habitus of specific medieval literary cultures—as in the work of Jocelyn Wogan-Brown and Elizabeth Tyler—we are in a position to see that one of the most vibrantly energizing aspects of a Latinate cultural continuum is precisely this sense of oscillation, this perception that the plenitude of a text's meaning is always only partially present in the utterance, that the text is always haunted by the absence of its

Doppelgänger—a gap that invites the active participation of the audience. But if this self-alienated phenomenology instilled into the reading experience of vernacular texts is celebrated variously in a wide range of texts, it also understandably gives rise to a pervasive anxiety, to a sense that the linguistic split consciousness of such a culture is a departure from original linguistic purity and self-presence.

Bede's account of Caedmon in *Historia ecclesiastica* 4.24 offers a vivid example. Despite Bede's assertion that the vernacular origin of the inspired cowherd's hymn in its absence betters the Latin prose paraphrase that he includes in his text, the episode is arguably driven by such an anxiety. For Bede, the hymn's miraculous origins render ostensibly unexceptionable the binary oppositions that he implies characterize its production—oppositions not only between Latin and vernacular, but between literate and illiterate, inspired and crafted, learned and unlearned, authorized and unauthorized. Bede acknowledges, accepts, and even implicitly celebrates the autonomy of the absent vernacular tradition, but that autonomy simultaneously represents an instability that must be controlled, and the elaborate apparatus that he sets up around the hymn's genesis attests in its own way to the discontents of split linguistic consciousness. Bede's earliest readership consisted of his fellow Northumbrians, yet he casts them rhetorically as denizens of a generalized Latin Christendom, as for example when he glosses proper names like *Hefenefeld*, the site of Oswald's great battle against his pagan adversaries, as though these require explanation in the acquired tongue of high culture in order to be rendered intelligible (Mehan and Townsend 2001). The Caedmon episode functions similarly as a highly elaborated gloss on a vernacular text already so familiar to Bede's early readers that it crept almost immediately into the margins of Bede's *Historia* as a spontaneous supplement (O'Brien O'Keefe 1990).

If eighth-century England was a particularly dramatic site for the relative novelty of a bilingual culture, and if that novelty registered as an uneasy recognition that one's own linguistic experience always lay in part abstracted from the present utterance, then we might venture to look for further indices of this frisson in intralinguistic as well as interlinguistic relations. The *opus geminatum*, the work written in deliberately twinned prose and verse versions explicitly announced, or at least strongly implied, as halves of a single unity (Wieland 1981; Godman 1981) might offer for future work a locus for exploration of this anxiety (and pleasure) of split consciousness. The celebrated precedent for such texts was the pairing of Sedulius's *Carmen Paschale* and *Opus Paschale*. It is perhaps misleading to say that the form enjoyed a vogue among early English writers: we have three eighth-century examples. Aldhelm's *De virginitate* is the first Anglo-Saxon instance of the form. Bede's prose and verse lives of Cuthbert are often adduced as the next important example, but this is complicated by the fact that Bede writes his verse life of Cuthbert not as a companion piece to his prose version, but as an adaptation of an earlier anonymous prose biography of the saint, and his own later prose represents a significant modification of the first prose version, arguably to current political ends (Goffart 1988). Anglo-Latin literature before the long hiatus of the Viking depredations of the early ninth century is nearly bookended by Alcuin's double life of Willibrord—a Carolingian production, but plausibly informed by the insular cultural preoccupations of Charlemagne's schoolmaster (Alcuin 1881 and 1920; Townsend 1995).

The obligatory declaration of unity in the prefaces of these works implies a structural or functional complementarity—the two halves of the work are likened to the walls and roof of a building; or the prose and verse are asserted to serve disparate purposes in different contexts (Wieland 1981, 114–17). But such assertions of unity do not address—nor have modern scholarly assessments seemed inclined to analyze in much detail—the fact that any interpretive crux is likely to spur the reader of these works into intensive cross-referencing to the text's self-declared other half. Aldhelm's verse is hardly the more challenging half of his work—it is a model of simplicity and clarity next to his willfully abstruse and precious prose. But furthermore, any chapter-by-chapter comparison of the prose and verse *De virginitate* quickly reveals the substantial extent to which the two versions diverge in content as well as in style. Alcuin's laconic verse version of the life of Willibrord often presents little more than an *aide-mémoire* to anecdotes more fully recounted in the prose, while occasionally the verse conversely supplements the prose in substantial detail (ibid., 117–19).

A fresh look at the phenomenology of reading the *opus geminatum*, equipped with the tools of deconstructive criticism and a sociolinguistic inflection of postcolonial studies, might open an integrative understanding of a peculiar literary vogue as an expression of paradoxes central to the multilingual milieu that engendered it. Such an approach would begin with the observation that early English *opera geminata* announce themselves as instantiations of unity and presence, whereas the reader's experience of these texts must necessarily emphasize disparity and absence. The reader of such texts is constantly driven back onto comparison with the twinned work, since the version present before the reader clearly demands supplementation; onto the quandary that the twinned versions of the bifurcated text turn out, upon comparison, not to be saying precisely the same thing at all. The more focused the reader of such texts becomes on establishing the unity of the two parallel texts of an *opus geminatum*, the more likely she is to unveil not the commonality that unites them, but the divergence that renders their unity problematic, even as it remains a foundational assumption informing one's entire reading practice.

*****

The prosecution of this, and of the other projects suggested above, would mark the participation of medieval Latin studies in a fundamental shift away from the recovery and representation of medieval cultural synthesis towards a heightened focus on the disruptions, conflicts, pluralities, problematically articulated identities, and internal contradictions evident both in the texts and in our present moment of scholarly interpretation. Such a reframing of the field's questions would answer calls issued a generation ago for increased metacritical awareness of the scholar's own ideological investment by Lee Patterson and Allen J. Frantzen in Middle English and Old English studies, respectively. If the lag is partly due to the institutional constraints outlined above, and partly to the skepticism of medieval Latinists towards the espousal of cultural theories imperfectly suited to the circumstances of the objects of our study, it is surely due as well, and perhaps chiefly, to the depth of medieval Latinity's own ideological investment in representing itself as the vehicle of universality: as the Tongue of the Fathers and the means by which, for a thousand years of European culture, the specificities of time, mother tongue, and space were putatively transcended. Medieval Latinity, so conceived, has presented its students with a particularly opaque resistance to their enquiries into its containment of cultural difference and contestation, the fault lines of that containment being so finely grained as they are, and so easily overlooked in the quest for a more foundational comprehension of texts and contexts.

At stake is more than the ongoing vitality of medieval Latin studies *per se.* There is indeed an argument to be made that the vexed boundaries of the medieval might plausibly be defined, at its inception, by the point when Latin, as the language of high culture, comes to be largely an artificially learned language, in ways traced by Roger Wright and Michel Banniard, and, at its close, by the point when, as an artificially learned language, it ceases to be the undisputed language of high culture. If Western European medieval culture as a whole defined itself around Latinity as its ideological fulcrum, then any understanding of medieval vernacular culture that takes the self-representations of Latinity at face value cannot fully evaluate vernacular texts' own implication in the same larger ideological structures. A commitment to the study of the instabilities at the Latinate heart of medieval ideologies of presence, unity, and continuity offers the promise of a fuller understanding not only of a central technology of indoctrination, but an enhanced critique of the divide between Latin and vernacular, natural and learned, local and universal, ephemeral and perdurative upon which medieval literary culture's larger signifying systems were founded.

SUGGESTIONS FOR FURTHER READING

While important studies in the field appear frequently in a range of journals, three periodicals are dedicated specifically to medieval Latin studies: *Journal of Medieval Latin, Mittellateinisches Jahrbuch,* and *Filologia Mediolatina*. The proceedings of five International Conferences on Medieval Latin Studies afford a sense of the state of the field over the last twenty-five years. For these, see Berschin (1991), Leonardi (1998), Herren (2002), Diaz y Diaz (2005), and Herren (2008). No extended treatment of the ideological dimension of medieval Latinity exists *per se*, but questions of medieval Latinity as a technology of cultural and social control and empowerment were early addressed by Ong (1959 and 1962), by Desmond (1994), and in the essays gathered in Townsend and Taylor (1998). The question of Latinity as an ideological mechanism since the sixteenth century is addressed by Waquet (2001).

BIBLIOGRAPHY

Primary sources

Abbo of St-Germain. 1899. "De Bello Parisiacae Urbis." In *Poetae Latini Aevi Carolini*, edited by Paul von Winterfeld, 72–121. Monumenta Germaniae Historica. Antiquitates. Poetae Latini Aevi Carolini 4.1. Berlin: Weidmann.

Aethelweard. 1962. *The Chronicle of Æthelweard*, edited by Alistair Campbell. Medieval Classics. London: Nelson.

Alcuin. 1881. "Vita sancti Willibrordi [prose]." In *Poetae Latini Aevi Carolini*, edited by Ernst Dümmler, 207–20. Monumenta Germaniae Historica. Poetae Latini Aevi Carolini 1. Berlin: Weidmann.

———. 1920. "Vita sancti Willibrordi archiepiscopi Traiectensis [verse]." In *Passiones vitaeque sanctorum aevi Merovingici*, edited by Bruno Krusch and Wilhelm Levison, 81–141. Monumenta Germaniae Historica. Scriptores Rerum Merovingicarum 7. Hannover, Leipzig: Weidmann.

Apollonius of Tyre. 1958. *The Old English Apollonius of Tyre*, edited by Peter Goolden. Oxford English Monographs 6. Oxford: Oxford University Press.

———. 1984. *Historia Apolloni regis Tyri*, edited by George A. A. Kortekaas. Mediaevalia Groningana 3. Groningen: University of Groningen.

Asser. 1959. *Asser's Life of King Alfred together with the Annals of St. Neot's erroneously ascribed to Asser*, edited by William Henry Stevenson. New impr. Oxford: Clarendon.

———. 1983. *Alfred the Great: Asser's Life of King Alfred and Other Contemporary Sources*, translated by Simon Keynes and Michael Lapidge. Penguin Classics. London: Penguin.

Byrhtferth of Ramsey. 2009. *The Lives of St. Oswald and St. Ecgwine*, edited and translated by Michael Lapidge. Oxford Medieval Texts. Oxford: Clarendon.

Eadmer. 1962. *The Life of St. Anselm Archbishop of Canterbury*, edited by Richard W. Southern. Medieval Classics. Oxford: Clarendon.

Earliest Life. 1968. *The Earliest Life of Gregory the Great, by an Anonymous Monk of Whitby*, edited by Bertram Colgrave. Lawrence, KS: University of Kansas Press.

Frithegod. 1950. *Frithegodi monachi Breuiloquium vitae beati Wilfredi et Wulfstani Cantoris narratio metrica de Sancto Swithuno*, edited by Alistair Campbell. Thesaurus Mundi 1. Turin: Thesaurus Mundi.

Hrotsvit. 2001. *Opera omnia*, edited by Walter Berschin. Bibliotheca scriptorum graecorum et romanorum Teubneriana. Munich: K. G. Saur.

Lantfred of Winchester. 2003. "Translatio et miracula s. Swithuni." In *The Cult of St. Swithun*, edited by Michael Lapidge, 217–333. Winchester Studies 4.2. Oxford: Clarendon.

Osbern. 1675. "Vita Sancti Elphegi." In *Acta Sanctorum Aprilis collecta, digesta, illustrata*, edited by Godefrid Henschen and Daniel von Papenbroek, 2: 628–40. Antwerp: Cnobarus.

———. 1874. "Vita Sancti Dunstani," edited by William Stubbs. In *Memorials of St. Dunstan, Archbishop of Canterbury*, 69–128. Rolls Series 63. London: Longman.

Widukind of Corvey. 1971. "Widukindi Res Gestae Saxonicae." In *Quellen zur Geschichte der Sächsischen Kaiserzeit*, edited by Albert Bauer and Reinhold Rau, 1–183. Ausgewählte Quellen zur Deutschen Geschichte des Mittelalters 8. Darmstadt: Wissenschaftliche Buchgesellschaft.

William of Malmesbury. 1998. *Gesta regum Anglorum*. Vol. 1: *Text and Translation*, edited and translated by Roger A. B. Mynors, Rodney M. Thomson, and Michael Winterbottom. Oxford Medieval Studies. Oxford: Clarendon.

———. 2002. *Saints' Lives: Lives of SS. Wulfstan, Dunstan, Patrick, Benignus and Indract*, edited by Michael Winterbottom and Rodney M. Thomson. Oxford Medieval Texts. Oxford: Clarendon.

Wulfstan the Cantor. 1950. "Narratio Metrica de Sancto Swithuno." In *Frithegodi monachi Breuiloquium Vitae Beati Wilfredi et Wulfstani Cantoris narratio metrica de Sancto Swithuno*, edited by Alistair Campbell. Thesaurus Mundi 1. Turin: Thesaurus Mundi.

Secondary sources

Archibald, Elizabeth. 1991. *Apollonius of Tyre. Medieval and Renaissance Themes and Variations*. Woodbridge: D. S. Brewer.

Bartlett, Robert. 1982. *Gerald of Wales, 1146–1223*. Oxford Historical Monographs. Oxford: Clarendon.

———. 1993. *The Making of Europe: Conquest, Colonization and Cultural Change 950–1350*. Penguin History. London: Penguin.

Baswell, Christopher. 1995. *Virgil in Medieval England: Figuring the Aeneid from the Twelfth Century to Chaucer*. Cambridge Studies in Medieval Literature 24. Cambridge: Cambridge University Press.

Berschin, Walter, ed. 1991. *Lateinische Kultur im X. Jahrhundert. Akten des I. Internationalen Mittellateinerkongresses, Heidelberg, 12.–15. IX. 1988*. Mittellateinisches Jahrbuch 24/25. Stuttgart: Hiersemann.

Bond, Gerald. 1995. *The Loving Subject: Desire, Eloquence, and Power in Romanesque France*. Middle Ages Series. Philadelphia: University of Pennsylvania Press.

Brown, Phyllis, Linda McMillin, and Katharina Wilson, eds. 2004. *Hrotsvit of Gandersheim: Contexts, Identities, Affinities, and Performances*. Toronto: University of Toronto Press.

Brownlee, Maria Scordilis. 1985. *The Status of the Reading Subject in the Libro de Buen Amor*. North Carolina Studies in the Romance Languages and Literatures 224. Chapel Hill, NC: University of North Carolina Press.

Burns, E. Jane. 1985. *Arthurian Fictions: Rereading the Vulgate Cycle*. Columbus, OH: Ohio State University Press.

———. 1993. *Bodytalk: When Women Speak in Old French Literature*. New Cultural Studies. Philadelphia: University of Pennsylvania Press.

Cohen, Jeffrey Jerome. 2004. "The Flow of Blood in Medieval Norwich." *Speculum* 79: 26–65.

———. 2000. "Hybrids, Monsters, and Borderlands: The Bodies of Gerald of Wales." In *The Postcolonial Middle Ages*, edited by Jeffrey Jerome Cohen, 85–104. New Middle Ages. New York: Macmillan.

Coffman, George, et al. 1924. "The Committee on Mediaeval Latin Studies." *Modern Philology* 21: 303–15.

Derrida, Jacques. 1976. *Of Grammatology*, translated by Gayatri Chakravorty Spivak. Baltimore: Johns Hopkins University Press.

Dinshaw, Carolyn. 1989. *Chaucer's Sexual Poetics*. Madison, WI: University of Wisconsin Press.

Desmond, Marilynn. 1994. *Reading Dido: Gender, Textuality, and the Medieval Aeneid*. Medieval Cultures 8. Minneapolis, MN: University of Minnesota Press.

Díaz y Díaz, Manuel C. and José M. Díaz de Bustamante, eds. 2005. *Actas del IV Congreso del "Internationales Mittellateinerkomitee" Santiago de Compostela, 12–15 de septiembre de 2002*. Millennio Medievale 55. Atti di Convegni 17. Florence: SISMEL.

Discenza, Nicole Guenther. 2001. "Wealth and Wisdom: Symbolic Capital and the Ruler in the Translation Program of Alfred the Great." *Exemplaria* 13: 433–67.

Dronke, Peter. 1984. *Women Writers of the Middle Ages: A Critical Study of Texts from Perpetua to Marguerite Porete*. Cambridge: Cambridge University Press.
Echard, Sian. 1998. "With Carmen's Help: Latin Authorities in the *Confessio Amantis*." *Studies in Philology* 95: 1–40.
Farmer, D.H. 1962. "William of Malmesbury's Life and Works." *Journal of Ecclesiastical History* 13: 39–54.
Frantzen, Allen J. 1990. *Desire for Origins: New Language, Old English, and Teaching the Tradition*. New Brunswick, NJ: Rutgers University Press.
Gellrich, Jesse. 1985. *The Idea of the Book in the Middle Ages: Language, Theory, Mythology, and Fiction*. Ithaca, NY: Cornell University Press.
Godman, Peter. 1981. "The Latin opus geminatum: From Aldhelm to Alcuin." *Medium Ævum* 50: 215–29.
Goffart, Walter. 1988. *The Narrators of Barbarian History, 550–800: Jordanes, Gregory of Tours, Bede, and Paul the Deacon*. Princeton, NJ: Princeton University Press.
Noah D. Guynn, Noah D. 2007. *Allegory and Sexual Ethics in the High Middle Ages*. New York; Palgrave Macmillan.
Herren, Michael et al., eds. 2002. *Latin Culture in the Eleventh Century: Proceedings of the Third International Conference on Medieval Latin Studies Cambridge, September 9–12 1998*. Publications of The Journal of Medieval Latin 2. Turnhout: Brepols.
Herren, Michael, ed. 2008. Proceedings of the Fifth International Congress of Medieval Latin Studies. *The Journal of Medieval Latin* 17/18.
Holsinger, Bruce. 1993. "The Flesh of the Voice: Embodiment and the Homoerotics of Devotion in the Music of Hildegard of Bingen (1098–1179)." *Signs* 19: 92–135.
———. 1998. "The Color of Salvation: Desire, Death, and the Second Crusade in Bernard of Clairvaux's Sermons on the Song of Songs." In *The Tongue of the Fathers: Gender and Ideology in Twelfth-Century Latin*, edited by David Townsend and Andrew Taylor, 156–86. Middle Ages Series. Philadelphia: University of Pennsylvania Press.
Hexter, Ralph J. 1986. *Ovid and Medieval Schooling: Studies in Medieval School Commentaries on Ovid's Ars amatoria, Epistulae ex Ponto, and Epistulae Heroidum*. Münchener Beiträge zur Mediävistik und Renaissance-Forschung 38. München: Arbeo-Gesellschaft.
Irvine, Martin. 1994. *The Making of Textual Culture: Grammatica and Literary Theory, 350–1100*. Cambridge Studies in Medieval Literature 19. Cambridge: Cambridge University Press.
Jankulak, Karen. 2003. "Alba Longa in the Celtic Regions? Swine, Saints, and Celtic Hagiography." In *Celtic Hagiography and Saints' Cults*, edited by Jane Cartwright, 271–84. Cardiff: University of Wales Press.
Jezierski, Wojtek. 2005. "Æthelweardus Redivivus." *Early Medieval Europe* 13: 159–78.
Jordan, Mark. 1997. *The Invention of Sodomy in Christian Theology*. The Chicago Series on Sexuality, History, and Society. Chicago: University of Chicago Press.
Kay, Sarah. 1990. *Subjectivity in Troubadour Poetry*. Cambridge Studies in French. Cambridge: Cambridge University Press.
Knapp, Fritz Peter. 1975. *Similitudo: Stil- und Erzählfunktion von Vergleich und Exempel in der lateinischen, französischen und deutschen Grossepik des Hochmittelalters*. Philologica Germanica 2. Vienna: W. Braumüller.
Lapidge, Michael. 1975. "The Hermeneutic Style in Tenth-Century Anglo-Latin Literature." *Anglo-Saxon England* 4: 67–111.
———. 1984. "Byrhtferth of Ramsey and the Early Sections of the *Historia regum* Attributed to Symeon of Durham." *Revue Bénédictine* 94: 326–69.

———. 1993. *Anglo-Latin Literature, 900–1066*. London, Rio Grande, OH: Hambledon.
———. 2003. *The Cult of St. Swithun*. Winchester Studies 4. Oxford: Clarendon.
Leonardi, Claudio. 1998. *Gli Umanesimi Medievali: Atti del II Congress dell'"Internationales Mittellateinerkomitee", Firenze, Certosa del Galluzzo, 11–15 settembre 1993*. Millennio medievale 4. Florence: SISMEL.
Leupin, Alexandre. 1989. *Barbarolexis: Medieval Writing and Sexuality*. Cambridge, MA: Harvard University Press.
Mantello, Frank A. C. and Arthur G. Rigg. 1996. *Medieval Latin: An Introduction and Bibliographical Guide*. Washington, DC: Catholic University of America Press.
Mehan, Uppinder and David Townsend. 2001. "'Nation' and the Gaze of the Other in Eighth-Century Northumbria." *Comparative Literature* 53: 1–26.
Nichols, Stephen G. 1983. *Romanesque Signs: Early Medieval Narrative and Iconography*. New Haven, CT: Yale University Press.
O'Brien O'Keefe, Katherine. 1990. *Visible Song: Transitional Literacy in Old English Verse*. Cambridge Studies in Anglo-Saxon England 4. Cambridge: Cambridge University Press.
Ong, Walter. 1959. "Latin Language Study as a Renaissance Puberty Rite." *Studies in Philology* 56: 103–24.
———. 1962. "Latin and the Social Fabric." In *The Barbarian Within and Other Fugitive Essays and Studies*, 206–19. New York: Macmillan.
Partner, Nancy F. 1977. *Serious Entertainments: The Writing of History in Twelfth-Century England*. Chicago: University of Chicago Press.
———. 1996. "Did Mystics Have Sex?" In *Desire and Discipline: Sex and Sexuality in the Premodern West*, edited by Jacqueline Murray and Konrad Eisenbichler, 296–311. Toronto: University of Toronto Press.
Pfaff, Richard. 1998. "Lanfranc's Supposed Purge of the Anglo-Saxon Calendar." In *Liturgical Calendars, Saints, and Services in Medieval England*, 95–108. Collected Studies 610. Aldershot: Ashgate Variorum.
Patterson, Lee. 1987. *Negotiating the Past: The Historical Understanding of Medieval Literature*. Madison, WI: University of Wisconsin Press.
Ratkowitsch, Christina. 1991. *Descriptio picturae: die literarische Funktion der Beschreibung von Kunstwerken in der lateinischen Grossdichtung des 12. Jahrhunderts*. Wiener Studien. Beiheft 15. Vienna: Österreichische Akademie der Wissenschaften.
Rigg, Arthur G. 1992. *A History of Anglo-Latin Literature, 1066–1422*. Cambridge, New York: Cambridge University Press.
Stein, Robert. 1998. "Making History English: Cultural Identity and Historical Explanation in William of Malmesbury and La͏amon's *Brut*." In *Text and Territory: Geographical Imagination in the Middle Ages*, edited by Sylvia Tomasch and Sealy Gilles, 97–115. The Middle Ages Series. Philadelphia: University of Pennsylvania Press.
———. 2006. *Reality Fictions: Romance, History, and Governmental Authority, 1025–1180*. Notre Dame, IN: University of Notre Dame Press.
Sticca, Sandro. 1970. "Hrotswitha's 'Dulcitius' and Christian Symbolism." *Mediaeval Studies* 32: 108–27.
———. 1973. "Hrotswitha's *Abraham* and Exegetical Tradition." In *Acta Conventus Neo-Latini Lovaniensis. Proceedings of the First International Congress of Neo-Latin Studies, Louvain 23–28 August 1971*, edited by J. Ijsewijn and E. Kessler, 633–38. Humanistische Bibliothek. Reihe I, Abhandlungen 20. Leuven: Leuven University Press.
———. 1984. "Sacred Drama and Comic Realism in the Plays of Hrotswitha of Gandersheim." In *Atti del IV Colloquio della Societé internationale pour l'étude du*

théatre médiéval, Viterbo, 10–15 luglio 1983, edited by Maria Chiabò, Federico Doglio, and Marina Mayome, 141–62. Viterbo: Centro studi sul teatro medioevale e rinascimentale.

Stock, Brian. 1983. *The Implications of Literacy*. Princeton, NJ: Princeton University Press.

Thompson, Rodney. 1987. *William of Malmesbury*. Woodbridge, Dover, NH: Boydell Press.

Townsend, David. 1991. "Anglo-Latin Hagiography and the Norman Transition." *Exemplaria* 3: 385–434.

———. 1993. "Alcuin's Willibrord, Wilhelm Levison, and the MGH." In *The Politics of Editing Medieval Texts*, edited by Roberta Frank, 109–30. New York: AMS Press.

———. 1995. "Omissions, Emissions, Missionaries, and Master Signifiers in Norman Canterbury." *Exemplaria* 7: 295–315.

———. 1998. "Sex and the Single Amazon in Twelfth-Century Latin Epic." In *The Tongue of the Fathers: Gender and Ideology in Twelfth-Century Latin*, edited by David Townsend and Andrew Taylor, 136–55. Middle Ages Series. Philadelphia: University of Pennsylvania Press.

———. 2008. "Cultural Difference and the Meaning of Latinity in Asser's *Life of King Alfred*." In *Cultural Diversity in the British Middle Ages: Archipelago, Island, England*, edited by Jeffrey Jerome Cohen, 57–73. New Middle Ages. New York: Palgrave Macmillan.

Townsend, David and Andrew Taylor, eds. 1998. *The Tongue of the Fathers: Gender and Ideology in Twelfth-Century Latin*. Middle Ages Series. Philadelphia: University of Pennsylvania Press.

Tyler, Elizabeth M. 2005a. "Fictions of Family: The *Encomium Emmae Reginae* and Virgil's *Aeneid*." *Viator* 36: 149–79.

———. 2005b. "Talking About History in Eleventh-Century England: the *Encomium Emmae Reginae* and the Court of Harthacnut." *Early Medieval Europe* 13: 359–83.

———. 2009. "From Old English to Old French." In *Language and Culture in Medieval Britain: The French of England c. 1100–c. 1500*, edited by Jocelyn Wogan-Browne. York: York Medieval Press.

Van Houts, Elizabeth. 1992. "Women and the Writing of History in the Early Middle Ages: the Case of Matilda of Essen and Æthelweard." *Early Medieval Europe* 1: 53–68.

Venuti, Lawrence. 1998. *The Scandals of Translation: Towards an Ethics of Difference*. London, New York: Routledge.

Waquet, Françoise. 2001. *Latin, or the Empire of the Sign: From the Sixteenth to the Twentieth Century*, translated by John Howe. London: Verso.

Wenger, Luke. 1982. "The Medieval Academy and Medieval Studies in North America." In *Medieval Studies in North America: Past, Present, and Future*, edited by Francis G. Gentry and Christopher Kleinhenz. Kalamazoo, MI: Medieval Institute Publications.

Whitbread, L. 1959. "Æthelweard and the Anglo-Saxon Chronicle." *English Historical Review* 74: 577–89.

Wieland, Gernot. 1981. "*Geminus Stilus*: Studies in Anglo-Latin Hagiography." In *Insular Latin Studies. Papers on Latin Texts and Manuscripts of the British Isles, 550–1066*, edited by Michael W. Herren, 113–33. Papers in Mediaeval Studies 1. Toronto: Pontifical Institute of Mediaeval Studies.

Winterbottom, Michael. 1967. "The Style of Æthelweard." *Medium Ævum* 36: 109–18.

Zumthor, Paul. 1972. *Essai de poétique médiéval*. Collection Poétique. Paris: Éditions du Seuil.

CHAPTER 2

CANONICITY

RALPH J. HEXTER

Medieval Latin Literary History?

We expect a literature, each and every literature, to have both a history and a canon. Medieval Latin literature is something of a scandal in that it has neither. This is of course an overstatement, certainly as far as the history is concerned. The scandal arises from the fact that, for a set of illuminating reasons, the history of medieval Latin literature does not fit neatly—if at all—the standard model of a literary history, based as it has been on a set of axioms: first, that the history of a literature itself maps onto the history of a language, understood as "a national language," and, second, that both language and literature map on to and "express" the nation itself in some mystical and mythical way. Before we can approach the splendors and miseries of medieval Latin as a literature in search of its canon, we must look more deeply into the problematics of its literary history, for the two—canon and literary history—are closely entwined, and together form the complex one might call "canonicity."

"Skandalon"—whence our word "scandal"—denotes a stumbling block, and insofar as a stumbling block impedes a pedestrian from going further down a wrong path, it may prove a very good thing. Indeed, coming to understand how we have stumbled, and that the seeming tangling or crossing of pathways makes possible a better mapping than an easy stroll up the straight and narrow, can provide important lessons. But one stumble, one *skandalon* at a time. Here, we observe only that over roughly the past fifty years the axioms that underpin conventional national literary histories have been widely discredited, and the concepts of "nation" and "literary history" shown to be all-too-evident constructs (Perkins 1992; Hexter 2005).

To be sure, all scholars in the field still need chronological accounts of literary activity in Latin through the medieval period. The few that exist serve as indispensable reference tools and guides among the still opaque forests of medieval

Latinity (Manitius 1911–31; Brunhölzl 1975–2009). While it is true that the histories of many a national language have to take into account the impact of other written traditions on the literature that is the object of study (e.g., via translation, the activity of readers, particularly readers who then write, etc.), few face the precise challenges medieval Latin literature does in this regard. For medieval Latin is not only later than classical Latin, medieval Latin recurs to its classical antecedent repeatedly and in a variety of ways. And while it is generally to classical Latin— both the *auctores* in common school use and the norms of the language as recorded by late antique grammarians (Priscian, Donatus)—to which writers of medieval Latin recur, with varying degrees of vigor and rigor, and to different effect in different eras, there are other norms and ideals that hold sway in its various registers and genres, whether it be a host of vernacular languages or the primarily translated corpora of scripture, liturgy, philosophy, and other sciences. Since the norm of classical Latin is there to be hailed and "revived" from time to time, it acts as a retarding mechanism on linguistic developments that might be taking place within the language, with this retardation likely more impactful on the written language (Stotz 1996–2004).

As Ruff and others discuss elsewhere in this volume, it is precisely this reversion to the classical norm that led, once classical orthography was taken as a guide to pronunciation, to the sundering of the romance vernaculars from hitherto evolving Latin. This had the significant effect of making it almost inevitable that medieval Latin (as primarily a written language, however much it was still spoken in certain milieux) would conform all the more insistently to classical Latin at the basic level. Regional differences in vocabulary and usage notwithstanding, it became generally more homogeneous across its catchment area. Nor does this deny the evolution of new and utterly nonclassical styles, both in prose and verse (see Hays and Tilliette in this volume), or the development of certain kinds of technical language (e.g., within fields as diverse as scholastic theology, speculative grammar, medicine, and law) with abundant neologisms and classically unattested structures. Things are of course more complex, as the case of secular (i.e., not canon) law, illustrates: though based on Roman jurisprudence, the language of the jurists, while ancient, reads nothing like the pleadings of a Cicero. At the level of orthography and morphology, however, there were few significant variations, and the great bulk of the medieval Latin lexicon remained close to classical usage. (Telling is the fact that important medieval lexical aids are often constructed to operate on the principle of only tracking what is not classical, e.g., Niermeyer 2002, Latham 1965.)

As a language taught now almost exclusively in schools or other closed institutions, the particular mixture of Latin texts presented to students had a supereminent effect on the textual universe in which the writers and speakers of medieval Latin led their Latinate existences. On top of a substrate of Latin composed, for almost all those who came into daily contact with the tongue, of the biblical language of the prayers and scriptural readings experienced through daily liturgical rituals, there came the set texts of the curricular canon. These included minor texts (like the *Disticha Catonis*), then biblical epics written in earlier centuries in imitation of Vergil above all (Juvencus, Arator, Proba), and other *auctores* with most of whom we are quite familiar.

While the *auctores* of medieval schooling were heavily weighted towards what we today consider classical authors (Vergil, Terence, Cicero, Sallust; more variously Horace, Ovid, Statius), they also included Christian authors of both prose and poetry (e.g., Augustine, Gregory, Ambrose, Prudentius) whom we do not consider "classical," not so much because they are "late" as because they were Christian. (Christianity plays a role in determining where modern scholars draw the boundary between "classical" and whatever follows, now generally "late antiquity"; on late antiquity, see Formisano in this volume.) For the Middle Ages in general, though, these foundational Christian Latin writers were full-fledged *auctores*, not only worth reading but worth emulating as stylistic models, and while it was rare for any student in medieval schools to be misinformed about whether a given author was pagan or Christian, what Sedulius, for example, had in common with Vergil was more important for school purposes than the fact that the one was Christian, the other not (cf. Hexter 2005).

Only rarely did a newly minted text enter these auctorial precincts. The *Ecloga Theoduli* (Theodulus 1997) did, although it is worth noting that the *accessus* (potted introductions) that describe it tend to read as if it were of hoarier vintage than its likely ninth- to tenth-century date. (The issue of the poem's date is discussed briefly by Otter in this volume.) The opening lines of the *accessus* in one well-known collection of such headnotes claim that the author traveled to Athens, where he not only learned Greek but heard Christians disputing with pagans [*gentiles*], a situation that obtained no later than the fifth century and would have been more likely in the second through fourth centuries (*Accessus ad auctores* 1970, 26–27). The few works admitted to auctorial status and simultaneously recognized as recent include, at the more elementary level, Matthew of Vendôme's *Tobias* and, at a more advanced level, Walter of Châtillon's *Alexandreis*. The latter can be said to have succeeded precisely because it embodied auctorial norms established by Vergil and Statius. Among grammatical works, high medieval productions like Eberhard of Béthune's *Grecismus* and Alexander of Villa Dei's *Doctrinale* entered the auctorial realm because they taught the same norms as Priscian and Donatus had, but did so in a new fashion. Two of Alain of Lille's works, the *Liber parabolarum* and the *Anticlaudianus*, also entered the teaching canon, the former at the elementary level, the latter for more advanced students.

Given the dominance of the classical, furnishing as it did both grammatical norms and a significant portion of the school curriculum, one might well say that medieval Latin literature does not need to have either its own literary history or canon. Medieval Latin would then be appropriately treated as a mere phase of Latin literary history. Certainly such an approach is possible, and recently there have been "experiments" at taking such a long perspective on Latin. This seems, in my view, to work more convincingly for Latin as a language than for the literature (Farrell 2001; Janson 2004), for what almost inevitably occurs is that works written in medieval Latin virtually disappear from sight. Perhaps new generations of scholars might right this imbalance, but for the moment classicizing biases seem still too strong. Certainly, from a perspective in which Augustan literature is the acme of Latin letters, it would be hard not to privilege those medieval works that most nearly approached this ideal (however it is constructed). It might just as well lead to an exoticization of what is most "medieval," in other words, quaintly different, and this is not so far from what one has found in published collections of medieval hymns or goliardic songs. Indeed, the two seemingly contradictory approaches can happily coexist.

An entirely different approach has been to refuse, explicitly or tacitly, "medieval Latin literature" as the entity that needs its history written. Simply by pronouncing the phrase "medieval Latin literature," we imply that there is a single and unified field such that its constituent elements, i.e., Latin texts labeled medieval, should be explicable within an account we could give of the category. But perhaps what Gregory of Tours and Peter of Blois have in common, or the *Waltharius* and the *Glossa ordinaria*, is so minimal and trivial that to construct such an account is an exercise in futility. Accordingly, some scholars have found it much more productive to focus on Latin texts written within a particular geographical demesne (e.g., Lapidge 1995 and 1993 and Rigg 1992 for Anglo-Latin literature; cf. Friis-Jensen for Scandinavia in this volume), to trace a poetic tradition (e.g., Raby 1953 and 1957 for Christian and secular poetry, respectively), to analyze the poetry of a cultural moment (e.g., Godman 1987 for the Carolingian period), or to describe a genre (e.g., Kinderman 1978 for satire, Lehmann 1963 or Bayless 1996 for parody, or Bernt 1968 for the epigram). These more focused studies are for this very reason frequently much more illuminating, and while they all belong to a larger history of medieval Latin, their authors cunningly sidestep the pitfalls involved in attempting that larger history. It may be that we can adapt some of this cunning and calculation as we attempt to devise a model for medieval Latin literature itself.

Canon and Authority

WITHIN each of these more focused studies, certain individual authors and works will inevitably loom larger than others, but one would hardly claim that this in itself made a significant author in one of these series canonical, whether the late twelfth- and early thirteenth-century Saxo Grammaticus among Scandinavian writers of Latin or the eleventh-century (pseudonymous) "Sextus Amarcius" among medieval satirists. Neither would one assume that even the most notable work of a given period or type belonged to the canon of medieval Latin for that reason alone. What, then, is a canon, and how is the canonical determined?

Most accounts of the canon begin by noting the etymology of the word itself. It is invariably recorded that the Latin *canon*—for it is the same as our English word—derives from the Greek κανών, "rod, measuring stick," itself related to κάννα, "reed" (e.g., Scholes 1992, 139–40). The Greek κάννα itself derives from Hebrew for "reed" or "cane": *kaneh*. Jerome, who learned Hebrew precisely to translate the Jewish scriptures, uses the word "canon" in what has become its most canonical sense, applying it to works that are regarded as of greatest authority. Given his project of translating scriptures from their original languages, he deployed the term to indicate whether a given book should be included in or excluded from sacred scripture. In the preface to his translation of Kings he wrote:

> Hic prologus Scripturarum quasi galeatum principium omnibus libris, quos de hebraeo vertimus in latinum, convenire potest, ut scire valeamus, quicquid extra hos est, inter apocrifa seponendum. Igitur Sapientia, quae vulgo Salomonis inscribitur, et Iesu filii Sirach liber et Iudith et Tobias et Pastor non sunt in canone. Macchabeorum primum librum hebraicum repperi, secundus graecus est, quod et ex ipsa φράσιν probari potest.
>
> [This prologue could fittingly serve (as if helmeted) to all the books of scriptures that we have translated from Hebrew into Latin, so that we are able to know what should be separated off as additional, in other words, apocryphal. For the book of Wisdom, which is commonly ascribed to Solomon, and the books of Jesus the son of Sirach, Judith, Tobias, and the Pastor [of Hermas] are not in the canon. The first book of Maccabees is found in Hebrew, the second, however, is Greek, which can be established on the basis of its style.] (Jerome 1983; my translation)

Jerome uses the adjectival form, too, for example in his letter to Dardanus, where, interestingly, he is not terribly exercised whether the Epistle to the Hebrews is actually by St. Paul or not. Jerome admits that "eam Latinorum consuetudo non recipit inter scripturas canonicas" [the custom of Latin speakers does not receive it among the canonical scriptures], but he nonetheless includes it (along with the Apocalypse of John, which he notes the Greeks generally exclude), because more important than the "custom" of current usage is the "veterum scriptorum auctoritatem" [authority of writers of old], who refer to it. Clearly, both these texts are "canonical and belonging to the church" ("*canonicis et ecclesiasticis*"; Epistle 129; Jerome 1996).

This usage may have been fairly recent in Jerome's day. While the so-called Muratorian fragment—a seventh-century copy of a list of the books of the "New Testament" datable to c. 170 CE—distinguishes between canonical and uncanonical, it does so without the use of the word "canon." (The term, as applied by scholars to this early document, dates from the modern period.) The word "canon" is so applied in the Greek of the Council of Laodicea (364 CE; *canon* 59), and will likely have appeared first in Latin as the translation of a Greek term, perhaps even earlier than the mid-fourth century. The application of "canonical" to church law, what we still to this day call "canon law," is likewise not a usage of the primitive church. It too dates back to the fourth century and refers to rules affirmed by greater church councils, like those of the aforementioned Laodicea, a usage Jerome would also have known.

To approach the historiography of the issue of how one ought to think about a canon of medieval Latin literature, we must acknowledge what canon and canonicity have come to mean in recent times. To that end, we cannot avoid a slight detour and a review of the culture wars of our own era.

Now culture wars involving literature are hardly new. One recalls the various "querelles" of early modern France, most famously "la querelle des anciens et modernes" in the seventeenth century, which along with other literary debates inspired Swift's satirical *Battle of the Books*. Even earlier, at the very opening of the fifteenth century, Christine de Pizan sparked a debate over the misogyny of Guillaume de Lorris and Jean de Meun's *Roman de la Rose*, inciting what became known as the *querelle des femmes* (Hult 2003).

There were notable redirections, or attempts at redirection, of the readings students learning Latin were assigned over the centuries. Some had little impact, like the fourteenth-century *Antiovidianus* (1929). The campaign of the humanists was, in the long run, massively effective, as the history of medieval Latin literature, the general reputation of medieval Latin, and the ultimate exile of the Christian Latin poets to nonclassical obscurity variously prove. Still, it took quite a long time before the traces of the basic medieval readings for elementary Latin students entirely disappeared. Catalogues of incunables reveal abundant printings of Donatus and other traditional collections—the *libri Catoniani*—aimed at students. (On medieval Latin texts in early print editions, see Chiesa in this volume.) The marketplace, too, at times has a role in determining the canonical.

While the humanists may seem to have little to do with our present cultural moment, we—at least those of us who work in humanistic and historical fields—live in the shadow of a far-reaching and momentous reorientation of the curriculum, one which exposes the cultural and social stakes of such battles in exemplary fashion. Education in the Greco-Roman classics had been a rite of passage for the elite leaders of society, and adherence to this fixed curriculum furthered the reproduction of these social, political, and economic elites, an argument advanced in classic fashion by Althusser (1970). But by the second half of the nineteenth century a host was forcing access to post-secondary education for a much broader spectrum of modern, industrialized societies and at the same time putting in question the assumption that the only course of study worthy of the name "higher education" was based on the reading of ancient Greek and Latin texts. Curricula in the natural sciences were created, and students could study and earn degrees in modern (i.e., post-classical national) languages and literatures.

These debates were conducted with explicit reference not only to class but to gender and race. Women had by and large not been expected to learn Latin or Greek, though quite a few had in every generation. Certainly, in the United States of the Reconstruction era, the question arose in the context of education of the now emancipated African slaves (on which see, i.a., Selden 1998 and Scarborough 2005). Initially, the universities and "polytechnics" founded to cater to the greater numbers of students were considered less prestigious than Oxford, Cambridge, or any other of the ancient institutions in England, or the Ivy League colleges in the United States, but at the same time these hoary institutions, not to be outdone by the newer ones, were creating degrees in the sciences and other new fields. The competition had, not surprisingly, national and economic overtones.

By the second half of the twentieth century, even the curricula in modern literatures (often with classics in translation—the so-called Great Books) came under fire, and as new groups gained entrance into the world from which they had once been excluded, they clamored for representation in reading lists in which the well-established elites were still overrepresented. The reading lists of introductory courses were criticized for being, so to speak, too male, too white, too European, too dead. The revision of these lists to include a much broader range of works, not to mention the creation of departments and programs in universities with names such as Women's Studies, African-American Studies, Chicano/a Studies, Gay Studies—to offer an incomplete list—inspired a fierce reaction among those who despised what they branded "political correctness." At this point, the word "canon" was on every culture warrior's lips, and both the canonical canon and the revisionist canons were seemingly under constant fire.

It is likely no accident of history that it was in 1970, but two years after European university students took to the streets to protest the conservatism of their curricula, that Günter Glauche used the word "canon" in the subtitle of his study of the school curriculum in the Latin Middle Ages ("Entstehung und Wandlung des Lektürekanons" [rise and development of the reading canon]). Glauche himself makes no explicit reference to events contemporary with the publication of his work, but notwithstanding the perfect applicability of the concept of a biblical canon to a comparably authoritative system, we know that after 1970 the words "canon" and "canonical" cannot be used as innocently and matter-of-factly as Jerome had done roughly 1,600 years earlier.

It is only to the good, I would argue, that the intensity of recent debates about the canon has reawakened our sensitivity to what has always been true about canons, whether biblical or educational. Momentous struggles over power and control are always at play when some texts are accorded authority, others denied it. "Als Kanon in diesem Sinne ist ein Korpus von Texten aufzufassen, an dessen Überlieferung eine Gesellschaft oder Kultur interessiert ist. Der Kanon ist 'gemacht' und hat in mehrfacher Hinsicht etwas mit Macht zu tun" [As a "canon" in this sense of the word is how one is to conceive a body of texts in the transmission of which a society or culture is interested. The canon is constructed and has from multiple perspectives something to do with power] (Winko 2002, 9). This was certainly true of the world of the fathers of the Church, seeking to draw a line between authoritative and non-authoritative texts, even if it is generally only specialists in the patristic and subsequent periods who understand the regional, political, classist, and sometimes gendered overtones of various exclusions, whether of the writings of Gnostics or Donatists, Monophysites or Eutychianists, Priscillianists or Cathars.

What of this is relevant for our concern here, namely, to see what shape a canon of medieval Latin literature might take today? Could such a selection be built upon the reading lists or anthologies of Latin texts compiled by medieval masters for their students? As they distinguished between the authoritative and non-authoritative, successive generations of medieval masters were concerned to select models of Latin usage and style, but their canon does not carry weight in that regard with the Latinists of today. Still less does it matter to the contemporary general reading public, a public who reads, here in America, almost exclusively in English, when it reads at all. (On the exceedingly small percentage of books that are translations into English published in any given year, see Ziolkowski in this volume.) One might stop right here with the drastic observation that since there is no body of medieval Latin texts that matters to any society or culture any more, there is no canon. End of essay.

Whiff of a Canon

Perhaps there is yet a medieval Latin canon, one that might still hover about in spectral form: the whiff of a canon. At the very least the complete or near nonexistence of such a canon or its evanescence might yet teach us something about canonicity.

We might begin by asking whether there was ever a society or culture that had an interest in the transmission of Latin literature of the Middle Ages. One such society is the Roman Catholic Church, but its medieval Latin canon is a very singular one, built on and in many cases constructed out of texts that belong to a superordinate canon. To be sure, some of these Latin texts are still alive, through liturgical repetition, but they are canonical as liturgical texts, not for being *medieval* Latin texts, and again, not for any significant reading public.

Of course, aesthetic values offer another possible set of criteria for placing works in the canon. "Einen Kanon in diesem Sinne bildet die Menge der besten Texte, basierend auf deren Eigenschaften" [A canon in this sense is constituted by the collection of the best texts, selected according to their characteristics] (Winko 2002, 10). Let us leave to one side the observation that there are political implications to an aesthetic canon, since the very existence of a given cultural agreement on what is "good" or "beautiful" reflects and in turn reinforces the existence of a culturally dominant elite.

Elsewhere in this volume Jean-Yves Tilliette eloquently and succinctly describes the aims of medieval poets as quite different from either ancient or modern poets. As he so rightly argues, they are fully in line with the values, practical and often ethical, which masters instructed students to seek out in the *auctores*. If works from earlier periods are to remain canonical or "evergreen" in the sense of perennially fascinating, they must fulfill to at least a certain extent contemporary readers' expectations for fine literature, good literature, literature of value. And for several centuries now, such judgments have involved aesthetic qualities. What works of medieval Latin literature can satisfy modern tastes?

In his contribution to the present volume, Jan M. Ziolkowski shows how changing tastes have guided the selection of medieval Latin texts to be published in English to no small degree, even as they have led translators to cast their renderings into different forms and styles according to the aesthetic of the time in which they lived. Ziolkowski's survey constitutes an important contribution to a full-bore study of the reception of medieval Latin literature since roughly 1800, a study that would profit, as his essay already suggests, from a comparative approach. Clearly, the range and shape, but also the historicity of a canon emerge from reception-oriented studies, and lingering biases against reception studies among classicists (or other students of literature) reflect persistent, if waning, resistance to understanding the historical relativity of their own position and field.

Such a study would join significant recent work on "medievalism," one of the fastest growing subfields within medieval studies. (Bloch and Nichols, 1995 and Fugelso 2009 are but two examples of the burgeoning secondary literature; there has been an annual bibliography of books and articles dealing with medievalism since 1979 compiled by the members of the Salzburger Symposion 1979–.) This reception history of medieval Latin would intersect at points with the Gothic novel and the Gothic revival in architecture, with neo- and Anglo-Catholicism, with the love for all things Arthurian, and with the tastes of the pre-Raphaelites, among many other currents. What already emerges from preliminary soundings is that medieval Latin is prized as exotic, precious, and obscure. This is perhaps nowhere better illustrated than in Huysmans' *À rebours* (1884), which contains what might be described as the decadent's guide to Latin literature (recently appreciated by Shanzer 2009). In chapter four, the narrator guides the reader along the main character des Esseintes's shelves of Latin poetry, heavy with late ancient and late antique texts and some unusual specimens of medieval Latin literature, such as the riddles of Aldhelm, Tatwine, and Euphonius, the life of Saint Radegund by Baudonivia, and Walahfrid Strabo's *Hortulus*. What Huysman concocted was deliberately outré, intended to define not so much a canon as an anti-canon.

While Huysmans had certain French aesthetes in mind as models for des Esseintes (the aristocrat Robert de Montesquiou in particular), some of the English translators of medieval Latin poetry had tastes running in comparable (if less extreme) directions. One thinks of Charles Algernon Swinburne, a highly popular poet in his day. John Addington Symonds constitutes a yet more interesting case. While he was a noted, and quite courageous, early defender of male-male love, interestingly, he is the creator of the long-lived anthology of translations of the goliardic poets *Wine, Women, and Song*, the example par excellence of muscular heterosexual medieval Latinity.

If there is any group of medieval Latin poets that have become canonical, it is the rowdy and randy (heterosexual) goliards. The emergence and popularization of the goliards through translations in the late nineteenth century, at the very moment when the homosexual was emerging as an identity (in Foucault's terms)—this canonization, in other words—constitutes a clear attempt to win back medieval Latin from the aesthetes and render it fit for the "common man."

The muscularity of this tradition reaches an apogee, with yet other and perhaps accidental overtones, in Carl Orff's popular *Carmina Burana* (1935–36; premiere 1937). Orff apparently first came upon the texts he would set for orchestra, chorus, and soloists in a copy of Symonds's anthology. The frequent performances of this work doubtless account for the most widely experienced selection of medieval Latin literature (with the possible exception of some hymns and liturgical texts heard by churchgoers, although since the Latin mass is said so infrequently, Orff probably has the upper hand). To what extent the muscular and percussive quality of these settings resonate with the time and place of their composition represents a more difficult question. The popularity of the work in general in Nazi Germany, and the suspicions one harbors about Orff's sympathies and actions, then and immediately after the war, are generally ignored, but they linger, providing odd overtones for these, the most popular of medieval Latin poems heard today, albeit with music radically different from the original medieval settings. These overtones make some listeners very queasy indeed.

Not that heterosexual love is uncommon, but it is perhaps noteworthy in this context that among the few other medieval Latin works that can possibly make a claim to popular readership are the letters of Heloise along with the calamitous story (*Historia calamitatum*) of Abelard and Heloises's love affair. The attraction of this pair—Paolo and Francesca *avant la lettre*—is of course older than the nineteenth century, running back well into the century of sentiment, the eighteenth, as Pope's "Eloisa to Abelard" (1717) indicates. (For the thematic in the "heroick epistle," the genre of poetry that gestures repeatedly to Ovid's *Heroides*—themselves widely read and imitated by medieval writers in Latin—see Dörrie 1968.)

The goliards, Abelard, Heloise: for all their brilliance and, in a way, "modernity" of spirit, they represent but a minuscule fraction of the Latin literature of the Middle Ages. Their aesthetic belongs, no doubt, to medieval Latinity, but medieval Latinity is home to so many other aesthetics. In seeking a broader canon, one that to a certain degree corresponds with the breadth of medieval Latin, one would have to engage in the kind of project Hans-Robert Jauss argued for and that he called *Rezeptionsästhetik* (Jauss 1977 and 1994). Jauss's project asks us, as learned and historically minded readers, to meld our expectations with those we reconstruct for the original audience. (It is the reception historian who does that work of reconstruction.) Only a relatively small number of readers in any generation will attempt to follow this program, and any canon that would emerge would be a canon for a tiny minority.

The very question whether there could today be an aesthetically based canon of medieval Latin literature leads us, then, to an embarrassed realization. An aesthetic judgment shared (even implicitly) by a group presupposes a community of readers, even a reading history, of the sort one would be hard-pressed to point to in the case of medieval Latin literature more broadly. Of course, given the narrowing of serious reading of a whole set of texts that had been until a generation or so ago regularly studied by a fair proportion of students in high school and college or university, are even Homer and Vergil, Dante and Milton canonical today in any real sense? Perhaps only Shakespeare remains, not only as frequent school text but because, as a dramatist, he is (re)presented on stage and screen over and over again—by actors who are featured by the popular media. Perhaps it is they who guarantee Shakespeare's continued canonical status. Amy Heckerling, the writer and director of *Clueless* (1995), implies as much when she has her heroine draw her knowledge of *Hamlet* from the movies ("I think I know my Mel Gibson"). "That Polonius dude" indeed. *Clueless*, as a version of Jane Austen's *Emma*, stands itself as a commentary on the state of the canon.

I referred above to the splendors and miseries of the medieval Latin canon. The ultimate misery, then, is the central problematic involved in searching for a canon in a tradition that is not living today much less in a language that requires a significant investment of time to master. There are the few isolated texts with a following of one sort or another, but they in no way amount to a canon of medieval Latin literature, and certainly do not match up with any recognizable canon within medieval Latinity.

Toward a New Model, a New Mode

The very unruliness of medieval Latin literary history, the tangled nature of our crisscrossing paths as we have attempted to come at it, its "monstrosity" when we try to push it into expected categories and publish its canon, might do more than highlight the specious order or "ruliness" of more tractable literary domains. Its very resistance—if I could apply such a term to a literature and its history—could challenge us to see whether in those very aspects we could not discern new modes of determining a canon. Not of course that we should necessarily feel compelled to issue a list. This would be a very uncanonical canon, a canon at once sensitive to its oddity and preternaturally aware of its constructedness.

For example, instead of regarding the recurrent bleed-through of a constantly recurring classical (or classical and early Christian) auctorial canon as problematic interference, we could embrace it as a defining characteristic of the medieval Latin canon, a canon expressly built with medieval reception in mind. By "medieval reception" I mean here what was received in the Middle Ages, so that earlier texts that were read and admired become an integral part of the canon we consider and call medieval. One would first add to what has become the modern standard (i.e., restricted and limited) "classical" canon the many works students of the classics today hardly ever read but that medieval readers admired deeply. This canon would include Statius, giving both the *Thebaid* and the *Achilleid* their rightful place not as second-rank epics read only by specialist students of "Silver Latin" but as absolute essentials. This canon would admit the Latin Josephus and (pseudo-)Hegesippus, Solinus, and Valerius Maximus, and of course Macrobius and Martianus Capella as well as Dares, Dictys, and the *Ilias Latina*. The medieval classical canon would require some excisions. For example, we would not include Catullus or Propertius, Livy (except as excerpted), or Tacitus, and were we to read Apuleius, we would read just about everything else by or attributed to him but the *Metamorphoses* (better known to English readers as *The Golden Ass*, a translation of its alternative Latin title *Asinus Aureus*).

We would include rather than exclude Latin texts by writers who professed the Christian faith. Minucius Felix's *Octavius* is a fascinating crossover text, Christian polemic in the guise of a classical dialogue. And certainly one should include Augustine well beyond the *Confessiones*, one of the few Christian texts that regularly make the list of world masterpieces. One would be hard-pressed to name a Latin patristic text more influential through the Middle Ages than Gregory's *Moralia in Job*, yet exceedingly few students of Latin ever read it, and certainly they do not attend to it to a degree proportionate to its impact.

Likewise, it would be somewhat unusual—yet fully in line with the reception-oriented approach urged here—to include translations from other languages when cataloging the canonical works of this literature (or literary period). For Latin, as is often noted (Farrell 2001; Szpiech and Burman in this volume), is a language and literature of translation par excellence. It becomes authoritative not least by transmitting writings authoritative, in multiple fields, in Greek, Hebrew, and Arabic. Jerome's Vulgate (or selections thereof) is often read in medieval Latin classes, but most often as background; it needs to be appreciated as fully contemporary throughout the medieval period, with special attention to those portions chanted and heard repeatedly in liturgy, e.g, the Psalms. Hardly ever read except by specialists but deserving of acknowledgment is the Greek pseudo-Dionysius the Areopagite rendered into Latin. This was, again, a text widely read and studied in the medieval West, and immensely productive of thought throughout medieval Latinity. The same could be said of some of the Greek philosophers and their Arabic commentators in their Latin form. These translated works should not only be studied with respect to their sources or as part of a story of intellectual history but as characteristic Latin works as well.

One might intentionally seek out other rocky pathways into a new medieval Latin canon, here using the very *skandala* or stumbling-blocks as veritable stepping-stones. For example, one could privilege precisely those texts that straddle divides that so often prove discomfiting, whether it be the Latin/vernacular or written/oral, two binaries that themselves often align. Or one could seek to explore and exploit articulations that do not map easily onto our modern expectations, for example, the continuum of authorial functions as opposed to the author alone with his genius and imagination. The former might lead us into an exploration of medieval preaching, a world that remains, with very few exceptions, largely untrodden by most students of medieval Latinity. Bernard of Clairvaux's sermons on the Song of Songs (discussed in this volume briefly by Scanlon) appear on reading lists, but there are many dozens of other preachers one could draw upon, especially the more popular ones, like Bernardino of Siena. As a matter of principle one would not exclude from our purview but rather seek out those sermons that might well have been delivered in the vernacular (sometimes on the basis of a Latin script, sometimes on the basis of a script already in Italian, German, or any one of several other vernaculars). The latter would lead us to examine, and regard as particularly important, a host of texts that are, in most traditional systems of literary history and canonization, regarded as merely parasitic: glosses, commentaries, paraphrases, abbreviations, adaptations, and rewritings. (See Copeland elsewhere in this volume.)

One could easily go on adding to the list, and of course such a "canon" would become impossibly large, in flagrant violation of the trend in recent years of producing a top hundred or even the top ten titles. (Hirsch 1987 constitutes one prime example of the contemporary mania for lists.) Certainly, such extreme culling presents readers with more manageable reading projects, but once reading lists have been reduced to the minimum—with no expectation that students will ever read more than the minimum—the stakes to defend the little that remains rise.

In the closing pages of this essay I will take a different path. I want to offer the possibility of a radically different conceptual framework with which we might begin to rethink some of the "unruly" facets of medieval Latin, medieval Latin literary history, and the challenges of defining—and pre- and proscribing—a medieval Latin canon.

In 1975 the French philosopher Gilles Deleuze, in collaboration with the psychoanalyst Félix Guattari, published a slight book entitled *Kafka: Pour une littérature mineure* (Paris: Les éditions de Minuit). Since 1986, an English translation (Deleuze and Guattari 1986) has amplified the impact of their study in the anglophone world, although it is still not nearly so widely influential as other critical writings to emerge from the France of the '60s, '70s, and '80s.

On the one hand, it is almost as if the authors chose the subtitle—in English, "toward a minor literature"—intentionally to minimize their claims. On the other hand, their tone is quite bold. Over nine chapters—loosely related essays, or "movements" one might almost say (as of an orchestral suite)—they explicate Kafka in a mode that is at once meditative and analytic, tentative and decisive, reading passages from all his writings (letters and journals as well as published stories and novellas) and exemplifying by these means the very rhizomatic pattern of connections they argue Kafka himself presents in his writings.

"How can we enter into Kafka's work?" they begin. "This work is a rhizome, a burrow. The castle has multiple entrances whose rules of usage and whose locations aren't very well known" (1986, 3). One could almost imagine these words and the paragraph they introduce applied to medieval Latin as a language and as a literature. Of course, one could not maintain that medieval Latin literature is commensurate with and exactly comparable to an individual author, although the translator of their study into English, Dana Polan, would almost give one the license to such a project, writing "*Kafka* is really a pretext, no more, or less, than one of the many ways to enter into the field of history" (Deleuze and Guattari 1986, xxiii). At times, Deleuze and Guattari seem to be analyzing something beyond a mere author, the human being named Franz Kafka who lived from 1883 to 1924 in Prague. They write, "A Kafka-machine is...constituted by contents and expressions that have been formalized to diverse degrees by unformed materials that enter into it, and leave by passing through all possible states" (7; on the machine in Deleuze's thought, see also Réda Bensmaïa in op. cit., xv).

For the specific purpose of this essay on the problematics of a medieval Latin canon and medieval Latin literary history, I want to focus specifically on the idea of "minor literature" that Deleuze and Guattari reference in their subtitle and that constitutes the subject of their chapter 3, "What is a Minor Literature?" (16–27). Although the idea has its ultimate roots in Kafka's own expansive and suggestive diary entry on the literatures of smaller nations (December 25, 1911, a small part of which is quoted in Deleuze and Guattari 1986, 17), Deleuze and Guattari's elaboration of the idea of "minor literature" moves it away from an application to Czech or Yiddish literature and renders it even more helpful as a possible tool with which to think about medieval Latin, for a minor literature is nothing other than a revision, reordering, and—to employ one of their key terms—"deterritorialization" of a major literature.

Deleuze and Guattari's concept of minor literature has spawned some excellent work, at once critical responses to and thought experiments inspired by their Kafka study. More often these works have been by scholars addressing authors and literatures in the modern period (Renza 1984; Bensmaïa 1985; Kronfeld 1996), but one finds among their number at least one medievalist, Jane Chance, who explicitly draws on Deleuze and Guattari's concept in her recent book on medieval women writers (2007).

Some of the women about whom Chance writes are textually represented in Latin, others in vernacular languages, but there remains, it seems to me, an open invitation fully to consider medieval Latin as a "minor literature" in the sense Deleuze and Guattari mean the term. Deleuze and Guattari themselves refer to the continuation of Latin after the classical period (1986, 24), but only in passing. Neither is a scholar of Latin, whether classical or medieval, and, more to the point, the linguistic and literary history of Latin is not their focus. For that reason, the project I have in mind—and whose first steps I can do no more than suggest here—would have to begin with the specifics of a minor literature as Deleuze and Guattari define it.

According to Deleuze and Guattari, a minor literature has three essential characteristics. First and foremost, "[a] minor literature doesn't come from a minor language; it is rather that which a minority constructs within a major language" (1986, 16). One immediately thinks of the followers of Christ in the first few centuries of the common era as creating a "minor literature" in Greek (the evangelists, Paul, etc.) and in Latin (e.g., Minucius Felix, Tertullian, Clement translated into Latin). A bit further along, Deleuze and Guattari gloss this first characteristic as "the deterritorialization of language" (18). In Deleuze and Guattari's duolect (if I might), "deterritorialization" connotes more than abandoning a territory or claims to a territory. It also has overtones of stripping away (one's) identification altogether, of a general "untethering." When they speak of Kafka's linguistic choice as "opt[ing] for the German language of Prague as it is and in its very poverty" (19), one ineluctably thinks of the *sermo humilis* [lowly style] prized by Christians for its rhetorical poverty. Many other examples suggest themselves. For example, when they describe how, in the everyday spoken dialogue in Godard's films, "[t]here...is an accumulation of stereotypical adverbs and conjunctions that form the base of all the phrases—a strange poverty that makes French a minor language within French" (23), an author like Egeria comes to mind. The fourth-century Galician pilgrim is no Godard, but the end effect is strangely similar.

Remaining with the early Christian writing in Greek and Latin, one can certainly see them fulfilling "[t]he second characteristic of minor literatures": "that everything in them is political" (17), rephrased as "the connection of the individual to a political immediacy" (18). This can, it seems to me, apply long after Christianity has become the dominant religion and has long since vanquished any real pagan rivals. Precisely because of the perennial recurrence of the classical, its ever-present reechoing in the school curricula, just as the *Ecloga Theoduli* stages a debate between pagan falsehood (Pseustis) and Christian truth (Alithia)—and even imagines it as contemporary in the "life" of the author fantasized by the *accessus* described above—so the Christian is always the minority. Or so one might frame the argument before developing it in a larger version of this project.

"The third characteristic is that everything has a collective value" (17) sounds as if it would also readily apply to the writings of the nascent Christian community, but that is not the sense in which Deleuze and Guattari mean "collective value." Rather, they explicate this final criterion as follows:

> Indeed, precisely because talent isn't abundant in a minor literature, there are no possibilities for an individuated enunciation that would belong to this or that "master" and that could be separated from a collective enunciation. Indeed, scarcity of talents is in fact beneficial, and allows the conception of something other than a literature of masters: what each author says individually already constitutes a common action, and what he or she says or does is necessarily political, even if others aren't in agreement. The political domain has contaminated every statement (*énoncé*). But above all else, because collective or national consciousness is "often inactive in external life and always in the process of break-down," literature finds itself positively charged with the role and the function of collective, and even revolutionary enunciation. It is literature that produces an active solidarity in spite of skepticism; and, if the writer is in the margins or completely outside his or her fragile community, this situation allows the writer all the more possibility to express another possible community and to forge the means for another consciousness and another sensibility... (17, quoting words from the December 25, 1911, diary entry referenced above).

This third criterion is highly suggestive, and one would want to work out exactly what it might mean to think of the Latin of the Middle Ages as "something other than a literature of masters." At first blush, it seems contradictory. Medieval Latin depends on a canon of *auctores*. Yet among the challenges of mapping medieval Latin literary history and its canon we have noted that there is no new and complete set of medieval Latin *auctores* or masters. Medieval Latinity is a literary culture content to have inherited the great majority of its masters and, further, one that, while affording the role of *auctor* supremacy, understands literary culture as involving a much more collective sense of authoring, including all the other functions involved or implicated in the processes of copying, annotating, and commenting. And, if we were to follow this logic through to its unspoken conclusion, reading as well.

Stepping back from these three characteristics, one sees more broadly the advantages of such an approach: beyond merely accommodating as an oddity the fact that Latin, over the long run, is indubitably a very major world language with an inarguably major literature, understanding medieval Latin as a "minor literature" as Deleuze and Guattari define it depends on and demands that very fact.

There are additional suggestive parallels between medieval Latin and the German of Kafka's Prague, for Kafka was not only in a minority as a Jew (with the formation of his own literary culture involving both Hebrew and Yiddish). In the context of rising Czech nationalism, he belongs to the Germanophone minority as well. In this context, it will be worth examining a bit more closely the remarks Deleuze and Guattari attach to the enunciation of the first criterion, that "a minor literature doesn't come from a minor language; it is rather that which a minority constructs within a major language." They explain:

> the first characteristic of minor literature...is that in it language is affected with a high coefficient of deterritorialization. In this sense, Kafka marks the impasse that bars access to writing for the Jews of Prague and turns their literature into something impossible—the impossibility of not writing, the impossibility of writing in German, the impossibility of writing otherwise. The impossibility of not writing because national consciousness, uncertain or oppressed, necessarily exists by means of literature...The impossibility of writing other than in German is for the Prague Jews the feeling of an irreducible distance from their primitive Czech territoriality. And the impossibility of writing in German is the deterritorialization of the German population itself, an oppressive minority that speaks a language cut off from the masses, like a "paper language" or an artificial language; this is all the more true for the Jews who are simultaneously a part of this minority and excluded from it...In short, Prague German is a deterritorialized language, appropriate for strange and minor uses...(16–17).

Leaving aside exactly what Deleuze and Guattari might mean by "strange" (and, throughout, they show no fear of making provocative asides, intended or unintended), it may be productive to think of Latin itself in the Middle Ages as ever more deterritorialized. Recall that for Deleuze and Guattari, this connotes more than a language without a territory: this is a language becoming untethered, alienated—even exiled—from its own identity, hollowed out. The value of this insight is not merely to provide a new and potentially productive framework for rethinking and rewriting medieval Latin literary history and its odd relation to the possibility of its own canon. It turns on its head the very canonicity Latin has regularly claimed for itself, indeed, as its very own alone. In the incisive words of Joseph Farrell,

> Latin culture tends to imagine itself and its language as universal and powerful beyond all competitors. It constructs an image of the Latin language as possessing similar qualities, along with definite canons of correctness conferring a stability

that other languages lack. Though the language does change, these canons remain, and the history of Latinity is marked by various "renascences" during which the language is "reformed" on ancient, "classical models" (2001, 5).

Even the major can modulate into the minor, including a major language and major literature. And as my own modulation into musical metaphorics suggests, the minor can have a relationship to the major very different from mere subordination. The major implies the minor, and vice versa. There would be no sense in which major is major without there being a minor. There is no value differentiation, no better or worse, not even—most shockingly—a temporality in this dialogic binary. These are dimensions that seem attractive and appropriate for any further meditations on medieval Latin, its scandalous literary history, and its disconcerting, discomfiting relationship with canonicity.

SUGGESTIONS FOR FURTHER READING

The canonical histories of medieval Latin literature have been in German, Manitius (1911–31), to be replaced some generations later by Brunhölzl (1975–2009), of which the second volume—after a seventeen-year gap—reached only the end of the eleventh century. D'Angelo (2009) is a recent overview, explicitly from the perspective of genres. It is hard to suggest a complete overview in English. Meanwhile, certain regions have received outstanding treatment; exemplary are the three volumes that offer accounts of Anglo-Latin Literature: Lapidge (1995 and 1993) and Rigg (1992) (to order them according to the periods of Latin literature in England they cover). For many years, for poetry, one consulted Raby (1953 and 1957); these still stand as models of literary histories that successfully track strands within the larger field of medieval Latin.

The problematics of literary history in general are well summarized in Perkins (1992); for medieval Latin, see Ziolkowski (1996) and Hexter (2005). On "nation" itself as construct, classic is Anderson (2006, first ed. 1983).

Perhaps the best study by a literary critic of the issues involved in the canon is Guillory (1993), though his focus is decidedly on neither Latin nor the Middle Ages. A range of perspectives and examples are offered in Assmann (1987). On the list of school curricular authors, Glauche (1970) is still valuable.

BIBLIOGRAPHY

Primary sources

Accessus ad auctores. 1970. *Accessus ad auctores, Bernard d'Utrecht. Dialogus super auctores, Conrad d'Hirsau*, edited by Robert B. C. Huygens. Leiden: E. J. Brill.

Antiovidianus. 1929. "Antiovidianus," edited by Richard Kienast. In *Aus Petrarcas ältestem deutschen Schülerkreise*, edited by Konrad Burdach, 81–111. Berlin: Weidmann.

Theodulus. 1997. *Teodulo, Ecloga: Il Canto della verità e della menzogna*, edited and translated by Francesco Mosetti Casaretto. Florence: SISMEL, Edizioni del Galluzzo.

Jerome. 1996. *Sancti Eusebii Hieronymi Epistulae*, edited by Isidorus Hilberg. 2nd ed. Vienna: Verlag der Österreichischen Akademie der Wissenschaften.

———, trans. 1983. *Biblia Sacra iuxta Vulgatam Versionem*, edited by Robert Weber and Bonifatius Fischer. 3rd ed. Stuttgart: Deutsche Bibelgesellschaft.

Secondary sources

Althusser, Louis. 1970. "Ideology and Ideological State Apparatuses (Notes towards an Investigation)." in *Lenin and Philosophy and Other Essays*, translated by Ben Brewster, 121–76. Modern Reader 213. New York, London: Monthly Review Press.

Anderson, Benedict. 2006. *Imagined Communities: Reflections on the Origin and Spread of Nationalism*. Rev. ed. New York: Verso.

Assmann, Aleida and Jan, eds. 1987. *Kanon und Zensur*. Archäologie der literarischen Kommunication 2. Munich: Wilhelm Fink

Bayless, Martha. 1996. *Parody in the Middle Ages: the Latin Tradition*. Recentiores. Ann Arbor, MI: University of Michigan Press.

Bensmaïa, Réda. 1984. "Traduire ou 'blanchir' la langue: *Amour Bilingue* d'Abdelkebir Khatibi." *Hors Cadre* 3: 187–206.

Bernt, Günter. 1968. *Das lateinische Epigramm im Übergang von der Spätantike zum frühen Mittelalter*. Münchener Beiträge zur Mediävistik und Renaissance-Forschung 2. Munich: Arbeo-Gesellschaft.

Bloch, R. Howard and Stephen G. Nichols. 1995. *Medievalism and the Modernist Temper*. Baltimore, London: Johns Hopkins University Press.

Brunhölzl, Franz. 1975–2009. *Geschichte der lateinischen Literatur des Mittelalters*. 3 vols. Munich: Fink.

Calin, William. 1999. "Making a Canon." *Philosophy and Literature* 23: 1–16.

Chance, Jane. 2007. *The Literary Subversions of Medieval Women*. New Middle Ages. New York: Palgrave Macmillan.

D'Angelo, Edoardo. 2009. *La letteratura Latina medievale. Una storia per generi*. Libri di Viella 95. Rome: Viella.

Deleuze, Gilles and Guattari, Félix. 1986. *Kafka. Toward a Minor Literature*, translated by Dana Polan. Theory and History of Literature 30. Minneapolis, MN: University of Minnesota Press.

Dörrie, Heinrich. 1968. *Der heroische Brief. Bestandsaufnahme, Geschichte, Kritik einer humanistisch-barocken Literaturgattung*. Berlin: De Gruyter.

Eckhardt, Caroline D. 2006. "Old, Fields, New Corn, and Present Ways of Writing about the Past." In *Comparative Literature in an Age of Globalization*, edited by Haun Saussy, 139–54. Baltimore: Johns Hopkins University Press.

Farrell, Joseph. 2001. *Latin Language and Latin Culture: from ancient to modern times*. Roman Literature and its Contexts. Cambridge: Cambridge University Press.

Fugelso, Karl, ed. 2009. *Defining Medievalism(s)*. Studies in Medievalism 17. Cambridge, Rochester, NY: D. S. Brewer.

Glauche, Günter. 1970. *Schullektüre im Mittelalter. Entstehung und Wandlung des Lektürekanons bis 1200 nach den Quellen dargestellt*. Münchener Beiträge zur Mediävistik und Renaissance-Forschung 5. Munich: Arbeo-Gesellschaft.

Godman, Peter. 1987. *Poets and Emperors: Frankish Politics and Carolingian Poetry*. Oxford: Clarendon Press.

Green, R. P. H. 1982. "The Genesis of a Medieval Textbook: The Models and Sources of the *Ecloga Theoduli*." *Viator* 13: 49–106.

Guillory, John. 1993. *Cultural Capital. The Problem of Literary Canon Formation*. Chicago: University of Chicago Press.

Herren, Michael. 2007. "Reflections on the Meaning of the *Ecloga Theoduli*: Where is the Author's Voice." In *Poetry and Exegesis in Premodern Latin Christianity: The Encounter between Classical and Christian Strategies of Interpretation*, edited by Willemien Otten and Karla Pollmann, 199–230. Supplements to Vigiliae Christianae 87. Leiden, Boston: Brill.

Hexter, Ralph J. 1987. "Medieval Latin: Horizons and Perspectives." In *Latinitas: The Tradition and Teaching of Latin = Helios* 14: 69–92.

———. 2005. "From the medieval historiography of Latin literature to the historiography of medieval Latin literature." *Journal of Medieval Latin* 15: 1–24.

Hirsch, Eric D. 1987. *Cultural Literacy: What Every American Needs to Know*. Boston: Houghton Mifflin.

Hult, David. 2003. "The *Roman de la Rose*, Christine de Pizan, and the *querelle des femmes*." In *The Cambridge Companion to Medieval Women's Writing*, edited by Carolyn Dinshaw and David Wallace, 184–94. Cambridge Companions to Literature. Cambridge, New York: Cambridge University Press.

Janson, Tore. 2004. *A Natural History of Latin*, translated by Merethe Darnsgård Sørensen and Nigel Vincent. Oxford: Oxford University Press.

Jauss, Hans Robert. 1977. *Ästhetische Erfahrung und literarische Hermeneutik*. Uni-Taschenbücher 692. Munich: W. Fink.

———. 1994. "Rezeptionsgeschichte als Provokation der Literaturgeschichte." In *Rezeptionsästhetik: Theorie und Praxis*, edited by Rainer Warning, 126–62. Uni-Taschenbücher 303. 4th ed. Munich: W. Fink.

Kindermann, Udo. 1978. *Satyra: die Theorie der Satire im Mittellateinischen. Vorstudie zu einer Gattungsgeschichte*. Erlanger Beiträge zur Sprach- und Kunstwissenschaft 58. Nürnberg: Hans Carl.

Kronfeld, Chana. 1996. *On the Margins of Modernism. Decentering Literary Dynamics*. Contraversions: Critical Studies in Jewish Literature, Culture, and Society 2. Berkeley, CA: University of California Press.

Lapidge, Michael. 1993. *Anglo-Latin Literature, 900–1066*. London, Rio Grande, OH: Hambledon Press.

———. 1995. *Anglo-Latin Literature, 600–899*. London, Rio Grande, OH: Hambledon Press.

Latham, Ronald E. 1965. *Revised Medieval Latin Word-List from British and Irish Sources*. London: British Academy and Oxford University Press.

Lehmann, Paul. 1963. *Die Parodie im Mittelalter*. 2nd ed. Stuttgart: A. Hiersemann.

Manitius, Max. 1911–31. *Geschichte der lateinischen Literatur des Mittelalters*. 3 vols. Handbuch der Altertumswissenschaft. 9. Abt., 2. T., 1–3. Munich: Beck.

Metzger, Bruce. 1987. *The Canon Of The New Testament: Its Origin, Development, and Significance*. Oxford: Clarendon Press.

Moog-Grünewald, Maria, ed. 1997. *Kanon und Theorie*. Neues Forum für allgemeine und vergleichende Literaturwissenschaft 3. Heidelberg: Winter.

Niermeyer, Jan Frederik. 2002. *Mediae Latinitatis lexicon minus/ Lexique latin medieval/ Medieval Latin Dictionary/ Mittellateinisches Wörterbuch*, edited by Jan F. Niermeyer and Co van de Kieft, revised by Johannes W. J. Burgers. Leiden, Boston: Brill.

Renza, Louis A. 1984. *"A White Heron" and the Question of Minor Literature*. The Wisconsin Project on American Writers. Madison, WI: University of Wisconsin Press.

Rigg, Arthur G. 1992. *A History of Anglo-Latin Literature, 1066–1422.* Cambridge, New York: Cambridge University Press.

Perkins, David. 1992. *Is Literary History Possible?* Baltimore: Johns Hopkins University Press.

Raby, Frederic J. E. 1953. *A History of Christian-Latin Poetry from the Beginnings to the Close of the Middle Ages.* 2nd ed. Oxford: Clarendon Press.

———. 1957. *A History of Secular Latin poetry in the Middle Ages.* 2 vols. 2nd ed. Oxford: Clarendon Press.

Salzburger Symposion. 1979–. *Mittelalter-Rezeption/ The Year's Work in Medievalism.* Göppinger Arbeiten zur Germanistik. Göppingen: Kümmerle.

Scarborough, William Sanders. 2005. *The Autobiography of William Sanders Scarborough,* edited by Michele Valerie Ronnick. African American Life Series. Detroit, MI: Wayne State University Press.

Scholes, Robert. 1992. "Canonicity and Textuality." In *Introduction to Scholarship in Modern Languages,* edited by Joseph Gibaldi, 138–58. 2nd ed. New York: Modern Language Association of America.

Selden, Daniel. 1998. "Aithiopika and 'Ethiopianism.'" In *Studies in Heliodorus,* edited by Richard L. Hunter, 182–217. Cambridge Philological Society. Supplementary Volume 21. Cambridge: Cambridge Philological Society.

Shanzer, Danuta. 2009. "Literature, History, Periodization, and the Pleasures of the Latin Literary History of Late Antiquity." *History Compass* 7: 917-54.

Stotz, Peter. 1996–2004. *Handbuch zur lateinischen Sprache des Mittelalters.* 5 vols. Handbuch der Altertumswissenschaft, 2. Abt., 5. T., 1–5. Munich: Beck.

Winko, Simone. 2002. "Literatur-Kanon als invisible hand-Phänomen." In *Literarische Kanonbildung,* edited by Heinz Ludwig Arnold. Text + Kritik. Sonderband. Munich: Edition Text + Kritik.

Ziolkowski, Jan M. 1996. "Towards a History of Medieval Latin Literature." In *Medieval Latin. An Introduction and Bibliographical Guide,* edited by Frank A. C. Mantello and Arthur G. Rigg, 505–36. Washington, DC: Catholic University of America.

PART II

LATINITY AS CULTURAL CAPITAL

CHAPTER 3

LATIN AS AN ACQUIRED LANGUAGE

CARIN RUFF

A Language at Arm's Length

To speak of acquiring a language—beyond first- or native-language acquisition in early childhood—presumes that that language is not already owned—that the target of acquisition is, in some sense at least, at a distance from the learner. That distance may be one of register, dialect, or linguistic background; it may result from a temporal, geographical, or cultural separation from the language in question. In the case of Latin, the characteristically medieval situation of language acquisition comes about at the point where we can say that all of Europe stands at a sufficient temporal, geographic, and cultural remove from Latin that anyone who wishes to use the language must acquire it through study. The modes of acquisition of Latin taken over by teachers and learners in the Middle Ages—the grammars of late antiquity—had developed in an environment in which it was still possible to have Latin as a native tongue or to acquire it by osmosis, by living in a Latin-speaking milieu. Formal language instruction in that period had been to a large extent a matter of artificial distancing. Native speakers had to be taught to stand back from the language they knew unconsciously, to apply an analytical vocabulary to it (grammar), and to make an informed choice about the use of its available registers (rhetoric). As Europe's distance from the spoken Latin of antiquity grew, the language-acquisition methodologies of antiquity were retained, but were turned to the new purpose of teaching Latin as a second language—and primarily a text language, not a spoken one.

This distancing from Latin can be detected in the attitudes of compilers and commentators who mediated the grammatical literature of antiquity to medieval audiences. They stand back from Latin, the target language, and contemplate the rationales behind how Latin is used as a descriptive language about itself. Latin mediates Latin—it becomes its own metalanguage.

Just when and in what places Latin grows distant enough from its would-be users to become a something that has to be acquired as a foreign language is a matter of contention. The question plays out differently in different places. In non-Romance-speaking countries newly converted to Christianity (the Celtic- and Germanic-speaking realms), Latin was obviously foreign, and the question is how far the modes of acquisition current in antiquity would serve these new populations. Was there a time when they had access to native speakers in a way that would have made acquisition by aural-oral immersion possible? If so, when did that moment pass? In the absence of native speaker informants or teachers, was it really possible to create an environment for oral learning that was comparable to what would have been available when it was still possible to go and live among native speakers? And, to the extent that it was necessary to learn Latin mainly through books, were those books adequate to the task, and can we tell how they might have been supplemented?

For populations who spoke languages that had developed or were developing out of the Latin of antiquity, the transition from Latin-as-native-language to Latin-as-acquired-language is masked by the nature of the textual evidence. In the fifth, sixth, and seventh centuries, literary Latin continued to be practiced in the former Roman Empire in an increasing variety of styles, genres, and registers, with varying degrees of what an ancient or modern educated person would recognize as "correctness." Interpreting the linguistic situation that underlies that textual corpus requires a subtle and inevitably controversial reading between the lines. Late Latin can be made to yield evidence of emerging Romance vernacular traits, or the persistence of pre-Classical or Vulgar Latin features; it can be collated with anecdotal evidence about who could understand whom at meetings, in commerce, at court, or in church (Banniard 1992; Derolez 1992). It would be extremely helpful if one could turn to the textbooks used to teach Latin in this period for evidence of the transition to foreign-language teaching, but grammars are the most conservative genre of all. The grammars of late antiquity were taken over as teaching tools by the masters of the early Middle Ages in the first instance with remarkably little change, and it is not until the eighth century in the Insular world that significant adaptations and additions were made to the inherited body of grammatical treatises to fit them for use by foreign-language learners (Law 1982). Change to accommodate the growing distance of late-Latin-speaking learners from the literary form of their language was incremental and took place mainly outside the canon of the *ars grammatica* proper.

GRAMMARS AS TOOLS OF CRITICAL DISTANCING

The grammars veil the situation of their changing audiences because they never addressed directly what the students (or teachers) who used them knew or didn't know. To a modern reader trying to imaginatively inhabit the learning experience of the medieval student, late-antique Latin grammars seem at once too close to their subject and too distant: too close, because they use the target language as the language of instruction, and too far because their subject matter has more to do with abstract categories than with specifics of accidence or practicalities of communication. (There is evidence that medieval readers were frustrated by that abstracting distance, too; see the discussion of metalanguage below.) The Latin grammars that medieval teachers and students used in their project of acquiring Latin were originally written to induce in native speakers a conscious awareness of analytical categories for describing their own language. (There is one important exception: the works of Priscian, who wrote for Greek-speakers in early sixth-century Byzantium who needed to learn Latin in order to work in the imperial civil service. Priscian's students, however, not only had access to Latin-speakers, they were already literate in their own language and thus familiar with the grammatical terminology of Greek, on which the description of Latin grammar was and is based. Their situation is thus not strictly comparable to that of Latin-speaking schoolboys acquiring elementary literacy, but it is farther still from Celtic- or Germanic-speakers who came both to Latin and to literacy as complete novices.)

The grammarians' grammarian for the medieval curriculum, Donatus (Holtz 1981), famously does not offer much that would be intelligible without interpretation to an absolute beginner in Latin. The language of instruction in Donatus's grammars is Latin, and his emphasis is on the presentation of analytical categories for talking about grammar, not on conveying the grammar of the language itself. He defines the smallest combinatory elements of language (sounds, letters, syllables); the eight parts of speech; and, in the larger of his two grammars, elementary rhetorical figures. This type of instruction derives from the place of grammar in the ancient curriculum, where grammar was preparatory to the study of rhetoric and was focused on providing students a common vocabulary for literary analysis. Linguistic categories and rhetorical figures could be used to explain why the poets had made the choices they had, how their figurative language worked, and what choices were available to the rhetor in his own compositions. Donatus exemplifies Latin words and forms only to the extent that he uses them to explain his grammatical terminology—that is, he gives just enough examples to support his taxonomy of grammatical categories, but does not systematically lay out the inflectional system of Latin or explain its syntax.

The categories Donatus and similar grammars treat are also sufficient to allow teachers to discuss with students the "correct" use of the literary language. It is hardly surprising that late antiquity saw a boom in Latin grammar-writing (Kaster 1988). This was the period when there were unquestionably thriving communities of Latin-speakers, but when the spoken language of even the educated classes in these communities would have begun to diverge noticeably from the literary language of antiquity. Grammar teaching in the late-antique Latin-speaking world, therefore, would have been very much analogous to formal instruction in grammar and literary analysis for modern English speakers, who are enabled both to conform to a written standard and to read and analyze literary texts dating back as much as four or five centuries. As with English, the conservatism of the written language would have allowed the speaker of Late Latin access to several centuries of literary Latin with only a fairly basic analytical toolkit and a certain amount of practice. As with English, too, some students and some communities would have a greater distance to travel between their spoken vernacular and the literary language they were expected to master. For a Romance-speaker, learning what we would call Latin—becoming literate in Latin—was thus analogous to a modern French- or English-speaker learning the rules of the formal, written form of his or her language. The student had to learn that crucial grammatical information was contained in morphemes that were not distinguished or not pronounced at all in everyday speech, and that spelling those morphemes correctly mattered. (Compare the great repertoire of homophonous or silent final letters and syllables in French, or the endless struggles over the apostrophe in English.) For Romance-speaking students being taught that kind of mastery over the written form of their language, the doctrine of the grammars of antiquity was a good fit: it provided teachers and students a metalanguage with which to discuss the standards of the written form of the language, and its emphasis on the units that make up words would have provided an intellectual framework for understanding what was not pronounced but still needed to be written.

Latin-Speakers Acquiring Latin

The extent of the distance between spoken and written forms of the language has been a topic of controversy among scholars of the development of the Romance languages and of Latin literacy. The question at stake is when, precisely, the spoken language in Latin-speaking areas diverged so far from the Latin of antiquity that we would no longer call it Latin. The implication for our purposes is that, at that point, whenever it came, learning Latin would have become more like acquiring a foreign language and less like mastering the educated or literary register of one's native language. The time when Latin "turned into" Romance is exceedingly difficult to pinpoint, because the answer depends on how one poses the question. The written record as far back as the lifetime of Cicero, or even earlier, preserves features that seem to anticipate the Romance languages as they eventually emerged. Conversely, signs of the persistence of the Classical language can be found well beyond the point where other evidence confirms that Romance vernaculars were being spoken.

The debate has been reframed for our time by Michel Banniard (1992) and Roger Wright (1982 and 2002). Banniard is primarily interested in the question of whether educated registers and the vernacular were mutually intelligible in the late-antique Latin-using world. His concern is with the realities of communication, and he argues that oral performance effectively bridged the gap between registers that would have been quite foreign to one another if encountered only in writing. Wright is more interested in the *awareness* of linguistic difference among users of various registers and dialects of Late Latin. He asks at what point speakers of Latin/Romance vernaculars came to see Latin as something apart from their native tongue. Wright and Banniard agree in locating the emergence of this diglossia, a consciousness of the presence of two separate languages operating in the culture, in the eighth century. For Banniard, the separation of Latin from Romance gathered speed in the Merovingian period. Wright pinpoints the moment of distinction more sharply, arguing that the Latin-vernacular disjunction was first crystallized for Romance-speakers around the year 800 as a result of the intervention of Alcuin. Alcuin, an Anglo-Saxon who had learned Latin from books and as a completely foreign language, came to the Continent to work for Charlemagne and was appalled by the way he heard Latin being pronounced by the Romance-speakers around him. (On this, Wright and Banniard agree.) The reform of pronunciation he initiated, which was crucial to the Carolingian program of standardizing the text and performance of the liturgy, specified the foreign-language learner's approach to reading Latin: every written letter was to be given a sound, and all grammatical distinctions present in the written language were to be clearly distinguishable in spelling and in oral performance.

For Wright, in Romance-speaking areas before the Carolingian educational reforms, Latin was merely the written register of the vernacular. In Wright's model, there was no need to call the various spoken and written forms of the language of Romance communities by different names. They were all Latin to their users. The situation in terms of *consciousness* of language difference was thus substantially similar to that of Latin-speaking communities in antiquity, except that linguistic evolution and the attenuation of the ancient educational system had widened the gap between the spoken and the written language. Incompleteness of education and the widening gap explain the distressing features to be seen in, for example, the Latin of Merovingian Gaul. For Wright, this non-normative Latin is not the result of foreign-language learners of Latin who have incompletely mastered the target language; rather, it is the result of native speakers of Latin who have not completely mastered the standard written form of their language. Moreover, interference from the spoken language is more likely to appear in the written language than is the case with foreign-language learners, precisely because Latin-users in Romance areas did not make a conceptual distinction between the language they spoke and the language they wrote. It would have been meaningless to tell them that some feature of their spoken language which was discouraged in the written standard was "not Latin"—it was all Latin.

The Foreign-Language Learner's Experience

Any appraisal of the Latin-acquisition process for communities that encountered Latin afresh with conversion to Christianity is to some extent complicated by the issues just mentioned. Take the Anglo-Saxons as an example, since their experience is critical to Wright's thesis about Alcuin. The distance between Old English and Latin is undisputed: they had almost no vocabulary in common, and while both are inflected languages, the inflectional systems and syntax are not such as to allow a speaker of one language to fake it in the other without immersion or instruction. The situation for speakers of Old Irish, who contributed their own expertise to the Anglo-Saxon acquisition of Latin, is even starker. We would want to know, to begin with, whether these new Celtic- or Germanic-speaking users of Latin would have had any meaningful opportunity to learn the language by oral immersion, from direct contact with native speakers or speakers possessing native fluency. Contemporary anecdotal evidence is colored by the ambiguities of what "Latin" meant on the Continent in the period when the Insular world was first coming to grips with the written form of Latin.

Latin was introduced into Ireland in the fifth century via Britain, where Latin was one among several spoken languages in a multilingual, multicultural context. There was never a sufficient population of native- or near-native Romano-British speakers of Latin in Ireland, however, to create a situation there that approximated that of any area that had been a Roman province. (For the truly multilingual situation of the Roman provinces, see Adams 2003.) By the time the Anglo-Saxons were grappling with Latin, Ireland seems to have cultivated a local tradition of writing Latin that was in many ways distinct from the Latin practiced in Latin/Romance-speaking areas of the same period. The Anglo-Saxons were converted by missionaries from Rome, whose Latin would presumably have been much like that of Cassiodorus—fluent, close enough to the traditional literary standard to make the oral-written switching relatively unproblematic, but far enough already that manuals of usage would come in handy. As with Ireland, however, a few missionaries do not effect the same sort of linguistic transfer as an army or a significant population of colonists. By the latter seventh century, three or four generations after the initial Roman mission to England, when both England and Ireland begin to produce significant amounts of written Latin, we are still talking about occasional Latin-speaking visitors rather than the importation of whole Latin-speaking communities. And as we approach the turn of the eighth century, we are well within the period in dispute by Wright and his critics, where the Latinity even of visitors from the Mediterranean is difficult to assess. Bede, who entered Monkwearmouth-Jarrow as a boy and may have been trained in Roman chant by John the Archcantor (Bede, *Historia ecclesiastica* 4.18 and *Historia abbatum* 6), would have come as close as any of his compatriots to learning the language orally from a native speaker. The students of Theodore and Hadrian's school at Canterbury described by Bede (*Historia ecclesiastica* 4.1, 5.23) as speaking Latin and Greek with native fluency probably also came close to this experience, in that they were exposed to teachers from the truly bilingual (Greek and Latin) culture of the eastern Mediterranean. Theodore came from Tarsus in the Greek-speaking eastern Mediterranean, studied in Antioch, and probably lived in a Greek-speaking community at Rome before coming to England late in life; Hadrian was most likely from Greek-speaking Libya and spent most of his career in Naples. But Aldhelm, the only product of this school whose own work survives, did not benefit from Theodore and Hadrian's school at Canterbury until he was an adult; his highly accomplished Latinity cannot be attributed to early oral immersion. Beyond these first two generations of Anglo-Latin studies, it becomes increasingly unlikely that Anglo-Saxons would have learned Latin from anyone—whether English, Irish, or other—who had not learned Latin in school.

Absent a significant Latin-speaking community to effect oral immersion, was there anything in the pedagogy of Latin in England and Ireland in the early Middle Ages to substitute for that experience? One possibility is the liturgy. For monastic students, especially those who entered religious life as children, memorizing and singing the Psalter began before or simultaneously with formal Latin instruction, and occupied significantly more of the student's time. Vivien Law suggested that this practice exposed learners to the aural shapes of Latin words, and thus provided a framework for and adjunct to formal grammar instruction (Law 1997, 129). We can go further: such a vast store of internalized Latin would have equipped students with an analogue to the native speaker's store of language, onto which the lens of grammar could then be turned. That is not to claim that a student who had the Psalter by heart but scarcely understood it *knew* Latin in anything like the way that native Latin speakers knew their mother tongue. Rather, the analogy merely helps explain how the grammars of antiquity could continue to function for an audience of foreign-language learners.

If the process of formally acquiring Latin as a written language meant turning the lens of grammar on a body of already incorporated but yet unanalyzed linguistic material, for foreign-language learners that process was complicated by the fact that grammar itself came packaged in Latin. Since Donatus's *Ars minor* was memorized as the very first step in formal Latin instruction, the structure of Donatus's text and the analytical categories it imposes were imprinted on the learner's mind even before very much of the language itself was known. Learning what Donatus was saying and learning what he was saying about Latin thus proceeded simultaneously. It is hardly surprising that "Donatus" and "grammar" and "Latin" were sometimes used interchangeably.

This leads to a recursive process in which the Latin-about-Latin in the grammars needs to become the object of the analysis that the grammars teach. Early medieval teachers of Latin as a foreign language eagerly took up that recursive imperative. Grammar, the tool for the exegesis of the poets in antiquity and for scriptural exegesis in the Middle Ages, itself became the object of exegesis. The *primae-inter-pares* status of Donatus's grammars made them a particular target for this kind of explication. Vivien Law (1981, 81) distinguishes two fundamental types of text among early Insular grammars of Latin: "elementary" grammars, texts on the model of Donatus's *artes*, which are elementary both in the sense of "basic" and in treating the elements of language; and "exegetical" grammars, those that take the form of a continuous commentary on Donatus.

Latin as Its Own Metalanguage

The special authority of Donatus is apparent in the exegetical grammar from an Irish-influenced milieu in Northumbria around the year 700 that goes under the name Anonymus ad Cuimnanum (1992, 18):

> Cuius auctoritatem ostendit Pompeius dicendo: Alii, inquid, scripserunt artem, sed illos non putes intellegere, nisi a Donato sumpserint principium.
>
> [Pompeius [another grammarian] shows Donatus's authority when he says: "Others have written grammars, but you would not imagine you could understand them if they had not started with Donatus."]

The Anonymus's method is, from one perspective, a practical response to the problem of an elementary grammar written in the target language. The commentator mines Donatus's text for every scrap of information about Latin. Beginning with the four-word sentence that opens the *Ars maior*, he delves into the hardest word, *oratio*:

> PARTES ORATIONIS SVNT OCTO. Oratio, id est eloquutio, et dicta oratio quasi oris ratio, et dictio est cum intuitu dicentis ad clausulam tendens.
>
> [THERE ARE EIGHT PARTS OF SPEECH. *Oratio*, that is speech, and it is called *oratio* as if from *oris ratio* [the mouth's reason], and it is a statement tending with the view of the speaker towards the end of the statement.]

The term *oratio* is explained with a synonym, an etymology (useful for mnemonic purposes), and a definition. Then we move on to the word "eight":

> Octo utrum perfectus an inperfectus uel plusquamperfectus est numerus, et in qua est forma, utrum origo an deductiuum est? Octo inperfectus est numerus, quod minus quam est ad se peruenit, quia demedia pars IIII, quarta II, octaua I, qui ad se iuncti non VIII, sed VII.
>
> [Is eight a perfect or imperfect or more than perfect number? What is its derivational status: is it an original or derived form? It is an imperfect number, because its factors add up to less than itself, since half of eight is four; a quarter is two, an eighth is one, and those added up do not make eight, but seven.]

What else do we know about nouns like "eight"?

> ... In forma aptoti est, ut sunt nomina numerorum et nomena literarum...
>
> [... It is in the form of an indeclinable, as are the names of numbers and letters...]

So far, the Anonymus is treating Donatus's grammar like a reader or an encyclopedia, but not engaging with the grammatical doctrine it contains. But the subject of "eight" leads, as it almost always does in grammatical commentaries, to the need to reconcile authorities:

> ...Ideo octo dicit, nam alii X, alii XI, Stoici autem V dicunt, alii duas, alii VIIII. Harum diuersitatum reddenda ratio est.

> X qui dicunt, articulum et gerendi uerba adieciunt. Qui XI, usurpantia adiciunt. Qui V, nomen et pronomen iungunt, uerbum et participium, aduerbium et interiectionem. Qui VIIII, articulum a pronomine seiungunt. Qui duas dicunt, ut est Aristotilis, nomen tantum et uerbum; nam aliae VI uelut apendices in duabus principalibus iunctae conuinciuntur.
> Donatus autem octo definit.
>
> [So he says (there are) eight (parts of speech), for some say ten, some eleven, but the Stoics say five, others say two, and still others say nine. We have to give a reason for these discrepancies.
> Those who say ten add the article and verbal nouns. Those who say eleven add the gerund as a separate category. Those who say five combine the noun with the pronoun, the verb with the participle. Those who say nine separate the article from the pronoun. Those who say two, like Aristotle, have the noun and verb alone; for the other six are joined like appendices in those two principal parts.
> But Donatus says eight.] (18-19)

Donatus wins. But the discussion is still about why Donatus structured his categories the way he did, rather than about what one does with those categories when reading or producing Latin. One has the sense that the grammatical text is simultaneously opaque, deflecting attention again and again from the target language that it is ostensibly about, and attractive, exerting a gravitational force on the exegetical energies of those who read it.

The need to make sense of why Donatus said what he said the way he said it does not go away as the grammatical culture of Celtic and Germanic Europe matures. In the ninth century, Sedulius Scottus, one of the expatriate Irishmen at the very forefront of later Carolingian intellectual developments, also wrote a Donatus commentary. The terms of the inquiry into Donatus's methods have shifted somewhat. As a result of the introduction of dialectic into the curriculum, commentators are more interested in the internal logical consistency of the authoritative text and why definitions are constructed the way they are. Still, the general tenor remains very similar to earlier commentaries like the Anonymus ad Cuimnanum. Here is Sedulius's discussion of the treatment of indeclinables in the *Ars maior*:

> SUNT PRAETER HAEC APTOTA, QUAE NEQUE PER CASUS NEQUE PER NUMEROS DECLINANTUR, UT FRUGI NIHILI NEQUAM FAS NEFAS NUGAS. Aptota dicuntur sine casu, id est incasualia, quae non declinantur. FRUGI, parcus; NIHILI, inutilis, nullius utilitatis; NEQUAM, quasi nequiquam; NEFAS, illicitum. Sed quaeritur cur Donatus, cum in substantiali definitione nominis dixerit: NOMEN EST PARS ORATIONIS CUM CASU, et difficile sit nomen reperiri sine casu quoniam omnem casum necesse est ostendere, cur in hoc loco ait aptotam esse, id est sine casu. Videtur enim in suis sibi contrarius esse verbis. Omne namque quod casu caret, nomen dici non valet. Sed animadvertendum, ut Donatus vera et non sibi contraria dixisse probetur, aptota nomina habere nominativum qui non proprie, sicut superious diximus, sed abusive, casus nuncupatur. Unde etiam, quia non cadit, rectus et stabilis appellatur.
>
> [BESIDES THESE, THERE ARE *APTOTA*, WHICH ARE DECLINED NEITHER BY CASE NOR BY NUMBER, AS FOR EXAMPLE *FRUGI, NIHILI, NEQUAM,*

> FAS, NEFAS, NUGAS. Nouns without case, that is, caseless, are called *aptota* ("indeclinable"). FRUGI, "frugal"; NIHILI, "useless," "of no use"; NEQUAM, like *nequiquam*, "in vain"; NEFAS, "forbidden." But it is asked why Donatus, when in the definition of the noun by substance he said, A NOUN IS A PART OF SPEECH WITH CASE—and it is difficult to find a noun without case, since it is necessary to show every case—why in this passage does he say that it is without case? For he seems to be contradicting himself in his own words. Anything that lacks case cannot be called a noun. But it should be noted—so that Donatus may be proven to have said true things that do not contradict one another—that indeclinable nouns have a nominative, which is not properly called a "case," as we said above, but inaccurately. For that reason, since it does not decline [lit. "fall"—"casus" is from the verb *cado*, "fall"], it is also called "upright" [sc. *casus rectus*]—that is, "stable".] (Sedulius Scottus 1975, 121; my translation)

Sedulius's analysis shows many of the complexities of using Latin to talk about how to talk about Latin. The sentence in capitals at the opening of the passage is the bit of Donatus's text that Sedulius will expound. That sentence from Donatus itself contains two kinds of "target" word: a technical grammatical term that is being introduced (and which is actually Greek), *aptota*, and a series of examples of *aptota* nouns, *frugi, nihili*, etc. (These are "nouns" because medieval grammar did not have a separate category for adjectives.) Then the whole quotation from Donatus, which itself contains two kinds of lemmata, becomes the lemma for Sedulius's gloss. Making sense of all this requires a lot of scribal help in setting apart lemma from gloss, target Latin from explanatory Latin, or the equivalent in the teacher's spoken performance, with the medieval equivalent of "air quotes." And that kind of scribal or teacherly performance presumes a deep familiarity with the modes of grammatical discourse.

Note, too, that the resolution to the apparent contradiction in the authoritative text depends on etymology, an explanatory strategy which in medieval grammars is mostly turned on the grammatical terminology itself. (See Amsler 1989 for a full treatment.) That is, etymology is a way of explaining the Latin about the Latin. The effect of using etymologies as the explanation of last resort is at once to distance the target language even further, and to burrow into it. The distancing effect comes from grammarians' habit of backing off from grappling with the way *Latin* works and focusing instead on the language their authorities use to talk *about* Latin. The burrowing is the result of the atomizing effect of etymological inquiry: a word is broken down into its smallest meaningful units, and at that level, everything is seen to make sense: the relationship of words to each other and to the words and world they describe.

Manifold Latins

The grammatical exegetes' obsessive need to reconcile authorities might suggest an intolerance for multiplicity in acquired Latinity, but in fact the opposite seems to be the case. To take two examples, Isidore of Seville and Virgilius Maro Grammaticus in the seventh century both acknowledge—one encyclopedically and the other playfully—that the corpus of Latin is large and various:

> Latinas autem linguas quattuor esse quidam dixerunt, id est Priscam, Latinam, Romanam, Mixtam. Prisca est, quam vetustissimi Italiae sub Iano et Saturno sunt usi…Latina, quam sub Latino et regibus Tusci et ceteri in Latio sunt locuti…Romana, quae post reges exactos a populo Romano coepta est…Mixta, quae post imperium latius promotum simul cum moribus et hominibus in Romanam civitatem inrupit, integritatem verbi per soloecismos et barbarismos corrumpens.
>
> [Some say that there are four kinds of Latin, that is the Ancient, the Latin, the Roman, and the Mixed. The Ancient is that which the very earliest inhabitants of Italy used…The Latin is that which the Tuscans and others in Latium used under Latinus and the kings…The Roman is that which was begun after the kings were driven out by the Roman people…The Mixed is that which, after the expansion of the empire, entered the Roman state along with customs and peoples, corrupting the integrity of the language with solecisms and barbarisms.] (*Etymologiae* 9.1.6–7)
>
> …tam multa sit et copiosa latinitatis totius regio et ut ita dicam pelagus inmensum, ut discerni omnino diuersitates ipsius et nouae adinuentiones et incognitae, ut putantur, a nemine ad liquidum possint.
>
> [… the realm of all of Latinity is so vast and abundant and, so to speak, an immense ocean, that no one would be able, as they might think, to discern clearly all its varieties and new and unheard-of innovations.] (*Epistulae* 2.119–22, translated in part in Law 1995, 53)

Isidore, the seventh-century Spaniard, sees himself at the tail of a long sequence of historical stages of the Latin language, over which some sort of intellectual control was desperately needed. Isidore's taxonomy in this passage echoes the value judgments of grammarians at the end of the ancient educational regime, who were trying to hold the tide against the decay, as they saw it, of the language they taught. But his practice throughout the *Etymologies* belies his judgmental tone here: Isidore assembles a multiplicity of names, authorities, and taxonomies and makes them both comprehensible and memorable through the universal solvent of etymology. If we read that approach back into his introductory account of multiple Latinities, it looks less like a lament for decline and corruption and more like a nod to the situation that prompted Isidore's encyclopedic labors. Meanwhile, Virgilius, an Irishman of the same century, belongs to a people who acquired the Latin tradition whole, without any sense of standing in a particular place in its development. All Latins were at his disposal, or so it must have seemed. It would not be surprising if its variety of styles and authorities made it appear at times a secret code partially deciphered.

Practitioners of medieval Latin inevitably confronted the fact that the best Latinity and the best authority did not always come in one convenient package. The contradiction had played out in the early Christian centuries with respect to the language of Scripture and the ancient decorum of styles, but it had constantly to be renegotiated as successive generations of medieval Latin-users chose and promulgated best practices for Latin and for life. The conflict, and the way it was handled, are made concrete in Saint Gall, Stiftsbibliothek MS 914, one of the two most important witnesses to the *Rule* of St. Benedict. The manuscript is generally agreed to be a copy at two removes of the (now lost) Monte Cassino manuscript that was believed to be Benedict's autograph (Meyvaert 1959). In the Middle Ages, Saint Gall 914 was understood to be a copy made directly from the autograph, and as such, the Latin text of the *Regula Benedicti* that it preserved carried special authority: Charlemagne ordered a copy made of Benedict's autograph precisely in order to propagate Benedict's own Latin as an authoritative form of the *Regula*, as an integral part of his reform of language and the regular life. Benedict's Latin, however, is highly problematic from the point of view of Carolingian reformers and grammarians. Benedict was a sixth-century Italian of incomplete education, and his Latin shows the features one would expect from that situation, including eccentricities of spelling and errors of case rection (Mohrmann 1952). Saint Gall 914 accommodates this situation by including a pre-planned set of glosses correcting Benedict's Latin. MS 914 helpfully includes a document explaining how the system of corrections works. This is a letter from Grimald and Tatto, the men commissioned to make the copy, explaining what they've done. Those words which Benedict did not write "according to art," they have corrected from other copies of the *Regula* corrected by modern masters; they have signaled those corrections with two dots. Words which Benedict dictated but which are not found in modern manuscripts they have marked with an obelus and two dots. As they wrote to their abbot, "Hoc egimus desiderantes uos utrumque et secundum traditionem pii patris etiam modernam habere" [We have done this desiring that you have both a text according to the tradition of the pious father and the modern text]. Saint Gall 914 is thus a direct witness to the promulgation from Aachen of an authoritative text with highly problematic Latinity, and also to the way that problematic Latinity was contextualized.

A similar negotiation between authority and style is to be seen in the twelfth century in William of Malmesbury's discussion of Aldhelm. William excused the style of the patriarch of Malmesbury, which was not to modern tastes, by correcting critics who were not aware that styles vary according to place and time:

> Sermones eius minus infundunt hilaritatis quam uellent hi qui rerum incuriosi uerba trutinant: iudices importuni, qui nesciant quod secundum mores gentium uarientur modi dictaminum.
>
> [His discourse instills less good cheer than would be liked by those who weigh words and care nothing for matter: demanding judges indeed, unaware as they are that style varies in type according to the character of a people.] (William of Malmesbury 2007, 5.196.5–6)

William's attitude towards Aldhelm's polarizing style is proof of an accommodation that weighs the demands of authority against those of taste.

William's recognition of the existence of national styles and tastes in Latin is also proof of a fully developed medieval regime of Latin. Five centuries earlier,

Isidore had surveyed a multiplicity of Latins and understood them as having arisen in historical sequence, yoked to the development and dissolution of a single state. In William's world, Latin is a distributed system. From the eighth century on, no one who writes Latin does so without having come to the language by conscious endeavor. There is, therefore, no default Latin, and there are no unmarked stylistic choices. All the literate communities of Europe in a sense occupy an even playing field. If Latin is no one's native language, no one has a better *a priori* claim than anyone else to correctness or authenticity. Anyone who has successfully acquired Latin through the medium of the grammatical curriculum is in a position to make judgments about what is *latinum* and what is *non latinum*; those terms, which in antiquity stood for a native speaker's judgment about grammaticality, are now common property. That Latin can be learned and taught to a very high degree of competence in the absence of any native informants; that local, national, and "house" traditions can flourish and self-perpetuate; that others can make judgments about those traditions: these are signs of a living, natural language. Yet Latin is always mediated, never unconsciously inhabited, always necessarily chosen in opposition to a native tongue. While it is far from dead, it cannot replicate by natural means, but must find new vessels to inhabit. It might best be called "differently alive"—a name for the undead preferred by those who are sympathetic to their plight.

SUGGESTIONS FOR FURTHER READING

Most of the grammars of antiquity known to the Middle Ages are to be found in Keil (1855–80), but those editions have in some important cases been superseded. Donatus's two grammars, in particular, are edited in Holtz (1981), where they are set authoritatively in the context of their reception. Kaster (1988) and Chin (2008) treat the late-Roman grammars in the social context of their composition. Law (1982), supplemented by the essays collected in Law (1997), offers a typology of grammars used in the early Middle Ages and an indispensable overview of which grammars were known in specific times and places. The best survey of linguistic doctrine from antiquity to the end of the Middle Ages is Law (2003). A wide-ranging selection of late-antique and medieval grammatical texts is available in translation in Copeland and Sluiter (2009), which includes an excellent bibliography and direction to individual editions.

For the early medieval reception of rhetoric, which was transmitted as part of basic grammar, see Schindel (1975); Baratin and Desbordes (1987); and Knappe (1996), the essentials of which are summarized in English in Knappe (1998). The most influential texts, besides Donatus's *Ars maior*, are Augustine's *De doctrina Christiana* (Augustine 1995) and Bede's *De schematibus et tropis*, edited by Kendall in Bede (1975).

The medieval grammatical genre that most directly engaged the choice amongst competing authorities was the *de orthographia* or usage handbook. The orthographic texts in Keil (1855–80) should be used only with great caution; use instead the edition of Bede's *De orthographia* in Bede (1975) and of Alcuin's *De orthographia* in Alcuin (1997), where Bruni sets out the textual problems.

BIBLIOGRAPHY

Primary sources

Alcuin. 1997. *De orthographia*, edited by Sandra Bruni. Millennio medievale 2. Florence: SISMEL, Edizioni del Galluzzo.

Anonymus ad Cuimnanum. 1992. *Expositio latinitatis*, edited by Bernard Bischoff and Bengt Löfstedt. Corpus Christianorum. Series Latina 133D. Turnhout: Brepols.

Augustine. 1995. *De doctrina Christiana*, edited by R. P. H. Green. Oxford Early Christian Texts. Oxford: Oxford University Press.

Bede. 1969. *Bede's Ecclesiastical History of the English People*, edited by Bertram Colgrave and Roger A. B. Mynors. Oxford Medieval Texts. Oxford: Clarendon Press.

———. 1975. *Bedae opera Didascalia*, edited by Charles W. Jones and Calvin B. Kendall. Corpus Christianorum. Series Latina 123A. Turnhout: Brepols.

Isidore of Seville. 1911. *Etymologiae sive origines*, edited by Wallace M. Lindsay. Scriptorum classicorum bibliotheca Oxoniensis. Oxford: Clarendon Press.

Keil, Heinrich, ed. 1855–80. *Grammatici Latini*. 7 vols. Leipzig: B. G. Teubner.

Sedulius Scottus. 1975. *Commentum Sedulii Scotti in Maiorem Donatum Grammaticum*, edited by Denis Brearley. Pontifical Institute of Mediaeval Studies. Texts and Studies 27. Toronto: Pontifical Institute of Mediaeval Studies.

Virgilius Maro Grammaticus. 1979. *Epitomi ed Epistole*, edited by Giovanni Polara. Nuovo Medioevo 9. Naples: Liguori.

Secondary sources

Adams, James N. 2003. *Bilingualism and the Latin Language*. Cambridge, New York: Cambridge University Press.

Amsler, Mark. 1989. *Etymology and Grammatical Discourse in Late Antiquity and the Early Middle Ages*. Amsterdam Studies in the Theory and History of Linguistic Science. Series III, Studies in the History of the Language Sciences 44. Amsterdam: John Benjamins.

———. 1990. "Commentary and Metalanguage in Early Medieval Latin Grammar." In *History and Historiography of Linguistics*, edited by Hans-Josef Niederehe and Konrad Koerner, 175–87. Amsterdam Studies in the Theory and History of Linguistic Science. Series III, Studies in the History of the Language Sciences 51. Amsterdam: John Benjamins.

Banniard, Michel. 1992. *Viva voce: Communication écrite et communication orale du ive au ixe siècle en Occident latin*. Collection des études augustiniennes. Série Moyen-age et Temps modernes 25. Paris: Institut des Études Augustiniennes.

Baratin, Marc, and Françoise Desbordes. 1987. "La 'troisième partie' de *l'ars grammatica*." In *The History of Linguistics in the Classical Period*, edited by Daniel J. Taylor, 41–66. Amsterdam studies in the Theory and History of Linguistic Science. Series III, Studies in the History of the Language Sciences 46. Amsterdam: John Benjamins, 1987.

Barwick, Karl. 1967. *Remmius Palaemon und die römische Ars grammatica*. Philologus. Supplementband 15.2. Hildesheim: G. Olms.

Bullough, Donald A. 1972. "The Educational Tradition in England from Alfred to Ælfric: Teaching utriusque linguae." *Settimane di Studio del Centro Italiano di Studi sull'Alto Medioevo* 19: 466–78.

Chin, Catherine M. 2008. *Grammar and Christianity in the Late Roman World*. Divinations. Philadelphia: University of Pennsylvania Press.

Copeland, Rita and Ineke Sluiter, eds. 2009. *Medieval Grammar and Rhetoric: Language Arts and Literary Theory, A.D. 300–1475*. Oxford: Oxford University Press.

Derolez, René. 1992. "Language Problems in Anglo-Saxon England: *barbara loquella* and *barbarismus*." In *Words, Texts and Manuscripts: Studies in Anglo-Saxon Culture Presented to Helmut Gneuss on the Occasion of his Sixty-Fifth Birthday*, edited by Michael Korhammer, 285–92. Woodbridge: D. S. Brewer.

Fontaine, Jacques. 1959. *Isidore de Séville et la culture classique dans L'espagne wisigothique*. 2 vols. Paris: Études Augustiniennes.

Gavrilov, Alexander K. 1997. "Techniques of Reading in Classical Antiquity." *The Classical Quarterly* N.S. 47: 56–73.

Gibson, Margaret. 1992. "Milestones in the Study of Priscian, circa 800–circa 1200." *Viator* 23: 17–33.

Gilissen, Léon. 1979. "Observations codicologiques sur le codex Sangallensis 914." In *Miscellanea codicologica F. Masai dicata MCMLXXXIX*, edited by Pierre Cockshaw, Monique-Cécile Garand and Pierre Jodogne, 51–70. Publications de Scriptorium 8. Ghent: E. Story-Scientia.

Gretsch, Mechthild. 1974. "Aethelwold's Translation of the *Regula Sancti Benedicti* and its Latin Exemplar." *Anglo-Saxon England* 3: 125–51.

Gwara, Scott. 1998. "Second Language Acquisition and Anglo-Saxon Bilingualism: Negative Transfer and Avoidance in Ælfric Bata's Latin Colloquia, ca. A.D. 1000." *Viator* 29: 1–24.

Hofman, Rijcklof. 1993. "The Linguistic Preoccupations of the Glossators of the St. Gall Priscian." In *History of Linguistic Thought in the Early Middle Ages*, edited by Vivien Law, 111–26. Amsterdam Studies in the Theory and History of Linguistic Science. Series III, Studies in the History of the Language Sciences 71. Amsterdam: John Benjamins.

Holtz, Louis. 1981. *Donat et la tradition de l'enseignement grammatical: étude sur l'Ars Donati et sa diffusion (IVe–IXe siècle) et édition critique*. Institut de recherche et d'histoire des textes. Documents, études et répertoires. Paris: Centre National de la Recherche Scientifique.

Irvine, Martin. 1986. "Bede the Grammarian and the Scope of Grammatical Studies in Eighth-Century Northumbria." *Anglo-Saxon England* 15: 15–44.

Jones, Christopher Andrew. 1998. "*Meatim Sed et Rustica*: Ælfric as a Medieval Latin Author." *Journal of Medieval Latin* 9: 1-57.

Kaster, Robert A. 1988. *Guardians of Language: The Grammarian and Society in Late Antiquity*. The Transformation of the Classical Heritage 11. Berkeley, CA: University of California Press.

Knappe, Gabriele. 1996. *Traditionen der klassischen Rhetorik im angelsächsischen England*. Anglistische Forschungen 236. Heidelberg: Universitätsverlag C. Winter.

———. 1998. "Classical Rhetoric in Anglo-Saxon England." *Anglo-Saxon England* 27: 5–29.

Lapidge, Michael. 1984. "Gildas's Education and the Latin Culture of Sub-Roman Britain." In *Gildas: New Approaches*, edited by Michael Lapidge and David Dumville, 27–50. Studies in Celtic History 5. Woodbridge: The Boydell Press.

———. 1995. "The Career of Archbishop Theodore." In *Archbishop Theodore: Commemorative Studies on his Life and Influence*, edited by Michael Lapidge, 1–29.

Cambridge Studies in Anglo-Saxon England 11. Cambridge: Cambridge University Press.

Law, Vivien. 1982. *The Insular Latin Grammarians*. Studies in Celtic History 3. Woodbridge: The Boydell Press.

———, ed. 1993. *History of Linguistic Thought in the Early Middle Ages*. Amsterdam Studies in the Theory and History of Linguistic Science. Series III, Studies in the History of the Language Sciences 71. Amsterdam: John Benjamins.

———. 1995. *Wisdom, Authority and Grammar in the Seventh Century: Decoding Virgilius Maro Grammaticus*. Cambridge: Cambridge University Press.

———. 1997. *Grammar and Grammarians in the Early Middle Ages*. Longman Linguistics Library. London, New York: Longman.

———. 2003. *The History of Linguistics in Europe from Plato to 1600*. Cambridge Textbooks in Linguistics. Cambridge: Cambridge University Press.

Meyvaert, Paul. 1959. "Problems Concerning the 'Autograph' Manuscript of St. Benedict's Rule." *Revue Bénédictine* 69: 3–21.

Mohrmann, Christine. 1952. "La latinité de S. Benoît." *Revue Bénédictine* 62: 108–39.

Norberg, Dag. 1958. "Le Développement du Latin en Italie de Saint Grégoire le Grand à Paul Diacre." *Settimane di studio del Centro italiano di Studi sull'alto medioevo* 5: 485–503.

Parkes, Malcolm B. 1991. "The Contribution of Insular Scribes of the Seventh and Eighth Centuries to the 'Grammar of Legibility'." In *Scribes, Scripts, and Readers: Studies in the Presentation and Dissemination of Medieval Texts*, edited by Malcolm B. Parkes, 1–18. London, Rio Grande, OH: The Hambledon Press.

Riché, Pierre. 1976. *Education and Culture in the Barbarian West, Sixth through Eighth Centuries*, translated by John J. Contreni. Columbia: University of South Carolina Press.

Saenger, Paul. 1997. *Space Between Words: The Origins of Silent Reading*. Figurae. Stanford: Stanford University Press.

Schindel, Ulrich. 1972. "Die Quellen von Bedas Figurenlehre." *Classica et Mediaevalia* 29: 169–86.

———. 1975. *Die lateinischen Figurenlehren des 5. bis 7. Jahrhunderts und Donats Vergilkommentar*. Abhandlungen der Akademie der Wissenschaften in Göttingen, Philologisch-Historische Klasse, Folge 3, 91. Göttingen: Vandenhoeck und Ruprecht.

Sullivan, Richard E., ed. 1995. *"The Gentle Voices of Teachers": Aspects of Learning in the Carolingian Age*. Columbus, OH: Ohio State University Press.

Traube, Ludwig. 1898. *Textgeschichte der Regula S. Benedicti*. Abhandlungen der Bayerischen Akademie der Wissenschaften. Philosophisch-Historische Klasse 25.2. Munich: Verlag der Königlich Bayerischen Akademie der Wissenschaften.

Waquet, Françoise. 2001. *Latin, or, the Empire of the Sign: From the Sixteenth to the Twentieth Century*, translated by John Howe. London, New York: Verso.

William of Malmesbury. 2007. *Gesta Pontificum Anglorum*. Vol. 1: *Text and Translation*, edited by Michael Winterbottom. Oxford Medieval Texts. Oxford: Clarendon Press.

Wright, Neil. 1984. "Gildas's Prose Style and its Origins." In *Gildas: New Approaches*, edited by Michael Lapidge and David Dumville, 107–28. Studies in Celtic History 5. Woodbridge: The Boydell Press.

Wright, Roger. 1982. *Late Latin and Early Romance in Spain and Carolingian France*. ARCA. Classical and Medieval Texts, Papers, and Monographs 8. Liverpool: F. Cairns.

———. 2002. A Sociophilological Study of Late Latin. Utrecht Studies in Medieval Literacy 10. Turnhout: Brepols.

CHAPTER 4

LATIN AS A LANGUAGE OF AUTHORITATIVE TRADITION

RYAN SZPIECH

In his work on language and signs, *De doctrina Christiana* (2.11), Augustine explains that the best remedy for uncertainty about literal meaning ("ignota signa propria") is knowledge of languages, and to resolve confusion in reading Scripture, one must turn to Hebrew and especially Greek rather than rely on the "latinorum interpretum infinita uarietas," [the endless diversity of the Latin translators] (Augustine 1962, 42). Augustine's unwavering support for the Greek Septuagint derived from his faith that it reflected the miraculous product of seventy men writing in unison—a unison that stood in stark contrast to the *infinita uarietas* of Latin translations. Because of this support, Augustine maintained a strident epistolary debate with Jerome over the latter's project to translate directly from Hebrew. He gave his Parthian shot against Jerome's translation in this debate in his late opus *De civitate Dei* (18.43), stating, "Ecclesiae Christi tot hominum auctoritati…neminem iudicant praeferendum" [The churches of Christ judge that no one is to be preferred to the authority of so many] (Augustine 1955, 2: 639).

In taking this position on the Septuagint, Augustine recalls the two foundational aspects of the concept of *auctoritas* that would persist throughout the Middle Ages. First, it is the power to initiate or create, the power of an *auctor*, a source or maker, ultimately ascribed to God; second, by extension, it is the imitability devolved by that maker to his heirs, the power given to God's vicar through prophecy or miracles to *authorize* through word and example. What was "authoritative" culled its power from both a legitimizing appeal to originality and a secondary appeal to the inheritance of that originality. Thus, authority could pertain, albeit unequally, to both the maker and the made, the originator and his epigone, the *auctor* whom all trusted and the authorized commentator whose authority depended on the *auctoritas* of his source.

It was in this double sense that Latin existed as a language of authoritative tradition in Augustine's time, and it was also in this sense that it faced repeated challenges over the long course of its medieval development. Although Latin *per se* was not the vehicle of original revelation, those who wrote it in the Church garnered authority for it by claiming that it represented an inheritance of God's law, just as the Septuagint, for Augustine, both followed the Hebrew Bible in prestige and was elevated in subsequent use to stand on equal prophetic footing with it. Similarly, through prescriptive and descriptive grammar in the works of Donatus and Servius (fourth century), Macrobius (fifth), and Priscian (sixth), among many other late-antique and early medieval grammarians, Latin's authority was established as a source of tradition by positing the unity of past expression and present understanding in terms of an unchanging grammatical code (Irvine 1994, 86). The authority of the Latin language in the Middle Ages stemmed from its own status as the inheritor of originality in three distinct but intersecting senses: as the language of Rome and its empire (implying also the authority of apostolic succession from the Church of Rome); as the language of learning and wisdom, first as embodied in a standard canon of trusted *auctores* and later, as a rival to Arabic, inherited from Greece; and, finally, as one of God's three holy languages, the companion of Hebrew and Greek. Authoritative as both a source and a derivative, the tongue of Rome and of its heirs, it became in the Middle Ages—in most cases, through deliberate and willful measures by its users to elevate and preserve its status—the language of science, learning, rhetoric, poetry, and imperium, but also of supersession, the language of the Church triumphant.

These aspects of Latin's authority emerged at different times roughly according to the evolution of medieval educational norms from monastery to cathedral school to university. This growth followed the pattern, established before the predominance of Christianity, of Latin as a language of *opposition* within a wider world of competing language communities. Classical Latin's competition against the prestige of Greek as a language of culture and philosophy was repeated in the early Middle Ages by ecclesiastical Latin's competition with the prestige of Hebrew as a holy language. This later gave way to a clerical competition against the status of Arabic as a language of learning and science and against the encroaching of written vernaculars as languages of poetry. Over the millennium following Augustine's defense of the authority of the Greek Septuagint, when Latin became de facto a Western, Christian language, the authority of Latin as a language of worship, poetry, and learning would be challenged both through multiple stages of vernacularization and through direct competition with Arabic, which came to be a dominant language of learning and cultural prestige across the Mediterranean after the ninth century.

The Last Shall be First: Latin and the Three Languages of the Cross

The thirteenth-century canonist and Bishop of Mende, Guillaume Durand (d. 1296), nicknamed "Speculator" for his encyclopedic treatment of canon law in the *Speculum iudiciale*, described the following familiar liturgical scene in his *Rationale divinorum officiorum*: "Post orationes, sacerdos crucem uelatam baiulat ad dextrum cornu altaris...Cantat autem sacerdos quasi hebraice in persona Saluatoris; acoliti cantant grece: 'Agyos o Theos,' quasi in persona grecorum; chorus respondet: 'Sanctus, sanctus' etc., in persona latinorum." [After prayers, the priest carries the veiled cross to the right corner of the altar...The priest then sings in Hebrew, as if in the role of the Savior; the acolytes sing "Agios o Theos" [Holy is God] in Greek, as if in the role of the Greeks; the Choir responds, "Sanctus, sanctus" [Holy, holy], etc., in the role of the Latins]. Just as each language is represented by the individual voices of the priest, acolytes, and chorus, respectively, so each language represents a figure in human history: "Sicque tribus linguis laudatur Deus, uidelicet hebraica, que propter legem omnium linguarum est mater; greca, que doctrix est; et latina, que imperatrix est propter Romani dominium imperii, et papatus" [Thus God is praised in three languages, namely Hebrew, which by law is the mother of all languages; Greek, which is the teacher; and Latin, which is the empress, on account of the dominion of the Roman Empire and of the Papacy] (Durand 1995, 2: 375). Latin, like Hebrew and Greek, is one of the holy languages of Christian worship, but it also plays a specific role in the history of the Church. Just as Hebrew is the mother and Greek the teacher, so Latin is the empress of all by virtue of the hegemony of the Roman Empire and of its heir, the papacy.

The connection of Latin with Hebrew and Greek hearkens back to the patristic notion of the three languages of the cross in which Jesus was mocked as "King of the Jews" (Jn 19:20). Although first elaborated in the writing of Hilary of Poitiers, this notion was quickly taken up by Augustine, for whom Latin appeared on the cross "propter Romanos multis ac paene omnibus iam tunc gentibus imperantes," [on account of the Romans, ruling many and, at that time, virtually all nations] (*PL* 35: 1946). In the patristic tradition to which Augustine gives voice, Latin is the newest and least prestigious of the three holy languages, yet it is also the rightful heir and keeper of its more illustrious forebears. On the basis of his formulation, Latin would be seen throughout the Middle Ages as the *imperatrix*, both worldly and spiritual, of all other tongues and nations.

The tradition of Latin as one of the three languages of the cross was an effective countermeasure to the very low place conceded to all languages but Hebrew by the Genesis accounts of the fall of man and the confusion of Babel (Gn 11:1–9). Latin, along with virtually all other languages, could not compete with the preeminent prestige of Hebrew as *omnium linguarum mater*, the only language uncorrupted by original sin. As God created things, says Petrus Comestor (d. 1178)—repeating an extremely widespread tradition that included Jerome, Cassiodorus, Bede, Remigius of Auxerre, Rupert of Deutz, and others—"imposuit eis nomina Adam hebraica lingua que sola fuit ab initio" [Adam gave them names in the Hebrew language, which was the only one at first] (Petrus 2005, 35). It was only after the confusion of languages at the Tower of Babel that other languages were born, and the tradition dating back at least to Irenaeus (*Adversus haereses* 3.22.3) specifies that seventy-two languages (seventy in some sources) resulted from the chaos (PG 7: 958). From this the diversity of nations was also born. Saint Isidore (d. 636) sums up in the *Etymologies* what was already a well-established tradition: "Linguarum diuersitas exorta est in aedificatione turris post diluuium. Nam priusquam superbia turris illius in diuersos signorum sonos humanam diuideret societatem, una omnium nationum lingua fuit, quae Hebraea uocatur.... ex una lingua multae sunt gentes exortae" [The diversity of languages arose with the building of the tower [of Babel] after the flood. Before the pride of that tower divided human society into the different sounds of signs, there was one language of all nations, which was called Hebrew...many nations arose from one language] (Isidore 1911, 9.1.1, 1:343). The division of languages was thus connected with the population of the world by the three sons of Noah (Shem, Ham, and Japheth) who came to occupy the Near East, Africa, and Europe, respectively, in the medieval T-and-O map.

This idea was repeated almost verbatim by the Frankish monk Rhabanus Maurus, and developed by many later writers such as Andrew of Saint Victor, Rodrigo Jiménez de Rada, and Lucas of Tuy (Grondeux 2005, 49–50; Richter 2006, 16). Such theories place Latin in an undistinguished position relative to Hebrew as a language of revelation. As Durand concluded, "hebrea lingua mater et nobilissima est omnium linguarum propter auctoritatem diuine Scripture; latina uero inferior quasi filia" [The Hebrew language is mother and noblest of all languages on account of the authority of divine Scripture, but Latin is inferior like a daughter] (Durand 1995, 2: 437). Based on this early patristic tradition, the idea persisted up until the late thirteenth century that Latin, like all languages except Hebrew, was the product of God confounding man's hubris and did not share in the supreme authority of Adam's language. Scholastic writers extended this idea by praising Hebrew as not only the original, prelapsarian language, but also as a more precise and perfect language of concrete realism. Thomas Aquinas (*De veritate* 18.4.5) thus praised Adam because, in giving Hebrew names to all things (Gn 2:9), "plene naturam rerum cognovit" [He recognized fully the nature of things] (Thomas Aquinas 1972, 541).

To trump Hebrew's prerogative as the only language to precede man's fall, ecclesiastical writers invoked the comprehension of tongues at Pentecost (Acts 2:1–4) to be the counterpoint to the chaos of Babel just as Christ was the counterpoint to Adam (Borst 1957–63, 224–26, 1989–92). Augustine, in his insatiable appetite for historical typology, would later extend this in his Psalms commentary (54.7) to see Pentecost as both a fulfillment of what began at Babel and a prefiguration of the future unity of the Church, which represents the unity of a perfect language of the spirit: "Volunt unam linguam, veniant ad ecclesiam; quia et in diversitate linguarum carnis una est lingua in fide cordis" (*PL* 36: 636) [Those who want a single language, let them come to the Church, since even in the diversity of the languages of the flesh, there is one language in the faith of the heart]. At the same time, although earthly Latin was more often relegated to the status of a distant epigone compared with Hebrew—much as it was repeatedly characterized in antiquity as an impoverished language next to Greek—the topos of Latin's inferiority, in both cases, contains within it a tacit claim to inheritance and even superiority. Just as Lucretius could praise Greek as having a more varied vocabulary but also imply that, for that reason, it was more confused and obscure, so medieval writers who invoked the status of Latin as a belated language of revelation could invert that idea to Latin's benefit by invoking the final supersession of Greek wisdom and Hebrew truth within the Latin tradition of the Western Church (Rubin 1998, 319).

The unity claimed by the Church, moreover, was also an adaptation of a familiar Roman topos of imperial unity out of linguistic diversity, such as in Martial's comments in his *Liber spectaculorum* praising Titus's dedication of the Coliseum: "Vox diversa sonat populorum, tum tamen una est, cum verus patriae diceris esse pater" [There sounds a diverse voice of the people, but nevertheless it is one when you are called the true father of the fatherland] (Farrell 2001, 3). This model of imperial unity transferred easily into patristic characterizations of Latin's prestige as the language of reunification, personified as an *imperatrix* under whose dominion the Church rules both Jews and Gentiles. This theme was particularly popular in Ireland. As Augustine Eriugena (fl. ca. 655) explains in *De mirabilibus sacrae scripturae*, "In eis crucis Christi titulus litteris hebraicis, graecis et latinis scriptus, euangelica auctoritate perhibetur" (*PL* 35: 2161) [The title written on the cross of Christ in those Hebrew, Greek, and Latin letters is asserted by evangelical authority]. Latin's ability to imperiously absorb the prestige of other, rival languages found apt expression in metaphors of war and conquest. As the abbot Baudri of Bourgueil (d. 1130) wrote in his "Ad dominam Constantiam," evoking the perennial topos of the beautiful captive woman of Deuteronomy 21:10–14, a prize of conquest "shorn" of her alterity by a Christian reading:

> Totus mundus velut unica lingua loquatur…
> Hostili preda ditetur lingua Latina,
> graecus et hebreus serviat edomitus…
>
> [The whole world speaks as if with one tongue…
> Let the Latin tongue be enriched by enemy booty;
> Let the vanquished Greek and Hebrew serve…]
> (Baudri 1979, 269–70; cf. Lubac 1959–64, 1.1: 298)

The attempt to claim for Latin the status of both a universal and revelatory language of reunification did not go unchallenged. In the late-antique rabbinical work of halakhic (legal) exegesis, *Sifre Devarim* (§ 343), Deuteronomy 33:2 is interpreted to mean that God "revealed Himself not in one language but in four… in Hebrew… Latin (*leshon romi*)… Arabic… [and] Aramaic." Yet all the nations are like dogs that cannot carry a burden, while Israel is like a sturdy ass that carries her own load plus that of the dogs (Neusner 2001, 161–62). Medieval Jewish texts attacked Christian views of authority close to the root by characterizing the Latin language itself as unfit to be a vehicle of revelation. The southern French philosopher Joseph Ibn Caspi (d. 1340) recounts a debate with a bishop over the relative merits of Hebrew and Latin:

> Once a bishop honored in our country, who was versed in the Holy Scriptures, asked me...what superiority and sanctity have the Hebrew language and writing over the Latin language (*leshon romi*) and writing, since the meaning intended in [both Hebrew and Latin] remains the same? My answer was...the writing of our books written in [Hebrew] is the Script of God and it is in this tongue that they were given. If a king gives us a letter of freedom and if he writes it with his own hand and in our own tongue, it will be more precious to us than anything else...Our books are written in the language of the King...[Secondly], the meaning intended by the metaphors has been changed [in Latin] and has so deteriorated in a number of passages that they cannot be understood even by the One who made them, God. The Book of Moses translated into another language and written in another writing is not at all the Book given to us by God. (Joseph 1996, 58–59; trans. in Sirat 1990, 326)

Ibn Caspi even quotes the opening of Genesis in Latin (but in Hebrew characters) to show that "the language of the Christians" lacks the "double sense" intended by God in the Hebrew original. Even if it serves as a language of translation, it lacks the capacity for the plenitude of God's original revelation. In Hebrew, Latin thus often goes unnamed and is referred to simply as *leshon romi* ("the language of Rome") or *laʿaz* ("a foreign language," which could include both Latin and Latinate vernaculars). (This usage is evident in medieval Hebrew exegesis in Christian lands [Banitt 2007] and also appeared in multilingual Hebrew pharmacological texts [Bos and Mensching 2005]. On the phenomenon of "Judeo-Latin" and Latin in Hebrew characters, see Wexler 1988 and Banitt 2007.) Arguments like Ibn Caspi's can be understood as responses to the persistent attempts to construct the authority of Latin as a supersessionist language of reunification within which are gathered the scattered fragments of truth left over from the loss of an edenic *Hebraica veritas*.

Between Our Fathers' *Latina* and Our Mother's *Ladino*

In the opening section of his Latin treatise, *De vulgari eloquentia*, Dante defines the spoken vernacular—a word meaning "of a *verna*, i.e., a home-born slave"—as implicitly domestic and female, a language "quam sine omni regula nutricem imitantes accipimus" [that we learn without any formal instruction, by imitating our nurses] (Dante 1996, 2). This common vernacular—as distinct from Dante's "illustrious vernacular," a learned and high register of (male) poetic expression not spoken natively by anyone—is contrasted with a "secondary," factitious but logical language, which the Romans call *grammatica*. Of these two, spoken vernacular and written *grammatica*, vernacular is more original, more universal, and more natural. Even so, this *materna locutio* is not to be confused with Hebrew, the proverbial "mother" of all languages that (as he later argued in *Paradiso* 26.124–38) was lost even *before* the chaos of Babel. (Dante changed his thinking on the question of Adam's Hebrew between the *De vulgari eloquentia* and *Paradiso*; Mazzocco 1993, 159–81.) Despite their nobility, the spoken vernaculars descend from the chaos of Babel each as "ydiomate in vindice confusione recepto" [a language received in vengeful confusion] (Dante 1996, 17), and are thus all among the wages of Eve's sin and subject to variation, development, and corruption. By contrast, *grammatica*—a Greek term that refers plainly to *writing*—"nichil aliud est quam quedam inalterabilis locutionis ydemptitas diversibus temporibus atque locis" [is nothing less than a certain immutable identity of speech in different times and places] (ibid., 20). As a grapholect, a language spoken by none but standardized through writing and rationalization, it is an artificial invention of men made to attenuate the fragmentation of Babel that is manifest in the permutations of spoken language. Latin is a man's language, learned only through long and arduous study, while the common vernacular is the natural language of all, taught by mothers and nurses and used by poets only to speak about love to women, who, as he says in the *Vita Nuova* (§ 25), might find "Latin verses difficult to comprehend." (Dante 1973, 55).

Dante here rehearses what was already a familiar distinction between the spoken vernacular as a *materna locutio* and written Latin as a *patrius sermo* (the language not of one's father, but of patriarchal tradition). Although he praises the former as "more noble," he unquestionably sees the latter as more authoritative. The origins of this topos, which fully emerged in the twelfth century, stretch back to Roman characterizations of Latin as the tongue of the Fathers, often in contrast with the effeminacy of Greek—and Horace's characterization of *Graecia capta* who retakes her Latin captor provides a felicitous parallel with the fair captive of Christian exegesis (Farrell 2001, 53). Such constructed gendering of language registers is obviously not unique to Latin or to Western Europe. As Walter Ong has pointed out, the learning of patriarchal languages including Latin and any other classical language (classical Arabic or Chinese, rabbinical Hebrew, and Sanskrit), involves in virtually all cases a distinction of prestige between the language of common currency and other "linguistic economies far removed from the hearth and from the entire world of infancy" (Ong 1977, 28). In the western Mediterranean, the precise relationship of natural and learned languages, of Hebrew as the exalted "mother of languages" alongside ignoble mother tongues, and of the place of Latin in these hierarchies, was a persistent topic of reflection in the later Middle Ages. The thirteenth-century Franciscan Salimbene de Adam (d. 1290) records among the "excesses" of Frederick II of Sicily his experiment to determine if children were born with innate ability in any language. Frederick had various newborns fed and cared for but isolated them from all language because "volebat enim cognoscere utrum Hebream linguam haberent, que prima fuerat, an Grecam vel Latinam vel Arabicam aut certe linguam parentum suorum ex quibus nati fuissent. Sed laborabat incassum, quia pueri sive infantes moriebantur omnes" [He wanted to know if they spoke Hebrew, which was the first language, or Greek or Latin or Arabic or some language of their parents from whom they were born. But he labored in vain, because the children—infants, rather—all died] (Salimbene 1998, 535).

In Latin's case the division between dialect and grapholect gradually took on a new, increasingly gendered connotation over the course of the Middle Ages. In his ninth-century encomium of Charlemagne, Einhard (d. 840) stated that "Latinam ita didicit, ut aeque illa ac *patria lingua* orare sit solitus" [He learned Latin so [well] that he used to speak it just as he would his *native tongue*] (Einhard 1947, 74, my emphasis). Here, his "native tongue" is a *patria lingua*, the spoken dialect of his fatherland against which his knowledge in Latin is measured. By the twelfth century, this "native tongue" appears as specifically feminized, as is evident in Guibert of Nogent's (d. 1124) description of Pope Urban II: "Non enim minor ei videbatur in Latinae prosecutione locutionis ubertas quam forensi cuilibet potest esse *in materno sermone* pernicitas" [The richness in his production of Latin speech did not seem any less than the fluency can be for any public speaker in his *mother tongue*] (Guibert 1996, 111, my emphasis). The evolving prestige of Latin in the Middle Ages is tied directly to the perpetuation and accentuation of this gendered contrast between, in Dante's words, the "natural" and the "artificial."

This contrast paralleled the widening gap between registers within Latin, slowly leading to a distinction, first in practice then in name, between different Latinate languages (Banniard 1992, 506–7; Grotans 2006, 16–17). Before the decisive moments, which varied by location, when written Latin began to acquire metalinguistic status as a language apart from its dialects (rather than remaining a high register on a single spectrum of *diglossia*), a systematic terminology to distinguish the unlettered spoken form from the learned written form emerged only very gradually, if at all. As the work of Roger Wright has proposed (1982, 112 and 2002, 138), and as Carin Ruff observes at length in the previous essay, it is not surprising that the attempt to reform norms of pronunciation and grammar patronized by Charlemagne at the turn of the ninth century was spearheaded by someone whose native tongue was not Latinate, Alcuin (d. 804), a Northumbrian for whom grammar was "custos recte loquendi et scribendi" [the guardian of correct speaking and writing] (PL 101: 857). The case of Iberia is especially instructive, where words distinguishing spoken and written forms in Ibero-Romance first appear around 1100 when written Latin came to be called "latín" while "latino" and "ladino" continued as variants meaning "Romance." A parallel double usage exists in Occitan and Old French, in which the phrase "en son latin" (often attributed to the warbling of birds) appears widely to mean "in his vernacular" (or jargon) even as it can be found to mean "in Latin" as well (Borst 1957–63, 713–14). In Ibero-Romance, we even see the survival of the word "ladino" as a multi-use term for both Latin and Romance as late as 1492, as in the

Latin-Castilian dictionary of Antonio Nebrija (Kramer 1998, 123–24), a usage that would partly survive even later among Sephardic Jews exiled from Spain (Wright 2002, 274).

A similar mixed use of the same word to mean both Romance and Latin persisted in Andalusi Arabic, in which *al-laṭīnī*, or *al-laṭīniyah* could refer to spoken and written forms of Latinate language, although most references are to spoken Ibero-Romance. Eleventh-century writer Ibn Ḥazm (d. 1064) mentions an enclave of the ancient Arabian Balī tribe living north of Cordoba, and notes, "they cannot speak *laṭīniyah* well, but only Arabic; [this is true both of] their women and of their menfolk" (Ibn Ḥazm 1962, 443; Wasserstein 1991, 9). While the term *laṭīniyah* (or *lāṭīniyah*) was common to denote spoken Ibero-Romance, Ibn Ḥazm uses the same term elsewhere to mean Latin (Thomas 2001, 98 n. 39).

The lack of distinction between written and spoken Latin among non-Christians—implying a lack of authoritative prestige of written Latin—is especially apparent in an anecdote recounted a century after Ibn Ḥazm by the Jewish poet Moses Ibn 'Ezra' (d. after 1138) in which the linguistic rivalry between Hebrew and Arabic is turned into a common opposition to Christian *laṭīnī*:

> When I was a young man in my native land (Granada), I was once asked by a great Islamic Scholar of law (*fiqh*), who was well versed in the religious disciplines of Islam and most kind towards me, to recite the Ten Commandments for him in Arabic. I realized his intention: he, in fact, wanted to belittle the quality of their language. So I asked him to recite to me the first *sūrah*—the *Fātiḥah*—of his Qur'ān in *al-laṭīnī*, a language he could speak and understood very well. When he tried to render the *Fātiḥah* in the above-mentioned language, it sounded ugly and was completely distorted. He noticed what was in my mind and did not press me further to fulfill his request. (Moses 1975, 43–45; translated in Rosenthal 1975, 19, with my changes)

Although the author clearly refers to some form of spoken Ibero-Romance, he puts it in contention with the classical languages of Scripture, a role logically played by Latin. Other twelfth-century Arabic sources, by both Jews and Muslims, make little conceptual distinction between spoken Romance and written Latin as separate languages, and if such a distinction is recognized (as in multilingual lists of plants), it is never maintained in a systematic way (Barceló 1997, 270–75; Dietrich 1988, 2: 67–70).

Among non-Christian intellectuals, Latin was, until very late, considered to be a commonly spoken (and thus "maternal") language, and it began to slough off this accrued infamy only after the twelfth century. Although recognized both by Christians and by non-Christians as a vehicle of authoritative Christian tradition, a language of vetted and venerated *auctores*, Latin defended its inveterate identity as a language of learning and acquired a broadly recognized status as a language of science after the twelfth century only by being distinguished as a predominantly written medium set apart from any spoken vernacular. Thus, Roger Bacon (d. 1294), who characterized Latin as his "mother tongue" along with English, affirmed that knowledge of *linguae sapientiae* depended not on speaking ability but only on knowledge of grammar: "Multi vero inveniuntur, qui sciunt loqui graecum, et arabicum, et hebraeum inter Latinos, sed paucissimi sunt qui sciunt rationem grammaticae ipsius, nec sciunt docere eam" [Among the Latins there are many who know how to speak Greek, Arabic, and Hebrew, but very few who know the structure of their grammar and are capable of teaching it] (Bacon 1859, 33–34; Bourgain 1989, 328). This emphasis on grammar in contrast to speech underscores the centrality of writing as the ongoing lodestone of authority throughout the Middle Ages. Martin Irvine's words, written about the early Middle Ages, hold true throughout: "The transition to medieval *grammatica* reveals that *auctoritas*, textual precedent or written authority, became the dominant criterion for *latinitas*" (Irvine 1996, 74). By the twelfth century, however, both *auctoritas* and *latinitas* came under substantial pressure from a rising vernacular and from competing written languages of learning, above all Arabic.

The Specter of Arabic

By the time Dante had formulated his theories of vernacular language, a willful blow had already been dealt to Latin's authority in the Iberian Peninsula with the ambitious projects of Castilian King Alfonso X, The Wise (d. 1284). He not only took steps to elevate the status of Castilian above other Romance dialects, but also explicitly worked to edge out Latin as the official language of his kingdom through use of Castilian for legal and historiographical writing and as the language of his chancery (Wright 1996). The ramifications of such policies on the construction of imperium in Alfonso's reign are nowhere more evident than on the tomb that Alfonso X had erected for his father, Fernando III, within the conquered mosque of Seville. The monument, now in the rebuilt cathedral, bears on each of its four sides an inscription in one of the languages of the kingdom—Hebrew, Arabic, Latin, and Castilian, respectively—that praises Fernando as the one "who conquered all of Spain" (Flórez 1754, 5–11). Physically as well as symbolically, Latin is made to share a crowded stage next to the vernacular as one of the official (i.e., written, *inscribed*) languages of the kingdom.

This monument, however, not only evinces the erosion of Latin as a language of empire in Alfonso's reign, but also signals the competition of both Latin and its vernaculars with Hebrew and Arabic. Alfonso patronized numerous translations from Arabic to Castilian, and the choice to bypass Latin was a deliberate attempt to stand apart from the first Arabic-to-Latin translation work of the preceding century (Márquez Villanueva 1994, 35–42). In contrast with the ambitious translating endeavor of the twelfth century, which infused the Latin language with new vitality as a viable language of learning, Alfonso's thirteenth-century translations into Castilian, along with his lyric production in Galician-Portuguese, enacted a double-pronged challenge to Latin's authority both as the language of learning in Western Christendom and also as the language of poetic and literary expression.

Alfonso's policies signal the ongoing standing of Arabic over Latin as the preeminent language of thought, science, and technology across the entire Mediterranean, but also intimate the inherent valence of Arabic as a language of empire and political prowess, one that had unified a continuous region of peoples and cultures stretching from Iberia to India since the eighth century. The sophistication and size of centers of learning across the Islamic world derived from the syncretism of a wealth of both ancient Greek sources and traditional Persian material along with some Sanskrit texts that had been absorbed into Middle Persian (Sassanian Pahlavi; Gutas 1998, 24–27). Such pooling of multiple traditions in Arabic dwarfed in quantity and variety even the greatest resources available to the monasteries and cathedral schools that peppered Western Latinity before the twelfth century. The rise of Latin into an authoritative language of scholasticism and science in the later Middle Ages depended greatly on the infusion into Latin through translation of this concentration of wealth in Arabic sources.

The fear within Latin cultures provoked by the Muslim conquest of North Africa and most of Iberia at the dawn of the eighth century slowly evolved into a marked ambivalence over Arabic learning and technology by the tenth. The specter of Arabic that hovered perpetually across the entire southern border of Latinity and occasionally wafted into it became a source of both polemical attack and fantasy and a reference point of self-evaluation. The famous and oft-touted remark of the Saxon nun Hrotsvit of Gandersham (fl. ca. 965) that "Partibus occiduis fulsit clarum decus orbis...Corduba famoso locuples de nomine dicta" [In the western regions of the world there shone a dazzling jewel...called by the illustrious name of Córdoba the rich], often taken as a paean to the celebrated Caliphal city in the ninth-century, in fact describes a pre-Islamic city of wealth and learning, a mythic conflation of Roman and Visigothic settlements whose Latin riches were arrogated by "Perfidia...Saracenorum gens indomitorum" [the perfidious race of untamed Saracens] (Hrotsvit 2001, 64). This evocation of physical and linguistic conquest was built on a long tradition. The famous, though often mistranslated, lament of Paul Alvarus (d. 861) casts the threat of Arabic in terms of a seduction away from Latin proficiency:

> Quis, rogo, odie sollers in nostris fidelibus laycis inuenitvr, qui scripturis sanctis intentus uolumina quorumquumque doctorum Latine conscripta respiciat?...Heu pro dolor, legem suam nesciunt Xpiani et linguam propriam non aduertunt Latini, ita ut omni Xpi collegio uix inueniatur unus in milleno hominum numero qui salutatorias fratri possit ratjonauiliter dirigere litteras, et repperitur absque numero multiplices turbas [sic] qui erudite Caldaicas uerborum explicet pompas.
>
> [Who, I ask, is found among our faithful laymen who is skilful enough to understand the book of Holy Scripture or anything written in Latin by any of [our] doctors?...Alas, what pain! The Christians no longer know their law, the Latins no longer pay attention to their own language, so that in the whole college

of Christ hardly one in a thousand can be found who reasonably is able to write a letter of greeting to his brother, while one finds uncountable throngs of those who explain with erudition Arabic displays of words.] (Gil 1973, 1: 314–15)

Alvarus wrote this lament in response to a situation particular to the Christian Mozarabs living in al-Andalus, but it is paradigmatic of a broader, albeit less articulated, Christian anxiety about Islam and Arabic that spread far beyond Iberia. Although, except in places like ninth- and tenth-century Cordoba, eleventh-century Palermo, or twelfth-century Toledo, Arabic wielded little immediate threat as a temptation away from Latin, it still remained an ineluctable, unsettling presence of foreignness on the horizon of Latinity. In the process of internalizing and domesticating this foreignness through translation in the twelfth and thirteenth centuries, however, Latinity acquired an awareness of both its own limitations and also of its place within a wider world of competing notions of authority.

One very telling example of the internalization of a sense of foreignness that accompanied an increased awareness of the authoritative prestige of Arabic can be found in a detail within the twelfth-century Latin translation of the Qur'ān undertaken by Robert of Ketton at the behest of Peter the Venerable, Abbot of Cluny (d. 1156). In verse 41:44, which addresses the importance of the Arabic language as the medium for God's words, God asks, "If we sent down a Qur'ān in a foreign language, they would have said, '[how can there be] foreign language and an Arab [speaker]?'" The word for "foreign language," 'aǧamīyah, is translated as *Latin* by Ketton, who adapts the whole verse slightly: "si *Latine* notaretur, fieret quaestio, cur Latinis et Arabicis litteris non distinguerentur" [If we had written it *in Latin*, he would ask why Latin and Arabic letters are not distinguished] (Bibliander 1543, 149; Ketton's Surah 51). This word choice was made again in the early thirteenth by Mark of Toledo in a different translation of the Qur'ān into Latin (Paris, Bibliothèque Mazarine Ms. 708, 86vb; Daniel 1993, 366 n. 32), and was quoted in the fourteenth century by John Wycliffe (d. 1384) in his *De veritate sacrae scripturae* (12) (Wycliffe 1905–7, 1: 269).

The choice to translate 'aǧamīyah as "Latin" followed a tradition that was evident as far back as the tenth-century translation of the Psalms into Arabic among Mozarab Christians of al-Andalus, characterizing speakers of Romance as non-Arab "foreigners" (a'ǧām) (Kassis 2006, 74; Versteegh 1997, 227). (In addition to being treated very often—but not always—as a synonym of laṭīnīyah, both usually to mean spoken Romance, the term 'aǧamīyah, "a non-Arabic/foreign language," had similarly functioned as a parallel term among Arabized Jews for the Hebrew term la'az, as we see in the statement by Maimonides in his Arabic commentary on *Pirkei Avot* that, because of Hebrew's holy status, it is more reprehensible to recite profane strophic poetry in Hebrew than in "Arabic or 'aǧam." In translating this text into Hebrew, Samuel Ibn Tibbon renders 'aǧam as la'az [Monroe 1988–89, 23, 29 n. 16].) The rendering of "'aǧamīyah" as "Latin" by Iberian Christians in the twelfth century reflects an internalization on the part of both translators, working in different moments, of the relative conceptual place of Latin from the perspective of revelation in Arabic. Even as they criticized the Qur'ān, both translators recognized the formidable concept of authority concomitant with the Arabic language itself, and as Thomas Burman has shown, Robert took steps to evoke "a particularly elevated Latin style" in order to render the solemn eloquence of the Qur'ān's language (Burman 2007, 34). The basis of this authority in Arabic, as both translators knew, rested principally on the Qur'ān itself, which was and is still considered among Muslims to be not simply a vehicle for divine expression but a miracle in itself, an exalted language that no man could equal or outdo. The status of Arabic within Islam is inseparable from the belief that God, the God of Abraham worshipped by Jews, Christians, and Muslims, repeatedly handed down his will to men through the prophets, including Moses and Jesus. The subsequent corruption and confusion of his message by both Jews and Christians necessitated the final revelation of Islam in "a clear Qur'ān" (15:1) given "in the clear Arabic language" (26:195). The Arabic language thus laid claim to an unparalleled uniqueness as being in itself a sort of theophany, a worldly manifestation of divine power and will preserved in a pure, transparent state.

The view in Islam of the Qur'ān as the very words of God existed among believers from the very beginning of its revelation in 610, and quickly became a universal belief among Muslims. This contrasts sharply with the slow development within Jewish belief of Hebrew as *Leshon ha-Qodesh*, "the holy language," a doctrine that is not evident within the biblical canon itself and that only seems to have emerged gradually within Hellenistic Jewish culture. The second-century BCE book of *Jubilees* contains the earliest references to Hebrew as a divine language, the original language of creation taught to Adam by God. Only in the rabbinical and medieval periods was Hebrew recognized widely as a holy language of creation, revelation, and mystical reflection, in addition to a language of ritual and liturgy (Aaron 2000, 270–72; Aaron 1999, 72-4). In contrast to Hebrew, Greek, and Latin which, despite their usage, were only gradually and belatedly *defined* by their users as holy languages, Arabic laid claim to a prestige within Islamic society as the preeminent holy language that was virtually synonymous with universal belief in Muḥammad and his prophecy from the very emergence of Islam (Kassis 2006, 62–63). Arabic's prestige can also be contrasted with Sanskrit, which originated as a language of sacred ritual and sacrifice restricted to an elite Brahman class and only later burst spontaneously across south Asia as a language of literary culture and then government (Pollock 2006, 28–29, 44–45). As the spread of Islam was as much, if not more, a political process as it was a religious one, this prestige naturally established Arabic as the most suitable imperial language as well (Gutas 2005, 104). Antonio de Nebrija's famous assertion in his *Grammar of the Castilian Language* (the first grammar of any Romance vernacular, published, not insignificantly, in 1492) that "language has always been the companion of power" (*compañera del imperio*, Nebrija 1980, 97), is nowhere more true in the Middle Ages than in the case of Arabic.

Even as the use of Arabic quickly permeated other spheres such as government and literature, the Qur'ān was always esteemed among Muslims as the standard benchmark of linguistic authority. The simultaneous spread of Arabic culture and Islam quickly produced a natural division between the many spoken Arabic dialects (*'āmmīyāt*) of each region and the single standard language of writing and formal expression (*fuṣḥā*) modeled according to these sources of authority. This classic *diglossia*, which still persists today, characterizes *fuṣḥā* as the natural heir of the combined prestige of Qur'ānic revelation and the purportedly "natural" language of the nomadic Bedouins. The definition and preservation of a pure Classical Arabic—not entirely separable from the standardization of a single written text of the Qur'ān after the death of Muḥammad under the third Caliph 'Uthmān—was one of the major endeavors of early Islamic civilization, producing the names of some 4,000 Arabic grammarians between 750–1500 CE (Versteegh 1997, 74). Most importantly, it represented the fulfillment of the mandate handed down in holy revelation itself.

In the context of this elevated sense of Arabic as the supreme language of creation, the language in which God chose finally to speak directly to all people, other languages could hardly figure within Arabic culture as valuable, let alone prestigious. In the ninth century, the Cordoban jurist Ibn Ḥabīb (d. 852) claimed that the three prophetic languages were Hebrew, Arabic, and Syriac, making no mention of Greek or Latin (Wilde 2007, 61–62, 80). His argument is all the more cutting because it is proffered by an Iberian Muslim for whom *laṭīnīyah* was a proximate reality. Among eastern Muslims, ignorance of Latin and Latinate Romance was a matter of course. The only direct reference to Latin as a written language found in medieval Arabic sources in the East is by the tenth-century bibliographer Ibn al-Nadīm, who set out in his *Fihrist* ("Catalogue") to classify the most important writers of his day, both Arabic and non-Arabic. He names a total of sixteen languages, three of which seem to refer to Western Christendom: Greek, the "writing of the Lombards and Saxons," and the language of the "Franks" (*ifranǧ*), which he claims to have seen on Frankish swords (Ibn al-Nadīm 1970, 28–30, 38). "Frankish," by which he probably means Latin, is not discussed in detail, but he does tell an anecdote, taken from an earlier source, about the arrival of an emissary from Queen Bertha of Rome to Baghdad in 906, bearing a letter whose "writing resembled the Greek [script] but was more straight." When none at the court were found to know the language, they found a Frank working in a clothing store who could translate it into Greek (Hamidullah 1953, 279–80).

Until the start of the Crusades in the eleventh century, what little was known in the 'Abbasid East about the people of Western Latinity (the *Ifranǧ*, or "Franks") or their language (*ifranǧī* or *al-luǧa al-ifranǧīya*, "Frankish language," a name connected with the later expression *lingua franca*) was often confused with Byzantium (Kassis 1999, 10-13). Western and Eastern Christians were regularly lumped together under the title *al-Rūm* (the "Romans"), a generic term used in the East to refer to Christians in general and Byzantines in particular (and in the West, sometimes also Iberian Christians). Arabic sources display a general disdain for the language and learning of the *Ifranǧ* and the *Rūm*, often in contradistinction to the more illustrious *Yūnān*, (the "Ionians"), the traditional Arabic term for ancient Greeks

(El Cheikh 2004, 104–8). While a few rare exceptions can be found in western Arabic sources, such as in the writing of Toledan jurist Ṣā'id al-Andalusī (d. 1070)—and such exceptions became more frequent after the twelfth century—Latin culture in general and Latin language in particular were so unimportant as to seem non-existent in eastern Arabic sources (Ṣā'id 1991, 32; Lewis 1982, 76–77).

The relative unimportance and total lack of authority of Latin in virtually any Arabophone worldview, whether Muslim or Jewish, east or west, was not lost on Latin scholars of the twelfth and thirteenth centuries. Roger Bacon saw Latin's low place in the world of learning as a call to learn the languages "a quibus tota Latinorum sapientia translata est, cujusmodi sunt Graecum, Hebraeum, Arabicum, et Chaldaeum" [from which all knowledge of the Latins is in some way translated, which are Greek, Hebrew, Arabic, and Aramaic] (Bacon 1859, 433; Bourgain 1989, 323–24). This need was all the more pressing because Latin was also comparatively poor in vocabulary and "translatores non invenerunt in lingua Latina vocabula sufficientia" [Translators do not find enough vocabulary in the Latin language] (Bacon 1859, 90). Moreover, "Latini nullum textum composuerunt, scilicet neque theologiae neque philosophiae" [The Latins have not composed a single text, that is, neither of theology nor of philosophy] (Bacon 1859, 465). Bacon's views resemble the opinion of twelfth-century Jewish poet and astronomer Abraham Ibn 'Ezra' (d. ca. 1164), who saw Hebrew as the primary language not only of creation and revelation, but of science as well. Although he wrote (or translated) a treatise on the Astrolabe in Latin, Ibn 'Ezra''s reflections on language express his hope that Hebrew be seen the first and richest language of science, certainly above Latin and even above Arabic (Sela 2003, 104–6, 140–43). A century after him, Bacon argued that Hebrew, along with Arabic, was the "primitivum vas" from which Latin scholars must draw the elixir of learning, if they are to compete with non-Latin traditions of science (Bacon 1859, 466).

At the same time, he affirmed that knowledge of language is useful for converting "infidels and schismatics" (Bacon 1859, 95), a view shared by his younger contemporary, the Mallorcan polymath Raymond Llull (d. 1315), who wrote, among his nearly three-hundred works in Catalan and Latin, polemical works in Arabic. Llull was one of numerous writers who took steps to adapt his use of Latin in order to incorporate characteristic expressions in Arabic, coining numerous Latin neologisms in an attempt to convey a "modum loquendi arabicum" [an Arabic mode of speaking]. In a telling passage from his *Compendium artis demonstrativae*, Llull even apologizes because "declinare namque terminos figurarum dicendo sub conditionibus bonitatis, bonificatium, bonificabile, bonificare bonificatum...non est multum apud latinos sermo consuetus..." [To decline the terms of the figures, saying on the basis of "goodness" [the terms] "good-ifying," "good-ifyable," "good-ify," "good-ified"... is not a way of speaking that is normal among the Latins..."] (Llull 1721–40, 3.6: 160; Hames 2003, 53). Despite Llull's conflicts of methodology with his contemporary, the Dominican Raymond Martini (d. after 1284), their approach to the adaptation of Latin into the form of their polemical enemies was not dissimilar. Martini had boasted that in his attack on Jews, "nec tolerabilem lingue Latine vitabo improprietatem" [I will not avoid the improper use, within tolerable limits, of the

Latin language] (Martini 1687, 4). This statement is similar to the claims of polemicist Juan of Segovia in the fifteenth century that in his translation of the Qur'ān, "minime dubitaui uerberare Priscianum, admodum incongrua persepe usus Latinitate" [I hesitated little to rough-up Priscian, [making] frequent use of incongruous Latin] (Martínez Gázquez 2003, 406; Burman 2007, 185).

As texts of Arabic learning, literature, and revelation began to be translated into Latin in the twelfth century, Latin scholars were faced not only with Arabic's unanswerable claims to divine authority but also with the reality of the vast wealth that had been absorbed into Arabic over the first centuries of Islam under the ʿAbbasid Caliphate. Moreover, such translations came at a time in the twelfth century when the very concept of *auctoritas* was in flux, not only in response to the increased attention to dialectic and rational argument, but also, in polemical writing, in response to the use of non-Christian sources as proof-texts. The tension between *ratio* and *auctoritas* that went back at least to John Scotus Eriugena seems to burst to the surface in the pointed remarks of Adelard of Bath (d. ca. 1152), in his *Quaestiones naturales* when, claiming he follows "ratione duce" [reason as a guide] he upbraids his nephew for following the "capistrum" [halter] of authority (Adelard 1998, 102–3). This sharp comparison between rational thought—learned, moreover, "a magistris arabicis" [from Arab masters]—was an opening salvo in what would become a much more pitched battle in the twelfth century, epitomized in the wry remark of Alan of Lille in his polemic against heretics, Jews, and Muslims [*paganos*] that "auctoritas cereum habet nasum" [authority has a nose of wax] (PL 210: 333). The impact of Arabic's monolithic prestige on Latin intellectual culture was all the deeper within the context of this internal uncertainty about the limits of *auctoritas*.

The ascendance of Latin as a language of learning, science, and wisdom depended on the usurpation of Arabic's prestige through translation and imitation in the twelfth and thirteenth centuries. The nature of the change can be gauged *in nuce* by the increasing respect commanded by Latin among non-Christian intellectuals. The fourteenth-century sociologist Ibn Khaldūn, in updating Ibn al-Nadīm's summary of scripts and languages, now names Latin (*al-Laṭīnī*), calling it the language of the *Rūm*, and even claims that it is one of the few languages (along with Arabic, Hebrew, and Syriac) even worth discussing (Ibn Khaldūn 1958, 3: 283–84). Latin makes his list because although "the intellectual sciences were shunned by" Romans when they became Christians, Latin has again in his time become a language of learning and wisdom: "We further hear now that the philosophical sciences are greatly cultivated in the land of Rome and along the adjacent northern shore of the country of the European Christians. They are said to be studied there again and taught in numerous classes" (ibid., 3: 115 and 118). A similar rise in Latin's status can be seen among Jewish intellectuals. By the fifteenth century, Jews living under Christian rule in Castile and Aragon no longer regarded Arabic as the exclusive and de facto language of thought. The Hebrew poet Solomon ben Reuben Bonafed (d. after 1448), praised and recommended the "straight path" of "the art of logic…in the Latin language," even as he harshly criticized Christian belief as a "path of death" (Sáenz-Badillos 2003, 17).

Despite this final flourishing of Latin as an authoritative language of wisdom and science, Arabic continued to hold a lingering prestige among Latin speakers long after it was eclipsed in Western Europe through translation. In the middle of the fourteenth century, the Dominican Alphonsus Bonihominis (d. 1353) proffered a pair of pro-Christian apologetic texts, the *Epistola Rabbi Samualis* and the *Disputatio Abutalib*, the former of which was destined to become one of the most widely circulated anti-Jewish texts of the later Middle Ages. In a statement found in the prologue to both texts, Alphonsus claims (dubiously, if we are to judge from the content) that he did not write the texts himself, but merely translated "libellum antiquissimum, qui nuper casu fortuito devenit in manus nostras, et fuit antea tot temporibus occultatus, nova translatione de Arabico in Latinum per me interpretatum" [a very old little book, which recently quite by chance came into my hands, and was hidden for so long in the past, interpreted by me in a new translation from Arabic to Latin] (PL 149: 335). Although already by his time, Arabic had ceased being the preeminent language of learning in the western Mediterranean, it still could be evoked as a framing device for his Latin text, providing a whiff of venerability and authority by virtue of its symbolic currency with past learning. Examples of such framing appear as late as the memorable rendition of Cervantes in 1605, claiming *Don Quixote* was the Arabic work of a Muslim author. Such tropes attest to the enduring prestige of Arabic in the fifteenth and sixteenth centuries when it enjoyed a rich afterlife as an imagined language of knowledge and authority at a time when Medieval Latin was increasingly derided as a foil of early modern humanism.

SUGGESTIONS FOR FURTHER READING

A popular and very accessible overview of the social history of Latin in all periods is Ostler (2007), who also offers a readable survey of notions of authority across multiple periods and languages (2005). A fine introduction to various concepts pertaining to Latin as a language of authoritative tradition is provided by Ziolkowski (2009). Chenu (1927) is still the starting point for all discussions of medieval concepts of *auctoritas* and Minnis (1988) offers the most in-depth and up-to-date analysis. Resnick (1990) and Richter (2006) are good starting points for exploring concepts of Latin as a holy language. Borst (1957–63) is the definitive source for the evolution of linguistic theories of authority and decadence connected with the myth of Babel. Irvine (1994) presents the important link between *latinitas*, *grammatica*, and *auctoritas* for the early medieval period through the eleventh century. On the notion of maternal and paternal language in medieval Latin, two short overviews are Grondeux (2008) and Spitzer (1948). There are numerous good studies of the relation between oral and written registers in Latin, including Farrell (2001), chapters 2 and 3, Banniard (1992), and Wright (1982). On various aspects of the intersection of Latin with Romance vernaculars, see Wright (1982), Lusignan (1986) and (1994), and Copeland (1991). For a survey of concepts of Latin as a language of learning and philosophy, see Bourgain (2005). There are numerous studies relating Latin in a context of multilingualism, including Adams (2003) for the late-antique period, Bishoff (1961), Grondeux (2005), Wright (2002), chapter 1, and Grotans (2006). Waquet (2001) offers a fascinating survey of the rise and persistence of Latin as a language of authority beyond the medieval period. For an overview of concepts of linguistic authority in Arabic, see Versteegh (1997), and for a general overview of such concepts in Hebrew, see Rubin (1998) and Aaron (2000). Wasserstein (1991) offers a short and lucid introduction to language use in al-Andalus, and Alfonso (2007) considers the competition of models of prestige between Hebrew and Arabic. Kassis (1999) gives a useful summary of the representation of Europeans in some medieval Arabic sources. Pollock (2006) provides both an in-depth analysis of such concepts in classical Sanskrit and a fruitful, if opaque, comparison with both classical and medieval theories of Latin (chapters 7 and 11). For a discussion of the authority of Greek within medieval Latinity, see Berschin (1988) and Lubac (1959–64, 2.1: 238–262). For studies comparing concepts of authoritative language in Latin, Hebrew, Arabic, and/or Greek, see Versteegh (1987) and Dahan et al. (1995).

BIBLIOGRAPHY

Primary sources

Adelard of Bath. 1998. *Conversations with His Nephew. On the Same and the Different, Questions on Natural Science, and On Birds*, edited by Charles Burnett. Cambridge Medieval Classics 9. Cambridge: Cambridge University Press.

Augustine of Hippo. 1962. *Sancti Aurelii Augustini De doctrina christiana. De vera religione*, edited by Klaus D. Daur and Josef Martin. Corpus Christianorum. Series Latina 32. Turnhout: Brepols.

———. 1955. *Sancti Aurelii Augustini de civitate Dei*, edited by Bernhard Dombart and Alphons Kalb. 2 vols. Corpus Christianorum. Series Latina 47–48. Turnhout: Brepols.

Bacon, Roger. 1859. *Opera quaedam hactenus inedita*, edited by John S. Brewer. 3 vols. in 1. London: Her Majesty's Stationery Office.

Bibliander, Theodor. 1543. *Machumetis Saracenorum principis, eiusque successorum vitae ac doctrina, ipseque Alcoran*. Basel: Nikolaus Brylinger for Johannes Oporin.

Baudri de Bourgeuil. 1979. *Baldricus Burgulianus Carmina*. Ed. Karlheinz Hilbert. Heidelberg: Carl Winter Universitätsverlag.

Baudri de Bourgueil. 1926. *Les oeuvres poétiques de Baudri de Bourgueil (1046–1130). Edition critique publiée d'après le manuscrit du Vatican*, edited by Phyllis Abrahams. Paris: Champion.

Dante Alighieri. 1996. *De vulgari eloquentia*, translated by Steven Botterill. Cambridge Medieval Classics 5. Cambridge: Cambridge University Press, 1996.

———. 1973. *Vita nuova*, translated by Mark Musa. 2nd ed. Indianapolis: Indiana University Press.

Dietrich, Albert, ed. 1988. *Dioscurides Triumphans. Ein anonymer arabischer Kommentar (Ende 12. Jahrh. n. Chr.) zur Materia medica*. 2 vols. Abhandlungen der Akademie der

Wissenschaften in Göttingen. Philologisch-Historische Klasse, 3. Folge, 172–73. Göttingen: Vandenhoeck & Ruprecht.

Durand, Guillaume. 1995–2000. *Guillelmi Duranti Rationale divinorum officiorum*, edited by Anselm Davril and Timothy M. Thibodeau. 3 vols. Corpus Christianorum. Continuatio Mediaevalis 140, 140A, 140B. Turnhout: Brepols.

Einhard. 1947. Vie de Charlemagne. Ed. Louis Halphan. 3rd ed. Paris: Les Belles Lettres.

Flórez, Enrique. 1754. "Elogios del santo rey don Fernando, puesto en el sepulcro de Sevilla." In *España Sagrada*, vol. 2. Madrid: Antonio Marín.

Gil, Juan, ed. 1973. *Corpus Scriptorum Muzarabicorum*. 2 vols. Manuales y anejos de "Emerita" 28. Madrid: Instituto Antonio de Nebrija.

Guibert de Nogent. 1996. *Dei gesta per Francos*, edited by Robert B. C. Huygens. Corpus Christianorum. Continuatio Mediaevalis 127A. Turnhout: Brepols.

Hamidullah, Muhammad. 1953. "Embassy of Queen Bertha to Caliph al-Muktafi Billah in Baghdad 293H./906." *Journal of the Pakistan Historical Society* 1: 272–300.

Hrotsvit of Gandersheim. 2001. *Hrotsvit Opera Omnia*. Ed. Walter Berschin. Munich and Leipzig: K. G. Saur Verlag.

Ibn Ḥazm. 1962. *Jamharat ansāb al-'arab*, edited by Abd al-Salām M. Hārūn. Cairo: Dar al-Ma'ārif.

Ibn al-Nadīm. 1970. *The Fihrist of al-Nadīm*, translated by Bayard Dodge. 2 vols. Records of civilization: Sources and Studies 83. New York: Columbia University Press.

Ibn Khaldūn. 1958. *The Muqaddimah. An Introduction to History*, translated by Franz Rosenthal. 3 vols. Bollingen Series 43. Princeton, NJ: Princeton University Press.

Isidore of Seville. 1911. *Isidori Hispalensis episcopi Etymologiarum sive Originum*, edited by Wallace M. Lindsay. 2 vols. Scriptorum classicorum bibliotheca Oxoniensis. Oxford: Clarendon.

Joseph Ibn Caspi. 1996. *Shulḥan Kesef*, edited by Hannah Kasher. Jerusalem: Ben-Zvi Institute.

Moses Ibn 'Ezra'. 1975. *Kitāb al-muḥāḍarah wa-l-mudhākarah*, edited by Abraham S. Halkin. Jerusalem: Mekize Nirdamim.

de Nebrija, Antonio. 1980. *Gramática de la lengua castellana*. Madrid: Editora Nacional.

Neusner, Jacob. 2001. *Sifré to Numbers and Sifré to Deuteronomy*, vol. 8 of *A Theological Commentary to the Midrash*. Studies in Ancient Judaism. Lanham, MD: University Press of America.

Petrus Comestor. 2005. *Petri Comestoris Scolastica historia. Liber Genesis*, edited by Agneta Sylwan. Corpus Christianorum. Continuatio Mediaevalis 191. Turnhout: Brepols.

Llull, Raymond. 1721–42. *Compendium artis demonstrativae*, vol. 3 of *Opera Omnia*, edited by Ivo Salzinger. Mainz. Reprint Frankfurt/Main: Minerva, 1965.

Martínez Gázquez, José. 2003. "El prólogo de Juan de Segobia al Corán (*Qur'ān*) trilingüe (1456)." *Mittellateinisches Jahrbuch* 38: 389-410.

Martini, Raymond. 1687. *Pugio Fidei adversus Mauros et Iudaeos*. Leipzig. Reprint Farnborough: Gregg, 1967.

Rosenthal, Franz. 1975. *The Classical Heritage in Islam*. The Islamic World Series. London: Routledge.

Ṣā'id al-Andalusī. 1991. *Science in the Medieval World. "Book of the Categories of Nations,"* edited and translated by Sema'an I. Salem and Alok Kumar. History of Science Texts 5. Austin, TX: University of Texas Press.

Salimbene de Adam. 1998. Cronica, ed. Giuseppe Scalia. Turhout: Brepols. Corpus Christianorum. Continuatio Medievalis vol. 125A.

Thomas Aquinas. 1972 [1882–]. *Quaestiones disputatae de veritate*. Vol. 22/2 of *Sancti Thomae de Aquino Opera Omnia*, edited by Leonine Commission. Rome: Vatican Polyglot Press.

Wycliffe, John. 1905–7. *John Wyclif's De Veritate Sacrae Scripturae*, edited by Rudolf Buddensieg. 3 vols. Wyclif Society Publications 29–31. London: Trübner & Co.

Secondary sources

Aaron, David. 1999. "Judaism's Holy Language." In *Approaches to Ancient Judaism XVI*, edited by. Jacob Neusner, 49-107. Atlanta GA: Scholars Press.

Aaron, David. 2000. "The Doctrine of Hebrew Language Usage." In *The Blackwell Companion to Judaism*, edited by Jacob Neusner and Alan Avery-Peck, 268–87. Blackwell Companions to Religion. Oxford: Blackwell.

Adams, James N. 2003. *Bilingualism and the Latin Language*. Cambridge: Cambridge University Press.

Alfonso, Esperanza. 2008. *Islamic Culture Through Jewish Eyes: Al-Andalus From the Tenth to the Twelfth Century*. Routledge Studies in Middle Eastern Literatures 20. London: Routledge.

Banitt, Menahem. 2007. "La'az." In *Encyclopaedia Judaica*, edited by Michael Berenbaum and Fred Skolnik, 2nd ed. Detroit: Macmillan. Vol. 12. pp. 405–6.

Barceló, Carmen. 1997. "Mozárabes de Valencia y 'Lengua Mozárabe.'" *Revista de Filología Española* 77: 253–79.

Banniard, Michel. 1992. *Viva Voce: communication écrite et communication orale du IVe au IXe siècle en Occident latin*. Collection des études augustiniennes. Série Moyen-âge et Temps modernes 25. Paris: Institut des études augustiniennes.

Berschin, Walter. 1988. *Greek Letters and the Latin Middle Ages*, translated by Jerold C. Frakes. Revised ed. Washington, DC: Catholic University of America Press.

Bischoff, Bernard. 1961. "The Study of Foreign Languages in the Middle Ages." *Speculum* 36: 209–24.

Borst, Arno. 1957–63. *Der Turmbau von Babel. Geschichte der Meinungen über Ursprung und Vielfalt der Sprachen und Völker*. 4 vols. in 6. Stuttgart: Anton Hiersemann.

Bos, Gerrit, and Guido Mensching. 2005. "The Literature of Hebrew Medical Synonyms: Romance and Latin Terms and Their Identification." *Aleph* 5: 169–211.

Bourgain, Pascale. 1989. "Le sens de la langue et des langues chez Roger Bacon." In *Traduction et traducteurs au moyen âge,* edited by Geneviève Contamine, 317–31. Institut de recherche et d'histoire des textes. Documents, études et répertoires. Paris: Centre nationale de la recherche scientifique.

———. 2005. "Réflexions médiévales sur les langues de savoir." In *Tous vos gens à latin. Le latin, langue savante, langue mondaine (XIVe–XVIIe siècles)*, edited by Emmanuel Bury, 23–46. Travaux d'humanisme et Renaissance 405. Geneva: Droz.

Burman, Thomas E. 2007. *Reading the Qur'ān in Latin Christendom, 1140–1560*. Material Texts. Philadelphia: University of Pennsylvania Press.

Cabanelas, Darìo. 1952. *Juan de Segovia y el problema islámico*. Madrid: Publicaciones de la Facultad de Filosofía y Letras de la Universidad de Madrid.

Chenu, Marie-Dominique. 1927. "Auctor, actor, autor." *Bulletin du Cange: Archivum Latinitatis Medii Ævi* 3: 81–86.

Copeland, Rita. 1991. *Rhetoric, Hermeneutics, and Translation in the Middle Ages: Academic Traditions and Vernacular Texts*. Cambridge Studies in Medieval Literature 11. Cambridge: Cambridge University Press.

Dahan, Gilbert, Irène Rosier, et al. 1995. "L'arabe, le grec, l'hébreu et les vernaculaires." In *Sprachtheorien in Spätantike und Mittelalter*, edited by Sten Ebbesen, 265–321. Geschichte der Sprachtheorie 3. Tübingen: G. Narr.

Daniel, Norman. 1993. *Islam and the West. The Making of an Image*. Oxford: Oxford University Press.

El Cheikh, Nadia Maria. 2004. *Byzantium Viewed by the Arabs*. Harvard Middle Eastern Monographs 36. Cambridge, MA: Harvard Center for Middle Eastern Studies.

Farrell, Joseph. 2001. *Latin Language and Latin Culture*. Roman Literature and its Contexts. Cambridge: Cambridge University Press.

Grondeux, Anne. 2005. "Le latin et les autre langues au Moyen Âge: contacts avec des locuteurs étrangers, bilinguisme, interprétation et traduction (800–1200)." In *Tous vos gens à latin. Le latin, langue savante, langue mondaine (XIVe–XVIIe siècles)*, edited by Emmaneul Bury, 47–68. Travaux d'humanisme et Renaissance 405. Geneva: Droz.

———. 2008. "La notion de langue maternelle et son apparition au Moyen Âge." In *Zwischen Babel und Pfingsten: Sprachdifferenzen und Gesprächsverständigung in der Vormoderne (8.–16. Jahrhundert)*, edited by Peter von Moos, 339–56. Gesellschaft und individuelle Kommunikation in der Vormoderne (GIK) 1. Zürich: Lit.

Grotans, Anna A. 2006. *Reading in Medieval St. Gall*. Cambridge Studies in Palaeography and Codicology 13. Cambridge, New York: Cambridge University Press.

Gutas, Dimitri. 1998. *Greek Thought, Arabic Culture. The Graeco-Arabic Translation Movement in Baghdad and Early 'Abbāsid Society (2nd–4th/8th–10th centuries)*. London: Routledge.

———. 2005. "Language and Imperial Ideology in Late Antiquity and Early Islam." In *The Contest of Language. Before and Beyond Nationalism*, edited by W. Martin Bloomer, 99–110. Notre Dame, IN: University of Notre Dame Press.

Hames, Harvey. 2003. "The Language of Conversion: Ramon Llull's Art as a Vernacular." In *The Vulgar Tongue: Medieval and Postmedieval Vernacularity*, edited by Fiona Somerset and Nicholas Watson, 43–56. University Park, PA: Pennsylvania State University Press.

Irvine, Martin. 1994. *The Making of Textual Culture. 'Grammatica' and Literary Theory 350–1100*. Cambridge Studies in Medieval Literature 19. Cambridge: Cambridge University Press.

Kassis, Hanna E. 1999. "Images of Europe and Europeans in Some Medieval Arabic Sources." In *From Arabye to Engelond. Medieval Studies in Honour of Mahmoud Manzalaoui on His 75th Birthday*, edited by A. E. Christa Canitz and Gernot R. Wieland, 9-23. Ottawa: University of Ottawa Press.

Kassis, Hanna E. 2006. "'We have sent it down as an Arabic Qur'an.' An Arabic Qur'an: An Examination of Sources and Implications." In *Language of Religion—Language of the People. Medieval Judaism, Christianity and Islam*, edited by Ernst Bremer et al., 61–76. MittelalterStudien 11. Munich: Wilhelm Fink.

Kramer, Johannes. 1998. *Die Sprachbezeichnungen Latinus und Romanus im Lateinischen und Romanischen*. Studienreihe Romania 12. Berlin: E. Schmidt.

Lewis, Bernard. 1982. *The Muslim Discovery of Europe*. London: W. W. Norton.

Lubac, Henri de. 1959–64. *Exégèse médiévale. Les quatre sens de l'écriture*. 4 vols. Théologie: études publiées sous la direction de la Faculté de théologie S. J. de Lyon-Fourvière 41, 42, 59. Paris: Aubier.

Lusignan, Serge. 1994. "Autorité et notoriété: langue française et savoir au XIVe siècle." In *Florilegium Historiographiae Linguisticae. Études d'historiographie de la linguistique et de la grammaire comparée à la mémoire de Maurice Leroy*, edited by Jan De Clercq and Piet Desmet, 185–202. Bibliothèque des Cahiers de l'Institut de linguistique de Louvain 75. Louvain-La-Neuve: Peeters.

———. 1986. *Parler vulgairement: les intellectuels et la langue française aux XIIIe et XIVe siècles.* Presses de l'Université de Montréal. Etudes médiévales. Paris, Montreal: J. Vrin and Les Presses de l'Université de Montréal.

Márquez Villanueva, Francisco. 1995. *El concepto cultural Alfonsí.* 2nd ed. Madrid: Mapfre.

Mazzocco, Angelo. 1993. *Linguistic Theories in Dante and the Humanists. Studies of Language and Intellectual History in Late Medieval and Early Renaissance Italy.* Brill's Studies in Intellectual History 38. Leiden, New York: E. J. Brill.

Minnis, Alastair J. 1988. *Medieval Theory of Authorship.* 2nd ed. Middle Ages Series. Philadelphia: University of Pennsylvania Press.

Monroe, James T. 1988–89. "Maimonides on the Mozarabic Lyric (A Note on the Muwaššaḥa)". *La Corónica* 17.2: 18–32.

Ong, Walter. 1977. *Interfaces of the Word: Studies in the Evolution of Consciousness and Culture.* Ithaca, NY: Cornell University Press.

Ostler, Nicholas. 2005. *Empires of the Word: A Language History of the World.* New York: HarperCollins.

———. 2007. *Ad Infinitum: A Biography of Latin.* New York: Walker & Co.

Pollock, Sheldon. 2006. *The Language of the Gods in the World of Men. Sanskrit, Culture, and Power in Premodern India.* Berkeley, CA: University of California Press.

Resnick, Irven M. 1990. "Lingua Dei, lingua hominis: Sacred Language and Medieval Texts." *Viator* 21: 51–74.

Richter, Michael. 2006. "Concept and Evolution of the *tres linguae sacrae.*" In *Language of Religion—Language of the People. Medieval Judaism, Christianity and Islam,* edited by Ernst Bremer et al., 15–24. MittelalterStudien 11. Munich: Wilhelm Fink.

Rubin, Milka. 1998. "The Language of Creation or The Primordial Language: A Case of Cultural Polemics in Antiquity." *Journal of Jewish Studies* 49: 306–33.

Sáenz-Badillos, Ángel and Arturo Prats. 2003. "Shelomo Bonafed y la lógica cristiana del siglo XV." *Revista Española de Filosofía Medieval* 10: 15–27.

Sela, Shlomo. 2003. *Abraham Ibn Ezra and the Rise of Medieval Hebrew Science.* Brill's Series in Jewish Studies 32. Leiden, Boston: Brill.

Sirat, Colette. 1996. *A History of Jewish Philosophy in the Middle Ages.* Paris: Cambridge University Press.

Spitzer, Leo. 1948. "Muttersprache und Muttererziehung." In *Essays in Historical Semantics,* 15–65. New York: S. F. Vanni.

Thomas, David. 2001. "The Doctrine of the Trinity in the Early Abbasid Era." In *Islamic Interpretations of Christianity,* edited by Lloyd Ridgeon, 78–98. New York: St. Martin's Press.

Versteegh, Kees. 1987. "Latinitas, Hellenismos, 'Arabiyya." In *The History of Linguistics in the Classical Period,* edited by Daniel J. Taylor, 251–74. Amsterdam Studies in the Theory and History of Linguistic Science. Series III. Studies in the History of the Language Sciences 46 Amsterdam, Philadelphia: John Benjamins.

———. 1997. *The Arabic Language.* New York: Columbia University Press.

Waquet, Françoise. 2001. *Latin, or The Empire of the Sign from the Sixteenth to the Twentieth Centuries,* translated by John Howe. London: Verso.

Wasserstein, David. 1991. "The Language Situation in Al-Andalus." In *Studies on the Muwaššaḥ and the Kharja,* edited by Alan Jones and Richard Hitchcock, 1–15. Oxford Oriental Institute Monographs 12. Reading: Ithaca Press for the Board of the Faculty of Oriental Studies, Oxford University.

Wexler, Paul. 1988. *Three Heirs to a Judeo-Latin Legacy: Judeo-Ibero-Romance, Yiddish and Rotwelsch.* Mediterranean Language and Culture Monograph Series 3. Wiesbaden: Otto Harrassowitz.

Wilde, Clare E. 2007. "*Lingua sacra? Some Reflections of Christian Discussions of faḍā'il al-suryāniyya and i'jāz al-Qur'ān.*" In *Eastern Crossroads: Essays on Medieval Christian Legacy,* edited by Juan Pedro Monferrer-Sala, 61–82. Gorgias Eastern Christianity Studies 1. Piscataway, NJ: Gorgias Press.

Wright, Roger. 1982. *Late Latin and Early Romance in Spain and Carolingian France.* ARCA, Classical and Medieval Texts, Papers, and Monographs 8. Liverpool: Francis Cairns.

———. 1996. "Latin and Romance in the Castilian Chancery (1180–1230)." *Bulletin of Hispanic Studies* 72: 115–28.

———. 2002. *A Sociophilological Study of Late Latin.* Utrecht Studies in Medieval Literacy 10. Turnhout: Brepols.

Ziolkowski, Jan M. 2009. "Cultures of Authority in the Long Twelfth Century." *Journal of English and Germanic Philology* 108: 421–48.

CHAPTER 5

THE CULTURES AND DYNAMICS OF TRANSLATION INTO MEDIEVAL LATIN

THOMAS E. BURMAN

A Culture of Translation

"Prima enim sunt hebrea, secundo greca translata de hebreis, tercio latina translata de grecis; unde latina maxime inemendata" [The first (Old Testament) texts are Hebrew, secondly Greek translated from Hebrew, thirdly Latin translated from Greek: hence the Latin are least correct] (Grosseteste 1982, 48). So wrote Robert Grosseteste (c. 1175–1253) in a commentary on Jerome's preface to the Vulgate Pentateuch. Here Jerome was defending his decision to make a translation of the Old Testament directly from Hebrew against those who considered the Septuagint, and hence the Old Latin versions of the Bible, to be more authoritative. Such critics, he pointedly observed, might as well assert that "emendatiora sunt exemplaria latina quam graeca, graeca quam hebraea!" [the Latin exemplars are more correct than the Greek, and the Greek than the Hebrew!] (Weber et al. 1994, 4). Lest the novice students for whom Grosseteste was writing be misled, he emphasized that Jerome was speaking ironically. Quite the opposite is true in reality: "the Latin are least correct."

Medieval European scholars often found themselves worrying over the reliability of their Latin texts, for medieval Latin Christendom was to an unusual degree a culture of translations, a culture whose core, canonical texts were translations of what was written, or even revealed, in other languages. Indeed, between Jerome's defense of his Biblical translation project and Grosseteste's commentary on it some eight hundred years later, the Latin tradition had become even more dependent on translated authoritative texts (Berschin 1991). As Latin sought to establish itself in the Mediterranean basin as a language of learning and sophistication alongside the more prestigious Greek and Arabic languages, and eventually against the rapidly developing European vernaculars (see Szpiech in this volume), more and more texts from those languages were, almost necessarily, translated into Latin and absorbed into the canon of works at the core of Latin education. Of course Latin culture had long been dependent on the outside influence of Greeks and Greek texts, but while ancient translators did make some Greek works available in Latin, much of the Hellenism of Rome was the result of the bilingualism of its elite who were educated in Greek and Latin and therefore read Homer and Plato in the original language. Medieval Latin civilization continued to be dependent on the Greeks and would later become profoundly reliant on Arab civilization as well, but, since knowledge of these languages was virtually nonexistent in Latin Christendom, translations were the primary vehicles of influence.

Of course, Latin Christendom was not the only civilization built in part on translated core texts, but the extent to which it was is remarkable. In the Byzantine world, while there were a few translations into Greek that were fundamental to Greek-Christian culture—especially the Septuagint, the Greek version of the *Codex iuris civilis*, and Pope Zecharias's Greek version of Gregory's works—for the most part the core texts, both pagan and Christian, of Byzantium had been written in Greek and were studied in Greek: Plato, Aristotle, the New Testament, the Greek Fathers, Pseudo-Dionysius, John of Damascus, Photius, Maximus the Confessor. Latin works, including some of Aquinas's, were translated into Greek from time to time, but none of these became deeply influential. Something similar could be said of Latin Christendom's other neighbor in the Mediterranean basin, Arab Islam. The Arabs had virtually no written language and no philosophical and scientific tradition before the time of Muḥammad. The Qur'an itself, therefore, was the founder of a written literary and intellectual tradition, serving not only as the final revelation of God to man, but as the inimitable exemplar of the Arabic language. As Islam developed, it produced a vast body of thoroughly Arabic works in addition to the Qur'an upon which the Islamic religion and Arab culture were constructed: the authoritative collections of Islamic tradition (the Hadith), the exhaustive Qur'an commentaries, the historical works, the anthologies of poetry. The well-known exception was the vast influence of the Greek and Persian scientific and philosophical texts translated into Arabic from the mid-eighth through mid-tenth century, Arab civilization in this regard becoming as Hellenized as its predecessors (Peters 1988, 77–91). Not only did this culminate in a sophisticated tradition of what might be called secular science and philosophy in the Arabic language, but a philosophical theology known in Arabic as *kalām* (debate) and inspired in part by Greek thought developed into a mainstream Islamic intellectual pursuit, while Neoplatonic mystical ideas took deep root in (far less mainstream) Sufi thought.

It is also true that translations from Persian such as *Kalilah wa-Dimnah* were influential in Arabic literature, but in general far fewer translations could be considered core texts of the Arab-Islamic world than in the Latin-Christian world. The basic Islamic educational curriculum consisted of the so-called Islamic sciences, and all its basic texts were originally Arabic—the Qur'an, Hadith, Qur'anic commentaries, legal texts, and the countless *responsa* or *fatwās* composed by jurisconsults. The "foreign" (Greek) sciences were of course studied in translation, but these texts never became standard in this curriculum, and had, in fact, to be studied apart from it. As a result Greek philosophy and science were never as central to Islamic education as Latin translations of both Aristotle and the Aristotelian commentaries of Ibn Rushd (Averroes) were to high-medieval Latin scholasticism. By the second half of the thirteenth century, the Bachelor of Arts curriculum of Latin universities—the basic university education that all students had to master—had essentially become a course on Aristotle's thought as interpreted by Ibn Rushd, both by way of Latin translations. Neither the Byzantine nor the Arab-Islamic world offered anything comparable to this.

While high-medieval universities represented Latin Christendom at its most dependent on translated canonical texts, Latin reliance on translation—and anxiety about that reliance—goes back to the beginning of the Middle Ages. Indeed, the Latin world faced a problem shared only in part by Byzantium and not at all by the Arab-Islamic world: its holy book in its entirety was a collection of translations. Jerome's prefaces to the books of the Vulgate made this all too apparent, for, in addition to being an aggressive defense of his decision to translate directly from the Hebrew and Greek, they amount to an extended reflection on both the danger and necessity of relying on translation in matters of revelation. He frequently reminds his readers that Hebrew, Aramaic, and Greek originals lie behind the Latin Biblical books that they read. There is a "silva hebraicorum nominum" [a forest of Hebrew names] that await even readers of the Old Testament in Latin, he points out, and the Hebrew alphabet itself crops up in the acrostic Psalms and the Lamentations of Jeremiah. Much of his preface to Samuel and Kings dwells at length on the Hebrew names of the Old Testament books. But more importantly, Jerome arrestingly (and influentially) asserts that his Latin version is meant to communicate the "hebraica veritas" [Hebrew truth] of the Old Testament, and challenges those who doubt the veracity of his translation "to ask the Hebrews" whether it is correct. Indeed, Jerome locates his own translation within a world seemingly overrun with different translations of the Hebrew Bible. The situation was especially serious for Latin readers, he notes, for among them "tot sint exemplaria quot codices" [there are as many versions [of the Bible] as there are manuscripts]. The book of Esther, for example, has been "vitiatus" [corrupted] by various translators, all this causing other contemporary Latin Christians such as Sophronius, to whom he addressed his preface to the Psalms, to be "interpretum varietate turbari" [disturbed by the variety of translations]. In the face of all this uncertainty, Jerome repeatedly defends his own Latin versions against *latrantes* [carpers] inclined to criticize, pointing out to his readers that he has taken important steps to achieve accuracy, such as correcting the order of Jeremiah's visions "qui apud Graecos et Latinos omnino confusus est" [which among Greeks and Latins has become intermingled] (Weber et al. 1994, 4, 285, 364, 365, 712, 731, 768, 1166).

Later medieval readers were reminded in countless ways that their Bible was a translation. For one thing, Jerome's Biblical prefaces frequently circulated with the Bible, and so also did his lexicon of Hebrew words that appear in the Vulgate. Moreover, Augustine's frequently copied guidebook on education and scriptural interpretation, *De doctrina christiana*, urged the same awareness on Latin Christians. Latin speakers, he observed, actually needed to know Hebrew and Greek to understand the Bible (though he knew no Hebrew himself). Short of that they must be prepared to compare as many Latin versions of the Bible as possible in order to arrive at the fullest awareness of the meanings of God's revelation (Augustine 1962, 42, 82). Hugh of St. Victor's twelfth-century blueprint for education, the *Didascalicon*, similarly stressed the non-Latin origin of the Bible (Hugh of St. Victor 1939, 71–80). As if to carry out Augustine's advice, medieval Latin scholars produced a large number of bilingual (Hebrew-Latin or Greek-Latin) manuscripts of the Psalms, Gospels, and Pauline epistles that circulated up through the Carolingian period, and while these became less common thereafter, bilingual Psalters continued to be copied till the end of the Middle Ages. Indeed it was probably the Psalter that raised the troubling issues of scriptural translation most pressingly, since it existed in three different Latin versions—Jerome's revision, based on the Septuagint, of the older Latin Psalms (*Psalterium Romanum*), his translation of the Hebrew original (*Psalterium iuxta Hebraeos*), and his third attempt, which amounts to a compromise methodologically between the first two (*Psalterium Gallicanum*). While the last, the Gallican Psalter, became predominant in the Christian West, the other two versions continued to circulate as well. Indeed, from time to time all three were copied side by side in the same codex to facilitate the sort of close comparison that Augustine had recommended (Berschin 1998, 38–39, 50–51).

As Greek-Latin bilingual Bibles became less common in the high Middle Ages, Biblical scholars in the twelfth century and later brought before their readers in striking new ways the limitations of their Latin Old Testament. Andrew of St. Victor's innovative fascination with the literal meaning of the Bible inspired him not only carefully to comb through Jerome's writings for insight into the historical meaning of Hebrew terms, but also compelled him to begin learning Hebrew himself and to consult with Parisian rabbis whose interpretations of important Biblical terms he sometimes preferred to the traditional Christian exegesis (van Liere 2005). This literal turn in Biblical exegesis culminated with Nicholas of Lyra in the fourteenth century, whose erudite *Postils* on the Bible minutely probed the relationships between the Vulgate Old Testament and the Hebrew and Aramaic source texts, relying on a large range of Jewish commentators in the process. To read this tremendously influential commentary was to be confronted at every juncture by the fact that the most important text in Latin Christian religion and culture was a not entirely satisfactory translation—especially if it was consulted in one of the many manuscripts that included the *additiones* to it composed by the *converso* Spanish bishop Pablo de Santa María who, in criticizing Lyra for excessive reliance on Rashi and failure to consult other Jewish thinkers such as Maimonides, raised even further concerns about the Vulgate's reliability (Szpiech 2010, 104 n. 16).

It is true that at the outset of the Middle Ages most of the other core educational texts of Western Christendom besides the Vulgate were not translations. The works of Augustine and Gregory and the other Western Fathers, the *Corpus iuris civilis*, the rhetorical works and orations of Cicero, Virgil's *Aeneid*, Priscian, and Donatus, the other textbooks commonly used to teach the seven liberal arts— all these were Latin products of a deeply Latin civilization, however dependent on Greek models and inspiration. But gradually throughout the following centuries, many of these key works were supplemented or entirely pushed aside by translations. Boethius's famous project to translate all of Plato and Aristotle into Latin never got beyond Aristotle's "old logic" supplemented by Porphyry's *Isagoge*, but this limited set of translations itself quickly became basic texts in the early Middle Ages. John Scotus Eriugena's translations of Greek works by pseudo-Dionysius were the vehicle through which non-Augustinian Neoplatonism significantly influenced Latin thought, while the vast Greek- and Arabic-to-Latin translation movement of the high Middle Ages introduced what became an entirely new educational curriculum to the Latin world. At about the same time, the European vernaculars had become powerful vehicles of literary culture as well, and while the intellectual and cultural resources that they contained were limited in comparison to what the Greek and Arabic languages offered, it occurred to an intriguingly large number of people to translate from French or German into Latin. Thus we find that the originally French *Travels of Sir John Mandeville* was known to a large readership in Latin translation, some fifty-four manuscripts of which are extant as well as four fifteenth-century printed editions (Higgins 1997, 20–23).

While Constantine the African attempted to conceal the Arab origins of the scientific works he translated in the eleventh century, most Greek- or Arabic-to-Latin translators did not imitate him. Indeed they often drew attention to the status of their texts as translations. Many, like Stephen of Antioch, another translator of Arabic scientific texts, echoed Jerome in urging potential detractors of their work to consult the Greek or Arabic original before criticizing (Burnett 2000, 28–29). Eriugena often expressed concern that the Greek passage he was translating spoke with greater meaning (*significantius*) than his Latin translation could capture (Théry 1931, 203), while Robert Grosseteste, bishop and translator, painstakingly elaborated, as we will see below, on the minute differences between Greek and Latin grammar, as if to emphasize the practical impossibility of completely adequate translation. In these circumstances, it is not surprising to discover scholars, concerned about the limitations of earlier translations, carefully revising scientific translations and consulting manuscripts of the Arabic original as they did so (Burnett 2001b). Moreover, many texts circulated in more than one independent translation. By the thirteenth century, many of Aristotle's works could be found in two or three translations, including versions made from both Greek and Arabic; five different translations of the works of pseudo-Dionysius were in circulation; and even the originally French *Mandeville* traveled in five Latin versions (Minio-Paluello 1972; Théry 1931, 185; Higgins 1997, 22). Just as Sophronius found himself disturbed by the variety of translations of the Psalms in the fourth century, so later medieval readers found themselves reckoning with multiple Latin versions of the same texts.

Scholastic thinkers were quite conscious of the challenges involved. Typically, while they closely followed Ibn Rushd as translated from Arabic as they worked their way through Aristotle, they nevertheless preferred to read Aristotle's works themselves in translations directly from Greek. That there were evident differences between the various translations of the same work, moreover, was by no means always seen as a problem. When, for example, Albert the Great cited readings from what he called the *vetus interpretatio* and *nova interpretatio,* he treated them, as Charles Burnett has suggested, rather as Augustine recommended treating the multiple translations of scripture—as "different ways of getting the 'truth' of Aristotle" (Burnett 2005, 375, 388 n. 17). Indeed, as Lorenzo Minio-Paluello pointed out many years ago, manuscripts of Aristotle's works were sometimes specifically designed to cultivate such line-by-line comparisons. Vatican City, BAV, MS Otto. lat. 2048 (Italian, mid-thirteenth century) offered readers different translations of the same work in parallel columns. *De Anima,* books 2–3, for example, appears in the Greek-to-Latin translation of James of Venice with the Arabic-to-Latin version of Michael Scot in a facing column, while the Arabic-to-Latin translation of *De generatione et corruptione* by Gerard of Cremona can be read in the same manuscript alongside an anonymous version from the Greek (Minio-Paluello 1972, 523–25).

Finding ways to make the variety of translations into an advantage was essential for the scholastic project, for by the thirteenth century the role of Latin versions of originally Greek and Arabic works was staggering. There were, of course, key areas of scholastic inquiry that were based for the most part on originally Latin works. Thus the study of law remained focused both on the *Corpus iuris civilis* and the *Decretum.* But for many subjects, scholastic thinkers had to work predominantly or entirely from translated sources, especially when we bear in mind that the Vulgate is itself a translation. When Aquinas, for example, discourses on God's perfection in the *Summa theologiae* (1.4), his most important source is pseudo-Dionysius's *Divine Names,* with six citations, followed by the Vulgate Bible with five. He quotes Aristotle's *Metaphysics* and Averroes's commentary on it once each. Of Latin thinkers only Gregory figures, and only once. His discussion of God's limitlessness (1.7) is built almost entirely around Aristotle's *Physics,* which he cites seven times. The other two works he cites, John of Damascus's *De fide orthodoxa* and the book of Wisdom, were likewise translations from Greek (Aquinas 1888, 50–54, 72–80).

Cultures of Translation

This culture so deeply dependent on translated canonical texts produced, and was itself a product of, a variety of individual cultures of translation. At the one extreme were the broad zones of linguistic, cultural, and (often) religious overlap, such as Spain or Sicily whose bi- or trilingual communities were at home with translation as a matter of practical necessity. At the other extreme were the small studies and libraries, such as that of Robert of Grossteste, where, far from any indigenous community of Greek speakers, the Bishop of Lincoln translated Aristotle's *Nicomachean Ethics* with remarkable learning.

The dense culture of translation that developed in Christian Spain benefitted from obvious advantages. To start with, there were books. Peter the Venerable, patron of the well-known collection of translated Islamic works assembled in the early 1140s, tells how his translators went carefully through more than one Arabic library in search of texts (Kritzeck 1964, 164). Indeed, just in Christian Toledo, which became an especially important center of translation after the middle of the twelfth century, there appear to have been several well-stocked libraries of Arabic texts, judging from an oft-quoted remark of Mark of Toledo, a translator at the court of the archbishop of that city, who mentioned his explorations in that city's Arabic libraries as he searched for another manuscript of a treatise he was translating (Burnett 2002, 151–52; Burnett 2001a, 249–51). These libraries, moreover, must have contained a wide range of texts. While the vast majority of translated works were scientific and philosophical, the three works of non-canonical Islamic tradition that were translated for Peter the Venerable's anthology were popular religious works, and the treatise, two statements of faith, and two hymns attributed to Ibn Tūmart (d. 1130) that Mark of Toledo translated had roots both in Islamic theology (*kalām*) and in the millenarian political traditions of North Africa (Fletcher 1991).

But abundant libraries were not the only advantage of Christian Spain. As important was the vital intellectual and cultural life of this still very Arab part of the world. Despite their continued use of the Latin liturgy, advanced knowledge of Latin appears to have become a rare thing among the Arabicized Christians (Mozarabs) of al-Andalus, most of whom came to live in and around Toledo during the course of the twelfth century. But the circulation among them of a Latin-to-Arabic dictionary in this period, as well as Latin manuscripts with Arabic marginalia, suggests that they were making efforts to master their historic learned language, even as Arabic continued to flourish among them. If the Mozarabs were Arab Christians re-embracing Latin culture, the non-Arab Christian population of Spain was actively cultivating things Islamic and Arabic. They attempted to capture some of the Arabic language's great prestige by carving and weaving fake Arabic, or pseudo-Kufic, into their precious objects, as in the case of the late eleventh or early twelfth century reliquary in the cathedral of Oviedo. Its front panel presents Jesus in majesty surrounded by angels and apostles, but it is bordered on all four sides by a meaningless pseudo-Arabic inscription (Harris 1995). The churches of Santa Cruz and San Román in Toledo were both remodeled extensively in the late eleventh or early twelfth centuries, and in both cases the repeated (and authentic) Arabic inscription *al-yumn wa-l-iqbāl*, or "good fortune and prosperity," played a key role in the decorative scheme (Dodd et al. 2008, 166–67). At times, moreover, even Arab-Muslim religious language was reworked to accommodate explicitly Christian purposes. When Queen Berenguela of Castile died in 1246, she was buried at the Convent of Las Huelgas with a gold and silk tapestry cushion adorned with the repeated Arabic inscription *la ilāh illā Allāh* (there is no god but God) (Shepherd 1978, 126), a phrase with close Qur'anic parallels that Muslims recited as part of their confession of faith.

The Jews of al-Andalus knew Arabic as well, and these populations of Latinizing Mozarabs, Arab-inclined Latin Christians, and Arabicized Jews were essential to this culture of translation because—though this is too often passed over or forgotten—there were actually very few Muslims living under Christian rule in Spain during the great age of Arabic-to-Latin translation (say, 1080–1220), especially in the areas where the translators largely worked—Leon, Castile, and Catalonia. Muslims, for example, had largely fled Toledo and its environs after its surrender to Castile in 1085 (O'Callaghan 1990, 18–21). Only after the great conquests of the period from 1220 to 1248 did enormous Muslim populations come to live under Christian rule. Toledo and other cities became centers of translation, therefore, because of their large populations of Arabic-speaking or at least Arabophilic Christians and Jews.

As a consequence, the many northern Europeans who came to Iberia in search of Arab learning, and sometimes became translators themselves, found a Christian and Jewish world where the Arabic language, Arabic books, and Arabic learning were held in particular esteem, and where native intellectuals were actively reading and discussing many of the Arabic texts that eventually were translated. This local scholarly and scientific culture must have been the basis upon which developed what Charles Burnett has shown to be a systematically coherent Arabic-to-Latin translation program in Toledo informed particularly by al-Fārābī's list of key philosophical texts in his *On the Classification of the Sciences* (Burnett 2001a). The specific character of this local Arabic scientific culture, moreover, shaped Western intellectual history profoundly, for the reading of Aristotle's works primarily through the interpretive lens of Ibn Rushd was "an isolated phenomenon" unique to al-Andalus in the Arab Muslim world, though it went on to flourish, as a result of translation, throughout Latin Christendom in the scholastic period (Burnett 2001a, 265).

So there were both abundant Arabic manuscripts and an active, very Arabic cultural and intellectual tradition in the (largely non-Muslim) cities of Christian Spain, and if we watch as a translator goes about his work in this richly endowed culture of translation, we cannot help being impressed by the results that could be achieved. Like many scientific translators, the Englishman Robert of Chester (fl. 1140–50) tended to follow the Arabic word order closely in his seminal translation of al-Khwārizmī's treatise on algebra. Yet he was hardly slavish about this. He clearly preferred, for example, to put the verb last or at least very late in the sentence in the interest of good Latin style, a position the Arabic verb virtually never occupies. He makes other adjustments in the interest of intelligibility. His Latin version of the first few words of a section discussing multiplication read "In primis ergo sciendum est quoniam ..." [First of all, it is to be known that...]. These words translate the much shorter Arabic phrase *i'lam anna-hu*, meaning simply "know that." Here Robert of Chester has provided his reader with a more elaborate transitional phrase intended to assist comprehension. Immediately afterward, moreover, we find Robert, when faced with a characteristic Arabic idiom, translating according to the sense rather than literally. In the Arabic we read that "For any number multiplied by another, there is no escape" from the fact that one of them must be compounded by the other. Now the phrase "there is no escape for *something* from *something*" (*lā budd li-...min...*) is a common way of saying in Arabic that some outcome is inevitable. Latin contains no such idiom, and, even though his readers might well have been able to work out the meaning of the Arabic idiom were it simply translated into Latin verbatim, Robert has here elected a more intelligible paraphrase: "numerus in numerum multiplicari non potest, nisi numerus multiplicandus tociens duplicetur quotiens in numero in quem ipse multiplicatur, vnitas reperitur" [a number cannot be multiplied by another number unless the number to be multiplied is compounded as often as unity is found in the number by which it is multiplied] (Hughes 1989, 45; al-Khwārizmī 1831, 15).

Neither this nor any other translation made in Christian Spain was without errors, and some had many, but the competency and sophistication of this translation cannot be denied. Robert is very much at home with both the grammar of Arabic and its characteristic modes of expression. He moves confidently through the source text, striking—at least in these examples—an effective compromise between cleaving to the word order of the Arabic and writing clear Latin. Indeed, the rich culture of translation in Christian Spain sometimes fostered exceptional feats of translation. Christian Qur'an translators, for example, had to reckon with enormous philological difficulties arising from that holy book's idiosyncratic vocabulary and its puzzlingly allusive style. The makers of both medieval Latin Qur'ans were able to solve many of these difficulties by consulting the Muslim tradition of Qur'an exegesis in the form of Arabic Qur'an commentaries or Muslim informants or, very likely, both. In Surah 96 (*al-'Alaq*, "The Clot") at verse 18, for example, they encountered *al-zabāniyah*. The root ZBN exists in Arabic, but this particular usage of it was puzzling enough that Muslim commentators felt obligated to explain it for their readers. Both Robert of Ketton's paraphrasing of the term as "aduocatis ipsum ad ignem" [the helpers who will guide [the inhabitants of hell] into the fire], and Mark of Toledo's "satellites" [guardians] draw directly on well-known Muslim explanations of this otherwise difficult word (Paris, Bibliothèque de l'Arsenal, MS 1162, fol. 137rb; Petrus Pons 2008, 408; Burman 2007b, 43).

Libraries, commentaries, and a living Arabic intellectual tradition were, therefore, seemingly essential for successful Arabic-to-Latin translations, and a comparison of these two Latin Qur'ans with Guillaume Postel's sixteenth-century attempt at Qur'an translation undertaken far from any of these things in Paris makes this seem especially so. Postel lacked both the competent grasp of Arabic grammar and vocabulary that Robert of Chester demonstrated and the impressive understanding of Muslim Qur'an exegesis that Robert of Ketton and Mark of Toledo had at their command, and his Latin attempt was therefore not remotely the equal of theirs (Bobzin 1994, 470–96).

Nevertheless, some of the most remarkable translations of the Middle Ages were made at places such as the court of Charles the Bald in the ninth century or the palace of the bishop of Lincoln in the thirteenth, places that, like Guillaume's Paris, lacked any of the ready-made advantages of Christian Spain. Latin had no meaningful competition from Greek as a language of learning in either place, nor were there substantial libraries of Greek texts. Yet John Scotus Eriugena and Robert Grosseteste attained knowledge of Greek sufficient to produce effective Latin versions of extremely difficult philosophical texts.

To a certain extent, this apparent poverty of resources is misleading. Though there were neither Greek speakers nor Greek manuscripts in abundance in the west, Latin-Christian dependence on a translated holy book, as we have seen, kept Greek alive, at least minimally, in the West, through bilingual manuscripts of New Testament books. Furthermore, connections with the Greek Christian world were by no means severed. As Michael McCormick has shown, "Eriugena's Hellenism was not a totally isolated phenomenon" at Charles the Bald's court. Byzantine influences on art and liturgy suggest ongoing interactions with Greek Christianity both through the intermediary of contemporary Italy, where such Byzantinism was widespread, and through the frequent diplomatic travel between Carolingian courts and Constantinople. McCormick calculates that the nine Frankish embassies to Byzantium and the seventeen Byzantine embassies to West Frankia ensured that at least 442 Franks traveled to and sojourned for some months in Constantinople while something like 936 Greeks traveled to various Frankish courts between 756 and 840 (McCormick 1994, 24–30).

Likewise, Robert Grosseteste undertook his Greek-to-Latin translations during a period of extensive interaction between Latin and Greek Christendoms. The establishment of the Latin Empire in Constantinople in 1204 brought many educated western Europeans to the Greek world, where they were exposed to both the language and texts of Byzantium. As it happens, at least one such scholar, John of Basingstoke, had become attached to Grosseteste's episcopal court and must have played a key role both in Grosseteste's learning of Greek and his acquisition of Greek manuscripts (Southern 1992, 185–86).

Despite the fact that there were more resources to hand in the worlds of Eriugena and Grosseteste than we might think, effective translation in their circumstances depended heavily on patrons willing to invest a great deal of money to create a culture in which such translation could flourish. Charles the Bald, like other Carolingian rulers, was an energetic patron of learning and culture who made a place for Eriugena at his court precisely because of his knowledge of Greek. His position at a royal court that was "a highly charged locus of cultural receptivity and innovation" (McCormick 1994, 20) made it possible for him to introduce, through his translations of pseudo-Dionysius, a tradition of non-Augustinian Neoplatonism that would put down deep roots in Latin philosophy and theology. Robert Grosseteste's position as bishop of Lincoln gave him the resources simply to buy Greek manuscripts in a way that would not have been possible for most scholars, very few of whom were church prelates.

The Dynamics of Translation

But resources—whether in the form of books, or an active scholarly tradition, or cultured patron—do not automatically lead to translation, which, as the translation theorist José Lambert has recently observed, is never an accident or the product of whimsy: "Translating may offer some excitement, some fun," he notes, "but fun is no sufficient explanation for the long lists of translated texts and books that have circulated between countries and centres of knowledge" (Lambert 2008, 5). Indeed, even along broad areas of overlap between civilizations, such as medieval Spain, translation was not a natural epiphenomenon of linguistic plurality, but rather the result of quite intentional decisions shaped by a complex range of factors. To understand the countless acts of laborious translation that helped create medieval Latin culture, therefore, we must be attentive to the powerful collective and individual incentives that persuaded scholars to take up the hard labor of making foreign texts speak Latin.

Translation theorists and historians have tended for the last decade or more to locate the motives for translation upon the field of power relations, seeing translation as the hegemonic tool of an aggressive ruler or aggrandizing culture. Surely this is true, at least in part. Sponsoring Greek translation at his court, alongside his cultivation of artistic and liturgical Hellenism, was an excellent way for Charles the Bald to project legitimacy as a ruler both within a Latin culture still acutely aware of its age-old debt to Greek civilization and to the outside world, especially to Byzantine rulers who had little regard for backward Frankish culture. That the Arabs likewise had little regard for Latin culture but commonly admired Greek civilization meant that in representing himself as patron of Greek culture he was projecting himself as a cultured ruler to the Muslim world as well. Translation from Greek to Latin at his court was, therefore, part of a broad program to acquire the kind of cultural capital that kings frequently found useful in projecting their worthiness to rule.

In some cases, the hegemonic motivations of translation are inescapable. The two principal medieval Latin versions of the Qur'an were made for patrons explicitly concerned to convert Muslims. Robert of Ketton, for example, described his patron, Peter the Venerable, as zealous for the destruction of Islam, and it is clear, moreover, that, once translated, his Latin Qur'an was often read in later centuries with specifically conversionary goals in mind (Burman 2007b, 88–98, 107–21). Much the same could be said of the immense mid-thirteenth century translation of Talmud excerpts extant today in Paris (BNF, MS lat. 16558) and intended to expose the "errors, obscurities, and blasphemies of the Talmud" (Loeb 1880, 248–49).

In the so-called Vulgate Latin Version of the *Travels of Sir John Mandeville* (surviving in no fewer than forty-four manuscripts), we can discern the urge to conquer and control a vernacular text. Its translator, in fact, revised and abridged it to make it conform to a more clerical and ecclesiastic vision of the world. This is especially true in sections dealing with religion. Where the French version is sympathetic to Greek Christians, this translator accentuates their differences from Roman Christianity, which he attributes to their ancestors' rejection of the Roman pope. He also tended to excise marvels that lacked religious value, and sometimes expresses skepticism about miracles. He omits, for example, the pyramids, which other versions claim were granaries erected by Joseph during the famine. He also leaves out the original's prophecy that Latin Christians will regain the Holy Land and disavows the belief that spots in a Bethlehem church are traces of Mary's milk. The translator even suggests that the spontaneous snuffing out of the fire in the Holy Sepulchre every Good Friday and its rekindling every Easter may have been an illusion created by Muslims to exploit Christian pilgrims' credulity (Higgins 1997, 82–84, 100–108; Tzanaki 2003, 64, 247).

So translation was often *une conquête des savoirs*, as the title of a recent collection of essays on medieval translation put it (Lejbowicz 2009); yet translation, like language itself, is a profoundly complex act that cannot be reduced simply to politics. Indeed, careful attention to how a translator works with his texts often reveals quite different dynamics at play. Certainly we might read Robert Grosseteste's creation of a culture of translation at his episcopal court as an attempt to gain symbolic and religious capital useful for a prelate with unpopular goals who found himself frequently in conflict with his diocesan underlings. By presenting himself as a learned scholar of Greek and Latin patristics and a translator of John of Damascus and Aristotle he no doubt gained a lot of religious and intellectual weight to throw around in an ecclesiastical fight. Yet if being both a patron of translation and a translator may have helped him predominate in ecclesiastical power struggles, politics alone does not explain the intensity of his scholarly and scientific efforts. Grosseteste's career as both intellectual and churchman had been unusual. Rather than being a product of the later twelfth-century scholastic education of northern France, his intellectual home had been a surprisingly independent and specifically English tradition of scientific thought going back at least to Adelard of Bath and Daniel of Morley. It was not until middle age that he was finally ordained and, in a remarkable departure, began to lecture on theology at Oxford. When he did so, he quickly realized the inadequacies of his education; yet rather than taking up the study of Peter Lombard's *Sententiae*, as other scholastics did, he began reading patristic authors directly and, most astonishingly of all, took up the study of Greek and, later, translation from Greek, with passionate dedication (Southern 1992, xvii–lxvi and passim).

While the group of Greek scholars that he assembled in Lincoln helped him learn that language and acquire Greek manuscripts, the translations attributed to him—sizeable in number—appear to be largely his own work. Modern scholars have criticized him for the extreme literalness of his Latin translations, but this method was rooted in his broader instincts as an intellectual: he had taken the fondness for direct observation that had characterized his scientific work and redirected it toward the founding texts of the Christian tradition. Indeed, his Latin translations were meant as much to illuminate the specific character and oddities of the Greek text as to deliver its deeper meaning. His approach, then, was profoundly philological and pedagogical, and this can best be seen in the many grammatical and textual observations that appear in the commentaries that accompany his translations. In the commentary on his translation of Aristotle's *Nicomachean Ethics*, for example, he noted at one point that

> Ubi autem ponitur *scire* in Greco habetur *fronein* quod est verbum sumptum ab hoc nomine: *fronesis*, id est, *prudencia*, quemadmodum hoc verbum: *videre* sumitur ab hoc nomine: *visus*; et sicut videre est operatio habitus qui est visus, ita *fronein* est operatio habitus qui est *fronesis*, id est prudencia; quia ergo apud latinos non est verbum sumptum a prudencia, compulit idiomatis penuria non proprie transferre.
>
> [Where (the word) *scire* appears, the Greek text has *fronein* which is a verb derived from the noun *fronesis*, that is, *prudencia*, just as the verb *videre* is derived from the noun *visus*. And just as *videre* is the action of the faculty of *visus*, so *fronein* is the action of the faculty of *fronesis*, that is "prudence." Therefore, because there is no verb in Latin derived from *prudencia*, the poverty of (that) language compels one to translate (it) inaccurately.] (cited in Franceschini 1933–34, 90)

That Grosseteste lingers here on the contrasting qualities of Greek and Latin is absolutely typical of his abundant notes. Like certain other translators, moreover, he frequently went so far as to adjust the Latin language as he translated to reflect the specifically Greek way of speaking—by using the dative, for example, with a Latin verb that normally does not require it when the Greek verb it translates does (Franceschini 1933–34, 81). All this urges us to recognize in Grosseteste's Greek translation project much more than the achievement of political power through cultural patronage, for surely there were other less laborious and time-consuming ways for a notoriously busy prelate to present himself as an authoritative scholar-bishop. To understand his efforts most fully, we need to recognize that they were informed by a serious thinker's own intellectual development, even as they garnered useful cultural capital for a political figure who no doubt needed it.

If the motivations for translation, even at a wealthy episcopal court, often transcended the realm of power relations, so also did the consequences of translation. Rodrigo Jiménez de Rada (c. 1170–1247), Archbishop of Toledo, almost certainly commissioned a new Latin Qur'an translation by Mark of Toledo as a tool to help convert, or at least subjugate, the enormous Muslim population that lived in areas under his spiritual jurisdiction. Yet it failed utterly in that task, all the while having a remarkable and unexpected legacy elsewhere. In fact, Mark's translation found virtually no readers that we know of in Rodrigo's Castile or elsewhere in Spain—Rodrigo did not even quote it in his own works on Islam. Rather it lived on in the later Middle Ages almost entirely in Italy. As a carefully literal translation that even maintained the Arabic word order when possible, Mark's Latin Qur'an turned out to be particularly useful to scholars who wanted a crib to use while they read the Qur'an in Arabic. We can actually follow the Dominican Riccoldo da Monte di Croce (c. 1243–1320), an impressively learned Arabist, as he read Mark's version side by side with his own copy of the Qur'an in Arabic (Paris, BNF, MS ar. 384). Quite often he wrote Mark's translation alongside the relevant passage of his Arabic manuscript, and then went on to quote some of these same passages in his *Contra legem Saracenorum*, the most influential Latin treatise against Islam of the later Middle Ages. His grappling with Mark's Latin version was remarkably intense, for as he copied portions of it in his Arabic Qur'an, he from time to time corrected it based on his own knowledge of Arabic. Verse 93 of Surah 3 (*Āl 'Imrān*, "The Family of 'Imrān"), for example, reminds the Prophet's followers of some of the food legislation of the ancient Israelites, concluding with this stirring challenge: "Bring forth the Torah and read, if you are truthful" [my translation]. Mark of Toledo had originally translated this exhortation as "Afferte legem Decalogi et sequimini eam, si ueraces estis" (Petrus Pons 2008, 48). When Riccoldo came to this passage as he went about his bilingual Qur'an reading, he noticed an error in Mark's version and proceeded to correct it as he copied it in the margin next to the relevant verse in his Arabic Qur'an. The word *Tawrāh* in the Qur'an means variously the five books of the Torah or all of the Hebrew Bible. It certainly doesn't refer to the Ten Commandments specifically. So Riccoldo changed "lex Decalogi" to "Pentateucum": "afferte Pentateucum et sequimini eum, si uos estis ueraces" (Paris, BNF, MS ar. 384, fol. 26v; Burman 2007a).

Riccoldo da Monte di Croce may not have been a Spaniard serving the hegemonic purposes of the Archdiocese of Toledo, but he was at least energetically engaged in the kind of anti-Islamic disputation that Rodrigo Jiménez de Rada had in mind. Another late-medieval Italian reader—this time anonymous—was not even doing this much. Rather, as he added interlinear notes to a copy of Mark's Latin Qur'an now in Turin (Biblioteca Nazionale Universitaria, MS F. V. 35), he appears to have been comparing it with the Arabic original together with a Qur'anic commentary in an attempt not to refute the Qur'an or attack Islam, but merely to answer quite basic textual questions. Several passages in Surah 2 (*al-Baqarah*, "The Cow"), for example, begin with the words "and when" immediately followed by a short account of the actions of one of the earlier prophets. Above the words "et quando" in these passages this reader frequently wrote "mementote"—transforming the Qur'anic phrase into "and *remember* when…" Remarkably enough, if we turn to standard Arabic Qur'an commentaries on this passage, we find that medieval Muslim scholars had long suggested that to understand them one must do the same thing: supply the verb *udhkurū*, a plural imperative, just like *mementote*, with exactly the same meaning, yielding "and *remember* when" as well. Rather than serving polemic, then, the Latin Qur'an that Rodrigo commissioned found itself in this case in the hands of a reader whose concerns appeared entirely philological (Burman 2007b, 131–32). A translation commissioned, therefore, to serve the purpose of reconquest and crusade in Spain found its most intent readers among Italians with a keen interest in the Arabic text of the Qur'an. Translated texts—like any other texts—have an amazing ability to evade the purposes, even the hegemonic ones, for which they were made.

Even if we prefer to examine the phenomenon of translation primarily as a kind of cultural politics, we are forced to recognize that a great deal of the time it was as much an act of surrender as of conquest. When we think of the names of the twelfth-century translators of Spain, so many of whom—Robert of Chester, Herman of Carinthia, Alfred of Shareshill, Plato of Tivoli—indicate their trans-Pyrenean origins, it is easy, but in fundamental ways misleading, to imagine them as participating in the intellectual equivalent of the contemporary crusades. In their decentralized organization, idealism, and ambition, the two movements certainly have much in common: both of them expressions of the self-confident and aggressive culture of the central lands of medieval Europe that could inspire free-booting crusaders like Tancred of Hauteville to undertake armed pilgrimage to Jerusalem and free-booting intellectuals like Gerard of Cremona to travel out to Toledo ready to commandeer astronomical texts.

But while the Arabic-to-Latin translation movement would, indeed, have never existed without the confident, ambitious, and—literally—expansive culture of the Twelfth-Century Renaissance, it is also true that this acquisition of foreign texts would not have come about, as its infantrymen made clear, without a powerful sense of insufficiency on the part of the same culture. Robert of Ketton and Gerard of Cremona moved to Spain precisely because they needed to learn from the Arabs, and to learn is, at least in part, to surrender. Indeed translators in Toledo, having been inspired to seek out scientific texts by the Twelfth-Century Renaissance's heavily Platonic fascination with natural philosophy, allowed the Arabs to teach them to prefer Aristotle; having set out to restock their libraries, they allowed themselves to be guided in what works to translate by the views of Ibn Sīnā (Avicenna); having surrendered enthusiastically to the Arab world's Aristotelian turn, they embraced the overwhelming authority of Ibn Rushd as his Commentator. So thoroughgoing was this surrender that Latin education was made over not just in the image of Aristotle, but in the image of Aristotle as interpreted by the Arabs, especially the Arab intellectuals of al-Andalus, all this culminating in what Jean Jolivet famously described as the "transformation of the quadrivium" (Jolivet 1982, passim).

The simultaneous overpowering and giving in to Greek and Arab culture in the twelfth-century translation movement was, therefore, profoundly transformative, its conquering surrender issuing in strikingly new cultural forms. This transforming potential of translation can be seen in many ways in the Latin Middle Ages, and perhaps nowhere is this clearer than in the case of John Scotus Eriugena. He would have fallen asleep, he commented, over the Latin works available to him in ninth-century Francia if Charles the Bald had not urged him to take up the Greek Fathers (John Scotus Eriugena 1969, 24), and eventually commissioned the translation of the works of pseudo-Dionysius, as well as texts by Maximus the Confessor, John of Damascus, and others. It was a shattering and inspiring experience. Like Grosseteste centuries later, Eriugena translated his Greek texts with a devoted literalness that resulted in Latin versions that amounted in many ways to a calque of the original. Indeed, the Latin words of his translation appear in the exact order in which they occur in the particular manuscript—still extant (Paris, BNF, MS gr. 437)—that Eriugena used as his source text (Théry 1931, 226–26). In the commentaries that he sometimes wrote to accompany his translation, we can see that his examination of the Greek text actually occurred in multiple stages. In some cases, he begins his commentary on a particular passage (which he had already literally translated) by, as Paul Rorem has observed, presenting four further translations of it:

> First, a straightforward paraphrase introduced by *inquit*: secondly, introduced by "it can also be translated thus," another paraphrase in the same word order but with alternative meanings to certain words; third, the announcement of a changed word order (*ut sit ordo uerborum*) involving the main verb and subject as well as an emphatic placement of a prepositional phrase; fourth and finally, the summary of the *sensus* of the passage in yet another, freer paraphrase. (Rorem 2005, 56)

But where in Grosseteste's case this sort of lavish attention to textual detail was itself an outgrowth of his intellectual predisposition toward direct observation, in Eriugena it was the medium of his metamorphosis from scholar of the seven liberal arts into brilliant philosopher and theologian, for while translating pseudo-Dionysius's works, he encountered the Neoplatonism derived from Proclus that would become the backbone of his own philosophical theology. Indeed, it would be difficult to imagine a better technique for mastering pseudo-Dionysius's demanding works than the minute grammatical and lexical analysis of the sort Rorem describes. His mastery, in fact, developed quickly, for immediately after translating the pseudo-Dionysian corpus (c. 862), he began writing his magisterial *Periphyseon*, the work of a mature Neoplatonist philosopher. "Before profiting future centuries," as Edouard Jeaneau observed, "John Scot's translation profited John Scot himself" (John Scotus Eriugena 1969, 28).

In the end, therefore, understanding both the mechanics of translation into Latin in the Middle Ages, and its motivations and consequences, requires greater interpretive flexibility than metaphors of conquest allow. Much better, perhaps, to think of translation as a powerful, but unstable and unpredictable, alchemy: an alchemy capable, yes, of changing Greek or Arabic or French into Latin; capable thus of achieving power and wealth for those who practiced or patronized it; but capable also of slipping out of those practitioners' and patrons' control and accomplishing transformations no one intended; capable, indeed, of redirecting its creative energies back on those who thought they were masters of it, changing them and their culture in unexpected ways.

SUGGESTIONS FOR FURTHER READING

Steiner (1998) and Eco (2003) are brilliant and irreplaceable discussions of translation in general while Kelly (1979) provides a vastly erudite survey of translation method in the West. Munday (2008) is the best introduction to the new interdisciplinary field of translation studies among whose leading scholars Toury (1995) probably has the most to offer historical scholarship on translation. Berschin (1988) exhaustively treats Greek studies in Latin Europe, and Gutas (1998) is by far the best work on the Greek-Arabic translation movement. D'Alverny (1982) is the best survey of Arabic-Latin scientific and philosophic translation while the many articles of Burnett (2000, 2001a, 2001b, 2002, 2005, etc.) present that movement with unmatched learning and insight. Glick's (1995, 2005) works provide the most searching analysis of the social bases of the Iberian translation movement while Dodds et al. (2008) and Mann et al. (1992) are fine presentations of the cultural *convivencia* in which it occurred. Minio-Paluello's (1972) remarkable articles on the manuscripts of the Latin Aristotle have not really ever been improved upon. On the impact of scientific translations on European education and culture see Jolivet (1982) and Grant (1996). For Jerome's views on the Hebrew Bible, Septuagint, and Latin Biblical translation, see Kamesar (1993). Jeauneau's charming and learned articles supplement the foundational work of Théry (1931) on Eriugena as translator. Franceschini (1933–34) and Dionisotti (1988) present detailed analyses of Grosseteste's translation method while Southern (1992) persuasively outlines its intellectual and institutional context. For translation at Rodrigo Jiménez de Rada's archepiscopal court see Pick (2004). Higgins (1997), and Tzanaki (2003) collectively provide an excellent overview of the nature and circulation of Mandeville in Latin and are models of what scholarship on the vastly understudied phenomenon of Latin translation of medieval vernacular works should be. On Latin Qur'an translation in medieval and early-modern Europe see D'Alverny (1947–48), Bobzin (1994), and Burman (2007b).

BIBLIOGRAPHY

Primary sources

Thomas Aquinas. 1888. *Opera omnia iussu impensaque Leonis XIII P. M. edita, t. 4: Pars prima Summae theologiae*. Rome: Ex Typographia Polyglotta S. C. de Propaganda Fide.

Augustine of Hippo. 1962. *De doctrina christiana. De vera religione*, edited by Klaus-Detlef Daur and Joseph Martin. Corpus Christianorum. Series Latina 32. Turnhout: Brepols.

Hugh of St. Victor. 1939. *Didascalicon*, edited by Charles Henry Buttimer. Washington, DC: The Catholic University Press.

Hughes, Barnabas B., ed. 1989. *Robert of Chester's Latin translation of al-Khwārizmī's al-Jabr: a new critical edition*. Boethius 14. Stuttgart: Franz Steiner Verlag.

John Scotus Eriugena. 1969. *Homélie sur le Prologue de Jean. Introduction, texte critique, traduction et notes*, edited by Edouard Jeauneau. Sources chrétiennes 151. Paris: Éditions du Cerf.

Al-Khwārizmī, Muḥammad ibn Mūsā. 1986. *The Algebra of Mohammed ben Musa*, edited and translated by Frederic Rosen. Reprint Hildesheim, New York: G. Olms.

Petrus Pons, Nadìa, ed. 2008. "Alchoranus latinus, quem transtulit Marcus canonicus Toletanus." PhD diss., Universidad Autónoma de Barcelona.

Robert Grosseteste. 1982. *Hexaëmeron*, edited by Richard C. Dales and Servus Gieben. Auctores Britannici Medii Aevi 6. Oxford: Oxford University Press.

Weber, Robert et al., eds. 1994. *Biblia sacra iuxta vulgatam versionem*. 4th ed. Stuttgart: Deutsche Bibelgesellschaft.

Secondary sources

Berschin, Walter. 1988. *Greek Letters and the Latin Middle Ages from Jerome to Nicholas of Cusa*, transcribed by Jerold Frakes. Washington DC: The Catholic University of America Press.

———. 1991. "Übersetzungen des XIII. Jahrhunderts ins Lateinische." In *Geist und Zeit: Wirkungen des Mittelalters in Literatur und Sprache. Festschrift für Roswitha Wisniewski zu ihrem 65. Geburtstag*, edited by Carola Gottzmann and Herbert Kolb, 191–200. Frankfurt/Main, Bern, New York, Paris: Peter Lang.

Bobzin, Hartmut. 1995. *Der Koran im Zeitalter der Reformation: Studien zur Frühgeschichte der Arabistik und Islamkunde in Europa*. Beiruter Texte und Studien 42. Beirut, Stuttgart: Franz Steiner Verlag.

Burman, Thomas E. 2007a. "How an Italian Friar Read His Arabic Qur'an." *Dante Studies* 125: 93–109.

———. 2007b. *Reading the Qur'ān in Latin Christendom, 1140–1560*. Philadelphia: The University of Pennsylvania Press.

Burnett, Charles. 2000. "Antioch as a Link between Arabic and Latin Culture in the Twelfth and Thirteenth Centuries." In *Occident et Proche-Orient: contacts scientifiques au temps des croisades. Actes du colloque de Louvain-la-Neuve, 24 et 25 mars 1997*, edited by Anne Tihon, Isabelle Draelants, and Baudouin van den Abeele, 1–78. Réminisciences 5. Turnhout: Brepols.

———. 2001a. "The Coherence of the Arabic-Latin Translation Program in Toledo." *Science in Context* 14: 249–88.

———. 2001b. "The Strategy of Revision in the Arabic-Latin Translations from Toledo: The Case of Abū Ma`shar's *On the Great Conjunctions*." In *Les Traducteurs au travail: leurs manuscrits et leurs methods: actes du colloque international organisé par le "Ettore Majorana Centre for Scientific Culture" (Erice, 30 septembre–6 octobre 1999)*, edited by Jacqueline Hamesse, 50–113, 529–40. Textes et études du moyen âge 18. Turnhout: Brepols.

———. 2002. "The Translation of Arabic Science into Latin: A Case of Alienation of Intellectual Property?" *Bulletin of the Royal Institute for Inter-Faith Studies* 4: 145–57.

———. 2005. "Arabic into Latin: The Reception of Arabic Philosophy into Western Europe." In *The Cambridge Companion to Arabic Philosophy*, edited by Peter Adamson and Richard C. Taylor, 370–404. Cambridge Companions to Philosophy. Cambridge: Cambridge University Press.

Dionisotti, Anna Carlotta. 1988. "On the Greek Studies of Robert Grosseteste." In *The Uses of Greek and Latin: Historical Essays*. Edited by Anna Carlotta Dionisotti, Anthony Grafton, Jill Kraye, 19–39. Warburg Institute Surveys and Texts 16. London: The Warburg Institute.

d'Alverny, Marie-Thérèse. 1947–48. "Deux traductions latines du Coran au Moyen Age." *Archives d'histoire doctrinale et littéraire du Moyen Age* 22–23: 69–131.

———. 1982. "Translations and Translators." In *Renaissance and Renewal in the Twelfth Century*, edited by Robert L. Benson and Giles Constable, 421–62. Cambridge, MA: Harvard University Press.

Dodds, Jerrilynn D., María Rosa Menocal, and Abigail Krasner Balbale. 2008. *The Arts of Intimacy: Christians, Jews, and Muslims in the making of Castilian culture*. New Haven, CT: Yale University Press.

Eco, Umberto. 2003. *Mouse or Rat?: Translation as Negotiation*. London: Weidenfeld & Nicolson.

Fletcher, Madeleine. 1991. "The Almohad Tawhīd: Theology which Relies on Logic." *Numen* 38: 110–27.

Franceschini, Ezio. 1933–34. "Roberto Grossatesta, vescovo di Lincoln e le sue traduzioni latine." *Atti del Reale Istituto Veneto di scienze, lettere ed arti* 93, 2: 1–138. Reprinted in *Scritti di filologia latina medievale*, 2: 409–544. Padua: Antenore, 1976.

Glick, Thomas F. 1995. *From Muslim Fortress to Christian Castle: Social and Cultural Change in Medieval Spain*. Manchester, New York: Manchester University Press.

——— . 2005. *Islamic and Christian Spain in the early Middle Ages*. 2nd ed. Medieval and Early Modern Iberian World 27. Leiden, Boston: E. J. Brill.

Grant, Edward. 1996. *The Foundations of Modern Science in the Middle Ages: Their Religious, Institutional, and Intellectual Contexts*. Cambridge History of Science. Cambridge, New York: Cambridge University Press.

Gutas, Dimitri. 1998. *Greek Thought, Arabic Culture: the Graeco-Arabic translation movement in Baghdad and early Abbāsid society (2nd–4th/8th–10th centuries)*. London, New York: Routledge.

Harris, Julie A. 1995. "Redating the Arca Santa of Oviedo." *The Art Bulletin* 77: 82–93.

Higgins, Iain MacLeod. 1997. *Writing East: The "Travels" of Sir John Mandeville*. The Middle Ages Series. Philadelphia: University of Pennsylvania Press.

Jolivet, Jean. 1982. "The Transformation of the Quadrivium." In *Renaissance and Renewal in the Twelfth Century*, edited by Robert L. Benson and Giles Constable, 463–87. Cambridge, MA: Harvard University Press.

Kelly, Louis G. 1979. *The True Interpreter: A History of Translation Theory and Practice in the West*. Oxford: Basil Blackwell.

Kamesar, Adam. 1993. *Jerome, Greek Scholarship, and the Hebrew Bible: A Study of the Quaestiones Hebraica in Genesim*. Oxford Classical Monographs. Oxford: Oxford University Press.

van Koningsveld, Pieter Sjoerd. 1977. *The Latin-Arabic glossary of the Leiden University Library: A Contribution to the study of Mozarabic manuscripts and literature*. Asfār 1. Leiden: New Rhine Publishers.

Kritzeck, James. 1964. *Peter the Venerable and Islam*. Princeton Oriental Studies 23. Princeton, NJ: Princeton University Press.

Lambert, José. 2008. "Medieval Translations and Translation Studies: Some Preliminary Considerations." In *Science Translated: Latin and Vernacular Translations of Scientific Treatises in Medieval Europe*, edited by Michèle Goyens et al., 1–10. Mediaevalia Lovaniensia, ser. 1, studia 40. Leuven: Leuven University Press.

Loeb, Isidore. 1880–82. "La controverse de 1240 sur le Talmud." *Revue des études juives* 1: 247–61, 2: 248–70, 3: 39–57.

Lejbowicz, Max, ed. 2009. *Un conquête des savoirs: Les traductions dans l'Europe latine (fin du XIe siècle–milieu du XIIIe siècle)*. Rencontres Médiévales Européennes 9. Turnhout: Brepols.

Mann, Vivian B., Thomas F. Glick and Jerrilyn D. Dodds. 1992. *Convivencia: Jews, Muslims, and Christians in Medieval Spain*. New York: G. Braziller in association with the Jewish Museum.

McCormick, Michael. 1994. "Diplomacy and the Carolingian Encounter with Byzantium down to the Accession of Charles the Bald." In *Eriugena: East and West. Papers of the Eighth International Colloquium of the Society for the Promotion of Eriugenian Studies, Chicago and Notre Dame, 18–20 October, 1991*, edited by Bernard McGinn and Willemien Otten, 15–48. Notre Dame Conferences in Medieval Studies 5. Notre Dame, IN: University of Notre Dame Press.

Minio-Paluello, Lorenzo. 1972. "Aristotele dal mondo arabo a quello latino." In *Opuscula: The Latin Aristotle*, 501–35. Amsterdam: Adolf M. Hakkert.

Munday, Jeremy. 2008. *Introducing Translation Studies: Theories and Applications*. 2nd ed. New York: Routledge.

O'Callaghan, Joseph F. 1990. "The Mudejars of Castile and Portugal in the Twelfth and Thirteenth Centuries." In *Muslims under Latin Rule, 1100–1300*, edited by James M. Powell, 11–56. Princeton, NJ: Princeton University Press.

Peters, Francis E. 1988. "Hellenism in Islam." In *Paths from Ancient Greece*, edited by Carol G. Thomas, 77–91. Leiden: E. J. Brill.

Pick, Lucy. 2004. *Conflict and Coexistence: Archbishop Rodrigo and the Muslims and Jews of Medieval Spain*. History, Languages, and Cultures of the Spanish and Portuguese Worlds. Ann Arbor, MI: University of Michigan.

Rorem, Paul. 2005. *Eriugena's Commentary on the Dionysian Celestial Hierarchy*. Studies and Texts 150. Toronto: Pontifical Institute of Mediaeval Studies.

Shepherd, Dorothy G. 1978. "A Treasure from a Thirteenth-Century Spanish Tomb." *The Bulletin of the Cleveland Museum of Art* 65: 111–34.

Southern, Richard W. 1992. *Robert Grosseteste: The Growth of an English Mind in Medieval Europe*. 2nd ed. Oxford: Oxford University Press.

Steiner, George. 1998. *After Babel: Aspects of Language and Translation*. 3rd ed. Oxford, New York: Oxford University Press.

Szpiech, Ryan. 2010. "Scrutinizing History: Polemic and Exegesis in Pablo de Santa María's Siete edades del mundo." *Medieval Encounters* 16: 96–142.

Théry, Gabriël. 1931. "Scot Erigène traducteur de Denys." *Archivum Latinitatis Medii Aevi* 6: 184–278.

Toury, Gideon. 1995. *Descriptive Translation Studies and Beyond*. Benjamins Translation Library 4. Amsterdam, Philadelphia: John Benjamins.

Tzanaki, Rosemary. 2003. *Mandeville's Medieval Audiences: A Study on the Reception of the Book of Sir John Mandeville (1371–1550)*. Aldershot, Burlington, VT: Ashgate.

Van Liere, Franz. 2005. "Andrew of St. Victor, Jerome, and the Jews: Biblical Scholarship in the Twelfth-Century Renaissance." In Scripture and Pluralism: Reading the Bible in the Religiously Plural Worlds of the Middle Ages and Renaissance, edited by Thomas J. Heffernon and Thomas E. Burman, 59–76. Studies in the History of Christian Traditions 123. Leiden.

CHAPTER 6

REGIONAL VARIATION: THE CASE OF SCANDINAVIAN LATIN

KARSTEN FRIIS-JENSEN

Christianity and Latin Culture

The anonymous author of the first major Latin text written in Norway, the *Historia Norwegie*, makes "the arrival of Christianity and the expulsion of heathendom" one of his main themes. He must have been a cleric and probably wrote his work during the period 1160–75 somewhere in southeastern Norway (Mortensen 2003, 23–24). It seems that even at that date, Christianity was not something to be taken for granted in Scandinavia:

> Circumsepta quidem [sc. Norwegia] ex occasu et aquilone refluentis Occeani, a meredie uero Daciam et Balticum Mare habet, sed de sole Swethiam, Gautoniam, Angariam, Iamtoniam. Quas nunc partes—Deo gratias—gentes colunt christiane. Uersus uero septemtrionem gentes perplures paganismo—proh dolor—inseruientes trans Norwegiam ab oriente extenduntur.

> [Norway is enclosed by the Ocean tides, to the south lie Denmark and the Baltic Sea, while to the east are Sweden, Götaland, Ångermanland and Jämtland. The peoples who live in these regions, thanks be to God, are now Christians. However, towards the north there are, alas, a great many tribes who have spread across Norway from the east and who are in thrall to paganism.] (*Historia Norwegie* 2003, 52)

In Scandinavia, Latin literacy is closely connected with the acceptance of Christianity as the official religion. This acceptance took place in Norway and

Denmark around the turn of the millennium and even later in Sweden. The Scandinavian kingdoms thus joined Latin Christendom at roughly the same time as Bohemia, Hungary, and Poland in central Europe (Berend 2007, 1). At first, regular maintenance of religious worship in Scandinavia was no doubt mainly in the hands of foreign clerics coming from Germany and England. The foreigners must have tried to educate some of the natives, but evidence of schools is only available from the twelfth century onwards, and the educational process was probably slow. Accordingly, the earliest known Latin texts produced in Scandinavia, apart from charters, were a series of biographies of royal saints from early twelfth-century Denmark written by English clerics (Gertz 1908–12). The longest of these texts is Ælnoth of Canterbury's *Vita et passio sancti Canuti regis* from c. 1115. Ælnoth was born, and probably educated, in Canterbury, but he spent at least twenty-four years as a member of the cathedral chapter at Odense in Denmark. His activities thus make a manifest link between the important literary centre of Canterbury and the beginnings of a Latin literary culture in Denmark. From the middle of the twelfth century onwards, longer Latin texts are known to have been produced by native Danes and Norwegians, but in this phase of literacy the Swedes were still behind the other Scandinavians.

One of the Danes belonging to the second generation of native writers in Latin was Saxo Grammaticus (c. 1200). Saxo explicitly connects Latin literacy with Christianity in several passages, although he sometimes also refers to a pre-Christian vernacular literacy in runic script. At the beginning of his preface, Saxo actually claims that when he accepted Archbishop Absalon's commission to write about Danish history in Latin, he was the first Dane to do so, thus ignoring two or three predecessors whom we know he had read and used:

> Quis enim res Danię gestas literis prosequeretur, quę nuper publicis initiata sacris ut religionis, ita Latinę quoque uocis aliena torpebat? At ubi cum sacrorum ritu Latialis etiam facultas accessit, segnicies par imperitię fuit, nec desidię minora quam antea poenurię uitia extitere. (*praef.* 1.1; Saxo Grammaticus 2005, 1: 72)

> [What man could have committed Denmark's history to writing? Only lately had it entered the Christian community, and still lay listlessly averse to religion as much as to the Latin tongue. Even when church worship brought Latinity, the Danes' sluggishness matched their former ignorance and they were as wretchedly slothful now as they were ill-educated before.] (Saxo Grammaticus, forthcoming, *praef.* 1.1)

There is isolated evidence that Scandinavians studied abroad before the mid-twelfth century. However, after c. 1150 a more regular pattern developed, and the schools of Paris seem to be the favorite destination, first frequented by Danes and Norwegians, and also by Swedes from the thirteenth century onwards. One of the most eloquent witnesses to this development is the writer Arnold of Lübeck, who wrote his *Chronica Slavorum* in the first decade of the thirteenth century. Arnold discusses the Danes as northern neighbors of the Germans, and he tells us that under the influence of the Germans the Danes have changed their practical sailors' clothes into fashionable furs and costly dyed cloth. But they have also made progress in the intellectual sphere:

> Scientia quoque litterali non parum profecerunt [sc. Dani], quia nobiliores terre filios suos non solum ad clerum promouendum, uerum etiam secularibus rebus instituendos Parisius mittunt. Ubi litteratura simul et idiomate lingue terre illius imbuti non solum in artibus, sed etiam in theologia multum inualuerunt. Siquidem propter naturalem lingue celeritatem non solum in argumentis dialecticis subtiles inueniuntur, sed etiam in negotiis ecclesiasticis tractandis boni decretiste siue legiste comprobantur.
>
> [The Danes have also become quite proficient in book learning, because the nobles of that country send their sons to Paris, not only in order to improve the clergy, but also to educate them in secular matters. There they are trained in learning and the language of the country, and they excel in the liberal arts as well as in theology. Because of their inborn quickness of tongue they are namely said to be subtle in dialectic discussions, and in the management of ecclesiastical affairs they also prove themselves to be good canon lawyers or legists.] (3.5; Arnold of Lübeck 1868, 147)

Early Norwegian Historiography

Two of the authors chosen to illustrate this first very productive phase of Scandinavian medieval Latin of the late-twelfth and early-thirteenth centuries have already been introduced by quotations, namely the author of the *Historia Norwegie* and Saxo Grammaticus. The *Historia Norwegie* as we have it today represents the substantial beginning of what was originally a very ambitious undertaking. As the preface shows, the original work extended into the writer's own times. Besides the preface, the transmitted text of about twenty-five printed pages comprises only Book 1. The work begins with a long topographical introduction and a survey of the legendary first kings of Norway, and it ends at the point (1015) where the future king and national saint, Olav Haraldsson, returned to Norway after years spent on Viking campaigns. The original work may easily have comprised another two or three books and a corresponding number of pages (Mortensen 2003, 9–10).

The Latin of the *Historia Norwegie* is stylistically ambitious as well. Rhetorical effects abound, including parallel phrasing of various kinds, alliteration and end-rhyme. The text example quoted above contains, for instance, two rhetorical exclamations (*Deo gratias! proh dolor!*) and a threefold alliteration (*perplures paganismo proh*). As early as 1930, the language of the *Historia Norwegie* was subjected to a very thorough analysis by Eiliv Skard. His pioneering work is still valuable. Skard points out that the author of the *Historia Norwegie* has learned his Latin by studying model texts and an ancient grammarian such as Donatus. His vocabulary is varied and includes rare words and poetic idioms. However, most of this learning is probably secondhand. He occasionally refers to ancient Roman writers as authorities, but in one case his source is in fact the twelfth-century writer Honorius of Autun, whose *De imagine mundi* also turns out to be an important source for factual information. Adam of Bremen (c. 1075) is the author's most important Latin source for historical information. The borrowings from the *Vulgate* are so numerous and pervasive that they point to systematic studies of the Bible.

The syntax of the *Historia Norwegie* is on the other hand close to the tradition marked by imitation of the ancient Roman writers. An example is the regular use of the accusative with infinitive as object of verbs of saying and feeling (Skard 1930, 42). The late antique and medieval trend was to replace the accusative with infinitive by a subordinate clause beginning with the conjunction *quod* (or *quia*)— a development which became the standard in the Romance vernaculars. Writers of classicizing Latin kept the accusative with infinitive alive by imitating the ancients. However, at the beginning of the thirteenth century the study of ancient models in the teaching of Latin was replaced with the study of freshly produced didactic treatises, such as the versified grammar *Doctrinale puerorum* of Alexander of Villa Dei. This shift paved the way for a scholastic Latin that became syntactically more standardized but very flexible in its coining of new words and derivatives of old ones.

On the basis of his survey of syntax, vocabulary, and style, Skard's conclusion was that the author of the *Historia Norwegie* must be an ecclesiastic who studied abroad in his youth, a view that is now generally accepted.

When the author of the *Historia Norwegie* wrote his work, the rivalry in Norway and Iceland between Latin and the vernacular as vehicles of written historical narratives was not yet an issue. The Icelandic magnate Sæmund the Learned, who died as an old man in 1133, had been educated in France in his youth and was the first Scandinavian known to have studied abroad. He wrote a now lost historical work in Latin about the Norwegian kings. Soon afterwards his relative Ari the Learned wrote a vernacular *Íslendingabók* (*Book of the Icelanders*), focusing on the chronology of the settlement of Iceland and of its history—he is the originator of the widely accepted claim that the Icelanders converted to Christianity collectively in the year 1000. Ari's treatise is the first work written in Old Norse and was followed in the second half of the twelfth century by a small number of Old Norse sagas of the Norwegian kings. In one instance a saga was in fact originally written in Latin, but only survives in a vernacular translation (Oddr Snorrason's *Óláfs saga Tryggvasonar*, cf. Friis-Jensen 1987, 40). In addition to these vernacular works and the *Historia Norwegie*, three other substantial historical writings exist in Latin from twelfth-century Norway, Theodoricus Monachus's *Historia de antiquitate regum Norwagiensium* and the anonymous works *Historia de profectione Danorum in Hierosolymam* and the *Passio et miracula Sancti Olavi* (in several versions, cf. Bibliographia Hagiographica Latina 6322–24; for the language see Skard 1932). Only in the beginning of the thirteenth century did Old

Norse, which previously gave voice to the oral tradition, become the primary language of historical writing in Norway and Iceland. The most famous vernacular author from the first half of the thirteenth century was the Icelandic magnate and politician Snorri Sturluson, who wrote the *Heimskringla*, a long, comprehensive history of the Norwegian kings.

Early Danish Historiography

The second author to illustrate the early phase of Scandinavian Latin is Saxo Grammaticus. He wrote his monumental *Gesta Danorum* during the period c. 1190–1208 at the request of Archbishop Absalon of Lund. Saxo decided to write a work that covered the entire history of the Danes and their kings from the earliest legendary times, up until his own day—an *origo gentis* in the manner of Paul the Deacon's history of the Lombards or Dudo of St. Quentin's history of the Normans. Saxo had a couple of forerunners in Denmark with similar projects, but only on a very modest scale. The anonymous *Chronicon Lethrense* and *Chronicon Roskildense* deal with legendary Danish history and the period 826–1140, respectively, whereas Sven Aggeson combines the two periods in his *Brevis historia regum Dacie* (Gertz 1918–22). Saxo seems to have included every kind of historical lore he could lay his hands on, and a peculiar feature of the first, legendary part of his work is a series of vernacular poems translated into classical Roman meters. In these poems Saxo also uses the traditional poetic language created by classical writers such as Vergil, Horace, and Ovid. However, a desire to imitate the Roman authors pervades not only the poems, but also the entire prose part of the work. In fact Saxo avoids the standard vocabulary of the Christian church and tries to restrict his language to the Latin of the pagan classics. Saxo shared this classicizing spirit with a group of other twelfth-century Latin authors. Saxo Grammaticus is the only Scandinavian, however, who may claim a place in the forefront of the literary classicism of the so-called renaissance of the twelfth century.

Saxo's classicizing Latin is atypical when compared with the language of other medieval Latin texts from Scandinavia. That said, we know more about Saxonian Latin than we do for most other Scandinavian texts: there even exists a separate dictionary of Saxo's language, which documents his large vocabulary and the syntactical range of single words, in particular the verbs (Blatt 1957). The introduction to Blatt's dictionary is the most comprehensive characterization so far of Saxo's language and style (German version: Blatt 1975). Unfortunately we have no systematic overall survey of Saxo's syntax, which makes it very difficult to establish qualified comparisons with other medieval texts, apart from a more superficial comparison of vocabulary. However, the question examined by Skard in the case of the *Historia Norwegie*, namely whether the use of the accusative with infinitive after verbs of saying and feeling is in accordance with classical standards, may be answered in the positive in the case of Saxo, after an investigation of the articles in Blatt's dictionary for the relevant verbs.

One aspect of Saxo's classicizing language is particularly well-documented, namely his allusive borrowings from a large number of Roman classics. The list of Saxo's classical models is long, but, not surprisingly, historians figure prominently among his favorite Roman models (Saxo Grammaticus 2005, 2: 550–625). They are first of all the writer of universal history, Justinus, and Alexander the Great's Roman historian Curtius Rufus. However, Saxo's absolute favorite is the now rather neglected author of a collection of historical *exempla*, Valerius Maximus, traces of whose work can be seen almost everywhere in Saxo's prose. A dozen borrowings from Sallust have also been identified, which is only to be expected, since in fact Sallust was the only Roman historian whose work belonged to the school curriculum of the eleventh and twelfth centuries.

So far only features that connect Saxo with the Roman classics have been mentioned. However, Saxo could not restrict his vocabulary to words found in the pagan classics, and isolated examples of Christian words occur, such as *ecclesia*. But characteristically enough, Saxo almost never uses *ecclesia* to refer to an actual structure devoted to worship; that is normally called *templum* or *aedes*. The previously mentioned Saxo dictionary operates with a third category of words, which do not occur before 600 CE. Saxo employs about a hundred such words, all marked in a special way. Most of Saxo's medieval neologisms are not common in medieval Latin. It is therefore possible that a systematic survey of this group of words and their dissemination in twelfth-century Latin texts might help us answer one of the important questions in Saxo scholarship: where was Saxo educated? In any case, scholars agree that Saxo's mastery of classicizing Latin must be the result of his studies abroad, most likely in France.

Scholasticism Arrives in Scandinavia

The last representative of the early phase of medieval Latin writing in Scandinavia is the fourth archbishop of Lund in Scania, Andrew Suneson, who succeeded his relative Absalon in 1202. He was the scion of a noble family with vast possessions of land, and, being a younger son, he was sent abroad to study in Italy, France, and England. As soon as he returned to Denmark, his education was put to the test, first when he was appointed royal chancellor, and then archbishop.

Andrew demonstrates that he acquired more than a smattering of legal education on his travels abroad. The Latin translation of the Scanian law, one of the provincial laws of Denmark, probably dates between 1200 and 1216. Andrew's lifetime spanned a fertile period for the codification of oral law in Denmark, and the Danish text of the Scanian law as we know it from medieval manuscripts likewise belongs to the early years of the thirteenth century. The Latin translation of the Scanian law

(*Lex Scaniae*) is ascribed to Archbishop Andrew in the oldest manuscript, and the ascription is supported by external evidence, but it is by no means secure. The Latin text takes the form of a paraphrase with comments interpolated where the author feels the need to explain specific points of local law. Some passages indicate that Andrew had studied Roman civil law somewhere abroad.

Andrew gives, for instance, a definition of the Latin term *praescriptio*, "prescription" or "right created by lapse of time," but in a way that makes it refer to a particular, corresponding term in Danish law, a vernacular word that he does not quote. In doing so he makes heavy use of a passage in the *Digest* of Justinian which introduces the definition and the justification of the term "usucaption," the term that was superseded in later Roman law and in canon law by the term "prescription" (*Digesta* 41.3.1–3; Andreas Sunonis 1933, chs. 36–37, cf. Andreas Sunonis 1846, 35). He must have felt that his application of definitions and explanations from Roman law would serve to make vernacular law more easily comprehensible. According to some scholars of medieval Scandinavian law, it is in fact possible to point out influences from Roman civil law in some parts of vernacular law (Fenger 1977). Therefore Andrew's paraphrase of the Scanian law is perhaps just a snapshot of a single phase in a very complex evolutionary process.

Andrew also used his legal training to explain and define vernacular terms that have no Roman equivalents. A famous example is his explanation of the vernacular term for "transfer of ownership of land," *skøtningh*, called *scotatio* by Andrew. Despite the fact that the term is used very often in Danish and other Scandinavian provincial laws, Andrew's explanation of it is the most complete one that survives. In this example, Andrew uses a Latinized version of the vernacular term:

> Quid sit scotacio. In uendicione terrarum ad translacionem dominii est necesse, ut interueniat quedam solemnitas, in qua terre modicum emptoris pallio, extento manibus assistencium, qui, si factum reuocetur in dubium, perhibere possunt testimonium ueritati, apponit uenditor, qui designans terram, quam distrahit, in emptorem ipsius se transferre dominium profitetur. Hec autem solemnitas ex uulgari nostro producto uocabulo competenter satis potest scotacio nominari.

> [What scotation is. When lands are sold, the transfer of ownership demands that a certain ceremonial is carried out, during which the seller puts a small quantity of earth into the buyer's mantle, which is stretched out by the hands of the bystanders. They can therefore bear witness to the truth if the transaction is contested. Meanwhile the seller defines the land which he is selling, and declares that he transfers the ownership of it to the buyer. And this ceremony may suitably be called "scotation," after a word taken from our vernacular.] (Andreas Sunonis 1933, ch. 38)

The central term *skøtningh* is etymologically related to the word for "a corner of a mantle," *skøtæ*. The Latinized noun *scotatio* and the corresponding verb *scotare* are found as technical terms in other Scandinavian countries in the Middle Ages (cp. Westerbergh and Odelman 1968–2002 s.v.).

A few other vernacular Scandinavian words in Latin disguise won general recognition in Scandinavia, for instance the word *bondo, bondones* (Old Danish *bondæ, bøndær*) for "freeholder" or "master of the house." Many other Latinized Scandinavian words are found in Scandinavian medieval Latin, but they almost all belong to rather restricted spheres, in terms of geography and occupation. However, Scandinavian Medieval Latin of course contained many of the Latinized vernacular words that were common in other parts of Europe, such as *feudum* and *guerra*. No comprehensive survey of Scandinavian medieval Latin exists, but Hammarström (1925, 3–73) and Maliniemi et al. (1965) are good introductions.

Andrew's paraphrase of the Scanian law clearly has a didactic purpose. It must have been written for young Danish clerics with no legal training as an introduction to the secular law of their province. The paraphrase does not try to discuss vernacular law from the point of view of Roman civil law, but now and then it tries to apply terms and definitions from Roman civil law in order to clarify difficult points. The paraphrase is kept on a much more elementary level than Andrew's other didactic work, the *Hexaemeron*, which could only be understood by advanced students of theology. This difference probably reflects two different student communities, such as the schools of Paris versus the cathedral school of Lund in Scania. But the difference may also tell something about Andrew's own education. His knowledge of scholastic theology was probably much more profound than his knowledge of Roman and canon law.

Andrew's main work is a huge didactic epic, the *Hexaemeron*, comprising more than 8,000 hexameters. It is in fact a versified commentary on the creation of the world, combined with a theological summa on some of the basic questions of theology, for example the Trinity, the nature of Christ, the fall of man and the human condition; this combination of commentary and summa seems to be unusual among the many twelfth-century works bearing the title "Hexaemeron." His main sources for biblical exegesis were the *Glossa ordinaria* and Peter Comestor's *Historia scholastica*, and for theological doctrine Peter the Lombard's *Sententiae* and not least Stephen Langton's theological *Summa* and *Quaestiones*. Andrew's very extensive use of texts by Stephen Langton makes it probable that Stephen was Andrew's teacher in Paris (Mortensen 1985).

Andrew's main challenge in the *Hexaemeron* was to forge a huge mass of disparate material, some of it very technical, into readable verse. Andrew is a competent versifier, and much points to his having studied some of the popular Roman classics. However, when he turns prosaic source-texts into verse, Andrew knows his priorities: faced with the choice of a rather clumsy, but close rendering on one side, and a more elegant, but freer paraphrase on the other, he often sacrifices elegance in order to adhere more closely to his source. One sign of such a compromise on Andrew's part is the preponderance of the heavy spondees in his hexameter lines compared with those of other writers. The Latin language abounds in heavy syllables, but this tendency was successfully curbed by classical hexameter poets. An example is the rather low frequency in classical hexameters of a line which contains only spondees in the first four feet. The average is six per hundred lines, 6 percent, whereas Andrew's average is almost 16 percent (Friis-Jensen 1985, 228).

It seems appropriate to give an example of how Andrew manages to handle the highly technical language of scholastic theology, in this case some important terms in the section on the Trinity. Each member of the Trinity is characterized by a number of *notiones*, relations or proprieties. These *notiones* originate in the teachings of the Church Fathers, but according to the latest editors of Andrew's poem Stephen Langton is the direct source of a long section on *notiones* in Andrew's *Hexaemeron*. Stephen gives a convenient summary of the doctrine at the beginning of his *quaestio* on *notiones*:

> Quinque sunt notiones: tres in patre (paternitas, innascibilitas, spiratio), duae in filio (filiatio et spiratio), una in spiritu sancto (processio).

> [There are five *notiones*: three in the Father—fatherhood, state of being unable to be born, ability to breathe forth (i.e., the Holy Spirit), two in the Son—sonship and ability to breathe forth (i.e., the Holy Spirit), and one in the Holy Spirit—ability to proceed (i.e., from the Father and the Son). Ebbesen and Mortensen 1985, 208; cf. ibid., 97–99]

Of these five *notiones*, only two fit into the meter, namely *spiratio* and *processio*. Consequently Andrew uses them freely in his verse. The other three he must somehow paraphrase, because they do not fit. Andrew's most recognizable paraphrase is that of *innascibilitas*, since the corresponding adjective *innascibilis* ("being unable to be born") may fit into the meter (used in line 1,317). The last two *notiones* or proprieties, *paternitas* and *filiatio*, have at least once been paraphrased as *Patris proprietas* ("the propriety of being father," line 1,237) and *notio Nati* ("the notion of being son," line 973). When the line of thought becomes just a bit complicated, and that is often the case in Andrew's *Hexaemeron*, we need little imagination to understand the difficulties that faced the uninitiated reader. The only preserved copy of Andrew's *Hexaemeron*, a handsome codex of the mid-thirteenth century, in fact carries a number of interlinear and marginal glosses, among others some discussing the *notiones* of *paternitas* and *filiatio* (Andreas Sunonis 1985–88, 1: 113). Such glosses will of course often offer welcome help, but their very existence throws the complicated nature of Andrew's poem into relief.

In his Proem, Andrew tells us that the purpose of his poem is to offer a wholesome substitute for the dangerous pagan poems that schoolboys read to improve their Latin. This statement cannot be taken quite literally. The reader of Andrew's *Hexaemeron* must already know a lot about scholastic theology in order to profit from his exposition. For that reason it is probably right to suggest that the poem was written when Andrew himself taught theology, probably in Paris in the early 1190s, and that his intended public consisted of Parisian students of theology.

Interestingly enough, Andrew's presumed teacher Stephen Langton also seems to have written a hexameter poem with the title *Hexaemeron*. The work is not known to survive, but two copies are attested, one of which was in Canterbury College, Oxford, in the early sixteenth century (Sharpe 1997, 631). A copy which was probably not identical with the Oxford one was spotted recently in a list of books donated c. 1230 to the library of Peterborough Abbey (Friis-Jensen and Willoughby 2001, 27). Stephen's *Hexaemeron* must have been a long poem, since it existed as a codex on its own, and the independent evidence from Peterborough, which most likely refers to a second copy, lays any suspicion of its being a ghost to rest.

However, common sense demands that we speculate a bit about this rather strange coincidence: Andrew Suneson wrote an 8,000-line-long *Hexaemeron* in hexameters, two-thirds of which are heavily influenced by Stephen Langton's scholastic theology, while Stephen wrote a long hexameter *Hexaemeron* that presumably also expressed Stephen's theological teachings. Are they two poems, or only one poem, and if only one, who wrote the poem: Andrew, Stephen, or both in collaboration? The problem cannot be solved on the basis of what we know today, but the existence of poem number two is undoubtedly endangered by Occam's razor. With respect to Andrew's authorship of the poem ascribed to him, the text itself does not contain any definite hints, but later thirteenth-century tradition in Denmark links him explicitly with the poem, as do the references to three now lost medieval manuscripts. However, the very fact that this question of attribution can arise emphasizes the international character of late twelfth-century scholasticism.

After Saxo's and Andrew's days a steady stream of Scandinavian students found their way to European universities, first of all to Paris. The Swedes, who at first had been rather slow on the uptake, made up for it later, and even founded a separate college in Paris for Swedish students. From the middle of the thirteenth century onwards, a number of Danish students in Paris made a name for themselves as scholastic philosophers and linguists. The most famous among them is Boethius de Dacia (c. 1240–c. 1280). He is credited with about thirty different works, many of which are commentaries on Aristotle; only a third of these titles have been identified and edited (Ebbesen 2002, 66–68). Critical editions of Boethius's and his compatriots' works are found in the monumental series *Corpus philosophorum Danicorum medii aevi* (Otto et al. 1955–). It goes without saying that these new branches of learning generated a whole new and complex terminology, which together with their students soon reached Scandinavia; the case of Andrew Suneson is an early example.

A Swedish Writer of Poetics

As long as northerners found their way to the centres of learning abroad, Scandinavian medieval Latin developed along the lines of European Latin. This almost organic growth was not broken until the rise of humanist Latin disturbed the unity of European Latin, as a harbinger of the finally triumphant vernaculars.

The last examples of Scandinavian Latin belong to fourteenth-century Sweden. Magister Matthias of Linköping (c. 1300–1350) was educated in France, probably

Paris, and when he returned to Sweden he obtained a canonry at the cathedral of Linköping. He also became father confessor to Saint Birgitta in the period before she traveled to Rome in 1349. Magister Matthias was a prolific writer, and his writings reflect the lively international exchange of texts and ideas in late medieval Europe. Most of his works have didactic purposes.

One example is his *Poetria* from the 1320s (Magister Matthias 1996; Kelly 1991, 12). The treatise is dedicated to the Archbishop of Uppsala, Olaf Björnsson, and it closes with a model poem, which praises the Swedish metropolis. Even if the text may have been written when Matthias studied abroad, it was probably intended as a handbook for the students of the cathedral school in Uppsala and their Swedish fellows. In his *Poetria*, Matthias most unusually attempts to combine in explicit terms two different poetological traditions: on the one hand Aristotle's *Poetics* (in Hermannus Alemannus's translation of Averroes's commentary from 1256), and on the other hand thirteenth-century treatises on poetics, as exemplified mainly in Geoffrey of Vinsauf's *Poetria nova*. This work Matthias classifies together with Horace's *Poetria uetus*, as he calls it; Geoffrey himself in fact represents a fusion of Horatian poetics with Ciceronian rhetoric.

Matthias differentiates between the *essentialia* and the *accidentalia* of poetry, the "essential" features belonging to all poetry in any language while the "accidental" features are specific to poetry in one language, as for instance a system of metrics. The dichotomy is Aristotelian, although not found in Aristotle's own *Poetics*. Matthias's work is only known in one rather poor manuscript, and it seems not to have had any influence on the development of later medieval poetics: in didactic writings a systematic juxtaposition of Aristotle and the Horatian tradition did not take place until the sixteenth century. However, it has been argued that Matthias with his Aristotelian point of view took a significant step towards recognizing cultural and linguistic difference, which is also a prerequisite for creating vernacular poetics (Mehtonen 2007, 137–38). Matthias's background for that was of course the multicultural and multilingual Europe of the fourteenth century. Besides the *Poetria*, Magister Matthias also wrote a handbook for preachers, a collection of examples to be used in preaching, and a commentary on the *Apocalypse*. Matthias's relationship with Birgitta found expression in his prologue to the first collection of her *Revelaciones*.

A Mystic Between Latin and the Vernacular

The most important work in Latin from fourteenth-century Scandinavia and our final principal textual example is St. Birgitta's *Revelaciones*. These texts are products of a complicated linguistic process, since they originated in reports in Old Swedish of the future saint's visions and underwent translation and various kinds of editing. However, their character as products of teamwork does not diminish their literary, theological, and linguistic interest.

Birgitta (c. 1303–73) came from an aristocratic family, related on her mother's side to the Swedish royal family. She married early and bore her husband eight children. At the same time she nurtured her literary and theological interests and read widely in texts accessible in the Scandinavian vernaculars, and perhaps also in German (Klockars 1966, 14–15). Her religious devotion also caused her to go on pilgrimages, and her first long journey abroad led her and her husband to Santiago de Compostela. Shortly afterwards she was widowed (1344). Her energy was then directed towards founding a new monastic order of nuns and monks, for which she chose Vadstena on Lake Vättern in Östergötland as site of the motherhouse. She also began to receive mystic experiences and visions, the material for some seven hundred written reports of her revelations. The 1340s probably also saw Birgitta's first systematic efforts to master Latin. There exist scattered pieces of information about her progress in the language. Moreover, an entire article in the documents of 1379 concerning her canonization discusses the ease with which Birgitta learned Latin, as a sign of her unusual powers:

> xxxviii articulus: Item quod dicta domina Brigida, dum esset totaliter rudis in sciencia gramaticali et iam esset seu attigisset quadragesimum annum etatis sue, ut melius intelligere posset sacram scripturam, cepit studere ex precepto Christi in gramaticalibus et infra non longum tempus ita profecit, quod in dicta sciencia et arte predicta bene erat instructa, ita quod bene intelligeret gramaticaliter loquentes, et ipsa eciam cum bonis latinitatibus longos eciam sermones gramaticaliter loqueretur. Et hoc est uerum, publica uox et fama.
>
> [Article 38: Likewise, when the said Lady Birgitta was completely unskilled in grammatical science and already had entered or approached the fortieth year of her life, she began to study [Latin] grammar on Christ's command, in order to understand the Bible better, and in a moderate span of time made such progress that she became well-instructed in the said science and art, so that she could understand people who talked together in correct Latin, and herself could hold even long conversations in good Latin. This is true, common saying and the general opinion.] (Collijn 1924–31, 24)

Among other things, this testimony shows that women who knew Latin well were still something of a rarity in fourteenth-century Europe. Likewise, the women who managed to get a Latin education were usually young, and, it must also be said, normally somehow connected with the ecclesiastical sphere, for instance as novices in monasteries. Birgitta herself wanted her nuns (and monks, too) to lead a contemplative life and to study. The copying of manuscripts and the translation of edifying texts filled a substantial part of their lives.

As long as Birgitta remained in Sweden, Magister Matthias was one of the confessors who supported her and her various religious activities. Concerning her visions, Birgitta's confessors translated and edited her own reports about her revelations, which were written in Swedish. These texts narrate how Christ, the Virgin Mary, a saint or an angel talked to her in her visions and presented her with messages to be mediated to her contemporaries, high and low, ecclesiastic and layman alike. Birgitta's texts therefore often touched upon controversial matters, both in terms of theological orthodoxy and of secular and ecclesiastical politics. It was the concern of Birgitta's confessors to present her revelations in a Latin text that was phrased as even-handedly as possible in order to avoid unnecessary conflict. Magister Matthias's Preface to Book One of Birgitta's *Revelaciones* mirrors these concerns:

> Nec suspicio ulla fallacis spiritus mentibus ista legencium obrepat. Non enim credendum est, quod spiritus malignus uel uere iustos decipiat, uel peccatores in melius conuertat, uel caritatem, quam non habet, frigidis cordibus infundere queat, uel in aliquo gloriam Dei, cui inuidet, promoueat. Sicut enim impossibile est, quod spiritus ueritatis uel loquatur mendacium, uel a iusticia quemquam auertat, uel superbiam et inuidiam cordibus sibi subditis inspiret, uel omnipotentis Dei contemptum adducat, sic spiritui falsitatis opposita horum malorum propter inolitam ei malignitatem et nequiciam omnino sunt interdicta. (Sancta Birgitta 1978, 231)

> [May those who read these revelations harbor no suspicions about a false inspiration. It is not to be believed that the evil spirit can deceive those who are truly just or convert sinners to the good or that he is able to infuse into cold hearts the love that he himself lacks or that he advances in any way the glory of God whom he envies. Just as it is impossible for the spirit of truth to utter a lie or turn anyone away from justice or inspire pride or envy in hearts that are subject to him, or induce anyone to the contempt of God almighty, so too, due to innate malice and wickedness, the spirit of falsehood is altogether incapable of producing the opposites of these evils.] (Sancta Birgitta 2006, 48)

Magister Matthias's worries about possible accusations of heterodoxy were not unfounded. The canonization of St. Birgitta in 1391 implicitly gave her writings the stamp of approval. However, at the councils of Constance and Basel the orthodoxy of the *Revelaciones* was discussed and the issue was only partially laid to rest in 1436 with Cardinal Juan de Torquemada's *Defensiones*.

In her later *Revelaciones* Birgitta often admonished kings, popes, and emperors in bold terms, but other subjects such as interpretations of the Bible were also frequent. An example is Birgitta's exposition of the passages in the New Testament about Lazarus's two sisters Mary and Martha who served Jesus, each in her own way, after he had raised the dead Lazarus to life; but Christ said that "Mary has chosen the best part, which shall not be taken from her" (Lk 10:38–42; Jn 11–12). Birgitta makes Christ give a very detailed exposition of the traditional interpretation that Mary and Martha are symbols of the two vocations, the contemplative life and the active life. Birgitta herself valued the contemplative life highly, as for instance seen in her instructions for her religious order. According to Christ, preaching (*predicacio*) is among the elements that belong to the contemplative vocation. Christ says:

Sed diligenter attendat Maria, quod ibi aperiat os predicacionis sue, ubi boni fiant feruenciores et mali efficiantur meliores, ubi iusticia possit augeri et praua consuetudo aboleri ... Si autem Maria non ualet predicare habens nichilominus uoluntatem et scienciam predicandi, faciat sicut uulpis, qui circuiens monticulos inquirit plura loca pedibus, et ubi reperiit loca meliora et apciora, ibi facit requiei sue fossam. Sic Maria attemptet uerbis et exemplis et oracionibus corda multorum.

[But let Mary consider carefully that she shall open her mouth to preach in places where the good may become more fervent and the bad may be made to mend their ways, where justice may be strengthened and vicious usage be abolished....But if there is no possibility for Mary to preach, but she nevertheless possesses the will and the knowledge to preach, let her act like the fox who circles the mounds, investigating the ground with his paws, and where he has found the best and most suitable places, he makes a den in which to rest. In this way let Mary try the hearts of the multitude with her words, her examples and her prayers.] (6.65. 54–56; Sancta Birgitta 1991, 216)

It is evident that the style of this passage is different from the rather elaborate rhetoric of Magister Matthias's preface to Book 1 quoted above. We can see the simile of the investigating fox as a truly Birgittine feature, a means of making the theological context more appealing. Interestingly enough the question of who possesses the right to preach the word of God had topical interest at the time. The right to preach belonged to priests and to monks who had a special license to do so, such as the Dominicans and the Franciscans. When laymen, and in some cases even lay women, dared to preach, heresy was afoot. Birgitta's Mary is a symbol of the contemplative life, and only incidentally a woman. However, it is probably not completely out of the question to think that Birgitta planted a seed here for the thought that ability and knowledge are more important for preachers than gender.

Birgitta's *Revelaciones* are the product of a collective process; their Latin, whether or not she understood it, is not Birgitta's own. Nevertheless the resulting language seems to be rather uniform and a supple vehicle for the many different moods, themes, and situations demanded by Birgitta. The corpus has received only limited linguistic analysis to date. An exception is an interesting survey of the proportion of accusative with infinitive constructions to *quod* clauses after verbs of saying and feeling (Karlsen 2001). Considering that the vernacular descendants of Latin verge towards the finite constructions (equivalents of *quod* clauses) while the infinitive construction is typical of classical Latin and the authors who imitate it, there are surprisingly many infinitive constructions in the *Revelaciones*, namely between 30 and 55 percent according to the type of the governing verb. In many cases, Karlsen is also able to pinpoint why a particular construction has been chosen. This interesting survey demands corresponding material for comparison in order to show its full research potential, so far lacking.

Unlike most of the Latin texts produced in medieval Scandinavia, Birgitta's *Revelaciones* became a huge international success, both in their Latin form and in a number of translations into the vernacular, including English and St. Birgitta's own Old Swedish. In this way Birgitta's ideas actually influenced the development of society, as she had wished. In particular Birgitta, as a visionary and as a writer, became a model for other medieval women. One of the Englishwomen who took inspiration from Birgitta was the visionary and autobiographer Margery Kempe; *Saint Bridget's Book*, as she once names it, was read to her (Boffey 1999, 632–33). In the early fifteenth century, Margery followed in the footsteps of Birgitta on extensive pilgrimages to Santiago de Compostela, Rome, and Jerusalem, and she also produced a record of her physical, social, and spiritual life called *The Book of Margery Kempe*. Since Margery herself probably could not read or write, she had to dictate the text to a scribe and collaborator. As it happens, Margery was once accused of preaching and had to defend herself before the Archbishop of York. Her famous answer is not unworthy of St. Birgitta: "I preche not, ser, I come in no pulpytt. I use but comownycacyon [*communication, talk*] and good wordys" (Margery Kempe 1996, 1.2975–76).

During the fifteenth century Scandinavians came only intermittently into contact with the new humanist movements of Italy, France, and Germany, and in Scandinavia the teaching of humanist Latin did not become an integral part of the educational system until after the Reformation. However, the kind of Latin that dominated fifteenth-century Europe was an organic development of medieval Latin, and Latin still held its position as the language of the Church and as the most important language of education and diplomacy. By then the Scandinavian kingdoms had been members of the religious, cultural, and educational community of Western Europe for at least three centuries. The few examples presented above of Latin texts written by Scandinavians in this period should suffice to show how quickly and how thoroughly this cultural assimilation took place. They also demonstrate that in some cases Scandinavians produced Latin works which bear comparison with those of their best-known European contemporaries; the historiographer Saxo Grammaticus, the philosopher Boethius de Dacia, and the mystic Birgitta of Sweden are such Scandinavians.

SUGGESTIONS FOR FURTHER READING

No large, comprehensive survey of medieval Latin language and literature in Scandinavia exists. Maliniemi et al. (1965) is a good article-length introduction, written in Scandinavian languages. A website in English of authors and anonymous works c. 1100–1530 is being established (Borgehammar, forthcoming); the entries have been written by a large group of specialists, and include sections on textual transmission and bibliography. Much of the older literature on the subject is written in Scandinavian languages. That also holds good for the three dictionaries of national Latin sources, Hammarström (1925) (charters from Sweden and Finland, with a useful introduction), Westerbergh and Odelman (1968–2002) (texts from Sweden), and Due and Terkelsen (1987–) (texts from Denmark). A survey of Swedish medieval Latin is found in the first chapter of Tengström (1973). Most medieval charters in Latin from Scandinavia have been edited in national cartularies which have been long in the making; an early survey is Nygren (1958). The old national serial editions of medieval Latin texts (Langebek et al. 1772–1878, Fant et al. 1816–76, Storm 1880) have to a large extent been replaced by modern critical editions, in recent years sometimes provided with a parallel translation. Some important editions have been listed in the bibliography below.

BIBLIOGRAPHY

Primary sources

Andreas Sunonis. 1846. *Lex Scaniæ antiqua latine reddita per Andream Sunonis*, edited by Janus L. A. Kolderup-Rosenvinge. Copenhagen: Gyldendal.

———. 1933. "Anders Sunesøns parafrase af Skånske lov." In *Danmarks gamle landskabslove med kirkelovene*, edited by Johannes Brøndum-Nielsen and Poul J. Jørgensen, 1: 467–667. Copenhagen: Gyldendal.

———. 1985–88. *Andreas Sunonis filius. Hexaemeron*, edited by Sten Ebbesen and Laurentius B. Mortensen. Corpus philosophorum Danicorum medii aevi 11:1–2. Copenhagen: G. E. C. Gad.

Arnold of Lübeck. 1868. *Arnoldus Lubecensis. Chronicon Slavorum*, edited by Johann M. Lappenberg. Monumenta Germaniæ Historica. Scriptores rerum Germanicarum 14. Hannover: Hahn.

Collijn, Isaak, ed. 1924–31. *Acta et processus canonizationis beate Birgitte*. Uppsala: Almqvist & Wiksell.

Ebbesen, Sten and Lars B. Mortensen. 1985. "A partial edition of Stephen Langton's Summa and Quaestiones with parallels from Andrew Sunesen's Hexaemeron." *Cahiers de l'Institut du moyen-âge grec et latin* 49: 25–224.

Fant, Eric M. et al., eds. 1818–76. *Scriptores rerum Svecicarum medii aevi*. 3 vols. Uppsala: Zeipel & Palmblad.

Gertz, Martin Cl., ed. 1908–12. *Vitae sanctorum Danorum*. Copenhagen: G. E. C. Gad.

———, ed. 1918–22. *Scriptores minores historiae Danicae*. 2 vols. Copenhagen: G. E. C. Gad.

Historia Norwegie. 2003. *Historia Norwegie*, edited by Inger Ekrem and Lars. B. Mortensen, translated by Peter Fisher. Copenhagen: Museum Tusculanum Press.

Langebek, Jakob, ed. 1772–1878. *Scriptores rerum Danicarum medii aevi*. 9 vols. Copenhagen: various publishers.

Magister Matthias. 1996. *Magister Matthias Lincopensis. Testa nucis and Poetria*, edited and translated by Birger Bergh. Arlöv: Berlings.

Margery Kempe. 1996. *The Book of Margery Kempe*, edited by Lynn Staley. Kalamazoo, MI: Medieval Institute Publications.

Otto, Alfred et al., eds. 1955–. *Corpus philosophorum Danicorum medii aevi*. Copenhagen: G. E. C. Gad.

Sancta Birgitta. 1978. *Revelaciones. Book I. With Magister Mathias' prologue*, edited by Carl-Gustav Undhagen. Stockholm: Almqvist & Wiksell.

———. *Revelaciones. Book VI*, edited by Birger Bergh. Stockholm: Almqvist & Wiksell.

———. 2006. *The Revelations of St. Birgitta of Sweden*, translated by Denis Searby, introduction and notes by Bridget Morris. Oxford: Oxford University Press.

Saxo Grammaticus. 2005. *Saxo Grammaticus. Gesta Danorum. Danmarkshistorien*, edited by Karsten Friis-Jensen, translated by Peter Zeeberg. 2 vols. Copenhagen: G. E. C. Gad.
———. Forthcoming. *Saxo Grammaticus. Gesta Danorum. History of Denmark*, edited by Karsten Friis-Jensen, translated by Peter Fisher. 2 vols. Oxford Medieval Texts. Oxford: Oxford University Press.
Storm, Gustav, ed. 1880. *Monumenta historica Norvegiæ. Latinske Kildeskrifter til Norges Historie i Middelalderen*. Kristiania: A.W. Brøgger.

Secondary sources

Berend, Nora, ed. 2007. Christianization and the Rise of Christian Monarchy. Scandinavia, Central Europe and Rus' c. 900-1200. Cambridge: Cambridge University Press.
Blatt, Franz, ed. 1957. *Saxonis Gesta Danorum*. Vol. 2: *Index verborum*. Copenhagen: Levin & Munksgaard.
———. 1975. "Einleitung zu einem Wörterbuch über die Latinität Saxos." In *Mittellateinische Philologie*, edited by Alf Önnerfors, 242–60. Wege der Forschung 292. Darmstadt: Wissenschaftliche Buchgesellschaft.
Boffey, Julia. 1999. "Middle English lives." In *The Cambridge History of Middle English Literature*, edited by David Wallace, 610–34. Cambridge: Cambridge University Press.
Borgehammar, Stephan et al. Forthcoming. *Medieval Nordic Literature in Latin. A website of authors and anonymous works c. 1100–1530*. Publications of the Journal of Medieval Latin. Turnhout: Brepols. Website: https://wikihost.uib.no/medieval/
Due, Otto S. and Peter Terkelsen. 1987–. *Ordbog over dansk middelalderlatin*. Aarhus: Aarhus University Press. [latest fascicle 2008, has reached *risibilitas*]
Ebbesen, Sten. 2002. *Dansk middelalderfilosofi. Ca. 1170–1536*. Copenhagen: Gyldendal.
Fenger, Ole. 1977. *Romerret i Norden*. Copenhagen: Berlingske Forlag.
Friis-Jensen, Karsten. 1985. "Hvordan omstøbes bibelshistorie i heksametre?" In *Anders Sunesen. Stormand teolog administrator digter*, edited by Sten Ebbesen, 221–31. Copenhagen: G. E. C. Gad.
———. 1987. *Saxo Grammaticus as Latin Poet. Studies in the verse passages of the Gesta Danorum*. Analecta Romana Instituti Danici. Supplementum 14. Rome: L'Erma di Bretschneider.
———. 1993. "Latin language and literature." In *Medieval Scandinavia. An encyclopedia*, edited by Phillip Pulsiano, 380–81. Garland Reference Library of the Humanities 934. New York, London: Garland Publishing.
Friis-Jensen, Karsten and James M. W. Willoughby, eds. 2001. *Peterborough Abbey*. Corpus of British Medieval Library Catalogues 8. London: British Library.
Hammarström, Magnus. 1925. *Glossarium till Finlands och Sveriges latinska medeltidsurkunder jämte språklig inledning*. Helsingfors: Finska Historiska Samfundet.
Karlsen, Espen. 2001. *The accusativus cum infinitivo and quod clauses in the Revelaciones of St. Bridget of Sweden*. Lateinische Sprache und Literatur des Mittelalters 33. Bern, New York: Peter Lang.
Kelly, Douglas. 1991. *The Arts of Poetry and Prose*. Typologie des sources du Moyen âge occidental 59. Turnhout: Brepols.
Klockars, Birgit. 1966. *Birgitta och böckerna. En undersökning av den heliga Birgittas källor*. Stockholm: Almqvist & Wiksell.
Maliniemi, Aarno et al. 1965. "Latin." In *Kulturhistorisk leksikon for nordisk middelalder*, edited by Georg Rona, 10: 327–43. Copenhagen: Rosenkilde & Bagger.

Mehtonen, Päivi. 2007. "Essential art: Matthew of Linköping's fourteenth-century Poetics." *Rhetorica* 25: 125–39.

Mortensen, Lars B. 1985. "The sources of Andrew Sunesen's Hexaemeron." *Cahiers de l'Institut du moyen-âge grec et latin* 50: 113–216.

———. 2003: "Introduction." In *Historia Norwegie*, edited by Inger Ekrem and Lars B. Mortensen, 8–47. Copenhagen: Museum Tusculanum Press.

Nygren, Ernst 1958. "Diplomatarium." In *Kulturhistorisk leksikon for nordisk middelalder*, edited by Georg Rona, 3: 82–86. Copenhagen: Rosenkilde & Bagger.

Sharpe, Richard. 1997. *A Handlist of the Latin writers of Great Britain and Ireland before 1540*. Publications of the Journal of Medieval Latin 1. Turnhout: Brepols.

Skard, Eiliv. 1930. *Målet i Historia Norwegiae*. Oslo: Jacob Dybwad.

———. 1932. *Sprache und Stil der Passio Olavi*. Oslo: Jacob Dybwad.

Westerbergh, Ulla and Eva Odelman. 1968–2002. *Glossarium till medeltidslatinet i Sverige*. Stockholm: Almqvist & Wiksell.

CHAPTER 7

THE IDEA OF LATINITY

NICHOLAS WATSON

The Reticence of Medieval Latin

My brief in this chapter, to explore medieval Latinity from a conceptual perspective, suggests two possible lines of enquiry. The first is sociolinguistic. It leads to a study of the ideological and cultural functions of Latinity in the medieval West that might feature subjects such as Latinity's identification with learning and the clerisy, association with ethical *habitus* and the transcendent (Breen 2010), and practical role in the slow societal transition "from memory to written record" (Clanchy 1993). A sociolinguistic enquiry into medieval Latin, in other words, is bound up with the study of Western pedagogy and learning on the one hand, intellectual and institutional history on the other: linked areas of study long of central interest to medievalists (Colish 1997). Indeed, such an enquiry is impossible to distinguish from these areas of study, even though explicit use of a sociolinguistic approach remains a rarity in the field (see Ong 1982; Stock 1983; compare Machan and Scott 1992; see also Burman and Szpiech elsewhere in this volume).

The second avenue, which I follow here, is metalinguistic. It focuses less on the functions of Latinity, moral or practical, than on the language's associations and meanings: on what *Latinitas* signified in the western Middle Ages, both in itself and, especially, in its relation to other languages. This topic is at once more restricted than its sociolinguistic neighbor and initially a good deal more elusive, since medieval Latin texts are, in most cases, noticeably reticent about how their use of Latin in preference to any other language is to be understood.

Medieval Latin texts are deeply self-conscious about style: whether this self-consciousness takes the form of the richly associative verbal and thematic patterns generated in that great collaborative art work, the liturgy, of a half-millennium of attempts by humanists to identify the acquisition of elegant Latinity with the practice of virtue (Grafton and Jardine 1986; Jaeger 1994), or of the distinctions among the *multiplices modi* of the Scriptures and other canonical texts made in scholastic *accessus ad auctores* (Minnis 1988; Minnis and Scott 1991). Medieval Latin texts also inherited from classical antiquity and developed into endless new forms a famously sophisticated understanding of the verbal arts of grammar, rhetoric, dialectic, and hermeneutics (Irvine 1994; Copeland 1991; Copeland and Sluiter 2009; Broadie 1993), as well as an intense semiotic awareness (Gellrich 1985; Biard 1989; Eco and Marmo 1989), whose engagements with lexis, grammar, and even orthography, among other subjects, are on display in texts as varied as Alain de Lille's *De planctu naturae*, Thomas of Erfurt's *De modis significandi*, and the *Ars generalis ultima* of Ramon Llull (Bardzell 2009; Sweeney 2006; Bursill-Hall 1971; Thomas of Erfurt 1972; Eco 1995, 53–72; Hames 2000). But if this intellectual activity qualifies as metalinguistic in the sense that its concern is with the nature and structure of language, it takes little interest in what makes Latin particular, behaving as though semiotic analysis of Latin were identical with analysis of language as such. The scholarship on medieval Latin's self-understanding, especially in relation to other languages, is slight and much no doubt awaits notice (although see Curtius 1953; Hexter 1987; Sheerin 1987; Ziolkowski 1991, 1996; Herren 1996; Minnis and Johnson 2005; Breen 2010, 43–121; again, see Berman and Szpiech elsewhere in this volume). But a crude survey of the vast array of prolegomena affixed to bellelettristic, scholastic, spiritual, pragmatic, and other texts suggests that medieval Latin writers were typically interested in almost everything having to do with literary theory and practice *other* than language choice.

This apparent reticence about language choice is striking because, despite the preponderance of Latin over other languages in the written record, such reticence was not characteristic of western medieval intellectual culture as a whole, even its Christian component. Prolegomena to texts in other languages written at any time between the tenth and the fifteenth centuries routinely feature metalinguistic comments, often in the form of apologias, sometimes written in Latin, for the decision to translate a given text from Latin. Despite a tradition of Old High German writing reaching back over two hundred years, the early eleventh century pedagogue, Notker, calls his ambitious translations of "ecclesiastici libri" (texts by Boethius, Martianus Capella, and others) "paene inusitatam" [almost unprecedented] and anticipates that his educated interlocutor "primum abhorrebitis quasi ab insuetis" [will recoil at first as if from something unfamiliar] when he looks at them (Hellgardt 1979, 172–73; Copeland 1991, 98). His prolific English contemporary, Ælfric, also justifies his many translations in ways at once socially nuanced and ethically open, appealing to the authorizing demands made on him by devout, high-born, and in one case notably learned lay patrons: "Non mihi inputetur quod diuinam scripturam nostrae lingue infero, quia arguet me praecatus multorum fidelium et maxime Æþelwerdi ducis et Æþelmeri nostri" [Let it not be charged against me that I turn divine scripture into our language, for the entreaty of many of the faithful clears me, especially that of ealdormann Æthelweard and our friend Æthelmer] (Ælfric 1994, 131–32).

Such justifications, and the bodies of reflection on what it is to write in a given language to which they give rise, are not limited to texts written early in that language's recorded history. Indeed, they are less likely to be present in earlier texts than in later ones. Ælfric, for example, is less publicly confident of vernacular translation than were his late ninth-century predecessors who produced the translations of King Alfred (Godden 2009); moreover, while differences of rank and status might account for this in part, Ælfric's overt self-consciousness is a sign of things to come (Stanton 2002, Watson 2008). The verse histories and fictions written in twelfth-century France and England are much preoccupied with their linguistic status as *romanz*, a status not that of Latin but still linked, as other languages are not, to the prestigious category of *Romanitas*. Religious *romanz* verse, especially in Anglo-Norman, features sophisticated musings on linguistic mediation as a form of theological mediation. By the end of the Middle Ages written English, French, Italian, German, Dutch, Spanish, and other languages all engaged routinely in a range of careful, if also strategic, modes of self-analysis. In the process, these languages developed bodies of what we call literary theory around the very question of language choice that is noticeably absent from Latin writings (Lusignan 1987, 2004; Haug 1997; Wogan-Browne et al. 1999; Minnis 2001, 2009; Somerset and Watson 2003). The very inadequacy that these languages attributed to themselves—especially in the hands of clerical writers concerned, perhaps for sound professional reasons, to show their linguistic home was elsewhere—acted as a powerful intellectual stimulus.

*****

From a certain point of view, then, it can be claimed that medieval Latin lagged behind other western languages when it came to metalinguistic reflection. Yet while this claim may at first seem as tendentious as Notker's German translations—and while we will later, admittedly, find some grounds to qualify it—the claim quickly brings us up against two familiar features of the medieval western European language situation: the high status of Latin in most institutional and intellectual contexts and its intimate association with textuality. If Latin writers did not often comment on their use of Latin, this was because no comment was felt necessary. Despite the complexity of practical language politics, within its own ambit Latin was symbolically superior to—or, one might equally say, more relevant than—the languages with which it most closely coexisted and had no reason to explain itself. Despite the oral or performed character of the liturgy and the widespread use of spoken Latin within the specialized community of *literati* or *clerici* (whose very names signify possession of literate skills), Latinity's relationship to textuality was normative, in linguistic terms "unmarked" (Trask 1999, 180). Latin's case for its own validity, utility, and cultural prestige was made on the manuscript page.

Conversely, the very fact that this case was always already made was potentially troublesome for texts written in languages other than Latin: languages symbolically associated with the unlearned and the oral, whose connections to textually oriented institutions in general tended to the informal. Members of the speech communities organized by these languages clearly had no daily sense of linguistic inadequacy and likely experienced contact with Latin (through the liturgy and other media) almost horizontally, understanding Latin as specialized or situational, not superior. The linguistic power imbalances that mattered—say, between French, Middle English, and Welsh or Cornish, or between French or German and that great exception, Hebrew (Kennedy and Meecham-Jones 2008; Fudeman 2010)—may have been those which reflected urgent sociopolitical realities, not abstract cultural ones. When they took written form, however, all these languages except Hebrew had no choice but to enter a discursive arena in which they were both "marked" or exceptional and subordinated: in a vertical or *hierarchic* relationship to Latin, to borrow a fashionable ecclesiological neologism from the period. To borrow two others, they were obliged to name themselves *vulgar* or *vernacular*: metalinguistic status terms often used casually to describe any medieval local or national language but that are properly meaningful only in the presence of their antonym, Latinity (Somerset and Watson 2003, ix–xiv). Prolegomena to vernacular works such as those by Notker and Ælfric exhibit public metalinguistic self-consciousness because they are enacting the recurring moment at which one of the intricately interconnected networks of local European languages submits to the ideological binarism that organizes its relationship to Latin, as the price of entry into textuality.

*****

Latinity's silent self-sufficiency and the vernacular's noisy, self-justifying self-analysis—whether conducted in the vernacular or in Latin, the language of authority, as it was by Notker and Ælfric—are thus at once contrasted and equivalent responses to a single phenomenon. They are both in their way acknowledgments, from opposite poles, of the symbolically diglossic character of medieval western European textuality: its organization around a notionally immemorial, systematic, and binary disparity of power (Ong 1984; Ziolkowski 1991; Trask 1999, 76). Despite the risks that attend any interpretation that rests partly on an absence, especially at such a level of generality, this equivalence is worth pressing, for two reasons.

First, it helps to explain why the search for metalinguistic reflection on Latinity so often leads to vernacular texts, or macaronic texts (in which Latin is juxtaposed with vernacular materials), or discussions of the vernacular, all of which prove rich resources with which to think about medieval Latinity. That is, it helps us to see that vernacularity, which I have suggested we understand as the product of a contractual arrangement between local languages and Latinity, was not the only linguistic condition defined by this arrangement: that, despite its silence on this point, medieval Latinity was also produced and defined, in part, by the shape of its relationship with the vernacular. Within this symbolically diglossic system, vernacularity's prolegomenal anxieties thus function, strangely, as an important site of metalinguistic self-consciousness for Latinity, as well as for the vernacular itself. This is why the present chapter looks so often to the constantly shifting and often regionally specific idea of the vernacular for help in interpreting developments that may seem internal to *Latinitas*.

Second, the self-deprecating chatter that arises from the *lingua materna* when it enters the textual domain of the father tongue irritates us into remembering what the effortless competence of *Latinitas* might soothe us into forgetting: that Latinity was not only defined by, but *dependent* on, the vernacular, both in socioeconomic practice and in a key symbolic sense. For by proclaiming its subordination, the vernacular was instrumental in enabling medieval Latin not only to translate its antique associations with the imperial into the fluid realm of the metalinguistic, but to face the threat looming from a second metalinguistic arena, in which it was Latin that ran the risk of subordination.

The Rise of Linguistic Binarism (to 1100)

As Ryan Szpiech also notes elsewhere in this volume, historically speaking, Latin was a latecomer among authoritative languages. It ran a distant third to Hebrew, a living European language that was also that of the Old Testament and, some thought, of Adam (Eco 1995). It came in second to Greek, the language of a rival church that was also that of the New Testament and the Septuagint, as well as the primal source of science, philosophy, arts, and letters (Berschin, 1998). As Rita Copeland has shown (1991), classical Latin literature, developing in tandem with an aggressive Roman ideology of empire in an Italic peninsula suffused with Greek influence, invented itself through a combination of scrupulous "grammatical" imitation of Greek texts and Greek canons of value and a competitive but never completed "rhetorical" displacement. This process of *translatio studii et imperii*, which set the agenda for the late republican and early imperial literary quadrumvirate, Cicero, Horace, Virgil, and Ovid, marked the Latin literary tradition with an abiding concern at once for stylistic purity and for universalizing power (Berschin 1998, 48): liable to denigrate less culturally central Latin idioms as barbarous (a word itself borrowed from Greek), and more than ready, when the time came, to take on the superior position in those diglossic pairings with other languages that caused the latter to be understood as "vernacular."

For Jerome and Augustine, who wrote in the wake of the fourth-century renaissance of *Romanitas* initiated by Diocletian and Constantine (Williams 1985), and who can take much of the credit for the emergence of Latin as a theological language equal to Greek, stylistic barbarity was an awkward but minor problem compared to the greater ones associated with the Latinizing of God's word: a process at once necessary and seemingly impossible, despite the promise of universal lucidity that was Pentecost. Only the long centuries of worship in which the somatic knowledge of divine presence was summoned into the temples and hearts of the faithful through movement, chant, image, light, incense, sacrament, and highly charged ritual language could sacralize Latin in the collective experience, compensating performatively for its failure to be numbered with the languages of revelation. In this area, the most important figure was Ambrose, both as a key player in the full Latinization of the western Catholic rite taking place at the end of the fourth century (Lafferty 2003) and as the most lyrical among the era's propagandists for that bodily purity which, through much of the Middle Ages, remained a precondition for full participation in the *opus dei* and, in theory, of entry into Latinity (Brown 2008).

Yet it was Jerome and Augustine who provided both many of the materials and a theoretical basis for understanding Latin as adequate to its sacred task. Jerome, loudly torn between his self-appointed role as a latter-day Cicero and his multilingual commitment to Christian learning, did so through his Latin Bible. So successfully did this translation and its many prefaces balance stylistic humility before the simplicity of the Bible's human authors—those shepherds and fishermen Moses, David, the apostles, and the rest—with well-funded contempt for the crudities of its rivals that Jerome's version slowly displaced its competitors to become "vulgate" (Williams 2006). Effectively monolingual in his thinking life, though not by birth or training, Augustine's greatest theoretical contribution to Latinity was his painstaking development, in *De doctrina christiana*, of a hermeneutics whose trust in the capacity of the divine word to reward even a relatively uneducated reader's loving intentions made it possible to circumvent the problem of rightly understanding the Holy Spirit in translation (Augustine 1987; Stock 1996; Bright 1999).

*****

Jerome's embattled translatorial stance and Augustine's acknowledgment (if only in principle) that the deep study of Scripture still requires knowledge of Greek and Hebrew suggest both the mobility of late antique Mediterranean language politics (Adams 2003) and the ways in which fourth- and fifth-century Latin, invested with the aura of imperial power though it was, had in other respects as near a kinship with the medieval vernacular as with medieval Latin. (This fact was not lost on vernacular translators, such as the Oxford scholars who produced the English Wycliffite Bible during the 1380s, loudly invoking Jerome and Augustine as their precursors; Dove 2007.) The foundations of Latin's emergence into the dignity of medieval *Latinitas* were laid only subsequently and elsewhere, at the extreme margent of the language's earlier sphere of influence: in the Christianization of Ireland from Britain during the fifth century and of Anglo-Saxon England from Celtic Britain, Ireland, and Rome in and after the sixth century (Hughes 1966, 1987; Blair 2005, 8–78).

Evidence of Old Irish, Breton, and Anglo-Saxon writing, and of the use of these languages in teaching Latin, suggests the seventh-century emergence around the Irish Sea of a binary but fluid written language system, in which Latin functioned as the language of liturgy and learning, while Irish and English served as aids and alternatives to Latin (Herren 1996; Wright 2001; Magennis 2001; Irvine 2001). This system allowed what we may begin to call the vernacular to stand in comfortably for Latin when necessary: as it does in the Alfredan translations of Gregory's *Cura pastoralis* and other texts in the late ninth century, written in West Saxon English in response to a perceived dearth of Latin literacy among the clergy, and as part of a royal strategy of using Christianity as an instrument of political unity (Godden 2009). It also encouraged the close technical attention to linguistic equivalence evidenced by the practice of glossing (Pulsiano 2001). But this system equally nourished Latin's distinct role as the language of collective worship—even, it seems, the worship of the laity (Tinti 2005)—and privilege as the caste language of those capable of rising to the lexically complex "hermeneutic" style developed in Ireland and given its headiest expression in Aldhelm's *Carmen de virginitate* (c. 690). The canonical status of this work among learned Anglo-Saxons was reaffirmed as late as the Benedictine reform of the tenth century (Orchard 1994).

This binary system, which was replicated in ninth-century Germany and later in Scandinavia, marks a major change from the late fourth century when—in parallel with the production of Jerome's Vulgate and Ambrose's establishment of a Catholic Latin rite at Milan—the Gothic Bible and liturgy were produced for the Arian Visigoths of Illyria, allowing them both to study and to worship in their own tongue (Thompson 2008). The system stands in equal contrast to the one set in place for the evangelization of the Slavs in the late ninth century, when a written Church Slavonic, devised by Saints Cyril and Methodius and taught in specially created schools, was again used as a standard language, not only for the initial process of evangelization but also for teaching the new Slavic clergy and for their liturgical rites, despite early protest from local Latinate bishops (Duichev 1985).

*****

Yet the system seems not to have begun its development into its more starkly diglossic later medieval shape until it was replicated in western and southern Europe as a result of the gradual, and partly managed, separation of spoken Latin and its written and liturgical counterpart. Until the eighth century, as Roger Wright has argued (1982, 1991a), Latin was at once a local and an educated language throughout most of what are now the Romance-speaking regions of Europe—those under neither Muslim nor Greek control, including those controlled by the immigrating Franks, who, unlike the Goths, had followed the Gauls by their early adoption, at least in most areas and for most purposes, of Latin as their own language (Herman 1997; McKitterick 1989, 1–22, 1991). In a manner not apparent to the modern Latinist, who is accustomed to read any form of the language phonetically, a single, broadly coherent spelling system was used to represent the range of regional dialects that would become the Romance languages, while written morphology, lexis and syntax were understood as formalizations of their spoken equivalents (Banniard 1992). From the reign of the Frankish king Charlemagne (771–814), however, the formal promotion of classicized forms of Latin pronunciation and syntax on the one hand, and the growth of a new awareness of linguistic regionalism on the other, gradually created a significant perceptual split between written and liturgical Latin and spoken proto-Romance (Van Uytfanghe 1991; Banniard 1991).

This split had a real relation to the binary language system of Ireland and England, not least because the new Latinity was evidently modeled on the learned Latin of England: the birthplace of one of the architects of the Carolingian language reform, Alcuin of York, whose teacher, Ecgbert, had himself been taught by the great early propagandist of Christian *Romanitas*, Bede (Wallach 1968; Godman 1986). The influence of Alcuin, the author of widely dispersed treatises on correct grammar, orthography, and speech, lies behind both Charlemagne's *capitulum* on the reform of spoken and sung Latin, *De litteris colendis*, and the royal insistence on correct grammar and copying of sacred texts in Carolingian monasteries and episcopal households in that most idealistic of social blueprints, the *Admonitio generalis* (Wright 1981).

Yet the split between Latin and Romance had more clearly marked hierarchic overtones than its earlier counterparts. The part played by Latinity in the Romanization of the Frankish kingdom, that polity's decision to see itself as the true western European heir to the empire of Constantine, elevated Latin by linking it to imperial authority and its universalizing and sacralizing claims. This resignification of Latin, motivated as it was not only by a desire to establish symbolic and administrative cohesion across an area that now included large tracts of Germany, but also by competitive cultural contact with Byzantine Greek, had the effect of reducing (proto-)Romance to the status of a set of mere local languages.

True, in one sense the symbolic situation of Romance was still equivalent to that of German, the language of the newly Christianized lands east of the Rhine. This equivalence was made famous by the chronicler Nithard's account of the Oaths of Strasbourg in 842, in which Charles the Bald and Louis the German are represented as swearing amity each in the language of the other's army: Charles in Old High German, Louis in a language historical linguists despairingly term "late Old Gallo-Roman." However, notwithstanding triumphant accounts of this scene by generations of French literary historians (Balibar 1985; Bloch 1989), the status of Romance between the ninth and eleventh centuries, at least in the hierarchy of written languages, was lower than that of either German or English and Irish. For where German, like English and Irish, rapidly established itself as a written language, Romance apparently did not, continuing for the most part to be represented by Latin. Despite its ostensible separation from the nascent Romance languages, Latin remained close enough to them to continue to function as their usual language of record, and so to put a strong brake on their independent literary development for a full three centuries after the death of Charlemagne.

The reason was not a lack of interest in representing the vernacular in writing. The first texts in French (the *Laudes regiae* of Soissons and a few others) are from as early as the late eighth century, while a very few highly worked texts from Italy, Spain, and France, such as the late ninth-century *Cantilène de sainte Eulalie*, provide sophisticated evidence of a specifically vernacular literary consciousness at the local level (Stock 1983, 25; Leupin 2003, 110–29). Yet it was not until the written vernacular was eagerly taken up by regional aristocracies in the early twelfth century because of its association with a sociopolitical ideal of *courtesie* (thus appropriating, in a sense, Latinity's own, long-standing identification with *curialitas*) that two Romance languages, Provençal and Anglo-Norman French, developed the relatively standardized written forms and the prestige necessary for the creation of significant literary traditions (Wright 1991; Kibbee 1991; Short 1992). (Continental French, not spurred on, as was Anglo-Norman, by an intimately aggressive language contact with Anglo-Saxon, seems to have been a few decades behind; Howlett 1996.) Even these works, moreover, which at first were generally in verse (*romanz*, romances), loudly declared themselves designed for oral performance and were anxiously aware of the paradox represented by their own textuality. By emerging into writing so slowly, it was thus the Romance vernaculars, the spoken descendants of the ancient and early medieval Latin language itself, not their Celtic and Germanic neighbors, that completed the development of the symbolically diglossic system of the late Middle Ages, by mapping the dichotomy between written and oral definitively onto that between Latin and vernacular.

Scholastic Latinity (1100–1300)

Medieval Latin, the international prestige language that was the birth tongue of nobody, was thus an ideological product at once of Latinity's increasingly powerful affirmation of its connection with the canonical Roman past and of its gradual denial of a significant part of its own history as a socially inclusive and constantly mutating regional language. This was the spoken Latin whose dialectal variability was sensitively registered by Augustine and whose ability to reach out towards the laity was exploited by homilists from Gregory the Great in the sixth century to Paul the Deacon in the eighth. It was also the Latin that, in tenth- and eleventh-century Italy, France, and Spain continued to give local inflection to liturgies performed, for the most part, by monks oblated to their houses in childhood, for whom the gap between birth tongue and the language of prayer and *conversatio* will have remained narrow indeed. Despite his secular upbringing, his international standing, and the careful grammaticality of his Latin, echoes of the vernacular are heard as late as Bernard of Clairvaux's sermons in the early twelfth century. The cadences of these sonorous masterpieces, shaped and reshaped with Horatian perfectionism by one of Europe's busiest men on delicate aural principles that yet remain obscure, seem still to evoke not only the liturgy but also the lift and fall of Bernard's native Bourgignon French (Leclercq 1955; Pranger 1994).

The echoes become inaudible, less through any final severing of the connection between Latin and Romance (a connection vital to the self-identity of Romance languages almost to the present), than with the development, from the twelfth century on, of the Latin of the schools: a lexically specialized spoken and written language, tailored to the needs of a new, multinational caste, clerks. After the flowering of monastic Latin in the eleventh and early twelfth centuries (from Peter Damian to Anselm to Bernard), and in symbiosis with the development of written Romance, school or university Latin became as dominant an influence on the idea of Latinity as on the language itself, and remained so until the fierce challenge from humanist Latinity over two hundred years later.

True, it was monasticism and its liturgies that continued to uphold Latin's symbolic association with the transcendent, such as it was. Yet where Carolingian and (from the early tenth century) Cluniac monasteries were viewed as communities whose worship was undertaken on behalf of the whole church, the new monasticism of the twelfth century was perfectionist: its conception of the spiritual life separated from, not representative of, the community as a whole (Constable 1996). Exploiting an association between allegoresis and the esoteric as old as the third-century exegete Origen, Bernard's *Sermones super cantica canticorum* assure Cistercian auditors, not of their fellowship with others, but of their status as a spiritual elite. The affective religiosity inherited in the thirteenth century by the friars found outlet in the promotion of personal religious praxis, as much as formal worship, and increasingly in the vernacular, not Latin. Given its interdependent relationship with the papacy, its ubiquity in the affairs of a Europe ever more reliant on texts, and an intellectual mandate that encompassed both the cosmos and its divine source, only scholasticism was placed to redefine the meanings of Latinity for the later Middle Ages (Southern 1995).

*****

At the heart of this redefinition was the reapplication of Latinity's now venerable tendency to evoke the universal and imperial in a new, abstract arena: *scientia*. *Scientia* was scholasticism's own *Romanitas* and a term as boundless for later medieval Latin Christian intellectuals as its linear descendant, "science," is for us now. A reach towards the universal already organizes the devout pedagogical program devised by Hugh of St. Victor in the second quarter of the twelfth century. By the mid-thirteenth century, a scholasticism in which dialectic, long regarded as the domain of philosophy, had also become central to theology, had developed the textual and lexical tools to address a far greater range of materials, whether encyclopedically or in the more systematic form of the *summa*. In the process, it had declared its intention to reexamine the Christian West's categories of understanding, albeit within the doctrinal framework provided by the deposit of Catholic faith, from the ground up (Colish 2000).

This program, moreover, was a direct corollary of the assertiveness with which Latin now claimed a place at the forefront of the group of sacred learned Mediterranean languages that (in two out of the three cases) had long been its familiar rivals, with whose intellectual traditions it established an intense set of imitative yet assimilative relationships clearly reminiscent in tone, if not genre, of those which early Roman intellectuals established with Greece. "Hostili preda ditetur lingua Latina; / Grecus et Hebreus seruiat edomitus" [Let the Latin tongue be enriched by enemy booty; let the vanquished Greek and Hebrew serve], as the lyricist Baudri of Bourgueil wrote at the end of the eleventh century (Baudri of Bourgueil 1979, 200.131–32; Bond 1987). With the help of Jewish converts, especially in Spain, Latin fought to achieve an intellectual, as well as a harsh political dominance, over Hebrew (Chazan 1992). As translations trickled in from Toledo and Sicily, it responded with excited anxiety to the threatening newcomer, Arabic, especially in the areas of medicine, alchemy, cognition theory, and cosmology (Burnett 2009). Besides engaging more deeply with Greek theology than at any time since John Scotus Eriugena, it used translations from Arabic and Greek to revive Boethius's great project of Latinizing Aristotle, whose categorizing approach to knowledge, despite bitter controversy, became the cornerstone of scholastic sciential rationalism (Dod 1988; Kretzmann 1988; Berschin 1998).

This rationalism was well aware of its limits, especially in the realm of theology. Here, the elevation of *scientia* helped precipitate, notably among thirteenth-century friars, a tense awareness that "Scientia inflat, caritas vero ædificat" (1 Cor 8:1) [knowledge puffs up, but charity edifies], and a careful theorization of the role of charity in *saving* knowledge or *sapientia* that built on an affective tradition derived from Victorine monasticism. Even before the rise of the radical epistemological skepticism associated with fourteenth-century Oxford, moreover, scholastic theology, again building on the Victorines, deployed an apophaticism derived from pseudo-Dionysius to insist upon what Mark Jordan, citing Aquinas, terms "the dispensability of particular theological utterances with regard to the truths they announce or recall" (2006, 26). Such an awareness, of obvious value to a Latinate scholasticism competing with more venerable peer languages, acknowledges both that theological utterances are translatable and that slippages between idioms are unavoidable and must thus be understood as incidental. As the late fourteenth-century treatise, *Cloud of Unknowing*, suggests—from the viewpoint of an emergent and, in this case, fiercely antirational theological vernacular—an apophatic semiotic system should in principle understand all languages as equal in their incapacity to describe a hidden God who can only be known, fleetingly, through unspeakable experience (Locke 2004).

Yet in practice Latin's privileged association with the universal category of Catholicity, and its need to maintain Catholic truth against not only the theological *errores graecorum* but the philosophical *errores gentilium*, long guaranteed both its special standing in its own eyes and its continued association with the rational: with the doctrinal considered as an object of dialectic proof, not saving faith. As Aquinas notes in his *Summa contra gentiles*, a work perhaps written as background preparation for Dominicans entering the mission field, in the absence of an agreed ground for argument in revelation, only the tools provided by reason could succeed (Jordan 2006, 89–115). Latin was the only western Christian language to have developed those tools; and it was scholastic Latin's great task to hone them more effectively than the competition.

*****

In reinterpreting Latinity's oldest project, *translatio studii et imperii*, by silently identifying itself with the universal, the sciential, and the authoritative or Catholic, scholastic Latin may seem to have felt secure in its diglossic relationship with a set of vernacular languages which, despite the rapid development of their own sciential prose traditions, were still much dependent on Latin. For the most part, this was no doubt the case, not least because so many vernacular instructional texts, encyclopedic (the *Lucidaires*), regulative (*Ancrene Wisse*), penitential (*Compileison*) or homiletic (*Somme le roi*), were themselves produced by highly educated friars (Fleming 1999; Honorius of Autun/Regensburg 2000), for whom the shift in mode involved in writing in the vernacular made language hierarchy into a felt experience: one akin to the simultaneous translation from Latin into local dialects expected of them on preaching tours (Waters 2004, 57–72).

When scholars did admit concern, however, it was Latin's status as a constructed language distant from ordinary speech that was uppermost in their minds. Giles of Rome's *De regimine principum*, written for Philip IV of France around 1280 by a major scholar of the new fraternal order of the Augustinian Hermits, holds that

Latin was created by philosophers dissatisfied by a common tongue that was incapable of formal analysis of natural science, ethics, astronomy or other topics:

> Videntes enim philosophi nullum idioma vulgare esse completum et perfectum, per quod perfecte exprimere possent naturas rerum, et mores hominum, et cursus astrorum, et alia de quibus disputare volebant, invenerunt sibi quasi proprium idioma, quod dicitur latinum, vel idioma literale: quod constituerunt adeo latum et copiosum, ut per ipsum possent omnes suos conceptus sufficienter exprimere.
>
> [Seeing that there was no complete and perfect vernacular idiom through which they could perfectly express the nature of things, or human behavior, or the course of the stars, or other subjects they wished to dispute, philosophers invented for themselves an idiom effectively their own, which is called Latin, or the lettered idiom, which they made so broad and copious that they could adequately express all their meanings through it.] (Giles of Rome 1607, 2.2.7, quoted in Briggs 1999, 78)

The pun on which this passage quietly turns, which links "latinum" to "latum" (broad), rather than "Latium" (the area around Giles's own birthplace, Rome, in which the language historically emerged), makes Latin the result of a mythical language reform much like that initiated by Charlemagne, but now oriented towards the rationalist exploration and articulation of knowledge through disputation.

It would seem that this language reform would condemn the vernacular to irrelevance. Yet no sooner has Giles underscored the unique virtues of Latin than the vernacular is reintroduced:

> Quare si hoc idioma est completum, et alia idiomata non possumus recte et distincte loqui nisi ab infantia assuescamus ad illa, ex parte eloquentiae—videlicet, ut recte et distincte loquamur idioma latinum—si volumus literas discere, debemus ab ipsa infantia literis insudare.
>
> [Therefore as this idiom [Latin] is complete, and as we cannot properly and distinctly speak other languages unless we have been used to them from infancy, if we wish to learn our letters fluently—i.e., so that we may speak in the Latin idiom properly and distinctly—we should sweat over our letters from infancy.] (Giles of Rome 1607, 2.2.7, quoted in Briggs 1999, 78)

Latin's lettered perfections render it particularly difficult even for the best-educated to achieve true fluency. The truly Latinate must be inducted into lettered culture at the same time others are learning their vernacular, both to master its idiom and to displace the rival sounds of Italian, French, or Spanish: those barbarously unreformed "idiomata" (a word whose meanings themselves slide illustratively between "idioms" and "languages") which haunt their learned counterpart. The "idioma literale" can fulfill its function only in so far as its acquisition successfully imitates that of the vernacular it was designed to correct.

Giles's concern over the porousness of the diglossic system separating Latin from vernacular is that of the worried pedagogue, anxious that Latin retain the fluency of a first language even as he celebrates its creation as a learned one. Yet there is something odd about his stance. For his defense of a Latin fully separated from, yet equivalent to, the vernacular is expressed in a language whose lexis and word order have themselves been deftly tailored to a reader habituated to French, as part of a work which was, for the most part, read in translation. Even as it describes a process moving in the opposite direction, Giles's Latin is ceding part of its lettered perfection in order to rejoin the wider speech communities accessed by the vernacular. For all the good it does for the production of specialized knowledge, the price extorted by the perfected "idioma literale," at least in the area of political science, has become too high. Despite the easy silence of scholastic Latin around its relationship with the vernacular, it seems that this relationship, too, was taut and competitive.

Towards A New Linguistic Order (1300–1530)

De regimine principum was written near the beginning of a period that saw the spread of a mode of Latin prose shorn of technical complexities and designed, above all, for mobility across a range of professions and educational levels. This was the Latin prose, both influenced by and influencing its vernacular equivalents, that allowed an ever broader circulation of religious guides (*Compendium theologicae veritatis*), devotional aids (*Meditationes vitae Christi*), saints' lives (*Legenda aurea*), encyclopedias (*Sophilegium*) and a great deal more, well into the age of print. Most of these (all those just mentioned included) were written by friars whose colleagues were engaged in producing similar works, many of them translations, in German, Italian, French, Spanish, and, latterly, English. The ubiquity and crudity of this Latin are signs at once of its usefulness as a medium of international communication, albeit in increasing competition with French (Dembowski 1986; Lusignan 1989), and of another shift in the relationships between western European languages, as the cultural prestige of Latin began, in conjunction with its ever wider dissemination, to be challenged by rapidly developing written vernaculars.

An important, if not representative, sign of this challenge is offered by the early fourteenth-century metalinguistic musings of Dante, a member of a still tiny class of learned intellectuals capable of working in a scholastic idiom whose first allegiance was to the vernacular. Dante admitted Latinity's prestige if it suited him, as when he describes his reasons for preferring the vernacular to Latin in writing an innovative scholastic commentary on his own Italian *cantiche* in *Convivio*:

> Latino...non era subietto ma sovrano, e per nobilità e per vertù e per bellezza. Per nobilità: perché lo latino è perpetuo e non corruttibile, e lo volgare è non stabile e corruttibile...[P]er vertù...Lo sermone, lo quale è ordinato a manifestare lo concetto umano, è virtuoso quando quello fa, e...lo latino molte cose manifesta concepute ne la mente che lo volgare far non può...[P]er

bellezza...Quello sermone è più bello ne lo quale più debitamente si rispondono le parole; e più debitamente si rispondono in latino che in volgare, però che lo volgare seguita uso, e lo latino arte.

[Latin is not subject but sovereign, through nobility and through virtue and through beauty. Through nobility: because Latin is perpetual and incorruptible and the vernacular is unstable and corruptible. Through virtue: language, which is designed to express human thought, is powerful when it does this and Latin articulates many things conceived in the mind that the vernacular cannot. Through beauty: that language is the most beautiful in which the words correspond most properly; and they correspond more properly in Latin than in the vernacular. For the vernacular follows custom and Latin art.] (Dante 1997, 1.5)

But while this self-derogatory praise of Latin trips (indeed, suspiciously well) off Dante's vulgar tongue, his real belief, expressed in *De vulgari eloquentia*, was in the vernacular's superiority to Latin ("Harum quoque duarum nobilior est vulgaris"; Dante 1968, 1.1.4). Significantly, given the anxieties expressed by Giles of Rome, this superiority was grounded, precisely, in the vernacular's integral connection with speech: a connection that, as a learned language, Dante believed Latin could never appropriate.

Although it has been in flux since the *confusio linguarum* of Babel, the vernacular, Dante argued, is natural ("naturalis"), drunk in with our nurse's milk and descended from the lost tongue spoken by Adam, which, even now, it can aspire to recreate. Cut off by its own abstraction and generality from the embodied concerns of the vernacular and not, here, granted any countervailing association with the philosophical, Latin is a language of a different order, devised for a different purpose. As an artificial ("artificialis"), not natural, language, whose grammatical character requires it to be formally learned and so delocalizes it in time and space ("gramatica nichil aliud est quam quedam inalterabilis locutionis ydemptitas diversibus temporibus atque locis"; Dante 1968, 1.9.11), Latin is the product of human ingenuity, invented to ensure that, despite the crisis of Babel, it would still be possible to learn from the past and communicate across language barriers in the present. Latin is thus useful, not least for such purposes as announcing the superior nobility of the vernacular, but is still a secondary ("secondaria") language with no special authority. Despite its corruption, the vernacular, on the other hand, emerges, not only as the language of human affairs (or, as *Vita nuova* has it, love) but as divine, integral to the original creation as Latin clearly was not (it is a "certam formam locutionis a Deo cum anima prima concreatam"; Dante 1968, 1.6.4). Like Hebrew, with which *De vulgari eloquentia* closely associates it, the spoken vernacular, not "lettered" Latin, is the language of the sacred (Eco 1995, 34–52).

Dante's downgrading of Latin to a transhistorical and supraregional common tongue was far from disinterested. Yet it was at the same time perceptive of the facts on the ground and an early instance of a rethinking of Latinity taking place in myriad forms in writings in and about the vernacular across western Europe. Justifying his English prose translation of Ranulph Higden's *Polychronicon* in his *Dialogue Between a*

Lord and a Clerk, the Oxford scholar John of Trevisa supported Dante's view of Latin as a post-Babelian international common tongue but argued that translation into local languages was necessary if its educational mission was to be completed (Wogan-Browne et al. 1999, 225–29). Vernacularizing Aristotle's *Ethics* for Charles V of France, the philosopher Nicole Oresme suggested that, just as it took time for Latin to acquire the capacity to express formal thought when it first encountered Greek, so it had been with French, whose increasing sophistication, combined with the advantage of its greater comprehensibility, would soon allow it to displace Latin, as Latin had Greek (Lusignan 1989, 306). Writing a guide to the astrolabe for his son, Lewis, the poet Geoffrey Chaucer, following Aquinas, asserted the equality of languages despite their different grammatical structures and implied a thought ubiquitous in late-medieval vernacular writings, that the process of *translatio studii et imperii* need not stop with Latin:

> This tretis...wol I shewe the under full light reules and naked wordes in Englissh, for Latin ne canst thou yit but small, my litel sone. But natheles suffise to the these trewe conclusions in Englissh as wel as sufficith to these noble clerkes Grekes these same conclusions in Grek; and to Arabiens in Arabik, and to Jewes in Ebrew, and to the Latin folk in Latin; whiche Latin folk had hem first out of othere diverse langages, and writen hem in her owne tunge, that is to sein, in Latin. And God woot that in alle these langages and in many moo han these conclusions ben suffisantly lerned and taught, and yit by diverse reules; right as diverse pathes leden diverse folk the righte way to Rome. (*Treatise on the Astrolabe* 25–40, in Chaucer 1987, 662)

Although the English vernacular is "full light" and "naked" compared to learned languages, it can also be said of it, not only that it "suffise" to its child-reader but that it "sufficith" to its complex subject matter. Much the same linguistic argument justified the contemporary translation of the Wycliffite Bible (Cole 2008).

*****

With the exception of Dante's, which aims to carve out a space for vernacular poetry, not prose, all these arguments for the standing of the vernacular are rationalistic, closely related to the educative and exploratory project of scholastic Latinity and, in most respects, as much a sign of its success as was the massive late-medieval vernacular borrowing of Latin lexis. The written vernacular's role as a local common tongue was continuous with, not in contradiction to, that of Latin. However, if Dante's specific rationale for holding the vernacular sacred was unique, his arguments for its difference from and superiority to Latin likewise found analogues elsewhere, notably in England.

The English understanding of Latin, like that of all non-Romance speakers, had always included a strong sense of its powerful incomprehensibility. By the fourteenth century, English worshippers were given private meditations to pursue as they heard mass, while learned theories about the *virtus verborum*, the power inherent in words (Delaurenti 2007), were deployed to justify the need for even the least Latinate to pay close attention to the reading of the gospel. Like the snake "whon thou hire enchauntes," who understands "nothing thy speche" but still obeys its trainer, so it is for the mass-goer "ther understanding failes": "The verrey vertu you alle availes" [the true power (of the gospel) is fully efficacious for you] (Simmons 1879, 140). With a similar implied belief in the intrinsic *virtus* of Latin, English religious writings routinely quote *auctori-*

tates in Latin before giving carefully tailored vernacular paraphrases, reiterating the epistemological gap between the global nature of Latinate authority and the situational character of the vernacular by repeatedly exposing the non-Latinate auditor to the mere sound of formal truth. In an aesthetic version of this effect, macaronic lyrics express not only the intimacy between liturgical Latin and vernacular as instruments of prayer but the aura that surrounds Latinity, irrespective of comprehensibility. Such lyrics typically use English as the language of narration and devotion while reserving Latin for resonant and theologically informative but finally nonessential filler:

> For on þat is so feir ant brist
> Velud maris stella,
> Bristore þen þe daiis list,
> Parens et puella;
> I crie þe grace of þe,
> Levedi, priie þi sone for me,
> tam pia,
> Þat I mote come to þe,
> Maria.

[For love of one who is so fair and bright as the star of the sea, brighter than the day's light, mother and maiden. I cry to you for grace from you, Lady, pray your son for me, so devoted, so that I may come to you, O Mary.] (Treharne 2004, 406)

The language of the liturgy here is syntactically dependent on English, not the other way around.

The gap between English and Latin, widened on the symbolic level by the former's long subordination to written Anglo-Norman, could be understood in different ways, some of them hostile to vernacularization. The arguments put forward against the Wycliffite Bible at Oxford by Thomas Palmer and William Butler in 1401, two learned friars who challenged the scholastic assumption that knowledge was *ipso facto* a good, turn on the incapacity not only of the "populus vulgaris" but of the ungrammatical, monosyllabic vulgar tongue itself to grasp clearly any thought about Christian truth (Watson 1995, 840–46). Despite deference towards Latin worthy of the *Convivio*, however, late-medieval English texts still found it advantageous to emphasize their vernacularity. The learned vernacular poets of the late fourteenth century were particularly interested in interlingual code-switching (William Langland's *Piers Plowman*; Machan 1994), marginal glossing (John Gower's *Confessio amantis*), and theories of *translatio* (Geoffrey Chaucer's *Legend of Good Women*) as resources for exploring the implications of the symbolic dichotomies that differentiated Latin and English. After all, these dichotomies had now moved well beyond the relative simplicity of *clericus-laicus*, transcendence-immanence, or father tongue-*lingua materna*, to incorporate *auctoritas-experientia*, *scientia-sapientia*, justice-mercy, and many others (Watson 1997a, 1997b; Copeland 1991, 179–220; Echard 1998). Indeed, for a brief, intense period, the relationship between Latin and vernacular seemed to sum up the key aesthetic, political, and theological concerns of an entire culture.

In the fifteenth century, interest grew in bringing the languages closer. The Benedictine poet, John Lydgate, taking as his starting point the neoclassicism of Chaucer and Gower, developed an "aureate" English so stiff with neologisms that one admiring contemporary characterized it as "half-chongid Latin" (Wogan-Browne et al. 1999, 54). Another, anonymous Benedictine worked in the opposite direction, importing common English phrases into his well-crafted but studiedly vernacular-sounding Latin sermons: "Dig doun in profundum sui cordis per debitam contemplacionem. Cogita intime de sua misericordia et gratitudine, de tua malici et ingratitudine, et be þi cor never so hard liquescet pre dolore" [Dig down into the depths of his heart through right contemplation. Think closely of his mercy and graciousness, of your malice and ingratitude, and, be your heart never so hard, let it melt with sorrow] (Horner 2006, 357). The wish to blend vernacular intimacy with Latinate authority and sophistication, to heal the separation between spoken and textual, local and universal, which underlies such experiments, associates them with that revival of a specialized mode of orality that was late-medieval humanism. From Francesco Petrarch in the mid-fourteenth to Desiderius Erasmus in the early sixteenth century, humanism is most famously associated with its ethical and philological challenge to scholasticism and its elevation of its own, rigorously classicized mode of Latinity above all existing languages and registers, Latin and vernacular, which in its view were, without exception, debased (Tunberg 1996; Fubini 2003, 9–42; Celenza 2005). Both in England and elsewhere, however, humanism was also manifested as the desire to reform vernacular languages forwards, to bring them, through partial Latinization, towards what Dante called *illustriousness* ("illustre volgare"). Although far less prestigious to this day, this process was more important to the establishment of the language systems of the sixteenth and seventeenth centuries, in which "horizontal" relationships between vernaculars loomed ever larger, than humanism's reassertions of Ciceronianism or revival of interest in Greek (although see Moss 2003).

Yet the legacy of the symbolic difference between Latin and English nonetheless survived into the modern era in the same, unusually powerful form it did in the German of Martin Luther's Reformation, as the vernacular again identified itself as sacred, this time in relation, not to Adamic language, but to Bible translation. Legislative attempts to ban the Wycliffite Bible in the early fifteenth and its successor, William Tyndale's New Testament, in the early sixteenth century did more than set back, however briefly, the continuing development of English as a vehicle of complex and potentially controversial written materials. It also generated a final set of symbolic dichotomies between the vernacular and Latin, in which the former functioned, as Latin had in Augustine's day, as the Pentecostal language of the gospel, while the latter's learned status tended to reposition it, within this rhetorical nexus, as the dark antonym of revelation: as a sign of the hidden, the hypocritical, the papist (Simpson 2007, 68–105).

For Tyndale himself, adding to a tradition of defenses of translation more than a century old in his *Obedience of Christian Man*, Latin is caught in a pincer movement between its old learned rivals and its vernacular successors, and has ceased even to have a role in a narrative of *translatio*:

> The sermons which thou readist in the Actes of the Apostles...were no doute preached in the mother tonge...Saynte Hierom also translated the Bible in to his mother tonge. Why maye not we also? They will saye it can not be translated into oure tonge it is so rude. It is not so rude as they are false lyers. For the Greke tonge agreeth moare with the English then with the Latyne. And the propirties of the Hebrue tonge agreth a thousande tymes moare with the English then with the Latyne. (Tyndale 1528, f. 15r–v)

As in Erasmus's polemical writings on language, which dismiss most of the thousand years between Jerome and himself as a period of linguistic barbarism (Erasmus 1993, 3–8; Vessey 1994), medieval Latin—the learned part of the diglossic system that was the engine of the intellectual life of western Europe for more than half a millennium—is already here in the process of being reclassified as a betrayal, a retreat, perhaps, at best, a mere *mistake*. For reasons still not that well separated from the strangely mingled legacies of humanism on the one hand, Protestantism on the other, not to mention our continuing cultural need to reaffirm the primacy of the mother tongue, this is a view that still dogs study of the field.

SUGGESTIONS FOR FURTHER READING

Convenient entry-points into the subject are Hexter (1987) and Ziolkowski (1991); Copeland (1990) and Minnis and Scott (2005) also contain much of immediate relevance. The mobility of the concept of "Latinity" itself, with respect to the earlier Middle Ages, is best tracked in Wright (1991); for the period in general, many essays in Mantello and Rigg (1996) remain fundamental. Stock (1983) is still the best study of medieval "textuality," Latin and otherwise. Jordan (2006) meditates astutely on Aquinas's understanding of Latinity. On "vernacularity" as an antonym to "Latinity," see Somerset and Watson (2003). On the practical interrelationship between Latin and vernacular in later medieval France, see Lusignan (1976); on their philosophical relation, see Dante's *De vulgari eloquentia* and the extensive literature that surrounds it: e.g., Eco (1995) (on "Adamic" language), Fubini (2003) (on humanistic appropriations of Dante and their aftermath). For discussions of Latinity in the context of the learning of grammar, see Breen (2010, chs. 2–3) (in contrast to the indifference to specifics in the "speculative" grammarians discussed in Bardzell 2009).

BIBLIOGRAPHY

Primary sources

Ælfric. 1994. *Aelfric's Prefaces*, edited by Jonathan Wolcox. Durham Medieval Texts 9. Durham: Durham Medieval Texts.
Augustine. 1987. *On Christian Doctrine*, translated by Durant W. Robertson. New York: MacMillan.

Baudri of Bourgueil. 1979. *Carmina*, edited by Karlheinz Hilbert. Editiones Heidelbergenses 19. Heidelberg: Winter.

Chaucer, Geoffrey. 1987. *The Riverside Chaucer*, edited by Larry Benson. 3rd ed. Boston: Houghton Mifflin.

Dante Alighieri. 1968. *De vulgari eloquentia*, edited by Aristide Marigo. 3rd ed. Florence: Le Monnier.

———. 1997. *Il Convivio*, edited by Gian Carlo Garfagnini. Diamanti. Roma: Salerno editrice.

Erasmus, Desiderius. 1993. *Patristic Scholarship: The Edition of St. Jerome*, edited by James F. Brady and John C. Olin. Erasmus. Works 61. Toronto: University of Toronto Press.

Giles of Rome. 1607. *Aegidij Columnae Romani, Archiepiscopi Bituricensis ... De regimine principum lib. III*. Romae: Apud Bartholomaeum Zannettum.

Honorius of Autun. 2000. *"Lucidaire de Grant Sapientie": Untersuchung und Edition der altfranzösischen Übersetzung 1 des "Elucidarium" von Honorius Augustodunensis*, edited by Monika Türk. Beihefte zur Zeitschrift für romanische Philologie 307. Tübingen: Max Niemeyer.

Horner, Patrick J., ed. and trans. 2006. *A Macaronic Sermon Collection from Late Medieval England, Oxford, MS Bodley 649*. Pontifical Institute of Mediaeval Studies. Studies and Texts 153. Toronto: Pontifical Institute of Mediaeval Studies.

Simmons, Thomas Frederick, ed. 1879. *The Lay Folks' Mass Book*. Early English Text Society. Ordinary Series 71. London: Oxford University Press.

Thomas of Erfurt. 1972. *Grammatica speculativa*, edited and translated by Geoffrey L. Bursill-Hall. The Classics of Linguistics. Harlow: Longman.

Treharne, Elaine M., ed. 2004. *Old and Middle English c. 890–c. 1400: An Anthology*. Blackwell Anthologies. Oxford: Blackwell.

Tyndale, William. 1528. *The Obedience of A Christian Man*. Antwerp: J. Hoochstraten.

Secondary sources

Adams, James N. 2003. *Bilingualism and the Latin Language*. Cambridge: Cambridge University Press.

———. 2007. *The Regional Diversification of Latin, 200 BC–600 AD*. Cambridge: Cambridge University Press.

Balibar, Renée. 1985. *L'Institution du Français: Essai sur le colinguisme des Carolingiens à la République*. Pratiques théoriques. Paris: Presses Universitaires de France.

Banniard, Michel. 1991. "Rhabanus Maurus and the Vernacular Languages." In *Latin and the Romance languages in the Early Middle Ages*, edited by Roger Wright, 164–74. Croom Helm Romance Linguistics Series. London, New York: Routledge.

———. 1992. *Viva Voce: Communication Écrite et Communication Orale du IVe au IXe Siècle en Occident Latin*. Collection des études augustiniennes. Série Moyen-âge et Temps modernes 25. Paris: Institut des Études Augustiniennes.

Bardzell, Jeffrey. 2009. *Speculative Grammar and Stoic Language Theory in Medieval Allegorical Narrative: From Prudentius to Alan of Lille*. Studies in Medieval History and Culture. New York: Routledge.

Berschin, Walter. 1998. *Greek Letters and the Latin Middle Ages: From Jerome to Nicholas of Cusa*, translated by Jerold C. Frakes. Washington, DC: Catholic University of America Press.

Biard, Joël. 1989. *Logique et Théorie du Signe au XIVe Siècle*. Études de philosophie médiévale 64. Paris: Vrin.

Blair, John. 2005. *The Church in Anglo-Saxon Society*. Oxford: Oxford University Press.
Bloch, Howard. 1989. "842: The First Document and the Birth of Medieval Studies." In *A New History of French Literature*, edited by Denis Hollier, 6–13. Cambridge, MA: Harvard University Press.
Bond, Gerald. 1987. "Composing Yourself: Ovid's *Heroides*, Baudri of Bourgueil and the Problem of Persona." *Mediaevalia* 13: 83–117.
Breen, Katharine. 2010. *Imagining an English Reading Public, 1150–1400*. Cambridge Studies in Medieval Literature 79. Cambridge: Cambridge University Press.
Briggs, Charles F. 1999. *Giles of Rome's De Regimine Principum: Reading and Writing Politics at Court and University, c. 1275–c. 1525*. Cambridge Studies in Paleography and Codicology 5. Cambridge: Cambridge University Press.
Bright, Pamela, ed. and trans. 1999. *Augustine and the Bible*. The Bible Through the Ages 2. Notre Dame, IN: University of Notre Dame Press.
Broadie, Alexander. 1993. *An Introduction to Medieval Logic*. 2nd ed. Oxford: Clarendon.
Brown, Peter. 2008. *The Body and Society: Men, Women, and Sexual Renunciation in Early Christianity*. Columbia Classics in Religion. New York: Columbia University Press.
Burnett, Charles. 2009. *Arabic into Latin In the Middle Ages: The Translators and Their Intellectual and Social Context*. Variorum Reprints. Farnham, UK: Ashgate.
Bursill-Hall, Geoffrey L. 1971. *Speculative Grammars of the Middle Ages: The Doctrine of the* Partes orationis *of the Modistae*. Approaches to Semantics 11. The Hague: Mouton.
Carruthers, Mary. 1998. *The Craft of Thought: Meditation, Rhetoric, and the Making of Images, 400–1200*. Cambridge Studies in Medieval Literature 34. Cambridge: Cambridge University Press.
Celenza, Christopher S. 2005. "Petrarch, Latin, and Italian Renaissance Latinity." *Journal of Medieval and Early Modern Studies* 35: 510–36.
Chazan, Robert. 1992. *Barcelona and Beyond: The Disputation of 1263 and Its Aftermath*. Berkeley, CA: University of California Press.
Clanchy, Michael T. 1993. *From Memory to Written Record: England 1066–1307*. 2nd ed. Oxford: Oxford University Press.
Cole, Andrew. 2008. *Literature and Heresy in the Age of Chaucer*. Cambridge Studies in Medieval Literature 71. Cambridge. Cambridge University Press.
Colish, Marcia L. 1997. *Medieval Foundations of the Western Intellectual Tradition, 400–1400*. Yale Intellectual History of the West. New Haven, CT: Yale University Press.
——— . 2000. *Remapping Scholasticism*. Etienne Gilson Series 21. Toronto: Pontifical Institute of Mediaeval Studies.
Constable, Giles. 1996. *The Reformation of the Twelfth Century*. Cambridge: Cambridge University Press.
Copeland, Rita. 1991. *Rhetoric, Hermeneutics, and Translation in the Middle Ages: Academic Traditions and Vernacular Texts*. Cambridge Studies in Medieval Literature 11. Cambridge: Cambridge University Press.
Copeland, Rita and Ineke Sluiter. 2009. *Medieval Grammar and Rhetoric: Language Arts and Literary Theory, AD 300–1475*. Oxford: Oxford University Press.
Curtius, Ernst Robert. 1953. *European Literature and the Latin Middle Ages*, translated by Willard R. Trask. Bollingen Series 36. New York: Pantheon Books.
Delaurenti, Béatrice, ed. 2007. *La Puissance des Mots, "Virtus Verborum": Débats Doctrinaux sur le Pouvoir des Incantations au Moyen Âge*. Cerf Histoire. Paris: Cerf.
Dembowski, Peter F. 1986. "Learned Latin Treatises in French: Inspiration, Plagiarism, and Translation." *Viator* 17: 256–69.

Dod, Bernard G. 1988. "Aristoteles Latinus." In *The Cambridge History of Later Medieval Philosophy: From the Rediscovery of Aristotle to the Disintegration of Scholasticism, 1100–1600*, edited by Norman Kretzmann, Anthony Kenny, and Jan Pinborg, 45–79. Cambridge: Cambridge University Press.

Dove, Mary. 2007. *The First English Bible: The Text and Context of the Wycliffite Versions*. Cambridge Studies in Medieval Literature 66. Cambridge: Cambridge University Press.

Duichev, Ivan, ed. 1985. *Kiril and Methodius: Founders of Slavonic Writing: A Collection of Sources and Critical Studies*, translated by Spass Nikolov. East European Monographs. New York: Columbia University Press.

Echard, Sian. 1998. "With Carmen's Help: Latin Authorities in Gower's *Confessio Amantis*." *Studies in Philology* 95: 1–40.

Eco, Umberto. 1995. *The Search For the Perfect Language*, translated by James Fentress. The Making of Europe. Oxford: Blackwell.

Eco, Umberto and Constantina Marmo, eds. 1989. *On the Medieval Theory of Signs*. Foundations of Semiotics 21. Amsterdam, Philadelphia: J. Benjamins.

Fleming, John. 1999. "The Friars and Medieval English Literature." In *The Cambridge History of Medieval English Literature*, edited by David Wallace, 349–75. New Cambridge History of English Literature. Cambridge: Cambridge University Press.

Fubini, Riccardo. 2003. *Humanism and Secularization: From Petrarch to Valla*, translated by Martha King. Duke Monographs in Medieval and Renaissance Studies 18. Durham, NC: Duke University Press.

Fudeman, Kirsten A. 2010. *Vernacular Voices: Language and Identity in Medieval French Jewish Communities*. Jewish Culture and Contexts. Philadelphia: University of Pennsylvania Press.

Gellrich, Jesse. 1985. *The Idea of the Book in the Middle Ages: Language Theory, Mythology, and Fiction*. Ithaca, NY: Cornell University Press.

Godden, Malcolm. 2009. "The Alfredian Project and its Aftermath: Rethinking the Literary History of the Ninth and Tenth Centuries. Sir Israel Gollancz Memorial Lecture." *Proceedings of the British Academy* 162: 93–122.

Godman, Peter. 1986. *Poets and Emperors: Frankish Politics and Carolingian Poetry*. Oxford: Clarendon.

Grafton, Anthony and Lisa Jardine. 1986. *From Humanism to the Humanities: Education and the Liberal Arts in Fifteenth- and Sixteenth-Century Europe*. Cambridge, MA: Harvard University Press.

Hames, Harvey J. 2000. *The Art of Conversion: Christianity and Kabbalah in the Thirteenth Century*. The Medieval Mediterranean 26. Leiden, Boston: Brill.

Haug, Walter. 1997. *Vernacular Literary Theory in the Middle Ages: The German Tradition, 800–1300, in Its European Context*. Cambridge Studies in Medieval Literature 29. Cambridge: Cambridge University Press.

Hellgardt, Ernst. 1979. "Notkers des Deutschen Brief an Bischof Hugo von Sitten." In *Befund und Deutung. Zum Verhältnis von Empirie und Interpretation in Sprach- und Literaturwissenschaft*, edited by Klaus Grubmüller et al., 169–92. Tübingen: Niemeyer.

Herman, József. 1997. *Vulgar Latin*, translated by Roger Wright. University Park, PA: Pennsylvania State University Press.

Herren, Michael W. 1996. "Latin and the Vernacular Languages." In *Medieval Latin. An Introduction and Bibliographical Guide*, edited by Frank A. C. Mantello and Arthur G. Rigg, 122–29. Washington, DC: The Catholic University of America Press.

Hexter, Ralph J. 1987. "*Latinitas* in the Middle Ages: Horizons and Perspectives." *Helios* 14: 69–92.

Howlett, David R. 1996. *The English Origins of Old French Literature*. Medieval Studies. Dublin: Four Courts Press.

Hughes, Kathleen. 1966. *The Church in Early Irish Society*. Ithaca, NY: Cornell University Press.

———. 1987. *Church and Society in Ireland, A.D. 400–1200*. Variorum Reprints. London: Variorum.

Irvine, Martin. 1994. *The Making of Textual Culture: 'Grammatica' and Literary Theory, 350–1100*. Cambridge Studies in Medieval Literature 19. Cambridge: Cambridge University Press.

Irvine, Susan. 2001. "Religious Context: Pre-Benedictine Reform Period." In *A Companion to Anglo-Saxon Literature*, edited by Philipp Pulsiano and Elaine Treharne, 135–50. Blackwell Companions to Literature and Culture 11. Oxford: Blackwell.

Jaeger, C. Stephen. 1994. *The Envy of Angels: Cathedral Schools and Social Ideals in Medieval Europe, 950–1200*. Middle Ages Series. Philadelphia: University of Pennsylvania Press.

Jordan, Mark D. 2006. *Rewritten Theology: Aquinas After His Readers*. Challenges in Contemporary Theology. Oxford: Blackwell.

Kennedy, Ruth and Simon Meecham-Jones. 2008. *Authority and Subjugation in Writing of Medieval Wales*. New Middle Ages. New York: Palgrave Macmillan.

Kibbee, Douglas A. 1991. *For to Speke Frenche Trewely: The French Language in England, 1000–1600: Its Status, Description, and Instruction*. Amsterdam Studies in the Theory and History of Linguistic Science. Series III, Studies in the History of the Language Sciences 60. Amsterdam, Philadelphia: J. Benjamins.

Kretzmann, Norman, Anthony Kenny, and Jan Pinborg, eds. 1988. *The Cambridge History of Later Medieval Philosophy: From the Rediscovery of Aristotle to the Disintegration of Scholasticism, 1100–1600*. Cambridge: Cambridge University Press.

Lafferty, Maura K. 2003. "Translating Faith from Greek to Latin: *Romanitas* and *Christianitas* in Late Fourth-Century Rome and Milan." *Journal of Early Christian Studies* 11: 21–62.

Leclercq, Jean. 1955. "Recherches sur les Sermons sur les Cantiques de S. Bernard." *Revue Bénédictine* 65: 228–58.

Leupin, Alexandre. 2003. *Fiction and Incarnation: Rhetoric, Theology, and Literature in the Middle Ages*, translated by David Laatsch. Minneapolis, MN: University of Minnesota Press.

Locke, Charles. "*The Cloud of Unknowing*: Apophatic Discourse and Vernacular Anxieties." In *Text and Authority: The Rhetoric of Authority in the Middle Ages*, edited by Marianne Børch, 207–33. Odense: University Press of Southern Denmark.

Lusignan, Serge. 1987. *Parler Vulgairement: Les Intellectuels et la Langue Française aux XIIIe et XIVe siècles*. 2nd ed. Études médiévales. Paris: J. Vrin.

———. 1989. "La Topique de la *Translatio Studii* et les Traductions Françaises de Textes Savants au XIVe Siècle." In *Traduction et Traducteurs au Moyen Age*, edited by Geneviève Contamine, 303–27. Institut de recherche et d'histoire des textes. Documents, études et répertoires. Paris: Editions du Centre national de la recherche scientifique.

———. 2004. *La Langue des Rois au Moyen Age: Le Français en France et en Angleterre*. Le nœud gordien. Paris: Presses Universitaires de France.

Machan, Tim William and Charles T. Scott, eds. 1992. *English in Its Social Contexts: Essays in Historical Sociolinguistics*. Oxford Studies in Sociolinguistics. New York: Oxford University Press.

Machan, Tim. 1994. "Language Contact in *Piers Plowman*." *Speculum* 69: 359–85.

Magennis, Hugh. 2001. "Audience(s), Reception, Literacy." In *A Companion to Anglo-Saxon Literature*, edited by Philipp Pulsiano and Elaine Treharne, 84–101. Blackwell Companions to Literature and Culture 11. Oxford: Blackwell.

Mantello, Frank A. C. and Arthur G. Rigg. 1996. *Medieval Latin: An Introduction and Bibliographical Guide*. Washington, DC: Catholic University of America Press.

McKitterick, Rosamond. 1989. *The Carolingians and the Written Word*. Cambridge: Cambridge University Press.

———. 1991. "Latin and Romance: An Historian's Perspective." In *Latin and the Romance Languages in the Early Middle Ages*, edited by Roger Wright, 130–45. Croom Helm Romance Linguistics Series. London: Routledge.

Minnis, Alastair J. 1988. *Medieval Theory of Authorship: Scholastic Literary Attitudes in the Later Middle Ages*. 2nd ed. Aldershot: Wildwood.

———. 2001. *Magister Amoris: The Roman de la Rose and Vernacular Hermeneutics*. Oxford, New York: Oxford University Press.

———. 2009. *Translations of Authority in Medieval English Literature: Valuing the Vernacular*. Cambridge: Cambridge University Press.

Minnis, Alastair J. and A. Brian Scott, eds. 1991. *Medieval Literary Theory and Criticism, c. 1100–c. 1375: The Commentary Tradition*. Oxford: Clarendon Press.

Minnis, Alastair J. and Ian Johnson. 2005. *The Cambridge History of Literary Criticism*. Vol. 2: *The Middle Ages*. Cambridge: Cambridge University Press.

Moss, Ann. 2003. *Renaissance Truth and the Latin Language Turn*. Oxford: Oxford University Press.

Ong, Walter. J. 1982. *Orality and Literacy: The Technologizing of the Word*. New Accents. London: Methuen.

———. 1984. "Orality, Literacy, and Medieval Textualization." *New Literary History* 16: 1–12.

Orchard, Andy. 1994. *The Poetic Art of Aldhelm*. Cambridge Studies in Anglo-Saxon England 8. Cambridge: Cambridge University Press.

Pranger, Marinus B. 1994. *Bernard of Clairvaux and the Shape of Monastic Thought: Broken Dreams*. Brill's Studies in Intellectual History 56. Leiden, New York: E. J. Brill.

Pulsiano, Phillip. 2001. "Prayers, Glosses and Glossaries." In *A Companion to Anglo-Saxon Literature*, edited by Phillip Pulsiano and Elaine Treharne, 209–30. Blackwell Companions to Literature and Culture 11. Oxford: Blackwell.

Pulsiano, Phillip and Elaine Treharne. 2001. *A Companion to Anglo-Saxon Literature*. Blackwell Companions to Literature and Culture 11. Oxford: Blackwell.

Shapiro, Marianne. 1990. *De Vulgari Eloquentia: Dante's Book of Exile*. Regents Studies in Medieval Culture. Lincoln, NE: University of Nebraska Press.

Sheerin, Daniel. 1987. "In Media Latinitate." *Helios* 14: 51–67.

Short, Ian. 1992. "Patrons and Polyglots: French Literature in Twelfth-Century England." In *Anglo-Norman Studies XIV: Proceedings of the Battle Conference 1991*, edited by Marjorie Chibnall, 229–49. Cambridge: D. S. Brewer.

Simpson, James. 2007. *Burning to Read: English Fundamentalism and Its Reformation Opponents*. Cambridge MA: Harvard University Press.

Somerset, Fiona and Nicholas Watson, eds. 2003. *The Vulgar Tongue: Medieval and Postmedieval Vernacularity*. University Park, PA: Pennsylvania State University Press.

Southern, Richard W. 1995. *Scholastic Humanism and the Unification of Europe*. 2 vols. Oxford: Blackwell.

Stanton, Robert. 2002. *The Culture of Translation in Anglo-Saxon England*. Cambridge: D. S. Brewer.

Stock, Brian. 1983. *The Implications of Literacy: Written Language and Models of Interpretation in the Eleventh and Twelfth Centuries*. Princeton, NJ: Princeton University Press.
———. 1996. *Augustine the Reader: Meditation, Self-Knowledge, and the Ethics of Interpretation*. Cambridge, MA: Harvard University Press.
Sweeney, Eileen C. 2006. *Logic, Theology, and Poetry in Boethius, Abelard, and Alan of Lille: Words in the Absence of Things*. New Middle Ages. New York: Palgrave Macmillan.
Tinti, Francesca. 2005. *Pastoral Care in Late Anglo-Saxon England*. Anglo-Saxon Studies 6. Cambridge: D. S. Brewer.
Thompson, Edward A. 2008. *The Visigoths in the Time of Ulfila*. 2nd ed. London: Duckworth.
Trask, Robert Lawrence. 1999. *Key Concepts in Language and Linguistics*. Key Concepts Series. London, New York: Routledge.
Tunberg, Terence O. 1996. "Humanistic Latin." In *Medieval Latin. An Introduction and Bibliographical Guide*, edited by Frank A. C. Mantello and Arthur G. Rigg, 130–36. Washington, DC: The Catholic University of America Press.
Van Uytfanghte, Marc. 1991. "The Consciousness of a Linguistic Dichotomy (Latin-Romance) in Carolingian Gaul: The Contradictions of the Sources and of Their Interpretation." In *Latin and the Romance Languages in the Early Middle Ages*, edited by Roger Wright, 114–29. Croom Helm Romance Linguistics Series. London, New York: Routledge.
Vessey, Mark. 1994. "Erasmus' Jerome: The Publishing of a Christian Author." *Erasmus of Rotterdam Society Yearbook* 14: 62–99.
Wallach, Luitpold. 1968. *Alcuin and Charlemagne: Studies in Carolingian History and Literature*. New York: Johnson.
Waters, Claire. 2004. *Angels and Earthly Creatures: Preaching, Performance, and Gender in the Late Middle Ages*. Middle Ages Series. Philadelphia: University of Pennsylvania Press.
Watson, Nicholas. 1995. "Censorship and Cultural Change in Late-Medieval England: Vernacular Theology, the Oxford Translation Debate, and Arundel's Constitutions of 1409." *Speculum* 70: 822–64.
———. 1997a. "Visions of Inclusion: Universal Salvation and Vernacular Theology in Pre-Reformation England." *Journal of Medieval and Early Modern Studies* 27: 145–88.
———. 1997b. "Conceptions of the Word: The Mother Tongue and the Incarnation of God." *New Medieval Literatures* 1: 85–124.
———. 2008. "Theories of Translation." In *The Oxford History of Literary Translation in English*. Vol. 1: *To 1550*, edited by Roger Ellis, 71–92. Oxford: Oxford University Press.
Williams, Megan Hale. 2006. *The Monk and the Book: Jerome and the Making of Christian Scholarship*. Chicago: University of Chicago Press.
Williams, Stephen. 1985. *Diocletian and the Roman Recovery*. London: Methuen.
Wogan-Browne, Jocelyn, Nicholas Watson, Andrew Taylor, and Ruth Evans, eds. 1999. *The Idea of the Vernacular: An Anthology of Middle English Literary Theory, 1280–1530*. University Park, PA: Pennsylvania State University Press.
Wright, Charles D. 2001. "The Irish Tradition." In *A Companion to Anglo-Saxon Literature*, edited by Philipp Pulsiano and Elaine Treharne, 345–74. Blackwell Companions to Literature and Culture 11. Oxford: Blackwell.
Wright, Roger. 1981. "Late Latin and Early Romance: Alcuin's *De Orthographia* and the Council of Tours (AD 813)." *Papers of the Liverpool Latin Seminar* 3: 343–61.
———. 1982. *Late Latin and Early Romance in Spain and Carolingian France*. ARCA. Classical and Medieval Texts, Papers, and Monographs 8. Liverpool: F. Cairns.

———. 1991a. "The Conceptual Distinction Between Latin and Romance: Invention or Evolution?" In *Latin and the Romance Languages in the Early Middle Ages*, edited by Roger Wright, 103–13. Croom Helm Romance Linguistics Series. London, New York: Routledge.

———, ed. 1991b. *Latin and the Romance Languages in the Early Middle Ages*. Croom Helm Romance Linguistics Series. London, New York: Routledge.

Ziolkowski, Jan. 1991. "Cultural Diglossia and the Nature of Medieval Latin Literature." In *The Ballad and Oral Literatures*, ed. Joseph Harris, 193–213. Harvard English Studies 17. Cambridge, MA: Harvard University Press.

———. 1996. "Towards A History of Medieval Latin Literature." In: *Medieval Latin. An Introduction and Bibliographical Guide*, edited by Frank A. C. Mantello and Arthur G. Rigg, 505–36. Washington, DC: The Catholic University of America Press.

PART III

MANUSCRIPT CULTURE AND THE MATERIALITY OF LATIN TEXTS

CHAPTER 8

READERS AND MANUSCRIPTS[1]

ANDREW TAYLOR

Obedient and Resistant Reading

Medieval scholars often described reading as the disinterested and impersonal pursuit of wisdom, deploring any markings of books that were not strictly scholarly. Part of the fascination old books hold today, however, lies in the hope that they may preserve traces of the idiosyncratic thoughts and feelings of some specific earlier reader. Far too often, however, books remain reticent, their pristine pages offering few indications of how they were read or even that they were read at all. As Robert Darnton notes, "If it is possible to recapture the great rereadings of the past, the inner experiences of ordinary readers may always elude us" (2009, 203). Instead of following the trail of some specific individual, then, more often we must settle for reconstructing general modes of textual apprehension. One of the dangers in doing so is to offer too sweeping an account. In particular, the history of medieval reading is often cast as a wholesale transition from a monastic culture, in which reading was essentially a form of prayer, to a clerical or scholarly culture, in which reading was a means of gathering information. While there is no doubt that the high and late Middle Ages saw the widespread adoption of new methods of reading, many of them designed to facilitate rapid consultation of books, nor that such methods were fostered by the schools, there has been a

---

1. I would like to thank Alexander Andrée, Jayna Brett, Isabelle Cochelin, Maura Nolan, and Lesley Smith for their generous responses to questions and the Social Sciences and Humanities Council of Canada for financial support which allowed me to consult the manuscripts.

tendency to telescope events that span many centuries and to suggest that one form of reading supplants another. Thus Paul Saenger describes the role of silent reading in the "transformation from an early medieval oral, monastic culture to a visual, scholastic one" (1997, 265) and goes so far as to claim that with "the general acceptance of separated script and the practices it made possible [that is, reading silently], Europe entered the modern world as we know it" (1997, 256). Even if we cannot fully capture their experiences, examples of specific readers, whether pious or worldly, diligent or feckless, may complicate such accounts of wholesale social transformation.

According to the fourteenth-century English bibliophile Richard of Bury, who used his position as keeper of the privy seal, treasurer, chancellor, and finally bishop of Durham to acquire the largest private collection of books in England, "Amorem...librorum amorem sapientiae constat esse" [The love of books is the same thing as the love of wisdom] (1960, 136–67). Books reprove vice and teach reverence for God (ibid., 138–39), and turn clerics into teachers, making them "in oculis laicorum mirabiles velut magna mundi luminaria" [marvellous in the eyes of the laity, like great lights in the world] (ibid., 36–37). But everywhere Bury finds books are abused by the clerics who should guard them.

Through his satirical account, Bury offers a glimpse of what some medieval readers actually did with their books. He rebukes

> iuvenes impudentes, qui cum litterarum figuras effigiare didicerint, mox pulcherrimorum voluminum, si copia concedatur, incipiunt fieri glossatores incongrui et ubi largiorem marginem circa textum perspexerint, monstruosis apparitant alphabetis; vel aliud frivolum qualecunque quod imaginationi occurrit celerius, incastigatus calamus protinus exarare praesumit.
>
> [shameless youths, who as soon as they have learned to form the shapes of letters, straightway, if they are allowed an abundance of the most beautiful books, become unsuitable commentators, and wherever they find an extra margin about the text, furnish it with monstrous alphabets, or if any other frivolity strikes their fancy, at once their promiscuous pen begins to plough away.] (ibid., 158–59; wherever possible, I have provided references to the most convenient or reliable editions and translations, to which I have occasionally made small modifications.)

Pledging books to moneylenders, doodling or testing one's pen on the margins, marking pages of personal interest by sticking in straws, pawing over books with filthy hands, eating fruit and cheese or drinking over an open book...all this Bury abhors. If he had had his will, the college he hoped to endow in Oxford would have been complete with a magnificent library—five carts were insufficient to move Bury's personal collection (Adam of Murimuth 1889, 171)—whose volumes would have circulated only under the most careful strictures.

Bury shares a recurring tendency in medieval culture to fuse the wise men of the past and the texts they bequeathed to us into *auctores*. Strictly speaking, as M. B. Parkes notes, "*Auctoritates* were texts rather than persons. They are *sententiae* or ideas excerpted from their immediate context in a work and divorced from the wider context of the writings of an *auctor*" (1976, 116, n. 1). But as A. J. Minnis observes, "in a literary context, the term *auctor* denoted *someone* who was at once a writer and an authority" (1984, 10, my emphasis). So, for Bury, in books we find "mortuos quasi vivos" [the dead as if they were alive] (1960, 16–17), and since "sint nobis commodissimi magistri...eisdem non immerito tam honorem quam amorem tribuere convenit magistralem" [they are the aptest teachers...it is fitting to bestow on them the honour and affection that we owe our teachers] (ibid., 28–29). Bury does reverse this paternal relationship once, when he briefly likens new copies of books that are worn out by age to the "propagationes recentium filiorum" [the begetting of fresh sons] (ibid., 146–47), gender coding that has been discussed by Carolyn Dinshaw (1989, 18–21). For the most part, however, he casts readers as pupils and books as benevolent masters "qui nos instruunt sine vergis et ferula" [who instruct us without the rod or ferrule] (ibid., 20–21).

Bury shares a prevailing medieval vision of the book as a metaphor for divine order (Gellrich 1985, 20). He has no sympathy for the idiosyncrasies of contemporary readers and wishes to present his own compulsive collecting—the subject of criticism in his own day and ours (Cheney 1973)—as merely the consequence of his desire for knowledge (Camille 1997, 35). (Efforts to assess Bury's psychological condition are complicated somewhat by residual uncertainty about the authorship of the *Philobiblon*. Courtenay (Oxford Dictionary of National Biography) suggests that Bury's clerk, the Dominican Robert Holcot, might have assisted in its composition. Denholm-Young 1950, xx, notes that Bury, in his younger days, before he could afford to collect books, was a no less dedicated collector of letters.) Bury's attitude is diametrically opposed to the tendency among recent book historians to champion readers against authors and celebrate individual acts of resistant reading, following on Roland Barthes's proclamation that "the birth of the reader must be at the cost of the death of the Author" (1977, 148). As Michel de Certeau writes, in a much cited passage, "Far from being writers—founders of their own place, heirs of the peasants of earlier ages now working on the soil of language, diggers of wells and builders of houses—readers are travellers; they move across lands belonging to someone else, like nomads poaching their way across fields they did not write, despoiling the wealth of Egypt to enjoy it themselves" (1984, 174). So the reader "escapes from the law of each text in particular, and from that of the social milieu" (ibid., 174). Similarly, for Roger Chartier, a reader's reception is always a form of "appropriation, which transforms, reformulates, and exceeds what it receives" (1991, 19). While the dynamic is obviously different for manuscript books, which were, as a rule, individually commissioned, many medievalists share this celebration of individual acts of appropriation, praising the medieval book for its open nature (Dagenais 1994, 18), noting the ways in which marginal comments can function as sites of subversion or contestation (Baswell 1992), and lamenting that medieval readers treated their books with too much respect and left them too clean.

Reading with the Lips and Reading with the Eye

For Bury, books offer the contemporary reader direct access to the wisdom of the past. Not only are readers thus consigned to a largely passive role, but their activity is presented as one without a history, as if good reading was always the same. Bury's description of reading is, nonetheless, very much of his period. As a late medieval cleric, he thinks of reading as essentially visual. Unlike the perishable truth of the voice,

> veritas scripta libri, non successiva sed permanens, palam se praebet aspectui et per sphaerulas pervias oculorum, vestibula sensus communis et imaginationis atria transiens, thalamum intellectus ingreditur, in cubili memoriae se recondens, ubi aeternam mentis congenerat veritatem.
>
> [the written truth of books, not transient but permanent, plainly offers itself to be observed, and by means of the pervious spherules of the eyes, passing through the vestibule of perception, and the courts of the imagination, enters the bridal chamber of the intellect, taking its place in the couch of memory, where it engenders the eternal truth of the mind.] (1960, 20–21)

But many people in the Middle Ages did not receive their books in this way. As Jean Leclercq put it, in his famous study of monastic reading practices, *The Love of Learning and the Desire for God*, "in the Middle Ages, as in antiquity, they read usually, not as today, principally with the eyes, but with the lips, pronouncing what they saw, and with the ears, listening to the words pronounced, hearing what is called 'the voices of the pages'" (1982, 15).

This form of monastic *lectio* was often associated with rumination and meditation. The approach was "to pronounce the sacred words in order to retain them; both the audible reading and the exercise of memory and reflection which it precedes are involved" (Leclercq 1982, 16). Peter the Venerable famously described how he would sit on the edge of his bed at night "os sine requie sacra verba ruminans" [chewing the Scriptures by turning them over in his mouth] (1854, 887). The twelfth-century mystic Christina of Markyate, while concealed in a dark closet so narrow she could barely move, repeated during the course of the day five verses from the thirty-seventh psalm, and the author of her vita tellingly refers to this recitation as her "leccionem" (Talbot 1998, 92).

Silent reading was not entirely unknown in late antiquity or the early Middle Ages, but it was unusual. Augustine found it remarkable that his teacher Ambrose read silently when he wished to avoid being asked questions or to rest his voice (Saenger 1997, 8 and 299, n. 41; cf. Carruthers 1990, 171). The classical practice of writing texts without word division in what is known as *scriptura continua* or *scriptio continua* made it difficult to read a text aloud without studying it in advance and encouraged those who were reading to themselves to sub-vocalize.

Scriptura continua introduced an element of ambiguity into texts and it was probably for this reason that English and Irish monks in the late seventh century began to introduce spaces between words (Saenger 1997, 83). The practice developed more slowly on the Continent, although Continental practice was itself informed by the presence of insular monks. Saenger argues that the move can be divided into four clearly delineated stages: full *scriptura continua*; "aerated script," in which spaces were introduced between some words but not all; "hierarchical word blocks," in which blocks of text of varying length were separated by larger spaces, with smaller spaces inserted indiscriminately between words or syllables; and finally full word separation (ibid., 35–37). But this precise grid is forced. In the case of Cluny, for example, Saenger locates the adoption of word division in about 1035 under the abbacy of Odilon (ibid., 215–17), although word division can also be found in much earlier Cluniac MSS (Atsma and Vezin 1997). One important example of early word division is St. Gall, Stiftsbibliothek, MS 914, a copy of Benedict's *Rule* dated to the first third of the ninth century, which is discussed elsewhere in this volume by Carin Ruff and is available in electronic facsimile (http://www.e-codices.unifr.ch/en/list/csg/Shelfmark/20/0).

It is silent reading, more than anything else, which has often been taken to mark a wholesale cultural transformation from monastic to clerical habits of reading. It is important, therefore, to note the temporal discontinuities. The methods developed by Irish monks in the seventh century took several centuries to prevail on the continent. When they were adopted, it was in part because of social changes, especially the dramatic increase in the use of writing in legal and administrative matters. A leading instance of this change is the reform and expansion of the papal chancery in the twelfth century, which permitted it to produce and house a much greater number of documents, giving it "an unparalleled advantage" over other institutions in legal disputes (Ullmann 1962, 262, 327–29; Stock 1983, 35–36). Michael Clanchy has traced a similar process in the royal chancery in England, where, to provide just one telling instance, the number of pounds of sealing wax used each week multiplied almost ninefold between 1226 and 1271 (1993, 59).

Scholastic Reading

As the number of books in circulation increased and people felt a pressing need for rapid access to information, reading habits shifted. So, Jacqueline Hamesse notes mournfully, "An uninterrupted reading of an entire work, one that took time and permitted assimilation of the whole (or at least the whole gist), was gradually replaced by a more fragmented, piecemeal reading style that had the advantage of providing a quick grasp of selections but no longer encouraged any deep contact with the text or any genuine assimilation of the doctrine it contained" (1999, 107). While this assessment scarcely does justice to the reading practices of the philosophers and theologians of the late Middle Ages, there is no doubt that the period saw major changes in book design and the production of a range of new finding aids, such as indices and catalogues, which permitted rapid consultation and cross-referencing. The new angular and compressed gothic script and the more extensive use of abbreviation allowed longer texts to be crammed into books, while the so-called *pecia* system, in which stationers rented out exemplars so that students could copy texts for themselves, made books more available (Destrez 1935; Bataillon, Guyot, and Rouse 1983). These new approaches were primarily associated with academic instruction, first in the schools and later in the universities. The development of scholastic theology and philosophy was thus paralleled by the development of what one might call scholastic reading, the primarily visual decoding of texts and their use as reference tools.

At the beginning of the twelfth century, the leading cathedral school, that at Chartres, was led by Bernard, chancellor until his death in 1124, who was praised by John of Salisbury in his *Metalogicon* as "exundantissimus modernis temporibus fons litterarum in Gallia" [the greatest font of literary learning in Gaul in recent times] (1991, 52; 1971, 67). John of Salisbury describes how this great teacher would work though passages line by line, commenting on the grammatical and rhetorical structures, not trying to teach everything at once but working "pro capacitate audientium" [according to the capacity of his hearers] (ibid.). Much of Bernard's commentary was directed to the great intellectual challenge of reconciling Plato's *Timaeus* with Christian doctrine, and his lectures and those of his pupil, William of Conches, formed the basis of their written glosses on the *Timaeus*. The Chartrian tradition continues in a number of manuscripts from later in the century, including one, the first part of Oxford, Bodleian Library, MS Digby 23, Calcidius's translation of the *Timaeus*, which has unusually perceptive and independent glosses (Dutton 1983). These glosses would have assisted a master in his teaching and reflect his own scholarly reading. At some point this text of the *Timaeus* was bound together with a copy of *The Song of Roland*. This conjunction would seem to offer a momentary glimpse of the intersection between clerical reading and leisure reading in the vernacular (Taylor 2002, 59–63). The trouble is that it is not clear when the conjunction occurred. Charles Samaran argued the two parts of Digby 23 were linked chiefly because he thought he could read the word "Calcidius" in a medieval hand on the flyleaf of the *Roland* (1933, 26–27), but Ian Short, examining the manuscript in preparation for his edition of 2005, could not make the word out (18). That the connection between the two texts should turn on a single word, whose very existence is questioned, exemplifies how precarious the history of reading can be.

Much more can be known about scholarly reading than leisure reading because strong efforts were made to direct it. One of the most forceful examples comes from the house of Augustinian canons of St. Victor, which was founded by Peter Abelard's teacher, William of Champeaux, just outside the medieval city walls of Paris. Here in the 1120s, Hugh, the brother responsible for the general program of studies, composed his *Didascalicon*, setting out a systematic program for pursuing various forms of knowledge, especially the proper reading of the Bible. For Hugh, the purpose of the arts is to undo the damage of the Fall "ut divina similitudo in nobis reparetur" [so as to restore within us the divine likeness] (1939, 23; 1961, 61)]. Reading, above all the reading of Scripture, must be conducted according to method and order or the reader will go astray: "[Q]ui ergo in tanta multitudine librorum legendi modum et ordinem non custodit, quasi in condensitate saltus oberrans, tramitem recti itineris perdit" [Whoever does not keep to an order and a method in the reading of so great a collection of books wanders as it were into the very thick of the forest and loses the path of the direct route] (1939, 103; 1961, 127).

For Hugh of St. Victor, a crucial part of disciplined study is memorization. He warns the student "ne nimium laeteris si multa legeris, sed si multa intellexeris, nec tantum intellexeris sed retinere potueris. Alioquin nec legere multum prodest, nec intelligere" [not to rejoice a great deal because you may have read many things, but because you have been able to understand them, and not because you have been able to understand them but because you have been able to retain them. Otherwise there is no profit in having read or understood much] (1939, 61; 1961, 94). Elsewhere, Hugh describes in detail his techniques for memorization, explaining how he committed the Psalms to heart (Caruthers 1990, 82; Harkins 2009, 14–18). In his attitude to memory and reading, Hugh is a transitional figure. He is the first writer since antiquity to offer a full account of architectural mnemonics, the construction of a mental grid in which mnemonic icons can be "placed" in order (Zinn 1974, 225; Carruthers 1998, 243–46), and in that sense paves the way for the accounts of Thomas Aquinas and Albertus Magnus a century later. At the same time, he "seems to be the last major figure to propose memory as the sole or principal means of retrieving information" (Rouse and Rouse 1982, 203), and in that sense preserves an older approach to books that assumed one would learn them thoroughly rather than consult them piecemeal.

For Hugh, reading is a form of personal development, like constructing a building. First one lays down the foundations by understanding the historical sense of Scripture and the basic principles of the faith on such matters as the Trinity (1939, 118–19; 1961, 141). This architectural model is one he develops in the late work, the *De arca Noe mystica*, or *Libellus de formatione arche*, to use the title favored by its most recent editor, Patrice Sicard, describing how by carefully studying and memorizing appropriate texts in an appropriate order one can build the house of God inside oneself (2001, 117).

A few decades before Hugh was teaching at St. Victor, two masters of the cathedral school of Laon in northern France, Anselm and his brother Ralph, began to compile glosses on the Bible from various Church fathers and theologians. Their work, significantly modified by Gilbert the Universal, deacon of Auxerre and Gilbert de la Porrée, also known as Gilbert of Poitiers (ca. 1080–1154), would form the core of what came to be known as the *Glossa ordinaria*, the "standard gloss" on the Bible. The very term *Glossa ordinaria* is a troublesome one. On the one hand, given the popularity and authority of this particular set of glosses, it is possible to claim, as Lesley Smith does, that "The Gloss, in some sense, had become the Bible" (2009, 1), a phrase which captures how influential glossing had become as a form of reading. On the other hand, the term *ordinaria* and even the use of a single term to designate what was actually a complex textual tradition, and one that is still only partially charted, can be very misleading. There were other glosses in circulation (Smalley 1961) and this "standard" text actually existed in numerous recensions, which differ from one book of the Bible to another (Smalley 1983, 65; Smith 2009, 73–76). The form in which the *Glossa ordinaria* is most easily available today, the first printed edition of 1480–81, now available in facsimile (Froehlich and Gibson, 1992), reflects further changes, above all the addition of the more literal commentary written by Nicholas of Lyra in the 1320s.

Although a complete set of glosses for the entire Bible was not available until about 1175—another way in which the term "Glossa ordinaria" can be misleading—(Smith 2009, 148), commercial copying of the Gloss began much earlier. Already by the second half of the twelfth century copies were much desired, and the demand fostered major developments in the book trade (Rouse and Rouse 2000). As Christopher de Hamel notes, the scriptorium at Laon was in no position to produce large numbers of copies (1984, 2–3). By about 1140, Paris had become the chief center for the production of glossed books of the Bible, the majority copied by professional scriveners (De Hamel 1984, 80, 87; Stirnemann 1994, 264).

The history of glossed Bibles is also a history of developments in layout. The early approach can be seen in Laon, Bibliothèque municipale, MS 74, a copy of the Gospel of St. Mathew that was once believed to be an autograph of Anselm but was probably copied several years after his death (Stirnemann 1994, 260). In Laon 74 the Biblical text is first copied in a central column with generous margins and the glosses added subsequently; in some cases, when they proved too long, in the form of L-shaped blocks that extend above or below the central column. During the 1130s, as the glossed books of the Bible began to be copied in large numbers, the design became more complex (De Hamel 1984, 18–20; Smith 2009, ch. 3).

According to the dramatic story told by Ivan Illich, it was in the abbey of St. Victor and under the personal supervision of the most influential of all Biblical commentators, Peter Lombard, that the new form of book design was developed, completing the transformation of the book from "a record of the author's speech" to a "repertory of the author's thought" (1993, 95). Here, in particular, it is tempting to think in terms of a complete shift from monastic to clerical reading, with the Augustinian canons regular of St. Victor playing the role of cultural middlemen (ibid., 79–81). Saenger, however, sees a very similar and equally fundamental transformation of book design occurring in the Insular compilations of Latin riddles from the late seventh century (1997, 98). There are further complications. Hugh himself may have resisted the copying of glossed texts, preferring students to concentrate on the originals, and his death in 1141 might actually have opened the way for large-scale copying, which seems to have begun about that time (Smith 2009, 132). The Cistercians, on the other hand, despite their reputation for being old-fashioned and hostile to scholastic learning, were enthusiastic patrons of the new glossed books of the Bible (Bouchard 2000).

As for the Lombard's alleged role, it seems that the new layout was probably developed after his death, when Parisian scribes began to set out the Biblical text in short blocks of a few lines written in a larger script, with generous spaces between the blocks, and then copied the glosses down in a smaller script in the spaces left within the same columns (cf. Brady 1962, 6; Smith 2009, 134). This is the format used for the earliest dated and surviving copies of the Lombard's Epistles, Cracow, Jagiellonian Library MS 318, and Psalms, Bremen, Focke-Museum, s.n. (De Hamel 1984, 21–22 and plate 9). De Hamel suggests that the Lombard was initially hesitant to publish what he regarded as notes or raw material (1984, 8). But once his glosses were finally released for copying, the changes happened quickly. As M. B. Parkes notes, in a manuscript such as Bodleian Library MS Auct. D. 2. 8, a copy of the Lombard's commentary on the Psalms that dates from the late twelfth century, "the whole process of indicating text, commentary, and sources was incorporated into the design of the page, presumably by a process of careful alignment worked out beforehand in the exemplar" (Parkes 1976, 116). Another copy of the Lombard's gloss on the Psalms, which was prepared by his pupil Herbert of Bosham and includes his own additions, survives in a manuscript no later than 1177, Bodleian MS Auct. E inf. 6, and its elaborate layout incorporates running headers, chapter numbers, and "a hierarchy of script and initial sizes" (Smith 2001, 46). Here one can see how far book design had progressed in the space of three generations since Anselm of Laon was copying his glosses. While few works equaled the complexity of the *Glossa ordinaria*, which even medieval scholars found challenging (Smith 2009, 138–39), the general approach of using a multi-columned layout with the commentary integrated into the design and an elaborate system of colored symbols for cross-referencing was extended to a wide range of scholarly books over the succeeding centuries. Among them were the numerous compilations of short excerpts from other texts, which offered one solution to the proliferation of scholarly material. As a result of these dramatic changes in design,

> [t]he late medieval book differs more from its early medieval predecessors than it does from the printed books of our own day. The scholarly apparatus which we take for granted—analytical table of contents, text disposed into books, chapters, and paragraphs, and accompanied by footnotes and index—originated in the applications of the notions of *ordinatio* and *compilatio* by writers, scribes, and rubricators of the thirteenth, fourteenth, and fifteenth centuries. (Parkes 1976, 135)

Professional Readers

During these three centuries there are numerous examples of dedicated professional readers, scholars who made it part of their job to annotate, cross-reference, and catalogue books. Some of these men were famous scholars. Robert Grosseteste, bishop of Lincoln, who supervised the education of the Franciscans at Oxford in the early thirteenth century, devised an elaborate code for cross-referencing books using small symbols in the margins (Hunt 1953). A copy of the Bible in the municipal library at Lyon contains his Biblical concordance, the "tabula Magistri Roberti lincolniensis episcopi cum addicione Magistri Ade de Marisco" [Table of Master Robert, bishop of Lincoln, with the addition of brother Adam of Marsh] (Thomson 1934, 140). Others are known only through their work on a single volume. In 1299 the Franciscan William of Tatewic (Todwick, Yorkshire) left to his friend Thomas and after him to the Friars in general a copy of Gregory's *Moralia in Job*, now Peterhouse, Cambridge, MS 89. The inscription on the flyleaf testifies to William's commitment to the book:

> Iste liber pertinet ad communitatem fratrum minorum de Lincolnia post decessum fr. Thome de quappelod per assignacionem fr. Willelmi de tatewic de licencia fr. Hugonis de hertelpoll provincialis ministri a.d. M.CC.XCIX quem dictus frater W. scribi fecit et de amicorum suorum elemosinis pro scriptura satisfieri procurauit et nichilominus manu sua a principio usque finem diligenter correxit et notablia specialia in marginibus titulauit et per decursum alphabeti in separatis per modum tabule designauit. et ideo quicunque huius libri usum habuerit tanquam gratus laboribus fructuosis orare dignetur pro anima predicti fratris Willellmi, et orent pro eo omnes sancti. Amen.

> [This book belongs to the Friars Minor of Lincoln, after the death of Brother Thomas of Whaplode (Lincolnshire), by the grant of Brother William of Todwick, and by the license of Brother Hugh of Hertelpoll (Hartlepool, Durham), the Provincial Minister in 1299 A.D. The said Brother William had the book made and by the charity of his friends got enough for it to be properly copied. Nevertheless, he corrected it diligently from start to finish and provided headings in the margins for matters of especial interest and then cross-referenced them individually with a table laid out alphabetically. And therefore anyone who may be using this book, in gratitude for so much fruitful labor, ought to pray for the soul of the aforementioned Brother William, and may all the saints pray for him. Amen].

Brother William was justifiably proud of his diligent labor; he had indeed corrected the volume extensively and so recorded his activity.

One of the most impressive of all these professional readers was Henry of Kirkestede, a monk at Bury St. Edmunds, who was at various times responsible for the novices and for the care of the books, and probably combined the two duties as precentor, before becoming subprior in 1361 (Rouse 1982, 481). He supervised the purchase of several volumes, including copies of Hugh of St. Victor's *Didascalicon* and *De arca Noe* and Richard of Bury's *Philobiblon*. He also devised a system of shelf marks for the books, annotated them, and noted *incipits* and *explicits* and missing sections, comparing various copies whenever possible. Furthermore, he produced what was in effect a union catalogue of religious books for all England, now Cambridge University Library MS Additional 3470, which listed alphabetically the names of all the books he knew of, including their various parts, their *incipits* and *explicits*, and their location, covering 674 authors in 195 libraries. He worked on this massive project, with a hand that latterly had a strong tremor, until his final years, dying some time after 1378.

Others had more modest ambitions but still wanted to pass on a book they had read and corrected. John de Glynton, a Gilbertine canon at Sempringham in Lincolnshire in the early fourteenth century, is one example. On his death, he bequeathed to his brothers a handsome collection of the works of Augustine, including the *Confessiones*, valued at 20 shillings, now London, British Library MS Royal 5 C.v. Several hands annotated the manuscript, one of them noting the donation. Another hand, quite possibly that of Glynton himself, provides a table of contents and numerous glosses to the *Confessiones* and other texts. In Book II, chapter 6, for example, when Augustine describes how the sins can pose as virtues, this glossator has carefully listed all the sins that do so in the margins (fol. 143v).

Such efforts were regarded as a pious legacy to a community and avoided personal revelations. A rare example of a glossator who left a more vivid record of his personality is John de Grandisson, bishop of Exeter from 1327 to 1369. As a student in Paris he acquired a copy of Augustine's *Confessiones*, now Lambeth Palace MS 203, which he annotated throughout his life. An opening inscription, which announces his gift of the book to his cathedral, casts his annotation as a conscientious clerical labor: "Damus ecclesiae nostre Exon: quia multum laborauimus in corrigenda parisius. Manu J. Ex." [We give to our church of Exeter [this book] since we have labored greatly over the corrections in Paris. In the hand of John of Exeter] (fol. 7r and Olson 1997, 241). But as Linda Olson has shown, the extensive annotations often reveal a more personal engagement with the text, and since his earlier annotations can be distinguished from his later ones, they provide "evidence of changes and developments in his sense of self over the years" (Olson 1997, 206, drawing on Steele 1994). Already as a student, Grandisson had an interest in the duties and dignity of the bishop: "Nota quod honor et dignitas episcopalis incomparabiliter excellit regiam dignitatem et quamcumque aliam" [note that episcopal honor and dignity incomparably surpass royal dignity and any other] (fol. 107r and Olson 1997, 233). As a student he was particularly interested in the discussions of the will and of education, worrying about the dangers of children reading pagan authors: "mirum valde est quod ecclesia patitur pueros audire in gramatica poetarum fabulas; quasi enim sacrificium demoniorum" [It is a great wonder that the church allows boys to hear the fables of poets when learning grammar, for it is like sacrificing them to demons] (fol. 11v and Olson 1997, 242). Later, he revealed his own love of church music, stressing those passages from Augustine that could be used to support its value, and struggled with pride, especially the desire for worldly praise (ibid., 221, 224, 229–30).

Women and Lay Readers

These kinds of clerical reading were largely confined to men and were based on youthful instruction in Latin, which Walter Ong has described as a male "puberty rite" (1959), and on the professional formation offered in the schools. Women were discouraged from annotating books, even if they were in religious orders. A telling colophon in an early fifteenth-century Middle English translation of the Benedictine Rule, probably from Lyminster, Sussex, specifically warns the nuns against leaving books lying around, cutting out pages, or writing in them, either to add or to excise text (Krochalis 1986; Tarvers 1992, 310). The *Ordinale* of the Benedictine nuns at Barking abbey similarly forbids them to mark their books (Bell 1995, 42; Tolhurst 1927–28, 68; Gambier 1927, 190). Of course young monks and scholars were also discouraged from casually marking books they had borrowed from a monastery or college library, but they often had copies of their own, and writing was an integral part of their professional formation.

In comparison, women's writing was less common and more eclectic, a series of individual triumphs over social norms. A striking case of this intellectual independence is that of the twelfth-century Benedictine Hildegard, abbess of Bingen, in the Rhineland. In addition to numerous letters and scientific, medical, and polemical works and her musical cycle, the *Symphonia*, Hildegard composed three major works of visionary theology, *Scivias*, the *Liber vitae meritorum* [*Book of Life's Merits*], and *De operatione Dei* [*On the Activity of God*]. Yet Hildegard herself never fully mastered Latin grammar and required a secretary "to correct her cases and tenses" (Newman 1987, 23). The "distinctions of the schoolmen" find no place in her work, which is as strongly individual in its prosody as in its themes (Newman 1987, 15, 24–25; Dronke 1970, 178–79). Her artistic work appears equally independent. The illuminated copy of *Scivias* produced at Bingen around 1165 contained a whole program of illuminations depicting her visions, in a manner "stylistically remote from the work of contemporary manuscript painters" (Newman 1987, 18). While the manuscript itself was lost during the bombing of Dresden in 1945, the facsimile produced in the 1920s survives, and is reproduced in the CCCM edition. What remains controversial is whether the illustrations reflect Hildegard's original sketches relatively directly or were modified after her death (Gerchow and Marti 2008, 139; Caviness 1997, 88–92; Saurma-Jeltsch 1998).

One of the recurring themes in the history of reading is that of the gradual adoption of monastic or clerical habits of reading by ever broadening circles of lay people. One instance is the way in which the techniques developed for annotating, rubricating, and indexing academic books were adopted for the lay market and for texts, both religious and secular, written in the vernacular, allowing the professional writers of the fourteenth and fifteen centuries "to filter the text for presentation to the patron or reading community" (Kerby-Fulton 2001, 8). Another instance of this process of cultural transmission is the way monastic meditative reading and the sustained visualization used in mnemonic exercises of the kind described by Hugh of St. Victor were fused and transformed into an intensely emotional form of devotion, often focused on Christ's passion. The most systematic manual for this practice is the *Meditaciones vite Christi*, a vivid account of Christ's life and Passion compiled from a variety of Biblical and apocryphal sources. In the Middle Ages, the text was attributed to Bonaventure. Modern scholarship has generally concluded that it is the work of the fourteenth-century Franciscan Johannes de Caulibus, from

San Gemignano in Tuscany, and that he compiled it for the devotional exercises of a Poor Clare nun. More recently, Sarah McNamer has argued that Johannes was actually reworking an Italian text that a woman, again possibly a Poor Clare nun, had composed herself, and that Johannes toned down the original work's insistence on Christ's vulnerability (McNamer 2009). The *Meditaciones* became one of the most popular works of the late Middle Ages, surviving in approximately 120 Latin manuscripts and a further 180 or so in English, French, Dutch, German, Italian, Spanish, and other vernaculars (Maxwell 2007, 19). In his prologue Johannes offers St. Cecilia's meditation as a model for devotional mediation, explaining that she chose certain aspects of Christ's life, "[i]n quibus meditabatur die ac nocte, corde puro et integro, attencione precipua et feruenti; et completa circulacione reincipiens iterum, dulci ac suavi gustu ruminans ea, in arcano pectoris sui prudenti consilio collocabat" [She mediated on these things day and night, with a pure and whole heart, with particular and zealous attentiveness; and when she had completed the cycle, beginning again, chewing them over with a sweet and pleasant appetite, she arranged them by wise counsel in the secret place of her heart] (Johannes de Caulibus 1997, 7). But the *Meditaciones* goes much further, urging its readers to engage in sustained exercises in visualization, imagining crucial scenes, such as Christ's Crucifixion, as if they were actually taking place and they were participating in them, deliberately visualizing the location and other participants and drawing on places and people they knew. This kind of intense meditative practice was to become a crucial component of late medieval lay piety (Marrow 1979, 20, 26).

While the professional annotations of clerics only allow occasional glimpses into their personality, lay readers most often leave no traces at all. One remarkable exception was Jean, count of Angoulême and son of the Duke of Orléans, who spent thirty-three years, from 1412 to 1445, as a prisoner of the English. During this period, "He forbade himself dice or cards. And he diverted himself, without really filling his long leisure hours imposed upon him, with music, study, and devotional exercises" (Dupont-Ferrier 1896, 52). At his death, Jean's personal library consisted of 167 volumes, not to mention a score of volumes, all in French, on loan to his daughter, and another dozen that had been mislaid (Ouy 2007, 55–100). Jean and his elder brother Charles drew upon the services of a number of copyists, including one John Duxworth, who copied *The Canterbury Tales* for him, among other works, and "who seems to have been an acquaintance or friend" of Jean and his brother Charles, rather than a professional scribe (Ouy 2000, 50). Jean collaborated with several others in copying works of Jean Gerson, which were not readily available in England (Roccati and Ouy 2000, 53–59). Jean also personally copied at least nine works in Latin, including Hugh's *Didascalicon*, the *Meditationes vite Christi*, and, of course, Boethius's *Consolatio Philosophiae*. He made one copy of the latter himself, Bibliothèque Nationale de France, lat 6733, and glossed another, Bibliothèque Nationale de France, lat 6405, as well as consulting two separate French translations. But all this labor has won him little credit. For Paul Strohm, Jean's praise of the Knight's Tale as "valde bona" and dismissal of the more experimental Squire's Tale and Canon Yeoman's Tale as "valde absurda" mark him as one of the conservative readers that characterize the "narrowed spectrum of taste" of the fifteenth century (1982, 28 and 1971). Yet Jean's pious reading and copying seems to have been a source of pride for him as well as of consolation. At any rate, the inventory taken after Jean's death carefully lists all the works copied "de la main de feu mon dit seigneur" [in the hand of my said late lord] (Ouy 2007, 55–69). Jean was not a subversive reader, but he was a powerful one. He engaged in a sustained reading of an entire work, a reading that stretched over many years and permitted assimilation, even internalization, of the whole text. Jean offers a very rare instance of a layman who has left a clear trail of his reading, and he did so because in many ways he read like a cleric.

Some medieval readers do leave signs that they have broken free from the yoke of the thought of others and have become nomads. One such is the owner of British Library MS Arundel 123, a modest compilation of Latin texts assembled in the early fourteenth century and copied by a single hand. The texts, often heavily revised, include a chapter on geographical regions from Bartholomeus Anglicus's *De proprietatibus rerum*, and a number of texts on Alexander the Great, with interpolations adding further details about the marvels he saw in India. The compiler, as Mary Hamel suggests, was probably a male cleric, "with an interest in foreign travel, exotic places, and adventure," who "omitted or sharply revised" whatever did not appeal to his curiosity (1997, 3). His editorial work suggests that his love of books was not so much a love of wisdom as a love of a very particular kind of knowledge. The man, if indeed he was a man, who compiled this collection, is otherwise completely unknown to us, but from his book we can extrapolate some sense of his interests and perhaps even of his character.

SUGGESTIONS FOR FURTHER READING

Jean Leclercq (1982) provides what is still one of the best introductions to monastic *lectio*. Paul Saenger (1997) has traced the development of word separation, which permitted silent reading, in Latin manuscripts from the seventh to the thirteenth centuries. Malcolm B. Parkes's essay on *ordinatio* and *compilatio* is an influential early study of these crucial concepts, and he has also written a valuable guide to medieval punctuation (1976, 1993). The development of book design in glossed Bibles and other theological works is traced by Christopher de Hamel (1984) and Lesley Smith (2001, 2009). Ivan Illich (1993) provides a stimulating account of the developments in reading at St. Victor, although several of his claims about developments in book design need to be modified in the light of the work of de Hamel, Smith, and others. Mary Carruthers has offered two major studies on medieval mnemonics used by Hugh and others (1990, 1998). Richard and Mary Rouse have provided numerous studies of the many finding tools that were developed in the later Middle Ages (1966, 1982). Raymond Clemens and Timothy Graham (2007, 39–43) provide a good general introduction to medieval glossing.

BIBLIOGRAPHY

Primary sources

Adam of Murimuth. 1889. *Adae Murimuth Continuatio Chronicarum Robertus de Avesbury, De Gestis mirabilibus Regis Edwardi Tertii*, edited by Edward Maunde Thompson. Rolls Series 93. London: Printed for Her Majesty's Stationery Office, by Eyre and Spottiswoode.

Bernard of Chartres. 1991. *The Glossae super Platonem of Bernard of Chartres*, edited by Paul Dutton. Studies and Texts 107. Toronto: Pontifical Institute of Mediaeval Studies.

Froehlich, Karlfried and Margaret T. Gibson, eds. 1992. *Biblia Latina cum Glossa Ordinaria*. 4 vols. Turnhout: Brepols.

Gilbertus Universalis. 2005. *Glossa Ordinaria in Lamentationes Ieremie prophete. Prothemata et Liber I*, edited by Alexander Andrée. Studia Latina Stockholmiensia 52. Stockholm: Almquist & Wiksell.

Henry of Kirkestede. 2004. *Catalogus de libris autenticis et apocrifis*, edited by Richard H. Rouse and Mary A. Rouse. Corpus of British medieval library catalogues 11. London: British Library in association with the British Academy.

Hildegard of Bingen. 1978. *Scivias*, edited by Adelgundis Führkötter. Corpus Christianorum. Continuatio Mediaevalis 43–43A. Turnhout: Brepols.

Hugh of St. Victor. 1939. *Hugonis de Sacto Victore, Didascalicon: De Studio Legendi*, edited by Charles Henry Buttimer. The Catholic University of America. Studies in Medieval and Renaissance Latin 10. Washington, DC: Catholic University Press.

———. 1961. *The Didascalicon of Hugh of St. Victor. A Medieval Guide to the Arts*, translated by Jerome Taylor. Records of Western Civilization. New York: Columbia University Press.

———. 2001. *De archa Noe Libellus de formatione arche*, edited by Patrice Sicard. Corpus Christianorum. Continuatio Mediaevalis 176–176A. Turnhout: Brepols.

Johannes de Caulibus. 1997. *Meditaciones vite Christi olim S. Bonaventuro attributae*, edited by Mary Stallings-Taney. Corpus Christianorum. Continuatio Mediaevalis 153. Turnhout: Brepols.

John of Salisbury. 1991. *Ioanne Sarisberiensis, Metalogicon*. Edited by John B. Hall and Katharine S. B. Keats-Rohan. Corpus Christianorum. Continuatio Mediaevalis 98. Turnhout: Brepols.

———. 1971. *The Metalogicon of John of Salisbury: A Twelfth-Century Defense of the Verbal and Logical Arts of the Trivium*, translated by Daniel D. McGarry. Gloucester, MA: Peter Smith.

Peter the Venerable. 1854. *Petri Cluniacensis Abbatis, De miraculis libri duo*. Patrologia Latina 189. Paris.

Richard of Bury, 1960. Philobiblon, edited and translated by E. C. Thomas. Oxford: Blackwell.

Short, Ian, ed. 2005. *Oxford version*, vol. 1 of *La Chanson de Roland: The French Corpus*, edited by Joseph J. Duggan. Turnhout: Brepols.

Tolhurst, John B. L., ed. 1927–28. *The Ordinale and Customary of the Benedictine Nuns of Barking Abbey*. Henry Bradshaw Society 65–66. London: Henry Bradshaw Society.

William of Conches. 1965. *Guillaume de Conches, Glosae super Platonem*, edited by Edouard Jeauneau. Textes philosophiques du Moyen Age 13. Paris: J. Vrin.

Secondary sources

Atsma, Hartmut and Jean Vezin. 1997. *Les plus anciens documents originaux de l'abbaye de Cluny.* Vol. 1. Monumenta Palaeographica Medii Aevi: Series Gallica 1. Turnhout: Brepols.

Barthes, Roland. 1977. "The Death of the Author." In *Image—Music—Text,* translated by Stephen Heath, 142–48. New York: Hill and Wang.

Baswell, Christopher. 1992. "Talking Back to the Text: Marginal Voices in Medieval Secular Literature." In *The Uses of Manuscripts in Literary Studies: Essays in Memory of Judson Boyce Allen,* edited by Charlotte C. Morse, Penelope R. Doob and Marjorie C. Woods, 121–60. Studies in Medieval Culture 31. Kalamazoo, MI: Medieval Institute Publications.

Bataillon, Louis J., Bertrand G. Guyot, and Richard H. Rouse, eds. 1988. *La Production du livre universitaire au moyen âge: Exemplar et pecia. Actes du symposium tenu au Collegio San Bonaventura de Grottaferrata en mai 1983.* Paris: Centre Nationale de la Recherche Scientifique.

Bell, David. N. 1995. *What Nuns Read: Books and Libraries in Medieval English Nunneries.* Cistercian Studies Series 158. Kalamazoo, MI: Cistercian Publications.

Bouchard, Constance B. 2000. "The Cistercians and the *Glossa Ordinaria*." *Catholic Historical Review* 86: 183–92.

Brady, Ignatius F. 1962. "The Rubrics of Peter Lombard's Sentences." *Pier Lombardo* 6: 5–25.

Camille, Michael. 1997. "The Book as Flesh and Fetish in Richard de Bury's *Philobiblon*." In *The Book and the Body,* edited by Dolores Warwick Frese and Katherine O'Brien O'Keeffe, 34–77. Ward-Phillips lectures in English language and literature 14. Notre Dame, IN: Notre Dame University Press.

Carruthers, Mary J. 1990. *The Book of Memory: A Study of Memory in Medieval Culture.* Cambridge Studies in Medieval Literature 10. Cambridge: Cambridge University Press.

———. 1998. *The Craft of Thought: Meditation, Rhetoric, and the Making of Images, 400–1200.* Cambridge Studies in Medieval Literature 34. Cambridge: Cambridge University Press.

Cavallo, Guglielmo and Roger Chartier, eds. 1999. *A History of Reading in the West,* translated by Lydia G. Cochrane. Amherst, MA: University of Massachusetts Press.

Caviness, Madeline H. 1977. "Gender Symbolism and Text Image Relationships: Hildegard of Bingen's *Scivias*." In *Translation Theory and Practice in the Middle Ages,* edited by Jeanette Beer, 71–111. Studies in Medieval Culture 38. Kalamazoo, MI: Medieval Institute Publications.

Chartier, Roger. 1991. *The Cultural Origins of the French Revolution,* translated by Lydia G. Cochrane. Bicentennial Reflections on the French Revolution. Durham, NC: Duke University Press, 1991.

Cheney, Christopher R. 1973. "Richard de Bury, Borrower of Books." *Speculum* 48: 325–28.

Clanchy, Michael T. 1993. *From Memory to Written Record: England, 1066–1307.* 2nd ed. Oxford: Blackwell.

Clemens, Raymond and Timothy Graham. 2007. *Introduction to Manuscript Studies.* Ithaca, NY: Cornell University Press.

Courtenay, William J. 2004. "Bury [Aungerville], Richard." In *Oxford Dictionary of National Biography.* http://dx.doi.org/10.1093/ref:odnb/4153.

Crow, Martin Michael. 1942. "John of Angoulême and His Chaucer Manuscript." *Speculum* 17: 86–99.

Dagenais, John. 1994. *The Ethics of Reading in Manuscript Culture: Glossing the Libro de buen amor.* Princeton, NJ: Princeton University Press.

Darnton, Robert. 2009. *The Case for Books: Past, Present, and Future.* New York: PublicAffairs.

De Certeau, Michel. 1984. *The Practice of Everyday Life,* translated by Steven Rendall. Berkeley, CA: University of California Press.

De Hamel, Christopher. 1984. *Glossed Books of the Bible and the Origins of the Paris Booktrade.* Woodbridge, Suffolk, Dover, NH: D. S. Brewer.

Denholm-Young, Noël. 1937. "Richard de Bury (1287–1345)." *Transactions of the Royal Historical Society,* 4th ser., 20: 135–68. Reprinted with an appendix in *Collected Papers on Mediaeval Subjects.* Oxford: Basil Blackwell, 1946, 1–25.

——, ed. 1950. *The Liber Epistolaris of Richard of Bury.* The Roxburghe Club 221. Oxford: Roxburghe Club.

Destrez, Jean. 1935. *La Pecia dans les manuscrits universitaires du XIIIe et du XIVe siècle.* Paris: J. Vautrain.

Dinshaw, Carolyn. 1989. *Chaucer's Sexual Poetics.* Madison, WI: University of Wisconsin Press.

Dronke, Peter. 1970. *Poetic Individuality in the Middle Ages: New Departures in Poetry, 1000–1150.* Oxford: Clarendon.

Dupont-Ferrier, Gustave. 1896. "La captivité de Jean d'Orléans, comte d'Angoulême." *Revue historique* 62: 42–74.

——. 1897. "Jean d'Orléans, comte d'Angoulême, d'âpres sa bibliothèque." In *Mélanges d'histoire du Moyen Âge publiés sous la direction de M. le Prof. Luchaire,* edited by Achille Luchaire, 53–54. Université de Paris. Bibliothèque de la Faculté des Lettres 3. Paris: Alcan. Reprint, Geneva: Slatkine, 1975.

Dutton, Paul Edward. 1983. "*Illustre ciuitatis et populi exemplum*: Plato's *Timaeus* and the Transmission from Calcidius to the End of the Twelfth Century of a Tripartite Scheme of Society." *Mediaeval Studies* 45: 79–119.

Gambier, P. 1927. "Lending Books in a Medieval Nunnery." *Bodleian Quarterly Record* 5: 188–90.

Gellrich, Jesse M. 1985. *The Idea of the Book in the Middle Ages: Language Theory, Mythology, and Fiction.* Ithaca, NY: Cornell University Press.

Gerchow, Jan and Susan Marti, 2008. "'Nun's Work,' 'Caretaker Institutions,' and 'Women's Movements': Some Thoughts about a Modern Historiography of Medieval Monasticism." In *Crown and Veil: Female Monasticism from the Fifth to the Fifteenth Centuries,* edited by Jeffrey F. Hamburger and Susan Marti, translated by Dietlinde Hamburger, 132–50. New York: Columbia University Press.

Hamburger, Jeffrey F. and Susan Marti, eds. 2008. *Crown and Veil: Female Monasticism from the Fifth to the Fifteenth Centuries,* translated by Dietlinde Hamburger. New York: Columbia University Press.

Hamburger, Jeffrey and Robert Sukale. 2008. "Between This World and the Next: The Art of Religious Women in the Middle Ages." In *Crown and Veil: Female Monasticism from the Fifth to the Fifteenth Centuries,* edited by Jeffrey F. Hamburger and Susan Marti, translated by Dietlinde Hamburger, 76–108. New York: Columbia University Press.

Hamel, Mary. 1997. "An Anthology for the Armchair Traveler: London, British Library, MS Arundel 123." *Manuscripta* 41: 3–18.

Hamesse, Jacqueline. 2003. "The Scholastic Model of Reading." In *A History of Reading in the West,* edited by Guglielmo Cavallo and Roger Chartier, translated by Lydia G. Cochrane, 103–19. Amherst, MA: University of Massachusetts Press.

Harkins, Franklin T. 2009. *Reading and the Work of Restoration: History and Scripture in the Theology of Hugh of St Victor.* Studies and Texts 167. Toronto: Pontifical Institute of Mediaeval Studies.

Hunt, Richard W. 1953. "MSS. Containing the Indexing Symbols of Robert Grosseteste." *Bodleian Library Record* 4: 241–55.

Illich, Ivan. 1993. *In the Vineyard of the Text: A Commentary to Hugh's Didascalicon.* Chicago: University of Chicago Press.

Kerby-Fulton, Kathryn. 2001. "Introduction: The Medieval Professional Reader and Reception History, 1292–1641." In *The Medieval Professional Reader at Work: Evidence from the Manuscripts of Chaucer, Langland, Kempe, and Gower*, edited by Kathryn Kerby-Fulton and Maidie Hilmo, 7–13. ELS Monograph Series 85. Victoria, BC: University of Victoria.

Krochalis, Jeanne. 1986. "The Benedictine Rule for Nuns: Library of Congress, MS. 4." *Manuscripta* 30: 21–34.

Leclercq, Jean. 1982. *The Love of Learning and the Desire for God: A Study of Monastic Culture*, translated by Catharine Misrahi. 3rd ed. New York: Fordham University Press.

Marrow, James H. 1979. *Passion Iconography in Northern European Art of the Late Middle Ages and Early Renaissance: A Study of the Transformation of Sacred Metaphor into Descriptive Narrative*. Kortrijk: Van Ghemmert.

Maxwell, Felicity. 2007. "Mapping the Mediations: A Survey of Recent Research on the Pseudo-Bonaventuran *Meditationes vitae Christi* and Nicholas Love's *Mirror of the Blessed Life of Jesus Christ*." *Bulletin of International Medieval Research* 13: 18–30.

McNamer, Sarah. 1990. "Further Evidence for the Date of the Pseudo-Bonaventuran *Meditationes vitae Christi*." *Franciscan Studies* 50: 235–61.

Minnis, Alastair J. 1984. *Medieval Theory of Authorship: Scholastic Literary Attitudes in the Later Middle Ages*. London: Scholar Press.

Morse, Charlotte C., Penelope R. Doob, and Marjorie C. Woods, eds. 1992. *The Uses of Manuscripts in Literary Studies, Essays in Memory of Judson Boyce Allen*. Studies in Medieval Culture 31. Kalamazoo, MI: Medieval Institute Publications.

Newman, Barbara. 1987. *Sister of Wisdom: St. Hildegard's Theology of the Feminine*. Berkeley, CA: University of California Press.

Olson, Linda. 1997. "Reading Augustine's *Confessiones* in Fourteenth-Century England: John de Grandisson's Fashioning of Text and Self." *Traditio* 52: 201–57.

Ong, Walter J. 1959. "Latin Language Study as a Renaissance Puberty Rite." *Studies in Philology* 56: 103–24.

Ouy, Gilbert. 2000. "Charles d'Orléans and his Brother Jean d'Angoulême in England: What their Manuscripts Have to Tell." In *Charles d'Orléans in England (1415–1440)*, edited by Mary-Jo Arn, 47–60. Cambridge, Rochester, NY: D. S. Brewer.

———. 2007. *La librairie des frères captifs: les manuscrits de Charles d'Orléans et Jean d'Angoulême*. Texte, codex & contexte 4. Turnhout: Brepols.

Parkes, Malcolm B. 1976. "The Influence of the Concepts of *Ordinatio* and *Compilatio* on the Development of the Book." In *Medieval Learning and Literature: Essays Presented to Richard William Hunt*, edited by Jonathan J. G. Alexander and Margaret T. Gibson, 115–41 and plates IX–XVI. Oxford: Clarendon.

———. 1993. *Pause and Effect: An Introduction to the History of Punctuation in the West*. Berkeley, CA: University of California Press.

———. 1999. "Reading, Copying and Interpreting a Text in the Early Middle Ages." In *A History of Reading in the West*, edited by Guglielmo Cavallo and Roger Chartier, translated by Lydia G. Cochrane, 90–102. Amherst, MA: University of Massachusetts Press.

Roccati, Giovanni Matteo. 1980. "A propos de la tradition manuscrite de l'œuvre latine de Gerson: les manuscrits Paris, B.N. lat. 3624 et 3638." *Revue d'Histoire des Textes* 10: 277–304.

Rouse, Richard H. 1966. "Bostonus Buriensis and the Author of the *Catalogus scriptorum ecclesiae*." *Speculum* 41: 471–99.

Rouse, Richard H. and Mary A. Rouse. 1982. "*Statim Invenire*: Schools, Preachers, and New Attitudes to the Page." In *Renaissance and Renewal in the Twelfth Century*, edited by Robert L. Benson and Giles Constable, with Carol D. Lanham, 201–25. Cambridge, MA: Harvard University Press.

———. 2000. *Manuscripts and Their Makers, Commercial Book Producers in Medieval Paris, 1200–1500*. 2 vols. Illiterati et Uxorati. Turnhout: Harvey Miller.

Saenger, Paul. 1997. *Space between Words: The Origins of Silent Reading*. Figurae: Reading Medieval Cultures. Stanford: Stanford University Press.

———. 1999. "Reading in the Later Middle Ages." In *A History of Reading in the West*, edited by Guglielmo Cavallo and Roger Chartier, translated by Lydia G. Cochrane, 120–148. Amherst, MA: University of Massachusetts Press.

Samaran, Charles. 1933. Introduction to *La Chanson de Roland: Reproduction phototypique du manuscrit Digby 23 de la Bodleian Library d'Oxford*, edited by Charles Samaran. Paris: Société des anciens textes français.

Saurma-Jeltsch, Lieselotte E. 1998. *Die Miniaturen im "Liber scivias" der Hildegard von Bingen: Die Wucht der Vision und die Ordnung der Bilder*. Wiesbaden: Reichert.

Sicard, Patrice. 1993. *Diagrammes médiévaux et exégèse visuelle: le Libellus de formatione arche de Hugues de Saint-Victor*. Bibliotheca Victorina 4. Paris and Turnhout: Brepols.

Smalley, Beryl. 1961. "Les commentaries bibliques de l'époque romane: glose ordinaire et glose périmées." *Cahiers de Civilisation Médiévale* 4: 15–22.

———. 1983. *The Study of the Bible in the Middle Ages*. 3rd ed. Oxford: Oxford University Press.

Smith, Lesley. 2001. *Masters of the Sacred Page: Manuscripts of Theology in the Latin West to 1274*. Medieval Book 2. Notre Dame, IN: University of Notre Dame Press.

———. 2009. *The Glossa Ordinaria: The Making of a Medieval Bible Commentary*. Commentaria 3. Leiden, Boston: Brill.

Steele, Margaret. 1994. "Study of the Books Owned or Used by John Grandisson, Bishop of Exeter (1327–1369)." Ph.D. diss., University of Oxford.

Stirnemann, Patricia. 1994. "Où ont été fabriqués les livres de la glose ordinaire dans la première moitié du XIIe siècle." In *Le XIIe siècle: Mutations et renouveau en France dans la première moitié du XII siècle*, edited by Françoise Gasparri, 257–301. Cahiers du Léopard d'or 3. Paris: Léopard d'or.

Stock, Brian. 1983. *The Implications of Literacy: Written Language and Models of Interpretation in the Eleventh and Twelfth Centuries*. Princeton, NJ: Princeton University Press.

Strohm, Paul. 1971. "Jean of Angoulême: A Fifteenth-Century Reader of Chaucer." *Neuphilologische Mitteilungen* 72: 69–76.

———. 1982. "Chaucer's Fifteenth-Century Audience and the Narrowing of the Chaucer Tradition." *Studies in the Age of Chaucer* 4: 3–32.

Talbot, Charles H., ed., 1959. *The Life of Christina of Markyate: A Twelfth-Century Recluse*. Reprint Toronto: University of Toronto Press, 1998.

Tarvers, Josephine Koster. 1992. "'Thys ys my mystrys boke': English Women as Readers and Writers in Late Medieval England." In *Uses of Manuscripts in Literary Studies*, edited by

Charlotte C. Morse, Penelope R. Doob, and Marjorie C. Woods, 305–27. Studies in Medieval Culture 31. Kalamazoo, MI: Medieval Institute Publications.

Taylor, Andrew. 2002. *Textual Situations: Three Medieval Manuscripts and Their Readers.* Material Texts. Philadelphia: University of Pennsylvania Press.

Thomson, S. Harrison. 1934. "Grosseteste's Topical Concordance of the Bible and the Fathers." *Speculum* 9: 139–44.

Ullmann, Walter. 1962. *The Growth of Papal Government in the Middle Ages: A Study in the Ideological Relation of Clerical to Lay Power.* 2nd ed. London: Methuen.

Zinn, Grover. 1974. "Hugh of Saint Victor and the Art of Memory." *Viator* 5: 211–34.

CHAPTER 9

GLOSS AND COMMENTARY

RITA COPELAND

MEDIEVAL thought leaves some of its richest records in glosses and commentaries on authoritative texts. Whether we want to know how medieval thinkers viewed their treasured inheritance of ancient philosophy and literature, or how they imbued their students with a love for the liberal arts, or how they studied sacred Scripture, our best access is often through their expositions of the texts that they read, taught, and copied. The present chapter surveys this field under the following topics: terminologies, formats, and character of gloss and commentary; the nature of large freestanding commentaries and examples of secular learned and literary texts that supported this particular form of critical approach; and interactions between text and commentary that gave rise to important theoretical understandings, including authorial intention and the interpretive control of the commentator.

TERMINOLOGIES AND FORMATS

The medieval Latin terminology for what we now call commentary or gloss is not precise or consistent, but the most common usages shed light on what was considered to be of greatest importance. In the eleventh and twelfth centuries, the terms most commonly encountered, either in definitions or as titles, are *glosa/glossa* and *commentum*; but we soon discover that these terms acquired different ranges of meaning from their modern equivalents "gloss" and "commentary." In the *Etymologiae*, Isidore of Seville defines *glossa* in a way that still carries the classical meaning of an obscure or foreign word that requires an explanation: Isidore says that *glossa* derives from the Greek for "tongue" because it denotes (*designat*) an obscure expression with one single word; that is, it explains a word by means of another word (*Etym.* 1.30.1–2). The classical definition of an obscure word needing explanation, hence also (in the plural) a collection of such explanations, is the ancestor of our modern definition of "gloss" as a vocabulary item ("glossary"). He also gives a definition of the classical Latin word *commentaria* (*commentarium*): "*commentaria* are so-called as if 'with the mind' (*cum mente*). They are interpretations, such as comments (*commenta*) on law, or comments on the Gospel" (6.8.5). By the High Middle Ages, the values of these terms have changed considerably, sometimes along with the term itself. The classical *commentarium* (or sometimes the masculine form *commentarius*) is still in use, but just as common, or even more so, is the word *commentum* (perfect passive participle of *comminisco* or the deponent *comminiscor*, to devise or invent), which in later Latin had taken on the same meaning as *commentarium* (cf. *TLL* 3, *commentum* II).

From medieval definitions we see how the scope of *commentum*/*commentarium* has narrowed while that of *glosa* has widened. In the first half of the twelfth century, William of Conches prefaces his *Glosae super Platonem* with a now classic distinction:

> Ut ait Priscianus in Preexercitaminibus puerorum, comminisci est plura, studio vel doctrina in mente habita, in unum colligere. Unde commentum dicitur plurium studio vel doctrina in mente habitorum in unum collectio. Et quamvis, secundum hanc diffinitionem, commentum possit dici quislibet liber, tamen non hodie vocamus commentum nisi alterius libri expositorium. Quod differt a glosa. Commentum enim, solam sententiam exequens, de continuatione vel expositione litere nichil agi. Glosa vero omnia illa exequitur. Unde dicitur glosa, id est lingua. Ita enim aperte debet exponere ac si lingua doctoris videatur docere.
>
> [As Priscian says in his *Praeexercitamina* for boys, *comminisci* (to devise) is to collect together many things that are held in the mind by study or teaching. Whence a collection of many things held together in the mind by study or teaching is called a *commentum*. While according to this definition any book can be called a *commentum*, nevertheless today we do not call it a *commentum* unless it is an exposition of another book. This is the difference between *commentum* and *glosa*: a *commentum* only pursues the sense, but is not at all concerned with the context (*continuatio*) or with exposition of the letter. A *glosa* deals with all these matters. Whence it is called *glosa*, that is, tongue. For truly a gloss ought to expound clearly, as if seeming to teach from the speech of the scholar.] (William of Conches 2006, 19; my translation)

While there are echoes here of the definitions given by Isidore, William of Conches underscores his own contemporary usage: "today we do not call it a *commentum* unless it is an exposition." But far more important to the contemporary understanding of the terms is that William sees the traditional definition of *commentum* as narrow in its application. *Commentum* designates what is held in the mind, but as such it is *limited* to what is held in the mind. It treats only the ideas (*sententiae*) contained in the authoritative text, and thus would be useful only as a précis of doctrine. *Glosa*, on the other hand, has widened in its application. While conserving Isidore's etymological link between *glosa* and *lingua*, William sees its rootedness in the letter of the text as its virtue, because from the letter it can expand to embrace context and then *sententia* (cf. Jeauneau 2007, 285–87; Munk Olsen 2009, 6). In the latter part of the twelfth century, a student or teacher who was very familiar with the work of William of Conches revisited the question of commentary and gloss in his own long commentary on Priscian's *Institutiones* (a commentary known now by its incipit, "Promisimus") in the rather self-conscious context of explaining Priscian's use of the word *commentarius*:

> OMNIA QUE SUNT RELICTA que non sunt emendata IN COMMENTARIIS ANTIQUORUM GRECORUM ARTIS GRAMATICE. Commentarius \vel commentum/ [1] dicitur liber continens sententiam et non littere expositionem, glosa vero continens sententiam et littere expositionem, et dicitur glosa quasi glossa, quia litteram plenarie exponit sicut lingua magistri...Dicitur autem "commentarius" a "comminiscor" quod est multa simul ad memoriam reducere et inde commentum collectio plurium ingenio et studio in unum reductorum. "Comminiscor" secundum quosdam est false invenire, sed nichil est.
>
> [EVERYTHING WHICH REMAINS, i.e., what has not been emended IN THE COMMENTARIES OF THE ANCIENT GREEKS ON THE ART OF GRAMMAR. A book comprising *sententia* but not an exposition of the letter of the text is called a *commentarius* \or *commentum*/, and "gloss" is so called from tongue [*glossa*], because it thoroughly explains the letter of the text as if it were the utterance of the master...*Commentarius* comes from *comminiscor*, which means to reduce many things at once to memory, whence *commentum* is a collection of many things concentrated in one place by intelligence or study. According to some, *comminiscor* means to fabricate falsely, but this is not so.] (Fredborg 1999, 93; my translation).

These remarks from the "Promisimus" commentary have the virtue of showing not only the long influence of the new definitions encountered in William of Conches's prologue, but also further awareness of terminological issues: the glossator (or copyist) adds the contemporary term *commentum* as an alternative to Priscian's antique term *commentarius*, and even attempts damage control on the worrying linkage between *commentum/commentarius* and *comminiscor*, which can indeed mean "to fabricate falsely," despite the glossator's protests. One further brief example can show how William of Conches's notion of "context" (*continuatio*) was subjected to more specification. Hugo of Pisa's *Derivationes*, from the very end of the twelfth century, explains that a *commentum* is an exposition that does not consider the "linking of words" (*verborum iuncturam*), but only the sense; it serves as an exposition of sense but not of the "construction" of the letter. But *glosa* is an exposition of the sense and of the letter itself that pays attention to words and not only to the sense: it is a kind of exposition of *sententia* that works by joining together and explaining the letter (*litteram continuans et exponens*) (Hugo of Pisa 2004, 2: 536; Munk Olsen 2009, 5). This definition points to why *glosa* is given privilege over *commentum*: it is precisely

---

1. The sign \.../ indicates an interlinear or marginal addition by the copyist, in this case most likely the author of the gloss himself.

its grammatical focus, its attention to words as they are "linked" together in context, that gives it greater authority than *commentum*, which is seen to hover above the work without ever quite immersing itself in the textual matter.

All of these definitions can show us what was valued in a textual exposition, no matter what term was used to designate that exposition. For indeed, the terminology varied considerably beyond the common terms *glosa* and *commentum*. In manuscript titles we find many words, including *enarrationes*, *tractatus* and *tractatulus*, *expositio*, *explanatio*, *adnotatio*, *interpretationes*, *opus*, and *postilla* (this last especially for exegesis of sacred texts) (Häring 1982, 174–77). In eleventh- and twelfth-century contexts, these were mostly specialized terms (Munk Olsen 2009, 7). Less often in the twelfth century, we meet the terms *notule* and *questiones* applied to Scriptural commentaries (Häring 1982, 177). From the period of the universities in the thirteenth century onwards, we continue to encounter some of these terms, especially *commentum* or *commentarius/commentarium* and *expositio*, as well as other terms such as *sententia*, *lectura*, and the specialized term *questiones* (Luscombe 1997, 322–24). Medieval Latin was not unique in its terminological variety. An even greater fluidity of terminology for scholarly genres is found in nearly contemporary Arabic commentary, which was produced in an environment without formalized institutional structures (Gutas 1993, 31; Jolivet 2000, 409).

The general *mise-en-page* of gloss-commentary descends to the Middle Ages from the codices of late antiquity. There one encounters two basic formats: commentary that is on the page of the manuscript with the author's text, and a freestanding commentary connected to the commented text by *lemmata* (*lemma*, the word or group of words from the original text that is quoted to refer back to the passage under consideration). In terms of transmission these had their own distinct characters. While a freestanding lemmatic commentary could be copied more or less as it was, protected by its mass, its internal logical progression (based on the structure of the commented text), and often its attribution to a scholarly authority, a manuscript containing marginal commentary was a personal item, specific to the teaching and interests of its owner, and was unlikely to be copied in exactly the same way (Holtz 2000, 104–5). However, as Louis Holtz suggests, the relationship between the forms was fluid: extracts from a lemmatic commentary could be inserted as marginal scholia in another manuscript of the text itself, and scholia could be copied from the manuscript containing the author's text to form the basis of a separate lemmatic commentary (Holtz 2000, 105; Zetzel 1975 and 1981).

Out of this late antique background, certain formal distinctions emerged more clearly in the Middle Ages. During the early Carolingian period, the newer necessity of teaching Latin as a foreign language is reflected in a division of functions in the layout of a canonical literary text with commentary: marginal glosses are used for discursive explanations of conceptual or historical meaning, while small interlinear glosses deal with grammatical and lexical questions, that is, *glosae* in the restricted sense of Isidore of Seville. But as marginal commentaries expanded, often incorporating the matter of existing lemmatic commentaries, achieving a canonicity of their own that was worth preserving in the copying of manuscripts, the very layout of manuscript pages had to change in order to ensure efficient visual correspondence between text and commentary. Towards the end of the tenth century, in a move that seems initially to be mainly concerned with the copying of the classical poets, the principle that determines the layout is no longer the commented text, but rather the accommodation of the commentary. Paris, Bibliothèque Nationale Ms. lat. 16236, from the end of the tenth century, possibly from Italy, is a copy of the works of Virgil with the lemmatic commentary of Servius (fourth century) in the margins. Here, what determines how much of the Virgilian text appears on a page, whether in one column of text or in two, is how much of the now marginal commentary has to be aligned with the text. This is in a period before the great copies of the biblical *Glossa ordinaria*, which perfected this layout system through the twelfth century. (On this, see Taylor in this volume.) The new technology of the page ensured that the marginal commentary was always in close proximity to the passage being commented, whether in sacred or secular writings (Holtz 2000, 108–14). Thus even marginal commentaries that were not imported from a preexisting lemmatic commentary, such as commentaries on grammatical texts that derive from the teaching in a particular school, will still have a clear layout. This is the case even where there is considerable variation in content from manuscript to manuscript, including annotations in different vernacular languages. Good examples of such consistency in layout are the heavily glossed manuscripts of Alexander Neckam's grammatical writings, which include Anglo-French and even English glosses (T. Hunt 1991, 1: 177–90, 235–73).

Characteristics of Freestanding Commentaries

The internal structure of the freestanding gloss or commentary tells us a great deal about the thoroughness of coverage. To illustrate the procedures of the twelfth-century glossator, there is no better example than the practice of William of Conches in his influential glosses on Boethius's *Consolatio Philosophiae*. Most freestanding lemmatic glosses would be equipped with an *accessus* or prologue which would introduce the author and work being studied by means of some conventional topics: the author's name and the title of the work; the subject matter and the author's intention (or why he wrote the work); the author's method of composition (*modus agendi* or *modus tractandi*); the "utility" of the work, or what value the work might serve, whether moral or philosophical teaching; and the place of the work among the divisions of knowledge (Munk Olsen 2009, 131–87; Minnis 1984, 19–28 and passim; R. W. Hunt 1980b). Arriving at the text itself, the gloss would proceed in three general stages: first, an overall summary of the teaching in the passage, the general meaning of the passage and the biggest ideas that the commentator wanted readers to grasp, usually quoting as a lemma the opening words of the passage; second, the *continuatio* (often indicated by this word), linking the opening summary to the rest of the passage and thus indicating the context; and third, a word-by-word examination or paraphrase, often introduced by the phrase "et hoc est quod ait" (or simply "et hoc est") which links the *continuatio* to the literal analysis which follows (Jeauneau 2007, 290–91).

We can see this structure at work precisely in the following passage from William's commentary on the opening of 1 *prosa* 1 of the *Consolatio*, connecting the end of the first sentence in that *prosa*, "statura discretionis ambiguae," with the following sentence "Nam nunc quidem ad communem":

> STATURA DISCRETIONIS AMBIGUAE. Statura illa est discretionis ambiguae in qua non est certus terminus, quia modo maior apparet, modo minor. Philosophiae ergo statura discretionis ambiguae est, quia modo parva videtur cum de parvis tractat ut de institutione morum in ethica, de dispensatione familiae in economica, de gubernatione reipublicae in politica. Maior vero videtur cum de caelestibus tractat, maxime de creatore. Et idcirco statura illius ambiguae discretionis est. Et hoc exponam postea. . .
>
> Continuatio. Vere statura illius erat ambiguae discretionis, NAM NUNC QUIDEM VIDEBATUR magna, modo maior, modo maxima. Et hoc est: NAM NUNC QUIDEM AD COMMUNEM SESE COHIBEBAT ETC., tractando de parvis ut de praedictis, NUNC VERO VIDEBATUR PULSARE CAELUM id est tractare de caelestibus ut in astronomia, et hoc CACUMINE SUMMI VERTICIS id est ratione et intellectu qui dicuntur vertex Philosophiae ut superius expositum est, et tunc quasi maior apparebat.
>
> [HER HEIGHT WAS DIFFICULT TO DETERMINE. That height is difficult to determine in that it has no definite limit, for at one time it appears greater, and at another time lesser. The "height" of philosophy is difficult to determine, because at one time it seems a small thing when it treats lesser matters such as the laws of morals in (the field of) ethics, the organization of the household in (the field of) economics, or the governing of the state in (the field of) politics. It seems larger when it treats the heavens, and greatest when it treats of the Creator. And so its height is difficult to determine. I will expound this later.
>
> Context. In fact her height was difficult to determine, FOR NOW ON THE ONE HAND SHE SEEMED big, or at times bigger, or at times biggest. And this is where he says FOR NOW ON THE ONE HAND SHE CONFINED HERSELF TO THE COMMON (SIZE OF HUMANS), in treating of the lesser things as described above, NOW ON THE OTHER HAND SHE SEEMED TO PUSH AGAINST THE HEAVENS, that is, to treat celestial matters such as in astronomy, and thus WITH THE VERY CROWN OF HER HEAD, that is, with reason and intellect which are called the "crown" of Philosophy, as was explained above, and then she appeared to be a greater being.] (William of Conches 1999, 23–24; my translation)

The gloss opens with a general statement, in this case a move immediately into the allegorical reading of the passage which William has set up earlier in the text by noting that Philosophy is an example of prosopopeia, philosophy represented "sub specie mulieris," "in the form of a woman." Thus the indeterminate height of Philosophy can be easily explained in terms of the various aspects of philosophical inquiry, whether worldly concerns of ethics, physics (astronomy), or metaphysics (the Creator). The *continuatio* develops the idea according to the syntax of the passage itself, and the exposition *ad litteram* alternately quotes and paraphrases the text, using the words themselves to support the allegorical reading. In this way the glossator demonstrates to students how he has pinned down his textual evidence.

During the thirteenth century, the commentaries produced by masters at the University of Paris took on a new standardized structure, under pressure of formal curricula and the homogeneity of the kinds of texts submitted to commentary in that milieu—logical, scientific, and theological texts, as opposed to the broad range of classical literary works that were taught by masters in earlier centuries. Through the first half of the thirteenth century, the commentary form associated with the teaching in the Faculty of Arts (the so-called Parisian commentary) was divided into sections (*lectiones* or "lessons"), the individual names for which denoted their function within the commentary as a whole: a *divisio textus*, which explains the logical structure of the text under discussion; the *sententia* (*in generali*), which deals with the *intentio* or meaning of the whole text; the *expositio*, or *expositio litterae*, or *sententia in speciali*, which gives close attention to the letter of the text, breaking words or syntactic units into their elements; a section called *notanda*, the position of which varies, but which complements the previous sections by returning to particular local issues; and then a section given over to *dubia* or *questiones*. This last section, the *questiones*, evolved into an autonomous commentary form after about 1260 (del Punta 1998; Weijers 2002, 17–18; Weijers 2000; Weijers 1996, chs. 3, 4). Manuscripts copied for university studies offer ample evidence of these formal divisions, as well as more informal notes for comprehension of the text (Hamesse 2002).

Freestanding lemmatic commentaries are signs that commentators felt in control of their textual material. Up until the fifth century, most commentaries on classical Latin authors were freestanding, although as noted above, such autonomous commentaries could also be incorporated into the margins of the author's text, where they might be abridged or intermingled with other authorities on the same text. We do not have good manuscript evidence of how this process of "marginalization" and "hybridization" took place, since few early exemplars survive. (Munk Olsen 2009, 11, lists three manuscripts from the fourth through sixth centuries which survive to show this process: Vatican Vat. Lat. 3236 [s. iv/v], the *Terentius Bembinus*, which has glosses from the fifth and sixth centuries; Verona, Bibl. Cap., XL [s. v], the works of Virgil with abundant contemporary glosses which cite various commentators by name; and Vatican Vat. Lat. 5750 [s. vi], which contains glosses on Juvenal.) Many such hybrid marginal commentaries must have survived into the Carolingian period, when they were copied and recombined, often to make new independent commentaries. But some freestanding lemmatic commentaries were transmitted to the Middle Ages in their original complete form, notably among them Servius's lemmatic commentaries on the works of Virgil (although there was also a hybrid form of the Servian commentary, the *Servius auctus*, which survives as marginalia or in various fragmentary forms) (Munk Olsen 2009, 11–12, 113), and the *Explanationes in Ciceronis rhetoricam* of Marius Victorinus (fourth century), which became in its own right an authoritative textbook on classical rhetoric (Ward 1995, 76–104; Copeland and Sluiter 2009, 104–24). In the cases of Servius and Victorinus, the antiquity of the commentary ensured its continuing prestige. But "modern" freestanding lemmatic commentaries could achieve similar success, especially if associated with a magisterial name: for example, Thierry of Chartres and William of Conches in the twelfth century; or Thomas Aquinas and Giles of Rome on the Latinized texts of Aristotle in the thirteenth century, presented in the highly regimented manner of scholastic commentaries, making them very easy to use even without the original text to hand (Lohr 1967–74). The existence of freestanding lemmatic commentaries gave medieval readers a certain advantage in mastering the original text, because the lemmatic format had the scope to develop extended, complex, and theoretically original responses to the work. The context in which a work was read and used might determine whether the commentary was marginal and interlinear, such as some of the schoolroom glosses on Ovid's lesser poems studied by Hexter (1986), or freestanding lemmatic, such as others studied by Hexter (1986) or the advanced readings of Cicero's rhetorical treatises in Thierry of Chartres's commentaries (Thierry of Chartres 1988).

The difference between the scope of freestanding commentaries and marginal or interlinear glosses can be seen in the reception of Priscian's *Institutiones grammaticae*. The *Institutiones* were copied and known through the early Middle Ages, but it is only in the Carolingian period that we see more energetic efforts to understand them. Up to the eleventh century, the main kind of commentary on this demanding text was the individual gloss on difficult terms or ambiguous words; the apparent exception during this early period was the commentary up to the beginning of book 3 by Sedulius Scottus (ninth century), which survives as a lemmatic commentary. But in the second half of the eleventh century, in the cathedral schools of northern France and the Rhineland, scholars began to strike out more courageously in their explorations of Priscian's conceptualization of speech, grammar, and language. The form in which they undertook these new investigations was a freestanding lemmatic commentary on books 1–16 of the *Institutiones* known as the *Glosule*, first identified by R. W. Hunt and named by him after the title given for the work in the *explicit* of one of the manuscripts (Hunt 1980a). This freestanding commentary survives (with variants and different interpolations) in five manuscripts from the eleventh and twelfth centuries; there is also an extension of this commentary devoted to books 17–18 of the *Institutiones*, which is found in four further manuscripts. Such a commentary assumes the availability (to hand) of a complete text of the *Institutiones*, but as a separate text the lemmatic commentary was easier to copy and circulate than if it had to be reproduced in the margins of the work itself.

The commentary seems to have gone through several generations of masters, the first unknown but the second associated with the teachings of William of Champeaux in the earliest years of the twelfth century (Gibson 1979 and 1992; Rosier-Catach 2005; Copeland and Sluiter 2009, 376–89). The early *Glosule* represents the first truly innovative grammatical thought in the Middle Ages, showing the impact of contemporary logic on the field of language theory. For these new interests, which really opened the window to linguistics, the masters turned from the straightforward teaching of Donatus's grammars (which had been the mainstay of grammatical study since the fourth century) to the massive, detailed, difficult, but theoretically rewarding text of Priscian. Yet they do not obediently accept all of Priscian's teachings. They assert their independence from many of his pronouncements, disputing and testing the validity of Priscian's premises, for example, on the materiality of *vox* (voice) or on the primary and secondary purpose of each part of speech. The only form in which this kind of independent, critical questioning could be undertaken and sustained over several generations was a freestanding lemmatic commentary which was not confined to the margins of a page and which could also grow to accommodate new views from later masters (interpolations). The proof of its historical importance lies in its influence. The *Glosule* stands directly behind the freestanding lemmatic commentary on Priscian's *Institutiones* by William of Conches (based on his classroom lectures), which took command of Priscianic grammatical theory and placed it at the center of twelfth-century intellectual debates. And via William of Conches, the *Glosule* extends its reach to the fullest medieval exposition of Priscian, Petrus Helias's *Summa super Priscianum* (ca. 1140–50), which dispensed altogether with the form of lemmatic commentary in favor of a new genre, the *summa*, which treats major theoretical questions organized by topics rather than by the order of the original text.

Interactions between Text and Commentary: Authorial Intention, Interpretive Claims, and the Test-Case of Statius's *Thebaid*

The vast territories of literary commentary on Ovid and other classical authors, notably Virgil, Juvenal, and Lucan, especially from the twelfth and thirteenth centuries, exemplify the whole range of commentary forms, from interlinear grammatical gloss and extended marginal gloss to freestanding commentary. The serious literary study of Ovid among the masters of Orléans in the twelfth and thirteenth centuries supplies a powerful case in point (McKinley 1996 and 2001; Hexter 1986 and 1987; Demats 1973). (The bibliography on classical literary commentary is extensive; several more items and overviews can be found in the Suggested Readings at the end of this essay.) The names of three late twelfth-century commentators on Ovid's poetry are known to us: Fulco, Arnulf, and William. Arnulf of Orléans was the most prolific and influential of these, producing two different commentaries on the *Metamorphoses* as well as on the *Amores, Ars amatoria, Remedia amoris*, and *Ex Ponto* (Engelbrecht 2008). Of Arnulf's two commentaries on the *Metamorphoses*, one is a running philological commentary appropriate to interlinear and marginal format (excerpt edited in Ghisalberti 1932, 180–89), and the other, the *Allegoriae*, is (as its name suggests) a series of allegorical readings of the Ovidian narratives, operating at a more synthetic level (edited in Ghisalberti 1932, 201–29). The *Allegoriae* was likely composed as a freestanding commentary, as befits its more experimental and innovative character. But the two commentaries were transmitted in various forms. While most later manuscripts containing Arnulf's philological glosses copy them into the margins of Ovid's text, some early witnesses copy them separately from the *Metamorphoses*; conversely, the *Allegoriae*, while commonly found as freestanding, was also integrated into marginal glosses along with the philological gloss (Hexter 1987, 65; Coulson and Nawotka 1993, 269, 281). Later Ovid commentators continued to borrow from Arnulf's work, and Arnulf's *Allegoriae* were copied in manuscripts along with the *Integumenta Ovidii* of the thirteenth-century master John of Garland, one of Arnulf's most important beneficiaries (McKinley 2001, 69). The reach of Orléannais *belles lettres* was large, extending down through the Ovidian tradition (Shooner 1981; Hexter 1987 and 1989; Coulson 1987 and 1991, 4–13; Coulson and Roy 2000; McKinley 1996 and 2001; Zeeman 2009) and to the study of other classical and classicizing authors (Arnulf of Orléans 1958; Löfstedt 1995; Geoffrey of Vitry 1973; Townsend 2008).

The tradition of commentary on Statius's *Thebaid* offers a relatively contained—though never simple—test case for the theoretical issues of authorial intention and the commentator's own interpretive claims. That the tradition of glossing and commenting on the *Thebaid* should be a limited one is surprising, given the fascination that the Thebes story held for medieval readers and the esteem accorded to Statius's epic. Compared to the commentary tradition on Virgil, which from its beginnings was complicated by the dominant Servian commentary subsuming earlier glosses, and later grammarians continuing to use Virgil as their subject matter, the story of *Thebaid* glossing is fairly straightforward. By late antiquity the *Thebaid* had not achieved the unquestioned canonical centrality of Virgil's *Aeneid*, and only one commentary comes down to us from the period, traditionally attributed to Lactantius Placidus, about whom nothing is known and whose date can only be fixed tentatively in the late fourth century (making him a near contemporary of the grammarian Servius). This commentary was not transmitted with the integral continuity of Servius's commentary on Virgil. If, as seems likely, the Lactantius commentary began as a freestanding lemmatic commentary, it was soon broken into marginal glosses, which were reassembled to form a new freestanding commentary at some point in the Carolingian period. Three early manuscripts (ninth through eleventh centuries) and at least one later copy attest to this latter stage, and these are not all complete. But marginalia remained the most common format for transmission, and many copies of the *Thebaid*, densely annotated, reflect the Lactantius tradition (Munk Olsen 2009, 103; Sweeney 1969; Clogan 1968). Two other distinctive commentaries are known, both of them from the twelfth century. The so-called *In principio* commentary (from its incipit), which modern scholarship has linked with Hilary of Orléans, was transmitted in both integral and marginal form, with many variants (de Angelis 1997, 94–106). A curious allegorical interpretation, freestanding but not lemmatic, survives in only one medieval manuscript of the twelfth century. (A third commentary in a unique manuscript, Vienna, Österreichische Nationalbibliothek 1757 II, of the twelfth century, apparently also distinctive, is noted by Munk Olsen 2009, 104. This commentary has not yet been studied or edited.) From the tenth century onwards, texts of the *Thebaid* with glossing are accompanied by a variety of *accessus* which fall into several distinctive groups (Munk Olsen 2009, 104–5; Anderson 2009, passim).

The Lactantius Placidus commentary does not, at least in its extant forms, attempt the breadth of coverage of Servius on the *Aeneid*. The glosses are devoted to explaining the sense of words or phrases, supplying mythological background and geographical or astrological information (both of crucial importance, given the density as well as allusiveness of Statius's style), and noting the variety of rhetorical figures. This commentary does not contain the grammatical teaching that we find in Servius on the *Aeneid*, suggesting that the glosses were aimed at general readers, not classroom instruction (Lactantius Placidus 1997, vii). However, the annotations often refer the reader back to passages in Virgil (with greatest frequency), Horace, Cicero, and other classical Latin writers to emphasize the rich intertextuality of Statius's style. The commentator rarely reads beyond the given narrative sense to offer broadly ideological or allegorical readings. (An interesting exception is at 4.516–17, "…et triplicis mundi summum, quem scire nefastum./ illum sed taceo," ["…(the one who is) the highest of the triple world, whom it is forbidden to know. Him – but I keep silent"], which the commentary develops into an extended astronomical, mythographical, philosophical [based on Pythagoras and Plato's *Timaeus*], and even religious account [citing Moses and Isaiah as well as Orpheus] of the Demiurge [*daemiourgon*] whose name must not be spoken [Lactantius Placidus 1997, 293–95].) The *In principio* commentary of the twelfth century finds in the ancient commentary an opportunity to develop this image in a new direction, taking the *triplicis mundi summum* as the "Demogorgon" which is identifiable with the *anima mundi* of the Calcidean *Timaeus*, and whose unpronounceability stimulated poetic invention. (For the text, see de Angelis 1997, 113–14.) In its extant forms, the commentary does not present an overarching vision of the poem, such as we find in Servius's famous prologue to the *Aeneid* or in his dilation on the opening lines of Virgil's epic. On the other hand, the Lactantius Placidus commentary gives great attention to the narrative architecture of the *Thebaid*: for most of the books of the *Thebaid*, the commentary supplies long head notes as readers' guides, reviewing the plot action. These help to keep the crowded but also diffuse plot of the *Thebaid* clear.

But given the complexity of Statius's text and the relatively modest scope of the Lactantius Placidus commentary, there was plenty of room for later commentators willing to brave the difficulties of the *Thebaid* to question and exceed the authority of the only ancient commentary. The author of the *In principio* commentary of the twelfth century finds many occasions to disagree with the Lactantius Placidus scholia on philological or mythographical matters, sometimes categorically pronouncing the earlier work wrong, and at other times couching his differences more neutrally (de Angelis 1997, 101–6). In this way he establishes his own interpretive supersedence. But his very dependence on the ancient commentary also opens the way for some interpretive excursions. At *Thebaid* 12.481–511, Statius describes the altar to Clementia built at Athens, so the tale goes, by the Heraclidae in gratitude for the refuge they found in Attica after their father's death. The Lactantius Placidus gloss on lines 497–98 restricts itself to the mythological background. The *In principio* gloss absorbs and reproduces the earlier gloss and then extends it in a new, Scriptural direction:

> FAMA EST [DEFENSOS ACIE POST BUSTA PATERNI/NUMINIS HERCULEOS SEDEM FUNDASSE NEPOTES]: determinat qui fuerunt illius templi positores. Hylus [sic], Deianire et Herculis filius, et reliqui ex eodem nati, postquam Hercules interiit pulsi ab Ericteo, Athenas confugerunt, a quibus facile impetrantes auxilium, hanc aram consecraverunt asserentes apud Athenas tantum misericordiam sedem posuisse.

> [He indicates who were the founders of this temple. Hyllus, son of Hercules and Deianira, and the others who were Hercules's children, driven out by Eurystheos after Hercules died, appealed to the Athenians, and easily winning their help, consecrated this altar, affirming in this way that Mercy made its dwelling among the Athenians.] (Cf. *Thebaid* 12.482–83: "mitis posuit Clementia sedem,/ et miseri fecere sacram.") (text in de Angelis 1997, 122; my translation)

Up to this point, the *In principio* commentary has followed the Lactantius gloss nearly word for word (Lactantius Placidus 1997, 652). But the commentator continues on a new theme:

> Ad eam igitur aram quicumque supplices accedebant misericordiam impetrabant. Cum beatus Paulus Athenas predicaturus advenisset, invenit Dionisium Ariopagitam, virum prudentissimum, quem cum non potuisset convincere, duxit eum per singulas aras deorum inquirendo cuius esset. Tandem ad hanc aram pervenit et inquisivit cuius esset. Cui Dionisius: "ara est ignoti dei." Tunc beatus Paulus: "Quem ignotum appellas solus ille notus est" et sermonem suum sic incipit "Notus in Iudea deus" et cetera.

> [Any suppliants would approach this altar and they would obtain mercy. When Saint Paul came to preach to the Athenians, he found Dionysius the Areopagite, a most prudent man; when Paul could not persuade him, he led him to every one of the gods' altars, asking whose altar it was. Finally he came to this altar and asked whose it was. Dionysius said to him, "This is the altar of the unknown god." Then Saint Paul said, "The one whom you call unknown, He alone is known," and then he began the sermon beginning "God is known in Judea."] (cf. Ps 75.2; text in de Angelis 1997, 122; my translation)

This identification of Statius's altar of Clementia in Athens with the altar of the "unknown god" on the Areopagus (Acts 17.23) which became the occasion for Paul's preaching to the Athenians and conversion of Dionysius the Areopagite (17.34) may seem unmotivated except for the Athenian setting. (De Angelis 1997, 122–23 notes that this gloss has a curious parallel in a passage in Abelard's *Theologia christiana*, where Abelard cites *Thebaid* 12. 482, "mitis posuit Clementia sedem" when expounding the preaching of Paul in Acts 17, and wonders whether Abelard may have seen the *In principio* commentary.) But in the apparent absence of motivation for this identification with sacred, Scriptural history also lies the power of the medieval exegete's claim upon the classical text. The exegete seizes Statius's text for his own Christian epoch, directing Statius's authorial intention to a new historical purpose, that of looking forward from the mythical prehistory of Athens to the revealed history of apostolic Christianity (on this passage cf. Anderson 1988, 162–63).

It is just such "unmotivated" appropriation that lies at the heart of allegorizing commentary in which the classical text is seen as an "integument" (*integumentum*), a covering of poetic fiction under which the author concealed his true philosophical purpose, and which awaits the skilled attention of the exegete who will draw back the covering to expose the true meaning that the author intended. We are familiar with this approach from the commentaries associated with the cathedral school of Chartres and its larger literary community in the twelfth century, especially the commentary by William of Conches on Plato's *Timaeus* and the commentaries on the *Aeneid* and Martianus Capella's *De nuptiis Philologiae et Mercurii* which have been linked to the poet-philosopher Bernardus Silvestris. The foundational studies of the term *integumentum* by Édouard Jeauneau, Winthrop Wetherbee, Brian Stock, and Peter Dronke have established the intellectual grounds for such allegorical understandings (Jeauneau 1957; Wetherbee 1972; Stock 1972; Dronke 1974).

It is out of this rich twelfth-century context of integumental reading that the short allegorical commentary on the *Thebaid*, extant in only one medieval copy, emerges. There is also a sixteenth-century transcript of this or a closely related manuscript by the humanist Pierre Daniel (Lactantius Placidus 1997, 694; Anderson 1998). In the twelfth-century manuscript, Paris, Bibliothèque Nationale MS lat. 3012, fols. 60v–64r, the commentary is attributed, fancifully, to the late antique bishop Fulgentius (the bishop of Ruspe, d. 532/33), who has also been identified with the late antique mythographer Fabius Planciades Fulgentius, author of the *Expositio Vergilianae continentiae* and of the *Mitologiae* (both influential allegorical expositions), a false connection which has now been conclusively demolished (Hays 2003). The assumption that the two Fulgentii were the same contributed, no doubt, to the ascription of the allegorical *Thebaid* commentary to "S. Fulgencius Episcopus" in the manuscript, given that the allegorical method in the commentary resembles that of Fulgentius the Mythographer. But it is beyond doubt a twelfth-century product that, like many other commentaries of that era, bears the influence of the mythographic Fulgentius's philosophical allegorizing (Stock 1971; Lactantius Placidus 1997, 694; Hays 2002).

The preemptive claim of the commentator to the "true" authorial intention is assumed from the start of the treatise, where the *accessus* sets forth a theory of allegorical reading in keeping with the ideas and vocabulary of twelfth-century commentary on classical myth:

> Poetarum investigabilem prudentiam ingeniique eorum venam inmarcescibilem non sine grandi ammiratione retracto, qui sub blanditorio poeticae fictionis tegumento moralium seriem institutionum utiliter inservuerunt. Cum enim teste Horatio:

> Aut prodesse volunt aut delectare poetae
> Aut simul et iocunda et idonea dicere vitae
> (Horace, *Ars poetica* 333–34)

[…] Quam ob rem, "si parva licet componere magnis," [Virgil, *Georgics* 4.176] non incommune carmina poetarum nuci comparabilia videntur; in nuce enim duo sunt, testa et nucleus, sic in carminibus poeticis duo, sensus litteralis et misticus; latet nucleus sub testa: latet sub sensu litterali mistica intelligentia; ut habeas nucleum, frangenda est testa: ut figurae pateant, quatienda est littera; testa insipida est, nucleus saporem gustanti reddit: similiter non littera, sed figura palato intelligentiae sapit. Diligit puer nucem integram ad ludum, sapiens autem et adultus frangit ad gustum; similiter si puer es, habes sensum literalem integrum nullaque subtili expositione pressum in quo oblecteris, si adultus es, frangenda est littera et nucleus litterae eliciendus, cuius gustu reficiaris. His itaque aliisque pluribus modis tam Graecorum quam Latinorum poemata possunt commendabilia probari, quorum summa poscit intentio ut nullos aut simplices aut peritos operum suorum utilitatis immunes relinquerent. Inter quos et Papinius Surculus[2] mirae strenuitatis vir evidentissime claruit qui Virgilianae Eneidis fidus imitator Tebaiden scribere adgressus est; cuius ut tegumentum pateat, historialis ordo seriei praemittendus est.

[Not without great admiration I reconsider the prudence of poets that is accessible to research and the inexhaustible vein of their genius; under a charming covering of poetic fiction, they have usefully inserted a series of moral instructions. Horace is witness to this:

> Poets aim to give profit or delight
> Or to speak what is both pleasing and proper to living.

On this account, "if one may compare small things to great," it is not uncommon to see the verses of poets as something like nuts. In a nut there are two things, the shell and the kernel, and so in poetic verses there are two things, the literal and mystical sense. The kernel is hidden beneath the shell; the mystical understanding is hidden under the literal sense; if you are going to have the kernel, the shell must be broken; so if the figurative sense is going to be revealed, the letter must be broken apart; the shell is tasteless, but the kernel delivers flavor to the tongue: likewise not the letter of the text but the figurative sense tastes good to the palate of understanding. The boy loves the whole nut for his play, but the one who is wise and mature breaks the nut so as to taste it. Likewise, if you are a child, you have the unbroken, solid literal sense, expressed without any subtle exposition, in which you might take pleasure. If you are mature, the letter is to be broken apart so as to draw out the nourishing kernel of the letter, so that you may be refreshed by its savor. Along these lines and many others, the poetry of the Greek as well as of the Latin authors can be tested and judged commendable; their principle intention was that no one, either simple or sophisticated, should go away without sharing in the utility of their work. Among these poets P. Papinius Statius stood

---

2. That is, Publius Papinius Statius. The designation "Surculus" was a tenth-century confusion with the name of another ancient writer. See Hays 2002, 203.

out most clearly as a man of remarkable vigor who set about composing the *Thebaid* in faithful imitation of Virgil's *Aeneid*. In order that the integument may be laid open (i.e., in order that the allegorical meaning beneath the integument be explained), it is necessary to present the literal narrative according to the order of its events.] (text in Lactantius Placidus 1997, 697–98; cf. Wolff and Graziani 2009, 69–81; my translation)

After giving a short summary of the plot, the treatise proceeds to its main purpose, the allegorical reading of the poem, accomplished in a terse 156 printed lines of prose. Thebes is the human soul: "*Thebes* is so called as if *theosbe*, that is, 'dei bonum.' This is the human soul" (99.53–54). Thebes is ruled by Laius, "id est lux sancta" (699.60), and Jocasta, "iocunditas casta" (699.65), but then comes under the rule of their son Oedipus, whose name is etymologized to mean *lascivia* (700.71–74). Polynices and Eteocles stand for *avaritia* and *luxuria* respectively (700–701) according to the etymologies offered for their names. The Seven Against Thebes (the seven kings of Greece) represent the Seven Liberal Arts, "who are aptly called kings because they are the regimen and the pillars of all the sciences" (702.125–27). The spring to which Hypsipyle leads the thirsty Greeks represents the human sciences, which are an insufficient guard against damnation (702–3). Creon, identified with *superbia*, "cremens [or premens] omnia" (703.160), takes over Thebes but is vanquished by Theseus, identified with deity, "quasi 'theos suus'" (704.170).

Since the author has given such a full textbook exposition of integumental theory, it is striking that the allegorical reading proves so labored—not that it is labored in its fancy, but rather that it is not fanciful enough. When compared to the celestial flights that William of Conches's glosses on Plato can take, this treatise barely rises above the floorboards of philosophy. The *Thebaid* is read as an allegory of ascent, the liberation of the soul, similar to contemporary approaches to the *Aeneid* (the commentary attributed to Bernardus Silvestris). But the treatise is curiously constrained by the story of the *Thebaid*. The bad characters (the sinful Oedipus, the warring brothers) remain bad, and the plot drives the philosophical logic. There is none of the aggressive structural revision, from artificial to natural order, that we see in the "Bernardus Silvestris" commentary on the *Aeneid*. But these relative deficiencies (when viewed against the standards of William of Conches and "Bernardus Silvestris") may also tell us something about the more humble contexts of commentaries on literary works.

While this treatise uses the exegetical devices familiar from commentaries by the most famous teachers in the prestigious cathedral schools, its survival in a unique manuscript may suggest that it was produced for more personal purposes, perhaps a schoolmaster's record of his own teaching in imitation of the more renowned masters of the day (with whom perhaps he had studied, or at least—and more certainly—whose works he had read). What would have inspired this unique effort? The *Thebaid* certainly had some presence in the grammar school curriculum by the twelfth century: Munk Olsen has noted sixty-six manuscripts of the work from this period (Munk Olsen 2005, 49). But unlike the works of Virgil, Horace, and

Ovid, the *Thebaid* was not a principal focus of literary commentary. One version of *accessus* often used for the *In principio* commentary (the most consistent medieval exegetical witness) places the poem under the aegis of politics, because it offers a negative lesson in statecraft (de Angeles 2007, 117; Anderson 1988, 232). And yet the poem was held in the greatest esteem, its Theban story an inexhaustible resource for medieval retellings as myth, epic, and history, and beyond this, for reflection upon the etiologies of history and redemption from its destructive cycles. Might this singular allegorical commentary represent an ambitious schoolmaster's effort to coax Statius's epic into an interpretive mainstream by furnishing it with the attributes of integumental writing? The *Thebaid* seems to be remarkably resistant to such an enterprise: its circular structure, woven through with dark allusions, unfathomable causes, and half-told stories, thwarts the valiant attempt of this interpreter to read it as a linear, self-consistent philosophical argument. But the attempt remains, as a record of one master's effort to equip the text with the kind of edifying moral meaning that would give it perhaps greater success as a classroom text.

Whether for schoolroom or scholar, general reader or specialist, glossing was the medium of experimentation, innovation, and renewal. Ancient commentaries achieved their own canonicity, copied in margins or as continuous freestanding texts, their prestige and value increasing in direct proportion to their elasticity. Newer glosses emerged to extend or contest the authority of their predecessors. From interlinear glosses that give Latin synonyms or even vernacular equivalents of the Latin words to freestanding texts that forge their own argumentative shape, the gloss is the signature of learned and literate culture in the Middle Ages.

SUGGESTIONS FOR FURTHER READING

The best resource for overviews of commentary on classical authors are the published and forthcoming volumes of Kristeller et al., eds. *Catalogus translationum et commentariorum*. The volumes of Munk Olsen (1982–89 and 2009) give a thorough guide to manuscripts of classical authors and the varieties of glossing in them. Literary studies of medieval Latin gloss and commentary on classical authors include Minnis (1982), Wieland (1983), D. Anderson (1988) (on the *Thebaid* tradition), Copeland (1991), and Baswell (1995). Pedagogical glossing is studied in Reynolds (1996) and Woods (2009). Volumes 17 and 18 of the *Journal of Medieval Latin* (2007–8) reflect much new work on the traditions of gloss and commentary.

BIBLIOGRAPHY

Primary sources

Arnulf of Orléans. 1958. *Arnulfi Aurelianensis Glosule super Lucanum*, edited by Berthe M. Marti. Papers and Monographs of the American Academy in Rome 18. Rome: American Academy in Rome.

Coulson, Frank T., ed. 1991. *The "Vulgate" Commentary on Ovid's Metamorphoses: the Creation Myth and Story of Orpheus.* Toronto Medieval Latin Texts 20. Toronto: Pontifical Institute of Mediaeval Studies.

Fredborg, Karin M., ed. 1999. "Promisimus: An Edition." *Cahiers de l'Institut du Moyen-Âge grec et latin* 70: 81–228.

Geoffrey of Vitry. 1973. *The Commentary of Geoffrey of Vitry on Claudian "De raptu Proserpinae,"* edited by Amy K. Clarke, Amy K. and Phyllis M. Giles. Mittellateinische Texte und Studien 7. Leiden, Cologne: E. J. Brill.

Hugo of Pisa. 2004. *Derivationes,* edited by Enzo Cecchini et al. 2 vols. Edizione nazionale dei testi mediolatini 11. Florence: SISMEL, Edizioni del Galluzzo.

Isidore of Seville. 1911. *Etymologiarum sive originum libri XX,* edited by Wallace M. Lindsay. 2 vols. Oxford: Oxford University Press.

Lactantius Placidus. 1997. *In Statii Thebaida commentum,* edited by Robert D. Sweeney. Vol. 1. Stuttgart, Leipzig: B. G. Teubner.

Löfstedt, Bengt, ed. 1995. *Vier Juvenal-Kommentare aus dem 12. Jh.* Amsterdam: J. C. Gieben.

Thierry of Chartres. 1988. *The Latin Rhetorical Commentaries by Thierry of Chartres,* edited by Karin M. Fredborg. Pontifical Institute of Mediaeval Studies. Studies and Texts 84. Toronto: Pontifical Institute of Mediaeval Studies.

Townsend, David, ed. 2008. *An Epitome of Biblical History: Glosses on Walter of Châtillon's Alexandreis 4.176–274, edited from London, British Library, MS. Additional 18217.* Toronto Medieval Latin Texts 30. Toronto: Pontifical Institute of Mediaeval Studies.

William of Conches. 1999. *Glosae super Boetium,* edited by Lodi Nauta. Corpus Christianorum. Continuatio Mediaevalis 158. Turnhout: Brepols.

———. 2006. *Glosae super Platonem,* edited by Édouard Jeauneau. Corpus Christianorum. Continuatio Mediaevalis 203. Turnhout: Brepols.

Wolff, Étienne and Françoise Graziani, eds. and trans. 2009. *Fulgence: Virgile dévoilé; Pseudo-Fulgence, Sur la Thébaide; Isidore de Séville, Étymologies (extraits); Bernard Silvestre, Commentaire à Martianus Capella (préface); Boccace, Interprétation de la Comédie de Dante (extraits).* Villeneuve d'Ascq: Presses Universitaires du Septentrion.

Secondary sources

Aertsen, Jan A. and Andreas Speer, eds. 1998. *Was ist Philosophie im Mittelalter?* Miscellanea Mediaevalia. Veröffentlichungen des Thomas-Instituts der Universität Köln 26. Berlin: Walter De Gruyter.

Anderson, David. 1988. *Before the Knight's Tale: Imitation of Classical Epic in Boccaccio's Teseida.* Middle Ages Series. Philadelphia: University of Pennsylvania Press.

Anderson, Harald J. 1997. "Medieval *Accessus* to Statius." PhD diss., Ohio State University.

———. 1998. "Note sur les manuscrits du commentaire de Fulgence sur la *Thébaïde.*" *Revue d'histoire des textes* 28: 235–38.

———. 2009. *The Manuscripts of Statius* (rev. ed.). 3: *Reception: The Vitae and Accessus.* Arlington, VA: CreateSpace.

de Angelis, Violetta. 1997. "I commenti medievali alla *Tebaide* di Stazio: Anselmo di Laon, Goffredo Babione, Ilario d'Orléans." In *Medieval and Renaissance Scholarship: Proceedings of the Second European Science Foundation Workshop on the Classical Tradition in the Middle Ages and the Renaissance,* edited by Nicholas Mann and Birger Munk Olsen, 75–136. Mittellateinische Studien und Texte 2. Leiden, New York, Cologne: Brill.

Baswell, Christopher. 1995. *Virgil in Medieval England: Figuring the Aeneid from the Twelfth Century to Chaucer*. Cambridge Studies in Medieval Literature 24. Cambridge: Cambridge University Press.

Benson, Robert L. and Giles Constable, eds. 1982. *Renaissance and Renewal in the Twelfth Century*. Oxford, Cambridge, MA: Harvard University Press.

Burnett, Charles, ed. 1993. *Glosses and Commentaries on Aristotelian Logical Texts: the Syriac, Arabic, and Medieval Latin Traditions*. Warburg Institute Surveys and Texts 23. London: The Warburg Institute.

Clogan, Paul M. 1968. "The Manuscripts of Lactantius Placidus' Commentary on the Thebaid (I)." *Scriptorium* 22: 87–91.

Copeland, Rita. 1991. *Rhetoric, Hermeneutics, and Translation in the Middle Ages: Academic Traditions and Vernacular Texts*. Cambridge Studies in Medieval Literature 11. Cambridge: Cambridge University Press.

Copeland, Rita and Ineke Sluiter, eds. 2009. *Medieval Grammar and Rhetoric: Language Arts and Literary Theory AD. 300–1475*. Oxford: Oxford University Press.

Coulson, Frank T. 1987. "The *Vulgate* Commentary on Ovid's *Metamorphoses*." *Mediaevalia* 13: 29–61.

Coulson, Frank T. and Krysztof Nawotka. 1993. "The Rediscovery of Arnulf of Orléans' Glosses to Ovid's Creation Myth." *Classica et Mediaevalia* 44: 267–99.

Coulson, Frank T. and Bruno Roy. 2000. *Incipitarium Ovidianum. A Finding Guide for Texts Related to the Study of Ovid in the Middle Ages and Renaissance*. Publications of the Journal of Medieval Latin 3. Turnhout: Brepols.

Demats, Paule. 1973. *Fabula. Trois études de mythographie antique et médiévale*. Publications romanes et françaises 122. Geneva: Librairie Droz.

Dorandi, Tiziano and Marie-Odile Goulet-Cazé, eds. 2000. *Le commentaire entre tradition et innovation*. Bibliothèque d'histoire de la philosophie. Nouvelle série. Paris: Vrin.

Dronke, Peter. 1974. *Fabula. Explorations into the Uses of Myth in Medieval Platonism*. Mittellateinische Studien und Texte 9. Leiden: E. J. Brill.

Edwards, Robert R. 2002. "Medieval Literary Careers: The Theban Track." In *European Literary Careers: The Author from Antiquity to the Renaissance*, edited by Patrick G. Cheney and Frederick A. De Armas, 105–28. Toronto: University of Toronto Press.

Engelbrecht, Wilken. 2008. "Fulco, Arnulf, and William: Twelfth-Century Views on Ovid in Orléans." *Journal of Medieval Latin* 18: 52–73.

van Engen, John H., ed. 2000. *Learning Institutionalized: Teaching in the Medieval University*. Notre Dame Conferences in Medievial Studies 9. Notre Dame, IN: University of Notre Dame Press.

Fera, Vincenzo, Giacomo Ferraù and Silvia Rizzo, eds. 2002. *Talking to the Text: Marginalia from Papyri to Print*. Messina: Centro Interdipartimentale di Studi Umanistici.

Fioravanti, Gianfranco, Claudio Leonardi and Stefano Perfetti, eds. 2002. *Il commento filosofico nell'occidente latino (secoli XIII-XV)*. Recontres de Philosophie Médiévale 10. Turnhout: Brepols.

Ghisalberti, Fausto. 1932. "Arnolfo d'Orléans: un cultore di Ovidio nel secolo XII." *Memorie del Reale istituto lombardo di scienze e lettere* 24: 157–234.

Gibson, Margaret T. 1979. "The Early Scholastic 'Glosule' to Priscian, 'Institutiones grammaticae': the Text and its Influence." *Studi medievali*, 3rd ser., 20: 235–54.

———. 1992. "Milestones in the Study of Priscian, circa 800–circa 1200." *Viator* 23: 17–33.

Gutas, Dimitri. 1993. "Aspects of Literary Form and Genre in Arabic Logical Works." In *Glosses and Commentaries*, edited by Ch. Burnett, 29–72. London: The Warburg Institute.

Hamesse, Jacqueline. 2002. "Les marginalia dans les textes philosophiques universitaires médiévaux." In *Talking to the Text: Marginalia from Papyri to Print*, edited by Vincenzo Fera, Giacomo Ferraù and Silvia Rizzo, 301–19. Messina: Centro Interdipartimentale di Studi Umanistici.

Häring, Nikolaus. 1982. "Commentary and Hermeneutics." In *Renaissance and Renewal in the Twelfth Century*, edited by Robert L. Benson and Giles Constable, 173–200. Cambridge, MA: Harvard University Press.

Hays, Gregory. 2002. "The Pseudo-Fulgentian *Super Thebaiden*." In *Vertis in usum: Studies in Honor of Edward Courtney*, edited by John F. Miller, Cynthia Damon and K. Sara Myers, 200–18. Beiträge zur Altertumskunde 161. Munich, Leipzig: K. G. Saur.

———. 2003. "The Date and Identity of the Mythographer Fulgentius." *The Journal of Medieval Latin* 13: 163–252.

Hexter, Ralph J. 1986. *Ovid and Medieval Schooling: Studies in Medieval School Commentaries on Ovid's Ars amatoria, Epistulae ex Ponto, and Epistulae Heroidum*. Münchener Beiträge zur Mediävistik und Renaissance-Forschung 38. Munich: Arbeo-Gesellschaft.

———. 1987. "Medieval Articulations of Ovid's *Metamorphoses*: from Lactantian Segmentation to Arnulfian Allegory." *Mediaevalia* 13: 63–82.

———. 1989. "The *Allegari* of Pierre Bersuire: Interpretation and the *Reductorium morale*." *Allegorica* 10: 51–84.

Holtz, Louis. 2000. "Le rôle des commentaires d'auteurs classiques dans l'émergence d'une mise en page associant texte et commentaire (Moyen Âge occidental)." In *Le commentaire entre tradition et innovation*, edited by Tiziano Dorandi and Marie-Odile Goulet-Cazé, 101–17. Paris: Vrin.

Hunt, Richard W. 1980a (originally published 1941–43). "Studies on Priscian in the Eleventh and Twelfth Centuries I: Petrus Helias and his Predecessors." In [Richard W. Hunt:] *The History of Grammar in the Middle Ages: Collected Papers (1941–1975)*, edited by Geoffrey L. Bursill-Hall, 1–38. Studies in the History of the Language Sciences 5. Amsterdam: John Benjamins.

———. 1980b (originally published 1948). "The Introductions to the 'Artes' in the Twelfth Century." In [R. W. Hunt:] *The History of Grammar in the Middle Ages: Collected Papers (1941–1975)*, edited by Geoffrey L. Bursill-Hall, 117–44. Studies in the History of the Language Sciences 5. Amsterdam: John Benjamins.

Hunt, Tony. 1991. *Teaching and Learning Latin in 13th-Century England*. 3 vols. Woodbridge, Suffolk: D. S. Brewer.

Jeauneau, Édouard. 1957. "L'usage de la notion d'*integumentum* à travers les gloses de Guillaume de Conches." *Archives d'histoire doctrinale et littéraire au moyen âge* 24: 35–100.

———. 2007 (originally published 1982). "Gloses et commentaires de textes philosophiques." In *"Tendenda vela." Excursions littéraires et digressions philosophiques à travers le Moyen Âge*, 285–99. Instrumenta patristica et mediaevalia 47. Turnhout: Brepols.

Jolivet, Jean. 2000, "Le commentaire philosophique arabe." In *Le commentaire entre tradition et innovation*, edited by Tiziano Dorandi and Marie-Odile Goulet-Cazé, 397–410. Paris: Vrin.

Kristeller, Paul Oskar, F. Edward Cranz, Virginia Brown, and Greti Dinkova-Bruun, eds. 1960–. *Catalogus translationum et commentariorum: Mediaeval and Renaissance Latin Translations and Commentaries. Annotated Lists and Guides*. Washington, DC: Catholic University of America Press.

Leclant, Jean and Michel Zink, eds. 2005. *La Grèce antique sous le regard du moyen âge occidental*. Paris: Académie des Inscriptions et Belles-Lettres.

Lohr, Charles H. 1967–74. "Medieval Latin Aristotle Commentaries." *Traditio* 23: 313–413; *Traditio* 24: 149–245; continued in volumes 26 (1970), 27 (1971), 28 (1972), 29 (1973), 30 (1974).

Luscombe, David E. 1997. "Commentaries on the *Politics*: Paris and Oxford, XIII-XVth Centuries." In *L'enseignement des disciplines à la Faculté des arts*, edited by Olga Weijers and Louis Holtz, 313–27. Studia artistarum 4. Turnhout: Brepols.

Mann, Nicholas and Birger Munk Olsen, eds. 1997. *Medieval and Renaissance Scholarship: Proceedings of the Second European Science Foundation Workshop on the Classical Tradition in the Middle Ages and the Renaissance*. Mittellateinische Studien und Texte 21. Leiden: E. J. Brill.

McKinley, Kathryn L. 1996. "The Medieval Commentary Tradition 1100–1500 on *Metamorphoses* 10." *Viator* 27: 117–49.

———. 2001. *Reading the Ovidian Heroine: Metamorphoses Commentaries 1100–1618*. Leiden: E. J. Brill.

Minnis, Alastair J. 1982. *Chaucer and Pagan Antiquity*. Cambridge: D. S. Brewer.

———. 1984. *Medieval Theory of Authorship: Scholastic Literary Attitudes in the Later Middle Ages*. London: Scholar Press.

Munk Olsen, Birger. 1982–2014. *L'étude des auteurs classiques latins aux XIe et XIIe siècles*. 4 vols. (1: 1982; 2: 1985; 3.1: 1987; 3.2: 1989: 4.1: 2009; 4.2: 2014). Paris: Éditions du Centre national de la recherche scientifique.

———. 2005. "La Grèce vue par l'école du XIIe siècle." In *La Grèce antique sous le regard du moyen âge occidental*, edited by Jean Leclant and Michel Zink, 39–49. Paris: Académie des Inscriptions et Belles-Lettres.

———. 2009. *L'étude des auteurs classiques latins aux XIe et XIIe siècles*. 4.1. Paris: Éditions du Centre national de la recherche scientifique.

del Punta, Francesco. 1998. "The Genre of Commentaries in the Middle Ages and its Relation to the Nature and Originality of Medieval Thought." In *Was ist Philosophie im Mittelalter?*, edited by J. A. Aertsen and A. Speer, 139–51. Miscellanea mediaevalia 26. Berlin: Walter De Gruyter.

Reynolds, Suzanne. 1996. *Medieval Reading: Grammar, Rhetoric, and the Classical Text*. Cambridge studies in medieval literature 27. Cambridge: Cambridge University Press.

Rosier-Catach, Irène. 2005. "The *Glosulae in Priscianum* and its Tradition." In *Flores Grammaticae: Essays in Memory of Vivien Law*, edited by Nicola McLelland and Andrew R. Linn, 81–99. Münster: Nodus.

Shooner, Hugues-V. 1981. "Les *Bursarii Ovidianorum* de Guillaume d'Orléans." *Mediaeval Studies* 43: 405–24.

Stock, Brian. 1971. "A Note on *Thebaid* Commentaries: Paris, B.N., lat. 3012." *Traditio* 27: 468–71.

———. 1972. *Myth and Science in the Twelfth Century: a Study of Bernard Silvester*. Princeton, NJ: Princeton University Press.

Sweeney, Robert D. 1969. *Prolegomena to an Edition of the Scholia to Statius*. Leiden: E. J. Brill.

Ward, John O. 1995. *Ciceronian Rhetoric in Treatise, Scholion, and Commentary*. Typologie des sources du Moyen Âge occidental 58. Turnhout: Brepols.

Weijers, Olga. 1996. *Le maniement du savoir: pratiques intellectuelles à l'époque des premières universités (XIIIe-XIVe siècles)*. Studia artistarum. Turnhout: Brepols.

———. 2000. "The Evolution of the Trivium in University Teaching: the Example of the Topics." In *Learning Institutionalized: teaching in the medieval university*, edited by John H. van Engen, 43–68. Notre Dame, IN: University of Notre Dame Press.

———. 2002. "La structure des commentaires philosophiques à la Faculté des Arts: quelques observations." In *Il commento filosofico nell'occidente latino*, edited by Gianfranco Fioravanti, Claudio Leonardi and Stefano Perfetti, 17–41. Rencontres de Philosophie médiévale 10. Turnhout: Brepols.

Weijers, Olga and Louis Holtz, eds. 1997. *L'enseignement des disciplines à la Faculté des arts (Paris et Oxford, XIIIe-XVe siècles)*. Studia artistarum 4. Turnhout: Brepols.

Wetherbee, Winthrop. 1972. *Platonism and Poetry in the Twelfth Century: the Literary Influence of the School of Chartres*. Princeton, NJ: Princeton University Press.

Wieland, Gernot Rudolf. 1983. *The Latin Glosses on Arator and Prudentius in Cambridge University Library MS GG.5.35*. Toronto: Pontifical Institute of Mediaeval Studies.

Woods, Marjorie C. 2009. *Classroom Commentaries: Teaching the Poetria nova across Medieval and Renaissance Europe*. Text and Context. Columbus, OH: Ohio State University Press.

Zeeman, Nicolette. 2009. "In the Schoolroom with the 'Vulgate' Commentary on *Metamorphoses* 1." *New Medieval Literatures* 11: 1–18.

Zetzel, James. E. G. 1975. "On the History of Latin Scholia." *Harvard Studies in Classical Philology* 79: 335–54.

———. 1981. "On the History of Latin Scholia II: The *Commentum Cornuti* in the Ninth Century." *Medievalia et Humanistica* 10: 19–31.

CHAPTER 10

LOCATION, LOCATION, LOCATION: GEOGRAPHY, KNOWLEDGE, AND THE CREATION OF MEDIEVAL LATIN TEXTUAL COMMUNITIES

RALPH J. HEXTER

Introduction: Access and Information

The work of paleographers and, more recently, codicologists has helped us appreciate the materiality of the books written in the Middle Ages. Literally handmade, each individual book tells a story. Few are the autographs that have come down to us. We know most texts from copies, indeed, usually copies of copies, and each instance of copying represents a fresh encounter with a text originally written at a distance, whether temporal, geographical, or both. Interlinear glosses and marginal comments, discussed by Rita Copeland (among others) in this volume, constitute traces of subsequent encounters. These interventions are so integral to the layered nature of medieval texts that medieval Latin usage assigned names to the functions involved in the production and consumption of medieval books. Rather than being divided into a simple writerly-readerly binary (Barthes 1974), the roles are arrayed along a continuum from *auctor* to *compilator, glossator* or *commentator, scriba* or *scriptor*, and *lector* (cp. Minnis 1988, 94–102; Reynolds 1996, 130–34), or in the other direction, depending on your perspective. This schema anticipates the opportunities that users—readers is too restrictive a term—of today's electronic media have to interact with textual resources: selecting, shaping, and even intervening in ways that are different from but to some degree approach the multiple modes of production and use in a manuscript culture.

The present study is inspired by the insistence of codicologists and other students of manuscript book production on the specificity of each exemplar. Without losing the keen interest in the specific, it looks beyond the covers of one book, beyond even the libraries in which the books were found—though such evidence is precious, as will appear—in search of discernible patterns of knowledge in the medieval period, knowledge which depended on the availability of texts. Whether writing is more reliable or more truthful than the spoken word is an open question, with an ancient and noble history (cp. Plato's *Phaedrus*), but writing can certainly transport information more reliably over distance. However conveyed, though, shared knowledge is part of what forms a community, and there are instances where access to texts, or lack of access to them, contributes to the formation of a community and, ultimately, the constitution of a culture.

My use of the term "geography" in the title of this essay is in the first instance literal. Where is certain knowledge available and being accessed, where not? (Availability is a precondition of being accessed but does not guarantee it.) I also intend geography in an extended sense, for my mapping is multidimensional, not merely physical but temporal and linguistic. Language competence is also requisite for access to information. Accordingly, one of the subordinate themes of this essay will be the state of knowledge of Greek in the Latin West.

It will make sense for my narrative to begin before the Middle Ages proper, since so much of what is known, or not known, was inherited (or not) from the ancient world. And while it is indeed true that much of our story of the transmission of knowledge in the Middle Ages will turn on the inaccessibility or highly localized availability of certain texts, if we go back to the ancient world, we will find a situation that again seems to anticipate our contemporary moment, when, with the worldwide web at our fingertips, we seem overwhelmed by information.

Great abundance of information only becomes "too much" when it overwhelms storage capacity. Without considering other moments of cultural culling it is appropriate to consider the sea change that occurred as the codex, no doubt gradually at first but then inexorably, replaced rolls as the preferred vehicle for Greek and Latin texts. This has been often discussed, and as I adduce it I wish only to highlight the "evolutionary" aspects of the transition, an uncanny cultural analogue to the mass species "die offs" paleontologists have identified via the fossil record. What is evolutionary are the significant changes in the "environmental niches" for the continued retransmission of inherited material. Choices had to be made about what would be copied, and texts—if I might personify them—had to compete for the allotment of finite resources of writing material and scribal time not only against other older texts but against new texts, many of which were for reasons of content considerably more relevant to now (mostly) Christian users. This obviously would impact what remained available, and how widely, for future generations, including our own.

Some texts and some authors disappeared altogether, but there were mitigating strategies. Abbreviations and epitomes were made, and anthologies and compilations of select shorter texts were created. Livy provides an instructive example. "*Ab urbe condita* was so monumentally large that it could only survive piecemeal" (Reeve in Reynolds 1983, 205). Of its original 142 books, we have only 1–10, 21–45, and a bit of 91. The separate transmission histories of these surviving decades and pentads and their various reemergences out of obscurity, now here, now there, exemplify many aspects of the localization of knowledge that constitutes the theme of this chapter. Illustrative here is that already at the beginning of the second century Florus epitomized Livy to create his history of 700 years of Roman wars (with admixtures of Sallust and Caesar). In the sixth century Florus's epitome was excerpted by Jordanes (P. K. Marshall in Reynolds 1983, 104–5). Likewise, in the third century Pompeius Trogus's forty-four book *Historiae Philippicae* were decimated (in the original Roman military sense of the term, i.e., "to something like a tenth of their original compass" [Reeve in Reynolds 1983, 197]) by M. Iunian(i)us Iustinus. This tithe is all of Trogus we possess.

Of course, the selection and incorporation—citation if one is being responsible about sourcing, certainly as current protocols require—of earlier writer's material into new works is not new. As Chaucer says in the prologue to his *Parlement of Fowles*,

> …out of olde feldes, as men seith,
> Cometh al this newe corn fro yeer to yere;
> And out of olde bokes, in good feith,
> Cometh al this newe science that men lere.
> (vv. 22–25)

Chaucer derived the analogy (as he himself tells us, v. 31) from Cicero's *Somnium Scipionis*, a portion of Cicero's *De re publica* he and the rest of the Middle Ages studied thanks to its selection by Macrobius, who made it the subject of a vastly influential commentary (Stahl in Macrobius 1966; Hüttig 1990). In premodern times it was often the case that this was the only way new readers gained access to earlier material; later, when there was a good chance that earlier works would survive along with later, consistent and honest sourcing was not only right, it was a matter of prudence. So Pliny the Elder, who wrote his *Historia naturalis* in the mid-first century CE, claims in his dedication to the emperor Titus that he read 2,000 volumes and collected 20,000 noteworthy facts from 100 authors into thirty-seven volumes. In fact, the number of authors consulted is much higher, but of them only a fraction survive, while we have the bulk of Pliny, along with—as one might have predicted—excerpts and epitomes. (Of these, the most important in the Latin Middle Ages was the *Collectanea rerum memorabilium* of Solinus, "probably of third-century date"; Reeve in Reynolds 1983, 308.)

Elsewhere in this volume Marco Formisano describes the literary qualities of compilations and epitomes as elements of a Late Antique aesthetic. Whether necessity or invention came first it may not be possible to decide, but there is no question but that there were practical aspects to the development of a taste for excerpting, fragmentation, and recombination. Here I wish to emphasize the institutional preconditions and pressures for selection and will use as a proxy for the wider topic of localized knowledge the transmission and availability of Latin texts, some "classical" by our standards, some late antique, some pagan, some Christian—not because this was the sum of important knowledge (though it is much of that sum) but because it is so well documented. At the same time, I will explicitly seek to correct for the tendency to focus more on "classical" than on patristic texts in tracing these patterns as well as highlight some common misperceptions that this tendency has only reinforced.

The collection and dissemination of information and the creation of such a complex text as Pliny's were enabled by the network of institutions, such as the book trade and schools, that the ancient elites patronized and that in turn reproduced them. (Lapidge reminds us that in the ancient and late antique world, book sellers—*librarii*—were in essence copy-on-demand operations: 2006, 22 n. 92.) These institutions appear to have been remarkably resilient for the first several centuries of the empire—at least from the distance of two millennia, for changes, subtle and not so subtle, in these networks would no doubt have struck contemporaries, and as economic supports, class structures, and even military frontiers shifted, the strains would have become ever more evident.

Let us focus on but one change that the expansion of the Christian religion effected as it became a more potent force—here an instance of the linguistic "geography" I referenced above. The learned bilingualism of the elite of Rome, who received tuition in Greek from early years and often enjoyed a "grand tour" to Athens, where they heard professors and philosophers expounding texts native to them, was a very different thing from the Greek Latin-speaking converts to Christianity heard from those who had proselytized them and in many areas constituted a significant portion of believers even in the West. What Greek meant to Cicero as he translated classical Greek philosophy, Athenian oratory, and Hellenistic poetry was vastly different from what it meant to Tertullian, say, or Ambrose, Christian writers who were quite expert in Greek in the second and fourth centuries, respectively, not to mention to the numerous individuals who took a keen interest in texts of far-from-elite status like the gospels and who would not have had access to much if any formal schooling. For them, Greek was important not for the cultural prestige its loftiest literature had long enjoyed but as the common tongue (*koine*) that transmitted "good news" and teachings they regarded as essential for living in the here-and-now and for salvation. For that reason, of course, they did not regard it as common at all but as sacred.

Meanwhile, the more learnèd Christians, especially those who were involved in the governance of the Church—and these are best known to us, for their writings have been disproportionately preserved—had a strong interest in the theological and homiletic tractates of their contemporaries in the East. The degree to which these were read in Greek as well as the degree to which they were translated into Latin—and that there were no lack of translators—bespeak the degree to which Greek language and thought were accessible, penetrating and inspiring the Latin world. All this not *despite* the Christianization of Rome but much more *because* of it.

Augustine makes an interesting "case study" in this context. In the second half of the fourth century Augustine had a privileged education in North Africa, progressing from his native Thagaste first to Madaurus, thence to Carthage, and eventually to Rome and Milan for advanced rhetorical and philosophical studies. This seems to suggest a comforting degree of continuity with what earlier provincials from comparably privileged backgrounds might have experienced. We know from his *Confessiones* that the early phases of his schooling offered him not only instruction in Roman classics—Virgil's *Aeneid*, most notably—but also Greek. The impression one gets, if one extrapolates from his comments on Greek literature in what is today the most widely read among Augustine's works, is that Greek did not stick.

Just as one can facilely observe that there was no trip to Athens for Augustine, so one can easily let Augustine's relative limitations in Greek stand as a portent of an East-West rift that will grow ever wider, both early symptom of and contributing factor to the virtually total ignorance of Greek that is supposed to have prevailed in the medieval West—a gross oversimplification importantly corrected by Berschin (1988) and discussed more extensively below.

What was always problematic about this story as far as Augustine is concerned is that he continued to champion the Septuagint as the authoritative base text for Latin biblical translations of what Christians call the "Old Testament" rather than Hebrew (and some Aramaic) originals, as Szpiech discusses elsewhere in this volume. To be sure Augustine was less fluent in Greek than some of his Western contemporaries; all the more did he press Jerome to translate patristic texts from the Greek, especially those of Origen (Berschin 1988, 51–53, esp. 54). One should not forget Augustine's own work as a translator from Greek. "Toward the end of his life, Augustine had a sufficient mastery of Greek to be moved to undertake the translation of an excerpt from Epiphanius's *Panarion*, since he held the work to be important and since no one else in the African Church could be found for the translation of the work" (Berschin 1988, 55). Whatever his "less Greek," then, it was more than the Greek of many others, enough for him also to render portions of the work of John Chrysostom.

Berschin's summary is worth quoting for its subtlety. Augustine's "activity" as a translator

> is not the most crucial in defining Augustine's importance as a mediator between Greek and Latin. It is rather a combination of three elements that already made Augustine, with his interests in Greek, a characteristic author of the Middle Ages: (1) the direct knowledge of Greek texts is restricted to only a few (although in Augustine quite significant) works; (2) otherwise he is dependent on translations; (3) even so his thought is allied to and participates in the Platonic tradition of Greek thought. (ibid.)

From Augustine to Alcuin and Alfred

Augustine responds in *De civitate Dei* as well as in several contemporary sermons to the turmoil caused even in North Africa by the Visigoths' sack of Rome in 410. But this incursion of Goths was merely temporary and did not have long-lasting effects. A hundred years later, the geopolitical landscape was utterly changed, with concomitant far-reaching alterations in the conditions for the transmission of and access to knowledge. One sees this clearly if one considers two important sixth-century Romans, Boethius and Cassiodorus, who both served the Gothic ruler of Italy, Theodoric.

One should not imagine Theodoric a barbarian for whom the ways of the Roman empire were utterly foreign, since as a young man he spent many years as a royal hostage in Constantinople at the court of, first, emperor Leo I and, subsequently, Zeno, where he held in turn the titles *magister militum* and *consul*, returning to the Ostrogoths at age 34. But for all that (and Roman rulers were hardly shy about exacting penalties), Theodoric had Boethius executed in 525, a year before his own death. Already in 523 ("almost indisputable"; O'Donnell 1979, 28) Cassiodorus succeeded Boethius as Theodoric's *magister officiorum*, and while Cassiodorus was only a few years younger than Boethius, he lived so long ("into his ninety-third year," O'Donnell 1979, 23) that he witnessed radical changes on the Italian peninsula. The sixth century in essence swept away the last vestiges of a cultural-educational complex that would have been familiar since at least the first century of the common era.

This is not to say there were not some survivals or, rather, surviving threads (cp. Riché 1976), a story in which Cassiodorus himself played a part. While the city of Rome had long since been marginal to imperial power, nostalgia and the papacy recommended Rome as a site for the "university" or at least the seat of study Cassiodorus, in concert with Pope Agapetus, sought to found in the 530s. (Although the Christian university did not come into being, it may be that an important collection of literary texts was assembled there [see O'Donnell 1979, 182].)

Cassiodorus's *Institutiones*, a work he wrote much later in life, is eloquent in conveying the tattered conditions for learning and study then prevailing. Cassiodorus wrote the *Institutiones* for the monks at the Vivarium, located on his Calabrian family estate. One of his chief concerns was the level of learning of the monks, and he intended the *Institutiones* to offer guidance on both sacred letters and the secular studies that were always to be subordinate to the sacred.

Telling are the number of times Cassiodorus refers to texts to which he no longer expected his monks to have access, and from that we can begin to take the measure of the fragmentation, and localization, of knowledge. For example, Cassiodorus had trouble finding Martianus Capella's *De nuptiis Philologiae et Mercurii*, a fairly recent book essential for the study of the liberal arts (whose importance is highlighted elsewhere in this volume in the contributions of Hicks, Formisano, and Wetherbee): "audivimus etiam Felicem Capellam aliqua de disciplinis scripsisse deflorata, ne talibus litteris fratrum simplicitas linqueretur ignara; quae tamen ad manus nostras adhuc minime pervenire potuerunt" (*Institutiones* 2.3.20; Cassiodorus 1963, 130) [We have heard that Felix Capella wrote a kind of anthology on the disciplines to enable the uneducated brothers to become acquainted with such literature. Nevertheless, up to now we have been able to acquire a small amount] (Cassiodorus 2004, 208).

This is not the only such instance. Cassiodorus has heard only rumors that Apuleius of Madaura, like Martianus an African author, had written on harmony ("fertur" [it is reported], *Institutiones* 2.5.10; Cassiodorus 1963, 149). Immediately before, in this same section on music, he writes:

> apud Latinos autem vir magnificus Albinus librum de hac re compendiosa brevitate conscripsit, quem in bibliotheca Romae nos habuisse atque studiose legisse retinemus. Qui si forte gentili incursione sublatus est, habetis Gaudentium, quem si sollicita intentione relegatis, huius scientiae vobis atria patefaciet (*Institutiones* 2.5.10; Cassiodorus 1963, 149)

> [Among the Latin writers Albinus wrote a book on this subject with summary brevity. I recall that we had this book in our library at Rome and read it eagerly. If by chance this work has been destroyed by the barbarian invasion, you have <here> Gaudentius, and if you should you read him with careful attention he will open for you the doors to this discipline] (Cassiodorus 2004, 222 [with slight modification]; cp. O'Donnell 1979, 183; Gaudentius was a Greek author whose work on harmony was translated by Mutianus [cp. *Institutiones* 2.5.1; Cassiodorus 1963, 142]).

Note that Cassiodorus appears to think that if this one exemplar has been destroyed, he would have to make use of another author. He does not say "look for another copy," for it seemed to him entirely likely that there was only one. How attenuated the threads of transmission, how near breaking the web. To have a book is not taken for granted. Concomitantly, scholarship can hardly be expected to be as systematic as it can be today. Cassiodorus writes "invenimus etiam Censorinum" [We have also come upon Censorinus] (*Institutiones* 2.5.1; Cassiodorus 1963, 143). One makes do with what one can get a hold of, what falls into one's hands.

Recopying, reducing, recombining: whatever beauties these offered the Late Antique eye, whatever opportunities for intertextuality, they were also the weapons—rearguard actions really—against the forces endangering transmission. Cassiodorus was himself a ferocious abbreviator and anthologist. He took what was already the summarizing introduction to the encyclopedic arts of Fortunatianus and abridged it. He assembled bits of Cicero and Quintilian into an anthology on rhetoric. Again in the *Institutiones* he tells us how he put together an anthology of philosophical—he calls them dialectical—texts. After listing Victorinus's translation of Porphyry's *Isagoge* and of Aristotle's *Categories*, *Perihermenias*, and Cicero's translation of Aristotle's *Topica*, he writes:

> auctoritatem vero eorum librorum in unum codicem non incompetenter fortasse collegi, ut quicquid ad dialecticam pertinent, in una congestione codicis clauderetur. expositiones itaque diversorum librorum, quoniam erant mutiplices,

sequestratim in codicibus fecimus scribi; quos in una vobis bibliotheca Domino praestante dereliqui (*Institutiones* 2.3.18; Cassiodorus 1963, 129).

[I thought it appropriate to collect these authoritative books not unsuitably into one manuscript so that whatever pertains to dialectic may be included in one codex. We have had the many commentaries on the different texts, since they are lengthy, written down in separate books and we have left them to you with the Lord's aid in one collection] (Cassiodorus 2004, 207).

What one notes in the later sixth and seventh centuries, and much of the eighth, is that there is not one cultural network but rather multiple centers arrayed around the periphery of the former western Roman Empire, and that they function for a time at least in relative isolation. On the Italian peninsula, in addition to whatever activity could be found in the Vivarium and a few other small sites, perhaps only Ravenna constituted an exception, but then Ravenna is *sui generis* in the period (as exemplified by Ieraci Bio 2003; cp. Reynolds 1983, xxx) on account of its links to Byzantium. (Constantinople is itself a special case: as the capital of the eastern empire, Latin language and knowledge persisted for some time in legal and governmental matters and court-related protocols.)

In North Africa, there was some continuation of cultural activity. These rich Roman provinces that had in earlier centuries produced Apuleius and Augustine and Martianus (whatever his precise date [cp. Hicks in this volume]) were still productive of talents, though ones hardly destined to become household names. Dracontius wrote in the late fifth century under a Vandal regime (which ultimately let him emigrate to Italy), and Corippus flourished in the sixth century under Byzantine protection.

Fifth- and sixth-century Gaul was home to a rich literary culture among a now Christian aristocracy. Among those who clearly had a significant education in Roman letters—following the better known fourth-century Claudian and Ausonius—are Rutilius Namatianus (fifth century), Sidonius Apollinaris (born c. 430), Caesarius of Arles (c. 470–542), and Avitus of Vienne (c. 470–523). In assessing the breadth as well as depth of this command of inherited culture, one can also point to the sisters and other female associates of some of these same men, whether Caesarius's sister Caesaria or the sister of bishop Hesychius of Vienne, Marcella, who wrote a poem in Sapphic meter (Stevenson 2005, 81–82). According to his recent translators, Avitus's "was perhaps the last generation for which the full pattern of education was available in Gaul, and he certainly took immense pride in the correctness of his pronunciation" (Shanzer and Wood in Avitus 2002, 7). Yet even later, the work of Venantius Fortunatus (c. 530–c. 609) bespeaks no little cultural competence; the same can be said of Fortunatus's female friend Radegund. In the seventh century, "[a]n abbess called Boba,... a German name, was exchanging Latin letters with Chrodibert, Bishop of Tours" (Stevenson 2005, 88).

Many of these latest antique/earliest medieval peripheral cultural centers were crucial for the transmission of material that would, once new networks were established, circulate more widely. Isidore of Seville (c. 560–636) is by no means the only figure we know from Visigothic Spain, but he is the most important because what he achieved, in numerous works but especially in the *Etymologiae sive Origines*, proved so vastly influential over the coming centuries. (Its place in the encyclopaedic tradition is discussed by Formisano in this volume; on his place in Visigothic Spain, see Fontaine 1983.) But while Isidore's impact spread across Europe, it was blunted on the Spanish peninsula when, in 711, Visigothic dominion there was terminated by the Muslim conquest.

There was no little traffic between Visigothic Spain and Ireland. Isidore's *Etymologiae* was known in Ireland within decades of its leaving Isidore's hands (Marshall in Reynolds 1983, 194–95); it was from Ireland that Isidore's encyclopedia made its way to England; and in Ireland a remarkably flourishing sprout of learning in both Latin and Greek took root. Irish masters—the most intriguingly named is Virgilius Maro Grammaticus—studied Latin intensively and developed highly distinctive forms and modes of expression (e.g., the *Hisperica famina*). Ireland, never part of the Roman Empire, would in the third quarter of the first millennium prove one of the most remarkable and influential repositories of classical learning.

Irish learning made its way to England and the Continent, and England was also the destination of a mission from Rome, Gregory the Great dispatching Augustine (soon "of Canterbury") in 595, and before long the school there had a very respectable library. The eighth archbishop of Canterbury (named 668) was Theodore of Tarsus, then in his late sixties, whose own pathway to the western marches of Latinity began in a Greek (and Syriac) speaking East. (On Theodore, see Lapidge 2006, 32–33; cp. also Lapidge 1986, Bischoff and Lapidge 1994, and Berschin 1988, 99–100 and 123–25). In his and Aldhelm's view, students ought to steer clear of pagan literature, and Aldhelm (d. 703) writes to Wihtfrith, one of his own pupils, a "letter [in which he]...objects fiercely to the young man's declared intention of going to study in Ireland, on the grounds that he would be studying pagan literature there" (Stevenson 2005, 70, with reference to Bischoff and Lapidge 1994 and Aldhelm 1919, 479).

It was, however, centers in the north of England, in Northumbria, at the monasteries of Wearmouth and Jarrow, and York, that the most significant "peripheral" cultural center coalesced, where Bede, Ecgbert, and above all Alcuin stand out as writers and masters. Again, rich treatments abound, and for the purposes of this essay it is enough to note that Alcuin represents an inflection point in this history, a point at which the centrifugal forces of fragmentation and peripheralization were effectively countered. Once, that is, Charlemagne summoned scholars from diverse parts of the Carolingian empire to his court: Alcuin and, eventually, the Franks Angilbert and Hrabanus Maurus, the Visigoth Theodolf (later of Orléans), and the Lombard Peter of Pisa (though he had been teaching at Pavia). This led ultimately to the development of a more standardized curriculum for those studying Latin letters, in an ever increasing number of locations on the Continent, as new monasteries and convents were founded and their libraries began to fill with texts. Certainly, if at first Anglo-Saxon scriptoria worked double time to provide books for new Continental foundations, the movement of texts and scholars soon became bidirectional. Lapidge describes "the restocking of English libraries" under Alfred, who, after becoming king in 878, "was...obliged to import scholars" (2006, 48).

Siting Books

The more scholars have discovered about individual books and their fates, the more we understand how deeply, and in how many complex ways, each book is the product of a location. Each book testifies to the state of knowledge out of which it was produced even as it becomes an element of the "geography of knowledge" for subsequent generations. For example, medieval texts were produced in scriptoria, and books traveled not only when missions were founded or monks were sent from a mother foundation to a daughter monastery but when masters in one location discovered gaps and asked brothers (and sometimes sisters) elsewhere to send exemplars to be copied. Styles of writing and master scribes traveled, too, so that what we know as "Carolingian" or "Caroline minuscule" over time replaced a variety of local hands such as the scripts of Luxeuil ("a-b") and Corbie within Merovingian France, as well as—ultimately—yet more distant insular or Beneventan local scripts. (This is a tremendously simplified version of a complex evolution, in which insular script itself and the scriptorium of Tours had important roles to play; indispensable is Ganz 1987; cp. also Bischoff 2004, 136–60 [or Bischoff 1990, 83–126]. Beneventan culture was so distant from the Carolingian "center" that as late as the tenth century a new branch, the Bari script, took shape; see Lowe 1980 and Newton 1995.)

The pre-Caroline scripts, uncial as well as minuscule, have each unique beauties beloved by teachers (and some students) of medieval palaeography. They are not just curiosities but artifacts of local, initially partially isolated cultures; as such they exemplify local traditions, embody local knowledge. Yet the variation of letter forms could cause problems for transcription, leading to the error textual critics classify as "confusion of letters" (Reynolds and Wilson 1974, 201; Lindsay 1914, 82–89). The Visigoth Theodulf would obviously have had no trouble reading the Visigothic script of Leiden, Voss. Lat. F. 111, c. 800, in which (and its first half, Paris, BN lat. 8093) he may well have read Ausonius (Reeve in Reynolds 1983, 26; see n. 3 for the possibility that Theodulf himself wrote the Paris manuscript). Yet as readers and scribes, and the texts themselves, began to circulate more widely, this very local variation proved problematic, and some errors in the transmission chain are best explained as simple transcription errors when a scribe accustomed to one script misread the exemplar written in a script with which he was less familiar. So, for example, in the case of Oxford, Bodleian Library Laud Misc. 141, copied at Lorsch from two extant exemplars, one in uncials (Bern A 91), the other in the characteristic minuscule of Luxeuil (Paris, BN lat. 9377), a transcription error arose when a scribe mistook a ligature in the Luxeuil exemplar (Ganz 1987, 28).

That the "standardization" represented by widespread adoption of Caroline minuscule reduced the chances of such "confusions of letters" in copying texts is indisputable, but one would be wrong in assuming that this was the reason for it—though, instructively, concern with readability in another context quite explicitly was. What mattered was that listeners not be hindered in their understanding of the gospel portions or other texts read aloud in churches and monasteries by readers who stumbled in pronouncing the holy words. Hence the conscious effort to add word division and punctuation as well as to offer universally recognizable letter forms, above all in evangelistaries and lectionaries (Ganz 1987).

The rationale for this change, then, is completely explicable within the value system of a Christian Carolingian empire and is not a reason that would motivate, or even likely occur to, a modern textual critic. Given the fact that so much work on the history of transmission has been done by classicists interested, not surprisingly, in the history of classical texts, it is very important to remind ourselves that, overwhelmingly, the business of writers, scribes, and readers was the furthering of the Christian faith and Roman Catholic Church. Accordingly, the greatest amount of scriptorial activity and vellum was invested in Christian texts, like that of Augustine's *De Genesi ad litteram* in which the transcription error noted above was made.

In his survey of "surviving manuscripts from the area of Anglo-Saxon mission in Germany" (2006, 77–81), Lapidge reviews 112 manuscripts and fragments. The overwhelming majority carry texts of patristic authors, and half of these are comprised by works from but four doctors of the church, Gregory, Isidore, Jerome, and Augustine (80). And while there are a few manuscripts with works used in the teaching of Latin,

> of the classical Latin literature which...was moderately well...represented by surviving Anglo-Saxon manuscripts, there is not so much as a trace from the scriptoria of the Anglo-Saxon mission in Germany....Was it that the pressures involved in establishing an incipient missionary church...imparted a tone of high seriousness to all reading and study, so that there was simply no time for the frivolities and delights of reading (say) Vergil or Lucan? The manuscript evidence would suggest so (81).

As long as we understand this context, the *relative* rarity of classical texts (in our sense of the term) *for that very reason* permits them to serve as "trace elements" to illuminate the narrowing of the transmission chain.

No student of any period of the Middle Ages can afford not to ask how something was known, or might have been known, in a given place and at a given time. Likewise, how an author was received depends very much on the texts and their presentation. To risk stating the obvious, Baudri of Bourgueil (say) did not read Ovid in a Teubner edition or Oxford Classical Text. He read his Ovid in a manuscript that was not the product of centuries of modern "scientific" textual criticism, had no *apparatus criticus*, and in addition to whatever "wayward" readings (by modern standards) that particular book exhibited, it might be lacking certain passages with which we are familiar (e.g., the *Heroides*; cp. Hexter 1986, 141–43)—obviously without any indication. Some readers would have encountered Terence in manuscripts that show by the disposition of text that his comedies were written in verse, others in manuscripts that represented Terence's plays as if they were prose (Reeve in Reynolds 1983, 417–18). And students of Terence or Ovid would have read these authors (and many others) with commentary and glosses that themselves usually varied greatly from one manuscript to another.

This is hardly a new insight. It undergirds the tradition of diplomatic editions by scholars dating from Bédier as well as the work of "new philologists," who have argued that an unthinking adoption of Lachmann's stemmatic methods of construction for many medieval textual traditions is tantamount to putting them on a procrustean bed. It is in a way the most extreme expression of the localization of knowledge: each book is a site, a *locus*. These manuscript *loci* change over time, not only gaining glosses (or having some scratched out and replaced with others), but in an extreme case, losing an entire text. The image and concept of the palimpsest is an evocative one. It is important to remember, though, when our colleagues in Classics, for example, refer in hushed tones to the fifth-century uncial codex of the first decade of Livy (siglum V), known to be at Verona by the ninth century, no one in ninth-century Verona was using it to read Livy. Of course not. V had already been "palimpsested at Luxeuil at the beginning of the eight century," its surface prepared, i.e., scraped clean, to receive Gregory the Great's *Moralia* (Reeve in Reynolds 1983, 206–7). It was, in that place and at that time, another copy of Gregory the Great, prized, in that time and place, above Livy. (However, "Palimpsesting was not limited to the pagan authors of classical antiquity," Lapidge 2006, 23–24 n. 99.)

While we have other manuscripts of Livy, our only direct witness of (parts of) Cicero's *De re publica* is the lower, uncial script of Vat. Lat. 5757. ("Direct" because the concluding portion of this work, the *Somnium Scipionis*, is transmitted along with Macrobius's commentary on the *Somnium*, as noted above.) That now precious book had made its way to Bobbio, where "in the seventh century the text of Cicero was washed off to make way for Augustine's commentary on the Psalms" (Reeve in Reynolds, 1983, 132). Until that moment, though, it was a witness to Cicero, as such underappreciated according to our standards, and of course not recognized as a text that needed preservation for the sake of scholars in some unimaginable future.

We know of a number of ancient works that were accessible to, and accessed by, at least a few readers in the late antique or even the early Middle Ages, which subsequently went missing. For example, Cassiodorus knew Seneca's *De forma mundi* (Reeve in Reynolds 1983, 358), no longer extant. Further:

> In the fifth century or later a reader of Orosius' *Historiae* was able to gloss his text with lines from the seventh book of Ennius' *Annales*. As late as the sixth century Johannes Lydus at Constantinople had more complete texts than we have of Seneca's *Natural Questions* and Suetonius' *De vita Caesarum*, in Africa Fulgentius could cite passages of Petronius which have not come down to us, and in Spain Martin of Braga could plagiarize one of Seneca's lost works. (Reynolds 1983, xv; on Seneca's *Naturales quaestiones*, see further Hine in Reynolds 1983, 376; and on Suetonius Tarrant in Reynolds 1983, 399).

The point of these examples is the extreme localization of the information available in, and represented by these books. Above I noted that material traveled from Visigothic Spain to Ireland. Visigothic Spain "was also a bridge by which the literature of North Africa could pass to northern Europe" (ibid., xviii), while other works came through Italy even in the sixth century (ibid., xix; note the subscription in manuscripts of Martianus that refer to "a recension made at Rome in 534 by the rhetor Securus Melior Felix"). The circulation of Celsus's *De medicina* seems to have been restricted to Italy (Reeve in Reynolds, 1983, 46–47). The Neronian bucolic poems known as the *Carmina Einsidlensia* "emerge" in the tenth century "in a unique copy at Fulda," Einsiedeln 266, from which they take their name (Reynolds 1983, xxxi). Caelius Aurelianus's fifth-century versions of works by the Greek methodist physician Soranus of Ephesus were available locally at the German monastery Lorsch in the ninth century (Reynolds and Rouse in Reynolds 1983, 33–34).

Monasteries with active scriptoria and growing libraries constituted the transmission nodes of texts, in these and other cases texts unknown elsewhere in medieval Europe. Fulda, further east than the imperial abbey Lorsch, seems to have been a center for the study of Cicero's oratorical treatises by some key Carolingian literati (e.g., Einhard, Hrabanus Maurus, Lupus of Ferrières), and we can in this case trace how Lupus of Ferrières wrote Einhard asking him to send him a copy of *De oratore* (Winterbottom, Rouse, and Reeve in Reynolds 1983, 104). In the mid-twelfth century, at Corvey, yet further north, Wibald assembles a manuscript that contains a great deal of the then extant Cicero, a great monument of learning. Yet it "sat on its shelf in Corvey, never copied so far as we can tell . . ." (Rouse and Reeve in Reynolds 1983, 93).

As in the case of Cicero's *De oratore*, texts traveled between monasteries, sometimes at great distances, to be shared, copied, and returned. In the late eighth and early ninth century Tiberius Claudius Donatus's *Interpretationes Vergilianae* were known in Luxeuil, Tours, and Bobbio. "The commentary is cited by name by Paul the Deacon in the *Historia Langobardorum*, written at Montecassino in the late eighth century. Given the contact between Bobbio and the two other houses, Montecassino and Luxeuil, perhaps the others were relatives, if not descendants, of the Bobbio codex" (Rouse in Reynolds 1983, 157). Between the ninth and eleventh centuries, Aelius Donatus's commentary on Terence seems to have been most readily accessible in and around Corvey, Reims, and Orléans (Reeve in Reynolds 1983, 154). On Orléans, more below. First, however, Greek.

The Case of Greek

I have discussed, both in this volume and elsewhere (Hexter 2005), the fact that the landscape of Latin authors looked different to our Latin-reading forebears in the Middle Ages than it does to us. No student today learns Latin literature without reading some Catullus, but his songs of love for Lesbia and Juventius were virtually unknown and unavailable to most Latin readers in the medieval period. The texts were, of course, theoretically accessible, and tantalizing echoes here and there resound. Not only is what we know as poem 62 found in the ninth-century French *Florilegium Thuaneum* (Tarrant in Reynolds 1983 45), but the fuller manuscript of Catullus that would "c[o]me to light shortly after 1300" (Tarrant in Reynolds 1983, 43) was apparently at Verona—near Catullus's original *patria*—several hundred years prior to its discovery. We know that Rather of Verona read Catullus there, whether in that manuscript or another, in 966.

Writers who were widely read over many centuries, like Terence, Vergil, Horace, Ovid, Lucan, and Statius among the poets (not to mention the Christian poets like Prudentius, Proba, Juvencus, et al., and the even greater number of prose authors), are extant in so many manuscripts that it is hard to say that they were unknown at any time, although there are variations, whether it is that Horace's *Carmina* are less widely known than his *Epistulae* and *Sermones*, or that Ovid's *Ibis* only began to be read in the twelfth century. (See Reynolds 1983, xxxv; Propertius and Seneca's *Quaestiones naturales* also come onto the scene in the twelfth century; for more detail on the former, see Tarrant in Reynolds 1983, 324.)

Lucretius makes an interesting case, since his Epicureanism and atomism were fundamentally incompatible with Christian doctrine. This notwithstanding,

> It would seem that Lucretius emerged towards the end of the eighth century, that the archetype of our manuscripts found its home in the Carolingian court, and that the text was disseminated from there, radiating westwards into the Low Countries and northern France and southwards along the Rhine. Excerpts show that the text was read and used, and it seems to have been well established in the area of Lake Constance. (Reynolds in Reynolds 1983, 220)

Consistent with this picture is the use of Lucretius documentable in the ninth century at Reichenau and St. Gall. We then lose sight of him and lack evidence that anyone read *De rerum natura* for centuries. All we know is that a copy of Lucretius (siglum "Q") came to the abbey of Lobbes (in what is now Belgium)

> probably in the early twelfth century, and he is listed in the twelfth-century catalogue of Corbie. The presence of Q at Saint-Bertin may well explain the echoes of Lucretius in the *Encomium Emmae* and the Lucretian gloss in Sigebert of Gembloux (c. 1030–1112) fits with the availability of his poem in the closely connected abbey of Lobbes. (ibid., 220–21)

Just as an exclusive focus on the fate of the modern classical canon can present a highly partial and misleading picture of the Latin textual universe in the Middle Ages, so classicists' unexamined expectations have contributed to the persistent underestimation of the knowledge of Greek in the West throughout the Middle Ages, a topic to which I have alluded above and that here deserves special, if necessarily brief, attention. Of course no one was reading the original Homer or the Attic dramatists, but as Walther Berschin succinctly put it, "[f]or the Latin Middle Ages, it was not Homer but Dionysius who was the 'seer' for whose sake it was thought worthwhile to undertake the study of Greek" (1988, 45).

Many Greek texts were important for intellectuals in the West over the centuries: the philosophers Plato and Aristotle, each with distinct accessibility patterns;

technical (e.g., medical) treatises; and of course the Bible, patristic texts, and other Christian tracts. But it would be hard to exaggerate the importance of (ps-)Dionysius the Areopagite, an author whose works rarely if ever appear on a Greek student's basic reading list today. The story of his arrival in the Latin West—truly *lux e oriente*, a transplant almost as exotic and maddening as the god Dionysus who once came to Thebes—is another example of the impact of a specific book that begins its western journey at a very precise moment:

> The decisive intellectual event of ninth-century Greco-Latin relations was set in motion by the Greek ambassadors of 827, who, while in Compiègne, presented Louis the Pious with the gift of Emperor Michael II: the four theological treatises and ten letters of Dionysius the Areopagite. The reception of the works of the Corpus Dionysiacum—as "a kind of sacred relic of Greek studies extending throughout the Middle Ages"—begins with this uncial codex presented at that time and preserved up to the present. Through Dionysius' works the apophatic element of Eastern thought, the consciousness of the unknowability of God, was opened up to the West. (Berschin 1988, 117, quoting Rädle 1984, 4)

This is not the place even to summarize the immense complex of translations of and commentaries on the pseudo-Dionysius, a Christian Neoplatonist who wrote in the late fifth or early sixth century, called "the Areopagite" because he was taken to be the Athenian whom Paul's preaching on the Areopagus (Acts 17:34) swayed. Over centuries it was to understand these difficult texts with such reputed antiquity and authority that scholars such as John Scottus Eriugena (discussed by Burman, above), Anastasius Bibliothecarius, and John Sarracenus mustered quite respectable and sometimes impressive knowledge of Greek.

The milieux in which these and other individuals gained their knowledge of Greek exemplify the linkage of knowledge and location, whether the site be Constantinople, Antioch, Sicily, Rome or the entire southern half of the Italian peninsula, where Greek monastic communities remained established. (One could tell shorter and more intermittent versions of this story, *mutatis mutandis*, about knowledge of Hebrew and Arabic among Western European Christians; cp. Szpiech and Burman in this volume.)

The presence of Greek-speakers and abundant Greek texts together make learning Greek easier, although no number of native speakers would have made understanding Dionysius simple. Ekkehard IV tells a story in the *Casus S. Galli* (eleventh century) about a young monk who sought out Hadwig so she could teach him Greek, a language she had purportedly learned from a eunuch (presumably from the Byzantine court, for Hadwig was affianced to Prince Constantine of Byzantium)—a pious eunuch, for Hadwig could translate Latin hymns into Greek (Stevenson 2005, 171; Berschin 1988, 18; Farrell 2001, 79–81). Yet it was not only in areas with Greek-speakers that Greek could be, and was learned. Bede, in Northumbria, seems to have learned Greek by studying bilingual manuscripts. Bede, Berschin claims, "was probably also the first to have approached the Greek language in what became the typical medieval manner—through the study of bilinguals," and we know of one such manuscript he used, a bilingual text of Acts ("Codex

Laudianus," "probably written in Sardinia c. 600," another interesting contact zone) in preparing his own commentary (Berschin 1988, 101 and 104–5).

Textual Communities

Ekkehard's anecdote about the young monk and Hadwig represents but one instance of a student traveling to a source of specialized knowledge. Students flocked to Bologna and Pavia to study law, or to Salerno and Toledo to study medicine, the preeminence of the latter two cities in that field directly related to their being loci for the transmission of Arabic learning (Berschin 1988, 213; at Salerno both Greek and Arabic learning were available). Even as Plato's star gradually faded in the new light of Aristotelianism, Chartres became the center for advanced and creative Platonism. (See Wetherbee in this volume.) Likewise, Orléans became renowned for its faithful championing of the liberal arts, especially study of the Roman poets, even as the universities seemed to be reducing the *artes* to mere prolegomenal status.

Orléans has long been recognized as a center of commentary attention on the works of Ovid, through at least three generations of masters: Fulco, Arnulf, and William (Engelbrecht 2008). This attention to ancient and non-Christian works is reflected in the unusually broad range of texts we can associate with Orléans, an interest that did not just spring forth in the eleventh and twelfth centuries. Consider, for example, Vat. Lat. 4929, a ninth-century manuscript of a sixth-century Ravenna collection including Censorinus, pseudo-Plautus (*Querolus*), Julius Paris's epitome of Valerius Maximus, and two important geographical works, Pomponius Mela's *De situ orbis* (also known as *De chorographia*), and Vibius Sequester's *De fluminibus*. What connection the manuscript might have had with the Irish Virgil, Bishop of Salzburg—at times speculated to be Aethicus Ister—is uncertain, but the sixth-century collection seems to have passed through the hands of Lupus of Ferrières and his student Heiric of Auxerre, who owned the ninth-century manuscript and annotated it (Rouse in Reynolds 1983, 290). The manuscript was in Orléans "[b]y the tenth century," where its text of *De situ orbis* "acquired extensive annotations in the early twelfth century" (291). We know that this copy is linked to the annotator of Berne 276, "who worked at and around Orléans in [the third quarter of the thirteenth century]" and who "cites Petronius at least eight times" (298). Both these first-century Roman authors were exceedingly rare. (On the annotator, see Rouse 1979; on Petronius in thirteenth-century England, see Colker 2007.) The survival of this one manuscript opens a window on the networks of usage and knowledge that ramified ten-thousand fold across Europe and at times beyond.

The reading and scholarly interests of the annotator of Berne 276 were remarkable for his time but perhaps not so uncommon at Orléans. He "reproduces in the margins of that manuscript two lines of Tibullus which were not available in the *Florilegium Gallicum* and which, hence, appear to represent a knowledge of the whole text" (Rouse and Reeve in Reynolds, 1983, 422). This and other evidence points to the presence and knowledge of Tibullus, one of Ovid's elegiac predecessors, in the Loire valley in and around Orléans.

One might well describe Orléans as a "textual community" and set it alongside other textual communities or transmissional niches, each with its own particular sets of resources and interests. Textual communities can also be extended by visitors who pass through or students who move on to other regions. The individual religious orders might themselves be considered textual communities, although their territories were discontinuous and their borders highly porous. Among the Augustinians, the Victorines, centered at the Abbey of St. Victor in Paris, comprised a particularly productive and distinctive textual community. Their founder was William of Champeaux (c. 1070—1121), but best known are Hugh, Richard, and Walter of St. Victor, active in the twelfth century. A fitting summary exceeds the bounds of this study, and the work of Victorine philosophers and commentators with mystical tendencies is well known, especially via the texts of Hugh of St. Victor. I wish here to instance the later Thomas Gallus (d. 1246) to serve as an example of how a textual community could extend its bounds far beyond the walls of one abbey. Even after Thomas left the Abbey of St. Victor in Paris for an Augustinian abbey in Vercelli (roughly midway between Turin and Milan in northern Italy), his commentaries on pseudo-Dionysius reveal a Neoplatonist whose thought (and vocabulary) is deeply rooted in that of Hugh and Richard (Lawell 2009, 175–78). "...Gallus lived and breathed the intellectual and verbal air of the Victorine school" and "clearly saw himself as continuing in the tradition of the Parisian Canons even if he was working from the north of Italy" (178, 179). His influence can be traced on later writers including Bonaventure, so that one might make the claim that commentators on the works of pseudo-Dionysius, or authors who are steeped in the Dionysiac world, themselves constituted textual communities of a different sort.

Montecassino shall serve as my last example, a uniquely important abbey ever since Benedict established himself and his monks there c. 529. Lying inland southeast of Rome and northeast of Naples, over the years it became home to a rich collection of texts and the source for copies, its scriptorium until well into the eleventh century one of the two key centers of the distinctive and beautiful Beneventan script (on which, see above). Again, Montecassino, its library and scriptorium, are richly documented (i.a., Newton 1999). Here I offer only a few glimpses of some of the least common texts it sheltered and helped bring into view. Among the "hitherto totally unknown texts" copied there in the eleventh century "are Apuleius (*Apologia, Metamorphoses, Florida*), Seneca (*Dialogues*), Tacitus (*Annals* 11–16, *Histories*), Varro (*De lingua Latina*) . . ." (Reynolds 1983, xxxiii). There must also have been a manuscript containing Tibullus there, for as Rouse and Reeve note, "There is only one body of medieval extracts from Tibullus that cannot be clearly explained in terms of the court library or Orléans: these appear in the florilegium (now Venice, Marc.

Lat. Z. 497 (1811)) compiled at Montecassino in the eleventh century by Lawrence of Amalfi, tutor of the future pope Gregory VII" (in Reynolds, 1983, 423).

Even more significant may be the emergence, as noted above, of Seneca's *Dialogi*, of which there is no trace between the sixth century, "when Martin, Bishop of Braga, quarried his own *De ira* from Seneca's treatise, and its emergence at Montecassino in the late eleventh century" (Reynolds in Reynolds, 1983, 367). We know from the "long list of texts copied on the instruction of Abbot Desiderius (1058–87)" preserved in the Montecassino Chronicle that in his own time "the *Dialogues*, which had lurked unknown since the sixth century, were used at this time by Guaiferius of Salerno, a local poet and hagiographer, who became a monk at Montecassino" (366).

Montecassino, with its unusually rich store of texts, plays a key role in a concluding narrative in which the very localization of knowledge is deployed as a secret weapon in a larger struggle. The story unfolds at the end of the ninth and beginning of the tenth century. Not for the last time would there be difficulties in papal succession. The hero of our story, Eugenius Vulgarius, was a staunch supporter of Pope Formosus. (I base my account on Pittaluga 1995.) Now Pope Formosus had had a very difficult career during the tumultuous closing years of the ninth century. Born c. 816, he was pope from 891 until his death in 896. One might assume that death would mark the end of his travails, but that was not the case. Formosus was succeeded by Boniface VI, but in 897, when Boniface had already been succeeded by Pope Stephen VI, Formosus's corpse was disinterred and put on trial. In what is called the "Cadaver Synod," Formosus was found to have been unworthy of the papacy and his memory damned.

Things were even more perilous for the living, and Stephen's papal reign was not much longer than Boniface's. Sergius III was made pope in 897 but was soon driven from Rome. After the rule of an "antipope," Christopher, Sergius's supporters used military force to reinstall him as of 904 to the See of Peter, which he then occupied until 911. Now some of the stories told about Sergius, and about his treatment of Formosus's corpse, lack credibility, but it is clear that he was always a bitter opponent of Formosus and those who supported him. It was during the second phase of his papacy that he received a deferential letter from Eugenius. The deference will have constituted a surprise, since Eugenius had hitherto been an unwavering member of the party of Formosus. (The fundamental monograph on Eugenius Vulgarius remains Dümmler 1866; for the letter, see Eugenius Vulgarius 1889, 416–18.)

In this letter Eugenius makes his peace with Sergius, or so it seems. In fact, his praise of Sergius is undercut by allusions to Seneca's tragedies that he had recently read in Teano, a town about 50 km south of Montecassino. How Eugenius Vulgarius came to Teano is a story in itself (Pittaluga 1995, 49–50). Seneca came to meet him, as it were, for monks from the abbey had taken refuge in Teano some years earlier in the face of marauding Muslims. Pittaluga posits that it was there that Eugenius would have read a manuscript of Seneca's tragedies the monks will have brought with them (ibid.)

> Nella lunga lettera indirizzata a Sergio III, ad esempio, questi motivi—il fato, il potere, la disperazione, la corruzione, la pace, la sicurezza, la vecchiaia—sono sviluppati sul filo di un susseguirsi fitto di citazioni desunte da tutte le tragedie di Seneca (peraltro mai indicate esplicitamente come fonte), che sollecitano il lettore a un continuo confronto con il modello. Ma quale lettore? Non certo Sergio III, il quale, se avesse conosciuto le tragedie, non avrebbe trovato opportuna una sua implicita identificazione con Bacco o con Fedra; si sarebbe vanificato l'apparento scopo panegiristico.
>
> [In the long letter addressed to Sergius III, for example, these themes—fate, power, desperation, corruption, peace, security, old age—are developed on a web of successive quotations drawn from all the tragedies of Seneca (even if these are never explicitly indicated as the source), that compel the reader to a continuous confrontation with the model. But which reader? Certainly not Sergius III, who, if he had known the tragedies, would not have found flattering an implicit identification with Bacchus or Phaedra—thus negating the letter's apparent panegyric aim.] (Pittaluga 1995, 50–51)

Eugenius could count on the fact that neither Sergius nor anyone else in the curia would know Seneca's tragedies. To cite Pittaluga again,

> In realtà il secondo fine cui mirava l'operazione di Eugenio si fondava proprio sulla ragionevole certezza dell'ignoranza di Seneca tragico da parte di Sergio. Ma, irriducibile formosiano, Eugenio doveva sapere che altri lettori di parte formosiana, o comunque avversari (occulti o palesi) di Sergio, certo non molti, cui le tragedie di Seneca potevano essere note—esponenti della cultura meridionale del tempo, colleghi maestri di grammatica, monaci cassinesi—non solo avrebbero identificato il papa con Bacco, con Fedro o con l'usurpatore Lico, ma possedendone la chiave di lettura, conoscendo il contesto dal quale derivano le citazioni, avrebbero anche scoperto, sotto la superficie dell'encomio e dell'apologia, la forte carica polemica dei suoi scritti.
>
> [In reality, the hidden aim of Eugenius's modus operandi is based precisely on the reasonable certainty that Sergius was ignorant of Seneca's tragedies. But, unrepentant partisan of Formosus, Eugenius must have known that other readers who were of the party of Formosus, or in some way enemies (whether hidden or declared) of Sergius, however few, to whom the tragedies of Seneca might have been known—representatives of the contemporary culture of the south, fellow teachers of Latin, monks of Montecassino—would not only have identified the pope with Bacchus, Phaedra or the usurper Lichas, but, in possession of the literary "key" and understanding the context from which the quotations derived, would also have discovered, beneath the encomiastic and apologetic surface, the strongly polemical nature of his writings.] (51)

If this is so—and I find Pittaluga's argument compelling—not only will Eugenius in the tenth century have anticipated the reception of Seneca's tragedies nearly 400 years later by the so-called Paduan prehumanists Lovato Lovati and Albertino Mussato, in particular the latter's revivification of Senecan tragedy in his Latin play *Ecerinis* (1311–15; Mussato 1975 and 2000). The ostensible subject of *Ecerinis* was Ezzelino III da Romano, but it was understood as an attack on the contemporary

Cangrande della Scala of Verona, then just threatening, but soon to take over Padua. Mussato carries Seneca on his shield's emblem, so to speak. Eugenius is more crafty, deploying his exclusive access to a text he knows is only available locally in the service of resistance and polemics that can only be appreciated by his nearest compatriots. It serves, then, as an exquisite example of the marginalized and the abject exploiting the very limits of knowledge available to the hegemonic center.

SUGGESTIONS FOR FURTHER READING

Foundational for tracing the manuscript traditions of Latin classical authors is Reynolds (1983); more broadly, with reference to the transmission of Greek classics, is Reynolds and Wilson (1974). Specifically for the medieval manuscripts in which the Latin classics are contained, see Munk Olsen (1982–2014). The broader accounts of the reception of each Latin classical author in Cancik et al. (2010) extend temporally beyond the medieval period but are up-to-date and authoritative. Extensive accounts of the medieval reception of many authors, with a focus on the relevant medieval commentary traditions, appear in the continuing series Kristeller et al. 1960–.

For the study of Greek in the West, Berschin (1988) is at once revisionary and foundational. For an illuminating and provocative study of the status of languages—Latin, Greek, and Arabic—in high medieval Sicily, see Mallette (2005). For an account of the contents of Anglo-Saxon libraries—a model of historical reconstruction—see Lapidge (2006). On the scriptorium and library collections of Montecassino, richly documented as a transmission vector, one may begin with Newton (1999).

For the "new philology" and the debates that ensued around it, carried out largely—but not exclusively—with reference to vernacular texts, see Cerquiglini (1989), Nichols (1990), and Busby (1993).

BIBLIOGRAPHY

Primary sources

Aldhelm. 1919. *Aldhelmi Opera*, edited by Rudolf Ewald. Monumenta Germaniae Historica. Scriptores 15. Berlin: Weidmann.
Avitus of Vienne. 2002. *Letters and Selected Prose*, translated by Danuta Shanzer and Ian Wood. Translated Texts for Historians 38. Liverpool: Liverpool University Press.
Cassiodorus. 1963. *Cassiodori Senatoris Institutiones*, edited by Roger A. B. Mynors. Oxford: Clarendon Press.
Cassiodorus. 2004. *Institutions of Divine and Secular Learning and On the Soul*, translated by James W. Halporn with an introduction by Mark Vessey. Translated Texts for Historians. Liverpool: Liverpool University Press.

Eugenius Vulgarius. 1889. "Eugenii Vulgarii sylloga cum appendice." In *Poetae latini aevi Carolini*, edited by Paul von Winterfeld, 406–44. Monumenta Germaniae Historica. Poeta latini aevi Carolini 4.1. Berlin: Weidmann.

Florilegium Gallicum. 1975. *Florilegium Gallicum: Prolegomena und Edition der Exzerpte von Petron bis Cicero, De oratore*, edited by Johannes Hamacher. Lateinische Sprache und Literatur des Mittelalters 5. Bern, Frankfurt/Main: Peter Lang.

Macrobius, Ambrosius Aurelius Theodosius. 1966. *Commentary on the Dream of Scipio*, translated by William Harris Stahl. Records of Civilization, Sources and Studies 48. New York: Columbia University Press.

Mussato, Albertino. 1975. *Albertino Mussato: Ecerinis. Antonio Loschi: Achilles*, edited by Luigi Padrin and Almerico da Schio, translated by Joseph R. Berrigan. Humanistische Bibliothek, Reihe 2: Texte, 17. Munich: W. Fink.

———. 2000. *Ecerinide, Tragedia*, edited by Luigi Padrin. Bologna: N. Zanichelli.

Secondary sources

Barthes, Roland. 1974. *S/Z*, translated by Richard Miller. New York: Hill and Wang.

Busby, Keith. 1993. *Towards a synthesis?: essays on the new philology*. Faux titre 68. Amsterdam, Atlanta, GA: Rodopi.

Berschin, Walter. 1988. *Greek Letters and the Latin Middle Ages. From Jerome to Nicholas of Cusa*, translated by Jerold C. Frakes. Rev. and expanded ed. Washington, DC: The Catholic University of America Press.

Bischoff, Bernhard. 1990. *Latin Palaeography. Antiquity and the Middle Ages*, translated by Dáibhí Ó Cróinín and David Ganz. Cambridge: Cambridge University Press.

———. 2004. *Paläographie des römischen Altertums und des abendländischen Mittelalters*. 3rd ed. Grundlagen der Germanistik 24. Berlin: E. Schmidt.

Bischoff, Bernard and Michael Lapidge, eds. 1994. *Biblical Commentaries from the Canterbury School of Theodore and Hadrian*. Cambridge Studies in Anglo-Saxon England. Cambridge: Cambridge University Press.

Cancik, Hubert, Manfred Landfester, and Helmuth Schneider, eds. 2010. *Rezeption der antiken Literatur: Kulturhistorisches Werklexikon*. Der Neue Pauly. Supplemente 7. Stuttgart: J. B. Metzler.

Cerquiglini, Bernard. 1989. *Éloge de la variante: histoire critique de la philology*. Paris: Seuil.

Chin, Catharine. 2008. *Grammar and Christianity in the Late Roman World*. Divinations. Philadelphia: University of Pennsylvania Press.

Colker, Marvin, ed. 2007. *Petronius rediuiuus et Helias Tripolanensi: id est Petronius rediuiuus quod Heliae Tripolanensis videtur necnon fragmenta (alia) Heliae Tripolanensis*. Mittellateinische Studien und Texte 35. Leiden, Boston: Brill.

Dümmler, Ernst. 1866. *Auxilius und Vulgarius. Quellen und Forschungen zur Geschichte des Papstthums im Anfang des zehnten Jahrhunderts*. Leipzig: Hirzel.

Engelbrecht, Wilken. 2008. "Fulco, Arnulf, and William: Twelfth-Century Views on Ovid in Orléans." *The Journal of Medieval Latin* 18: 52–73.

Fontaine, Jacques. 1983. *Isidore de Séville et la culture classique dans l'Espagne wisigothique*. 2 vols. 2nd ed. Paris: Études Augustiniennes.

Ganz, David. 1987. "The Preconditions for Caroline Minuscule." *Viator* 18: 23–44.

Hexter, Ralph J. 1986. *Ovid and Medieval Schooling. Studies in Medieval School Commentaries on Ovid's Ars Amatoria, Epistulae ex Ponto and Epistulae Heroidum*. Münchener Beiträge zur Mediävistik und Renaissance-Forschung 38. Munich: Arbeo-Gesellschaft.

———. 2005. "From the medieval historiography of Latin literature to the historiography of medieval Latin literature." *Journal of Medieval Latin* 15: 1–24.

Hüttig, Albrecht. 1990. *Macrobius im Mittelalter: ein Beitrag zur Rezeptionsgeschichte der Commentarii in Somnium Scipionis*. Freiburger Beiträge zur mittelalterlichen Geschichte 2. Frankfurt/Main, New York: Peter Lang.

Ieraci Bio, Anna Maria. 2003. "Fonti alessandrine del *De natura hominis* de Melezio." *Quaderni medievali* 55: 25–44.

Kristeller, Paul Oskar, F. Edward Cranz, and Virginia Brown, eds. 1960–. *Catalogus translationum et commentariorum: Mediaeval and Renaissance Latin translations and commentaries; annotated lists and guides*. Washington, DC: Catholic University of America Press.

Lapidge, Michael. 1986. "The School of Theodore and Hadrian." *Anglo-Saxon England* 15: 45–72. (Reprinted in Michael Lapidge, *Anglo-Latin Literature, 600–899*. London: Hambledon Press, 1996, 141–68.)

———. 2006. *The Anglo-Saxon Library*. Oxford: Oxford University Press.

Lawell, Declan. 2009. "*Ne de ineffabili penitus taceamus*: Aspects of the Specialized Vocabulary of the Writings of Thomas Gallus." *Viator* 40: 151–84.

Lindsay, Wallace M. 1896. *An Introduction to Latin Textual Emendation, Based on the Text of Plautus*. London: Macmillan and Co.

Loew, Elias A. 1980. *The Beneventan Script. A History of the South Italian Minuscules*. 2nd ed., prepared and enlarged by Virginia Brown. Sussidi eruditi 33–34. Rome: Edizioni di Storia e Letteratura.

Mallette, Karla. 2005. *The Kingdom of Sicily, 1100–1250. A Literary History*. Middle Ages Series. Philadelphia: University of Pennsylvania Press.

Minnis, Alastair J. 1988. *Medieval Theory of Authorship: Scholastic Literary Attitudes in the Later Middle Ages*. 2nd ed. London: Aldershot.s

Munk Olsen, Birger. 1982–2014. *L'Étude des auteurs classiques latins aux XIe et XIIe siècles*. 4 vols. (1: 1982; 2: 1985; 3.1: 1987; 3.2: 1989; 4.1: 2009; 4.2: 2014). Paris: Editions du Centre national de la recherche scientifique.

Newton, Francis. 1999. *The Scriptorium and Library at Monte Cassino, 1058–1105*. Cambridge Studies in Palaeography and Codicology 7. Cambridge: Cambridge University Press.

Nichols, Stephen G., ed. 1990. *The New Philology. Special Issue of Speculum. Speculum* 65: 1–108.

O'Donnell, James J. 1979. *Cassiodorus*. Berkeley, CA: University of California Press. [N.b.: author offers text with updates at http://www9.georgetown.edu/faculty/jod/texts/cassbook/toc.html].

Pittaluga, Stefano. 1995. "Memoria Letteraria di Seneca Tragico." In *Mediaeval Antiquity*, edited by Andries Welkenhuysen, Herman Braet, and Werner Verbeke, 45–58. Mediaevalia Lovaniensia 74. Louvain: Louvain University Press.

Rädle, Fidel. 1984. "[review:] Walter Berschin, Griechisch-Lateinisches Mittelalter." *Anzeiger für deutsches Altertum und deutsche Literatur* 95: 1–6.

Rouse, Richard H. 1979. "Florilegia and Latin Classical Authors in Twelfth- and Thirteenth-Century Orléans." *Viator* 10: 131–60.

Reynolds, Leighton D., ed. 1983. *Texts and Transmission. A Survey of the Latin Classics*. Oxford: Clarendon Press.

Reynolds, Leighton D. and Nigel G. Wilson. 1974. *Scribes and Scholars. A Guide to the Transmission of Greek and Latin Literature*. 2nd ed. Oxford. Clarendon Press.

Reynolds, Suzanne. 1996. *Medieval Reading: Grammar, Rhetoric, and the Classical Text*. Cambridge Studies in Medieval Literature 27. Cambridge: Cambridge University Press.

Riché, Pierre. 1976. *Education and Culture in the Barbarian West, sixth through eighth centuries*, translated by John J. Contreni. Columbia, SC: University of South Carolina Press.

Rigg, Arthur G. 1996. "Anthologies and Florilegia." In *Medieval Latin. An Introduction and Bibliographical Guide*, edited by Frank A. C. Mantello and Arthur G. Rigg, 708–12. Washington, DC: The Catholic University of America Press.

Stevenson, Jane. 2005. *Women Latin Poets. Language, Gender, and Authority from Antiquity to the Eighteenth Century*. Oxford: Oxford University Press.

PART IV
STYLES AND GENRE

CHAPTER 11

PROSE STYLE

GREGORY HAYS

The French novelist Raymond Queneau's best-known work, *Exercices de style*, consists of ninety-nine different versions of the same pointless anecdote. Each version of the story is composed in a different style or foregrounds a different grammatical feature or rhetorical device: *Litotes, Anagrammes, Passé simple, Hellénismes, Macaronique, Médical, Précieux*... Taken as a whole, the work playfully subverts notions dear to modern aesthetics: style as the expression of a unique authorial voice (*le style c'est l'homme même*), or as inseparable from the content it expresses. Queneau's variations imply a more arbitrary relationship: style as a set of hats that an author can don or doff at will, a garment that clothes content but is not inseparable from it. (Compare Norden 1909, 1: 12: "Der Stil war im Altertum nicht der Mensch selbst, sondern ein Gewand, das er nach Belieben wechseln konnte" [In antiquity style was not *l'homme même* but a costume that he could change at will].)

Queneau's little book is not without relevance to the topic of this chapter. In analyzing medieval Latin prose we should think not in terms of a monolithic "medieval" style, but rather of a wide *range* of styles and stylistic devices, which an author may employ or discard from work to work, or even within a single work. The choice of a style may be influenced by content, but is not dictated by it. Above all, the use of a given stylistic feature is meaningful only within a system of conventional expectations that links author and audience. It is this shared sense of stylistic propriety that makes Queneau's variations amusing. We do not normally use Alexandrines to recount an altercation on a public bus, any more than we would wear a tuxedo to a baseball game.

The Shaping of Style

How did a medieval Latin prose writer develop a style? Not, for the most part, from handbooks or manuals. Late antique grammarians identified rhetorical figures and laid down rules on spelling and usage, but their focus was on verse rather than prose. Ancient rhetorical manuals (the *Rhetorica ad Herennium*, Cicero's *De inventione*, and Quintilian's *Institutio oratoria*) continued to be copied and read, but they taught one how to construct a speech, not a chronicle or a saint's life. Augustine's *De doctrina Christiana* adapted ancient rhetorical theory to Christian ends. It was widely read, but it is not clear how much it actually influenced writers. Medieval handbooks of prose composition are late and limited to particular genres. Epistolary theory is covered by the tradition of the *ars dictaminis*, the earliest examples of which date from the twelfth century (Rockinger 1863; Camargo 1991). For the thirteenth century some insight can be gained from texts like John of Garland's *Parisiana poetria* or the *Ars versificatoria* of Matthew of Vendôme, though these are primarily oriented toward verse (Kelly 1991). Other manuals instructed late medieval preachers in sermon composition (Charland 1938; Briscoe 1992). For the most part, however, medieval writers learned by reading and imitating what they read.

It is traditional and tempting to see medieval prose style, like the medieval period itself, as defined by the two poles of "classical" and "Christian." These are not irrelevant terms, but each is more complicated than may at first appear. In evaluating "classical" aspects we should keep in mind that the classical canon of the Middle Ages differed in many ways from our own. Cicero and Sallust, cornerstones of the imperial curriculum, remained key authors in the medieval period. Caesar's *Bellum Gallicum* was known (though not as a school text), as were many of the works of the younger Seneca. Livy was less popular than Valerius Maximus's collection of historical exempla or Justin's epitome of Pompeius Trogus. Authors and texts we now think of as important (e.g., Tacitus, Apuleius's *Metamorphoses*, Cicero's letters to Atticus) were virtually unknown. By contrast, some technical authors were widely read, for style as well as substance: Vitruvius on architecture, for instance, or Vegetius on military tactics. At least as influential as classical prose, at least on some authors, was the late antique tradition of *ornatus*, the prose equivalent of the "jeweled style" affected by late antique poets (Roberts 1989; see also Formisano in this volume). Characterized by exotic vocabulary and contorted word order, the style is canonized in writers like Martianus Capella, Ennodius, Avitus, Sidonius, and Venantius Fortunatus. (A strangely persistent theory [going back to Sittl 1882] has tried to connect this style with the North African origin of several of its prominent practitioners. This idea has been repeatedly debunked [see Kroll 1897; Norden 1909; Lancel 1985; Petersmann 1998], but still staggers on, zombie-like, even in quite recent literature.)

The other pole, Christianity, is obviously centered on the Latin Bible. Here we tend to think first of the narrative portions in the Pentateuch, the historical books of the Old Testament, the Gospels and Acts. But as Christian critics were well aware, the Bible contains more than one kind of writing. The Psalms provided a model for a densely metaphorical and expressively subjective style. (Their influence is palpable, for example, in Augustine's *Confessiones*.) Almost as influential was the prose poetry of the Song of Songs. The Old Testament prophets offered a useful persona for critics of society or the church. The New Testament epistles offered a model for theological instruction quite unlike Cicero, but equally distinct from Old Testament wisdom books like Proverbs or Sirach.

Beyond the Bible itself lies a wider circle of Christian texts. Medieval readers approached scripture through the lens of patristic interpretation. Commentators like Cassiodorus and Gregory drew attention to rhetorical elements in the Bible. They also sketched out the elaborate metaphorical systems that inform much medieval prose. Medieval texts are filled with images of storms, clouds, rain, light and darkness, wine, water, milk, oil, honey, doves, ravens, lions, sheep, shepherds, wolves, snakes, fish, springs, dew, rocks, trees, thorns, fruit, fields, gardens, vineyards, mountains, seas, ships, harbors, pearls, and treasure houses. When a medieval writer invokes clouds of ignorance, honeyed words, or the pure fount of scripture he touches upon complex networks of scriptural and typological allusion (see, for example, Rahner 1964 and the ageing but still useful bibliography of Pöschl et al. 1964). Finally, we should not overlook the influence of the liturgy, to which all medieval writers were exposed regularly—some many times a day (see Mohrmann 1957).

Early Christian literature also established models for imitation in various genres. Martyrial *acta* and saints' lives set the pattern for later hagiography. Patristic writers—especially Jerome and Augustine—provided models for letters, sermons, or theological polemic. Orosius and the Latin translations of Josephus and Eusebius established a distinctively Christian historiographical voice. Inevitably, genre had an influence on style. Hagiography, for example, had strong conventions of structure and content, enforced by canonical models like Sulpicius Severus's *Vita sancti Martini*. Along with them came certain stylistic features, such as the rhetorical questions (*quid plura?*) that introduce a miracle accomplished or a prediction fulfilled. Yet despite their family resemblance, hagiographical texts cover a wide stylistic range, even crossing the boundary between prose and verse. Similarly, would-be historiographers had an array of potential models. An ambitious work like Otto of Freising's *Gesta Friderici imperatoris* will follow different conventions than a local chronicle. And there are texts that break the boundaries of genre altogether: Rather of Verona's *Phrenesis*, for example, or Abelard's *Historia calamitatum*. In creating a new kind of text, these authors also had to create a new style or styles.

Also important is the self-positioning of the authorial subject. Does he write to praise? To instruct? To petition? To express anger? Grief? Contrition? Gratitude? Does he speak as scholar, priest, prophet, father? What if "he" is a she? Naturally, the addressee will be a factor too. A bishop will write differently to his colleagues than he does to his own clergy or a secular ruler. And of course the ostensible addressee of a text is not necessarily the only one, or even the main one, envisaged by the author. A charter that grants its nominal recipient title to a few hides of land also conveys another, more important message to a broader audience—a message about power and authority that is communicated largely through style.

The Stylistic Toolkit

The medieval Latin stylist had a variety of tools at his—or her—disposal. Of these, one of the most important is word choice. English-speakers recognize that particular words can be restricted in their stylistic register: we do not expect "phenylephrine" and "wimp," or "roseate" and "dialectical" to appear in the same sentence. The same is true of medieval Latin. Words and formations associated with hexameter epic could lend a poetic flavor: *ensis* for *gladius*, *crinis* for *capillus*; abstracts in *-men*, compounds in *-fer* and *-ger* (see Axelson 1945). Authors striving for a satiric tone looked to the Roman satirists and comic playwrights for archaisms, morphological oddities, and onomatopoeic words (e.g. *topper, grunnire, poppyisma*). Greek loan-words and coinages attested to the author's learning, particularly in early insular prose. Writers might collect words casually, from their own reading, or deliberately, from glossaries and lexicographical works like Isidore's *Etymologiae*. Some types of words may be significant by their absence. Authors who aim for a classicizing style may avoid obvious Christianisms, or translate medieval administrative terms into Roman equivalents. Circumlocution can be used for sexual parts, undignified bodily functions, or for everyday objects too ordinary to feature in high-style prose. Circumlocution may also be employed simply for pleasure, as a display of virtuosity or a challenge to the reader (Curtius 1953, 275–78).

Medieval authors did not always follow the modern injunction to "omit needless words" (Strunk and White 1979, 23–25). Where modern taste sees redundancy, medieval readers might see more positive qualities: *abundantia* or *ubertas*. Pleonasm can be used to add emphasis or to heighten emotional tone. In high-style passages a noun's meaning may be emphasized by a redundant adjective (*tranquilla quies*) or a dependent genitive synonymous with the noun itself (*furor insaniae; seminum germina*). A particular idea may be reiterated in a new form without significantly changing the meaning. This "theme and variation" structure is a feature both of biblical poetry (e.g., Ps 29:9 *ad te, Domine, clamabo et ad Deum meum deprecabor* [To thee, Lord, will I cry, and to my God will I appeal]) and in classical verse (e.g., Vergil, *Aen.* 12.318 *has inter uoces, media inter talia uerba* [Amidst these utterances, in the midst of words such as these]; see Henry 1873, 745–51).

A prose work may be divided by verse interludes, in the mixed form known as *prosimetrum* (Pabst 1994). Or a writer's own Latin may be mixed with that of others, in the form of quotations or uncredited borrowings. Scriptural echoes provide one sort of texturing, a constant reinforcement by appeal to the ultimate authority. Classical works are also drawn on, sometimes in very unexpected ways. It is naïve to dismiss such borrowings as plagiarism, but it is no less misguided to try to make each one yield a subtle "allusion." Sometimes the borrowing's original context is less significant than its genre or author. A Sallustian tag establishes a historian's credentials; a Vergilian phrase can transform a patron into a new Aeneas. The order of words is also important. It is question-begging to speak of "natural" word order, particularly in a highly inflected language like Latin. Even so, one expects that words with a close relationship to one another (e.g., an adjective and its noun) will be found in proximity. Separation of such words (the figure known as "hyperbaton") is common in verse, for metrical reasons. Consequently, its use in prose texts can confer a poetic flavor. The flexibility of Latin word order can also be exploited in the larger structuring of sentences. Classical Latin authors learned to place the most syntactically critical element—the governing verb—in final or penultimate position, thus withholding crucial information from the listener until the remaining content of the sentence has been filled in. To be most effective, a "periodic" sentence of this sort will have a single main verb, all other actions being expressed by subordinate clauses of various sorts, or by ablative absolutes.

Latin sentences can be categorized as (more or less) "paratactic" or "hypotactic," the former implying a low, the latter a high degree of grammatical subordination. The overall level of hypotaxis in a work can be an indication of its stylistic level and intended audience. The same holds for average sentence length. At the same time, analysis has to take account of context and be sensitive to local variations. We experience sentences as "long" or "complex" not only in absolute terms but also by comparison with surrounding sentences. An author's ability to mix long and short, paratactic and hypotactic, is a measure of his compositional skill.

Most medieval prose was meant to be read aloud, and many writers make good use of sound effects. Often quoted is the opening of Aldhelm's letter to Eahfrith: "Primitus pantorum procerum praetorumque pio potissimum paternoque praesertim privilegio panagericum poemataque passim prosatori sub polo promulgantes..." (Aldhelm 1919, 488). [Principally, with particularly pious and paternal privilege, publicly proffering beneath the pole panegyric and poems promiscuously to the Procreator of all princes and praetors...] (Aldhelm 1979, 160). This is a playful *tour de force*, but less obtrusive alliteration is found everywhere. Authors also exploit the potential of assonance, especially at the ends of phrases and sentences. This can range from simple consonance of grammatical endings to full multisyllabic rhyme (Polheim 1925).

Medieval writers inherited from their classical predecessors an attraction to particular rhythms (initially quantitative, later stress-based) at major pauses or sentence-end (Norberg 1968, 86–89; Tunberg 1996, 114–18). The *cursus* system, as it is called, privileged four patterns in particular. (See Table 11.1)

Deliberate use of the *cursus* is demonstrated not simply by isolated examples of such endings, but by their greater-than-normal frequency (Janson 1975). In later medieval usage certain patterns of word break become standard, and the final word is normally three or four syllables. As a result, authors employing the *cursus* tend to avoid both monosyllables and very long words at sentence-end, and to privilege certain patterns of word order in the same position.

Table 11.1

planus	ó o o ó o	e.g.... mánibus nóstris.
tardus	ó o o ó o o	e.g.... heréditas dómini.
velox	ó o o o o ó o	e.g.... grátia caritátis.
trispondaicus	ó o o o ó o	e.g.... ésse uideátur.

THEORY AND PRACTICE

We have had little to say thus far about medieval stylistic theory. Medieval critics inherited from antiquity the notion of a hierarchy of styles (typically "low," "middle," and "high"), with the choice of level influenced by factors such as genre, audience, and subject matter (Quadlbauer 1962). Yet such models seem inadequate to the range and variety of medieval Latin prose, particularly in the hands of its greatest stylists. Medieval writers' comments on their own styles are often misleading, being influenced by topoi of conventional modesty that go back to antiquity (Hagendahl 1959; Janson 1964; Bambeck 1993). Central to many such statements is the claim to offer a plain narrative of facts (*res, ueritas*...) devoid of verbal decoration (*ornatus, pompa uerborum*, etc.). Yet those texts that claim to eschew ornament are often the most ornate.

As at other periods, it may be more useful to observe what an author actually does than what contemporary critics (or even the author himself) have to say about it. In the remainder of this chapter we will look closely at some short individual passages, chosen to illustrate both the range of medieval Latin prose and some of the specific factors discussed above. For each passage I offer a brief introduction, followed by a stylistic analysis. The translations are meant as guides to construing the Latin, not as substitutes for it.

1. Zeno of Verona, *Sermons* 1.4.13–15

Manuscripts preserve ninety-two sermons ascribed to Zeno, bishop of Verona in the late fourth century. (For orientation see Di Berardino 1986, 127–30.) They appear to have been collected after his death, probably for liturgical use. Many of the sermons are short (as brief as a single paragraph) or fragmentary. Our passage occurs about two-thirds of the way through a longer sermon on *patientia*.

> Nunc mihi Abrahae memoranda est mira illa temptatio, quae eum aut sacrilegum fecerat, si contemneret deum, aut crudelem, si occideret filium, nisi quadam singulari ac uere diuina patientia inter religionem pietatemque negotium temperaret, in spe non denegans deo, quod contra spem acceperat a deo. Igitur Isaac sibi dulcissimum filium, deo uictimam dulciorem contemnit, ut seruet, destinat iugulare, ne iugulet, securus illo se non posse displicere facinore, quod deo gerebatur auctore. O nouum spectaculum ac uere deo dignum, in quo

definire difficile est, utrum sit patientior sacerdos an uictima! Non percussoris, non percutiendi claudicat color; non membra tremore uibrantur; non dimissi, non torui sunt oculi. Nemo rogat, nemo trepidat, nemo se excusat, nemo turbatur. Ne uere sit parricidium, ille lignum quo inuratur sibi praeportat, ille aram struit. Ille exserit gladium, ille ceruicem. Vno uoto, una deuotione, ne quid profanum sit, diligenter ac patienter geritur, quod ab altero celebratur. Sub tanto, non dicam humanitatis, sed ipsius naturae metu laeti sunt soli. Cedit affectus pietati, pietas religioni, fauet utrisque religio. Medius stupet gladius nullo impedimento suspensus mactatione terribili gloriam se praestitisse, non crimen. Quid hoc est? Ecce immanitas in fidem et scelus transit in sacramentum; parricida incruentus redit et qui immolatus est uiuit. Ambo sibi gloria, ambo claritatis exemplum, ambo dei cultus admirabile saeculis testimonium. Felix orbis fuerat, fratres, si omnes sic fierent parricidae.

[Now I must make mention of that miraculous temptation of Abraham, which would have meant impiety if he had refused God, or pitiless cruelty if he had killed his son, had he not by some singular and truly divine patience struck a balance between piety and gentleness, not refusing to God in hopefulness what he had received from God against all hope. Thus he relinquishes Isaac—sweet to him as a son but sweeter to God as a sacrifice—in order to preserve him, he determines to slaughter him so as to avoid slaughtering him, confident that he could not displease God through an action performed at God's instigation. An unprecedented performance, and one truly worthy of God, in which it is hard to decide if the priest or the victim displayed more patience. From the face of the slayer and that of his victim no color drained. Their limbs did not tremble, their eyes were not downcast or grim. No one begged, no one hesitated, no one asked for forgiveness, no one was distraught. To prevent the crime from being committed, one carried the wood with which he was to be burned, the other filled the altar with it. One bared his sword, the other his neck. With a single will, a single devotion, lest there be any profanation, that which the other performs is borne diligently and patiently. When not just humanity, but nature itself trembled, they alone were joyful. Love gave way to piety, piety to reverence, reverence sustained both. In midstroke the sword, held in suspense, with nothing to keep it from falling, was stunned to find that it conferred by its terrible stroke not guilt but glory. But what is this? Lo, cruelty is transformed into faith and a crime into a sacrament. A child-murderer emerges unbloodied and his victim still lives. Both were a glory to themselves, an example of brilliance, an admirable testimony of devotion to God for ages to come. It would have been a happy world, brothers, if all murderers were such.] (Zeno of Verona 1971, 34–35)

A stylistic analysis might begin by noting some of the obvious—indeed, positively ostentatious—rhetorical figures: rhyme (*facinore/auctore*; *redit/uiuit*) and "grammatical rhyme" (*gladium/ceruicem*; *fidem/sacramentum*), apostrophe (*o nouum spectaculum…!*), rhetorical question (*quid hoc est?*) and alliteration (*felix orbis fuerat, fratres…*). Anaphora of *nemo* links the four verbs *rogat…trepidat…excusat…turbatur*. Another sentence features a *tricolon crescens*: **Ambo** sibi gloria, / **ambo** claritatis exemplum, / **ambo** dei cultus admirabile saeculis testimonium.

Structurally, the passage is built around a series of verbal and conceptual contrasts. Our attention shifts back and forth between Abraham and Isaac (*sacerdos/victima*; *percussoris/percutiendi*; *gladium/cervicem*). Pairings also point to Isaac's dual role (*filium/victimam*) and to the paradoxical identity of the horrific act purposed by Abraham with the pious obedience it constitutes: *sacrilegum/crudelem*; *gloriam/crimen*; *immanitas/fidem*; *scelus/sacramentum*. Such paired contrasts can be traced as a rhetorical device back to the Greek rhetorician Gorgias (c. 483–376 BCE). Their frequency in preaching owes something to sheer rhetorical effectiveness, but it also reflects a deeper pattern inherent in Christian discourse. Scriptural episodes are regularly framed as contrasts between two figures (Cain/Abel; Abraham/Lot; Jacob/Esau; Mary/Martha; Dives/Lazarus…). The individual Christian must choose between salvation and eternal torment. The crucifixion transforms defeat into victory. The New Testament fulfils the Old.

The basic elements and sequence of the biblical narrative remain dimly discernible: wood and altar, the knife descending, the last-minute intervention. But the passage is curiously static, as if Zeno is an observer in a museum, walking around a statue and marveling at it from all sides. The event is *admirabile*, a *spectaculum*, like a nineteenth-century *tableau vivant*. What is described is only what would be visible to a third-party observer: actions and facial expressions, not the thoughts or emotions of the participants. The human participants are once described as joyful (*laeti*), but the emphasis is otherwise on their *lack* of emotion: they do not beg, tremble, etc. Only the sword, paradoxically, feels a "human" emotion; its astonishment mirrors Zeno's and, by implication, our own.

The passage raises many questions. Clearly, this is not the only way the story could be (or has been) told. Why is it told here in this way? The passage was designed for public performance, and the audience is once explicitly addressed (*fratres*). Yet we do not sense the close connection between preacher and hearer that characterizes many of Augustine's sermons. Does this reflect a difference in the two men's oratorical training? Or in their audience? (Did the inhabitants of Verona expect something grander than their counterparts in provincial Hippo?) The circumstances of preservation and transmission may also be relevant. Many of Augustine's sermons appear to have been recorded by shorthand writers from his impromptu delivery (Deferrari 1922). How far does Zeno's text correspond to what was actually delivered? Did he speak from a prepared or memorized text? Did he revise and expand his sermon after the fact? Such questions can only be answered by comparison with other contemporary sermon collections, as well as external evidence about preaching practice.

2. Bede, *Historia Ecclesiastica* 4.13

Bede (672/73–735) spent most of his life at the twin monasteries of Wearmouth and Jarrow in Northumbria. (On his career and output see, e.g., Brown 2009; DeGregorio 2010.) His extant works range over many genres: biblical commentary, grammar, hagiography, chronology, verse. His *Historia ecclesiastica gentis Anglorum*, in five books, surveys the growth of the English church from the earliest missionaries to Bede's own day. It looks back to a Christian tradition of historiography represented by the *Historia contra paganos* of Orosius and Rufinus's translation of Eusebius's *Historia ecclesiastica* (Shanzer 2007). In our passage, Bede describes the conversion of Sussex by Wilfrid of Ripon (d. 709 or 710).

> Euangelizans autem genti episcopus Uilfrid, non solum eam ab aerumna perpetuae damnationis, uerum et a clade infanda temporalis interitus eripuit. Siquidem tribus annis ante aduentum eius in prouinciam, nulla illis in locis pluuia ceciderat, unde et fames aceruissima plebem inuadens impia nece prostrauit. Denique ferunt quia saepe XL simul aut L homines inedia macerati procederent ad praecipitium aliquod siue ripam maris, et iunctis misere manibus, pariter omnes aut ruina perituri, aut fluctibus absorbendi deciderent. Verum ipsa die, quo baptisma fidei gens suscepit illa, descendit pluuia serena sed copiosa, refloruit terra, rediit uiridantibus aruis annus laetus et frugifer. Sicque abiecta prisca superstitione, exsufflata idolatria, cor omnium et caro omnium exultauerunt in Deum uiuum: intellegentes eum, qui uerus est Deus, et interioribus se bonis et exterioribus caelesti gratia ditasse. Nam et antistes, cum uenisset in prouinciam, tantamque ibi famis poenam uideret, docuit eos piscando uictum quaerere. Namque mare et flumina eorum piscibus abundabant; sed piscandi peritia genti nulla nisi ad anguillas tantum inerat. Collectis ergo undecumque retibus anguillaribus, homines antistitis miserunt in mare, et diuina se iuuante gratia mox cepere pisces diuersi generis trecentos: quibus trifariam diuisis, centum pauperibus dederunt, centum his a quibus retia acceperant, centum in suos usus habebant. Quo beneficio multum antistes cor omnium in suum conuertit amorem, et libentius eo praedicante caelestia sperare coeperunt, cuius ministerio temporalia bona sumserunt.

> [In converting the people, Bishop Wilfrid rescued them not only from the sufferings of perpetual damnation, but also from an unspeakable misfortune of mortality in this world. For in the three years prior to his arrival in the region, no rain had fallen in the area, so that a dreadful famine had attacked the people and laid them low with terrible destruction. Indeed, they report that groups of forty or fifty people, consumed by hunger, regularly made their way to some high place or to the sea's edge, and taking hold of one another's hands in a pitiable fashion, leapt forth to perish from the fall or drown in the waves. But on the very day on which the people underwent the baptism of faith, a calm and copious rain descended, the earth flowered once more, a happy and fruitful season returned to the blossoming fields. And thus with the old superstition cast off, idolatry swept away, everyone's heart and everyone's flesh rejoiced in the living God, recognizing that he who is the true God had enriched them through celestial grace with goods within and without. For when the bishop came into the region, and saw how great was their suffering from hunger, he also taught them to make their living by fishing. For the sea and their rivers abounded in fish, but the people had no idea how to catch anything except eels. So having collected eel nets from all sides, the priest's people cast them into the sea, and as it pleased divine grace, soon they caught three hundred fish of different kinds. And dividing them three ways, they gave a hundred to the poor, a hundred to those from whom they had received the nets, and kept a hundred for their own use. By this service, the priest turned the

hearts of all to love of him, and they began to hope for celestial things more willingly as they listened to this man, at whose hands they had received earthly goods.] (Bede 1969, 372, 374)

Bede, like Zeno, is describing miraculous events. But in contrast to Zeno's static description, Bede's narrative draws us steadily forward. Each sentence explains the previous one or adds a new element. Each is linked by a particle or connecting relative: *Siquidem...Denique...Verum...Sicque...Nam...Namque...sed...ergo...quibus trifariam diuisis...Quo beneficio...* The passage as a whole shows a masterful mix of classical and biblical stylemes. Bede's skill at constructing an effective period can be seen in the sentence in which the starving inhabitants throw themselves into the sea:

> Denique ferunt quia
>   saepe
>   quadraginta simul aut quinquaginta homines
>   inedia macerati
>   procederent   ad praecipitium aliquod
>   sive ripam maris,
>   et iunctis misere manibus,   pariter   omnes
>   aut ruina perituri,
>   aut fluctibus absorbendi
>   deciderent.

The use of *quia* to introduce indirect statement is a late and medieval development, but the sentence shows a firm grasp of classical construction (note the ablative absolute *iunctis...manibus,* one of several in this passage). Bede here pays out information item by item. By *ad praecipitium* most readers will guess what is coming, but the tension is effectively maintained until the final verb.

Verum in the next sentence marks a turning point in the narrative, and here Bede shifts into a more scriptural and poetic voice. At one point we hear an actual hexameter line-end: *rĕdĭīt uĭrĭdāntĭbŭs ārūs.* Events are framed as straightforward subject-plus-predicate—*descendit pluvia, refloruit terra, rediit annus*—and the connections between them left to be deduced, as in the famous passage from Ct 2:11–12: "iam enim hiems transiit; imber abiit, et recessit; flores apparuerunt in terra nostra" [For now the winter is past, the rain is over and gone; flowers appear on the earth]. A near-verbatim scriptural echo lends solemnity (Ps 83:3: "cor meum et caro mea exultavit in Deum uiuum" [My heart and my flesh have rejoiced in the living God]).

The next few sentences shift back to a more prosaic register, in keeping with the subject matter. But the needle jumps once or twice: at *famis poenam* (where a simple *famem* would have done) and *piscandi peritia...nulla...inerat* (more stately than, e.g., *piscari non nouerunt*). But here too we should not neglect scriptural undertones. By writing an ecclesiastical history "of the English people," Bede was implicitly inviting the reader to draw parallels with the history of the early church. His readers will not have missed the symbolism of a spiritual teacher who instructs his converts in fishing, or who directs them to cast their nets and pull in a substantial haul. And the division of the resulting catch into three equal portions will hardly have seemed to them accidental. The audience has been prepared for such a subtext by the more explicitly scriptural style of what precedes.

Taken as a whole, the passage is a useful reminder that medieval Latin works are not always stylistically homogenous; even a text by a single author may vary in register from section to section and even from one sentence to the next (Ogle 1926). Not all authors are capable of this kind of versatility, but for those who are it is an extraordinarily effective tool. Straightforward narrative may alternate, as here, with more highly charged or reflective passages. Ornamentation tends to cluster in certain types of passage: prefaces, for example, or set-piece descriptions (a *locus amoenus*, a storm at sea, the sufferings of a besieged city). Bede's mastery of multiple styles is one of his particular gifts as a writer (Sharpe 2005).

3. Atto of Vercelli, *Polipticum* 13

Atto served as bishop of Vercelli in Northern Italy in the mid-tenth century (for a general study see Wemple 1979). His surviving works are extant in two manuscripts, one preserved in his native city and one in the Vatican; they include sermons, letters, and commentaries on the Pauline epistles. The Vatican codex also contains two distinct redactions of a text variously entitled *Polipticum* (roughly "A Manifold Work") or *Perpendiculum* ("The Plumbline") (Atto of Vercelli 1922; see also Frova 1982/83). One of the two versions employs a more straightforward word order than the other, and includes glosses, which may or may not derive from the author. The "hard" version (from which our passage comes) seems to be primary, with the easier version meant to serve as a guide to it. Whether or not the simplified and glossed version of the text goes back to Atto himself, it usefully illustrates the kind of work any reader must do to understand the passage.

> Desine nunc ceptos et sensibus utere nostris. Sic *fabre* nunc eos suggilare iuuat *pecuatos* memet: O quos sat est uestris effusa distrahere emicadiis. Quorsum? ut possitis fore uel *simbolones* magnatum. Dumtaxat nugae quorum in talione redduntur. *Delenifici!* Pleumon non durat dum angitur panagerica uester *tuccetis* exprimere solum. Elluones! *Edulio* conclaue uos si suspendat ab uno, mox *catillando* procul *lentaculum* uel insectari, temetum exteriusque libare *ferculum* et inde gyrando uel obolam in *ganea*, deficiat si hoc parare curatis. Abscessu remota si praeda sit uel auctoritate priuetur, non crapula differtur utcumque praegrauidus acerbum reppellat dum aqualiculus fascem. Fraternitas in uobis *arualis* quae sola est fatetur a uobis. Iam quibus sarchian staret ut *neferendis* sed uergitur quod pectore uulnus haec in tenui licore consumens, hinc faetare bilem non desinit atrum. Sarcophaga *polinctos* quam nunc o tantum caperent uos *subgrundaria* prius. Et *silicernios* obtat in istis si pegaso uos protrahi ad usque non capulum spectat tum sed ora iocunda *uispillones* et neque sublustrat. *Manalibus* nam licet ualidum esset caeli uobis faciem non uiri est inficere sensum. Rictibus bachantes quid tristibus cassare minamini uerum ad leuem aemula ducentes *ualgias* et ora baubatum? *Aritina* cacabant ut humida cum <h>auserint ignem, sic temulentia stultis stitiat in ipsis. Quid taciti respuo *nictent*, quorum et *frigultire* contemno garrireque *nauci* pono.

[Renounce your original views and adopt mine. Now it is my delight cunningly to humiliate fools as follows: O you who are satisfied to peddle the effusions of your half-filled oil-jugs. And to what end? So that you can become the hangers-on of the great, in reciprocation of whom only worthless trifles are awarded. Flatterers! Your chest cannot endure it when, craving savories, it is constrained to express only panegyrics. Spendthrifts! If a locked pantry (?) should defer you from a single tidbit, at once by cadging abroad you strive to pursue an *hors d'oeuvre* and pour out wine in foreign parts and from there, making the rounds, to obtain a main course or, failing that, at any rate a coin or two in a tavern. If prey is denied you by its absence or prohibited by authority, your drinking is not adjourned until your overladen belly expels its sour burden. The only "brotherhood" you will admit to is the feasting kind. You would already have a paunch as castrated animals do, but it is lessened because the wound in your slender breast, consuming these things with its moisture, does not cease to generate black bile from it. Ah, if only an infant's grave received you, sooner than the sarcophagi that now hold your anointed bodies. And if a jester hopes that you will enjoy such pursuits until you are old men, he sees only happy faces and does not pay heed to the funeral bier or the undertakers. For though you may be able to alter the appearance of the sky with rain-stones, you cannot change the nature of a man. Rejoicing in shameful riotings, why do you boast that you will make invalid what is true, distorting your envious faces into sneers and shallow chortling? As clay pots bubble when they absorb the fire, so drunkenness chatters in fools. I spew out of my mouth what people sneer *sotto voce*; I disdain their blathering and care not a fig for their babbling.] (Atto of Vercelli 1922, 21–22)

This is a difficult passage by any standard; the rendering above draws on both the glossed version and Goetz's German translation, but the interpretation remains doubtful at more than one point. Two features stand out immediately here. One is word order, which in this version is deliberately disrupted, and to an extreme degree. Even for readers used to the flexible word order of classical verse, Atto's text would have had a crossword-puzzle quality. The other source of obscurity is the mass of arcane vocabulary employed. A number of these items (they are italicized above) come from Fulgentius's *Expositio sermonum antiquorum*, a collection of archaic words with illustrative quotations compiled in the mid-sixth century. In Fulgentius the words occur as discrete entries, and in no very obvious order; Atto has stitched them together into a connected discourse, as an exercise in "contextualized lexicography" (Lendinara 2005).

The passage (and the work as a whole) draws on several distinct but related generic traditions. One is diatribe, the kind of popular sermonizing attributed to ancient philosophers, in which the speaker upbraids the society around him for its failure to behave moderately or rationally. Typical of this mode is the creation of a dialogic relationship between speaker and audience. Here the use of apostrophe (*o quos…! elluones!*) and second person forms (*uos…uestris…*) establishes and maintains such a connection.

Elements of diatribe play an important role in verse satire, going back to Horace, Persius, and Juvenal. Atto's debt to this tradition is made explicit in the hexametric opening sentence, with its echo of Horace's *Epistulae* 1.6.68 (*…si nil, his utere* *mecum*). The description of the gluttons, fawning on the great in exchange for meals, evokes the stock character of the parasite, a staple of Roman satire and comedy (Damon 1997). Much of the vocabulary here is also satiric. Many of Fulgentius's items come from comedy and satire, and Atto has added other borrowings from the same register. We find colorful, archaic, or onomatopoeic words like *crapula, neniae, garrire, baubatum, <h>elluones*. Atto imitates Persius and Juvenal in his incorporation of Greek loan-words: *pleumon, panagerica, obola, sarchian (?)*. Some items can even be traced back to specific classical passages. *Aqualiculus*, for example, is found once in Persius (*Sat.* 1.57) and nowhere else. The verb *cassare* is attested only in Plautus, where it is coupled with *bacchari*, just as it is here (*Miles Gloriosus* 856: "ubi bacchabatur aula, cassabant cadi" [When the pot was reveling, the casks tottered]).

What motivated Atto to write in this style? His modern editor suggests a desire to veil his critique of contemporary potentates (Atto of Vercelli 1922, 8, 10). But this ignores the comic and satiric aspects of the text. Atto's targets are as conventional as Horace's; no names are named, and no identifying details given. It is hard to believe that contemporary individuals could have recognized themselves in (assuming they bothered to read) even the simplified version of the *Polipticum*. It seems more likely that Atto's purpose was literary: to display his own linguistic mastery and challenge his readers to demonstrate theirs. The *Polipticum*, in both its original and simplified form, testifies to the existence of a larger interpretive community that it simultaneously helps to create and maintain. In this respect, it invites comparison with a number of other medieval texts, notably the highly artificial prose of the seventh-century *Hisperica famina* (1974), the peculiar grammatical treatises of Virgilius Maro (Law 1995), and the "hermeneutic" strand in Anglo-Latin that runs from Aldhelm (Winterbottom 1977) to the tenth century (Lapidge 1975; for more general thoughts see Ziolkowski 1996).

4. Hildegard of Bingen, *Scivias* 2 visio 1

Hildegard (1098–1179) was born to an upper-class family in the Rhineland. Handed over to the church at an early age, she rose to become head of her community. She reports experiencing visions as a young child, and these continued throughout her life. Through her role as visionary and prophet she achieved ecclesiastical and even political influence to a degree unusual in a male-dominated society. (For orientation to her life and works see Burnett and Dronke 1998; Flanagan 1998.) Her *Scivias* (a shortening of *Scire uias*, "Know [the] ways") is a description of twenty-six visions accompanied by commentary and interpretation.

> Vidique de eodem fulgore praefatae aurorae serenissimum hominem egredientem, qui claritatem suam ad praedictas tenebras effundens ita ab eis reuerberatus est quod in ruborem sanguinis et in albedinem palloris uersus tanta fortitudine easdem tenebras repercuteret, quod ille homo qui in eis iacebat per eum tactus apparens fulgeret atque ita erectus exiret. Et sic idem serenus homo qui de praedicta aurora egressus est in tanta claritate apparens ultra quam

humana lingua effari possit, in acutissimam altitudinem innumerabilis gloriae tetendit, ubi in plenitudine magnificae fructuositatis et odoris mirifice radiabat.

Et audiui ex praefato uiuente igne uocem dicentem mihi: "O quae es misera terra et in nomine femineo indocta de ulla doctrina carnalium magistrorum, scilicet legere litteras per intellegentiam philosophorum, sed tantum tacta lumine meo, quod tangit te interius cum incendio ut ardens sol, clama et enarra ac scribe haec mysteria mea quae uides et audis in mystica uisione. Noli ergo esse timida, sed dic ea quae intellegis in spiritu, quemadmodum ea loquor per te, quatenus illi uerecundiam habeant qui populo meo deberent rectitudinem ostendere, sed de petulantia morum suorum recusant iustitiam aperte dicere quam nouerunt, nolentes se abstrahere de malis desideriis suis, quae illis ita adhaerent quasi sint magistri eorum facientia eos fugere a facie Domini, ita ut erubescant loqui ueritatem."

[And I saw from the same blazing of the aforementioned sunrise a most serene figure emerging, shedding his brightness upon the aforementioned shadows, who was so beaten by them that, transformed to the redness of blood and the whiteness of pallor, he fought back against those same shadows with such strength that that person who lay within them, touched by him, shone forth visibly and so came forth, standing upright. And thus that same serene figure who emerged from the aforementioned sunrise, made visible in such brightness, more than the human tongue can express, attained to the topmost height of uncountable glory, where in the fullness of magnificent fruitfulness and fragrance he wondrously shone forth. And I heard from the aforementioned living fire a voice saying to me: "O you who are wretched earth and, as a woman, untutored in any learning of fleshly teachers, so as to read with the intelligence of the philosophers, but only touched by my light, which touches you within with fire like a burning sun, cry out and tell and write these mysteries of mine which you see and hear in mystical vision. Do not be afraid, but say those things which you understand in the spirit, as I say them to you, so that those may be ashamed who ought to show my people uprightness, but out of the arrogance of their characters refuse to speak plainly of the justice which they know, being unwilling to tear themselves from their evil desires, which so adhere to them as if they were their teachers, making them to flee from the face of the Lord, so that they are ashamed to speak the truth."] (Hildegard of Bingen 1978, 111–12)

Hildegard's visions draw on existing traditions of vision literature, which have their own characteristic styles and tropes. The ultimate model for such descriptions is scriptural: most obviously the visions of Revelation but also passages such as Jacob's dream (Gn 28:12), Ezekiel's vision of the wheel (Ez 1:4) or Peter's vision of permitted food (Act 10:10–16). But there were other sources too. An important model for the *Scivias* is the Latin version of the second-century *Shepherd of Hermas*, which like Hildegard's work is structured as a series of discrete visions followed by explications (Liebeschuetz 1930, 51–56).

The basic structure of the passage is consistent with those found throughout the work: an initial vision (*et uidi...*) is followed by an auditory experience (*et audiui...uocem dicentem*). The vision is regularly expressed as a past experience, with perfect and imperfect verbs. The scene is narrated neutrally; we are not told Hildegard's reactions if any. Sight is the primary sense employed; the vision is described as if seen through glass, though it sometimes becomes more abstract and synaesthetic toward the end, as here with *in plenitudine...fructuositatis et odoris...radiabat*.

We are regularly reminded that the verbal description is an inadequate approximation of the actual experience. Here, for example, the brightness is *ultra quam humana lingua effari possit*. Superlatives (*serenissumum*; *acutissimam*) stress the indescribability of what is seen. The same instinct perhaps motivates the unnatural phrasing: a figure is said to be "beaten" (*reuerberatus*) by shadows and "transformed into the whiteness of pallor" (*in albedinem palloris uersus*), while the inherently plural *innumerabilis* modifies the indivisible noun *gloria*. At such moments one feels Latin being wrenched almost beyond its capacity. Yet these features are balanced by the almost lawyerly precision of other parts of the passage (*de eodem fulgore*; *ad praedictas tenebras*; *idem...homo qui...egressus est*). This combination of ecstasy and order is symptomatic of a larger discourse within medieval Christianity and, indeed, the *Scivias* itself. From its earliest days the Church was conscious of the need to "manage" revelation and direct it into appropriate channels. Hildegard's prose recapitulates this process.

The passage places a good deal of emphasis on Hildegard's gender and consequent lack of education: she is unlearned (*indocta*), her words are not the product of painstaking study but "only" (*tantum*) of an inward fire "like a burning sun." Those inclined to take this statement at face value can point to apparent stylistic awkwardness, like the clumsy double result clause in the vision (*ita...reuerberatus...quod...tanta fortitudine...repercuteret, quod...*), or the rather straggly final sentence. But this ignores more stylistically ambitious features: the high-style combination of abstract noun + genitive (*in albedinem palloris*; *in plenitudine...fructuositatis*), or the skillful playing off of polysyllabic words (*per intellegentiam philosophorum*) against short, simple ones (*clama et enarra ac scribe...quae uides et audis*). Despite its own claims, there is nothing artless about such prose.

Is Hildegard's gender relevant to the evaluation of her style? Here caution is indicated. For one thing, Hildegard is known to have worked with a male amanuensis (her confessor Volmar) and we cannot be sure how far she herself is responsible for the *ipsissima uerba* we read. One suggestion is perhaps worth making, however. Medieval writers needed to establish an authoritative voice, and the need was perhaps even more pressing for women writers. From this perspective, the disproportionate prominence of the visionary mode in medieval literature by women (both in Latin and in the vernacular) is not accidental. Hildegard's visions conferred upon her an authority that, as a woman, she could not have achieved through other channels. It is perhaps in this context that we should approach the auditory portions of the visions. Hildegard's disembodied voice is, above all, authoritative. It echoes scriptural visitations (e.g., Lc 1:30, Dn 10:12) in instructing Hildegard to "be not afraid" (*noli...esse timida*). It indicts false teachers in the accents of Old Testament prophets or of St. Paul. Woven into its discourse are actual scriptural phrases (*fugere a facie domini*; cf. Jonah 1:3 *ut fugeret...a facie domini*), as well as phrasing that sounds scriptural but is not (*nolentes se abstrahere de malis desideriis suis*). Hildegard's chosen form enables her to experiment here with a stylistic identity that would not have been available to her in other genres—or, indeed, in real life.

5. Alexander Neckam, *Commentum super Martianum* 1.63–64

Alexander Neckam (1157–1217) studied in Paris, taught theology in Oxford, and ended his life as Abbot of the Augustinian abbey of St. Mary's, Cirencester. His extant works include poetry and scriptural commentary. (On his life and output see Hunt 1984.) His commentary on Martianus Capella's *De nuptiis Philologiae et Mercurii* is representative of an active twelfth-century industry of explication of the classical *auctores*. For medieval readers that category included Martianus (fl. c. 500; see also Hicks, Formisano, and Wetherbee in this volume), whose work consists of an encyclopedic treatment of the seven liberal arts, set in an allegorical frame. Our passage comprises the commentary on two sentences from the opening book (supplied here with commented words underlined):

> Tunc Ianus in limine militesque Iovis ante fores regias constiterunt; ingressuros etiam cunctos nominatim vocabat Fama praeconans. at intra consistorium regis quaedam femina, quae Adrastia dicebatur, urnam caelitem superamque sortem inrevocabilis raptus celeritate torquebat excipiebatque ex volubili orbe decidentes sphaeras peplo inflexi pectoris Imarmene. (Martianus Capella 1983, 19)

> TUNC IANUS, quia omne initium Iano est consecratum. MILITESQUE, id est stipatores siue angeli. ANTE FORES. Inter fores et ualuas hec distantia est, quod fores sunt hostia que foris aperiuntur, ualue autem que intrinsecus; dicte sunt, quod se uelent uel uallent. PRECONANS, id est uociferans. CONSISTORIUM locus est, ubi rex consistit. ADRASTRIA interpretatur petrosa siue dura; nam adria Grece petra Latine interpretatur. Hinc Adriaticum mare dicitur, quod sit saxosum et periculosum. Adrastria autem signat sortem, que dura et inexorabilis; siue Adrastria dicta est a Greco quod est 'adranes', id est infirmitas uel impotentia. Sortes enim propter impotentiam humanam reperte sunt, quod per se nesciebant homines quid uitandum uel quid eligendum esset. URNAM, eo quod sors in urnam iaciebatur. TORQUEBAT, id est uoluebat, SPERAS id est giros. YMARMENHE est quasi proprium nomen femine, que hoc agebat. Interpretatur autem Ymarmenhe ex Greco *cronu sineches*, id est temporis continuatio; *sineche* enim Grece continuum; hinc et *sinecha* passio uocatur febris continua. Omni enim tempore et nascuntur homines et in fata, id est <in> mortem, succidunt.

> [Then Janus took up his position at the threshold and Jove's guards theirs before the doors; and Fama, acting as herald, announced each of the arrivals by name. Inside the king's council hall (consistorium), a certain woman, who was called Adrastia, was rotating a celestial urn and whirling heavenly fate with the celerity of irrevocable speed and the stony-hearted Imarmene caught in the folds of her garment the spheres which were ejected from the spinning orb.

> THEN JANUS because all beginnings are sacred to Janus. AND THE SOLDIERS, that is his bodyguard or angels. BEFORE THE DOORS (*FORES*).

Between *fores* and *ualuae* the distinction is that *fores* are gates that open outward (*foris*), *ualuae* those that open inward; so-called because they veil (*uelent*) or wall off (*uallent*). ACTING AS HERALD, that is, shouting. The CONSISTORIUM is the place where the king takes his seat (*consistit*). ADRASTRIA means "rocky" or "hard"; for the Greek *adria* means "stone" in Latin. Hence we speak of the Adriatic Sea, because it is rocky and dangerous. But Adrastria signifies Fate (*Sors*), which is inexorable. Alternatively she is called Adrastria from the Greek word *adranes*, that is, "weakness" or "inability." For lots (*sortes*) were invented because of human inability, since humans did not know on their own what to select or avoid. URN because the lot was placed in the urn. WAS ROTATING, that is, was turning. SPHERES, that is, circles. YMARMENHE is treated as the proper name of a woman, who did this. But Ymarmenhe is derived from the Greek *cronu sineches*, that is "continuity of time"; for *sineche* in Greek means continuous; hence a continuous fever is called a *sinecha* illness. For men are constantly being born and succumbing to their fates, that is, death.] (Neckam 2006, 156)

Medieval commentaries on the *auctores* look back to late antique models, notably to the massive Virgilian commentary of Servius. Neckam's commentary draws substantially on Martianus's earlier interpreters, especially the ninth-century polymath John Scottus Eriugena and the slightly younger Remigius of Auxerre, as well as on contemporary mythographic texts. It is also informed by a central tradition of medieval thought, the analysis of etymology as a guide to meaning and the world (Curtius 1953, 495–500).

As with other specialized areas (e.g., scholastic philosophy, canon law, medicine), commentary on the *auctores* developed its own idioms and technical formulae, many of which are on display here: *x (Grece) interpretatur y (Latine); x dicitur y; x uocatur y; y dicta est a Greco quod est x; hinc x dicitur; id est (quasi) y*. These remained stable over hundreds of years; all can be found in the fountainhead of medieval etymology, the *Etymologiae* of Isidore of Seville. These phrases can appear singly but can also be combined into more elaborate structures, as in the comment on Ymarmenhe: <u>Interpretatur</u> autem Ymarmenhe <u>ex Greco</u> "cronu sineches," <u>id est</u> temporis continuatio; "sineche" enim <u>Grece</u> continuum; <u>hinc et</u> "sinecha" passio uocatur febris continua. Equally conventional is the formula for distinguishing a word from a near-homonym or synonym (here *fores* from *ualuae*): *inter x et y hoc interest quod...* Such *differentiae* are found scattered through commentaries and grammatical works, and are also preserved in separate collections (see Brugnoli 1955). Another feature prominent even in this short extract is the commentator's habit of glossing a target word with more than one equivalent: *petrosa siue dura; saxosum et periculosum; dura... et inexorabilis; infirmitas uel impotentia*. Since terms in different languages are seldom exactly synonymous, the intent seems to be to cover the original term's range with two equivalents (rarely more); often these are a literal term followed by a more figurative one.

The commentary shows marks of its probable origins in oral teaching. Syntactically it is built up of short sentences and sentence fragments, with little subordination beyond the ubiquitous *quia...* or *(eo) quod...* For comments longer than a sentence, however, there is a clear attempt at sentence connection. Discourse particles are typically explanatory (*enim*, *nam*) or resumptive (*ergo*); rather than adversative (*autem* does not mark an objection, but simply a new topic).

The exegesis oscillates uneasily between two poles. At the lower end of the spectrum are straightforward *id est*-type glosses. Such comments can be seen as striving toward a commentary that (at an extreme) would consist of a verbatim recitation of the original text expanded with explanatory paraphrases. This format is suggestive of oral instruction, the teacher translating and construing the text in front of him for the benefit of his students. The longer comments fall into several types. Sometimes the lemma stands in isolation, followed by an independent sentence (so in the comment on *ANTE FORES*): here syntax enforces a distinction between lemma and comment. In other cases the lemma is woven into the syntax of the comment (*CONSISTORIUM locus est ubi*...), and is distinguishable from it only graphically (by a difference in script, like the modern editor's capitals, or by underlining or rubrication). Both types of comment seem to presuppose a reader with independent access to a written source text.

Functionally the passage has something in common with the Zeno excerpt with which we began. But the emotional and rhetorical level of the passage is much lower here; we find no rhetorical figures, no use of the second person or other acknowledgment of the audience. We are being talked at, not to. Neckam conducts us through Martianus's text as if it were a long corridor with a series of rooms opening off it. The guide may leave some doors closed (here, e.g., *Fama* or *inflexi pectoris*), open others and gesture briefly from the threshold (CONSISTORIUM or URNAM), or invite the group to enter and have a closer look at the contents (ADRASTRIA). But always the next room beckons, and the guide's monologue resumes its unwearying course.

Neckam's authorship of the commentary is attested by the manuscripts, and there is no reason to doubt it. But on the basis of internal evidence, it would be hard to ascribe this text to him, or indeed to anyone in particular. This cannot be said to be a personal style at all. It might better be described as the articulation of a discourse or social practice that *speaks through* Neckam, rather than being *spoken by* him. The ability to generate text in this medium is a marker of membership in a group, and the status that such membership confers. Neckam's use of it can be compared to the use of distinct professional styles in other areas, such as scholastic philosophy, law, imperial or papal chanceries, as well as to the technical styles of medicine or cookery.

Conclusion

Ludwig Traube famously observed that there is no such thing as "medieval Latin" and consequently there can be no grammar or dictionary of it. The same is true of medieval Latin prose style. The passages above should not be taken as representative of a given period (or even of their authors' total output). A different choice of passages would present different features, and raise different problems. Nor do they support any model of continuous development or periodization. Rather, they represent initial soundings from a vaster sea of material, much of which still remains unexplored.

SUGGESTIONS FOR FURTHER READING

The approach to style taken here has its roots in Auerbach (1953 and 1965) and in von Albrecht (1989). Though their concerns are broader, Norberg (1968) and Bourgain (2005) present a useful array of commented passages for readers who wish to explore further. The most detailed synchronic view of the topic to date is Stotz (1998, 430–519). For diachronic surveys see Norden (1909, 2: 573–731) and (more briefly) Tunberg (1996, 111–14). Useful introductions to the conventions of individual genres will be found in the series *Typologie des sources du moyen âge occidental* (represented below by Camargo 1991, Kelly 1991, and Briscoe 1992).

BIBLIOGRAPHY

Primary sources

Aldhelm. 1919. *Opera*, edited by Rudolf Ehwald. Monumenta Germaniae Historica. Auctores Antiquissimi 15. Berlin: Weidmann.
———. 1979. *The Prose Works*, translated by Michael Lapidge and Michael Herren. Cambridge: D. S. Brewer.
Atto of Vercelli. 1922. *Attonis qui fertur Polipticum quod appellatur Perpendiculum*, edited by Georg Goetz. Abhandlungen der philologisch-historischen Klasse der Sächsischen Akademie der Wissenschaften 37.2. Leipzig: B. G. Teubner.
Bede. 1969. *Ecclesiastical History of the English People*, edited and translated by Bertram Colgrave and Roger A. B. Mynors. Oxford Medieval Texts. Oxford: Clarendon Press.
Hildegard of Bingen. 1978. *Hildegardis Scivias*, edited by Adelgundis Führkötter and Angela Carlevaris. Corpus Christianorum. Continuatio Mediaevalis 43. Turnhout: Brepols.
Hisperica Famina. 1974. *The Hisperica famina: I. The A-text*, edited by Michael Herren. Studies and Texts 31. Toronto: Pontifical Institute.
Martianus Capella. 1983. *Martianus Capella*, edited by James Willis. Bibliotheca scriptorum Graecorum et Romanorum Teubneriana. Leipzig: B. G. Teubner.
Neckam, Alexander. 2006. *Commentum super Martianum*, edited by Christopher McDonough. Millennio medievale 64. Florence: SISMEL, Edizioni del Galluzzo.
Zeno of Verona. 1971. *Tractatus*, edited by Bengt Löfstedt. Corpus Christianorum. Series Latina 22. Turnhout: Brepols.

Secondary sources

von Albrecht, Michael. 1989. *Masters of Roman Prose*, translated by Neil Adkin. ARCA classical and medieval texts, papers and monographs 23. Leeds: Francis Cairns.

Auerbach, Erich. 1953. *Mimesis. The Representation of Reality in Western Literature*, translated by Willard R. Trask. Princeton, NJ: Princeton University Press.

———. 1965. *Literary Language and its Public in Late Antiquity and the Middle Ages*, translated by Ralph Manheim. Princeton, NJ: Princeton University Press.

Axelson, Bertil. 1945. *Unpoetische Wörter. Ein Beitrag zur Kenntnis der lateinischen Dichtersprache*. Lund: C. W. K. Gleerup.

Bambeck, Manfred. 1993. "Fischer und Bauern gegen Philosophen und sonstige Großkopfeten: ein christlicher Topos in Antike und Mittelalter." *Mittellateinisches Jahrbuch* 18: 29–50.

Bourgain, Pascale. 2005. *Le latin médiéval*. L'atelier du médiéviste 10. Turnhout: Brepols.

Briscoe, Marianne G. 1992. *Artes Praedicandi*. Typologie des sources du moyen âge occidental 61. Turnhout: Brepols.

Brown, George. H. 2009. *A Companion to Bede*. Anglo-Saxon Studies 12. Woodbridge: Boydell.

Brugnoli, Giorgio. 1955. *Studi sulle Differentiae Verborum*. Rome: Angelo Signorelli.

Burnett, Charles S. F. and Peter Dronke, ed. 1998. *Hildegard of Bingen. The Context of her Thought and Art*. London: Warburg Institute.

Camargo, Martin. 1991. *Ars Dictaminis. Ars Dictandi*. Typologie des sources du moyen âge occidental 60. Turnhout: Brepols.

Charland, Thomas M. 1938. *Artes Praedicandi. Contribution à l'histoire de la rhétorique au moyen âge*. Paris: J. Vrin.

Curtius, Ernst R. 1953. *Latin Literature and the European Middle Ages*, translated by Willard R. Trask. Princeton, NJ: Princeton University Press.

Damon, Cynthia. 1997. *The Mask of the Parasite. A Pathology of Roman Patronage*. Ann Arbor, MI: University of Michigan Press.

Deferrari, Roy J. 1922. "St. Augustine's Method of Composing and Delivering Sermons." *American Journal of Philology* 43: 97–123, 193–219.

DeGregorio, Scott, ed. 2010. *The Cambridge Companion to Bede*. Cambridge Companions to Literature. Cambridge: Cambridge University Press.

Di Berardino, Angelo, ed. 1986. *Patrology. Volume IV. The Golden Age of Latin Patristic Literature*, translated by Placid Solari. Westminster, MD: Christian Classics.

Flanagan, Sabina. 1998. *Hildegard of Bingen. A Visionary Life*. 2nd edition. London: Routledge.

Frova, Carla. 1982/3. "Il *Polittico* attribuito ad Attone vescovo di Vercelli (924–960 ca.): tra storia e grammatica." *Bullettino dell' istituto storico Italiano* 90: 1–75.

Hagendahl, Harald. 1959. "Piscatorie et non Aristotelice." In *Septentrionalia et Orientalia. Studia Bernhardo Karlgren...dedicata*, 184–93. Kungl. Vitterhets historie och antikvitets akademiens handlingar 91. Stockholm: Almqvist and Wiksell.

Henry, James. 1873. *Aeneidea, or Critical, Exegetical and Aesthetical Remarks on the Aeneis*, vol. 1. London: Williams and Norgate.

Hunt, Richard W. 1984. *The Schools and the Cloister. The Life and Writings of Alexander Nequam (1157–1217)*. Oxford: Clarendon Press.

Janson, Tore. 1964. *Latin Prose Prefaces. Studies in Literary Conventions*. Acta Universitatis Stockholmiensis. Studia Latina Stockholmiensia 13. Stockholm: Almqvist and Wiksell.

———. 1975. *Prose Rhythm in Medieval Latin*. Acta Universitatis Stockholmiensis. Studia Latina Stockholmiensia 20. Stockholm: Almqvist and Wiksell.

Kelly, Douglas. 1991. *The Arts of Poetry and Prose*. Typologie des sources du moyen âge occidental 59. Turnhout: Brepols.

Kroll, Wilhelm. 1897. "Das afrikanische Latein." *Rheinisches Museum* 52: 569–90.

Lancel, Serge. 1985. "Y-a-t-il une Africitas?" *Revue des Études Latines* 63: 161–82.
Lapidge, Michael. 1975. "The Hermeneutic Style in Tenth-Century Anglo-Latin Literature." *Anglo-Saxon England* 4: 67–111.
Law, Vivien. 1995. *Wisdom, authority and grammar in the seventh century. Decoding Virgilius Maro Grammaticus*. Cambridge: Cambridge University Press.
Lendinara, Patrizia. 2005. "Contextualized Lexicography." In *Latin Learning and English Lore. Studies in Anglo-Saxon Literature for Michael Lapidge*, edited by Katherine O'Brien O'Keeffe and Andy Orchard, 2: 108–31. Toronto Old English series 14. Toronto: University of Toronto Press.
Liebeschuetz, Hans. 1930. *Das allegorische Weltbild der heiligen Hildegard von Bingen*. Leipzig: B. G. Teubner.
Mohrmann, Christine. 1957. *Liturgical Latin. Its Origins and Character*. Washington, DC: Catholic University of America Press.
Norberg, Dag. 1968. *Manuel pratique de latin médiéval*. Collection Connaissance des langues 4. Paris: Picard.
Norden, Eduard. 1909. *Die antike Kunstprosa*. 2 vols. Leipzig: B. G. Teubner.
Ogle, Marbury B. 1926. "Some Aspects of Mediaeval Latin Style." *Speculum* 1: 170–89.
Pabst, Bernhard. 1994. *Prosimetrum*. 2 vols. Ordo 4. Cologne: Böhlau.
Petersmann, H. 1998. "Gab es ein afrikanisches Latein?" In *Estudios de lingüística latina*, edited by Benjamin García-Hernandez, 125–36. Madrid: Ediciones Clásicas.
Pöschl, Viktor, et al. 1964. *Bibliographie zur antiken Bildersprache*. Bibliothek der klassischen Altertumswissenschaften, n. F., 1. Heidelberg: Carl Winter Universitätsverlag.
Polheim, Karl. 1925. *Die lateinische Reimprosa*. Berlin: Weidmann.
Quadlbauer, Franz. 1962. *Die antike Theorie der genera dicendi im lateinischen Mittelalter*. Sitzungsberichte der Österreichischen Akademie der Wissenschaften. Philosophisch-Historische Klasse 241, 2. Abhandlung. Vienna: Österreichische Akademie der Wissenschaften.
Queneau, Raymond. 1947. *Exercices de style*. Collection Soleil. Paris: Gallimard.
Rahner, Hugo. 1964. *Symbole der Kirche*. Salzburg: Otto Müller Verlag.
Roberts, Michael. 1989. *The Jewelled Style*. Ithaca, NY: Cornell University Press.
Rockinger, Ludwig, ed. 1863. *Briefsteller und Formelbücher des elften bis vierzehnten Jahrhunderts*. Quellen und Erörterungen zur bayerischen und deutschen Geschichte 9. Munich: Franz.
Shanzer, Danuta. 2007. "Bede's Style: A Neglected Historiographical Model for the Style of the *Historia Ecclesiastica*." In *Source of Wisdom. Old English and Early Medieval Latin Studies in Honour of Thomas D. Hill*, edited by Charles D. Wright, Frederick M. Biggs, and Thomas N. Hall, 329–52. Toronto Old English Series. Toronto: University of Toronto Press.
Sharpe, Richard. 2005. "The Varieties of Bede's Prose." In *Aspects of the Language of Latin Prose*, edited by Tobias Reinhardt, Michael Lapidge and James N. Adams, 339–55. Proceedings of the British Academy 129. Oxford: Oxford University Press.
Sittl, Karl. 1882. *Die lokalen Verschiedenheiten der lateinischen Sprache mit besonderer Berücksichtigung des afrikanischen Lateins*. Erlangen: Andreas Deichert.
Stotz, Peter. 1998. *Handbuch zur lateinischen Sprache des Mittelalters. Vierter Band: Formenlehre, Syntax und Stilistik*. Handbuch der Altertumswissenschaft, 2. Abt., 5. T., 4. Bd. Munich: C. H. Beck.
Strunk, William, Jr. and Elwyn B. White. 1979. *The Elements of Style*. 3rd edition. New York: Macmillan.

Tunberg, Terence. 1996. "Prose Styles and Cursus." In *Medieval Latin. An Introduction and Bibliographical Guide*, edited by Frank Mantello and Arthur G. Rigg, 111–21. Washington, DC: Catholic University of America.

Wemple, Suzanne F. 1979. *Atto of Vercelli*. Temi e testi 27. Rome: Edizioni di storia e letteratura.

Winterbottom, Michael. 1977. "Aldhelm's Prose Style and its Origins." *Anglo-Saxon England* 6: 39–76.

Ziolkowski, Jan. 1996. "Theories of Obscurity in the Latin Tradition." *Mediaevalia* 19: 101–70.

CHAPTER 12

VERSE STYLE[1]

JEAN-YVES TILLIETTE

Translated by Emily Blakelock

DOES verse style exist in medieval Latin literature? As strange as this question seems, it is legitimate for two main reasons. The first is linked to the singular linguistic status of medieval Latin. From the time when Latin ceases to be a mother tongue (a progressive process), its nature as a learned language paradoxically confers great freedom upon its most competent users. Liberated from the demands of simplicity and immediacy associated with everyday usage, they can give freer rein to the whims of invention, to the dazzling qualities of artifice in both prose and verse. For example, the two versions of the *Life of St. Christopher*, one in hexameters and one in prose, composed just before the year 1000 by Walter of Speyer (Walter of Speyer 1937), both employ scholarly, complex, and obscure language, replete with the play of homophones, internal rhymes, and parallelisms also found abundantly in eleventh-century narrative chronicles and formally related to writing techniques used in the lyric poetry of the same period (Bourgain 2002).

The second reason the identification of typical poetic modes of expression is not a simple process is related to content rather than to form. As we have just suggested in the case of Walter of Speyer's double *Vita et passio Sancti Christophori* (and hagiographic literature offers many other examples), the same theme can be developed in an equally effective way in both prose and verse (Dolbeau 2002, 128–32). This suggests that, strictly speaking, there is no exclusive province reserved for poetry, and more explicitly that poetry has the right to treat any possible subject in verse. Compared to the categories inherited from Hegel's *Aesthetics*, which posit

---

1. I should especially like to thank Emily Blakelock for her work both on the translation of this essay and on the technical aspects of presentation–JYT

only epic, lyric, or dramatic poetry, there is something disconcerting about seeing verse treat subjects like Latin grammar (Alexander of Villedieu, Eberhard of Bethune), botany (Walahfrid Strabo), pharmacopeia (the *Macer floridus*), mineralogy (Marbod's lapidary), pedagogy (Abelard, *Carmen ad Astrolabium*), the history of ideas (John of Salisbury, *Entheticus maior*), and so on. Frederick J. E. Raby's classic volumes on medieval Latin poetry (1953 and 1957) thus record an astonishing diversity of linguistic objects under the single title of "poetry."

Indeed, grammatical instruction passed down from the teachers of late antiquity continues to contrast prose, *prosa,* which is defined etymologically as "that which goes forwards (*proru[i]t*), which follows a continuous forward motion," with verse, *versus,* "that which turns back on itself (*revertitur*), which doubles back to the margin of the page" (Isidore of Seville, *Etymologiae* 1.38.1, 1.39.2). But does this opposition describe a reality other than the obvious one of codicological layout (Bourgain 1989)? It is uncertain that medieval authors could rely on precepts as reassuring as the one Molière's "bourgeois gentilhomme" learns from his philosophy master, for whom "all which is not verse is prose," and vice versa. Instead, a system with multiple terms is outlined in the *artes dictaminis* which begin to flourish in the eleventh and twelfth centuries. Following a trajectory begun by Bede the Venerable in his *De arte metrica,* they usually enumerate three forms of *dictamen,* understanding this term to mean "writing governed by the rules of art," rather than the more frequent, but stricter, definition "epistolary writing." Defined in this way, *dictamen* can be *prosaicum, metricum,* or *rythmicum* (see Conrad of Hirsau's *Dialogus super auctores* for a twelfth-century definition, and for the thirteenth century see Bene of Florence's *Candelabrum*). The last two correspond to what we would call "verse" or "poetry," but are subject to different methods of composition: *dictamen metricum* follows the rules of classical versification, which is based on the opposition between long and short syllables, and their organization into feet, while the *dictamen rythmicum* is based on the number of syllables, the regular occurrence of tonic accent, and to a lesser extent on rhyme, *consonantia dictionum* [sounding similar] or *similiter desinens* [with a similar ending] (Norberg 1958, 87–94). Some Italian theorists of the thirteenth century will add *prosimetricum* and *prosirythmicum* to these two models, which designate prose which is so measured and rhythmical that it resembles poetry without actually being poetry, rather than the alternation of prose and metrical or rhythmic poetry, as is often assumed (Turcan-Verkerk 2003, 136–56). And what can be said of the psalm versicles, which St. Jerome calls *versus,* or of the primitive Notkerian sequence, which modern editions print in verse format, but which contains no metrical or accentual regularity because of the extent to which the verse is subordinated to the music to which it is set, the modulation of the alleluia? (See Boynton and Fassler in this volume.)

The purpose of these preliminary remarks is to emphasize the diverse and fluid character of medieval Latin poetry. It would certainly be presumptuous to attempt to situate it in a framework of universal and constraining stylistic rules. Our goal here is only to make some sense of this diversity, and to identify a few major characteristics of a corpus with such vast and uncertain limits. With this in mind, we will follow a path from the concrete to the abstract, from the role of form to its intended effects, from the aural resonance of words to their spiritual resonance.

The Constraints of Form

Starting in the third or fourth century, the system which had formed the basis of Latin versification, a system of phonetic opposition between long and short syllables, begins to weaken: in his apocalyptic epic entitled *Carmen de duobus populis*, the Syrian writer Commodian (second half of the third century), a native speaker of a Semitic language, is completely indifferent to it, and only preserves the recurrence of the six marked beats, or *ictus*, of hexameter. It is curious to note that in the ninth century, in a similar eschatological context, Paul Alvarus of Cordoba will give the name *versus heroici* to hexameters that are equally awkward (Norberg 1958, 10). From the end of the fourth century, there is a marked divide between scholarly usage and direct aural perception, at least in some areas of the Roman Empire: according to Augustine, "Afrae aures de correptione vocalium vel productione non iudicant" [African ears do not discern the shortening or lengthening of vowels] (*De doctrina Christiana* 4.10.24), and the disciple to whom he teaches pronunciation in his dialogue *De musica* admits ignorance of the quantity of syllables ("syllabarum longarum vel brevium cognitionem non habeo," 3.3.5), while in Cicero's day, even the uneducated public was well aware of syllabic quantity and would copiously heckle any actor who pronounced a short syllable as long, or vice versa (*De oratore* 3.196). By the beginning of the Middle Ages, this process is complete: even the most educated are deaf to the music of antique verse. Ennodius, bishop of Pavia at the beginning of the sixth century and one of his day's most sophisticated and erudite writers of Latin, trusts his eyes, not his ears, to guarantee the metrical accuracy of his poetry: "non enim possunt esse solidata versuum vestigia luminis officio destituta" [the workings of verse cannot be assured if the function of the eye is absent] (Polara 1995, 64–65).

Yet metrical poetry continues to be produced. The prestige attached to a form perfected by illustrious classical models surely plays a role in explaining its continued popularity. But the persistent success of the poetic formats and genres transmitted by the Latin tradition can also be explained by the inertia of educational institutions. The school of the *grammaticus* (which should be translated "teacher of literature") is the descendant of Late Antique schools, and is characterized by a remarkably stable curriculum, in which the work of the poets predominates, and by great consistency in its pedagogical methods. The exercise of *lectio*, the glossed reading of classical *auctores* and their Christian imitators, is at its foundation. This can be amplified by the exercise of imitation: in the Ottonian empire, the most gifted students are set the task of transposing the life of a venerated saint into verse, as a final record of the end of their studies (like the metrical *Vita et passio Sancti*

Christophori by Walter of Speyer, for example) (Dolbeau 2002, 136–37). The music of verse is no longer perceived intuitively and becomes the subject of a technical apprenticeship. Manuals for prosody, starting with those of ancient grammarians like Sacerdos or Servius, number by the dozens throughout the Middle Ages (Leonhardt 1989, 196–235). Theory can also be demonstrated through practical examples: numerous prosodic florilegia survive in which the verses of the *auctores* serve as models for the analysis of syllabic quantity and of the respective patterns of various metrical feet. In manuscripts, these last are often underlined with diacritical marks, like commas, which separate the feet between words or even in the middle of a word. In the same spirit, an author like Aldhelm, in his *De metris et enigmatibus ac pedum regulis* (ca. 700), describes Juvenal's verse "Omenta? ut video nullum discrimen habendum est" (Juvenal, *Saturae* 13.118) in the following way: "scanditur omen spondeus, tautvide dactilus per sinalipham, onul spondeus, lumdis spondeus, crimenha dactilus, bendum est spondeus per sinalipham" [*omen* should be scanned a spondee, *t(a)utvide* a dactyl with a synalepha, *onul* a spondee, *lumdis* a spondee, *crimenha* a dactyl, *bendum(e)st* a spondee with a synalepha] (Aldhelm, *De metris* 9).

This tendency to dismantle verse is evidence of the decidedly artificial character of metrical versification in the Middle Ages, whose rules are then made even more rigid by theorists: thus, through a process of hypercorrection, purists do not hesitate to banish all use of elision, or to recommend a monotone system of breaks overwhelmingly dominated by the penthemimeral caesura (after the first syllable of the third foot) (Orlandi 1988, 161–65). The overall effect of these rules is that word order becomes mechanical. Rigidification is due as well to the almost universal adoption of dactylic verse by medieval metrical poets. With very few exceptions, such as the Sapphic stanza, only a few virtuosos write Aeolic verse. Dactylic hexameter and pentameter, moreover, are badly suited to Latin phonetics, being in origin an importation from the Greek tradition. Their triumph manifests itself in the invasion of seemingly formulaic expressions into medieval Latin poetry, or at least into the poetry that claims to derive from classical models.

But this judgment would benefit from a more nuanced perspective. At a very modest level of competence are the hagiographic *Legends* of Hrotsvit of Gandersheim, who is more inspired when she takes on the task of composing drama in rhythmical prose. The hexameters of the *Legends* are riddled with words like *itaque, etenim, porro, quoque*, empty of any semantic significance, but intended to provide the short syllables that are indispensable for the construction of dactyls (Leotta 1995, 208–9). At the other extreme, some of Hildebert of Lavardin's epigrams (ca. 1100) are so well-crafted that they were long considered to be the work of Late Antique poets, and were classed as such in the editions of the *Anthologia latina* until the end of the nineteenth century; critics remain hesitant about the date of the *Bucolics*, written by the mysterious Marcus Valerius in either the sixth or twelfth century (Dolbeau 1987, 167–68). Most commonly, classicizing medieval poetry, like the Christian epic of the fifth or sixth century, which is its chief inspiration, gives the impression of a patchwork since it is woven from remembrances, be they conscious or unconscious, of formulas borrowed from classical models. Its masterpiece, the *Alexandreis* of Walter of Châtillon, thus contains, according to the meticulous accounting of its editor Marvin Colker, a classically inspired *junctura* in almost half its verses (Walter of Châtillon 1978).

In both medieval and classical literary theory, *imitatio* is a virtue. Nevertheless, it is threatened by the risk of sterility and servility, especially when under the severe constraints just mentioned. This is probably one of the factors which pushed medieval poets to explore an alternative solution, that of *rythmus*, which, as opposed to the *metrum*, is based entirely on the judgment of the ear, since its chief organizational principle is the regular tonic accent of the words (to be distinguished from the metrical *ictus*), and secondarily consonance at the ends of periods, assonance or rhyme. The processes by which metrical versification evolved into a rhythmic system are complex, and are the subject of extremely technical analyses by specialists (Burger 1957, 82–106; Norberg 1958, 87–135). We will illustrate them with a simple example, that of the hymn classified as "Ambrosian."

It was in dramatic circumstances, as reported by Augustine in his *Confessiones* (9.7.15), that Ambrose, the bishop of Milan, perfected the use of the liturgical hymn in 386. This poetry arises from a religious observance marked by a threefold character: musical, doctrinal, and communal, with the goal of affirming the morals and faith of its hearers. To this end, he employs a very simple metrical structure, one almost never used in pagan poetry, that of iambic dimeter, the succession of four iambs each composed of one short and one long syllable, with the stress on the *ictus*, or marked beat of the long syllable. These verses are grouped into quatrains, according to a model destined to become canonical. Here is an example of an Ambrosian stanza:

> Aeterne rerum conditor
> Noctem diemque qui regis
> Et temporum das tempora
> Ut alleves fastidium.
>
> [Eternal creator of all things,
> who rules both night and day,
> and gives time its meaning,
> to lift our hardship.] (Raby 1961, 8)

Ambrose was a very cultured man, and the meter of these verses is perfectly correct, both in the arrangement of long and short syllables and the placement of the *ictus*. But one can also observe that this structure usually allows the "natural" tonic accent of the words to coincide with the metrical *ictus* (aetErne rErum cOnditor), a phenomenon rare in dactylic poetry. Ambrose's verse is more easily imprinted on the memory and heart of an audience with little literary education because it is closer to the structure of everyday language. And this audience was quick to interpret Ambrose's perfect iambic dimeters as proparoxytonic octosyllables, accented on the antepenultimate syllable. Already in 475, bishop Auspicius of Toul writes:

> Magnas caelesti domino
> Rependo corde gratias
> quod te Tullensi proxime
> Magnum in urbe vidimus.
>
> [I offer from my heart great thanks
> to the celestial Lord
> that I saw your greatness
> in the city of Toul.] (Raby 1961, 43)

Perhaps he thought he was composing an Ambrosian stanza, but his metrically flawed verses bear no relation to iambic dimeter (Norberg 1958, 106–9).

This same process will cause the various metrical schemes to evolve to form "verses" (even if some theorists hesitate to give this name to rhythmic periods) characterized first by their number of syllables, second, by the accent which falls on their last word, as either proparoxytonic or paroxytonic (on the third-last or second-last syllable, respectively). In any case, it is certain that rhythmic versification is the child, albeit the bastard child, of metrical versification. Some models are particularly fruitful, especially iambic and trochaic verses, which are considered the closest to ordinary spoken language: these are the verses of dramatic dialogue, comic or tragic (Nougaret 1956, 60–63). Should the "learned" *metrum* be considered the opposite of a *rythmus* which is termed "popular"? Certainly not. Their difference lies in their usage and function. If metrical poetry, in the image of its classical models, is intended for individual reading—an assertion we will refine shortly—rhythmical poetry spreads through oral, musical, and communal means. This is true of liturgical poetry (addressed by Susan Boynton and Margot Fassler elsewhere in this volume), which is preserved in tens of thousands of witnesses, but also of its parodies, the most complete collection of which is the famous *Carmina Burana* (not to mention battle songs, attested by very old examples). But for every inexpert poet who wields hexameters heavily and awkwardly, there is a virtuoso of rhythmical verse. Among such adepts, Adam of St. Victor's liturgical sequences wed an absolute mastery of word order and sound to a deep doctrinal significance. He writes thus about divine love:

> Lumen carum, lumen clarum
> internarum tenebrarum
>   effugas caliginem.
> Per te mundi sunt mundati,
> tu peccatum, tu peccati
> destruis rubiginem.
>
> [Dear light, clear light
> you drive out the fog
> of inner darkness.
> Through you the good are purified,
> You banish both sin and its stain.] (Adam of St. Victor 2008, 335)

The play on sound that characterizes this stanza, with its repetition of *lumen*, the paronomasia of *carum-clarum*, the etymological figure *mundi—mundati*, the polyptoton *peccatum—peccati*, the richness of the rhymes (*caliginem—rubiginem*), including internal rhymes (*internarum tenebrarum*), overall make up a work in which each phoneme has weight, reminding us that medieval poetry, even Latin poetry, is most of all carried by the breath and the voice (see Grosfillier's detailed commentary on this text, Adam of St. Victor 2008, 642–48). This literature, like its vernacular sibling, is an oral literature.

Such orality applies even to medieval Latin poetry's most "written" forms. We have several witnesses to the fact that metrical poetry was also intended to be recited. Baudri of Bourgueil (ca. 1100) concludes his massive encyclopedic poem (almost 700 distichs of unusually great difficulty) with the injunction, addressed to the bearer of these verses, "reddat recitetque" [let him recite and declaim] them to their recipient, the countess Adela of Blois (Tilliette 2002, 43). Some treatises on the art of poetry, like Geoffrey of Vinsauf's *Poetria nova*, give advice (which is itself difficult to interpret) on how to articulate these declamations aloud. There are even musical notations associated with excerpts of the classical epics of Virgil, Lucan, and Statius (Ziokowski 2007, 1–37).

It is in this spirit that medieval culture will treat traditional versification with a fair amount of disrespect (an attitude the Renaissance will in turn prohibit), imagining forms that can almost be considered to be halfway between the *metrum* and the *rythmus*. Assonance, starting in the sixth century, then rhyme, from the ninth century, punctuate rhythmical verses more and more frequently. But even hexameter will begin to admit rhyme under the form called "leonine verse," which uses consonance between the word placed at the penthemimeral caesura of the verse and that which ends it. This practice, attested sporadically since the Carolingian era (as in Gottschalk of Orbais's poem for Ratramnus), comes increasingly into vogue by the turn of the twelfth century, as in the work of Marbod, the first author of a medieval *ars poetica*, *De ornamentis verborum* (Marbod 1998). It has the effect of dividing verses into two asymmetrical parts of 5–7 and 8–10 syllables respectively, linked by their last syllables, which assimilates their vocal effect to that of rhythmical poetry. This effect is even more marked as poets begin to imagine more complex systems that combine internal and final rhymes. The most spectacular example is the poem *De contemptu mundi* (Bernard of Cluny 2009), composed in the mid-twelfth century. Each of its 2,966 hexameters not only links the end of the second and fourth foot with a rhyme, often a disyllabic one, but also the last syllables of two successive verses:

> Aurea temp*ora* primaque rob*ora* praeteri**erunt**
> Aurea gens f*uit* et simul haec r*uit*, illa ru**erunt.**
> Flebilis in*cipit* aurea, sus*cipit* aurea **metas**
> Transiit oc*ius* et studium pr*ius* et prior a**etas**…
>
> [The golden age and early vigour have passed by
> The golden race thrived, and just like them, fell away.
> Gold begins to be mourned, gold comes to an end;
> Earlier customs and the previous age have both slipped away so quickly.]
> (*De contemptu mundi* 2.1–4)

It is hardly necessary to outline the other devices that reinforce this obsessive cadence, like the paronomasia *aurea—area*, the polyptota *ruit—ruerunt* and *prius—prior*, the etymological figure *incipit—suscipit*. Verses like this, called *tripertiti dactylici* because they are divided into three parts and are composed only of dactyls, resolutely shatter the mold of classical hexameter, whose system of breaks is totally annihilated. These verses are diametrically opposed to the fluidity of Ovid's verses. Still, do they trespass against the language itself? The morphology of Latin, which places heavily marked grammatical inflexions at the ends of words and which very often tends towards suffixal derivation, authorizes this approach. And the poet can adapt it to his topic: the heavy hammering of rhymes can underline the gravity of the message, parallelisms can emphasize its obviousness, or constant repetition with variations can drive home its urgency. Thus, in a preface with a lofty tone, Bernard claims to have put beauty (*decor*) at the service of efficiency (*utilitas*). His contemporary audience must have agreed with him, since the manuscript tradition of *De contemptu mundi* bears evidence of its wide distribution.

In a lighter register, poetry is a favorite site for plays on the words, graphemes, and phonemes that constitute it: acrostics, palindromes, *vers rapportés* (which can be read vertically), retrograde verses (which can be read both forwards and backwards), echo effects like that which reproduces the first hemistich of a hexameter in the second hemistich of a pentameter (this is *epanalepsis,* so dear to Sedulius Scottus), or concatenation (the repetition of the end of one verse at the beginning of another). These are highly characteristic of the art of writing in the Middle Ages. We will cite only one extreme example of this playful use of language from the *Ecloga de calvis* [praise of bald men] by the poet Hucbald of St. Amand, who was also one of the greatest medieval music theorists. His 136 hexameters contain only words that start with the letter C, the first initial of the poem's dedicatee, the emperor Charles the Bald (Carolus Calvus):

> Carmina, clarisonae, calvis cantate, Camenae.
> Comere condigno conabor carmine calvos,
> Contra cirrosi crines confundere colli...
>
> [Muses, sing a boisterous song for bald men.
> I will try to adorn bald heads with a fitting song,
>   and, conversely, to muss the hair of those with ample curls...]
> (*Ecloga de calvis* 4–6)

We will soon see that what seems at first glance to be word-fueled intoxication has other causes. We will content ourselves in the meanwhile with invoking a few less staggering examples of the pleasure the ear takes in the musicality of words. The first of the late twelfth-century poetry manuals, the *Ars versificatoria* by Matthew of Vendôme (ca. 1175), advocates a sharp return to classicism. To that end, it condemns all use of rhyme as pointless and puerile, most likely because it is not attested by the classical tradition. Matthew devotes no less than one whole book of his manual to the choice of words, and underlines the poetic effect of long, sonorous adjectives ending in *-alis* (*effugialis, favoralis, exsequialis,...*), -*osus* (*officiosus, imperiosus, deliciosus,...*), -*ivus* (*responsivus, incentivus, petitivus,...*), -*atus* (*illaqueatus, orbiculatus, primiciatus,...*), -*aris* (*articularis, exemplaris,...*), and also of comparatives in -*ior* (*floridior, sordidior, cognitior,...*), at the same time forbidding the use of short atonal adverbs and conjunctions (*porro, quoque, itaque,...*) (Matthew of Vendôme 1988, 140–50). One can see parallels with Dante, who, in *De vulgari eloquentia* (2.7.6), praises those resounding polysyllables which confer harmony upon speech, *speranza, gravitate, alleviato, impassibilità, beneventuratissimo, inanimatissimamente....* Even the poetic work that appears to be the pinnacle of classicizing medieval Latin verse, Walter of Châtillon's *Alexandreis*, which was destined to replace the *Aeneid* as a canonical text in the schools of the thirteenth century, makes constant (and not very Virgilian) use of poetic devices that depend on the impact of resonance and homophony, such as paronomasia and polyptoton, while it is otherwise reminiscent of the traditional epic formula (Tilliette 2008, 269–74). In short, even if the melody of hexameter, which was once carried by the *ictus* and the alternation of long and short syllables, has been lost, poetry has not completely abandoned the realm of the voice.

Intertextual Games

The poetic style of the Middle Ages is therefore the site of a subtle dialectic between self and other. Emblematic of this idea is the first example of the medieval revival of epic, a poem composed around 800 to celebrate Charlemagne, known as *Paderborn epos* [the epic of Paderborn] or *Karolus Magnus et Leo Papa* [Charlemagne and Pope Leo] (*Karolus Magnus et Leo Papa* 1881). One of the extant fragments depicts the future emperor presiding over the construction of his new capital at Aix-la-Chapelle. It does so in the form of a very faithful paraphrase of the passage in Book 1 of the *Aeneid* in which Virgil depicts the Tyrians in the midst of building Carthage, and the poet does not hesitate, following his model, to equip the Germanic city with a theatre, and even a port, contrary to all geographic reality. Must we view this as evidence of foolish *naïveté*, or of the medieval poet's slavish devotion to his source? Certainly not. When describing the "second Rome" which is Aix, the anonymous poet found in his literary memory, and more precisely in the most prestigious work of Latin literature, an image of the ideal city, the only one worthy to embody Charlemagne's ambition of building a local counterpart to the city of God. Compared to this ambition, the mediocre demands of "realism" have no importance. It is even possible that the poet was conscious that Virgil had done the same thing, providing his imaginary Carthage with the splendors of Augustus's Rome.

The same poet describes a deer hunt led by the king in which Charles proves his mastery of the noble sport *par excellence*, and perhaps by extension his ability to beat back the enemies of the faith, who are symbolized by the black, hairy, and ferocious beast. The model for this passage does not come from the *Aeneid* but from

Book 3 of Venantius Fortunatus's hagiographic epic devoted to the life and miracles of St. Martin, written around 575. In it, we see the bishop of Tours, using only the power of charisma, save a hare that is being pursued over the fields by a band of horsemen and their pack of furious hounds. Here, we witness a semantic inversion along with the word for word repetition of quite a few expressions. The tenderness of Martin, the Roman saint, is contrasted with Charlemagne's Germanic bravery: on one side lies a domesticated rural landscape and a small inoffensive animal, on the other, the thickets of the vast forest which still covers pagan Europe, and a wild and dangerous beast. These depictions are highly indicative of the ideals of two different eras and of two opposite figures of Christian heroism, the bishop who protects the weak, who is a peacemaker and missionary, and the warrior who yearns to conquer Evil. A powerful contrast emerges from these intertextual echoes.

Thus the practice of literary imitation arises from anything but a timid and lazy attitude. Although our own post-Romantic era tends to prize originality above all else, medieval poets were only following in the footsteps of their classical predecessors: after all, Terence's comedies, Virgil's *Bucolics*, and Horace's *Odes* are nothing other than fantastic re-creations of the works of Menander, Theocritus, and Pindar, respectively, fully Roman despite their translation from Greek, and fully responsive to the expectations of their audience. In the same way, the selection of prized models by medieval poets and their various methods of using these models reflect their aesthetics. According to an old cliché, not totally deprived of relevance, the history of medieval Latin poetry can be divided into three periods, each one characterized by a favorite author whose work gives it its "color." The Carolingian era, engaged in the praise of the sovereign and his exploits and prone to the didactic, is the *aetas virgiliana* [age of Virgil]; the monastic movement of the tenth and eleventh century will appropriate the mistrust of the world found in Horace and other satirists such as Terence, Persius, and Juvenal (*aetas horatiana*); the renaissance of the twelfth century, which revives love poetry and a kind of naturalism, prizes the reading of Ovid (*aetas ovidiana*) (Traube 1911, 113). This narrative is corroborated by reception history: according to extant manuscripts, the peaks in popularity of the three classical poets correspond to the periods assigned to them. All the same, we must take a nuanced view of such a summary periodization. When Ovid was rediscovered, appreciation of Virgil and Horace did not cease. Each writer, according to his temperament, the affinity he feels with various models, the literary genre he writes or the audience he seeks, takes his inspiration wherever he finds it. Rather than basing our argument on dangerous historical generalizations, we would instead propose a phenomenology (rather than a typology) of intertextual encounters and their stylistic consequences.

As we have already shown, the first and most widespread technique of imitation is unattributed word-for-word citation. Since we have already described this practice, we will not dwell on it. An effect of education, it often arises out of a more or less conscious remembrance, and occurs most often in parts of the verse where lexical choices are limited by the demands of prosody: in hexameter, the first foot or the last two feet. Many authors have begun a verse with the words *Me miserum*, and finished another with *lumina solis* or *lumina somno* without having the slightest awareness that they are citing Ovid on one hand, Virgil on the other (see Schumann 1979–83 for a collection of these formulas and the data provided in Mastandrea and Tessarolo 2010). Such borrowings confer an antique patina on a medieval text, ornamenting it with "gems drawn from a quarry of precious stones" (Vinay 1978, 481), which make the poem sparkle, just as antique gems and cameos were mounted on reliquaries that preserved the bodily remains of saints—and on this subject, it is surely not a coincidence that the lives of saints make up a substantial part of the poetry written in epic verse between the ninth and twelfth century. More intentional borrowings can also coincide with sense, as is the case with the most learned and competent poets. Baudri of Bourgueil, whose inspiration is extremely varied, thus makes use of the *Bucolics* and *Georgics* of Virgil, and to a lesser extent Horace's *Satire* 2.6, in the poem *De sufficientia votorum suorum* [On the fulfilment of his desires] (*Carm.* 126), which praises the charms of a country retreat, while his description of the battle of Hastings is a veritable cento of selections from the *Aeneid*, Lucan's *Pharsalia*, and Statius's *Thebaid*. And the brilliant mid-thirteenth-century poet Henry of Avranches starts his metrical lives of saints Oswald and Hugh of Lincoln, which are intended to extol the former's thaumaturgical power and the latter's victorious battles against the devil, with the words *In nova fert animus* and *Arma virumque cano*, the respective incipits of the *Metamorphoses* and the *Aeneid*.

The mimetic ability of medieval poets can inspire them towards pastiche. The *Alexandreis* of Walter of Châtillon makes no secret of its aim to rival the *Aeneid*. In fact, it contains a description of a shield, that of Darius (*Alex.* 2.494–539), which corresponds to that of Aeneas's shield (*Aen.* 8), and, in a considerable extension of an episode barely mentioned in the poem's historical source, Quintus Curtius, the daring exploits of two young Macedonian warriors, Symmachus and Nicanor (*Alex.* 10.77–147), whose story parallels that of Nisus and Euryalus in *Aeneid* 9. The poet even includes a descent to the underworld, that of the goddess Nature (*Alex.* 10.6–162). Still more faithful to his favorite poet, Baudri of Bourgueil rewrites Ovid's *Heroides* 16 and 17 (the exchange of letters between Paris and Helen) in his own style. These are not merely brilliant exercises in style: the reuse of ancient forms carries with it meaningful contemporary concerns. By pretending to walk in the footsteps of Virgil, Walter of Châtillon radically reorients the historical and human message of the original: while the iconography of Aeneas's shield heralded the future glories of Rome, that of Darius's shield prefigures the crumbling of the Persian empire, and while Aeneas's descent to the underworld ended with a grandiose vision of the triumphs of Augustus, that of Nature announces the inglorious death of Alexander, a symbol of the fleeting and provisional character of all earthly glory. It is no accident that Walter, by dividing his poem into ten books like the *Pharsalia* and not twelve like the *Aeneid*, places himself under the authority of Lucan, the anti-Virgil, who makes men and their passions the mere toys of the whims of Fortune. Baudri writes in a lighter register, but reveals equal poetic mastery. His Helen is certainly not the impish coquette described by Ovid, but instead bears a certain resemblance to the distant lady praised by the troubadours. It is not so much that the medieval poet was a bad reader. On the contrary, he fully understood the Roman poet's humor, which was based on the anachronistic transposition of Achaean heroes into a sphere that is in no way epic. The proof lies in another pair of epistles composed by Baudri, but this time the protagonists are the author himself and a young nun named Constance. The spiritual friendship that seems to be the focus of this probably fictitious correspondence disguises an obscene undertone, emphasized by ample Ovidian references (Tilliette 1992, 148–57).

With this example, we slide from pastiche to parody. The ironic relationship between medieval poems and the authoritative texts that are their source seems to have been a dominant characteristic of that great era of Latin literature, the renaissance of the twelfth century. Goliardic poetry offers innumerable examples. The flavor is already there in the mid-ninth-century work of the Irish master Sedulius Scottus. His poem 41 recounts in epic style the plight of a ram torn to pieces by a hound—and therefore, from the poet's perspective, the loss of a promising Irish stew—drawing equally from the battle scenes of the *Aeneid* and the account of Christ's passion through the precise use of textual allusions. A burlesque, or even carnivalesque, dimension tends to emerge, especially in beast poetry, and most of all in the main work of this genre, an epic in seven books called *Ysengrimus* (ca. 1150). With an understanding of the epic genre as certain and masterful as that of Walter of Châtillon, the author retells the (often obscene and scatological) tales of the struggle between the wolf and the fox, thus killing two birds with one stone, since he mocks both the corrupt clerics symbolized by these animals and the principles of the noblest of genres. (On *Ysengrimus* and its connections to vernacular literatures, see Murdoch in this volume.)

In the case of rewriting, the author does not limit himself to the use of an arsenal of formulas or a stylistic model, but decides to remake an entire work. This can take place in various ways. A good example of stylistic transformation is the *Iliad* by the English poet Joseph of Exeter (ca. 1180). His epic in six books is an exact paraphrase of a text which adopts the blandest and flattest writing style in all of Latin literature, the *Historia destructionis Troiae* by Dares the Phrygian, but Joseph's verses are laden with gaudy rhetorical devices (Sedgwick 1930, 49–59). On the other hand, a thematic transformation occurs when a text is faithful to the letter, but opposed to the spirit, of its model. The scenes composed by Hrotsvit of Gandersheim (d. 975) for the edification of her sisters echo the comedies of Terence, but the delights of sacred love stand in for the poisons of profane love. Less renowned but even more astonishing, Metellus of Tegernsee (d. 1160), a worthy predecessor of Jorge Luis Borges's Pierre Menard, takes up the characters, situations and structure of Virgil's ten eclogues in his *Quirinalia*, but for the purpose of celebrating the miracles of St. Quirin, the protector of his monastery (Metellus 1988).

We will close this catalogue with a discussion of transposition, which aims to adapt a canonical work to the tastes and requirements of the present day. Around the year 1210, the very title of Geoffrey of Vinsauf's *Poetria nova* proclaims his intention to dethrone Horace's *Ars poetica*, or *Poetria vetus*. Both works are written in hexameters, thus giving verse itself the task of enunciating the rules of poetic composition—otherwise they seem to have as little in common as James Joyce's *Ulysses* and Homer's *Odyssey*. But a closer analysis can uncover very precise replies in Geoffrey's work to the questions which, according to the grammar teachers of the twelfth century, are raised by Horace's rambling and seemingly disordered reflections. Geoffrey's goal is to found an authentically Christian poetics, a marked break with the great classical models. As is often the case, theory here comes after practice, and Geoffrey is only reassembling and synthesizing the (often very novel) poetic experiments to which the renaissance of the twelfth century is devoted. So what is this new poetics and this new poetry?

The Poetic Turning Point of the First Half of the Twelfth Century

Geoffrey of Vinsauf was perhaps not wrong in reclaiming "novelty" for the poetic writing of his time. Over the two generations from 1130 to 1180, medieval Latin poetry produced its greatest masterpieces: the comedies of Vitalis of Blois, the *Ysengrimus*, Peter Riga's biblical paraphrase *Aurora*, the *Alexandreis* by Walter of Châtillon and the *Iliad* by Joseph of Exeter, Alan of Lille's philosophical allegory *Anticlaudianus*, and, in rhythmic poetry, the liturgical work of Adam of Saint Victor and the satirical and erotic works of Hugh the Primate, the Archpoet, Walter of Châtillon, and Peter of Blois. For all their variety, these authors share their decided break from classical style. Whatever models continue to be invoked and used—Plautus for Vitalis of Blois, Lucan and Claudian for Walter of Châtillon, Prudentius for Alan of Lille…—the era of imitation is entirely in the past. Poetry is now exploring new stylistic territory.

The poetry of the Carolingian era and the two centuries following stays faithful, for the most part, to the methods of late antique Christian poetry, which consisted of reappropriating words and formulas from canonical works to express original content. The fullest expression of this ideal was the cento, the prime example of which was provided by the biblical paraphrase the noblewoman Faltonia Proba confected in the mid-fourth century out of hexameters drawn from the works of Virgil. (On centos and other features of late antique poetics, see Formisano in this volume.) Without going too far into the practice of literary vampirism, the Christian poets of late antiquity, Juvencus, Sedulius, Avitus, and Arator, scatter many expressions lifted from classical authors throughout their versified adaptations of the holy books, which thus appear as embedded citations: the description of the storm calmed by Christ in Juvencus's *Evangelica historia* (2.25–42), for example, owes much to that of the gale Juno inflicts on the Trojans in the first book of the *Aeneid*. These authors, who are little remembered today, constitute the core of poetic culture for the writers of the Carolingian era even more than the pagan classics: they are at the top of the lists of *auctores* drawn up by Alcuin and Theodulph, the two most talented poets of Charlemagne's court, well before Virgil, Ovid, or Terence (Glauche 1970, 10–37). Late antique Christian epics comprise four-fifths of Cambridge University manuscript Gg. 5.35, copied in the eleventh century for use in the classroom and most famous for containing the *Carmina Cantabrigiensia* (Rigg and Wieland 1970).

Inspired by these models, the Latin poetry of the early Middle Ages fully justifies the architectural terminology of reuse we have used to describe it. But to reuse does not mean to copy. In the same way that Eginhard, the architect of the palace at Aix-la-Chapelle, builds an entirely medieval monument using columns, marble, and capitals the emperor has had brought from Rome, the author of the *Paderborn epos* (which, indeed, others would like to identify as the same Eginhard) constructs, using citations drawn from Virgil, Venantius Fortunatus, and perhaps the Byzantine Latin poet Corippus, a strikingly original portrait of a king, combining the traits of Augustus, St. Martin, and the Greek emperor Justin (Ratkowitsch 1997, 17–59). Writers of the Carolingian renaissance and their successors thus sought to "medievalize" Latin poetry, though they were not always conscious of doing so.

But remarkably, by the same means they were also able to "classicize" oral traditions whose origin lies in folklore. We will treat only two examples. The *Waltharius*, in my opinion written in the ninth century, records a tale linked to the cycle of the Nibelungen, whose first attestations in German do not predate 1200. Nevertheless, it is told in well-crafted heroic verses that are literally stuffed with implied citations of the *Aeneid*, Statius's *Thebaid*, and Prudentius's *Psychomachia*. This choice of models is far from random: Statius's poem serves to describe the ferocious clash of two worlds in the form of successive duels, that of Prudentius explains the battle between Virtue and Vice, and Virgil's masterpiece helps the poet to fill out the psychological portrait of his hero, a fugitive like Aeneas, and like him a melancholy and pensive warrior (Vinay 1978, 458–73). The other example is the *Ecbasis captivi*, composed in the second half of the eleventh century. This is an animal epic which elaborates considerably on the famous fable of the sick lion and transposes it humorously into the context of monastic culture. This text is studded with citations of Horace, drawn mostly from the *Satires* and *Epistles*, which aim to confer a moral and didactic value on a folk tale that is very old and attested almost everywhere. This is further suggested by the full title of the work, *Ecbasis cuiusdam captivi per tropologiam*—tropology, in the vocabulary of exegesis, is the moral sense of a work (Quint 1988, 125–39). The borrowing of epic formulas appears to be the main stylistic trait of Latin poetry as it was written until about 1100. Yet this practice does not preclude originality. One might well say that the poetry of Baudri, abbott of Bourgueil between 1079 and 1107, is extremely personal in nature, even though it is a sort of massive expansion of the syntagma *musa jocosa*, which he borrows from his favorite author, Ovid (Bond 1986; Tilliette 1994, 73–101).

But Baudri, with his strict fidelity to the aesthetic principles we have just described, seems to have been behind his times. His culture, acquired or developed in the monastery, is traditional in its inspiration. The urban cathedral schools that were vigorously blossoming at that time were developing new models for writing. Marbod, a pupil at Angers and a friend of Baudri's, is the first to recommend the systematic use of rhetorical figures in poetic discourse in his brief treatise *De ornamentis verborum*. To be sure, Latin poetry had not been indifferent to the seductions of the decorative style ever since the works of Ovid, Lucan, and Statius. From about 1100 onwards, this becomes a matter not simply of taste, but of instruction: the poetic value of a work seems to be measured according to the density of the figures it contains. Poems composed this way renounce the practice, common from the late antique period onward, of unacknowledged or disguised borrowing of *juncturae* or *clausulae* from classical phraseology in favor of rules governing artistic, or mannered, writing. In a manner characteristic of the attitude of the "renaissance of the twelfth century," there seems to be a conscious rupture with classical models, which poets now feel capable of rivaling, going much further than their predecessors along the path they began. After Marbod, the great *artes poeticae* of the late twelfth and early thirteenth century, that of Matthew of Vendôme and even more so that of Geoffrey of Vinsauf (ca. 1210), will take on the task of formulating poetic doctrine and submitting poetry to the laws of persuasive discourse (Faral 1924, 55–98). Before trying to understand their intention in doing this, we must first examine the stylistic effects of their teaching.

It is possible to identify two characteristic traits of the poetic writing of this era (Tilliette 2006, 78–86). Following the treatises which recommend them, we will call them *zeugma* and *transsumptio*, although in other systems both these terms can have other meanings. The first, called by Matthew zeugma, with its variant hypozeuxis, pertains to word order and has the effect of disarticulating syntax. It consists in making a series of juxtaposed subjects, verbs, and complements, often in threes, so that the first subject is associated with the first verb and the first complement, the second subject with the second verb and complement, and so on. Matthew of Vendôme has a specific interest in this rhetorical device, which seems for him to represent the touchstone of poetic expression, since he devotes the first pages of the *Ars versificatoria* to describing it. Moving from theory to practice, he provides some particularly scintillating examples in his poem *Tobias*, a paraphrase of the biblical book of Tobias in elegiac distichs, a work that, starting in the thirteenth century, was very often included in the *libri catoniani*, collections of school texts for young students. The following verses speak for themselves:

> Odit [*sc.* Tobias], amat, reprobat, probat, execratur, adorat
>   Crimina, iura, nefas, fas, simulacra, Deum;
> Fas, simulacra, Deum probat, execratur, adorat;
>   Odit, amat, reprobat crimina, iura, nefas.
> Seminat, auget, alit, exterminat, arguit, arcet
>   Dogmata, iura, decus, scismata, probra, dolos;
> Scismata, probra, dolos, exterminat, arguit, arcet;
>   Seminat, auget, alit dogmata, iura, decus.

> [He (Tobias) hates, loves, condemns, approves, loathes, worships
> crimes, laws, sins, morality, idols, God;

He approves, loathes, worships morality, idols, God;
he hates, loves, condemns crimes, laws, sins.
He preaches, honors, cherishes, banishes, denounces, prevents
doctrines, laws, virtue, schisms, disgraceful acts, deceit;
He banishes, denounces, prevents schisms, disgraceful acts, deceit;
He preaches, honors, cherishes doctrines, laws, virtue.]
(*Tobias* 89–96)

An example like this borders on caricature. However, it is important to note that the most popular—to judge from the abundant manuscript tradition—biblical epic of the Middle Ages, *Aurora*, composed around 1200 by Peter Riga, makes very frequent use of this literary device.

Transsumptio could be translated "a semantic transfer or displacement" and communicates poets' taste for metaphorical language. It is theorized in the *Ars poetica* composed by Gervase of Melkley around 1210. (This grammarian was the pupil of John of Hauville, the author of the allegorical epic *Architrenius*, one of the best examples of *ornatus difficilis* [difficult ornamentation], a device characterized by the use of tropes.) It was the literary doctrine of the twelfth and thirteenth centuries that made metaphor the poetic figure of speech *par excellence*, which it remains even today. A particularly original feature of the poetic language of this time is that it gives the verb, not the noun, the role of creating an image. While in prose its grammatical role is merely to establish the relationship between the subject and predicate, here it has a substantive value. These verbs of action, which are often transitive, from the first conjugation, and are sometimes neologisms, shed a new light on their subject and complement in the absence of any semantic relationship, shifting the attention of the reader and refocusing all of the suggestive power of the sentence onto themselves. Matthew of Vendôme gives no fewer than 61 examples in Book 2 of his *Ars versificatoria*. For example:

Intumulat pallor divitis oris opes

[Pallor buries the treasure of a rich complexion]
(Matthew of Vendôme 1988, 157)

(In short, the face in question blanches: the ugliness of such a physiological reaction, according to medieval aesthetic standards, which prize a florid complexion, is emphasized by the implied image of a miser who buries his treasure) or:

Fimbriat egregium lingua maligna decus

[A malicious tongue fringes glorious honor]
(Matthew of Vendôme 1988, 159)

If I understand it correctly, this means that malicious gossip stays peripheral to glory, at its margins, and is incapable of attacking its true heart, though it may appear to do so. These very compact expressions clearly defy translation.

We will now attempt to hypothesize the historical reasons for the phenomenon we have named "the poetic turning point," suggesting that one writer, perhaps involuntarily, played a decisive role in the success of the linguistic traits we have just identified. Hildebert of Lavardin (1056–1133), pupil at and then bishop of Le Mans, eventually becoming the archbishop of Tours and highly respected for his moral treatises, letters, and sermons, was also considered to be the prince of poets of his time. Just as his letter collection provides a model for later collections and serves as a reference for the practice of the art of prose, so his poems, dispersed in numerous anthologies, elicit so much admiration and imitation that to this day it is difficult to establish a precise canon of his work. In contrast to his contemporary and compatriot Baudri of Bourgueil, ever faithful to the late antique aesthetic of reuse, Hildebert seems to have acquired a taste for linguistic experimentation and a marked predilection for zeugma and *transsumptio*. The beginning of his famous elegy *De exilio suo* provides a splendid example of the first device:

> Nuper eram locuples multisque beatus amicis.
> > Et risere diu fata secunda michi.
> Larga Ceres, deus Archadie Bachusque replebant
> > Horrea, tecta, penum, farre, bidente, mero.
> (Hildebert of Lavardin 1969, *carmen* 22.1–4)

> [Once I was rich and blessed with many friends;
> > for a long time the Fates smiled favorably upon me.
> Generous Ceres, the god of Arcadia and Bacchus filled up
> > my granaries, my barns, my cellar, with wheat, with livestock, with wine.]

(Of course we are to interpret "Ceres filled my granaries with wheat, the god of Arcadia [sc. Pan, patron deity of shepherds] filled my barns with livestock, and Bacchus filled my cellar with wine.")

As for the second device, it is the very subject of his sacred epigrams, which attempt to explain the allegorical meanings of Scripture. Indeed, it is not impossible that Matthew of Vendôme, who studied at Tours, met the elderly Hildebert there, or at least that the still-vivid memory of Hildebert served as the inspiration for his *Ars versificatoria*. Whatever the value of these conjectures, it is clear that the optimistic, contagious humanism of the twelfth century is nevertheless confident enough in its own strengths and methods to free itself from a strict fidelity to the ancients in order to explore new literary horizons.

In Search of the Ineffable

All the same, novelty gets bad press in the Middle Ages. The question is whether a change in taste alone can justify the adoption of a new poetic style. Indeed, one might at first be tempted to attribute the formal innovations we have described to the exhaustion of inspiration: increasingly aging Latin poetry could only offer the allure of an overworked writing style, which gazes complacently back at its own effects, reflecting only itself, as an alternative to the conquering dynamism of the new vernacular literatures, which gradually encroach on its monopoly. (It is worth recalling that the first *romans* in French are paraphrases of the *Thebaïd* and the *Aeneid*.) But such a hypothesis seems anachronistic, although its premise cannot be utterly set aside. The literature of the time turns up its nose at the notion of art for art's sake. Prefaces and *accessus* repeat *ad nauseam* that a work's only *raison d'être*, and the only standard for judging its success, lies in its intellectual, moral, or spiritual benefit (*utilitas*) to the reader. From this perspective, what is the benefit that can be drawn from poetic expression?

The answer to this question depends on the intention that motivates the work and the genre to which the work belongs (if the notion of "genre" has any meaning in the Middle Ages), on one hand, and on the other on the degree of stylistic creativity it manifests. This is where we must return to the branching "moment" in our chronology. As we discussed above, the medium of verse can convey all kinds of content in the Latin Middle Ages. Because of this, one can legitimately wonder whether its use denotes any particularly significant intention. In fact, the use of the *opus geminum*, which was quite widespread in the first centuries of the Middle Ages, seems to suggest that poetry did not have a specific purpose at that time. Without going as far as Ernst Robert Curtius, who affirms that the two narratives in prose and verse are "interchangeable" (Curtius 1953, 147–48), the difference between them can be seen as functional, but not intrinsic. In the preface to his double *Vita* of St. Willibrord, Alcuin specifies that the prose version is intended for public recitation, while the verse is to serve as a focus for meditation and as an intellectual stimulus for *scolastici* (*Ep*. 120). The pedagogical virtue of the verse form is underlined once again in the early thirteenth century, in a gloss to Eberhard of Béthune's *Graecismus*: the "lucida brevitas" [enlightening brevity] of the *sermo metricus* allows for "levior acceptio" [easier learning] and "memoria firmior" [firmer memorization] of the rules of grammar which are the subject of this poem—a poem that is hardly poetic in our estimation, but which was widely diffused in the schools of the later Middle Ages (Grondeux 2000, 37).

Compared to the claims made by both ancient and modern poets, the ambitions of the verse-makers of the Latin Middle Ages seem modest. Still, in the early Middle Ages, the breath of inspiration can be found in works that demonstrate a form that is the least restrictive and the most novel: the sequence. The gorgeous "sequence of the swan" (inc. *Clangam filii*, Norberg 1968, 174), composed in the ninth century in the abbey of St. Martial de Limoges, articulates (in language that is both awkward and meticulous) the plaint of a large bird, stranded in darkness on a stormy sea:

> Angor inter arta
> gurgitum cacumina,
> gemens alatizo
> intuens mortifera,
> non conscendens supera.

[Trapped between the high crests of the waves, I beat my wings, gasping, I see death all around me, I cannot raise myself towards the heavens.]

The arrival of the scintillating dawn (...*venit aurora rutila*) will restore his hope and his strength:

> Ovatizans
> iam agebatur
> inter alta
> et consueta nubium
> sidera,
> hilarata
> ac iucundata
> nimis facta
> penetrabatur marium
> flumina.

[And now, triumphant, he rises between the lofty stars and clouds, where he is at home. Brought to the peak of happiness and joy, he cuts through the waves of the sea.]

With the exception of the final invocation "Regi magno sit gloria!" [Glory to the supreme King!], the poem only depicts the swan's anguished struggle against the harsh elements, and his happiness at reaching the delights of dry land ("amena arida") at long last. But its form is still liturgical, as is shown by its organization into symmetrical verses and the obsessive rhyming of -*a*, which echoes the final vowel of the alleluia. And this image, as implied by an understated use of words borrowed from the Bible, refers to a fundamental anthropological reality of the Christian worldview: for Augustine and Gregory the Great, the bird lost over the water symbolizes the exile of the soul in the darkness of sin and the dawn symbolizes its return to the celestial homeland. Far from being a mere stylistic ornament, this metaphor is revealed *in fine* as the bearer of a message with great spiritual significance. The assiduous reading of sacred texts, especially in the monastic setting, the exploitation of their fruitful imagery by Gregorian-style exegesis, and the simple example of the Psalms all confer a significance and power upon the words of religious poetry that infinitely surpasses their own meaning.

Could this model be applied to other forms of poetic expression? In other words, does the medieval poet see himself as the master of a language which, beyond its performative effects, can communicate better, more completely, or differently than prose? "Qui prosam conferre metro contendit, et antra / Deserti poterit domibus componere regni" [Whoever wishes to compare prose to meter might as well be comparing desert caves to the palaces of kings] writes Henry of Avranches in the mid-thirteenth century (1878, ll. 15–16). And he adds, in even more explicit terms: "Suntque modi duo: prosa—metrum, quibus omnia constant / Que loquitur vel que scribit homo. Sine pondere prosam / et sine mensura profert humana voluntas; / est autem species divina loquendi." [There are two modes, prose and meter, to which all oral and written expression refers. Prose, deprived of weight and measure, is produced by the human will; but as for meter, it is God's means of expression] (1878, ll. 3–6). However bold and boastful Henry's claim, it suggests that the status of poetry, like that of the poet, has evolved since the early Middle Ages.

Here again the turn of the twelfth century stands as the point of rupture. As Gerald Bond has argued, the spread of written culture among urban elites prompted the formation of "textual communities," or at least of literate circles which fostered a passion for poetry, especially that of Ovid, which was gradually rediscovered (Bond 1986). These informal groups, like the famous "Loire valley school" (Marbod, Baudri, Hildebert), constitute a propitious environment for the hatching of a new kind of poetic consciousness, even a love of literature for its own sake. Baudri of Bourgueil, above the example of an earlier world, is strikingly self-conscious about his métier, extolling with devoted and touching attention the humble instruments of his craft—his stylus and wax tablets. Significantly, Baudri also endeavored, with the help of the scribes in his monastery, to produce a complete edition of his poetic works, a codex we are lucky to possess since it alone preserves his oeuvre. He even goes so far as to declare: "quicquid volui dicere musa fuit" [everything I wanted to say became poetry] (*Carm.* 98, 122). Characteristically, he is here paraphrasing a famous verse from Ovid's autobiographical elegy (*Trist.* 4.10.26).

This pride in being a poet resurfaces a generation later, in the extremely novel stylistic forms created by a compatriot of Baudri's, Hugh of Orléans, who provides himself with a surname, Primas, which says quite a lot about his confidence in his own abilities. The first model for those who would later be called the Goliards, he provides us with an image of himself as a wicked subject, poor and proud, humiliated by Philistines, but sovereign in his inspiration (Hugh of Orléans 1907). He seems to have taught the arts of the trivium. Indeed, it is as a consummate master of grammatical knowledge and a connoisseur of the *auctores* that he forges his own rhythmical methods out of the remnants of older forms, while putting the cacophonic leonine hexameter, so dear to metrical hagiography, at the service of invective:

> Pontificum spuma,   fex cleri, sordida spuma,
> Qui dedit in bruma   michi mantellum sine pluma!

[You scum of a prelate, you discard of the clergy, disgusting pustule, who gave me, in the cold, a cloak with no lining!] (2.1–2)

or when he confers a tone of anxious urgency, hammered home by an obsessive chorus of rhymes, upon the peaceful octosyllable of sacred hymns:

> Dives eram et dilectus
> inter pares preelectus.
> Modo curvat me senectus
> et etate sum confectus.
> Unde vilis et neglectus
> a deiectis sum deiectus,
> quibus rauce sonat pectus,

> mensa gravis pauper lectus,
> quis nec amor nec affectus
> sed horrendus est aspectus.
>
> I was rich, I was beloved,
> preeminent amongst my peers,
> now I am an old man, hunched
> and hobbled by old age.
> Reviled, neglected,
> rejected with society's rejects,
> who have creaky lungs,
> dreary tables and the beds of paupers,
> they are neither cherished nor loved,
> but their appearance is horrific. (23.1–10)

It is in the same spirit and using the same stylistic devices that another poet with an equally modest pseudonym, the Archpoet of Cologne, composes vengeful verses, but these are even more steeped in eschatological urgency. Under his pleasant and pleading pen the spirit of poetry, which he claims to extract from wine, becomes a spirit of prophecy—as is clear in the "confession" (inc. *Fama, tuba dante sonum*, Archipoeta 1958, 54–56) where he makes a parallel between himself and Jonah, the recalcitrant messenger, but also with the typological figure of Christ reincarnated (Cairns 1983). If, as *accessus* insist, poetry "relates to ethics," this is certainly the case with the poetry of Hugh Primas and the Archpoet, for beneath their clownish exterior, they only demonstrate the corruption of their vices in order to hold up a mirror to the vices of the *hypocrite lecteur*.

In the twelfth century, the renewal of poetic forms of expression is accompanied by an equally new ambition for poetry to announce itself as the unique bearer of the truth—in other words, as something other than an elegant and delightful repetition of content that could be expressed in prose. In a nobler and more intellectual register than that of the Goliards, this explanation of the virtues proper to poetic language must, in our opinion, be credited to the masters of the school of Chartres. Following the lessons of Macrobius in his *Commentarii in Somnium Scipionis*, the masters of Chartres decide, in an abruptly forceful move, to apply the interpretive techniques of exegesis, up until now reserved for the elucidation of sacred texts, to the great pagan works. The commentary by Bernard Sylvestris on the first six books of the *Aeneid* (1977) and the *Allegoriae* elicited from Ovid's *Metamorphoses* by Arnulf of Orléans (Ghisalberti 1932) suggest that "fabulous narratives" can cover a second sense, of a scientific, philosophical, or spiritual kind, with an alluring veil. But as soon as poetry earns the right to be the subject of allegorical reading, it also earns the legitimate right to practice allegorical writing, to become the clothing (*integumentum, involucrum*) of a secret truth (Wetherbee 1972, 28–73 and elsewhere in this volume). The figurative language proper to poetry takes up a project that is not only aesthetic but cognitive in nature—that of revealing objects that are inaccessible in rational discourse. It has been quite well established that the great *artes poeticae*, especially those of Matthew of Vendôme and Geoffrey of Vinsauf, are steeped in Chartrian thought (Kelly 1991, 57–68). The latter, from the beginning of his *Poetria nova*, underlines poetry's capacity to bring the superhuman reality of archetypal ideas into the perceptible world. It is surely no accident that he illustrates the poetic function of the *figurae verborum* and *figurae sententiarum* of classical rhetoric using examples which attempt to verbally represent the Christian mysteries of the Incarnation and the Redemption (Tilliette 2000, 135–60).

A few decades earlier, the work of the theologian Alan of Lille, whose allegorical epic entitled *Anticlaudianus* was destined to serve as an indirect inspiration for Dante's *Divina Commedia*, had already set this new poetics into practice, putting rhetoric at the service of sense rather than style. Pascale Bourgain (1997) has shown convincingly the way in which the rules that govern poetic expression in the *Anticlaudianus*, especially the emphasis on metaphor, express the fundamental inadequacy of human language when it comes to naming the essence of things, but nevertheless authorize its ability to communicate some idea of the incomprehensible divine. The editor of the poem, Robert Bossuat, rightly notes that Alan, "familiar with school exercises and the practice of the art of poetry since childhood,…applies certain rhetorical devices with a special *insistance*, and this repetition perhaps constitutes the essential characteristic of his style" (Alan 1955, 48)—for example *expolitio* (the accumulation of synonyms), oxymoron, paronomasia, and zeugma. These "artifices" are not free, but must agree with the construction of meaning. Thus, when the heroine of the poem, Wisdom (*Fronesis*), travels amongst the stars and admires the extraordinary equilibrium of the elements which constitute them (fire and water), oxymorons, which cannot be considered referential to any reality, are most expressive of the prodigious miracle of divine creation:

> Nec iam natiuos querunt memorare tumultus
> Quos ligat assensus discors, discordia concors,
> Pax inimica, fides fantastica…
>
> [They no longer seek to remember the conflicts inherent in their natures, they join in a discordant agreement, a harmonious discord, a warlike peace, an imaginary certitude…] (*Anticl.* 5.315–17)

Elsewhere (*Anticl.* 6.412–15), zeugma, repetition, antithesis, and alliteration express the mercy of the Redeemer.

The case of Alan of Lille is perhaps not emblematic. During his time and in the centuries following him, people continue to versify various subjects without necessarily considering themselves poets. Still, it seems that what begins in the twelfth century, and is borne out by the literary theory of the time, is the glorification of poetic function. The Latin Middle Ages, as instructed by Isidore of Seville, remain hesitant for a long time about the identity of the poet, *vates*. Is he, according to the two competing etymologies Isidore proposes, an artisan, laboring to weave ("viere") words together, or a visionary carried by the strength of his spirit ("vi mentis") (*Orig.* 8.7.3)? The first option seems to have predominated in the early Middle Ages. We would cautiously suggest that a higher conception of poetic speech arose little by little, at least in the most talented authors, from the time of Alan of Lille and the Archpoet. But what was its foundation or its justification? Henry of Avranches, with his characteristic subtle humor, suggests an answer. In the passage cited above, in which he contrasts the prestige of poetic language, defined as divine, with that of prose, he refers to the famous verse in the biblical book of Wisdom (11:21), according to which God has organized everything *in mensura et numero et pondere*: the world created by God is thus...a metrical (*metrum id est mensura*) or rhythmical (*rithmus id est numerus*) poem, and the voice of the poet, because of these same formal constraints imposed upon it, echoes that of the Almighty.

SUGGESTIONS FOR FURTHER READING

This material is so vast and diverse that it seems advisable to begin with a historical approach, by way of the two magisterial syntheses by the *amateur éclairé* Frederick J. E. Raby (1953 and 1957). He identifies all of the most important texts and illuminates them with precise critical judgment. Joseph Szövérffy (1992–95), more erudite but less inspiring, provides a rich array of bibliographical information. Among Peter Dronke's numerous works, the collection of articles in Dronke (1984) outlines a sensible yet original approach to the main poetic genres and to some of the major authors. From a technical standpoint, Dag Norberg's work on versification (Norberg 1958) and Edmond Faral's work on poetics (Faral 1924) are still the best authorities. More recent on these two topics are Klopsch (1972) and Klopsch (1980), respectively. Finally, the texts themselves, with good English translations, can be found in the anthologies of Frederick Raby (1961) and Peter Godman (1985).

BIBLIOGRAPHY

Primary sources

Adam of St Victor. 2008. *Les Séquences d'Adam de Saint-Victor: étude littéraire (poétique et rhetorique), textes et traductions, commentaires*, edited by Jean Grosfillier. Bibliotheca Victorina 20. Turnhout: Brepols.

Alan of Lille. 1955. *Anticlaudianus*, edited by Robert Bossuat. Textes philosophiques du Moyen âge 1. Paris: J. Vrin.

Alcuin. 1920. "Vita Willibrordi archiepiscopi Traiectensis," edited by Wilhelm Levison. In *Passiones vitaeque sanctorum aevi Merovingici*, edited by Bruno Krusch and Wilhelm Levison, 81–141. Monumenta Germaniae Historica. Scriptores rerum Merovingicarum 7. Hannover, Leipzig: Hahn.

Aldhelm. 1919. "De metris et enigmatibus ac pedum regulis." In *Aldhelmi Opera*, edited by Rudolf Ehwald, 59–204. Monumenta Germaniae Historica. Auctores antiquissimi 15. Berlin: Weidmann.

Archipoeta. 1958. *Die Gedichte des Archipoeta*, edited by Heinrich Watenphul and Heinrich Krefeld. Heidelberg: C. Winter.

Baudri of Bourgueil. 1998, 2002. *Poèmes*, edited by Jean-Yves Tilliette. 2 vols. Auteurs latins du Moyen âge. Paris: Belles Lettres.

Bene of Florence. 1983. *Candelabrum*. edited by Gian Carlo Alessio. Thesaurus Mundi 23. Padua: Antenore.

Bernard of Cluny. 2009. *De contemptu mundi. Bernard le Clunisien: une vision du monde vers 1144*. edited and translated by André Cresson. Témoins de notre histoire. Turnhout: Brepols.

Bernard Sylvestris. 1977. *Commentum quod dicitur Bernardi Silvestris super sex libros Eneidos Virgilii*, edited by Julian W. Jones and Elizabeth F. Jones. Lincoln, NE: University of Nebraska Press.

Conrad of Hirsau. 1970. *Dialogus super auctores*. edited by Robert B. C. Huygens. Leiden: E. J. Brill.

Ghisalberti, Fausto. 1932. "Arnolfo d'Orléans, un cultore di Ovidio nel secolo XII." *Memorie del Reale Istituto Lombardo di Scienze et Lettere* 24: 201–29.

Godman, Peter, ed. and trans. 1985. *Poetry of the Carolingian Renaissance*. London: Duckworth.

Henry of Avranches. 1878. *Carmen ad Fridericum imperatorem*. In "Drei Gedichte Heinrichs von Avranches," edited by E. Winkelmann. *Forschungen zur deutschen Geschichte* 18: 482–92.

Hildebert of Lavardin. 1969. *Hildeberti Cenomannensis episcopi Carmina minora*, edited by A. Brian Scott. Bibliotheca scriptorum Graecorum et Romanorum Teubneriana. Leipzig: B. G. Teubner.

Hucbald of St-Amand. 1899. "Ecloga de calvis." In *Poetae latini aevi Carolini*, edited by Paul von Winterfeld, 267–71. Monumenta Germaniae Historica. Poetae Latini medii aevi 4.1. Berlin: Weidmann.

Hugh of Orléans. 1907. *Die Oxforder Gedichte des Primas Magister Hugo*, edited by Wilhelm Meyer. Nachrichten von der königlichen Gesellschaft der Wissenschaften zu Göttingen, Phil.-Hist. Kl. 2. Berlin: Weidmann.

Karolus Magnus et Leo Papa. 1881. "Karolus Magnus et Leo Papa." In Poetae latini aevi Carolini, edited by Ernst Dümmler, 366–79. Monumenta Germaniae Historica. Poetae Latini medii aevi 1. Berlin: Weidmann.

Marbod of Rennes. 1998. *De ornamentis verborum, Liber decem capitolorum: retorica, mitologia e moralità di un vescovo poeta (secc. XI–X)*, edited and translated by Rosario Leotta. Per verba 10. Florence: SISMEL, Edizioni del Galluzzo.

Matthew of Vendôme. 1988. *Mathei Vindocinensis opera*. Vol. 3: *Ars Versificatoria*, edited by Franco Munari. Storia e letteratura 171. Rome: Edizioni di Storia e Letteratura.

Metellus of Tegernsee. 1988. *Die Quirinalien des Metellus von Tegernsee. Untersuchungen zur Dichtkunst und kritische Textausgabe*, edited by Peter Christian Jacobsen. Mittellateinische Studien und Texte 1. Leiden, Cologne: E. J. Brill.

Norberg, Dag, ed. 1968. *Manuel practique de latin médiéval*. Collection Connaissance des langues 4. Paris: A. et J. Picard.

Raby, Frederick, ed. and trans. 1961. *The Oxford Book of Medieval Latin Verse*. Oxford: Clarendon Press.

Walter of Châtillon. 1978. *Galteri de Castellione Alexandreis*, edited by Marvin L. Colker. Thesaurus Mundi 17. Padua: Antenore.

Walter of Speyer. 1937. "Vita Christophori." In *Die lateinischen Dichter des deutschen Mittelalters*. Vol. 5: *Die Ottonenzeit. Erster Teil*, edited by Karl Strecker, 10–79. Monumenta Germaniae Historica. Poetae Latini medii aevi 5.1. Leipzig: Hiersemann.

Secondary sources

Bond, Gerald A. 1986. "'*Iocus amoris*': The Poetry of Baudri of Bourgueil and the Formation of the Ovidian Subculture." *Traditio* 42: 143–93.

Bourgain, Pascale. 1989. "Qu'est-ce qu'un vers au Moyen Âge?" *Bibliothèque de l'École des Chartes* 147: 231–82.

———. 1997. "La conception de la poésie chez les Chartrains." In *Aristote, l'école de Chartres et la cathédrale*, edited by Monique Cazeaux, 165–79. Chartres: Association des Amis du Centre Médiéval Européen de Chartres.

———. 2002. "La *compositio* et l'équilibre de la phrase narrative au onzième siècle." In *Latin culture in the Eleventh Century: Proceedings of the third international conference on medieval Latin studies*, edited by Michael W. Herren, Christopher J. Mcdonough, and Ross G. Arthur, 83–108. Publications of the Journal of Medieval Latin 5. Turnhout: Brepols.

Burger, Michel. 1957. *Recherches sur la structure et l'origine des vers romans*. Société de publications romanes et françaises. Publications 59. Geneva: Droz.

Cairns, Francis. 1983. "The Archpoet's 'Jonah-confession' (poem II): Literary, exegetic and historical aspects." *Mittellateinisches Jahrbuch* 18: 168–93.

Curtius, Ernst Robert. 1953. *European literature and the Latin Middle Ages.* translated by Williard R. Trask. Bollingen Series 36. Princeton, NJ: Princeton University Press.

Dolbeau, François. 1987. "Les 'Bucoliques' de Marcus Valerius sont-elles une oeuvre médiévale?" *Mittellateinisches Jahrbuch* 22: 166–70.

———. 2002. "Un domaine négligé de la littérature médiolatine: les textes hagiographiques en vers." *Cahiers de Civilisation Médiévale* 45: 129–39.

Dronke, Peter. 1984. *The Medieval Poet and his World*. Storia e letteratura 164. Rome: Edizioni di Storia e Letteratura.

Faral, Edmond. 1924. *Les arts poétiques du XIIe et du XIIIe siècle: Recherches et documents sur la technique littéraire du Moyen Âge*. Bibliothèque de l'Ecole des hautes études. IVe section, Sciences historiques et philologiques 238. Paris: Honoré Champion.

Glauche, Günter. 1970. *Schullektüre im Mittelalter: Enstehung des Lektürekanons bis 1200 nach den Quellen dargestellt*. Münchener Beiträge zur Mediävistik und Renaissance-Forschung 5. Munich: Arbeo-Gesellschaft.

Grondeux, Anne. 2000. *Le Graecismus d'Evrard de Béthune à travers ses gloses: Entre grammaire positive et grammaire speculative du XIIIe au XVe siècle*. Studia artistarum 8. Turnhout: Brepols.

Kelly, Douglas. 1991. *The arts of poetry and prose*. Typologie des sources du moyen âge occidental 59. Turnhout: Brepols.

Klopsch, Paul. 1972. *Einführung in die mittellateinische Verslehre*. Darmstadt: Wissenschaftliche Buchgesellschaft.

———. 1980. *Einführung in die Dichtungslehren des lateinischen Mittelalters*. Lateinisches Mittelalter. Darmstadt: Wissenschaftliche Buchgesellschaft.

Leonhardt, Jürgen. 1989. *Dimensio syllabarum: Studien zur lateinischen Prosodie- und Verslehre von der Spätantike zur frühen Renaissance*. Hypomnemata 92. Göttingen: Vandenhoek & Ruprecht.

Leotta, Rosario. 1995. "La tecnica versificatoria di Rosvita." *Filologia mediolatina* 2: 193–232.

Mastandrea, Paolo and Luigi Tessarolo. 2010. *PoetriaNova: A CD-ROM of Latin Medieval Poetry (650–1250 A.D.)*. 2nd ed. CD-ROM. Florence: SISMEL, Edizioni del Galluzzo.

Norberg, Dag. *Introduction à l'étude de la versification latine médiévale*. Acta Universitatis Stockholmiensis. Studia Latina Stockholmiensia 5. Stockholm: Almqvist & Wiksell.

Nougaret, Louis. 1956. *Traité de métrique latine classique.* Paris: Klincksieck.
Orlandi, Giovanni. 1988. "Caratteri della versificazione dattilica." In *Retorica e poetica tra i secoli XII e XIV,* edited by Claudio Leonardi and Enrico Menestò, 151–69. Quaderni del "Centro per il collegamento degli studi medievali e umanistici nell'Università di Perugia" 18. Florence: La Nuova Italia.
Polara, Giovanni. 1995. "La metrica latine medievale." In *Il verso europeo,* edited by Francesco Stella, 59–74. Florence: Fondazione Franceschini.
Quint, Maria-Barbara. 1988. *Untersuchungen zur mittelalterlichen Horaz-Rezeption.* Studien zur klassischen Philologie 39. Frankfurt/Main: Peter Lang.
Raby, Frederic J. E. 1953. *A History of Christian Latin Poetry From the Beginnings to the Close of the Middle Ages.* Oxford: Clarendon Press.
———. 1957. *A History of Secular Latin Poetry in the Middle Ages.* 2 vols. Oxford: Clarendon.
Ratkowitsch, Christine. 1997. *Karolus Magnus: alter Aeneas, alter Martinus, alter Iustinus: zum Intention und Datierung des "Aachener Karlsepos."* Wiener Studien. Beiheft 24. Arbeiten zur mittel- und neulateinischen Philologie 4. Vienna: Verlag der österreichischen Akademie der Wissenschaften.
Rigg, Arthur G. and Gernot R. Wieland. 1975. "A Canterbury classbook of the mid-eleventh century (the 'Cambridge songs' manuscript)." *Anglo-Saxon England* 4: 113–30.
Schumann, Otto. 1979–83. *Lateinisches Hexameter-Lexikon. Dichterisches Formelgut von Ennius bis zum Archipoeta.* 6 vols. Monumenta Germaniae Historica. Hilfsmittel 4. Munich: Monumenta Germaniae Historica.
Sedgwick, Walter B. 1930. "The *Bellum Troianum* of Joseph of Exeter." *Speculum* 5: 49–76.
Szövèrffy, Joseph. 1992–95. *Secular Latin lyrics and minor poetic forms of the Middle Ages: A historical survey and literary repertory from the tenth to the early thirteenth century.* 4 vols. Publications of the Archives for Medieval Poetry 25–27. Concord, NH: Classical Folia Editions.
Tilliette, Jean-Yves. 1992. "Hermès amoureux ou les métamorphoses de la Chimère: Réflexions sur les *carmina* 200 et 201 de Baudri de Bourgueil." *Mélanges de l'École française de Rome, Moyen âge* 104: 121–61.
———. 1994. "Savants et poètes du moyen âge face à Ovide: les débuts de l'*aetas ovidiana* (v. 1050–v. 1200)." In *Ovidius redivivus: von Ovid zu Dante,* edited by Michelangelo Picone and Bernhard Zimmermann, 63–104. Stuttgart: Metzler & Poeschel.
———. 2000. *Des mots à la parole: une lecture de la Poetria Nova de Geoffroy de Vinsauf.* Recherches et rencontres 16. Geneva: Droz.
———. 2006. "Le latin de la poésie médiévale." *Filologia mediolatina* 13: 67–90.
———. 2008. "La poétique de Gautier de Châtillon." In *Dichten als Stoff-Vermittlung: Formen, Ziele, Wirkungen, Beiträge zur Praxis der Versifikation lateinischer Texte im Mittelalter,* edited by Peter Stotz and Philipp Roelli, 265–78. Medienwandel, Medienwechsel, Medienwissen 5. Zurich: Chronos.
Traube, Ludwig. 1911. *Einleitung in die lateinische Philologie des Mittelalters.* Vol. 2 of *Vorlesungen und Abhandlungen.* Munich: Beck.
Turcan-Verkerk, Anne-Marie. 2003. "Le *Prosimetrum* des *Artes dictaminis* médiévales (XIIe–XIIIe s.)" *Archivum Latinitatis Medii Aevi* 61: 111–74.
Vinay, Gustavo. 1978. *Alto Medioevo latino: conversazioni e no.* Naples: Guida.
Wetherbee, Winthrop. 1972. *Platonism and Poetry in the Twelfth Century: the Influence of the School of Chartres.* Princeton, NJ: Princeton University Press.
Ziolkowski, Jan. M. 2007. *Nota Bene: Reading Classics and Writing Melodies in the Early Middle Ages.* Publications of the Journal of Medieval Latin 7. Turnhout: Brepols.

CHAPTER 13

CROSSING GENERIC BOUNDARIES

A. G. RIGG

MEDIEVAL Latin literature flouts the boundaries between the expectations of one genre and another in many ways, but the present essay concentrates, by way of example, on three: the presence of humor in contexts where it might seem incongruous; the uncertain negotiations of meter, rhythm, and rhyme as principles of poetic form; and the importation of vernacular vocabulary and structure and crosslinguistic puns into Latin texts.

UNEXPECTED HUMOR

Despite the general assumption that because Latinity presupposes an author's clerical status it must involve piety and seriousness, it is in Latin that we most often find a touch of irony or "subversive" laughter, perhaps because the clerical classes were more alert, better trained, and even more skeptical about too much piety. No one could doubt that Alexander Neckam (1157–1217), abbot of Cirencester, was "one of the most remarkable scholars of the second half of the twelfth century" (Raby 1957, 118), a grammarian, encyclopedist, theologian, homilist and commentator, but he had his lighthearted side. In the *De lapidibus*, on the bestiary tradition of the *rhinoceros* captured in a maiden's lap, he writes:

> Rhinoceros capitur amplexu virginis. At quis
> Consimili renuat proditione capi?
> [The unicorn succumbs in maiden's lap—

> but who'd decline a similar defeat?]
> (Neckam 1863, 490.167–68)

In the *De commendatione vini* he engages in a praise of wine familiar from Hugh Primas and many so-called Goliardic poets, but adds a new twist—he honors it for its part in the Eucharist:

> Que sit in altari panis, que Gloria vini,
> Vera fides retinet. Perfide Fauste, tace!...
> In verum calicem que sit conversio vini,
> Quis verbis possit enucleare? Tace!

> [The glory of the altar bread and wine
> True faith preserves, so Faustus hold your tongue!...
> The turning of the wine to chalice true
> No one could put in words, so now be still!]
> (Neckam 1965, 121.151–52, 165–66)

The preference for (French) wine over beer is a frequent topos of Anglo-Latin literature, but it also introduces a lighthearted tone into Reginald of Canterbury's *Vita Malchi* (see Rigg 1992, 24–30 for an introduction): Malchus is stirred from his inertia by the sight of industrious ants, but they are discriminating ants:

> Frumentum cernunt, praedantur, at hordea spernunt:
> Hoc dedignantur, frumenti farre cibantur!

> [They spot and plunder stores of wheat, but barley they disdain:
> They don't like this—they'd rather feed on spelt of other grain.]
> (Reginald of Canterbury 1942, 97.4.27–28)

Henry of Avranches, another verse hagiographer who likes to enliven his saints' lives with some humor, also uses the anti-beer topos. The pious Roman Birin is sent on a mission to Britain, where he will have to face the enormity of this brew:

> Nescio quod Stigie monstrum conforme paludi—
> Ceruisiam plerique vocant. Nil spissius illa
> Dum bibitur, nil clarius est dum mingitur, unde
> Constat quod multas feces in uentre relinquit.

> [A hellish brew of mudlike hue
> That they call beer is rather queer,
> For though it's thick when in the glass
> You'll find that when you come to pass
> Water, there is nothing thinner
> Than that which comes out from your inner
> Parts. You see, it must be true:
> It left the dregs inside of you.]
> (Townsend 1994, 324.253–56)

For Neckam, however, the whole of creation is God's joke:

> En dum naturae considero ludicra, ludos
> Eius maturos seria jure voco...
> Lusit ab aeterno summi sapientia patris,
> Singula disponens, ars, noys, ordo, decor.
>
> [Now when I think of Nature's quirks, I say
> Her solemn works are simply grown-up jokes...
> For outside time, God's wisdom played: his mind
> His art, design and grace disposed all things.]
> (Neckam 1863, 426.252–57)

Neckam is here playing on Ovid's more sinister idea that humans are the playthings of the gods:

> Ludit in humanis diuina potentia rebus
> Et certam praesens uix feret hora fidem.
>
> [With human life the gods just play a game;
> The present moment gives no surety.]
> (*Ex Ponto* 4.3.49–50)

Lawrence of Durham (see Rigg 1992, 54–61 for an introduction) also noted God's sense of humor when Joseph's brothers, who had sold him into slavery, were forced to come to beg his aid (Gn 37–45):

> Tales sepe iocos diuina potentia ludit,
> Utitur et nostris hec bene sepe malis.
>
> [Such jokes are often played by God's great might,
> Which often makes good use of our mishaps.]
> (Lawrence of Durham 2002, 117.587–88)

It is also Lawrence who compares his own frustration at not having time to write to that of a eunuch who catches a beautiful girl:

> Et velut apprensa pulcra spado virgine triste
> Suspirat tristis pectora, sic et ego.
>
> [And just as when a eunuch grabs a fair
> Young girl he grieves at heart, so now do I.]
> (ibid., 83.15–16)

Examples so far have been of incidental lighthearted humor (though some have theological implications about God's apparent frivolity). Another category includes humorous scenes (often burlesque) introduced to provide variety. Martianus Capella sometimes, rather heavy-handedly, breaks into the solemnity of the assembly of gods attending the wedding of Mercury and Philology. At the arrival of Geometry Jupiter scans the earth to see if there are any pretty girls:

> Ipse etiam Iuppiter curiosius totius terrae latebras vellet exquirere, credo necubi decentes puellas isto quoque saeculo is versiformis etiam cupitor audiret.
>
> [Jupiter himself wanted to investigate hiding-places throughout the world, in case, I suppose, that lustful shapeshifter might hear of some comely girls somewhere in that world.] (Capella 1983, 206.589)

In the introduction to the entry of Arithmetic, Pleasure mocks Mercury for his lack of interest in sex:

> Nec te cura tori, nec te puer ambit herilis,
> Nec mea mella rapis? Quaenam haec hymeneia lex est?
>
> [So does no thought of bed nor Cupid's play enthrall?
> My honey doesn't please? What kind of marriage law is this?]
> (ibid., 269.16–17)

There are similar squabbles elsewhere in VII and VIII, and the drunkenness of Silenus is described in VIII.803–9 (ibid., 302–7).

Someone else who manipulated a genre—but with more humor and imagination—was the poet-historian Henry of Huntingdon (d. 1156/64). His verse *Herbal* (written 1118–35) was based on the verse herbal by Macer Floridus (i.e., Odo of Meun) and other herbals, but Henry imposes an elaborate structure of a four-sided garden, each side containing twenty-five herbs, with a theater and fountain, and two additional books containing sixty more "Eastern" herbs. Henry goes beyond the usual lists of cures of everything from gonorrhea to gout to construct a lighthearted and literary concatenation. Some plants answer him back (e.g., elecampane):

> "Menstrua tam leuiter purgat quam pectora sanat."
> "Turpe loquax mulier! Vates odere loquaces."
>
> ["It lightly cures the monthly flow and soothes the breast"—
> "A prating woman is a pest: such women poets hate!"]
> (Rigg 2003, 270.13–14)

Many descriptions are embellished by classical myths (e.g., periwinkle 1.23, dittany 3.1) and 4.1–2 (hyacinth and narcissus) are based on them:

> Hic igitur Iacincte nites; Narcissus adheret;
> Nunc flores, olim pueri…
>
> [Here, Hyacinth, you shine; close by Narcissus grows;
> You once were boys but now as flowers bloom…]
> (ibid., 273.14–15)

Henry often sprinkles autobiographical details in the *Herbal*: England produced the plant baldmoney and the poet himself (1.5), and he recalls attending the lectures of Anselm of Bec at Laon (1.12) and the late Queen Matilda's care for her pot of basil (1.2). Most ingeniously, in 5.2.1–6 Henry has himself interrupted by a cook (the medieval soubriquet for Martial) who wants to know why Henry has not included vegetables:

> Qui porrum, cepas, caules—wulgaria certe
> Sed prorsus valde gratissima—conticuisti.
>
> [You didn't write at all of leeks or onions
> Or cabbages—low class, for sure, but very good.]
> (ibid., 281.9–10)

Thus he creates the opportunity to link six more plants in his dramatic scheme. Unfortunately, Henry's bold attempt to transform the genre of herbals had no followers—no one else had the talent—and some scribes actually cut out his embellishments, reducing his poems back to the bare botanical and medicinal information.

More intriguing are cases where the detection of humor is difficult, particularly where irony is involved, as it requires us to decide whether our sense of the ridiculous is the same as that of antiquity or the Middle Ages. In the absence of a laugh-track or a notice to the audience saying "laugh" or a marginal note *ironice*, we have no way of knowing if an utterance is serious, and we may see irony where none was intended. In the *Vera historia de morte Arthuri* (ed. by Lapidge 1981) an alternative version is given on the fate of Arthur. While in Geoffrey of Monmouth he is taken to Avalon *ad salvanda vulnera*, here Arthur is killed by a young man with a poisoned spear of yew, but the body disappears. As this leaves the eventual fate of Arthur undetermined, one wonders if the word *vera* was intended ironically (modern usage would put a *sic* after it). Sarcasm is rare, but Walter Map has an extended attack on the Cistercians for their expropriation of lands, which they excuse by alluding to Exodus 12:36 and the prayer in the Missal "O truly blessed night which despoiled the Egyptians and enriched the Hebrews." Thereafter, for thirteen pages of Latin, wherever Map refers to the Cistercians he calls them "Hebrews" and the rest of us "Egyptians." Reginald of Canterbury records with pleasure the reply he had from Hildebert of Le Mans, who expressed delight that Reginald had made use of some of Hildebert's lines (Reginald of Canterbury 1942; PL 171.292 *Epist.* 15.7). Was Hildebert being serious or was this a polite way of pointing out the plagiarism? If the latter, was Reginald aware of it?

Even modest self-deprecation cannot be assessed with complete confidence. After writing several thousand lines of poetry on the first three ages of the world, Adam of Barking decides to omit the stories of Jacob and Esau and to go straight from Abraham to Joseph. In an apology for the omission he writes:

> De Abraham et Loth satis hactenus est. Non iterabo que dixi. Inhonestum est aures hominum longis onerare sermonibus, ne tedium inferat auditori sermo prolixus.
>
> [That's enough for now about Abraham and Lot. I will not repeat what I have said. It is wrong to burden men's ears with lengthy sermons, lest an overlong sermon should cause boredom in the listener.] (Rigg 2009, 238)

At the end of his epic on the fall of Troy, after inventing dozens of episodes and battles involving entirely fictitious names (not even in his source Dares Phrygius), Joseph of Exeter says that he had been "etsi quando auctor, rarus tamen" [even if sometimes an augmenter, only rarely] (1970, 210.6.961).

It finally rests with our own judgment. On purely stylistic grounds we may assume comic intent in the constant repetition of the names of the three knights in the *Historia Meriadoci*: "scilicet Nigrum Militem de Nigro Saltu, Roseum Militem de Roseo Saltu, et Candidum Militem de Candido Saltu" [namely the Black Knight of the Black Forest, the Red Knight of the Red Forest and the White Knight of the White Forest] (*Historia Meriadoci* 1988, 100; Echard 1998, 185). I mention below the problem of Burchard's *In Defence of Beards*.

The transformation of genre and the uncertainty of interpretation are both apparent in Walter Map's *De nugis curialium* (ca. 1180). Map tells us that he is a hunter:

> Siluam uobis et materiam, non dico fabularum sed faminum appono; cultui sermonum non intendo...Singuli lectores appositam ruditatem exculpant, ut eorum industria bona facie prodeat in publicum. Venator uester sum: feras uobis affero, fercula faciatis (2.32; Map 1983, 208.)
>
> [I am presenting you with the wood and material, not of stories but of sayings; I am not aiming at cultivated prose...Individual readers should shape the roughness placed before them, so that by their hard work it may become public with a fine appearance. I am your hunter; I bring you the game and it is up to you to make the meals.] (ibid., 209)

In fact, although the *De Nugis* is clearly in an unfinished state, he has often done the polishing (or cooking) for us, and it is in these transformations that genre-busting takes place. He transforms the *famina* into political satire (Herla), historical fiction (Godwin) and, if I am right, parody of scholastic disputations.

The story of Herla comes unannounced at the end of a long, learned, and witty satire on life at the court of Henry II, its torments, frustrations and peregrinations (a topos used also by Peter of Blois, *Epist.* 4). Herla, an ancient British king, is invited by a pigmy king (who had provided all the entertainment for Herla's recent wedding) to visit his underground kingdom. When he and his retinue leave, they are told that they must not dismount from their horses until a small bloodhound, a present from the pigmy, has jumped down; some men disobey and are turned into dust. Thus Herla and his men are condemned to ride forever and have been seen often—until finally they disappeared into the River Wye and their ridings ceased: "Quievit autem ab illa hora fantasticus ille circuitus, tanquam nobis suos tradiderunt errores, ad quietem sibi" (1.11; Map 1983, 30) [From that hour their fantastic wanderings came to a stop, as if they have passed on to us their wanderings to give themselves a rest] (ibid., 31). Thus, the classic folktale of a troop of riders condemned to wander eternally has been reduced to the punch line of a shaggy-dog story. The technique of the delayed punch line—apparently a feature of Welsh story-telling—is common in Map, as we will see. It is also the main structural device of the Latin romance *Arthur and Gorlagon* (ed. by Kittredge 1903), in which Arthur is constantly urged to dismount and eat; in response to Arthur's desire to learn the mind of a woman, Gorlagon agrees to continue his story (about a werewolf) but repeats, like a refrain, "Magnum est quod queris... et cum tibi retulero parum inde doctior habeberis" [What you ask for is a great matter, and when I have finished, you will be none the wiser] (Kittredge 1903, 152, 154, 156–61). In his lengthy introduction to his diatribe against monastic orders (1.15–32), Map is even more devious. Beginning with an account of the *annus nubileus* of 1187 when Jerusalem was captured by Saladin, he goes on to deplore human follies in comparison with the wisdom of wild and even tame animals; he then, apparently without purpose, quotes Hildebert's opening couplet of Epigram 66 on the miraculous raising from death of Jairus's daughter, the widow's son, and Lazarus, but Map ignores Hildebert's interpretation, writing instead:

> Suffecerunt due femine mouere Dominum paucis etiam precibus ad suscitationem quatriduani; tot autem hominum et feminarum milia noui uel ueteris ordinis quem suscitant? (1.15; Map 1983, 48)

> [It took only two women to move God by a few prayers to raise from death a man dead for four days. But who has been revived by so many thousands of men and women of both old and new orders?] (ibid., 49)

This is followed by a long series of tales about religious orders, to show how some (such as the Templars) had good beginnings but have declined, and others (especially the Cistercians) are thoroughly bad. The whole series occupies about forty-five pages of Latin.

The origin of Godwin, Earl of Wessex and later father of Harold, future king of England, was unknown in the Middle Ages (and uncertain even now); apart from a couple of allusions to his being in Denmark in 1019, he first appears in the English chronicles after the death of Cnut in 1035 (Rigg 2001, 1001–10). Map seems to have dug around in popular tales and spun together a remarkable prequel to his career, describing how King Ethelred chanced to seek shelter at the home of a cowherd and was entertained lavishly, mainly by the cowherd's son Godwin (paralleling a story in the *Cnytlinga saga*), who thereafter rose in favor and (mainly by trickery) secured for himself eight earldoms, marriage to Cnut's sister, and control of Denmark. Although deriving history from local legends was probably the normal process of historiography, Map's dramatization of the stories and attempts at character analysis of his hero put it in the literary genre that we would now call "historical fiction."

Map did not set out to transform genres: he simply used stories for his own purposes, satirical, historical, or literary. The following examples, however, seem to point to a deliberate intention to subvert, or at any rate undercut, tales of the supernatural, of which there are many in the *De nugis*. One of the most dramatic (4.9; Map 1983, 344–48) is that of Henno-with-the-teeth, who found his beautiful future wife abandoned after a storm. She bears him children and is an ideal wife, but Henno's mother observes that she avoids holy water and leaves church before the consecration of the host. A priest is brought and the wife (with her maid) is sprinkled with holy water, at which the wife and her maid fly up through the roof. Map's comment is astonishing:

> Ne miremini si Dominus ascendit corporaliter, cum hoc pessimis permiserit creaturis, quas eciam necesse sit deorsum inuitas trahi. (4.9; ibid., 348)

> [Do not be surprised if the Lord ascended physically, seeing that he allowed this to his lowest creations, who are inevitably going to be dragged downwards against their will.] (ibid., 349)

Several stories of the supernatural are drawn into the ambit of the scholastic disputation (using technical terms): 2.30 (ibid., 206) concerns the post-mortem absolution of the father of a Northumbrian knight: "Nouus his casus nouam diuine pagine disputacionem intulit" [this new event introduced a new disputation into theology] (ibid., 207); another concerns attempts at last-minute repentance, which are frustrated by a merciless bishop, resulting in the suicidal death of Eudo:

> Lector et auditor disputent si miles rectum habuit zelum et secundum scienciam, qui precipitatam indiscreti pontificis et iracundi secutus est sentenciam. (4.6; ibid., 340)

> [Let the listener and reader dispute whether the knight, who followed the rash sentence of an indiscreet and angry bishop, had a proper zeal in full knowledge of the facts.] (ibid., 341)

In 4.7 a recidivist monk who breaks his vow not to bear arms, as he lies dying asks a temporary confessor to pray that he be tormented in Hell until Judgment Day. When Map revised this, he added the words:

> Quomodo potuit hic ingemiscere, et non fecit? Si quid ex contingentibus omisit, inter nos sit disputatio, anime illius misereatur Deus. (1.14; ibid., 40)

> [How could he have lamented and not done so? If he omitted any of the details, let us do the disputing and may God have mercy on his soul.] (ibid., 41)

It is possible that Map believed these supernatural or (to us) farfetched stories and that for him there were real theological problems to be addressed, but in the story of Triunein (2.11) Map's sense of humor seems to be dominant as he narrates a shaggy-dog story par excellence. Gwestin Gwestiniog saw some women dancing on the shores of Lake Brekeniauc, into which they later submerged. One night he caught and married one of them; she left him, as she had threatened, on the day that he struck her with a bridle, but he was able to catch one of his sons, Triunein Vagelauc. Triunein went to serve the king of Deheubarth. One day the king boasted that he could raid anyone's land with impunity. Triunein retorted that his own king, Brychan, would resist and was thrown in prison for his impertinence. Eventually a raid was planned with Triunein as its guide. News is brought to Brychan in his bath, despite some trepidation, as Brychan was known to strike messengers who brought bad news; Brychan rides off to challenge the raiders. Despite a temporary interruption by a woman who tells him to loosen a shackle from his horse, Brychan and his men wipe out the invaders and pile up their mutilated bodies under a heap of stones. Triunein, however, was not found.

> Quod autem aiunt Triunein a matre sua seruatum et cum ipsa in lacu illo unde supra mencio est, imo et mendacium puto, quod de non inuento fingi potuit error huiusmodi. (2.11; ibid., 154)

> [The suggestion that he was preserved by his mother and lives with her in that lake that I mentioned before, is, I think, a lie, since an error of this kind could easily have been made up about someone who was not found.] (ibid., 155)

The rambling story with its elaborate digressions (the argument between Brychan in his bath and the messenger, the delays over the loose shackle and the old woman, and the cairn built over the right hands and penises of the defeated raiders) can hardly be intended to be anything but comic. But what is the punch line? It is surely in the word *error* in the explanation of the disappearance of Christ's body from the tomb where it had been placed by Joseph of Arimathea; to the Jews the "error" was the story that Jesus had ascended to heaven; to the Christians it was the story that the soldiers were bribed to circulate, that Christ's disciples had stolen the body (Mt 28:11–15; *Evangelium Nicodemi* 13.3, 14.3). Map's equation of the disappearance of Christ's body with that of Triunein might (in a different age) seem blasphemous, but this is Walter Map. We have seen already his parallel between the ascensions of Christ and Henno-with-the-teeth's wife; in his antimatrimonial *Epistola Valerii* (4.3; Map 1983, 294) he cites the eclipse of Apollo because of his infatuation with Leucothoe (from Ovid's *Metamorphoses* 4) and warns his friend "ne lumen quod in te est tenebre fiat, Leucotoen fugito" [Flee Leucothoe lest the light that is within you become darkness], embedding Christ's word's in Luke 11:35.

From Meter to Rhythm and Rhyme

One of the most striking literary developments involving Latin is Henry of Huntingdon's Latin version of the Old English poem on the *Battle of Brunanburgh*, in which Henry employs various combinations of quantitative or rhythmical adonics, trochaics or dactyls, together with rhyme and/or alliteration to produce a kind of heroic verse, as the final six lines show:

Non fuit bellum	hac in tellure
Majus patratum	nec caedes tanta
Praecessit istam	postquam huc venerunt
Trans mare latum	Saxones et Angli
Brittones pulsuri	clari Martis fabri:
Walenses vicerunt,	reges fugaverunt,
	regna susceperunt.

[In all this kingdom was never a conflict
Greater accomplished, nor did such a slaughter
Surpass that fought here, ever since the time
That across the broad sea the Angles and Saxons,
Splendid war-smiths, came in conquest
To banish the Britons and won against Welshmen,
Drove out their kings and claimed their kingdoms.]
(Rigg 1991, 70)

Henry's experiment (like that of his *Herbal*) had no followers, though there had been a couple of earlier attempts. On the other hand, the native (English) popularity of alliteration was often extended into Latin poetry for decorative effects, as in Walter of Wimborne:

> Multi mortalium   in mundi stadio
> certatim cursitant   sed casso studio.
>
> [Many the mortal on mundane tracks:
> They run the race but reward they lack.] (Walter of Wimborne 1978, 40.1.1–2)
>
> Multi mortalium   per mundi maria
> solent Mercurii   mercari precia.
>
> [Many mortals on mundane seas
> Pursue their profits by trading deals.] (ibid., 3.1–2)

In the north of England, where English alliterative verse was still thriving, the fourteenth-century religious writer Richard Rolle (see Rigg 1992, 248–53 for an introduction) used alliteration as a structural device in his *Melos amoris* (ed. by Arnould 1957), and one of his poems is rightly called a "carmen prosaicum":

> O paruulorum pater, qui punis potentes,
> Pactum pepigi properare pacifice
> Ad panem paradisi.
> Tu pastum pretende ne peream pergendo.
> Porta pingatur ut pareat perpure,
> Quia puto quod paries pie perdurabit.
>
> [O protector of the little ones, who punish the powerful,
> I have pledged a promise to proceed peacefully
> To the provisions of paradise.
> Provide the provender, lest I perish on the pilgrimage.
> Let the portal be painted, that its appearance may be pure,
> For I predict that the protecting wall will be permanent in piety.]
> (Liegey 1957, 31)

Historians of the "renaissance" of the twelfth and thirteenth centuries rightly stress such developments as the rise of universities, the rediscovery of Aristotle and Arabic science, the spread of new religious orders like the Franciscans, new and enthusiastic forms of Christian devotion (pathos, the cult of the Virgin), the secular love lyric, and so on. I want to concentrate here on the metrical developments, which, combined with the kind of playfulness described above, manifested themselves in many new verse forms (Norberg 1958; Rigg 1992, 320–21; Mantello and Rigg 1996, 106–110), an explosion of new types, which multiplied without restraint. The new developments (widespread in medieval Latin) arose from (a) the replacement of quantity by rhythm in lyrical poetry, and (b) rhyme, which was ubiquitous in rhythmical verse but also very common in traditional dactylic verse (hexameters and pentameters), where it took advantage of the possibility of new line divisions. For example, in addition to the traditional caesura, which gave rise to the very common leonines,

> Linquo coax ranis,   cra corvis vanaque vanis;
> Ad logicam pergo   que mortis non timet ergo,
>
> [To frogs I leave the croak, to crows the caw, the vain to vain,
> And go to Logic, where Death's "therefore" holds no pain,]
> (Serlon of Wilton 1965, 121)

and their many multiplications (single-sound couplets, collaterals, *cruciferi*, etc.), there were *dactylici tripertiti, hexametri tripertiti, trinini salientes,* and many others. Although simple leonines were used for ordinary narrative and even religious verse, there is no doubt that a multiplicity of rhymes produces a comic effect and is often used for vituperation or satire, as in Michael of Cornwall's complex run-over rhymed hexameters:

> Eris collector,   lector non historiarum
> Harum   quas recito. Cito   cessa, false relator!
> Lator   rumorum, morum   corruptor, omissis
> Missis,   inmensis mensis   vis sepe vacare.
>
> [Money-grubber, you're no lover of such histories
> As these I read, so now concede, you lying teller,
> Seller of rumor, the soul's doomer, and then having missed
> The eucharist at vast repast you want to sate yourself.]
> (Hilka 1926, 153; see also Rigg 1992, 197)

Incidentally, this type of rhyming structure is similar to the Irish *devi* (i.e., the end of one line rhyming with the beginning of the next), perhaps another example of hybridization.

The second wheel on the bicycle of the New Versification (the first being rhyme) was rhythm. The best illustration of the shift from classical quantity (i.e., syllable length) to stress is the trochaic tetrameter catalectic, which is scanned classically as

> $-\smile-\,\_\,/\,\_\quad\smile\,\_\_/\,\smile\,-\,\_/\_\smile\smile$
> Da puer plectrum, choreis ut canam fidelibus
> [Give me my quill, page, that in loyal trochees I may sing] (Prudentius 1962, 76–7).

In rhythm this becomes the rhythmical trochaic septenarius (8p7pp):

>   /   / /   /
> Apparebit repentina dies magna domini.
> [That mighty day of God will suddenly appear.] (Raby 1959, 14)

Subsequently the first half of the line (8p) was divided in two, producing 4p4p7pp, rhyming in couplets aabccb; the a- and c-rhymes could be extended to three or four lines. This was the Victorine Sequence, extremely popular for hymns and also parodies, as in (at its simplest) Walter of Wimborne:

> Mundi uolo uanitatem
> Et fortune leuitatem
>   Breuiter describere,
> Que non habent firmamentum

>   Sed fugacem uincunt uentum
>   Fugiendo propere.
>
> [The world's vain emptiness
> And fortune's fickleness
>   I wish to briefly say:
> They have no solid base;
> The wind they can outpace
>   And quickly pass away.]
> (Walter of Wimborne 1978, 73.1)

Another classical lyric meter that was widely adapted and adopted, mainly for satire, was the Lesser Asclepiad. Classically this was scanned

> $\_\_ \_ / \_ \smile\smile \_ / \_ \smile\smile \_ / \smile \smile$
> Maecenas atavis edite regibus
> [Maecenas, born of ancient kings].
> (Horace, *Carmina* 1.1)

Rhythmically this became the rhythmical asclepiad, 6pp6pp, which is almost always found in quatrains aaaa, as in

>   /   /
> Vxorem ducere quondam volueram
>   /   /
> Vt vitam sequerer multorum miseram
>   /   /
> Decoram virginem, pinguem et teneram,
>   /   /
> Quam inter alias solam dilexeram.
>
> [I once had planned to take a wife
> (to follow others' wretched life),
> A tender, juicy winsome maid—
> By her alone my heart was swayed.]
> (*De coniuge non ducenda* 1986, 66.2)

Other examples could be given of shifts from quantity to rhythm, but some new forms have no classical antecedent, notably the Goliardic line, 7pp6p usually in quatrains:

>   /   /
>   Meum est propositum in taberna mori,
>   /   /
>   Ut sint vina proxima morientis ori.
>   /   /
>   Tunc cantabunt letius angelorum chori:
>   /   /
>   "Sit Deus propitius huic potatori."

> [It's my design to end my time against a tavern bar—
> A flask of wine (just there'll be fine) at hand and not too far.
> Angelic hosts will raise a toast and give a happy cheer:
> "May God's great mind be sweet and kind to one who loved his beer."]
> (Archipoeta 1958, 75.10.12)

It may be sung to the tune of "Good King Wenceslas."

Alien Influences

By the twelfth and thirteen centuries Latin was once again a living language—alive not artificially (as it is now), but alive in its capacity to change in response to its environment. In England the environment was clerical: Latin was used by people whose native language was English (or Welsh) and who may also have been bilingual in French (or other European languages). In religious services Latin was used for all offices; in school and university, students were expected to speak Latin at all times (a rule not always observed, as we see from its frequent repetition). In professional life, clerics might be lawyers, drafting wills and property deeds. If they were employed as agents or diplomats, they might be communicating with non-English speakers with whom they shared only Latin; like their forebears after 1066, they would simplify grammar and syntax and would adopt new vocabulary. In short, they produced a pidgin or creole, and this is evident in some literary Latin of the age. There were, of course, restraints: Latin still had its rules when it was first learned. (It should be noted that not all translators of Latin could actually understand it correctly: the Middle English version of the Letter of Alexander to Aristotle is notable for its "literal-mindedness and outright incompetence," exhibiting an "almost entirely deficient knowledge of Latin" [Hahn 1979, 106 and 109]. But most of those who chose to write in Latin could understand it.)

In the comic Latin verse satire, there is often evident a linguistic fluidity between Latin and the vernaculars. In the *Descriptio Northfolchie* the peasants often use English, but the rhyme and rhythm are controlled by Latin:

> Dicitque sepius ob hanc leticiam
> "Ha ha, mi swete brid, ego te comedam."
>
> [In all his joy he'd constantly repeat
> "My pretty little bird, you're mine to eat."]
> (Rigg 2004, 587.180–81)
>
> Bufonem intuens statim interrogat,
> "How, gossyb, quid est hoc?" et ille recitat…
>
> [He asks, while staring in the toad's big eyes,
> "How neighbor, what is this?" and he replies…]
> (ibid., 587.188–89)

Similarly, in a satire on the people of Stoughton, the rhymes are Latin-English:

> Rustice <u>Willelme</u>, causam tibi supplico <u>tel me</u>.
> [Tell me, rustic William, just what is the problem?]
> (Wright 1864, 24)

> Quilibet ex <u>illis</u> sibi dicit, "do that ti <u>will is</u>".
> [They say, each one of these, "well do just what you please".]
> (ibid., 74)

Intralinguistic wordplay is common in political polemic, especially in the fourteenth-century English poet I have called the Anonymous of Calais, who wrote about the beginning of the Hundred Years War, on France and Scotland (see Rigg 1999, 169–211). He puns frequently on proper names:

> In Cressi creuit laus Anglica, Francia fleuit.
> [In Crecy English honor grew and Frenchmen wept.]
> (Rigg 1999, 185.228)

> Mentif mentitur.
> [Mentieth is a liar (from *mentior*).]
> (ibid., 158.17)

> Acies fortes penetrauit.
> [(Percy) pierced the fierce force.]
> (ibid., 191.66.2)

The French king's lack of the first element of his name (*Valois*—*valere*) is often mocked:

> Te faciet maleys Edwardus aper polimitus.
> [Edward will put you ill at ease, the multicolored boar.]
> (ibid., 177.24)

Vernacular words appear frequently (*coir* = Middle French *cuir*; *alle* = English "all"), and rhyme neatly:

> In proprio climat tibi dicit aper cito "Chekmat".
> [Now soon, in your climate, the Boar will say "Checkmate."]
> (ibid., 179.71)

Such word play is not, of course, a genre, but it illustrates the self-confidence in several languages that in our own age James Joyce displays (Perce O'Reilly = *perce-oreille* "earwig").

Another form of wordplay in historical poetry is the chronogram. Thomas Elmham (early fifteenth century) employs *apices numerales* (i.e., M, D, C, L, X, V, I) to spell out the date in many hexameter lines, e.g.,

> Hic Ion Oldcastel Christi fuit insidiator.
> [This year Christ's foe, John Oldcastle, intrigued.]
> (Rigg 1992, 299–301)

That is, the date of 1413 can be extracted as a Roman numeral (DDCCCLLVIIIIIII) from the letters of the line.

Simpler but more amusing is a popular poem in mock-Latin, *Quondam fuit factus festus* (English in origin), in which an abbot, prior, and canon argue about whether more drink should be served. The meter is the Victorine stanza; inflections, number, tense, mood, declensions, and conjugations are all distorted:

> Abbas dixit: ut senectus
> ego bipsi cum affectus.
> Vadi queri promtum lectus
>   ubi sum iacencia.
> Dixit abbas serviatis:
> Date vinum nostris fratris.
> Bene legunt et cantatis
>   Ad nostra solempnia.
> Dixit prior ad abbatis:
> bene bibunt, habent satis.
> Non est bonum ebriatis;
>   eant ad claustralia.
> Unus cano iuniorum,
> bonus lectus et cantorum,
> irascatus ad priorum
>   dixit ista folia.
>
> [The abbot said: "As age befits
> I drunken was with loving fits.
> I'm off to find a ready pits
>   To lay my body down."
> The abbot said to servant kind:
> "To brethren mine give drink of wine.
> They read and sing good all the time
>   At all our solemn sounds."
> The prior to the abbot said:
> "They've drunk quite well, they're very fed.
> Such drinking isn't godlihead—
>   Be off to cloister town."
> A canon of the younger ones,
> A fluent read and tuneful song,
> At the prior angered strong,
>   Said these foolish clown.]
> (Meyer 1908, 412–13.5–8)

Throughout the poem the rhymes and rhythm are preserved; towards the end the number of lines per stanza and syllables per line increase, but this may plausibly be attributed to the drunken state of the participants.

In one of its manuscripts, the *Quondam fuit* is followed by the unique copy of a superhybridization, the *Stores of the Cities*, listing the principal features of seven English cities, with three lines each in leonine hexameters, e.g.,

> Hec sunt Lincolne: bow, bolt et bellia bolne,
> Ad monstrum scala, rosa bryghta, nobilis ala,
> Et bubulus flatus—hec sunt staura ciuitatis.
>
> [At Lincoln: bow, bolt, swollen bells,
> The minster stairs, bright rose, fine aisle,
> The cattle's farts—the city's wealth.]
> (Rigg 1967, 128)

Latin rhymes with English (Lincolne: bolne "swollen") and Latin forms are changed (*monstrum* = monasterium); *ciuitatis* changes its ending throughout for the sake of rhymes.

Such frivolities did not start new genres, but they do indicate the literary possibilities in the linguistic dexterity of the clerical class. Hidden puns appear in Walter of Wimborne's *mors surda* "deaf death" (Walter of Wimborne 1978, 129, 132.100, 129–30) and he can hardly have been unaware that the conspiracy to put out the sun (ut solis lampadem tollant de medio *MC* 434/4) is also one to remove the Son of God, as *sun* and *son* were homophones by this date.

If there was linguistic trading between English, French, and Latin in poetry, this was even more true of music, where tunes were interchanged between Latin and English, and thus between sacred and profane. In the *Red Book of Ossory* the religious poems of Bishop Richard Ledrede are sometimes supplied with a vernacular "cliche" indicating the tune to which it was to be sung, e.g., "Haue mercy of me frere," "Mayde yn the moore lay," "Alas, hou scholdy synge," etc. (Rigg 1977). This was not a new phenomenon: some of the eleventh-century Cambridge Songs are given headings indicating the original German tune to which they were to be sung, e.g., *Modus Ottinc, Modus Liebinc, Carmina Cantabrigiensia* 1955). There are many other medieval examples (see Ledrede 1974, xxxviii–xxxix).

A final case for generic shifts in medieval Latin literature might be parody: the parodist selects a form to mimic, for satire or just for fun. There are parodies of anything that was common and popular. The Bible was the most popular target, producing mock-gospels satirizing the church, the *Nemo* gospel, which is a new version of Odysseus's joke at the expense of the Cyclops (Nobody was a contemporary of the Creator, he ascended to heaven and saw God, etc.). There were parodies of the Mass (for drinking) and of hymns such as Venantius Fortunatus's *Pange lingua*, one of which celebrated the death of the hated Piers Gaveston. There is Burchard of Bellevaux's *Defense of Beards*, based on scriptural citations; the only evidence that this is parodic is the reader's sense that it can hardly be anything else. There were also parodic letters (including some from Satan, congratulating the church on its good work on his behalf) and parodic grammars (based on Donatus and satirizing peasants).

In the fifteenth and sixteenth centuries a shift in literary taste began that had the effect of a pedagogical contraceptive pill. By reverting to classical standards of Latin grammar, style, orthography, meter, and textual criticism, Humanism put the brake on and eventually stopped most of the inventiveness of late medieval Latin literary endeavors and frivolities. Such experimentation now found its outlet in the vernacular, the future vehicle for metrical innovation.

BIBLIOGRAPHIC NOTE

I must begin with an apology for the frequent recurrence of my own name in the parenthetical notes and bibliography. When seeking examples of genre shifting, I found it easier to go to works that I have edited or studied myself. I am sure that there are other (and probably better) works and studies, which I do not know.

There are many (perhaps too many) studies of the nature and function of humor and comedy. Not surprisingly, there are none of mere lightheartedness, which simply needs to be observed and smiled at. In addition to the authors discussed here (Alexander Neckam, Reginald of Canterbury, Lawrence of Durham and Henry of Avranches), see my remarks on Walter Map and the Shaggy Dog Story (Rigg 1998). Other likely places for such humor are letters (like those of Peter of Blois) and the more garrulous historians, such as Gerald of Wales and Matthew Paris. Naturally, writers known for their wit like Walter Map have more incidental humor. For contrast between Map and Gerald, see Bate (1972).

On meter, the spread of rhyme, and the shift from quantity to rhythm, the standard work is Norberg (1958). There are summaries by Mantello and Rigg (1996) and Rigg (1992). Norberg's work is the summation of many earlier scholars such as Meyer. It is worth noting that outrageous rhymes, especially between one word and two, are themselves a source of humor, as in Alexander Pope and Ogden Nash.

The affect of Latin on English language and literature is probably to be found discussed in every linguistic or literary history of English, but there are few discussions of the reverse process, the penetration of Latin itself by the vernaculars. On vernacular lexical intrusions into Latin, see Sharpe in Mantello and Rigg (1996). I do not know of any studies of the literary use of the vernaculars (particularly English and French) in Latin such as I have outlined here. A start has been made by M. C. Davidson (2002) in her study of code-switching from one language to another. The word "macaronic" is usually applied to the formal and structured juxtaposition of English and Latin in hymns and poems, but the more casual use of French or English in the middle of a Latin text (as seen here in the poems on Norfolk, Stoughton, and the *Stores of the Cities*) has not been studied: it is certainly not susceptible of a rigorous statistical methodology. The best place to see this kind of linguistic juxtaposition is in miscellanies such as the *Glastonbury Miscellany* (1968) and similar late Middle English collections.

BIBLIOGRAPHY

Primary sources

Archipoeta. 1958. *Die Gedichte des Archipoeta*, edited by Heinrich Watenphul and Heinrich Krefeld. Heidelberg: C. Winter.

Burchard of Bellevaux. 1985. *Apologia de Barbis*, edited by Robert B. C. Huygens. Corpus Christianorum. Continuatio Medievalis 62. Turnhout: Brepols.

Capella, Martianus. 1983. *De Nuptiis Mercurii et Philologiae*, edited by James Willis. Bibliotheca scriptorum Graecorum et Romanorum Teubneriana. Leipzig: B. G. Teubner.

Carmina Cantabrigiensia. 1955. *Carmina Cantabrigiensia*, edited by Karl Strecker. Monumenta Germaniae Historica. Scriptores 40. Berlin: Weidmann.

De coniuge non ducenda. 1986. *Gawain on Marriage: the textual tradition of the De coniuge non ducenda*, edited by Arthur G. Rigg. Studies and Texts 79. Toronto: Pontifical Institute of Mediaeval Studies.

Elmham, Thomas. 1858. *Memorials of Henry V*, edited by Charles A. Cole. London: Rolls Publications.

Glastonbury Miscellany. 1968. *A Glastonbury Miscellany of the Fifteenth Century*, edited by Arthur G. Rigg. Oxford English Monographs. London: Oxford University Press.

Hahn, Thomas. 1979. "The Middle English *Letter of Alexander to Aristotle*." *Medieval Studies* 41: 106–60.

Hilka, Alfons. 1926. "Eine mittellateinische Dichterfehde. *Versus Michaelis Cornubiensis contra Henricum Abrincensem*." In *Mittelalterliche Handschriften: Paläographische, kunsthistorische, literarische und bibliotheksgeschichtliche Untersuchungen. Festgabe zum 60. Geburtstag von Hermann Degering*, ed. by Aloys Bömer and Joachim Kirchner. Leipzig: Hiersemann. Reprint Hildesheim: Olms, 1973.

Historia Meriadoci. 1988. *The Story of Meriadoc, King of Cambria*, edited and translated by Mildred Leake Day. Garland Library of Medieval Literature, Ser. A, 50. New York: Garland Publishing.

Joseph of Exeter. 1970. *Joseph Iscanus: Werke und Briefe*, edited by Ludwig Gompf. Mittellateinische Studien und Texte 4. Leiden: Brill.

Kittredge, George L. 1903. "Arthur and Gorlagon." *Harvard Studies and Notes in Philology* 8: 149–62.

Lapidge, Michael. 1981. "An edition of the *Vera Historia de morte Arthuri*." *Arthurian Literature* 1: 79–93.

Lawrence of Durham. 2002. *Gottes Heilsplan—verdichtet: Edition des Hypognosticon des Laurentius Dunelmensis*, edited by Susanne Daub. Erlangen: Palm & Enke.

Ledrede, Richard. 1974. *The Latin Poems of Richard Ledrede OFM*, edited by Edmund Colledge. Studies and Texts 30. Toronto: Pontifical Institute of Mediaeval Studies.

Liegey, Gabriel M. 1957. "Richard Rolle's *Carmen prosaicum*." *Mediaeval Studies* 19: 15–36.

Map, Walter. 1983. *De Nugis Curialium*, edited and translated by Montague R. James, revised by Christopher N. L. Brooke and Roger A. B. Mynors. Oxford Medieval Texts. Oxford: Clarendon Press.

Meyer, Wilhelm. 1908. "*Quondam fuit factus festus*: Ein Gedicht in Spottlatein." *Nachrichten von der königlichen Gesellschaft der Wissenschaften zu Göttingen. Phil.-Hist. Klasse.* [1908:] 406–29.

Neckam, Alexander. 1863. *De Naturis Rerum*, edited by Thomas Wright. Rerum Britannicarum Medii Aevi Scriptores 34. London: Longman, Green, Longman, Roberts, and Green.

Prudentius. 1962. *Prudentius. With an English Translation*, translated by Henry J. Thomson. 2 vols. Loeb Classical Library 387, 398. London, Cambridge, MA: Harvard University Press.

Reginald of Canterbury. 1942. *The Vita sancti Malchi of Reginald of Canterbury*, edited by Levi R. Lind. Illinois Studies in Language and Literature 27:3–4. Urbana, IL: University of Illinois Press.

Rigg, A. G. 1967. "The Stores of the Cities." *Anglia* 85: 125–37.

———. 1999. "Propaganda on the Hundred Years War: poems on the battles of Crecy and Durham (1346)." *Traditio* 54: 169–211.

———. 2004. "*Descriptio Northfolchie*: a critical edition." In *Nova de Veteribus: mittel- und neulateinische Studien für Paul Gerhard Schmidt*, edited by Andreas Bihrer and Elisabeth Stein, 577–94. Munich: K. G. Saur.

———. 2003. "Henry of Huntingdon's Herbal." *Mediaeval Studies* 65: 213–92. A new edition is forthcoming by Winston Black.

Rolle, Richard. 1957. *The Melos Amoris*, edited by Emile J. Arnould. Oxford: B. Blackwell.

Serlon de Wilton. 1965. *Poèmes latins*, edited by Jan Öberg. Acta Universitatis Stockholmiensis. Studia Latina Stockholmiensia 14. Stockholm: Almquist & Wiksell.

Townsend, David. 1994. "The Vita Sancti Birini of Henry of Avranches." *Analecta Bollandiana* 112: 309–38.

Walter of Wimborne. 1978. *The Poems of Walter of Wimborne OFM*, edited by Arthur G. Rigg. Studies and Texts 42. Toronto: Pontifical Institute of Mediaeval Studies.

Walther, Hans. 1965. "Zu den kleineren Gedichten des Alexander Neckam." *Mittellateinisches Jahrbuch* 2: 111–29.

Wright, Thomas, ed. 1844. *Anecdota literaria: a collection of short poems in English, Latin, and French*. London: J. R. Smith.

Secondary sources

Bayless, Martha. 1985. *Parody in the Middle Ages: the Latin tradition*. Recentiores. Ann Arbor, MI: University of Michigan Press.

Echard, Siân. 1998. *Arthurian Narrative in the Latin Tradition*. Cambridge studies in medieval literature 36. Cambridge: Cambridge University Press.

Lehmann, Paul. 1963. *Die Parodie im Mittelalter*. 2nd ed. Stuttgart: Hiersemann.

Mantello, Frank A. C. and Arthur G. Rigg. 1996. *Medieval Latin: an Introduction and Bibliographical Guide*. Washington, DC: Catholic University of America Press.

Norberg, Dag L. 2004. *An Introduction to the Study of Medieval Latin Versification*, translated by Grant C. Roti and Jacqueline de La Chapelle Skubly, edited by Jan Ziolkowski. Washington, DC: Catholic University of America Press.

Raby, Frederic J. E. 1957. *A History of Secular Latin Poetry in the Middle Ages*. 2 vols. 2nd ed. Oxford: Clarendon.

———, ed. 1959. *The Oxford Book of Medieval Latin Verse*. Oxford: Clarendon Press.

Rigg, A.G. 1977. "The Red Book of Ossory." *Medium Aevum* 45: 269–78.

———. 1991. "Henry of Huntingdon's metrical experiments." *Journal of Medieval Latin* 1: 60–72.

———. 1992. *A History of Anglo-Latin Literature 1066–1422*. Cambridge: Cambridge University Press.

———. 1998. "Walter Map, the Shaggy Dog story, and the *Quaestio Disputata*." In *Roma Magistra Mundi*, edited by Jacqueline Hammesse, 723–35. Textes et études du moyen âge 10. Louvain-la-Neuve: Fédération des Instituts d'Etudes Médiévales.

———. 2001. "Historical Fiction in Walter Map: the construction of Godwin of Wessex." In *Scripturus vitam: lateinische Biographie von der Antike bis in die Gegenwart*, edited by Dorothea Walz, 1001–10. Heidelberg: Mattes.

———. 2009. "Adam of Barking: work in progress." *Journal of Medieval Latin* 19: 219–49.

Strayer, Joseph R., ed. 1982–89. *The Dictionary of the Middle Ages*. New York: Macmillan Publishing.

CHAPTER 14

TEXTUAL FLUIDITY AND THE INTERACTION OF LATIN AND THE VERNACULAR LANGUAGES

BRIAN MURDOCH

The Status of the Vernacular

It took time for literatures in the vernacular languages to acquire sufficient status to be preserved in writing and thus to develop beside and away from Latin, the language of the Vulgate and that of an already established literature, of scholarship and of science. In the cases of the Celtic (especially Irish and Welsh) and West-Germanic (continental High and Low German and Anglo-Saxon) cultures in particular, Latin was a completely distinct language which had to be learned (Ponert 1975). Accordingly, these cultures often provide the clearest examples of the interpenetration with Latin at all levels—linguistic, thematic, and aesthetic. Possibly the most physical sign of textual integration is the practice of bilingual glossing, namely writing a word-equivalent in the other language above, in the margin, or close to the Latin word concerned, and, when a glossed text was copied, sometimes rewriting the vernacular words side by side with the Latin ones. An early secular example of a slightly different integration of Latin and the vernacular is found where Roman legal codification was applied to the customs of very different cultures. The Lombardic *Edict of Rothar* of 643 is in Latin, but it incorporates Germanic terms (Lombardic was a High German dialect which died out fairly early), sometimes in

Latinised form and usually explained, though the integration is not always clear. In a section about illicit wood-cutting we find in one manuscript the curious phrase *si... sinaidam fecerit*. The noun is Germanic *snaida*, Old High German *snita*, "a cut," with a Latin accusative ending: worse, other manuscripts have *sanaidas* and even *signaidam*, hard to interpret in any language (Bluhme 1868, 3–90). One version of the Latin *Lex Salica*, the laws of the Franks, also contains a number of probably Low German words, each preceded with the term *mal(lo)bergo*, a Latinised form of the word for a place of judgment, signaling a local legal term. There are also interlanguage curiosities, such as the enigmatic Old High German-Latin phrasebook (it has the German text first, with the Latin beside or above it) known as the *Pariser Gespräche*. Beside useful words and phrases based on the Graeco-Latin *Hermeneumata* tradition are some intriguing and occasionally abusive extras. The document might relate to a Romance-speaking traveler venturing into Germanic territory, and both the German and the Latin show influences of the developing Gallo-Roman vernacular, such as the writing of Germanic bilabial *w*- as *gu*- (see William/Guillaume), or the frequent loss of initial *h*- (*abeo* for Latin *habeo*, *erro* for German *hērro*, "Lord"). However, in what context "Vndes ars in tine naso" the German for "canis culum in tuo naso" [dog's ass up your nose], delivered with a French accent, might *ever* have been appropriate is debatable (Haubrichs and Pfister 1989; Penzl 1985).

In more formal literary contexts, assertions of the superiority of Latin are common, but precisely how these are to be taken is another matter. Otfrid, a monk from Weissenburg, composed in the ninth century a substantial rhymed Gospel-poem in German (Otfried of Weissenburg 1973) which will serve later to exemplify a great many aspects of the interaction of Latin and vernacular. He justified his choice of language in an explanatory and apologetic Latin letter to his superior, Archbishop Liutbert of Mainz (Otfried of Weissenburg 1943). He sandwiched this between two prefatory poems in German in strophes of two long-lines, in which acrostics and telestichs spell out Latin greetings to the king and to the Bishop of Constance. In the letter he says that German is a foreign, uncultivated, and undisciplined language; *barbaricus* is used normally for "a language other than Latin," although a pejorative meaning is developing. Otfrid worries that German words have different genders from Latin, and he refrains from giving examples in the letter "lest they give occasion for laughter." The Irish *Auraicept na n-Éces*, the scholar's primer, a grammatical guide for poets based upon Latin grammars such as that of Donatus, composed probably a century before Otfrid, took a different line. While acknowledging that Latin and Irish did not match, it stressed the superiority of Irish, claiming a richer vocabulary; the Gael, it asserts, is wider in words and letters than the Latinist (*Auraicept na n-Éces* 1907, 83). Even Otfrid, however respectful he might have sounded when addressing his ecclesiastical superior, strikes a different note within the poem itself: the Franks are just as good as the Greeks and Romans, so why should Christ not be praised "in our language"? Over a century later another monk, the educator Notker III of St. Gall (ca. 950–1022), apologizes to Bishop Hugo of Sion (Sitten), in a Latin letter from around 1015, for using German in his writings, but assures the bishop that he will get used to the idea (Copeland 1991, 98–103).

Notker III, who acquired the unflattering physical soubriquet *labeo*, thick-lipped, as well as the appellative *teutonicus*, the German, provides an important illustration of interaction. Notker developed what is termed in German a *Mischsprache*, a mixed language, which he applied to a wide range of books on the monastic syllabus, from the Psalter to Boethius, Martianus Capella, and others. His pattern was to give the Latin and then translate it fairly freely, adding a German commentary. Key Latin words are either explained, or deliberately left untranslated (sometimes attracting later German glosses). As a simple example, Notker translates and comments upon the phrase *cathedra pestilentiae* in Psalm 1:1, and then adds: "Pestis chît latine pecora sternens. Sô pestis sih kebrêitet. sô ist iz pestilentia." The mid-twelfth-century St. Gall manuscript has the gloss *fiêo nider slahinde* over *pecora sternens*. An imitation might be, with the German italicised: "Plague *means* in Latin felling animals [gloss: *animals/ striking down*]. *When* plague *spreads, then it is* pestilence" (Notker 1935–55 and 1972–, 8:9). Notker's skill, accuracy, and variation remain impressive, and the use of these texts in the classroom is easily imagined. His integral technique had a successor a generation or so later in the tripartite *Expositio in Cantica Canticorum* by Williram of Ebersberg (ca. 1020–85), a work of some complexity at all levels. The text is a commentary on the Canticles, but mixes prose and verse as well as German and Latin. In the manuscripts (there are several) the work is written in three columns, sometimes separated decoratively. In the center is the Vulgate in large letters, with the exposition (based principally upon a commentary by Haimo of Auxerre) in the outside columns. On the left, this is in Latin verse; on the right is a prose commentary using Notker's *Mischsprache*, with the verse usually given in full in a free German version, then a prose commentary in mixed German and Latin (Williram of Ebersberg 2004; Schupp 1978). Williram's *Expositio* is really an *opus geminatum*, a double work like Sedulius's *Carmen Paschale*, which is accompanied by a separate prose *Paschale opus*, and Williram's Latin verse commentary is more difficult and aesthetically more significant than the German prose, which has the lowest status. Williram wrote otherwise in Latin, and some manuscripts of the *Expositio* have only the biblical text and the Latin verse, while elsewhere the German part is translated into Latin. There are also, to be sure, cases of a far more *ad hoc* mixing of the languages outside the theological context; the languages seem to be used indiscriminately in charms and in the closely related medical recipes.

The Sermon

Of major significance in the consideration of vernacular and Latin interaction is the sermon, that part of Church ritual where the vernacular was encouraged. In the early period spoken Latin sermons appear to have been translated orally on the spot:

Walahfrid's ninth-century life of St. Gall tells us not only that the Irish missionary had a good command *barbaricae locutionis* [of foreign—in this case German—speech] which was exploited by his superior, Columbanus, but that on a later occasion Gall himself preached a Latin sermon which was orally translated *ad utilitatem barbarorum* [for the benefit of non-Latin speakers] by his own deacon, Johannes (Krusch 1902, 289 and 303 = *Vita* 1.6 and 1.25; see Murdoch 2001). Occasionally, it is true, miracles rendered this unnecessary. Gerald of Wales, never overly modest, tells us in his *Itinerarium Cambriae* of 1191 (1.11) how he preached in Latin and French at Haverfordwest, aware that most of the extensive audience understood neither, in spite of which large numbers were still persuaded by him to take the cross (Gerald of Wales 1978).

Once homiletic material is committed to writing the position becomes more complex. Vernacular texts may be translations of Latin sermons or may be original (Tristram 1995). They range from brief *aides-mémoire* for preachers to full-scale structured sermons intended for delivery, as models, or as edifying reading for nuns or for *conversi* and *illiterati* attached to monastic institutions. Full-scale *homiliaria* might contain sermons in Latin, or a vernacular, or in both. Of interest too are the *reportationes*, notes on sermons (for example those preached by the Paris masters in the early thirteenth century) in Latin with or without some vernacular comments, or in the vernacular itself. Some survive in rough, others in polished and analyzed versions (Bériou 1992; D'Avray 1985). Handbooks on technique, the various *artes praedicandi*, are mostly Latin, however, and thus the structure of vernacular sermons continues to be dictated by Latin models, and it is worth remembering at this point that Latin collections of saints' lives or of edifying tales not only provided a wealth of *exempla*—narrative moral examples—for sermons, but supplied material for all kinds of vernacular writing. The best-known collections are James of Varazzo's *Legenda Aurea*, and the *Gesta Romanorum*, both translated into most European vernaculars, and others by Caesarius of Heisterbach, Odo of Cheriton, Johannes Herolt, and James of Vitry were also widely used. Individual tales in these collections might in any case have had a vernacular oral source in the first place.

The precise balance between Latin and vernacular in sermons can vary considerably. Some vernacular examples contain very little Latin apart from an indication of the feast—*Epiphania Domini*, say,—or a formula in the exordium. The pericope for a homily, and biblical or patristic quotations are usually retained in Latin, often (though not always) with a following translation in the vernacular. Such Latin quotations may, however, be abbreviated, sometimes to a few guide-words and an *et cetera*. One of the earliest examples of Irish prose, the so-called *Cambrai Homily* from the seventh or eighth century, mixes Latin and the vernacular fully, with Irish formulas introducing the biblical passages, which are themselves perhaps sometimes cited from memory and not always translated (Murdoch 2001). Translations of Latin sermons with biblical and other material left in Latin are familiar in German. The Quadragesima sermon in the twelfth-century collection known as the *Speculum Ecclesiae*, which has a somewhat defective Latin inscription, opens with a (curtailed) quotation which is not translated, but cites other biblical passages (sometimes confused), which *are* translated, and the whole piece is based on a Latin sermon by Hildebert of Le Mans (*Speculum Ecclesiae* 1944, 41–48). A major Irish collection, the (originally eleventh-century) homilies in the Royal Irish Academy MS 23 P. 16 (the *Leabhar Breac*), exhibits all permutations: Latin followed by Irish translations of each sentence, Latin left untranslated, Irish material for which there is no Latin equivalent. The interesting *Sermo ad reges* (based on Proverbs 17:7), largely in Irish, has abbreviated Latin quotations and occasional formulaic inserts (*ut dixit*...), usually translated; but there is also a Latin version of the same sermon which is briefer than the Irish. That sermon is in any case based on a (variously ascribed) seventh-century Hiberno-Latin treatise *De duodecim abusivis seculi* (PL 40: 1079–88), which was used in its turn in continental homilies (Mac Donncha 1976).

Vernacular preaching reached a peak with the Franciscans and Dominicans in the thirteenth century. Substantial written collections of the work of the mendicants survive, as well, incidentally, as evidence of sermons preached in the vernacular *against* the friars by Richard FitzRalph, Archbishop of Armagh, delivered in English but preserved in Latin, then translated back into English not long after FitzRalph's death by John Trevisa (Dolan 1989). But there is still a great deal of fluidity between languages. The sermons of the Florentine Dominican Giordano da Pisa (da Rivalto, ca. 1255–1311) are reported to have been extremely vigorous and indeed long, and he comments occasionally on the Tuscan words he is using; Latin sermons of his seem not to have survived. In Germany the Franciscan Berthold of Regensburg (ca. 1210–72) was also reportedly able to command enormous audiences for his vernacular sermons, even if some of the numbers mentioned (200,000) may be a touch exaggerated. Although Berthold preached in German, his sermons (or those attributed to him) were written down after his death for reading purposes, possibly initially in (glossed) Latin, and then reworked (and excerpted) in German. His own Latin sermons are patently for a clerical audience and demand biblical knowledge, but the moralizing German sermons have a distinctive style, in which the use of German is sometimes conscious, as when he discusses different possible renderings of a Latin word (Berthold of Regensburg 1862; Banta 1995).

OTFRID OF WEISSENBURG, THE VERNACULAR AND THE BIBLE

When Karl Müllenhoff and Wilhelm Scherer produced in the nineteenth century the first major collection of Old High German texts (with a title meaning "monuments of German poetry and prose from the eighth to the twelfth century") they included five riddles, a poem on the life of St. Gall, seven further poems, and a collection of proverbs, all of which are in Latin. Just after the Latin riddles, however, comes a piece which *is* in Old High German. Two lines, each rhymed at the half-line, under the modern title of *Ein Spielmannsreim* (minstrel rhyme) tell us that a certain Uodalrich lost his honor. Recourse has to be had to the very full notes (which became a bulky separate volume by the third edition in 1892) to establish that the slight verse is not extant in German at all, but in Latin, in a chronicle of the deeds of Charlemagne, where it is described as a *scurra* (Pertz 1829, 736). The original could have been in Old High German, but what we actually have is in Latin. However, those same notes contain a far more spectacular illustration. In an account in a Latin chronicle of the building of the monastery of Admont in Austria by Bishop Gebhard in the eleventh century, we are told that a deaf-mute suddenly exclaims "divino nutu coram omnibus haec verba in Teutonico eleganter…Tu debes inchoare, Deus debet consummare" [in public by God's will these words in elegant German…You may begin, God will complete]. The "elegant German" presumably implies a verse, which would rhyme on *beginnen* and *vollebringen*, "begin" and "complete," and God clearly spoke in Old High German verse through the deaf-mute so that those around could understand (Pertz 1854, 54–55). The incident is recorded in Latin, but depends upon the reader, too, "hearing" it in the vernacular. Many other examples bear witness to small-scale literary interaction. The Latin riddles can be reconstructed convincingly in German, and MS Cotton Faustina A. x in the British Library has two Latin proverbs, one rhymed, which are then matched in Anglo-Saxon. Notker Labeo's Latin *Rhetoric*, finally, contains illustrations in German for figures of speech. Once presumably well-known, these can now be enigmatic, especially a brief but much-discussed rhymed example of hyperbole about a giant boar with bristles the size of a forest.

The exemplary case of Otfrid's ninth-century German Gospel-poem (*Evangelienbuch*) offers a number of perspectives on the interaction of Latin and the vernacular. Otfrid gave as one of his reasons for writing his poem the not unfamiliar clerical desire to counter the *cantus obscenus*, which probably meant only German popular (oral) secular poetry. Although Otfrid's substantial poem *is* in German, its contextualization, as we might expect from a monk, is Latin: titles, sub-headings explaining the content and nature of sections and sub-sections, marginal references, the letter to Liutbert, and even the acrostics. The idea for the work as such derives from Latin literature; in his letter to the Archbishop, Otfrid cites Arator, Juvencus, and Prudentius as models (Green 2006, 359–72). So too, Otfrid's revolutionary use of end-rhyme may have had Latin origins (Patzlaff 1975; Klopsch 1966). His is a very early vernacular text to use end-rhyme on a large scale (rather than the Germanic alliterative long-line, which persisted for far longer in Anglo-Saxon), but thereafter it becomes firmly established in German, soon spreading to nonreligious poetry. At Charlemagne's court, Alcuin had declared in 799 his intention to establish an *Athena nova*, by which he really meant a new Rome, and advocated as formal models the classical Latin poets and Christian poets of late antiquity, with verse based on syllabic quantity rather than stress. For all that, the Carolingian Latin poets did also use the Leonine hexameter, with a rhyme at the caesura and the cadence, and accentual, stress-based verse with (sometimes coincidental) end-rhyme makes a fairly early appearance in Latin poetry in the so-called Ambrosian hymns. (See further the contribution of Tilliette in this volume.) Finally, and perhaps most significantly, end-rhyme within Latin *prose* composition was a rhetorical device, *homoteleuton*, and Otfrid mentions this in his Latin letter. Rhymed verse is found even earlier in Irish, and there have been similar debates as to the origins. Certainly, Hiberno-Latin writers use rhythmic and rhymed verse; an early example of the latter is the *Altus prosator* ascribed to Columcille, and Old Irish verse uses rhyme early and with considerable skill, even small lyrics containing end-rhyme and internal rhymes as well as alliteration. An early and highly skilled continental practitioner, perhaps influenced by Irish examples, is the Saxon Gottschalk, who in his grammatical writings incidentally manifests an interest in various vernacular languages. Nor need the process have been entirely one-way; Cuthbert's obituary letter on Bede tells us that he "erat doctus in nostris carminibus" [was skilled in our (Anglo-Saxon) poetry] and Bede's Latin paraphrase of Caedmon's hymn in the *Historia ecclesiastica* has alliterations which may echo native style (Howlett 1997, 268).

One final point about Otfrid's work reinforces, moreover, another major aspect of the interaction of Latin and the vernacular. While the Gospel is the main content, Otfrid, like Sedulius, Juvencus, and others, does more than retell the story. Possibly the most prolific of all literary activities in medieval Latin was the writing of biblical commentaries, usually deriving from the works of Augustine and Gregory the Great, offering a detailed exegesis of every verse of the Bible according to the various senses of Scripture, literal, allegorical-typological, moral, or anagogical. This huge body of Latin writing exerts an equally great influence on vernacular presentations of the Bible in all genres, helping to create, in effect, a medieval popular Bible, that is, the biblical story plus a great deal of material which is not actually in the Bible, but which is implicitly given equal status for an audience that could not distinguish what was original and what was not. Some of it is commonplace, a familiar literal instance being the apple eaten in the Garden of Eden, still universally accepted, quite unbiblical, and deriving from a pun on *malum*, meaning "apple" and "evil." Latin biblical commentaries and compilations such as the *Glossa ordinaria* have a lasting influence on vernacular writing throughout the Middle Ages (Murdoch 2003). Otfrid, like many subsequent writers in various vernaculars, merges biblical material and commentary (McKenzie 1946; see also Michel and Schwarz 1978). Sometimes he has whole sections headed *moraliter* or *allegorice*, and in other places he will break off and signal (occasionally somewhat patronisingly) that he is going to explain something. Occasionally, however, he incorporates exegesis so succinctly that if the Latin commentary were not familiar to the reader, the passage would be thoroughly obscure. Thus when he refers in his *Evangelienbuch* (Otfried of Weissenburg 1973, 3.4.17) to the man in John 5:5 who has been crippled, according to the Vulgate, for thirty-eight years, he gives the number as "forty less two." There is no explanation in the poem for this awkward formulation in German, but it implies knowledge of the Latin interpretation (in Bede and elsewhere) in which forty represents perfection, and the cripple thus symbolizes mankind as being less than perfect. A great deal of Latin has to be read into a single line of German. Although later writers, addressing an audience outside the monastery, would not make the same kind of assumptions, the use of commentaries in a less succinct form continues; the German *Wiener Genesis*, the French rhymed *Bible* of Macé de la Charité, the Irish *Saltair na Rann* and many other works show the same technique. Later on, particular Latin commentaries come to the fore, most strongly of all the *Historia scholastica* of Peter Comestor, itself a compilation from all kinds of other sources, and later still such texts as the *Speculum historiale* of Vincent of Beauvais. That the serpent of paradise was the devil in disguise is a nonbiblical commonplace of great antiquity, but that it had a woman's face, for example, is probably from the Comestor, though he blames the motif on Bede. Vernacular biblical writings such as the massive *Cursor Mundi* in English, or Jacob van Maerlant's *Rijmbijbel* in Dutch, or Rudolf von Ems's *Weltchronik* in German, all reflect the Comestor (Sherwood-Smith 2000; Thompson 1998). Prose story-Bibles, too, mix actual biblical (or apocryphal) narrative with material from the Comestor or elsewhere, and there are examples of these in many European languages well into the nineteenth century. In the fourteenth, the introductory material to the Old Norse *Stjórn* ("governing"), a little-known but much copied text which uses biblical material, the *Historia scholastica,* and Vincent's *Speculum*, tells us how Haakon V Magnusson (king of Norway 1299–1319) commissioned it specifically for those who "eigi skilia edr vndirstanda latinu" [do not know or understand Latin] (*Stjórn* 1862, 2). Vernacular literary texts quite frequently assert or imply that a motif is biblical when it is not, and although they do occasionally flag up the fact that they are following a commentary, more often they render the distinction invisible by complete integration, especially for interpretations in the literal or historical sense.

Latin library catalogs provide evidence of lost material in the vernacular, and Latin writers from Tacitus to Venantius Fortunatus and beyond testify to the existence of vernacular heroic poetry (Naumann 1931, 1–16). Charlemagne's biographer Einhard famously refers to the emperor's having collected *barbara et antiquissima carmina* [early German songs], and in England William of Malmesbury equally famously talks about having gathered material for his chronicles from historical poetry in the vernacular (Frank 1993). The knowledge or assumption of a lost vernacular original by reference to surviving versions or descriptions in Latin goes well beyond the small pieces noted already, and again German provides some substantial examples, including the *Galluslied*, a panegyric to St. Gall, composed by Ratpert (d. ca. 900), monk, chronicler, and teacher at St. Gall. Ratpert, we are told, *fecit carmen barbaricum*, as well as Latin hymns and litanies, and his German poem was based on an early Latin *vita* and possibly also on oral traditions regarding the saint. Crucially, however, his *carmen* is not extant in German, but in Latin, having been translated by Ekkehart IV of St. Gall, the continuator of his chronicle, the *Casus Sancti Galli*. Ekkehart's version is found in three codices from the ninth to the eleventh century (plus a seventeenth-century copy) with rather different texts, and an introduction (also varied in the manuscripts) describes the background and claims that it was translated so that the sweet melody of the piece could be preserved and used in Latin (Osterwalder 1982; von Unwerth 1917). The text as we have it consists of seventeen rhythmic five-line strophes, each line rhyming at the half-line, and Ekkehart's Latin may reflect the original closely; reference to the use of the melody would support this. Otfrid's Gospel-poem and other early German works use strophes of two and three lines, which might be reflected in this five-line pattern, and the Leonine rhymes resemble German half-line rhymes in any case. One is inclined to agree with the only slightly patronizing judgment that the "wild growth of the German form" was simply being more carefully cultivated here (Plenio 1918, 83–86). Precisely why Ekkehart translated the text is unclear, but his own context was Latin, and insecurity perhaps still obtained about writing in German.

Ysengrimus and *Waltharius*

We possess, however, even longer literary works in Latin based upon material which was clearly widespread, probably orally, and two such texts—there are others—demonstrate the point well. The Latin texts do not necessarily derive from specific vernacular versions, but simply represent part of a large tradition. The first is the beast-epic *Ysengrimus* (ca. 1150), attributed to a Flemish writer Nivard of Ghent, a lively version of the tales of the wolf Ysengrim and Reinardus, Reynard, the crafty fox who regularly outwits him, and whose (perhaps originally German) name becomes the common noun for a fox in French (Nivard of Ghent 1884). Nivard's poem (of which there was also an abbreviated version) is the earliest in a broad written tradition which includes French material as well as much-read later versions in Dutch, German, and English. The second case is that of *Waltharius*, a substantial Latin poem about a Germanic hero. It tells how Waltharius, a Visigoth from Aquitaine, is given as a hostage to Attila together with Hagano, a Frank (who is a substitute for Guntharius, the king's son), and Hildegunda (Hiltgunt), a Burgundian princess. Some of the characters and incidents can be matched with the (distorted) fifth and sixth century history of the Germanic tribes and the Huns, albeit with names associated with the wrong tribes. Waltharius establishes himself as a warrior for Attila, but when his friend Hagano flees after the Franks stop paying tribute, he and Hildegunda get Attila and his men drunk, and escape with a great amount of treasure. The Franks, now ruled by Guntharius, waylay them and Waltharius fights with twelve Franks, defeats Guntharius, and is (reluctantly) engaged at the last by his old friend Hagano. After much damage to the three men, Hildigunda stops the fight and the Hun gold is shared. A purely Germanic epic might have demanded the killing of Waltharius by his duty-driven friend.

Waltharius is a poem of approaching fifteen hundred hexameters with many Virgilian echoes (Strecker 1951, 1–83; see also *Waltharius* 1892). The precise date and authorship is disputed; it has been attributed to Ekkehart I, Dean of St. Gall, who died in 973, and Ekkehart IV the chronicler does refer to him as having written about a Waltharius, which may or may not be the same text. However, a preface to the poem in some manuscripts claims authorship for an otherwise unknown monk called Gæraldus, perhaps writing in the ninth century, although dates between 800 and 1020 have been confidently proposed. At all events, we have a Latin poem on a classical model dealing with vernacular material. There is a reference at one point to what must be the Nibelungen, and the German *Nibelungenlied* indeed alludes to the story. Hagano means "hawthorn" in German, and this is played upon in the poem, although the pun does not work in Latin; and there are unclassical words and phrases, including at one point possibly the least Virgilian of hexameter openings with the exclamation "*Wah! Sed quid dicis…*" [Uh! What do you say…]. The author is clerical, however, and there are also many biblical references. The Germanic names of the main characters and of the Frankish warriors stand out, perhaps especially that of Hiltgunt, though it works well as a spondee, and are sometimes found in mixed German and Latin forms. All in all, the work is an oddity, a Germanic heroic saga in Latin, probably with an ending modified by Christianity. On the other hand, it is unlikely to be a translation, but rather an independent work within a complex tradition which is represented by a number of analogues, in Anglo-Saxon, Middle High German, Old Norse, and Polish, as well as in Latin prose chronicles.

Macaronics

The Cambridge University Library manuscript containing the misleadingly named *Cambridge Songs* was probably copied at Canterbury in the middle of the eleventh century from a German original. It includes several Latin songs with Germanic themes and Latin poems based apparently upon the melodies of Germanic poems, and Müllenhoff and Scherer's ostensibly German monuments included seven Latin songs, *modi*, from this manuscript, most of which seem to reflect German oral tradition. In one comic poem a *Suevulus*, "a chap from Swabia," gets his own back on a not-too-faithful wife, while others feature characters called Lantfrid and Cobbo, a nun named Alfrâd, and the genuine tenth-century Bishop Heriger of Mainz (albeit in the context of a comic anecdote). A praise-poem to Christ seems to be based on a German song, and there is a panegyric to the three Saxon emperors named Otto. In the collection too, however, are two pieces which go even further in terms of integration, and actually mix Latin with the vernacular; these are the macaronic poems known usually as *De Heinrico* and *Suavissima nonna*, the latter of which has barely survived (*Carmina Cantabrigiensia* 1998, 82–85 and 94–97).

Both of the poems are more or less secular. In *De Heinrico*, most of the twenty-seven long lines, each falling into two parts divided by a caesura and linked by rhyme or assonance, begin with a Latin half-line, with the second in Old High German. Some of the German parts are repeated or are formulas, which might imply that the underlying basis for the whole is German, with the Latin (which may have been based on a prose chronicle) adapted to fit. The balance of the two languages is consistently handled, and there are only a few lines (including, however, the first) where there is a less clear division. The dialect is probably of the Rhineland, though this is disputed, and the content is anything but clear. It is a eulogy on a Duke of Bavaria named Henry as an imperial advisor, possibly Henry II of Bavaria ("the Quarrelsome") or his son, Henry IV. In the poem he is welcomed by an Emperor Otto, who perhaps (the meaning is disputed) welcomes "two of the same name." There are three Saxon emperors called Otto, too many dukes named Henry, and not enough historical details to let us work out exactly what is going on, although predictably there have been plenty of suggestions (Dittrich 1952–53; Herweg 2002, 181–270). The poet writes competently in both languages, and was probably a cleric, since the opening invokes Christ to help him tell the story. This is an historical or panegyric piece, possibly written as Bavarian propaganda, but the reason behind the use of the two languages is equally uncertain; the theme is a serious one and it has to be presumed that the audience would have been able to understand both languages and judge it precisely as a bilingual piece, rather than fitting it into a Latin or Germanic genre.

The second macaronic poem in the manuscript, now usually known as *Suavissima nonna*, "sweetest nun," from the putative opening words, is even more problematic. The text was damaged in the Middle Ages presumably because its content was felt to be improper, and in the nineteenth century because it was treated with chemicals supposed to make it easier to read, but which damaged it further. In spite of a virtuoso reconstruction after ultraviolet inspection, it is again hard to be sure what the poem is about (Dronke 1965, 2: 353–56). It again combines a Latin and then a German half-line linked by assonance, and again many views have been voiced about the theme. What survives evokes a pastoral, with a love theme in which a man seems to urge a nun to love him and is rejected.

The whole concept of macaronic poetry requires an excursus. The term was first applied to late medieval poetry which mixes Italian words into the Latin, but it is more generally applied to writings which use two (or more) languages, and there is a long tradition of verse in which Latin is merged structurally with a vernacular. One of the earliest examples is an Irish poem called *Sén Dé* [The Blessing of God], based on a Breviary prayer and attributed to Colmán moccu Clúasaig, who was *fer légind*, the lector or Latin scholar in Cork in the later part of the seventh century. After ten strophes in Irish, Latin makes a sudden and significant appearance, pointing up the conscious use of different languages:

> Regem regum rogamus
> in nostris sermonibus
> *anacht Nóe a luchtlach*
> diluui temporibus.

[We beseech the King of Kings / in our languages / *who protected Noah and his crew* / in the times of the flood.]

Later stanzas continue the mixture, the Latin fitting metrically with the Irish, and the languages seem to have a quite explicitly equal status (Byrne 1965, 33; Greene 1969, 14–15).

There is considerable variation in the relative extent and structural interaction of the two languages in verse. The simple embedding of Latin phrases in vernacular poems, sometimes made to fit into the form and rhyme-scheme and sometimes not, is a feature of much early religious poetry in particular. One of the earliest recorded (tenth-century) religious poems in Welsh opens with the words *Omnipotens auctor*, and a twelfth-century poem in the same language, known in two versions, fits Latin into its opening alliteration: *Deus Duw delwat...* [*Deus*, God the creator...]. Later in this work, *Deus* is rhymed in one version with a Welsh word, in the other with Latin (Lewis 1931, 11–17). While some vernacular religious poetry, such as Norse skaldic verse, rarely introduces Latin, early German religious poetry, by monks or by secular canons, frequently includes Latin lines, sometimes biblical or liturgical quotations, and often they are rhymed in as part of the poetic structure (Grünewald 1908). Thus *Ezzos Gesang* in the mid-eleventh century: "in principio erat uerbum / daz was der ware gotes sun" [in the beginning was the word / that was the true son of God], and it is not difficult to find parallel examples in other cultures. In English religious poetry individual Latin lines may again occur in isolation, or as a repeated refrain, or they may be integrated. In one case the lines of the Latin *Ave maris stella* alternate with rhymed English lines (and there is a German poem which does the same thing). Marian poems in particular use Latin for this effect in English, German, and even in Romance languages, as in the eleventh-century Provençal *Mei amic...* from Limoges, which offers *u so noel* [a new song] *de virgine Maria* (Dronke 1968, 50–51). Two later English Marian poems in a nine-line strophic form, both in Trinity College Cambridge MS 323, may exemplify the skill with which Latin lines may be integrated. *Of on* [= one] *that is so fayr and bright* and *Seinte Mari moder milde* also have the Latin written in red, adding a graphic distinction. English rhymes with English and Latin with Latin, but the Latin lines become shorter and more striking and the strophes end on brief or single word Latin lines (Chambers and Sidgwick 1907, 89–93 and 345–46) A final familiar and effective later example in which a repeated concluding line in Latin is always rhymed in with the vernacular (in this case Scots) is William Dunbar's fifteenth-century *Lament for the Makars*. Each of the twenty-five strophes ends with a rhyme-anticipated and hence terrifyingly cumulative fear of death, *timor mortis conturbat me*, the liturgical authority and solemnity of the Latin (a response in the third nocturn for the Breviary Office of the Dead) being used to augment what is a finality in every sense. The build-up is underscored by the poetic voice, who announces in the penultimate quatrain that *he* will be the next victim, and thus literalizes the motif.

As far as nonreligious material is concerned, the *Carmina Burana* collection (which contains purely German pieces amongst the Latin majority) provides well-known macaronics, again with different levels of integration. The little love-poem *Floret silva nobilis* has a strophe in Latin, with a final rhymed-in line of Middle High German, followed by four lines of German which translate the Latin; the four strophes of *Stetit puella* move gradually into German; *Audientes audiant*, finally, alternates Latin and German more or less consistently, rhyming one with the other (*Carmina Burana* 1991, 476, 530, 636–38). Here the mixture of languages is more likely to be a scholarly *jeu d'esprit*. Elsewhere, religious macaronic songs include the still-sung hymn *In dulci jubilo*, of which there is also a familiar Latin-English version.

The use of some Latin within the vernacular continues. In the fourteen century a major poet, John Gower, produced works in Latin (*Vox clamantis*), French (*Speculum meditantis*), and English (*Confessio amantis*), but the last-named has Latin verse summaries and marginal glosses. The words of the Vulgate or of the liturgy can still be used for effect, too, within a vernacular context, as when, in the Visitation play of the English mystery cycle known as the *Ludus Coventriae* or the N-Town plays, Mary pronounces the Magnificat in Latin, two lines at a time, which is then translated into English by Elizabeth. Given the supposed origins of the (religious) drama in the *Quem quaeritis* trope, it is hardly surprising that Latin continues to play its part for a very long time. God frequently opens the vernacular drama with the *Ego sum alpha et omega* formula, and aspects of the liturgy remain influential; the lyrical effect of the hymns of the *Planctus Mariae* tradition on the medieval vernacular dramatic tradition is well-documented (Sticca), and there are plenty of individual cases, too, such as the use of the processional antiphon *Christus resurgens* in the Cornish *Ordinalia* (Longsworth 1967, 102–21). The Cornish *Ordinalia* (which has stage directions in Latin, as sometimes happens) also contains, incidentally, a diabolical mock mass, and there is, in fact, a generically more widespread tradition of Latin, vernacular, and macaronic parodies of the liturgy or the Psalms.

The *Vita Adae et Evae* and the Legend of *Gregorius*

Two final case-studies of less familiar works can illuminate the fluidity between Latin and vernacular texts in terms of translation and influence across Europe. The works in question are rather different, though they are both theological and literary in varying degrees. The first is a prose work known in a range of Latin versions, translated and adapted into almost all the languages of Western and some of Eastern Europe over many centuries, and into all genres. The Latin *Vita Adae et Evae*, a Christian-Latin apocryphon with vernacular versions from Ireland to Russia, is part of a complex of works about Adam and Eve which contains motifs possibly of Hebrew origin; its closest antecedent is a Greek version with a number of major differences, but over a hundred very varied manuscripts of the Latin text are known. The work describes how Adam and Eve try to return to paradise by the penance of fasting whilst immersed in a river, which sometimes stands still as a gesture of support, but Eve is tempted a second time by the devil, now disguised as an angel. Later we hear how Adam and Eve cope with such novelties as childbirth and death. The *Vita Adae et Evae* is not really a single text, but rather an accumulation of episodes, and there is, further, a close link, clear in some versions, with the equally widespread and flexible Latin legends of the Cross before Christ, the Holy Rood, since the *Vita Adae et Evae* ends with a journey by Eve and Seth to paradise, where they sometimes are given the seeds that will grow into the Cross.

The Latin life of Adam and Eve was translated into languages as far apart as Welsh and Polish, was adapted into verse, incorporated as prose or verse into biblical poems and chronicles, and dramatized in Italian, German, and Breton, often with changes along the way when the vernacular writers did not understand what was happening, needed to adapt to fit the new genre, or simply wanted to expand an idea, as when the Austrian Lutwin introduces the first marital disagreement: Eve insists that the newly discovered act of love is better than paradise, but Adam demurs. An English metrical version (with the title *Canticum de creatione*) even mentions a Latin original, though it claims a Hebrew text before that, which is not likely, and virtually none of the vernacular texts even mentions the Greek version (see Murdoch 2009 for all examples).

It is hard to correlate vernacular adaptations with specific Latin sources, particularly as some of the vernacular versions predate many of the Latin manuscripts. Later, too, there are incunabula versions of the *Vita Adae* both in Latin and in the vernacular, and the (printed) Polish translation, for example, is clearly from a printed Latin text. The earliest adaptation is probably the Irish poem *Saltair na Rann*, which resembles in some places the Greek text rather than the Latin one, although the use of Latin words in the Irish indicate a Latin source. The discovery of a variant version in Latin (though with later manuscript representation) has clarified this source issue and some of the problems in the Irish text, where, for example, Adam is placed after death in the third heaven, which is given the entirely opaque name *Ficconicia*. However, a Latin text in a manuscript now in Paris also has another odd-looking name, *economia*, at this point, and it seems that a reference to God's creation of everything in the phrase *feci(t) omnia* has been corrupted in both versions, to *economia* in Latin and *Ficconicia* in Irish. Close comparisons of the Latin texts with those in the vernacular reveal how the apocryphal story as such can change or develop apparently new and sometimes confusing motifs. Thus in most Latin versions Adam is taken into heaven in a "chariot like the wind with fiery wheels": "vidi currum tamquam ventum et rotae illius erant igneae…" One Latin text from England, however, seems to have turned the chariot into several (angelic) choirs: "choros tamquam uentos et rota illius erat ignea," presumably through a miscopying of *currum* (or more probably *currus*) as *choros*. The reading *currus* is grammatically problematic, even if it is taken as an accusative plural, but the original fiery wheels (now reduced) are even harder to fit. Two discrete English versions follow this Latin text. One has: "I sawe ordres of aungeles as thikke as mots in the son, being in a feire cercle." The winds have been replaced by motes in the sun.

However, that adjective *feire* "fair" must be an extra corruption from an earlier *English* version, which had something like *fier-*, for fiery. A second English version combines everything, correct or otherwise: "I say [= saw] ordris of aungels as Þicke as wynd beynge in a fair cercle, and I say a chare, and Þe whelis Þerof as fier." These English texts seem, therefore, to introduce new motifs based on Latin *and* English misreadings.

A German example provides evidence of a different kind of error. Hans Folz (ca. 1435–1513) made a prose translation of the Latin, which he then adapted into a vernacular poem and published himself in Nuremberg in 1480. In the Thüringische Landesbibliothek, Cod. Weimar 566 is Folz's own draft prose translation, something not intended for publication. We cannot identify his precise source, but it must have been a manuscript rather than a printed text, because at the end, St. Michael takes "ein zweiglin der sun der erden geprochen von dem paum dez wissens" [a twig of the sons of the earths, broken from the Tree of Knowledge]. The line comes in one of the sections which overlap with the Holy Rood legends, making source-identification even more complex, but makes no sense in any case. However, the Latin which lies behind this reads "ramusculum trium foliorum fractum der arbore scientiae," and it can be assumed that in Folz's source *trium foliorum* "of three leaves" was abbreviated as something like *trm flrm* and wrongly expanded to read *terrarum filiorum*. Folz clearly spotted the mistake when he came to compose his poetic version, but it does remind us that the written form of medieval Latin could lead to the introduction of new and apparently peculiar motifs, much as (in a purely Latin example) the 11,000 virgins who customarily accompany St. Ursula sprang either from a confusion between *miles* (soldier) and *mille* (thousand), or a misreading of an abbreviated XI MV, *undecim martyres virgines* [eleven virgin martyrs] as *undecim millia virgines* [eleven thousand virgins]. After the discovery of a burial ground in Cologne in 1155 which could, with commercial possibilities for pilgrimages, be identified as their last resting place, the existence of the virgins was further supported with forged materials.

The second case—and this time we do not know if there ever *was* a single Latin original—is a theme which is itself balanced between the secular and the religious, the legend of the fictitious incestuous pope and Saint Gregorius, sometimes referred to inaccurately and unhelpfully as the medieval Oedipus (see Plate 1983, 2–3). A French metrical *Vie du Pape Saint Grégoire*, which perhaps originated in England and which exists in several different versions from the late twelfth and early thirteenth centuries is the earliest text we have. The generic concept of the saint's *vita* as such is a Latin tradition, and some manuscripts of the French text have the title "incipit uita sancti Gregorii papae" (*Vie du Pape Saint Grégoire* 1977). There are thematic links with other incest-narratives involving both saints (Albanus) and sinners (Judas) which are known in Latin, as indeed was the Oedipus story through Statius. This story is of double incest: Gregorius, the product of a brother and sister relationship, unwittingly marries his mother, and after an extraordinary penance, becomes pope. There are strong biblical/theological parallels between the invisible sin of incest and the passing on of original sin through the act of reproduction. The story was adapted from French into German in a poem by Hartmann von Aue in about 1190 (Hartmann von Aue 1984), and a Middle English poem, also based on French, came just over a century later.

In terms of language interaction, Hartmann's German was soon freely adapted into Latin rhythmic and rhymed couplets by the chronicler Arnold, Abbot of St. John's in Lübeck, for the use of Wilhelm of Lüneburg and perhaps his court (Arnold of Lübeck 1968: Murdoch 2012, 91–108). Arnold adds theological material and moralizing which is more direct than Hartmann's. Later on, a German prose version from Hartmann's poem was incorporated into a much-copied (and also printed) collection of lives of the saints, and it also found its way into Icelandic, again into a collection of saints' lives. By the middle of the fourteenth century the tale (derived from the French poem) had already returned to Latin prose in the well-known moralizing story-book, the *Gesta Romanorum*. Not all manuscripts of the *Gesta* have the story, or they have it in a truncated form, but that popular collection was in its turn widely translated and adapted into most western and a good many eastern European languages, indeed, even into Neo-Aramaic and Coptic. Folktales and degenerated versions are known in even more languages, and the story of Gregorius became one of the most widely-known of the Middle Ages. By the time it reaches the folktale stage the hero may become a patriarch or catholicos rather than pope, or indeed, in a late but still recognizable Hassidic version, a rabbi.

Most of the traffic between Latin and the vernaculars in the Middle Ages—and there is a great deal of it—is one-way, in the sense that Latin texts form the basis for vernacular translations and adaptations on a large and—as in the two exemplary cases cited—complex scale. Movement in the other direction is harder to establish in detail. We do not know precisely what Ratpert's panegyric on St. Gall really looked like, and the vernacular material immediately behind major works like *Waltharius* remains even more conjectural. Later on there is more complex two-way traffic, and both with the *Vita Adae et Evae*, where there was a Latin original, and with the tale of *Gregorius*, where there may or may not have been, vernacular texts are adapted into Latin and back, Latin and the relevant vernaculars mix, change positions, and can exist side by side.

SUGGESTIONS FOR FURTHER READING

The standard general work on the interaction of Latin and European vernacular writing remains Curtius (1953), which has been much reprinted. Also useful is Laistner (1931), revised in 1957. Two additional general studies may also be noted, one older, one more recent: Bolgar (1963) and Waquet (2001), first published in French in 1998, which focuses on the post-medieval period, but has much of interest. The topic, however, is so broad that relevant studies usually concentrate on a single genre: love lyric (Dronke 1965) and his briefer study of medieval lyric (1968); Fletcher and Gillespie (2001), a collection of essays on *Irish Preaching 700–1700*; or the collection *Die deutsche*

Predigt im Mittelalter, edited by Mertens and Schiewer (1992) (not exclusively about German); Brian Murdoch (2003) on *The Medieval Popular Bible*. Other studies are specific to a particular culture: Rupp (1958) on the relationship between German and Latin poetry and Langosch (1964), Bertau (1973), and Ponert (1975) on German medieval literature are all useful, and there is a specialist study of some breadth by Wolf (2006) on Latin and German writings in Vienna in the later Middle Ages. Many collections of essays contain valuable material, such as Minnis (1989), Henkel and Palmer (1992), or Haubrichs et al. (2000). Individual aspects—such as macaronic poetry—are covered both in relatively recent works, such as Diehl (1985), or even in still-useful studies of much greater age, as in the appendix (*In dulci jubilo*) attached to Hoffmann von Fallersleben (1861), reprinted in 1965.

BIBLIOGRAPHY

Primary sources

Arnold of Lübeck. 1968. *Gesta Gregorii Peccatoris*, edited by Johannes Schilling. Palaestra: Untersuchungen zur europäischen Literatur 280. Göttingen: Vandenhoeck und Ruprecht.

Auraicept na n-Éces. 1907. *Auraicept na n-Éces. The Scholar's Primer*, edited and translated by George Calder. Edinburgh: Grant.

Berthold of Regensburg. 1862. *Berthold von Regensburg. Vollständige Ausgabe seiner Predigten*, edited by Franz Pfeiffer. Vol. 1. Wien: Braumüller. Reproduction with introduction and appendix by Kurt Ruh, Berlin: de Gruyter, 1965.

Bluhme, Friedrich and Alfred Boretius, eds. 1868. *Leges Langobardorum*. Monumenta Germaniae Historica 17. Leges 4. Hannover: Hahn.

Carmina Cantabrigiensia. 1998. *The Cambridge Songs (Carmina Cantabrigiensia)*, edited and translated by Jan M. Ziolkowski. Medieval and Renaissance Texts and Studies 192. Tempe, Ar.: Medieval and Renaissance Texts and Studies.

Chambers, Edmund K. and Frank Sidgwick. 1907. *Early English Lyrics*. Reprint London: Sidgwick and Jackson, 1947.

Dolan, Terence. P. 1989. "English and Latin versions of FitzRalph's Sermons." In *Latin and Vernacular. Studies in Late-Medieval Texts and Manuscripts*, edited by Alastair. J. Minnis, 27–37. York Manuscript Conferences 1. Cambridge: D. S. Brewer.

Gerald of Wales. 1978. *A Journey through Wales*, translated by Lewis Thorpe. Harmondsworth: Penguin.

Hartmann von Aue. 1984. *Gregorius*, edited by Hermann Paul and Burghart Wachinger. 13th ed. Altdeutsche Textbibliothek 2. Tübingen: Niemeyer. First published Halle/Saale: Niemeyer, 1882.

Haubrichs, Wolfgang and Max Pfister, eds. 1989. *"In Francia fui". Studien zu den romanisch-germanischen Interferenzen und zur Grundsprache der althochdeutschen "Pariser (Altdeutschen) Gespräche" nebst einer Edition des Textes*. Abhandlungen der Geistes- und Sozialwissenschaftlichen Klasse, Jahrg. 1989, Nr. 6. Mainz: Steiner.

Carmina Burana. 1991. *Carmina Burana. Die Lieder der Benediktbeurer Handschrift*, edited by Alfons Hilka, Alfons, Otto Schuhmann, and Bernhard Bischoff, translated by Carl Fischer and Hugo Kuhn. 5th ed. Munich: Deutscher Taschenbuch Verlag.

Krusch, Bruno, ed. 1902. *Passiones vitaeque sanctorum aevi Merovingici*. Monumenta Germaniae Historica. Scriptores rerum Merovingicarum 4. Hannover, Leipzig: Hahn.

Lewis, Henry, ed. 1931. *Hen Gerddi Crefyddol*. Cardiff: University of Wales Press. Reprint Cardiff: University of Wales Press, 1974.

Müllenhoff, Karl, Wilhelm Scherer, and Elias von Steinmeyer, eds. 1892. *Denkmäler deutscher Poesie und Prosa aus dem VIII.–XII. Jahrhundert*. 2 vols. 3rd. ed. Berlin: Weidmann. Reprint Berlin: Weidmann, 1964.

Naumann, Hans. 1931. *Frühgermanisches Dichterbuch*. Trübners philologische Bibliothek 13. Berlin and Leipzig: de Gruyter.

Nivard of Ghent. 1884. *Ysengrimus*, edited by Ernst Voigt. Halle/Salle: Waisenhaus.

Notker III. 1935–55, 1972–. *Die Werke Notkers des Deutscxhen*, edited by Edward H. Sehrt, Taylor Starck, James C. King, and Petrus Tax. Altdeutsche Textbibliothek. Halle/Saale: Niemeyer (1933–55), then Tübingen: Niemeyer (1972–).

Osterwalder, Peter, ed. 1982. *Das althochdeutsche Galluslied Ratperts und seine lateinischen Übersetzungen durch Ekkehart IV*. Das Althochdeutsche von St. Gallen 6. Berlin and New York: de Gruyter.

Otfried of Weissenburg. 1943. "Otfrid's *Ad Liutbertum*," edited by Francis P. Magoun. Publications of the Modern Language Association of America 58: 869–90.

———. 1973. *Otfrids Evangelienbuch*, edited by Oskar Erdmann and Ludwig Wolff. 7th ed. Tübingen: Niemeyer. First published Halle/Saale: Waisenhaus, 1882.

Pertz, Georg Heinrich, ed. 1829. *Scriptores rerum Sangallensium. Annales, chronica et historiae aevi Carolini*. Monumenta Germaniae Historica. Scriptores 2. Hannover: Hahn.

———, ed. 1854. *Historiae aevi Salici*. Monumenta Germaniae Historica 13. Scriptores 11. Hannover: Hahn.

Plate, Bernward, ed. 1983. *Gregorius auf dem Stein: frühneuhochdt. Prosa (15. Jh.) nach dem mittelhochdeutschen Versepos Hartmanns von Aue*. Darmstadt: Gesellschaft zur Förderung von Wissenschaft, Bildung und Kultur.

Speculum Ecclesiae. 1944. *Speculum Ecclesiae: eine frühmittelhochdeutsche Predigtsammlung (Cgm. 39)*, edited by Gert Mellbourn. Lunder germanistische Forschungen 12. Lund: Gleerup, Copenhagen: Munksgaard.

Stjórn. 1862. *Stjórn: Gammelnorsk Bibelhistorie*, edited by Carl R. Unger. Oslo: Feilberg and Landmark.

Strecker, Karl, ed. 1951. *Nachträge zu den Poetae aevi Carolini. Erster Teil*. Monumenta Germaniae Historica. Antiquitates 6:1. Weimar: Böhlau.

Thompson, John J. 1998. *The Cursor Mundi. Poem, Texts and Contexts*. Medium Aevum monographs, N.S., 19. Oxford: Society for the Study of Medieval Languages and Literature.

Vie du Pape Saint Grégoire. 1977. *La Vie du Pape Saint Grégoire. 8 versions francaises médiévales de la légende du bon pécheur*, edited by Hendrik B. Sol. Amsterdam: Rodopi.

Waltharius. 1892. *The Saga of Walther of Aquitaine*, edited by Marion Dexter Learned. Publications of the Modern Language Association of America 7:1. Baltimore: Modern Language Association of America. Reprint Westport, CO: Greenwood, 1970.

Williram of Ebersberg. 2004. *Expositio in Canticum Canticorum und das "Commentarium in Cantica Canticorum" Haimos von Auxerre*, edited and translated by Henrike Lähnemann and Michael Rupp. Berlin and New York: de Gruyter.

Secondary sources

Banta, Frank G. 1995. *Predigten und Stücke aus dem Kreise Bertholds von Regensburg*. Göppinger Arbeiten zur Germanistik 621. Göppingen: Kümmerle.

Bériou, Nicole. 1992. "Latin and the Vernacular. Some Remarks about Sermons Delivered on Good Friday During the Thirteenth Century." In *Die deutsche Predigt in*

Mittelalter, edited by Volker Mertens and Hans-Jochen Schiewer, 268–84. Tübingen: Niemeyer.

Bertau, Karl. 1973. *Deutsche Literatur im europäischen Mittelalter*. Vol. 2. Munich: Beck.

Bolgar, Robert R. 1963. *The Classical Heritage and its Beneficiaries*. Cambridge: Cambridge University Press.

Byrne, Francis John. 1965. "Latin Poetry in Ireland." In *Early Irish Poetry*, edited by James Carney. Thomas Davis Lectures. Cork: Mercier.

Copeland, Rita. 1991. *Rhetoric, Hermeneutics and Translation in the Middle Ages*. Cambridge Studies in Medieval Literature 11. Cambridge: Cambridge University Press.

Curtius, Ernst Robert. 1953. *European Literature and the Latin Middle Ages*, translated by Willard R. Trask. Bollingen Series 36. London: Routledge.

D'Avray, Donald L. 1985. *The Preaching of the Friars*. Oxford: Oxford University Press. Reprint Oxford: Oxford University Press, 2000.

Diehl, Patrick S. 1985. *The Medieval European Religious Lyric: an ars poetica*. Berkeley, Los Angeles, London: University of California Press.

Dittrich, Marie-Luise. 1952–53. "De Heinrico." *Zeitschrift für deutsches Altertum* 84: 274–308.

Dronke, Peter. 1965. *Medieval Latin and the Rise of the European Love-Lyric*. 2 vols. Oxford: Clarendon.

———. 1968. *The Medieval Lyric*. London: Hutchinson.

Fletcher, Alan J. and Raymond Gillespie, ed. 2001. *Irish Preaching 700–1700*. Dublin: Four Courts.

Frank, Roberta. 1993. "The Search for the Anglo-Saxon Oral Poet." *Bulletin of the John Rylands University Library of Manchester* 75: 11–36.

Green, Roger P. 2006. *Latin Epics of the New Testament. Juvencus, Sedulius, Arator*. Oxford: Oxford University Press.

Greene, David. 1969. "Irish as a Vernacular Before the Norman Invasion." In *A View of the Irish Language*, edited by Brian Ó Cuív, 11–21. Dublin: Stationery Office.

Grünewald, August. 1908. *Die lateinischen Einschiebsel in den deutschen Gedichten von der Mitte des 11. bis gegen Ende des 12. Jahrhunderts*. Göttingen: Huth.

Haubrichs, Wolfgang et al., eds. 2000. *Theodisca. Beiträge zur althochdeutschen und altniederdeutschen Sprache und Literatur in der Kultur des frühen Mittelalters*. Ergänzungsbände zum Reallexikon der germanischen Altertumskunde 22. Berlin, New York: de Gruyter.

Henkel, Nicholas, and Nigel F. Palmer, eds. 1992. *Latein und Volkssprache im deutschen Mittelalter, 1100–1500*. Tübingen: Niemeyer.

Herweg, Matthias. 2002. *Ludwigslied, De Heinrico, Annolied. Die deutschen Zeitdichtungen des frühen Mittelalters im Spiegel ihrer wissenschaftlichen Rezeption und Erforschung*. Imagines Medii Aevi 13. Wiesbaden: Reichert.

Hoffmann von Fallersleben, A. Heinrich. 1861. *Geschichte des deutschen Kirchenliedes bis auf Luthers Zeit. Anhang. In dulci jubilo (Kurze Geschichte der lateinisch-deutschen Mischpoesie)*. 3rd ed. Hannover: Rümpler. Reprint Hildesheim: Olms, 1965.

Howlett, David R. 1997. *British Books in Biblical Style*. Medieval Studies. Dublin: Four Courts.

Klopsch, Paul. 1966. "Prosa und Vers in der mittellateinischen Literatur." *Mittellateinisches Jahrbuch* 3: 9–24.

Laistner, Max L. W. 1931. *Thought and Letters in Western Europe AD 500–900*. London: Methuen. New, revised edition London: Methuen, 1957.

Langosch, Karl. 1964. *Die deutsche Literatur des lateinischen Mittelalters in ihrer geschichtlichen Entwicklung*. Berlin: de Gruyter.

Longsworth, Robert. 1967. *The Cornish Ordinalia. Religion and Dramaturgy*. Cambridge, MA: Harvard University Press.

Mac Donncha, Frederic. 1976. "Medieval Irish Homilies." In *Biblical Studies. The Medieval Irish Contribution*, edited by Martin McNamara, 59–71. Proceedings of the Irish Biblical Association 1. Dublin: Dominican Publications.

McKenzie Donald A. 1946. *Otfrid von Weissenburg: Narrator or Commentator?* Stanford University Publications. University series. Language and literature 6:3. Stanford: Stanford University Press.

Mertens, Volker and Hans-Jochen Schiewer, eds. 1992. *Die deutsche Predigt im Mittelalter*. Tübingen: Niemeyer.

Michel, Paul and Alexander Schwarz. 1978. *unz in obanentig. Aus der Werkstatt der karolingischen Exegeten Alcuin, Erkanbert und Otfrid*. Studien zur Germanistik, Anglistik und Komparatistik 79. Bonn: Bouvier.

Minnis, Alastair J., ed. 1989. *Latin and Vernacular. Studies in Late-Medieval Texts and Manuscripts*. York Manuscript Conferences 1. Cambridge: D. S. Brewer.

Murdoch, Brian. 2001. "Preaching in Medieval Ireland: the Irish Tradition." In *Irish Preaching 700–1700*, edited by Alan J. Fletcher and Raymond Gillespie. Dublin, Portland, OR: Four Courts, 40–55.

———. 2003. *The Medieval Popular Bible: expansions of Genesis in the Middle Ages*. Cambridge: D. S. Brewer.

———. 2009. *The Apocryphal Adam and Eve in Medieval Europe: vernacular translations and adaptations of the* Vita Adae et Evae. Oxford: Oxford University Press.

———. 2012. *Gregorius. An Incestuous Saint in Medieval Europe and Beyond*. Oxford: Oxford University Press.

Patzlaff, Rainer. 1975. *Otfrid von Weissenburg und die mittelalterliche versus-Tradition*. Hermaea, N.F., 35. Tübingen: Niemeyer.

Penzl, Herbert. 1985. "Stulti sunt Romani." *Wirkendes Wort* 35: 240–48.

Plenio, Kurt. 1918. "Bausteine zur altdeutschen Strophik, 8." *Beiträge zur Geschichte der deutschen Sprache und Literatur* 43: 56–99.

Ponert, Dietmar Jürgen. 1975. *Deutsch und Latein in deutscher Literatur und Geschichtsschreibung des Mittelalters*. Studien zur Poetik und Geschichte der Literatur 43. Stuttgart: Kohlhammer.

Rupp, Heinz. 1958. "Über das Verhältnis von deutscher und lateinischer Dichtung im 9. bis 12. Jahrhundert." *Germanisch-romanische Monatsschrift* 39: 19–34.

Schupp, Volker. 1978. *Studien zu Williram von Ebersberg*. Bibliotheca Germanica 21. Berne and Munich: Francke.

Sherwood-Smith, Maria C. 2000. *Studies in the Reception of the Historia Scholastica of Peter Comestor*. Medium Aevum monographs, N.S., 20. Oxford: Society for the Study of Medieval Languages and Literature.

Sticca, Sandro. 1988. *The Planctus Mariae in the Dramatic Tradition of the Middle Ages*, translated by Joseph R. Berrigan. Athens, GA, London: University of Georgia Press.

Tristram, Hildegard C. 1995. *Early Insular Preaching: Verbal Artistry and Method of Composition*. Sitzungsberichte der Österreichischen Akademie der Wissenschaften, Philosophisch-Historische Klasse 623. Veröffentlichungen der Keltischen Kommission 11. Vienna: Verlag der Österreichischen Akademie der Wissenschaften.

von Unwerth, Wolf. 1917. "Vers und Strophe von Ratperts Lobgesang auf den Heiligen Gallus." *Beiträge zur Geschichte der deutschen Sprache und Literatur* 42: 111–21.

Waquet, Françoise. 2001. *Latin, or, The Empire of a Sign: from the sixteenth to the twentieth century*, translated by John Howe. London, New York: Verso.

Wolf, Klaus. 2006. *Hof-Universität-Laien*. Wissensliteratur im Mittelalter 45. Wiesbaden: L. Reichert.

PART V
SYSTEMS OF KNOWLEDGE

CHAPTER 15

MARTIANUS CAPELLA AND THE LIBERAL ARTS

ANDREW HICKS

> Gram loquitur; Dia vera docet; Rhet verba colorat;
> Mus canit; Ar numerat; Ge ponderat; Ast colit astra.
>
> [Gram(mar) speaks; Dia(lectic) teaches truth; Rhet(oric) colors words; Mus(ic) sings; Ar(ithmetic) counts; Ge(ometry) weighs; Ast(ronomy) cultivates the stars.]

So goes one schoolboy's mnemonic for the seven liberal arts, here neatly divided between hexameters into the three verbal arts of the trivium and the four mathematical disciplines of the quadrivium. The quaint simplicity of a mnemonic, however, deliberately belies the complexities and tensions within the long-standing tradition of the *artes liberales*. Adumbrated in countless encyclopedias, handbooks, and treatises that detail the content of and epistemological approaches to the various disciplines, the liberal arts were an all-pervasive presence, ever differently realized in disciplinary configurations and institutional programs. The various schemata of the seven disciplines have been dismissed as (for instance) a "scholastic detail, a notice transmitted from one author to another, which each may contaminate or modify from his own point of view, yet without any correspondence to real-life teaching" (Díaz y Díaz 1969, 46). But the system of the liberal arts was more than a seven-part schema; it established itself as a dynamic discursive apparatus and pedagogical paradigm that shifted continuously to accommodate different cultural contexts and philosophical viewpoints. A comprehensive history of the liberal arts, however, would quickly become a Borgesian map, a representational surface as broad and expansive as the cultural, literary, and philosophical terrain it overlays (see, for instance, the nearly one hundred contributions to *Arts libéraux et philosophie au Moyen Age* 1969). It is, perhaps, an impossibility.

The commentary tradition on Martianus Capella's fifth-century allegorical encyclopedia of the liberal arts, *De nuptiis Philologiae et Mercurii*, provides an enclosed, if still rugged, terrain through which to map the differing conceptual frameworks within which the liberal arts gained pedagogical and philosophical traction. Martianus remained *the* ancient authority on the liberal arts from his "re-discovery" at the beginning of the ninth century through to the close of the twelfth. And despite the continuity ostensibly guaranteed by the nearly uninterrupted use of a single text, the interpretative mutability of the *De nuptiis*'s elaborate allegorical frame provided a site for the continual renegotiation of the liberal arts, even after Martianus's seven treatises had fallen by the wayside as outdated and outmoded. (All references to the *De nuptiis* are keyed to book number and Kopp's paragraph numbering to facilitate easy cross-reference with the various translations and editions; page and line number/s from Willis's Teubner edition [Martianus Capella 1983] follow in brackets when necessary.) The first part of the present chapter introduces the lively panoply of Martianus's *disciplinae cyclicae* (9.998 [385.5]; cf. Greek ἐγκύκλιος παιδεία) in the company of the other divisions of knowledge within which the liberal arts were differently subsumed at different periods in the reception of Martianus's text: the divisions of Boethius, Cassiodorus, and Isidore of Seville. The second part charts the trajectory of the *De nuptiis* through its medieval commentary tradition, primarily focusing on its Carolingian and twelfth-century reception. (On late-ancient encyclopedism in general, see Formisano in this volume; on the literary influence of Martianus, see Wetherbee in this volume.) At issue throughout is the discursive framework for the liberal arts and not their institutional or practical application as an actual program of study; hence, the topographical survey closes just before the rise of university curricula in the thirteenth century, when the tension between the old scheme(s) of the liberal arts and the new exigencies of university-based educational structures wrought significant changes, and Martianus's *De nuptiis* largely fell out of favor.

Much remains uncertain about Martianus Minneius Felix Capella's allegorical encyclopedia. Dates proposed for its composition have swung between the fifth century's early decades (410–39, the *communis opinio* most recently defended by Jean-Yves Guillaumin in Martianus Capella 2003) and its later decades (470s or 480s, as argued by Shanzer 1986a, Barnish 1986; as late as 496–523 according to Grebe 2000); we know next to nothing about its author save for the work's possible autobiographical glimmers, e.g., 1.2 (2.6–7), 6.577 (203.8–11), 9.999–1000 (385.11–386.4); and its original intent and audience remain shrouded in obscurity. But one thing can be said with absolute certainty: it is a difficult text. Replete with recondite syntax and *hapax legomena*, it has taxed generations of editors, medieval and modern alike. As early as 534, its first editor, a certain Securus Melior Felix, lamented the corrupt state of the manuscripts (Cameron 1986; Préaux 1975), and any emendations that Felix might have provided seem still insufficient, for the proliferation of medieval copies stem from a single Merovingian archetype that itself was of suspect authority (Martianus Capella 1983a, vi; Shanzer 1986b). The complaints of the medieval commentators—"locus iste corruptus scriptorum vitio" [this passage has been corrupted by scribal error] noted Remigius of Auxerre (1962, 195.17–18)—still echo as "locum pro desperato reliqui" in the apparatus of J. Willis's Teubner edition (Martianus Capella 1983), and even more passages not obelized by Willis may drive readers to despair (see the list in Shanzer 1986b, 78–79).

The syntactical and lexical abstruseness of the *De nuptiis* is not merely a matter of historical curiosity; it is central to one of its most puzzling aspects: how and why did such a formidable text seize the medieval literary imagination and establish itself as one of the most important medieval school-texts, surviving in no less than 244 copies? On one level, as Mariken Teeuwen observes, the "intricate Latin was seen as a good test case for one's knowledge of the language (on an 'expert level'), and a good opportunity to expand one's vocabulary and grammatical skills" (2003, 186). Indeed there are abundant examples of scholars mining the *De nuptiis* for its lexographical riches—the annotations of Rather of Verona (890–974) are one such instance (see Leonardi 1959; Rather of Verona 1984; Teeuwen 2005). But Martianus's text was more than just a whetstone for sharpening linguistic competence, and it was as much the *De nuptiis*'s allegorical form as its scholastic content that recommended it to its medieval readers.

The *De nuptiis* consists of two parts: the first and second books establish a framing allegory, the eponymous marriage of Philology and Mercury, and the seven subsequent books comprise short treatises on the seven liberal arts, diegetically framed as Mercury's wedding gifts. Briefly, the story runs thus: Mercury has come of age and thus must take a wife (1.3–5). When Sophia, Mantice, and Psyche are all dismissed as unsuitable (1.6–7), Mercury, accompanied by Virtue, looks for advice to his brother Apollo (1.8–21), who suggests the learned though mortal Philology (1.22–24). Jupiter and Juno are sought to confirm the betrothal (1.25–40), and they convene the celestial senate to approve Philology's apotheosis (1.41–97). Book two opens on earth, as Philology performs arithmological calculations to confirm that her forthcoming marriage is indeed auspicious (2.98–108) and begins to prepare her mortal body for the celestial ascent (2.109–13). Phronesis, Philology's mother, dresses her appropriately (2.114–16), and the Muses come to sing her praises (2.117–30). Athanasia (Immortality), the daughter of Apotheosis, then gives Philology an emetic (2.131–35), which causes her to vomit forth a stream of writings; the Muses and maidens—some called Disciplines, some called Arts—collect the writings, each according to her need (2.136–38). Philology then drinks from the cup of immortality, described as a cosmic egg (2.139–40), and after performing other preparatory rites (2.141–42), she mounts a litter borne aloft by Labor, Epimelia (Application), Agrypnia (Wakefulness), and Periergia (Curiosity) to begin her ascent through the celestial spheres (2.143–99). Upon arrival at the heavens' outermost periphery (2.200–201), she offers a silent, mystical prayer to "quaedam fontana virgo" [a certain Maiden of the Source] and to the "ἅπαξ καὶ δὶς ἐπέκεινα potestates" [the powers once and twice beyond] (the Chaldean hypostases known to Martianus through a Neoplatonic intermediary), before finally approaching the celestial assembly (2.202–8). As the bridal party draws close, Jupiter summons the groom (2.209–14), and Philology follows soon after, modestly declining Jupiter's offer of a seat at his right hand and taking her place in the company of Athena (2.215–16). Phronesis requests that Mercury's wedding gifts be conferred before the full assembly (2.217–18), and here begins the procession of the seven learned "dotales virgines" [dowry maidens]: "nunc ergo mythos terminatur; infiunt/ artes libelli qui sequentes asserent" [now the fable is done; here begin the subsequent books, which will set forth the arts] (2.220 [57.24–58.1]).

But Martianus's liberal arts are not the *sobriae disciplinae* stripped of fictitious embellishments, as promised in the last metrum of book two (2.220 [58.3]), for Martianus's muse protests: "vestiantur Artes" [let the Arts be clothed!] (3.222 [59.7]). The muse has her way, and far from sober, Martianus's arts are loud, boisterous, even comic personifications (see Cristante 2005), whose nuptial offerings to the bride take the form of seven orations on the liberal arts, declaimed in the order: grammar, dialectic, rhetoric (later the trivium), geometry, arithmetic, astronomy and music (later the quadrivium). Accounting for the number and order of Martianus's arts is tricky business, especially since it seems likely that any preexistent system was modified to suit Martianus's literary purposes, e.g., music comes last to occasion Hymenaeus's epithalamium (9.902–3; Hadot 2005, 149). But let the classicists worry about Martianus's antecedents. Whether Martianus had before him Varro's lost *Disciplinarum libri* (the traditional opinion upheld most recently by Shanzer 1986a, 2005; Bovey 2003) or a later, Neoplatonic, Porphyrian source (maintained by Hadot 1984; rev. ed. 2005) is immaterial for the later medieval commentators. And regardless of whether Martianus's summary dismissal of medicine and architecture as "having nothing in common with heaven or the gods" (9.891 [339.5–6]) departs deliberately from Varro's ninefold scheme (Shanzer 1986a, 15) or reflects a Middle Platonic unease with their propaedeutic value (Hadot 2005, 150), the dismissal highlights one important theme that strongly recommended the *De nuptiis* throughout its long reception history: the ascent from the corporeal to the incorporeal, from the terrestrial to the celestial (cf. Aug., *De ord.* 2.5.14, 2.14.39–15.43; *Retr.* 1.6).

This (Neoplatonic) *reditus* is allegorized by Philology's apotheosis in book two, and it remains discernible within the ascent through the individual *disciplinae* of the seven subsequent books, the quadrivium in particular. The first of the quadrivial maidens, *Geometria*, whose (notably Grecian) sandals are worn thin from her globetrotting (6.581), offers primarily a compendium of terrestrial geography. Geometry's closest sister, the second maiden, *Arithmetica*, introduces herself to the assembly by requesting that Jupiter himself acknowledge her as the "source of his own unique and originary nature" (7.730 [262.7–8]), as indeed the mother of the entire celestial throng. The third maiden, *Astronomia*, appears enclosed in a globe of ethereal light (9.810), and her numinous presence startles the lesser deities of the aerial, terrestrial, marine, and subterranean realms. Finally *Harmonia*, the last maiden, enters the celestial senate to the melodious strains of the *musica caelestis*, and all stand in reverence and awe of the extramundane intelligence (9.910 [348.1–2], cf. 2.202), a gesture of respect accorded *Harmonia* alone. The Christianization of this avowedly pagan, Neoplatonic ascent, and its implications for the arrangement and purpose of the liberal arts, remained a primary theme throughout the commentary tradition.

Boethius, Cassiodorus, and Isidore

The commentators did not approach Martianus empty-handed, nor were the seven liberal arts the only or even primary schema handed down from antiquity for the organization of knowledge. There were other basic divisions, known primarily through the works of Boethius, Cassiodorus, and Isidore of Seville: (1) a bipartite division into *theoretica–practica* allied with the Peripatetic tradition, and (2) a tripartite division into *logica–ethica–physica* associated with Stoic and Academic traditions, though both Cicero (*Acad.* 1.5.19) and Augustine (*De ciu. Dei* 8.4–6) attribute the tripartition directly to Plato (an attribution that probably extends back to the Hellenistic Academic, Antiochus of Ascalon). Boethius knew both divisions, but he alludes to the Stoic tripartition only three times: twice as a heuristic approach to the Aristotelian corpus (*In Cat.* 161B; *In Perih.* 2.79.18–20) and once in the course of presenting the Stoic case for logic as a part of philosophy (*In Isag.* II, 140.18–141.19; page and line numbers here and following refer to Boethius 1906). Although the Stoic tripartition is not without utility, it is not Boethius's preferred position; his primary allegiance—in accord with the Alexandrian Neoplatonist Ammonius (Ammonius 1891), long presumed (probably wrongly) to be Boethius's source (e.g., Weisheipl 1965, 59, no doubt influenced by Courcelle 1943, 268-78)—lies with the Peripatetic bipartition (e.g., *In Isag.* I, 8.1–3; *In Isag.* II, 140.18–19; *De trin.* 2; *Cons.* 1.1.4; cf. Ammon., *In Isag.* 11.6ff.).

The practical side of the division (*practica*) is presented only once (*In Isag.* I, 9.13–21), periphrastically and oddly ordered (ethics, politics, economics, though nowhere named as such; cf. Ammon., *In Isag.* 15.2–3: ethics, economics, politics). The theoretical division (*theorica*), Boethius's primary concern, is presented twice, as both a descending Platonic ontology and an ascending Aristotelian epistemology. The ontological formulation, set out in the first *Isagoge* commentary (8.3–5), departs from the standard subdivision of theology, mathematics, and physics (e.g., Ammon., *In Isag.* 11.22–23: πάλιν τὸ θεωρητικὸν διαιρεῖται εἰς θεολογικὸν μαθηματικὸν καὶ φυσιολογικόν [the theoretical divides into theology, mathematics, and physics]) and offers in its stead: (1) *intellectibilia* (=θεολογικά), (2) *intellegibilia* (=?), (3) *naturalia* (=φυσιολογικά). The difficulty here lies in the specification of the second rung. If the presumed parallel with Ammonius were to hold, *intellegibilia* should comprise mathematics or Neoplatonic "mathematicals" (μαθηματικά), and if Boethius were to have countenanced the separate subsistence of mathematicals, we would expect to find them here. Yet he makes no such identification. *Intellegibilia* hover between lower and higher realities: through corporeal contagion (*corporum tactu*: cf. *Cons.* 3.12.1) they degenerate from *intellectibilia* and become a lower reality; through contemplation of *intellectibilia* they become *beatiora* (*In Isag.* I, 9.2–6). Boethius then concludes by noting that the *intellegibilium substantia* rightly holds the medial position since it has the dual role of animating bodies and contemplating the *intellectibilia* (9.10–12). It seems unavoidable that this second rung is closer to psychology than to mathematics, even if it is, in the final analysis, neither. In

Boethius's *De trinitate*, however, Neoplatonic ontology gives way to an ascent through a sober Aristotelian epistemology (cf. *Met.* 1026a13–16): *naturalis*, the lowest rung, is "in motu inabstracta" [changeable and inabstract], glossed ἀνυπεξαίρετος [inseparable]; *mathematica* is "sine motu inabstracta" [unchangeable and inabstract]; *theologica*, the highest rung, is "sine motu abstracta atque separabilis" [unchangeable, abstract, and separable] (*De trin.* 2). The tension between the two divisions of theoretical philosophy appears irreducible.

The division of mathematics is harvested from the "first fruits" of Boethius's intellectual labors, the *De institutione arithmetica* (cited hereafter from Boethius 1999), a loose translation of Nicomachus of Gerasa's *Introductio arithmetica* (Nicomachus 1866), which Boethius seems to have undertaken early in his career (probably during the same period as the first *Isagoge* commentary). In line with Nicomachus, and in many ways similar to the first *Isagoge* commentary, Boethius begins his *De institutione arithmetica* with an account of *philosophia* and *sapientia* from the standpoint of ontology. Although the objects of *sapientia* are themselves incorporeal and immutable, through their participation in bodies and the contagion of changeable things they necessarily share in bodily, material flux (1.1 [9.8–22]). The similarity of this language to the description of the second ontic category in the first *Isagoge* commentary is striking: both are intermediaries "degraded" by *tactu corporum* (*In Isag.* I, 9.3) or *tactu uariabilis rei* (*Inst. ar.* 1.1 [8.17–18]); though themselves incorporeal, they are both incorporated; and *qua* intermediaries, they are both a conduit from the lower to the higher. For as Boethius concludes later in the prooemium, the mathematical disciplines are (famously) a "quadruuium...quo his uiandum sit, quibus excellentior animus a nobiscum procreatis sensibus ad intellegentiae certiora perducitur" [a fourfold road that must be journeyed by those whom a more excellent soul leads away from the senses inborn within us to the greater certainties of understanding] (1.1 [11.64–66]). Hence, in its ontological focus in general, its Platonic ontology in particular, the *De institutione arithmetica* is closer to the first *Isagoge* commentary than it is to *De trinitate*.

Boethius divides the objects of mathematics into discrete quantity (*multitudo*, τὸ ποσόν) and continuous quantity (*magnitudo*, τὸ πηλίκον). Each of these has a second bipartition (*Inst. ar.* 1.1 [10.31–38] = *Intr. ar.* 1.3.1–2 [6.1–7]): multitude into *per se* = καθ' ἑαυτό (arithmetic) and *ad aliquid* = πρὸς ἄλλο (music); magnitude into *immobilis* = ἐν μονῇ καὶ στάσει (geometry) and *mobilis* = ἐν κινήσει καὶ περιφορᾷ (astronomy). Hence, arithmetic is the science of multitude in itself, whereas music the science of multitudes in relation to each other; geometry is the science of immobile magnitudes, but astronomy the science of magnitudes in motion. The order is not arbitrary, for the mathematical sciences are not, strictly speaking, coordinate. Rather, they demonstrate a clear sequence of priority, and this priority takes the tidy form of two parallel priorities—the absolute (arithmetic) is prior to the relative (music) just as stasis (geometry) is prior to motion (astronomy)—nested within the single overarching priority of arithmetic to the other mathematical sciences (*Inst. ar.* 1.1 [12.73–14.130] = *Intr. ar.* 1.4–5 [9.5–11.23]).

Such are the divisions and subdivisions scattered throughout Boethius's œuvre, and the sources do not easily cohere. The first *Isagoge* commentary casts a Peripatetic division in distinctly Platonic terms but conspicuously avoids any engagement with the mathematical or numerical realities that might underpin such a world-view. *De trinitate* 2, by contrast, maintains a strict Aristotelian division where mathematical objects are fundamentally *inabstracta*, even if they are considered "sine materia ac per hoc sine motu" [without matter and consequently without change]. Hence, Boethius's account of the mathematical sciences, the quadrivium, concords from an ontological standpoint with the first *Isagoge* commentary where mathematics is absent, but it is not easily subsumed within the Aristotelian epistemology of *De trinitate* 2, where mathematics is explicitly included.

After the complexities presented by Boethius, the Peripatetic division of philosophy in the *Institutiones* of Cassiodorus is comparatively straightforward. The second book of the *Institutiones* is devoted to the liberal arts, which are dealt with in the order: grammar, rhetoric, dialectic, arithmetic, music, geometry, and astronomy. Cassiodorus knew of the *De nuptiis* but had failed to procure a copy (*Inst.* 2.3.20, cf. 2.2.17; the Martianus interpolations in the Φ recension, subsequently expunged from the Δ recension, have nothing to do with Cassiodorus, see Shanzer 1984, 299–301). At the beginning of his chapter *De dialectica*, Cassiodorus remarks that it is traditional to include a division of philosophy amongst the prolegomena to an exposition of Porphyry's *Isagoge* (2.3.3; *PL* 70: 1168b). Though he doubtless knew Boethius's translation and commentaries (2.3.18; *PL* 70: 1202d-3a), the terminology and presentation of Cassiodorus's division suggests a closer connection in many respects to Ammonius's *Isagoge* commentary (or more likely another commentary within the same tradition; cf. Courcelle 1969, 341–44; Hadot 2005, 199–202), though the Peripatetic scheme is lightly recast within the Neoplatonic framework of Origen's commentary on the Song of Songs (see Hadot 2005, 299–301). Philosophy divides into *inspectiua* (=θεορητική) and *actualis* (=πρακτική); these divide respectively into *naturalis–doctrinalis–diuina* and *moralis–dispensatiua–ciuilis*. Of the three theoretical sciences, *doctrinalis* (a literal rendering of μαθηματική) includes the quadrivial subdivision of *arithmetica–musica–geometria–astronomia*, enumerated in their Nicomachean order and with similar criteria for division (*quantitas secundum se, numerus ad aliquid, magnitudo immobilis*—only astronomy lacks the Nicomachean specification of *magnitudo mobilis*). Similarly Nicomachean is Cassiodorus's claim that arithmetic is the *fons et mater* of all the mathematical sciences (2.4.1; *PL* 70: 1204c).

The first three books of Isidore of Seville's *Etymologiae* likewise encompass the liberal arts: grammar (I), rhetoric and dialectic (II), arithmetic, geometry, music, and astronomy (III). In line with Boethius and Cassiodorus, Isidore also prefaces his compendium of dialectic with the definition and division of philosophy (2.24), which he presents according to both the Stoic (primarily via Augustine, *De ciu. Dei* 8.4–6) and Peripatetic (cribbed from Cassiodorus) traditions. Within the Stoic classification, physics is further subdivided into the mathematical sciences, which Isidore attributes to Plato and lists in the distinctive order: arithmetic, geometry, music, astronomy (see Jean-Yves Guillaumin's comments in Isidore of Seville 2009, xvi–xviii); logic is subdivided into rhetoric and dialectic; and ethics comprises the four principle virtues (cf. *De ciu. Dei* 19.4). The Peripatetic division (2.24.10–14) tacitly follows Cassiodorus, with only minor differences (again music is generally presented as the third of the mathematical sciences). Isidore's *De differentiis verborum* (2.39.148–58), however, offers an idiosyncratic tripartite division whereby physics includes *seven* disciplines: astrology, mechanics, and medicine are appended to the four quadrivial sciences (*Diff.* 2.39.150–52; *PL* 83: 94ab; cf. *Liber numerorum* 8.44; Isidore of Seville 2005, 133–134). It was Isidore's tripartite division, in its various and contradictory formulations, that was favored by the *Scotti peregrini* of the Carolingian Renaissance (see Díaz y Díaz 1969).

The Ninth-Century Commentary Tradition

In the ninth century, both the allegorical and the encyclopedic components of the *De nuptiis* fueled and shaped the pedagogical programs of the Carolingian Renaissance (on which see Contreni 1995, esp. 725–47; Fried 1997). The *De nuptiis*, as Préaux has speculated, may have first been copied in the Loire valley and further disseminated from Corbie during the reign of Louis the Pious (Préaux 1978, esp. 92–104), reaching the peak of its popularity in the period of Charles the Bald. The importance of the *De nuptiis* in Carolingian schools is abundantly witnessed by the nearly fifty manuscript copies surviving from the ninth century, many studiously glossed (see Teeuwen 2003). Within the extraordinarily complex textual transmission of these glosses, three traditions can be recognized but only two securely attributed: those of John Scotus Eriugena (reworked throughout the mid-ninth century) and Remigius of Auxerre (composed in the last decade of the ninth century or the beginning of the tenth). There exist at least two distinct recensions of Eriugena's glosses on the *De nuptiis* (Paris, Bibliothèque nationale, lat. 12960, edited by Cora Lutz in John Scotus Eriugena 1939; and Oxford, Bodleian, Auct. T.2.19, partially edited by Edouard Jeauneau in John Scotus Eriugena 1978; on the relationship between the two, see Herren 1986, 268–71), in addition to numerous partial or hybrid versions that often unite the Eriugenian tradition with material from the earliest glosses (see Teuween 2002 for a conspectus of the scholarship). The later, more stable commentary of Remigius (edited by Lutz in Remigius of Auxerre 1962, 1965) is demonstrably dependent upon both Eriugena and the oldest known corpus of glosses, and Remigius seems also to have known other commentaries not yet identified. The third and oldest corpus has been variously attributed to Dunchad and Martin of Laon, among others (partially edited by Lutz in Dunchad of Laon 1944; Teuween 2002; O'Sullivan 2010), but the recent research of Mariken Teuween (et al.) has cast serious doubt on all attributions. Teuween has collectively described the fifteen known manuscripts that bear witness to the oldest tradition as "scholarly works," probably compiled by more than one scholar, with two distinct goals: the establishment of a solid text of the *De nuptiis* and the explication of its encyclopedic content through the accumulation of "as much surrounding knowledge as possible" (2007, 48). These earliest glosses, perhaps taking shape around the third decade of the ninth century, clearly formed the basis for Carolingian Capellan scholarship (see Eastwood 2007, 303–8). Because of the complexity of the ninth-century commentary tradition, the three traditions are here discussed jointly as evidence for the Carolingian reception of Martianus.

At Lady Philosophy's first entrance in the *De nuptiis* (2.131 [41.6]), she boasts that "per ipsam Iuppiter ascensum cunctis in supera tribuerit" [through her, Jupiter granted everyone ascent into heaven]. Eriugena, followed by Remigius, radically Christianizes this claim: "nemo intrat in celum nisi per philosophiam" [no one enters into heaven except through philosophy] (John Scotus Eriugena 1939, 64.24; cf. Remigius of Auxerre 1962, 171.22–24). This claim, a deliberate echo of Jn 14:6 ("nemo venit ad Patrem nisi per me" [no one comes to the Father but by me]), encapsulates Eriugena's theological application of the liberal arts, as developed in his commentary on the Ps.-Dionysian *Celestial Hierarchy*. As Rene Roques and Edouard Jeauneau have thoroughly demonstrated, Eriugena's (mis)understanding of Ps.-Dionysius's phrase ἀτεχνῶς ἡ θεολογία ταῖς ποιητικαῖς ἱεροπλαστίαις ἐχρήσατο [theology *simply* used sacred symbols] as valde artificialiter *theologia factitiis sacris formationibus usa est* [theology *supremely artfully* used sacred symbols] (*In coel. hier.* 2.124–26) gave biblical and even Christological precedent to the liberal arts (Roques 1975, 45–98; Jeauneau 1996, 357–61): the liberal arts converge upon Christ, the supreme fount of all wisdom (*In coel. hier.* 1.550–60; see Jeauneau 1996, 359–61). Eriugena continues: "nulla enim sacra scriptura est que regulis liberalium careat disciplinarum" [for there is no part of Holy Scripture that lacks the rules of the liberal arts] (*In coel. hier.* 1.560–61; cf. Alcuin, *De grammatica*; PL 101: 853bc; see d'Alverny 1946, 245–47; Holtz 1997, 57–59). Hence, the arts are not just of propaedeutic value, not solely a means to (Christian) wisdom: they are a path to salvation (Contreni 1992, 4: 4).

Instruction in the arts, moreover, does not come from without but from within, for Eriugena finds in Martianus's phrase, "Philologia had shown Psyche so much affection that she strove constantly to make her immortal" (1.23 [11.10–11]), proof that the *studia sapientiae* are innate within the human soul. If the study of philosophy (*sapientia*) renders the soul immortal, and all souls are immortal, thus (Eriugena concludes) the individual arts are innate within everyone, even if they are not equally exercised by all (John Scotus Eriugena 1939, 27.15–22; cf. Remigius of Auxerre 1965, 26.23–29; *Periphyseon* 1, 486bd). The immanence of the arts—a position characteristic of Augustine's early dialogues (*Sol.* 2.20.35; *De quant. anim.* 20.34; *De lib. arb.* 1.12.24; but cf. *Retr.* 1.4.4, 1.8.2)—is a theme repeatedly stressed by both Eriugena and Remigius, but this view predates both. A gloss found in the earliest corpus (as edited by Lutz and present in the earliest known manuscript, Leiden, Universiteitsbibliotheek, Vossianus lat. F.48, f. 32r) argues for a strikingly similar interpretation:

> Omnis igitur naturalis ars in humana natura posita et concreata [*scripsi cum Voss.*, concreta *Lutz*] est. Inde conficitur ut omnes homines habeant naturaliter naturales artes, sed quia poena peccati primi hominis in animabus hominum obscurantur [*scripsi cum Voss.*, obscurantur *om. Lutz*] et in quandam profundam ignorantiam devolvuntur, nihil aliud agimus discendo nisi easdem artes quae in profundo memoriae repositae sunt in praesentiam intellegentiae revocamus, et cum aliis occupamur curis, nihil aliud agimus artes neglegendo nisi ipsas artes iterum dimittimus ut redeant ad id a quo revocatae sunt.
>
> [Every natural art is therefore present in and co-created with human nature. Consequently, everyone naturally possesses natural arts, but because, as punishment for the sin of the first man, they are obscured in the souls of men and sunk deep in ignorance, in learning we only recall into the presence of our understanding those same arts, which are stored deep in our memory; in neglecting them when our minds are occupied with other concerns, we only let go of them again such that they return to the place from which we recalled them.] (Dunchad of Laon 1944, 23.8–17; cf. Remigius of Auxerre 1965, 26.12–19)

Eriugena and Remigius also emphasize that the knowledge of the arts has been clouded by the Fall and that it is their recovery through study and learning that helps to restore the soul to its pristine state. Exemplary is their explication of the mirror bestowed upon Psyche by Uranie: "Uranie autem praenitens speculum, quod inter donaria eius adytis Sophia defixerat, quo se renoscens etiam originem vellet exquirere, clementi benignitate largita" [Urania, with kind generosity, bestowed upon her a gleaming mirror, which Sophia had placed amongst her gifts in her rooms, so that Psyche, recognizing herself, would also desire to seek her origins] (1.7 [4.20–22]). The correct reading, "Uranie," however, was first restored in Grotius's critical notes to Martianus Capella (1599), a conjecture later confirmed by modern collations of Parisianus 8670 (ninth century), which stands alone against the vulgate "Anie" (a product of faulty word division). Both Eriugena and Remigius read "Anie," and both make sense of it by interpreting Anie as yet another deity among Martianus's Greek and Latin pantheon, etymologically glossed as *recognitio* or *libertas*, which well suits the account of Neoplatonic reminiscence.

> ANIE dicitur quasi ἀνὰ ἔννοια, id est recognitio. Potest etiam Anie quasi ἀνιεῖσα, id est libertas, intelligi. Virtus quippe recognitione originis suae qua ad imaginem et similitudinem creatoris sui condita est, seu liberi arbitrii notitia, quo velut maximo dono et nobilitatis suae indicio prae ceteris animalibus ditata est, rationabili nature ex divinis thesauris concessa est atque donata. In qua virtute dico veluti in quodam speculo clarissimo lumine renidenti dignitatem naturae suae et primordialem fontem humana anima, quamvis adhuc merito originalis peccati ignorantiae nebulis circumfusa, perspicit, et quoniam ex sapientiae studiis et donis virtus recognitione originis suae et libertatis notitia humane distribuitur nature, pulchre Sophia aditis Aniae speculum spiritualis notitiae et donasse et immutabiliter fixisse [*scripsi*, finxisse *Lutz*] describitur.

[ANIE derives from "re- (ἀνὰ) cognition (ἔννοια)", that is "recognition". And it can also be understood as "liberating" (ἀνιεῖσα), that is "freedom". A natural capacity [for the liberal arts] (*virtus*),[1] in fact, by the recognition of its origin, in which it was fashioned according to the image and likeness of its creator, or by the knowledge of its free will, with which as a great gift and indication of its nobility it has been enriched more than the other animals, has been offered and bestowed upon a rational nature from the divine treasury. In this natural capacity, I say, as if in a kind of clear mirror gleaming with light, the human soul sees the dignity and primordial font of its own nature, although it is still, on account of original sin, enveloped by the clouds of ignorance. Because, as a result of the study and gifts of philosophy, this natural capacity has been distributed to human nature by the recognition of its origin and the knowledge of its freedom, Sophia is beautifully described as having bestowed and immutably fixed within Psyche's rooms Ania's mirror of spiritual knowledge.] (John Scotus Eriugena 1939, 12.26–37; Remigius of Auxerre 1962, 79.1–6)

Both Remigius and Eriugena identify Philology with *ratio* or *sapientia* and Mercury with *sermo* or *facundia sermonis*: the marriage of the two is preparatory to the knowledge of the liberal arts (John Scotus Eriugena 1939, 3.16–22; Remigius of Auxerre 1962, 65.17–29). And although both group the *liberales artes* into the three verbal arts (the term *trivium*—first attested in the ninth century—is nowhere used by either) and the four mathematical arts (*quadrivium* is used in Boethius's sense only by Remigius), neither explicitly links Philology with the mathematical arts and Mercury with verbal arts (an interpretation that was to gain force in the twelfth century). At the end of book two's transition to the orations on the arts, Phronesis, Philology's mother, asks that Mercury bestow his wedding gifts in the sight of all, after which "a dowry would be given by the maiden" (2.217 [57.9]). This promised gift is never mentioned again, and both Eriugena and Remigius offer the following solution (John Scotus Eriugena 1939, 74.20–21; cf. Remigius of Auxerre 1962, 208.11–13): "ac si dixisset: Postquam Mercurius dederit septem liberales artes, tunc virgo dabit septem mechanicas" [as if he had said: after Mercury has given the seven liberal arts, the maiden will then give the seven mechanical arts]. In the Oxford recension of Eriugena's glosses, knowledge of the *artes mechanicae* is likewise ascribed to Philology: "Sciens enim Mercurius Philologiam peritam esse septem mechannicae artis partium... inuenit septem liberales disciplinas, quas compararet septem mechannicis disciplinis, singulas singulis comparans" [Mercury, knowing that Philology was skilled in the seven parts of the mechanical art, discovered the seven liberal disciplines, which he matched, one to one, to the seven mechanical

---

1. On the meaning of *virtus* here, cf. John Scotus Eriugena 1939, 65.20–23: "inter artem et disciplinam hoc interest, quod quando discitur, disciplina vocatur, quando perfecta in habitu mentis est, ars nuncupatur. Ars dicta est ἀπὸ τῆς ἀρετῆς, hoc est a virtute" [This is the difference between "discipline" and "art": when something is in the process of being learnt, it is called a discipline; when it is perfected as a mental disposition, it is called an art. The Latin word "art" derives from the Greek word ἀρετή, which means "virtue"]. Cf. *Periphyseon* 4, 767c; *In coel. hier.* 2.129–31; the etymology derives from Isidore, *Etym.* 1.1.2.

disciplines] (John Scotus Eriugena 1978, 143). Neither Eriugena (the first to employ the *septem artes mechanicae*) nor Remigius specify these seven mechanical arts (cf. Hugh of St. Victor, *Didascalicon*, 2.20–27), but the references suggest that there is a larger scheme in play, of which the liberal arts form only a part.

There are several hints that this underlying rationale is Isidorian. At the outset of book four, *De dialectica*, Eriugena and Remigius both explain the presence of "quoque" ("also") in its first sentence as follows: "HAEC QVOQVE ideo dixit quia grammatica quam laboriose inter dotales virgines recepta est, quia inter duos parvam potestatem habet litteratoria ars; tamen, quia dialecticae brachium fuit, recepta est" [SHE ALSO. He said this because Grammatica was rather laboriously received among the dowry maidens, since, of these two (i.e., grammar and dialectic), the grammatical art has little power; nevertheless, she was allowed in because she was a branch of dialectic] (John Scotus Eriugena 1939, 88.10–13; Remigius of Auxerre 1965, 9.9–12). The location of grammar as a branch of dialectic reflects the Isidorian division of the sciences, witnessed throughout the Carolingian period. The *Schemata* associated with Alcuin's works are directly indebted to Isidore's *Differentiae* (see Bischoff 1966, 286–87), as is, several generations later, Martin of Laon's *De proprietate philosophiae et de vii liberalibus artibus* (edited in Contreni 1992, 6: 18–20), which offers the Isidorian tripartition and describes grammar as "adhering" to rhetoric and dialectic. Remigius too alludes to the tripartite division of philosophy in his Martianus commentary, glossing the typically Capellan, obscurantist *trigarium germanitatis* and *trigeminam feminam* (9.895 [340.14, 18]), as *triplicem feminam*, whom "putant... esse physicam ethicam, et logicam" [they think to be physics, ethics, and logic] (Remigius of Auxerre 1965, 301.33), but without further comment. A fuller version of the Isidorian division is found in Remigius's commentary on the *Disticha Catonis*, where logic comprises grammar, rhetoric, and dialectic (Mancini 1902, 180), and it is also alluded to in his commentary on Sedulius (Huemer 1885, 321). Perhaps it is not surprising, then, that a later reader added a diagram of the Isidorian tripartition (with the sevenfold division of *physica* from the *Differentiae*) to a copy of Remigius's commentary on the *De nuptiis* (Berne, Burgerbibliothek, B 56, f. 183v; see the plate in Mostert 1987, 164).

A similiarly Isidorian scheme is suggested in book five of Eriugena's *Periphyseon*. His argument that "finis enim totius motus est principium sui" [the end of all motion is its own beginning] (866c; cf. 1, 515c–516a) is illustrated through both sensible and intelligible examples, "ut sunt disciplinae quas philosophi liberales uocant" [such as the disciplines that philosophers call liberal] (868c). But Eriugena offers examples only from dialectic, arithmetic, geometry, music, and astronomy (note the Isidorian order). When his interlocutor fails to see why grammar and rhetoric are omitted, Eriugena replies: "quia ipsae duae artes ueluti quaedam membra dialecticae a multis philosophis non incongrue existimantur" [because these two arts are rightly thought by many philosophers to be, in a manner of speaking, the limbs of dialectic] (869d). As Contreni has noted, "while John's observation that the arts return to their principles reflects his Neoplatonism, his view of grammar and rhetoric as divisions of logic resembles the Hiberno-Latin versions of Isidore's *Differentiae*" (1992, 6: 7). Eriugena's division of philosophy in book three of the *Periphyseon* (705b), however, synthesizes the Isidorian division with the division he knew from Maximus the Confessor (ethics, physics, and theology: *Ambigua ad Iohannem* 6, 422–45) to forge a "quadriformis sophiae diuisio" [a fourfold division of wisdom]: πρακτική (ethics), φυσική (physics), θεολογία (theology), and λογική (logic). This division of philosophy is unique to Eriugena, and it anticipates the more expanded Boethian divisions employed in the twelfth-century commentary tradition.

THE TWELFTH-CENTURY COMMENTARY TRADITION

The twelfth century inaugurated a new focus on Martianus's introductory allegory. Both Mercury's ascent in quest of a wife in book one and Philology's apotheosis in book two offered, in the words of Winthrop Wetherbee, "an authoritative presentation of the stages of intellectual fulfillment" (1972, 91). Several of the individual books on the arts continued to be copied, read, and commented upon, primarily books five on rhetoric (included in Thierry of Chartres's *Heptateuchon* and cited several times as the "Rethorica Marciani" in William of Conches's *Glosae super Priscianum*) and eight on astronomy (on which there are several anonymous commentaries, see Lutz 1971, nos. 9 and 11; Jeauneau 1973, 17–23). But these later books were often divorced from the allegory and circulated separately in thematic collections, though a mid-century Chartrian manuscript (now the second part of Paris, Bibliothèque nationale, lat. 14754, fols. 92–255) includes the full text of the *De nuptiis* alongside other, more current, astronomical texts (e.g., the *Preceptum Canonis Ptolomei* also found in Thierry's *Heptateuchon*). Of the numerous twelfth- and (perhaps) early thirteenth-century commentaries on books one and two (see the list in Lutz 1971, 376–80, with the *addenda* in Westra 1986b, 185–86; cf. Westra 1994, ix–xxxi) only a few have modern editions: a mid-century, incomplete commentary (through 1.37) ascribed to Bernard Silvestris (Westra 1986a; henceforth the Cambridge commentary), an anonymous commentary, related to the Cambridge commentary, from the late twelfth- or early thirteenth-century (Westra 1994, 1998; henceforth the Berlin commentary), and the commentary of Alexander Neckam, perhaps composed between 1177 and 1190 (Neckam 2006). These commentaries all owe a profound debt to Remigius of Auxerre, who was clearly the primary authority (though not one above reproach) for the entire twelfth-century tradition.

Despite the nuanced, if often *ad hoc*, attention devoted to the intricate subtleties of Martianus's allegory, its broad sweep was sketched in ever broader strokes. Following a cue from Remigius (1962, 66.23–26; cf. John Scotus Eriugena 1939, 9.29), all these commentators cite Cicero's *De inventione* (1.1.1) as an expression of the ideal union of *sapientia* and *eloquentia*: "eloquentiam sine sapientia multum obesse, sapientiam vero sine eloquentia parum prodesse" [eloquence without wisdom is greatly harmful, but wisdom without eloquence is hardly useful] (as cited in Westra 1986a, 2.125–27; cf. Westra 1994, 3; Neckam 2006, 4; cf. Nuchelmans 1957). This Ciceronian passage, however, has far greater repercussions in the twelfth-century interpretations of the allegory. The marriage of eloquence and wisdom is not just preparatory to the liberal arts (as in Eriugena and Remigius), but at a fundamental level the marriage embodies the liberal arts: Mercury (*eloquentia*) is the trivium and Philology (*sapientia*) the quadrivium (cf. Thierry of Chartres's *Prologus in eptatheucon* [Jeauneau 1973, 90]). This theme is articulated at the very outset of the Cambridge commentary's accessus: "Tractaturus itaque philosophus de septem liberalibus artibus, quarum quatuor spectant ad rationem, tres ad sermonem, premittit de coniuctione rationis et sermonis. Doctrinam etenim artium ideo horum precedit coniunctio, quia oportet et comprehendere ratione et comprehensa ratione sermone exprimere." [The philosopher, as he begins his treatise on the seven liberal arts, of which four pertain to reason and three to speech, deals first with the union of reason and speech. For the conjunction of these precedes the teaching of the arts, since it is necessary both to understand through reason and to express through speech things rationally understood] (Westra 1986a, 2.1–3).

But Philology's sapiential persona was simultaneously more than just the quadrivium: it was philosophy in all of its manifestations (cf. Westra 1986a, 9.228–314; Westra 1994, 166–169). The division of the sciences in both the Cambridge (Westra 1986a, 3.889–1018) and Berlin (Westra 1994, 27–30) commentaries rehabilitates the Boethian bipartite division, but with crucial changes. *Scientia*, the "agnitio rerum comprehensibilium" [the knowledge of all things conceivable] is the genus of all disciplines, and it has *four* species: *sapientia, eloquentia, poesis*, and *mecania*. This expanded division finds room for the trivium under the banner of *eloquentia*, which has three species: grammar, dialectic, and rhetoric. *Eloquentia*, however, is not a part of philosophy (cf. Westra 1986a, 9.22–23), which is limited to *sapientia*, the "divinorum et humanorum agnicio" [the knowledge of divine and human matters]. It is *sapientia* that encompasses the Boethian bipartition of theoretical and practical philosophy, with their various subdivisions discussed above. But the commentators enumerate the order of the theoretical sciences differently than did Boethius, for whom (as already noted) mathematics held the medial position between theology and physics. For the Cambridge and Berlin commentators, however, theology and physics are both "higher" theoretical sciences than the mathematical sciences. Their rationale synthesizes Boethius's ontological and epistemological approaches: the three theoretical sciences, from an ontological standpoint, descend from theology (invisible substances), through physics (invisible causes of the visible world), to mathematics (visible forms of the visible world); from an epistemological standpoint (deemed by the Cambridge commentator the *ordo discendi* [the order of learning]), human knowledge must ascend from the visible to the invisible. The Cambridge commentator buttresses this re-ordering with the language of Boethius's *De institutione arithmetica*, reminding us that the mathematical sciences of the quadrivium both lead the mind from sense perception to "the greater certainties of understanding"—by which (according to the commentator) Boethius intends theology—and re-illuminate the eye of the mind (Westra 1968,

1.14–23; cf. Wetherbee 1972, 112–13). Thus all theoretical knowledge has as its starting point the *sapientia* of the quadrivium, the bride of *eloquentia*. Martianus and Boethius are brought into harmony.

This same division is found in several other related texts (e.g., the *Ysagoge in theologiam* and a commentary on the *Aeneid* also ascribed to Bernard, see Evans 1991), and it has clear affinities with Hugh of St. Victor's division in his *Didascalicon*, although in Hugh's version, the trivium is included under the more expected heading of *logica* or *logica sermonicalis*. Although the broad *eloquentia–sapientia* division may have originally been inspired by Cicero's *De inventione* (e.g., the tenth-century diagrammatic colophon in Leiden, Bibliotheek der Rijksuniversiteit, Voss. Lat. Q. 33, fol. 56r; on which see Evans 1991, 8), its twelfth-century proliferation was more indebted to Martianus. The division of *scientia* into *eloquentia* and *sapientia* is standard within the commentaries and treatises of William of Conches (see Rodnite Lemay 1977), who may himself have composed a Martianus commentary ("sed interim taceamus, quia super Martianum hoc exponemus," *Glosae super Boetium* 5 pr. 4.24–26). In the prologue to his *Philosophia*, William directly connects the Ciceronian passage quoted above (*De inv.* 1.1.1) to the marriage of Mercury and Philology. To divorce *eloquentia* and *sapientia*, he claims, "est Mercurii et Philologiae coniugium tanta cura Virtutis et Apollinis quaesitum, omni conventu deorum approbatum, solvere" [is tantamount to nullifying the marriage of Mercury and Philology, sought with such great effort by Virtue and Apollo and approved by the full assembly of the Gods] (*Philosophia* 1. prol. 1).

Though Remigius remains an ever-present source for the Cambridge commentator, the liberal arts are the threads in a discursive fabric cut from a new cloth. The immanence of the arts, their study as a process of reminiscence from within instead of acquisition from without, has been thoroughly expunged from the tradition— this perhaps because of a deep suspicion of the soul's celestial preexistence (cf. Westra 1986a, 6.513–53). In the place of Platonic reminiscence is a Christianized Vergilian and Boethian journey to the *summum bonum* (Westra 1986a, 2.114–19) and an equally Pauline epistemology (cf. Rom 1:20) of the ascent *per creaturas ad creatorem* (cf. Westra 1986a, 8.10–15). Already deeply ingrained in the commentator's rationale for the division of knowledge, the point is driven home by his comments on Mercury's rejected brides. Mercury is denied Sophia's hand in marriage because eloquence cannot unite directly with theology (symbolized by Sophia): "notandum est in disciplinis certum ordinem statutum" [there is a fixed and established order to the disciplines] (6.3–4). Theology is the final stage of the epistemological ascent: it represents the point beyond which no one can ascend (6.43). The emphasis on the proper *ordo discendi* even seeps into the individual disciplines. The Cambridge commentator's extensive remarks on the opening metrum, "Tu quem psallentem," are organized around the Boethian tripartite division of music (*Inst. mus.* 1.2; Boethius 1867, 187.18–89.12: *musica instrumentalis, humana, mundana*), but the commentator tacitly revises Boethius's ordering of the subdivision and interprets the metrum as an ascent from *musica instrumentalis*, through the intermediary of *musica mundana*, to the apex of *musica humana* (Westra 1986a, 3.36–65; on which see Hicks 2008). The passages that prompted remarks from Eriugena and Remigius on the immanence of the arts are accordingly reinterpreted within this new framework. The comment (*ad* 1.23) that Philology made Psyche immortal is not interpreted as the immortality bestowed by the arts; rather, it teaches us that reason both permits the distinction between good and evil and counsels us to embrace the former while rejecting the latter; thus reason (Philology) leads the soul (Psyche) to the immortal good (Westra 1986a, 9.350–52). Likewise, the mirror that Anie bestowed on Psyche (1.7) is recast as the mirror of scripture bestowed by Wisdom ("Anie enim id est sine nouitate dicitur sapientia" [Anie, i.e., 'without novelty,' is said to be wisdom]) and infixed upon the soul by Theology (Sophia). Hence, it is scripture—in which we see the eternal good as if through a glass darkly (cf. 1 Cor 13:12)—that teaches the soul of its origin and creator (Westra 1986a, 6.768–91).

In the later twelfth century, the focus of Martianus commentaries shifted again, from the epistemological implications of Martianus's myth to its mythological texture. Both Alexander Neckam's *Commentum super Martianum* and an anonymous (unedited) Florentine commentary are exemplary of this last phase. In comparison with the Cambridge commentator, as Christopher McDonough notes, Neckam "is less concerned with creating an overarching philosophical or religious system than he is with mythography" (Neckam 2006, xxii). The mythological focus is immediately apparent in Neckam's lengthy response to *De nuptiis* 1.3–4, Martianus's opening summary of the various celestial nuptials that prompted Mercury's own quest for a wife. Here Neckam begins: "Videamus ergo quid sint illi dei, que coniugia eorum, que etiam progenies eorum et quomodo Mercurius inuitatus sit ab eis coniugem ducere" [Let us examine what these gods are, what sort of marriages they have, who their children are, and why Mercury has been inspired by them to seek a wife of his own] (Neckam 2006, 17–18). Neckam then launches into fifty-seven pages of mythographic material (much of it independent of Eriugena, Remigius, and the Cambridge commentator, and reliant instead upon the Third Vatican Mythographer), enumerating and discussing numerous figures never directly mentioned by Martianus (e.g., the Titans, Tantalus, Phineus, Diana, Endymion, etc.) Though many of Remigius's and Eriugena's formulations on the liberal arts remain in Alexander's text—e.g., Neckam 2006, 89–90 (following Remigius) and 134 (following Eriugena)—such passages are, as McDonough rightly remarks, "the residue of Neckam's appropriation" of the earlier commentary traditions (xxiii). Neckam compresses Martianus's elaborate allegory into an even more simplified and streamlined interpretation, in which Philology has lost the lofty, sapiential implications of the Cambridge and Berlin commentaries: when we marry Philology to Mercury, we unite the liberal arts, and only then can we ascend to philosophy: "prius enim Philologiam Mercurio per artes copulamus, deinde ad philosophiam, id est sapientiam ascendimus" (Neckam 2006, 5).

This flattening of the allegory and the concomitant shift to the mythological is apparent as well in an anonymous set of notes on the *De nuptiis* contained in a late fourteenth-century Florentine manuscript (Biblioteca Nazionale Centrale, Conv. Soppr. I.1.28). Here the allegory receives even shorter shrift and the focus is overtly mythological. The third section (fols. 49r–64v) of the manuscript (on its history and structure, see Ullman 1973, esp. 135–45, 173–175) begins with an anonymous

Quedam geneologia deorum (inc.: "Celius ab inenarrabili patre ortus genuit saturnum"), and the remarks on Martianus (fols. 50r–64r) first begin under the heading *Allegoria et expositio quarumdam fabularum poeticarum*. Although fol. 55r begins a seemingly new, second text headed *Expositio super librum Martiani Capelle de Nuptiis Phylologie*, Peter Dronke (1974a, 169; 1974b, 224–25) first noted the continuity of the two texts, which in fact constitute a set of continuous notes on *De nuptiis* 1.1–2.100 interrupted by an incomplete accessus (printed below as an appendix), which immediately follows upon the new heading at fol. 55r.

The Florentine text makes little attempt to engage, much less explicate, Martianus's narrative and rarely connects its comments explicitly to the *De nuptiis*. Rather, it is (as its initial title suggests) a collection of mythological notes— introduced by "nota quod..." [Note that...]—on the gods in Martianus's pantheon, and the comments often parallel the Third Vatican Mythographer. It is difficult to determine when the notes acquired their present form (certainly prior to the copying of the manuscript), but there are several hints that they were mined from an earlier lemmatic commentary. Several striking points of overlap with the thought of William of Conches led Dronke to suggest, albeit cautiously, that the redactor of the Florentine notes, perhaps a "disciple" of the Chartrian master, had quarried William's "lost commentary" on Martianus (Dronke 1974a, 179; 1974b, 232). Recent scholars have not been so circumspect. Claudio Leonardi subtitled a discussion of the Florentine glosses "The Interpretation of William of Conches," and deemed the author "Der Carnotenser" (Leonardi 1987, 84–88); Jane Chance likewise describes it with confidence as "almost certainly a set of notes by one of [William's] students" (1998, xxxi), and refers throughout to "William's 'Martianus commentary'" (418–20): *uires adquirit eundo*. Dronke's caution was well founded, for the commentary upon which the Florentine text is dependent is still (partially) extant, though heretofore unrecognized, in a late twelfth- or early thirteenth-century Cistercian manuscript, Zwettl, Stiftsbibliothek, 313, fols. 142v–179v (see Westra 1998, xi–xiv for a full codicological description), which from fol. 151ra31 onward is itself identical to the Berlin commentary (hence Florence fol. 60r.2–5 = Westra 1994, 153.9–12; 60r.5–8 = 153.13–16; 60r.8–12 = 154.14–21, etc.). Florence, Conv. Soppr. I.1.28, however, was not excerpted directly from Zwettl 313, and the Florentine redactor had access to a more complete copy than what now remains in Zwettl 313, which lacks both the accessus and beginning of the commentary (entering at 1.3: Cum inter deos). The Zwettl commentary is not by William of Conches.[2] The accessus in Conv. Soppr. I.1.28,

---

2. The accessus in Conv. Soppr. I.1.28 does not follow William's usual formula (on which see the remarks of Édouard Jeauneau in William of Conches 2006, li), nor does the Zwettl commentary evince any of William's stylistic trademarks (*continuatio, quandoquidem... ergo, uere... nam, dicet aliquis...*, etc.). The parallels with William's thought noted by Dronke should not, however, be discounted, but at most they indicate the influence of William's writings on the Martianus commentary tradition (a fact already evident in the Cambridge commentary). The existence of William's presumed *Glosae super Martianum* (though it may yet be found) cannot be securely deduced from the Florentine notes.

assuming it is drawn from the same commentary, is closely related—though not identical—to the more scholastic accessus in the Berlin commentary (see the critical notes in the appendix), and its approach to Martianus's allegory parallels the streamlined reading of Neckam: Mercury is equated with *eloquentia* and Philology with *sapientia*, but only quadrivial *sapientia* ("non pro qualibet sapientia, sed pro illa quae in quadriuio continetur").

In the final throes of the Capellan commentary tradition, the philosophical sweep of Martianus's allegory, itself the foundation for an even more elaborate exegesis of its epistemological and philosophical implications for the *artes liberales*, was finally upstaged by its mythological actors. The continued market for manuals on the arts (e.g., the *De communibus artium liberalium* and the *Accessus philosophorum VII artium liberalium*, on which see Lafleur 1995, 1988), as well as the numerous references to the trivium and quadrivium in thirteenth- and fourteenth-century philosophical texts, confirm that the rise of university curricula in the thirteen century did not eliminate the liberal arts; the curriculum, after all, began with the *facultas artium* or *ordo artistarum*. But it did obviate the continued need for Martianus Capella's *De nuptiis Philologiae et Mercurii*. The commentary tradition lived on in the various scriptoria of the thirteenth, fourteenth, even fifteenth centuries (see the manuscript lists in Lutz 1971, 367–81), but it was no longer a vibrant, living tradition.

Appendix

Printed here is the partial accessus to Martianus's *De nuptiis* from Florence, Biblioteca Nazionale Centrale, Conv. Soppr. I.1.28, fol. 55r–55v (*F*). The odd placement of the accessus, in the middle of an otherwise continuous set of mythological notes, led Dronke to conclude that the leaves of the exemplar were faulty in their order (Dronke 1974a, 169; 1974b, 225). This may have been the case, but there is yet a quasi-logic to the placement of the accessus: it interrupts a set of notes on Mercury (*ad* 1.5–7), who is also the primary focus of the accessus (as excerpted in *F*). It is at least possible that the placement was intentional. The text has clear affinities with the accessus in Berlin, Staatsbibliothek Preussischer Kulturbesitz, lat. fol. 25, fol. 1r (*B*). The notes indicate some places where *F* improves *B* or vice versa, but the reader should not conclude that where the notes are silent, the texts are in full agreement.

Expositio super librum Martiani Capelli de nuptiis phylologie

<E>x tituli inscriptione concluditur[3] quod in hoc libro de nuptiis Mercurii et Phylologie[4] tractatur. Vt ergo quod dictum est planius explanemus, et fabulosam

---

3. concluditur] perpenditur *B*
4. phylologie *scripsi*, phylogie *F (hic et alias)*

narrationem et ueram eius intelligentiam componamus.⁵ Mercurius, solus ex adulterinorum numero nouercalem Iunonis gratiam adeptus, eius uberibus nutritus perhibetur. Phylologiam Fronesis⁶ filiam duxit, Virtute ac Phebo paranimphis, Ioue ac Iunone consentientibus⁷. Huic fabulose narrationi hec subest intelligentia. Mercurius eloquentiam significat, quod ex omnimoda nominis interpretatione habetur. Quia

"laudat uenales⁸ qui uult extrudere⁹ merces¹⁰",

sic dictus quasi 'mercatorum kirius', id est deus,¹¹ quoniam eis sit magnis in negotiis necessaria eloquentia.¹² Vel Mercurius 'mentis currus', eo quod uehiculum nostri intellectus sermo est ad audientem. Vel Mercurius quasi 'medius currens' inter loquentem et audientem.

Per illius etiam planete naturam¹³ qui Mercurius dicitur, bene proprietas¹⁴ eloquentie exprimitur. Ille enim per se nec bonus nec malus est nobis. Sed si in domicilio beniuoli planete, ut Iouis uel Veneris, ei coniungatur, salutem nostram cooperatur; si uero alicui nociuo societur, ut Saturno uel Marti, mortiferam pestem ab illo expectamus. Sic eloquentia per se nullius efficacie dicitur, sed quasi gladius in manu furiosi, eloquentia in animo maligni,¹⁵ quasi gladius in manu principis, eloquentia sapientis in animo.

Et ut nulla pretermittatur interpretatio, Mercurius dicitur quasi 'mercatorum chere', id est aue. Illi in principio sermonis adiuti eloquentia¹⁶ pace salutationis <homines>¹⁷ alliciunt. Principium enim amicitie bonus sermo.¹⁸

Hic Iouis et Maie filius, Iunonis priuignus dicitur, ut per Iouem ethera, per Iunonem aera intelligamus. Sermo enim noster oritur quia in umecto¹⁹ <aere>²⁰ ether ille superior ad nos coniungitur. Vnde phylosophi diffiniunt uocem esse aerem tenuissimum ictum.²¹ Quia ergo ether ille superior per quosdam occultos meatus

---

5. componamus] exponamus B
6. fronesis *scripsi*, frenesis F
7. consentientibus] fautoribus B
8. uenalem *ante corr.*
9. extrudere *scripsi*, excludere F
10. laudat – merces] Horace Ep. 2.2.11; Walther, Sprichw. 13566, 13536 with refs; *om.* B
11. deus] dominus (*recte*) B
12. eloquentia] affabilitas B
13. naturam] *om.* B
14. proprietas] prosperitas B
15. sed quasi gladius – in animo maligni] *om.* B
16. illi in principio – eloquentia] illi enim ad rerum venalium coemptionem B
17. homines *scripsi cum* B
18. principium – sermo] *om.* B
19. in umecto *scripsi cum* B, nomini inuecto F
20. aere *scripsi cum* B
21. Priscian, Inst. 1.1

huius inferioris attrahitur nobis,[22] quasi lac uberibus, sic Iuno uberibus propriis eum nutriuisse perhibetur. Sed hoc inuentum satis bene exprimit[23] quare Maie[24] filius uel Iunonis dicatur priuignus.

Ideo eiusdem fabule alia ponitur expositio, ut Iupiter dicatur quilibet sapiens et eloquens, ut Orpheus, qui congregauit homines ad bene uiuendum. Per Maiam[25] intelligitur illa hominum collecta pluralitas ad iure uiuendum, | 55v | que peperit eloquentiam qua hominibus bonum persuadetur et ciuitates legibus refrenantur.[26] Iuno uero actiuam uitam significat, unde in fabulis Paridi promittit diuitias. Que similiter Iouis uxor dicitur, quia uir sapiens et eloquens bene operando plurimas de se gignit utilitates. Quod enim in alio docet, bone operationis exemplo persuadet. Ideo eius priuignus est Mercurius,[27] quoniam alterius uxoris filius, sed gratum est ei. Quid enim est melius quo in agendo perficiatur quam per eloquentiam? Vnde eam diligenter amplectuntur homines et quasi immortaliter produci faciunt.

Hic Mercurius Phylologiam ducit uxorem, id est sapientie legitimam coniunctionem petit eloquentia. Phylologia autem Fronesis filia dicitur, quia Fronesis prudentia interpretatur, que homini a primeua creatione cum anime potentiis data est, et ipsam propria industria et exercitatione ad sapientiam inducit, unde eadem 'se[28] gignens' dicitur. Phylologia autem dicitur a 'phylos', quod est amor, et 'logem' quod est ratio, quasi amor rationis. Hoc autem intellige non pro qualibet sapientia, sed pro illa que in quadriuio continetur. De paranimphis et fautoribus in his nuptiis, operis executio plene docebit.

Ostenso de quo tractet, utilitatem ostendamus, que in hoc consistit, ut scias[29] quibus gradibus ab eloquentia uenias ad sapientiam. Quod[30] maxime ideo fecit, quia uidit Latinos, omissis gradibus sapientie, soli studere eloquentie, et illud Tullii[31] sepe approbat, quia eloquentia....[32]

An Exposition on the book by Martianus Capella on the marriage of Philology

From the title, we conclude that this book is about the marriage of Mercury and Philology. In order, therefore, that we may more clearly explain what we have said, let us set out both the mythic tale and its true meaning. Among Jupiter's many

---

22. nobis *scripsi*, modo F
23. exprimit *scripsi*, exprimitur F
24. maie *scripsi*, male F
25. maiam *scripsi*, malam F
26. refrenantur *scripsi*, referentur F
27. *Hic explicit pars communis cum B*
28. se *scripsi*, si F
29. scias *scripsi*, sciam F
30. quod *scripsi*, quia F
31. tullii *scripsi*, iulii F
32. *fortasse continuandum* sine sapientia multum obest *etc.*; Cic., *De inv.* 1.1.1.

illegitimate children, only Mercury received Juno's stepmotherly favor and is supposed to have been nourished at her breasts. He married Philology, the daughter of Fronesis, with Virtue and Apollo as groomsmen, Jupiter and Juno giving their blessing. This is the hidden meaning in the mythic tale: Mercury signifies eloquence, which is clear however you may derive his name. Because "he who wishes to palm off his goods hypes the praise of his wares," Mercury is called, so to speak, the "merchants' *kyrios*" (*kyrios* means 'God'), since eloquence is the merchants' necessity in big business. Or Mercury is a "mental curricle," because speech is the vehicle for our meaning to reach the listener. Or Mercury is the "mediating courier" between the speaker and listener.

The property of eloquence is also well expressed through the nature of the planet we call Mercury. For that planet by itself is neither useful nor harmful to us. But if, on the one hand, a conjunction should occur in the house of a benevolent planet (such as Jupiter or Venus), then Mercury contributes to our well-being; if, on the other, Mercury be allied with a harmful planet (such as Saturn or Mars), then we dread from it deadly plague. So too eloquence by itself is said to be of no efficacy; but like a sword in the hand of a mad man, so is eloquence in the mind of the malicious; like a sword in the hand of a prince, so is eloquence in the mind of the wise.

Also (so as not to omit any interpretation) Mercury is, as it were, the "merchants' *chere*" (*chere* means 'hello'), for they, by employing eloquence at the outset of their speech, win <men> over with the favor of their greeting. After all, friendship begins with good conversation.

He is said to be Jupiter and Maia's son but Juno's stepson so that through Jupiter we understand the aether, through Juno the air. For our speech arises because that upper aether is joined to us in the humid <air>. Whence philosophers define voice as most subtle air that has been struck. Because, therefore, that upper aether is drawn to us through certain hidden passages in this lower air, like milk to breasts, thus Juno is said to have nourished him at her own breasts. This contrivance sufficiently explains why he is called Maia's son or Juno's stepson.

Another explanation of this same myth is posited: Jupiter stands for any wise, eloquent man, such as Orpheus, who gathered men together for the purpose of right living. By Maia we understand the collected plurality of men gathered for lawful living, which gave birth to eloquence through which men are persuaded to good and cities are checked by laws. Juno, however, signifies the active life; whence, in myths she promises Paris riches. She likewise is called Jupiter's wife because the wise, eloquent man begets of himself many useful things through his right action. For he persuades through the example of right action what he teaches in another. Mercury is her stepson because he is the son of another wife; but this pleases her. For what is better for completing a work actively in progress than eloquence? Whence men lovingly embrace her and make her immortal.

Mercury takes Philology as his wife, that is, eloquence seeks a lawful union with wisdom. Philology is called the daughter of Fronesis because Fronesis means 'prudence,' which was bestowed upon men as one of the soul's powers from the very moment of creation, and it leads the soul by its own industry and exercise to wisdom; whence it is called 'self-begetting.' Philology takes her name from *phylos*, which means 'love,' and *logos*, which means 'reason'; she is, as it were, 'love of reason.' But understand this not as any reason whatsoever, but as that which pertains to the quadrivium. Concerning the attendants and patrons in the wedding, our discussion of the work will give a full account.

Since we have shown the work's subject matter, let us reveal its utility. The utility consists in this: that you know by what steps you may proceed from eloquence to wisdom. He [*sc.* Martianus] did this for the following reason, because he saw that the Latins omitted the steps of wisdom and strove only for eloquence. And he often approves this passage from Cicero, that eloquence…

SUGGESTIONS FOR FURTHER READING

On Martianus's *De nuptiis*, the standard English translation and commentary by Stahl (1971) (which predates Willis's 1983 Teubner edition, Martianus Capella 1983) must be corrected and supplemented by consulting the more recent translations and commentaries by Shanzer (1986a, book one only), Ramelli (Martianus Capella 2001), and Zekl (Martianus Capella 2005) (the latter with only minimal notes), as well as the ongoing Budé edition, which thus far has published books four (Martianus Capella 2007a), six (Martianus Capella 2007b), and seven (Martianus Capella 2003). For Martianus's treatment of individual arts, see Scarpa (1983) on geometry, the commentaries of Gasparatto (1988) on arithmetic, and Cristante (1987) on music. Ramelli's appendix on the fortunes of the *De nuptiis* from the sixth to the fifteenth century (Martianus Capella 2001, 1013–67) is marred by an almost exclusive and uncritical reliance on older studies (primarily Lutz and Stahl). Better is Ramelli (2006), which collects in one volume many—though not all—of the edited medieval commentaries on Martianus, some printed in both Latin and Italian, others printed only (and less usefully) in Italian. For a census of known commentaries, see Lutz (1971), with addenda and corrigenda in Lutz and Contreni (1976) and Westra (1986a). Teeuwen (2002, 27–57; 2003) provides a generally reliable guide to the considerable bibliography on the ninth-century commentary tradition. The manuscript studies by Leonardi (1959–60) and Préaux (1978) remain fundamental; Lutz (1956) on Remigius's commentary, Mathon (1969) on Eriugena's commentary, Roques (1975) on Eriugena's theory of the arts, and Contreni (1992) on Eriugena and Martin of Laon can still be consulted with profit. O'Sullivan's edition of the oldest gloss tradition on books one and two (O'Sullivan 2010) has appeared after the time of this writing. Scholarship on the twelfth-century commentary tradition is more dispersed; valuable information can be gleaned from Jeauneau (1973, 5–49), Wetherbee (1972), and Dronke (1974a), as well as the introductions in Westra (1986 and 1994) and Neckam (2006). On the liberal arts, Hadot (2005) (a revised and expanded version of Hadot 1984) offers a rich and polemical approach to the ancient and early medieval arts tradition, and the many (if uneven) contributions to *Arts libéraux et philosophie au Moyen Âge* (1969) convey the wide range and reach of the topic in the Middle Ages; cf. also the articles collected in Koch (1959), Wagner (1983), and Craemer-Ruegenberg and Speer (1994). On the relation between the liberal arts and the educational structures introduced by Carolingian reforms, see Brunhölzl (1965), Riché (1989, esp. 246–84), and Holtz (1997); on the fortune of the liberal arts within university curricula, see Leff (1968, esp. 138–60), Glorieux (1971, esp. 11–58), and Lafleur (1988 and 1995).

BIBLIOGRAPHY

Primary sources

Ammonius. 1891. *In Porphyrii Isagogen sive V voces*, edited by Adolf Busse. Commentaria in Aristotelem Graeca 4.3. Berlin: Reimer.

Boethius. 1867. *Anicii Manlii Torquati Severini Boetii De institutione arithmetica, libri duo. De institutione musica, libri quinque*, edited by Godfrey Friedlein. Bibliotheca scriptorum Graecorum et Romanorum Teubneriana. Leipzig: B. G. Teubner.

———. 1906. *Anicii Manlii Severini Boethii In Isagogen Porphyrii commenta*, edited by Samuel Brandt. Corpus Scriptorum Ecclesiasticorum Latinorum 48. Vienna: F. Tempsky.

———. 1999. *De institutione arithmetica*, edited by Henry Oosthout and Iohannes Schilling. Corpus Christianorum. Series Latina 94A. Turnhout: Brepols.

Cassiodorus. 1937. *Cassiodori Senatoris Institutiones*, edited by Roger A. B. Mynors. Oxford: Clarendon Press.

Dunchad of Laon. 1944. *Dunchad Glossae in Martianum*, edited by Cora E. Lutz. Philological Monographs 12. Lancaster, PA: American Philological Association.

Isidore of Seville. 1911. *Isidori Hispalensis episcopi Etymologiarum siue Originum libri XX*, edited by Wallace M. Lindsay. Oxford: Clarendon Press.

———. 2005. *Le livre des nombres*, edited and translated by Jean-Yves Guillaumin. Auteurs latins du moyen âge 14. Paris: Belles lettres.

———. 2009. *Étymologies, livre 3 (la mathématique)*, edited and translated by Jean-Yves Guillaumin. Auteurs latins du moyen âge 18. Paris: Belles lettres.

John Scotus Eriugena. 1939. *Iohannis Scotti Annotationes in Marcianum*, edited by Cora E. Lutz. Cambridge, MA: Mediaeval Academy of America.

———. 1978. "Le commentaire érigénien sur Martianus Capella (*De nuptiis*, lib. I) d'après le manuscrit d'Oxford (Bodl. Libr. Auct. T.2.19, fol. 1-31)" [=*Glosae Martiani*], edited by Édouard Jeauneau. In *Quatre thèmes érigéniens*, 91–166. Montréal, Paris: Institut d'études médiévales Albert-le-Grand.

Martianus Capella. 1599. *Martiani Minei Felicis Capellæ carthaginiensis viri proconsularis Satyricon, in quo De nuptiis Philologiæ & Mercurij libri duo & De septem artibus liberalibus libri singulares*, edited by Hugo Grotius. Lugdunum Batavorum: Ex officina Plantiniana.

———. 1983. *Martianus Capella*, edited by James Willis. Bibliotheca scriptorum Graecorum et Romanorum Teubneriana. Leipzig: B. G. Teubner.

———. 2001. *Le nozze di Filologia e Mercurio*, translated by Ilaria Ramelli. Il pensiero occidentale. Milan: Bompiani.

———. 2003. *Les noces de Philologie et de Mercure. Livre VII. L'arithmétique*, edited and translated by Jean-Yves Guillaumin. Paris: Belles lettres.

———. 2005. *Die Hochzeit der Philologia mit Merkur*, translated by Hans Günter Zekl. Würzburg: Königshausen & Neumann.

———. 2007a. *Les noces de Philologie et de Mercure. Livre IV. La dialectique*, edited and translated by Michel Ferré. Paris: Belles lettres.

———. 2007b. *Les noces de Philologie et de Mercure. Livre VI. La géométrie*, edited and translated by Barbara Ferré. Paris: Belles lettres.

Neckam, Alexander. 2006. *Commentum super Martianum*, edited by Christopher McDonough. Millennio Medievale 64. Florence: SISMEL, Edizioni del Galluzzo.

Nicomachus of Gerasa. 1866. *Nicomachi Geraseni Pythagorei Introductionis arithmeticae libri duo*, edited by Richard Hoche. Leipzig: Teubner.

O'Sullivan, Sinéad, ed. 2010. *Glossae aeui Carolini in libros I-II Martiani Capellae "De nuptiis Philologiae et Mercurii."* Corpus Christianorum. Continuatio Mediaevalis 237. Turnhout: Brepols.

Ramella, Ilaria, trans. 2006. *Tutti I commenti a Marziano Capella*. Il pensiero occidentale. Milan: Bompiani.

Rather of Verona. 1984. *Notae et glossae autographicae Ratherii Veronensis*, edited by Claudio Leonardi. Corpus Christianorum. Continuatio Mediaevalis 46A, 293–303. Turnhout: Brepols.

Remigius of Auxerre. 1962. *Remigii Autissiodorensis Commentum in Martianum Capellam Libri I–II*, edited by Cora E. Lutz. Leiden: E. J. Brill.

Remigius of Auxerre. 1965. *Remigii Autissiodorensis Commentum in Martianum Capellam Libri III–IX*, edited by Cora E. Lutz. Leiden: E. J. Brill.

Westra, Haijo Jan, ed. 1986a. *The Commentary on Martianus Capella's De nuptiis Philologiae et Mercurii Attributed to Bernardus Silvestris*. Studies and Texts 80. Toronto: Pontifical Institute of Mediaeval Studies.

———, ed. 1994. *The Berlin Commentary on Martianus Capella's De nuptiis Philologiae et Mercurii. Book I*. Mittellateinische Studien und Texte 20. Leiden: E. J. Brill.

Westra, Haijo Jan and Tanja Kupke, eds. 1998. *The Berlin Commentary on Martianus Capella's De nuptiis Philologiae et Mercurii. Book II*. Mittellateinische Studien und Texte 23. Leiden: E. J. Brill.

William of Conches. 2006. *Guillelmi de Conchis Glosae super Platonem*, edited by Édouard Jeauneau. Corpus Christianorum. Continuatio Mediaevalis 203. Turnhout: Brepols.

Secondary sources

Arts libéraux et philosophie au Moyen Âge. 1969. Montreal: Institut d'études médiévales.

Barnish, Samuel I. B. 1986. "Martianus Capella and Rome in the Late Fifth Century." *Hermes* 114: 98–111.

Bischoff, Bernhard. 1966. "Eine verschollene Einteilung der Wissenschaften." In *Mittelalterliche Studien. Band I. Ausgewählte Aufsätze zur Schriftkunde und Literaturgeschichte*, 273–288. Stuttgart: Hiersemann.

Bovey, Muriel. 2003. *Disciplinae cyclicae: l'organisation du savior dans l'œuvre de Martianus Capella*. Polymnia 3. Trieste: Edizioni Università di Trieste.

Brunhölzl, Franz. 1965. "Der Bildungsauftrag der Hofschule." In *Karl der Grosse. Lebenswerk und Nachleben. Band II. Das geistige Leben*, edited by Bernhard Bischoff, 28–41. Düsseldorf: L. Schwann.

Cameron, Alan. 1986. "Martianus and His First Editor." *Classical Philology* 81: 320–28.

Chance, Jane. 1994. *Medieval Mythography: From Roman North Africa to the School of Chartres, A.D. 433–1177*. Gainesville, FL: University Press of Florida.

Contreni, John J. 1992. "John Scottus, Martin Hiberniensis, the Liberal Arts and Teaching." In *Carolingian Learning, Masters and Manuscripts*, 6: 1–22. Collected Studies 363. Hampshire, Brookfield, VT: Variorum.

———. 1995. "The Carolingian Renaissance: Education and Literary Culture." In *The New Cambridge Medieval History: Volume II c. 700–c. 900*, edited by Rosamond McKitterick, 709–57. Cambridge: Cambridge University Press.

Courcelle, Pierre Paul. 1943. *Les lettres grecques en Occident. De Macrobe à Cassiodore*. Bibliothèque des Écoles françaises d'Athènes et de Rome 159. Paris: E. de Boccard.

———. 1969. *Late Latin Writers and their Greek Sources*, translated by Harry E. Wedeck. Cambridge, MA: Harvard University Press.

Craemer-Ruegenberg, Ingrid and Andreas Speer, ed. 1994. *Scientia und ars im Hoch- und Spätmittelalter*. Miscellanea mediaevalia 22. Berlin: W. de Gruyter.

Cristante, Lucio, ed., trans., and comm. 1987. *Martiani Capellae De nuptiis Philologiae et Mercurii Liber IX*. Medioevo e Umanesimo 64. Padova: Editrice Antenore.

Cristante, Lucio. 2005. "*Spectaculo detinemur cum scripta intellegimus aut probamus*. Per un riesame della rappresentazione delle Artes in Marziano Capella." *Incontri triestini di filologia classica* 4: 375–90.

Díaz y Díaz, Manuel C. 1969. "Les arts libéraux d'après les écrivains espagnols et insulaires aux VIIe et VIIIe siècles." In *Arts libéraux et philosophie au Moyen Âge*, 37–46. Montreal: Institut d'études médiévales.

Dronke, Peter. 1974a. *Fabula. Explorations into the Uses of Myth in Medieval Platonism*. Mittellateinische Studien und Texte 9. Leiden: E. J. Brill.

———. 1974b. "William of Conches's Commentary on Martianus Capella." In *Études de civilisation médiévale (IXe–XIIe siècles). Mélanges offerts à Edmond-René Labande*, 223–35. Poitiers: Centre d'Etudes Supérieures de Civilisation Médiévale.

Evans, Michael. 1991. "The *Ysagoge in Theologiam* and the Commentaries Attributed to Bernard Silvestris." *Journal of the Warburg and Courtauld Institutes* 54: 1–42.

Fried, Johannes. 1997. "Karl der Große, die Artes liberales und die karolingische Renaissance." In *Karl der Grosse und sein Nachwirken. Band I: Wissen und Weltbild*, edited by Paul Butzer, Max Kerner, and Walter Oberschelp, 25–43. Turnhout: Brepols.

Gasparotto, Giovanni, ed., trans., and comm. 1983. *Marziano Capella. Geometria. De nuptiis Philologiae et Mercurii Liber sextus*. Verona: Libreria universitaria editrice.

Glorieux, Palémon. 1971. *La Faculté des Arts et ses maîtres au XIIIe siècle*. Études de philosophie médiévale 59. Paris: J. Vrin.

Grebe, Sabine. 1999. *Martianus Capella De nuptiis Philologiae et Mercurii. Darstellung der Sieben Freien Künste und ihrer Beziehungen zueinander*. Beiträge zur Altertumskunde 119. Stuttgart, Leipzig: Teubner.

———. 2000. "Gedanken zur Datierung von *De nuptiis Philologiae et Mercurii* des Martianus Capella." *Hermes* 128: 353–68.

Hadot, Ilsetraut. 1984. *Arts libéraux et philosophie dans la pensée antique*. Paris: Etudes augustiniennes.

———. 2005. *Arts libéraux et philosophie dans la pensée antique: contribution à l'histoire de l'éducation et de la culture dans l'Antiquité*. 2nd ed. Texts et traditions. Paris: J. Vrin.

Herren, Michael. 1986. "The Commentary on Martianus Attributed to John Scottus: Its Hiberno-Latin Background." In *Jean Scot écrivain: actes du IVe colloque international, Montréal, 28 August–2 September 1983*, edited by Guy-H. Allard, 365–86. Cahiers d'études médiévales. Cahier spécial 1. Montreal: Bellarmin.

Hicks, Andrew. 2008. "*Musica speculativa* in the Cambridge Commentary on Martianus Capella's *De nuptiis*." *Journal of Medieval Latin* 18: 292–305.

Holtz, Louis. 1997. "Alcuin et la renaissance des arts libéraux." In *Karl der Grosse und sein Nachwirken. Band I: Wissen und Weltbild*, edited by Paul Butzer, Max Kerner, and Walter Oberschelp, 45–60. Turnhout: Brepols.

Jeauneau, Édouard. 1973. *"Lectio philosophorum". Recherches sur l'Ecole de Chartres*. Amsterdam: Hakkert.

———. 1996. "Artifex Scriptura." In *Iohannes Scottus Eriugena. The Bible and Hermeneutics. Proceedings of the Ninth International Colloquium of the Society for the Promotion of Eriugenian Studies held at Leuven and Louvain-la-Neuve, June 7–10, 1995*, edited by Gerd van Riel, Carlos Steel, and James McEnvoy, 351–365. Ancient and Medieval Philosophy, ser. 1, 20. Leuven: Leuven University Press. [Reprinted in *"Tendenda Vela." Excursions littéraires et digressions philolophiques à travers le Moyen Âge*, 69–83. Instrumenta patristica et mediaevalia 47. Turnhout: Brepols.]

Koch, Josef, ed. 1959. *Artes liberales. Von der antiken Bildung zur Wissenschaft des Mittelalters*. Studien und Texte zur Geistesgeschichte des Mittelalters 5. Leiden: E. J. Brill.

Lafleur, Claude. 1995. "Les 'guides de l'étudiant' de la Faculté des arts de l'Université de Paris au XIIIe siècle." In *Philosophy and Learning. Universities in the Middle Ages*, edited by Maarten J.F.M. Hoenen, Jacob H. J. Schneider, and Georg Wieland, 137–99. Education and Society in the Middle Ages and Renaissance 6. Leiden: E. J. Brill.

———. 1988. *Quatre introductions à la philosophie au XIIIe siècle: textes critiques et étude historique*. Université de Montréal. Publications d'études médiévales 23. Montréal: Institut d'études médiévales.

Leff, Gordon. 1968. *Paris and Oxford Universities in the Thirteenth and Fourteenth Centuries. An Institutional and Intellectual History*. New Dimensions in History: Essays in Comparative History. New York: John Wiley & Sons, Inc.

Leonardi, Claudio. 1987. "Der Kommentar des Johannes Scotus zu Martianus Capella im 12. Jahrhundert." In *Eriugena redivivus. Zur Wirkungsgeschichte seines Denkens im Mittelalter und im Übergang zur Neuzeit*, edited by Werner Beierwaltes, 77–88. Abhandlungen der Heidelberger Akademie der Wissenschaften, Philosophisch-Historische Klasse, Jahrg. 1987, 1. Heidelberg: C. Winter.

———. 1961. "Nuove voci poetiche tra secolo IX e XI." *Studi medievali*, 3a serie, 2: 139–68.

———. 1959. "Raterio e Marziano Capella." *Italia Medioevale e Umanistica* 2: 73–102.

———. 1959–60. "I codici di Marziano Capella." *Aevum* 33: 443–89 and *Aevum* 34: 1–99, 411–524.

Lutz, Cora. 1971. "Martianus Capella." In *Catalogus translationum et commentariorum: Mediaeval and Renaissance Latin Translations and Commentaries*, edited by Paul O. Kristeller and Ferdinand E. Cranz, 2: 367–81. Washington: Catholic University of America Press.

———. 1956. "Remigius' Ideas on the Classification of the Liberal Arts." *Traditio* 12: 65–86.

Lutz, Cora and John Contreni. 1976. "Martianus Capella: Addenda et Corrigenda to Volume II." In *Catalogus translationum et commentariorum: Mediaeval and Renaissance Latin Translations and Commentaries*, edited by Paul O. Kristeller and Ferdinand E. Cranz, 4: 449–52. Washington: Catholic University of America Press.

Mancini, A. 1902. "Un commento ignoto di Remy d'Auxerre ai *Disticha Catonis*." *Rendiconti della Reale Accademi dei Lince, classe di scienze morali, storiche e filologiche*, Ser. V, 11: 175–98.

Mathon, Gérard. 1969. "Les formes et la signification de la pédagogie des arts libéraux au milieu du IXe siècle. L'enseignement palatin de Jean Scot Érigène." In *Arts libéraux et philosophie au Moyen Âge*, 47–64. Montreal: Institut d'études médiévales.

McInerny, Ralph. 1983. "Beyond the Liberal Arts." In *The Seven Liberal Arts in the Middle Ages*, edited by David L. Wagner, 248–72. Bloomington, IN: Indiana University Press.

Mostert, Marco. 1987. *The Political Theology of Abbo of Fleury: A Study of the Ideas about Society and Law of the Tenth-Century Monastic Reform Movement*. Middeleeuwse studies en bronnen 2. Hilversum: Verloren.

Préaux, Jean. 1978. "Les manuscrits principaux du *De nuptiis Philologiae et Mercurii* de Martianus Capella." In *Lettres latines du moyen-âge et de la renaissance*, edited by Guy Cambier, Carl Deroux, and Jean Préaux, 76–128. Collection Latomus 158. Brussels: Latomus.

———. 1975. "Securus Melior Felix, l'ultime Orator Urbis Romae." In *Miscellanea patristica, historica et liturgica Eligio Dekkers O.S.B. XII lustra complenti oblata*, 2: 101–121. Bruges: Sint-Pietersabdij.

———. 1953. "Le Commentaire de Martin de Laon sur l'oeuvre de Martianus Capella." *Latomus* 12: 437–59.

Riché, Pierre. 1989. *Écoles et enseignement dans le Haut Moyen Âge. Fin du Ve siècle—milieu du XIe siècle*. 2nd ed. Paris: Picard.

Rodnite Lemay, Helen. 1977. "Guillaume de Conches' Division of Philosophy in the *Accessus ad Macrobium*." *Mediaevalia* 1: 115–29.

Roques, Rene. "*Valde artificialiter*: le sens d'un contresens." In *Libres sentiers vers l'erigenisme*, 45–98. Lessico intellettuale europeo 9. Rome: Edizioni dell'Ateneo.

Scarpa, Luigi, ed., trans., and comm. 1988. *Martiani Capellae De nuptiis Philologiae et Mercurii Liber VII (Arithmetica)*. Padova: CLEUP.

Shanzer, Danuta R. 1984. "Tatwine: an Independent Witness to the Text of Martianus Capella's *De Grammatica*?" *Rivista di filologia e d'istruzione classica* 112: 292–313.

———. 1986a. *A Philosophical and Literary Commentary on Martianus Capella's De Nuptiis Philologiae et Mercurii Book 1*. University of California Publications. Classical Studies 32. Berkeley, CA: University of California Press.

———. 1986b. "Felix Capella: *Minus sensus quam nominis pecudalis*." *Classical Philology* 81: 62–81.

———. 2005. "Augustine's Disciplines: *Silent diutius Musae Varronis*?" In *Augustine and the Disciplines: From Cassiciacum to Confessions*, edited by Karla Pollman and Mark Vessey, 69–112. Oxford: Oxford University Press.

Stahl, William Harris. 1971. *Martianus Capella and the Seven Liberal Arts*. 2 vols. Records of Civilizations: Sources and Studies 84. New York: Columbia University Press.

Teeuwen, Mariken. 2008. "The Pursuit of Secular Learning: The Oldest Commentary Tradition on Martianus Capella." *Journal of Medieval Latin* 18: 36–51.

———. 2005. "The Vocabulary of Martianus Capella Commentators of the Ninth Century. Some Observations." *Archivum Latinitatis Medii Aevi* 63: 71–81.

———. 2003. "The study of Martianus Capella's *De nuptiis* in the Ninth Century." In *Learned Antiquity. Scholarship and Society in the Near-East, the Greco-Roman World, and the Early Medieval West*, edited by Alasdair A. MacDonald, Michael W. Twomey, and Gerrit J. Reinink, 185–94. Groningen Studies in Cultural Change 5. Leuven: Peeters.

———. 2002. *Harmony and the Music of the Spheres. The ars musica in Ninth-Century Commentaries on Martianus Capella*. Mittellateinische Studien und Texte 30. Leiden: Brill.

Ullman, Berthold L. 1973. "The Composition of Petrarch's 'De vita solitaria' and the History of the Vatican Manuscript." In *Studies in the Italian Renaissance*, 135–175. 2nd ed. Storia e letteratura 51. Rome: Edizioni di Storia e letteratura.

Wagner, David L., ed. 1983. *The Seven Liberal Arts in the Middle Ages*. Bloomington, IN: Indiana University Press.

Weisheipl, James A. 1965. "Classification of the Sciences in Medieval Thought." *Mediaeval Studies* 27: 54–90.

Westra, Haijo Jan. 1986b. "Martianus Capella: Addenda et Corrigenda to Volume II." In *Catalogus translationum et commentariorum: Mediaeval and Renaissance Latin Translations and Commentaries*, edited by Paul OskarKristeller and Ferdinand E. Cranz, 6: 185–86. Washington: Catholic University of America Press.

Wetherbee, Winthrop. 1972. *Platonism and Poetry in the Twelfth Century. The Literary Influence of the School of Chartres*. Princeton: Princeton University Press.

CHAPTER 16

LEARNED MYTHOGRAPHY: PLATO AND MARTIANUS CAPELLA

WINTHROP WETHERBEE

Perhaps the first thing to be said about medieval mythography is that it assumed as its implicit context the universe of Plato's *Timaeus*. Within this cosmic framework the Olympian gods of the classical poets coexisted with a host of personifications, philosophical concepts, natural forces, or attributes of the divine, giving rise to the tradition of "learned" mythography which emerged in late Carolingian commentary on Martianus Capella and Boethius, and culminated in the allegorical poems of Bernardus Silvestris and Alan of Lille. Classical poetry, too, was read against this background: The *Aeneid* modeled the ascent to Neoplatonist wisdom, and the *Metamorphoses*, centerpiece of the *aetas ovidiana*, was introduced to the twelfth century as embodying the Platonist cosmological tradition.

This chapter will be concerned mainly with the twelfth century, when the Latin mythographic tradition came to fruition. Thereafter the living tradition survived only in vernacular poetry, and Latin mythography was largely reduced to compendia of standardized allegorizations of myth which no longer bore any significant relation either to ancient poetry or to contemporary poetic practice.

Learned Mythography: Plato and Martianus Capella

With the rise of philosophy in ancient Greece, "the idea emerged that the soul is somehow akin to the stars and the sky, while the divine enters into more and more direct relations with the cosmos" (Burkert 1985, 199). The definitive representation of this view was the *Timaeus*, the one Platonic dialogue known to early medieval Europe. In Plato's cosmogony cosmos and man are living, rational beings, each informed by a divine soul. The "gods" are heavenly bodies distinct from the Olympian gods, though they will be fused allegorically by Hellenistic writers, as in the Stoic cosmology outlined, with frequent reference to mythology, in Cicero's *De natura deorum*. Stoic mythography and the synthesizing labors of Neoplatonist scholars carried forward the ancient tradition of reading the myths of Homer and Hesiod allegorically as vehicles of profound knowledge (Buffière 1956, 9–31; Pépin 1958, 85–124). Calcidius, to whose partial translation and commentary medieval scholars owed their knowledge of the *Timaeus*, refers several times to Homer's scientific knowledge (Lamberton 1986, 250–56). Vergil is similarly idealized in Macrobius's *Saturnalia* and the commentary of Servius. Servius's exposition of the "deep learning" of *Aeneid* 6 and Macrobius's commentary on Cicero's *Somnium Scipionis* (c. 430) established the Neoplatonic myth of the soul—its divine origin, its descent into the "prison" of the body, its post-bodily return to the realm of the undying—as a fundamental theme of great literature. Macrobius's definition of the *narratio fabulosa* in his commentary on the *Somnium Scipionis* solemnized the mythical ancestry and deeds of the gods as presenting sacred truths in allegorical form (*sub pio figmentorum velamine*), while dismissing as beneath consideration tales which show the gods guilty of wickedness or immorality (*Commentarii* 1.2.10–11). This distinction between profoundly meaningful and merely impious myth was perhaps an act of deference to the famous strictures of Plato's Socrates (*Republic* 377–82); it was not strictly observed by Macrobius himself, and would prove difficult to maintain.

The *Timaeus* defines the scope of serious mythography and many of its major themes. The dialogue is continually cited in Macrobius's commentary on the *Somnium Scipionis*. A brilliant poetic distillation of the Timaean cosmology is the centerpiece of Boethius's *Consolation of Philosophy* (3, metr. 9), and this poem was frequently glossed in the early medieval period (Troncarelli 1981). From the *Timaeus*, as mediated by these *auctores*, the Middle Ages learned a distinctively Platonic conception of myth and its function: myths need not be borrowed from the poets, but can be created for a philosophical purpose "to translate the truths of intellect into sensible terms" (Pépin 1958, 118–21).

Thus the poetic and "philosophical" uses of myth were perceived as largely complementary. But before proceeding to the medieval period we must consider the text most immediately responsible for ensuring that perception, the *De nuptiis Philologiae et Mercurii* of Martianus Capella (late fifth century).

The *De nuptiis* is a manual of the Liberal Arts prefaced by an allegorical narrative of the quest of Mercury, or eloquence, for a bride; the election of Philology, or earthly knowledge, as his mate; and the preparation of the bride for marriage through an initiation into divine wisdom. The overarching theme, announced in the opening poetic address to Hymen, is marriage, understood as including the interaction of the agents of cosmic order, and the correspondences between the paradigms and symbolic languages of earthly knowledge and the universal principles they express. A host of classical deities are encountered and described in terms of their attributes and cosmic functions. Philology's ascent to knowledge of the causes of things, and ultimately to a vision of "that truth which exists by virtue of powers beyond existence" (*De nuptiis* 2.206), provides the occasion for a thorough review of the organization of knowledge and its relation to the order of the universe.

Martianus's self-consciously learned style is seasoned with a pedantic humor which, without excluding moments of real beauty and religious feeling, prevents our taking its mystical aspect too seriously. It is the work of a teacher, and might be described as commentary turned inside-out. The theme of human life as an intellectual and spiritual journey, for Macrobius and earlier Neoplatonists latent in virtually all epic poetry, itself becomes Martianus's "fabulous narrative," and his treatment of the gods is similarly schematic. Cosmology and mythology are precisely correlated, and mythographical analysis involves no more than translation from one set of terms to the other. Under Martianus's influence, the Olympian gods, the Muses, and other mythical beings would descend to the medieval schools invested with a rich orthodoxy of cosmological, pedagogical, and ethical associations.

The importance of Martianus as model is clear if we compare the *De nuptiis* with the *Mitologiae* of Fulgentius (early sixth century), where the traditional tendency to treat meaning as virtually independent of authorial intention reaches its logical extreme. The *Mitologiae* offer a series of allegorical readings of myth in which its doctrinal content is expounded *in vacuo*, without reference to text or system. Moralization, euhemerism, contrived etymologies and vestiges of Stoic and Neoplatonic mythography are presented simply as alternative and occasionally contradictory possibilities, in no order and with no perceptible emphasis. Myth is an occasion for exercises in allegorizing; "meaning" has become wholly independent of context.

Nonetheless the *Mitologiae* would enjoy great respect and a long life; Fulgentius's glosses provided a repertory of basic prompts for more probing analyses by later commentators, and his exotic vocabulary, with its uncertain grasp of Greek terms and etymologies gleaned from Martianus, Servius, and the scholia, is still alive in the astronomy and divine mythology of the *Carmina Burana*. Equally long-lived was Fulgentius's *Expositio* of Vergil, a reading of the first six books of the *Aeneid* as a progression from birth through youth to the attainment of learning and a knowledge of God and human destiny.

The early medieval centuries produced no real literary criticism. Carolingian court poets compose skillful imitations of Vergil and Ovid, and Theodulf of Orleans discusses the rudiments of mythography (Godman 1985, 168–71), but the glosses of John Scotus Eriugena (810–77) on Martianus's *De nuptiis* are perhaps the first instance of a medieval reader approaching an ancient text in full awareness, both of the errors to which its pagan Platonism gives rise, and of all that it can nonetheless offer to the Christian scholar. Eriugena saw a profound connection between philosophical and Christian studies: a deliberate and crucial misreading of the Pseudo-Dionysius enabled him to assert that the Liberal Arts are not only fundamental for understanding Scripture, but immanent in human nature and symbolic of Christ (*In Ier. coel.* 1.540–68; 2.124–58; Roques 1975, 45–98). To gain knowledge of the Arts is to discover divine wisdom latent in oneself. The *De nuptiis* affirms this, for the immortalizing of Philology represents the return of the soul to its true home through a self-realization made possible by the Arts (Eriugena 1939, 27).

This responsiveness to both Platonism and poetry, and Eriugena's great respect for the *ingenium acutissimum* of Martianus, appear plainly in his readings of Martianus's mythology. When Martianus, describing the gifts bestowed on Psyche, the human soul, speaks of Sophia-Minerva's gift of the "speculum Aniae" (*Uraniae*; Shanzer 1986, 73), Eriugena, guided by a dubious Greek etymology and a sensitive appreciation of Martianus's purpose, discovers in the mirror a reflection of "the natural dignity and primordial fountain" of the human soul (Eriugena 1939, 12). Vulcan, whose gift of "unquenchably enduring fires" is balanced against Venus's infusion of the pleasurable itch of lust, becomes, in the light of what Eriugena calls "higher natural theory," a figure of the *ingenium* or natural orientation present in all rational beings, which keeps alive the memory of their original dignity and its divine source (Eriugena 1939, 13).

Virtually every feature of Eriugena's engagement with Martianus reappears, along with a renewal of interest in cosmological questions, in the twelfth century. Much has been made of the twelfth-century "renaissance" and the discovery of man and nature by the group of scholars connected in various ways with the cathedral school at Chartres. These scholars pursued their investigations in a scientific spirit and produced new kinds of knowledge, but much of their work remained a kind of literary criticism. The *Timaeus*, which continued to frame their investigations, was by its own account a literary text, a "likely story" of the nature of things, and engaging it philosophically required penetrating its mythic surface. The *ornatus elementorum* must be read like a text; the philosophy of nature "involves and embodies a transcendent form of rhetoric" (Cadden 1995, 10).

Study of the *Timaeus* generated reflection on the role of mythic or figurative elements in other authors, along with "integumental" reading of a broader range of myth. William of Conches, glossing Macrobius, meets head-on that author's strictures on the use of myth in philosophy. Fables of divine violence or sexual intrigue can harbor a "beautiful and honorable" meaning, as he demonstrates by explaining the "true" significance of the myths of Jove and Semele and the castration of Caelus by Saturn. Commenting on Macrobius's association of "fabulous narrative" with religious ceremony, William imagines a pagan priest expounding the meaning of the winnowing-fan in the temple of Bacchus: as Bacchus, dismembered by the

Giants and placed in the winnowing-fan, reappeared wholly restored on the third day, so the soul is subjected to a winnowing which purges it of fleshly contamination. William has borrowed from Servius's gloss on the "mystic fan of Iacchus" (*Georgics* 1.166) and Calcidius's on the fan image in *Timaeus* 52e; concerned only with the meaning latent in non-Christian myth, he significantly ignores the obvious Christian associations of the violation and resurrection he describes (Dronke 1974, 21–23).

William's glosses on Boethius's *Consolation* are largely concerned with its psychological complexity. The tone is set in his gloss on the *lacerae Camenae* of the opening elegy: "They are 'wounded' because they tear apart men's hearts and render them inconstant by recalling pleasure or sorrow to the memory, rather than guiding or consoling" (William of Conches 1999, 10). Reading Boethius's lyric of Orpheus and Eurydice (*Cons.* 3. m. 12), he speaks of "a certain god called a 'genius' who is born with each of us.... This genius is our natural desire. It is rightly called Eurydice or 'judgment regarding good' because each of us desires what he judges to be good whether it is truly so or not" (William of Conches 1999, 201). But Eurydice is coltish and intractable, and Orpheus, the philosopher, powerless to extricate his mind from its involvement with her, comes to resemble the prisoner of the opening book, whose heart is torn by the faithless Muses of memory and lost joys.

William's confidence in the underlying integrity of what he considers authentic myth enables him to practice a kind of archetypal criticism, in a serious attempt to demonstrate how a particular myth could plausibly generate philosophical meaning. A gloss on the god Hymenaeus, in a fragmentary commentary on Martianus which almost certainly reproduces William's teaching, provides an unusually full illustration of the faith in the integrity of myth that this criticism requires.

The commentator summarizes Hymenaeus's mythical role, then explains the function of the physical hymen. The mythic and the physiological come together in an account of how Hymenaeus prepares for the procreative union of the bridal chamber, and his parents, Bacchus and either "Camena" (as in Martianus's proem) or Venus, are glossed as figures of the desire and "proportionate commingling" necessary to procreation. A comparison of this proportionality to that of the elements, which constitute the universe at large, introduces an extended gloss *secundum philosophiam*. Here Hymenaeus stands for the larger force that encompasses and informs all mutual loves, identified first as the Boethian love that rules the earth, sea, and heavens, then as the effect of "the holy spirit which infuses a certain ardor of charity into all things," and finally as the activity of the world soul (Dronke 1974, 114–15).

Whatever implications of Christian pantheism or sexual mysticism such a passage may harbor, its importance is in the plausibility of the chain of associations it forms between Martianus's mythic imagery and what William sees as the true substance of Martianus's narrative. Both the strengths and the limitations of his criticism are reflected in two commentaries clearly written under his influence, and clearly by a single author, on Vergil and Martianus. The earlier of these, ascribed in one late manuscript to Bernardus Silvestris, reads the first six books of the *Aeneid* as an allegory of "what the human soul, placed for a time in a human body, achieves and undergoes" (Jones and Jones 1977, 3), emphasizing Aeneas's growth in philosophical and spiritual understanding, and reworking Fulgentius's tracing of the hero's passage from youth to maturity in the light of Macrobius's conception of the poet as a Neoplatonist sage. The commentary breaks off as Aeneas and the Sibyl approach Elysium, the point at which, "the visible universe having been traversed, it remains to explore the invisible" (Jones and Jones 1977, 114). His reading of the *Aeneid* is mainly a compilation from earlier commentators and mythographers, harmonized and occasionally elaborated to conform to his allegory of philosophical education. But like the work of Fulgentius, its interpretative model of the *Aeneid* enjoyed a long life, and left its mark on the *Inferno*.

The Martianus commentary explores Martianus's mythic imagery with an intuitive boldness more like William's, and conveys a similar sense of engaging the archetypal aspect of the text, though in a less probing way. The *accessus* includes a precise distinction between two kinds of *involucrum*: *allegoria*, the figural mode proper to Scripture, and *integumentum*, the mode employed by philosophy. Each harbors a hidden meaning (*misterium occultum*), and they are two ways of expressing truth (Westra 1986, 45–46). In a gloss on Martianus's opening paean to Hymenaeus, the "sacred bond" of cosmic marriage, whereby the divine unites with mortal life "just as mortal is united with divine in eternity," is compared to the bond whereby Pollux accepted mortal existence in order to confer immortality on his brother Castor, an act explained in effectively Christian terms: "the god underwent mortal death that he might confer his godhead upon mortality; for spirit dies temporally that flesh may live eternally" (Westra 1986, 64). Glossing Martianus's Vulcan as a figure of human *ingenium*, the commentator borrows a gloss by William on Vulcan's abortive pursuit of Pallas and develops it in virtually Pauline fashion, making him an image of fallen man, seemingly powerless to realize his aspirations or control his desires, though endowed with the capacity for vision, and perhaps, like the Vulcan of Eriugena's commentaries, subliminally aware of his original dignity and its divine origin (Westra 1986, 156–57). The presiding deities, Jove, Pallas, and Juno are explained as "mystical" (i.e., mythical) representations of *pater*, *nois*, and *anima mundi*, and both groupings are equated, with a directness which recalls the earlier pairing of *allegoria* and *integumentum*, to the Persons of the Christian Trinity (Westra 1986, 245–47).

The ease with which the anonymous commentator ignores distinctions between "pagan" and Christian terms, above all that between *anima mundi* and *spiritus sanctus*, which had aroused serious controversy when William had seemed to disregard it (Gregory 1955, 150–52), may indicate that commentary of this type was coming to be taken less seriously, regarded as literary rather than philosophical, as the twelfth century moved forward. Similarly reductive, as though adapted for less advanced students, is a comment in the *accessus* to the commentary which compares Martianus's *intentio* with Vergil's: "For just as in that poet's work Aeneas is led through the underworld attended by the Sibyl to meet Anchises, so Mercury here traverses the universe attended by Virtue, to reach the court of Jove. So also in the book *De Consolatione* Boethius ascends through false goods to the *summum bonum* guided by Philosophy." (Westra 1986, 47) Thus, the commentator concludes, these three *figurae* express virtually the same thing, reduced to a single paradigm in a context of quasi-spiritual but essentially pedagogical allegory.

The same tendency is present in the highly sophisticated treatise of the third of the Vatican Mythographers (Bode 1834), the so-called *Poetria*, attributed to Alberic of London and dated to the later twelfth century, though parts are older and may have been known to William and "Bernardus." Far more selective and coherent than earlier treatises of its kind, it brings together the myths associated with each of the major classical deities and the heroes Hercules and Perseus. Its review of the classical underworld includes what amounts to a treatise on the soul in the form of a commentary on several passages from Vergil (*Poetria* 3.6, 8–20), but its focus is almost exclusively literary. It quotes continually from the poets, reviews and compares the views of earlier commentators, and more than any work of the period gives the impression of having been conceived as a companion to the study of poetry. Its influence can be seen in the work of virtually all later mythographers.

The mid-twelfth century also produced a body of Latin poetry "learned" in its use of myth, and at times scarcely intelligible without a knowledge of Martianus and the commentators. One anonymous poet managed to produce a love lyric so faithful to Martianus's praise of Hymenaeus that it scarcely mentions human love:

> Omnis nexus elementorum
> legem blandam sentit amorum.
> sed Hymenaeus eorum
> iugalem ordinat torum
> votis allubescens deorum
> piorum.

[Every joining of the elements knows the sweet bond of love. But Hymen ordains the conjugal bed, favoring the wishes of the kindly gods.] (*Carmina Burana* 57)

The *Metamorphosis Goliae Episcopi* (Wright 1841) was written by someone close to the schools of central France in the early 1140s. It shows the ancient gods and prominent *magistri* of the day convening to celebrate the marriage of Philology and Mercury in a palace created and richly adorned with mythic and cosmological imagery, "totum sub involucro, totum sub figura," by Vulcan (45–52):

> Hic sorores pinxerat novem Heliconis,
> et coelestis circulos omnes regionis;
> et cum his et aliis eventum Adonis,
> et Gradivi vincula et suae Dionis.
> Ista domus locus est universitatis,
> res et rerum continens forma cum formatis,
> quas creator optimus, qui praeest creatis,
> fecit et disposuit, nutu bonitatis.

[Here Vulcan had depicted the nine sisters of Helicon, and all the spheres of the celestial region, and, amid these and other details, Adonis's fate, and the fettering of Mars and his Dione. This mansion is the seat of the universe, containing things and the forms of things with what is formed from them, which that best creator who exists beyond creation made and disposed as an expression of his goodness.]

The importance of the marriage is explained, and Philology is crowned. But the ceremony is interrupted by Silenus and a mob of satyrs, who usher in Venus and Cupid. Their appearance raises the question of the place of love in a universe ruled intellectually by Pallas, sponsor of the marriage: Pallas and Venus confront each other, and a dispute breaks out among their supporters. The poet offers four instances of the power of love borrowed from Martianus (161–64; cp. *De nupt.* 1. 4, 6, 7):

> Nexibus Cupidinis Psyche detinetur;
> Mars Nerinae coniugis ignibus torretur,
> Ianus ab Argyone disiungi veretur,
> Sol a prole Pronoes diligi meretur.

[Psyche is caught by the snares of Cupid; Mars is inflamed by his bride Nerina; Janus fears to be divided by Argione; Apollo earns the love of the daughter of Providence.]

The following stanza provides a gloss on each (165–68):

> Psyche per illecebras carnis captivatur;
> sors in Marte fluctuat, Nereus vagatur;
> opifex in opere suo gloriatur;
> quid fiat in posterum Deo scire datur.

[Psyche is captured by fleshly temptation; the fortunes of war shift; Nereus ebbs and flows; the maker rejoices in what he has made; what may one day come to pass is known only to God.]

Psyche's plight is plain enough, and those who know their Martianus will know that *Mantike* (Prophecy) is the daughter of Providence. But the trite glosses on Mars and "Nereus" are clearly makeshift; the poet did not know what to make of *Nerinae coniugis*. And the glorification of Janus and Argyone must have puzzled anyone unfamiliar with the "Bernardus Silvestris" commentary on Martianus, where "*Janus*, ille archetypus mundus, *miratur Argionem*, miratur sensilem speram" [Janus, the universal archetype, marvels at the sensible (i.e., material) world] (Westra 1986, 123).

We are somehow to understand that Pallas and Venus will engage in a debate. A host of witnesses appear: the great philosophers; ancient poets, each accompanied by his beloved; and contemporary scholars, many of them students or associates of Peter Abelard. But the debate never takes place. Philology laments that Abelard, her beloved protégé, is absent, provoking the schoolmen to inveigh against conniving monks, presumably the Cistercians William and Bernard, who caused Pope Innocent II to forbid Abelard to teach after the Council of Sens (1141). In the final stanzas the gods declare the monks forever banished from the schools.

Awkward and occasionally obscure, the *Metamorphosis* deals astutely with its mythological material. That Vulcan's divine *involucra* include his capture of Venus and Mars recalls the glosses of Eriugena, where he counters the force of Venus by preserving the memory of the soul's divine origin and a vestigial impulse to return home. The treatment of the high gods, if more discreet than that of the "Bernardus Silvestris" commentary, conveys a similar sense of transcendent significance: Jove may not be the *creator optimus* who exists beyond creation (51), though the poet hints that he represents something more than a cosmic power (66), but Pallas is explicitly the *mens altissimi divinitatis* (73–76), beyond our power to understand.

A lyric from the same period reopens the dispute which the *Metamorphosis* had left suspended. An opening description of the beauties of spring provokes satyrs to wanton merriment. Contention breaks out, and quickly turns to conflict (Dronke 1968, 367–69):

> 1b. Nunc contendunt
> Venus et Minerva.
> Pugnat Pallas egide
> proterva;
> clamat: Iovis me paterne
> serva!

2a. Tonat, prestat ille Parcas	2b. Iuvant partes Citharee
et decanas et tetrarchas,	Ceres, Bachus, natus
Musas ducit Stilbon Arcas,	Ree, omnes simul fere dee
anxiat Apollo.	adiuvant in bello.
3a. Bello fera dat innumera	3b. Terga dat plane
Venus vulnera;	pompa Diane,
tenet ethera,	capto Titane,
perimit Tartara.	teque, bifrons Iane.
4a. Fles tu, o dia	4b. casus Limitane.
Filologia,	Catenato Pane
flesque, Talia,	rides, Volicane.

[1b. Now Venus and Minerva clash. Pallas fights with her fearsome shield. She cries out "Father Jupiter, protect me!" 2a. He thunders, he reveals the Fates, and the decans and the tetrarchs; Arcadian Stilbon leads the Muses, Apollo is troubled. 2b. Ceres, Bacchus, and the son of Rhea help Cytherea's side; at once almost all the goddesses join the battle. 3a. Venus, fierce in war, inflicts countless wounds. She holds sway in heaven and ravages hell. 3b. Diana's host turns tail entirely once Titan is captured, and you, two-faced Janus. 4a. You weep, Goddess Philology, and you, Thalia, weep 4b. at the calamities of Diana. And you laugh, Vulcan, because Pan is chained.]

Cosmic order, represented by Pallas and Jove, is overthrown; Mercury and the Muses are powerless; Apollo foresees trouble; Philology weeps at the plight of chaste Diana. Venus's triumph seems complete.

In the final lines Pan is chained and Vulcan laughs. Whether we see Pan as simply lust or as the whole of Nature (William of Conches 1999, 109; *Mythographus tertius* = Bode 1834, 8.2), his capture by Vulcan suggests that Venus's ascendancy will not produce sheer anarchy. But Vulcan's role is ambiguous. As controller of lust, he recalls Vulcan the artist, creator of the cosmic palace of the *Metamorphosis Goliae*, the tutelary presence of Eriugena and "Bernardus Silvestris." But he is also Vulcan the husband of Venus, first person of the bourgeois trinity, and in this light his fettering of Pan, like his chaining of Venus and Mars, may remind us that the power of sensuality is capable of eluding his control and mocking his orientative impulse. In a lyric that seems closely related, but makes no mention of Vulcan, essentially the same scene is disrupted by Bacchus, Pan, and their followers, but order is restored by "the King, the Law, *opifex archetyporum*," and Mercury and Philology are duly married (Dronke 1968, 369–71).

The response of vernacular poets to the work of the Latin schools appears mainly in their adoption of the rhetorical precepts of the *artes poeticae*, but the *Roman d'Eneas* (c. 1160; *Eneas* 1925–29) incorporates one mythological pattern which recalls the texts we have been considering, centered on the arms forged for Aeneas by Vulcan at the instigation of Venus. As in the *Aeneid*, Venus gains her request by sexual means, and the poet adds that she has denied herself to Vulcan for seven years, angered by his exposure of her relations with Mars. After a digression to recall this episode, the poet describes the arms themselves, but omits the engraving on the hero's shield, which occupies nearly all of the corresponding passage in Vergil. Instead he tells the story of a standard affixed by Venus to the hero's lance (4524–36):

> [It had long been in the possession of Mars, and he had given it to her as a token when first she became his mistress...It was worth a hundred pieces of any other kind of cloth. Pallas had made it in a spirit of rivalry: she worked it with great skill when Arachne had provoked her...And because Arachne produced a superior piece of work, she changed her to a spider.]

The allusions to Ovidian tales which bracket the account of Vulcan's work illustrate the ambiguous relation of Vulcan and Pallas to the action of the *Eneas*, and, as in the Latin poems, suggest parallel subversions of the qualities associated with the two deities. Vulcan, responding to the *losengerie* of Venus, succumbs to the sensuality which in his nobler role he aims to control. Pallas, replying in kind to the *anvie* of Arachne, becomes involved in a web as complex as Arachne's. Their subversion is the *Eneas* poet's own ironic comment on the pattern of divine rivalry and animosity that overshadows the narrative of the *Aeneid*, and will be recalled again at the very conclusion of the Vergilian action, when the names of Vulcan and Pallas are again, as if fortuitously, juxtaposed. Eneas discovers the ring of the dead prince Pallas on the hand of Turnus (4523–27):

> ... sailli avant,
> se l'a feru de maintenant,
> o le branc que Vulcans forja
> an prist lo chief: Pallas vanja.

[He moved forward and struck him down at once. With the sword which Vulcan had forged he cut off his head. Thus he avenged Pallas.]

A possible link between the *Eneas* and the mythographic complex we have seen in the *Metamorphosis Goliae* and its lyric pendant is a well-known *Streitgedicht* clearly influenced by the *Metamorphosis*, the *Altercatio Phyllidis et Florae* (Bömer 1919), the first of many poetic debates on the relative merits of knights and clerics as lovers. When the two maidens decide to travel to the court of Cupid and present their dispute for his judgment, Flora, who speaks for the cleric, rides a magnificent stallion, a consummate expression of the creative zeal of Nature, crowned by an ivory saddle carved by Vulcan and adorned by Pallas/Minerva with beautifully woven fabrics (sts. 53–57). Vulcan's carving includes the marriage of Mercury, and the court of Cupid where Phyllis and Flora present their case is clearly modeled on the divine court appropriated from Martianus by the poet of the *Metamorphosis*. But it seems clear that the standards of the *Metamorphosis* have been compromised. Vulcan has laid aside the shield of Achilles to fashion Flora's saddle, and Minerva too has abandoned all other pursuits for this work (sts. 56–57). Like the *Eneas* poet's substitution of the spear and its standard for Vergil's great shield as the centerpiece of the arming of Eneas, this removes us from the world of epic to a lesser, courtly world whose values are treated with a less than tragic irony. At court the maidens find a Cupid surrounded by drunken satyrs and attended by "Graces" who administer his drinking cup; he quickly refers the matter to *usus* and *natura* who decide in favor of the cleric.

The *Altercatio* leaves us at an impossible distance from the world where Vulcan forges the shields of heroes; and the *Eneas*, too, after its reductive version of the Vergilian finale, wholly abandons its epic model. Within twenty lines Eneas has named his wedding day, and the poem turns to the anxieties of a very Ovidian Lavine, as visible and vocal as her Vergilian counterpart had been silent and remote.

A New Mythology: Nature and Genius

During the later 1140s appeared the *Cosmographia* of Bernardus Silvestris, a new mythic cosmogony in the spirit of the *Timaeus*, written in the prosimetrum form of the *De nuptiis*, and in a richly allusive style which synthesizes Martianus, the Hermetic *Asclepius*, Eriugena, and other models.

The *Cosmographia* virtually ignores traditional mythology. The first of its two books, *Megacosmus*, reaches beyond the gods to reimagine the work of the divine *Noys*, the shaping of *hyle* or unformed matter, and the infusion into the created world of its vital principle, *endelechia*, the *anima mundi*. In *Microcosmus*, the second book, *Urania*, at the behest of *Natura*, unites a soul provided by *Noys* to a body fashioned from the four elements by *Physis* to create man, the lesser universe.

In Bernardus's universe, where Platonic principles have displaced the gods, Nature, ceaselessly concerned with the continuation and well-being of universal life, assumes the role of heroine. The *Cosmographia* opens with her passionate appeal to Noys on behalf of matter, which yearns to be endowed with form, and her voice echoes many others: in Claudian's *De raptu Proserpinae*, for example, Jupiter recreates for the gods the ceaseless complaints of Nature at the sorry state of a humankind deprived of agriculture (3.33–45); she recalls as well Vergil's Venus, beseeching Jove to grant rest to her son and his Trojan followers; and the abandoned lovers of Ovid's *Heroides*. Nature voices a desire which remains constant in the *Cosmographia*, where human life is both modeled on and starkly contrasted to the orderly cycles of the universe at large, a constant struggle to withstand the effects of passion and error. The complement to Nature is the "Genius" figure, who appears in several forms in the *Cosmographia*. When Nature ascends through the spheres to seek Urania, who will provide man's soul, she encounters a Genius whose office is to "compose and assign the forms of all creatures," and it is he who brings them together, uniting natural understanding with the power that imparts both form and, as in Martianus, knowledge of man's divine origin. And at the poem's conclusion the description of the newly created human body includes a vivid account of the work of twin Genii who govern the work of the male genitalia (2.14.157–64):

> Cum morte invicti pugnant genialibus armis:
> Naturam reparant, perpetuantque genus.

[They fight unconquered against death with life-giving weapons, renew our nature and perpetuate our kind.]

In Bernardus's new, more existential mythology, Noys, Nature, and Genius effectively displace the Pallas and Vulcan of the *Metamorphosis Goliae*. In another *Streitgedicht*, the *Altercatio Ganymedis et Helenae* (Lenzen 1972), the case is judged in what is still vestigially Martianus's court of Jove, but by new authorities:

> 12 Iovis in palacio genetrix Natura
> De secreta cogitat rerum genitura;
> Ilem multifaria vestiens figura...

[In Jove's palace procreating Nature plans the mysterious generation of things, clothing matter in many different shapes...]

Once the excitement of the Olympian gods at the arrival of the litigants has been calmed, judgment is passed in favor of Nature, Helen and heterosexual, procreative love.

In the *De planctu Naturae* of Alan of Lille (Häring 1978), the gods return, but only as a topic in the long dialogue of Nature and the unhappy poet, with whose lament over mankind's abandonment of heterosexual love the poem begins. As Nature seeks to explain the proper relation of humanity to the natural order and the human failings which have caused a divorce between them, the poet interrupts to ask why humanity alone should be censured, when poetry shows the gods, too, pursuing homosexual love. After her Macrobian dismissal of such stories has failed to satisfy him, Nature attempts to distinguish Cupid's "original" nature, intimately linked with her own, from a new, perversely cupidinous desire which she can only explain by resorting to the same deceitful mythology she has urged the poet to repudiate, and explaining that Venus has committed adultery with "Antigenius" and given birth to "Jocus," a perverse counterpart to Cupid.

In the final scene, the true Genius appears; he combines the roles of Bernardus's cosmic and sexual Genii and Nature honors him as her "priest." Together they recall a time when love was pure, though neither recognizes it as the prelapsarian state of humanity. Genius pronounces excommunication on all who reject the sexual behavior Nature prescribes, but it is clear that the problem is beyond Nature's power to resolve. In Alan's second major poem, the *Anticlaudianus*, an epic account of the creation of a new man who, with divine aid, renews mankind and restores the natural order, sexual desire is present only as a vice, and the traditional gods are reduced to conventional labels, cited mainly to identify the planets that bear their names.

Aetas Ovidiana

Though other works of Ovid were known in the Carolingian period, the *Metamorphoses* descended to the Middle Ages unaccompanied by a tradition of ancient scholia, and early manuscripts are very rare (Hexter 1987, 69–78). The charming tenth-century Eclogue of "Theodulus" contains a surprising number of echoes of the *Metamorphoses*, but the first major step forward is marked by the poetry of Baudri of Bourgueil (1046–1130). (Otter elsewhere in the volume references debate about the date of the *Ecloga Theoduli*.) Baudri knew the full Ovidian corpus, and is probably the first medieval poet to have attempted to emulate the grandeur of the *Metamorphoses*. In a long poem addressed to Countess Adela of Blois, the Countess's bedchamber becomes an eleventh-century encyclopedia (*Carmen* 134). Silken hangings are adorned with an Ovidian account of the creation, panoramas of world history, pagan and biblical, and a lengthy account of the conquest of England by William, the father of Countess Adela. The ceiling displays the order of the heavens, the pavement that of the natural world, and statues of the Liberal Arts as described by Martianus surround the bed. Cumbersome and formulaic, the poem nonetheless includes such Ovidian touches as that whereby the work of embroidering maidens overseen by Adela is imperceptibly transformed into that of cosmic powers governed by the supreme *Opifex* (103–8). Its very grandiosity reveals a new awareness of the potential capacities of poetry, as it seeks to integrate the role of Ovid the celebrant of urban-courtly culture with a gesture toward the totalizing ambition of the poet of the *Metamorphoses*.

A second long poem is a series of allegorizings of myth based on Fulgentius's *Mitologiae*. These are largely pedestrian, but Baudri seems to see in his project something like the program that Marie de France will announce in the Prologue to her *Lais* (154, 651–52):

> Credo, uiuit adhuc nobiscum fabula lecta;
> Viuit enim quidquid fabula significat.

> [When a fable is read among us, I believe, it still lives; for whatever the fable signifies gives it life.]

A similar sense of the great tradition emerges in Baudri's one startlingly original allegorization: Fulgentius had glossed "Pegasus" as *fons aeternus*; Baudri merges the fountain Hippocrene, brought forth by Pegasus's hoof and sacred to the Muses, with the fount of living water offered by Jesus to the Samaritan woman (154, 1075–78):

> Hec immortales hauserunt flumina uates,
> Hoc uiuunt magni flumine philosophi.
> Non patitur uiuos hec unda perire poetas;
> Hec est quam semper non sitiens sitiat.

> [The immortal bards have drunk these waters; it is from this stream that the great philosophers draw life. This spring grants poets an imperishable life. For this one may always thirst yet feel no thirst.]

In southern Germany in the early twelfth century appears perhaps the first critical engagement with Ovid's masterpiece. A commentary evidently based on the teaching of Manegold of Lautenbach introduces the *Metamorphoses* as the work of a monotheist, explaining Ovid's outward polytheism as a political necessity, and viewing such metamorphoses as Jove's reduction to a lustful bull as signs of his scorn for the pagan gods. Ovid's cosmogony displays the Platonist trinity of "Good" (*togaton*, i.e., *to agathon*), "Mind" (*Nous*), and "World Soul" (*anima mundi*), and the "better nature" of *Metamorphoses* 1.21 is "the will of God, the son of god" (Meiser 1885, 50–52). As in even the most sophisticated later commentaries, there is no attempt to engage Ovid's irony; the *Metamorphoses* aims to instruct by pleasing ("delectare et delectando tamen mores instruere"), and its *utilitas* is in the many gracefully told fables it makes available.

A single Tegernsee manuscript offers a clerk-poet's carefully anonymous advice to nuns concerning the poet who speaks of the loves of the gods through "the metaphor of changing forms" (Dronke 1968, 232–38, 452–63). This mock-sermon moves from censure of divine lust and its corrupting influence to a reading in which such *mystica fabula* becomes inspirational: clerks and nuns can emulate the unions of gods and goddesses. ("Cum deliramus, ea numina significamus!" (72) [when we rave, we represent the gods]. The gods' descents into the world are also meaningful. Jove's begetting of Hercules is treated with a religious solemnity (51–54): Three days were required "that conception might be recognized as more glorious, and heavenly seed be bestowed to creating something so great, such a progeny" (52–54).

The poet dwells at length on Ovid's cosmology. Cosmic harmony can draw us away from the erratic and violent world, inspiring pure thoughts of transcendence, yet its vitality infuses our wills with a lustful energy we cannot control. And it is finally this, the uncertainty of our situation amid the complex of cosmic forces, that myth represents:

> quicquid in hec operantur,
> Ex quibus omne genus rerum constare videmus,
> Quod sapis et sentis, quod ab his fit et ex elementis,
> Hoc opus istorum coitum dixere deorum.

[whatever has influence on those forces through which every kind of created thing has life that you know and feel, that comes to be through them and from the elements—this great work, men said, was the sexual union of the gods.]

Whether we hear in it the ostentatiously cynical *magister amoris* or an affirmation of the unity between earthly and heavenly love (Dronke 1968, 236), the poem makes plain with remarkable prescience the liability of myth to manipulation by a virtuoso interpreter when the dogmas of traditional criticism are set aside. There will clearly be no reducing the *Metamorphoses* to a Neoplatonic Bildungsroman, and the Tegernsee poet provides a distant foreshadowing of the subversion of all such projects by Jean de Meun.

These two Ovidiana are isolated phenomena. For most of the twelfth century awareness of the *Metamorphoses* appears mainly in *pseudo-antike* school poetry on Ovidian themes, chiefly tales of human lovers (Lehmann 1927; Faral 1936, 115–17). But the poem itself continued to be regarded with a certain mistrust, and seems always to have existed in an uneasy relation to the curriculum of the schools. At length its complexities were subjected to methodical treatment in the *Allegoriae super Ovidii Metamorphosin* of Arnulf of Orleans (c. 1170; Ghisalberti 1932) and the *Integumenta Ovidii* of John of Garland (c. 1134; John of Garland 1933).

Arnulf had strong ties to the tradition of William of Conches; his commentary on Lucan deals at length with the philosophical background of the *Pharsalia*. John, too, though by his time the humanism of the twelfth-century schools had suffered the defeat reported in the *Bataille des vii ars* of Henri d'Andeli (c. 1240), saw himself as the embattled defender of the literary standards of an earlier time. But by providing Fulgentian guides to the *Metamorphoses* they effectively neutralized its poetic qualities, and under their influence mythography ceased to be in dialogue with the poetry it was ostensibly intended to explain.

Arnulf's *accessus* adopts the cosmic analogy of the *Timaeus* to explain metamorphosis; Ovid's representations of moral elevation or degeneration correspond to "the stability of heavenly things and the changeableness of things on earth" (Ghisalberti 1932, 181). In practice his reading is less coherent. He briefly considers other types of metamorphosis: natural (the combining or dissolution of the elements), "spiritual" (loss or recovery of sanity), and magical. Stories read in these varied terms and those read euhemeristically far outnumber those treated as images of moral transformation. Many interpretations are based, not on Ovid, but on the mythographers, or are drawn from commentary on other authors. Repeatedly, the metamorphosis on which an Ovidian story turns is ignored, rationalized, or reduced to the status of an emblem. Thus Europa was abducted by Jupiter, king of Crete, in a boat named "the Bull" or with a bull painted on its prow; Iphis at first behaved like a woman, but afterwards like a man; sailors took on board not Bacchus, but wine; they were not turned to fish, but became drunk and fell overboard.

John's *Integumenta Ovidii* provide theoretical discussions of metamorphosis and allegory, a description of the physical universe, and allegorizations of the entire *Metamorphoses* in 260 terse elegiac couplets. Like Arnulf's *Allegoriae* (on which they largely depend), the *Integumenta* begin with gestures toward a Platonist reading, but they too reduce transformation to metaphor and emblem, and give scant attention to the particulars of Ovid's poem. As for Arnulf, the *Metamorphoses* are reduced to a mythographic compendium.

The allegorizations of Arnulf and John became a standard feature of *Metamorphoses* manuscripts. They provide much of the allegorical material in the so-called Vulgate commentary compiled in central France around 1250 (Coulson 1987). But they remain something other than commentary, which as Dante says must be either servant or master of its text; Ovid's poem is the mere occasion for their common project.

Arnulf and John brought traditional mythography into wider circulation than ever before, but it would be difficult to show that they significantly influenced literary creation. In the continuation of the *Roman de la Rose* by Jean de Meun, a shrewd student of twelfth-century humanism, the reduction of mythography to allegory and moral euphemism has become a joke. *Raison*, seeking to draw the effete lover out of his unproductive preoccupation with *amors*, refers him to the *integumanz aus poetes* to explain her reference to the castration of Saturn (*Rose* 7123–50), but allegory cannot withstand a growing materialism that will dismantle the delicate courtly world of Guillaume de Lorris and muster the forces of desire in full armor. In response to the mythographic dilemma faced by Nature in Alan's *De planctu naturae*, Jean's Nature will send forth her priest Genius to urge this army forward to besiege the castle that holds the Rose, convinced that in doing so they will be recovering their prelapsarian dignity. Two Ovidian figures represent the poles of the lover's situation: Narcissus, his early adolescent suspension; Pygmalion, the transformative power of active desire which will lead to the winning of the Rose. Both are emblems, but emblems charged with the psychological complexity lacking in the allegories of Arnulf and John.

Dante's use of Ovid, as of classical poetry generally, is remarkably unaffected by the commentary tradition. Metamorphosis is a fundamental and constantly recurring motif in the three *cantiche* of the *Commedia*, and Ovid is allowed to be ethically and psychologically profound on his own terms. It is not hard to imagine a commentary on Dante's poem that would actually follow the guidelines of an *accessus* not unlike that of Arnulf.

The *Fulgentius metaforalis* of John Ridevall (c. 1330; Ridevall 1926) introduces an important reorientation of mythography in that its explicit purpose is to adapt the *Mitologiae* of Fulgentius to the purposes of the preacher (Smalley 1960, 110–13). Earlier mythographers, including Fulgentius and the Third Vatican Mythographer, had spoken of the traditional attributes of the gods and goddesses as "painted" by the ancient poets, and Ridevall develops this idea systematically, first identifying the chief Olympian gods with virtues, then compiling their traditional attributes in the form of mnemonic verses, then imagining paintings of the gods that illustrate these attributes, which then become the texts for extended homilies filled with material from Christian authors. Illuminators proved unable to produce satisfactory counterparts to Ridevall's imaginings (Ridevall 1926, pl. 1–15), but later mythographers followed Ridevall in prefacing their treatises with descriptions of the images of the gods.

After Ridevall, mythography will be largely directed to the needs of the preacher, and the *Fulgentius metaforalis* is as utterly dissociated from poetry, ancient or modern, as the *Mitologiae* of Fulgentius himself. But another significant change occurred with the appearance of a vernacular text, the *Ovide moralisé* (1316–28; ed. 1915–38), whose 72,000 octosyllables incorporate a full translation of the *Metamorphoses* and a double commentary, "historical" and allegorical. The poet will not attempt to fully explain every myth (1.53–55):

> Mes les mutacions des fables
> qui sont bones et profitables
> Se Dieus me l'otroie, esclorrai.
>
> [But if God is willing, I will set forth the transformations of the fables, which are good and profitable.]

It is the *mutacions*, not the *fables*, which are good and profitable. As told, *grossement*, by Ovid, the tales are lies, and the failure to recognize them as such is dangerous (15.2525–31, 2552–57). But in the hands of the French poet they prefigure biblical history, the lives of Christ and the Virgin, the Sacraments and Christian doctrine.

But while Ovid's intention as author appears to count for little in the *Ovide*, basing a work so explicitly Christian in its concerns on a fully rendered pagan text—in effect, giving the *Metamorphoses* the status of the Hebrew Bible—is an extraordinary gesture. And despite the poet's obligatory dismissal, Ovid's poem is treated with the utmost respect. The translation abbreviates and amplifies, and incorporates myth and legend from other classical and postclassical sources, but it is accurate and often remarkably sensitive in rendering the details of Ovid's metamorphoses: Acteon's human awareness of becoming a stag (3.468–89); Iphis's becoming male in both body and mind (9.3082–95); Lycaon's body adapting to his wolfish character (1.1371–88). When the poet inserts the term *martire* into his account of the sufferings of an Oedipus or Acteon, or suggests that *vertu divine* transformed Daphne and saved her from the relentless desire of Apollo, he is not only preparing for the Christian allegory to come, but showing himself aware of Ovid's own deep sympathy with his human characters.

The *Ovide* is also a remarkable poem in its own right, one whose riches we are only beginning to appreciate. It is rich in borrowings from the *romans d'antiquité*, Chrétien, and the *Roman de la Rose*, and reproduces their style as well. Far from a dogged moralist, the *Ovide* poet is "un veritable conteur" (Possamaï-Pérez 2006, 235–56) whose poem is a virtual *summa* of romance in the classical tradition, an artist who takes pleasure in his art. His portraits of Callisto, Europa, and even Pasiphaë are finely wrought, and he can pursue a narrative for its own sake without regard to its future allegorization: savage Achilles resurfaces as Christ, noble Hector as Satan (12.4092–145; 4184–268).

The poet of the *Ovide* was almost certainly a Franciscan, and certainly had an audience of preachers in mind (Possamaï-Pérez 2006, 726–30). This is clearly the case with the *Ovidius moralizatus* of Pierre Bersuire (1340, 1350–62; Ghisalberti 1933a), which draws on Ridevall and the Third Vatican Mythographer, and found the initial impetus for its introductory description of the "forms and figures" of the gods in the *Africa* of Bersuire's friend Petrarch (*Africa* 3.138–264). In its final form, Bersuire's treatise follows the pattern of the *Ovide* and acknowledges its indebtedness to the *volumen gallicum*, though it exhibits none of the French poet's appreciation of the *Metamorphoses* as poetry, and offers only brief summaries of Ovid's tales as the basis for its allegories.

Bersuire views interpretation as a test of *ingenium*, what can be "adduced" or "affirmed" (*potest allegari*) about a text (Hexter 1989, 66–68), and his address to his fellow religious (*karissimi*) is full of little urgings to exercise a similar inventiveness ("dicas," "vel si vis dic," "vel verte folium et dic," "applica si vis"). His justification for this use of the *Metamorphoses* is a highly dubious reading of 1 Timothy 4:1 in which "the teachings of demons" become "fables," enabling him to compare their moralization to the similar treatment of such biblical fables as Jotham's tale of the trees seeking to choose a king in Judges 9 (Ghisalberti 1933a, 87–88).

Bersuire's moralized Ovid circulated widely, and became sufficiently notorious to be banned by the Counter-Reformation Church in 1559 (Gillespie 2005, 206). But the *Ovide* is the fundamental work. A literary *summa*, it is also a *summa* of mythology, and it was so regarded by poets and scholars alike. As such it performed a double task. By providing a full and appreciative rendering of the *Metamorphoses*, while maintaining a clear distinction between that text and the interpretative *mutacion* to which he would subject it, the *Ovide* poet released Ovid's great poem from the commentary tradition of Arnulf and John of Garland. And by making a major classical text the basis for a poetic commentary unprecedented in scope and explicitness of doctrine, with full respect for the ancient text but following the poet's own inspired *ingenium*, he made mythography available to a range of new purposes.

I have said nothing about the Italian mythographic tradition, which followed a separate path from that of northern Europe. A convenient starting point for considering its development is the work of Giovanni del Virgilio, classical scholar and friend of Dante, who lectured on classical poetry at Bologna in 1322–23 and apparently produced his *Allegorie* on the *Metamorphoses* at this time (Ghisalberti 1933b,

4–8). Giovanni employs both prose and verse, borrowing from but often correcting Arnulf and John, frequently substituting his own allegorizations, and interpolating occasional Christian readings. But whatever cultural exchanges may have taken place at the papal court in Avignon, Giovanni's sophisticated commentary, like the works of Dante (with whom Giovanni engaged in a learned correspondence; see Witt in this volume) and the *Genealogiae deorum gentilium* of Boccaccio, seem to have been virtually unknown outside of Italy. Only in the fifteenth century would the achievements of the *trecento* cross the Alps.

SUGGESTIONS FOR FURTHER READING

There exists no comprehensive and reliable history of medieval mythography, but the following specialist studies may provide a general view. Lamberton (1986), primarily concerned with ancient critics of Homer, includes chapters on the Latin tradition and its medieval versions. Demats (1973) studies medieval readings of Ovid as illustrating the development of medieval mythography. On this subject see also Hexter (1987). Dronke (1974) studies the twelfth-century assimilation of ancient theories of myth. On the place of mythography in medieval literary studies, see Wetherbee (2005) and Gillespie (2005).

BIBLIOGRAPHY

Primary sources

Baudri of Bourgueil. 2002. *Carmina*, edited by Jean Yves Tilliette. Vol. 2 (poems 134–256). Auteurs latins du Moyen âge. Paris: Les Belles Lettres.
Bernardus Silvestris, 1978. *Cosmographia*, edited by Peter Dronke. Textus minores 53. Leiden: Brill.
Bode, Georg Heinrich, ed. 1834. "Mythographus Tertius." In *Scriptores Rerum Mythicarum Latini Tres Romae nuper reperti*, 152–256. Celle: E. H. C. Schulze. Reprint, Hildesheim: Georg Olms, 1968.
Bömer, Aloys, ed. 1919. "Das vagantenlied von Phyllis und Flora nach einer niederschrift des ausgehenden 12. jahrhunderts." *Zeitschrift für deutsches Altertum* 56: 217–39.
Eneas. 1925–29. *Eneas*, edited by Jean-Jacques Salverda de Grave. 2 vols. Paris: Honoré Champion.
Fulgentius. 1898. *Opera*, edited by Rudolf Halm. Leipzig: Teubner.
Godman, Peter, ed. 1985. *Poetry of the Carolingian Renaissance*. Norman, OK: University of Oklahoma Press.
Häring, Nikolaus, ed. 1978. "Alanus ab Insulis, De planctu Naturae." *Studi medievali* 19: 797–879.
John Scotus Eriugena. 1939. *Annotationes in Marcianum*, edited by Cora E. Lutz. Cambridge, MA: Medieval Academy of America.
———. 1975. *Expositiones in Ierarchiam coelestem*, edited by Jeanne Barbet. Corpus Christianorum. Continuatio Medievalis 31. Turnhout: Brepols.

John of Garland. 1933. *Integumenta Ovidii*, edited by Fausto Ghisalberti. Messina: Principato.

Jones, Julian W. and Elizabeth F. Jones, eds. 1977. *The Commentary on the First Six Books of the* Aeneid *of Vergil Commonly Attributed to Bernardus Silvestris*. Lincoln, NE: University of Nebraska Press.

Ovide moralisé. 1915–38. *Ovide moralisé*, edited by Cornelis de Boer. 5 vols. Verhandelingen der Koninklijke Akademie van Wetenschappen te Amsterdam. Afdeeling Letterkunde. Nieuwe reeks 15, 21, 30 no. 3, 37, 43. Amsterdam: J. Müller etc.

Kulcsár, Péter, ed. 1987. *Mythographi Vaticani. I et II*. Corpus Christianorum. Series Latina 91C. Turnhout: Brepols.

Lenzen, Rudolf, ed. 1972. "'Altercatio Ganimedis et Helene'—Kritische Edition mit Kommentar." *Mittellateinisches Jahrbuch* 7: 161–86.

Macrobius. 1963. *Commentarii in Somnium Scipionis*, edited by James Willis. Leipzig: Teubner.

Martianus Capella. 1983. *De nuptiis Philologiae et Mercurii*, edited by James Willis. Leipzig: Teubner.

Ridevall, Joannes. 1926. *Fulgentius metaforalis*, edited by Hans Liebeschütz. Studien der Bibliothek Warburg 4. Leipzig: Teubner.

Westra, Haijo Jan, ed. 1986. *The Commentary on Martianus Capella's* De Nuptiis Philologiae et Mercurii *attributed to Bernardus Silvestris*. Toronto: Pontifical Institute of Mediaeval Studies.

William of Conches. 1999. *Glosae super Boetium*, edited by Lodi Nauta. Corpus Christianorum. Continuatio Mediaevalis 158. Turnhout: Brepols.

Wright, Thomas, ed. 1841. "Metamorphosis Goliae Episcopi." In *Latin Poems Commonly Attributed to Walter Mapes*, edited by Thomas Wright, 21–30. London: J. B. Nichols.

Secondary sources

Buffière, Félix. 1956. *Les mythes d'Homère et la pensée grecque*. Études anciennes. Série grecque 11. Paris: Les Belles Lettres.

Burkert, Walter. 1985. *Greek Religion*. Cambridge, MA: Harvard University Press.

Cadden, Joan. 1995. "Science and Rhetoric in the Middle Ages: The Natural Philosophy of William of Conches." *Journal of the History of Ideas* 56: 1–28.

Coulson, Frank T. 1987. "The Vulgate Commentary on Ovid's *Metamorphoses*." *Mediaevalia* 13: 29–61.

Demats, Paule. 1973. *Fabula: Trois études de mythographie antique et médiévale*. Publications romanes et françaises 122. Geneva: Librairie Droz.

Dronke, Peter. 1968. *Medieval Latin and the Rise of European Love-Lyric*. 2nd ed. 2 vols. Oxford: Oxford University Press.

———. 1974. *Fabula: Explorations into the Uses of Medieval Platonism*. Mittellateinische Studien und Texte 9. Leiden: Brill.

Faral, Edmond. 1936. "Le manuscrit 511 du 'Hunterian Museum' de Glasgow." *Studi medievali* 9: 18–119.

Ghisalberti, Fausto, ed. 1932. "Arnolfo d'Orleans, un cultore di Ovidio nel secolo XII." *Memorie del Reale Istituto Lombardo di Scienze e Lettere. Classe di Lettere* 24: 157–234.

———, ed. 1933a. "L'Ovidius moralizatus di Pierre Bersuire." *Studi romanzi* 23: 5–133.

———. 1933b. "Giovanni del Virgilio espositore delle *Metamorfosi*." *Giornale dantesco* 34: 1–110.

Gillespie, Vincent. 2005. "The Study of Classical Authors: From the twelfth century to c. 1450." In *The Cambridge History of Literary Criticism*. Vol. 2: *The Middle Ages*, edited by Alastair J. Minnis and Ian Johnson, 145–235. Cambridge: Cambridge University Press.

Gregory, Tullio. 1955. *Anima mundi. Guglielmo di Conches e la scuola di Chartres*. Florence: Sansoni.

Hexter, Ralph J. 1987. "Medieval Articulations of Ovid's *Metamorphoses*: From Lactantian Segmentation to Arnulfian Allegory." *Mediaevalia* 13: 63–82.

———. 1989. "The *Allegari* of Pierre Bersuire: Interpretation and the *Reductorium Morale*." *Allegorica* 10: 51–84.

Lamberton, Robert. 1986. *Homer the Theologian: Neoplatonist Allegorical Reading and the Growth of the Epic Tradition*. Berkeley, CA: University of California Press.

Lehmann, Paul. 1927. *Pseudo-antike Literatur des Mittelalters*. Leipzig: Teubner.

Meiser, Karl. 1885. "Über einen Commentar zu den Metamorphosen des Ovid." *Sitzungsberichte der Königlichen bayerischen Akademie der Wissenschaften. Philosophisch-philologische und historische Classe* [1885]: 47–89.

Pépin, Jean. 1958. *Mythe et allégorie: les Origines grecques et les contestations judéo-chrétiennes*. Paris: Études augustiniennes.

Possamaï-Pérez, Marylène. 2006. *L'Ovide moralisé. Essai d'interprétation*. Paris: Honoré Champion.

Roques, René. 1975. *Libres sentiers vers l'érigénisme*. Lessico Intellettuale Europeo 9. Rome: Edizioni dell'Ateneo.

Shanzer, Danuta. 1986. *A Philosophical and Literary Commentary on Martianus Capella's De Nuptiis Philologiae et Mercurii Book 1*. University of California Publications. Classical Studies 32. Berkeley, CA: University of California Press.

Smalley, Beryl. 1960. *English Friars and Antiquity in the Early Fourteenth Century*. Oxford: Blackwell.

Wetherbee, Winthrop. 2005. "The Study of Classical Authors: From late Antiquity to the twelfth century." In *The Cambridge History of Literary Criticism*. Vol. 2: *The Middle Ages*, edited by Alastair J. Minnis and Ian Johnson, 99–144. Cambridge: Cambridge University Press.

CHAPTER 17

BIBLICAL THEMATICS: THE STORY OF SAMSON IN MEDIEVAL LITERARY DISCOURSE

GRETI DINKOVA-BRUUN

It is impossible to present the influence of the Bible on medieval literary discourse comprehensively in a single short essay. The Bible was practically ubiquitous in medieval writing, shaping arguments and providing inspiration for a variety of literary endeavors, from commentaries and sermons to biblical epic and versification, historical accounts, and liturgical reenactments. Seen as an encyclopedia of divine and human knowledge, the Bible was understood to contain undeniable truths about the entire world and the meaning of human existence. It was a guide of faith, a testimony of history, a record of geography, a code of moral conduct. It explained the meaning of the past, influenced the experience of the present, and shaped expectations for the future. Because of the central role it played in the lives of all medieval men and women, the Bible was studied and taught, interpreted and memorized, versified and dramatized. This multifaceted flurry of activity reveals that Holy Scripture was indeed the heart and soul of medieval literary life; it is also our key to understanding many, if not most, of the complexities of medieval literary expression.

In order to exemplify the various modes of biblical discourse in medieval Latinate culture, I concentrate in this essay on one biblical story, the life and death of the Old Testament hero Samson. Since a comprehensive survey even of the literature dependent on this one biblical episode is clearly impossible, a few representative medieval works here illustrate the multifaceted role the Bible played in medieval literary imagination. These works can be divided into two groups: first, prose texts which interpret the Bible for either scholarly or preaching purposes; and second, biblical poetry which comprises a large variety of verse compositions, from narrative versifications to liturgical pieces to poetic expressions of devotion and piety. These poetic compositions are all inspired by the Bible but in unique and often surprising ways. It is worth stressing, however, that there is no sharp divide between the two groups of texts as outlined above.

The wondrous life of Samson is told in Judges 13–16. This relatively straightforward but dramatic story was read and understood differently during the Middle Ages: as a historical account, as a Christological allegory and typology, as a cautionary tale for moral behavior. In each of these interpretative modes the Bible had a different meaning and encouraged a multilayered intellectual involvement with its text. The four senses of scripture (literal, allegorical, tropological, and anagogical) are fully embraced and internalized by medieval readers of Holy Scripture in their search for truth, wisdom, and complete understanding of the Word of God (de Lubac 1959; Smalley 1983; Evans 1984; Dahan 1999; Dahan 2009, among many others). A clear definition of these four senses is found in a teacher's preface to Petrus Riga's famous biblical versification, the *Aurora*:

> Est autem historia quasi quedam testis temporum, lux ueritatis, magistra uite, uita memorie, nuntia uetustatis. Allegoria est misticus sensus qui fit in littera de Christo et ecclesia. Quedam bona allegorie species est anagoge. Inter hanc autem et illam distinguitur, quod allegoria dicitur misticus sensus pertinens ad militantem ecclesiam, anagoge uero misticus sensus pertinens ad triumphantem ecclesiam uel Dei Trinitatem. Tropologia est sermo conuersus ad edificationem anime et bonorum morum informationem.
>
> [History is, so to speak, the witness of the times, the light of truth, the teacher of life, the life of memory, the herald of antiquity. Allegory is the mystical sense, which is found in the letter referring to Christ and the Church. A positive type of allegory is called anagogy. The difference between allegory and anagogy is that allegory is the mystical sense referring to the militant Church, while anagogy is the mystical sense referring to the triumphant Church or God's Trinity. Tropology is a discourse intended for the edification of the soul and the formation of good morals.] (Petrus Riga 1965, 1.6: 43–50)

Here I will not discuss in much detail the reading of the Bible as history *ad litteram*, even though this first level of discernment reveals the medieval preoccupation with the time continuum as preordained by God and constitutes the required scholarly preparation for uncovering the deeper significance of Sacred Scripture. Among the biblical histories that enjoyed a vast popularity during the Middle Ages are the Latin translations of the *Antiquitates Iudaicae* and the *De bello Iudaico* by Flavius Josephus (37–ca. 100 CE), and the *Historia Scholastica* by Petrus Comestor (d. 1179). For countless medieval exegetes the literal understanding of the Bible was only the starting point in the path to true enlightenment, an intellectual attitude epitomized in Paul's famous words: "littera enim occidit, Spiritus autem vivificat" [the letter kills but the spirit gives life] (2 Cor 3:6). The meaning of this statement and the basic methods of medieval biblical interpretation are explained by Gregory the Great (540–604) in the preface to his treatise *Moralia in Job*:

> Sciendum uero est, quod quaedam historica expositione transcurrimus et per allegoriam quaedam typica inuestigatione perscrutamur, quaedam per sola allegoricae moralitatis instrumenta discutimus, nonnulla autem per cuncta simul sollicitius exquirentes tripliciter indagamus. Nam primum quidem fundamenta historiae ponimus; deinde per significationem typicam in arcem fidei fabricam mentis erigimus; ad extremum quoque per moralitatis gratiam, quasi superducto aedificium colore uestimus. Vel certe quid ueritatis dicta nisi reficiendae mentis alimenta credenda sunt?.

> [But let it be known that some parts we go through in a historical exposition, some we examine through allegory in a figurative investigation, some we discuss through the exclusive use of moral teaching, conveyed allegorically, while there are some other parts which we investigate with more particular care in all these ways together, exploring them in a threefold method. For first, we lay the historical foundations; next, by pursuing the figurative sense, we erect the fabric of the mind into a citadel of faith; and finally, by the grace of moral instruction, we, as it were, clothe this edifice with additional embellishment. For surely, what are the words of truth if not food for the refreshment of the mind?] (Gregorius Magnus 1979, 4: 106–15)

Without undermining the importance of the literal sense to the understanding of the biblical message, it becomes apparent that the central tenet in the medieval Latin hermeneutic engagement with the Bible is the belief that the Old Testament (as it came to be called by Christians) must be understood as a prefigural allegory for the coming of Christ and his Church. The spiritual layers of biblical signification are exemplified brilliantly in two medieval works: the *Quaestiones in Vetus Testamentum* by the Spanish encyclopedist and bishop Isidore of Seville (d. 636) and the fourth homily for Palm Sunday by Abbot Gottfried (d. 1165), founder of the renowned "school of Admont" in Central Europe. (Gottfried's authorship of the sermons published in vol. 174 of the *Patrologia Latina* was questioned by Borgehammer 1993, who proposes as author Gottfried's brother Irimbert. For an illuminating essay on the history of Admont's library holdings, see Stammberger 2005.) Isidore's text is an exegetical treatise directed to scholars, while Gottfried's composition is a sermon for delivery to a congregation; in both, the meaning of Samson's story is not only elevated above the mere recitation of glorious deeds performed by a long-dead hero, but also transformed into a tale of cosmic significance.

One thing is certain when one reads the two works in question: nothing is what it seems to be. At the literal level, Samson is a mighty defender of his people and a tragic victim of treachery and deceit; allegorically, he is Christ. Isidore's text is basically a summary of the most popular typological connections between the two heroes advanced by previous patristic scholars. Thus it presents all major events in Christ's incarnation as prefigured in Samson's tragic yet glorious life. The inventiveness of this typological analysis is worth presenting in detail.

Samson's birth is announced by an angel; so is the birth of Jesus. Both men are called Nazaraeus and both are described as "sol" [the sun] because of the crucial role they play in the lives of their people. Samson kills the lion; Jesus defeats the devil. By destroying the temple of Dagon, Samson exterminates many enemies; by shattering the temple of his body, Christ snatches many nonbelievers from the grave of infidelity. Even Samson's hair has a deep significance; it is Christ's grace. When Samson loses his locks, a sinner loses Christ's grace, but when Samson's hair regrows, the sinner has repented and has been forgiven by our gracious Lord. Finally, a typology of gender is also proposed: the man (Samson) signifies reason, while the woman (Delilah) denotes flesh, lust, and deceit (see Isidore 1850). Isidore's exegetical analysis was adopted in its entirety by Hrabanus Maurus (d. 856) in his *Commentaria in Librum Iudicum* and partially in the eleventh-century biblical glossing enterprise known as the *Glossa Ordinaria*.

To a modern reader these connections might seem strange and arbitrary. Not so to the medieval audience. The Christian covenant was believed to have superseded the Jewish one; the blindness of the Jews and their limited understanding of Scripture was often belabored in Christian writings; the Old Testament was seen as the letter of the law, whose true meaning could be uncovered only through its fulfillment in the New Testament. Or, in the words of Alexander of Ashby (d. 1208/14), who explains this in the prologue to his *Breuissima comprehensio historiarum*:

> Hoc credunt Iudei et tamen in tenebris sunt quia a fide incarnacionis Christi, sine qua salus esse non potest, et a mistici intellectus lumine alieni existunt. Procedunt quidem ad audiendam uocem Moysi, sed eius faciem sensus moralis et allegorici lumine choruscantem intueri refugiunt.
>
> [The Jews believe this, but still live in darkness, because they exist alienated both from the belief in the incarnation of Christ, without which there can be no salvation, and from the light of mystical understanding. They continue to hear the voice of Moses, but fail to see his face shining with the light of the moral and allegorical sense.] (Alexander of Ashby 2004, 6–7, 36–40)

As an example of performative rhetoric, Gottfried of Admont's sermon for Palm Sunday paints a more dramatic and emotional picture than does Isidore's scholarly prose. Gottfried concentrates on the final episodes in Samson's life, in which the hero brings destruction upon himself as a result of his foolish love for Delilah (various exegetical approaches to Judges 16 are outlined in Dahan 2004). Gottfried wrote as many as five sermons for Palm Sunday, all inspired by passages from the Old Testament which could be read *mystice* as prefiguring Christ's passion and his triumphant victory over death.

Within this liturgical frame the abbot from Admont strives to make the story of the ancient judge of Israel relevant to the Christian sensibilities of his listeners. The mystical parallels drawn by Gottfried are complex indeed. He is not satisfied with simply establishing the typological relationship between Samson and Christ; for him, this seems to be an obvious association. Instead, Gottfried moves to the level of tropology, that is, to edification of the soul and spiritual instruction.

Gottfried starts by calling the literal Samson *verus Samson* and *Samson noster* in order to link him with the Savior. After establishing the connection between the two heroes he presents an array of striking examples to strengthen the bond further. One can read the entire story of Christ's life in the Samson narrative in the Book of Judges: the incarnation, the passion, the harrowing of Hell, and finally the resurrection. For example, Samson being bound by seven fresh bowstrings signifies Christ being born into the world and strapped down by his human nature (*natus et ligatus humana natura*). When Samson snaps effortlessly, first, the seven bowstrings (Jgs 16:9) and, then, the new ropes (Jgs 16:12), this is understood as a prefiguration of two events: first, the sacrament of Christ's passion, through which he breaks the chains of both original and actual sin, and second, Christ's descent to Hell, which shatters the chains of punishment by saving the elect and leaving the doomed to their tragic fate. The supernatural strength needed for the accomplishment of these deeds is underscored by Gottfried through a multiple repetition of words for "breaking, smashing, and shattering":

> In prima *ruptione*, qua Christus *rumpebatur* in corpore suo per passionem et mortem, *rupta sunt* uincula peccatorum; in secunda *ruptione*, qua anima eius descendit ad inferos, *rupta sunt* uincula poenarum. Qui mystice dicitur *rupisse* uincula.
>
> [In the first breaking, in which Christ was broken in his body by his passion and death, the chains of sins were shattered; in the second breaking, in which his soul descended to Hell, the chains of punishment were smashed. So, when it is said that he 'broke the chains', this statement has to be understood mystically.]
> (Gottfried of Admont 1854, 279B)

In addition, Christ's suffering on the cross is foretold by Samson standing between the two columns in the temple of Dagon, because the two columns are actually the two arms of the cross (*duo cornua crucis*) upon which the body of the Savior was stretched out and suspended. Finally, Christ's glorious resurrection is prophesied in Samson's waking up from his sleep and pulling free his seven locks from the pin and the web with which Delilah had bound them together (Jgs 16:14). These seven locks should not be seen as regular hair; they stand for the blessed soul of Christ (*beata anima Christi*), which abounds with countless virtues after being filled with the sevenfold grace of the Holy Spirit. The moment Samson's hair is removed, all good intentions, devout thoughts, and divine meditations leave the human heart.

As with his hair, Samson's eyes are also imbued with rich symbolism. When the Philistines succeed in blinding their feared enemy, Christ also loses his sight. And we need to be aware of the fact that the eyes of the Savior signify three different pairs of people: first, the Jews and the gentiles; then, Adam and Eve; and finally, Peter and Judas. Or, in Gottfried's own words:

> Duo oculi Iesu duo erant populi, Iudaei et gentes. Duo oculi eius Adam et Eua siue duo oculi Petrus et Iudas. Duo oculi eius Adam et Eua euulsi sunt, quando Adam, qui dexter oculus Dei erat, peccare in paradiso non extimuit. Erutus est ei sinister oculus Eua, dum quae pridem rectis luminibus ad Deum respexerat, ad sinistram serpenti obaudiendo respexit. Amisit oculum dextrum, quando Petrus

in uoce ostiariae ter illum negauit; amisit sinistrum, quando Iudas, qui tradidit illum, laqueo sese suspendit.

[The two eyes of Jesus were two peoples, the Jews and the gentiles. They are also Adam and Eve or Peter and Judas. His two eyes Adam and Eve were gouged out when Adam, who was the right eye of God, was not afraid to commit sin in paradise (Gn 3:6). His left eye, Eve, was gouged out for him when she, who previously was looking at God with eyes turned to the right, looked to the left after listening to the serpent (Gn 3:1–5). Jesus lost his right eye when Peter denied him three times in the voice of the woman who guarded the gate (Mt 26:69–74; Mk 14:66–71; Lk 22:55–60; Jn 18:17). He lost his left eye when Judas, who betrayed him, hanged himself (Mt 27:5).] (Gottfried of Admont 1854, 284B)

In all of the examples presented above we can see the numerous and multifaceted ways in which Samson can be seen as a type of Christ. And yet this is not all. Gottfried presents even more surprising prefigurative links in the figure of Delilah. We saw in Isidore's text that she was presented as a typical symbol of womanly evils, carnal desire, and treachery. Yet, in Gottfried's discussion Delilah's portrayal is much more nuanced. In the very beginning of the sermon we are told that she has to be understood as representing *omnis natura humana*, that is, human nature in its full complexity. This statement opens up a wealth of exegetical possibilities that are often unexpected for the modern reader.

Because she is a personification of the human soul, with its contradictory impulses and conflicting desires, Gottfried's Delilah is simultaneously good *and* evil, Virgin Mary *and* Eve, Ecclesia *and* Synagoga. She is Eve when she is lured by the Philistines (or the evil spirits) to betray Samson (Jgs 16:5). Thus, the cunning Philistine in Sorek signifies the deceiving serpent in paradise; both the Philistine and the snake are in fact the devil. In contrast, Delilah is Mary, the blessed Mother of God, when she begs Samson for the fourth time to tell her his secret and he finally does so (Jgs 16:16–17). Delilah's persistence in this instance can be compared to Mary's when she begs her son for the kiss of love (Sg 1:1). The more she pleads with him, the more he envelops her in the delicate scent of his affection. All of this leads to the conclusion that Delilah must be seen as the bride of Christ and a symbol of his all-encompassing Church, which from the very beginning seeks to understand where his unsurpassed strength is hidden. But Delilah is also the Synagogue when she refuses to believe in the Savior and calls the Philistines to seize and bind him, even though he had opened his heart to her (Jgs 16:18). For that reason, she is a symbol of the Jews who capture Jesus and tie him to the cross (a detailed discussion of Delilah as a figure of the Synagogue is found in Dahan 1988).

Gottfried's complex understanding of Delilah's character gives him the opportunity to present a moral lesson to his listeners. Delilah is really an image of all of us who both love Christ in our souls and betray him in our flesh. How many times have we promised to be faithful to him and how many times have we been seduced by evil spirits and have failed to keep our promises? It is easy to turn against a reprobate, not so easy to look into our own hearts and admit to our own transgressions:

Multi nostrum Dalilam istam propter malitiam suam detestamur. Sed si nosipsos intueamur, quod illa semel uisibiliter Samsoni fecit, nos Samsoni nostro Christo frequenter fecisse et quotidie, proh dolor!, agere negare non possumus. O quotiens post dulcia oscula et foedera amoris eius ipsum abiicimus et a nobis repellimus, Philisthaeos, hoc est malignos spiritus, aduocantes eis superiorem locum damus, ad decipiendum et perdendum in cordibus nostris amatorem animae nostrae multas impietatum machinationes construimus!

[Many of us curse this Delilah because of her malice. But if we look at ourselves, (we will realize) that what she clearly did to Samson once, we, alas, cannot refrain from doing to our Samson, that is Christ, frequently and every day. How many times, after kisses and tokens of love, we cast him off and push him away; or, invoking the Philistines, that is the evil spirits, we grant them a higher station; or create numerous impious intrigues for deceiving and destroying in our hearts the lover of our soul!] (Gottfried of Admont 1854, 287BC)

In the end, insists Gottfried, we must remember that God loves us, flawed and imperfect as we are, just like Delilah whom he also loved. And because of this compassionate love we will be forgiven if we suffer and die with the Lord so that we might be resurrected with him and reign by his side in heaven for eternity.

The discussion above makes it apparent that the biblical text, as understood by its medieval readers, is an intricate system of interconnected meanings. Various, often contradictory, typologies are not only masterfully interwoven in Gottfried's sermon but also stretched over the entire span of human history, from Adam and Eve to the day of the second coming of Christ and the general resurrection. The real focal point of these past and future events, furthermore, is the moment of the sermon's delivery when the audience is made to understand its own place in the drama of human existence. Gottfried's sermon, only one among countless examples of how the Bible was read in the Middle Ages, treats even a single episode from Holy Scripture as containing everything a Christian needs to know about history, faith, and morality.

Poetic Retelling of the Bible

Biblical commentaries are the main source of exegetical ideas for the biblical poets, but while the commentators and preachers, as we saw, strive to elucidate the various meanings of the biblical narrative, the versifiers seek to make their insights more easily accessible to a wider audience of readers, whether students, monks, or lay congregations. Latin biblical versification from its beginning in late antiquity to its apogee in the twelfth and the thirteenth centuries represents a most fruitful amalgamation of exegetical wisdom, didactic purpose, and poetic inspiration.

Jean-Yves Tilliette elsewhere in this handbook points out the close linkage of medieval intellectual pursuit to poetic expression. This is to say that an astonishing variety of medieval verse compositions are dedicated to topics that might not immediately be regarded as "poetic": grammar, canon law, biblical exegesis, mineralogy, martyrology, flora, fauna, and science are only a few that need to be mentioned here. The majority of these poems were composed with didactic and mnemonic purposes, as we are repeatedly told in the works' prefaces. The usefulness of *sermo metricus* was indisputable for the medieval reader; its brevity, orderliness, and melodic rhythm helped the mind, pleased the intellect, and delighted the soul. Young and old, unschooled and learned, students and masters could all profit from it (Dinkova-Bruun 2008; Dinkova-Bruun 2010).

Biblical versification, sometimes also called biblical epic, is a poetic genre with a long history. Starting in late antiquity, Christian poets faced the problem of how to reconcile in their poetry the fluidity of poetic convention with the immutability of scriptural truth. Their answers to this question varied according to the poets' cultural milieu and poetic sensibilities. In late antiquity, poets such as Juvencus, Avitus, Sedulius, and Arator wrote biblical epics in order to express the significance of the Christian message in a poetic form, which their contemporaries considered the high point of literary sophistication (Green 2006). In the subsequent periods, when the social and cultural context changed fundamentally, the biblical versifiers were not concerned with converting unbelievers. Their aims were to use the universal appeal of poetry both to help the memorization of the vast new biblical scholarship and to facilitate understanding of the complexity of scriptural truth. Thus, numerous examples of biblical versifications in the later Middle Ages were written for purposes of teaching and memorizing, and it suffices to mention here the names of poets such as Hildebert of Le Mans, Lawrence of Durham, Alexander of Ashby, Leonius of Paris, Petrus Riga, and Guido Vicentinus, even though we should not forget that many pieces were composed also by anonymous authors (for an overview of the development of the genre, see Dinkova-Bruun 2007a).

So how do the medieval poets deal with the Samson story? It is immediately apparent that, since poetry is so closely defined not only by content but also by form, the treatment of any theme will vary accordingly. For example, an epigram and an epic are *a priori* imbued with very different poetic force that is not unrelated to the pieces' very different length. What a sweeping epic is able to portray is not what is captured by the few chosen lines of an epigram. Thus in poetry the dialectic relationship between meaning and form is always much stronger than in prose.

Among the smaller types of biblical verse, also called *tituli*, three representatives can serve here as examples: the *Tituli historiarum* (or *Dittochaeon*) of Aurelius Prudentius (d. ca. 413), the biblical epigrams of Hildebert of Le Mans (d. 1133), and the anonymous *Pictor in Carmine* (written probably in the late twelfth century). To these also the elusive *Ecloga Theoduli* can be added, for even though the eclogue is a long poem in its entirety (352 verses), each chosen biblical character is treated there in a quatrain of hexameters, an approach that is clearly inspired by the epigrammatic genre.

It is intriguing to observe how these short biblical compositions not only capture the essence of Samson's story but also succeed in placing it in entirely different intellectual contexts. Prudentius and Hildebert, even though separated by a number of centuries, exhibit a similar attitude towards the biblical text. Thus both poets include their short *tituli* on Samson in a larger collection of independent poetic pieces that aim to explicate the meaning of Scripture. Among Prudentius's 48 *tituli historiarum* we find two epigrams about Samson (Prudentius 1966, 393, nos. 17, 18). Especially interesting is the second one (no. 18), where Prudentius compares the episode of Samson setting on fire the fields of the Philistines by sending into them 300 burning foxes or jackals (Jgs 15:4–6) with the way the cunning fox, that is heresy, scatters flames of vice in the lands: "Sic calida uulpes || nunc heresis flammas uitiorum spargit in agros." It is clear that for Prudentius, who is writing in the late third or early fourth century, the problem of heretical movements within the Christian faith is a burning issue, which the poet illustrates compellingly with a burning story from the Old Testament.

Hildebert's four-line epigram entitled "Quid significat quod Sanson euerso templo in morte sua multos interfecit" [What it signifies that Samson slew many at his death when the temple was destroyed] underlines three key Christological parallels in the Samson story, all known from the treatise of Isidore previously discussed: first, Samson is Christ; second, the destruction of the temple of Dagon means the shattering of Christ's body; and third, the many enemies killed by Samson in his death prefigure all the faithful saved from vice after Christ's death (Hildebert 1985, 280, no. 8).

The anonymous *Pictor in Carmine* takes the established typological parallels between Samson and Christ to a new level. The various links between the two extraordinary men are expressed in crisp couplets (*bini uersus*) that could be employed as captions for images suitable for church decoration (*Pictor in Carmine* 2006, 110, 119–23). The work comprises 138 chapters or antitypes that represent events narrated in the New Testament. Each antitype is in turn elucidated by more than one type (or events of the Old Testament and rarely of the natural world), which is the reason why for the 138 antitypes we have as many as 510 types. In addition, each type is almost always illustrated by multiple hexameter distichs, amounting to about 6,000 verses. In this maze of types, antitypes, and descriptive couplets, there are multiple references to Samson: thirteen antitypes and types, within which we have thirty-nine distichs. All of them explicate Christological links well known from exegetical sources, but which have never been organized in such an ingenious way. To give one example, antitype CI entitled "Crucifigitur Christus" has seventeen explanatory types, among them one that relates to Samson called "Samson concussis duabus columpnis moritur et opprimit principes Philistinorum" [Samson with the collapse of the two columns dies and oppresses the chiefs of the Philistines] (Jgs 16:29–30). Under this typological rubric four *tituli*-couplets are presented in rapid succession (*Pictor in Carmine* 2006, 235, no. 14):

(1) Vi quatiens postes Samson ruit et necat hostes.
    Sic tua, Christe, reos mors in cruce uicit Hebreos.
(2) Gens datur erumpne duplicis sub mole columpne.
    Que perit est frendens plebs, qui quatit est cruce pendens.

(3) Fit mors Samsonis Gaze pressura colonis.
   Sic genus in laqueum crux Christi ducit Hebreum.
(4) Plures dum cecidit perimens quam quando cecidit
   Samson, ob mortem te, Christe, notat mage fortem.

[(1) Breaking the doorposts Samson falls and kills his enemies.
   Thus your death on the cross, Christ, conquered the guilty Jews.
(2) People are subjected to suffering under the heap of the two columns.
   He dies who is lamenting; he breaks the columns who hangs on the cross.
(3) Samson's death becomes affliction for the dwellers in Gaza.
   Thus Christ's cross puts the Jewish people in fetters.
(4) When he fell, Samson killed more people than when he was slaughtering them. In his death he denotes you, Christ, who are the mightiest.]

Even though they basically convey the same message, these four epigrams introduce different nuances. As paintings inspired by the same theme are nevertheless never identical, such is also the case with this "pictorial" poetry. By capturing subtle variations in the typology, the poet offers the artist a choice of verses that would best suit the tenor of his work.

In contrast with the texts discussed above, the *Ecloga Theoduli* provides a completely different context for the Samson narrative, which is for the first time detached from its Christological signification. The *Ecloga*, a typical example of a "Streitgedicht" or literary debate between opposing views (Walther 1920), pits Pseusis (Falsehood), which represents classical mythology, against Alithia (Truth), which defends Christian belief. In this context Samson is paired with Hercules, since each man is a symbol of bravery and a fighter for the good of his people. However, strong and invincible as they were, both heroes were in the end defeated by treacherous women, Deianira and Delilah (*Ecloga Theoduli* 1997, vv. 173–80).

After examining the minimalist creations of the epigrammatic genre, let us look at some of the more extensive biblical versifications that deal with the Samson narrative. The best examples here are the *Aurora* of Petrus Riga (d. 1209), the *Historie ueteris testamenti* of Leonius of Paris (d. after 1201), and the *Vetus Testamentum uersibus latinis* of Petrus Episcopus (d. 1219). In each of these ambitious compositions the story of Samson forms just one episode in the poetic fabric of the work. These versifications are of different length, as well as of varying focus. The least popular (preserved in only one manuscript) and the least original is Petrus Episcopus's *Vetus Testamentum* (Petrus Episcopus 1995). This composition, which in 4,058 hexameters deals with the biblical narrative from Genesis to Maccabees, is truly a versification, but not of the biblical text, as one might expect. Rather, it is a faithful verse rendition of Isidore's influential commentary on the Old Testament, the *Quaestiones in Vetus Testamentum*, discussed above. The story of Samson is told in forty-five unrhymed hexameters of somewhat unremarkable quality (vv. 3228–72). The typologies are enumerated one by one in the order in which they appear in Isidore's text and often in the same language. For example, the Isidorian passage "Vere enim hic sol iusticiae est qui omnium credentium mentes coelesti lumine clarificat. Hic vere Nazaraeus et sanctus Dei, in cuius similitudinem ille Nazaraeus est nuncupatus" [For truly, he is the sun of justice that illuminates the minds of all believers with celestial light. He truly is the Nazarite and saint of God, in whose similarity he is called Nazarene] (Isidore 1850, col. 389C) is versified by Petrus as follows: "Est sol iusticie, celesti lumine mentes/ credentum illustrans, Sanctusque Dei et Nazareus" [He is the sun of justice that brightens the minds of the believers with celestial light; he is the saint of God and a Nazarite] (vv. 3234–5). The wording is so similar that the reader realizes immediately that Petrus Episcopus is using the verse medium not for intrinsically poetic ends but to render Isidore's important treatise even more useful to the reader by turning it into its verse counterpart in a form potentially easier to memorize.

Leonius of Paris takes a different approach. Of his enormous *Historie ueteris testamenti*, which versifies the Octateuch in a staggering 14,065 hexameters, only small sections have ever been edited (Schmidt 2000 [Joseph and the wife of Potiphar, 143 vv.], Dinkova-Bruun 2005 [*Liber Ruth*, 259 vv.], Dinkova-Bruun 2009 [Cain and Abel, 100 vv.], and Dinkova-Bruun 2010 [the destruction of Sodom, 55 vv.]). Leonius's *Historie* is found in eight manuscripts, all of French origin. The poem is divided into twelve books, starting with a prologue and ending with an epilogue which mentions the poet's intentions of finishing the versification of the Old Testament in a second volume. However, such a codex has not yet been discovered. The tale of Samson is found in Book 12 of the *Historie*, just preceding Ruth. The account is 515 verses long, which is an impressive length when one considers the fact that the following Book of Ruth (also four biblical chapters like the Samson narrative) is versified in half that number of lines, 259. Another feature of Leonius's version of the Samson story, apart from its verbosity, is the total lack of allegory and typology. Leonius is truly a master of literal interpretation. His poem presents all minute twists and turns of the biblical account and then surpasses it by adding even more detail. The expansions are often subtle, providing motivation for the action, explaining away inconsistencies in the plot, and filling in gaps in the story. Occasionally, the presence of the poet is felt more acutely, especially in the instances when he decides to include his personal comments on the unfolding events. For example, in the beginning of his versification of Judges 16 Leonius cannot resist expressing his amazement that such a great hero as Samson could be defeated by foolish love and shameful lust (Biblioteca Apostolica Vaticana, Ms. Reg. Lat. 283, fol. 232v):

> Post tot tam pulcre tam gesta insigniter, immo
> Virtutis post tanta sue miracula Sanson
> Legis non timuit diuine turpiter esse
> Trangressor, posuitque illi quam feda libido,
> Incidit in laqueum meretricis captus amore.

> [After so many deeds performed beautifully and nobly,
> or rather after such great miracles of bravery,
> Samson was not afraid to shamelessly transgress
> the law of God: a horribly filthy lust descended upon him
> and, captivated by love, he fell into the snares of a prostitute.]

Leonius's approach to the biblical text, even though not unusual among the biblical exegetes, is rather unique among the biblical versifiers. His pronounced interest in the literal level of interpretation can be linked to the influence of the exegetical ideas of the scholars at the School of St. Victor in Paris for whom the understanding of the literal sense of the Bible was the necessary basis for any advanced study. As I have suggested elsewhere, Leonius, a Victorine himself, subscribes to this historical approach to the biblical narrative which aims at making the authority of Sacred Scripture even more profound and meaningful (Dinkova-Bruun 2009).

The last poet to be examined here is Petrus Riga, the most popular and the most remarkable of the three. His poem, the *Aurora*, comprises about 15,000 verses covering the historical books of both the Old and the New Testament. The popularity of Riga's *magnum opus* is witnessed by the fact that we still find it in over 450 manuscripts in libraries around the world. The poem was included in the medieval school curriculum, mined for examples by various lexicographers and grammarians, revised and commented upon by countless readers and teachers. In addition, it provided inspiration for numerous poetic imitations both in Latin and the vernacular. The impact of the *Aurora* on the medieval consciousness cannot be overstated (Petrus Riga 1965, 1: xxi–xlvii; Dinkova-Bruun 2007b).

What is fascinating in Riga's poem is that it deals with Samson's story twice: first, at the end of the *Liber Iudicum* where the reader would expect to find it (Petrus Riga 1965, 1: 241–43, vv. 254–324), and second, in the *Recapitulationes*, a book which Petrus wrote at a later stage and appended to his revised version of the *Aurora* (Petrus Riga 1965, 2: 616–17, vv. 275–302). The account in the *Liber Iudicum* is sixty-eight verses (or thirty-four elegiac couplets) long. It contains many of the Christological typologies which we know so well from Isidore and which were also at the heart of Petrus Episcopus's *Vetus Testamentum*, but here they are not versified in the same mechanical and uninspired way. Riga exhibits much higher poetic aspirations than his colleagues in both his rhetorical language and his carefully planned composition. The poet and the reader are both present in the story: the poet through an opening remark declaring that he will now turn his attention to the great Samson (*magnus Samson*), whose great triumphs will be described with a simple song (*tenui carmine magna loquens*, v. 258), and the reader, by being directly addressed by the poet and urged to consider carefully the holy words of the Bible (vv. 297–98). Samson's misfortune is indeed what happens to each and every one of us, for our flesh can so easily succumb to temptation. Thus the traditional interpretation of Delilah as evil is preserved by Riga. Samson is blinded and his hair is shaved off; we too are blinded by the blackness of sin and God's grace is snatched away from us (*gratia rapta tibi*, v. 304). However, if we repent in earnest, grace will make our hope for forgiveness increase like the hero's growing hair (*crescere spem uenie gratia prima facit*, v. 314). Finally, just as Samson conquers his enemies, so also we will triumph over the demons that constantly torment us (*sic ex demonibus multa trophea refers*, v. 320). Thus, Riga's versification of the Samson story clearly summarizes the traditional exegetical ideas developed by the poet's predecessors, but at the same time also succeeds in making Sacred Scripture relevant to the poet's contemporary readers by both issuing a warning against wickedness and providing hope for salvation. It is no wonder that the *Aurora* was such a popular work during the Middle Ages. Its text represents a skillful amalgamation of scholarly content, poetic mastery, and moral signification.

The sense of relevance for the reader is preserved also in the *Recapitulationes*, even though in this book Riga includes only an excerpt of twenty-eight verses from the original text dedicated to Samson. What is interesting, though, is what the poet does with these lines. Because the *Recapitulationes* is a lipogrammatic or letter-dropping poem, containing twenty-three sections, each missing one letter of the Latin alphabet, Riga had to revise his verses in order to make them suitable for the appropriate letter-missing divisions (Petrus Riga 1965, 1: xix). Samson's narrative is reworked for the last four lines of the "Sine M" section and for the entirety of "Sine N." It is fascinating to observe the ingenuity with which the poet succeeds in finding alternative ways to express the same idea and convey the same message while avoiding words that contained the letters "M" or "N". This is a virtuoso performance that probably was meant to make the reading and memorizing of a long list of biblical characters (which is what the *Recapitulationes* are) a bit more fun.

The various texts examined above, from the epigrammatic to the epic in length, have revealed that medieval biblical versifiers did not approach the text of the Bible mechanically. Sacred Scripture was their point of departure but also their font of inspiration.

Biblical *Planctus*

In addition to narrative biblical versifications, medieval biblical poetry comprises a vast number of devotional compositions, some of which were meant for use in the liturgy, while some others were clearly expressions of personal piety. From this vast corpus of poetry I have chosen to examine only the genre of the lament, or *planctus*, a poetic form that contains elements of both the lyrical and the dramatic and aims at channeling feelings of sorrow, anguish, and torment caused by the loss of a loved one. As such, it possesses universal appeal.

As a narrative whose entire meaning is defined by the most dramatic event in human history, i.e., Christ's sacrifice on the cross, the Bible is in itself a *planctus* of cosmic proportions. Within its all-encompassing frame, laments for various biblical personages were composed during the Middle Ages. The most notable is, however, the influential and often imitated *Planctus Mariae* that captures the suffering of Mary at the crucifixion of her beloved son (Sticca 1988).

Two *planctus* exist about our hero Samson. The first is written by Peter Abelard (d. 1142) and entitled *Planctus Israel super Samson*; the second is anonymous, composed in the thirteenth century and called *Planctus Samsonis*. Both place the hero in a new, emotionally charged context.

Abelard's lament over Samson is included in a series of six *planctus* in which various biblical personages mourn the tragic faith of people close to them. Thus, in addition to the Samson lament, we have the *Planctus Dine filie Iacob* (Dina laments the death of her lover Sichem), *Planctus Iacob super filios suos* (Joseph and Benjamin are the two sons in question), *Planctus uirginum Israel super filia Iepte Galadite*, *Planctus Dauid super Abner filio Ner quem Ioab occidit*, and *Planctus Dauid super Saul and Ionatha* (Vecchi 1951). The lament over Samson was examined by Peter Dronke (1986, 114–49), who outlines the structure of the poem and discusses in detail its misogynic second half, where Samson's ruin is compared to that of Adam, David, and Solomon. "Sinum aspidi || uel igni prius aperi, || quisquis sapis, || quam femineis || te conmittas illecebris [it is preferable to anyone to bare his breast to snakes and flames rather than to entrust himself to the wiles of a woman] is the sentiment expressed in the final verses of the *planctus*. It is worth noting here that even though the usual typological exegesis is missing from Abelard's lament, there is still a sense that the biblical narrative is clothed in mystery so deep that it is often difficult to comprehend its meaning (Otten 2007). The frustration of not always being able to grasp God's providential plan underlines Abelard's treatment of Samson. This is why the *planctus* starts with words of awe and despair (text and translation Dronke 1986, 121):

Abissus vere multa	Truly a great abyss
iudicia, deus, tua,	are your judgments, God,
eo plus formidanda	to be feared the more
quo magis sunt occulta	the more they are mysteries,
et quo plus est ad illa	the more that, faced with them,
quelibet vis infima!	all other strengths are weak!

The feelings of betrayal, suffering, and ultimate victory are captured more clearly in the thirteenth-century anonymous *planctus* printed in the *Analecta Hymnica*, 21: 169–71, no. 239. This lament is structured differently than the one by Abelard. It starts with two stanzas that ask a number of questions of the mighty biblical hero about why is he in jail and who was the one able to conquer him. The answer is also given: *fraus mulieris* [a woman's deception] betrayed the man who was in consequence taken, subdued, blinded, and tormented. After this introduction that sets the tone for the entire *planctus*, Samson personally gives a brief account of his life (stanzas 3–7): how he married a girl from among the Philistines, ate honey from the killed lion, destroyed the fields of the enemy, was given to the Philistines after slaughtering many of their compatriots with the jaw-bone, and was ambushed unsuccessfully by the citizens of Gaza. Then things started going wrong, because he fell in love with Delilah. Thus the first half of stanza 8 reads:

Post amavi Dalidam	Then I fell in love with Delilah,
Virginem pulcherrimam	a most beautiful maiden,
Corpore iuvenculam,	in body a young girl,
Fraudibus vulpeculam.	in deceitfulness a little fox.

The following seven stanzas (9–15) recast Delilah's repeated attempts to discover Samson's secret and her success at the end, while the last five (16–20) tell the story of the hero's captivity and self-sacrifice. The two final verses of the poem call Samson's death a great and glorious victory, thus linking him implicitly with Christ ("Pro tali victoria || Samson sit in gloria").

The two *planctus* discussed here enrich even further our insight into the multi-faceted meaning of the Samson story. If the biblical versifiers provided us with Christological typology, the lyrical laments give us human sentiment. Samson, the spiritual *figura*, has been transformed into Samson, the man of flesh and bone. His victory at the end is still applauded but we have been made aware of how much suffering that victory had caused the hero. This approach strips away from the story its traditional *allegoria* but definitely stretches wider its *littera*.

Biblical Parody

The last poem to be examined in this essay is the highly unconventional *Cena Cypriani* (edited from one manuscript, London, British Library, Harley 2773 in Doležalová 2007, 502–10) composed by John the Deacon in the ninth century on the basis of an earlier prose text with the same title written in late antiquity and attributed in the Middle Ages to Cyprianus Cecilius, the third-century bishop of Carthage. (This attribution is quite likely incorrect.) The genre of the piece is also a matter of debate but it is undeniable that the text shows a flair for the grotesque and the parodic. The original prose text and its medieval reception was studied recently by Lucie Doležalová, who outlines and attempts to solve many of the problems connected with this fascinating literary creation (Doležalová 2007). In addition to John's version, which is a very close rendition of the prose original, there are two late eleventh or early twelfth-century poems of the *Cena*: first, the so-called *Cena Azelini*, and second, the *Cena* of Codex Atrebatensis 557; both are fragmentary, even though lengthy (Modesto 1992; Mosetti Casaretto 2005). These poems are not examined here since they propose a different reorganization of the original and thus represent a completely different tradition in the reception history of the text.

So what is this *Cena* about, and how does Samson figure in it? The original *Cena*, as well as John the Deacon's verse rendition of it, describes a long wedding banquet in Cana of Galilee to which many biblical characters are invited. The host of the feast is "quidam rex nomine Iohel" [a certain king named Johel], the guests are numerous, the seating arrangements precise, the dishes lavish, the presents from and to the king numerous, and the amusements manifold. The only thing that disturbs the good cheer is the discovery on the second day of the feast that some precious objects have been stolen. As a result, the king orders that all guests be interrogated. Some are tortured, some are blinded, and some are killed, while others are just exiled or frightened. At the end, the only one who is blamed for the theft is

Camri's son Achan. Because of his crime, he is executed and buried. If this is a strange scenario to begin with, everything becomes even more unusual when the reader realizes that all of these events merely serve as pretext to provide lists of names of biblical personages who are paired with objects, locations, or actions that are strongly associated with them. As an example, here are the seating arrangements in John the Deacon's poetic version (Modesto 1992, 178–201, esp. 180, vv. 13–32):

> Adam pater sedit primus cunctorum in medium,
> Eua mater heu lasciua fici super folium,
> Et Cain super aratrum, Abel in mulctrarium,
> Super archam sedit Noe, Iafet super laterem,
> Isaac super altare, Abraham sub arbore,
> Iacob sedit supra petram et Loth secus hostium,
> Moyses super lapillos, Helias in pellibus,
> Daniel super tribunal, Tobias in lectulum,
> Beniamin sedit in saccum, Ioseph super modium,
> Ionathan in terram sedit, Dauid in monticulum,
> Pharao rex in arenam, Lazarus in tabulam,
> Zacheus in sicomorum, Iesus super puteum,
> Matheus sedit in scammum, Rebecca in ydriam,
> Thecla sedit in fenestra, Ruth in stuppa recubat,
> Susanna sedit in orto, in ramis Abessalon,
> Petrus sedit in cathedra, Iudas super loculum,
> Samson sedit in columpnas, super rete Iacobus,
> Heli senex super sellam, Rachel super sarcinam.
> Patienter stabat Paulus, murmurabat Esau,
> Et dolebat Iob, sederet quod solus in stercore.

> [Father Adam, first of all, sat down in the middle,
> Mother Eve, oh so impudent, on a leaf of fig,
> Cain on a plough and Abel on a milk churn.
> Noah sat on top of an ark, Japheth on a hillside,
> Isaac on an altar, and Abraham under a tree.
> Jacob sat on a rock, Lot beside a gate,
> Moses on stones, Elijah on furs,
> Daniel on a tribunal, and Tobias on a bed.
> Benjamin sat on a sack, Joseph on a bushel.
> John sat on the ground, David on a small mountain,
> The King Pharaoh on sand, Lazarus on a table,
> Zacheus on a mulberry-tree, and Jesus on top of a well.
> Matthew sat on a bench, Rebecca on a water jug.
> Tecla sat by a window, Ruth reclined on hemp.
> Susanna sat in a garden, Absalom in branches.
> Peter sat on a cathedra, Judas on a money box.
> Samson sat on columns, James on a net,

The old Eli on a chair, Rachel on a bundle.
Paul stood patiently, Esau grumbled,
And Job was grieved because he was sitting by himself on a dung heap.]

Few of these seats are conventional, and lounging on some of them must have been really uncomfortable. The way the seating arrangements are handled represents a typical example of the *Cena*'s approach to the biblical material. In the excerpt presented here, each person is perched on an object that clearly relates to a well-known episode in his or her story and to a precise biblical verse. The lists of people that are attached to each event of the unfolding narrative vary in length, and nobody, not even Jesus, appears in every single one of them. Samson is mentioned seven times altogether. In addition to sitting on columns (v. 29), he also keeps his portion of the meat which comes from hunting a lion (*Samson tenet leoninam, sc. partem*, v. 121), takes the jaw of the animal that all the guests have prepared together for their meal (*maxillam fortis Samson, sc. sustulit*, v. 130), fetches for himself a sun-fish (*pellionem Samson fert*, v. 157), offers sweet honey when Pilate asks for water to wash his hands (*Samson favi dulcia, sc. ministrat*, v. 197), brings a lion as a present to the king (*Samson leonem fert bestiam*, v. 244), and finally is tied up in chains when the interrogation is instigated (*vinculis Samson ligatur*, v. 274). All of these references are perfectly understandable to the reader because they remind him of the key elements in Samson's story: the killing of the lion, the sweet honey in the lion's carcass, the jaw-bone used as a weapon, the capture and death of the hero. Even the more obscure reference about Samson eating a "sun-fish" is not difficult to figure out when one remembers that Samson's name means "sun" (*sol ipsorum*). Many other texts stress the same connections. However, no other medieval composition achieves the effect of the *Cena*. It is funny and instructive, parodistic and earnest, mnemonic and memorable. The biblical characters are introduced here both in their usual context and in a setting that is completely surprising. The humorous tone of the piece is unmistakable, but so also is its serious engagement with the biblical text. One can only marvel at its ingenuity.

Conclusion

The various modes of expression discussed in this essay show unequivocally that understanding and explaining the message of the sacred page was the defining feature of medieval literary discourse. Whether in prose or verse, the medieval writers dedicated their efforts to finding the meaning of creation and to establishing how the human relates to the divine. In this quest, they followed different paths, from academic inquiry to emotional self-examination to humoristic parody, but ultimately, their goal was the same: to glorify God through study and teaching, preaching and writing, word and image, faith and morality. The variety of approaches to Scripture (in our case the story of Samson) exhibited by the writers examined in this essay demonstrates that their relationship to the truth and mystery of the Bible was not dogmatic and uniform; rather, it was an impetus for intellectual curiosity and an inspiration for literary creativity. The text of the Bible opened many doors of understanding and showed a multitude of paths to enlightenment. Sacred Scripture, albeit inerrant, did not imply one meaning for the medieval thinkers. How different from the way many people view the Bible today!

SUGGESTIONS FOR FURTHER READING

A good general introduction on biblical exegesis is found in de Lubac (1959), with further elaboration in Dahan (2009). For a stimulating discussion on the characteristics of the late-antique biblical epics, see Roberts (1985). The best study of biblical poetry in the Carolingian period is Stella (1993). The later developments in the genre of biblical versification are outlined in Dinkova-Bruun (2007a and 2008). An engaging collection of essays on the relationship between poetry and exegesis may be found in Otten and Pollmann (2007), while Berndt (2009) contains a range of superb essays on the importance of the Bible in the scholarly program of the School of St. Victor in Paris. Stotz (2008) is an excellent attempt to capture the various modes of medieval poetic expression. The importance of the verse Bible as aide-mémoire is stressed in Dinkova-Bruun (2010).

BIBLIOGRAPHY

Primary sources

Alexander of Ashby. 2004. *Alexandri Essebiensis Opera Poetica*, edited by Greti Dinkova-Bruun. Corpus Christianorum. Continuatio Mediaevalis 188A. Turnhout: Brepols.

Ecloga Theoduli. 1997. *Teodulo Ecloga: il canto della verità e della menzogna*, edited by Francesco Mosetti Casaretto. Per verba 5. Florence: SISMEL, Edizioni del Galluzzo.

Gottfried of Admont. 1854. "Homiliae Dominicales, Homilia 42 In Dominicam in Palmis Quarta." In *Patrologia Latina*, edited by Jacques P. Migne, 174: cols. 275D–288D. Paris.

Gregorius Magnus. 1844. *Morals on the Book of Job, by S. Gregory the Great, the First Pope of That Name*. 4 vols. Library of Fathers of the Holy Catholic Church 18, 21, 23, 31. Oxford: J. H. Parker.

———. 1979. *Moralia in Iob*, edited by Marc Adriaen. Corpus Christianorum. Series Latina 143. Turnhout: Brepols.

Hildebert. 1985. "The *Biblical Epigrams* of Hildebert of Le Mans: A Critical Edition," edited by A. Brian Scott, Deirdre F. Baker and Arthur G. Rigg. *Mediaeval Studies* 47: 272–316.

Isidore. 1850. "Quaestiones in Vetus Testamentum" and "In librum iudicum," ch. 8: "De Samson." In *Patrologia Latina*, edited by Jacques P. Migne, 83: cols. 207B–424D, 389B–90C.

Petrus Episcopus. 1995. "Vetus Testamentum uersibus latinis," edited by A. Emery. Ph.D. thesis, École Nationale des Chartes. (I thank Dr. Emery for giving me a copy of her thesis and for granting me permission to use her work.)

Petrus Riga. 1965. *Aurora Petri Rigae Biblia Versificata*, edited by Paul Beichner. 2 vols. Publications in Mediaeval Studies 19. Notre Dame, IN: University of Notre Dame Press.

Pictor in Carmine. 2006. *Pictor in Carmine. Ein Handbuch der Typologie aus der Zeit um 1200. Nach MS 300 des Corpus Christi College in Cambridge herausgegeben*, edited by Karl-August Wirth. Veröffentlichungen des Zentralinstituts für Kunstgeschichte, München 17. Berlin: Gebr. Mann.

Prudentius. 1966. *Carmina*, edited by Maurice Cunningham. Corpus Christianorum. Series Latina 126. Turnhout: Brepols.

Secondary sources

Berndt, Rainer, ed. 2009. *Bibel und Exegese in der Abtei Sankt Viktor zu Paris. Form und Funktion eines Grundtextes im europäischen Raum*. Corpus Victorinum. Instrumenta 3. Münster: Aschendorff.

Borgehammer, Stephen. 1993. "Who Wrote the Admont Sermon Corpus—Gottfried the Abbot, His Brother Irimbert, or the Nuns?" In *De l'homélie au sermon: Histoire de la predication médiévale*, edited by Jacqueline Hamesse and Xavier Hermand, 47–53. Publications de l'Institut d'études médiévales. Textes, études, congrès 14. Louvain-la-Neuve: Institut d'études médiévales de l'Université catholique de Louvain.

Dahan, Gilbert. 1988. "Les 'figure' des Juifs et de la Synagogue. L'example de Dalila. Functions et méthodes de la typologie dans l'exégèse médiévale." *Recherches augustiniennes* 23: 125-150.

———. 1999. *L'exégèse chrétienne de la Bible en Occident médiéval: XIIe–XIVe siècle*. Patrimoines. Christianisme. Paris: Cerf.

———. 2004. "Samson and Dalila. Le chapitre 16 des Juges dans l'exégèse chrétienne du XIIe et du XIIIe siècle." *Graphe* 13: 97-118.

———. 2009. *Lire la bible au moyen âge: essais d'herméneutique médiévale*. Paris: Droz.

de Lubac, Henry. 1959. *Exégèse médiévale*, 2 vols. in 4. Théologie. Etudes publiées sous la direction de la Faculté de théologie S. J. de Lyon-Fourvière 41. Paris: Aubier.

———. 1998. *Medieval Exegesis*, translated by Mark Sebanc. 3 vols. Ressourcement. Grand Rapids, MI: Eerdmans.

Dinkova-Bruun, Greti. 2005. "Leonius of Paris and his *Liber Ruth*." In *Schrift, Schreiber, Schenker. Studien zur Pariser Abtei Sankt Viktor und den Viktorinern*, edited by Reiner Berndt, 243–66. Corpus Victorinum. Instrumenta 1. Berlin: Akademie Verlag.

———. 2007a. "Biblical Versifications from Late Antiquity to the Middle of the Thirteenth Century: History or Allegory?" In *Poetry and Exegesis in Premodern Latin Christianity. The Encounter between Classical and Christian Strategies of Interpretation*, edited by Willemien Otten and Karla Pollmann, 315–42. Supplements to Vigiliae Christianae 87. Leiden.

———. 2007b. "Additions to Peter Riga's *Aurora* in Paris, Bibliothèque National de France, Lat. 13050." *Mediaeval Studies* 69: 1–57.

———. 2008. "Rewriting Scripture: Latin Biblical Versification in the Later Middle Ages." *Viator* 39: 263–84.

———. 2009. "*Autor*, Authorship and The Literal Sense of The Bible: The Case of Leonius of Paris." In *Bibel und Exegese in der Abtei Sankt Viktor zu Paris. Form und Funktion eines Grundtextes im europäischen Raum*, edited by Rainer Berndt, 259–77. Corpus Victorinum. Instrumenta 3. Münster: Aschendorff.

———. 2010. "The Verse Bible as Aide-mémoire." In *The Making of Memory in the Middle Ages*, edited by Lucie Doležalová, 115–31. Later Medieval Europe 4. Leiden: Brill.

Doležalová, Lucie. 2007. *Reception and its Varieties. Reading, Re-Writing, and Understanding* Cena Cypriani *in the Middle Ages*. Bochumer altertumswissenschaftliches Colloquium 75. Trier: Wissenschaftlicher Verlag Trier.

Dronke, Peter. 1986. *Poetic Individuality in the Middle Ages. New Departures in Poetry 1000–1150*. 2nd ed. Westfield Publications in Medieval Studies 1. London: Westfield College, Committee for Medieval Studies.

Evans, Gillian R. 1984. *The Language and Logic of the Bible: The Earlier Middle Ages*. Cambridge, New York: Cambridge University Press.

Green, Roger. 2006. *Latin Epics of the New Testament: Juvencus, Sedulius, Arator*, Oxford, New York: Oxford University Press. (With further useful bibliography.)

Heinzer, Felix. 2008. "*Samson dux fortissimus* – Löwenbändiger und Weiberknecht vom Dienst? Funktionen und Wandlungen eines literarischen Motivs in Mittelalter." *Mittellateinisches Jahrbuch* 43: 25–46.

Modesto, Christine. 1992. *Studien zur* Cena Cypriani *und zu deren Rezeption*. Classica Monacensia 3. Tübingen: Günter Narr.

Mosetti Casaretto, Francesco. 2005. "Intorno alle corna della 'Cena' di Arras." In *Poesía latina medieval (siglos V–XV): actas del IV Congreso del "Internationales Mittellateinerkomitee", Santiago de Compostela, 12–15 de septiembre de 2002*, edited by Manuel C. Díaz y Díaz, 801–15. Millennio medievale 55. Florence: SISMEL, Edizioni del Galluzzo.

Otten, Willemien. 2007. "The Poetic of Biblical Tragedy in Abelard's Planctus." In *Poetry and Exegesis in Premodern Latin Christianity. The Encounter between Classical and Christian Strategies of Interpretation*, edited by Willemien Otten and Karla Pollmann, 245–61. Supplements to Vigiliae Christianae 87. Leiden, Boston: Brill.

Otten, Willemien and Karla Pollmann, eds. 2007. *Poetry and Exegesis in Premodern Latin Christianity. The Encounter between Classical and Christian Strategies of Interpretation*. Supplements to Vigiliae Christianae 87. Leiden, Boston: Brill.

Roberts, Michael. 1985. *Biblical Epic and Rhetorical Paraphrase in Late Antiquity*. ARCA. Classical and Medieval Texts, Papers, and Monographs 16. Liverpool: F. Cairns.

Schmidt, Paul G. 2000. "Die Bibeldichtung des Leonius von Paris." in *Als das wissend die meister wol. Beiträge zur Darstellung und Vermittlung von Wissen in Fachliteratur und Dichtung des Mittelalters und der frühen Neuzeit: Walter Blank zum 65. Geburtstag*, edited by Martin Ehrenfeuchter und Thomas Ehlen, 253–60. Frankfurt/Main, New York: Peter Lang.

Smalley, Beryl. 1983. *The Study of the Bible in the Middle Ages*. 3rd, rev. ed. Oxford: B. Blackwell.

Stammberger, Ralf. 2005. "The Works of Hugh of St. Victor at Admont: A Glance at an Intellectual Landscape in the Twelfth Century." In *Schrift, Schreiber, Schenker. Studien zur Pariser Abtei Sankt Viktor und den Viktorinern*, edited by Reiner Berndt, 233–61. Corpus Victorinum. Instrumenta 1. Berlin: Akademie Verlag.

Stella, Francesco. 1993. *La poesia carolingia latina a tema biblico*. Biblioteca di "Medioevo Latino" 9. Spoleto: Centro italiano di studi sull'Alto Medioevo.

Sticca, Sandro. 1988. *The* Planctus Mariae *in the Dramatic Tradition of the Middle Ages*, Athens, GA: University of Georgia Press.

Stotz, Peter, ed. 2008. *Dichten als Stoff-Vermittlung. Formen, Ziele, Wirkungen*. Medienwandel, Medienwechsel, Medienwissenschaft 5. Zürich: Chronos.

Vecchi, Giuseppe. 1951. *Pietro Abelardo. I "Planctus."* Modena: Società tipografica Modenese.

Walther, Hans. 1920. Das Streitgedicht in der lateinischen Literatur des Mittelalters. Quellen und Untersuchungen zur lateinischen Philologie des Mittelalters 5.2. Munich: Beck.

CHAPTER 18

THE LANGUAGE, FORM, AND PERFORMANCE OF MONOPHONIC LITURGICAL CHANTS

SUSAN BOYNTON AND MARGOT FASSLER

INTRODUCTION

THE Latinity of medieval sung liturgical texts depends fundamentally on their performance, for the style of a chant is determined by the parameters of genre, local and regional traditions, and by the liturgical context within which it was sung. As a result, diverse stylistic layers and forms of Latin verse and prose coexisted within the medieval Mass and Office. The basic structures of these daily services were established by the mid-ninth century. Some of their elements, such as the proper chants of the Mass, were fairly fixed, while others, such as tropes, sequences, and liturgical dramas, changed over time and varied by region or ecclesial affiliation. Singing the liturgy was thus an embodied experience of group identity, both because it was performed in choir and because religious communities and urban centers had their own distinctive traditions. Singing was also a process of linguistic assimilation. The clergy internalized the Latin of the Bible by singing it day after day, year after year. The Psalms, which were central to the medieval liturgy, were a primary point of reference for medieval writers, whose readings of Scripture were often influenced by their experience of the liturgy.

All the texts studied here functioned intertextually with other genres brought into contact with them through various kinds of juxtaposition. The very moments in the liturgy in which they were sung conditioned the meanings of their performance. The idiom of each genre was determined both by its function and by its mode of singing, and therefore the style of performance dictated the nature of chant texts and their melodies.

It is often overlooked that most of the genres studied today as texts were actually rendered musically. Not only were biblical and poetic texts sung to more or less elaborate melodies, but also prayers and many other prose texts were intoned or chanted, such as the homilies, epistles, commentaries, and hagiographic narratives that served as lessons in the Divine Office.

Singing the Divine Office

Of all genres of liturgical texts, the most numerous are antiphons. In general, antiphons are short verses designed for singing before and after the intonation of a particular psalm or canticle; antiphons predominate not only in the night office, but also in every other hour of prayer. This kind of singing established community, as singers sat in the same place in choir, heard the same voices beside them, and looked across at the same faces, year in, year out, as they sang verses of the psalmody in alternation (antiphonally). By the tenth century, office antiphons were sung both before and after the psalms and canticles. The repetition of the antiphon followed the lesser doxology "Gloria Patri, et filio, et spiritui sancto; Sicut erat in principio et nunc et semper, et in secula seculorum Amen" [Glory be to the Father, and to the Son, and to the Holy Spirit; as it was in the beginning, now and always and unto the ages of ages, Amen]. Antiphons sung on ferial days (when there was no major feast) constituted a form of exegesis on the meaning of the psalms with which they were sung. On major feasts, the antiphons chosen from psalm texts were proper to the day, their texts providing the reason that particular psalms were proper to the feast; other antiphons had been newly composed for the feast itself.

Antiphons created to accompany the intoning of the canticles are generally longer than Psalter antiphons, and of special importance are those antiphon texts designed for the singing of the Benedictus (Lk 1:68–79) at Lauds and the Magnificat (Lk 1:46–55), the canticle of Mary, at Vespers. The antiphon commonly sung with the Magnificat at Vespers on Christmas Day artfully combines and layers several different phrases from Scripture, with the constant return to the word "hodie" [today], to emphasize the immediacy of this liturgical recreation of an historical event. The most important source for this antiphon is Luke 2:11, the angels' announcement to the shepherds that "natus est vobis hodie salvator qui est Christus

Dominus in civitate David," but the antiphon also echoes Luke 2:14: "gloria in altissimis Deo et in terra pax in hominibus bonae voluntatis." The melody shapes the text, with the cadences parsing the lines as follows:

> Hodie Christus natus est; hodie Salvator apparuit; hodie in terra canunt Angeli, laetantur Archangeli; hodie exsultant justi, dicentes: Gloria in excelsis Deo, alleluia.
>
> [Today, Christ is born; today the savior has appeared; today angels sing on earth and archangels rejoice; today the just exult singing, "Glory to God in the highest, Alleluia."] (*Corpus antiphonalium officii* [hereafter *CAO*] no. 3093; Hesbert 1963–79)

This antiphon text would make the Magnificat (sung every day at Vespers) proper to Christmas, joining the choirs of angels and the rejoicing of shepherds to Mary's own song of joy.

Antiphon texts were usually chosen to be a form of commentary on the psalms or canticles with which they were sung. (For the ways in which a set of antiphons composed by Hildegard of Bingen relates to a particular group of Psalms, see Fassler 2003.) Some antiphons stood alone, however, and were used as processional chants, or as points of repose in the office. The famous set of Marian antiphons, which came to be sung at Compline, one for each season of the year, reflect a Mariology that was developing in the course of the late eleventh century with its emphasis on Mary as the mother of mercy. These four antiphon texts also were endlessly quoted in the miracle literature, and phrases from them filled the prayer lives of ordinary Christians as well as of the clergy and monastics. Of these antiphons, the "Salve Regina" was most often a focus for processions, especially in the later Middle Ages and among the Dominicans and Franciscans. The text of "Salve Regina" is neither regularly metrical nor rhythmic, although some of the lines rhyme. The music shapes the phrases to emphasize words with like endings (*gementes* and *flentes*; *illos tuos* and *oculos*; and *Jesum, benedictum fructum*), and makes the declamation of this pleading prayer powerfully dramatic.

> Salve, Regina, Mater misericordiae,
> vita, dulcedo, et spes nostra, salve.
> Ad te clamamus, exsules filii Evae,
> ad te suspiramus, gementes et flentes
> in hac lacrimarum valle.
> Eia, ergo, advocata nostra, illos tuos
> misericordes oculos ad nos converte;
> et Jesum, benedictum fructum ventris tui,
> nobis post hoc exsilium ostende.
> O clemens, O pia, O dulcis Virgo Maria

[Hail, holy Queen, Mother of Mercy, our life, our sweetness and our hope. To you we cry, poor banished children of Eve; to you we send up our sighs, mourning and weeping in this valley of tears.

> So, most gracious advocate, turn your merciful eyes toward us;
> and after this our exile, show us the blessed fruit of your womb, Jesus. O clement,
> O loving, O sweet Virgin Mary.]

Great responsories (distinct from the short responds that punctuate brief capitula) are long chants that accompany reflection following the readings of the night office. They were different in liturgical function from antiphons, with a correspondingly different textual structure and performance practice. Responsories consist of two parts, a respond and a soloistic verse; their performance practice varied in the Middle Ages, and in many places half of the doxology was also sung at the conclusion of a set of readings. Because the final section of the respond was used as a refrain, the various parts of the texts needed to be constructed so that they made a harmonious entity.

One of the most beloved of all medieval responsories was "Stirps Jesse," whose text and melody are usually attributed to Fulbert of Chartres (d. 1028). It exemplifies many features of the responsory texts composed in the tenth and eleventh centuries for feasts of the saints, and, as was common, was created to complement a particular saint's vita or other proper reading, in this case, Fulbert's sermon *Approbate Consuetudinis* for the feast of the Nativity of the Virgin Mary (see Fassler 2010). It can be seen that the *repetendum* of this responsory (which begins with the asterisk) follows neatly upon the verse so as to express and refine its meaning further. The responsory draws upon imagery from Isaiah 11:1–2 "et egredietur virga de radice Jesse et flos de radice eius ascendet et requiescet super eum spiritus Domini." But the flowering rod is also that of Aaron in the tabernacle from Numbers 17. The responsory text transforms these Old Testament images, calling up as well the new tabernacle of Hebrews 8, and making a thickly descriptive statement that comments upon the sermon and the feast of the day:

> Stirps Jesse uirgam produxit uirgaque florem *et super hunc florum requiescit spiritus almus (*CAO* 7709) V. Virga dei genetrix uirgo est flos filius eius. (*CAO* 7709a)
>
> [The shoot of Jesse produced a rod, and the rod a flower; and now over the flower rests a nurturing spirit. V. The shoot is the virgin Genetrix of God, and the flower is her Son.]

From the ninth century onward, the antiphons and responsories written for the office reflect developments in liturgical poetry more generally. Prose texts, often following scriptural models with balanced phrases, were supplemented by versified forms of various types, some metrical, some semi-metrical. Various early experiments with rhythmic verse forms led ultimately to the rhymed offices of the later Middle Ages, some of which were created as fully integrated sets of antiphons and responsories.

Some new versified offices were composed as alternatives or replacements for earlier prose ones. The office of Saint Benedict provides an instructive example. Most of the chants in the Benedict office were taken from the account of the saint's life and miracles in book II of the *Dialogues* of Gregory the Great. These prose chants exist in various configurations (as the ordering of the office varied from place to place), with the result that the events recounted in their texts did not always follow the order of Gregory's narrative. A versified office from the twelfth century instead creates a continuous verse narrative in which sections of iambic dimeter are interspersed with Sapphic strophes. The first two antiphons of Matins, both in iambic dimeter, refer to the interpretation of Benedict's name as "blessed," his origins in Nursia, his prominent family, and his parents' decision to send him to Rome to study.

> Benedictus tam nomine
> quam gratiarum munere
> e nursia progenitus
> claris fulsit parentibus

[Benedict shone as much in name as in the gift of grace; he was born in Nursia to distinguished parents.] (*Analecta Hymnica* [hereafter *AH*] 25: 146; Dreves 1886–1922)

(second antiphon of Matins, first two lines):

> Hic ergo Romae traditus
> disciplinis scholaribus.

[Therefore, he was sent to Rome for academic training.] (*AH* 25: 146)

These two antiphons are clearly based on the prose antiphons of the night office, which quote from the opening of the prologue of Book II of the *Dialogues:* "Fuit vir vite venerabilis gratia Benedictus et nomine" [There was a man of venerable life, blessed both by grace and in name] (*CAO* 2906) and "Liberiori genere ex provincia Nursiae ortus Romae liberalibus litterarum studiis traditus a parentibus fuerat" [Of noble birth, from the province of Nursia, he had been sent to Rome by his relatives for liberal studies of letters] (*CAO* 3626).

A similar transformation occurs in the responsories of the night office. One of the responsories usually sung in the first part of Matins is taken from the section of the *Dialogues* (2.3.23) that relates the attempted assassination of Benedict by his monks, who offered him a cup of poison mixed with wine. When he made the sign of the cross over it, it shattered: "Inito consilio venenum vino miscuere; quo oblato ex more ad benedicendum patri, vir Dei signo crucis edidit, et vas pestiferi potus ita confractum est, ac si pro signo lapidem dedisset" [They decided to mix the poison into the wine; when, according to custom, it was offered to the father for the benediction, the man of God performed the benediction with the sign of the cross, and thus the vessel of the poisonous drink was shattered, as if he had struck it with a stone instead of (making) the sign] (*CAO* 6968). In the twelfth-century versified office, a responsory in approximately the same liturgical position tells the story more tersely, using some of the same words as in the prose responsory (*patri, signo, lapidem*) but varying the lexicon slightly. The cup containing the poisonous drink is called both *poculum* and *vas*, and *mortiferum* is substituted for *pestiferum*. Referring to the community as Benedict's *grex* aptly conveys the irony of the situation: using the sacred wine of communion, his own flock sought to assassinate the abbot they had elected.

> Electo grex mortiferum
> patri ferebat poculum
> sed vir dei signo vitae
> vas rupit tamquam lapide.

[The flock bore a mortal cup to their chosen father, but with the sign of the cross the man of God broke the vessel as if with a stone.] (*AH* 25: 146)

In the late twelfth century, rhymed offices began to predominate, in which the individual chants of the office are composed in strophes that often look as if they were parts of hymns or rhymed sequences. (For an introduction to the genre see Hughes 2001.) Many of the strophes of the antiphons and responsories for later rhymed offices are set in trochaic verse, and frequently in couplet form: 887/887 or 87/87, although unlike the sequences, the music for each half strophe would not usually be the same. The use of these familiar verse patterns made it easy to create numerous contrafacta (that is new texts for preexisting music) for the most popular rhymed offices. The rhymed office for Francis of Assisi by Julian of Speyer (d. 1250) was certainly one of the most influential examples of the genre written in the later Middle Ages. Music written for this particular set of texts served for numerous other offices, thus drawing together several sets of rhymed office texts into a Franciscan sphere of influence.

The structure followed in the office for St. Louis is modeled upon the earlier office of St. Francis; further details include parallels in meter and word choice (see Gaposchkin 2008). Rhythmic verse reflects patterns employed in classical meters, transformed so that the number of syllables in the line takes precedence over accent (Norberg 2004). The antiphon below from the St. Louis office is a contrafactum of a chant written earlier for St. Francis. In these related examples, classical dactylic trimeter provides a fundamental formal understanding, but the number of syllables and rhyme shape the lines.

The fifth antiphon of the night office from "Franciscus vir catholicus" for St. Francis (written in 1232):

> Iam liber patris furie
> non cedit effrenati
> clamans se voluntarie
> pro Christo mala pati

[Now free, he no longer
yields to the unbridled fury of his father,
proclaiming that he is free to suffer
punishment for the sake of Christ.]

The fifth antiphon from "Francorum Rex magnificus" for St. Louis (written in the early fourteenth century):

> Populi princeps furie
> non cedit effrenati
> monstrans se voluntarie
> pro Christo mala pati

> [The leader no longer yields
> to the unbridled fury of the people,
> showing that he is free to suffer
> punishment for the sake of Christ.]

Hymns

Each of the eight daily services of the medieval divine office included a hymn with a nonscriptural poetic text. Every strophe of the text was sung to the same melody, usually simple in style, which followed the syntax of the verse line, foregrounding the verbal structure of the hymn text. Most texts exhibit a thematic progression from proclaiming the occasion in the first strophe, to elaborating on the subject in the body of the hymn, finally concluding with a verse doxology. Within this broad outline, rhetorical and syntactic strategies vary widely. Recurrent patterns of accentuation and syllable count were inherent features of the strophic form, which also allowed the relationship between word and melody to change from line to line. The flexibility of the form extended to the music: most hymn texts could be sung to any of several different melodies; conversely, a melody that fit a text with a given form of versification would at least in theory be suited to another text with the same prosodic structure.

Much of the medieval hymn repertory results from the close imitation of venerable models. Most hymn texts are composed in one of three meters: iambic dimeter, Sapphic strophes, or trochaic tetrameter. The principal model for iambic hymns is Ambrose's Vespers hymn "Deus creator omnium"; many hymns are rhythmic rather than quantitative, and thus imitate the accentual pattern of iambic dimeter without observing the quantities of the syllables. Some rhythmic hymns do not derive from a quantitative model at all; "Ave maris stella," for example, has strophes with four lines of six syllables. Since the final accent falls on the penultimate syllable, the conventional notation for this verse form is "6p."

While analyses of hymn texts often center on date and attribution, both the manuscript tradition and the conventional character of hymns makes it difficult to establish even a relative chronology. We therefore focus here on stylistic and thematic conventions. Comparing different hymns for the same general liturgical function (in this case, the office of Matins, on different days of the week) highlights their shared characteristics. Hymns frequently refer to the act of singing, which the Matins hymns place specifically in the dark hours of the late night and early morning, when the night office (often called "nocturns") took place. The hymn for Matins on Sundays in winter, "Primo dierum omnium," extends the temporal symbolism to the day of the week. In the first strophe, a string of dependent clauses introduce Sunday as the first day of creation, prefiguring the day of the Resurrection.

> Primo dierum omnium,
> Quo mundus exstat conditus,
> Vel quo resurgens conditor
> Nos morte uicta liberat

[On the first of all days, when the world stands created, and when the creator, arising again, liberates us, death having been vanquished.] (Walpole 1922, 262)

The use of the present tense here establishes the special dimension of time that characterizes liturgical poetry: it situates the hymn simultaneously in the recurring, weekly Sunday office and in salvation history. The present time of the singers' experience encompasses both the beginning of earthly time and the annually commemorated occasion of Easter. The second strophe completes this all-embracing typology by linking the act of rising to celebrate the night office not only to the Resurrection but also to the words in Psalm 118:62 ("In the middle of the night I arose to give you praise") that were traditionally attributed to David ("the prophet"), words which were conventionally cited as the basis for the night office:

> Pulsis procul torporibus
> Surgamus omnes ocius
> Et nocte queramus pium
> Sicut prophetam nouimus

[With torpors thrust far away, let us all rise eagerly and by night let us seek out the holy one just as we know the prophet to have done.]

The hymn for Matins on Mondays begins by presenting singing explicitly as a form of supplication and also as the path to salvation:

> Somno refectis artubus
> Spreto cubili surgimus:
> Nobis, Pater, canentibus
> Adesse te deposcimus

[Bodies refreshed by sleep, spurning the bed, we arise: Father, we entreat you to assist those singing to you.] (Walpole 1922, 267)

In the Matins hymn for Tuesday, singing metaphorically breaks through the darkness of night, and the first strophe plays with the theological associations of light:

> Consors paterni luminis
> Lux ipse lucis et dies
> Noctem canendo rumpimus;
> Adsiste postulantibus

> [Companion of the paternal light, very light of the light and day, we break the night by singing: Come to the aid of those entreating you.] (Walpole 1922, 268)

In the second strophe, each of the first three lines begins with an imperative, resulting in a simpler and more repetitive construction than that of the first strophe. The lines occasionally approximate end-rhyme (mentium/-entiam), but mainly employ alliteration:

> Aufer tenebras mentium,
> Fuga cateruas daemonum,
> Expelle somnolentiam,
> Ne pigritantes obruat

> [Lift the shadows from our souls; put the crowds of demons to flight; expel somnolence, lest it overpower those who are slackening.]

Likewise, in the penultimate strophe, which invokes the spiritual efficaciousness of singing, the first three lines end in -*ibus*:

> Sic, Christe, nobis omnibus
> Indulgeas credentibus,
> Ut prosit exorantibus
> Quod praecinentes psallimus

> [Thus, Christ, be kind to all of us believers, so that the fact we sing before you may profit those praying to you.] (Walpole 1922, 269)

Unlike the other Matins hymns considered thus far, the hymn for Sunday Matins during the summer is in Sapphic meter and presents the familiar themes more concisely. The strophes are more tightly constructed and feature enjambment between at least the second and third line of each strophe. The first strophe describes the night office through allusion to communal wakefulness animated by meditation on the psalms and vigorous singing of hymns (the term *hymni* encompassing both psalms and other songs of praise). In the second strophe the heavenly realm to which the singers aspire is called a palace (*aula*). The doxology, which is transmitted together with the two strophes of the hymn in most manuscripts, explicitly names the three persons of the Trinity.

> Nocte surgentes uigilemus omnes,
> Semper in psalmis meditemur, atque
> Viribus totis Domino canamus
> Dulciter hymnos,
>
> Ut pio regi pariter canentes
> Cum suis sanctis mereamur aulam

> Ingredi caeli, simul et beatam
> Ducere uitam.
>
> Praestet hoc nobis deitas beata
> Patris ac nati pariterque sancti
> Spiritus, cuius reboatur omni
> Gloria mundo

[Rising at night, let us all stay awake; let us always meditate on the psalms, and with all our strength let us sweetly sing hymns to the Lord, so that, singing together to the holy king, we may, along with his saints, deserve to enter the palace of heaven, and at the same time to lead a blessed life. May we be granted this by the blessed divinity of the Father, and the Son, and equally of the Holy Spirit, whose glory resounds in the whole world.] (Walpole 1922, 265)

Tropes and Prosulae for the Mass Liturgy

The Mass liturgy, like the Office, was a composite of many kinds of Latin verse and poetry, creating constant interplay between chronologically distinct layers. There are essentially two kinds of Mass chants: the propers, whose texts are different for every feast or category of feast; and texts for the ordinary, whose texts remain the same. Beginning in the late ninth century, chant texts of both the proper and the ordinary were often troped, or added to, and in a variety of ways. Texts were added to chant melismas (and such a text is called a prosula); some chants were expanded upon through the use of prefatory or interpolated verses of chanted texts (most often called tropes); and some chants were transformed by the use of added melismas (the neuma), usually at the end, to make them longer and more splendid. So it is that many Mass chant texts existed along with their sung commentaries throughout the central Middle Ages.

A Set of Introit Tropes

As proper chants of the Mass often had texts taken from Scripture, especially from the Psalms, the tropes added to them resemble interlinear glosses. Tropes for the introit, which comprise the majority of the repertory, existed in all regions of Europe throughout the central Middle Ages; they began to die out as a genre in the twelfth century (although many survived east of the Rhine). Several sets of introit tropes that were sung at Chartres Cathedral in the twelfth century demonstrate the variety in such texts. Both sets discussed here were created for the introit chant for the feast of the Purification, the text of which is Psalm 47:10–11, chosen for the sake of the feast with its reference to "the midst of the temple" and the reception by the prophet Simeon of the baby Jesus. The two sets of introit tropes flesh out the meanings that the psalm would have for the particular feast of the Purification, bringing it into the time of the New Testament. As is the case with so many tropes for the Mass introit, the emphasis here is on prophecy and entrance, themes well suited to the liturgical function of the introit, the entrance chant. The ways in which introit texts were divided up for receiving trope texts were traditional, and the sets of tropes may be narrowly regional, or widespread. The first set, for example, can be found in a variety of centres, not only in the North, but in Italy as well, although the elements may be combined in different ways. The second set, on the other hand, divides the psalm text somewhat differently, and was unique to Chartres. As is often the case with introit tropes, the first set is in hexameters. In the example below, the Psalm text of the introit is in capital letters, and the trope was likely sung by a soloist whereas the introit chant was sung by the choir:

O nova res, en virgo venit, partum gerit, et nos
SUSCEPIMUS, DEUS, MISERICORDIAM TUAM,
Quod non visuri patres cupiere, videmus
IN MEDIO TEMPLI TUI
Rex pie Christe, tuum sit nomen semper honestum
SECUNDUM NOMEN TUUM, DEUS, ITA ET LAUS TUA IN FINES
TERRAE, IUSTITIA PLENA EST DEXTERA TUA.

[O novel thing, behold, a virgin comes bearing a child, and we
WE HAVE RECEIVED YOUR MERCY, O GOD
We see what the fathers desired but were not to see
IN THE MIDST OF YOUR TEMPLE.
O King, Merciful Christ, may your name be ever honored
AS YOUR NAME DOES, O GOD, SO TOO MAY YOUR PRAISE GO TO
    THE ENDS
OF THE EARTH; YOUR RIGHT HAND IS FULL WITH JUSTICE.]

Ecce venit ad templum sanctum suum
Christus natus ex virgine
Gaudeamus omnes dicentes
SUSCEPIMUS, DEUS, MISERICORDIAM TUAM
quem senex iustus Simeon gaudens suscipit
IN MEDIO TEMPLI TUI SECUNDUM NOMEN TUUM,
DEUS, ITA ET LAUS TUA.
Anna vidua Christum agnovit advenisse
IN FINES TERRAE
Laus, virtus et honor deo nostro
in his sacris sollemniis
IUSTITIA PLENA EST DEXTERA TUA.

[Behold Christ born from a virgin comes to His holy temple: Let us all rejoice saying:
WE HAVE RECEIVED YOUR MERCY, O GOD
Whom the righteous old man Simeon received rejoicing
IN THE MIDST OF YOUR TEMPLE AS YOUR NAME DOES, O GOD, SO TOO MAY YOUR PRAISE
Anna the widow knew that Christ had come
TO THE ENDS OF THE EARTH
Praise, power, and honor to our God on these holy solemnities
YOUR RIGHT HAND IS FULL WITH JUSTICE.] (Fassler 2010, 223–41)

A Troped Kyrie, with Prosulae

Ordinary chants for the Mass liturgy also were troped, and each genre had its own style. Kyries could be graced with two kinds of tropes, the interlinear kind, and also the prosula, texts set to syllables of these highly melismatic chants, the latter being the more common for this genre of chant. "Tibi Christi supplices" is one of the oldest Kyries, and the most magnificent; it was composed at the end of the ninth century, and survived into the late twelfth century, when it quite swiftly disappeared, probably because of its complex and somewhat (by then) archaic style. It is a useful text to examine, however, because it contains both types of Kyrie commentary, tropes and prosulae. The introductory trope encourages the choir to sing, rightly, with understanding, as is customary in many introductory tropes regardless of genre; it was sung to music that was independent of the Kyrie itself (Bjork 2003, 101–20). The prosula texts are not metrical, but nonetheless they are tightly structured and rhythmical, forming a kind of heightened prose found in sequences composed in the late ninth and tenth centuries. The prosula speaks of the nature of pleading itself and is sung to the same notes as the melismatic chant that follows, line by line, defining the song, allowing the music to exist in two separate but interrelated modes of expression, with text and without. The example below provides only the introductory trope and the first line of the ninefold Kyrie with its prosula, but the manuscripts show that this Kyrie was sung in a variety of ways, sometimes with other introductory tropes.
Introductory trope:

> Christe redemptor miserere nobis, Kyrie eleison, eia omnes dicite:
> [Christ, Redeemer, have mercy on us, Kyrie eleison, all say eia!]

First Line of the chant with its prosula:

> 1. Tibi Christe supplices exoramus cunctipotens, ut nostri digneris eleison.
> [v.1 prosula: To you, Christ almighty, we suppliants plead that you deign to show us mercy].
> (Melismatic singing of Kyrie eleison, without the prosula.)

The Sequence

The sequence is a catch-all term for a wide-ranging group of works that developed in that part of the Mass liturgy between the singing of the Alleluia, a responsorial proper chant, and the intoning of the Gospel. Already by the mid-ninth century, the Alleluia was sometimes decorated with long, wordless melismas, called neumata, jubilii, or (in the words of Notker Balbulus, d. 912) *longissimae melodiae* (see Haug 2008). By the time of Notker, the custom had developed both east and west of the Rhine of adding texts to the very long melodies; these pieces, sequences, are commonly also called prosae, especially by French scholars. (On the early sequence see Crocker 1977.) Because sequences developed after the partition of Verdun (843), they are fairly distinct regionally, at least until the eleventh century, when the barrier between East and West became more porous (Kruckenberg 1997). Although they may have started out as prosulae, sequences had become a genre in their own right by the later ninth century, forming a kind of commentary on the meaning of the Alleluia, and more generally on the relationships between the temporal liturgy on earth and the parallel liturgy sung for eternity in heaven. The ninth and tenth-century East Frankish sequences, the greatest and most beloved of which were written by Notker and collected as a presentation copy in his *Liber Hymnorum*, often are characterized by a learned and sophisticated exegesis. The sequences created west of the Rhine tend to be simpler, with a great emphasis on the use of "a" at the end of lines to call up the sense of an alleluia prosula. In southern Francia, a mystical language developed for the expression of the sequence, one that played upon the differences between music with and without texts, and that also speculated about the meanings of language used for praise, and the nature of worship itself.

"Aureo flore," which was widely transmitted beginning in the tenth century, offers a good example of the early sequence. As in the early Notkerian sequences, the lines are paired by their melodies and the text is prose-like. Here only the final line stands alone, but in many early sequences both the first and last line are independent melodically. A number of lines end in "a," creating somewhat more assonance than in most East Frankish sequences, but the rhyme and clearly defined rhythmic accent characteristic of the late sequence are absent here. Instead, the early West Frankish/Aquitanian sequence luxuriates in its own beauty, combining lush imagery with allusions to theological commonplaces expressed in loose and florid prose.

The poem begins with the patristic interpretation of Mary as the new Eve, a flowering rose described in terms reminiscent of the Song of Songs:

> Aureo flore prime matris Eue florens rosa processit sicut sol
> Oritur ut Lucifer inter astra decorate polorum sidera
>
> Flauescunt campi eremi collocassia germinantque lilia
> Odore nouo acantu roscida nectarea rorantque arua

[From the golden flower of the first mother, Eve, came forth the flowering rose like the sun. She rises like the morning star, beautiful among the stars, the stars of the heavens. Arid fields become golden with collocassia and sprout lilies, the dewy elecampane and the fields exude the new odor of acanthus.] (Boynton 1994, 37)

The language is richly evocative, echoing not only the Song of Songs but also classical and late-Latin texts. The term *collocassia* (the Egyptian bean) also appears in close proximity to *acantho* in Vergil's fourth *Eclogue*, which was interpreted in the Middle Ages as a prophecy of the birth of Christ. "Aureo flore" focuses on the Annunciation, the Incarnation, and Mary's virginity *in partu* rather than exploring the mystery of the Assumption. The Annunciation is described in classicizing terms, the account of the Incarnation recalls the *Paschale Carmen* of Sedulius, and only the conclusion of the text refers explicitly to the Assumption by quoting a refrain in Martianus Capella's *De nuptiis Philologiae et Mercurii* ("scande caeli templa uirgo digna tanto foedere"):

Velut sol migrans cuncta conscendisti globorum luminaria lucerna nitens inter
angelorum castra
Hodie celi templum scandens beata dei genitrix alma cum celicolis exorare regem regum

[You descended like the sun passing over all the lights of the spheres, a lamp gleaming among the hosts of angels, today ascending to the temples of heaven, blessed propitious mother of God, to prevail upon the king of kings, with those dwelling in heaven.] (Boynton 1994, 37)

Many characteristics of the early sequence continued for centuries, especially the formal convention of couplets whose lines were paired by the use of the same melodic phrase. But in the later tenth and eleventh centuries, creators of sequence texts increasingly experimented with rhyming, accentual poetry. This "new song" of shifting stylistic approaches appeared in many sequences, an example of which is the Christmas sequence "Sonent regi," which was composed in the eleventh century (Arlt 1992). The first and last lines of the sequence stand alone, and continue to demonstrate the affinity for the "a" at the end of lines to evoke the relationship to the Alleluia. But the shifting interest toward experimentation with rhyme and word accent can be seen from just one strophe. The poet was determined to make the paired half-strophes mirror images of each other, at least in regard to rhyme, especially at the ends of verses, but sometimes at the caesura as well; words not part of the rhyming will at least match each other in accent, as with "omnia" and "feminam." The poetry is filled with the tricks of versification that would become the hallmark of the rhymed sequence in the twelfth century, as can be seen in the final lines of the first half strophes, with the playful rhyming of "virgo" and "viro," the one in the nominative case and the other in the ablative. Indeed, a "virgo" is by definition "sine viro"!

1. Sonent regi nato nova cantica

2.1 Cuius pater fecit omnia
mater est
uirgo sacratissima

2.2 Generans nescit hic feminam
illa est
sine uiro grauida

[1. Let us sound forth with a new song to the newborn king. 2. Whose father made all things and whose mother is a most holy virgin; the begetter knowing no woman and she pregnant without a man.]

By the twelfth century, the desire for rhymed accentual verse with a regular syllable count (rather than variable, as in quantitative poetry) manifested itself in a large group of sequences written in Paris. The apparent master of the style was Adam of St. Victor, now believed to have been the precentor of the Cathedral of Notre Dame, who moved to the Abbey of St. Victor around 1133 and died there around 1146. We cannot say exactly which sequences in the Parisian/Victorine repertory were actually written by Adam, but we can describe the style of poetry created in his school (Grosfillier 2008). The opening strophes of "Prunis datum" for St. Lawrence exemplify the various kinds of word play that are characteristic of the style. The poet has worked to fill not only every line but every phrase of a given line with various kinds of repetition, bringing varying degrees of rhyming into the ends of smaller and larger units. In strophe three, for example, the opening two phrases of each half-strophe rhyme, and in two syllables, but there are related parallels as well, as in "Sicut" and "Sic in," the openings of the two half-strophes. Rhyming within phrases was also employed consistently and often, as in "exultaret" et "sonaret," which sports three "et" sounds, in addition to the rhyming "… taret" and "… naret." Polyptoton is highly favored in this poetry, as can be seen in the first half-strophe with "laureatum" and "laurentium." There are also various uses of chiasmus, as can be seen in the first strophe: the rhymes "admiremur" and "veneremur" create a cross relationship with the opening phrases of the second half strophe: "veneremur" and "deprecemur."

In Victorine sequences, the poetic unit of the three verse lines, which typically comprise a half-strophe, have become tightly controlled cells of rhyme and rhythm, and the musical phrases that sustain them reflect this structure as well. The rhymes of the verse are often captured in the music, especially given the sameness of the cadential phrases that often sustain the large-scale structure of the massive, through-composed works, often thirteen strophes long (Fassler 2011, 72–78). As with rhymed offices, the use of particular textual forms in the late sequence repertory encouraged the creation of contrafacta. The Victorines were especially skilled in this art, and the sequence "Prunis datum," for example, was part of an enormous complex of sequences, interrelated by common melodies and melodic material, and interconnected by theme.

1.1 Prunis datum admiremur; laureatum ueneremur; laudibus laurentium.
1.2 Veneremur cum tremore; deprecemur cum amore; martyrem egregium.

2.1 Accusatus non negauit; sed pulsatus resultauit; in tubis ductilibus.
2.2 Cum in penis uoto plenis; exultaret et sonaret; in diuinis laudibus.

3.1 Sicut corda musicorum; tandem sonum dat sonorum; plecti ministerio.
3.2 Sic in cheli tormentorum; melos christi confessorum dedit huic tensio.

[1. Let us admire the one given to the hot coals; let us venerate Lawrence with praise. 1.2 Let us venerate with trembling; let us pray with love to the excellent martyr. 2.1 The accused did not deny, but, struck, resounded in long trumpets; 2.2 when in torments full of prayers he exulted and sounded in divine praise. 3.1 Just as the musician's string at length gives the sonorous tone by the action of the quill; 3.2 thus stretching out on the harp of torments this man gave the song of the confessors of Christ.]

The highly wrought rhetorical techniques of the Parisian/Victorine sequence repertory exercised a profound influence on the development of liturgical poetry in the later Middle Ages, but other styles of writing sequences continued from earlier times, and new experiments abounded. The highly imagistic sequences of Hildegard of Bingen kept the loosely paired versicle formulae typical of all sequences but spilled over their formal bounds. Her sequences generally were not accentual and rhythmic, although she often flavored a poem with uses of these strategies. The fluidity of form found in her sequences can be discerned in the first three strophes of her sequence for the feast of Ursula and the 11,000 Virgins. Hildegard joins the openings of the first three strophes by setting them to the same music, but the musical parallels are far from exact. Through this tactic, she places the strophes in parallel, making them part of a mega-strophe that constitutes the opening of the sequence as a whole (Fassler 2004). Hildegard thus makes a statement about the mystical relationship between the church, the virgin martyr Ursula, the bride of the Song of Songs, and the Virgin Mary, who was assumed into Heaven as its queen:

> O ecclesia
> oculi tui similes
> saphiro sunt,
> et aures tue monti Bethel,
> et nasus tuus est
> sicut mons mirre et thuris,
> et os tuum quasi sonus
> aquarum multarum.
>
> In visione vere fidei
> Ursula Filium Dei amavit
> et virum cum hos secula reliquit
> et in solem aspexit
> atque pulcherrimum iuvenem
> vocavit, dicens

> In multo desiderio
> desideravi ad te venire
> et in celestibus
> nuptiis tecum sedere,
> per alienam viam ad te currens
> velut nubes que in purissimo aere
> currit similis saphiro

[O Church, your eyes are like sapphire, and your ears like Mount Bethel, your nose like a mountain of incense and myrrh, and your mouth like the sound of many waters. In a vision of true faith, Ursula fell in love with the Son of God and renounced a husband along with this world. She gazed upon the sun and called to the fairest youth, saying: In great yearning I have yearned to come to you and sit with you at the heavenly wedding feast, racing to you by a strange path like a cloud that, in the purest sky, races like sapphire.] (Hildegard of Bingen 1998, 243)

Sequences were often dramatic, and were components of liturgical plays as well. The eleventh-century sequence "Victimae Paschali Laudes" for Easter features the discovery by Mary Magdalene of the empty tomb, and itself became a text often incorporated into Easter drama. The Easter sequence "Epithalamica" is one of Abelard's most complicated and beautiful compositions (if indeed it is by him). The piece is composed in rhythmic verse, exhibits a variety of accentual patterns, and incorporates a refrain. The sequence seems both to express Abelard's love for his wife and to praise God's redeeming love. Its very title speaks of love, for it is a wedding song in which the poet fuses several images from Scripture: the lovers in the Song of Songs, the Wise and Foolish Virgins of Matthew 25, and various female figures he associates with the Resurrection: Miriam, who sings and plays in the Old Testament, the Virgin Mary, and Mary Magdalene at the tomb and in the garden. In this theological love song, the singers grieve when the beloved slips from out of their arms into the bonds of death, only to return for a joyful reunion that features a refrain. The refrain's text comes from Psalm 118:24, "haec est dies quam fecit dominus" [this is the day the Lord has made], also the text of the Gradual for the Easter mass. In the opening few lines the poet quotes from this work to cement the festive relationship, just as he also references the popular eleventh-century Easter sequence melody "Victimae paschali laudes," bringing Mary Magdalene into a new, more jubilatory context (see Waddell 1986).

On yet another level, this sequence is a miniature Easter drama, created to interact intertextually with other elements of the liturgy. If indeed originally written for the Paraclete, the nuns played a significant role, as did Heloise, who lost her husband through their forced separation but could regain him through a love that transcends and justifies loss. In a singing at the Paraclete, the sequence would have joined composer, solo singer, and choir of nuns into one, a performative exegesis rooted in the community and its unique circumstances.

From the penultimate strophes of "Epithalamica":

> Eia nunc comites et Sion filiae,
> Ad sponsae cantica psalmum adnectite,

> Quo moestis reddita sponsi praesentia
> Convertit elegos nostros in cantica:
>
> Quam fecit Dominus haec est dies;
> Quam exspectavimus haec est dies;
> Quae vere risimus haec est dies.
>
> Quae nos eripuit haec est dies;
> Hostes quae subruit haec est dies;
> Quam psalmus praecinit haec est dies.
>
> [And now, companions and daughters of Zion
> Add your psalms to songs for the bride
> For the restored presence of the bridegroom
> Has turned our dirges into carols:
>
> This is the day that the Lord has made;
> This is the day we have awaited;
> This is the day we have truly laughed.
>
> This is the day that has rescued us;
> This is the day that has vanquished the foe;
> This is the day [of which] the psalm sings.]

Liturgical Drama

The body of texts usually called "liturgical drama" (for lack of a better term) offers another window onto the creative process of compilation and adaptation in this period, and thus illustrates other ways in which musical performance could re-present material originally conceived for different purposes. One particularly rich example is the Massacre of the Innocents in the collection known as the "Fleury Playbook" (contained within the twelfth-century miscellany manuscript Orléans, Bibliothèque Municipale, MS 201 because it once belonged to the abbey of Saint-Benoît-sur-Loire [Fleury]). The play of the Innocents weaves together preexisting texts with new compositions in prose and in a variety of verse forms. The opening rubric specifies that "Ad interfectionem puerorum induantur innocentes stolis albis, et gaudentes per monasterium, orent deum dicentes" [for the killing of the children, let the innocents put on white stoles, and rejoicing through the nave of the church, let them pray to God, saying]. The text they are to sing is "O quam gloriosum est regnum in quo cum christo gaudent omnes sancti amicti stolis albis; sequuntur agnum quocumque ierit" [O how glorious is the kingdom in which all the saints, clothed in white albs, rejoice with Christ; they follow the lamb wherever it goes] (*CAO* 4063), an antiphon for the divine office that was traditionally sung on the feasts of All Saints, Holy Innocents, and for several martyrs. The antiphon text combines two quotations from Revelation 7:13: "hii qui amicti sunt stolis albis" and 14.4 "virgines enim sunt hii qui sequuntur agnum quocumque abierit," both of which were commonly cited in anagogical readings of Matthew 2 that interpreted the Holy Innocents as the souls of the elect who stand adoring the Lamb of God at the end of time. The rubric clearly associates the child singers of the first antiphon with this tradition of exegesis and readily links them with the feast of All Saints. The performance both describes and represents the apocalyptic scene, and the next rubric makes the intention of visual symbolism even clearer: "Tunc agnus ex improuiso ueniens, portans crucem, antecedat eos huc et illuc, et illi sequentes cantent" [Then a lamb, arriving suddenly, carrying the cross, precedes them here and there, and they, following it, sing]. This rubric introduces the antiphon, "Emitte agnum, Domine dominatorem terrae, de petra deserti ad montem filiae Sion" [Lord, send forth the Lamb, the ruler of the earth, from the rock of the desert to the mountain of the daughter of Sion] (*CAO* 2642), which quotes directly from Isaiah 16:1, typologically identifying the processioning figure representing the Lamb with the figure of Christ. The beginning of the Fleury play demonstrates the dense semiosis created by the performance of scriptural chant texts: singing each antiphon links its biblical text and the relevant interpretations to the liturgical occasion, deepening the meaning of the Innocents' procession.

A large part of the Innocents drama consists of the lament of Rachel over her slaughtered children, in dialogue with two consolers. After seventeen lines of dialogue in leonine hexameters, the consolers address Rachel with the words of the Notkerian sequence "Quid tu, uirgo." This poem illustrates the prose-like form of the early East Frankish sequences: the lines are of variable length, there is no end-rhyme or meter, and the text is structured around the musical form. Paired lines have the same syllable count because they are sung to the same melody; the first and last verses are sung to melodies that are not repeated. The text is laid out with spaces to show the separation between pairs and independent lines. Each pair of lines is semantically self-sufficient, except for the enjambment between the first line and the first pair.

> Quid tu, uirgo
>
> mater Rachel ploras formosa
> cuius uultus Jacob delectat?
>
> Seu sororis aniculae
> lippitudo eum iuuet.
>
> Terge, mater, fluentes oculos.
> Quam te decent genarum rimulae? (von den Steinen 1978, 86).

[Why do you weep, lovely virgin mother Rachel, whose face delights Jacob? As if the bleariness of your little sister's eyes could please him. Dry, mother, your flowing eyes, how do your cheeks' rivulets become you?]

The fact that "Quid tu, uirgo" was intended to be sung during mass on the feast of a martyr reflects the widespread interpretation of Rachel's lament for her children (in Matthew 2) as the Church's lament for her martyrs, and for the Innocents in particular (Boynton 1998). This symbolism operates on multiple levels: Rachel is a figure of the Church and a type of Mary (as a virgin mother), while Jacob is a type of Christ. At the same time, Rachel is a mourning mother who is admonished for not realizing that her loss is redeemed in heaven. The compiler of the Innocents drama, who understood the layering of meanings in the traditions of commentary on Rachel, reinforced the Marian typology already present in "Quid tu, uirgo" by concluding Rachel's lament with the Good Friday antiphon "Anxiatus est super me spiritus meus in me turbatum est cor meum" [My spirit is troubled and my heart is disturbed within me] (*CAO* 1442). Singing this antiphon, with its text from Psalm 142:4, enacted the typological reading of the Psalms as prophecies of the life of Christ. Having Rachel sing it (along with Christ, and by implication, with Mary) reinforces the Christian idea of fulfillment that stood behind the reference to Rachel's lament in Matthew 2.

The innovative ways that dramatic compositions drew upon preexisting music and liturgical traditions can be seen in numerous other liturgical plays. The reuse of the traditions of the *Ordo Prophetarum* (play of the prophets) in three later works is an example that must stand in here for many comparable families of interrelated liturgical plays. Plays of the prophets were created for the Christmas season, and they featured a singing row of typological figures from the Old and New Testaments, and sometimes from Vergil as well as a Sibylline prophecy. These characters, and sometimes even their texts, were drawn from a sermon by the fifth-century Carthaginian writer Quodvultdeus, a portion of which was read in the night office on Christmas Eve. The *Ordo Virtutum* by Hildegard of Bingen is the first medieval morality play. In order to create this innovative work, Hildegard drew upon the tradition of the prophets' plays. Hildegard turns the tradition on its head, supplanting the patriarchs at the beginning of her work with an ordo of female characters. Each female character embodies a virtue, and, as a group, they war against the devil for the salvation of Anima, the leading character, a kind of "everysoul" with a strong female monastic bent. The play is written in free and lofty imagistic poetry, which relates to Hildegard's other liturgical texts in a variety of sophisticated ways. Chastity is a major character, and her hailing recalls the poetry Hildegard wrote for the liturgical celebration of St. Ursula and the 11,000 Virgins. The Virtues sing to Chastity:

"O Virginitas, in regali thalamo stas. O quam dulciter ardes in amplexibus regis, cum te sol perfulget ita quod nobilis flos tuus numquam cadet" [Maidenhood, you remain within the royal chamber. How sweetly you burn in the King's embraces, when the Sun blazes through you, never letting your noble flower fall] (Dronke 1994, 169).

The tradition of the prophets' plays can be seen operating in *Ordo Representacionis Ade*, a cross-over dramatic work which features a number of sung responsories borrowed from the Lenten liturgy to punctuate scenes from the Fall in Genesis. The play, probably written in the late twelfth or early thirteenth century, depicts Adam, Eve, and the Devil, as well as Cain and Abel. All speak their parts in Old French, while the liturgical texts are sung in Latin, and the whole is concluded by a prophets' play with a strong Marian emphasis; the vernacular play text thus forms an elaborate performed gloss on the Latin responsories and prophecies. In the *Ludus Danielis*, written in Beauvais in the early thirteenth century for the Feast of the Subdeacons (January 1), we encounter another kind of reversal. The prophet Daniel, who was regularly featured in the tradition of the prophets' plays, is a type of Christ. Daniel occasionally speaks in Old French, showing his humility, while the dramatic world around him is filled with the raucous pomposity of the Babylonian court. It is indeed a world turned upside-down, as the Song of the Ass, "Orientis Partibus," is incorporated into speeches for the kings and their counselors (Fassler 1992). The goliardic strophe of 8 and 6 trochaic syllables is used in the stirring song of the satraps, who bear cups to the king:

Iubilemus Regi nostro	magno ac potenti!
Resonemus laude digna	voce competenti!
Resonet iocunda turba	sollempnibus odis!
Cytharizent, plaudant manus,	mille sonent modis!

[Let us jubilate for our King, the great and mighty one! Let us proclaim the praise he merits, with harmonious voice! Let the joyous crowd proclaim it in ceremonial songs! Let their zithers play it, their hands clap it, making it sound in a thousand ways!]

The melody has been adapted from a drinking song also found among the *Carmina Burana*, "Istud vinum bonum vinum generosum" [Such wine, good wine, noble wine], and the youth of Beauvais surely delighted in having goliardic verse in their cathedral, as they sported with the very liturgical vessels it was their custom to steal on January 1. *Ludus Danielis*, January 1, and its traditions refer back to the Feast of Holy Innocents, December 28, on which the elegant Innocents play in the Fleury playbook would have been performed. It too must have had other levels of meaning, one of which was related to the performance by the children who were acolytes. During the week of Christmas, each of the clerical orders celebrated their own identities on a particular day, and the performative exegesis of the dramatic works and other chants was part of a larger celebration that made the Christmas Octave the most musically splendid and textually intricate of the entire liturgical year.

SUGGESTIONS FOR FURTHER READING

Harper (1991) provides a general introduction to the medieval liturgy. For texts of liturgical poetry, the *Corpus Troporum* and von den Steinen (1978) give reliable critical editions. The texts in the *Analecta Hymnica* are sometimes questionable, but this massive collection has not yet been superseded. Editions of both texts and melodies are found in Borders and Brunner (1996–), Planchart and Boe (1989–), Planchart (1977), and Hiley (2001). The classic studies of the early sequence are Crocker (1977) and Planchart (1977). For recent overviews of the manuscript transmission of sequences see Kruckenberg (2006a, 1997). Björkvall and Haug (2000) show the influences of textual and musical forms on each other. On the various ways that sequence texts were sung with and without their melismas, see Kruckenberg (2006b). Fassler (2010) situates liturgical texts in their historical and artistic contexts. Boynton (2004, 2005, 2001b) demonstrates the function of hymns in the teaching of grammar. For editions and studies of liturgical chants by Hildegard of Bingen, see Hildegard of Bingen (1998), Fassler (2003), and Fassler (2004).

BIBLIOGRAPHY

Primary sources

Borders, James and Lance Brunner, eds. 1996–. *Early Medieval Chants from Nonantola*. Recent Researches in the Music of the Middle Ages and Early Renaissance 30–. Madison, WI: A-R Editions.

Corpus Troporum. 1975–. Acta Universitatis Stockholmiensis. Studia Latina Stockholmiensia 21–22, 25–26, 31, 34. Stockholm: Almqvist & Wiksell.

Dreves, Guido Maria et al., eds. 1886–1922. *Analecta Hymnica Medii Aevi*. 55 vols. Leipzig: O. R. Reisland.

Dronke, Peter, ed. and trans. 1994. *Nine Medieval Latin Plays*. Cambridge Medieval Classics 1. Cambridge: Cambridge University Press.

Hesbert, René-Jean, ed. 1963–79. *Corpus Antiphonalium Officii*. 6 vols. Rome: Herder.

Hildegard of Bingen. 1998. *Symphonia*, edited and translated by Barbara Newman. 2nd ed. Ithaca, NY: Cornell University Press.

Hiley, David, ed. 2001. *Das Repertoire der normanno-sizilischen Tropare*. Vol. 1: *Die Sequenzen*. Monumenta monodica medii aevi 13. Kassel, New York: Bärenreiter.

Planchart, Alejandro Enrique and John Boe, eds. 1989–. *Beneventanum Troporum Corpus*. Recent Researches in the Music of the Middle Ages and Early Renaissance 16–28. Madison, WI: A-R Editions.

von den Steinen, Wolfram, ed. and trans. 1978. *Notker der Dichter und seine geistige Welt*. 2 vols. Bern: A. Francke.

Walpole, Arthur S., ed. 1922. *Early Latin Hymns*. Cambridge: Cambridge University Press.

Secondary sources

Arlt, Wulf. 1992. "Sequence and Neues Lied." In *La sequenza medievale: Atti del Convegno internazionale, Milano, 7-8 aprile 1984*, edited by Agostino Ziino, 3–18. Quaderni di San Maurizio 3. Lucca: Libreria Musicale Italiano.

Bjork, David. 2003. *The Aquitanian Kyrie Repertory of the Tenth and Eleventh Centuries*, edited by Richard Crocker. Aldershot: Ashgate.

Björkvall, Gunilla and Andreas Haug. 2000. "Performing Latin Verse: Text and Music in Early Medieval Versified Offices." In *The Divine Office in the Latin Middle Ages*, edited by Margot E. Fassler and Rebecca A. Baltzer, 278–300. New York: Oxford University Press.

Boynton, Susan. 1994. "Rewriting the Early Sequence: Aureo flore and Aurea uirga." *Comitatus* 25: 21–42.

———. 1998. "Performative Exegesis in the Fleury *Interfectio Puerorum*." *Viator* 29: 39–64.

———. 2001a. "Glosses on the Office Hymns in Eleventh-Century Continental Hymnaries." *The Journal of Medieval Latin* 11: 1–26.

———. 2001b. "Hymn, II. Monophonic Latin." In *The New Grove Dictionary of Music and Musicians*, edited by Stanley Sadie, 12: 19–23. 6th ed. London: Macmillan.

———. 2004. "The Didactic Function and Context of Eleventh-Century Glossed Hymnaries." In *Der lateinische Hymnus im Mittelalter: Überlieferung-Ästhetik-Ausstrahlung*, edited by Andreas Haug, 301–29. Monumenta monodica medii aevi. Subsidia 4. Kassel, New York: Bärenreiter.

———. 2005. "The Theological Role of Office Hymns in a Ninth-Century Trinitarian Controversy." In *In principio erat verbum. Mélanges P. Tombeur*, edited by Benoît-Michel Tock, 19–44. Textes et études du Moyen âge 25. Turnhout: Brepols.

Crocker, Richard. 1977. *The Early Medieval Sequence*. Berkeley, CA: University of California Press.

Fassler, Margot. 1992. "The Feast of Fools and *Danielis Ludus*: Popular Tradition in a Medieval Cathedral Play." In *Plainsong in the Age of Polyphony*, edited by Thomas Forrest Kelly, 65–99. Cambridge Studies in Performance Practice. Cambridge: Cambridge University Press.

———. 2003. "Hildegard and the Dawn Song of Lauds: an Introduction to Benedictine Psalmody." In *Psalms in Community: Jewish and Christian Textual, Liturgical, and Artistic Traditions*, edited by Harold W. Attridge and Margot E. Fassler, 215–39. Society of Biblical Literature. Symposium Series 25. Leiden: The Society of Biblical Literature.

———. 2004. "Music for the Love Feast: Hildegard of Bingen and the Song of Songs." In *Women's Voices across Musical Worlds*, edited by Jane A. Bernstein, 92–117. Boston: University Press of New England.

———. 2010. *The Virgin of Chartres: Making History through Liturgy and the Arts*. New Haven, CT: Yale University Press.

———. 2011. *Gothic Song: Victorine Sequences and Augustinian Reform in Twelfth-Century Paris*. 2nd ed. Notre Dame, IN: University of Notre Dame Press.

Gaposchkin, M. Cecilia. 2008. *The Making of* Saint Louis: *Kingship, Sanctity, and Crusade in the Later Middle Ages* Ithaca, NY: Cornell University Press.

Grosfillier, Jean. 2008. *Les Séquences d'Adam de Saint-Victor: Étude littéraire (poétique et rhétorique), textes et traductions, commentaires*. Bibliotheca Victorina 20. Turnhout: Brepols.

Harper, John. 1991. *The Forms and Orders of Western Liturgy from the Tenth to the Eighteenth Century: A Historical Introduction and Guide for Students and Musicians*. New York: Oxford University Press.

Haug, Andreas. 2008. "Re-Reading Notker's Preface." In *Quomodo cantabimus canticum? Studies in Honor of Edward H. Roesner*, edited by David Cannata et al., 65–80. Publications of the American Institute of Musicology. Miscellanea 7. Middleton, WI: American Institute of Musicology.

Hughes, Andrew. 2001. "Late Medieval Plainchant for the Divine Office." In *Music as Concept and Practice in the Late Middle Ages*, edited by Reinhard Strohm and Bonnie J. Blackburn, 45–96. Oxford: Oxford University Press.

Kruckenberg, Lori. 1997. "The Sequence from 1050-1150: The Study of a Genre in Change." Ph.D. diss. University of Iowa.

———. 2006a. "Making a Sequence Repertory." In *The Sequences of Nidaros: A Nordic Repertory and It European Context*, edited by Lori Kruckenberg and Andreas Haug, 5–44. Norges teknisk-naturvitenskapelige universitet. Senter for middelalderstudier. Skrifter 20. Trondheim: Tapir Academic Press.

———. 2006b. "Neumatizing the Sequence: Special Performances of Sequences in the Central Middle Ages." *The Journal of the American Musicological Society* 59: 243–317.

Norberg, Dag. 2004. *An Introduction to the Study of Medieval Latin Versification*, translated by Grant C. Roti and Jacqueline de La Chapelle Skubly, edited and with an introduction by Jan M. Ziolkowski. Washington, DC: Catholic University of America Press.

Planchart, Alejandro Enrique. 1977. *The Repertory of Tropes at Winchester*. 2 vols. Princeton, NJ: Princeton University Press.

Waddell, Chrysogonus. 1986. "Epithalamica: An Easter Sequence by Peter Abelard." *The Musical Quarterly* 72: 239–71.

PART VI

MEDIEVAL LATIN AND THE FASHIONING OF THE SELF

CHAPTER 19

REGIMENS OF SCHOOLING

MIA MÜNSTER-SWENDSEN

While we are reasonably well informed on *what* was taught in medieval schools and which texts were used in teaching, we know far less about *how* teaching was conducted in medieval classrooms and what daily interaction was like between teachers and pupils. This chapter aims to provide a sketch of medieval teaching and learning as a lived experience, concentrating on practice rather than pedagogic theory and hence on a select number of texts that contain vestiges of this practice. The focus here is on the formative period of the medieval schools from the late tenth to the twelfth century, that is, the period before the emergence of universities, and on those stages in which the chief concern was the arts of language—grammar and rhetoric in particular.

Medieval primary education sought to teach linguistic skills while at the same time instilling a moral *habitus* through imitation of textual as well as human examples. The school was a consciously disciplinary system with an ethical purpose beyond the teaching of intellectual skills. As the French sociologist Émile Durkheim states in the chapter on medieval schools in his classic work on the development of French pedagogy, education engenders self-reflection, enjoining its participants to "prendre conscience de soi" (Durkheim 1938, 61). For students *disciplina* became internalized through emulation in a setting where the persona of the magister, demonstrating a living *exemplum* of learning and cultivation, occupied the center of attention.

Frameworks of Pedagogy

In one of the most frequently quoted passages of the *Metalogicon*, John of Salisbury (c. 1115–80) addresses the actual practice of classroom teaching and presents a detailed norm for the division of the activities of a school-day modeled upon the methods of one of the most celebrated teachers of the early twelfth century, Bernard of Chartres (d. 1130). According to John, the grammar master should not only present *his* analysis for the students, but encourage them to analyze the texts themselves, identify the various tropes and rhetorical colors, recognize metrical forms, and uncover the layers of hidden meanings behind the veil of words, the *involucrum verborum*. The teacher should also provide alternative suggestions on how to express meaning, and by repeating them, impress them on the minds of his listeners. He should proceed slowly and make sure that his teaching is equal to the level of discernment of his students. In turn, the students should imitate the teacher's example and produce their own original materials (short pieces in verse or prose), commit parts of texts or precepts to memory, and recite them the day after. John calls this exercise *debitum*, that is, the "debt" to the master. In order to have his students do his bidding Master Bernard uses encouragement, fatherly exhortation, and, only as a last resort, the rod. This pedagogy combines repetition and recitation, mnemotechnical exercises, written composition, and active participation in discussions. John of Salisbury explains: "…prosas et poemata cotidie scriptitabant, et se mutuis exercebant collationibus, quo quidem exercitio nichil utilius ad eloquentiam, nichil expeditius ad scientiam, et plurimum confert ad uitam, si tamen hanc sedulitatem regit caritas, si in profectu litteratorio seruetur humilitas" [… they composed prose and poetry every day, and exercised their faculties in mutual conferences. Nothing serves better to foster the acquisition of eloquence and the attainment of knowledge than such conferences, which also have a salutary influence on practical conduct, provided that charity moderates assiduity, and that humility is preserved during the progress in learning] (John of Salisbury 1929, 57). The school day in Bernard's classroom ended with an "evening exercise" called *declinatio* or a "philosophical collation." This functioned as an opportunity to sum up the lessons, which concluded with a spiritual communion, comprising prayers for the departed and the singing of hymns, before closing with the recitation of the Lord's Prayer. For a concerned twelfth-century humanist like John of Salisbury, this constituted proper *disciplina*: an education that combined the teaching of intellectual skills with the inculcating of an ethical and moral system—the *litterae* and *mores* described so vividly in the work of C. Stephen Jaeger (Jaeger 1994; Jaeger 2002).

John's vignette from Bernard of Chartres's classroom represents the ideal ordering of a school day, yet nothing suggests that the framework and teaching methods depicted do not reflect actual practice or that they were unique to the famous French school. The pedagogic approach and the elements of classroom teaching that John describes can be found in other European schools at the time (and earlier) for which we have at least some evidence of daily practice. For example, a longer passage in the *vita* of Burchard of Worms provides a picture of the cathedral school of Worms around the year 1000. It shows that the same general pedagogic principles employed in Bernard's classroom were applicable to a German school a century earlier. Its students were taught according to their individual capabilities and they were expected daily to prepare a written piece or an oral recitation delivered to the teacher for correction. The *vita* even includes two examples of the so-called *quaestiunculae*, longer and more advanced written exercises, clearly an attempt of the anonymous author to highlight the intellectual sophistication of the early eleventh-century school of Worms. As in John of Salisbury's model school, the pedagogic success of the teacher depended upon his maintaining an open and friendly attitude "so that students are not afraid to have their work examined by him" (*Vita Burchardi*, Waitz 1841, 840–43). In short, the schoolteacher should aim to make himself loved rather than feared, as was generally acknowledged by medieval pedagogues who modeled their pedagogic thinking on Quintilian's *Institutio oratoria*, according to which students "do not seek to imitate those whom they do not love" (for a discussion of this and similar statements, see Münster-Swendsen 2006, 308–9). The key word here is *imitatio*—the main principle of both intellectual and moral formation, in which the set texts and the teacher's person would serve as paradigmatic models for emulation (on the role of *imitatio* in medieval literary culture, see Ziolkowski 2001, 293–308).

So who were these students, and how old were they? In principle, they could come from any social background, though some schools obviously tended to be more exclusive and aristocratic than others. Some of these students may even have been female. According to the standard model of the educational life cycle, school education would start around the age of seven. Medieval pedagogic writers commonly divided childhood and adolescence into three parts consisting of seven years each, and to each part pertained a specific type of discipline. The first seven years of a child's life were devoted to bodily, "natural discipline." During this period the child would become acquainted with the rudiments, such as learning the letters of the alphabet. The next seven years, until children reached the age of fourteen, marked the gradual transition from *pueri* to *scolares*. During this stage of learning schooling would focus primarily on grammar and composition, that is, mastering the learned language while concurrently absorbing moral doctrine. The third stage broadened the scope to the full extent of the seven *artes liberales*, but commonly the main focus would still be on the arts of language: grammar, dialectic, and rhetoric. This arrangement, which played on the heavily symbol-laden number seven, also known as the "Pythagorean" model, is described in a particularly informative twelfth-century pedagogic manual, the *Dragmaticon philosophiae* of William of Conches (c. 1080–1154). In William's ideal classroom, students should "listen and believe" (*audire et credere*) for seven years (commencing at the age of seven) and then "question" (*interrogare*) for the next eight, though, as this pedagogue complained, no one followed that precept anymore: contemporary students were annoyingly demanding and would not only question but begin passing judgment—the master's prerogative—from the outset (William of Conches 1997, 4). In practice, the model based on age-divisions was not followed rigidly, and indeed, it is often difficult to determine the students' age or that of the teachers for that matter. The Latin terminology for age groups was fluid—the term *puer* (boy) could sometimes, according to context or whim, denote a teenager or even a young man in his twenties. Moreover, different age groups were often taught together in the same classroom where the teacher would assign different tasks to his students according to their level of comprehension.

Poetry and versification remained at the core of teaching and learning in medieval schools, both at the primary and the more advanced levels. While the earliest stage in schooling was dominated by rote learning and the recital, repetition, and memorizing of dicta and distichs, which usually contained moral messages, the method of teaching would quickly demand a more active participation of students. *Imitatio* thus transcended mere repetition as students were gradually taught to compose their own texts ranging from a few sentences to longer versified "dissertations" on a wide range of subjects. Most frequently, these subjects would be based upon themes from the classical Roman literary canon (Virgilian or Ovidian themes were particularly popular), but hagiography, letters, the teacher's homemade materials, or even his own student exercises might also serve as a basis for the written works of students. Teaching manuals aside, the everyday practices of teaching and learning are perhaps most clearly reflected in the varied writings that were the products of daily school routines. To give the reader a sense of how teaching was conducted I have selected two examples that stem directly from teaching: one consisting of teaching materials from a monastic school milieu and one from a cathedral school representing the work of a student. Both are from the decades around the year 1000 and from the German Empire, but they reflect practices representative of medieval schools throughout the period with which this chapter is concerned.

A Teacher's Personal Handbook

Among the numerous treasures in the *Stiftsbibliothek St. Gallen*, there is a remarkable manuscript which merits closer scrutiny than it has hitherto received, particularly from the perspective of the history of education: the *Codex Sangallensis 393*, an autograph collection of texts by Ekkehard IV of St. Gall (c. 980–c.1060), the last in a long line of celebrated teachers of this important school. The main text consists of a variety of versified material of varying length touching upon a wide array of topics. Added to these are the author's own numerous erasures and additions, along with an extensive apparatus of interlinear and marginal glosses. The manuscript begins with two prologues, one in prose followed by one in verse. In the prose prologue, Ekkehard alludes to his position as schoolmaster at the cathedral of Mainz, which he held from the early 1020s until 1031, when his patron, Archbishop Aribo, died. The text includes a self-portrait of the author as a master interpreter, explaining to the Archbishop the complex hermeneutics of the liturgical phrase "iube, domne, benedicere" through references to the Roman classics. Having thus struck the initial chord by an allusion to the central part of the work, the so-called *benedictiones* (blessings), and the principle of the co-existence of multiple and differing interpretations, the text breaks off rather abruptly, seemingly because there is no empty space left. The verse prologue is wholly different, being a dedication to a friend and colleague John, deacon, monk, and later abbot of St. Maximin in Trier

(d. 1035), who is cast in the role of the author's muse. After the prologues and until page 184 (St. Gall manuscripts are paginated rather than foliated), the codex contains the *Benedictiones* covering the main features of the whole church year. On pages 185–97 follow the *Benedictiones ad mensas*, blessings for the dinner table. The pages 197–238 are taken up by the *Versus ad picturas domus Domini Moguntine*, comprising the *tituli* designed to accompany the new paintings at the cathedral of Mainz. Pages 239–46 contain similar versified accompaniment to images adorning the monastery of St. Gall, and after this the codex is a miscellany of songs, epitaphs, and other material connected to the school of St. Gall. Among these is a song of the schoolboys addressed to Notker, Ekkehard's former teacher, celebrating the special school holiday after Epiphany (7 January). Mirroring the three gifts of the Magi, on this day the boys are granted an extra supply of torches because of the seasonal darkness, a bath, and last but not least wine. The students play various sports and, asked to "let Parnassus sleep," the teacher lays aside his seriousness and joins the celebration. There shall be no punishments and misdemeanor should be gracefully overlooked. The tradition of this particular holiday is common to medieval schools and found too at the thirteenth-century University of Paris, as illustrated, for example, in the *exemplum domesticum* [homely example] of a song on the liberties of students at the feast of Epiphany from John of Garland's teaching manual of verse and prose composition, the *Parisiana poetria* (John of Garland 1974, 188–91).

As a whole, the manuscript represents the interconnectedness of orality and textuality in several aspects. A reader can almost hear the voice of the teacher between the lines, especially in the glosses, which are likely to have served as lecture notes. A number of verses also carry neumes, and musical terms and musical metaphor consistently play a large role in the text. The system of reading cues that Ekkehard employs likewise points towards the text forming the basis of oral performance. Such cues were meant to guide the speaker in modulating the pitch of his voice and thus draw attention to central parts of the content. (For an analysis of the systematic use of reading cues especially by Ekkehard's teacher, Notker of St. Gall, see Grotans 1997; for a larger study of reading and annotation techniques, see Grotans 2006.)

Despite what the titles and choice of themes seem to suggest, the purpose of the annual cycle of *benedictiones* was clearly not liturgical: the texts are too long, too hermeneutically dense, too "scholastic" and the learned glosses would serve no purpose in a liturgical context. Without excluding other uses of the manuscript, I would therefore suggest that it should be regarded primarily as a collection of home-made teaching materials. It seems Ekkehard wished the reader to understand the title *benedictiones* to contain a pun: these are the teacher's "good sayings" akin to the distichs or *sententiae* forming the textual basis of emulation by students. Single sentences have a distinctly proverbial flavor, and they could easily be taken out of context and used as examples in teaching, exemplifying meter, versification, and moral precepts at the same time. Classical pagan authors are mentioned and quoted extensively, both explicitly and implicitly, even in the most pious contexts. And most importantly, all of the *benedictiones* contain one or more parts marked with the marginal note *dictamen* or *debitum magistro*, thus providing a clue to the origin and use of the text, which is otherwise rarely found even among manuscripts of a similar type. The final *benedictio* (on the Eucharist) carries a further gloss to the *dictamen debitum magistro* mark that explains the purpose of the verse collection: these are the school exercises that Ekkehard was assigned by his teacher, Notker—this is Notker III "Teutonicus," c. 950–1022, author of a large number of Old German translations and commentaries on canonical Latin school texts for use in teaching—which Ekkehard wrote down on parchment and later, to his surprise, discovered preserved among Notker's belongings after the master's death. As Ekkehard explains, he has collected them here for the use of his own students (Codex Sangallensis 393, p. 183; Egli 1909, 279). Furthermore he mentions that the said pieces of parchment were given to him by the teacher, and while schoolboys' *dictamina* would normally have been consigned to wax tablets and thus to impermanence, Notker's gift of precious parchment underscores a special, privileged relationship between this master and his student—a theme that Ekkehard would revisit again and again. Indeed the manuscript is as much a tribute to Notker as to its author's pedagogic ingenuity.

Ekkehard's *dictamina* examples reflect not only the method but the broadness of the content of his teaching, touching upon the whole scope of the *artes liberales* and ranging from the mysteries of faith to the minute technicalities of monastic chant. Hints and more or less hidden allusions to a vast body of classical texts are scattered throughout the whole manuscript. (As was common for the schoolmaster of a community, Ekkehard was also the librarian at St. Gall and hence had a direct access to its remarkable collection. Several extant manuscripts are meticulously corrected and annotated in his highly distinctive hand and in some he even inserted copies of his own poems.) At several places such references occur in somewhat surprising contexts, for example in the *benedictio* for Easter (*In Pascha*), Ekkehard provides the gloss "read Virgil" (Codex Sangallensis 393, p. 81; Egli 1909, 118).

For Ekkehard all types of knowledge are thoroughly interconnected. Thus, even while he elaborates upon strictly religious and liturgical topics, he frequently adds explicatory scientific notes and remarks on the content of the *artes liberales*. For instance, in the middle of the hymn for Epiphany, Ekkehard inserts a note on astronomy and discusses its relation to divination and the art of magic (Codex Sangallensis 393, p. 34; Egli 1909, 49); and in the verses on "the Twelve Pillars of the Church," the longest part in this numerological exposition is taken up by the number seven, and glosses refer the reader to the *artes liberales* (Codex Sangallensis 393, p. 40; Egli 1909, 55). The glosses to the verses celebrating the nativity of John the Baptist revisit the symbolism of the number seven, while in the main text on the page, Ekkehard swiftly changes focus from the Biblical theme to the way the St. Gall choir sing *osanna* instead of *osianna*—"incorrectly, but aptly" as he infers—since this piece of local knowledge also serves as an example of when linguistic rules must yield before the demands of aesthetic impact. He then proceeds directly to the difference of languages and the problems of translation, retorting with a quotation: "Torqueat Erculeam manibus sibi quis, rogo, clavam?" [Who, I ask, turns the Herculean club in his hands?] to which he adds the gloss "responsum Virgilii, quod Democritum non integre latinasset in eglegis incusati" [the response of Virgil, when he was criticized for not having Latinized Democritus completely in his Eclogues] (Codex Sangallensis 393, p. 104; Egli 1909, 15; "Democritum" seems likely a mistake for "Theocritum," but when this confusion arose is uncertain). In the *benedictio* commemorating the beheading of John the Baptist, Ekkehard sees an opportunity to add a moralizing sermon on the temptations of women which then jumps to the question of kinship and parentage. In this context, he alludes to contemporary incest prohibitions, as the glosses make explicit, but the theme shifts suddenly to the hierarchy of languages and the notion of changing one's "nation" by abandoning the rusticity of native mores and attaining civilization through the learned Classical languages:

> Si mare, si terras male conciliatus oberras,
> Captum feminee mersant mulcendo Syrene.
> Ecce modernus Adam, si forte novam petit Aevam,
> Spernit gente paris gener amplexus mulieris.
> Teutonus affinis sordet, studet ergo Latinis
> Extolli soceris seu, quod mage nobile, Grecis.

[If you wander ill-favored by sea or by land, the female Sirens will capture and drag you down by soothing you. Behold! A modern Adam! If he, perhaps, seeks a new Eve, he, as son-in-law, despises the embraces of a woman who is his equal in kin. A German affinity appears coarse, therefore he seeks to be raised on high by Latin parents-in-law, or which is nobler, by Greek ones.] (Codex Sangallensis 393, p. 122; Egli 1909, 175)

This multilayered moral lecture also carries the *dictamen diei magistro* mark. Let me give a final example of Ekkehard's attempt to teach several subjects at once. In the fortieth *benedictio*, entitled *Confutatio rhetorice in facie ecclesie et sanctorum* [*The Confutation of Rhetoric confronted by the Church and the Saints*], the religious theme of confession becomes a vehicle for explaining rhetorical doctrine—or rather both are fused into one, merging language, law, textual composition, and penitence:

> Causa pro nostris si fors sit agendaque rostris,
> Translativa statum lapsis dabit actio gratum.
> Que scripsit pretor, transscribit crimina censor
> Aut genus aut finem renotans, nomen quoque mutans.
> Quale sit exquirens, interdum singula vertens.
> Hic pius ipse deus censor, concessio, pretor.
> Pretor dat signum, censor cruce laudeque dignum.
> Transfert peccata censor pretore notata.
> Ipse Satan quoque sit pretor, transfert ea censor:
> Si fletur, cito transcribit, translatus abibit
> Nullus eritque reo terror, si penitet error.

[If, perchance, a case shall be brought forth on our speaker's podium, a process of appeal will give the disgraced a favorable position. Those accusations, which the *praetor* has written, the censor rewrites, while he redefines their origin or denotation, and also changes their name, as he examines how it is, and sometimes changes the details. The affectionate *censor* is the Lord himself, confession is *praetor*. *Praetor* gives a sign and censor gives with crosses and praise what is deserved. *Censor* transfers the misdeeds which have been noted by *praetor*. Even if Satan himself is praetor, censor revises: If tears are shed, he quickly rewrites, and one will leave delivered of a burden. There will be no terror for an accused, if the error is regretted.] (Codex Sangallensis 393, p. 142; Egli 1909, 206)

The paragraph is heavily glossed. It seems mainly intended to introduce students to Roman legal terminology through an example that combines the themes of courtroom, classroom, and confession that merges Christian and legal doctrine. The text continues with similar expositions of the arts of dialectics and grammar, situating both in a religious context and presenting their precepts as homologous to the doctrines of the Faith, although, paradoxically, the divine mysteries defy all disciplinary rules. Through these often cryptic examples, Ekkehard was teaching students to make similar associations and analogies linking different types of knowledge together while honing their linguistic and hermeneutical skills.

Along with the vestiges of a highly expressive teaching style, Ekkehard's handbook occasionally provides a glimpse of private emotions. In the part of *In Palmis*, which is marked with *dictamen magistro*, Ekkehard glossed the term *doctor* with an impassioned exclamation: "ó Notker" and in the same passage ("Doctor, quod canto Iudeum narrasse memento…" [Doctor, what I sing I recall the Jew told…]) *narrasse* carries the interlinear gloss *mihi et tibi* (Codex Sangallensis 393, p. 66; Egli 1909, 98). In a later series of marginal and interlinear glosses he dwells upon the subject of the student's grief at the loss of his teacher. In Notker's classroom, affection was reciprocal. As Ekkehard explains in a gloss to a poem about the luminaries of St. Gall, the teacher wrote his translations of the great works of the Latin canon "because of his love for his students" (Codex Sangallensis 393, p. 155–56; Egli 1909, 230). These pages are among the most glossed and emended by Ekkehard himself in the whole manuscript. In the epitaph Notker is praised for being *apertus*, open and accessible, which also connotes that his great contribution consisted in opening up the meaning of texts, explaining obscurities by his meticulous expositions (Codex Sangallensis 393, p. 262; Egli 1909, 405). Judging from the manuscript, Ekkehard's teaching, which presumably copied Notker's style, revolved around such *dictamina*, serving as the textual background both for the oral exposition by the teacher (hence the glosses) and the student's reciprocation either orally or in writing. Much of the more intimate interaction between teachers and students would have centered on written and/or recited "homework." It is therefore in the context of the exchange of such assignments that the nature of the daily interaction between teacher and student stands out most clearly.

The Student's Work

As students progressed they would move from minor composition exercises to arranging and completing whole, complex narrative structures. As long as there was no formal ritual to mark the end of education, and thus the transition from student to master, it looks as if these longer works of composition served as a rite of passage, similar to today's dissertations.

François Dolbeau has recently called for an appraisal of the impressive number of versified renditions of saints' lives originally in prose that have been much neglected by scholarship, though they take up a considerable part of the *Monumenta Germaniae Historica*, the *Acta Sanctorum*, and the *Patrologia Latina* collections (Dolbeau, 2002). Dolbeau convincingly argues that the majority of these *vitae* should be viewed in the context of "the classroom exercise of poetic paraphrase." Their often abstruse and hyper-embellished Latinity underscores their function as literary showpieces, and their prologues, which often describe the conception and recipient of the work, point towards their school context. Indeed, such texts were often commissioned by and dedicated to a *magister* of a school, and in the cases where the author can be identified, it appears that the writer was often young and the versified *vita* would usually be his debut work.

One of the most illuminating examples of such student "dissertations" is the highly elaborate work of Walther of Speyer—a student from the school of Balderich, also known by the nickname Palzo of Speyer. In 984, he completed his education at the cathedral school with a rewritten *vita* of St. Christopher in prose and verse versions (Walther of Speyer 1937–39, 10–79). The unique manuscript consists of a compendium of materials, including two introductory letters, one to a female former co-student, Hazecha, and another to three colleagues of the school in Salzburg, Liutfred, Benzo, and Friderich; two prologues, one to each version of the *vita*, in which he informs the reader further about the circumstances of the work's composition; a general preface for readers; and on top of it all, remarkably, a versified "autobiography," the *Libellus scolasticus*, in which Walther presents us with a description of his education within the framework of a highly elaborate and abstruse allegory (for a most helpful German translation of the *Libellus scolasticus* see Walther of Speyer 1962). Interwoven within the rhetorical colors and classicizing imagery we get a rare precise recounting of his educational progress from toddler to teenager. Walther was born in 967 and, as a small child, he was taught to read by his parents. In his seventh year he enrolled in the cathedral school of Speyer, where for the first two years he was taught singing, reading, and writing. In his third school year he embarked upon the study of *grammatica*, which, as Walther states, "for the first time, let me gaze upon the halls of the Romans." He was taught through exercises in composition based upon the imitation of set examples for a period of four years, after which two years were devoted to the remainder of the *artes liberales*. Walther asserts, with a tinge of regret it seems, that nearly eight years of schooling were an extraordinarily short time to complete the whole curriculum. Thus this student was 14–15 years old when he received from Master Balderich/Palzo the terrifying assignment of composing the life of St. Christopher "in the prose of Cicero and the verse of Virgil" (Walther of Speyer 1937–39, 65)—a work it took him three years to complete.

After the death of his teacher in 986, Walther decided to publish his work, which until then had shared a fate similar to that of Ekkehard's *dictamina* to

Notker: languishing among the teacher's belongings. To paraphrase his statement in the preface to readers: why should one write things that no one reads, that no one finds valuable? (Walther of Speyer 1937–39, 12). Thus, the great versified *vita* in six books of hexameters accompanied by its prose version was prepared to be circulated among people within Walther's personal network of learned colleagues. To the *vitae* he added the two letters, the prologues and an allegorized portrait of the author as a young scholar. The prologues and letters depict the young author's insecurity during the writing process and his relationship to his teacher and reveal that the composition was written under close, ongoing supervision (Walther of Speyer 1937–39, 11). To Hazecha, now treasurer at Quedlinburg, he wrote that the teacher's corrections had improved the work, and that the master had also added glosses to it (Walther of Speyer 1937–39, 64). Interestingly, Walther's letter reveals that near the end of her own studies, during the latter half of the 970s, Hazecha had herself composed a work on St. Christopher in verse of *inaudita dulcedine* (unheard-of sweetness), but unfortunately an incompetent librarian lost the manuscript somewhere and Master Balderich was thus unable to return his corrections to his student. How she reacted to receiving Walther's text (if she ever did) is impossible to guess. To the three Salzburg colleagues he wrote that after the grievous death of the master he had found much solace in getting back to the work, in which he found so many traces of the lost paragon. Walther's description of how he completed his task is strongly emotional, stressing the toil of composition, his struggle to please the master, and the fear of disappointing him. The master is a beloved yet awe-inspiring and imposing figure, and the student suffers a mounting anxiety in the anticipation of the teacher's corrections. As an act of appeasement, Walther depicts himself kneeling at the master's feet in supplication, begging him to lead the way. In the prose prologue, the student mentions that he begged the master to leave his habitual friendliness behind when he undertook the correcting and amending of his work (Walther of Speyer 1937–39, 66). Now and then he addresses the deceased teacher directly, as when he introduces his work as "te duce concepta et te interprete lumen adepta accubet ingenuis vel in imo margine biblis" [that which was conceived under your guidance and illuminated by your interpretations, to achieve among noble books its place in the lowest margin] (Walther of Speyer 1937–39, 11). In several places Walther dramatizes the relationship by shifting to dialogue, in which the teacher, as the student's conscience or superego, exhorts him to persevere (Walther of Speyer 1937–39, 12, 15, 65). Elsewhere he addresses the dead *magister* as his "shining star and radiant sun"—metaphors of illumination that highlight the master's charisma which shines from beyond the grave and is now embodied in the student's text.

On the last page of the manuscript, as a sort of conclusion, Walther sketched a curious little figure framed by four hexameters that make up a square and titled it *De sizzugiis*. A *syzygy* is an astronomical term derived from Greek *suzugia* (union) which covers several configurations of celestial bodies (most commonly a conjunction in which earth, moon, and sun are aligned), but it is also a rhetorical term for the combination of two feet within a single metrical unit. Furthermore, it generally connotes the pairing of complementary entities (such as male-female). Here, the master's and the student's names are woven into a figure presenting cosmic harmony and the conjunction of opposites ending with the dedication: "Quas tibi Waltherus, Baldrice, coegit ephoebus" [These, Balderich, Walther the youth joined together for you] (Walther of Speyer 1937–39, 79). Thus the figure may be read as a deliberate symbol of the contemporary ideals surrounding the intimate relationships of teachers and their chosen students.

Learning and Teaching as an Emotional Experience

In the intimate environment of these early schools, *disciplina* became second nature when absorbed by a process of osmosis through the imitation of literary masterpieces and of the provider of knowledge, the teacher-paragon. It is no coincidence that in medieval animal symbolism, the parrot was the embodiment of eloquence, yet imitation is not mere repetition. Both Ekkehard of St. Gall and Walther of Speyer show creative, individual solutions to assigned tasks—and in Ekkehard's case an almost idiosyncratic approach to the learned canon, blending religious and secular elements in an often startling fashion. Despite his assurances of humility, Walther conceived of a place for his work among "those most noble books"—even if his contribution would only be a gloss reflecting the original splendor of its textual and human models. Within their works both portray their former teachers and their teaching styles.

The immense importance placed upon the teacher's person gave rise to a veritable teacher cult and a literary industry aimed at preserving the memory of past masters. Far from being merely sentimental meditations upon private emotions, the teacher portraits found in the literature of the tenth and eleventh centuries, not least the epitaphs included in the circulating mortuary rolls, served an important function of upholding intellectual genealogies that lent prestige to a school and its members. After all, the value of a student's education, in an era before formalized academic degrees or titles, depended upon the master's reputation. Hence, students had an essential, self-serving interest in preserving the master's name and prestige, or even enhancing it through their own literary activities, and reciprocally, the teachers who had managed to make themselves loved could expect to be immortalized in writing (Münster-Swendsen 2008).

The foundation histories of the medieval European schools thus revolve around the personalities of great teacher-paragons. Some of the best examples of early teacher portraits come from the Lotharingian area in the tenth century, notably of such majestic founding fathers as Bruno of Cologne (925–65) (on Bruno and his intellectual circle, see Mayr-Harting 2007) and Ebracher of Liège (d. 971). Here is the condensed portrait of the latter depicting Ebracher as imperial administrator, bishop, and schoolmaster teaching from beyond the classroom:

> …quas ipse vicissim non indignum duxit frequentare, lectiones maiusculis tradere, si quid minus in lectione intelligerent, benignissime identidem inculcare, spondens, quae non tam facile paterent intellectu, se eis vel cencies enodare. Si quando autem eum contingeret, aut ad palatium, aut in expeditionem longius ab hac urbe discedere, quos reliquisset scolarum magistros, litteris animare, ipsis crebro dulci carmine alludere solebat, adeo quibus praesens congaudere non poterat, uti erat imperialibus edictis obnoxius, sepe ab Italia, sepe a Calabria, ut caros filios ad studia incendebat. Nec ante a tam praeclaro labore destitit, donec multos ex rudibus tam spiritualibus quam saecularibus disciplinis brevi perfectos reddidit.
>
> […he in turn did not consider it beneath him to visit them frequently and give lectures to the older students, and if there was something in the lecture that they did not quite understand, he would most kindly inculcate it again and again, assuring them that he would explain even a hundred times that which was not so easily accessible to their understanding. But when it happened that he left this town for a prolonged time to go to court or on a military campaign, he used to encourage the schoolmasters he left behind with letters, frequently joking with them in pleasant verse, so that those with whom he could not enjoy himself in person, as he was obedient to the emperor's orders, he roused to study like dear sons, often from Italy, often from Calabria. Nor did he cease from this admirable work, until he had swiftly made many of the ignorant perfect in the spiritual as well as the secular disciplines.] (Anselm of Liège 1844, 201–2)

Teaching is here presented as a high-status occupation, on par with managing the realm and consorting with the emperor himself. Its driving force is the love of learning and the affection for students and colleagues. This ideal schooling was based upon an affective pedagogy which sometimes found its expression in a strongly eroticized discourse of mutual attraction, playing with a variety of performative stances as seducer, enticer, or as the lover scorned (Jaeger 1999; Münster-Swendsen 2006, 308–17). Medieval teachers would consciously use both negative and positive emotions as instruments of education, and they frequently selected teaching materials that contained emotionally stirring images—for example, choosing the more colorful and sexually suggestive parts of a text as the basis of school exercises. The psychological impact of such texts, particularly those containing more or less explicit sexual violence, on early levels in schooling has been perceptively studied by Marjorie Woods (Woods 1996). Equally, clever pedagogues would use their students' taste for bawdiness, as in the grossly scatological early eleventh-century colloquies of Aelfric Bata, or as in Matthew of Vendôme's wordy late twelfth-century meditation upon a revolting old woman's body in his *Ars versificatoria*. Medieval teachers recognized that just as rhythm helps memory, extreme imagery impresses itself much more readily upon the recipient's mind. Such imagery may also serve to introduce laughter into a potentially conflict-ridden educational milieu, soften the severity of discipline, and, in some cases such as Aelfric Bata's rants, it may allow the students to play with roles of authority, and even challenge the master verbally.

Yet on the other side of the coin we find the less gentle means of persuasion. These are less often encountered in the source material, possibly because they do not fit into the ideal of the cool, calm, and collected schoolmaster. A particularly nasty example of a teacher-student relationship gone awry is found in a letter collection from twelfth-century St. Albans. The correspondents are close friends and ex-schoolmates, though the recipient is also at times addressed as a former teacher of the sender, so presumably the letter-writer attended school at the time when his friend, an older student, was embarking upon a teaching career. In a series of letters, the sender narrates the terrifying school experience of a third friend who as a boy went to a French school accompanied by a private teacher (letters 18–20; *Epistolae ad amicum* 1975, 131–39). This teacher turned out to be a rather cruel character, beating the boy so ruthlessly that at one time he was confined to bed for several months. Furthermore, the horrible teacher—the letter-writer gets the opportunity to exercise his vilifying vocabulary when describing him—tried to ruin the good relationship that the boy had achieved with the renowned Master T, the head of the French school. The stories of the cruel treatment circulate and eventually reach the boy's parents, who promptly demand his return. On his homecoming, the boy's mother is appalled to see the change wrought upon her son, now malnourished, dressed in rags, and with his face distorted by excessive consumption of wine. The boy explains that this is the way of life in the French schools: too little solid food and plenty of booze. Defamed for his mistreatment, the evil teacher takes revenge and continues his torture of the young man, now by means of magic incantations and the tormenting of a wax doll. Though the effect of this voodoo stops after he becomes a canon, the unfortunate student never fully recovers, but is haunted by periods of depression and dies prematurely without fulfilling a promising career. Whether real or fictional, the sad tale of Benedict (the student's name is disclosed in the last letter) is a reminder that despite the meticulously cultivated affective discourse between master and disciple, not all students would recall their schooldays with fondness. The letter-writer's recollection of his own education, too, is full of mental anguish as he inundates his friend with bad school memories, centering on his emotional and intellectual insecurities. It is perhaps no coincidence that another, more famous example of a perversely violent teacher-student relationship, that of Guibert of Nogent (c. 1060–1125), who also suffered damaging physical and emotional abuse by his teacher, also involves a privately hired, semi-learned tutor (1.6; Guibert of Nogent 1981, 38). The most celebrated *magistri*, on the contrary, would typically be remembered for their leniency—being adept pedagogues, so revered and loved that the application of the rod was rarely necessary. It appears to have been generally accepted that excessive punishment was the surest way of destroying a student's character. In fact I have not yet encountered a single instance in which beatings are described in positive terms; on the contrary, they are regarded as a necessary evil. Indeed nothing suggests that medieval schooling was significantly more severe when it comes to physical punishment than what might be encountered in schools well into the twentieth century. The vision of a medieval classroom should not automatically conjure up the brutalizing spectacle of a Dickensian public school regime. The frequency of the use of the rod depended very much on the temperament of individual schoolmasters and the minimizing of its use was a measure of pedagogic success.

Twelfth-Century Renewal or Decline?

Let us for a moment reflect upon a time and its learned milieus, such as the late tenth-century cathedral school of Speyer or Ekkehard's St. Gall, in which the highest intellectual exercise consisted in composing the most elaborate, abstruse verse, playing with ambiguity and a multiplicity of interpretations in a meticulously (and painfully) acquired artificial language. In this intellectual environment, learning is conceived as a unity of all knowledge expressed preferably through the medium of poetry. Now compare this with the misgivings about the schools found in the later literature; in particular the worry about specialization of twelfth-century humanists such as John of Salisbury here singling out the main culprit: "Laudat Aristotilem solum, spernit Ciceronem. / et quicquid Latiis Graecia capta dedit. / Conspuit in leges, vilescit phisica, quaevis/litera sordescit, logica sola placet" [He praises Aristotle alone, he scorns Cicero / and whatever captive Greece gave to the Latins. / He spits upon laws, physics comes to seem worthless, all / literature filthy, logic alone pleases]. For such semi-learned dimwits, John contends, "tormenti genus est, saepe videre librum" [it is a kind of torture often to see a book] (John of Salisbury 1987, 113–12).

The sense of a crisis or decadence of learning is prevalent in later twelfth- and thirteenth-century literature, especially voiced by writers claiming to be defending an "old" approach usually exemplified by these writers' own education. The question remains how much we should take such laments *ad litteram*; how much this topos of the demise of an earlier harmony reflects real circumstances; and to what extent such pessimism was deliberately exaggerating the case to stress the author's point about what comprised true *disciplina*. Like medieval students, modern historians are habitually drawn towards the dramatic and colorful, and I would suggest here that we might have been misled by an explosion of sustained polemical rhetoric concerning the schools. Such rhetoric ranges from the voices of monastic traditionalists since the time of Peter Damian (c. 1007–72), via anti-scholastic satires such as Walter of St. Victor's *Contra quattuor labyrinthos Franciae* [Against the Four Labyrinths of France (i.e., Peter Abelard, Gilbert de la Porrée, Peter Lombard, and Peter Poitiers)], to exasperated secular humanists such as Peter of Blois.

Today's academic discourse still maintains a preference for certain narratives and finds nonlinear structures and plotless, inconclusive developments difficult to describe. The obsession with origins and decline haunts Western historical consciousness perhaps nowhere more than in intellectual history. Equally, in the general history of the Middle Ages, the twelfth century has long figured as the great turning point, and in this historiography, learning and its institutions have played a major role. It has been seen as an age in which reasoning reached a new level of sophistication, marked by increasing technicality and by the triumph of specialization and professionalization, resulting in a burst of creativity and prosperity, the rediscovery of classical philosophies, and, eventually, the rise of the universities. In short, the twelfth century has been presented both as the genesis of the new and as a "renaissance." (There are numerous studies that take this perspective. For a comprehensive survey of the literature and a study of the origins of the concept of a Twelfth Century Renaissance, see Novikoff 2005.) In retrospect, from this pinnacle in the grand narrative, the learning of the preceding centuries appears odd, hermetic, ambiguous, random, or if one judges it by thirteenth-century standards of systematic philosophy, incomplete and flawed. This grand narrative has come under critical scrutiny during the past three or four decades, not by denying that a major change, a series of significant shifts occurred, but by turning the image of progress on its head. R. I. Moore's pessimistic vision of the emergence of an increasingly intolerant "persecuting society," a closing rather than an opening of the mind, provided a new perspective on the century. Since then there has been an increasing tendency among medievalists, if not to discard, then at least to revise the notion of a progressive twelfth century, which sustained the work of great twentieth-century medievalists such as Charles Homer Haskins and Sir Richard Southern. Instead, the twelfth century is viewed as an age of crisis within social, political, and cultural spheres—this with the underlying supposition that crises are often creative. Stephen Jaeger's tantalizing shift between old and new learning and the demise of an old humanist "charismatic" paradigm belong to this category of reevaluation from an age of progress to one of decline. Hence, the works of John of Salisbury or Alan of Lille can be seen alternately as representing the culmination or "swan song" of an old paradigm or as a new departure. Whether the perspective has been the collapse of the old or the arrival of the new, no one denies that this was an era of profound changes within the political, social, and cultural setup of European societies. Yet regarding the manner in which these changes refracted upon the daily practices within the educational system, there is still much work to do.

Historians tend to seize upon what is visible, and before the emergence of the modern research-based university, the vast majority of teachers left no texts. Comparing the diverse and often fragmentary picture gained from the frequently polemical literature about the schools is fraught with methodological pitfalls, particularly when we are dealing with different levels of learning, such as a broad, primary approach and a more technical one reserved for a minority of devoted specialists. It should be obvious that these two are not readily comparable and that it is problematic that intellectual historians have tended to focus on the latter.

If we are searching for profound changes in intellectual and educational norms, they should perhaps be sought on the foundational levels of schooling that had an impact on the largest number of educated people, among those textual products that were most plentiful and most frequently copied. In these contexts the proposed major landslide and historiographical caesura around 1200, whether interpreted as decadence or renewal, becomes increasingly tenuous. Granted, the obsession with the Aristotelian corpus from the thirteenth century on changed the entire focus of certain parts of the university curriculum, yet it does not appear to have affected the methods of teaching the foundational arts of language to any significant degree. (As C. Stephen Jaeger has recently argued, the overwhelming focus on Aristotle and logic among generations of intellectual historians has given rise to major flaws in their evaluation of the learning of the tenth to twelfth centuries; see Jaeger 2009.) On the contrary, on the quotidian level of schooling as experienced by the vast majority of students and teachers, the "old" system was surprisingly durable. If we are to judge from the teaching manuals that were used in the later medieval centuries, poetry remained central to the teaching of Latin composition; learning was still based upon imitation of set examples; the school-year was still structured as in the earlier monastic and cathedral schools, with its special holidays and their accompanying rituals; and pedagogues still recommended that teaching should be based on *amor* rather than *timor*. Learning—as *disciplina*—still consisted of both *litterae* and *mores*.

Let me, as a conclusion, try to illustrate these notions of continuity and change with the help of a thirteenth-century schoolbook: The *Laborintus* of Eberhard the German—a propaedeutic manual for teaching grammar and composition. Next to nothing is known about this Eberhard, and the work cannot be dated precisely: it is thought to have been written between 1218 and 1280. Though relatively little studied, the work is in no way marginal, but was still found in the university curriculum in the late Middle Ages and among the early printed schoolbooks (see Murphy 1984 and Murphy and Davies 1997, 355–62). The text represents an interesting example of the longevity of the pedagogic approaches described above. The content of learning, comprising the unity of the seven liberal arts, is explained through an elaborate allegory. The daily *dictamen* is a main feature of teaching practices, the manual is written in verse, grammatical and moral doctrine are thoroughly entwined, and the focus is still on language and the composition of poetry as the foundation of all learning. For this thirteenth-century schoolmaster, poetry is still the domain that contains everything and explains everything. Even philosophy herself—as personified Poetry contends in Eberhard's allegory—is under her sway and subject to her games (Eberhard the German 1924, 346). Regarding the teacher's attitude, he is exhorted to teach students according to their individual level and skills, and he should represent an example worthy of emulation: "Verba monent, movet exemplum; verbum ferit aures, / Exemplum cordis interiora subit" [Words admonish, the *exemplum* moves, the word strikes the ears, the example sinks into the depths of the heart] (Eberhard the German 1924, 344: 215–16). The sentence implicitly plays on the *verba-verbere* similitude—a topical word play that is repeated again in a more explicit manner when the teacher is told to discipline wayward students with words rather than beatings (Eberhard the German 1924, 345: 231). In its recommendations for teachers, the *Laborintus* stresses an affective and affectionate pedagogy: the teacher teaches by example and the manual thus echoes the general pedagogic precepts of the earlier centuries.

If anything distinguishes Eberhard's picture of schooling from the earlier examples it is its pessimism: the author's bitter irony and sarcasm with regard to the schoolmaster's position. In Eberhard's allegory, Lady Nature even considers whether or not it is charitable to let unborn children destined to become schoolteachers develop. Then follows a list of authors and works that the schoolteacher-to-be will *not* get to read because he has to concentrate on Donatus, whose tiresome propaedeutic textbooks on grammar and rhetoric are truly a "fount of tears." Teachers' complaints about their profession are relatively rare before this period, though already in the late twelfth-century intellectual milieus there is evidence of concern with the loss of social status. Eberhard's thirteenth-century schoolmaster finds himself lost in the labyrinth of learning. In her long tirades, personified Poetry complains of the ills of the day, in particular that teaching licenses are bought for money. Moreover, there is something wrong with the students: "Non placet his cera, sed nummus; non stylus, immo / Talorum jactus;... / Pro studio cauponam, pro doctore tabernae / Provisorem, pro codice scorta colunt... Jurgia dictamen, convicia lectio, pugna / metrum, lis norma talibus esse solet" [They do not find pleasure in the writing tablet, but in money, not the stylus but dice they cast,... they care not for study but for the innkeeper, the tavern rather than the teacher, they worship whores rather than books,... their *dictamen* is abuse, their *lectio* insults, their *metrum* is battle, their *norma* is quarrel] (Eberhard the German 1924, 367: 875–88). Teaching composition to small boys is unbearably tedious and the colleagues are intolerable, pompous dimwits (Eberhard the German 1924, 369: 955–60). Is this simply crass realism finally emerging to tear away the tinsel of the charismatic cult of the *magistri*? For Eberhard's schoolmaster, teaching is, as is implied by the pun in the title, *labor*—a term with negative and demeaning connotations of menial work. Furthermore, teaching is tainted by money matters. Contrary to teachers of the earlier monastic and cathedral schools, Eberhard's teacher is dependent upon a salary. Not that money, in the shape of donations to the communities that housed schools, or patronage of individual scholars, or the existence of privately paid teachers, had no impact before, but now schoolmasters (including those with university affiliation) themselves increasingly needed to cash in their livelihood from reluctant debtors. Hence, Eberhard's manual introduces a new element in the master-student relationship: the lawyers hired by the student's parents. Instead of the idealized conception as an ennobling spiritual gift, learning becomes a commodity to be bought and sold on a competitive market, immediately likened by critics to being nothing short of a prostitution of *Philosophia* herself. Maybe this quotidian economic element, the teacher being dependent upon fees directly from the recipients of their services, marks a much greater cultural shift than any curricular change, inasmuch as it inevitably changes the balance of power within the classroom. The magniloquent, emotionally high-charged cult of the *magister* eventually receded into the background. Neither because of Aristotelianism or scholasticism, nor because of the emergence of a "new" learning, but because of money.

SUGGESTIONS FOR FURTHER READING

In the past two decades there has been a growing interest in the social and psychological implications of school discipline among medievalists, especially following the seminal work of C. Stephen Jaeger (see in particular Jaeger 1994). There is still no major scholarly monograph on medieval pedagogic practice and teacher-student relationships before the universities, but a number of anthologies contain studies that focus particularly on the subject: for the Carolingian period see Sullivan (1995) and for the central Middle Ages see Vaughn and Rubenstein (2006). Numerous studies by literary scholars and intellectual historians on individual school texts and authors shed light on the more intimate aspects of teaching methods and disciplinary practices as well. A good starting point is the expanding scholarship on the twelfth- and thirteenth-century *artes poetriae*—for an overview see Kelly (1991) and Camargo (2003). For the later Middle Ages the work of Rita Copeland and Marjorie C. Woods concerning the teaching of rhetoric and composition is particularly illuminating (Copeland 2001; Woods 1996 and 1999). Regarding the more general social history of medieval education, especially the later Middle Ages, there is a large research literature in German, see Classen (1983); Fried (1986); Kintzinger et al. (1996), and Miethke (2004). In French, Riche (1999) and Verger (1999) provide broad introductions to the European school and university milieus in the early and late Middle Ages. On the transformation from schools to universities, see Ferruolo (1985); van Engen (2000); and Ridder-Symoens (1992).

BIBLIOGRAPHY

Primary sources

Aelfric Bata. 1997. *Anglo-Saxon Conversations. The Colloquies of Ælfric Bata*, edited and translated by David Porter and Scott Gwara. Woodbridge, Rochester, NY: Boydell.

Anselm of Liège. 1844. "Gesta episcoporum Tungrensium, Traiectensium et Leodiensium [Deeds of the Bishops of Tongres, Utrecht, and Liège (Anselm's continuation)]." In *Annales, chronica et historiae aevi Carolini et Saxonici*, edited by Georg Heinrich Pertz et al., 189–234. Monumenta Germaniae Historica. Scriptores 7. Hannover: Hahn.

Eberhard the German. 1924. "Laborintus." In *Les arts poétiques du XIIe et du XIIIe siècle*, edited by Edmond Faral, 336–77. Bibliothèque de l'Ecole des hautes études. IVe section, Sciences historiques et philologiques 238. Paris: Honoré Champion.

Egli, Johannes, ed. 1909. *Der Liber Benedictionum Ekkeharts IV. nebst den kleineren Dichtungen aus dem Codex Sangallensis 393*. Mitteilungen zur vaterländischen Geschichte 31. St. Gall: Fehr.

Ekkehard IV. *Stiftsbibliothek St. Gallen, MS Codex Sangallensis 393*. Also online: http://www.e-codices.unifr.ch/en/description/csg/0393, accessed December 11, 2009.

Epistolae ad amicum. 1975. In *Analecta Dublinensia*, edited by Marvin L. Colker. Mediaeval Academy of America: Publications 82. Cambridge, MA: The Medieval Academy of America.

Guibert of Nogent. 1981. *Autobiographie*, edited by Edmond-René Labande. Classiques de l'histoire de France au Moyen Âge 34. Paris: Belles Lettres.

John of Garland. 1974. *The 'Parisiana poetria' of John of Garland*, edited and translated by Traugott Lawler. Yale Studies in English 182. New Haven, CT: Yale University Press.

John of Salisbury. 1987. *John of Salisbury's Entheticus maior and minor*, edited and translated by Jan van Laarhoven. Studien und Texte zur Geistesgeschichte des Mittelalters 17. Leiden, New York: E. J. Brill.

———. 1929. *Ioannis Saresberiensis episcopi Carnotensis Metalogicon libri III*, edited by Clement C. I. Webb. Oxford: Clarendon.

Walther of Speyer. 1937–39. "*Passio metrica sancti Christophori.*" In *Poetae Latini aevi Carolini*, edited by Karl Strecker and Norbert Fickermann, 10–79. Monumenta Germaniae Historica. Poetae 5.1–2. Leipzig: Hiersemann.

———. 1962. *Der Libellus Scholasticus des Walther von Speyer*, edited and translated by Peter Vossen. Berlin: Walter de Gruyter.

Waitz, Georg, ed. 1841. "Vita Burchardi episcopi Wormatiensis." In *Annales, chronica et historiae aevi Carolini et Saxonici*, edited by Georg Heinrich Pertz, 829–46. Monumenta Germaniae Historica. Scriptores 4. Hannover: Hahn.

William of Conches. *Dragmaticon*, edited by Italo Ronca. Guillelmi de Conchis opera omnia 1. Corpus Christianorum. Continuatio Mediaevalis 152. Turnhout: Brepols, 1997.

Secondary sources

Camargo, Martin. 2004. "Defining Medieval Rhetoric." In *Rhetoric and Renewal in the Latin West 1100–1540. Essays in Honour of John O. Ward*, edited by Constant J. Mews, Cary J. Nederman and Rodney M. Thomson, 21–34. Disputatio 2. Turnhout: Brepols, 2004.

Classen, Peter. 1983. *Studium und Gesellschaft im Mittelalter*, edited by Johannes Fried. Schriften der Monumenta Germaniae Historica 29. Stuttgart: A. Hiersemann.

Copeland, Rita. 2001. *Pedagogy, Intellectuals, and Dissent in the Later Middle Ages. Lollardy and Ideas of Learning*. Cambridge Studies in Medieval Literature 44. Cambridge: Cambridge University Press.

Durkheim, Émile. 1938. *L'Évolution pédagogique en France*. Bibliothèque de philosophie contemporaine. Reprint Paris: Presses Universitaires de France, 1969.

Dolbeau, François. 2002. "Un domaine négligé de la littérature médiolatine: Les textes hagiographiques en vers." *Cahiers de Civilisation Médiévale* 45: 129–39.

van Engen, John, ed. 2000. *Learning Institutionalized. Teaching in the Medieval University*. Notre Dame Conferences in Medieval Studies 9. Notre Dame, IN: University of Notre Dame Press.

Ferruolo, Stephen C. 1985. *The Origins of the University. The Schools of Paris and Their Critics 1100–1215*. Stanford: Stanford University Press.

Fried, Johannes, ed. 1986. *Schulen und Studium im sozialen Wandel des hohen und späten Mittelalters*. Vorträge und Forschungen 30. Sigmaringen: Thorbecke Verlag.

Grotans, Anna. 1997. "'Sih dir selbo lector'—Cues for reading in tenth- and eleventh-century St. Gall." *Scriptorium* 51: 251–302.

———. 2006. *Reading in Medieval St. Gall*. Cambridge Studies in Palaeography and Codicology 13. Cambridge: Cambridge University Press.

Jaeger, C. Stephen. 1994. *The Envy of Angels: Cathedral Schools and Social Ideals in Medieval Europe 950–1200*. Middle Ages Series. Philadelphia: University of Pennsylvania Press.

———. 1999. *Ennobling Love: In Search of a Lost Sensibility*. Middle Ages Series. Philadelphia: University of Pennsylvania Press.

———. 2002. *Scholars and Courtiers: Intellectuals and Society in the Medieval West.* Variorum Collected Studies. Aldershot: Ashgate.
———. 2009. "Philosophy, ca. 950–ca. 1050." *Viator* 40: 17–40.
Kelly, Douglas. 1991. *The Arts of Poetry and Prose.* Typologie des sources du moyen âge occidental 59. Turnhout: Brepols.
Kintzinger, Martin, Sönke Lorenz, and Michael Walter, eds. 1996. *Schule und Schüler im Mittelalter.* Beihefte zum Archiv für Kulturgeschichte 42. Cologne: Böhlau.
Mayr-Harting, Henry. 2007. *Church and Cosmos in Early Ottonian Germany. The View from Cologne.* Oxford: Oxford University Press.
Miethke, Jürgen. 2004. *Studieren an mittelalterlichen Universitäten. Chancen und Risiken.* Education and society in the Middle Ages and Renaissance 19. Leiden, Boston: Brill.
Münster-Swendsen, Mia. 2006. "The Model of Scholastic Mastery in Northern Europe c. 970–1200." In *Teaching and Learning in Northern Europe 1000–1200*, edited by Sally N. Vaughn and Jay Rubenstein, 306–42. Studies in the early Middle Ages 8. Turnhout: Brepols.
———. 2008. Medieval "'Virtuosity'—Classroom Practice and the Transfer of Charismatic Power in European Scholarly Culture c. 870–1200." In *Negotiating Heritage: Memories of the Middle Ages*, edited by Mette Birkedal Bruun and Stephanie A. Glaser, 43–63. Ritus et artes 4. Turnhout: Brepols.
Murphy, James J. 1984. "Rhetoric in the Earliest Years of Printing 1465–1500." *Quarterly Journal of Speech* 70: 1–11.
Murphy, James J. and Martin Davies. 1997. "Rhetorical Incunabula: A Short-Title Catalogue of Texts Printed to the Year 1500." *Rhetorica* 15: 355–65, 367–443.
Novikoff, Alex. 2005. "The Renaissance of the Twelfth Century before Haskins." *Haskins Society Journal* 16: 104–16.
Riché, Pierre. 1989. *Écoles et enseignement dans le haut Moyen Âge fin du Ve siècle–milieu du XIe siècle.* 2nd ed. Reprint Paris: Picard, 1999.
de Ridder-Symoens, Hilde, ed. 1992. *Universities in the Middle Ages.* The History of the University in Europe 1. Cambridge: Cambridge University Press.
Sullivan, Richard E., ed. 1995. *"The Gentle Voices of Teachers": Aspects of Learning in the Carolingian Age.* Columbus, OH: Ohio State University Press.
Verger, Jacques. 1999. *Culture, enseignement et société en Occident aux XIIe et XIIIe siècles.* Collection "Histoire". Rennes: Presses Universitaires de Rennes.
Woods, Marjorie C. 1996. "Rape and the pedagogical rhetoric of sexual violence." In *Criticism and Dissent in the Middle Ages,* edited by Rita Copeland, 56–86. Cambridge: Cambridge University Press.
Woods, Marjorie C. and Rita Copeland. 1999. "Classroom and Confession." In *The Cambridge History of Medieval English Literature*, edited by David Wallace, 376–406. New Cambridge history of English literature. Cambridge: Cambridge University Press.
Ziolkowski, Jan M. 2001. "The Highest Form of Compliment: *Imitatio* in Medieval Latin Culture." In *Poetry and Philosophy in the Middle Ages—A Festschrift to Peter Dronke*, edited by John Marenbon, 293–308. Mittellateinische Studien und Texte 29. Leiden, Boston: Brill.

CHAPTER 20

GENDER

SYLVIA PARSONS AND DAVID TOWNSEND

THE pervasively male authorship and audience of medieval Latin literary culture powerfully naturalizes an ideology that allows the relativity of the tradition's gendered constructions to masquerade as given and unexceptionable. That ideology, moreover, has often just as profoundly constrained modern studies of how gender matters in the primary texts. Yet like all ideological formations, medieval Latinity's self-understanding as the tongue of the fathers *par excellence* depends upon continued discursive performances that carry the seeds of their own undoing. A literary tradition that represents itself as a celebration of disembodied yet normatively male authority, it risks with surprising frequency the unmanning of its own gendered identifications.

This essay explores the ways that intertextual and reflexive constructions of authority and textuality both enable and circumscribe medieval Latin authors as they develop and critique models of gender. Thus we focus neither upon sociohistorical description nor principally upon analysis of concepts of gender as applied to represented characters. Rather, we address implicit (or more rarely explicit) metacritical self-understandings of textuality. The rhetoric of gender as deployed in medieval Latin of course reflects and in turn shapes extratextual realities; but at a prior level, it depends upon a system of palimpsested, specifically textual cultural markers bounded within the constraints of quintessentially Latinate expectations of diction and genre. Prior to the syntagmatic relations of text to social environment lie the paradigmatic requirements of gender as dictated by ubiquitous classical and patristic models, and as expressed not merely in the specifics of a male or female character's representation but in the very constraints of generic expectation.

This is not to say that such genre-determined models of gender are narrowly reductive or unsusceptible of internal contradiction. But it is to say that the range of possible tensions is itself contained within limits set by prior expectation. Given the artificiality of interpretive competency in Latin as a learned language of high culture, continuously reinforced by the regimen of the schoolroom and by the high value placed on successful imitation of models (on which see Münster-Swendsen in this volume), modification or subversion of generic expectation is no more likely to derive from the representation of contemporary life outside the text than from intertextual relationships with recognizable models. Traditional Benedictine praxis inculcated in authors ruminative styles of reading that in turn shaped an approach to texts as attentive to their internal world as to their relationship to extratextual realities.

The investment of specific genres and reading environments in concomitant models of gender suggests that switching from one identifiable generic code to another implies a switch from one code of gender to another. Likewise, the hybridization of genre within a given text involves as well an exploration of hybrid models of gender. Thus, the scandal of textual incongruity is likely to offer a site of exploration for the scandal of incongruously juxtaposed models of gender. The monastic literary environment offers an apt field of analysis, not only for its distinctive reading praxis but because the uniformity of monastic rules and customaries created a space of intensified homosociality in which codes of gender difference were necessarily devised and performed primarily within the theater of the text. This is emphatically *not* to say that the profound artificiality of gender, and of gendered desire, in a monastic context is equivalent to its abstraction from the lived subjectivity of those who produced and received these texts. The imagination of gender as a textual performance, rather, is bound up inextricably with the *Latinitas* of that performance, as a technology of lived experience. The artifice of such a technology of experience stands in full congruence with the monastic *regula* as itself the primary force that both shaped monastic life and determined the desirous possibilities of monastic imagination—for celibate culture was at no point exclusive of discourses of desire. Thus we concentrate below on monastic texts, in order to demonstrate the quintessential intertextuality of their Latinate encoding of gender and its hybridizations. We address Benedictine texts of the tenth through the early twelfth century, namely, the dramas and narrative poems of Hrotsvit of Gandersheim, the *Waltharius*, Reginald of Canterbury's *Vita Sancti Malchi*, and the lyrics of Baudri of Bourgeuil.

Hrotsvit and the Dialogization of Genres

Hrotsvit's negotiations of the dialectic between gender and the implications of genre-specific conventions and diction are pervasive throughout her corpus. Such issues are central to the *recusationes* of her prefatory letters to the dramas of Book 2. There, however, the conventions of the modesty topos might lead us to discount the seriousness of her meditation on the burdens of writing as a woman in genres whose constructions of masculinity and femininity variously privilege the former. In the

Gesta Ottonis she likewise exploits the heightened rhetorical self-consciousness of the *recusatio* to explore the gendered implications of genre: here she suggests that a woman sequestered from martial experience and values is by the very circumstances of her life ill suited to the practice of epic. In both these cases, *recusatio* arguably functions not so much as the denial of Hrotsvit's qualifications that it purports to be, but rather as a sort of *praeteritio*, asserting her qualifications by implicitly inviting from her readers a reconsideration of the naturalized mapping of gender onto genre. But both these passages, and the ways they raise issues recurrent throughout the corpus, are perhaps best addressed after a consideration of her most radical single foray into the metacriticism of gender and genre, the play *Pafnutius*.

Pafnutius stands out among Hrotsvit's dramas not only for its length but for its striking amalgamation of contrasting generic conventions and expectations. Presupposing the underlying template of Hrotsvit's explicitly declared imitation of Terentian comedy, the opening scene invokes as well the homosocial conventions of the schoolroom dialogue. This disproportionate episode, whose sheer *copia* threatens to swamp the remainder of the play, grounds its staging of the classroom in late antique treatments of theoretical music, and particularly in the *De institutione arithmetica* of Boethius (Chamberlain 1980). In the context of Hrotsvit's emulation of Terence, the entirely fictive dramatic conventions of the academic colloquy here playfully cross over to the possibility of a literalized performance. The disembodied abstractions of the dialogue would only be heightened by a fully realized staging. Its gratuitous length is dramatically justified only by its final perfunctory transition from macrocosmic music and its microcosmic human counterpart to the specificity of one shameless and notorious courtesan plying her trade in a nearby city. The unprepared abruptness of the shift from the sublimity of earlier preoccupations to obsession with an arbitrarily singled-out flaw in the cosmic harmony threatens to undercut the scandalized earnestness of Pafnutius and his followers.

> *Pafnutius.* Sed quid moror in istis que vobis minimum afferunt delectationis?
> *Discipuli.* Enuclea nobis causam tui meroris . ne diutius frangamur pondere curiositatis.
> *Paf.* Si quando experiemini . auditu non delectabimini.
> *Disc.* Haut raro contristatur qui curiositatem sectatur . sed tamen hanc nequimus superare . quia familiaris est fragilitati nostre.
> *Paf.* Quedam inpudens femina moratur in hac patria.
> *Disc.* Res civibus periculosa.
> *Paf.* Hec miranda prenitet pulchritudine . et horrenda sordet turpitudine.
> *Disc.* Miserabile. Quid vocatur?
> *Paf.* Thais.
> *Disc.* Illa meretrix?
> *Paf.* Ipsa.
>
> [*Paf.* But why do I linger on these matters that bring you so little satisfaction?
> *Disc.* Unlock the cause of your discomfort. Don't crush us any longer under the weight of curiosity.
> *Paf.* If you find out, hearing it won't please you.

Disc.	One who chases his curiosity often enough comes to grief; yet we can't overcome it, innate as it is to our fragile condition.
Paf.	A shameless woman dwells in this land.
Disc.	There's a menace to the citizenry!
Paf.	She glitters with wondrous beauty—and wallows in horrific turpitude.
Disc.	O wretched circumstance! What's her name?
Paf.	Thais.
Disc.	That whore?
Paf.	The very one.] (Hrotsvit 2001, 225)

To be so deeply preoccupied by late antique formulations of a liberal art is itself incongruous with the conventions of early monastic discourses of eremitic spirituality, as voiced in the *Vitae patrum* and in the works of Cassian, and as such arguably constitutes a shift from transcendent *sapientia* into secular *curiositas*—a curiosity explicitly named as such once the conversation turns to Thais herself. (Thus Hrotsvit's dialogization of generic expectations includes the literature of the desert as a third element implicitly framing the play as a whole.) Pafnutius's further descent from theoretical speculation into obsessive concern for the transgressions of a single whore in turn represents a distraction from the purity of his withdrawal from a world of libertine urbanity—a withdrawal upon which his entire life is already predicated. At the end of the dialogue, with the announcement of his plan to impersonate one of Thais's suitors and in that guise to approach her with a call for repentance, he crosses the boundary from a masculinity whose spiritual purity is expressed precisely as a regimen of renunciatory abstraction into an impersonation of the bathos of lustful obsession.

Hrotsvit here presents Pafnutius less as a character than as mouthpiece for a discourse that enacts a model of gender precisely in and through its performance of generic expectation. Thus his descent to the level of the particular *eo ipso* destabilizes the credibility of his gendered purity, all the more so because that purity is already cast as a confused amalgam of Neoplatonic speculation and desert spirituality. If all this is strongly implied by the conclusion of the play's first scene, it is confirmed to playful but unmistakable effect in the transition to the second. There, Pafnutius is transported instantaneously to the square before Thais's house and, simultaneously, squarely into one of the most stereotypically Terentian moments in Hrotsvit's entire corpus, complete with a group of sexually frustrated suitors eager to share with a newcomer the depths of their passion for a woman whose full devotion remains unattainable. Pafnutius's cluelessness in asking them to point out which of the nearby houses belongs to Thais does more than convey him by stages from his hermitage to her boudoir. It serves as well to establish in a few short lines, with a ham-fisted emphasis that is itself part of the humor of the scene, the implicit dramaturgy of the Terentian streetscape. It further jeopardizes the abstracted, renunciatory authority of Pafnutius's masculinity—not in the first instance by calling into question the purity of his motives, which remain implicit, but by his complicit co-performance of the fallible, comic, and sexually obsessed masculinity of his much younger fellows in the marketplace. We fully enter the hagiographic core of the play, the ostensible excuse for its existence, with the scene in which Thais welcomes Pafnutius into her house. But by this point, Pafnutius is in a double bind, not only as a minimally realized character who must convey his outrage towards the woman he hopes to convert, but at a prior level as the embodied performance of linguistic conventions dependent on the generic expectations of reader or audience. At this point in the play, those generic expectations are confusingly manifold indeed, including not only the classroom dialogue and the Terentian comedy, but hagiographical romance and the colloquies of the desert fathers.

This uneasy amalgam creates one of the edgiest, least reverent moments in the entire drama: the point at which Pafnutius's continued request to retreat further and further into Thais's private space finally results in her declaration that she will take him to a place so secret it's known only to her and God:

Pafnutius.	Secretum nostre confabulationis . desiderat solitudinem loci secretioris.
Thais.	Ecce cubile stratum . et delectabile ad inhabitandum .
Paf.	Estne hic aliud penicius . in quo possimus colloqui secretius?
Thais.	Est etenim aliud tam occultum . tam secretum . ut eius penetral nulli preter me nisi deo sit cognitum .
[*Paf.*	The secret of our exchange wants the solitude of a more secret spot.
Thais	Here's a nicely made bed to hop into.
Paf.	Isn't there someplace further inside where we can talk more privately?
Thais.	Oh, yes. There's another spot so hidden, so secret, that only God and I know its depths.] (Hrotsvit 2001, 229)

The comedy of the exchange is ribald if fleeting comedy indeed. In the midst of his impersonation of the love-struck client, he even manages to deliver an outrageously suggestive, and painfully sophomoric, homophony in "penicius." For this brief moment only, the joke is dependent upon the fact that Pafnutius wants it all ways at once, as a performer in turn of the generic masculinities of the school dialogue, the desert adept, and the Terentian suitor. Reading his performance as embodying the last of these, Thais responds with an innuendo upon which Pafnutius immediately capitalizes. He turns her blasphemously irreverent quip into the occasion for his rebuke of her harlotry, in the process apparently pulling her in the course of a few shorts lines from the space of her own Terentian performance into the discourse of hagiographical renunciation that will dominate the remainder of the play.

The most trenchant of Hrotsvit's metacritical evaluations of how gender is performed through the reproduction of generic expectation is, however, yet to come. The severity of the penance imposed by Pafnutius on the repentant Thais brings her up short—as it does as well the abbess of the house to which Pafnutius leads her. The evaluative purchase that the text accords to the women's resistance transcends the question of their motivation as two-dimensional characters. The feat of asceticism imposed by Pafnutius upon Thais, before it constitutes a representation of her motivation as a character, maps the conventions of desert spirituality onto those of more moderate Benedictine hagiographical models far closer to the lived experience of Hrotsvit's own house of Gandersheim. It also projects onto the body of the reformed prostitute the radically embodied desert spirituality that Pafnutius has abjected in favor of the abstract preoccupations of the schoolroom. In this contest of discourses, the resistance of the abbess functions as a "reading interlude"—appealing from within the text to receptions it might have elicited among a privileged and notably empowered community of aristocratic and highly educated women, many of them canonesses with at least a nominal option of leaving the house and returning to secular life (Goetting 1973).

Finally, in one last jarring stylistic shift, the text concludes with Pafnutius's prayer of consolation in the presence of the dying Thais. Delivered in a single convoluted periodic sentence, it returns to abstract contemplation of humanity as a microcosmic harmony of opposites. Here Thais, as Pafnutius prays for her, is no longer *femina* nor *muliercula*, but, three times in close succession, *homo*, her gender marked only by the grammatically feminine modifier that denotes her imminent death in the phrase "huius solvende hominis." In thus hearkening back to the generic conventions of the opening scene, the prayer's abstractions drive home one last time the play's relativization of masculinist models of sanctity as contingent upon the generic conventions that support them.

In light of *Pafnutius*'s exuberant staging of gender as a contest between the discursive expectations of disparate genres, Hrotsvit's subversive explorations are palpable throughout the corpus, as her imposition of Terentian comic form onto hagiographical content necessarily sets alternative gender constructs into contestative relation with one another. Debates about the meaning of Hrotsvit's assertion of Terentianism generally turn on the palpable departures of her texts from her avowed models (Coulter 1929; Burgess 1968; De Luca 1974; Talbot 2004). Yet at the level of generically determined representations of gender, the grafting of a masculinity risibly fallible in its obsessive subordination to the disempowering demands of lust—the stock in trade of Terentian comedy—remakes the stories of virgin martyrs into a gynocentric critique of masculinist projections of femininity. No scene in Hrotsvit's plays exemplifies this so vividly, or so entertainingly, as that in which one of three incarcerated sisters watches through the chinks in a door, narrating to the others the details of their captor Dulcitius's self-defilement with a kitchen's worth of sooty pots and pans (Hrotsvit 2001, 168–69). The dramatic convention of offstage narration here serves to reverse the nearly ubiquitous scopic economy of martyrial *acta*, in which the suffering body of the heroine becomes the object of the text's unflinching gaze.

To return from these dialogized enactments to Hrotsvit's self-conscious meditations on genre and its gendered implications in her *recusationes*, it is in these, with their explicit meditations on the gendered implications of genre, that she most self-consciously disengages her authorial voice from the presumptively male generic voice implicit in her intertexts. Fully conscious of the potential destabilizations inherent in speaking from a marginal position, she declares in the *Praefatio* to the dramas of Book 2 that she exults particularly in imposing the plots of female martyrdom on the Terentian model. Her modest boast—"triumphantium victoria probatur gloriosior presertim cum feminea fragilitas vinceret et virilis robur confusioni subiaceret" [the victory of the triumphant is in particular proven all the more glorious when womanly fragility conquers and manly strength lies low]—conflates the victory of the female martyrs she celebrates with her own achievement in overthrowing the "turpia lascivarum incesta feminarum" [shameful disgrace of lustful women] with the "laudabilis sacrarum testimonia virginum" [praiseworthy witness of holy virgins] (Hrotsvit 2001, 132). Likewise, she draws back from the traditional martial matter of epic in the *Gesta Ottonis* with the declaration, "Sed nec hoc fragilis fas esse reor mulieris/Inter cenobii posite secreta quieti,/Ut bellum dictet, quod non cognoscere debet." [But neither do I claim that it is the part of a weak woman, sheltered in the quiet of an abbey's privacy, to write of war, which she has no business knowing] (*Gesta Ottonis*, ll. 243–45, Hrotsvit 2001, 284). She sets aside battle as the sphere for the "perfectorum...virorum sudori" [the labor of perfect men] (*Gesta Ottonis*, ll. 246 and 249, Hrotsvit 2001, ibid.). While Hrotsvit demurs that as a female monastic she risks encroaching on the masculine space of epic, she thereby frees herself to focus on dynastic concerns that emphasize the dependence of epic's aristocratic warrior ethos on the continuities of marriage and reproduction guaranteed by women. When she refers in the poem's opening lines to her "vilis textum monialis" [the weavings of a meager nun] (*Gesta Ottonis* l. 5, Hrotsvit 2001, 275), she associates her enterprise with the textile arts traditionally symbolic of women's work. In the male authors to whom we now turn we will see other interweavings of gendered voices within the fabric of genre: Hiltgund's ironic counterpoint to epic masculinity in the *Waltharius*; Malcha's textually significant textile expertise in the *Vita Sancti Malchi*; Dido's voice haunting Baudri of Bourgueil's invocation of a fantasized reproductive domesticity spliced into the world of monastic celibacy and poetic industry. In all of these texts, male authors ventriloquize female voices. Like Hrotsvit's subversive *recusationes*, however, these counter-voices suggest that even for male authors, gaps exist between the masculine identifications of individual authorial personae and the normative idealizations encoded in the generic models. The ensuing tensions undermine monologic gendered identifications.

Ironic Intertextuality in the Waltharius

The *Waltharius*, a short anonymous epic of the ninth or tenth century directly addressed in its opening lines to an audience of *fratres*, overlays a celebration of the vernacular heroic masculinity of Germanic legend with a dense network of Vergilian allusion. The Vergilian intertext, however, does not so much translate the Germanic hero into classical terms as destabilize epic masculinity itself. Peter Dronke has pointed out the collocation of references to the bereaved Dido in the poem's description of Attila searching in vain for the departed Walther, the Aquitanian hostage to the Pannonian court who has escaped with his fellow-hostage and betrothed, the Burgundian princess Hiltgund (Dronke 1971, 159–64). The intense irony of the passage depends upon readerly expectations of gendered representation, expectations shaped less by contemporary social circumstance than by the codes of a canonical model. Only in relation to such codes does the Hunnish despot's transgression of gendered norms come into sharp focus:

> Iam princeps nimia succenditur efferus ira,   380
> Mutant laetitiam maerentia corda priorem.
> Ex humeris trabeam discindit ad infima totam
> Et nunc huc animum tristem, nunc dividit illuc.
> Ac velut Aeolicis turbatur arena procellis,
> Sic intestinis rex fluctuat undique curis,   385
> Et varium pectus vario simul ore imitatus
> Prodidit exterius, quicquid toleraverat intus,
> Iraque sermonem permisit promere nullum.
> Ipso quippe die potum fastidit et escam,
> Nec placidam membris potuit dare cura quietem.   390
> Namque ubi nox rebus iam dempserat atra colores,
> Decidit in lectum, verum nec lumina clausit,
> Nunc latus in dextrum fultus nunc inque sinistrum.
> Et veluti iaculo pectus transfixus acuto
> Palpitat atque caput huc et mox iactitat illuc,   395
> Et modo subrectus fulcro consederat amens.
> Nec iuvat hoc, demum surgens discurrit in urbe,
> Atque thorum veniens simul attigit atque reliquit.
> Taliter insomnem consumpserat Attila noctem.

[Now the fierce prince is enflamed with excessive rage, a grieving heart transforms his earlier happiness. He rends his whole cloak from shoulder to hem and divides his sad spirit now to this side, now to that. And just as the sand is stirred up by Aeolic storms, so the king tossed on waves of inner care, and matching his changing countenance to his changing heart, he revealed without whatever he endured within, and wrath allowed no speech to come forth. That day he spurned both food and drink, nor could his anxiety give him easy rest. When black night leached color from all things, he fell abed but did not close his eyes. Propped now on his right side, now on his left, fixed through the heart as with a sharp javelin, he trembled and soon tossed his head this way and that and now sat up distracted against the bedpost. Nor did this help, but, rising up at last, he ran through the city, and coming again to his couch touched it only to leave it again at once. So Attila spent the night without sleep.] (*Waltharius* 1951, ll. 385–99)

The entire passage is rife with verbal echoes of the *Aeneid*, but three are particularly telling for their direct evocation of Aeneas's liaison with Dido: just three lines after Attila is presented as an *efferus princeps* in his rage, line 383 closely imitates *Aeneid* 4.285, "Atque animum nunc huc celerem nunc dividit illuc," where Aeneas vacillates upon first hearing the divine directive to leave Carthage to seek his destiny. Line 390 follows *Aeneid* 4.5, "...nec placidam membris dat cura quietem," where the line refers to Dido's first lovesick obsession with her Trojan guest. The sense of line 397 recalls the substance though not so exactly the wording of *Aeneid* 4.68–69: "Uritur infelix Dido totaque vagatur/ Urbe furens."

Ironic intertextuality has already come into play a little differently almost immediately before this passage, in Walther's arming scene as he and Hiltgund prepare to set out (ll. 326–38). Here, context overturns implicit gendered expectations of a broader narrative arc. The arming scene, which follows the comic subterfuge of a banquet in which Walther renders the Pannonian nobility senseless with drink on the night of the escape, does not lead to the combat that epic convention suggests should ensue. Rather, it takes place as a preparation for flight. We begin with four lines (326–29) in which the hero leads forth his mount, appropriately named "Leo." But immediately thereafter, the first incongruous note is struck in lines 330–31 with a descent to pragmatic details of loading the steed with contraband and provisions. The diversion proves as brief as it is abrupt. The passage moves back into a detailed description of Walther's arms (ll. 333–38) that would suggest to a reader competent in the conventions of epic the commencement of an *aristeia*. Our hero, however, having seized spear and shield, now makes his escape rather than joining battle. He departs not *intrepidus* as convention would demand, but just the opposite:

> Tunc hastam dextra rapiens clipeumque sinistra
> Coeperat invisa trepidus decedere terra.

[Then seizing the spear with his right hand and the shield with his left, he fearfully began to take leave of that hateful land.] (ll. 339–40)

In the immediately ensuing description of flight through the countryside by night, narrative attention to Walther's now-pointless weapons is dropped with the single comment that, weighed down as he is, Hiltgund must take up the practical equipment for the journey. No longer mentioned, the weapons presumably now constitute an encumbrance as the escaping couple move through a landscape whose generic reflexes owe something to bucolic as well as to epic convention, in particular the "montibus intonsis" [unshorn mountains] of line 356 recalling those of Vergil's *Eclogae* 5.63, and where the most sustained parallel of thought with the *Aeneid* is not with a martial scene, but of lines 347–53 with Aeneas's fearful escape from Troy in *Aeneid* 2.725–29.

The articulation of gender as a collocation of generic expectations of diction, specific textual reference, and narrative patterns is nowhere more vividly in evidence than in the peculiar scene in which Hiltgund responds to Walther's initial proposal of flight with a remonstrative outburst:

> Provocat et tali caram sermone puellam:
> "Exilium pariter patimur nam tempore tanto,
> Non ignorantes, quid nostri forte parentes
> Inter se nostra de re fecere futura.
> Quamne diu tacito premimus haec ipsa palato?"
> Virgo per hyroniam meditans hoc dicere sponsum

Paulum conticuit, sed postea talia reddit:
"Quid lingua simulas, quod ab imo pectore damnas,
Oreque persuades, toto quod corde refutas,
Sit veluti talem pudor ingens ducere nuptam?"
Vir sapiens contra respondit et intulit ista:
"Absit quod memoras, dextrorsum porrige sensum!
Noris me nihilum simulata mente locutum,
Nec quicquam nebulae vel falsi interfore crede.
Nullus adest nobis exceptis namque duobus..."

[And he addressed the dear girl with words like this: "We have long suffered exile together, aware of what our parents decided between them about our affairs. How long shall we suppress all this with a mute tongue?" The maiden, thinking her betrothed was speaking ironically, was silent for a little while, but then answered thus: "Why do your words counterfeit what deep in your heart you abhor, and urge with your lips what you reject with all your heart, as though it were great disgrace to wed such a bride?" The wise man answered to the contrary and responded thus: "God forbid what you imply! Direct your understanding rightly! Know that I've spoken nothing with feigned intent. Do not suppose any murky falseness is involved. No one is present except us two.] (ll. 230–44)

Hiltgund's apparently ungrounded accusation of Walther's duplicity—that he speaks *per hyroniam* in proposing that they flee together—makes little immediate sense. But the passage introduces the resolve of the hero to end a long exile. It is more or less unavoidable, given the density of Vergilian echoes already shot through the poem for over 200 lines, that the reader should immediately juxtapose Walther's circumstances with those of Aeneas in his resolve to quit Carthage. In the ensuing passages already cited, Attila's parodic distraction at the news of Walther's disappearance will soon establish that the Dido to Walther's Aeneas is not Hiltgund, but Attila. Walther's flight, unlike Aeneas's, will not reassert martial homosociality after a heterosexual liaison but rather overturn it (on the levels of diction and narrative expectation as well as on that of content) in a reversal of the Vergilian pattern.

To make sense of Hiltgund's apparently unprepared response to Walther's opening line, "Exilium pariter patimur nam tempore tanto," it is necessary to understand her words as more than the speech of a character within the text. She also speaks, in transgression of the text's fictive frame, for a reader deeply steeped in Vergilian generic expectations, who without prior knowledge of how the plot will unfold might imagine that the end of the hero's exile entails the abandonment of his love interest. Thus Hiltgund functions simultaneously within the frame of narrative fiction as represented character and outside it as a metafictional cue to the reader. Her speech both invokes and subverts genre-based cues upon which the poem's construction and representation of gender depend. In light of this uneasy, outlandishly Borgesian amalgamation of fictional and metafictional voice, the fact that Walther's response to her initial suspicion begins with a tag borrowed from Juno's response to Venus in Book I of the *Aeneid* ("Absit quod memoras") would do nothing to allay the fears of such a character/reader (Townsend 1997).

Ascetic Fecundity and Cohabitation in Reginald of Canterbury

Another monastic narrative of a couple in flight from a hostile master, Reginald of Canterbury's late eleventh-century hagiographic romance the *Vita Sancti Malchi* (hereafter *VSM*), versifies and expands a brief prose *vita* by Jerome. A sprawling narrative in six books rife with digressions and generic hybridizations, the poem invokes epic, hagiography, and didactic literature. Its impulse toward encyclopedic didacticism harks back both to Vergil's *Georgics* and to late antique sensibilities addressed elsewhere in this volume by Marco Formisano. As we shall see, Reginald's medieval Benedictine revision of this patristic tale of chaste marriage imagines a heterosocial collaborative alternative both to solitary ascesis and to homosocial cenobitic models of monastic *habitus*. In the source text, Jerome claims to have heard the story from Malchus himself. In Jerome's version the hero's nameless female companion figures less as character or agent than as catalyst for Jerome's initial inquiry into Malchus's anomalous domestic circumstances. Reginald, by contrast, gives the heroine a name, albeit the perfunctorily eponymous "Malcha," and makes of her an active collaborator in the formation of the couple's unique quasi-monastic praxis. Reginald ends his poem with this scene of meeting between Malchus and Jerome. Jerome, one of the fathers of the Western celibate monastic ethos, passes on an edifying narrative that he himself heard from an older, male ascetic, thus grounding the poem literally in the discourse of the fathers. Yet this discourse is occasioned by the startling appearance of a woman living with a man in an ascetic household. It is when Jerome sees Malcha in Malchus's house and asks about her that Malchus tells him the story of his adventures. The etiological heart of the poem lies neither in the Benedictine context of Reginald's authorial voice nor in the homosocial encounter of Jerome and Malchus, but in the anomalous partnership of Malchus and Malcha. Reginald's own narrative voice situates itself within the world of Benedictine community: his prefatory *Epistola ad Monachos* begins "O monachi cari, quos non sinit ordo vagari" [O beloved monks, whom the order does not permit to wander].

The prefatory epistle goes on to describe the prosperity Reginald wishes for his monastic brothers in terms of agricultural fecundity, terms that will recur thematically throughout the poem. The fertile crops, bees distilling honey, goats rich with milk, and sheep with fleece initiate in the prefatory epistle this strain of imagery, which will return near the poem's end to ratify Malchus and Malcha's alternate quasi-monastic way of life—and Reginald's poetic enterprise as well, which he conceives as fruit offered to the Muse ("poma Thaliae," *VSM* 5.565). Reginald's emphasis on the chaste pair's domestic economy (*VSM* 5.502–65), which includes agricultural labor in garden, vineyard, and orchard, connects this unusual form of life to the idealized productivity of the Benedictine community in the opening *epistola*. At the same time, human artifice intervenes in the reproductive imagery of the gardening passage, notably in the description of grafting. As we shall see, such a detail parallels the double queering of Malchus and Malcha's household, where praxis is denaturalized in relation both to normative heterosexual domesticity and to the alternatively fertile world of Reginald's idealized Benedictine cenobitic monasticism. The intertextual relationship to Vergil's *Georgics* established in these agricultural references and in the lengthy description of the habits of bees connects both traditional forms of monastic life and the alternative improvised by Malchus and Malcha to a canonical depiction of human industry in a world of natural production and reproduction.

The *Vita Malchi* moves from an initial dichotomy between heterosexual marriage and a competing monastic option to a hybridization that combines and reinvents the two alternatives. Malchus's monastic life begins as a rebellion against an arranged marriage. Worldly considerations, however, tempt him to stray from a communal monastic setting to which he never returns. Captured and enslaved to a pagan master, he proves successful in the increase of his master's herds, "fructus bidentum" (*VSM* 2.382), another instance of the poem's leitmotif of agricultural and natural fertility. He next faces the very situation he initially sought to avoid: an arranged marriage. His fellow captive Malcha, in her uncertainty whether or not her husband is alive, is equally reluctant. This time, however, the solution is not flight from marriage into monastic life but transformation of marriage into monastic life. Malchus and Malcha agree to live together chastely, and the establishment of their household consists of mutual instruction in monastic and domestic practice. Malchus teaches Malcha the principles and rule of monastic life (*VSM* 3.516–41), but Malcha in turn teaches him the practical skills of the preparation of fiber, spinning, and the weaving of cloth (*VSM* 3.542–67). In one respect this mutual instruction constitutes a balanced diptych of *oratio* and *labor*: Malchus teaches Malcha to celebrate the liturgical hours, while Malcha teaches Malchus to work with his hands. But the longstanding association of textile arts with women's work—the *VSM* explicitly tags such work as the *usus mulierum* (*VSM* 3.546)—in the context of a household also suggests that what Malchus and Malcha are establishing is not a Benedictine community of two but a hybrid fusion of a gendered heterosexual domestic economy with a celibate communal monastic praxis.

Yet this provisional solution remains haunted by nostalgia for the cenobitic life that lies behind Malchus. He resolves to flee his pagan master when two encounters with insect life remind him of the traditional cenobitic community he abandoned. Reginald's description of the common life of ants and bees rehearses a canonical image of monastic life: both insects appear, for instance, in a poem that has been attributed to Reginald's contemporary Marbod, the *Laus monasticae vitae* (Marbod of Rennes [attr.], PL 171, 1657C–D). Reginald dwells in loving detail on the habits of both creatures. His bee passage is virtually a Vergilian cento, drawing on the extensive discussion of apiculture in the fourth book of the *Georgics*. His account of ants, however, shows a fascination with reproduction that brings images of sociality founded on gendered, reproductive sexuality into contact with the ideal of homosocial, celibate community.

> Pars parit arte nova spem prolis; pars fovet ova.
> Edendo coitu pars instat perpete ritu.
> Corporis et motu generat pars compote fotu.

[Some bear the promise of offspring by a novel art; some cherish the eggs. Some with continuous usage are eager at performing coitus. And some with the motion of their body procreate with shared warmth.] (*VSM* 4.48–50)

The ensuing conversation between Malchus and Malcha, in which they resolve to escape from slavery and flee to Malchus's monastery, amply displays the gendered dynamics of their relationship. Curious parallels obtain with the exchange we have already considered between Walter and Hiltgund in the *Waltharius*. Neither female character responds unproblematically to escape plans sprung on her by her male companion. As in the *Waltharius*, a hermeneutically weighted communications glitch underlines the complex questioning of gender dynamics introduced into the masculinities of ascetic romance, as much as into those of epic, when a male author gives voice to a female character.

Neither Hiltgund nor Malcha acquiesces immediately to her partner's plans; neither at first takes the man's statement at face value. Just as Hiltgund presumes that Walther speaks ironically, *per hyroniam*, Malcha's hesitation also has hermeneutic overtones: "Audiit illa fugas; incredula sed quasi nugas/Primo fugas reputat et secum multa volutat" [she hears "flights," but not believing she at first thinks "flights" is a joke, thinking over many things with herself] (*VSM* 4.147–48). *Nugae* is a weighted term in Reginald's poetics. The poet uses it and its cognates to denote playful activity involving simulation. It occurs in the prelude to the *VSM*, where he develops the fictive aspects of Jerome's image of a mock sea battle (*Preludium Reginaldi super Malchum* 5), and it returns when Malchus's captors celebrate their successful raid with pagan games, Reginald's major epic set-piece (*VSM* 2.132). If in the *Waltharius* Hiltgund is responding to Vergilian cues, standing in for a shrewd reader of the tradition of which she is a part, Reginald's Malcha responds to problematic authorial self-identifications in Reginald's own poem.

Like Hiltgund, Malcha follows her moment of doubt with a promise of full cooperation. Indeed, she goes beyond her predecessor in explicitly endorsing Malchus's masculine privilege of decision-making. Yet Reginald also rewrites the gender dynamics of the scene in ways that return some of the balance of power to Malcha. Walther, in the *Waltharius*, shows a commendable grasp of the practicalities of escape, instructing Hiltgund to bring not only a hefty supply of treasure and weapons for him but also fish-hooks so that they do not starve on the journey. Reginald found in Jerome's account of Malchus's escape a similar example of good sense: Jerome's Malchus providently kills two well-grown goats, taking the meat for food and turning the hide into water skins. Reginald assigns this piece of practicality to Malcha. Even as she assures

Malchus that he, the man, is in charge of all important decisions, she assigns to herself the measures that will make the flight a practical reality. "Cetera curabis quia vir sine cortice nabis" [You take care of the rest, since, as a man, you swim without a cork] (*VSM* 4.168) is the image she uses to affirm patriarchal supremacy. When, later in the story, the two survive a dangerous river crossing by using the well-sealed water skins that Malcha provided as flotation devices, the reader may wonder whether Reginald himself has employed a touch of *hyronia* there.

The last sections of the poem provide another pairing of *oratio* and *labor*, in this case the planting of garden, orchard, and vineyard that concludes Book 5, followed by the composition of Malchus's prayers and hymns which make up the bulk of Book 6. It is the former that concern us here. The work is initially presented as a joint undertaking of Malcha and Malchus (*insumant operam*; *VSM* 5.505). Though the verbs from thereon are singular and only Malchus is named in connection with the horticultural undertakings, the imagery of the passage connects Malchus's tasks to marriage and reproduction:

> Luxuriant plantae postquam Iove conciliante
> Imbre maritantur vites acinisque gravantur.
> Gemmae pubescunt et pampinus uvaque crescunt.
> Mittit ager florem, spondet vindemia prolem.

[Afterwards the plantings burgeon; by Jove's favor the vines are married with rain and they grow heavy with grapes. Buds ripen, the foliage and grapes grow, the field puts forth flowers, the vintage promises offspring.] (*VSM* 5.535–38)

Malchus's horticultural activities culminate in an orchard in which grafting supplements the natural fertility of vegetation; the *ars* of the cultivator allows the trees to bear fruits not their own (see *Georgics* 2). Reginald ends the orchard section and Book 5 with the promise that he will give fruit to the Muse, *poma Thaliae* (*VSM* 5.565). The imagery of natural fertility, rife with Vergilian allusion, clusters around Reginald's representation both of monastic life and of poetic craft.

The natural intersects with the unnatural in these passages, in the *arte nova* with which the ants bring forth the *spem prolis* and the grafting whereby the *ars* of the gardener intervenes in the natural reproductive strategies of trees. As we shall also see in Baudri of Bourgueil, agricultural fecundity connects both with monasticism's alternative to biological productivity and with heterosexual marriage's alignment between human and natural rhythms of reproductive potential. Malchus and Malcha's union and their eventual establishment on Malchus's ancestral land partake of both the "natural" sociological/biological unit of marriage and the "unnatural" alternative of celibate asceticism. Theirs is a marriage queered by celibacy and a celibacy queered by heterosexual marriage. The anomalous nature of the relationship, "cur femina virque moratur/Insimul hoc habitu non lege nec ordine ritu" [Why a woman and a man tarry together in this way of life in a usage not from law or social order] (*VSM* 6.506–7) is the question which in turn generates Malchus's narrative to Jerome, Jerome's writing of the original prose *vita*, and Reginald's inventively fertile versification. The recurring leitmotif of agricultural imagery, pointing as it does to the intertext of the *Georgics,* invokes the canonical classical depiction of human life as part of the natural world in order to endorse the "unnatural" monastic life. At the same time, the Vergilian backing for Malchus and Malcha's anomalous experimentation denaturalizes the monastic alternative in its turn, suggesting that more than one reading of Vergil could support more than one version of the performance of gender difference in a monastic context.

Utopian Bucolic and Domestic Fantasy in the Lyrics of Baudri of Bourgeuil

Baudri of Bourgueil, like Reginald, belonged to a late eleventh-century Benedictine context, though he studied at Angers before he entered St-Pierre at Bourgeuil. There he was abbot (elected in 1089) during the years he flourished as a poet. He became bishop of Dol in 1107. He lived until 1130, but he seems to have almost entirely completed his poetic corpus during his years at Bourgeuil. Baudri is the poster child for the contemporary revival of interest in Ovid known as the *aetas ovidiana.* The poems in which he ventriloquizes Ovid himself or a Helen of Troy modeled on the *Heroides* would be legitimate objects for the study of gendered Latin poetics. The critical literature has also addressed Baudri's poetic engagement with female contemporaries both within and beyond the monastic world. (On the controversy over the authorship of the Constance poems see Bond 1986 and 1995, and Tilliette 1992 and elsewhere in this volume.) Our focus, however, will be on gendered imaginings of the monastic life voiced through intertextual involvement with Vergil. We have seen Reginald chiefly focused on the *labores* and entomology of the *Georgics* in his meditations on the gendered productivity of ascetic life. Baudri's invocations of Vergil, by contrast, run through the full *rota Vergilii* (on the *rota,* which schematizes the range of Vergilian genres and diction, see John of Garland 1974) from the poetic, eroticized landscape of the *Eclogues* to the agricultural realism of the *Georgics* to a disconcerting allusion to Dido's thwarted desires in the *Aeneid.*

Baudri's poem to the *puer* he calls Avitus, perhaps after the late antique poet of that name, inviting him to join Baudri in the idyllic space of Bourgeuil, puts us squarely in the world of the Vergilian pastoral:

> Nos ut nostrorum dulcedine colloquiorum
> Condelectemur, letum quoque tempus agamus
> Est locus, est ortus herbis conserta odoris,
> Quem rosa, quem viola cithisusque timusque crocusque,
> Lilia, narcissus...venustant...
> Huc ades ergo, puer, ut iocundemur in orto
> Iocundoque situ recreentur pectora nostra.

> Vel tua cantabis vel ego mea carmina cantem.
> Et fidibus lentis aptabimus organa nostra.
> Multaque composui, sunt et michi carmina multa,
> Multa reservo tibi, que tu recitabis Alexi...

[So that we may delight ourselves with the sweetness of our talks and pass happy times, there is a place, there is a garden planted with fragrant herbs, which rose, violet, clover, thyme, crocus, lily, narcissus [and a long list of other flowers] beautify... Come to this place, boy, so that we may enjoy ourselves in the garden, and refresh our hearts in the pleasant place. Either you will sing your songs or I mine, and we will fit our voices to leisured lyres. I have composed and also have many songs, many I am saving for you, which you will recite to Alexis...] (Baudri of Bourgeuil 1979, 129.5–9, 11, 25–30)

Baudri borrows the name Alexis for the recipient of Avitus's recitations, and the invitation *huc ades* that he himself addresses to Avitus, from Corydon's apostrophe to the beautiful Alexis in Vergil's second *Eclogue*. The intertextual choice and the eroticization of the chain of homosocial monastic bonds it conveys are conceived in terms of a landscape of desire, where relationships are conducted through a leisured exchange of poems. In this bucolic world, the *labor* of agricultural life is elided into the emotional entanglements and literary activities of the inhabitants of the pastoral landscape. The seduction into a shared landscape and shared language fuses Baudri's invitation to monastic life with the fictional allurements of the pastoral landscape. In so doing, it transforms a notoriously homoerotic school text into an inducement to a homosocial monastic praxis poised continuously at the threshold of desire. The seductive male voice of the teacher speaks through the shared culture of a scandalous classical text to incorporate the addressee into monastic culture conceived as a poetic landscape.

Carmen 77, *Ad eundem ut monachus fiet*, as Tilliette's commentary notes *ad. loc.*, recalls the invitation to Avitus in its depiction of Baudri's environment as a *locus amoenus*. Also in its way a poem of seduction addressed to a male addressee, though it is not cast in the playfully erotic terms of 129, its rhetoric aims to woo Godfrey from the world of the schools to that of the monastery. Its imagery establishes a geographically specific and concrete landscape: instead of the pointed Vergilian allusions of *Carmen* 129, we find here only the most general sense of the traditional vocabulary of the *locus amoenus*. This is the least explicitly gendered of the Baudri poems we are here considering. The imagery of fecundity partakes neither of the erotic landscape of eclogue nor the pervasive sexuality of the *Georgics*. The *floridus* setting begets the leisure that is the condition of literary activity, fusing the attractions of the landscape with the activities the place enables. Moreover, it also produces books and parchment, the material conditions of scholarly activity. Like Reginald, Baudri conflates agricultural fecundity with both monastic prosperity and literary productivity.

Thus far we have not seen much in the way of domesticity in these two invitational poems of landscaped felicity. *Carmina* 129 and 77 do not engage their settings in socio-economic terms. Human relationships and activities are imagined in terms of leisured exchange, not function. Carmen 126 by contrast organizes its landscape around a functioning, socially stratified household that incorporates a peculiar sidelong version of a traditional reproductive family, as Baudri imagines a child, a *parvus Iulus*, the offspring of his bailiff and sister, playing in his courtyard. The gendering of the passage is intertextually complicated by Vergilian alllusion. The male householder with his surrogate family speaks in the voice of Dido, lamenting the absent possibility of the child she never conceived by Aeneas.

Baudri's fantasy revolves around property and status as well as gender: "Atque situ proprio domus ipsa suos recrearet/ Et statio dominis esset amoena suis." [And in its proper site the house itself would refresh its owners, and the abode would be pleasant to its masters] (ibid., 129.25–26). The household unit that includes a woman and a child is a solid sociological entity in a way that Baudri's landscapes of poetic exchange and scholarly productivity are not. Baudri's depiction of himself as master drinking out of a silver cup emphasizes even further his sense of ownership: "Argenti puri crater michi misceat haustum/ Ut, quando bibero, conspiciar dominus." [A vessel of pure silver would mix my drink, and, when I drink, I will be visible as the master] (ibid., 129.81–82). As in Carmen 77, the abundance of the manufactured material supports of literary activity is paradoxically represented as a function of nature rather than of culture (ibid., 77.71–74), but here the requirements of scholarly and poetic activity include secretarial help.

> Sit procurator puer ad mea vota paratus,
> Qui properus tabulas praeparet et calamos,
> Qui domui praesit, ne nobis ocia desint.

[There would be a manager slave ready for my wishes, who would hastily prepare wax tablets and pens, who would be in charge of the household, so that leisure would not be lacking for me.] (ibid., 129.19–21)

The function of the *puer* includes both a supporting role in the mechanics and materials of Baudri's poetic activity and the management of the domestic affairs that might otherwise distract the master from his literary *otium*, a very different *puer* from the eroticized figure of *Carmen* 129. This awareness of social status brings a Horatian touch to the Vergilian landscape; the male Vergilian lover has become the male householder.

While the speaker endows himself with the manufactured cultural paraphernalia of master and head of household as the setting for his alternate family unit, his agricultural surroundings are freighted with sexual reproduction and sexuality.

> Hi michi ludentes coitu sua proelia temptent
> Frontis adhuc levis et pedis instabilis
> Oblectentque meas gratis balatus aures
> Cum totidem matres utraque gens revocet.
> Atque bis ad multram veniant ex gramine sponte
> Distentae matres ubera lacte gravi.

[These [goats] playing at coitus would try their battles, still without horns and unsteady on their feet, and their pleasing bleating would delight my ears, while just as many of either kind would call back their mothers, and would come from the grass to milking twice a day of their own will, mothers with their udders swollen with heavy milk.] (ibid., 129.41–46)

> Unus in ede mea gallus bis quinque maritet
> Uxores, noctis excubias celebrans.

[In my establishment one rooster, celebrating the watches of the night, would marry ten hens.] (ibid., 129.57–58)

Like Reginald's interest in the reproductive strategies of ants, Baudri's goats and rooster read into a natural world mediated by Vergilian intertext an imaginative range of possibilities for gendered sexuality. The oddest moment in Baudri's idyll, however, is the scheme that supplies him with a female companion and a child without involving him in sex or reproduction:

> Sitque soror mulier carum paritura nepotem
> Qui michi post annum sit iocus et cithara.
> Preludat vacua michi parvulus Iulus in aula
> Quem soror atque meus villicus ediderint.
> Sit michi casta domus, mens casta, cubile pudicum;
> Deturpet thalamum nulla libido meum.

[And there would be a sister-woman to give birth to a beloved nephew, to be my entertainment and music after a year. A little Iulus, whom my sister and my bailiff would have brought forth, would play before me in my empty court. My home would be chaste, my mind chaste, my bedchamber undefiled; no desire would foul my chamber.] (ibid., 126.105–10)

Here the Vergilian allusions, which we have traced through the *Eclogues* and *Georgics*, extend to the *Aeneid*, namely to Dido's words to her departing lover:

> Saltem si qua mihi de te suscepta fuisset
> ante fugam suboles, si quis mihi paruulus aula
> luderet Aeneas, qui te tamen ore referret...

[At least, if I'd received from you some offspring before your flight, if a little Aeneas played in my hall whose face could yet recall you...] (*Aen.* 4.327–29)

Baudri also recalls the *parvus Iulus* of *Aen.* 2.677 and 723. While the speaker takes care to assert his chastity, he does so in the voice of a Dido who notoriously lost her own *pudor*. The compromise between monastic chastity and a household that includes a heterosexual reproductive relationship that benefits without including the speaker is haunted by Dido's hypothetical counterpoint to patrilineal succession.

Baudri's conflation of Dido's imaginary love-child with the *parvus Iulus* who, in the *Aeneid*, is the actually existing heir confounds some of the distance that Baudri is establishing between himself and his oblique surrogate family. At the same time imagining the child playing *in aula* connects family structure to the domestic architecture of Baudri's fantasy. Baudri's poetic entry into the *Aeneid* through the voice of Dido is perhaps a similarly sidelong integration of his ludic poetics into the central text of the medieval schoolroom, an oblique and hypothetical poetic heirship. The speaker who is established as a solid male householder is also intertextually a sidelined female lover. The imagined integration of heterosexual, reproductive relationships into monastic identity is simultaneously a negotiation with the gendered voices of Vergilian epic.

Our discussion of monastic voices that engage gender and gendered desire as functions of intertext, genre, and authorial persona suggests that the easy binaries of male and female, homoerotic and heteroerotic, ascetic celibacy and marriage, are insufficiently nuanced tools of analysis. The authors we have surveyed queer gender in ways that invoke the broader category of the queer as defined by Carolyn Dinshaw, as well as the more varied and concrete models of gender and sexuality developed by Eve Sedgwick. Codes of gender inherent in the generic patterning of the formative texts emulated by these authors intersect with their lived experience of the homosocial world of monastic education and reading. When Hrotsvit and Baudri invoke classroom dialogue and pedagogical relationships in works modeled on these canonical precedents, they remind us that studying the gender constructs of medieval Latinity is not an alternative to, but an aspect of, the study of gender in actual social contexts. Texts are lived experience. The alterity of the classical models our monastic authors engaged itself contributed to their experience and understanding of gender. Difference and familiarity are another pair of opposites complicated and confounded by the fact that texts marked by cultural alterity shaped the literary milieu that questioned, experimented with, and transformed inherited norms.

The ironies, cognitive dissonances, and imaginative experiments that mark the hybridized texts we have examined represent understandings of gender that are enabled as well as circumscribed by the intersection of conflicting codes. As when Reginald or the author of the *Waltharius* voice metacritical questioning through the female characters of their poems, or when Hrotsvit examines the gap between the discourse of classroom dialogue in which Pafnutius and his companions engage and that of desert asceticism which he projects and imposes on Thais's female body, medieval authors used the gendered codes implicit in genre-coded texts to construct chimerical masculinities and femininities that conform neither to any single concrete social model nor to any univocal authorial voice. Pafnutius is neither a Terentian suitor, a philosophical teacher, or a desert ascetic, but an intersection of the conflicting masculinities of all three discourses. Malchus and Malcha constitute neither a heterosexual couple nor a monastic unit nor two independent male and female ascetics living side by side, but an experimental queering of all three possibilities and their literatures. Baudri inflects an imagined masculinity built on domestic rather than monastic structures with an allusion to Dido's unrealized familial fantasies. The *Waltharius* poet deploys intertextual allusion in narrative description and in dialogue between male and female characters to voice a metacritical reflection on epic models of gender. Rather than seeing these texts as voices of alternative subcultures existing independently of the texts themselves, it is better to see them as instantiations of the gendered experience of reading and writing, inhabiting texts and authorial personae in the acts of reading and writing themselves. The lived experience of medieval Latinity is no less concrete and no less elaborately interwoven with and constructive of gender than is any extratextual social environment.

SUGGESTIONS FOR FURTHER READING

A brief treatment of four authors cannot begin to address the wealth of medieval Latin literary matter that invents and reinvents gender in dialogue with canonical models of genre. Nor will these few suggestions for further reading provide an exhaustive entrée into the subject, only a limited selection of possible next steps. In parallel with Hrotsvit the reader might consider Aldhelm's *opus geminatum*, the *De virginitate*. A male author addressing highly educated nuns and drawing on the same patristic materials that Hrotsvit would later mine, Aldhelm makes demands on the erudition of his audience that conflate feats of Latinity with feats of asceticism and martyrdom. Latinity and ascesis become related performative theatres shared by male author and female readers.

Hildebert's verse life of Mary of Egypt forms a potential bridge between Hrotsvit and the *VSM*. Hildebert's *vita*, like the *Pafnutius*, addresses the projection of extremes of both pollution and ascetic purification onto the female body. At the same time, Hildebert's Zosimas behaves almost like an elegiac lover in his pursuit of Mary, recalling both Hrotsvit's reworking of the gender conventions of Roman comedy and Reginald's invocation of a marriage plot to constitute ascetic romance.

If the *Waltharius*, as we have suggested, parallels the *VSM* at certain points, its generic positioning can also be juxtaposed with later medieval experiments with Latin epic. Walter of Châtillon's *Alexandreis*, like the *Waltharius*, is profoundly skeptical of epic masculinity. In Walter's poem, lack marks the gap between an imagined plenitude of canonical heroic masculinity and Alexander's never fully adequate emulation. Joseph of Exeter's Troy epic, the *Ylias*, takes a different approach, making the narrative dependence of epic action on female figures the lynchpin of its poetics. The metacritical references to poetry integrated into his rhetorical version of the Judgment of Paris recall the junctures in the *Waltharius* and the *VSM* where female characters voice moments of hermeneutic crisis. Albert of Stade in his *Troilus* dwells on the martial body of Penthesilea, exploring the paradox of an epic femininity.

Finally, while the reader could profitably juxtapose Baudri to other authors of the so-called Loire school (Bond 1986), Marbod, Hildebert, and Rudolfus Tortarius, another approach would draw on different elements of his oeuvre and relate them to these epic questionings and reinventions. *Carmina* 7 and 8, the epistles of Paris to

Helen and Helen to Paris, constitute a double questioning of gender in genre. Ovid's *Heroides*, their model, already reimagine the matter of epic as a series of epistolary exchanges between lovers. By giving his own medieval rendition of Ovid's highly gendered and strongly intertextual genre, Baudri leaves no doubt that the masculinities and femininities of medieval Latin literature are artifacts of a profoundly textual lived experience.

Detailed secondary expositions of gender in medieval Latin works—like detailed readings of medieval Latin works in general—are rare. The readings of gender in monastic and ascetic texts we have been discussing draw on the cultural history of the body explored in the work of Peter Brown (1988) and Caroline Walker Bynum. Given the importance of classical intertexts, readings of gender in classical Latin literature such as Ellen Oliensis (1997) and Alison Keith's (1999, 2000, 2002) work on epic are also essential background to the study of gender in medieval Latinities, as are Erik Gunderson's wonderfully revisionist assessments of the masculinity of classical rhetoric (2000, 2003). Baswell (1995) and Desmond (1994) on the medieval *Aeneid* deal as much with vernacular as Latin texts, but offer valuable insight into gendered medieval readings of the classical canon. Hexter (2007) discusses Bond, Ratkowitsch, and Tilliette's assumptions about Baudri's persona and sexuality. Both of the current authors have dealt with the particular problems of gender in medieval Latin epic (Parsons 2005; Townsend 1995 and 1997). For general discussions of female authorship in the Latin Middle Ages, see Dronke (1984) and Stevenson (2005).

BIBLIOGRAPHY

Primary sources

Albert of Stade. 2007. *Troilus*, edited by Thomas Gärtner. Spolia Berolinensia 27. Hildesheim: Weidmann.

Aldhelm of Malmesbury. 1919a. "De virginitate. I. Prosa." In *Aldhelmi Opera*, edited by Rudolf Ehwald, 226–323. Monumenta Germaniae Historica. Scriptores. Auctores Antiquissimi 15. Berlin: Weidmann.

———. 1919b. "De virginitate. I. Carmen." In *Aldhelmi Opera*, edited by Rudolf Ehwald, 350–471. Monumenta Germaniae Historica. Scriptores. Auctores Antiquissimi 15. Berlin: Weidmann.

———. 2001a. *Aldhelmi Malmesbiriensis Prosa de virginitate: cum glosa latina atque anglosaxonica*, edited and translated by Scott Gwara and Rudolf Ehwald. Corpus Christianorum. Series Latina 124. Turnhout: Brepols.

Baudri of Bourgueil. 1979. *Carmina*, edited by Karlheinz Hilbert. Editiones Heidelbergenses 19. Heidelberg: Carl Winter.

———. 1998. *Poèmes*, edited and translated by Jean-Yves Tilliette. 2 vols. Paris: Belles Lettres.

Hildebert of Lavardin. 2007. *Vie de Sainte Marie l'Égyptienne*, edited and translated by Charles Munier. Miroir du Moyen Age. Turnhout: Brepols.

Hrotsvit. 1902. *Hrotsvithae opera*, edited by Paul Karl Rudolf von Winterfeld. Monumenta Germaniae Historica. Scriptores rerum Germanicarum in usum scholarum separatim editi 34. Berlin: Weidmann.

———. 2001. *Opera omnia*, edited Walter Berschin. Bibliotheca scriptorum graecorum et romanorum Teubneriana. Munich: K. G. Saur.
John of Garland. 1974. *The Parisiana Poetria of John of Garland*, edited and translated by Traugott Lawler. Yale Studies in English 182. New Haven, CT: Yale University Press.
Joseph of Exeter 1970. *Werke und Briefe*, edited by Ludwig Gompf. Mittellateinische Studien und Texte 4. Leiden, Köln: E. J. Brill.
Marbod of Rennes (attr.) 1854. *Laus Monasticae Vitae*, edited by Jacques Paul Migne. Patrologia Latina 171: 1656–68.
Reginald of Canterbury. 1942. *The Vita Sancti Malchi of Reginald of Canterbury*, edited by Levi Robert Lind. Illinois Studies in Language and Literature 27: 3–4. Urbana, IL: University of Illinois Press.
Walter of Châtillon. 1978. *Alexandreis*, edited by Marvin L. Colker. Thesaurus mundi 17. Padua: Antenore.
Waltharius. 1951. "Waltharius." In *Die lateinischen Dichter des deutschen Mittelalters. Sechster Band: Nachträge zu den Poetae aevi Carolini*, edited by Karl Strecker and Peter Vossen, 1–83. Monumenta Germaniae Historica. Poetae Latini Aevi Carolini 6.1. Weimar: Hermann Böhlaus Nachfolger.

Secondary sources

Baswell, Christopher 1995. *Virgil in Medieval England: Figuring the Aeneid from the Twelfth Century to Chaucer*. Cambridge Studies in Medieval Literature 24. Cambridge: Cambridge University Press.
Bond, Gerald A. 1986. "Iocus amoris: the poetry of Baudri of Bourgueil and the Formation of Ovidian Subculture." *Traditio* 42: 143–93.
———. 1995. *The Loving Subject: Desire, Eloquence and Power in Romanesque France*. Middle Ages Series. Philadelphia: University of Pennsylvania Press.
Boswell, John. 1981. *Christianity, Social Tolerance, and Homosexuality*. Chicago: University of Chicago Press.
Brown, Peter. 1988. *The Body and Society: men, women, and sexual renunciation in early Christianity*. Lectures on the History of Religions, N.S., 13. New York: Columbia University Press.
Brown, Phyllis, Linda McMillin, and Katharina Wilson, eds. 2004. *Hrotsvit of Gandersheim: Contexts, Identities, Affinities, and Performances*. Toronto: University of Toronto Press.
Burgess, Henry E. 1968. "Hroswitha and Terence: A Study in Literary Imitation." *Proceedings of the Pacific Northwest Conference on Foreign Languages* 19: 23–29.
Bynum, Caroline Walker. 1987. *Holy Feast and Holy Fast: The Religious Significance of Food to Medieval Women*. New Historicism. Berkeley, CA: University of California Press.
———. 1995. *The Resurrection of the Body in Western Christianity, 200–1336*. Lectures on the History of Religions, N. S., 15. New York: Columbia University Press.
Chamberlain, David. 1980. "Musical Imagery and Musical Learning in Hrotsvit." *Studies in Philology* 77: 319–43.
Coulter, Claudia. 1929. "The 'Terentian' Comedies of a Tenth-Century Nun." *Classical Journal* 24: 515–29.
De Luca, Kenneth. 1974. "Hrotsvit's 'Imitation' of Terence." *Classical Folia* 28: 89–102.
Desmond, Marilynn 1994. *Reading Dido: Gender, Textuality and the Medieval Aeneid*. Medieval Cultures 8. Minneapolis, MN: University of Minnesota Press.
Dinshaw, Carolyn. 1999. *Getting Medieval: sexualities and communities, pre- and postmodern*. Series Q. Durham, NC: Duke University Press.

Dronke, Peter. 1984. *Women Writers of the Middle Ages: A Critical Study of Texts from Perpetua († 201) to Marguerite Porete († 1310)*. Cambridge: Cambridge University Press.
Goetting, Hans. 1973. *Das Bistum Hildesheim. I. Das reichsunmittelbare Kanonissenstift Gandersheim*. Germania sacra, N.F., 7. Berlin, New York: de Gruyter.
Gunderson, Erik. 2000. *Staging Masculinity: The Rhetoric of Performance in the Roman World*. The Body, in Theory. Ann Arbor, MI: University of Michigan Press.
———. 2003. *Declamation, Paternity, and Roman Identity: Authority and the Rhetorical Self*. Cambridge: Cambridge University Press.
Hexter, Ralph J. (2007). "Ovid and the Medieval Exilic Imaginary." in *Writing Exile: The Discourse of Displacement in Greco-Roman Antiquity and Beyond*, edited by Jan Felix Gaertner, 209–36. Mnemosyne, bibliotheca classica Batava. Supplementum 283. Leiden, Boston: Brill.
Keith, Alison 2000. *Engendering Rome: Women in Latin Epic*. Roman Literature and its Contexts. Cambridge: Cambridge University Press.
———. 1999. "Versions of Epic Masculinity in Ovid's *Metamorphoses*." In *Ovidian Transformations: Essays on Ovid's Metamorphoses and its Reception*, edited by Philip Hardie, Alessandro Barchiesi, and Stephen Hinds, 214–39. Cambridge Philological Society. Supplementary Volume 23. Cambridge: Cambridge University Press.
———. 2002. "Ovid on Vergilian War Narrative." *Virgilius* 48: 105–22.
Kong, Katherine. 2004. "Chapter 1: 'Letting the Game be in the Pen': The Verse Epistles of Baudri of Bourgueil and Constance of Angers." In "Epistolary Positions: Gender and Authority in Medieval and Early Modern French Letters." Ph.D. Dissertation, University of Michigan.
Kratz, Dennis. 1980. *Mocking Epic: Waltharius, Alexandreis, and the Problem of Christian Heroism*. Madrid: J. P. Turanzas.
Oliensis, Ellen 1997. "Sons and lovers: sexuality and gender in Virgil's poetry," in *The Cambridge Companion to Virgil*, edited by Charles Martindale, 294–311. Cambridge Companions to Literature. Cambridge: Cambridge University Press.
Parkes, Ford B. 1974. "Irony in *Waltharius*." *Modern Language Notes* 89: 459–65.
Parsons, Sylvia 2004. "The Representation of the Body in Medieval Latin Epic: the Alexandreis of Walter of Châtillon and the Ylias of Joseph of Exeter." Ph.D. Dissertation: University of Toronto.
Ratkowitsch, Christine. 1990. "Europa und Io bei Baudri von Bourgueil." In *Arbor amoena comis*, edited by Ewald Könsgen, 155–61. Stuttgart: Steiner.
Schumann, Otto. 1931. "Baudri von Bourgueil als Dichter." In *Studien zur lateinischen Dichtung des Mittelalters, Ehrengabe für Karl Strecker*, edited by Walter Stach and Hans Walther, 158–70. Schriftenreihe zur Historischen Vierteljahrschrift 1. Dresden: Wilhelm und Bertha von Baensch-Stiftung.
Sedgwick, Eve. 2008. *Epistemology of the Closet*. Rev. ed. Berkeley, CA: University of California Press.
Stevenson, Jane. 2005. *Women Latin Poets: language, gender, and authority from antiquity to the eighteenth century*. Oxford, New York: Oxford University Press.
Talbot, Robert. 2004. "Hrotsvit's Dramas: Is There a Roman in These Texts?" in *Hrotsvit of Gandersheim: Contexts, Identities, Affinities, and Performances*, edited by Phyllis Brown, Linda McMillin, and Katharina Wilson, 147–59. Toronto: University of Toronto Press.
Tilliette, Jean-Yves. 1992. "Hermès amoureux, ou les métamorphoses de la Chimère: Réflexions sur les Carmina 200 et 201 de Baudri de Bourgueil." *Mélanges de l'Ecole française de Rome. Moyen Age* 104: 121–61.
Townsend, David. 1997. "Ironic Intertextuality and the Reader's Resistance to Heroic Masculinity in the Waltharius." In *Becoming Male in the Middle Ages*, edited by Jeffrey

Jerome Cohen and Bonnie Wheeler, 67–86. Garland Reference Library of the Humanities. New Middle Ages 4. New York: Garland Publishing.

———. 1998. "Sex and the Single Amazon in Twelfth-Century Latin Epic." In *The Tongue of the Fathers: Gender and Ideology in Twelfth-Century Latin Literature*, edited by David Townsend and Andrew Taylor. The Middle Ages Series. Philadelphia: University of Pennsylvania Press.

Wilson, Katharina, ed. 1987. *Hrotsvit of Gandersheim: Rara Avis in Saxonia?* Medieval and Renaissance Monograph Series 7. Ann Arbor, MI: Medieval and Renaissance Collegium.

CHAPTER 21

SEX AND SEXUALITY

LARRY SCANLON

The Normal, the Natural, the Medieval

Any discussion of sex and sexuality in medieval Latin culture must contend with two tenacious misconceptions: first, the claim that medieval culture, because of its pervasive devotion to Christianity, had little interest in sex and sexuality; second, the claim that Latin was the language of authority. To demonstrate the inaccuracy of the first one need look no further than a few of the most venerable features of medieval culture, its love literature, for example, or its many innovations in marriage doctrine, or its institutionalization of sexual abstinence in the orders of the Church. The last of these usually provides the rationale for ignoring the others. While it certainly is possible to interpret abstinence as an absence of interest in sexuality, the fact remains that it is a form of sexual behavior, a fact medieval writers never forgot, even if modern scholars all too often have.

If the first claim is simply inaccurate, the second is too reductive. It allows neither for the complexity of medieval forms of authority nor for the complexity of Latin's relation to them. Latin was the language of authority because it was the language of the Church. But the *auctoritas* of the medieval Church, undeniable though it was, ultimately derived from a theological tenet which was by definition dispersive, inclusive, and democratizing—namely, the radical equality of all sinners before God. To make this point denies neither the social dominance of the medieval Church, its enmeshment in the power relations of its society, nor the elitism, repressiveness, or violence, structural or otherwise, that frequently characterized its institutional behavior and the attitudes of its leadership. Even less does it suggest that these aspects of the medieval church simply constituted a failure to live up to its own ideals. On the contrary, these were as central to the complex reality of the medieval Church as was its theological commitment to the radical equality of sinners. But one always needs to keep the latter in mind, for it constituted an ideological necessity which the medieval Church could seldom evade entirely even in its most exclusionary or hierarchical aspects or practices. This necessity also meant that the Church's authoritativeness was never pure and not always evenly distributed. At surprising points, it could be relatively open or inclusive. Paradoxical as it may seem, the role of Latinity in relation to the Church's sexual teachings was as often dispersive and inclusive as it was repressive.

Linguistically, as in many other ways, Christianity originated on the margins. It did not remain there, to be sure. But there is a dispersiveness to Christianity's discursive structures that never completely disappears in the medieval Church, even at its most hegemonic moments. The first language of Christian sacred writings was koine Greek, the common colloquial idiom of the Hellenic world, a "colonial equalizing language" (Binder 2011). In producing the Vulgate, Jerome self-consciously chose a popular idiom over the more Ciceronian Latin of the schools. Augustine famously cites the vulgar (*indigna*) quality of the *Vetus Latina* as one of the primary stumbling blocks to his conversion (*Confessions* 3.5). After his conversion, Augustine would come to use the stylistic simplicity of Scripture as the model for a distinctively Christian, and anti-classical rhetorical principle, the *sermo humilis*, which sought to convey the most transcendent of truths in the plainest of styles. What is crucial here is the crossing of sorts: Scripture's deployment of popular idioms in the name of its transcendent truths, and the inevitable preservation of this dispersive impulse in every subsequent return of Christian thought to Scripture as the ultimate source of authority. Thus, to the extent one can identify a single summary feature of the authority of medieval Latinity, that feature has to be the translatability of such authority rather than its inherent hegemony. Modern scholarship has long recognized this feature of Latinity in a different but related context, that is, the *translatio studii*, the transmission, preservation, and dissemination of the traditions of classical antiquity. In spite of its venerability, this concept remains vital and useful, precisely because of its flexible and nuanced depictions of traditional authority. At its supplest, what the *translatio studii* describes is the productive interchange between past and present or Latin and vernacular or both. This process is sometimes defined against the putatively more restrictive traditions of the Church as if the *translatio studii* were a strictly lay phenomenon. Ironically, the very centrality of the Church as an institution to Latinity's cultural preeminence makes this possibility unlikely. On the contrary, because of Latin's pedagogical function as the central vehicle of Church learning, it is much more plausible to ally it with Christianity's dispersive tendencies than with its hegemonic ones. That is certainly the case with sex and sexuality.

This chapter will sketch the treatment of sex and sexuality in medieval Latin culture by concentrating on the ideal of *natura*, its peculiarly double discursive structure and its parallel articulations in two quite distinct ecclesiastical traditions, the contemplative (or mystical), and the penitential. Both of these traditions emerge largely though not exclusively out of monasticism. They arguably constitute the most individuated of medieval clerical discourses. However, their individuating tendencies operate in antithetical directions. The contemplative tradition aspires to become the most rigorous and self-consciously elite, while the penitential tradition aspires to become the most widely disseminated. They also both raise the issue of *translatio*, the penitential because the exchange between Latin and vernacular is an irreducible element of lay confession, the contemplative because its vernacular dispersion is one of the most striking features of lay piety in the later Middle Ages and early modernity. Michel Foucault defined the historical "experience of sexuality... as the correlation between fields of knowledge, types of normativity, and forms of subjectivity in a particular culture" (Foucault 1985, 4). In the past forty years medieval studies has moved well beyond the stark opposition of medieval to modern assumptions in its investigations of sex and sexuality, and a wealth of scholarship has definitively put paid—one hopes forever—to the notion that the Middle Ages had no real interest in erotic life. At the same time, most of this recent work has focused either on the first of Foucault's triad, that is, "fields of knowledge," or the third, "forms of subjectivity." (The latter is especially true of work in literary studies.) As a result even some of the most adventurous new studies define the material they investigate against some purely repressive, anti-erotic cultural core.

The only way past this conundrum is to address the second of Foucault's categories, "types of normativity." I hope to do just that by exploring the ideal of the natural. The medieval mystic has long been a figure of modern fascination; perhaps inevitably that fascination has settled in particular on the mystic's singularity, his or her apparent transcendence of the institutional structures and intellectual traditions that make the contemplative project possible. By contrast, medieval penance continues to be treated largely as entirely communal, an instrument of social control—a view that has not changed all that much since Luther nailed his ninety-nine theses to that church door in Wittenberg. These lacunae are symptomatic. A continuing challenge facing all of contemporary medieval studies is how to understand the social and communal functions of the spiritual exemplarity which medieval culture assigned to its religious leaders, the empowering aspects of the spiritual obedience expected of the laity, and the dialectical relations between the two. The challenge is particularly pointed in this case.

Simply seeking a medieval norm raises a historiographical problem. As Karma Lochrie notes, the notion of the norm is itself a purely modern product. It emerged in the middle of the nineteenth century. The word *normal*, which, deriving from the Latin *norma*, "T-square," had meant simply "perpendicular," acquired a much broader range of meaning, one that continues to color current "popular... understandings of the term." The notion of the norm came to encapsulate the wholesale attempt to quantify human social behavior, and to place the study of such behavior on a more scientific footing. It enabled moral evaluation to be redefined and re-presented as if it were simple fact. "On the one hand, the normal is that which is usual, in the sense of being most prevalent, most quantifiable as common, and susceptible to averaging. On the other, it is a rule or standard, a type that defines an ideal as well as deviations from that ideal" (Lochrie 2005, 3). In spite of its scientific pretensions, the modern norm is an ideal. Yet because of those pretensions it presents itself not as an ideal but as pure *datum*. The transcendent ecstasies of the contemplative or any of the other medieval ascetic ideals explicitly acknowledge their status as exceptions. To this extent, they are dispersive and double where the modern norm is convergent and always aspires to uniformity. To put the difference in more polemical terms: in this case, contrary to type, it is the modern notion that is mystified, unself-conscious, and a matter of pure, unquestioning faith, while the medieval notion is self-reflexive and rationative.

Natural is the closest medieval approximation to *normal*. Indeed, modern sexual attitudes often employ the two interchangeably and the notion of a natural sexuality provides a substantial portion of the unacknowledged traditional background to modern notions of sexual normality. Yet in medieval usage, the natural is also dispersive and double. In its most common use, especially in penitential tradition and related contexts it refers to reproductive sexuality, where it is opposed to sex *contra naturam*. Yet, especially in contemplative contexts, *natural* also conveys the more properly theological sense which originates with Augustine, that is the unfallen state to which humanity aspires to return. There is another difference. The norm is by definition synchronic and timeless. It admits of historical variation but has no way of recognizing its own past, that is, its own historical constitution. The opposite is true of the notion of the natural. The ideals of a natural sexuality come to Christianity with a distinguished pedigree. Plato makes the first extant appeal to nature as the governing principle for human sexual behavior in the course of his last dialogue, *The Laws*. As the Athenian (playing the role usually played by Socrates) advocates removing the future leaders of his ideal city from their families in order that they be educated as a cohort, he also suggests facilitating the process by developing a taboo on homoeroticism as strong as the taboo on incest. He then supports this suggestion by describing homoeroticism as unnatural inasmuch as it is not reproductive. Philo will adapt this passage in one of his commentaries on Genesis and the Sodom story (*On Abraham*, 26.133–36; Philo 1935, 68–71). Paul may not have had direct knowledge of Philo's writings, but this notion of the natural clearly forms part of the intellectual horizon for Romans 1:18–32, as does the Sodom story which Philo is glossing. Paul begins what will become Christianity's first major ecclesiological statement by disavowing the idolators (presumably the polytheistic Greeks and Romans) whom God has abandoned to sex *contra naturam* (παρὰ φύσιν; Rom 1: 26). From the beginning then, Christianity's disavowal of sex *contra naturam* can be separated neither from its transcendental quest for the divine, nor from the constitution of its community. This passage from Paul will be cited liberally in medieval Latin writings dealing with sexuality. While in most practical respects, its effect would have been no different from modern homophobia, its conceptual structure differs considerably. Paradoxical as it may seem, even in their harshest forms, medieval idealizations of natural sexuality also always harbored utopian strivings, however repressed. And the explicit commitment to their own past evidenced in the very fact of the citation of scriptural authority meant these strivings could never be repressed completely. In the case of the contemplatives, they were given pride of place.

The Erotics of Christian Contemplation

The erotic aspects of Christian mysticism have long been obvious to outside observers. Jacques Lacan put the matter with characteristic, if somewhat anachronistic, bluntness, once declaring of Bernini's statue of Teresa of Avila, "you only have to go and look at Bernini's statue in Rome to understand immediately that she's coming, there is no doubt about it" (Lacan 1982, 147). Medievalists have been more reticent, largely because of an understandable desire to avoid just this sort of anachronism. Fortunately, acknowledging the obvious erotic element in Christian mysticism does not require dismissing mystic ecstasy as nothing more than a repressed alibi for orgasm. Indeed, one of the most frankly and consistently erotic works in the medieval contemplative tradition is also the single most influential, Bernard of Clairvaux's *Sermones super Cantica canticorum*. These eighty-six sermons constitute a massive commentary on the Song of Songs, focusing almost entirely on the poem's opening sections. They amplify and redefine an exegetical strategy that begins with Origen, a tradition which uses Paul's notion of Christ as the Bridegroom to transform Solomon's erotic *epithalamium* into an allegory for the soul's passionate longing for God and for the foundation of the Christian community. Paul's metaphor first occurs in the Letter to the Ephesians. Paul advises the Ephesians, as a way of giving thanks to God, to be "subject to each other in the fear of Christ" and in particular that

> mulieres viris suis subditae sint sicut Domino, quoniam vir caput est mulieris sicut Christus caput est ecclesiae, ipse salvator corporis. Sed ut ecclesia subiecta est Christo, ita et mulieres viris suis in omnibus. Viri diligite uxores, sicut et Christus dilexit ecclesiam et se ipsum tradidit pro ea ut illam sanctificaret, mundans lavacro aquae in verbo, ut exhiberet ipse sibi gloriosam ecclesiam non habentem maculam aut rugam aut aliquid eiusmodi, sed ut sit sancta et inmaculata. Ita et viri debent diligere uxores suas ut corpora sua. Qui suam uxorem diligit, se ipsum diligit. Nemo enim umquam carnem suam odio habuit sed nutrit et fovet eam sicut et Christus ecclesiam, quia membra sumus corporis eius, de carne eius et de ossibus eius. Propter hoc relinquet homo patrem et matrem suam et adhaerebit uxori suae et erunt duo in carne una. Sacramentum hoc magnum est, ego autem dico in Christo et in ecclesia.

> [women be subject to their husbands, as to the Lord: Because the husband is the head of the wife, as Christ is the head of the church. He is the saviour of his body. Therefore as the church is subject to Christ, so also let the wives be to their husbands in all things. Husbands, love your wives, as Christ also loved the church, and delivered himself up for it: That he might sanctify it, cleansing it by the laver of water in the word of life: That he might present it to himself a glorious church, not having spot or wrinkle, or any such thing; but that it should be holy, and without blemish. So also ought men to love their wives as their own bodies. He that loveth his wife, loveth himself. For no man ever hated his own flesh; but nourisheth and cherisheth it, as also Christ doth the church: Because we are members of his body, of his flesh, and of his bones. For this cause shall a man leave his father and mother, and shall cleave to his wife, and they shall be two in

one flesh. This is a great sacrament; but I speak in Christ and in the church.] (Eph 5:21–33)

In noting the ultimate origin of this metaphor I am less concerned to specify its meaning for Paul and his immediate audience than to note the rich possibilities it offered to subsequent tradition. Indeed, while the metaphor's most obvious function, that is, the justification of women's subordination to men, would certainly prove durable, its use of the purely human institution of marriage to define the Christ's relation to His Church would have a wide variety of other effects, including, ironically enough, the capacity to reverse symbolically the gender subordination Paul uses to enforce it literally. To make Christ a bridegroom and His Church a bride is to impute to Him an interrelated set of qualities with no clear significance beyond the network of sexual, gender, and social relations within which the purely human institution of marriage constitutes itself. Obviously, the metaphor does not automatically sexualize the relationship in any straightforward way; yet that complexity is precisely the source of its rhetorical power. For while marriage is a form of sexual relationship, it can by definition never be entirely reduced to pure sexuality. That is to say, it is a social relationship which derives its plasticity from the plasticity of sexuality, that is, from sexuality's capacity to shape and define itself in response to nonsexual categories, discourses, and social formations. To put the point more theologically: marriage is an institution with both carnal and spiritual dimensions. Yet there is no conceptual point where the spiritual can float entirely free of the carnal. On the contrary, the spiritual specificity of marriage consists of its revaluation and management of carnal desire. Paul insists on this aspect of the metaphor with his paraphrase in verse 31 of Gn 2:24. Moreover he also uses the plasticity of the sexual body to define Christianity's capacity to create human community: "we are members of his body, of his flesh, and of his bones."

Origen appeals to Paul's metaphor of the Bridegroom in the very first sentence of his *Commentary*. Yet his inspiration for this allegorical move came in large part from rabbinic tradition, which already read Solomon's *epithalamium* "as the song of love between God and Israel" (Matter 1990, 26–29, 51). Translated by Rufinus in 410, Origen's *Commentary* (240) was destined to be much more influential in the Latin West than the Greek East. (Indeed, the Greek original is now lost.) Bernard comes to a thriving tradition already several centuries old. However, his focus on individual contemplation—in Astell's felicitous phrase, "personal brideship" (Astell 1990, 73–104)—activates a "secondary possibility" in "the long tradition" and moves it to the foreground (Matter 1990, 123). At the same time Bernard is completely faithful to the authority of Paul in that in his repeated, extensive deployments of the metaphor he never dismisses or disavows either the carnal or the social elements of human marriage. As he explains in his fifth sermon:

> ...nos vivimus quidem post corpus, sed ad ea quibus beate vivitur nullus nobis ascensus vel accessus patet, nisi per corpus. Senserat hoc qui dicebat: "Invisibilia Dei per ea quae facta sunt intellecta conspiciuntur." Ipsa siquidem quae facta sunt, id est corporalia et visibilia ista, nonnisi per corporis instrumentum sensa in

nostram notitiam veniunt. Habet igitur necessarium corpus spiritualis creatura quae nos sumus, sine quo nimirum nequaquam illam scientiam assequitur, quam solam accepit gradum ad ea de quorum sit cognitione beata. (1.1; Bernard of Clairvaux 1957–58, 1: 21–22)

[...we live after the death of the body. Nevertheless, only through the body does the way, the ascent to the life of blessedness, lie open to us. He who said, "The invisible things of God are understood through the things he has made" (Rom 1:20) realized that. Those things which are made, that is, those bodily and visible things, come to our knowledge only through the bodily senses. The spiritual creature which we are has a body which is necessary to it, and without which it cannot reach that knowledge which is the only way to the knowledge the blessed have.] (Evans, 226)

Learning through the senses necessarily includes learning through sexual feeling. Bernard's general mode of exegetical procedure is to treat the Song of Songs as a gloss on the Bride/Bridegroom conceit, which he understands both in ecclesiological and individual terms. That approach enables him to use his rhetorical explication of the erotic imagery of the Song as the basis of a wide-ranging encyclopedic exposition of all of theology relevant to the contemplative life, as well as extensive commentary on monasticism, ecclesiology generally, and a number of current controversies. A "'*summa*' on contemplative theology" (Leclercq 2008, 310), the *Sermones super Cantica canticorum* are also an exegetical *tour de force*. Much of the interpretation is allegorical in a conventional sense, as Bernard absorbs the erotic significances of Solomon's poem into purely theological concepts. But the rest cannot be so easily pigeon-holed. The collection derives much of its rhetorical energy—and I would argue, its beauty—from a much more associative, ambiguous, and syntagmatic treatment of its erotic original. Bernard often leaves the exact boundary between the sexual and the transcendent unclear. A particularly spectacular instance occurs at the collection's conclusion.

Bernard devotes his final twelve sermons (75–86) to verse 3:1 of the Song of Songs, "In lectulo meo quaesivi per noctes quem diligit anima mea" [In my bed I sought at night him whom my soul loves] (citing Bernard's version; in the Vulgate "per noctes" precedes "quaesivi"). Such an extended quantity of exposition is unusual even by Bernard's generous standards. Though he never loses contact with the verse, these twelve sermons contain some of the densest, most sustained philosophical argumentation in the entire cycle. Bernard uses this verse to gloss both the general ontological relation between Divine consciousness and the fallen human soul and the ecstasy of the mystical union. He saves the latter for the very end. In Sermon 84 he explains that the soul, having succumbed to worldly temptations, returns to God as an adulterous spouse to a loving husband. Sermon 85 pursues an elaborate analogy between clerical vocation and maternity. Thanks to the pioneering work of Caroline Bynum, medievalists have long recognized Cistercian interest in metaphors of maternity (Bynum 1982, esp. 115–18). However, they have been slower to recognize the plasticity of these metaphors, especially in Bernard. Citing Paul's invocation from Gal 4:19, "Filioli mei, quos iterum parturio, donec formetur

Christus in vobis" [My sons, to whom I have given birth again, until Christ is formed in you], Bernard explains two types of parturition in "spiritual matrimony," each producing different offspring: first, there is preaching, when "holy mothers" give birth to souls, and, second, meditation, when they give birth to "spiritual understandings" (4.13; Bernard of Clairvaux 1957–58, 2: 315). Both are important, but the latter is more pleasurable.

> Aliter sane afficitur mens fructificans Verbo, aliter fruens Verbo: illic sollicitat necessitas proximi, hic invitat suavitas Verbi. Et quidem laeta in prole mater, sed in amplexibus sponsa laetior. Cara pignora filiorum; sed oscula plus delectant. Bonum est salvare multos; excedere autem et cum Verbo esse, multo iucundius.
>
> [Sometimes the Word inspires the mind to enrich, sometimes to be enriched: sometimes one looks after the needs of neighbors, sometimes one welcomes the sweetness of the Word. And indeed there is the mother's pleasure in her children, but there is the wife's greater pleasure in embraces. Dear are the tokens of progeny; but kisses please more. To save many is good; to withdraw and be with the Word much more delightful.] (4.13; Bernard of Clairvaux 1957–58, 2: 316)

In this passage Bernard returns sexuality to the letter. He returns motherhood to its larger social context, drawing on the conventional expectation that a mother is also a wife, and as a wife, a lover. He then makes sense of the distinction between preaching and meditation by comparing the first to the maternal love of children and the second to an erotic embrace. As he does throughout the *Sermones*, Bernard effects a gender reversal, identifying male clerics with the bride to Christ's bridegroom. But he also offers erotic pleasure as an unglossed simulacrum to contemplative ecstasy, allowing it to retain its carnal specificity. It is hard to see how this figurative choice could be anything but self-conscious and intentional, especially if we recall Bernard's own claim that spiritual knowledge depends on the body. Bernard uses erotic pleasure and gender reversal to make mystic ecstasy more intelligible; these rhetorical deployments also demonstrate that Christian spirituality can reshape all things of the body to its own end, including the gender roles through which erotic pleasure is conventionally imagined. His insistence on situating his erotic analogies within marriage recalls the social plasticity of the sexual, its amenability to institutional structuration even as it extends and celebrates the Bride/Bridegroom metaphor.

The erotic analogies form a rhetorical counterpart to the theological expositions of Christian psychology in the sermons immediately preceding. At the same time, the parallel paradoxically depends on the difference between the two conceptions of nature governing each counterpart. In his philosophical rationale for the brief, mysterious, transcendent unions of the contemplative with God, Bernard appeals to the notion of nature as the unfallen state to which the soul longs to return. His erotic analogies, framed as they are in marital terms, depend on nature as reproductive *telos*. Yet the transcendent, theological notion of nature ultimately lies behind the erotic rhetoric as well. Moreover, the erotic rhetoric enacts the superiority of the theological concept precisely by allowing Bernard to transgress the worldly notion of nature as reproductive *telos*. In its momentary return to its true, unfallen nature, the contemplative soul can transcend all human markers of gender and sexual identity. The male preacher can become a holy mother giving birth to souls, the male contemplative an adulterous woman returning to her husband's embrace. Paradoxically, transcendence becomes intelligible, at least metaphorically, as a form of transgression.

This paradoxical mode of transgression would come to constitute one of Bernard's major legacies to the subsequent contemplative tradition. Among other things it facilitated the explosion in vernacular female spirituality which recent scholarship has increasingly recognized as a central feature of later medieval contemplative tradition. However, my interest here concerns what Bernard's figurative pyrotechnics reveal about the ideal of nature as a form of "normativity"—namely, that it exerts its transcendent authority transgressively; that such authority seeks as much to reshape sexual convention as to escape it; and that its transgressiveness is socially and cultural productive. One could trace these transgressive, productive energies in a wide variety of medieval Latin traditions: in canon law and its treatment of marriage formation, for example, or in medieval science. Much such work has already been done in connection with literary texts, as for example particularly on the enigmatic prosimetrum *De planctu Naturae* of Alan of Lille (another prominent Cistercian), which bequeathed a model of poetic authority to most subsequent vernacular traditions. As Thomas Moser (2004, 17–65) has shown, Alan was working in a clerical tradition of Ovidian poetry already a century old. However, I focus below on penitential tradition because it remains under-studied and because of its aspirations to disperse its own authority as widely as possible within medieval society as a whole.

Penance: Nature and Silence

There is no doubt that from the very beginning penitential discourse concerned itself with social order as well as with Christ's grace and His endless forgiveness. Nevertheless the doctrinal and devotional significances of penance reside in the latter. Moreover, in the penitential approach to the sexual, the social and the transcendent are very difficult to separate. That is because the centrality of sexual renunciation to Christian asceticism drove the Church's reshaping of the institution of marriage, and because this same ascetic practice defined the institutional origins of the most individuated aspects of lay penance. Private confession began as a form of monastic self-examination. Not surprisingly, penitential tradition concerns itself mainly with natural sexuality in the teleological sense. Nevertheless, penitential writings draw on the transcendent, Augustinian notion of nature as well. They also make this doubleness the source of significant semantic instability and complexity. Sex *contra naturam* constitutes the ultimate boundary against which penitential texts define all the other, natural forms of sexual behavior. But there is little obvious or self-evident about this boundary. On the contrary, penitential writing typically treats the distinction between natural and unnatural sex as a discursive structure rather than a simple fact. Not only does this structure retain traces of the transcendent yearnings one can find in the contemplative tradition, but it retains them as part of its interplay with the distinction between clerical and lay.

Penitential traditions can claim the center of medieval regulation of sexuality in at least two respects. First, to the extent that there was a single institution that regulated sexual behavior, it was the Church. Penance, while probably a less prominent and influential sacrament than either baptism or the Eucharist, was nevertheless the most broadly individuated, especially after 1215, when the Fourth Lateran Council made annual confession a universal obligation. Second, penitential tradition provided much of the basis for canon law, fundamentally shaping its treatment of marriage, among other things. Penitential tradition takes its ultimate meaning from the salvific mission of the Church. As the later medieval formulation would have it, there are three parts of penance: contrition, confession, and satisfaction. In confession the lay believer comes in direct contact with a member of the ecclesiastical hierarchy, who also sets the terms for satisfaction. Clerics licensed to hear confession from the laity were distinguished from their confessants in two ways: by the moral exemplarity and ritual purity inhering in their celibacy and by their literacy in Latin. The confessional encounter thus constitutes a *translatio studii* of a very particular sort. Literally translating a body of Latin learning to lay believers, the confessor grants access to confessants to the authority of this learning for the purposes of reconceptualizing their experience according to penitential doctrine. This linguistic encounter is simultaneously an encounter with an embodied spiritual ideal, an embodied ideal whose most material sign of exemplarity is sexual abstinence. In the confessional exchange, confessants encountered a sexual ideal constructed according to the dictates of ecclesiological rule, and that ideal was part of the spiritual guidance they took away with them. How, then, should we understand this encounter? Was it, as one of the most influential of recent accounts of late medieval penance has argued, an ideological subordination, an exercise in "social control," limited only by "the fear that excessive severity would make compliance impossible," its consolatory features functioning only to secure compliance (Tentler 1977, xvi–xviii)? Or was it, as medieval clerics viewed it, a form of empowerment, a dispersion of Church authority and clerical knowledge to the less spiritually privileged laity? Obviously it was both.

Penitential tradition alone among the major forms of medieval Christian devotion originated on the periphery and moved to the center. The penance recognized and consolidated in 1215, when the Fourth Lateran Council ordained annual confession for all believers, began in the sixth century in Britain and Ireland. From there it spread to the Continent and the Carolingians. An early reformer, Burchard, Bishop of Worms, produced a definitive recapitulation of this tradition in the *Corrector*, the nineteenth book of his massive *Decretum*. Notoriously frank and direct, early penitential tradition made sexuality a prominent concern from its inception. A particularly famous canon from the mid-sixth century, *Praefatio de poenitentia Gildae adscripta* [Preface of Gildas on Penance], begins: "Praesbiter aut diaconus faciens fornicationem naturalem sive sodomitam praelato ante monachi voto .iii. annis peniteat" [A presbyter or a deacon committing natural or sodomitical fornication who has previously taken the monastic vow shall do penance for three years] (*Irish Penitentials* 1963, 60–61). The canon will leave no doubt about the severity of this sin, calling upon the sinner to "seek pardon every hour," fast once a week ("Veniam omni hora roget, superpositionem faciet in unaquaque hebdomada") and restrict his diet other times, "at all times deplore his guilt from his inmost heart," and show himself obedient "above all things" ("Semper ex intimo corde defleat culpam suam; obedientiam prae omnibus libentissime excipiat") to compensate for the gross disobedience of committing fornication. At the same time the article is remarkably dispassionate and spends more time discussing the details of the sinner's diet than it does his other expressions of contrition. It also shows little interest in policing social order. As Allen Frantzen notes, "penance was not a punishment: it was a cure" (Frantzen 1983, 3). Most strikingly, the article treats natural and unnatural sexual misconduct as almost entirely equivalent. The phrase it uses, "fornicationem naturalem siue sodomitam," clearly implies that readers have assimilated the conflation of unnatural sexuality with Sodom and understand natural and sodomitic fornication as two variants of the same general sin.

After 1215, penitential tradition will increasingly distinguish between the natural and unnatural. Yet this basic equivalence never disappears: the natural forms of fornication are ultimately sins just as deadly as the unnatural. Unrepented, they will get one sent to hell just as quickly. Moreover, natural though it may be with respect to reproduction and the political structures of human society, "natural" sexual misbehavior is still unnatural in the Augustinian sense, that is, with respect to humanity in its pre-lapsarian state. The quest to return to that state is communal no less than individual. Although the canon begins by specifying three years of penance, it concludes by advising "Post annum et dimedium eucharistiam summat, ad pacem veniat, psalmos cum fratribus canat, ne penitus anima tanto tempore caelestis medicinae intereat" [After a year and a half he may receive the eucharist and come for the kiss of peace and sing the psalms with his brethren, lest his soul perish utterly from lacking so long a time the celestial medicine] (*Irish Penitentials* 1963, 60–61). Perhaps the inconsistency is simply a mistake; or perhaps the *Preface* assumes the penitent will continue the other aspects of his penance even after his period of excommunication is ended. Either way, the *Preface* characterizes the return to full devotional participation as "celestial medicine," as if the Eucharist itself were a form of therapeutic penance. The phrase reminds its readers that every human being is a sinner, a condition of which the Eucharist is at once memorial and remediation. The canon ends by imagining the penitent restored to the community, that is, as restored to spiritual health through ministrations to the body connected directly to communal spiritual health, which, it reminds its readers, is founded on the broken, but salvific, body of Christ.

This emphasis on the therapeutic is a legacy of ancient monasticism and particularly of the writings of John Cassian, the primary intellectual influence on early medieval penitential tradition. Yet, this therapeutic legacy also continues past 1215. Indeed it appears prominently in Canon 21 of the Fourth Lateran Council itself, *Omnis sexus utriusque*, the canon which declares the obligation of yearly confession. Though the fact is rarely noted, Canon 21 spends as much time discussing the obligations of the confessor as it does those of the confessant. It frames that discussion in therapeutic terms, describing the confessor as "a skilled doctor" pouring "wine and oil over the wounds of the injured one." It also imposes very strict sanctions on any confessor who betrays a confessant's confidence: deposition and perpetual penance in a "strict monastery" (*arctum monasterium*, Tanner 1990, 244–45). In this way the canon makes secrecy an extension of the confessor's therapeutic, quasi-medicinal role. It becomes constructive as well as regulative, conveying to the Christian community as a whole a spiritual privilege originally confined to monasticism, and opening a new forum, private confession, wherein that privilege can exercise itself. Whatever regulative, disciplinary role the new forum was to play, its most fundamental aspiration was inclusion. Secrecy played an irreducibly double role in relation to that aspiration, that is, as guarantor no less than monitor. Perhaps because of that doubleness, secrecy functioned pivotally in the more general sexualization that defined, as I have already noted, the social boundaries of the confessional encounter. In 1898, when Lord Alfred Douglas described homosexuality as "the love that dare not speak its name," he bequeathed to subsequent modern thought a postulate about past sexualities that has rarely been questioned—namely, that homosexuality has always been unspeakable, or at least that Christianity has always treated it that way. The evidence of the Middle Ages suggests this trajectory can be made more precise.

Allen Frantzen has called the treatment of homoeroticism in the Anglo-Saxon penitentials "straightforward"; he memorably describes the early Middle Ages as a time "before the closet" (Frantzen 1998, esp. 1–29, 111–228). Burchard's *Corrector* is entirely typical in both its colloquial tone and nearly clinical detachment. Composed in the form of interrogatories, it advises the confessor to ask,

> Fecisti fornicationem sicut Sodomitae fecerunt, ita ut in masculi terga et in posteriora virgam tuam immitteres, et sic secum coires more Sodomitico?
>
> [Have you committed fornication as the Sodomites committed it, have you thus inserted your rod in male backsides and posteriors, and have you thus coupled with them in the Sodomitical custom?] (Burchard of Worms 1853, col. 967)

Indeed, though the fact is not widely acknowledged, homoeroticism became unspeakable at the very moment when, according to Foucault, "Western man became a confessing animal," that is, in the wake of the Fourth Lateran Council (Foucault 1980, 59). In contrast to the frankness of penitential writing before 1215, the *topos* of unspeakability becomes widespread for the first time. The most influential, most widely disseminated penitential work of the later period are the twin *Summae virtutum ac vitiorum* of the Dominican William Peraldus (ca. 1236). Where Burchard is straightforward, Peraldus warns of the sin against nature,

> De quo vitio cum magna cautela loquendum est: et praedicando: et interroga-
> tiones in confessionibus faciendo: ut nihil hominibus reveletur quod praestat
> occasionem peccandi.
>
> [This vice is to be spoken of with great caution, both in preaching and in the
> inquiries made during confessions, so that nothing be revealed to men that might
> give them occasion to sin.] (2.3.2.2; Peraldus 1585, 2: 47)

This warning makes the sin against nature unspeakable. Yet it does not make of that unspeakability an absolute condition. On the contrary, Peraldus treats the unspeakability of the sin against nature as entirely a function of pastoral duty. As an extension of pastoral discretion it also becomes an extension of pastoral privilege. While Burchard and the tradition he recapitulates took the confessor's duty to require the explicit explanation of all forms of sexual sin, including the sin against nature, Peraldus takes it to require the withholding or careful management of that knowledge. This change constitutes a fairly radical shift. Yet it also defines itself against an equally radical continuity: the therapeutic knowledge and discretion of the confessor. In what does this knowledge inhere? How can Burchard know the details of the fornication of the Sodomites, and even its pleasures, without being tainted by them himself? Why is Peraldus so confident that the knowledge of the sin against nature possessed by preachers and confessors will not tempt them with the same occasion for sin as it might the lay auditor or confessant? In part, this privilege proceeds from clerical Latinity: the cleric's exclusive access to the Latin traditions of the Church. But in part it also proceeds from the mastery of sexuality embodied in clerical celibacy. That is, as we have already seen in the case of Bernard, sexual abstinence means much more than a simple renunciation. It is a transcendence and a sublimation that enables the revaluing, reshaping, and redeploying of human sexual practice in its entirety.

That leads us to an even more paradoxical continuity implicit in Peraldus's warning. On the one hand, it intensifies the distinction between the sin against nature and other forms of sexual transgression. On the other hand, that very intensification takes place within an encyclopedic taxonomy, so that it must ultimately reflect on all the other forms. It becomes exemplary in Agamben's sense, a limit case marking the boundary of the class to which it belongs (Agamben 1998, 15–29). To put the paradox in more concrete terms, Peraldus actually retains the equivalence between natural and unnatural fornication assumed by Gildas, and defines his heightened distinctions accordingly. He accomplishes this paradoxical feat in a variety of ways. He frames his discussion of sin as a whole with the ideal of nature in its transcendent sense that was so important to Bernard. Citing Bernard among others, he declares all sin unnatural (*innaturale*, 2.1.4.3; Peraldus 1585, 2: 25). He then interweaves this larger, transcendent ideal with his use of the specifically sexual opposition between natural and unnatural. Peraldus lists five kinds (*species*) of *luxuria*: 1) simple fornication; 2) rape or *stuprum*, which he defines solely as "the illicit defloration of a virgin"; 3) adultery; 4) incest; and 5) the *peccatum contra naturam*. These five subcategories are implicitly unified by their relation to the institution of marriage and the degree to which they violate it. In his *summa* on virtue, traditionally placed first, though compiled later (ca. 1250), Peraldus makes marriage the precondition for any licit sexual activity. The first and predominant case is for the purpose of generation. (The other two are marriage debt, and the avoidance of sin, 1.3.3.17; Peraldus 1585, 1: 369.) The *peccatum contra naturam* is obviously the most antithetical to marriage understood as the institutional vehicle of reproductive sex. But Peraldus discusses it first and then continues in reverse order. Incest and adultery follow the sin against nature, and in both cases, Peraldus reiterates their essential unnaturalness in the transcendent sense. He suggests that in Leviticus, God classed incest with the sin against nature, giving them both the same punishment: "omnis anima quae fecerit de abominationibus his quippiam peribit de medio populi sui" [every soul that shall commit any of these abominations, shall perish from the midst of his people] (Lv 18:19). Adultery he declares a violation of natural law on the grounds that natural law holds that one should not do unto others what one does not want done to oneself, and that no one wants another to sin with his wife. In this way Peraldus literally brackets the *peccatum contra naturam* between the general claim that all sin is unnatural and his discussion of these lesser, ostensibly natural, sexual sins. He seems intent on frustrating any attempt to contain the unnatural within a clearly recognizable hierarchy. It is at once the worst of the sexual sins and entirely typical. This taxonomic ambiguity might be said to reinforce its unspeakability, but only by dispersing the category of the unspeakable across the subdivisions of *luxuria*, or at least the more serious of them.

That leads us to Peraldus's discussion of the *peccatum contra naturam* itself. Like the rest of his treatment of the deadly sins and their subcategories, this one is a combination of taxonomy and exhortation. That is, he offers his exposition of a sin's features as a series of reasons to avoid it. His mode of analysis is exegetical. In this case he offers eight ways to demonstrate the "magnitudo" (seriousness) of the *peccatum contra naturam*. The first is the Sodom story itself and the clamor that ascended to God's hearing. The next six he also derives from scripture, citing Genesis, Leviticus, Joel, Romans, Judges, and Isaiah, and adding such relevant *auctoritates* as Augustine, Methodius, and Bernard. He also draws on a wide variety of other exegetical material he does not name. His eighth point notes the sin's "multiplicem effectum impium" [manifold impious effect], chief among these rending the bond between God and humanity, for it makes men into women, contrary to God's creation of them. The sin destroys what humanity is in itself, and transforms it into inferior beasts. He even repeats one of the most curious and extreme pieces of medieval homophobic lore: Peter the Chanter's claim that Christ was so horrified by the sin against nature that He postponed His own Incarnation. (However, Peraldus mentions this notion parenthetically and attributes it only to an anonymous "authoritas," unlike Peter who falsely attributes it to both Augustine and Jerome.) Then he ends his discussion with a gloss.

> Ideoque Sodoma bene muta interpretatur: quia hoc peccatum reddet homines mutos in die Iudicii. Non poterunt enim excusare se per ignorantiam, quum ipsa natura legem docuerit ipsa bruta animalia, quam isti transgrediuntur. (2.3.2.2; Peraldus 1585, 2: 49)

> Sodom is thus fitly interpreted to mean "mute," because this sin will render men mute on the Day of Judgment. They will not be able to excuse themselves on the

grounds of ignorance, when nature herself taught the law to brute animals which these men transgress.

The gloss obviously plays on the figure of *clamor* with which Peraldus opens his discussion. It just as obviously recalls the discretion Peraldus enjoined on preachers and confessors a little earlier. The opposition also frames the discussion with a schematic trajectory of Christian salvation history, that is, from the Sodom story as a foil to Abraham's covenant, through Paul's juxtaposition of the unnatural pagans to his new Christian community on to Judgment Day. All three of these exegetical and rhetorical effects complicate the pure exclusion this ending seems to want to enforce. For they remind us of both the strong pastoral cast which informs Peraldus's discussion, and of the extent to which he identifies the pastoral with the exegetical. In this respect, perhaps the most important point about this passage is what it does not say. It locates the *peccatum contra naturam* on the outer limit of the Christian community, and on the very edge of the economy of salvation: it is the sin that rends the bond between God and man. Yet Peraldus does not say the *peccatum contra naturam* is unforgivable. Paradoxical—perhaps even hypocritical—as it may seem, the ultimate aim of all the imprecations, including the brief vision of Judgment day, is pastoral. To imagine this sin as the rejection of a sexual identity God Himself has created may well collapse the distinction between the two ideals of nature Peraldus works so hard to maintain nearly everywhere else. Or the distinction may remain in the very subjection of sexual identity to human choice, so long as we recall that for Christian ethics such choice is itself a gift from God. But even if the distinction collapses, the ideal of the natural remains tied to the unnatural in a way that the normal is never tied to the abnormal. The norm presents itself as an unmotivated, purely transparent signifier. As an ideal, the norm represses its reproductive teleology; indeed such repression may well constitute its essence. By contrast, the natural makes its teleology overt, especially when deployed by a Christian cosmology. And with his exegetical framework, Peraldus makes the teleology especially insistent. The final paradox of the *peccatum contra naturam* is that however liminal it becomes, its liminality will also always remain typical. The silence of the unnatural sinner before God on Judgment day is an image that must haunt all sinners, for that is the condition toward which all sin tends.

SUGGESTIONS FOR FURTHER READING

The foundational work on medieval sexuality remains Boswell (1980). The recent collection edited by Kuefler (2006) offers valuable explorations of his continuing influence. A concise recent study that nevertheless attempts to survey the whole field is Karras (2005). These works do not focus on Latin traditions *per se*, and, in general, studies of medieval sexuality, especially the more speculative and conceptually daring, have tended to approach linguistic tradition very eclectically. As a result, Latin texts and traditions have been treated in chapters in monographs or critical anthologies with comparative or thematic focuses. These include Baldwin (1994); Bernau, Evans, and Salih (2003); Bulloch and Brundage (1996); Burgwinkle (2004); Cohen and Wheeler (1997); Frantzen (1998); Harper and Proctor (2008); Kiefer (2009); Lochrie (2005); Lochrie, McCracken, and Schultz (1997); Murray (1999); Murray and Eisenbichler (1996); Salisbury (1990); Sautman and Sheingorn (2001). Archibald (2001) treats a wide variety of Latin materials. Works dealing exclusively with Latin texts and traditions include Jordan (1997), Moser (2004), Taylor and Townsend (1998). On sex and the early penitential tradition, see Payer (1984). For an authoritative and exhaustive account of sexuality and canon law, see Brundage (1987). For a more selective treatment of sexuality and medieval theology, see Payer (1993). On sexuality in medieval medicine and science, see Cadden (1993). On Bernard's *Sermones super Cantica canticorum*, see Astell (1990) and Matter (1990). Hagiography offers very fertile ground for sexuality studies. Jordan (1997) discusses a single transvestite saint. However, as no medievalist has yet devoted a full length study to this topic, those interested in it will find very rewarding Burrus's (2004) study of ancient hagiography. No clear line separates gender studies from studies of sexuality. Of the wealth of feminist medieval scholarship produced in the last four decades, readers interested in sexuality and Latinity will find particularly relevant works by Bynum (1982 and 1991), Elliott (1993 and 1999), and Newman (2003). As in every other field, scholarship on medieval sexuality was profoundly transformed by Foucault's three-volume *History of Sexuality*. Its projected fourth volume *Les aveux de la chair* (Confessions of the Flesh) concerned ancient and medieval Christianity. Nearly complete at his death, at his request it remains unpublished. An overview can be found in Foucault (1999).

BIBLIOGRAPHY

Primary sources

Bernard of Clairvaux. 1957–58. *Sancti Bernardi Opera*. Vol. 1: *Sermones super Cantica Canticorum, 1–35*. Vol. 2: *Sermones super Cantica Canticorum, 36–86*, edited by Jean Leclercq, Charles H. Talbot, and Henri M. Rochais. Rome: Editiones Cistercienses.
Burchard of Worms. 1853. "Decretorum libri viginti." In *Patrologiae Latina*, edited by Jacques Paul Migne, 140: cols. 537–1057. Paris.
Irish Penitentials. 1963. *The Irish Penitentials*, edited by Ludwig Bieler. Scriptores Latini Hiberniae 5. Dublin: Dublin Institute for Advanced Studies.
Peraldus, William. 1585. *Summae virtutum ac vitiorum*. Lyons: Rouillium, sub scuto Veneto.
Philo. 1935. "On Abraham." In *The Works of Philo*, edited and translated by Francis H. Colson and George H. Whitaker, 6: 4–135. Loeb Classical Library. Cambridge, MA: Harvard University Press.

Secondary sources

Agamben, Giorgio. 1998. *"Homo Sacer": Sovereign and Bare Life*, translated by Daniel Heller-Roazen. Meridian. Stanford: Stanford University Press.

Archibald, Elizabeth. 2001. *Incest and the Medieval Imagination*. Oxford, New York: Oxford University Press.

Astell, Ann. 1990. *The Song of Songs in the Middle Ages*. Ithaca, NY: Cornell University Press.

Baldwin, John. 1994. *The Language of Sex: Five Voices from Northern France around 1200*. The Chicago Series on Sexuality, History, and Society. Chicago, London: University of Chicago Press.

Bernau, Anke, Ruth Evans, and Sarah Salih, eds. 2003. *Medieval Virginities*. Toronto: University of Toronto Press.

Binder, Vera. 2011. "Koine." In *Brill's New Pauly*: Antiquity volumes edited by Hubert Cancik and Helmuth Schneider. Leiden: Brill.

Boswell, John. 1980. *Christianity, Social Tolerance, and Homosexuality: Gay People in Western Europe from the Beginning of the Christian Era to the Fourteenth Century*. Chicago, London: University of Chicago Press.

Brundage, James A. 1987. *Law, Sex, and Christian Society in Medieval Europe*. Chicago, London: University of Chicago Press.

Bulloch, Vern L., and James A. Brundage, eds. 1996. *Handbook of Medieval Sexuality*. Garland Reference Library of the Humanities 1696. New York: Garland Publishing.

Burgwinkle, William. 2004. *Sodomy, Masculinity, and Law in Medieval Literature: France and England, 1050–1230*. Cambridge Studies in Medieval Literature. Cambridge: Cambridge University Press.

Burrus, Virginia. 2004. *The Sex Lives of Saints: An Erotics of Ancient Hagiography*. Divinations. Philadelphia: University of Pennsylvania Press.

Bynum, Caroline Walker. 1982. *Jesus as Mother: Studies in the Spirituality of the High Middle Ages*. Publications of the Center for Medieval and Renaissance Studies 16. Berkeley, CA, Los Angeles, London: University of California Press.

———. 1991. *Fragmentation and Redemption: Essays on Gender and the Human Body in Medieval Religion*. New York: Zone Books.

Cadden, Joan. 1993. *The Meanings of Sex Difference in the Middle Ages: Medicine, Science and Culture*. Cambridge History of Medicine. Cambridge: Cambridge University Press.

Cohen, Jeffrey J. and Bonnie Wheeler, eds. *Becoming Male in the Middle Ages*. Garland Reference Library of the Humanities 2066. New York: Garland Publishing.

Elliot, Dyan. 1993. *Spiritual Marriage: Sexual Abstinence in Medieval Wedlock*. Princeton, NJ: Princeton University Press.

———. 1999. *Fallen Bodies: Pollution, Sexuality and Demonology in the Middle Ages*. The Middle Ages Series. Philadelphia: University of Pennsylvania Press.

G.R. Evans, tr. and ed., *Bernard of Clairvaux: Selected Works*. New York and Mahwah, NJ: Paulist Press, 1987.

Foucault, Michel. 1980. *The History of Sexuality*. Vol. 1: *An Introduction*, translated by Robert Hurley. New York: Vintage Books.

———. 1985. *The History of Sexuality*. Vol. 2: *The Use of Pleasure*, translated by Robert Hurley. New York: Vintage Books.

———. 1999. *Religion and Culture*, edited by Jeremy R. Carrette. New York: Routledge.

Frantzen, Allen. 1983. *The Literature of Penance in Anglo-Saxon England*. New Brunswick, NJ: Rutgers University Press.

———. 1998. *Before the Closet: Same-Sex Love from Beowulf to Angels in America*. Chicago, London: University of Chicago Press.

Harper, April and Caroline Proctor, eds. 2008. *Medieval Sexuality: A Casebook*. Medieval Casebooks. New York: Routledge.

Jordan, Mark D. 1997. *The Invention of Sodomy in Christian Theology*. The Chicago Series on Sexuality, History, and Society. Chicago, London: University of Chicago Press.

Karras, Ruth Mazo. 2005. *Sexuality in Medieval Europe: Doing Unto Others*. New York and London: Routledge.

Kiefer, Frederick, ed. 2009. *Masculinities and Femininities in the Middle Ages and Renaissance*. Arizona Studies in the Middle Ages and the Renaissance 23. Turnhout: Brepols.

Kuefler, Mathew, ed. 2006. *The Boswell Thesis: Essays on "Christianity, Social Tolerance, and Homosexuality"*. Chicago, London: University of Chicago Press.

Lacan, Jacques. 1982. "God and the *Jouissance* of Woman." In *Feminine Sexuality: Jacques Lacan and the "école freudienne,"* edited by Juliet Mitchell and Jacqueline Rose, translated by Jacqueline Rose. New York, London: W.W. Norton.

Leclercq, Jean. 2008. "Introduction to Saint Bernard's Doctrine in the Sermons on the Song of Songs." *Cistercian Studies Quarterly* 43: 309–25.

Lochrie, Karma. 2005. *Heterosyncrasies: Female Sexuality When Normal Wasn't*. Minneapolis, MN: University of Minnesota Press.

Lochrie, Karma, Peggy McCracken, and James A. Schultz. 1997. *Constructing Medieval Sexuality*. Medieval Cultures 11. Minneapolis, MN: University of Minnesota Press.

Mantello, Frank A. C. and Arthur G. Rigg. 1996. "Medieval Latin, Past and Present." In *Medieval Latin: An Introduction and Bibliographical Guide*, edited by Frank A. C. Mantello and Arthur G. Rigg. Washington, DC: The Catholic University of America Press.

Moser, Thomas C. 2004. *A Cosmos of Desire: the Medieval Latin Erotic Lyric in English Manuscripts*. Studies in Medieval and Early Modern Civilization. Ann Arbor, MI: University of Michigan Press.

Matter, E. Ann. 1990. *The Voice of My Beloved: The Song of Songs in Western Medieval Christianity*. Middle Ages Series. Philadelphia: University of Pennsylvania Press.

Murray, Jacqueline, ed. 1999. *Conflicted Identities and Multiple Masculinities: Men in the Medieval West*. Garland Medieval Casebooks. New York: Garland Publishing.

Murray, Jacqueline and Konrad Eisenbichler, eds. 1996. *Desire and Discipline: Sex and Sexuality in the Pre-Modern West*. Toronto: University of Toronto Press.

Newman, Barbara. 2003. *God and the Goddesses: Vision, Poetry, and Belief in the Middle Ages*. Middle Ages Series. Philadelphia: University of Pennsylvania Press.

Payer, Pierre J. 1984. *Sex and the Penitentials: The Development of a Sexual Code 550–1150*. Toronto: University of Toronto Press.

———. 1993. *The Bridling of Desire: Views of Sex in the Later Middle Ages*. Toronto: University of Toronto Press.

Salisbury, Joyce E. 1990. *Medieval Sexuality: A Research Guide*. Garland Medieval Bibliographies 5. Garland Reference Library of Social Science 565. New York: Garland Publishing.

Sautman, Francesca Canadé and Pamela Sheingorn. 2001. *Same-Sex Love and Desire among Women in the Middle Ages*. New Middle Ages. New York: Palgrave.

Taylor, Andrew and David Townsend. 1998. *The Tongue of the Fathers: Gender and Ideology in Twelfth-Century Latin*. The Middle Ages Series. Philadelphia: University of Pennsylvania Press.

Tanner, Norman P. 1990. *Decrees of the Ecumenical Councils Vol. 1: Nicaea I to Lateran V*. London, Washington, DC: Sheed and Ward.

Tentler, Thomas N. 1977. *Sin and Confession on the Eve of the Reformation*. Princeton, NJ: Princeton University Press.

CHAPTER 22

MEDIEVAL LATIN SPIRITUALITY: SEEKING DIVINE PRESENCE

ANNE L. CLARK

L<small>IKE</small> sex and gender (the subjects of other chapters in this section of the *Handbook*), spirituality was not a type of text, Latin or otherwise. Rather, medieval spirituality was a practice that could be shaped, articulated, and constrained by the reading and writing of texts and, as a practice, it resonates with the materials discussed in the essay on embodied performance. Medieval Latin spirituality can be characterized as the Christian practice of cultivating the self—through reading, hearing, seeing, singing, meditation, often institutionalized and experienced communally—so as to experience the objects of this world—books, architecture, images, nature, other people—as leading one into the divine presence. This characterization accords with recent developments in "spirituality studies" in framing spirituality as a conscious involvement in an ongoing project of transformation (Schneiders 2005).

An immense variety of Latin texts supported medieval spirituality and they cannot be reduced to a single genre, style, or even subject matter, and attempts to categorize them by religious affiliation ("Cistercian," "beguine"), or gender (e.g., "female spirituality"), or era ("twelfth-century"), while often highlighting salient characteristics, usually point to the permeable boundaries of the chosen category. The focus here on Latin spirituality illuminates a domain that was largely limited to professed religious: men and women who lived in institutions that trained them for literacy and the practice of literate spirituality. This does not imply a lack or inferior quality of lay spirituality but rather acknowledges that medieval Latin spirituality was for most of the Middle Ages a religious practice of the educated.

This "professional" or elite constituency opened up in the fourteenth and fifteenth centuries with increased literacy and the creation of texts offering versions of Latin spirituality for lay practice.

Regulating Spirituality

One of the most significant works of Latin spiritual literature, whose influence would be felt directly or indirectly throughout the Middle Ages, is the text known as *Regula monachorum* (Rule of Monks) or *Regula Benedicti*, the *Rule of St. Benedict* (Benedict 1980, hereafter *RB*; Latin texts are cited by chapter enumeration from the critical editions listed in the bibliography). Written in the mid-sixth century, it shares with other contemporary religious literature (e.g., that of Cassiodorus and Gregory the Great) the task of shaping and translating the venerable traditions of the "fathers" for monastic audiences of Western Europe. It was not the only such attempt to lay down regulations for monastic life, but it was often recommended by bishops, was imperially promoted in the ninth century, and was adapted by later monastic legislators even as they devised their own rules.

The influence of the *RB* on Latin spirituality is due to two closely entwined aspects of the text itself: its clear, practical program for organizing cenobitic (i.e., communal) monastic life and the spiritual perspective that Benedict strove to inculcate through this program. For example, the rule required uncompromising obedience to the abbot (or abbess, when the rule was adopted by nuns), which enabled the efficient running of the monastery with a clear chain of authority and sanctions to enforce it. Obedience was one of three vows made upon formal profession of monastic life, and all commands of the abbot or abbess, even the manifestly impossible, were to be met with immediate, wholehearted compliance. Although tyrannical rule by the abbot was condemned and leadership was to be loving, wise, and discrete, the authoritarian tenor of monastic life undergirds the *RB*.

This authoritarian tenor—easily understood as simply pragmatic—was in fact deeply integrated into a spiritual vision that made obedience a critical technique for the realization of the highest religious goals. The Prologue announces this connection:

> Ad eum per oboedientiae laborem redeas, a quo per inoboedientiae desidiam recesseras. Ad te ergo nunc mihi sermo dirigitur, quisquis abrenuntians propriis voluntatibus, Domino Christo vero regi militaturus, oboedientiae fortissima atque praeclara arma sumis.
>
> [Through the work of obedience you may return to Him whom you have abandoned through the idleness of disobedience. Therefore, my word is now directed at you, whoever you are, as you renounce your own will, ready to fight for the true king, the Lord Christ, taking up the strongest and shining weapons of obedience.] (*RB*, Prologue 2–3)

The pairing of obedience and disobedience as the means of relationship to God inserts every monk or nun into the primal story of Adam and Eve, and offers obedience as the means to salvation. What is silent here—the equation of obedience to God (or Christ) and obedience to the abbot—becomes explicit in the following chapters (*RB* 2.2, 5.4, 63.13). The pairing of abandoning God/returning to God (*recesseras/redeas*) characterizes the spiritual life as one of movement rather than stillness, a movement that, while enacted in submission to the abbot, is nonetheless agonistic. And obedience, the chief weapon in this battle, is defined as renouncing self-will (*abrenuntians propriis voluntatibus*; see also *RB* 5.7: *voluntatem propriam deserentes*). Thus obedience is envisioned not as mere compliance with authority but as a reconfiguration of the self, the creation of a being not enlivened by personal desire or will. The saying of Jesus from the Gospel of Matthew, "If anyone wishes to come after me, let him renounce himself (*abneget semetipsum*), and take up his cross and follow me" (Mt 16:24), is explicitly evoked by Benedict as one of the tools of spiritual craft (*instrumenta artis spiritualis*, *RB* 4.10), pointing to the crafting or even chiseling of self. In this context, the Gospel words take on the specific monastic meaning of obedient submission to the abbot as part of the dismantling of the autonomous self. So for example, Benedict stipulates the conditions in which the monk may own any object:

> Praecipue hoc vitium radicitus amputandum est de monasterio, ne quis praesumat aliquid dare aut accipere sine iussione abbatis, neque aliquid habere proprium, nullam omnino rem, neque codicem, neque tabulas, neque graphium, sed nihil omnino, quippe quibus nec corpora sua nec voluntates licet habere in propria voluntate.
>
> [This vice especially must be cut out by the roots from the monastery, lest someone presume to give or receive anything without the command of the abbot, or have anything of one's own—not anything at all, not a book nor writing tablets nor a stylus, absolutely nothing. Indeed, they are not allowed to have control over their own bodies or their wills.] (*RB* 33.1–4)

Although Benedict calls this a vice, there is no noun that corresponds to it—not greed or pride (cf. "the vice of private ownership," *RB* 55.18, *vitium peculiaris*). It is not a characteristic but a series of actions (giving, receiving, having, controlling) that is being regulated. The usually sober language of the *RB* escalates with the attempt to communicate that nothing, whether small (a tablet) or large (self-will), should be entrusted to the monk's independent judgment.

This dismantling of the autonomous person who wills is accompanied by the reconstruction of that being into a member, a limb of a larger body, the monastic community itself. The subjective center of this monastic being is not the will (*voluntas*), but the emotions of love (*caritas* and *amor*). The stipulations of the rule are techniques for accomplishing and maintaining this reprogramming of the self: each monk must take his turn in kitchen work and serving food to the others because thereby "charity is acquired" (*caritas acquiritur*, *RB* 35.2); younger monks are to obey their elders "in all charity" (*omni caritate*, *RB* 71.4); guests are to be met "with every duty of charity" (*cum omni officio caritatis, RB* 53.3). Charity, of course, is not a spontaneous emotional response but a subjectivity cultivated by and for being in community.

The community itself is instrumental in the pursuit of eternal beatitude, and it is the communal activity par excellence—the Divine Office—that offers the monk the most intense experience of the presence of God in this lifetime (*RB* 19.1–2). The Divine Office or "work of God" (*opus Dei*), comprised of eight offices or services of communal prayer to be celebrated in the oratory, provides the temporal structuring of monastic day and night. Directions for the celebration of the Divine Office constitute the largest single topic in the text (*RB* 8–19). The primary element in the office is the chanting of the psalms, and while Benedict allows for some flexibility in the arrangement, he insists that the whole collection of 150 psalms be sung each week. Perhaps the driest part of reading the *RB*, the chapters on the Divine Office laid the foundation for the emotional core of monastic spirituality. Eight times throughout the day and night, the full community gathered in the oratory to sing a collection of haunting poems that were to be learned by heart. Benedict spends but one terse sentence addressing the subjective experience of being emotionally colonized by the melodic recitation of these poems: "Ergo consideremus qualiter oporteat in conspectu divinitatis et angelorum eius esse, et sic stemus ad psallendum ut mens nostra concordet voci nostrae" [Let us consider, then, how we should be in the presence of the Divine and his angels, and in this way, let us stand to sing the psalms in such a way that our mind is in harmony with our voice] (*RB* 19.6-7). But he has drawn upon, and directs his monks to, the *Collationes* or *Conferences* of John Cassian (*RB* 42.3; 73.5), thus canonizing it along with the Psalter as foundational to the spiritual enterprise of the monastery. Written in the 420s, the *Collationes* (Cassian 1886) is Cassian's attempt to create a coherent picture of the monastic traditions practiced in the Egyptian desert. For Cassian, the properly prepared monk

> omnes quoque psalmorum adfectus in se recipiens ita incipiet decantare, ut eos non tamquam a propheta conpositos, sed velut a se editos quasi orationem propriam profunda cordis conpunctione depromat.... eundem namque recipientes cordis affectum, quo quisque decantatus vel conscriptus est psalmus, velut auctores eius facti praecedemus magis intellectum ipsius quam sequemur, id est ut prius dictorum virtutem quam notitiam colligentes, quid in nobis gestum sit vel cotidianis geratur incursibus superveniente eorum meditatione quodammodo recordemur, et quid nobis vel neglegentia nostra pepererit vel diligentia conquisierit vel providentia divina contulerit vel instigatio fraudauerit inimici vel subtraxerit lubrica ac subtilis oblivio vel intulerit humana fragilitas seu inprovida fefellerit ignoratio, decantantes reminiscamur.

> [taking into himself all the emotions of the psalms, will begin to sing them in such a way that he draws them forth from the deep compunction of his heart, not as compositions of the prophet, but as if produced by himself as his very own prayer.... For if we take into ourselves the same heartfelt emotion by which each psalm was sung or composed, then we become like its author, anticipating its meaning rather than following it. That is, rather than an idea of what was said, we

first get the force of it and, adding meditation, we somehow remember what was done within us or what should be done about the daily assaults, what negligence has brought upon us and what diligence has overcome or divine providence has conferred, how the urging of the enemy has deceived us or slippery and subtle forgetfulness has undermined us, or how human weakness or careless ignorance has tricked us. Singing, we are reminded of all this.] (*Collationes* 10.11)

The memorization of the psalms—like so many other aspects of monastic life—is not simply a means of facilitating the smooth operation of communal life but is part of the larger working of the monastic machinery for transforming the self to experience the presence of God. The emotions of David are tried on and recognized as one's own. This internalization is shared, shaping the emotional milieu of community and mitigating potential tension between the desire to "dwell in the tabernacle of the Lord" and the actual dwelling with a number of other all too human monks. And the emotions shared are constructed by the idiom of the late antique Latin of the biblical text, which will in turn inflect spiritual texts throughout the Middle Ages. Thus, through the monastic training for liturgy, Latin became an emotionally charged means of natural expression even when acquired by Germanic language speakers.

Bridging between the goal of the religious life and the everyday world of monastic life is also effected by the retraining of vision. The mundane utensils of the kitchen are to be seen as if they were sacred vessels of the altar (*RB* 32.10). Even more powerfully, not only can the monk see the Lord in the abbot (thus reinforcing the abnegation of self-will in obedience), but also the sick and visitors to the monastery are to be treated "as Christ" (*sicut Christo, RB* 36.1; *tamquam Christus, RB* 53.1), thus offering a simulacrum of divine presence in the community's daily routines. This retraining of vision requires the monk not only to see differently, but to be seen differently:

> Non solum corde monachus sed etiam ipso corpore humilitatem videntibus se semper indicet, id est in opere Dei, in oratorio, in monasterio, in horto, in via, in agro vel ubicumque sedens, ambulans vel stans.
>
> [Not only in his heart but also in body let the monk always manifest humility to those seeing him, whether in the Divine Office, in the oratory, in the monastery, in the garden, on the road, in the field, whether sitting, walking, or standing.] (*RB* 7.62–63)

Accomplishing this total embodiment of humility (the twelfth and final step on the ladder leading heavenward) transforms the emotional charge of abnegation and *memoria Dei*, the continual mindfulness of God:

> Monachus mox ad caritatem Dei perveniet illam quae perfecta foris mittit timorem, per quam universa quae prius non sine formidine observabat absque ullo labore velut naturaliter ex consuetudine incipiet custodire, non iam timore gehennae, sed amore Christi et consuetudine ipsa bona et delectatione virtutum.
>
> [The monk will quickly arrive at that perfect love of God which casts out fear, through which everything that he had previously done with dread he will

begin to observe without any struggle, as if naturally from habit, no longer from fear of hell but from love of Christ, good habit, and delight in virtue.] (RB 7.67–69)

Despite his flexibility in some details, Benedict strove to ensure that his whole vision of monastic life was kept intact by mandating frequent communal reading of the rule (*RB* 66.8). With this deep embedding of the text of the rule in monastic culture, the *RB* itself, like the Psalms, became an authoritative model of Latin expression. Furthermore, the explicitly prescriptive form of the rule served to authorize the norms it prescribed, enshrining in medieval Christian spirituality the suspicion of autonomy, the need for self-abnegation, the internalization of biblical emotions as one's own, and the communal life as the setting for serious movement toward God, naturalizing the belief that connection with God was a matter of degree that could be cultivated through specific techniques.

Women, Ecstasy, and Vision

The perdurance of these views can be seen about six centuries later, when another monk sought to adapt the *RB* to two circumstances different from those Benedict had envisioned: the life of a solitary woman, rather than a cenobitic man. Around 1160–62, Aelred of Rievaulx composed his *De institutione inclusarum* [About the Regulation of Recluses], which he described as written for his sister who had requested a formula for her life so that she could organize her daily habits and spiritual exercises (*De inst.* 1.3–5, in Aelred 1971). The belief in the spiritual life as something to be cultivated through the establishment of habits and exercises introduces another attempt at regulation, the composition of an overtly prescriptive text. Aelred was a Cistercian abbot, a member of a monastic order dedicated to the strict observance of the *RB*. Although he doesn't explicitly invoke the *RB* in his *De institutione inclusarum*, its influence powerfully shaped his views about the type of life his sister had embraced.

Unlike cenobitic monks, recluses were men and women who undertook a solitary life dedicated to God. The ideal of the solitary life haunted the *RB*, explicitly acknowledged in the first and last chapters. Benedict referred to the existence of anchorites or hermits, emphasizing that they had only moved into that mode of living after a long period of training in the communal life (*RB* 1.3–5). But he offers no mechanism for movement from communal to solitary life; rather, he recommends that those yearning for the perfection of monastic life should *read about* the great desert solitaries of the past. Those texts are tools of virtue for obedient monks living in a community (*RB* 73.5–6). For where is the place for obedience, self-abnegation, and authoritative structure when one is alone? As Aelred notes, even some of those ancient solitaries did not consider themselves safe "propter solitudinis libertatem et vagandi potestatem" [in the liberty of solitude and the possibility of wandering] (*De inst.* 2.11–12). Living a life pursued in community, first as monk and then as abbot, Aelred admits he has no experience of the solitary life on which to base his rule (*De inst.* 1.8–9).

Aelred's uneasiness with the solitary life is compounded by the fact that he is writing for women. Even his praise of his sister's virtue is tinged with suspicion that she will fail (*De inst.* 32.1333–37), and that suspicion is given full reign when he envisions other women or young girls following his rule (*De inst.* 7.177–78). This leads Aelred to a position markedly different from Benedict's: an almost obsessive focus on the preservation of virginity as the hallmark of the spiritual life. Every activity of the recluse's life is subsumed in this effort:

> Cogitet semper virgo omnia sua membra sanctificata Deo, incorporata Christo, Spiritui sancto dedicata. Indignum iudicet quod Christi est tradere Satanae, et virginea eius membra erubescat vel simplici motu maculari. Ita proinde in virginitatis suae custodiam totum animum tendat, cogitationes expendat, ut virtutis huius perfectionem esuriens, famem delicias putet, divitias paupertatem. In cibo, in potu, in somno, in sermone, semper timeat dispendium castitatis, ne si plus debito carni reddiderit, vires praebeat adversario, et occultum nutriat hostem.

> [Let the virgin always be mindful that all her members are consecrated to God, incorporated in Christ, dedicated to the Holy Spirit. She should judge it unworthy to hand over to Satan what is Christ's, and she should blush if her virginal members are stained by even a simple movement. Therefore, let her extend her whole effort toward the guarding of her virginity, let her expend her thoughts so that, thirsting for the perfection of this virtue, she will judge hunger a delight and poverty riches. In drink, in food, in sleep, in words, let her always fear the loss of her chastity, lest by giving the flesh more than its due, she grant strength to the Adversary and nourish a hidden enemy.] (*De inst.* 15.494–503)

Aelred does acknowledge that the recluse's physical integrity remains insufficient without humility (*De inst.* 23.663–66), but his repeated address to his audience as "virgin" reinforces the sense that the whole spiritual life is condensed in the preservation of virginity. This leaves open the question of whether the life of the recluse is even an option for women who are not physical virgins, even though Aelred openly describes sexual debauchery as part of his own past (*De inst.* 32.1278–1325).

One of the fundamental differences between the communal life as prescribed in the *RB* and the solitary life for women as prescribed in *De institutione inclusarum* is the space envisioned for the experience of the presence of God. While Benedict sought to retrain the eye of the monk to see Christ in the abbot, the sick, and the guest, Aelred has no comparable technique. Rather, he is vehement that every human being poses a threat to the recluse. Even as she is walled in her cell—and he would have no other material condition for her life—she is vulnerable to harm. Through the window of the cell, the words of a widow, wife, or young girl "[o]s interea in risus cachinnosque dissoluitur, et venenum cum suauitate bibitum, per viscera membraque diffunditur" [loosen the recluse's mouth in laughter and cackles, and poison—slurped in with the sweetness—spreads throughout her guts and limbs] (*De inst.* 2.30–32). She must also ignore the poor who seek alms at her window (*De inst.* 4.75–79). While some recluses teach children, Aelred forbids it because children inevitably stimulate a variety of emotions:

> Nunc irascitur, nunc ridet, nunc minatur, nunc blanditur, nunc percutit, nunc osculatur, nunc flentem pro verbere vocat propius, palpat faciem, stringit collum, et in amplexum ruens, nunc filiam uocat, nunc amicam.

> [Now she is annoyed, now she laughs, now warns, now flatters, now strikes, now kisses, now calls the crying child close, strokes her face, touches her neck and, sinking into an embrace, now calls her daughter, now sweet friend.] (*De inst.* 4.118–22)

Conceding that she must have some—albeit rare—conversation with an elderly priest-confessor, Aelred ominously refers to the mutual danger lurking even in this relationship (*De inst.* 6.164–75). Aelred, who elsewhere argued that spiritual friendships—between men—can actually lead one closer to God (*De spiritali amicitia* 3.88, in Aelred 1971), here envisions no possibility of human relationship that does not send the recluse into a swirl of illicit affections that could lead to even greater damage. Discussing Cistercian monks, he could poignantly elaborate the emotional benefits of "habere quem tibi affectu quodam intimo et sacratissimi amoris unire possis amplexu" [having someone you can join to yourself in a certain intimate feeling and embrace of most holy love] (*Speculum charitatis* 3.39.109, in Aelred 1971). But the only embrace he grants to the recluse is both impersonal and symbolic: she must "totum mundum uno dilectionis sinu complectere...Omnibus pectus tuae dilectionis aperias" [embrace the whole world in the bosom of compassion...open the breast of her love to everyone] (*De inst.* 28.850–58). Those others are never to be seen or conversed with; the loving engagement takes place solely in her solitary prayer.

Aelred's unsettling equation of the recluse's life with virginity reflects his constricted assumptions about women. His view of the dangerously open bodies of women and their seething sensual impulses leads him to construct the cell as a second body enclosing the first, a kind of carapace that enforces her isolation. But the recluse's total withdrawal from the world leaves her without the demands of obedience as a means of self-abnegation, and without being enmeshed in a community of shared striving and reciprocal scrutiny. By refusing the life of professed obedience to a superior, she has thereby left behind the possibility for any positive human relationship. This not only illuminates the centrality of conceptualizing human relationships in terms of dominance and subordination in monastic spirituality shaped by the *RB*, but it also opens up a rich realm for articulating relationships not bound by human limitations of time and space.

When Aelred described the recluse as being stimulated by anyone who comes to her window, he builds his picture of her emotional flux, culminating in a question: "Qualis inter haec memoria Dei, ubi saecularia et carnalia, etsi non perficiantur, moventur tamen, et quasi sub oculis depinguntur" [Amidst all this, what is the memory of God where the secular and carnal, even if they are not acted upon, nevertheless move as if as painted right under her eyes?] (*De inst.* 4.123). Aelred's worry is not simply about what the recluse will do when encountering other people; he is also worried about the damage to her memory when it is impressed with images of what she has seen. Influenced by ancient mnemonic theories as they have passed through Augustine and others, Aelred knows that the internal impress of what has been seen remains long after the visual experience. The pictures in the recluse's mind are the real threat to what should be there, the continuous memory of God.

So in addition to the stipulations designed to protect that inner space by regulating her physical existence, Aelred also tries to regulate her interior experience. While Benedict relied on the emotional life of the psalms to engender a monastic subjectivity thoroughly stripped of self-will, Aelred offers his own blueprint to orchestrate emotion and imagination. This blueprint is a meditation guide that concludes the rule, reflecting Aelred's view that the mind and eyes must first be cleansed (*purgata; defaecatos*) by the practice of the ascetic life that he has outlined. Enduring the mandated seclusion, fasts, and vigils, the recluse can move from the life of deprivation to ecstasy, from isolation to reveling in the mutual delight between herself and Christ that the meditation guide seeks to stimulate almost as a kind of aphrodisiac: "Itaque ut ille dulcis amor Iesu in tuo crescat affectu, triplici meditatione opus habes" [So that that sweet love of Jesus might grow in your affections, you need a threefold meditation] (*De inst.* 29.883–85). Although the meditation is structured in three parts (past, present, and future) with the ultimate goal of a future dwelling in heaven, Aelred offers the recluse the possibility of present sweetness (*dulcedine*), nourished primarily by her imaginative recreation of the life of Jesus and insertion of herself into his story. The text gives a selective overview of Jesus's life, retelling poignant episodes to elicit a strong emotional response from the recluse. Including an admittedly apocryphal episode, Aelred emphasizes that the authenticity of the legend is not as important as its use as an "incentive of love" (*incentivum amoris, De inst.* 30.949).

This emotional arousal is heightened by a blurring of conventional lines between interior and exterior, mental and physical. When Aelred describes the meeting of Mary and Elizabeth, he tells the recluse to run and prostrate herself at their feet and embrace their fertile wombs (*De inst.* 29.917–20). At the bed of the newborn Jesus, the recluse is exhorted to embrace the crib and lovingly kiss the baby's feet (*De inst.* 39.925–27). She is to wash the adult Christ's feet with her tears, rub them with her hair, and caress them with her kisses (*De inst.* 31.988–91). She must lick up Christ's sweated blood as well as the dust from his feet on Mount Olivet (*De inst.* 31.1109–10). And at the crucifixion, she must gaze at his pale face and the tears of his mother and cry at their shared grief (*De inst.* 31.1179–83).

Thus, while confined in her cell, the recluse is ecstatically transported to another time and place and enacts the emotionally charged role of lover of Christ. She is guided not just to visualize but to participate in these scenes; the commands to sing, kiss, prostrate herself, lick the dust, and weep script a fully embodied performance. The emotionality is further stoked by personalizing Jesus's own actions as being done specifically for her, as the love-motivated actions in which his humanity almost eclipses his divinity: "Ita compateris mihi te exhibens hominem, ut quodammodo videaris nescire quod Deus es" [You have such compassion for me in showing yourself as human to me that you almost seem to not know that you are God] (*De inst.* 31.1105–7). Aelred encourages the recluse to take full advantage of this proffered body of Christ. When blood and water pour from the wound in Christ's side, Aelred exhorts her:

> Festina, ne tardaueris, comede fauum cum melle tuo, bibe uinum tuum cum lacte tuo. Sanguis tibi in uinum uertitur ut inebrieris, in lac aqua mutatur ut nutriaris. Facta sunt tibi in petra flumina, in membris eius uulnera, et in maceria corporis eius cauerna [cf. Sg 2:14], in quibus instar columbae latitans et deosculans singula ex sanguine eius fiant sicut uitta coccinea labia tua, et eloquium tuum dulce [cf. Sg 4:3].

> [Hurry, do not delay, eat the honeycomb with your honey; drink your wine with your milk. The blood was turned into wine for you to inebriate you; the water was changed into milk to nourish you. Rivers have been made for you in the rock, in the wounds of his limbs, and holes in the walls of his body (cf. Sg 2:14). Hide in them like a dove, kissing each one so that your lips are made like a scarlet band from his blood, your speech made sweet (cf. Sg 4:3).] (*De inst.* 31.1188–94)

Adapting the erotic imagery of the Song of Songs, Aelred transforms the crucifixion into an opportunity for mystical incorporation; the wounds that perforate Christ's body are the intimate sanctuary for inebriation and entering into the body of the beloved. In the emerging use of the Song of Songs, especially among Cistercian authors writing for male audiences, to articulate the relationship between the soul (bride) and Christ (bridegroom), allegory made space for possible homoerotic investment. For the female recluse, Aelred literalizes the heterosexual yearning of the Song. This consolidates the significance he attaches to virginity, even as he suggests that perhaps it is the male lover of Christ who most fully experiences the mystical delights that go beyond the connection to the humanity of Christ:

> Quisnam ille est, rogo te, qui supra pectus eius recumbit, et in sinu eius caput reclinat [Cf. Jn 13:23]? Felix quicumque ille est. O, ecce video, *Ioannes est nomen eius* [Lk 1:63]. O Ioannes, quid ibi dulcedinis, quid gratiae et suauitatis, quid luminis et deuotionis ab illo haurias fonte edicito.... Iam nunc exulta, virgo, accede proprius, et aliquam tibi huius dulcedinis portionem vendicare non differas. Si ad potiora non potes, dimitte Ioanni pectus, ubi eum uinum laetitiae in diuinitatis cognitione inebriet, tu currens ad ubera humanitatis, lac exprime quo nutriaris.

> [Who is that one, I ask you, who is lying upon his breast, and leans his head in his bosom (Cf. Jn 13:23)? Happy he is, whoever he may be. O look, I see; John is his name (Lk 1:63). O John, tell us what delight, what grace and sweetness, what light and devotion you are drinking there from that fountain!... Now hurry, virgin, go quickly, and do not delay to claim some portion of this sweetness for

yourself. If you cannot drink the stronger things, leave the breast to John where the wine of gladness inebriates him with the knowledge of divinity. You, run to the breasts of humanity, and squeeze out the milk by which you are fed.] (*De inst.* 31.1079–94)

Milk rather than wine, humanity rather than divinity, is the more likely fulfillment of her desire. Aelred offers the female recluse a path for visceral connection with a loving Christ, and he teases her with the possibility of something beyond, something that the disciple especially loved by Christ was able to reach. Like his circumscribed view of women's spiritual friendships, his vision of women's relations to Christ is a much paler version of what he imagines for men and seems to long for himself.

While Aelred's rule codified instructions for cultivating visionary spirituality, women at least did not need his directions to pursue the possibilities of sensing the presence of the divine through extraordinary experience. By the time Aelred composed his rule for recluses, at least four visionary works of Elisabeth of Schönau were completed and probably in circulation. Elisabeth, who lived in a Benedictine monastery from the age of twelve, offers an exemplary case for seeing how the life prescribed in the *RB* set up conditions that for some individuals were conducive to the cultivation of visionary experience. Elisabeth was thoroughly immersed in the ritual life of the Divine Office and, like all children given to the monastic life by their parents, she was educated to meet the ritual demands of literacy and performance (Boynton 2000).

The liturgical character of Elisabeth's visionary spirituality is evident throughout her works, which are comprised of accounts of extraordinary encounters that she experienced, usually in the context of the various services of the Divine Office or the celebration of the Mass (cf. Palazzo 2010). The agonistic quality of the monastic life envisioned by Benedict dominates the earliest visions. In these episodes, Elisabeth is taunted by "my Adversary" (*adversarius meus, Liber visionum primus* 2; in Roth 1884), "the Betrayer" (*ille perfidus, Liber visionum primus* 2), "a small phantom clothed in a monk's cowl" (*fantasma parvulum, quasi cuculla monachi indutum, Liber visionum primus* 3), or a figure "in humana effigie, statura brevis, et spissus, et horribilis aspectu, facies eius ignea, lingua flammea, et longe ab ore eiecta, manus eius et pedes similes unguibus avium rapacissimarum" [in human shape, short in stature and stocky, and dreadful in appearance. Its face was fiery and its flaming tongue stuck far out of its mouth, and its hands and feet were like the talons of greedy birds of prey] (*Liber visionum primus* 4). The apparitions themselves are unsettling, but more profound is the effect on Elisabeth's spirituality. The usually uplifting liturgy left her melancholy and weary: "Psalterium, quod iocundum semper mihi fuerat, quandoque vix uno psalmo perlecto, longe a me proieci" [The Psalter, which had always been a great joy to me, I threw far from me when I had hardly finished reading one psalm] (*Liber visionum primus* 2). She doubted the truth about Christ written in scripture and she considered ending her life. In the midst of this turmoil, Elisabeth also claimed to see something quite different from the demonic tormentors:

Deinde cum inchoaretur missa de beata virgine domina nostra, sabbatum enim erat, collapsa sum in extasim, et apertum est cor meum, et vidi super aerem istum rotam magni luminis similem lune plene, sed quasi duplo maiorem. Et introspexi per medium rote, ac vidi similitudinem regalis femine, stantem in sublimi quasi candidissimis indutam vestimentis, ac purpureo amictu circumdatam. Continuo intellexi, hanc esse sublimem celi reginam, matrem salvatoris nostri, cuius semper desideravi aspectum. Cunque intenderem in eam cum desiderio, procidit in faciem suam ter adorans coram divino quodam lumine, quod erat ante illam... Convertit ad me faciem et modicum progressa est in inferiorem aerem contra me... Stans autem domina mea signo crucis me consignavit et hec verba menti mee nescio qualiter inseruit: Ne timueris, quia nihil tibi ista nocebunt.

[Afterward, on Saturday, when the Mass of our Lady the blessed Virgin had begun, I sank into ecstasy and my heart was opened, and I saw above our atmosphere a wheel of great light like the full moon, but almost twice as large. And I looked through the center of that wheel and I saw the likeness of a regal woman standing on high, dressed in the whitest garments and wrapped in a purple mantle. I immediately understood that this woman was the exalted Queen of heaven, mother of our Savior, whom I had long desired to see. While I looked at her with longing, she prostrated herself three times, worshiping in the presence of the divine light... She turned her face to me and came forward toward me, into the lower atmosphere a little... Standing there my Lady marked me with the sign of the cross and implanted—I don't know how—these words in my mind, "Do not fear because those things will not harm you at all."] (*Liber visionum primus* 5)

In the context of a celebration of the Eucharist—a ritual believed to create a physical connection between this world and the next and that particularly commemorates the role of the Virgin Mary in making that connection—Elisabeth claims to have "sunk into ecstasy," and in this altered state of consciousness, to have seen a very specific extension of the heavenly world into this earthly realm. This vision of the Virgin at prayer reinforces the significance of the structured communal prayer life of the monastery as a mirror of the heavenly realm, confirmed by the presence of St. Benedict accompanying the Virgin as she approaches Elisabeth. In a subsequent vision, Elisabeth describes how "my Comforter" (*consolatrix mea*) responded to her cries and again descended to her as she was tormented by "my Waylayer's evil" (*nequitia insidiatoris mei, Liber visionum primus* 11). The cosmic forces of good and evil are fully personalized and, in these most intimate confessions of experience, Elisabeth acknowledges the role of her own desire for visionary connection to the heavenly realm, unconcerned with suspicions that human desire or need might create the illusion of supernatural experience (cf. Newman 2005b).

Elisabeth's acknowledgment of the role of her desire—that is, of her own agency—as well as her confidence in the objective reality of her extraordinary experience led to the creation of a new genre of spiritual literature, the visionary memoir. Accounts of visionary experience had long existed: third-person narratives of one-time "out of the blue" experiences (Dinzelbacher 1981), or first-person testimonies in biblical texts such as Ezekiel or Revelation, or even the *Scivias* of Elisabeth's contemporary, Hildegard of Bingen. But none of these are truly autobiographical beyond the brief, usually introductory sketches that offer a narrative frame for the visions that follow. With the works of Elisabeth, however, a dramatic persona emerges, narrating her religious aspirations and articulating a spirituality in which the distance between heaven and earth was radically diminished.

Desire, devotion, and prayer were her tools for cultivating ecstasy, but unlike the ecstasy Aelred encouraged for recluses, Elisabeth's ecstatic life was the basis for developing prophetic teaching authority and a spirituality of connection with the world. Connection or affirmation of community pervades Elisabeth's works. Not only was the communal liturgy the site for ecstatic encounter with the sacred presence, but the monks and nuns of her monastery were deeply implicated in the unfolding of her experience. Their shared sin impedes her visions (*Liber visionum secundus* 11); their shared prayer enables visions (*Liber visionum primus* 9); and throughout, her inspired speech becomes authoritative in their own spiritual formation. Despite the efforts of her brother Ekbert, who edited her works, to emphasize that Elisabeth's extraordinary experience was purely the result of divine grace pouring into a passive receptacle, Elisabeth's accounts portray a complicated world of human and divine agencies at work in the process of human seeking for divine presence. In editing her works, Ekbert used textual introductions and interrogations of her visions to attempt to bring her visions in line with what he understood to be edifying for the church, but her own more complicated spirituality is still traceable in the textualization of Elisabeth's dialogic meditation on her experience.

Elisabeth's accounts also indicate a widening of the significance of her visions beyond her immediate monastic community to a belief in their relevance for the entire Christian world. She portrays herself receiving a divine mandate, reminiscent of that of the biblical prophets, to share with the world the content of her visions. Some of these visions have specific pastoral demands, but even the visions of ostensibly only personal value are included in her efforts to edify and console the world. Elisabeth's experience of being strengthened by the Virgin Mary, her *consolatrix*, in her time of personal distress is thus constructed as consoling to all Christians. And this universalizing tendency is further developed when Elisabeth articulates a more universalized understanding of the Virgin Mary in some of her later visions, where, for example, she claims a redemptive role for the Virgin who restrains her Son from destroying the world. This meditation upon Mary's role is part of a complex vision in which Elisabeth first claims that the resplendent *virgo* that she saw sitting in the sun was a figure of the humanity of Christ. Her retention of an explicitly feminine image (*in specie virginis et non in forma virili*) to represent Christ, while layering it with an affirmation of Mary's soteriological power (*Liber visionum tertius* 4), evokes her sense of her own transformation into a divinely inspired prophet in the tradition of Moses and Paul, her femaleness notwithstanding.

Elisabeth's spirituality crystallizes many of the aspects of monastic life that Benedict sought to institutionalize, particularly the centrality of liturgy and the role of other members of the monastic community in the shared pursuit of the spiritual life. And like Aelred of Rievaulx, Elisabeth explored the cultivation of ecstasy as a means of transcending the limitations of physical time and space. But Elisabeth's experience of transcendence led her not to the containment that Aelred envisioned as particularly necessary for women, but to an emboldened sense of the impossibility for her to live according to what the world expected a humble handmaid of the Lord to be. The new type of spiritual text created to express this experience, the visionary memoir, will become one of the characteristic modes of spiritual writing in the later Middle Ages, particularly among women. Gertrude of Helfta and Birgitta of Sweden, for example, also crafted accounts of visionary experience in which they represented themselves as agents of mystical connection between heaven and earth, and as divinely empowered to share the fruits of their experience with others. Anonymous nuns of Helfta and nuns such as Katherina von Gebersweiler (Unterlinden) and Anna von Munzingen (Adelhausen) wrote about the experiences of their fellow sisters, transforming the autobiographical memoir into *vitae* of mystical monastics. These Latin memoirs and *vitae* enshrined descriptions of women's personal experience within the authoritative language of spiritual instruction at a time in which women's claims about extraordinary experience were becoming increasingly suspect as heretical or demonically inspired.

Passion and Compassion

Although Elisabeth of Schönau expressed a sense of the divine diffused throughout a heavenly world and most palpably experienced in connections with the Virgin Mary, the saints, and the angels, the Christocentric piety evident in Aelred's *De institutione inclusarum* would come to dominate later medieval spirituality. Aelred's guide reflects a practice of meditating on the passion of Christ that emerged in the eleventh century with the millennial anniversary of the Passion (Fulton 2002). The cultivation of emotion directed toward the humanity of Christ, emotion modeled by the Virgin Mary, continued to be the hallmark of much spiritual writing of the later Middle Ages, such as the *Lignum vitae* of Bonaventure, the *Planctus Mariae* probably by Ogier of Locedio, and the *Vita Christi* of Ludolphus of Saxony. The *Meditationes vitae Christi* (Stallings-Taney 1997), a fourteenth-century text frequently attributed to Bonaventure, was the most popular of these passion texts and is particularly noteworthy for a consideration of medieval Latin spirituality because—as has been convincingly argued by Sarah McNamer—it is based on a text written in Italian by a nun. The male, probably Franciscan, author "corrected" the excessively carnal and affective piety of the nun's vernacular spirituality and contained it in a more conservative, exegetical framework (McNamer 2009). Not only does this point again to women creating significant contributions to spiritual traditions, but it also testifies to the influence of vernacular texts on authors of Latin works and the use of Latin to authorize orthodox spirituality.

In adapting the nun's work, the anonymous author of the *Meditationes* (hereafter *MVC*) created a text that, like Aelred's *De institutione inclusarum*, was written for a female religious audience—this time Franciscan. And like Aelred, the author admonishes his addressee to make herself literally present to everything done in the life of Christ so as "tuis auribus audires et oculis ea uideres, toto mentis affectu diligenter, delectabiliter et morose" [to hear with your own ears and see with your own eyes, lovingly, delectably, mournfully, with the total emotion of your mind] (*MVC* Prologue, 105–7). The author elaborates many of his themes with lengthy citations from other texts, especially the works of Bernard of Clairvaux, and offers a long series of episodes in Christ's life, even including "certain imaginary scenes" (*quasdam imaginarias representaciones*) to heighten his effect (*MVC* Prologue, 92–94). For example, one "meditacio ualde pulchra de qua tamen scriptura non loquitur" [exceedingly beautiful meditation not mentioned in Scripture] is Mary Magdalene's invitation to the Lord to spend Passover at her house (Mary Magdalene is identified with Mary of Bethany). While Jesus is later sitting entwined in an embrace with his mother, the Magdalene tells his mother of her son's intention. Jesus explains to his mother that it is his Father's will for him to celebrate Passover in Jerusalem as part of the plan for redemption. His mother's immense grief leads her to pray that God will offer "de alio modo redempcionis sine tua morte" [some other means of redemption without your death]. The verbal picture presented here is to be imaginatively visualized to enable mimetic performance: "O si uideres inter uerba hec Dominam plorantem, modeste tamen et plane, ac Magdalenam tanquam ebriam de Magistro suo largiter et magnis singultibus flentem, forte nec tu posses lacrimas continere!" [Oh, if in all these words you could see this Lady weeping, softly and yet openly, and the Magdalene crying profusely with huge sobs as if she were intoxicated with the Master, indeed you could not contain your own tears!] (*MVC* 72) The devout nun must use the intimate connection of the Marys to the person of Jesus in order to elicit her own emotional reaction to the cost of her redemption. Although democratized and no longer valued as the spiritual charism it once had been (Nagy 2000), weeping here becomes a technique for creating identification with Mary and, through her, with Jesus.

For the author, such meditating on the life of Christ is the most necessary and beneficial of all spiritual exercises. But herein lies a tension. Its effectiveness is ostensibly in learning the life of Christ, "que fuit absque omni defectu perfectissima" [which is most perfect without any defect] and thus serves to strengthen and teach the soul "quid facere quid ue fugere debeat" [what to do and what to avoid] (*MVC* Prologue 17–21). Blessed Francis achieved this: "ad tantam uirtutum copiam et ad tantam luculentam intelligenciam Scripturarum…peruenerit…per impressionem sacrorum stigmatum, fuit in eum totaliter transformatus" [he arrived…at such an abundance of virtues and such a lucid understanding of Scripture…that through the impression of the sacred stigmata, he was totally transformed into Him] (*MVC* Prologue 59–73). And yet, in the meditations themselves, the author primarily emphasizes compassion—a deeply felt pity for the suffering of Christ as his mother experienced it, rather than an imitation of Christ's virtues that might lead to a transformation into Christ as Francis experienced it. Like Aelred, the author felt that the proper place for a religious woman enclosed behind walls precluded the active life of full imitation of Christ that Francis achieved, and so he did not even include what he called the second part of the active the life, the life dedicated to serving others. His addressee was indeed to imitate Jesus's model of virtue to purify herself for compassionate contemplation, but without the possibility of imitating the active life of Jesus that would lead to the divinizing transformation experienced by Francis (*MVC* 47.121–27).

Even with the gendered nature of this spiritual path, the *Meditationes vitae Christi* circulated broadly and compassion was not limited to the spiritual aspiration of women. One aspect of compassion spirituality in the *MVC*, which was powerfully developed elsewhere as well, was a certain "passionizing" of the life of Christ. Not only did the scenes associated with the trial and death of Jesus garner greater and greater attention, often with graphic focus on the physical details of his torment and execution, but even ostensibly non-Passion scenes were read through the prism of his bloody death. For example, in an anonymous thirteenth-century life of Christ in verse, Jesus's circumcision begins the blood sacrifice of redemption:

> Qui sub lege nasceris legem observasti
> Circumcisus precium nostrum inchoasti
> Dum pro nobis sanguinem patri immolasti
> Quos cruoris precio culpis expiasti.
>
> [Born under the Law, you observed it
> Circumcised, you began to pay our price
> Sacrificing blood to the Father for us
> Whom you expiated from guilt by the price of bloodshed.]
> (Kauffmann 2007, 281, fig. 1)

Like other passion texts (Bestul 1996), this poem was variously adapted—abridged, lengthened, revised—and circulated in manuscripts owned by monks and friars as well as lay people. One extensively illustrated version included in a devotional book for a lay owner couples this quatrain with a picture of Mary suckling her naked baby as the Jewish priest approaches him with a huge knife, and together with an assistant begins to pull his legs apart to ready him for the cutting of flesh. The poem connects the circumcision with the crucifixion and redemption, and the image adds details from other parts of the poem: Mary's compassionate love for her son as he faces pain and the role of Jews as torturers of Jesus (Kauffman 2007). While countless Latin and vernacular texts harnessed words to vividly describe the suffering of Jesus and his mother, this particular example of the poem illustrates a crucial feature of compassion piety of the later Middle Ages. The textual evocations of pain and pity were read and meditated upon by individuals who had already absorbed pictorial representations of these scenes and may even have been pondering the text while simultaneously gazing at images, either as part of the book or in the furnishings of their immediate environment. While all spiritual literature was located in a visual world, the late medieval profusion of images, particularly those associated with Christ's suffering and death, powerfully inflected the spirituality of compassion (Biernoff 2002; Camille 1998; Marrow 1979).

This pairing of text and image crystallizes another potent feature of "passionized" spirituality: tensions about guilt and responsibility. Even though the sins that are expiated are "ours," the obvious wrong-doers in the passion story are Jews, who are represented as responsible for the death of Jesus. Embedded in the pity to be engendered by Jesus and his suffering mother was a heightened imagination of the tortures inflicted by Jews who were often represented as brutal and depraved (Bestul 1996; Bynum 2002). The development of compassion spirituality shaped and was shaped by the growing anti-Semitism and outbreaks of violence against Jews in the later Middle Ages (Rubin 1999).

BEYOND VISION AND COMPASSION

Despite the emergence of compassion as a spiritual path, there remained other powerful strains in medieval piety, hinted at by Aelred in his suggestion that the recluse should be satisfied with the milk of Christ's humanity while the beloved disciple drank the wine of the Godhead. This possibility, a taste of divinity beyond reveling in the visions stimulated by liturgy and meditation, can be seen in what some monastic authors describe as contemplation. In a letter on the monastic life written in the 1180s but remaining popular throughout the later Middle Ages, Guigo II, a Carthusian monk, succinctly summarized the "scala claustralium qua de terra in coelum sublevantur" [ladder by which monks are lifted up from earth into heaven] (*Scala* 2.21). Four rungs compose the ladder: reading of Scripture, meditation, prayer, and contemplation. The final stage of contemplation differs from the preceding three in being not the action of the spiritual striver but the reward for the three previous labors. *Contemplatio* is beyond all senses: beyond the external exertions, the interior intellect, and even beyond desire, although desire inflamed by reading and meditation cries out in prayer for it (*Scala* 12.294–98). It is an ecstatic experience that Guigo calls contemplation: "Contemplatio est mentis in Deum suspensae quaedam supra se elevatio, eternae dulcedinis gaudia degustans" [Contemplation is the elevation of the mind, suspended above itself in God, tasting the joys of eternal sweetness] (*Scala* 2.36–38). The effect of this experience is a total transformation of the whole person: "In hac superna contemplatione ita superantur et absorbentur carnales motus ab anima ut in nullo caro spiritui contradicat, et fit homo quasi totus spiritualis" [In this supernal contemplation, carnal movements are overcome and drawn away from the soul in such a way that the flesh in no way opposes the spirit and the person is rendered as completely spiritual] (Guigo 1970, 7.171–74).

Guigo's view of contemplation gave voice to a need to express the ultimate otherness of God, even though this is far from a thoroughgoing *via negativa*. The otherness expressed here is not cast in theological terms of the unknowable essence of divine nature, but in the experiential terms of the human inability—despite all desire—to propel oneself into union with God. The sensual language of the Song of Songs invoked by Guigo as by so many others was, after all, a language of desire, of the impossibility of assured satisfaction. This existential abyss lay at the heart of various medieval attempts to create hierarchical categories of experience culminating in something beyond human comprehension. Not every spiritual text expressed a hierarchy culminating in heaven, but usually some trace of Guigo's sense of the incommensurability between human and divine lurks within otherwise pragmatic programs of spiritual progress or ecstatic claims of extraordinary experience. But it is the latter—the confidence in progress through tuning the body, intellect, and emotion (as in the programs offered by Benedict, Aelred, the *Meditationes vitae Christi*, and countless other passion meditations) and the authority of having experienced being lifted up or invaded by the divine (as in the works of Elisabeth of Schönau and other visionary and mystical nuns)—that dominates the Latin spiritual literature of the Middle Ages.

SUGGESTIONS FOR FURTHER READING

Classics of Western Spirituality, a series published by Paulist Press, provides modern translations of many primary sources, some only newly characterized as "classic." Groundbreaking work defining new themes in medieval spirituality can be found in Bynum (1982, 1987, 1991, and 2007) and Newman (1995 and 2005a). On monastic spirituality in general, see Leclercq (1961). For the mnemonic practices that shaped cognition and spiritual creativity, see Carruthers (1998). On the relationship between art and spirituality, see especially Hamburger (1998). For the use of the Song of Songs, see Matter (1990) and Turner (1995). A fruitful debate on affective spirituality is emerging, signaled by two major contributions, Fulton (2002) and McNamer (2010). Suspicions about unorthodox spirituality are analyzed in Caciola (2003) and Elliott (2004).

BIBLIOGRAPHY

Primary sources

Aelred of Rievaulx. 1971. *Opera Omnia*, edited by Anselm Hoste and Charles H. Talbot. Corpus Christianorum. Continuatio Mediaevalis 1. Turnhout: Brepols.
Benedict. 1982. *RB 1980: The Rule of St. Benedict*, edited by Timothy Fry. Collegeville, MN: Liturgical Press.
Cassian, John. 1886. *Conlationes XXIIII*, edited by Michael Petschenig. Corpus Scriptorum Ecclesiasticorum Latinorum 13. Vienna: Geroldus.
Guigo II the Carthusian. 1970. "Scala Claustralium." In *Lettre sur la vie contemplative (L'échelle des moines); Douze meditations*, edited by Edmund Colledge and James Walsh. Sources Chrétiennes 163. Paris: Les Éditions du Cerf.

Kauffman, C. M. 2007. "An Illustrated Life of Christ in Verse." In *Tributes to Lucy Freeman Sandler*, edited by Kathryn A. Smith and Carol H. Krinsky. London: Harvey Miller Publishers.

Roth, Friedrich Wilhelm Emil, ed. 1884. *Die Visionen der hl. Elisabeth und die Schriften der Aebte Ekbert und Emecho von Schönau*. Brünn: Verlag der Studien aus dem Benedictiner- und Cistercienser Orden.

Stallings-Taney, M., ed. 1997. *Meditaciones vite Christi*. Corpus Christianorum. Continuatio Mediaevalis 113. Turnhout: Brepols.

Secondary sources

Bestul, Thomas H. 1996. *Texts of the Passion: Latin Devotional Literature and Medieval Society*. Middle Ages Series. Philadelphia: University of Pennsylvania Press.

Biernoff, Suzannah. 2002. *Sight and Embodiment in the Middle Ages*. The New Middle Ages. New York: Palgrave Macmillan.

Boynton, Susan. 2000. "Training for the Liturgy as a Form of Monastic Education." In *Medieval Monastic Education*, edited by George Ferzoco and Carolyn A. Muessig, 7–20. London: Leicester University Press.

Bynum, Caroline Walker. 1982. *Jesus as Mother: Studies in the Spirituality of the High Middle Ages*. Publications of the Center for Medieval and Renaissance Studies 16. Berkeley, CA: University of California Press.

———. 1987. *Holy Feast and Holy Fast: The Religious Significance of Food to Medieval Women*. New Historicism. Berkeley, CA: University of California Press.

———. 1991. *Fragmentation and Redemption: Essays on Gender and the Human Body in Medieval Religion*. New York: Zone Books.

———. 2002. "Violent Imagery in Late Medieval Piety." *GHI Bulletin* 30 (Spring): 3–36.

———. 2007. *Wonderful Blood: Theology and Practice in Late Medieval Northern Germany and Beyond*. Middle Ages Series. Philadelphia: University of Pennsylvania Press.

Caciola, Nancy. 2003. *Discerning Spirits: Divine and Demonic Possession in the Middle Ages*. Conjunctions of Religion & Power in the Medieval Past. Ithaca, NY: Cornell University Press.

Camille, Michael. 1998. "Mimetic Identification and Passion Devotion in the Later Middle Ages: A Double-Sided Panel by Meister Francke." In *The Broken Body: Passion Devotion in Late-Medieval Culture*, edited by Alasdair A. Macdonald, H. N. Bernhard Ridderbos, and Rita M. Schlusemann. Mediaevalia Groningana 21. Groningen: Egbert Forsten.

Carruthers, Mary. 1998. *The Craft of Thought: Meditation, Rhetoric, and the Making of Images, 400–1200*. Cambridge Studies in Medieval Literature 34. Cambridge: Cambridge University Press.

Clark, Anne L. 1992. *Elisabeth of Schönau: A Twelfth-Century Visionary*. Middle Ages Series. Philadelphia: University of Pennsylvania Press.

Dinzelbacher, Peter. 1981. *Vision und Visionsliteratur im Mittelalter*. Monographien zur Geschichte des Mittelalters 23. Stuttgart: Hiersemann.

Elliott, Dyan. 2004. *Proving Woman: Female Spirituality and Inquisitional Culture in the Later Middle Ages*. Princeton, NJ: Princeton University Press.

Fulton, Rachel. 2002. *From Judgment to Passion: Devotion to Christ and the Virgin Mary, 800–1200*. New York: Columbia University Press.

Hamburger, Jeffrey F. 1998. *The Visual and the Visionary: Art and Female Spirituality in Late Medieval Germany*. New York: Zone Books.

LeClercq, Jean. 1961. *The Love of Learning and the Desire for God: A Study of Monastic Culture*. Translated by Catherine Misrahi. New York: Fordham University Press.

Marrow, James H. 1979. *Passion Iconography in Northern European Art of the Late Middle Ages and Early Renaissance: A Study of the Transformation of Sacred Metaphor into Descriptive Narrative*. Ars Neerlandica 1. Kortrijk: Van Ghemmert Publishing Company.

Matter, E. Ann. 1990. *The Voice of My Beloved: The Song of Songs in Western Medieval Christianity*. Philadelphia: University of Pennsylvania Press.

McNamer, Sarah. 2009. "The Origins of the *Meditationes vitae Christi*." *Speculum* 84: 905–55.

———. 2010. *Affective Meditation and the Invention of Medieval Compassion*. Philadelphia: University of Pennsylvania Press.

Nagy, Piroska. 2000. *Le Don des larmes au Moyen Âge: Un instrument spirituel en quête d'institution (Ve–XIIIe siècle)*. Paris: Albin Michel.

Newman, Barbara. 1995. *From Virile Woman to WomanChrist: Studies in Medieval Women and Literature*. Philadelphia: University of Pennsylvania Press.

———. 2005a. *God and the Goddesses: Vision, Poetry, and Belief in the Middle Ages*. Philadelphia: University of Pennsylvania Press.

———. 2005b. "What Did It Mean to Say 'I Saw'? The Clash Between Theory and Practice in Medieval Visionary Culture." *Speculum* 80: 1–43.

Palazzo, Eric. 2010. "Visions and Liturgical Experience." In *Looking Beyond: Visions, Dreams, and Insights in Medieval Art & History*, edited by Colum Hourihane. Index of Christian Art, Occasional Papers 11. Princeton, NJ: Trustees of Princeton University.

Rubin, Miri. 1999. *Gentile Tales: The Narrative Assault on Late Medieval Jews*. New Haven, CT: Yale University Press.

Schneiders, Sandra M. 2005. "Approaches to the Study of Christian Spirituality." In *The Blackwell Companion to Christian Spirituality*, edited by Arthur Holder, 15–33. Malden, MA: Blackwell Publishing.

Turner, Denys. 1995. *Eros and Allegory: Medieval Exegesis of the Song of Songs*. Cistercian Studies Series 156. Kalamazoo, MI: Cistercian Publications.

CHAPTER 23

MODES OF SELF-WRITING FROM ANTIQUITY TO THE LATER MIDDLE AGES

GUR ZAK

HISTORIANS of autobiography have generally skipped through the Middle Ages, or else have viewed autobiographical works from the period as somehow lacking or incomplete, primordial precursors of a future mode of writing that will bloom only centuries later (Misch 1949–69; Zumthor 1973; Weintraub 1978; Gusdorf 1980). The teleological nature of such studies explains this tendency. From its coinage in the early nineteenth century as a composite of three Greek words, the term "autobiography" has been strongly related to specific formal expectations and a particular conception of the self. Formally, "autobiography" was conceived as a complete narrative description and interpretation of the author's life, composed from the vantage point of the present moment of writing (Lejeune 1975, 14; Weintraub 1978, xviii; Gusdorf 1980, 35). Behind this expectation resides the modern conception of the self as an authoritative agent able to fashion one's life more or less freely and then to construct a narrative of this process. From this perspective, the medieval period indeed offers us a mere handful of works that point to the later development of autobiography, yet even these fail to live up to the ideal, being either too heavily based upon prior models, or else failing to provide a complete narrative account of the author's life.

This chapter examines the history of medieval Latin practices of self-writing from a different perspective, exploring them on their own terms. The choice of the term "self-writing" rather than "autobiography" here underscores the fact that people wrote—and indeed still write—about themselves in various ways and for various reasons that often do not conform to our modern assumptions about the nature of the self and the act of writing about it. Furthermore, the term "self-writing"—taken from Michel Foucault's article by that name (Foucault 1997a)—stresses that the act of writing about oneself was often perceived in the pre-modern period not only as descriptive, or mimetic, but also as a practice, a "technology of the self," that actively shaped the writer.

Three dominant modes of self-writing developed in the centuries between Ovid and Petrarch: self-examination, self-portrait, and confessional narrative. The classification carries with it a taxonomy both of authors' aims in writing as they emerge from the texts, and of dominant thematic and formal characteristics. In order to analyze the central features of these modes and their evolution, I present below a close analysis of central works in each mode, beginning with Ovid, Seneca, and Augustine, continuing with Guigo I, Guibert of Nogent, and Peter Abelard, and culminating in the fourteenth century with Petrarch. A central aim of this essay is to show that the uniqueness of Petrarch resides largely in the way he absorbs and develops all of the modes of self-writing available in the Latin tradition he inherited and presupposed.

To be sure, other modes of self-writing were employed, such as the *consolatio*, the soliloquy, and mystical accounts of dreams and visions. I will refer to some of these, but will focus on the former three as arguably most prevalent and influential. Below, I also explore the tensions and internal contradictions that dominate the works I take as exemplary, especially between the ethical use of writing for self-cultivation and the realization of the aesthetic and public nature of writing (on which see Stock 2007). These tensions reveal the tenuous lines that at times separate these modes, and the often fluid boundaries between them. Such indeterminacies, however, do not nullify the value of analyzing these different modes and their evolution over time, if only due to the fact that ancient and medieval authors were strongly aware of these modes and consciously applied them for their purposes.

The Ancient Models

Seneca and Ovid: Self-examination and Self-portrait

One central mode of self-writing, which emerged in antiquity and had a crucial impact on the Middle Ages, is self-examination. The most important exponent of this mode was Seneca, particularly in his *Ad Lucilium epistulae morales*. For Seneca, written (as well as unwritten) self-examinations played a crucial part in the ethical formation of the self (Foucault 1997b, 236–38; Ker 2010). In the eighty-third of his *Epistulae morales*, Seneca responds to Lucilius's request to provide him with an account of his everyday actions, stressing that self-observation is a necessary part of ethical life, and that this observation is particularly beneficial when performed before everyone (i.e., in writing): "Sic certe vivendum est tamquam in conspectu vivamus, sic cogitandum tamquam aliquis in pectus intimum introspicere possit...Faciam ergo, quod iubes, et quid agam et quo ordine libenter tibi scribam" [It is thus that we should live, as if we lived in plain sight of all men, and it is thus that we should think, as if there were someone who could look into our inmost souls...I shall therefore do as you bid, and shall gladly inform you by letter what I am doing, and in what order] (*Epistulae morales* 83.1–2; edition: Seneca 1965; translation: Seneca 1953).

Seneca goes on to provide an account of his day, listing mundane activities such as a running contest with a slave, a bath in cold water, a scanty breakfast, and a short nap. Such a public review of his daily activities ensures that his actions accord with the precepts of right conduct handed down mostly, but not solely, from the Stoic tradition. As Foucault noted, Seneca does not thus serve as a judge accusing himself of evil intentions, but rather as an administrator making sure that his actions correspond to precepts of virtuous conduct (Foucault 1997b, 237). Among the foremost precepts in letter 83 are the need to live in accordance with nature (as is evident from Seneca's depiction of his eating and sleeping habits), and to be in full control of one's time. Inspecting his behavior in light of these precepts, Seneca corrects false actions and thus advances on the road to virtue, the state of complete self-mastery.

Whereas Seneca provided the Middle Ages with a model of self-writing aimed at the cultivation of the self, Ovid had earlier presented future generations with a practice of self-writing aimed above all at leaving behind a carefully constructed literary monument of the self. Ovid fashions his self-portrait in *Tristia* 4.10. Placing the portrait at the end of the fourth book as a form of appendix—as was common in Alexandrine poetry collections (Misch 1949–69, 1: 308)—Ovid opens the poem with a direct address to posterity: "Ille ego qui fuerim, tenerorum lusor amorum,/ quem legis, ut noris, accipe posteritas" [I, whom you read, I, fond love's witty poet,/ Learn who I was, you of the years to come] (edition: Ovid 1995; translation: Ovid 1988). Ovid then turns to narrate his life chronologically, beginning with his birth and culminating with his present condition as an exile.

In constructing his self-image for posterity, Ovid is particularly concerned with his life as a poet and establishing his poetic greatness (Fredericks 1976). Opening the poem with his poetic "I"—*Ille ego*—Ovid immediately introduces himself as *tenerorum lusor amorum* and then describes how poetry was for him a sort of destiny, a divine calling (l. 19–20). Near the middle of the poem, Ovid fashions a genealogy of elegiac poets that leads directly to himself: "Successor fuit hic [Tibullus] tibi, Galle, Propertius illi;/ quartus ab his serie temporis ipse fui" [He [Tibullus] was Gallus's successor, his, Propertius;/ Fourth in time's order after them I came] (l. 53–54). The self-portrait thus serves Ovid as a means to claim his place in literary history.

While addressing his portrait to posterity, Ovid undoubtedly also directs the poem to his contemporary audience, attempting to proclaim his innocence and perhaps to alter his condition (Fairweather 1987; Claassen 1999, 139–53, 214–19). Over the course of the poem, Ovid emphatically addresses his departed parents, writing that his exile was decreed in error (l. 81–90), and blames his banishment on *comitumque nefas* (friends' wickedness, l. 101) and *famulosque nocentes* (injuring slaves, l. 101). Through such declamations, Ovid clearly appeals to the mercy of his Roman readers.

Near the end of the poem, Ovid reveals another possible motivation for its writing—therapy. His ability to withstand exile, he declares, is primarily due to the comfort and solace he receives from writing (l. 111–18). This therapeutic use of writing, we should note, is very different from Seneca's: for Ovid, writing serves as a means to allay his grief, not to lead him to virtue. In the closing lines of the poem, Ovid thanks his Muse, as well as his *candide lector*, for providing him with an immortal name. This conclusion takes us back to the opening address to posterity and shows that the portrait aims above all to secure the literary afterlife of its author, to guarantee the survival of the self *as* text.

Augustine and the Birth of the Confessional Narrative

The third central mode of self-writing that emerged in the ancient world comes to the fore in Augustine's *Confessiones*, the first full-length attempt at a complete prose narrative of the author's life. Written between 397 and about 400, the work recounts the story of Augustine's life up to his conversion in Milan in 386 and the ensuing death of his mother. Augustine's groundbreaking practice of self-writing combines ethical, epistemological, and rhetorical goals, many of these shared with the two previously discussed modes.

Like Seneca, Augustine stresses the value of writing, and particularly of written self-examinations, for the ethical formation of the self. In the opening of Book 2 of the *Confessiones*, Augustine states:

> Recordari volo transactas foeditates meas, et carnales corruptiones animae meae, non quod eas amem, sed ut amem te, deus meus. Amore amoris tui facio istuc, recolens vias meas nequissimas in amaritudine recogitationis meae, ut tu dulcescas mihi, dulcedo non fallax, dulcedo felix et secura, et colligens me a dispersione, in qua frustatim discissus sum. (Augustine 1992, *Conf.* 2.1.1)

> [I intend to remind myself of my past foulness and carnal corruptions, not because I love them but so that I may love you, my God. It is from love of your love that I make the act of recollection. The recalling of my wicked ways is bitter in my memory, but I do it so that you may be sweet to me, a sweetness touched by no deception, a sweetness serene and content. You gathered me together from the state of disintegration in which I had been fruitlessly divided.] (Augustine 1991, *Conf.* 2.1.1)

The act of writing his past sins, this passage suggests, is for Augustine a reminder of his guilt and former falsehoods and of the benevolence God has shown him. This recollection, in turn, secures his resolution to abandon his past falsehoods, "put aside the old person," and place his trust solely in God.

In Book 10, Augustine moves from his past sins to his present ones, inspecting his susceptibility to sins related to the senses, such as excess in food and drink and enjoyment of beauty and music. Here, he focuses on his fornications against God, times in which he is too attached to earthly objects. He confesses the sin of pride, his insurmountable attachment to praise and ultimately to self-love. He declares that although writing itself does not aid in his understanding of the source of his attachment to praise, it does lead him to the cure: "Egenus et pauper ego sum, et melior in occulto gemitu displicens mihi et quaerens misericordiam tuam, donec reficiatur defectus meus" [I am poor and needy (Ps 108:22), but am better if, secretly groaning, I am vexed with myself and seek your mercy, until my defect is repaired] (*Conf.* 10.38.63).

Although retaining the Senecan emphasis on the ethical value of self-writing, Augustine's self-examination departs from that of Seneca in crucial ways: whereas Seneca concentrates on a list of daily *actions*, Augustine reflects on his entire life, searching for evil deeds and intentions. Furthermore, whereas the aim of Seneca's self-examination is the perfection of the self, the attainment of inner virtue and self-control, Augustine's self-cultivation is paradoxically based on the progressive denial of his attachment to his earthly self.

Alongside the goal of self-cultivation, Augustine's portrayal of his life-story also has an epistemological end—serving as a means to gain knowledge and understanding of self. For Augustine, since we are creatures existing in time and dependent upon language for the acquisition of knowledge, we can know ourselves only as a process, a continuum. As he demonstrates in his great meditation on the nature of time in Book 11, just as the understanding of a psalm requires reading through its entire sequence of words, so the understanding of a person's life—or the whole of human history—requires the consideration of the whole sequence of that life's events: "Et quod in toto cantico, hoc in singulis particulis eius fit atque in singulis syllabis eius, hoc in actione longiore, cuius forte particula est illud canticum, hoc in tota vita hominis, cuius partes sunt omnes actiones hominis, hoc in toto saeculo filiorum hominum, cuius partes sunt omnes vitae hominum" [What occurs in the psalm as a whole occurs in its particular pieces and its individual syllables. The same is true of a longer action in which perhaps that psalm is a part. It is also valid of the entire life of an individual person, where all actions are parts of a whole, and of the total history of "the sons of men" (Ps 30:20) where all human lives are but parts] (*Conf.* 11.28.38). The ordered sequence of his life's events is thus the means by which Augustine gains self-knowledge (Ricoeur 1985, 5–30; Stock 1996, 21–121; Olney 1998, 1–83).

This attainment of self-knowledge through self-narration also has considerable therapeutic value. As Augustine declares, the constant change that characterizes human existence in time is a source of an ongoing experience of fragmentation: "Sed quoniam melior est misericordia tua super vitas, ecce distentio est vita mea…pater meus aeternus es. At ego in tempora dissilui quorum ordinem nescio" [Because your mercy is more than lives (Ps 62:4), see how my life is a distension in several directions…You are my eternal Father, but I am scattered in times whose order I do not understand] (*Conf.* 11.29.39). The ability to structure the narrative of his life thus has a healing value for Augustine, providing him with a sense of unity and order. Nonetheless, the question that hovers over the *Confessiones* is how Augustine can guarantee the objective veracity of his narrative. The answer, of course, lies in divine grace. It is only in the reception of grace that he realizes the meaning of his past life and becomes capable of narrating it as the journey of the prodigal son on the way back home.

To these ethical and epistemological motivations for Augustine's self-portrayal we should add a third one—the rhetorical. In narrating his life story, Augustine aims to cure not only his own self, but also that of his reader. As a professional rhetorician, Augustine knows that the depiction of his personal story will likely affect his readers more directly than would an elaborate philosophical analysis—a point demonstrated at length in Book 8, when he shows how hearing a series of conversion stories finally facilitated his own.

Although Augustine asserts the ethical, epistemological, and rhetorical value of recounting the narrative of his salvation, his self-writing is not free from tensions— tensions relating in particular to the public and aesthetic aspects of writing. In his confession of present sins in Book 10, as we have seen, Augustine focuses on his ongoing attachment to praise. The danger of pursuing praise, he states, is especially acute when one makes his actions publicly known: "Sermo autem ore procedens et facta quae innotescunt hominibus habent temptationem periculosissimam ab amore laudis" [But the word proceeding out of the mouth and the actions which become known to people contain a most hazardous temptation in the love of praise] (*Conf.* 10.38.63). The confession of his sins in writing thus contains for Augustine an insurmountable earthly and sinful element. Writing, the cure applied to the malaise, emerges in itself as part of the problem.

Augustine's concern with his proud attachment to praise is closely related to the question of style and aesthetics. As Eugene Vance points out, Augustine's narrative of his life is largely a description of his journey through the realm of fallen language and texts back to the Word (Vance 1973). What characterizes these fallen texts is especially their captivating style, which arouses earthly desires and leads Augustine to vainly reject the Bible. Already in Book 1 we learn how the story of Dido in the *Aeneid* caused him to identify with her sorrow to such an extent that he forgot himself completely (*Conf.* 1.13.21). In Book 3, Augustine describes how his acquaintance with Ciceronian eloquence caused him to look down upon the humble style of the Bible, preventing him from realizing its hidden treasures (*Conf.* 3.5.9). It is this concern with style that also led him to identify with the empty but elegant words of the Manichees (*Conf.* 3.6.10).

Eloquent style is therefore presented as problematic throughout the *Confessiones* and is persistently associated with pride and vainglory. Augustine's concern with his ongoing attachment to praise is thus no doubt related to the polished and elaborate style of his own text, with its predilection for rhyming, antithesis, and, at times, a Ciceronian sentence structure (Augustine 1991, x; Mohrmann 1961, 308-23). Excessive concern for style is inevitably associated with pursuit of praise, and might also jeopardize its intended effect upon readers: just as Augustine himself was captivated by the Ciceronian eloquence of the Manichees, his readers may be captivated by his style rather than imitate his saintly behavior. In Book 5, Augustine appears to address such concerns when he claims that writing style does not determine the truthfulness of the content: "Rursus nec ideo verum, quia impolite enuntiatur, nec ideo falsum, quia splendidus sermo est" [A statement is not true because it is enunciated in an unpolished idiom, nor false because the words are splendid] (*Conf.* 5.6.10). Yet despite this assurance, as Book 10 reveals, the tension between the ethical, public and aesthetic aspects of writing is not completely resolved in the work. As we shall see, this tension will become one of the central legacies of Augustine to future practices of self-writing.

THE TWELFTH CENTURY AND THE REVIVAL OF SELF-WRITING

The centuries following Augustine's *Confessiones* have left relatively few examples of self-writing. Such practices begin anew in the eleventh century, alongside the general contemporary transformation of European society (Duby 1988, 2: 511–14; Le Goff 1988, 56–105), from which time onwards we witness a steady growth in practices of self-writing; the twelfth century presents us with a revival of the three central ancient modes previously discussed.

The rise of the monastic reform movements is particularly relevant to this renaissance of self-writing. Critical of the lax morals and the growing riches of Benedictine monasteries of the time, reform groups like the Cistercians and the Carthusians called for a new, stricter monastic spirituality (Lawrence 1989, 149–205). In this new spiritual program, the practices of reading and writing in general, and self-writing in particular, received a central role (Lawrence 1989, 115–19; Stock 2001, 52–70; van 'T Spijker 2004). William of St. Thierry, in his *Epistola ad fratres de Monte-Dei*, for example, emphasized the value of writing as a spiritual exercise: "Sic cum in adjutorium spiritualis studii necessaria sint, non tamen in hoc semper aeque convenire videntur omnia corporalia exercitia, sed quae cum spiritualibus propiorem habere videntur similitudinem, et affinitatem propiorem; sicut ad aedificationem spiritualem, meditari quod scribatur, vel scribere quod legatur" (William of Saint-Thierry 1975, 208–10) [physical exercise is necessary as a help to spiritual pursuits. But not all its forms are of the same value in this respect. Those are to be preferred which have the greater likeness and kinship to the spiritual; for example, meditating on something to be written or writing something to be read for spiritual edification] (William of Saint-Thierry 1976, 40). Within this emphasis on the spiritual value of writing in the monasteries, the practice of self-examination held special importance.

Guigo I and the Medieval Self-Examination

An example of a written self-examination from that period is provided by Guigo I, Prior of the Charterhouse, in his *Meditationes* written in the first half of the twelfth century. Guigo's *Meditationes* comprise 476 sections, which range from concise aphorisms to page-length theological reflections. A significant number of the meditations are dedicated to an examination of Guigo's everyday experiences. In meditation 265, for example, he writes: "Laesis spectaculis doles. Tibi et errori tuo hoc imputa, qui laesibilibus inhaesisti" (Guigo 1983, 186) [Your reading glass has been broken, and you are upset. Blame yourself for this, and your own error, in attaching yourself to breakable things] (Guigo 1995, 120); or again in meditation 282:

> Vide quomodo, cum nuper coram fratribus cecidisses, aliam pro alia antiphonam dicendo, quaerebat animus tuus qualiter culpam ipsam in aliud aliquid devolveret, sive in librum ipsum, sive in aliud. Nolebat enim se tale videre cor tuum, et ideo se sibi aliud simulabat, declinans in verba malitiae, excusando peccatum. (Guigo 1983, 190)

> [Notice how, when you recently tripped up in front of the brethren by singing one antiphon instead of another, your mind tried to think of a way of putting the blame on something else—on the book, or on some other thing. Your heart was reluctant to see itself as it really is, and so it pretended to itself that it was different, inclining itself to evil words to excuse its sin.] (Guigo 1995, 124)

In his self-analysis Guigo concentrates on his mundane experiences and his *reactions* to them, discerning the instances in which his reactions are motivated by sinful earthly attachments. Such examination of isolated everyday experiences, aimed at shaping and transforming its author, clearly relates the work to the Senecan tradition of self-examination, yet Guigo's work is evidently Christian: like Augustine, Guigo aims to excavate his guilt and reproach himself for his falsehoods in order to lead himself to renounce his worldly attachments, and above all that to his own self: "Facile est iter ad Deum, quoniam exonerando itur... In tantum ergo te exonera, ut, dimissis omnibus, te ipsum abneges" (Guigo 1983, 122) [The way to God is easy, for it is travelled by unburdening oneself... So, unburden yourself to the extent that, having left everything, you may deny your own self] (Guigo 1995, 75).

The practice of written self-examination will become increasingly widespread in the later Middle Ages. The official prescription of the sacrament of penance in the Fourth Lateran Council of 1215, as well as the rise of lay devotional groups such as the *Devotio Moderna*, brought the practice of reviewing one's sins in writing to the wider lay literate public (Zimmerman 1971; Van Engen 2008, 266–304). Florentius Radewijns, one of the founders of the *Devotio Moderna*, gave the novices in his *Tractatulus devotus* the following advice: "Alicui viro spirituali... bis vel ter in anno, loquatur de profectu et defectu suo, de temptacionibus, et modum suum vivendi ostendat et in scriptis" [Speak to a certain spiritual man... about your triumphs and defects and about your temptations at least twice or thrice a year, and show to him *in writing* your way of life] (quoted in Staubach 1991, 433 n. 48; emphasis mine). Thomas à Kempis's *De imitatione Christi*, the most popular book to come out of the movement, notably emphasizes the revelation of sins: "Confitebor tibi, Domini, infirmitatem meam. Saepe parva res est quae dejicit et contristat" (à Kempis 1982, 3.20.1) [I will confess my weakness to you, Lord. Often it is such a small thing that makes me downcast and sad] (à Kempis 1963, 3.20.1).

Guibert and the Collapse of the Confessional Narrative

Alongside the emergence of the practice of self-examination, the twelfth century also provides the most evident attempt in medieval Latin to imitate Augustine's confessional narrative—Guibert of Nogent's *Vita*, or *Monodiae* ("songs for one voice"), as he himself referred to his work (Guibert 1970, 11 n. 16). However, although Guibert explicitly attempts to follow in Augustine's footsteps, his *Vita* departs from his model in significant ways that manifest the challenges inherent in his undertaking.

Guibert begins his work, written probably in 1121, with a clear allusion to the *Confessiones*: "Confiteor amplitudini tuae, Deus, infinitorum errorum meorum decursus, et creberrimos ad te miserationis internae, quos tamen inspirasti, recursus" (Guibert 1907, 1) [I confess to Thy Majesty, O God, my endless wanderings from Thy paths, and my turning back so often to the bosom of Thy mercy, directed by Thee in spite of all] (Guibert 1970, 35). Like Augustine, Guibert addresses God directly and declares his intention to look back from the present moment of writing upon his past wanderings. The reference to "decursus" (wanderings), and "recursus" (returns), indicates the wide scope of the reflection, the attempt to reveal both the many wrongdoings the author committed and the many remedies provided him by God. Through such a revelation, as Guibert states, he is able to "know himself"—to realize his inherent wickedness—and is thus inspired to alter his ways and devote himself completely to God: "Dignum ac singulariter salutare est, ut obscuritas rationis meae per hujusmodi confessiones crebra tui luminis inquisitione tergatur" (Guibert 1907, 4) [It is a worthy act and singularly for my soul's good that through these confessions the darkness of my understanding should be dispersed by the searching rays Thy light often casts upon it] (Guibert 1970, 37). The very writing of his confession is for him—as it was for Augustine—a spiritual exercise aimed to strengthen his self-denial and secure his attachment to God.

Following his introductory statements, Guibert turns, like Augustine, to describe his birth and early childhood. Yet the description of his birth soon turns into a lengthy portrayal of the beauty and the many virtues of his mother, which begins to direct our attention to the differences between the two accounts: whereas Augustine's self-portrayal is calculated and coherent, Guibert's is scattered and full of digressions. Guibert continuously breaks his life-story to speak about his mother, provide fantastic stories of divine retribution, or describe major events that took place in his lifetime. In fact, following his self-portrayal in Book 1, the second and third books become a lively historical account of the events of his time, with the author himself now almost completely forgotten.

This difference between Augustine's and Guibert's accounts might be explained by the most crucial discrepancy between the two texts: in contrast to the *Confessiones*, Guibert's *Vita* does not entail a clear point of conversion, a climax, which defines and gives meaning to both self and text. Instead of one unmistakable transformation, Guibert's presents several "minor" ones, all ending with a relapse: one when in his youth he entered the monastery of his teacher and decided to become a monk, another when he abandoned the composition of profane literature, and a third near the end of Book 1, when he describes the waning of his political ambitions and his newfound commitment to God. Yet even this last transformation, as he declares, was short lived: "Quid dicam, Domine, quam momentaneus iste paradisus extiterit" (Guibert 1907, 78) [What shall I say, Lord, of how fleeting was the existence of that paradise] (Guibert 1970, 100). This portrayal of a repetitive process of ascent and descent—implied already in the reference to "decursus" and "recursus" at the beginning of the work—gives the work a circular structure that clearly departs from the linearity of Augustine's account, and indicates his inability to reach a vantage point that would give his past life clear order and purpose. It is this inability, therefore, that might account for the scattered nature of Guibert's narrative.

Guibert acknowledges that his failure to attain the calm port of conversion stems from his susceptibility to pride, and particularly to pride associated with reading and writing. Describing his early dedication to the study of letters, he states: "Et tu, Jesu pie, non nesciebas qua intentione id facerem, conquirendae utique gratia laudis, et ut praesentis saeculi honorificentia major occurreret" (Guibert 1907, 54) [And Thou, Holy Jesus, didst know with what motive I did this, chiefly to win glory and so that greater honor in this present world might be mine] (Guibert 1970, 78–79). This sinful desire did not wane with time but rather increased. While at an early age the study of Scripture led him to tearful meditation, nowadays, he declares, he reads Scripture only in the search for "jactantiam et verba" (Guibert 1907, 55) [vocabulary and matter for display] (Guibert 1970, 79). The tension that dominated Augustine's *Confessiones* between the ethical and aesthetic aspects of writing thus dominates Guibert's work as well: while serving as an ethical tool, the writing of his *Vita* is also tainted for him by a desire to display his talents and win praise. Yet Guibert is palpably less confident in his ability to "put aside the old person" than Augustine, much less secure about his power to detach his practice of writing from his worldly ways. At the time of writing he still tosses in stormy seas, far from port, hoping that writing will provide him with the remedy he seeks.

In addition to the absence of a clear conversion, the work's many digressions might be explained by Guibert's different understanding of the development of the self. As Aviad Kleinberg argues, whereas Augustine understands and portrays his development as an interior process, Guibert gives considerable attention to the impact of society upon the self (Kleinberg 1996, 62). For example, when he portrays his mother's decision to become a nun, Guibert considers it necessary to describe the religious renewal taking place in the monasteries of his day and the many famous religious conversions that fueled this renewal. And yet, this attention to context cannot explain all the work's digressions, given that many of them consist of fantastic stories with moral overtones. Guibert's scattered narrative thus seems a combined result of his hermeneutics of self, his inability to reach the authorial point of conversion, and his sense—perhaps due to the very lack of conversion—that in the face of his own story's insufficiency he must insert other exempla to make his account useful. As he states near the beginning of the work, he decided to insert such discussions due to "the poorness of his subject" (Guibert 1970, 49) (*pro sui tenuitate*, (Guibert 1907, 17). Despite his imitation of Augustine, Guibert's confessional narrative ultimately collapses amid his wavering feelings of insurmountable pride and profound unworthiness.

Abelard and the Medieval Self-portrait

Peter Abelard probably completed his *Historia calamitatum* in 1132 at the age of 53. Abelard's "account of misfortunes" is in many respects *sui generis*. Nonetheless, Abelard's self-representation also shares crucial characteristics with the Ovidian self-portrait, making it a prime example of the revival of this classical mode in the twelfth century. Although Abelard does not address posterity explicitly, his repetitive attempts to glorify his abilities, justify his actions, and proclaim his innocence turn his work into a self-portrait in the Ovidian fashion, aimed above all at providing present and future readers with a carefully constructed image of its author.

Abelard states at the outset that he writes in consolation of the troubles of his unnamed addressee—whom he then almost completely forgets. In the second paragraph Abelard turns to his life-story. In the fashion of Ovid and the Roman biographical tradition—and unlike the Augustinian confessional narrative—Abelard begins his self-portrayal with a description of his birthplace and his early upbringing, as well as his early dedication to the study of philosophy: "Martis curie penitus abdicarem ut Minerve gremio educarer" (Abelard 1967, 63) [[I] withdrew from the court of Mars in order to kneel at the feet of Minerva] (Abelard 1974, 58). His language here echoes Ovid's description of his choice of poetry over arms in *Tristia* 4.10.17–20. Furthermore, just as Ovid focuses from the outset of his poem on his poetic career, Abelard directs our attention from the beginning to the fact that his account will concentrate on Abelard the philosopher.

Abelard next asserts his greatness in his chosen profession, repeatedly emphasizing the superiority of reason and talent over empty reliance upon tradition, particularly in describing his meeting with one of the leading theologians of his time—Anselm of Laon (Kleinberg 1996, 56). Abelard limns his portrayal of Anselm with images of barrenness and infertility: "Cum ignem accenderet, domum suam fumo implebat, non luce illustrabat. Arbor ejus tota in foliis aspicientibus a longe conspicua videbatur, sed propinquantibus et diligentius intuentibus infructuosa reperiebatur" (Abelard 1967, 68) [The fire he kindled filled his house with smoke but did not light it up; he was a tree in full leaf which could be seen from afar, but on closer and more careful inspection proved to be barren] (Abelard 1974, 62). Abelard attributes this infertility to Anselm's reliance solely upon the knowledge of past authorities (*longevus usus*), with no allowance for his own talent and inventiveness (*ingenium*). Unlike Anselm, Abelard portrays himself as the mark of fertility, relying only upon his own intelligence. Boasting to Anselm's students that he is able to comment upon Scripture without any instruction from teachers, Abelard accepts their challenge to comment on an especially difficult passage of Ezekiel; when they advise him to take time to prepare his exposition, he declares that "non esse mee consuetudinis per usum proficere sed per ingenium" (Abelard 1967, 69) [it was not my custom to benefit by practice, but I relied on my own intelligence] (Abelard 1974, 63). Abelard views the ability to rely upon one's intelligence and wit rather than memorization and the aid of others as a mark of fertility and abundance, a proof of his greatness. Given the physical castration about which we will soon learn, it is tempting to consider this emphasis on intellectual fertility as a form of compensation on his part.

After this demonstration of his philosophical abilities and success, Abelard describes his downfall, portraying the two major calamities that befell him—his castration by the uncle of his lover, Heloise, and the burning of his book. In describing these calamities, Abelard employs language reminiscent of Augustine, depicting his downfall as a just retribution from God for his sins of pride and lust: "Cum igitur totus in superbia atque luxuria laborarem, utriusque morbi remedium divina mihi gratia licet nolenti contulit" (Abelard 1967, 70) [Since therefore I was wholly enslaved to pride and lechery, God's grace provided a remedy for both these evils, though not one of my choosing] (Abelard 1974, 65). Although he refers to Augustine and describes his calamities as a "remedy from God," in his actual description of the events Abelard rarely blames himself or perceives his downfall as just and remedial. Instead, he repeatedly emphasizes the injustice of his punishments, especially in the case of the burning of his book (Abelard 1967, 89; 1974, 84–85). Rather than reproaching himself for his sins in the Augustinian fashion, Abelard is concerned mainly to proclaim his innocence and to bemoan the jealousy of others (McLaughlin 1967; Spence 1996, 66–72; Clanchy 1999, 124). At the same time, the strong apologetic strain in the work continues to turn on the trope of reason's superiority over blind adherence to tradition.

In sum, as in the case of Ovid, Abelard's practice of self-writing is primarily aimed at providing readers with an image of himself that would assert his greatness and proclaim his innocence. Significantly, near the end of his account, while portraying his present condition as an abbot at the remote monastery of St. Gildas, Abelard describes himself in language closely reminiscent of Ovid: "Terra quippe barbara (cf. *Tristia* 3.1.18) et terre lingua mihi incognita erat,..., et gens terre illius inhumana atque incomposita" (Abelard 1967, 98) [The country was wild and the language unknown to me, the natives were brutal and barbarous] (Abelard 1974, 94–95). Whether Abelard is drawing directly upon Ovid or only exploiting a common topos, it is without a doubt revealing that both describe their condition at the time of writing as that of an exile in a dangerous land, hoping that the act of writing will provide present and future readers with the authors' side of the story and perhaps help them out of their present misfortunes.

Petrarch

The spread of the practice of self-examination between the twelfth and the fourteenth centuries and the revival of the modes of the confessional narrative and the self-portrait were accompanied by several other important developments in practices of self-writing, among them the rise of the vernacular lyric tradition culminating in Dante's *Vita nuova*, and the proliferation of visionary literature, particularly by female mystics. (On the latter, see Clark in this volume.) However, the central development in practices of self-writing in Latin in the later Middle Ages emerged from Petrarch's tireless experiments with practically all the modes of self-writing discussed thus far. It is the adoption and transformation of all these modes that defines to a large extent Petrarch's enormous contribution to European practices of self-writing.

In his massive collections of Latin letters, the *Familiares* and the *Seniles*, assembled throughout his adult life, Petrarch often writes to friends about his own condition, reviewing his everyday activities much as Seneca does in his *Letters to Lucilius*. Petrarch similarly inspects his mundane activities in light of Stoic precepts, such as the need to use time well and to live in accordance with nature. In *Familiares* 21.12, written to his friend Francesco Nelli, Petrarch explicitly refers to Seneca's admonition of the need to save time before turning to portray his own efficiency in daily life: "Augustum sequens et inter tondendum radendumque legere aut scribere aut legentes audire et scribentibus dictare soleo" (Petrarch 1933–42, 4: 86) [I, too, following in Augustus's footsteps, usually read or write or listen to someone reading or dictate to scribes while combing my hair and shaving] (Petrarch 1975–85, 3: 195). In the following letter, written again to Nelli, Petrarch describes his eating and dressing habits, praising his satisfaction with simple meals and reproaching himself for his predilection for fancy outfits (Petrarch 1933–42, 4: 90; 1975–85, 3: 198). Such an elaborate portrayal of his daily habits, with particular emphasis on areas for improvement, turns Petrarch's accounts into a Senecan self-examination, aimed at shaping and transforming his own self (Zak 2010, 105–6).

Alongside his revival of this Senecan mode in letters to friends, Petrarch develops, in works like the *Secretum*, a more medieval analysis of one's sins. In his imaginary dialogue with the figure of Augustinus, written and revised between 1347–53 (Baron 1985), Petrarch echoes Augustine's self-examination in Book 10 of the *Confessiones* and the recommendations of late medieval authors such as Radewijns to explore one's sins in writing. The penitential aspect is particularly evident in the second book of the work, in which the two go through the list of the seven cardinal sins and explore the extent to which "Franciscus" is guilty of each one.

Although Petrarch's examination of his sins in the *Secretum* is indebted to the Augustinian medieval tradition, the work also departs from it. To begin, the figure of Franciscus is not simply a sounding-board that passively accepts the accusations of his spiritual advisor Augustinus, but rather fiercely contests the accusations made against him. At times, the figure of Augustinus is even led to affirm anti-Christian values such as the pursuit of earthly glory. For Petrarch there is no one indisputable truth in light of which he examines and reproaches himself, and the aim of the writing is thus not only to excavate his guilt, as it was for Augustine and Guigo, but also to externalize his inner conflict and to reach conclusions about the required course of action (Celenza 2005, 512–13; Kircher 2006, 145–84; Ascoli 2010). Furthermore, the dominant ascetic view represented by the figure of Augustinus contrasts markedly with that of the historical Augustine: in opposition to the Augustinian focus on self-denial, the figure of Augustinus advances the Senecan emphasis on the need to attain the state of reason, the full control over the passions: "Quod tum demum excidisse tibi noveris, cum, calcatis passionibus humanis, totus sub virtutis imperium concesseris" (Petrarch 2000, 146) [You will know that you have finally cut off this yoke when, having scorned human passions, you have submitted wholly to the rule of virtue] (Petrarch 2003, 83). The medieval form of self-examination is thus employed in the *Secretum* in order to attain clear classical goals.

Whereas the *Secretum* and his letters on his own condition from the *Familiares* follow the mode of the self-examination, Petrarch's *Letter to Posterity* is his most evident attempt to revive the Ovidian mode of the self-portrait. Written sometime between 1370 and 1374 (the year of his death), Petrarch intended the letter to be a kind of appendix to his second collection of Latin letters—the *Seniles* (*Letters of Old Age*) (Bernardo 1986; Enenkel 1998). His decision to use the letter as an appendix and to address it to posterity leaves no doubt that Petrarch is using Ovid's *Tristia* 4.10 as his model. Petrarch's decision to open the letter with a "synchronic" description of his origins, appearance, and character, points to the central impact of another ancient model—Suetonius's *Life of Augustus*. Already in the opening description of his family background Petrarch directly alludes to Suetonius's description of Augustus, declaring that he, like Augustus, came from "familia antiqua" ("old family," Petrarch 1998, 256–57, referring to *familia...vetere* in Suetonius 1958, 47). Furthermore, Petrarch's elaborate portrayal of his appearance, which gives special attention to individual attributes such as the complexion of his skin, is also based upon the Suetonian model. Medieval authors such as Abelard, Guibert, and even Dante refrained from providing a description of their physical appearance. Yet the element of "individualism" implied in such a description should not be exaggerated: even the portrayal of his own unique physical attributes follows convention. For example, when Petrarch describes his complexion as "colore vivido inter candidum et subnigrum" [between light and dark] (Petrarch 1998, 258–59), he directly imitates Suetonius's description of Augustus—"colorem inter aquilum candidumque" (Suetonius 1958, 93) [between swarthy and fair]. The specificity of Petrarch's individual attributes is always mediated through literary antecedents.

While combining the Suetonian and Ovidian forms of self-portrayal, Petrarch's account also departs from his models. Significantly, Petrarch's account of his character at the beginning of his letter is based upon the Christian taxonomy of sins—the same ones mentioned in the *Secretum*. Petrarch describes his disdain of wealth, his release from the torments of lust, his freedom from pride, as well as his dedication to sacred letters later in life. Even while addressing posterity and explicitly reviving the ancient Ovidian mode of the self-portrait, the image of himself that Petrarch strives to leave behind is that of the devout Christian. Just as the *Secretum* employed a medieval form of self-examination in order to advance classical goals, so the *Letter to Posterity* uses a classical form to advance a Christian self-image. In both cases, Petrarch synthesizes classical and Christian values and forms of writing (on which see also Witt 2003, 239–60).

Yet the letter itself demonstrates the complexity of this fusion. In direct opposition to his models Ovid and Suetonius, Petrarch ends his portrait abruptly with his decision to leave Padua and return to France to alleviate his condition by a change of scene "in the manner of invalids" (*more egrorum*, Petrarch 1998, 280–81). Petrarch's self-portrait here becomes finally a self-reproach not very different from that of the *Secretum*, and the character trait that comes to dominate the work is the author's inconstancy, his "inability to stay still" (*stare nescius*, Petrarch 1998, 280–81). The attempt to combine the Ovidian form of the self-portrait, which inevitably contains an element of pride, with Christian content that esteems humility and simplicity of style, thus proves to lie beyond Petrarch's powers as an insurmountable contradiction of terms.

The abrupt ending of his life story in the *Letter to Posterity* connects us to the third and final mode of self-writing discussed here—the confessional narrative. The intertextual presence of Augustine's *Confessiones* pervades Petrarch's works, and in his celebrated letter portraying his ascent of Mount Ventoux (*Familiares* 4.1) Petrarch expresses his desire to write a healing narrative of his past like his mentor. After his slow and circuitous ascent to the top of the mountain, which is contrasted with the direct and easy climb of his brother, the Carthusian monk Gherardo, Petrarch takes in the view and then turns his reflection from space to time:

> Hodie decimus annus completur, ex quo, puerilibus studiis dimissis, Bononia excessisti; et, o Deus immortalis, o immutabilis Sapientia, quot et quantas morum tuorum mutationes hoc medium tempus vidit! Infinita pretereo; nondum enim in portu sum, ut securus preteritarum meminerim procellarum. Tempus forsan veniet, quando eodem quo gesta sunt ordine universa percurram, prefatus illud Augustini tui: 'Recordari volo transactas feditates meas et carnales corruptiones anime mee, non quod eas amem, sed ut amem te, Deus meus'. Michi quidem multum adhuc ambigui molestique negotii superest. (Petrarch 1933–42, 1: 157)

> [Today completes the tenth year since you departed from Bologna after completion of your youthful studies. Oh, immortal God, oh immutable wisdom, how extensive and how many changes within me during this interim! I shall skip an infinitude of them since not yet being in port I cannot recall in security the storms through which I have passed. The time will perhaps come when I shall enumerate all of these storms that beset my life in their appropriate order, prefacing it with the words of your Augustine: "I wish to recall all my past foulness and the carnal corruption of my soul not because I love them but so that I might love you, my God." As for me,

there still remains indeed a great deal that is uncertain and troublesome.]
(Petrarch 1975–85, 1: 176)

The remedy for the cycles of earthly desires that plague him—allegorized in his circuitous ascent up the mountain—resides in the linearity of the Augustinian narrative, the discovery of the order and meaning that underlie the many changes he went through. However, in order to construct such a narrative, Petrarch declares, he must reach the vantage point of conversion like Augustine and renounce all that is *ambigui molestique.*

When he wrote the letter—probably in the early 1350's (Billanovich 1947, 193–98)—Petrarch was evidently not yet in port. Unable to structure the narrative of his past, Petrarch can only dramatize the conflict that plagues him and use writing as a form of confession that will perhaps facilitate the conversion he seeks. Near the end of the letter, Petrarch refers to it directly as a confession, telling his addressee—the Augustinian monk Dionigi da Borgo San Sepolcro (who gave Petrarch his copy of the *Confessiones*)—that he opened his heart completely to him as in a confession: "Vide itaque, pater amantissime, quam nichil in me oculis tuis occultum velim, qui tibi nedum universam vitam meam sed cogitatus singulos tam diligenter aperio; pro quibus ora, queso, ut tandiu vagi et instabiles aliquando subsistant" (Petrarch 1933–42, 1: 160–61) [See, therefore, beloved father, how I wish that nothing of me be hidden from your eyes, having carefully opened not only my entire life to you but even my single thoughts. I beg you to pray for them so that having been rambling and unstable for so long, they may sometime find rest] (Petrarch 1975–85, 1: 180). The entire letter, from this perspective, should be considered another of Petrarch's written self-examinations aimed at transforming his condition.

As the letter makes clear, the main obstacle that prevents Petrarch from reaching the port of conversion is his earthly desires, and above all his desire for glory through his writings. Descending the mountain, Petrarch describes his withdrawal to a hidden portion of the inn to write an account of the day: "hec tibi, raptim et ex tempore, scripturus; ne, si distulissem ... scribendi propositum deferveret" (Petrarch 1933–42, 1: 160) [In order to write this [account] to you hastily and extemporaneously lest with delay ... my determination to write might subside] (Petrarch 1975–85, 1: 179–80). At the end of the letter we therefore receive the impression that what is particularly important for Petrarch is to leave behind a written account of the event—a captivating portrait of his inner conflict reflected in the climb—both to his addressee and to his present and future readers. The inner conflict that characterizes Petrarch's life thus becomes one that revolves around the very practice of self-writing: between desiring to leave behind an absorbing portrait of himself and using such an account for the ethical goal of self-transformation. A similar conflict between the ethical and aesthetic aspects of writing, as we have seen, also dominated Guibert's *Vita,* yet while Guibert was certain of the evil nature of his pride and used the writing to reproach himself for it, Petrarch presents in the letter—as in the *Secretum*—the two conflicting approaches—the ethic and the aesthetic—without fully adhering to either one. (On Familiares 4.1, see also Ascoli 1992.)

Petrarch's inability to reach the authorial point that will allow him to structure a narrative of his life led him to develop a new mode of self-writing. Both in the *Familiares* and the *Seniles* and in his collection of vernacular poems, the *Rerum vulgarium fragmenta*, Petrarch gathers together the fragments of his past written through the years into collections that reflect the linear passage of time. Nonetheless, what defines these collections is above all the absence of a clear vantage point from which the author recounts his past life (Mazzotta 1993, 58–60). Rather than conveying the meaning of his past life, the author juxtaposes the fragments in a continuum, without giving any of these states primacy over the others. The task of providing the thread that binds these *disiecta membra* together is left for the reader.

Furthermore, while Petrarch's collections do allude to the linear passage of time, they are also marked by circularity and repetition: successive letters stand in direct contradiction to one another or repeat themes already discussed. For example, the final letter of the *Familiares* deals with the same topic of the opening letter of the collection—the incredible flight of time—and is written to the same correspondent (Ludwig van Kempen). The end of the collection thus takes us back to the beginning and creates a sense of circular motion (Antognini 2008, 115–310). This sense of circularity and repetition militates against the very linearity the collection attempts to convey, and thus depicts more realistically, according to Petrarch, the indeterminate, contradictory, and shifting nature of the development of the self than the Augustinian confessional narrative. It is this type of fragmentary self-representation that will continue to evolve in the early modern period in the letters of Angelo Poliziano, the *Essays* of Montaigne, and countless other letter collections and sonnet sequences. The modern secular autobiography, in which the author "securely" recounts his or her past life from the vantage point of the present, thus emerged in spite of—rather than, as is generally assumed, because of (Weintraub 1978, 93–114; Scaglione 1989)—Petrarch's obsessive experiments with the variety of ancient and medieval modes of self-writing at his disposal.

SUGGESTIONS FOR FURTHER READING

For studies of autobiographical writing in the Middle Ages, see especially Misch (1949–69). The first volume is translated in Misch (1973). Other useful studies are Zumthor (1973) and Weintraub (1978). On the practice of self-writing as a technique of self-care in Seneca's letters, see Foucault (1997a). The fortunes of Seneca's letters in the Middle Ages are discussed by Reynolds (1965). On Ovid's self-portrait in *Tristia* 4.10, see the seminal articles by Fredericks (1976) and Fairweather (1987), as well as Claassen (1999 and 2008). For the medieval reception of Ovid's exile poetry, see Hexter (2007 and 2010). The best general introduction to Augustine's *Confessiones* is Brown (1967). On the impact of the *Confessiones* in the Middle Ages, see Courcelle (1963). On Augustine's practice of self-writing, see Vance (1973), Stock (1996), and Olney (1998). On Guigo I's *Meditations*, see Mursell's introduction in Guigo (1995), as well as Stock (2001). Valuable discussions of Guibert's *Vita* are Benton's introduction in Guibert (1970), Ferguson (1983), and Lerer (1990). The literature on Abelard's *Historia calamitatum* is large. The best introductory works are Gilson (1948) and Clanchy (1999). For the debate over the authenticity of Abelard's correspondence, see Zerbi (1981). On the *Historia calamitatum*, see McLaughlin (1967), and Spence (1996). For Petrarch's biography, see Dotti (1987). On his humanism, see Witt (2003) and Kircher (2006). Petrarch's practice of writing is discussed by Greene (1982), Mazzotta (1993), Stock (1995), Ascoli (1992, 2010), and Zak (2010).

BIBLIOGRAPHY

Primary sources

Abelard, Peter. 1967. *Historia calamitatum*, edited by Jacques Monfrin. Bibliothèque des textes philosophiques. Textes et commentaires. Paris: Vrin.
———. 1974. *The Letters of Abelard and Heloise*, translated by Betty Radice. Penguin Classics. New York: Penguin.
à Kempis, Thomas. 1963. *The Imitation of Christ*, translated by Betty I. Knott. Glasgow: Collins.
———. 1982. *De imitatione Christi: libri quatuor*, edited by Tiburzio Lupo. Storia e attualità 6. Città del Vaticano : Libreria Editrice Vaticana.
Augustine. 1991. *Confessions*, translated by Henry Chadwick. Oxford: Oxford University Press.
———. 1992. *Confessions*, edited by James J. O'Donnell. 3 volumes. Oxford: Clarendon Press.
Guibert of Nogent. 1907. *Histoire de sa vie (1053–1124)*, edited by Georges Bourgin. Collection de textes pour servir à l'étude et à l'enseignement de l'histoire 40. Paris: Picard.
———. 1970. *Self and Society in Medieval France: The Memoirs of Guibert of Nogent*, translated with an introduction by John F. Benton. Harper Torchbooks 1471. New York: Harper & Row.
Guigo I. 1983. *Les méditations (recueil de pensées)*, edited and translated by "un chartreux." Sources chrétiennes 308. Sources chrétiennes. Série des textes monastiques d'Occident 51. Paris: Editions du Cerf.
———. 1995. *The Meditations of Guigo I, Prior of the Charterhouse*, translated by A. Gordon Mursell. Cistercian Studies Series 155. Kalamazoo, MI: Cistercian Publications.
Ovid. 1988. *Sorrows of an Exile*, translated by Alan D. Melville. Oxford and New York: Oxford University Press.
———. 1995. *Tristia*, edited by John Barrie Hall. Bibliotheca scriptorum Graecorum et Romanorum Teubneriana. Stuttgart, Leipzig: B. G. Teubner.
Petrarch, Francesco. 1933–42. *Le Familiari* [*Familiarium Rerum Libri*], edited by Vittorio Rossi (vols. 1–3) and Umberto Bosco (vol. 4). 4 vols. Edizione nazionale delle opere di Francesco Petrarca 10–13. Florence: Sansoni.
———. 1975–85. *Rerum Familiarium Libri* [*Letters on Familiar Matters*], translated by Aldo S. Bernardo. 3 volumes. Albany: State University of New York Press.

———. 1998. "Posteritati," edited and translated by Karl Enenkel. In *Modelling the Individual: Biography and Portrait in the Renaissance*, edited by Karl Enenkel, Betsy de Jong-Crane and Peter Liebregts, 243–81. DQR Studies in Literature 23. Amsterdam, Atlanta: Rodopi.

———. 2000. *Il mio segreto [Secretum]*, edited by Ugo Dotti. Classici della BUR 1334. Milan: Rizzoli.

———. 2003. *The Secret*, translated by Carol E. Quillen. Bedford Series in History and Culture. Boston and New York: Bedford/St. Martin's.

Seneca. 1953. *Ad Lucilium Epistulae Morales*, translated by Richard M. Gummere. 3 vols. Loeb Classical Library. Latin Authors 75–77. Cambridge, MA: Harvard University Press.

———. 1965. *L. Annaei Senecae Ad Lucilium Epistulae Morales*, edited by Leighton D. Reynolds. 2 vols. Scriptorum classicorum bibliotheca Oxoniensis. Oxford: Clarendon Press.

Suetonius. 1958. *De Vita Caesarum libri VIII*, edited by Max Ihm. Bibliotheca scriptorum Graecorum et Romanorum Teubneriana. Stuttgart: B. G. Teubner.

William of Saint-Thierry. 1975. *Lettre aux frères du Mont-Dieu: lettre d'or*, edited and translated by Jean Déchanet. Sources chrétiennes 223. Sources chrétiennes. Série des textes monastiques d'Occident 45. Paris: Editions du Cerf.

———. 1976. *The Golden Epistle*, translated by Theodore Berkeley. Cistercian Fathers series 12. Kalamazoo, MI: Cistercian Publications.

Secondary sources

Antognini, Roberta. 2008. *Il progetto autobiografico delle Familiares di Petrarca*. Studi e ricerche. Milan: LED.

Ascoli, Albert Russell. 1992. "Petrarch's Middle Age: Memory, Imagination, History, and the 'Ascent of Mount Ventoux.'" *Stanford Italian Review* 10: 5–43.

———. 2010. *'Favola fui': Petrarch Writes his Readers*. Bernardo Lecture Series 17. Binghamton, NY: Center for Medieval & Renaissance Studies, State University of New York at Binghamton.

Baron, Hans. 1985. *Petrarch's Secretum: Its Making and Its Meaning*. Medieval Academy Books 94. Cambridge, MA: Medieval Academy of America.

Bernardo, Aldo S. 1986. "Petrarch's Autobiography: Circularity Revisited." *Annali d'Italianistica* 4: 45–72.

Billanovich, Giuseppe. 1947. *Petrarca letterato: I. Lo scrittoio del Petrarca*. Storia e letteratura 16. Rome: Edizioni di Storia e letteratura.

Brown, Peter. 1967. *Augustine of Hippo: a biography*. Berkeley, CA: University of California Press.

Celenza, Christopher. 2005. "Petrarch, Latin, and Italian Renaissance Latinity." *Journal of Medieval and Early Modern Studies* 35: 509–36.

Claassen, Jo-Marie. 1999. *Displaced Persons: The Literature of Exile from Cicero to Boethius*. Madison, WI: University of Wisconsin Press.

———. 2008. *Ovid Revisited: The Poet in Exile*. London: Duckworth.

Clanchy, Michel T. 1999. *Abelard: A Medieval Life*. Oxford: Blackwell.

Courcelle, Pierre. 1963. *Les Confessions de Saint Augustin dans la tradition littéraire*. Paris: Etudes Augustiniennes.

Dotti, Ugo. 1987. *Vita di Petrarca*. Collezione storica. Rome: Laterza.

Duby, George. 1988. "Solitude: Eleventh to Thirteenth Century." In *A History of Private Life*, edited by Georges Duby, translated by Arthur Goldhammer, 2: 509–34. Cambridge, MA: Harvard University Press.

Enenkel, Karl. 1998. "Modelling the Humanist: Petrarch's Letter to Posterity and Boccaccio's Biography of the Poet Laureate." In *Modelling the Individual: Biography and Portrait in the Renaissance*, edited by Karl Enenkel, Betsy de Jong-Crane, and Peter Liebregts, 11–49. DQR Studies in Literature 23. Amsterdam, Atlanta: Rodopi.

Fairweather, Janet. 1987. "Ovid's Autobiographical Poem, *Tristia* 4.10." *Classical Quarterly* 37: 181–96.

Ferguson, Chris D. 1983. "Autobiography as Therapy: Guibert de Nogent, Peter Abelard, and the Making of Medieval Autobiography." *Journal of Medieval and Renaissance Studies* 13: 187–212.

Foucault, Michel. 1997a. "Self Writing." In *Ethics: Subjectivity and Truth*, edited by Paul Rabinow, translated by Robert Hurley et al., 207–22. New York: New Press.

———. 1997b. "Technologies of the Self." In *Ethics: Subjectivity and Truth*, edited by Paul Rabinow, translated by Robert Hurley et al., 223–52. New York: New Press.

Fredericks, Betty R. 1976. "*Tristia* 4.10: Poet's Autobiography and Poetic Autobiography." *Transactions of the American Philological Association* 106: 139–54.

Gilson, Etienne. 1948. *Héloïse et Abélard*. Essais d'art et de philosophie. Paris: J. Vrin.

Greene, Thomas M. 1982. *The Light in Troy: Imitation and Discovery in Renaissance Poetry*. Elizabethan Club Series 7. New Haven, CT: Yale University Press.

Gusdorf, Georges. [1956] 1980. "Conditions and Limits of Autobiography," translated by James Olney. In *Autobiography: Essays Theoretical and Critical*, edited by James Olney, 28–48. Princeton, NJ: Princeton University Press.

Hexter, Ralph J. 2007. "Ovid and the Medieval Exilic Imaginary." In *Writing Exile: The Discourse of Displacement in Greco-Roman Antiquity and Beyond*, edited by Jan Felix Gaertner, 209–36. Mnemosyne, bibliotheca classica Batava. Supplementum 283. Leiden, Boston: Brill.

———. 2010. "Ovidius Naso, Publius (Ovid). Exildichtung," translated by Uwe Vagelpohl. In *Rezeption der antiken Literatur: Kulturhistorisches Werklexikon*, edited by Hubert Cancik, Manfred Landfester, and Helmuth Schneider, 585–608. *Der Neue Pauly*, Supplemente, vol. 7, edited by Christine Walde with Brigitte Egger. Stuttgart: J. B. Metzler.

Ker, James. 2010. "Seneca on Self-Examination: Rereading *De ira* 3.36." In *Seneca and the Self*, edited by Shadi Bartsch and David Wray, 160–87. Cambridge: Cambridge University Press.

Kircher, Timothy. 2006. *The Poet's Wisdom: The Humanists, the Church, and the Formation of Philosophy in the Early Renaissance*. Brill's Studies in Intellectual History 133. Leiden, Boston: Brill.

Kleinberg, Aviad. 1996. "Three Autobiographies from the Middle Ages." *Alpayim* 13: 44–64 (in Hebrew).

Lawrence, Clifford H. 1989. *Medieval Monasticism: Forms of Religious Life in Western Europe in the Middle Ages*. 2nd ed. London, New York: Longman.

Le Goff, Jacques. 1988. *Medieval Civilization, 400–1500*, translated by Julia Barrow. Oxford: Blackwell.

Lejeune, Philippe. 1975. Le Pacte Autobiographique. Paris: Seuil.

Lerer, Seth. 1990. "*Transgressio studii*: Writing and Sexuality in Guibert of Nogent." *Stanford French Review* 14: 243–66.

Mazzotta, Giuseppe. 1993. *The Worlds of Petrarch*. Duke Monographs in Medieval and Renaissance Studies 14. Durham, NC: Duke University Press.

McLaughlin, Mary M. 1967. "Abelard as Autobiographer: The Motives and Meaning of His 'Story of Calamities.'" *Speculum* 42: 463–88.

Misch, Georg. 1949–69. *Geschichte der Autobiographie*, 3rd ed. 4 vols. Frankfurt/Main: Schulte-Bulmke.

———. 1973. *A History of Autobiography in Antiquity*. translated by Ernest W. Dickes. Westport, CT: Greenwood Press.

Mohrmann, Christine. 1961. "Considerazioni sulle 'Confessioni' di sant'Agostino." In *Études sur le Latin des Chrétiens*, 2: 277–323. Rome: Edizioni di Storia e letteratura.

Olney, James. 1998. *Memory & Narrative: The Weave of Life-Writing*. Chicago: University of Chicago Press.

Reynolds, Leighton D. 1965. *The Medieval Tradition of Seneca's Letters*. Oxford Classical and Philosophical Monographs. Oxford: Oxford University Press.

Ricoeur, Paul. 1985. *Time and Narrative*, translated by Kathleen McLaughlin and David Pellauer. 3 vols. Chicago: University of Chicago Press.

Scaglione, Aldo. 1989. "Classical Heritage and Petrarchan Self-Consciousness in the Literary Emergence of the Interior 'I.'" In *Petrarch*, edited by Harold Bloom, 125–37. Modern Critical Views. New York: Infobase Publishing.

Spence, Sarah. 1996. *Texts and the Self in the Twelfth Century*. Cambridge Studies in Medieval Literature 30. Cambridge, New York: Cambridge University Press.

Staubach, Nikolaus. 1991. "Pragmatische Schriftlichkeit im Bereich der Devotio Moderna." *Frühmittelalterliche Studien* 25: 418–61.

Stock, Brian. 1995. "Reading, Writing, and the Self: Petrarch and his Forerunners." *New Literary History* 26: 717–30.

———. 1996. *Augustine the Reader: Meditation, Self-knowledge, and the Ethics of Interpretation*. Cambridge, MA: Harvard University Press.

———. 2001. *After Augustine: The Meditative Reader and the Text*. Material Texts. Philadelphia: University of Pennsylvania Press.

———. 2007. *Ethics Through Literature: Ascetic and Aesthetic Reading in Western Culture*. The Menahem Stern Jerusalem Lectures. Hanover, NH, London: University Press of New England for Brandeis University.

Vance, Eugene. 1973. "Augustine's *Confessions* and the Grammar of Selfhood." *Genre* 6: 1–28.

Van Engen, John. 2008. *Sisters and Brothers of the Common Life: The Devotio Moderna and the World of the Later Middle Ages*. Middle Ages Series. Philadelphia: University of Pennsylvania Press.

van 't Spijker, Ineke. 2004. *Fictions of the Inner Life: Religious Literature and Formation of the Self in the Eleventh and Twelfth Centuries*. Disputatio 4. Turnhout: Brepols.

Weintraub, Karl J. 1978. *The Value of the Individual: Self and Circumstance in Autobiography*. Chicago: University of Chicago Press.

Witt, Ronald G. 2003. *In the Footsteps of the Ancients: The Origins of Humanism from Lovato to Bruni*. Studies in Medieval and Reformation Thought 74. Leiden, Boston: Brill.

Zak, Gur. 2010. *Petrarch's Humanism and the Care of the Self*. Cambridge, New York: Cambridge University Press.

Zerbi, Piero. 1981. "Abelardo ed Eloisa: il problema di un amore e di una corrispondenza." In *Love and Marriage in the Twelfth Century*, edited by Willy van Hoecke and Andries Welkenhuysen, 130–61. Mediaevalia Lovaniensia, ser. 1, studia 8. Leuven: Leuven University Press.

Zimmerman, T. C. Price. 1971. "Confession and Autobiography in the Early Renaissance." In *Renaissance Studies in Honor of Hans Baron*, edited by Anthony Molho and John A. Tedeschi, 119–40. DeKalb, IL: Northern Illinois University Press.

Zumthor, Paul. 1973. "Autobiography in the Middle Ages?" *Genre* 6: 29–48.

PART VII

PERIODIZATIONS

CHAPTER 24

LATE ANTIQUITY, NEW DEPARTURES*

MARCO FORMISANO

I. A Matter of Premises: "What are we worrying about?" or The Pleasure and Pain of Late Antiquity

When taking lunch with colleagues, Arnaldo Momigliano often posed the question, "Tell me, what are you worrying about?" (Brown 2004, 103). With his question he was asking about current projects and perhaps also about the inner torment accompanying many scholarly activities. Peter Brown, who tells of Momigliano's favorite question, applies it to the study of history in general, but if we apply it to the field of classics, we could say that late antique literature nowadays represents not only a possible source of delight and "pleasure" because of its novelty and freshness (Shanzer 2009), but also the true worry for studies of the ancient world. On the one hand, symptomatically for the end of the twentieth and early twenty-first centuries, late antique studies are experiencing a boom: recent years have seen a mass of publications (journals, companions, and monographs), and universities are gradually beginning to acknowledge this growing scholarship by institutionalizing it within programs and curricula. On the other hand, "late antiquity" is by definition that field of ancient studies which is most deeply and intrinsically subject to historical

---

* I wish to express my warm thanks to the volume's editors Ralph Hexter and David Townsend as well as to Michael Roberts, Craig Williams, and Cristiana Sogno for their generous comments, and to Friderike Senkbeil for assistance with the bibliography.

distortions: the very impossibility of naming this age without recurring to a more or less negative term ("late") is representative of how this basic distortion has ended up shaping and unconsciously framing the study of late antiquity. Thus every discussion, review or book devoted to late antique texts unavoidably starts with the same subtle refrain: this was not an age of decline and fall but rather of change, growth, and transformation. Of course this style of argumentation is closely connected with scholarship on the emergence of medieval culture, with which late antique studies entertain an ambiguous relationship: on the one hand they share the necessity of looking differently at certain cultural and literary phenomena; on the other hand, late antiquity risks being overshadowed by medieval studies, which represent an autonomous and well-established discipline within current academic systems all over the world.

More than thirty years ago, Reinhart Herzog described late antiquity as "the most un-read period" of Western culture (Herzog 1977, 13), and this dictum is arguably still valid. Late antiquity has over the last decades achieved recognition as a prominent field in *historical* research, which has taken advantage of the linguistic and textual turn (Martin and Miller 2005), but late antique *textuality* continues in general to be investigated (with few but promising exceptions) with the hermeneutical tools stemming from the dominant historical paradigm, or to be read from the perspective of "classical" literature (exemplary cases of this approach are Bowersock, Brown, and Grabar 1999 and Rousseau 2009, while sustained attention to specifically literary aspects characterizes Scourfield 2007). While the rationale for exclusion may vary between Britain, North America, and the Continent, late antique texts are generally marginalized and left out of course syllabi and university reading lists. Late antique texts are believed not to have the same aesthetic or historical value as texts of the classical canon. Cast as non-normative or nonconforming, they are rarely read in the classroom. The aesthetic of this literature, which, like medieval textuality, is unfamiliar and appears strange, bizarre, even exotic both to general readers and more experienced scholars of the classical world, is under-valued.

In reading and interpreting late antique texts we should, to the extent possible, avoid the unquestioning use of the interpretive tools and aesthetic categories which we normally apply to "classical" texts; we might thus wonder to what extent being a classicist helps or impedes the discussion of these texts, since classicists arguably tend to look for aspects with which they are familiar and which they prize. Interpreters of the *cento* or of late Latin epic poetry, for example, very much insist on Virgil's influence on these texts rather than shedding light on the sorts of cultural and aesthetic paradigms which lie behind the obvious fact of Virgil's dominating presence in late antique literature. To transfer this question to the Middle Ages: the influence of Virgil on Dante has of course been carefully investigated, but does not represent a *Leitmotiv* of Dante studies in the way it has been for the study of late antique literature. One might wonder whether this insistence on the past as such, which is commonly shared within late ancient studies, has not been influenced by the very fact that those who study this epoch are generally classicists. But does late antique literature share "classical" conceptions of textuality at all? And, even more importantly, how different are our own modern categories and expectations from those of late antiquity? Is there an ontological difficulty for us as we attempt to understand late antique literature independent of its classical past?

As Danuta Shanzer has argued, the kind of textuality produced in late antique literature is intrinsically *non-canonical*, because it does not form a canonical corpus of texts (as, for instance, Augustan literature did), and *metaliterary*, since it constantly reflects on itself, on its being a matter of writing and the book (Shanzer 2009, 921). The reading of authors such as Prudentius, Augustine, Claudian, Venantius Fortunatus, Jerome, or Cassiodorus might remind us of Flaubert's or Borges's parallel worlds of books and written words: they all show a different possibility for conceiving textuality, a way which often clashes with the expectations of modern classicists since it configures a new concept of literature by defamiliarizing our perception of "classical" literature (cp. Hinds 2005).

In short, the study of late antique literary discourse compels us to conceive of another kind of textuality, one which our usual interpretive categories are not equipped to accommodate. As a result, the reading of late antique texts has both the beneficial effect of reflecting on literature itself as such and representing a foundational moment for literary theory and textual analysis. In the eyes of a modern reader, late antique textuality can acquire the mission of putting in question common views of what "literature" is; at the same time, it invites being put in productive comparison with literature produced in other ages. This will have not only the effect of tracing the reception of this often neglected textuality, but also, and perhaps more importantly, of challenging the various clichés which characterize the reading of late antiquity.

Of the topics that would deserve detailed treatment in a more extended essay, here I mention but one, and that briefly: the issue of periodization. Late antiquity seems to be *the* age that challenges the very concept of clearly defined periods. Since Peter Brown's influential *The World of Late Antiquity* (1971), historians have insisted on the expansion or "elephantiasis" of the period, whose beginning and end have been variously located from the third to the eighth centuries (Giardina 1999, cp. Averil Cameron 2002, Bowersock 2004, and Marcone 2008). Some medievalists have even claimed that the very category of late antiquity as such is an artificial creation of "classicists and their adepts," introduced and maintained for academic reasons (cp. Leonardi 2002, xxx).

In any case it is important to emphasize that historical periodizations do not necessarily correspond to the needs of literary history. In what follows, instead of the traditional focus on individual genres and authors, I consider characteristic features of late antique literature which on the one hand represent a novelty in respect to previous ages, and on the other were further developed in the multiform and heterogeneous Latin textuality of the Middle Ages and beyond. I organize my discussion around three textual aspects which, although not comprehensively describing the entire late antique literary production, are new and specific to late antiquity in comparison with earlier periods. In the first section, dedicated to knowledge, I will briefly discuss the mass of textuality—usually considered to be typically late antique but simply documentary, not really "literary"—devoted to the transmission of knowledge of any kind. The second section is dedicated to panegyric, another characteristic element in late ancient discourse. The third section will discuss fragmentation, dislocation, and replacement, facets of late antique intertextuality that detach texts and their meanings from their original contexts by reconfiguring them within new frames and re-coding them through a process of resemanticization. At the same time, these processes fragment the text by parceling it up into discrete images and meanings. These three features are frequently intertwined within any given text or genre, and their combination bespeaks a new and uniquely late antique literary culture.

II. Knowledge

In our modern perception the transmission of knowledge is something different from literary imagination. In fact, we tend not to describe as "literature" treatises, encyclopedic works, documentary texts, or commentaries, since they do not correspond to the idea of literature that since Romanticism has shaped the tastes and expectations of Western readerships. Within the history of knowledge, late antiquity is often cited as *the* epoch of exegesis, encyclopedism, and related texts normally appreciated for the service they perform in the mechanisms of the transmission of knowledge. But those texts also demand to be read on their own terms and compel the interpreter to set aside predefined concepts of what "literature" can be. Literature and the transmission of knowledge can be intimately connected, and in some phases of the history of Western culture, such as in late antiquity, they seem to jointly respond to common needs of readerships. Even after the Romantic idea of literature became established, some authors in the nineteenth and twentieth centuries nonetheless created a literary universe in which knowledge and its transmission were heavily thematized and stood at the center of literary imagination (cp. Clark 1990). Foucault, for example, describes Flaubert's *La tentation de Saint Antoine* (1874) as a "monument to meticulous erudition" (Foucault 1977, 89), putting it in relation to his posthumously published *Bouvard et Pécuchet* (1881). Both works, Foucault writes, share a status as "a book produced from other books; the encyclopedic learning of a culture" (Foucault 1977, 105). Another author whose work constantly challenges the borders between literature and knowledge is Borges. One of his most intense stories, "Tlön, Uqbar, Orbis Tertius" (1940), contained in the collection *Fictions*, tells the story of an entire region whose existence is given only within the written universe of an encyclopedia and whose aspiration is "destined to be deciphered by men."

Recent decades have seen a growing interest in the literary dimension of "encyclopedism"; in particular, Roman encyclopedic works such as Pliny the Elder's *Naturalis historia* can now be seen from a new perspective. (Although it is not appropriate to apply the term "encyclopedia" to texts before early modernity—when the genre arises as such with this name—the concept of "encyclopedism" is widely used to describe antique, late antique, and medieval works which aim to present a systematization of knowledge in general or within a particular field.) Rather than merely a source of knowledge, Pliny's work has become an ordered universe of words presented within the political frame given by the Roman Empire (Beagon 1992, Conte 1994, Naas 2002, Murphy 2004, and Doody 2009). Scholarship on ancient encyclopedism has also drawn attention to Vitruvius's *De architectura*—no longer understood as (merely) a "manual" for architects and constructors, but as a titanic attempt at rationalizing and institutionalizing the knowledge of architecture within Latin literary culture (Romano 1987, Geertman 1989, Vitruvius 1997, and Novara 2005). In fact, the "encyclopedic" mode is one of the most powerful and significant impulses for late Latin textuality, which tends on the one hand to collect, select, and systematize the cultural heritage from previous eras, on the other to exalt the verbal nature of existence and to launch any kind of discourse into the universe of written words.

Three late antique works continuing and developing Pliny's project in particular had an immense *Nachleben* through the Middle Ages. In the first of these, *De nuptiis Philologiae et Mercurii* (first half of the fifth century), Martianus Capella presents the traditional apparatus of knowledge of the liberal arts within an allegorical frame. The work is dedicated to his son Martianus, a traditional aspect present already in the oldest Roman encyclopedist Cato the Elder (second century BCE), and presented in the mixed form of prose and verse in the tradition of Menippean satire. The allegory is introduced in the first two books with the *fabula* telling the mythical circumstances of the wedding, which are followed by the remaining seven books, each dedicated to one of the liberal arts (grammar, dialectics, rhetoric, geometry, arithmetic, astronomy, and harmony), personified by women slaves given to Philology as a gift (cp. Shanzer 1986; see also Hicks in this volume). In this work the knowledge of the seven liberal arts is presented as a fiction: it has, in other words, undergone an explicit process of narrativization. (For mythographical aspects in Martianus, see Wetherbee in this volume.)

An analogous impulse characterizes Boethius's *De consolatione philosophiae*. Boethius's work differs in many respects from *De nuptiis* and is one of the most sophisticated texts of late antiquity, but like Martianus Capella, he recurs to the *prosimetrum*, a form variously used by several other authors, e.g., Ausonius and Sidonius Apollinaris. (Ennodius's sixth-century prosimetric *Paraenesis didascalica* also uses the technique of personification, adding the Christian Verecundia, Castitas, and Fides to Grammatica and Rhetorica; cf. Schröder 2007, 52–53 and 86–88.) Furthermore, many of these texts, along with such works of Augustine as *De magistro* and *De musica*, make use of the dialogue form, which characterizes much late antique prose. The literary value of these texts has rightly been emphasized (Augustine 2002), although the dialogical quality of late antique literary culture has been recently questioned (Goldhill 2008).

The second major figure in late ancient encyclopedism is Cassiodorus (c. 485–c. 585), who lived under the Ostrogothic Theodoric the Great, founded a monastery called Vivarium, and wrote the *Institutiones divinarum et saecularium litterarum*, intended as a guide for those living in the monastery. The writings of Cassiodorus represent "the construction of an ideal type of higher culture" (Cassiodorus 2004, 11), and the *Institutiones* constitutes an important step towards the establishment of a Christian system of learning in particular. Cassiodorus's work was destined to become a standard part of curricula through the Middle Ages, since it offers a synthesis of pagan knowledge and Christian doctrine combined with practical instructions for everyday life.

The text that demonstrates with particular exemplarity the late antique tendency toward combining a fundamental attention to the written word with the transmission of knowledge is no doubt the dictionary composed in the seventh century by Isidore of Seville. Transmitted in more than a thousand manuscripts, Isidore's *Etymologiae, sive Origines* can be described as one of the most widely read Latin works of all time. The work consists of twenty books, each devoted to an *ars* or field of knowledge; it draws on many texts, with Cassiodorus's *Institutiones*, the late antique exegetical tradition, and the Church fathers as primary influences.

Eschewing a general foreword or theoretical introduction, Isidore starts *in medias res*. Readers are immediately confronted with the particular universe created by the author: a universe that is entirely self-referential and based on words and their "true meanings," as the title *Etymologiae* has it. In order to appreciate the kind of intellectual project pursued by Isidore, it might be useful to quote the opening of the first book, devoted to Grammar, i.e., language, which is, appropriately, the first art treated:

> De disciplina et arte. Disciplina a discendo nomen accepit: unde et scientia dici potest. nam scire dictum a discere, quia nemo nostrum scit, nisi qui discit. aliter dicta disciplina, quia discitur plena. ars vero dicta est, quod artis praeceptis regulisque consistat. alii dicunt a Graecis hoc tractum esse vocabulum ἀπὸ τῆς ἀρετῆς, id est a virtute, quam scientiam vocaverunt. (*Etymologiae* 1.1.1–2)

John Henderson has recently offered an unusual translation which evokes the intellectual density of Isidore's style by drawing attention to words and sounds:

> DISCIPLINE + ART. Disciplearne got its name from learning: ergo it can also be called science: you see, sci-earnce is short for psychal learning, because none of us plies sciernce without applied learning. On another line disciplearne's the word because it does plenary learning. The etymo-logy of Art is arid artillery, a combo of "heartily" and "dictates" (*sc.* rules). Others bespeak the word's importation from the Greek "<à la arête>," i.e. "from the complete article," the perfection they dubbed science. (Henderson 2007, 27)

Isidore's linguistic grand tour through knowledge gives a good sense of how important textuality was in this period; this text implies an absolute correspondence between *res* and *verba*, things and words, knowledge and *litterae* in their broadest sense. When one wants to understand the world, one has first to understand the word used to define the things out there. See for instance this passage:

Nomen dictum quasi notamen, quod nobis vocabulo suo res notat efficiat. Nisi enim nomen scieris, cognitio rerum perit (*Etymologiae* 1.7.1).

[The noun is so called as if it were "denoter," because by its designation it makes things known to us. Indeed, unless you know its name, the knowledge of the things perishes.] (Isidore of Seville 2006, 42)

Martianus Capella, Cassiodore, and Isidore heavily influenced medieval culture and its exemplary possession of what Jacques LeGoff has called the "ésprit encyclopédique" (LeGoff 1994). A long series of medieval authors used these authors in their own systematizations of knowledge, both in method and in content. The "Venerable" Bede (seventh to eighth century), Hrabanus Maurus (eighth to ninth century), Lambert of St. Omer, Hildegard of Bingen, Honorius von Autun, Hugh of St. Victor, Alexander Neckam (twelfth century), Thomas of Cantimpré, Bartholomeus Anglicus, and Vincent of Beauvais (thirteenth century)—all represent one of the most intellectually lively of genres, whose models were found in late antique encyclopedism.

It has been argued that it was precisely this kind of textuality—a "literature of knowledge" exemplified by encyclopedic works, grammatical treatises, technical manuals, herbaria, medical handbooks, etc.—that was key to the preservation and spread of the Latin language all over medieval Europe (cp. Bischoff 1981 and Meier 1994). But these works need to be seen not only as sources for the history of the Latin language. The patient and open-minded reader who approaches texts like the anonymous treatise *De rebus bellicis* (fourth or fifth century), Vegetius's *Epitoma rei militaris* or his veterinary handbook *Mulomedicina* (both fourth century), or Palladius's *Opus de agri cultura*, will be rewarded not only by an appreciation of the formative contribution these works made to medieval culture, but more importantly by the discovery of a sophisticated kind of literary communication. Precisely by continuing certain ancient traditions of the rhetoric typical of the transmission of knowledge, authors within this textual universe not only establish some peculiar traits of the communication of knowledge, but clearly challenge the problematic dialectic between rhetoric and knowledge, between language and practice, which lies at the very core of "technical" discourse (Formisano 2001). Because of the new culture of this age, the discourse of *utilitas*, which has of course a long history within the Greco-Roman tradition, becomes more complex and connects itself to the specific religious and cultural needs of Christianity (Roberts 1989, 130 and 137). Within the late antique reconfiguration of cultural and moral values, *eloquentia*, i.e., the whole possession of technical skills required in order to master knowledge of the spoken word, takes on a new form. Jeffrey Schnapp observes, "Rhetoric was an *institutio* in the Latin sense: at once a method of organizing speech to achieve consensus within the city, an established body of customs and norms (linguistic, literary, and other), and a system for transmitting these customs from one generation to another" (1995, 101).

On the other hand, the Christian refusal of *eloquentia* as the main mark of culture can be seen in connection with the growing practice of silent reading, as attested in a famous and debated passage from Augustine (*Conf.* 6.3.3, see also Taylor in this volume): silent reading marks "the transition from a literary system anchored in the institution of rhetoric to one founded on the 'careful reading' and exegesis of a written artifact" (Schnapp 1995, 104). *The* written artifact is of course the Bible, which is used by readers as an encyclopedic text in which it is possible to find the sum of all human and divine knowledge. As Schnapp again puts it, "The antirhetorical manner in which this knowledge is conveyed constitutes a new model of eloquence which disrupts the varying functional, performative and situational criteria that formerly tied the production and consumption of texts to public performance" (1995, 105). It is within this cultural reconfiguration of rhetoric that we need to observe and appreciate the vast production of "technical" books of various kinds, especially in Latin, during late antiquity. As the fourth book of Augustine's *De doctrina Christiana* shows, language in general has been recast in a new interpretation of knowledge and of the world. Late antiquity offers a particular theater for observing how literature and the production and transmission of knowledge (including knowledge we would describe as highly "technical") have been tightly connected (Formisano, forthcoming).

How intensively "literary" this textuality was—though to many modern eyes it seems very far removed from literature—is shown with exemplarity by the verse insertions found within various prose texts. This is the case for instance with Marcellus Empiricus, who at the end of his pharmacological treatise *De medicina* adds a hexametric poem on medical virtues and the perils of plants, and of Palladius, who, after having treated agricultural knowledge, describes grafting techniques in a *Carmen de insitione* (Book 15), which also invites being read metapoetically as a statement about "grafting" poetry onto prose (Formisano 2005). We also find the encyclopedic mode in poetic texts. Ausonius's fourth-century *Ephemeris* couples descriptions of his everyday life with an impressive number of references to erudite knowledge; this collection of poems has been compared to the *Cathemerinon* of Prudentius (fourth to fifth century), a collection of twelve hymns dedicated to the daily liturgical schedule and the most important Christian festivities (Charlet 1980, 125–26).

The anti-rhetorical bookish mode represents the principal impetus behind the most richly diversified late antique textual production, namely the exegetical tradition, a kind of textuality produced in order to explain and comment on other texts. This tradition was of course deeply rooted in Hellenistic literary culture, but it ends up being *the* cultural mark of late antique literary sensibility. There has been a growing awareness that late antique exegesis needs to be reconsidered not just in itself, but also more broadly as a pervasive cultural and literary dimension. Exegesis offers a lens, for example, through which poetry, philosophy, and religion can be observed and investigated (Otten and Pollmann 2007; Moretti 2003 questions whether it is possible to consider biblical exegesis a literary genre, defining it instead as a "supra-genre"). In this regard exegetical work appears as strictly connected to the approach to texts characteristic of the grammarians, rightly defined as "guardians of language," since their work had the function of keeping alive certain linguistic aspects considered as normative (Kaster 1988 and Irvine 1994; we will return to grammar below, in the section on fragmentation and displacement). A specific type of exegesis, the commentary or *poetarum enarratio*, is a peculiar product of the fourth and fifth centuries (Marrou 1958, still valuable). Within profane literature, Virgil is by far the most studied author, followed by Cicero.

Commentaries on the Virgilian corpus were composed by Aelius Donatus (whose work included the most influential grammatical handbook *Ars maior* and a commentary on Terence's comedies) and by Tiberius Claudius Donatus, author of the *Interpretationes Vergilianae*. The oldest entirely preserved exegetical work on a Latin author are the fifth-century Virgilian commentaries by Servius (with the so-called Servius Danielis, Marshall 1983), who comments in detail on almost every single word, describing Virgil's language and style but also treating poetological and cultural problems not always strictly connected with the Virgilian texts.

Both Virgil's and Cicero's works were also thematized in Macrobius's *Saturnalia*, very probably composed in the first half of the fifth century and placing itself within a number of different literary traditions: the Platonic and Ciceronian dialogue, the encyclopedic treatise, and the commentary. Macrobius is also the author of the *Somnium Scipionis*, a philosophical commentary devoted to the last part of the sixth book of the Ciceronian *De re publica* and heavily influenced by Neoplatonic philosophy. This work was widely read and used as a handbook throughout the Middle Ages.

Finally, the massive presence of Cicero, Virgil, Varro, and many other classical authors pervades the pages of the most imposing theological treatise in Latin, the *De civitate Dei* of Augustine (written between 413 and 426), which is not only the expression of a Christian philosophy of history but a *sui generis* encyclopedia of pagan knowledge. *De civitate Dei* is a book made of other books, and according to its author the world itself is a textual construction: "Augustine's own big book is a city of books, built up from 'their' classics of Roman culture and from 'our' scripture, from his own work of exegesis and reflection on human society and from earlier Christian apologetic and reflection on Rome" (Clark 2007, 133). As for biblical exegesis, Church Fathers such as Jerome, Ambrose, Augustine, and Isidore produced a formidable ocean of textuality (Herzog 1989, 32). Particularly interesting in this regard is the figure of the grammarian and rhetorician Marius Victorinus, who according to Jerome converted to Christianity in very old age. He wrote an *Ars grammatica* as well as commentaries both on classical texts (his commentary on Cicero's *De inventione* enjoyed an immense popularity during the Middle Ages) and on Paul's letters, applying the same classical hermeneutical method to both, despite the differences in style and content. Similarly, Boethius's *Opuscula theologica* applies to Christian theology a method stemming from Aristotelian logic.

Reminding us of the different uses and purposes of commentaries, Karla Pollmann notes that "we cannot confine the notion of 'late antique exegesis' to the narrow intellectual genre of a learned commentary: it begins to pervade every mode of communication" (2009, 259). On the one hand, commentaries and exegetical works had a practical aim, i.e., to help the reader find his or her way through the reading of a "sacred" text (the Bible, Homer, or Virgil) by commenting on grammar and style; on the other hand, they render explicit and exalt an attachment to the written word and an emphasis on literalness. Furthermore, as Glenn Most has observed, a commentary—and I would add, more generally the culture of commentary—might also offer a subversive view on a given text (Most 1999, x), while Kraus 2002 describes the commentary "as a map, or an adventure, in which nature and artifice combine not only to elucidate the text but also to make it new" (p.16).

This quality of late antique textuality has certainly been noted by scholars (e.g., Döpp 1988, 27; Gualandri 1995, 155; Averil Cameron 1991, 19) but still awaits a fuller analysis in its own terms. Both commentary on pagan poetry, such as Servius's or Donatus's, and biblical exegesis practice a grammatical analysis leading to a sort of fragmentation of the original text, which profiles itself as something needing to be taken apart and disassembled in order to be first understood, then recomposed for other purposes (see below). This way of creatively using models was of course present in preceding ages (Hexter 2010, for instance, shows how Virgil read Homer not only directly but also through contemporary interpretations), but this mode literally exploded during late antiquity, especially in connection with tireless investigations of the universe contained in the Bible. Moreover, biblical exegesis invites being seen as a creative source for the formation of a specifically Christian "mythology," which—according to Reinhart Herzog—was not present in the Bible itself but was created by biblical commentary in order to productively assimilate and contrast itself with Greek myth (Herzog 1971). Within this varied textual realm, Jewish exegesis, especially what is now described as rabbinic literature (including the Midrash, i.e., commentary on the Hebrew Bible, and other strands increasingly textualized after the destruction of the second temple in 70 CE), also had a significant influence on Christian exegetical practices.

In any case, it is worth emphasizing that the mass of textuality produced by literary criticism can itself be considered a literary genre. Literary criticism, to cite Genette, has not only a "critical" and "scientific" function—the former related to contemporary texts and the literary tastes of the readership, the latter to the work of scholars within the academic institution—but also a literary function that is valid in itself (Genette 1982, 3). This leads to a consideration that becomes central for a treatment of late antique textuality as a kind of literature which needs interpretive categories that are *sui generis*: "There is no literary object strictly speaking, but only a *literary function*, which can invest or abandon any object of writing in turn" (Genette 1982, 4).

The encyclopedic and exegetic mode is found not only in texts such as treatises, manuals, and commentaries, but in other genres as well. Worth singling out is one that has deservedly received a good deal of scholarly attention over the past decades, whose essence derives from a knowledge of the two most read texts of this period: Virgil and the Bible. From the point of view of classical education, the Bible was a new text, one which needed to be discovered. It offered manifold possibilities for experimentation, and according to the approach to the Bible developed by Northrop Frye and his school, the Fathers represent an important step within the Western hermeneutical tradition, for "Christian discourse was fundamentally intertextual. The writings of the New Testament constantly quote, mirror or allude to the Jewish Scriptures" (Young, Ayres, and Louth 2004, 491). The so-called biblical epic, i.e., a treatment of biblical stories in hexameters (about evenly divided between the Hebrew Bible and New Testament, but epics on the latter were more influential in the Middle Ages), deserves special mention here for two reasons: it heavily influenced medieval literature both in Latin and in the vulgar languages, and it exemplifies the tension with the classical and pagan past which marks late antique literary culture and aesthetics. In this genre exegetical work on classical poetry (principally Virgil, but also Ovid, Lucan, and Statius) meets and converges on the Scriptures as well as on Christian doctrine and aesthetic values. Different styles are combined—the sophistication of Virgilian language and meter with the simplicity of the Bible—but also different narrative patterns and structures. In order to describe the kind of textual mechanism present in the biblical epics and Christian Latin poetry in general, philologists have created the term *Kontrastimitation*, which can be defined as "the taking over of collocations, of words (*iuncturae*), with the aim of making contrary statements" (Thraede 1962, 1039, translated in Green 2006, 59).

Juvencus, the author of the *Evangelia* in four books, probably composed 329–30, generally counts as the first Latin Christian poet to write a substantial work in classical meters (Herzog 1989, 332). Juvencus's pioneering work was continued by many other poets: in addition to Proba, whose cento will be discussed below, these include Paulinus of Nola, who composed paraphrases on both Old and New Testament subjects (see the *Laus Iohannis*); Cyprianus Gallus (probably early fifth century), who wrote a *Heptateuchos*; Sedulius (first half of the fifth century), author of a *Carmen paschale*; Claudius Victor (first half of the fifth century), who narrated the events of Genesis up to the destruction of Sodom and Gomorrah in a biblical poem with the title *Alethia*; Avitus, author of the late fifth-century *De spiritalis historiae gestis*; and Arator (sixth century), who versified the book of Acts in *De actibus apostolorum*. This new genre shows not only a lively cross-fertilization between Christian religion and pagan culture, but also another possibility of conceiving literature itself. And, as is of course true for all Christian literary activity, exegesis both of classical texts and of the Bible plays a central role in shaping the literary tastes and expectations of the readers (cp. Averil Cameron 1998, 672). Although Ernst Robert Curtius notoriously condemned the fusion of biblical content and the classical form as a "genre faux" (1953, 462), biblical epic proved to be one of the most successful genres of Western literature, through the Middle Ages to Tasso, Vida, Milton, Vondel, Blake, Klopstock, Rilke, and Péguy, among others (cp. Stella 2001, 18; on biblical poetry, see also Dinkova-Bruun in this volume).

From another perspective, apparently critical of this Christian poetry, Jerome emphasized the difference between a classical and a Christian writer: the first is an imitator of classical forms, while the second is "an interpreter (*interpres*) of the biblical text itself, one who cleaves to its letter and fastens on its sense" (Vessey 2004, 321). The biblical commentary, i.e., knowledge of the Book in its otherness, represents now "the main burden of the Christian literatus" (ibid.). Jerome provides us an exemplary case of the late Latin culture of the commentary, since he constantly underlines not only the importance of grammar for understanding the biblical text, but also the many possibilities offered by this kind of text to the imagination of a Christian reader. Catherine Chin has well described Jerome's attitude through his letters, which depict the commentary as "the only place in which the imagined Christian landscape appears" (Chin 2007, 102).

III. Panegyric

Late antique culture shows a strong tendency toward preferring the epideictic, both the celebratory and the denunciatory, to telling a story in terms of narrative or even aiming to persuade. Panegyric, understood both as literary genre and as a more broadly defined textual dimension, offers a key to appreciating and understanding important aspects of late antique textuality that seem far removed from the tastes and expectations of a modern readership. Although the panegyric genre has its own "archaeology" within Greco-Roman literature, it represents an especially characteristic product of the culture of late antiquity (McCormack 1976).

The technique of praising someone, especially the *princeps*, had already been subject to the scrutiny of Greek theorists and rhetorical masters who systematized rules and types of praise (see Menander 1981 and Russell 1998), and panegyrics were composed in both prose and verse. It would be hard to overemphasize the role played by textuality in the construction of imperial power. The figure of the emperor pervades and shapes many texts and genres; he is the protagonist not only in those speeches in which his omnipotence is publicly acknowledged, i.e., panegyric, but also in historical texts, biographies, letters, poetry, and technical treatises.

The corpus of the *Panegyrici latini* contains twelve speeches written between the ages of Trajan and Theodosius I that were probably gathered in Gaul at the end of the fourth century in order to offer a canonical corpus, or even a handbook intended to instruct young rhetoricians on how to deliver a speech in honor of the emperor or an important person. The speeches were delivered on a variety of occasions such as the birthday or the marriage of an emperor, the anniversary of the foundation of Rome, or the celebration of a victory. The language is highly formal and literary, quoting and alluding to a large repertory of classical texts, but also very inventive and baroque, full of imaginative descriptions of events and persons. Particularly interesting features are the use of mythology in order to describe historical events such as the victories of the honorand, the comparison of the emperor with both good and bad predecessors and with heroes, and the panegyrists' claim on sincerity.

A passage from Pacatus's Panegyric for Theodosius shows with exemplarity the sensationalism coupled with a vertiginous mixture of reality and fictionality that is typical in this genre:

Ego vero, si caeleste studium pro dignitate causarum aestimandum sit, iure contenderim equites tuos Pegasis, talaribus pedites vectos ac suspensos fuisse. Neque enim quia se divina mortalibus dedignantur fateri, idcirco quae visa non fuerint dubitabimus facta, cum facta videamus quae dubitaverimus esse facienda. (*Pan.* 2.39.5)

[If the favor of the gods is to be measured by the worthiness of the cause, I for one would contend with good reason that your cavalry were carried along, born aloft, by Pegasuses, your infantry on winged feet. Simply because divine things disdain to show themselves to mortals, we shall not on that account doubt that things that were not seen were done, since we see things done which we would have doubted could have been done.] (*Panegyrici latini* 1994, 507)

Much that can offend the tastes of a modern readership—adulation, falsification of history, verbosity—are at the core of this kind of speech, yet unless we appreciate the way panegyric functions and what it represents, we cannot truly understand late antique literary taste.

An intriguing aspect of the speeches contained in the corpus of the *Panegyrici latini*, but which has a broader relevance to late antique literature, is that in many cases the text was never actually delivered in front of the imperial court but remained a written record. Self-fashioning, joined with the desire for an (absent) interlocutor, is the most significant drive of the "panegyric dimension" just described, present also in verse encomia as well as in a broad spectrum of texts of different kind. One of the most representative authors of panegyric poetry is Claudian, born in Alexandria in 370 and often described as the "last classical poet" (Fo 1982, 19–20). In 395 he gave a speech in Rome in honor of the consuls Olibrius and Probinus, with which he acquired popularity as a panegyrist. Other encomia he authored include the *Laus Stilichonis* and the *Laus Serenae*. The high quality of his art as poet is found not only in his metrical perfection but also in the relationship he was able to develop between traditional epic and panegyric, which marks his work in a very particular way.

The panegyric mode also pervades the specifically Christian genres, and encomium informs an important part of Christian literary production of this period, such as martyr acts, hagiography, and the new Christian genre of "universal" or ecclesiastical history. As Michael Roberts reminds us, "Christian poetry as a whole could be conceived of as *Laudes Domini*, 'praises of the Lord'" (2007, 162). And as Averil Cameron has emphasized, the educational system based on grammar and rhetoric was the same for the followers of the new religion, so that secular oratory deeply influenced all kinds of Christian public writing, such as encomia, hymns, and hagiography, the last representing the most interesting case of interaction between pagan and Christian rhetoric (1998, 675). Not only does there seem to have been an expectation among the readerships of panegyric for details about the "private" lives of the emperors (Rees 1998), but more generally, biography experienced a boom during late antiquity. As Ammianus Marcellinus (28.4.14) suggested, readers were eager to read sensationalistic biographies (Averil Cameron 1998, 685), and sensationalism was a quality not only of panegyric but of hagiography in all its forms, from martyr acts to the lives of the saints, such as the *Vitae eremitarum* by Jerome or the *Vita Martini* by Sulpicius Severus, put into hexameters by Venantius Fortunatus.

Biography also informs historiographical discourse, of course, and the boundaries between the genres are fluid. Biographical and historiographical genres often incorporate a strong panegyric dimension as well. Here we might recall the set of emperors' biographies contained in the *Historia Augusta* (perhaps end of the fourth century) as well as the *Liber prodigiorum* by Julius Obsequens (also fourth century), containing sensational and prodigious events. The central figure of Ammianus Marcellinus's *Res gestae* is the emperor Julian; Ammianus's writing is characterized by a strong tendency towards (auto-)biographical aspects, and Julian's virtues are depicted much as Christian authors like Jerome and Sulpicius Severus represent the saints in their *Lives* (cp. Sabbah 2003, 63). The historical epitomes are also intended to please the emperor: Eutropius and Festus address and dedicate their *breviaria* of the history of Rome to Valens (Momigliano 1963). (Autobiography is discussed at greater length by Zak in this volume.)

Addresses to the emperor also inform texts that can be called "administrative acts," such as the *Relationes* by Symmachus, the most famous being the *Relatio III de ara Victoriae* (384), in which the orator asks that the altar of Victory, representing the pagan tradition of the empire, not be removed from the curia. The speech is of course primarily a work of persuasion, but the panegyric mode is one of its key elements. Similarly, some "technical" authors address the emperor in support of the realization of their ideas and proposals (Formisano 2003): this is the case with Vegetius's *Epitoma rei militaris*, which heavily influenced medieval culture (Richardot 1997), and the anonymous treatise *De rebus bellicis*, which was also widely read from the late Middle Ages through Voltaire (*De rebus bellicis* 1989).

Places too can be subjects of praise. Rutilius Namatianus's *De reditu suo*, narrating a journey back to his native Gaul, sings the beauty of the city in the so-called "Hymn to Rome" (cp. Rutilius Namatianus 2007, 51–53), and Ausonius's *Mosella* describes a journey along that river, not without some political panegyric (cp. Roberts 1984 and 2009, 73–75). Self-promotion, too, can be seen as employing the panegyric mode: networking and advertising are important characteristics of the diverse epistolary corpora of Jerome, Symmachus, Ambrose, Sidonius Apollinaris, and Ennodius (Ebbeler 2009 and Shanzer 2009, 936).

IV. Fragmentation, Dislocation, Replacement

The emphasis on the demonstrative and the epideictic, on the figural qualities of textuality and ecphrasis, on "showing and telling" (Averil Cameron 1991), can be related to another characteristic tendency of late antique literature: the disintegrating and fragmenting of form. Tendencies toward the abandonment of the chronological order traditionally constitutive of narrative and even of a logical order (a *pendant* to the kind of "irrationality" ostensibly practiced by Christian authors; Averil Cameron 1991, 67) accompany, favor, and nurture the fragmentation of literary discourse. Coupled with this aspect is the highly figural and visual quality of virtually every late antique text, profane and religious, pagan as well as Christian. Michael Roberts's book on the "jeweled style" systematically draws attention to the following set of tendencies within late Latin poetry, many of which are found in prose genres as well: to fragment literary discourse into short units of composition; to recur to variation and figures of parallelism; to abandon attention to the symmetry of the overall structure in favor of careful composition of smaller units, so that "the individual word, its choice and position, receives greater emphasis than would be the case in other styles of composition" (1989, 44).

Late antique textuality shows a strong tendency to conceive composition in visual terms: Roberts analyzes a wide range of texts in which words are presented as flowers, gems, and jewels. As Roberts observes:

> Poetry of the period is often criticized as episodic, but what is involved is no more than the application of the principle of *variatio* to large units of composition ("episodes"). Late antiquity preferred juxtaposition and contrast to logical interrelationship; contiguity no longer required continuity. The impression of an organic whole, the sense of proportion, is lost, but it is compensated for by the elaboration of the individual episode. Late antique poetry has its own unity, but it is conceptual and transcends the immediate historical content of narrative. (1989, 56–57)

Roberts compares visual aspects of textuality to the mosaic technique of composition—something of a refrain in previous scholarship, but one that needed discussion in greater detail, and more comparison of artifacts and texts. Visual aspects are particularly characteristic of early Christian discourse, which through images aimed to present a higher truth (Averil Cameron 1991, 57).

This attention to detail and short units can easily be seen as a consequence of a certain kind of study of classical texts. As we have already seen, commentary and exegesis of all kinds are not only significant literary products of this period in their own terms, but they also provide a different way of reading and hence writing texts. As Martin Irvine as shown in detail, grammar and the culture practiced by grammarians pervaded late antique and medieval culture (Irvine 1994). Grammar also influenced the production of texts and shaped a new literary sensibility, the most important surface feature of which is precisely a strong dependence on traditional texts such as Virgil, Cicero, and other classical authors, along with a ludic dimension. Ausonius, for instance, is an author who is very aware of his own identity as *litteratus* and likes to display his *savoir-faire* in bravura pieces which heavily depend on an attention to short units. In the *Technopaegnion*, lines start or finish only with monosyllabic words, and the *Griphus ternarii numeri* is a poem dedicated exclusively to the number three. This kind of experiment might not appear so strange to modern readers, accustomed to literary currents such as the French *Oulipo* and such texts as Georges Perec's lipogrammatic novel *La Disparition* (translated into English as *Void*), written entirely without the letter "e," the most commonly used vowel in French. (Roughly 800 years after Ausonius, Peter of Riga would employ the same device; see Dinkova-Bruun elsewhere in this volume.)

In late antiquity, Virgil and the Bible were texts that could now be disassembled and recomposed into new unities, and the work of recomposition or *bricolage* (to use a metaphor created by Claude Lévi-Strauss) does not necessarily follow a logical path, but can also be associative and evocative, especially in poetry (Gualandri 1995, 172). The most prominent example of this way of conceiving the production of a literary text is no doubt the *cento*, a phenomenon peculiar to late antiquity. A *cento* ("patchwork") is a poem consisting entirely of rearranged verse units stemming from another text, usually Homer in Greek and Virgil in Latin. Within Latin literature a wide range of Virgilian centos have come down to us, with both secular (especially mythological) and Christian content. In the first category are Ausonius's *Cento nuptialis*, Luxurius's *Epithalamium Fridi* (both of them belonging to the genre of epithalamium as well; see Hortsmann 2004) and the anonymous *De alea* and *Narcissus* (McGill 2005, with the most complete list). Among Christian centos, the one composed by Faltonia Betitia Proba bearing the title *Cento Virgilianus de laudibus Christi* has received a good deal of attention (Proba 1981; Pollmann 2004; McGill 2007; Harich-Schwarzbauer 2009).

The major challenge in reading the cento is of an aesthetic nature: this kind of text has long been seen as a derivative product of low or even nonexistent poetic quality. But it is possible to read and enjoy this kind of text by abandoning classicist prejudices, understanding the cento within its specific late antique literary culture context, and appreciating that its creativity lies in its ingenuity. (For linkages of cento technique with other poetic experiences, such as the various modern European avant-gardes, which systematically recurred to textual montage in order to assert and deconstruct their relation to the literary tradition, see Formisano and Sogno 2010.) The cento in fact represents an extremely sophisticated form of textual manipulation, since on the one hand it is the result of a process of recomposition of a given text, i.e., the author is confronted with a relatively limited number of options stemming from another text (e.g., Virgil), while on the other hand a radical subversion of meaning is enacted. Ausonius for instance gives a strongly erotic and at times even obscene reading of the "sacred" Virgilian hypotext, and Proba consciously Christianizes *the* classical pagan text, transforming the Latin *vates* into a Christian prophet. More generally, fragmentation seems on the one hand to challenge our ways of understanding and reading ancient literature, and it may represent the major factor in the (often negative) evaluation of any texts which do not fully respond to a drive for unity (see Sharrock 2000 on "intratextuality"); on the other hand, fragmentation is necessary from the point of view of readers and commentators (see Shuttleworth Kraus 2002, 10 ff.).

This eminently textual approach to the classical tradition is not only illustrated by the extreme case of the cento but also characterizes a strand of late antique textuality represented by epitomes, breviaria, and florilegia of all sorts

(Herzog 1989, 32, who also includes chronicles, scholia, and commentaries). I have already mentioned historical compendia such as the *breviaria* by Eutropius and Festus, the *Epitome de Caesaribus*, and epitomes that contain knowledge within a specific field, such as Vegetius's *Epitoma rei militaris* and Marcellus's *De medicina*. Vegetius's *Epitoma* in particular was one of the most widely read Latin texts during the Middle Ages, undergoing various kinds of rewriting in the form of florilegia, quotations, and eventually translations. In this way the *Epitoma* was deeply influential not only within the specific tradition of military literature, but also within the encyclopedic tradition from Hrabanus Maurus to Vincent of Beauvais. Even works of moral philosophy and theology such as Thomas Aquinas's *Summa theologiae* show the influence of Vegetius (Richardot 1997, 93–99 and passim). In fact, I would argue that the *Epitoma rei militaris* is more interesting for literary than for technical reasons. It aims to reintroduce to the contemporary system the ancient rules applied in Rome during the first stage of empire; this project was to be implemented through writing, which thus acquires a key role in the process of transmitting the knowledge of war. Even the title *Epitoma rei militaris*, which might best be translated into modern languages as "The Roman art of war" or "The ancient art of war" (*pace* Milner in Vegetius 1996), is a reminder of the close relationship the author wishes to have with the past. Vegetius's logic is circular: he begins from writing, substantiates actions with exempla that also derive from a world of books, only to return inexorably to writing. His work inherits, justifies, and sets up a system of profound interaction between "literary" past and present action, which becomes the axiom of the art of war for the future. In Vegetius's *Epitoma* the reader encounters a language that establishes a continuity between the written word and action that will never cease to influence the way we think about war in the West. This is the reason why Vegetius requires literary attention; he establishes a literary genre with its own style, structure, and argumentative technique that was to be continually used throughout the Middle Ages and the Renaissance (see Wisman 1986 and Vegetius 2003).

This approach to textuality and tradition is of course not unique to Vegetius. In the prologue to his *Saturnalia*, Macrobius describes his mode of writing, which consists precisely of creating an orderly and organic corpus from various sources (*Sat.* 1, *praef.* 3):

> nec indigeste tamquam in acervum congessimus digna memoratu; sed variarum rerum disparilitas, auctoribus diversa, confusa temporibus, ita in quoddam digesta corpus est, ut quae indistincte atque promiscue ad subsidium memoriae adnotaveramus, in ordinem instar membrorum cohaerentia convenirent.

> Nor have I haphazardly deployed these items that are worth remembering, as though in a heap: I have organized the diverse subjects, drawn from a range of authors and a mix of periods, as though in a body, so that the things I initially noted down all a jumble, as an aide mémoire, might come together in a coherent, organic whole. (Macrobius 2011, 5)

In his pharmacological text *De medicamentis* (*praef.* 1) Marcellus Empiricus uses a similar argument, recurring to a metaphor especially appropriate to his subject, that of Asclepius recomposing Hippolytus's/Virbius's body into a new and different one (cp. Formisano 2001, 64–66):

> libellum hunc de empiricis quanta potui sollertia diligentiaque conscripsi, remediorum physicorum sive rationabilium confectionibus et adnotationibus fartum undeunde collectis. Nam si quid umquam congruum sanitati curationique hominum vel ab aliis comperi vel ipse usu adprobavi vel legendo cognovi, id sparsum inconditumque collegi et in unum corpus quasi disiecta et lacera Asclepius [aut] Virbii membra composui.

> [I have composed this book on practical remedies with as much care and diligence as possible, having filled it with the means of preparing cures both natural and man-made, along with instructions for their use, gathered from many different sources. If I have ever picked up from others, verified by my own experience, or learned by reading anything that is suited to human health and therapy, I have taken what was scattered and hidden from sight, gathered it together and rearranged it into a single body, like Asclepius with the scattered and torn limbs of Virbius.]

The *De medicamentis* is not only a compendium of medical knowledge, but also an epitome of different literary genres: the author includes epistles from other authors, adding at the end of the treatise a 78-line hexametric poem that claims for itself the double function of rendering sweet the reading of the medical material and at the same time of bringing the laboriousness of a long work to an end with a more personal and ludic touch (cp. *De medicamentis*, pr. 6–7). We might also compare the practice of grammarians, whose work consisted precisely of dismantling a text—indeed, the most prestigious texts of the Latin literary tradition—and analyzing them by decontextualizing gobbets from their original context. Catherine Chin has well shown how the techniques applied by grammarians in their work of extracting linguistic knowledge from texts, of dislocating and placing it in a new constellation, offered Augustine a method for the creation of ideological representations of "paganism" and "Christianity" in the *De doctrina Christiana* (cf. 2.40.60, where Augustine compares the gold of the Egyptians, stolen by the Jewish people for a better use [Ex 3:21–22], to the use of the liberal arts practiced by Christians). "Augustine," comments Chin, "like his grammarian contemporaries, is interested in changing the signification of previously existing signs by 'literally' removing them from their symbolic signifying contexts" (Chin 2008, 90).

The mechanisms of recollecting past textual traditions, fragmenting and dislocating their content, and giving them a new form—like Hippolytus's body after the mythical *sparagmós*—is of course very familiar to our postmodern tradition, which has frequently been compared to late antique culture. Tellingly, both have been described as periods of "decadence" (cp. Herzog 1987 for an essay with the thought-provoking title "Wir leben in der Spätantike" [We live in late antiquity]). Precisely this image, however, seems to characterize the textual culture of a very different period of Western culture that has only very rarely been put in relation to late antiquity. Angelo Poliziano, considered one of the fathers of humanistic philology, recurs in the *Centuria secunda* of his work *Miscellanea* to the image of the lacerated body of Hippolytus and the restoring work of Asclepius, comparing it with his own philological work of restoring the text of Cicero's *De natura deorum*:

> Ciceronis liber secundus de deorum natura non minus lacer in omnibus novis, vetustis etiam exemplaribus reperitur quam olim fuerit Hippolytus turbatis distractus equis; cuius deinde avulsa passim membra, sicuti fabulae ferunt, Aesculapius ille collegit, reposuit, vitae reddidit; qui tamen deinde fulmine ictus ob invidiam deorum narratur. Me vero quaenam deterrebit invidia, quod fulmen, quominus restituere ipsum sibi coner Romanae vel linguae vel philosophiae parentem, nescio equidem a quo rursus Antonio truncatum capite et manibus? (Poliziano 1978, 3)

> [The second book of Cicero's *De deorum natura* is no less mangled in all manuscript copies, both old and new, than Hippolytus once was, torn apart by the frenzied horses. As the stories have it, Asclepius gathered up all the torn-apart pieces of his body, put them back together, and restored them to life; but it is said that Asclepius was subsequently struck by lightning because of the gods' ill-will. As for me, though: what ill-will, what lightning-bolt will keep me from attempting to restore to himself the father of the Latin language and Latin philosophy after some other Antonius has once again cut off his head and hands?] (my translation)

It is not only very tempting but perhaps even historically correct to place Poliziano's "hymn to philology and poetry" (Branca 1983, 239) in continuity with late Latin textuality. The Middle Ages took up the Latin "classics" not only through specific late antique texts but also, and more relevantly, through the optic of late antiquity, whose intellectual style and textual production represent one of the most fascinating and extreme experiences in the realm of Western literature.

SUGGESTIONS FOR FURTHER READING

For an outline of late Latin literary production, see Herzog (1989) and more recently Shanzer (2009). Roberts (2007) offers an overview of late Latin poetry; see also Scourfield (2007). Important steps towards the definition of a specifically late antique literature are also taken by the collections contained in Fuhrmann (1977) and *Philologus* 132:1 (1988), a number of this journal devoted entirely to late antique literature. For biblical epic, see Herzog (1975), Kartschoke (1975), Roberts (1985), Nazzaro (2001), Stella (2001), and the more recent Green (2006). For the relationship between exegesis and biblical poetry in particular, see Nodes (1993) and the critical review in Consolino (2005). On medieval encyclopedism, see the collective volumes edited by Picone (1994) (including LeGoff's important article), Binkley (1997), and Meier (2002). On panegyric, see the collection of papers edited by Whitby (1998); especially relevant for the corpus of the *Panegyrici latini* is Rees (2002). Modern scholarship on Claudian starts with Alan Cameron (1970); see also Cameron's revision of his own work in Alan Cameron (2000) along with Ehlers, Felgentreu, and Wheeler (2004). The book to read on the interactions between pagans and Christians within a common "rhetoric of empire" is Averil Cameron (1991). For Ammianus, see Matthews (1989), and for late antique historiography in general, see the collective volume edited by Marasco (2003).

BIBLIOGRAPHY

Primary sources

Augustine of Hippo. 2002. *Augustinus. Opera/Werke*. Vol. 11: *De magistro—Der Lehrer*, edited and translated by Therese Fuhrer. Paderborn: Schöningh Verlag.
Cassiodorus. 2004. *Cassiodorus: "Institutions of Divine and Secular Learning" and "On the Soul,"* translated by James W. Halporn and introduced by Mark Vessey. Translated Texts for Historians 42. Liverpool: Liverpool University Press.
De rebus bellicis. 1989. *Le cose della guerra*, edited and translated by Andrea Giardina. Scrittori greci e latini. Milan: A. Mondadori.
Isidore of Seville. 2006. *The Etymologies of Isidore of Seville*, translated by Stephen A. Barney et al. Cambridge: Cambridge University Press.
Macrobius. 2011. *Saturnalia*, edited and translated by Robert Kaster. Loeb Classical Library. Cambridge and London: Harvard University Press.
Menander. 1981. *Menander Rhetor*, edited and translated by Donald A. Russell and Nigel G. Wilson. Oxford: Oxford University Press.
Panegyrici latini. 1994. *In Praise of Later Roman Emperors: The Panegyrici Latini*, edited and translated by Charles E. V. Nixon and Barbara S. Rodgers. Transformation of the Classical Heritage 13. Berkeley, CA: University of California Press.
Poliziano, Angelo. 1978. *Miscellaneorum centuria secunda*, edited by Vittore Branca and Manlio Pastore Stocchi. Florence: L. S. Olschki.
Proba, Faltonia Betitia. 1981. *The Golden Bough, the Oaken Cross: The Virgilian Cento of Faltonia Betitia Proba*, edited by Elizabeth A. Clark and Diane F. Hatch. American Academy of Religion. Texts and Translations Series 5. Chico, CA: Scholars Press.
Rutilius Namatianus. 2007. *Rutilius Namatianus: Sur son retour*, edited and translated by Etienne Wolff. Paris: Collection des Universités de France.
Vegetius. 1996. *Epitome of Military Science*, translated by N. P. Milner. Translated Texts for Historians 16. Liverpool: Liverpool University Press.
———. 2003. *L'Arte della guerra romana*, translated by Marco Formisano. Milan: Rizzoli.
Vitruvius. 1997. *De architectura*, edited by Pierre Gros, translated by Antonio Corso und Elisa Romano. Turin: Einaudi.

Secondary sources

Beagon, Mary. 1992. *Roman Nature: The Thought of Pliny the Elder*. Oxford Classical Monographs. Oxford: Clarendon Press.

Bischoff, Bernhard. 1981. "Die Überlieferung der technischen Literatur." In *Mittelalterliche Studien. Ausgewählte Aufsätze zur Schriftkunde und Literaturgeschichte*, 3: 277–97. Stuttgart: A. Hiersemann.

Bowersock, Glen W. 2004. "Centrifugal Force in Late Antique Historiography." In *The Past Before Us. The Challenge of Historiographies of Late Antiquity*, edited by Carole Straw and Richard Lim, 19–24. Bibliothèque de l'antiquité tardive 6. Smith College Studies in History 54. Turnhout: Brepols.

Bowersock, Glen W., Peter Brown, and Oleg Grabar, eds. 1999. *Late Antiquity: A Guide to the Postclassical World*. Harvard University Press Reference Library. Cambridge, MA: Belknap Press of Harvard University Press.

Branca, Vittore. 1983. *Poliziano e l'umanesimo della parola*. Saggi 655. Turin: G. Einaudi.

Brown, Peter. 2004. "Conversion and Christianization in *Late Antiquity*: The Case of Augustine." In *The Past Before Us: The Challenge of Historiographies of Late Antiquity*, edited by Carole Straw and Richard Lim, 103–17. Bibliothèque de l'antiquité tardive 6. Smith College Studies in History 54. Turnhout: Brepols.

Cameron, Alan. 1970. *Claudian. Poetry and Propaganda at the Court of Honorius*. Oxford: Clarendon Press.

———. 2000. "Claudian Revisited." In *Letteratura e propaganda nell'occidente latino da Augusto ai regni romanobarbarici: atti del Convegno internazionale, Arcavacata di Rende, 25–26 maggio 1998*, edited by Franca Ela Consolino, 127–44. Saggi di storia antica 15. Rome: L'Erma di Bretschneider.

Cameron, Averil. 1991. *Christianity and the Rhetoric of Empire: The Development of Christian Discourse*. Sather Classical Lectures 55. Berkeley, CA: University of California Press.

———. 1998. "Education and Literary Culture." In *The Cambridge Ancient History*. Vol. 13: *Late Empire, A.D. 337—425*, edited by Averil Cameron and Peter Garnsey, 665–707. Cambridge: Cambridge University Press.

———. 2002. "The 'long' Late Antiquity. A Late Twentieth-Century Model." In *Classics in Progress. Essays on Ancient Greece and Rome*, edited by Timothy P. Wiseman, 165–92. Oxford, New York: Oxford University Press.

Carrié, Jean-Michel and Aline Rousselle. 1999. *L'Empire romain en mutation. Des Sévères à Constantin. 192–337*. Nouvelle histoire de l'antiquité 10. Paris: Éditions du Seuil.

Charlet, Jean-Louis. 1980. *L'influence d'Ausone sur la poésie de Prudence*. Publications de l'Université de Provence. Aix-en-Provence, Paris: H. Champion.

Chin, Catherine M. 2007. "Through the Looking Glass Darkly: Jerome Inside the Book." In *The Early Christian Book*, edited by William E. Klingshirn and Linda Safran, 101–16. Catholic University of America Studies in Early Christianity. Washington, DC: Catholic University or America Press.

———. 2008. *Grammar and Christianity in the Late Roman World*. Divinations. Philadelphia: University of Pennsylvania Press.

Clark, Gillian. 2007. "City of Books: Augustine and the World as Text." In *The Early Christian Book*, edited by William E. Klingshirn and Linda Safran, 117–38. Catholic University of America Studies in Early Christianity. Washington, DC: Catholic University of America Press.

Clark, Hilary. 1990. *The Fictional Encyclopaedia: Joyce, Pound, Sollers*. Garland Studies in Comparative Literature. New York: Garland Publishing.

Compagnon, Antoine. 2004. *Literature, Theory, and Common Sense*, translated by Carol Cosman. New French Thought. Princeton, NJ: Princeton University Press.

Consolino, Franca Ela. 2005. "Il senso del passato: generi letterari e rapporti con la tradizione nella 'parafrasi biblica' latina." In *Nuovo e antico nella cultura greco-latina di IV–VI secolo*, edited by Isabella Gualandri, Fabrizio Conca, and Raffaele Passarella, 447–526. Quaderni di Acme 73. Milan: Università di Milano.

Conte, Gian Biagio.1994. *Genres and Readers: Lucretius, Love Elegy, Pliny's Encyclopedia*, translated by Glenn W. Most. Baltimore: Johns Hopkins University Press.

Curtius, Ernst Robert. 1953. *European Literature and the Latin Middle Ages*, translated by Willard Trask. Bollingen Series 36. Princeton, NJ: Princeton University Press.

Doody, Aude. 2010. *Pliny's Encyclopedia: The Reception of the Natural History*. Cambridge, New York: Cambridge University Press.

Döpp, Siegmar. 1988. "Die Blütezeit lateinischer Literatur in der Spätantike (350–430 n. Chr.). Charakteristika einer Epoche." *Philologus* 132: 19–52.

Ebbeler, Jennifer V. 2009. "Tradition, Innovation, and Epistolary Mores." In *A Companion to Late Antiquity*, edited by Philip Rousseau, 270–84. Blackwell Companions to the Ancient World. Ancient History. Chichester, Malden, MA: Wiley-Blackwell.

Ehlers, Widu-Wolfgang, Fritz Felgentreu, and Stephen M. Wheeler, eds. 2004. *Aetas Claudianea: Eine Tagung an der Freien Universität Berlin vom 28. bis 30. Juni 2002*. Munich, Leipzig: Saur.

Fo, Alessandro. 1982. *Studi sulla tecnica poetica di Claudiano*. Studi e ricerche dei "Quaderni Catanesi" 4. Catania: C. Tringale.

Formisano, Marco. 2001. *Tecnica e scrittura. Le letterature tecnico-scientifiche nello spazio letterario tardolatino*. Ricerche. Lettere classiche 95. Rome: Carocci.

———. 2003. "*Auctor, utilitas, princeps. L'Epitoma rei militaris e il De rebus bellicis* tra tecnica e letteratura." Voces (Salamanca) 14: 155–64.

———. 2005. "Veredelte Bäume und kultivierte Texte. Lehrgedichte in technischen Prosawerken der Spätantike." In *Wissensvermittlung in dichterischer Gestalt*, edited by Marietta Horster and Christiane Reitz, 295–315. Palingenesia 85. Stuttgart: Franz Steiner.

———. 2008. "*Speculum principis, speculum oratoris*. Alcune considerazioni sui *Panegyrici Latini* come genere letterario." In *Amicitiae templa serena. Studi in onore di Giuseppe Aricò*, edited by Luigi Castagna and Chiara Riboldi, 581–99. Letteratura greca e latina. Milan: V&P.

———. 2013. "Late Latin Encyclopaedism: Towards a New Paradigm of Practical Knowledge." In *Encyclopaedism from Antiquity to the Renaissance*, edited by J. König and G. Woolf, 197–215. Cambridge: Cambridge University Press.

Formisano, Marco and Sogno, Christiana. 2010. "*Petite Poésie Portable*. The Cento in its Late Antique Context." In *Condensed Texts—Condensing Texts*, edited by Marietta Horster and Christiane Reitz, 375–92. Stuttgart: Franz Steiner Verlag.

Foucault, Michel. 1977. "Fantasia of the Library." In *Language, Counter-Memory, Practice: Selected Essays and Interviews*, translated by Donald F. Bouchard and Sherry Simon, 87–109. Ithaca, NY: Cornell University Press.

Gardini, Nicola. 2010. *Rinascimento*. Piccola biblioteca Einaudi. Mappe 18. Torino: Einaudi.

Geertman, Herman and de Jong, Jan J., eds. 1989. *Munus Non Ingratum. Proceedings of the International Symposium on Vitruvius' De Architectura and the Hellenistic and Republican Architecture*. Bulletin Antieke Beschaving. Supplement 2. Leiden: Stichting Bulletin Antieke Beschaving.

Genette, Gérard. 1982. *Figures of Literary Discourse*, translated by Alan Sheridan. European Perspectives. New York: Columbia University Press.

Giardina, Andrea. 1999. "Esplosione di Tardoantico." *Studi Storici* 40: 157–80.

Goldhill, Simon, ed. 2008. *The End of Dialogue in Antiquity*. Cambridge: Cambridge University Press.

Green, Roger P. H. 2006. *Latin Epics of the New Testament: Juvencus, Sedulius, Arator*. Oxford: Oxford University Press.

Gualandri, Isabella. 1995. "Prassi esegetica e stile letterario: alcuni problemi." In *Esegesi, parafrasi e compilazione in età tardoantica: atti del terzo*, edited by Claudio Moreschini, 147–74. Collectanea 9. Naples: D'Auria.

Harich-Schwarzbauer, Henriette 2009. "Von Aeneas zu Camilla. Intertextualität im Vergilcento der Faltonia Betitia Proba." In *Jeux de voix. Enonciation, intertextualité et intentionnalité dans la littérature antique*, edited by Danielle van Mal-Maeder, Alexandre Burnier, and Loreto Nuñez, 331–46. Université de Lausanne. Institut d'archéologie et des sciences de l'antiquité. Echo 8. Bern, New York: Peter Lang.

Heather, Peter J. 2005. *The Fall of the Roman Empire*. London: Macmillan.

Henderson, John. 2007. *The Medieval World of Isidore of Seville. Truth from Words*. Cambridge, New York: Cambridge University Press.

Herzog, Reinhart. 1971. "Metapher—Exegese—Mythos. Interpretationen zur Entstehung eines biblischen Mythos in der Literatur der Spätantike." In *Terror und Spiel. Probleme der Mythenrezeption*, edited by Manfred Fuhrmann, 157–86. Poetik und Hermeneutik 4. Munich: W. Fink.

——. 1975. *Die Bibelepik der lateinischen Spätantike: Formgeschichte einer erbaulichen Gattung*. Theorie und Geschichte der Literatur und der schönen Künste 37. Munich: Fink.

——. 1977. "Probleme der heidnisch-christlichen Gattungskontinuität am Beispiel des Paulinus von Nola." In *Christianisme et formes litteraires de l'antiquité tardive en occident*, edited by Manfred Fuhrmann, 373–411. Entretiens sur l'antiquité classique 23. Geneva: Fondation Hardt.

——. 1987. *"Wir leben in der Spätantike". Eine Zeiterfahrung und ihre Impulse für die Forschung*. Thyssen-Vorträge 4. Bamberg: Buchner.

Herzog, Reinhart and Peter L. Schmidt. 1989. *Handbuch der lateinischen Literatur der Antike*. Vol. 5: *Restauration und Erneuerung: die lateinische Literatur von 284 bis 374 n. Chr.* Handbuch der Altertumswissenschaften 8.5. Munich: C. H. Beck.

Hexter, Ralph J. 2010. "On First Looking Into Vergil's Homer," in *A Companion to Vergil's Aeneid and its Tradition*, edited by Joseph Farrell and Michael Putnam, 26–36. Blackwell Companions to the Ancient World. Literature and Culture. Oxford: Blackwell.

Hinds, Stephen. 2005. "Defamiliarizing Latin Literature. From Petrarch to Pulp Fiction." *Transactions of the American Philological Association* 135: 49–81.

Horstmann, Sabine, 2004. *Das Epithalamium in der lateinischen Literatur der Spätantike*. Beiträge zur Altertumskunde 197. Munich: Saur.

Irvine, Martin. 1994. *The Making of Textual Culture: 'Grammatica' and Literary Theory, 350—1100*. Cambridge Studies in Medieval Literature 19. Cambridge, New York: Cambridge University Press.

Kartschoke, Dieter. 1975. *Bibeldichtung: Studien zur Geschichte der epischen Bibelparaphrase von Juvencus bis Otfrid von Weißenburg*. Munich: Fink.

Kaster, Robert A. 1988. *Guardians of Language: The Grammarian and Society in Late Antiquity*. The Transformation of the Classical Heritage 11. Berkeley, CA: University of California Press.

Leonardi, Claudio. 2002. *Letteratura latina medievale (secoli VI–XV): un manuale*. Millennio medievale 31. Società internazionale per lo studio del Medioevo latino. Strumenti 2. Florence: SISMEL, Edizioni del Galluzzo.

Marcone, Arnaldo. 2008. "A Long Late Antiquity? Considerations of a Controversial Periodization." *Journal of Late Antiquity* 1: 4–19.

Marrou, Henri I. 1958. *Saint Augustin et la fin de la culture antique*. Bibliothèque des écoles françaises d'Athènes et de Rome 145. Paris: E. de Boccard.

Marshall, Peter K., 1983. "Servius." In *Texts and Transmission. A Survey of the Latin classics* edited by Leighton D. Reynolds, 385-388. Oxford: Clarendon Press.

Martin, Dale B. and Patricia Cox Miller, eds. 2005. *The Cultural Turn in Late Ancient Studies: Gender, Asceticism, and Historiography*. London, Durham, NC: Duke University Press.

McCormack, Sabine. 1975. "Latin Prose Panegyric." In *Empire and Aftermath: Silver Latin II*, edited by Thomas A. Dorey, 143–205. London, Boston: Routledge & K. Paul.

———. 1981. *Art and Ceremony in Late Antiquity*. Transformation of the Classical Heritage 1. Berkeley, CA: University of California Press.

McGill, Scott. 2005. *Virgil Recomposed: The Mythological and Secular Virgilian Centos in Antiquity*. American Classical Studies 48. Oxford, New York: Oxford University Press.

———. 2007. "Virgil, Christianity, and the *Cento Probae*." In *Texts and Culture in Late Antiquity: Inheritance, Authority, and Change*, edited by J. H. D. Scourfield, 173–94. Swansea: Classical Press of Wales.

Meier, Christel. 1994. "*Pascua, rura, duces*. Verschriftungsmodi der *Artes mechanicae* in Lehrdichtung und Fachprosa der römischen Kaiserzeit." *Frühmittelalterliche Studien* 28: 1–50.

Momigliano, Arnaldo, ed. 1963. *The Conflict Between Paganism and Christianity in the Fourth Century*. Oxford-Warburg Studies. Oxford: Clarendon Press.

Moreschini, Claudio, ed. 1995. *Esegesi, parafrasi e compilazione in età tardoantica: atti del terzo convegno dell'Associazione di Studi Tardoantichi*. Collectanea 9. Naples: D'Auria.

Moretti, Paula Francesca. 2003. "L'esegesi biblica: un genere letterario? Un tentativo di approccio al problema." In *Forme letterarie nella produzione latina tra IV e V secolo: con uno sguardo a Bizanzio*, edited by Franca Ela Consolino, 127–45. Studi e testi tardoantichi 1. Rome: Herder.

Most, Glenn W., ed. 1999. *Kommentare/Commentaries*. Aporemata 4. Göttingen: Vandenhoeck & Ruprecht.

Murphy, Trevor M. 2004. *Pliny the Elder's Natural History: The Empire in the Encyclopedia*. Oxford, New York: Oxford University Press.

Naas, Valérie. 2002. *Le Projet encyclopédique de Pline l'ancien*. Collection de l'Ecole française de Rome 30. Rome: Ecole française de Rome.

Nazzaro, Antonio V. 2001. "Poesia biblica come espressione teologica: fra tardoantico e altomedioevo." In *La Scrittura infinita. Bibbia e poesia in età medievale e umanistica: atti del convegno di Firenze, 26-28 giugno 1997*, edited by Francesco Stella, 119–53. Millennio medievale 28. Florence: SISMEL, Edizioni del Galluzzo.

Nodes, Daniel J. 1993. *Doctrine and Exegesis in Biblical Latin Poetry*. ARCA. Classical and Medieval Texts, Papers, and Monographs 31. Leeds: F. Cairns.

Novara, Antoinette. 2005. *Auctor in bibliotheca: essai sur les textes préfaciels de Vitruve et une philosophie latine du livre*. Bibliothèque des études classiques 46. Louvain, Dudley, MA: Peeters.

Otten, Willemien and Karla Pollman, eds. 2007. *Poetry and Exegesis in Premodern Latin Christianity: the Encounter between Classical and Christian Strategies of Interpretation*. Supplements to Vigiliae Christianae 87. Leiden, Boston: Brill.

Pernot, Laurent. 1993. *La Rhétorique de l'éloge dans le monde gréco-romain*. Etudes augustiniennes. Série Antiquité. Paris: Institut d'Etudes Augustiniennes.

Pollmann, Karla. 2009. "Exegesis without End: Forms, Methods, and Functions of Biblical Commentaries." In *A Companion to Late Antiquity*, edited by Philip Rousseau, 258–69. Blackwell Companions to the Ancient World. Ancient History. Chichester, Malden, MA: Wiley-Blackwell.

Rees, Roger. 1998. "The Private Lives of Public Figures in Latin Prose Panegyric." In *The Propaganda of Power. The Role of Panegyric in Late Antiquity*, edited by Mary Whitby, 77–101. Mnemosyne, bibliotheca classica Batava. Supplementum 183. Leiden, Boston: Brill.

———. 2002. *Layers of Loyalty in Latin Panegyric, AD 289–307*. Oxford: Oxford University Press.

Richardot, Philippe. 1997. *Végèce et la culture militaire au Moyen Âge: Ve- XVe siècles*. Bibliothèque stratégique. Paris: Institut de stratégie comparée, EPHE IV-Sorbonne.

Roberts, Michael. 1984. "The *Mosella* of Ausonius. An interpretation." *Transactions and Proceedings of the American Philological Association* 114: 343–53.

———. 1985. *Biblical Epic and Rhetorical Paraphrase in Late Antiquity*. ARCA. Classical and Medieval Texts, Papers, and Monographs 16. Liverpool: F. Cairns.

———. 1989. *The Jeweled Style: Poetry and Poetics in Late Antiquity*. Ithaca, NY: Cornell University Press.

———. 2001. "Rome Personified, Rome Epitomized: Representations of Rome in the Poetry of the Early Fifth Century." *American Journal of Philology* 122: 533–65.

———. 2007. "Bringing Up the Rear: Continuity and Change in the Latin Poetry of Late Antiquity." In *Latinitas Perennis*. Vol. 1: *The Continuity of Latin Literature*, edited by Wim Verbaal, Yanick Maes, and Jan Papy, 141–67. Brill's Studies in Intellectual History. Leiden, Boston: Brill.

———. 2009. *The Humblest Sparrow: The Poetry of Venantius Fortunatus*. Ann Arbor, MI: University of Michigan Press.

Romano, Elisa. 1987. *La capanna e il tempio. Vitruvio o Dell'architettura*. Letteratura classica 15. Palermo: Palumbo.

Rousseau, Philipp, ed. 2009. *A Companion to Late Antiquity*. Blackwell Companions to the Ancient World. Ancient History. Chichester, Malden, MA: Wiley-Blackwell.

Russell, Donald. 1998. "The Panegyrist and their Teachers." In *The Propaganda of Power. The Role of Panegyric in Late Antiquity*, edited by Mary Whitby, 17–50. Mnemosyne, bibliotheca classica Batava. Supplementum 183. Leiden, Boston: Brill.

Sabbah, Guy. 2003. "Ammianus Marcellinus." In *Greek and Roman Historiography in Late Antiquity. Fourth to Sixth Century A.D.*, edited by Gabriele Marasco, 43–84. Leiden: Brill.

Schnapp, Jeffrey T. 1992. "Reading Lessons: Augustine, Proba and the Christian Détournement of Antiquity." *Stanford Literature Review* 9: 99–123.

Schröder, Bianca-Jeanette. 2007. *Bildung und Briefe im 6. Jahrhundert. Studien zum Mailänder Diakon Magnus Felix Ennodius*. Millennium-Studien 15. Berlin: De Gruyter.

Scourfield, J. H. D., ed. 2007. *Texts and Culture in Late Antiquity: Inheritance, Authority, and Change*. Swansea: Classical Press of Wales.

Shanzer, Danuta. 1986. *A Philosophical and Literary Commentary on Martianus Capella's De Nuptiis Philologiae et Mercurii, Liber 1*. University of California Publications. Classical Studies 32. Berkeley, CA: University of California Press.

———. 2009. "Literature, History, Periodization, and the Pleasures of the Latin Literary History of Late Antiquity." *History Compass* 7: 917–54.

Sharrock, Alison. 2000. "Intratextuality: Texts, Parts, and (W)holes in Theory." In *Intratextuality. Greek and Roman Relations*, edited by Alison Sharrock and Helen Morales, 1-39. Oxford: Oxford University Press.

Shuttleworth Kraus, Christina. 2002. "Introduction." *Reading Commentaries/Commentaries as Reading in The Classical Commentary. Histories, Practices, Theory* edited by Roy K. Gibson and Christina Shuttleworth Kraus, 1-27. Leiden: Brill.

Stella, Francesco, ed. 2001. *Poesia e teologia: l'Occidente latino tra IV e VIII secolo*. Eredità medievale 18. Milan: ISTeM.

Thraede, Klaus P. 1962. "Epos" in RAC 5, 983-1042.

Vessey, Mark. 2004. "Jerome and Rufinus." In *The Cambridge History of Early Christian Literature*, edited by Frances M. Young, Lewis Ayres and Andrew Louth, 318–27. Cambridge: Cambridge University Press.

———. 2007. "Theory, or the Dream of the Book (Mallarmé to Blanchot)." In *The Early Christian Book*, edited by William E. Klingshirn and Linda Safran, 241–74. Catholic University of America Studies in Early Christianity. Washington, DC: Catholic University of America Press.

Ward-Perkins, Bryan. 2005. *The Fall of Rome and the End of Civilization*. Oxford, New York: Oxford University Press.

Wisman, Josette A. 1986. "Flavius Renatus Vegetius." *Catalogus Translationum et Commentariorium: Medieval and Renaissance Latin Translations and Commentaries*, vol. VI, edited by F. Edward Cranz, Virginia Brown, and Paul Oskar Kristeller, 175–184. Washington, D.C.: The Catholic University of America Press and the Pontifical Institute at the University of Toronto.

Young, Frances, Lewis Ayres, and Andrew Louth, eds. 2004. *The Cambridge History of Early Christian Literature*. Cambridge, New York: Cambridge University Press.

CHAPTER 25

RENAISSANCES AND REVIVALS

MONIKA OTTER

THAT "renaissances" are even a recognizable issue in medieval studies depends on two well-known, deeply engrained notions of European historiography and the Western historical imagination. First, the Latin Middle Ages, so fundamentally identified as Christian, nonetheless inherited their language, their literature, and much of their scholastic culture from pagan Rome. Medieval intellectuals saw Roman civilization as their powerful and defining ancestor and Other, both distant and near, taken for granted and strange, authorizing and superseded. Second, the "Middle Ages" themselves were defined, from the first uses of that term, as modernity's Other, an exclusionary move that permitted the humanists, and succeeding generations almost until the present day, to reattach themselves directly to the high-prestige classical period (Greene 1983, 3, 32–35). Thus, the "Renaissance" marks the end of what we call "the Middle Ages"; and Renaissance spells modernity and progress, paradoxically, by way of a return to earlier cultural and political patterns.

As the bipartite title of this chapter suggests, we have two separate (but of course not unconnected) issues on our hands, each aligned more closely with one of the two terms of the title, "renaissances" and "revivals," respectively. On the one hand, we are concerned with "RENAISSANCES" writ large, that is, a modern historiographical concept that seeks to isolate periods of particular cultural vibrancy and innovation, albeit always innovation of the backward-looking sort noted above, with explicit reference to the Classics. There may be more or less strong, or even predominant, political elements to these renaissances: a revival or invocation of Roman ideas of governance and empire. The Carolingian renaissance is directly tied to, and in fact consciously managed by, Charlemagne's court. The twelfth-century renaissance can plausibly be linked to the investiture controversy that preceded it, the dramatic confrontation of secular and religious sovereignty (Schramm 1929; Garrison 1994). Other historians have tended not so much to deny those political backgrounds as to discuss the cultural innovations in their own right, as part of an intellectual history thought to exist almost in isolation from political forces, or even in contradistinction to them.

A renaissance is generally designated *ex post facto* as a modern (or at any rate later) attempt at characterizing, categorizing, and interpreting the cultural documents that have come down to us. Certain movements, such as the Italian humanists or the intellectuals assembled at the Carolingian court, did perceive themselves as a cultural as well as a political revival. A good example is the panegyric poem *Karolus Magnus et Leo Papa*, which, apart from praising Charles as a champion and eager student of all the liberal arts as well as a great conqueror, also has him build Aachen as a "Roma secunda" [second Rome], indeed "ventura Roma" [the Rome to come] (Beumann et al. 1966; for Italian humanism, see Greene 1982, 28–53).

No modern historian would proclaim a renaissance if there were not some signs in the contemporary sources of a sense of new departures, of renewed intellectual vigor. But it is not until later, in retrospect, that such claims harden into historical periods and epochal divides. This was famously done, for the end of the Middle Ages, by Jacob Burckhardt's influential *The Civilization of the Renaissance in Italy*, the Renaissance with the capital R that can stand alone without further qualifications (Burckhardt 1958; first German edition 1860). Whether that Renaissance is best seen as an absolute epochal divide, a paradigm shift that fundamentally altered the worldview and even the psychological constitution of Europeans, or whether we would do better to de-emphasize or even abandon that notion, has been and still is a matter of lively debate (Dannenfeldt 1974; Nichols 1991; von Moos 1988). The so-called Twelfth-Century renaissance was proposed, in direct reaction to the Burckhardtian paradigm-shifting Renaissance, as a "revolt of the medievalists" tired of being relegated to the dark ages that came before. Its most influential proponent was Charles Homer Haskins (1927), but the 1982 collection of essays edited by Benson, Constable, and Lanham, *Renaissance and Renewal*, has also attained the status of a classic. The notion of a Carolingian renaissance is of slightly longer standing, partly because Carolingian historiography itself suggested an orchestrated cultural reform, partly because that awakening played a role in the nationalistic rivalries of modern scholarship, as Germans and French both claimed Charlemagne and the Carolingians for themselves. As if to demonstrate the instability of such postulated epochal markers, it has since been suggested that we also need a Tenth-Century renaissance, although there has been some debate on whether this is a freestanding movement or merely the Carolingian renaissance finding its second wind; perhaps also a Late-Antique one, circa 400 CE. Byzantinists also have identified renaissances in the Eastern Empire, but those are beyond the scope of this chapter. (For a useful overview of the historiography, as well as specialist essays on each of these renaissances, see Treadgold 1984.) Inasmuch as the concept of RENAISSANCE attempts to single out certain historical moments as positively asserting something new (albeit by looking back), it is closely related to the larger problem of historical periodization.

"Revivals," on the other hand, or smaller-scale renaissances—or sometimes "renascences"—with a small "r," concern a renewed interest in a particular author, or with a cluster of ideas, such as Aristotle and Aristotelianism, Cicero, or Ovid. Of the epochs identified by Ludwig Traube in 1911, the "aetas Virgiliana" of the ninth and tenth centuries, the "aetas Horatiana" (tenth and eleventh centuries") and the "aetas Ovidiana" of the twelfth and thirteenth, it is the last that has been most readily accepted in subsequent scholarship. (For a somewhat sceptical assessment of that idea, and a discussion of the manuscript evidence, see Tilliette 1994; also Hexter 2011, Orbán 2004. Hexter 1986 is fundamental on the scholastic reception of Ovid in the Middle Ages.) Interest in Ovid certainly rose sharply in the later eleventh and twelfth centuries, and additional Ovidian works were added to the list of those regularly read and studied. Cicero's rhetorical works, particularly the introductory *De Inventione* (and the *Rhetorica ad Herennium*, erroneously attributed to Cicero) become much more widely available at around the same time (Ward 1995). Other authors enjoyed a more continuous reception, especially in the classroom; but even for Virgil or Terence, there are periods of more intense engagement—starting with the late classical period, which produced the standard commentaries and even pictorial programs for illustrated manuscripts that remained influential throughout the medieval and early modern periods. Other authors, perhaps never actually forgotten, seem to come to the forefront as they resonate with a given era's political concerns and intellectual temperament. (Moos 1979 makes this case for Lucan in the twelfth century.) Where the renaissances typically involve philosophy, the sciences, and other disciplines, we are here more closely focused on literature (in the modern sense), although there are analogous phenomena in art history. And we are more likely to deal with cultural phenomena directly experienced, articulated, and sometimes discussed by those who lived through them, rather than with later rationalizations. The question of "revivals" is thus closely linked to the larger issue of the reception of the Classics.

Whether "renaissance," along with other period designations and boundaries, is still a useful term today is much debated. (See, for instance, Peter von Moos's incisive 1988 critique of the term in general, and the twelfth-century renaissance in particular; LeGoff 2001; Treadgold 1984; Colish 2003 and 2004.) In the first place, as all these critics concede, the term can be unproblematic and useful as long as one remembers that, like all terminology, it is heuristic. It is designed to organize and more clearly focalize certain ideas about intellectual history and put them forward for discussion. A renaissance is not a datum or an event on a timeline, but a historiographical concept and interpretive model. In Karlheinz Stierle's happy formulation, it is not a fact but a "system of propositions" ("Aussagesystem," Stierle 1979, said by him not only of meta-historiographical concepts such as "renaissance" but of the very notion of historical "event"). Like any analytical concept, the term "renaissance" will favor certain insights and hinder others, highlight certain data and obscure others from view. As long as it is not taken as an absolute, there is nothing wrong with using it. For instance, an alternative and equally helpful and/or problematic view of the medieval engagement with classical civilization stresses continuities over ruptures, the *longue durée* over the dramatic change. E. R. Curtius's influential *European Literature and the Latin Middle Ages* (1953; first German edition 1948) tends in that direction. One could also cite Rita Copeland (1991), Martin Irvine (1994), and other students of medieval rhetoric, who favor a relatively continuous, although not static, transmission of classical learning, and slow shifts rather than sudden changes. As long as one remains open to both models (and others besides), as long as one sees "renaissance" as a useful abstraction, as long as one is willing to critique it, there should be little harm in continuing to use the term.

Yet, compared to other epoch markers ("Romanticism," for instance), the RENAISSANCE concept is particularly charged, fraught with powerful but often unstated value terms, and there is a real danger of confusing our values with those of the period under consideration. The "Classics," arguably the single most important constitutive term of a renaissance, are a high prestige concept then as now. But "renaissance," as we have already noted, is also closely aligned with notions of modernity and progress. This makes the various renaissances markedly proleptic, teleological. We want them to predict and anticipate that which we value most, or most wish we had, in our own culture: enlightenment, rationality, secularity, "humanism," individualism, pluralism, independence and freedom of thought and expression, historical and philological sophistication in encounters with the past. Some such projection is both unavoidable and legitimate. Enquiring after the prehistory of our own cultural and political values is a central task of all cultural history. To encounter the Middle Ages entirely "on their own terms" is not only an unattainable ideal, but perhaps not even an ideal at all. It is largely the confrontation of perspectives, the negotiation of terms, the dialogue that make the encounter fruitful.

Yet if it is used uncritically, the proleptic view can lead us not only to overstate certain elements of the "renaissances," such as their secularity or freedom of thought, but also factors as basic as the availability of the very Classics on which the renaissance is supposedly founded, or the depth of engagement with those classics. Garrison (1994) asks these skeptical questions about the Carolingian renaissance. Edouard Jeauneau (2009) famously challenged the "School of Chartres," long held to be central to the twelfth-century renaissance. As described by John of Salisbury, did it really operate at the university-like level we like to imagine, or was it far more modest in its educational aims? We may, conversely, understate, neglect, or explain away other factors that do not chime well with our definition of terms, or we may facilely assume homologies or identities where, on closer inspection, the underlying concepts are rather different. For instance, Carolyn Bynum's influential essay "Did the Twelfth Century Discover the Individual?" (1982) sought to sketch a sense of self-fashioning, of choice of life-plan, that might be more congenial to the twelfth-century than the notions of individuality we tend to take for granted.

A related example (in fact implicit in Bynum's essay) concerns the role of Christian religion, which is of course a massively important cultural force throughout the medieval period. Our own post-enlightenment preference for secularism leads us by and large to treat religious reform movements as something categorically different from the classicizing renaissances. A partial exception is the Protestant reformation of the sixteenth century, which is generally seen as a major contributing factor in the Renaissance—but, paradoxically, chiefly insofar as it is seen as a secularizing movement, not *qua* religious reform. (Brian Stock's *The Implications of Literacy* [1983] and the Benson, Constable and Lanham collection [1982] are among those that do look at religious and secular innovations together.) This division may be largely defensible and conducive to historical arguments we wish to make, but one wonders if people at the time might have drawn different dividing and connecting lines, might have sorted the cultural phenomena that surrounded them differently than we are inclined to do. Was "rationality" or personal or political liberty at the top of their agenda, as it is for us? Did they see the secular part of their renaissance as an end in itself? Would they have automatically privileged the religious revival and considered the reinvigorated study of the pagan classics simply as a means to an educational end? Did they, as several of the examples further on suggest, conceive of their renaissance primarily as a *Christian* rewriting of their pagan antecedents? And if so, did they, consciously or not, explicitly or covertly, rebel against that formulation? These are questions that do not call for a blanket answer but, in the first place, a careful, sensitive reading of each movement, each author, each text.

Moreover, some of the parameters by which we diagnose a renaissance are themselves vague and of doubtful analytical value. We have already noted that it is not immediately obvious what the term "individual" might mean in a phrase like "the discovery of the individual" (Morris 1972). Whether the term "humanism" is sharp enough to serve a useful function, let alone an epoch-dividing one, is also open to doubt. Another example, which may at first glance seem less problematic, is "literacy." Most often renaissances are also seen to be accompanied (or perhaps even caused) by a change in intellectual style, or in the available technologies for producing and transmitting knowledge. That the invention of the printing press spelled the end of the Middle Ages and helped usher in the Renaissance is part of our most basic, large-scale narrative of Western history, part of what is considered indispensable general knowledge for any educated person. But similar claims have been made for the renaissance of the twelfth century (Stock 1983, Clanchy 1993), and to a lesser extent the Carolingian renaissance (McKitterick 1989). Indeed, the linguistic medium of the Carolingian renaissance has itself been described as a "renaissance" phenomenon: according to Roger Wright's somewhat controversial account, "medieval Latin" is the product of Alcuin's and other intellectuals' classicizing attempt to reestablish a (largely illusory) continuity with Roman civilization (R. Wright 1982, 1991; see also Farrell 2001, 16–18). But it should be noted that the notion of literacy as a "cognitive divide," as proposed perhaps most influentially by Walter Ong, has itself been challenged, even for those situations where literacy is introduced from the outside in cultures that previously had no writing (Frake 1983; Bloch 1998). These objections would seem to apply *a fortiori* to the Christian

Middle Ages, which never experienced this state of "primary orality," having inherited from both its classical and its Jewish ancestry not only the practical skills of reading and writing, but a very strong cultural orientation towards the written word. Both Stock and Clanchy (1993) (who nevertheless strongly argue for an epochal literacy divide in the twelfth century) note that "literacy" in this sense is not simply a given individual's ability to decipher written language, but a general participation in what Stock calls "textuality." Such a measure may lend itself more to a sliding scale—what proportion of the population was "textual" in that broad sense and in what situations, and how central were those interactions with writing to the lives of individuals and communities?—than to sharply demarcated shifts, or even to a steady, linear evolution.

Perhaps most seriously, as a value term, RENAISSANCE is exclusionary. It is almost necessarily predicated on the corollary notion of "dark ages" (Treadgold 1984). A renaissance depends on dismissing the immediately preceding age as static or retrograde, denying it all those good things that make a renaissance. As the only half-joking designation "revolt of the medievalists" acknowledges, it moreover depends, institutionally, on the acquiescence of those who study that preceding period. Occasionally, there is a variant: studies that maintain a strong epochal divide but attach more value to the earlier age, or even absolutely privilege the "before" over the "after." E. R. Curtius and the Princeton school headed by D. W. Robertson (perhaps more familiar to Middle English scholars than to Latinists) belonged in that camp, as does, in a less ideologically conservative way, C. Stephen Jaeger's important study, *The Envy of Angels* (1994; see also Colish's quietly provocative suggestion that there is greater intellectual freedom and experimentation in the Middle Ages, and that it is in fact the Renaissance that closes down the medieval mind [2004]). But more commonly, the model is one of progress: the "after" is privileged over the "before." Many of the renaissances we now recognize in medieval history were formulated in reaction to such exclusions. Once medievalists were tired of seeing themselves relegated to a dark age, they asserted precursors to the Renaissance. Each of these earlier renaissances in its turn has been critiqued on similar grounds, challenged as to its substance, as to its pervasiveness (does a renaissance, or even the Renaissance, ever really involve more than a relatively small, elite portion of the population? [Farrell 2001, 124]), and above all as to its newness. If an entire argument is essentially based on the unprecedented novelty of a phenomenon, either relatively concrete and circumscribed ("literacy") or vague and enormous ("individuality"), it throws itself open to quick and easy falsification: other scholars are bound to point out earlier instances of the same thing. Even more fundamentally, as Farrell has noted, the ebb-and-flow, boom-and-bust, renaissance-and-dark-ages model is predicated on a much too unitary, monological view of "Latin culture," or of civilization generally. "Latinity" (what other language even has a totalizing abstract noun of this sort attached to it?) is more adequately described, even in classical times, as a multifarious, contentious concert of voices, languages, registers, texts, and intellectual endeavors, whose history is far more complex than a single, linear graph (Farrell 2001, 123).

None of this necessarily means that these periodizations, or the concept of renaissance as such, are worthless. For one thing, change does happen, even large-scale change that shifts the entire culture. The intellectual climate of, say, the thirteenth century is manifestly quite different from that of the tenth, and we must ask ourselves how, when, and why this happens. (See Giardina's [1999] eloquent plea in favor of periodization: it is what historians do!) In practice, of course, no one suggests that a renaissance happens overnight. It is always a softer transition, in the vein of Malcolm Gladwell's "tipping points." Elements previously present in the culture (such as a desire to shape one's own life and person, such as the orientation towards written models, or an interest in the works of Ovid) reach critical mass, gather momentum, and become recognizable as cultural paradigm shifts, whether to contemporaries or, in retrospect, only to later generations. In that sense, the renaissance as a sharp dividing line is in any case an abstraction, a simplification, and few serious students of history are confused about that fact. Moreover, each renaissance proposed by literary and cultural historians has given rise to new insights, offered new perspectives by drawing different dividing lines, and highlighted texts, ideas, and witnesses previously neglected. For this reason, scholarly debates about various "renaissances" do not necessarily indicate a weakness in the concept. As long as we see them as propositions to be debated, defended, contested, abandoned if necessary and sometimes re-proposed if that seems useful; if we see them not as static dividers but as challenges to scholars, on both sides of the dividing line, to marshal arguments and evidence, to shore up the divide, reach across it, or even erase it, to find what distinguishes and what unites, what changes and what stays the same, the terms are functioning as intended.

If we turn to "revivals," the conscious and deliberate reception of classical authors in the medieval period, it is worth paying close attention to the flavor of these interactions, the terms on which old and new meet, the negotiations that take place. There is no dearth of contemporary statements to guide us. Older scholarship especially tended to see such encounters, once diagnosed, as relatively unproblematic. In that older view, the question of whether it is permissible for Christians to interact freely with pagan works had been very largely settled in the earliest Christian centuries. The ancients served as "sources." The moderns imitated the ancients, sometimes ineptly, sometimes so successfully that their works were mistaken for classical (as happened, for instance, to Hildebert of Lavardin's "Hermaphrodite" epigram, as well as various pseudo-Ovidiana, on the latter of which see Hexter 2011). Yet no cultural reception is as straightforward as this; medieval Latin writers' engagement with classical culture was both more conflicted and more energizing than this flat picture suggests. Despite their reverence for the Classics, medieval readers often experienced them as alienating, and not only for the reason most frequently articulated, namely the ancients' paganism. (For two magnificent case studies of this alienation, see Barkan 1991 and Rankin 2010.)

Yet the estrangement was fruitful. Medieval teaching of literature and composition relied heavily on the imitation of classical models, and this educational practice left its mark on the larger literary culture (Stotz 1981; Greene 1982). Yet medieval literature, and medieval Latin literature above all, derived surprising strength and vitality from what might at first blush appear to be a rather limiting dependence on cultural predecessors, that is to say, from its own derivativeness and its own sense of belatedness. Of the two pillars on which their literary edifice rested, the first—Biblical and Patristic literature—had the aura of the sacred and ceremonial. (See both Dinkova-Bruun, and Boynton and Fassler in this volume.) Classical literature, devoid of that unshakable truth claim and unassailable seriousness, permits creative engagement and experimentation, as the Bible generally does not (some hybrid, tellingly classicizing Bible epics notwithstanding). Forcing their voices into the received, authoritative language and poetical forms prescribed by the Classics gives medieval Latin writers an almost automatically parodic stance. "Parody," in the sense I intend it here, does not necessarily or primarily mean satire or send-up, or even anything humorous at all; but it does mean a certain distancing, a framing and setting apart, a self-conscious sense of speaking not quite in one's own voice or with full commitment. (A classic definition of parody in this broader sense is found in Hutcheon 1985.) And that distanced, heightened authorial voice is, as I shall argue, also one of the preconditions of fictionality. It is not much of an overstatement to say that the chief effect of the continuous reception and reworking of the Classics in the Middle Ages is that playful freedom of the authorial voice, that setting-aside of truth claims, that we call "fiction."

Even in the decontextualizing, dehistoricizing setting of the classroom, where so much reception of antiquity takes place, the classical author is both familiar and strange, beloved and loathed, oppressively authoritarian and easily dismissed. To every new generation of pupils, the classical author is absolutely contemporary (we read Virgil because that is what one does in school) and age-old (…and it has been that way as long as anyone can remember). There could be no better illustration of this simultaneous presence and absence than the fragmentary little classroom skit known as *Delusor Terentii* (1965; "Terence and his Critic," variously dated between the eighth and tenth centuries, or even as far back as the seventh). This little drama opens with a rebellious schoolboy mouthing off about having to read Terence. "Terence" then appears in person to make the boy come up on stage and debate him openly. The boy, clearly feeling himself to be in hot water, bravely soldiers on but cannot muster much except to reiterate that he is young and Terence is so very, very old. There may have been more, but the fragment breaks off at that point. As far as we have it, the play is devoid of any Terentian comical content besides the meta-literary situation of a reader encountering the author; but it does imitate some of Terence's stagecraft, such as the comic aside to the audience.

Terence had indeed been a classroom presence continuously since the fourth century, an author of indisputable canonicity. Since the medieval manuscripts generally came complete with Terence's combative, defensive prologues, which considerably exercised the medieval imagination, he could also serve as a model for discussing the role of the author and the conditions of literary production generally. He was also, of course, a model of comic writing. These factors together almost invite his medieval writers to test their wit against his. Another medieval writer to confront Terence, and to comment on the experience of doing so, is Hrotsvit of Gandersheim (tenth century), who produced a series of short plays formally inspired by Terence but filled with new, hagiographic content. Her prologue to these plays discusses her ambivalence towards her own project, while anticipating and disarming possible criticism. Like the schoolboy, she half-humorously underlines the courage required to take on a literary giant of Terence's stature, calling herself, in a somewhat fanciful Latinization of her German name, the "Clamor Validus" (Strong Voice, or Brave Shout) of Gandersheim. The prologue is a little masterpiece of polemics and defensiveness, directness, and equivocation, all in a very brief, highly crafted piece of art prose (Hrotsvit 2001, 132–33). If others may enjoy reading Terence, savoring his polished style despite the objectionable focus on love and sex, she argues defiantly that she may surely write like him, especially if it is in the service of "celebrating the laudable chastity of sacred virgins." She would never presume to equate herself with the master, or with his more official, academic (male) students; yet there is no arrogance in her decision to take up the pen. On the contrary, to abstain from writing merely in order to escape criticism would be a selfish act. ("Ideoque non sum adeo amatrix mei . ut pro vitanda reprehensione...cessem praedicare." [Nor am I so much a lover of myself, that in order to avoid censure I should cease to preach.]) If she is suspiciously good at writing the love scenes she professes to abhor, that is (she argues) necessary to throw into relief the fortitude of the heroines, for there is not much glory in resisting a temptation that is unattractive in the first place. In sum, if she has succeeded in her literary efforts, good; if not, she has at least contributed to turning her readers' minds against the shameful things found in Terence.

It is hard to assess the tone of such an authorial statement today. I suspect it is fundamentally serious. But there is parody, and that is not at all inconsistent with such seriousness. The plays are parodic in the most fundamental definition of parody, of filling a recognized form with new, often incongruous content, and not necessarily for comic purposes. Her prologue echoes Terence's prologues, which, on the evidence of illustrations and commentaries, fascinated medieval readers almost as much as the plays themselves (D. Wright 1993). Finally, there is Hrotsvit's playful equivocation as she describes her writerly activity alongside, underneath, and above her textual model, celebrating, critiquing, and subverting it all at once.

Hrotsvit's prologue and the *Delusor*, perhaps not coincidentally, show two figures that are somewhat marginal to the intellectual establishment of their time: a schoolboy still apprenticed to it and an educated woman excluded from full membership and eyed with suspicion. Both find a parodic voice over against the solidly canonical figure of Terence. Other medieval texts that directly stage an encounter with classical antiquity make similar parodic discoveries. The *Ecloga Theoduli* was also a canonical school text well into the modern era. Its date of composition is uncertain; Michael Herren (2007) recently put it as late as the early eleventh century, whereas its most recent editor, Francesco Mosetto Casaretti (1997), retains the more traditional Carolingian dating. The pseudo-pastoral debate polemically pits Biblical truth against the "lies" of the ancients. The debate is of course rigged: the

Biblical maiden "Alithia" stands, even in her name, for Truth, while her classical opponent is from the start saddled with the name "Pseustis" (Liar). But, as Herren notes in his recent article, not only does Pseustis score points in the fight, but the whole poem is predicated on at least the outside possibility that Pseustis might win; and the poet, whose authorial voice remains unmoored and floating, at least partially embraces the poetic and fictional possibilities of the "Liar" for himself (Herren 2007; see also Mosetto Casaretti's introduction [1997], particularly on the question of the almost certainly pseudonymous author's name; and Hexter 2011 on pseudonymy in medieval writing generally).

Something analogous, I would argue, occurs in two "archeological" poems of the late eleventh, or the turn of the twelfh century. In a letter poem to Abbot Odo, Foulcoie of Beauvais describes the accidental discovery of the head of a gigantic ancient statue at Meaux (Colker 1954, no. IV). He is both attracted and repelled by the find: anticipating Bernard of Clairvaux's celebrated formula, "deformis formositas et formosa deformitas" ["deformed beauty and beautiful deformity"] (Bernard 1990, 282–83), he observes:

> Horrendum caput et tamen hoc horrore decorum
> Lumine terrifico, terror et ipse decet,
> Ritibus, ore fero, feritate sua speciosum,
> Deformis formae forma quod apta foret.

(ll. 11–14) [The head was horrible and yet beautiful in that horror: with its terrifying eye, yet the terror itself is fitting; with its savage rituals, its savage mouth, yet beautiful in its savagery, because the misshapen beauty of its shape was fitting.]

Foulcoie does put his classical learning to work, inferring by some quite plausible mythological and toponymical reasoning that the statue likely depicted Mars, since the place is popularly known as "Martis Fanum." He then takes the discovery as a starting point for an exercise in Christian apologetics against Ovidian mythology. But in denouncing the *Metamorphoses* he implicitly recognizes and adopts its poetic principles. Foulcoie is highly exercised by the gods' sex life—which, to him, suffices to disqualify them as divinities—and more particularly by the unnatural, species-bending modes of procreation, such as the admittedly unsettling image of a human Leda laying an egg and hatching human or semi-divine offspring from it. But the generativity of the lustful gods is of course also a poetic fecundity: if there is one thing the gods bring forth it is stories, absurd and fantastic stories, and in Foulcoie's poem they are breeding wildly. The multitude of mythical stories, and Ovid's wonderfully fluid form in particular, permit endless *amplificatio*, glossing, riffing. Foulcoie's joy in doing so is evident, a playfulness I seek to match by attempting a verse translation:

> Iupiter et Iuno, deus et dea, si uir et uxor,
> Sunt soror et frater: nil deitatis inest.
> Mugiat atque tonet, uolitet, pluat aureus imber:

Non coeunt deitas et deitatis amor.
Factus olor, conuersus homo, cum uirgine mixtus,
Fallit olor specie, ledit homo coitu.
Sic iuxta uolucrem genitrix duo protulit oua;
Sic hominem iuxta fit generatus homo.
Ledam ledit homo, fiunt cum Castore Pollus.
Falsus olor genitor, sic genitura fuit.

[Juno and Jupiter, goddess and god, are wife and husband,   35
Sister and brother too: nothing divine in that.
Let him thunder and moo, or flutter, or rain down golden:
This god's famous amours do not smack of a god.
Made a swan, or turned into man and mixing with virgins,
This swan's whiteness is false; this man is far from pure.   40
Insofar as he's bird, his mother produced two eggs;
He was born human style insofar as he's man.
Leda's led on by a man, and this brings forth Castor and Pollux,
Fathered by a fake swan: thus stood the stars at their birth.]

Foulcoie resists this freewheeling fictionalizing. He wants species boundaries to remain intact and everything to remain in its allocated place. The framing project, of finding a name for the fragmentary statue, and, conversely, finding a "res," a thing, that gives substance to the traditional place name, indicates his desire to match words to things, clearly and unequivocally. Yet, whether he meant to or not, he has not only understood how Ovidian fiction works but he plays along, for the duration of the poem. It is precisely because the mythological figures have no real referents, because they are "empty" images, not anchored in the stable one-name, one-referent relations that Foulcoie demands, that they can be manipulated, shifted around, blended, recombined, morphed from one thing into another in this dizzying and exhilarating whirl of interconnected narratives. Foulcoie is disturbed by this fluidity, yet it also spurs him to a poetic attempt of his own. Just as he grudgingly admits the fascination, the power, even the perverse beauty of that savage head, perhaps he has here discovered, and briefly inhabited, a space for fiction—even though he has to shut it down at the end.

The far better-known "Rome Elegy" by Hildebert of Lavardin (ca. 1100; Hildebert of Lavardin 2001, no. 36) has inspired several important discussions of medieval "humanism" and the nature of the "Twelfth-Century Renaissance" (Jaeger 1997; Smolak 2002; Tilliette 1995; for a summary of earlier discussions and a response, see Otter 2010). In "Par tibi, Roma, nihil," the poet first laments the ruin of Rome and its great art; then, in a companion poem ("Dum simulacra mihi," Hildebert of Lavardin 2001, no. 38), he has Rome herself reply that in her current ruined state, far from her former greatness ("I barely remember myself") she has found a new and greater (Christian) fulfillment. This is neither a bigoted Christian rejection of classical antiquity nor a "humanistic" awarding of a consolation prize to modernity. It is a true dialectic, asserting simultaneously modern respect and modern triumphalism in the adoption of the ancient, and acknowledging how deeply the culture of Latin Christianity is suffused with its ancient heritage. The English chronicler William of Malmesbury, who quotes "Par tibi, Roma, nihil" in its entirety in his *Gesta Regum Anglorum* (1125), makes it part of an extended excursus on Rome that, as David Rollo has suggested, subtends his entire historiographical enterprise and his representation of his own Christian civilization (Rollo 2000, 1–31).

In the process, Hildebert proposes a complicated and deeply insightful play on the ancient statues that so intrigued twelfth-century visitors to Rome. Turning on its head the ancient anti-pagan polemic that cultic images are merely made by human hands, and therefore invalidate *qua* deities, he expresses profound admiration for the artists' skill: so well are the statues made, he says, that the very gods admire their own representations. This of course declares the images idols, empty of any true divinity. (The gods are, after all, *outside* their own statues and contemplating them.) It also has the statues' referents shrink towards zero. In Hildebert's Christian world, there *are* no pagan gods; they are only called into a brief, fictional existence by the very statues that represent them, and by the words of the poet recreating the statues. The statues do not refer to any true referent; yet here they are, concrete, material survivals of a prized cultural past, and themselves solidly part of the cultural imaginary of Hildebert's time. He simultaneously hollows out the statues (or words) and ascribes to them a kind of self-sufficient plenitude that can not only survive the absence of its referent, but create its referent. This is as good a description of fictionality as one could hope for.

Perhaps the most committed Ovidian of the *aetas Ovidiana* is Baudri of Bourgueil. He not only imitates Ovid but derives an entire sophisticated poetics from him (Bond 1995). The *Heroides* seem to have been more present and more widely read even in the earlier Middle Ages than their rather slim manuscript tradition suggests (Reynolds 1983, 268–72; Hexter 1986; Tilliette 1994), perhaps because they tie nicely into one of the standard school exercises of imitative poetry, memorably attested in Augustine's *Confessions* (1.18): the prosopopeia, the composed speech in the voice of a historical or mythological figure. Gerald Bond (1987) has shown how Baudri made use of Ovidian impersonation to forge his own poetic voice. Baudri offers three pairs of *Heroides*-like letter poems, at increasing distances from the Ovidian model: one recreating, and varying, Ovid's own exchange between Paris and Helena; one in which he actually takes the role of Ovid himself, as well as a fictional interlocutor named "Florus," discussing Ovid's exile, his guilt or innocence of the charges brought against him; and one exchange between Baudri, writing in his own name, and Constance, a pupil and presumably nun in the aristocratic convent of Le Ronceray. (On these poems, see also Tilliette 1994 and elsewhere in this volume; Hexter 2011.) It is not clear whether what we have is in fact by Constance, or by Baudri speaking in her voice, or some mix thereof; at any rate, the exchange is playfully risqué, bordering on outright flirtation. Other letter poems, mostly to young men, imply an exchange of letters, although the other half of the correspondence is missing, and perhaps existed only in the fiction of the poem we have.

But Baudri also reflects and comments on his practice of writing such poems, insisting that they are a literary game. He says as much, somewhat defensively, in the poem "Qua intentione scripserit" (*carmen* 85; Baudri of Bourgueil 1998–2002, 1: 80–81), arguably one of the most impressive and bold theorizations of poetic voice from the Middle Ages. One could almost describe it as a self-*accessus*, that exercise of literary criticism of the high Middle Ages that concisely summed up the genre of the work, its time and place, and its author's *intentio*. Baudri characterizes his verse (partly in imitation of the classical epigrammists) as a minor art, as "nugae" (trifles) and playful jokes, not the heavy matters that would perhaps suit his standing better but might not find a readership. He characterizes his poems as youthful, even childish. Yet he emphatically embraces the label of youthfulness, and partially turns it around: yes, it is poetry for "boys and girls"; but as long as they read and reread it, his works will live. Youth, rather than a sign of immaturity, becomes a bold assertion of newness and a promise of new and always self-renewing life:

> Ergo, quod pueros demulceat atque puellas
> Scripsimus, ut pueris id consonet atque puellis,
> Sique meum relegatur opus volitetque per orbem,
> Illud dum relegent pueri relegentque puellae.

[Therefore, I have written to please boys and girls, to have my poetry resonate with boys and girls, and thus my work is reread and flutters around the globe, as long as boys reread it and girls reread it.]

Finally, Baudri directly tackles the problem of fictional persona. If he speaks of his loves and hatreds in the first person,

> Crede michi: non uera loquor, magis omnia fingo.
> Nullus amor foedus michi quidlibet associavit.

[Believe me: I do not relate true things, but rather make it all up. No shameful love has bound me to anyone.]

Love poetry is a literary genre, and a particularly pleasing one ("genus...iucundius"), a generator of literary subject matter ("semen materiei"). The first person is not a true first person but an index for "many." The "intention," then (perhaps in multiple senses: the intentionality of the writing, as well as its reference, the thing "intended") resides not in him but in the words:

> Quodcirca sodes mea sit sententia uerbi
> Et sua, non mea sit intentio materiei.

[Therefore, I pray, let the word's meaning be my responsibility; and let it in turn be responsible for the "intentio" of the matter.]

In the last lines of the poem, he turns the responsibility for that "intentio" over to the reader's frame of mind:

> Non sis uerborum scurrilis leno meorum.
> Perlege, quidquid erit, sine suspitione sinistra.

> [Do not be a scurrilous pimp of my words; read whatever it is without sinister suspicions.]

However tentative its formulation, Baudri's ambitious statement clearly goes beyond mere defensiveness; he is not merely deflecting criticism. Nor is Baudri dismissing his own poetry as entirely unserious; the "youthful" poetry of the latter-day Ovidian and the feigned persona have their own seriousness. In a remarkable late poem, "Voces ambiguas," which either is or purports to be a reply to a confused and hesitant love letter by a young monk ("ignoro, nolo, laboro, volo" [I don't know, I don't want, I am struggling, I want], in Baudri's mocking paraphrase), Baudri gives a nuanced account of the poetic license he wishes to take, and to give to others. Absolutely, he tells his young interlocutor: if you love me, say so. Do understand that nothing physical or sexual will come of it; we are both priests and monks, sworn to chastity. But, as he permits himself and the young writer the "verba iocosa" [joking words] that have characterized his entire poetic career, and even suggests that their priestly status and personal integrity is a protection against anything evil they might bring on, Baudri encourages both of them to embrace their poetic voice, but also to recognize its artifice. There is nothing false or insincere about it, quite the contrary (the "ambiguities" of the sly fox being the rejected alternative); a poet does and does not speak in his own voice. If, as Bond persuasively argues, Baudri has learned his literary role-play from Ovid, founds it on Ovid, and justifies it with reference to Ovid, then his interaction with the Classics seems to have given him the gift of literary fiction.

In an important 1977 essay, Peter Haidu argued that vernacular literature in the Middle Ages is always "parodic," always being a restating and distancing of the Latin that preceded it, emptied of Latin's religious truth-claims and its high-culture seriousness, and thereby set free to practice fiction. Yet there is no need, as I have argued elsewhere (Otter 1996), to exclude medieval Latin literature from this assessment; quite the contrary. Medieval Latin is "always parodic," not in the sense of being facetious or satirical, but in the sense of restating, citing, celebrating, and fighting the Classics, and in the sense of filling old cultural forms with new content. "Renewals" are, then, not only a sporadic event in medieval Latin culture but part of its intellectual foundation. As they build on the ruins of Rome and make them the underpinning of their own intellectual culture, medieval writers are always conscious of also being readers, always responding to a prior culture that enriches and authorizes their own. And even where the prior culture seems overwhelming or stifling, it pushes medieval writers to forge a literary idiom that is authentically theirs.

SUGGESTIONS FOR FURTHER READING

The "classics" on the subject of renaissances include Jacob Burckhardt's *The Civilization of the Renaissance in Italy* (1958; first German edition 1860; conveniently excerpted, with useful supplemental materials, in Dannenfeldt 1974) and Haskins's *The Renaissance of the Twelfth Century* (1927); on the twelfth-century renaissance, one must also consult the collaborative volume *Renaissance and Renewal* edited by Benson, Constable, and Lanham (1982). There is no equally obvious classic for the Carolingian renaissance; an excellent starting point is Michel Rouche's chapter on "The Carolingian 'Renewal'" in *The Cambridge Illustrated History of the Middle Ages*, Vol. 1 (1989) and McKitterick 1994, particularly Garrison's chapter. Treadgold (1984) offers a good overview of the scholarly history as well as the problematics of "renaissances," and a chapter on each major renaissance, with a good, though no longer quite up-to-date, introductory bibliography. Of the theoretical discussions, I would especially recommend von Moos (1988) and the two essays by Colish (2003, 2004). Indispensable reference tools for tracing the reception of classical authors in the Middle Ages are Munk Olsen (1982–89) and Reynolds (1983).

BIBLIOGRAPHY

Primary sources

Baudri of Bourgueil. 2002. *Carmina*, edited by Jean-Yves Tilliette. Auteurs latins du Moyen âge. Paris: Belles Lettres.

Bernard of Clairvaux. 1990. "Apologia ad Guillelmum Abbatem." In *The "Things of Greater Importance": Bernard of Clairvaux's Apologia and the Medieval Attitude Towards Art*, edited and translated by Conrad Rudolph, 227–337. Philadelphia: University of Pennsylvania Press.

Beumann, Helmut, Franz Brunhölzl, and Wilhelm Winkelmann, eds. 1966. *Karolus Magnus et Leo Papa: Ein Paderborner Epos vom Jahre 799*. Paderborn: Verein für Geschichte und Altertumskunde Westfalens.

Colker, Marvin L. 1954. "Fvlcoii Belvacensis Epistvlae." *Traditio* 10: 191–273.

Delusor Terentii. 1965. In *Hrotsvithae Opera*, edited by Paul von Winterfeld, xx–xxiii. Monumenta Germaniae Historica. Scriptores rerum Germanicarum in usum scholarum separatim editi 34. Berlin: Weidmann.

Ecloga Theoduli. 1980. In *Seven Versions of Carolingian Pastoral*, edited by Roger P. H. Green. Reading University medieval and Renaissance Latin texts. Reading: Department of Classics, Reading University.

———. 1997. *Ecloga: Il canto della verità e della menzogna*, edited by Francesco M. Casaretto. Florence: SISMEL.

Hildebert of Lavardin. 2002. *Carmina Minora*, edited by A. Brian Scott. 2nd ed. Bibliotheca Teubneriana. Munich, Leipzig: K. G. Saur.

Hrotsvit. 2001. *Opera Omnia*, edited by Walter Berschin. Bibliotheca scriptorum Graecorum et Romanorum Teubneriana. Munich, Leipzig: K. G. Saur.

William of Malmesbury. 1998. *Gesta regum Anglorum = The history of the English kings*, edited by Roger A. B. Mynors, Rodney M. Thomson, and Michael Winterbottom. Oxford medieval texts. Oxford: Clarendon Press.

Secondary sources

Barkan, Leonard. 1991. "Rome's Other Population." *Raritan* 11: 66–81.

Benson, Robert L., Giles Constable, and Carol D. Lanham, eds. 1982. *Renaissance and Renewal in the Twelfth Century*. Cambridge, MA: Harvard University Press.

Bloch, Maurice. 1998. *How We Think They Think: Anthropological Approaches to Cognition, Memory, and Literacy*. Boulder, CO: Westview Press.

Bond, Gerald A. 1987. "Composing Yourself: Ovid's *Heroides*, Baudri of Bourgueil, and the Problem of Persona." *Mediaevalia* 13: 83–117.

———. 1995. *The Loving Subject: Desire, Eloquence, and Power in Romanesque France*. Middle Ages Series. Philadelphia: University of Pennsylvania Press.

Burckhardt, Jacob. 1958. *The Civilization of the Renaissance in Italy*, translated by Samuel G. C. Middlemore. New York: Harper and Row. First German edition Basel: Schweighauser, 1860.

Bynum, Caroline Walker. 1982. *Jesus as Mother: Studies in the Spirituality of the High Middle Ages*. Publications of the Center for Medieval and Renaissance Studies 16. Berkeley, CA: University of California Press.

Clanchy, Michael T. 1993. *From Memory to Written Record: England 1066–1307*. 2nd revised ed. Oxford: Blackwell.

Colish, Marcia L. 2003. "Haskins's *Renaissance* Seventy Years Later: Beyond Anti-Burckhardtianism." *Haskins Society Journal* 11: 1–15.

———. 2004. "When Did the Middle Ages End? Reflections of an Intellectual Historian." In *Schooling and Society: The Ordering and Reordering of Knowledge in the Western Middle Ages*, edited by Alasdair A. MacDonald and Michael W. Twomey. Groningen Studies in Cultural Change 6. Leuven: Peeters.

Copeland, Rita. 1991. *Rhetoric, Hermeneutic, and Translation in the Middle Ages*. Cambridge Studies in Medieval Literature 11. Cambridge: Cambridge University Press.

Dannenfeldt, Karl H., ed. 1974. *The Renaissance: Basic Interpretations*. 2nd ed. Problems in European Civilization. Lexington, MA: Heath.

Farrell, Joseph. 2001. *Latin Language and Latin Culture from Ancient to Modern Times*. Roman Literature and its Contexts. Cambridge: Cambridge University Press.

Frake, Charles O. 1983. "Did Literacy Cause the Great Cognitive Divide?" *American Ethnologist* 2: 368–71.

Garrison, Mary. 1994. "The Emergence of Carolingian Latin Literature and the Court of Charlemagne." In *Carolingian Culture: Emulation and Innovation*, edited by Rosamond McKitterick. Cambridge, New York: Cambridge University Press.

Giardina, Andrea. 1999. "Esplosione di tardoantico." In *Prospettive sul tardoantico: Atti del Convegno di Pavia (27–28 novembre 1997)*, edited by Giancarlo Mazzoli and Fabio Gasti. Biblioteca di Athenaeum 41. Como: New Press.

Greene, Thomas M. 1982. *The Light in Troy: Imitation and Discovery in Renaissance Poetry*. Elizabethan Club Series 7. New Haven, CT: Yale University Press.

Haidu, Peter. 1977. "Repetition: Modern Reflections on Medieval Aesthetics." *Modern Language Notes* 92: 875–87.

Haskins, Charles H. 1927. *The Renaissance of the Twelfth Century*. Cambridge, MA: Harvard University Press.

Herren, Michael. 2007. "Reflections on the *Ecloga Theoduli*: Where is the Authorial Voice?" In *Poetry and Exegesis in Premodern Latin Christianity: The Encounter between Classical and Christian Strategies of Interpretation*, edited by Willemien Otten and Karla Pollmann. Supplements to Vigiliae Christianae 87. Leiden, Boston: Brill.

Hexter, Ralph J. 1986. *Ovid and Medieval Schooling: Studies in Medieval School Commentaries on Ovid's Ars Amatoria, Epistulae ex Ponto, and Epistulae Heroidum.* Munich: Arbeo-Gesellschaft.

———. 2011. "Shades of Ovid: *pseudo- (and para-) Ovidiana* in the Middle Ages." In *Ovid in the Middle Ages,* edited by James G. Clark, Frank T. Coulson, and Kathryn L. McKinley, 284–309. Cambridge: Cambridge University Press.

Hutcheon, Linda. 1985. *A Theory of Parody: The Teachings of Twentieth-Century Art Forms.* New York: Methuen.

Irvine, Martin. 1994. *The Making of Textual Culture: 'Grammatica' and Literary Theory, 350–1100*. Cambridge Studies in Medieval Literature 19. Cambridge: Cambridge University Press.

Jaeger, C. Stephen. 1994. *The Envy of Angels: Cathedral Schools and Social Ideas in Medieval Europe, 950–1200*. Middle Ages Series. Philadelphia: University of Pennsylvania Press.

———. 1997. "Charismatic Body—Charismatic Text." *Exemplaria* 9: 117–37.

Jeauneau, Edouard. 2009. *Rethinking the School of Chartres*, translated by Claude P. Desmarais. Rethinking the Middle Ages 3. Toronto: University of Toronto Press.

Le Goff, Jacques. 2001. "What Did the Twelfth-Century Renaissance Mean?" In *The Medieval World*, edited by Peter Linehan and Janet L. Nelson. London: Routledge.

McKitterick, Rosamond. 1989. *The Carolingians and the written word*. Cambridge: Cambridge University Press.

———, ed. 1994. *Carolingian Culture: Emulation and Innovation*. Cambridge: Cambridge University Press.

Moos, Peter von. 1988. "Das 12. Jahrhundert—eine 'Renaissance' oder ein 'Aufklärungszeitalter'?" *Mittellateinisches Jahrbuch* 23: 1–10.

Morris, Colin. 1972. *The Discovery of the Individual, 1050–1200*. New York: Harper and Row.

Munk Olsen, B. 1982–89. *L'étude des auteurs classiques latins aux XIe et XIIe siècles*. 3 vols. Documents, études et répertoires. Paris: Editions du Centre national de la recherche scientifique.

Nichols, Stephen G. 1991. "The New Medievalism: Tradition and Discontinuity in Medieval Culture." In *The New Medievalism*, edited by Marina S. Brownlee, Kevin Brownlee, and Stephen G. Nichols. Parallax. Baltimore: Johns Hopkins University Press.

Otter, Monika. 1996. *Inventiones: Fiction and Referentiality in Twelfth-Century English Historical Writing*. Chapel Hill: University of North Carolina Press.

———. 2010. "Vultus adest (The Face Helps): Performance, Expressivity and Interiority." In *Rhetoric Beyond Words: Delight and Persuasion in the Middle Ages*, edited by Mary Carruthers. Cambridge Studies in Medieval Literature 78. Cambridge: Cambridge University Press.

Rankin, Susan. 2010. "*Terribilis est locus iste*: The Pantheon in 609." In *Rhetoric Beyond Words: Delight and Persuasion in the Middle Ages*, edited by Mary Carruthers. Cambridge Studies in Medieval Literature 78. Cambridge: Cambridge University Press.

Reynolds, Leighton. D. 1983. *Texts and Transmission: A Survey of the Latin Classics*. Oxford: Clarendon.

Rollo, David. 2000. *Glamorous Sorcery: Magic and Literacy in the High Middle Ages*. Medieval Cultures 25. Minneapolis: University of Minnesota Press.

Rouche, Michel. 1989. "The Carolingian 'Renewal'." In *The Cambridge Illustrated History of the Middle Ages, I: 350–950*, edited by Robert Fossier. Cambridge: Cambridge University Press.

Schramm, Percy E. 1929. *Kaiser, Rom und Renovatio: Studien und Texte zur Geschichte des römischen Erneuerungsgedankens vom Ende des karolingischen Reiches bis zum Investiturstreit*. 2 vols. Studien der Bibliothek Warburg 17. Leipzig: B. G. Teubner.

Stierle, Karlheinz. 1979. "Erfahrung und narrative Form: Bemerkungen zu ihrem Zusammenhang in Fiktion und Historiographie." In *Theorie und Erzählung in der Geschichte*, edited by Jürgen Kocka and Thomas Nipperdey. Beiträge zur Historik 3. Munich: Deutscher Taschenbuchverlag.

Stock, Brian. 1983. *The Implications of Literacy*. Princeton: Princeton University Press.

Stotz, Peter. 1981. "Dichten als Schulfach: Aspekte mittelalterlicher Schuldichtung." *Mittellateinisches Jahrbuch* 16: 1–16.

Tilliette, Jean-Yves. 1994. "Savants et poètes du moyen âge face à Ovide: Les débuts de l'*aetas Ovidiana*." In *Ovidius Redivivus: Von Ovid zu Dante*, edited by Michelangelo Picone and Bernhard Zimmermann. Stuttgart: Metzler & Poeschel.

———. 1995. "Tamquam lapides vivi: Sur les 'élégies romaines' d'Hildebert de Lavardin (ca. 1100)." In *'Alla Signorina': Mélanges offerts à Noëlle de la Blanchardière*, edited by Claude Nicolet. Collection de l'Ecole française de Rome 204. Rome: École française.

Traube, Ludwig. 1911. *Vorlesungen und Abhandlungen*, edited by Paul Lehmann. Vol. 2. Munich: Beck.

Treadgold, Warren. 1984. "Introduction: Renaissances and Dark Ages." In *Renaissances Before the Renaissance: Cultural Revivals of Late Antiquity and the Late Middle Ages*, edited by Warren Treadgold. Stanford: Stanford University Press.

Ward, John O. 1995. *Ciceronian Rhetoric in Treatise, Scholion and Commentary*. Typologie des sources du moyen âge occidental 58. Turnhout: Brépols.

Wright, David H. 1993. "The Forgotten Early Romanesque Illustrations of Terence in Vat. Lat. 3305." *Zeitschrift für Kunstgeschichte* 56: 183–206.

Wright, Roger. 1982. *Late Latin and Early Romance in Spain and Carolingian France*. ARCA, Classical and Medieval Texts, Papers and Monographs 8. Liverpool: F. Cairns.

———. 1991. "The Conceptual Distinction Between Latin and Romance: Invention or Evolution?" In *Latin and the Romance Languages in the Early Middle Ages*, edited by Roger Wright. Croom Helm Romance Linguistics Series. London: Routledge.

CHAPTER 26

HUMANISM AND CONTINUITIES IN THE TRANSITION TO THE EARLY MODERN

RONALD G. WITT

LATIN humanism began in Italy in the mid-thirteenth century as a literary movement dedicated to the restoration of the texts of ancient Latin literature, their study, and their use as models for imitation. The defining goal of the humanists was to recapture in their own writings, inspired by these texts, the beauty of the poetry and prose of antiquity. By the sixteenth century this movement was to have a transformative effect on Western European society. The humanists articulated for the first time in European history the modern lay ethic in which the life of lay people had at least equal value to that of clerics in God's sight. They created the secondary school curriculum focused on ancient Greek and Roman authors that dominated Western European education down to the twentieth century. The philological techniques and hermeneutical methods the humanists developed proved fundamental to the wave of religious reform movements that swept over the subcontinent in the sixteenth century, while ancient geographical and astronomical works that it made available, beginning with the translation of Ptolemy's *Geography*, provided vital spurs for the exploration of the earth. Finally, the humanists' highly developed sense of historical perspective not only helped Europeans gain control of the past by seeing it as a time-differentiated series of social, political, economic, religious, and intellectual changes, but also, against that backdrop, to objectify the present with a view to the reform of society and politics.

Latin humanism began in that part of Italy known as the *regnum*, the northern third of the Italian peninsula that formed the southern part of the Holy Roman Empire. Before the thirteenth century this area can scarcely be said to have had a literary tradition (the summary account of the intellectual character of the *regnum* until the early thirteenth century is taken from Witt, 2011). Roughly twenty Latin poems survive from the twelfth century, among them Mosè del Brolo's *Liber pergaminus* (Gorni 1970, 440–56) and *Carmen de gestis Frederici I Imperatoris in Lombardia* (Schmale-Ott 1965). Warfare between the Italian cities and between them and the emperor constituted the major topic for the larger share of what production there was. With the exception of the poetry of Pietro Damiani (d. 1073) (Damiani 1964), even less poetry survives from the preceding 300 year period. Of the poems, the most outstanding are *Il canto delle scolte modenesi* (Godman 1985, 324–27) and *O admirabile Veneris idolum* (Giovini 1999, 261–62) from the ninth and tenth century, respectively.

As for prose, in the course of the twelfth century, manuals of *ars dictaminis* became the textbooks for prose composition and all but obviated the possibility of a further range of stylistic choices. Crucial to the expansion of the Latin-literate population had been the propaganda wars of the Investiture Struggle (1075–1122) in which pro-imperial and pro-papal publicists argued for the justice of their cause. These propaganda campaigns served to awaken in the urban populations, deeply involved in the struggle at the local level, to the importance of the written word. By offering instruction in writing highly formulaic Latin letters, composed according to well-defined structural divisions with a simple vocabulary and sentence structure, the manuals were designed to meet the demand of a new public with minimal training in Latin grammar (Witt 2008, 70–72). Although the authors proclaimed their allegiance to Cicero in the introduction to their manuals, the models that they provided had much in common with legal documents.

The formal, legalistic character of Latin epistolography fits well with the new interest in reviving Roman law. In a society where the suzerain was rarely in residence, Roman law appealed to Italians because it promised to provide a legal network for the whole kingdom, overriding local laws and customs. For the same reason *ars dictaminis* proved congenial to the growing interest in canon law, a direct outgrowth of the fifty-year conflict over investiture, in which rival parties sought out statements to support their position by citing biblical passages, decrees of church councils, writings of Latin and Greek fathers, and the like.

The intellectual life of the *regnum* in the twelfth century, consequently, was dominated by legal/rhetorical interests inimical to literary creativity. Grammar instruction was streamlined to provide enough Latin to enable the student to write formulaic letters and begin legal studies. Disciplines associated in the north with a clerical intelligentsia, theology and biblical exegesis, also fared badly in such a climate. Several theological treatises remain from the middle decades of the century, but the discipline only began to enjoy attention in the 1220s with the arrival of mendicant friars trained north of the Alps. No exegetical works survive after the death of Bruno of Asti (1123) for the rest of the century. The mediocre character of the liturgical sequence, so richly developed north of the Alps in this century, exemplifies the lack of innovation in liturgical performance.

The stepchild of both the Carolingian and Ottonian empires, the *regnum* lacked the patronage that offered rewards for literary and scholarly work. The burst of production of such work linked to the support of Matilda of Tuscany (1046–1115), the single princely patron identifiable in the *regnum* since the destruction of the Lombard kingdom in 773, suggests what a catalyst patronage could have been in inspiring intellectual life.

After 1100, in northern Europe, however, the formation of a clerical audience proved a more important source of inspiration for literary and scholarly production than patronage. An important proof of its existence resides in the scrolls of the dead, the scrolls carried sometimes across the whole of Francia by representatives of monasteries and churches in search of prayers from ecclesiastical establishments along the way for the soul of a dead churchman or important lay figure connected with their institutions. By 1100, these scrolls had become something akin to literary journals on which individuals inscribed poetic creations in honor of the dead man or woman.

Nothing like a clerical public existed in the *regnum*. Much of the writing by clerics that survives celebrates individual cities and their triumphs in war. Loyalty to the city and religious faith appear inextricably linked for clerics and laymen alike. Given the proliferated nature of the *regnum*'s ecclesiastical organization and the strong sense of local patriotism, the clergy lacked the kind of textual community that existed among their counterpart in northern Europe, which provided an audience for works of biblical exegesis, theology, liturgy, and religious poetry. Until the advent of the Dominicans and Franciscans in the first quarter of the thirteenth century and a growing divide between the intellectual concerns of laymen and clerics, it is possible to affirm that compared with northern Europe the *regnum* had no clerical culture.

Granted that Italian humanism represented a sharp break with prior intellectual life in its place of origin, what did this movement, drawing inspiration from ancient Roman literature and history, have in common with what has come to be called "medieval humanism" (Southern 1970, 29–60) and to what extent were the earliest Italian humanists inspired by its influence? We must begin with the fact that the early Italian humanists were almost without exception laymen compared to their clerical counterparts in medieval humanism. Members of the first two generations were city dwellers, notaries or judges, and most were deeply committed to communal politics and/or active in city administrations. Their civic experience led them to impose a very different template on the works of the ancient Romans from that of the proponents of medieval humanism, that is, northern European clerics.

The advent of lay writers by the mid-thirteenth century, skilled enough in Latin to collate ancient manuscripts and to emulate ancient Latin style, as well as the existence of a body of readers sufficient to encourage their enterprise, requires an explanation, albeit brief. Throughout the medieval centuries many of the everyday actions taken in the *regnum*, such as buying, selling, and leasing property, taking oaths, judicial processes, and governmental decisions, were recorded in documents written by notaries with practical knowledge of Latin. Although in earlier centuries some of these notaries had been clerics, after 1150 only lay notaries appear in the documents.

Some laymen, however, possessed a knowledge of Latin beyond that required to capture legal actions in appropriate legal form. Already in the eleventh century, laymen with legal training began the ambitious task of reconstructing the texts of ancient Roman law. The greatest philological achievement of the European Middle Ages, the reconstruction required not only legal training but also a good foundation in Latin grammar far beyond practical Latin literacy. Laymen also dominated another new scholarly activity, the translation of Greek theological and scientific works into Latin. Of the five men from the *regnum* identified as translators in the twelfth century, four were definitely laymen and, until his emigration to Spain, the fifth, Gherardo of Cremona, had probably been a layman as well.

The number of notaries in the *regnum* multiplied dramatically after 1200 and the demand for schooling in grammar, the necessary preparation for study of the *ars notaria*, grew correspondingly. Not counting older centers of advanced education at Bologna, Modena, and perhaps Reggio, at least six universities were founded in the *regnum* between 1204 and the 1240s. Preparation in grammar was the basic requirement for entry. By the 1220s the appearance of local communal histories in Latin, written largely by laymen and containing classical citations and original poetry by the authors or their friends, suggests an urban intellectual milieu in which grammatical knowledge was relatively widespread. By the second half of the thirteenth century we have enough evidence to affirm that the vast majority of the teachers in the grammar schools were laymen, mainly notaries.

An early indication of the new orientation that laymen gave to the interpretation of the works of ancient Roman literature and history is found in the writings of Albertano of Brescia (fl. 1226–53), a notary. He was the first to draw on his reading of ancient Roman writers to formulate a code of conduct specifically designed to guide the daily lives of the citizens of urban communes in the *regnum* (Nuccio 1994, 95–155). Although writing in the prose style of *ars dictaminis*, Albertano drew his justification for the active life of the merchant population of the city primarily from the works of Cicero and Seneca. Whereas a limited number of Cicero's writings, primarily his *De inventione*, had been quoted by Italian authors for centuries, references to Seneca had appeared in a work authored in the *regnum* only in the 1190s. As for Albertano, he gained his knowledge of the Roman Stoic by reading an unglossed manuscript of Seneca's *Epistulae ad Lucilium*, now Brescia, Biblioteca civica, MS Queriniano B II, which he probably found in the local cathedral library.

Consequently, by its very nature Italian humanism, a movement fostered by laymen, made a fundamental contribution to the transition of Europe from medieval to early modern in that it broke with northern medieval humanism by emphasizing a new focus for the study of the ancients, that is, the needs of contemporary lay society. What continuities, then, were there? Despite the frequent exchange of students and teachers with transalpine Europe, especially with Francia during most of the twelfth century, intellectual life in the *regnum* remained largely immune to external influence. By contrast, northern Europeans profited in this period from Italian innovations in Roman and canon law as well as in rhetoric (*ars dictaminis*). In the 1190s, however, the situation changed to such an extent that something akin to a French invasion occurred in certain disciplines of knowledge.

Despite the fact that Justinian's corpus might have offered at least scholars of Roman law—all laymen—an opportunity to appreciate the character of ancient society, the traditional Italian approach to the corpus through glosses tended to discourage a general view of the texts and of the society that they reflected. Only after 1190 did Bolognese jurists borrow the more synthetic French approach involving analysis of the *Code*, *Institutes*, and *Digest* as whole works. In the 1190s as well, Italian jurists followed the lead of French jurists in undertaking the interpretation of the *Tres Libri*, that part of the *Code* (Bks. 10–12) that dealt primarily with ancient Roman administrative law and required a broad appreciation of ancient and late-ancient Roman history and society. Beginning with Azzo (fl. 1190–1220), references to ancient literature and works of history decidedly increased in Italian legal treatises.

By the 1190s the French approach to *ars dictaminis* also had become popular in Italy. Although still formulaic, the ornateness of the French model letters presupposed more intensive training in grammar and literature than the traditional Italian approach required. In the same decade recent French teachings on Latin syntax, a subject cursorily treated in ancient manuals, made their first appearance in a grammar written by Bene of Florence (fl. 1190s–1240), an Italian grammarian at Bologna. As his and subsequent Italian grammars were to show, the effect was to revolutionize the teaching of the subject in the *regnum*'s schools. Introduced into Italy a decade or so later, French manuals of *ars praedicandi* offered a consistent formal structure for sermon composition designed to help clerics meet Innocent III's new emphasis on preaching.

The relationship of early Italian humanism to French innovations was complex. The numerous grammars authored in the *regnum* in the thirteenth century reflect the concern of Italians to improve the teaching of Latin for an expanding body of students by devising practical applications of French theorizing on Latin syntax. Almost paradoxically, the interest in the more complex style of French *dictamen*, essentially unclassical in character, encouraged an emphasis on sentence construction and biblical and classical allusions. As a consequence, the growing body of lay literates presumably left grammar school with a better knowledge of Latin grammar than was generally available in the twelfth century and with some acquaintance with biblical and classical sources. It is important to stress, however, the almost total absence of evidence that the writings of authors associated with twelfth-century medieval humanism had any discernible influence on the new classicizing movement.

By contrast, the origins of Italian humanism were intimately connected with the introduction of Provençal poetry into the *regnum* in the 1180s and 1190s, and the growing popularity of French epics and romances late in the twelfth century.

Principally these works contributed to a new appreciation of the poetic voice as reflected in the widespread textual community that they enjoyed. The very success of the new poetry, however, depended on the expansion of education then in progress. In southern Francia the fact that music appears to have accompanied the recitation of the poetry suggests that it tended to be presented orally. In Italy the poems were not only performed orally but circulated as texts without musical accompaniment. In fact, the corpus of Provençal poetry along with the *vidas* and *rasos*, that is the biographies of the troubadour and commentaries on the poetry, was created almost entirely in the *regnum* (Witt 2000, 47–49). Skills acquired in elementary school might have been sufficient to read the poems, but most readers were probably trained in grammar schools where they would already have been acquainted with literary texts.

Italians very quickly assimilated the formulas and language of the troubadours, and while in areas of Lombardy and the Veneto, including Padua, Provençal remained the dominant vernacular for lyric, after about 1230 Italian vernacular poets increasingly wrote in their local dialect. I am suggesting that contact with vernacular poetry by the Latin literate produced an aesthetic awakening to the emotive power of poetry in general and in the long run encouraged creative emulation in Latin. The poetry of Lovato dei Lovati (1240–1309), the first Italian humanist, was clearly influenced by Provençal literature, and it is likely that he also composed poetry in Provençal that has not survived.

The inspiration of Provençal poetry did not have an immediate effect. Over fifty years separate the last significant Latin poem of the twelfth century, the *Elegia* by the Tuscan cleric Enrico of Settimello, composed in 1192/93 (Enrico of Settimello 1949) and the first of the thirteenth century, the Latin epic *De victoria quam Genuenses ex Friderico II retulerunt* (Urso 1853 and 1857), composed shortly after 1245 by the Genoese notary Urso of Genoa. The brief poetic efforts that appear in the communal histories from the 1220s, however, which indicate knowledge of poetic techniques and a growing receptivity for poetic expression, constituted steps preparatory to the flowering of ambitious poetic compositions beginning with Urso's work. In the quarter century that followed Urso's poem at least six other writers, five of them laymen, composed Latin poetry. Lovato dei Lovati (1240/41–1309), notary and judge of Padua, was the youngest and most radical of the group.

At least by sixteen, Lovato di Rolando di Lovato of Padua was a notary, as had been his father and grandfather before him, but his father had higher ambitions for his talented son. Because the university had remained closed from 1237 and 1260/61, it was only after about 1261 that the young man could begin the six years of legal training necessary to become a judge. Joining Padua's College of Judges in 1267, he served numerous terms as a judge in the communal courts and played an active role in communal government. He was honored with communal knighthood and, thus ennobled, became an attractive candidate for the office of *podestà* in neighboring cities. We know only that he held that office in Vicenza in 1291 and perhaps in Treviso in 1290 (Weiss 1951, 5–11).

The time that remained to him from professional and political responsibilities he devoted to studying the ancients and writing poetry. He read voraciously and sought out forgotten manuscripts. His marginal notes to Justin's *Epitome* in British Library, Add. 19906, indicate that he matched the account given in the text to comparable passages in Livy's *Decades* I, III, and IV. The third and fourth *Decades* were almost unknown in previous centuries, and Lovato's now lost manuscript of Livy, probably taken by him from the monastery at Pomposa, played an important role in the revival of Livy's work (Billanovich 1981, 1: 6–10).

His manuscript of Seneca's *Tragedies*, created by him on the basis of the medieval "A" and the superior and hitherto neglected "E" version of Pomposa, served as a fundamental text in the revival of Seneca's works. Lovato's brief essay on Seneca's complicated metric scheme in the plays, which he appended to his Seneca manuscript, was perhaps the first comprehensive analysis in the Middle Ages of an ancient author's meters (Megas 1967, 105). He was the first in three or four centuries to cite Tibullus, Propertius, Horace's *Carmina*, and Statius's *Silvae* in his poetry, and he also reintroduced Ovid's *Ibis* and Martial's *Epigrammata* to Western Europe (Reynolds 1974, 110–11).

Even more momentous than Lovato's textual scholarship, however, was his introduction of a classicizing approach to Latin style that was to become dominant in Europe in succeeding centuries. Lovato's four surviving epistolary poems represent the first Latin poetry written by an Italian since antiquity to employ classical diction for the expression of private thoughts and feelings. Strongly opposed to the current domination in the *regnum* of poetic composition by French vernacular models and driven to rival the personal, if formalized, voice articulated in the Provençal lyric, Lovato cast back to the ancient tradition for models. His intimate acquaintance with major authors of the late Roman republican and early imperial periods and his innate talent for creative imitation enabled him, as he put it, to follow *veterum vestigia vatum* [the footsteps of the ancient poets]—echoing Horace, *Epistulae* 2.2.80, *sequi vestigia vatum*, by appropriating not only their techniques, but also their modes of expressing a range of nuanced attitudes and feelings. As a result, through cultivating the style by which ancient writers expressed their emotional and intellectual life, Lovato provided the key to exploring the mentality and sensibility of antiquity. Essentially, Lovato's poetry sought to celebrate the aesthetic realm of antiquity as a contrast with that articulated by contemporary vernacular literatures.

The first two surviving examples of Lovato's epistolary poetry were written in 1267–68, when Conradin and Charles of Anjou were struggling for possession of the Hohenstaufen Italian inheritance (Foligno 1906–7, 51–55). The earlier letter was addressed to Lovato's friend Compagnino, a Paduan legist, who apparently was not living in Padua at the time. Lovato had been ill, and the sick man reported his illness to his friend in 228 lines of elegiac verse. The second letter, composed in dactylic hexameter, was probably sent days later. By this time, the poet felt well enough to think of marrying his fiancée.

From the outset of the first poem, the poet's voice resonates with echoes of antiquity:

> Accipe quam patria tibi mittit ab urbe salutem,
> Compagnine, tui cura secunda, Lupus.
> Scire voles, sic te socii iactura pericli
> Exagitat, quali est mea cumba lacu.
> (Foligno 1906–7, 51, vv. 1–4; Sisler 1977, 56)

[Accept the greeting which Lupus, your second charge, sends to you from his home town, Compagnino. Your friend's dangerous illness so disturbs you that you'll want to know on what sort of sea my skiff is sailing.] (Sisler 1977, 82)

Here the "tui cura secunda, Lupus" draws either on Propertius 2.1, vv. 25–26, or Statius, *Silvae* 4.4, v. 20; and "socii iactura...exagitat" recalls either Propertius 3.7, vv. 41–42, or Ovid, *Amores* 2.14, vv. 31–32. This is learned poetry, densely interspersed with ancient poetic fragments and mythological and biblical reminiscences. Intensely referential verses, such poems must have delighted his small audience, charmed by familiar literary associations set in a new context and intrigued regarding the origin of some of the expressions and imagery drawn from rare ancient texts and so classical in character but unfamiliar.

Wasted by a fever lasting many days, despairing of help from his doctors, bedridden and desperate, Lovato described in the first poem how he finally resorted to magic. The scene may have been imagined or in any case embellished. After describing the gyrations of the sorceress, a wrinkled old woman, who was about to administer a secret potion to him, Lovato elaborately described the contents of the magical mixture:

> Postmodo secrete *Circaeas* aggerat *herbas*,[1]
> *Quas* dederat *Pindos, Othrys, Olympus*, Athos,
> Quas Anthedonii gustarunt intima Glauci.
> *Nec* desunt monti *gramina lecta Rubro*
> Nec quae refovent ictam serpente, Galanthi,
> Nec Florentini stamina fulva croci
> Additur his *myrrhae* facinus, gummique Sabaeum,
> *Et quae* cum *casiis cinnama mittit Arabs*.
> His oculis lyncis, renovataque *cornua cervi*
> *Et* candens refugo *concha relicta mari*,
> Neu teneam verbis animum, *miscentur* in unum
> *Singula Thessalici* quae docuere *magi*.
> (Foligno 1906–7, 53, vv. 83–94; Sisler 1977, 60–61)

---

1. The words borrowed from ancient authors are italicized: represented are Tibullus, Ovid (*Meta.*), Propertius, Statius (*Silv.*), Martial, Virgil (*Ecl.*), and Horace (*Car.*).

[Afterwards, she secretly piles up the herbs of Circe which Pindos, Othrys, Olympus, and Athos had provided for her, and which the inner parts of Anthedonian Glaucus had tasted. Nor are herbs collected from Mount Rubrus lacking, nor those which renew you, bitten by a serpent, Galanthis, nor the tawny fibers of the Florentine crocus. To these are added the working of myrrh and Sabaean gum and twigs of cinnamon, which, with cinnamon bark, the Arabs send. Also added to these are the eyes of a lynx and the regrown horns of a deer, and a glistening white conch, left behind at low tide. And to make sure that I cannot keep my mind[2] through magic words, all the individual things which the Thessalian wizards taught are mixed into one.] (Sisler 1970, 85–86)

In thirteen lines, Lovato took the occasion to intermingle lavish borrowings from well-known works, Ovid's *Metamorphosis* and Virgil's *Eclogues*, with newly revived authors like Tibullus, Propertius, and Martial, and rare works by familiar authors like Horace's *Carmina* and Statius's *Silvae* (Sisler 1977, 68–81).

At times, Lovato struggled unsuccessfully to bend the language to his thought. A few passages read like prose (e.g., vv. 53–64). The work's antique facade was occasionally blemished by biblical references and, at one point, by the mention of Tristan wounded for love of Isolde (vv. 221–22). The overall effect, however, was impressive. The vocabulary was classical throughout, the metric quantities were generally correct, and rhetorical figures were used with restraint. In the first poem, Ovid was the presiding genius of Lovato's creation, from the opening section describing the ravaging fire of Lovato's disease (akin to the love pangs of the ancient heroines of the *Heroides*) to the elegiac character of the conclusion, where the poet, seeking consolation in his writing, invoked, among other examples, the scene of the exiled Ovid relieving his misery through song on the shores of the Black Sea:

> Naso Tomitana metro spatiatus in ora
> Flebilis exilii debilitabat onus.
> (Foligno 1906–7, 55, vv. 215–16; Sisler 1977, 67)

[Ovid, walking around on the shores of Tomis, used to lessen the burden of his wretched exile with verse.] (Sisler 1977, 91)

In the second poem, Ovid shared with Propertius the honor of providing the most subtexts.

The intimate nature of Lovato's letter of 1267/68 broke new ground. Enrico of Settimello, the only Italian medieval poet in the twelfth century to approach the lyrical quality of Lovato's composition, began his *Elegia* (1192/93) on a personal note, but the didacticism of the ensuing furious debate between the author and Fortune ended by drowning out the voice of intimacy. By contrast, Lovato had no apparent didactic purpose in mind. His only concern was to articulate his suffering in poetry and, by sharing it with his good friend Compagnino, to temper the agony

---

2. As opposed to Sisler, I read the phrase "Neu teneam animum" to mean "keep control."

coursing through his body. The second, shorter letter to Compagnino, written days later as the disease had somewhat abated, was equally personal in tone and equally classicizing (Foligno 1906–7, 55–56; Sisler 1977, 92–96).

Despite his intention to classicize Latin, both the form and content of Lovato's work exhibit the influence of the *langue d'oïl* and the *langue d'oc*. The inclusion of Tristan among a series of ancient examples in the first letter to Compagnino hints at the effect of epic French literature on the poet, and at some time in his life Lovato composed a Latin poem, of which only six verses survive, that celebrated the romance of Tristan and Isolde while incorporating parts of the narrative tradition connected with Lancelot (Billanovich 1976, 139–42). The project suggests that Lovato thought that the material could be more elegantly expressed in Latin than in French.

Provençal poetry also inspired Lovato and other members of his group to assume *seghals*, that is, code names for themselves: Lovato called himself *Lupus* (wolf) and Mussato took the name *Asellus* (little ass) (Witt 2000, 101). Lovato's letter of circa 1290, to Bellino Bissolo, concluding with an address to the letter itself in the last two lines (vv. 106–7), is a borrowing from the Provençal *renvois* (Weiss 1951, 17). Several fourteen-line hexameter compositions, Latin versions of the vernacular sonnet form, are found among Lovato's late poems (Padrin 1887, 1–4 and 26–27), while he and other members of the Paduan group were given to poetic debates probably inspired directly by the Provençal *tenso*. Most importantly, however, Lovato's rivalry with the vernacular led him to develop a poetic form alien to the narrow Latin verse tradition of northern Italy just as more than seventy years earlier, Provençal influence had inspired Enrico of Settimello to write the first lines of lyric surviving in the *regnum* since the tenth century (Bianchini 1989, 855–63).

The collection of short poems exchanged late in life by Lovato with members of his circle, however, shows that poetic fashions of the day still detained them, at least when circulating poetry within their own group. Whereas Lovato's four long epistle poems had been based on the poetic letters of Ovid and Horace, the poetry in this collection seems alien to any ancient model. Overall, the poverty of figurative language, the taste for end-rhyme, and the frequency of word-games in these poetic exchanges reveal that on the threshold of a new aesthetic, these scholars could not help reverting to the old from which they still derived pleasure.

A man of immense personal magnetism, Lovato created a small circle of contemporaries and younger men dedicated to the study of ancient history and literature. Of other Paduans of his generation, Ugo Mezzabati, a fellow Paduan jurist (Foligno 1906–7, 47), Bovetino Bovetini, a cleric (De Angelis 1985, 57–69), and Giambono di Andreae, a notary (Padrin 1887, 6–11 and 31–34), only a handful of metric poetry survives, all of it pedestrian in quality. Another member of the Paduan Guild of Judges, Geremia da Montagnone (1250/60–1320/22), writing in dictaminal prose, displayed knowledge of a wide range of ancient authors in his *Florilegia* (*Epytoma Sapientie*; Geremia da Montagnone 1505), composed in the first years of the fourteenth century. His classification of the poets prior to approximately 600

CE as *poetae* and all those after as *versilogi* (versifiers) probably reflects a widely diffused judgment among learned circles in the Veneto of the superior quality of ancient literature.

A contemporary foreign scholar also reflected Lovato's influence on his work. In two periods late in Lovato's life (1293 and 1305–8), Padua played host to Riccobaldo of Ferrara (1251–1318), the author of a series of histories. Already the author of a universal history entitled *Pomerium* and a series of shorter works, during his four years in Padua he wrote his *Historiae*, which, like the *Pomerium*, was a universal history, but one placing more emphasis on the ancient Roman period. A third major work, *Compendium Romanae historiae*, probably composed mostly at Verona in 1317–18, summarized the material covered in the *Historiae*.

During his two residences in the city, Riccobaldo was likely associated closely with Lovato's circle. He may already have been acquainted with Livy's fourth *Decade* before his arrival in Padua in 1293, but during his second, longer sojourn, like Lovato he studied Livy intensively and became interested in other ancient authors such as Josephus and Justin, apparently ignored in the *regnum* before his generation. The writings of Riccobaldo's last fifteen years indicate an increasing critical faculty and a reluctance to take medieval authorities at their word. Although his *Historiae* and *Compendium* rely heavily on Vincent of Beauvais when treating the period from the ninth century on, they utilize ancient and late ancient sources for the earlier period. Nevertheless, while Riccobaldo's histories reflect humanist tendencies, his fidelity to universal history and apparent lack of interest in expressing himself in classicizing style make him more like Geremia da Montagnone than an early humanist.

When Lovato died in 1309, the mantle of leadership in the new literary movement fell on Albertino Mussato (1261–1329). In 1315, Mussato's most famous work, *Ecerinis*, a play heavily influenced by Seneca's tragedies, initiated Renaissance theater. Designed to remind his fellow citizens of the dangers of tyranny in a time when Padua's freedom was being threatened by Cangrande della Scala, the plot recounted the rise and fall of the tyrant of the Romagna, Ezzelino da Romano, who had ruled Padua with a heavy hand between 1237 and 1256. By Mussato's time, the tyrant's reputation for evil had reached mythic proportions.

Thanks to their master Lovato's pioneering study of Seneca's tragedies, Mussato's plays were highly prized by Lovato's circle of disciples, who admired the profuse moral instruction encoded in the writer's aphoristic language. Seneca's portrayal of the miseries of life, the instability of fortune, and the grim fate of those who transgressed universal laws revitalized the moralists of the period. No other Latin writer known to them equaled Seneca's force in describing powerful human personalities infused with a demoniacal energy. The influence of Seneca's *Thyestes*, the principal stylistic model for the *Ecerinis*, appears early in the description of the Da Romano castle:

> *Arx* in excelso sedet
> Antiqua colle, longa Romanum vocat
> aetas; in altum porrigunt *lectum trabes*

> *Premit*que turrim contingua *ad austrum domus*
> Ventorum et omnis cladis aërea *capax*.
> (Mussato 1900, 23–24, vv. 9–12)

[On an ancient hill sits a fortress that for ages has been called Romano. Columns hold the roof on high and on the south the house joins a tower, where it is exposed to the winds and all the airy forces of destruction.] (my translation)

The relevant passage of Seneca's work reads as follows (vv. 641–47):

> In *arce* summa Pelopiae pars est *domus*
> conversa *ad austros*, cuius extremum latus
> aequale monti crescit atque urbem *permit*
> et contumacem regibus populum suis
> habet sub ictu; fulget hic turbae *capax*
> immane *tectum*, cuius auratas *trabes*
> variis columnae nobiles maculis ferunt. (Seneca 1917, 2:144)

Mussato's greatest contribution to Italian humanism was his creative imitation of ancient Latin prose style. While Lovato initiated classicizing Latin poetry, he followed tradition by writing prose in *ars dictaminis* style. The new prose style is first found in Mussato's *Historia augusta* published in 1315. In Mussato's brilliant account of Emperor Henry VII's Italian expedition during the years 1310–13, the author successfully melded stylistic concerns with his grasp of detail. Seizing the expedition as his central principle of organization, Mussato chronicled the three years of political history, in which he himself played a minor role as the leading representative of the commune to the emperor. In describing Henry VII's attack on Brescia, for example, Mussato writes:

> Nec remissus ad incumbentia Caesaris animus aggrediendi montani castri, quod moeniis civitatis contiguum est, fortunam tentare in sequentem diem constituit. Iam primum illuscesceret. Ordinatis itaque in ipso crepusculo centuriis peditum, militumque suis singulis ordinibus totam veluti insulturus civitatem, ne intrinseci in castri succursum convolarent, fundibularios, levisque armaturae pedites, quorum fere quingentos et mille Januenses direxerant, ceterosque ad expugnationem cum balistarum, tormentorumque omnis generis apparatibus ingeniosos ad castri oppugnationem sero praeordinat, summoque mane lituum ac tubarum clamoribus universi exercitus copias moenia circumeduxit. Perterriti tanto fremitu Brixiani per propugnacula quaeque assilientes, muros corona cinxere. Ad castri munitionem solitas bellicosorum excubias misere, seque ad sua quisque loca coaptavit. Assurgentes itaque Galli, Germani, Tuscorum Longobardorumque distincti ordines cum tegmentis, caeterisque instrumentis accessere ad castri foveas citeriores, excisasque rupes circumquaque. (Mussato 1636a, 389–90)

[Relentlessly making plans for attacking the mountain castle, which is near the walls of the city, the mind of Caesar decided to test fortune on the following day as soon as it was light. Thus, at dusk he drew up the ranks of infantry and the several ranks of his knights as if he were about to attack the city, in order that those inside not hasten to bring aid to the castle. In the darkness, however, he organized for an assault on the castle the stone-throwers and lightly armed infantry, of which the Genoese had sent fifteen hundred, and other men skilled in attacking with all kinds of slings and stone-throwers. At daybreak, with the clamor of trumpets and horns, he led the forces of the whole army around the walls. Thoroughly frightened at such noise, the people of Brescia, springing up on whatever ramparts they could, fortified the walls in crowds. They sent the usual guard of warriors to protect the fortress and each one took his assigned place. Thus, rising up with covering roofs and other devices, the French, Germans, and different ranks of Tuscans and Lombards approached the nearer ditches of the fortress and the hewn rocks protecting it on all sides.] (my translation)

Mussato's account of Henry VII's attack on the fortress of Brescia offered a tightly woven, logically developed description of the succession of events. In a complicated period that moved from an ablative absolute (*ordinatis...centuriis*) to a future participle (*insultaturus*), then to a purpose clause (*ne...*), and finally to a relative clause (*quorum*), Mussato provided an ordered account of the preparations from twilight until dawn. He concluded the period, however, with a declarative clause announcing the beginning of the assault at daybreak (*summoque mane...circumeduxit*). This sequence had been prepared in the first line of the passage by a psychological portrayal of the emperor restlessly searching for a plan of attack, ending in his resolution to take the field on the following day (*Nec remissus...constituit*).

The use of the syncopated perfects in the following two periods, i.e., *cinxere*, *misere*, and *accessere*, hastened the action, whereas the perfect *coaptavit* conveyed the defenders' response, which had become second nature for them since the start of the siege. The author adroitly communicated the terror roused in the inhabitants, causing them to rush to the ramparts (*perterriti...cinxere*), and the difficulty of scaling the walls of the fortress defended by ditches and "hewn rocks protecting it on all sides" (*excisasque rupes circumquaque*).

Contemporaries of Mussato, who read more than a brief passage like the text cited above, would have been struck not only by the comparative difficulty of the syntax, but also by the author's failure to comply with the standard rules of the Italian *cursus*, that is, a series of accented and unaccented patterns of syllables used in *dictamen* to conclude a clause or a sentence. Although in the preface to the *Historia augusta* he compared himself to Livy as a foot soldier to a knight (Mussato 1636b, 2, vv. 25–28), Mussato nevertheless tried to approximate the ancient periodic sentence. He was not always successful. At times, his periods failed to integrate the various clauses with the main verb. At other times, perhaps unwittingly, he introduced unnecessary neologisms and twisted the Latin to conform to a vernacular sentence structure. Nevertheless, the overall effect of the prose was classicizing.

In Mussato's generation, Padua boasted a second foreign scholar whose compositions demonstrate allegiance to Lovato's classicizing style. Pace da Ferrara taught logic and grammar in the Paduan *studium* around the beginning of the fourteenth century. While in the city, he composed at least two long poems. The first, celebrating the Venetian festival of the Purification of the Virgin, *Descriptio festi gloriosissime Virginis Marie*, written about 1299–1300, was dedicated to the doge of Venice, Pietro Gradenigo, and provided a fulsome description of one of the major festivals of the city. The second, written about 1302–4 for the newly elected bishop of Padua, Pagano della Torre, celebrated the recovery of Milan by members of the bishop's family in 1302. In later years, with his *Evidentia Ecerinidis*, an *accessus* for Mussato's play, he helped transform the work into a school text (Megas 1967, 203–4).

The dedicatory verses of Pace's poem for Pagano show him explicitly suggesting that a gulf separated him from the literary achievements of the ancients and implicitly condemning the mediocrity of the poetry of the previous millennium. While claiming that the muse has been in hiding since ancient times, Pace presented himself as a "new poet" composing "new verses":

> Tu, Dea, Maeonio quondam celeberrima cantu
> Aoniis educta iugis, ducente Marone
> In Latium, doctisque diu venerata poetis
> Romuleas dum sacra domos arcesque teneres
> Caesareas, scenis famosa, et nota cothurnis
> Calliope...
> Non ultra latuisse velis; assume sonorae
> Plectra chelis, vatisque novi dignare virenti
> Nectere fronde comas...
> Ergo novos dignare gravi modulamine versus
> Fingere, meque tuo deductum remige portu
> Siste, precor, placido, viresque impende canenti.
> (Ferrari 1893, 330–31, vv. 6–11, 15–17, 22–23)

[O you, Goddess, once wondrously celebrated by Homeric song, brought by Virgil from the Aonian mountains to Latium, and long venerated by gifted poets when, O Calliope, you as a sacred being inhabited the houses of Romulus and the Caesarian fortresses, and were well-known on the stage and distinguished for your tragedies... hide yourself no longer; take up the pick of the sweet-sounding harp and deign to bind the hair of a new poet with the living leaf... Accordingly, be willing to invent new verses full of grave melody, and place me, led by your oar, in a calm port, I pray, and provide power to the singer.] (my translation)

By Mussato's generation, it becomes difficult to assess the extent to which classicizing works appearing in other cities of the *regnum* were directly influenced by the Paduans or had local origins. In the case of the Vicentine scholar Ferreto Ferreti (1294–1337), however, Mussato's historical works were a major source of inspiration. In his *Historia rerum in Italia gestarum* (ca. 1330), Ferrato reverently mentions Mussato in the introduction and inserts passages of Mussato into his work. Ferreto's style was less periodic than Mussato's. He tended to develop his narrative by accumulating clauses, following the temporal succession of events:

> His iactatus Cesar animi pressuris, equo subiectus, per castra, visendi causa, cardinales secum ducit, utque suorum languentes impetus ad pugnam audentius erigat, dein sumpto cibo, hora pene sexta, paratis Wandalorum Ytalorumque copiis et armis, hostes impeti telis imperat.... (de' Ferreti 1908–20, 1: 347–48)

> [Disturbed by these worries, mounting a horse, Caesar led the cardinals with him through the camp for an inspection, so that he might stimulate the failing energies of his troops more boldly for an attack, and then, after eating, at almost the sixth hour, with the forces and arms of the Germans and Italians made ready, he ordered an attack on the enemy with weapons.] (my translation)

The sometimes tortured, exuberant structures of Mussato's text have been unpacked and simplified. While Ferreto's Latin had shed many of its associations with *dictamen*, he remained loyal to the medieval *cursus*, and his lexicon was less classical than Mussato's. Although easier to read, Ferreto's style lacked Mussato's immediacy and concentrated vigor.

Although not humanists inasmuch as they were unconcerned with stylistic imitation of the ancients, scholars in Verona utilized philological techniques in their approach to ancient texts similar to those of Lovato and Mussato. Relying on various patristic works, the acts of councils, and ancient and early medieval historical writings, Giovanni de Matociis compiled his *Historia imperialis* in the second decade of the fourteenth century in an unadorned Latin. He realized that the books of the ancient *Historia augusta*, on which he based relevant chapters, were out of order and the text corrupt. He refuted those who claimed that Constantine had only been baptized at the end of his life, and he demolished a number of saints' legends. His greatest philological feat was his *Brevis adnotatio de duobus Pliniis*, composed between 1320 and 1328 (Avesani 1976, 2: 119–20). In that short work, he proved that the single Pliny of the Middle Ages was actually two, uncle and nephew.

Benzo da Alessandria is usually associated with Verona, although he lived in Verona only from 1328 until his death in 1333. His immense *Cronica*, a history of the world from the creation down to Henry VII, like that of Riccobaldo's earlier, was modeled on Vincent of Beauvais's *Speculum historiale* (Berrigan 1967, 125–92). Like Petrarch, Benzo had spent many years searching in various cities for manuscripts that he needed for his research. He had already visited the cathedral library at Verona sometime before 1328 and had found, among other rare works, Catullus, Ausonius, and the *Historia augusta*. Despite his *Cronica*'s diction and its encyclopedic approach, so medieval in character, Benzo, like de Matociis, developed rigorous techniques in textual criticism. He endeavored to find the most reliable witnesses for his account and when they contradicted one another, he discussed the disagreements and then chose the most likely position. He also entertained the possibility that some of the contradictions were conscious distortions on the part of the writers. Historians for him were more reliable than poets. He did not hesitate to compare readings from different manuscripts and to admit obscurity in his sources when he found it. He scrupulously quoted from ancient and medieval texts.

Like Geremia da Montagnone in Padua, de Matociis and Benzo should not be considered humanists because of their lack of interest in classicizing. All three men, however, and especially the latter two, exhibit a new critical mentality toward their sources and an incipient sense of anachronism. As humanists developed this new mentality, ancient Rome with its thought and way of life would emerge as a "cultural alternative" to contemporary Italy and encourage objectification of the humanists' own society and its examination (Greene 1982, 90). While the mental flexibility afforded by the intensifying critical mentality led initially to calls for ethical and political reform, its focus, when subsequently redirected toward early Christian society and the sources of Christian truth, had explosive effects on the Christian establishment.

Outside the Veneto, there were very few northern Italian scholars and writers in Mussato's generation who contributed to humanism. In fact, the only one was Giovanni da Cremenate (d. ca. 1344) (Cremenate 1889). Like Mussato and Ferreto, he was inspired by Henry VII's arrival in Italy to write history. Giovanni's narration of world history from Noah down to modern times (Cremenate 1889, 5–19), finished by 1322, demonstrated his affinity with the traditions of medieval historiography. Psychological factors, prominent in Mussato and Ferrato, figured very little in Cremenate's explanation of events, and he often impeded the narrative with needless details. Nevertheless, his extensive borrowing from the first decade of Livy in the sections dealing with the early history of Rome indicates a commitment to reforming current Latin prose, albeit a heavy-handed one. His main innovation, though, was his aggressive effort to eliminate the *cursus* from his prose. Otherwise, however, when he wrote independently without Livy as his model, his style was marked by the frequent use of the present participle and minimal reliance on the subjunctive characteristic of *ars dictaminis* prose.

In central Italy three scholars stand out as second-generation Latin humanists, Giovanni del Virgilio (d. ca. 1327), Dante d'Alighieri (1265–1321), and Geri d'Arezzo (ca. 1270–ca. 1337). Professor of poetry in the Bolognese *studium* and probably of Paduan origin, Giovanni is best known for his correspondence with Dante d'Alighieri between 1319 and 1321. His verse epistle written to Dante in Ravenna encouraged the Florentine to undertake a Latin epic and assured him that such a poem would win him the laurel in Bologna.

Within the year, Dante replied—not, however, with the requested epic, but in a humorous vein—with a "humble" (the word is Dante's) bucolic. Dante began in the allegorical code traditional with pastoral poetry:

> Vidimus in nigris albo patiente lituris
> Pierio demulsa sinu modulamina nobis.
> (Dante, *Ecl.* 1, vv. 1–2, Bolisani and Valgimigli 1963, 12)

[In black letters imposed against a white background, I see a song milked for me from a Pierian breast.] (Wicksteed and Gardner 1902, 152)

He realized Giovanni's scorn of the vernacular:

> Comica nonne vides ipsum reprehendere verba,
> tum quia femineo resonant ut trita labello
> tum quia Castalias pudet acceptare sorores? (Dante, *Ecl.* 1, vv. 52–54, Bolisani and Valgimigli 1963, 16)
>
> [Do you not see that he blames the words of comedy, because they sound so trite on women's lips, and the Castalian sisters are ashamed to accept them?] (Wicksteed and Gardener 1902, 156).

In expectation that he might change Giovanni's mind, he intended to send him ten cantos of his *Paradiso*.

Giovanni explained in his reply, written later in the same year, that, inspired by Dante's revival of the bucolic cipher, he too would "sing as a herdsman in the woodlands":

> Nec mora, depostis calamis maioribus inter
> arripio tenues et labris flantibus hisco.
> (del Virgilio, vv. 31–32, Bolisani and Valgimigli 1963, 22)
>
> [And without more delay, casting the greater reeds aside, I seize the slender ones and part my lips to blow.] (Wicksteed and Gardener 1902, 161)

Whereas all the pastoral names in both poems were taken from Virgil's *Eclogues*, Dante had preserved the Virgilian subtext in his work with sparing citation of the original, while Giovanni borrowed generously.

Dante's second bucolic, probably written the following year, may have been sent only after his death. Less inspired than the first, it may have been completed by his literary heirs. In the letter, Dante reassured his various friends, anxious for him to accept Giovanni's invitation, that he would not abandon them. He praises the place of his current residence:

> ...herba
> Trinacride montis, quo non fecundior alter
> montibus in Siculis pecudes armentaque pavit.
> (Dante, *Ecl.* 2, vv. 70–72, Bolsani and Valgimigli 1963, 36)
>
> [...on the soft grass of a Trinacrian mount than which no other of Sicilian mountains has given richer pasturage to flocks and herds.] (Wicksteed and Gardner 1902, 171)

Thus, he would not desert "the dewy country of Pelorus" (v. 46). Besides, he dare not visit Bologna for fear of his life.

While Giovanni's classicizing can be explained by his probable Paduan origin and his deep admiration for Mussato, it is something of a surprise that Dante, dedicated to vernacular poetry throughout his whole life, would demonstrate both the willingness and capacity to write what would be the first bucolic Latin poetry of the

Renaissance. The roughly eight years of his exile spent moving between Verona, Padua, and Treviso, which gave Dante access not only to the North's rich libraries, but also to men dedicated to unlocking the secrets of ancient literature, provide at least a partial explanation.

Enough survives of the work of Geri d'Arezzo to credit him with classicizing the personal letter, for centuries the domain of *ars dictaminis* (Weiss 1949, 109–15 and 118–25). Mussato had classicized historical prose, but Geri initiated the century-long humanist practice of using two styles, one for personal correspondence and the other for *ars dictaminis* in official letters. His citation of hitherto rare Latin authors such as Apuleius and the younger Pliny put him in the literary avant-garde. His allusion in one letter to the two Plinys points to contact with Veronese humanism.

Until recently the first two generations of Italian humanists have curiously been regarded as "pre-humanists," rather than simply "pre-Petrarcan humanists." Although their classicizing Latin and their philological studies were not equal to his, Petrarch knew their work and built on it, even if he blatantly obscured his debt by claiming to be the pioneer. Nonetheless, in many respects Petrarch deserves the title "father of humanism." Not only did Petrarch's compelling writings, dramatized by a life lived self-consciously, serve to create, at least temporarily, an international movement and to win broad respect for humanistic endeavors among the powerful, but they also provided humanists with a clear conception of the goal of their enterprise. Neither Lovato nor Mussato did this. At the same time, while for them antiquity was confused with mythology, Petrarch focused primarily on Roman history and literature. His addition of the writings of the Latin Church Fathers to the ancient pagan sources previously studied by humanists broadened the focus of the movement and tempered the distinctively secular orientation given it by the first two generations of the movement. Beginning with Petrarch, Italian humanism faced up to the challenge of integrating the traditional reverence for ancient pagan authors with the Christian values of contemporary society.

SUGGESTIONS FOR FURTHER READING

Until recently, Novati (1926) offered the only synthetic account of the history of Latin literature in Italy down to 1200. The work, however, is largely descriptive and indicates no interest in exploring the interrelationships between literary developments and other aspects of Italian society. Witt (2011) endeavors to remedy this omission but only in regard to one geographical area of the peninsula, the *regnum*, and by defining the striking differences between the society and culture of the medieval *regnum* and those in the rest of contemporary Western Europe. The object is to explain the origins of Renaissance humanism.

Two works of Roberto Weiss (1947, 1949) are fundamental for the study of early Italian humanism. Billanovich (1976) provides a rich analysis of their writings. Witt (2000) discusses the influence of early humanism on later developments in the movement.

I have used the more accurate edition of Lovato's poetry by William Sisler (1977) rather than the earlier one of Foligno (1906–7).

BIBLIOGRAPHY

Primary sources

Berrigan, Joseph R. 1967. "Benzo d'Alessandria and the Cities of Northern Italy." *Studies in Medieval and Renaissance History* 4: 125–92.

Bolisani, Ettore and Manara Valgimigli, eds. 1963. *Corrispondenza poetica di Dante Alighieri e Giovanni del Virgilio*. Settimo centenario della nascita di Dante 1. Florence: Olschki.

Cigogna, Emmanuele. 1843. *La festa delle Marie descritta in un poemetto elegiaco latino da Pace del Friuli*. Venice: G. Cecchini.

Damiani, Petrus. 1964. *Opera poetica di S. Pier Damiani*, edited by Margareta Lokrantz. Acta Universitatis Stockholmiensis. Studia Latina Stockholmiensia 12. Stockholm, Göteborg: Almqvist & Wiksell.

Enrico of Settimello. 1949. *Elegia*, edited by Giovanni Cremaschi. Bergamo: Istituto Italiano Edizioni Atlas.

Ferrai, Luigi A. 1893. "Un frammento di poema storico inedito di Pace dal Friuli." *Archivio storico lombardo*, 2nd ser., 10: 322–43.

de' Ferreti, Ferreto. 1908–20. *Historia rerum in Italia gestarum*. In *Le opere di Ferreto de' Ferreti vicentino* 1, edited by Carlo Cipolla. Fonti per la storia d'Italia 43/1. Rome: Forzani E. C. Tipografi del Senato.

Foligno, Cesare. 1906–7. "Epistole inedite di Lovato de' Lovati e d'altri a lui." *Studi medievali* 2: 37–58.

Geremia da Montagnone. 1505. *Epytoma Sapientie*. Venice: Petrus Liechtensteyn Coloniensis.

Giovanni of Cermenate. 1889. *Historia Johannis de Cermenate, notarii mediolanensis*, edited by Luigi Alberto Ferrai. Fonti per la storia d'Italia 2. Rome: Tipografi del Senato.

Giovini, Marco. 1999. "'O admirabile Veneris ydolum,': Un carme d'amore paidico del X secolo e il mito di Deucalione." *Studi medievali* 3rd ser., 40: 261–78.

Godman, Peter. 1985. *Poetry of the Carolingian Renaissance*. Norman, OK: University of Oklahoma Press.

Gorni, Guglielmo. 1970. "Il *Liber Pergaminus* di Mosè de Brolo." *Studi medievali*, 3rd ser., 11: 409–60.

Megas, Anastasios. 1967. *Ho prooumanistikos kyklos tes Padouas (Lovato Lovati—Albertino Mussato) kai hoi tragodies tou L.A. Seneca*. Parartemata 11. Thessaloniki: [s. n.].

Mussato, Albertino. 1636a. "Historia augusta." In *Albertini Mussati: Historia augusta Henrici VII Caesaris et alia quae extant opera*, edited by Lorenzo Pignori et al. Venice: Typographia Ducali Pinelliana. (internal pagination)

———. 1636b. "Epistolae." In *Albertini Mussati: Historia augusta Henrici VII Caesaris et alia quae extant opera*, edited by Lorenzo Pignori et al. Venice: Typographia Ducali Pinelliana. (internal pagination)

———. 1900. *Ecerinide tragedia*, edited by Luigi Padrin. Bologna: Zanichelli.

Padrin, Luigi, ed. 1887. *Lupati de Lupatis, Bovetini de Bovetinis, Albertini Mussati necnon Jamboni Andreae de Favafuschis carmina quaedam ex codice veneto nunc primum, edita: Nozze Giusti-Giustiniani*. Padua: Tipografia del Seminario.

Riccobaldo of Ferrara. 1984. *Riccobaldi ferrariensis Compendium romanae historiae*, edited by A. Teresa Hankey. Fonti per la storia d'Italia 108, 1–2. Rome: Istituto Storico Italiano per il Medioevo.

Schmale-Ott, Irene, ed. 1965. *Carmen de gestis Frederici I Imperatoris in Lombardia*. Monumenta Germaniae Historica. Scriptores 62. Hannover: Hahn.

Seneca, Lucius Annaeus. 1917. *Seneca's Tragedies*, edited by Frank J. Miller. 2 vols. Loeb Classics. New York: Harvard University Press.

Sisler, William P. 1977. "An Edition and Translation of Lovato Lovati's Metrical Epistles." PhD Diss., Johns Hopkins University.

Urso da Genova. 1853. *Historia de victoria quam Genuenses ex Friderico II retulerunt*. In *Historia patriae monumenta. Chartarum*, edited by Tommaso Vallauri, 2: 1741–64. 3 vols. Turin: Ex officina regia.

———. 1857. *Vittoria de'Genovesi supra l'armata di Federico II: carme di Ursone notaio del secolo XIII*, edited and translated by Giovanni B. Graziano. Genoa: Tipografia di Gaetano Schenone.

Wicksteed, Philip H. and Edmund G. Gardner. 1902. *Dante and Giovanni del Virgilio*. Westminster: A. Constable.

Secondary sources

Avesani, Rino. 1976. "Il preumanesimo veronese." In *Storia della cultura veneta*, edited by Gianfranco Folena and Girolamo Arnaldi, 2: 111–41. Vicenza: Pozza.

Bianchini, Simonetta. 1989 "Arrigo da Settimello e una sua fonte oitanica." *Studi medievali*, 3rd ser., 30: 855–63.

Billanovich, Giuseppe. 1976. "Il preumanesimo padovano." In *Storia della cultura veneta*, edited by Gianfranco Folena and Girolamo Arnaldi, 2: 19–110. Vicenza: Pozza.

———. 1981. *La tradizione del testo di Livio e le origini dell'umanesimo*. Studi sul Petrarca 8, 1–2. Padua: Editore Antenore.

Greene, Thomas M. 1982. *The Light in Troy: Imitation and Discovery in Renaissance Poetry*. Elizabethan Club Series 7. New Haven, CT, London: Yale University Press.

Novati, Francesco. 1926. *Le origini, continuate e compiute da Angelo Monteverdi*. Milan: F. Vallardi.

Nuccio, Oscar. 1994. "I trattati ed I sermoni di Albertano da Brescia: fonti inesplorate dell'Umanesimo economico." In *Albertano da Brescia. Alle origini del Razionalismo economico, dell'Umanesimo civile, della Grande Europa*, edited by Franco Spinelli, 95–155. Brescia: Grafo.

Reynolds, Leighton D. and Nigel G. Wilson. 1974. *Scribes and Scholars. A Guide to the Transmission of Greek and Latin Literature*. Oxford: Clarendon.

Stadter, Philip A. 1973. "Planudes, Plutarch, and Pace of Ferrara." *Italia medioevale e umanistica* 16: 137–62.

Weiss, Roberto. 1947. *The Dawn of Humanism in Italy*. London: H. K. Lewis. Reprint, New York: Haskell House Publishers, 1970.

———. 1949. *Il primo secolo dell'umanesimo: Studi e testi*. Storia e letteratura 27. Rome: Edizioni di storia e letteratura.

———. 1950. "Lovato Lovati. 1241–1309." *Italian Studies* 6: 3–28.

Witt, Ronald G. 2000. *"In the Footsteps of the Ancients": The Origins of Humanism from Lovato to Bruni*. Leiden, New York: Brill.

———. 2011. *The Two Latin Cultures and the Foundation of Italian Humanism in Medieval Italy*. Cambridge, New York: Cambridge University Press.

CHAPTER 27

MEDIEVAL LATIN TEXTS IN THE AGE OF PRINTING

PAOLO CHIESA
TRANSLATED BY AMYROSE MCCUE GILL

THE INTRODUCTION OF PRINT AND THE DEVELOPMENT OF EDITORIAL METHODS

It is commonly held that the introduction of movable type printing (which occurred, in the West, around the middle of the fifteenth century) had revolutionary consequences for the production and circulation of literary texts. Even if the effects of this technological innovation were felt on a large scale only decades later, the replacement of a manual with a mechanical process—namely printing—for book reproduction immediately brought long-term mechanisms and methods into play and laid the groundwork for a series of radical transformations. The uniqueness of manuscript copies—each, inevitably, distinct from every other—was superseded by a system of serial reproduction, in which all published copies of a given work were, in principle, identical—exceptions aside—because they were produced by the same print matrix. (The exceptions, however, were in fact quite frequent; they are nonetheless worthwhile precisely as exceptions.) Printed books usually appeared in more readable and accurate form than those copied by hand: printed characters had their own uniformity, and texts were reviewed by an editor before passing beneath the press, which ensured the elimination of obvious errors. The time required for the printing process was considerably less than that required for manuscripts, and the number of copies could be considerably larger. Besides a broader availability of titles, this made for a drastic drop in book prices and a corresponding expansion of the market for literature and for culture more generally.

In the long term, the consequences were incalculable: one could say that the introduction of print was, if not the cause, then certainly an enabling factor of and essential ingredient in the intellectual development of Europe from the sixteenth through the eighteenth centuries. As with all innovations, however, even this one had its price. In the first place, the printing process involved the use of machines, whose acquisition or construction required a fairly consistent expenditure of capital. A printer was therefore first and foremost an entrepreneur whose goals included earning money, even if he might have more noble motivations like the advancement of culture; his editorial choices (particularly in terms of which works to publish and which to reject) were thus contingent upon the book market. In the second place, the printing process required specific technical knowledge and necessitated a clear division of labor within a complex chain of operations involving people with diverse qualifications and duties (the caster who forged the metal characters; the compositors who arranged the characters in the press mould; the press operators who physically created the ink impressions; the proofreaders—all these are of course in addition to the actual manager who owned the machines and frames). As a result, the author or editor (in the case, for instance, of texts by ancient writers) of a printed work lost much of his opportunity to oversee the process and to intervene when necessary. In the third place, a work thus produced was distributed via many identical and to all appearances good-quality copies; this meant that a published text soon established itself as authoritative, even when it was intrinsically flawed and its accuracy merely specious and illusory.

Latin texts composed during the Middle Ages were also, inevitably, caught up in these transformations. We will examine their specific circumstances as well as the most important consequences affecting them, both immediately and over the course of the following centuries.

The Selection of Medieval Latin Works

The introduction of movable type printing, however much it may have triggered profound transformations, was in fact less destructive than the previous revolution in print materials that occurred in the West in the last centuries of antiquity, when papyrus ceded its place to parchment. In that case, the literary works that were not transferred onto the new material—which was considered more elegant, more convenient, and physically more durable—were inevitably doomed to be lost, with few exceptions. Papyrus was a perishable material that only poorly withstood the passage of time; the cultural decay that consumed a large part of Western Europe, especially during the seventh and eighth centuries, did the rest. In the 1400s, in contrast, books were considered a precious good and were carefully conserved; thus manuscript works that were not immediately printed were not, for the most part, lost. It is nonetheless the case that such works remained at the margins of cultural life and lost all influence, both at the time and until their eventual publication, while printed works—above all those that circulated in a high number of copies—came to constitute the cultural foundation of subsequent centuries.

A brief census of medieval Latin works printed in the fifteenth and early sixteenth centuries is therefore quite instructive. Such an overview provides a snapshot of the book market's interests in terms of medieval Latin works since, as noted above, the selections made by editors and printers were first and foremost commercially driven. In addition, it enables us to see which works, independent of their merit, became available to libraries in printed form, and further indicates which among them made the greatest contribution to the shaping of subsequent centuries. A census of this kind was attempted in the mid-1900s by Ernst Philip Goldschmidt (Goldschmidt 1943). We will take up and refine several of his conclusions regarding medieval Latin texts, taking advantage of the best cataloguing of incunabula available today (*Gesamtkatalog* 1925–; Hain and Copinger 1926).

In general, medieval Latin literature seems not to have enjoyed the particular favor of the first printers, undoubtedly an indication of a certain lack of interest on the part of the fifteenth-century book market in literature produced during the centuries immediately preceding. Of the works that could rightfully be reinstated in any canon of medieval Latin authors today, only the fewest appear in incunabula, and some were never printed at all. Bede's *Historia ecclesiastica*, for instance, is recorded in only one fifteenth-century edition, published at Strasbourg between 1475 and 1478; the same is true of the *Alexandreis* by Walter de Châtillon (Rouen 1487–90) and even of *Policraticus* by John of Salisbury (Brussels, date unknown), which was, moreover, the only one of his works published within the century. Similarly, one sole incunabulum (from 1500) of the *Historia Francorum* by Gregory of Tours exists, as is the case for the *Historia Langobardorum* by Paul the Deacon (Lyon 1492), which today remains the most popular and valued "barbarian history" of the early Middle Ages. *De natura rerum* by Rabanus Maurus fared only a little better: it was published twice in the fifteenth century under the arbitrary title *De universo*, a name by which it is still frequently referenced today. Other authors—for instance Abelard, Einhard, Hildebert of Lavardin, Marbod of Rennes, and Liutprand of Cremona, whose names figure prominently in every history of medieval Latin literature published today—are entirely absent from the catalogue of incunabula. Still others had a few works printed, but in selections that would not be considered adequately representative today. In the case of Cassiodorus, for example, the *Historia ecclesiastica tripartita* was published (in four incunabula) as it was much used at the time as a manual for ancient Christian history. Yet neither his *Variae* nor his *Institutiones* saw print, though in our view they are much more important in their cultural and literary significance. For other works, vernacular and translated versions were preferred over Latin originals. Such was the case for Andreas Cappellanus's *De Amore*, which was only printed (in two incunabula) in the German translation of Johannes Hartlieb; for the *Ludus schacorum* of Jacopo da Cessole (four Latin incunabula, twelve in the vernacular); and also for various late antique Latin romances such as the *Historia*

Apollonii regis Tyrii, which was published only once in Latin and thirteen times in the vernacular. A similar argument could be made for the texts of the Epic Cycle and of the Alexander romance.

Among the works produced between the sixth and fourteenth centuries, didactic texts seem to have been of most interest to the first printers and their market. To this interest is owed the relatively good fortune of the *Facetus* (twenty-two incunabula of the Latin text), the *Pamphilus* (twenty-four incunabula), the *Doctrina dicendi et tacenti* by Albertanus of Brescia (thirty-three incunabula) and the dictionary by Johannes Balbus (twenty-four incunabula); also popular was the *Ecloga Theoduli*, which was printed in a collection of didactic aphorisms that included the *Disticha Catonis*, a Latin version of Aesop, as well as the *Liber parabolarum* by Alain de Lille (twenty-three incunabula). The verse treatises that had constituted the basis for grammatical and rhetorical education in previous centuries also proliferated: not so much the *Grecismus* by Eberhard of Béthune (of which, nonetheless, nineteen incunabula are recorded), but certainly the various works of John of Garland (160 incunabula in all) and above all the *Doctrinale* by Alexander of Villedieu (of which there are as many as 291 incunabula). It appears that every printer found it advantageous to produce a run of this last work, which was used as a scholastic grammar and thus had a dependable market.

Alongside teaching tools, legal texts from the thirteenth and fourteenth centuries have a substantial presence: works on canon law, for instance, and legal commentaries, like those by Bartolus de Saxoferrato (192 incunabula) and Baldus de Ubaldis (98 incunabula). Regarding religious texts, those best represented in fifteenth-century print production are also the most recent, which were evidently most applicable to the issues and needs of the period (nearly 150 incunabula of the *Imitatio Christi* in either Latin or the vernacular are recorded, for instance). In addition, the foundational theological texts of the Latin Middle Ages continued to be in use: the exegetical treatises by Nicholas of Lyra (ninety-seven incunabula), Peter Lombard's *Sententiae* (forty incunabula), and Peter Comestor's *Historia scholastica* (nineteen incunabula), for instance, enjoyed great success. A genuine best-seller was the *Legenda aurea* by Jacobus de Voragine, the most important hagiographical collection of the early Middle Ages: 123 incunabula of this work are recorded in Latin, thirty-two in German, twenty in Dutch, thirty-one in French, fourteen in Italian, four in English, four in Spanish and three in Czech. One could argue that the widespread circulation of this work established the foundation of the hagiographical tradition for all of modern Europe.

Also well represented in the oldest print editions are philosophical and scientific works from the last centuries of the Middle Ages, which were welcomed by the academic market: from Latin versions of works either rightly or wrongly attributed to Aristotle (165 incunabula in all) to texts by scientists and encyclopedists like Pierre d'Ailly (fifty-eight incunabula), Albertus Magnus (203 incunabula) and, above all, Thomas Aquinas (309 incunabula) and to works by numerous logicians (like Paolo Veneto and Gualtiero Burleo, who are represented by fifty-four and twenty-nine incunabula, respectively). Other classics of religious thought—like

Bonaventure (181 incunabula) and Bernard of Clairvaux (173 incunabula)—enjoyed great success as well and benefited enormously from the support of their associated religious orders (Franciscan and Cistercian, respectively)—or, rather, from the market for print copies secured by their presence. The founder of the single most important order of the Middle Ages, Benedict of Nursia (or, as he is sometimes regarded, of Montecassino), had a scant presence on this list (his Latin *Regula* was published in only three incunabula, and another five contain vernacular versions), an indication of the modest cultural importance of his order in the 1400s and of a more conservative attitude among Benedictines towards the then new means of book production.

Valued by the first printers and their customers for its grammatical, philosophical, juridical, and religious production, the Latin Middle Ages were not, however, thought highly of for works more narrowly defined as literary. It must be understood that the vast majority of books published during the 1400s were recently written works, many of which were destined from their very creation for print, and which aimed at practical ends: many devotional works (breviaries, penitentials, and clerical manuals), for example; a few collections of laws; the occasional collection of medical remedies; and so on. Aside from these, much space was granted classical works: more than 250 Virgilian incunabula and over 330 incunabula (more than eight per year during the period from 1460 to 1500) from the various works of Cicero are recorded, for instance. One could argue that the canon which has kept the Latin Middle Ages at the margins of literary history until the present day has its origins in this moment. When printing was invented, medieval literature suffered from a poor reputation, and even those texts that were printed in the period were little appreciated—or, as occurred in Italy, were explicitly condemned for stylistic reasons—by the humanists, who constituted the first market for printers. Much medieval Latin literature was not published at all or was published only in few copies and, as a consequence, would continue to be little known in the following centuries.

The selection process was also influenced, at times, by censorship. Because of the wide circulation it assured works, print production provoked the most distrust—and reprimands—on the part of church authorities, who were worried that the new books might facilitate the diffusion of unorthodox ideas. This distrust increased in the Catholic world after the Protestant reformation and brought with it the development of instruments of control and prohibition like the preventative pre-approval of publications (*imprimatur*) and the Index of Prohibited Books (*index*). The writers of the Latin Middle Ages were not particularly affected by censorship, which did, however, have an impact on many contemporary writers; a few exceptions include medieval authors suspected of doctrinal deviation, such as Berengar of Tours, Abelard, Claudius of Turin, and William of Ockham, all of whose names appear from the beginning on the Index of Prohibited Books in 1559. Among the affected was even a Latin work by Dante Alighieri, the *Monarchia*, which argued for the legitimate and autonomous nature of imperial government against the universal claim of the papacy. Condemned by the church a few years after the death of its author, the *Monarchia* was on the Index of Prohibited Books until the 1800s. The work was not printed in the fifteenth century; when it finally appeared in print (in Basel, in Protestant territory, in 1559), the editor—the humanist Johannes Herbst (Oporinus)—published it with a note claiming that the author was not the famed Dante Alighieri of Florence but a more recent author of the same name (Dante 1965, 19 n. 2), who in reality did not exist and against whom there were therefore no restrictive measures. In so doing, the editor likely sought the best way to ensure the broadest dissemination of the work, even though we cannot exclude the possibility that the pseudo-attribution may have already been present in the original manuscript as a means of masking the author so as to prevent the destruction of the codex by censorship.

On occasion, the printing press saved medieval Latin works from a destruction that would otherwise have been their likely fate. This is the case with the *Relatio de legatione Constantinopolitana* by Liutprand of Cremona, which is among the most original and interesting political pamphlets of the entire Middle Ages. The booklet, preserved in a codex at Trier Cathedral, came to the attention of the highly learned German printer Henricus Canisius, who procured himself a copy and published it in Ingolstadt in 1600 (Chiesa 2004, 274–75). Today, the Trier codex is nowhere to be found, probably because it was destroyed during the Thirty Years' War, and we owe the survival of the work to the *editio princeps*. An analogous incident occurred regarding the works of the ninth-century Spanish hagiographer and polemicist Eulogius of Córdoba, which were preserved until the 1500s in a codex at Oviedo Cathedral. The codex disappeared after Ambrosio Morales made an edition (published in Madrid in 1574). In this case it is disputed whether, aside from the manuscript *Ovetensis*, others existed at the time that were also accessible to the editor, and whether these too were subsequently lost (Mellado Rodríguez 2004, 118–26). Print reproduction thus sometimes permitted the survival of works that were only preserved in the fewest of copies, but other, less fortunate circumstances are also recorded. The *Metrum de vita sancti Galli* by Notker Balbulus (tenth century), for instance, was preserved in a single manuscript at the Abbey of Saint Gall. Even though it aroused the interest of sixteenth-century scholars, it was never printed and this sealed its fate: the codex eventually disappeared and today the work is lost (Berschin 2004, 309–10).

The preservation of texts (not only medieval Latin texts—similar cases are also recorded for classical literature) exclusively in printed editions poses a philological problem of some interest: was the intervention of the first print editors of the same nature as that of the earlier hand-copyists or was it different? Can we liken the text of an *editio princeps* to that of any given manuscript or do we need to use it with more caution? To answer this question, a thorough investigation of the philological strategies of the first printers in relation to the copies available to them would be required, an investigation that has not as yet been undertaken systematically. We can, however, observe that the print edition, given its commercial objectives, had to guarantee a certain "external" quality with respect to properties classified as "accidental" by bibliographers (correct orthography, respect for standard grammatical norms, consistent use of punctuation). On this level, we might imagine that the revisions of the person preparing the text for print and of the proofreaders who intervened a second time were relatively substantial—on average more substantial than those that occurred during the creation of a single manuscript copy.

The Birth of Bibliographical Information and Medieval Latin Texts

Medieval manuscripts did not exhibit the standard format of textual presentation we are accustomed to seeing in a modern book. In handwritten codices, a true frontispiece was generally lacking, even though the first page usually included certain bibliographical particulars. Useful information for identifying the work, like the author's name and the title, could usually be found in the *incipit*, but rarely did it form a paratextual element in a different position, as occurs today; only occasionally would a table of contents appear at the beginning or end of a codex. The introduction of printing, with its entrepreneurial and commercial requirements, favored the gradual development of placing bibliographical information at the beginning (and at the end) of the text. Over the course of a few decades, publishers commonly began presenting a well-defined frontispiece that incorporated the author's name; the title of the work (or works) included; the name of the printer and, sometimes, of editors, patrons, and dedicatees; the year and date of publication; and, at times, yet other details. The contents of the volume could thus be quickly identified, and the person who produced it could also append his own imprint.

The introduction of the frontispiece—the easiest means of identifying printed editions as opposed to works that circulated as manuscripts—also brought certain oversimplifications in content description, however. If a printed work was substantial enough to warrant its own volume, all was well. However, when one wanted to publish more modest works (texts which might better be united, for practical reasons, under a single cover), the frontispiece, due to its nature as a summary, might well neglect to mention several of these. The risk, therefore, was that the principal author could have attributed to him secondary works that he did not in fact compose. Previously, in manuscripts, short works had also normally circulated in anthologies. While for the most part relatively homogeneous (in theme, literary genre and, if possible, also authorship) in earlier medieval centuries, during the fourteenth and fifteenth centuries, when codices for personal use proliferated, these compendia became somewhat more irregular, so much so that, in a given manuscript, it was possible to find texts of very diverse genres brought together solely by the interests of an individual reader. These codices were precisely those that the first printers had to hand and which they therefore used as models. The possibility of endowing a book with a frontispiece (or at least with more precise bibliographical information) rendered common the error of attributing a *corpus* of texts from different sources but collected under a single title to a single author. We cannot dismiss the possibility that, at times, this had less to do with error and more to do with purposeful mystification because the attribution of an anonymous text to an important author could entail commercial advantages for the printer, as is certainly still the case today. As long as book production was done by hand—and also for some of the oldest incunabula—the absence of a frontispiece acted as an antidote to oversimplification because the reader was aware that the codex he had in hand could contain works by several authors. When bibliographical information became all but obligatory, however, its apparent authority clearly and conveniently (but also dangerously, if it provided misleading information) "fixed" the contents of the volume under a single label.

In general, this problem affected any work that came to be printed, but for medieval Latin works the problems were perhaps greater. Many medieval Latin works, in fact, have limited literary originality (*centos*, *catenae*, anthologies, collections of *excerpta*, rewritings and compendia of previous texts, etc.), and even among the most original works many were strongly imitative with respect to previous models. In the high Middle Ages when these texts were composed, the author's name was not considered particularly important; moreover, there are no few instances in which the very notion of an "author" seems to have become very fluid, even to the point of being inapplicable. Many works, therefore, circulated in anonymous form, and it was considered unnecessary to establish their authorial origins, except in the case of an already-attributed work or of one that could be attributed to a recognized *auctoritas*. For entire literary genres—for instance hagiographies or annals—anonymous works constituted the norm rather than the exception. In the 1400s (and even more so in subsequent centuries), however, the concept of an author became substantially more important, so that it became commonplace to attempt to attribute as many anonymous texts as possible to a known writer, deservedly or not. Indeed, the introduction of print—and the resulting standardization and presentation of bibliographical information—motivated the first discussions regarding the ownership of literary texts (Brown 1995). The fact that missing authorial information was seen as a serious failure in the new frontispieces engendered many pseudo-attributions, which were added to yet other, medieval, pseudo-attributions. Once these were accepted by the first print editions, they acquired an undeserved authority and, finally, became traditional.

The Emergence of the Vulgates (and of the "New Vulgates")

Though innovative in both theory and practice, the introduction of print in Europe maintained a certain continuity with earlier techniques employed for book preparation. In terms of their physical characteristics, the first incunabula strongly resembled the manuscript books in use at the time. Pagination (or, more often, foliation), format, materials, and scripts were either identical or very similar—so much so that in some cases, it is difficult to distinguish at first glance a handwritten from a printed book of the period. As a consequence, fifteenth-century scholars seem not to have coined a specific term for printed books that distinguished them from manuscripts: all books were referred to as *codices*, *volumina*, and *exemplaria*, independent of the technique by which they were created. If, indeed, one wanted to be more specific, expressions such as *codex calamo scriptus*, "a book copied by hand," or *codex impressus*, "a printed book," were employed. But *codices* remained the term in use, and the type of production was considered to have constituted no more than a specific difference within a general category (Rizzo 1973, 69–71). Tellingly, in one of the most famous documents concerning the Gutenberg Bible, the letter of March 1455 in which Enea Silvio Piccolomini describes having seen copies of the work for sale in Frankfurt, the Italian humanist praises the beauty and the legibility of the writing but does not comment on the novelty of the technical procedure, as though this had escaped his attention or was considered of little importance (Braida 2000, 15). To the learnèd of the era, print apparently seemed a simple technical innovation that neither required any changes in the traditional classification of book products nor altered the mechanisms governing literary circulation—or if it did, then only quantitatively, and that alone brought with it, obviously, enormous advantages.

Indeed, it was lost on no one that printed books were in many ways more convenient than manuscripts, and this was not only due to the wider availability of titles or because of the resulting economic advantages which became greater and greater with the passage of time. Teachers and jurists soon realized that it was easier to teach lessons and to administer laws with printed books, seeing as everyone had an identical text at their disposal and quibbles over content could thus be avoided. Scholars discovered that it was possible to cite the classics without misunderstandings by adopting the edition available in print as the only authoritative version. Clerics noticed that it was all but effortless to guarantee the doctrinal conformity of circulating texts because it was enough to inspect the printing plate only once in order to control the entire run.

One of the strengths of the printed—in comparison with the handwritten—text was that, when published, it had about it an air of high quality. Before appearing in print, the text passed through the hands of many people, among whom might be skilled proofreaders—actual editors, as we might say today—who verified and, when necessary, modified and improved it. Unavoidably, printing errors always escaped, and these could be numerous. The result, however, was enormously better—at least in appearance—than in typical handwritten copies, which were assigned to scribes of varying abilities, were much more haphazard and, in general, contained far more superficial errors. The printing process, in part owing to the commercial ends it pursued, ensured a superior standard; the purchaser of a printed book could rest assured regarding its accuracy and readability.

If a work that came to be published was written by a living author, he or she often had the opportunity to oversee the printing process, and in many cases did so.

In these cases, the edition could be said, in a certain sense, to be "authorized": the version that came to be published was the one the author wished printed, and it could be considered both authorially guaranteed and definitive, at least until a future print run of the work. Of course, a publisher could go against the wishes of the author—either for commercial reasons or for practical ones—no differently than is done today, when an editor arbitrarily changes the text approved for publication. In general, however, an agreement was reached. Whether or not it fully reflected the wishes of the author, a text published in print appeared "fixed": the presence of many identical copies ensured this stability—something that, in the earlier era of inevitable variation in manuscript copies, was unthinkable.

In contrast, the works of the past—both ancient and medieval—were necessarily brought to print by people other than those who had written them; their authors no longer had control over what was published. The fact that a scholar reorganized an ancient text and presented it to the reading public in revised form—thus creating an "edition"—was not in itself a new thing: we know, for instance, of numerous "editions" of the classics beginning in late antiquity, and similar approaches were taken in the preparation of books used by medieval universities. With the introduction of print, however, the responsibilities of the person editing a new version of an ancient work increased: the textual revision was done only once, yet it echoed through tens and hundreds of copies—establishing, yet again, a standard. It was at this time that the figure of the *editor* of a publication—someone who prepared someone else's text for print and ensured its quality—was born.

A printed text thus appeared superficially "better" than a handwritten one. However, for ancient and medieval works—over which the author no longer had control—was it in fact better also at a more profound level? Did superior typographic quality and the elimination of obvious errors also correspond to greater textual accuracy from a philological point of view, in other words, to a more faithful representation of what had originally been written by the author? Edited texts *seemed* good, but in reality they were full of arbitrary corrections and debatable conjectures, especially when they were prepared in haste and overly influenced by commercial concerns. Various scholars of the time voiced doubts (Kenney 1974, 17–18). The most famous case involves the criticisms aimed at Giovanni Bussi—the pioneer of classical editions, who prepared numerous texts for publication that were later printed by the German publishers Konrad Sweynheym and Arnold Pannartz at Rome between 1468 and 1471. Niccolò Perotti, a fellow humanist and an editor of the classics in his own right, who was therefore also driven by some degree of professional rivalry, challenged Bussi with having twisted the words of his authors, going against the very letter of the manuscripts (Mercati 1925). What most interested learnèd men of the period, however, was whether editions presented texts that were structurally and linguistically correct; with rare exceptions, few seemed to feel the necessity of having an "exact" text—one that represented, as much as possible, the words originally dictated by the author. This explains why, even though at the time there already existed codices by classical writers that were known, available, relatively ancient, and potentially "better" than fifteenth-century exemplars, it was these last—produced in a more "civilized" era than the previous ones and therefore usually less marred with errors caused by the ignorance of the copyist, but on the other hand often strewn with conjectures and unjustified corrections—that were most often employed for new editions. Philological editing was thus limited to eliminating obvious errors and to ensuring that grammar was correct by current standards, but did not extend to asking whether the published text was the best possible. Even the most philologically sophisticated and attentive editors rarely succeeded in printing editions based upon first-rate copies, to judge from the case of the best-studied Venetian printer, the great Aldus Manutius (Lowry 1979).

Accustomed to the modes of distribution and circulation of handwritten copies (which seemed, to the humanists, substantially analogous to those of printed copies, aside from the fact that the latter type were much more numerous), the humanists did not perceive an important consequence of the introduction of print: the emergence of the so-called vulgates. The first print edition of a work (*editio princeps*) tended to become "official" immediately, not only because of the aura it acquired from a new format, but also—and above all—for the fact that it had the numerical advantage and hence a widespread presence. Manuscript copies of a given work that still existed and circulated became immediately obsolete in the face of the printed version, which was easily available, clearer to read, less inaccurate, and, most importantly, familiar to everyone; the manuscripts became antiquarian objects during an era in which, however, an antiquarian mindset had not yet been developed. The domination of the printed version was entirely independent of the intrinsic value of the published text, which was, after all, rather difficult to adjudicate at the time. The first edition, then, constituted the basis for the second—usually with the correction of obvious errors and sometimes with other emendations based on other manuscripts (*ope codicum*) or on editorial conjecture (*ope ingenii*)—and this gave the impression that the text was progressively becoming better and better. But where the basis for future editions remained the *princeps* and the manuscript used for the *princeps* had been of poor quality, this produced the mere illusion of textual improvement—based upon rotten foundations. This is true, for instance, of one of the few well-studied cases of the fifteenth century, that of Virgil. The Bussi edition, though subject to criticism, remained the basis for most successive editions, even though it would not have been difficult to use manuscripts of higher quality (Venier 2001).

The emergence of printed vulgates (the *textus receptus*, the "common text" with which everyone was familiar) had, on a philological level, contradictory consequences. According to Edward J. Kenney, "the early printed editions, however much they left to be desired philologically, at all events represented from the textual point of view a fixed point, an *ubi consistam*. ... There now appeared, for the first time, the possibility of an effective, because permanent, control over the textual evidence" (Kenney 1974, 19). But when—starting in the eighteenth century and even more so in the first half of the nineteenth—a scientific philological method slowly began to develop, the primary objective of scholars became to free themselves from the hindrance of the "received texts"—seeing as how these had evolved from the first print editions—and to turn instead to older codices.

For the works of classical antiquity, however, an ideal tension between the acquisition of a quality text and its gradual improvement was always maintained. The former desire—for correctness limited to the level of form—was slowly replaced by the aspiration to possess an "authentic" text, and scholars began to have recourse, in great measure, to quality scholarship on specific readings and on the manuscript witnesses that transmitted them. For these works, the new eighteenth- and nineteenth-century philology could benefit from centuries' worth of reflection, which had set a remarkable course towards textual improvement. But for medieval Latin texts, which did not reenter the literary canon, the preoccupation with a "better" text was rather less pressing: the important thing was that it be possible to read such texts in any form, given that only the content (informational or doctrinal) was of interest, and the use to which it was put was neither literary nor aesthetic.

For medieval Latin texts, the philological bottleneck created by the first print editions and by the emergence of the vulgates was thus lengthier and, in some ways, more dramatic than that of other literatures—for instance classical or vernacular. In the seventeenth and eighteenth centuries, valuable editions based upon broad research and documentary analysis were produced even in the field of medieval Latin: the *Collectio veterum scriptorum* published by Luc D'Achery, Étienne Baluze, and Edmond Martène between 1655 and 1700 with texts taken from French libraries; the *Rerum Italicarum scriptores*, the medieval Italian chronicles, published by Ludovico Antonio Muratori between 1723 and 1738; the *Acta sanctorum*, launched in 1643 by Jean Bolland, which presented a critical evaluation of ancient and medieval hagiographic texts. But the method and objectives of scholarly historiography and of scientific philology in the seventeenth-century tradition were different. Historiography aimed at the rediscovery of documents and sought the accumulation of data; scientific philology strove to uncover the "exact text" via the ordering and selection of material. Medieval Latin literature, insofar as it was primarily ecclesiastical, was not reexamined in this new methodological light, for while the philologists of the Enlightenment were very sensitive to the problem of exactness in Scripture, they were much less so in works deriving from it.

This impediment to scholarship escalated in the middle of the nineteenth century. Precisely when the vulgates of classical texts (those prevailing between the fifteenth and eighteenth centuries) were declared obsolete and were gradually replaced with newer and more reliable critical texts, the works of the Latin Middle Ages were published in the *Patrologia Latina* by the French abbot Jacques-Paul Migne (Bloch 1994). In the 217 monumental volumes that constituted the *Patrologia*, which was issued beginning in 1844, works by ecclesiastical Latin writers from before the 1200s were systematically reprinted, with rare exceptions, as reproductions of previous editions without critical revision. The *Patrologia* was explicitly addressed to the clerical market—primarily seminarists and their instructors—and did not therefore have specific philological goals. (The parallel series—the *Patrologia Graeca*, which was issued beginning in 1856—initially planned only the publication of texts in Latin translation, and thus without philological value; only later was the choice made to publish the Greek text beside the Latin.) The goal was to make available in a single series works otherwise dispersed in myriad volumes that were often impossible to find. In this sense, the project can be said to have fully succeeded and also to have had considerable consequences for academe, because it enabled generations of scholars to conduct their research more smoothly and rapidly. In addition, the considerable nineteenth- and twentieth-century advancements in the fields of late antique and medieval literature can be explained by the availability of this resource. From a strictly philological point of view, however, the *Patrologia*—by re-presenting nonempirical or, worse still, pseudo-empirical editions—simply produced a reiteration of the vulgates. While dismantled and rendered obsolete in the fields of classical and vernacular literatures, these vulgates instead acquired a new legitimacy for the literature of the Latin Middle Ages.

In comparison, it might be interesting to note the different methods and objectives pursued by the group of German scholars who, under the guidance of Georg Wilhelm Pertz, worked on the *Monumenta Germaniae Historica* during these same decades. Having identified a field of study of national interest—works that had a connection with the historical development of medieval *Germania*, understood in the broadest sense—the Monumentists proposed to publish the relevant texts in revised form, employing the "scientific" method that was slowly being developed at the time. Not unlike the classical philologists of the period, the Monumentists also had recourse to ancient manuscripts and did not settle for preexisting printed editions (which, instead, they treated with suspicion). Their published texts were thus critical editions, produced by means of a broad and generally intelligent interrogation of source material and accompanied by original critical essays, which have remained the basis for subsequent research and more in-depth study to the present. This model was emulated in the national historiography of other countries (the *Rolls Series* in England, conceived in 1857; the *Fonti per la Storia d'Italia*, published beginning in 1887; *Les classiques de l'histoire de France au Moyen Âge*, published even later, in the 1900s), even though these later publications were not always of the quality of the German series. Of course, not even the editions of the *Monumenta*—then as now—are free from error. Nonetheless, the effort made to revise the available editions according to criteria agreed upon by a community of scholars produced—then as now—a series of superior academic quality.

This same quality, however, is not one of the virtues of the *Patrologia*, prone as it is to accepting, unquestioned, whatever had previously existed. The errors present in earlier editions were thus passed into this new collection, multiplied by the inevitable typographical errors produced in the reprinting and, in some ways, guaranteed new authority. (The situation worsened further due to the fire that devastated the *Ateliers catholiques* of Montrouge, where the work was printed, in 1868, which destroyed the print matrices that had until then been jealously guarded. The subsequent reprintings were based upon recreated matrices, with a resulting increase in errors.) Though Abbot Migne and his collaborators were not entirely undiscerning in choosing which editions to publish when different versions were available—for some texts, for example, the first editions of the *Monumenta Germaniae* were employed, since they were already available—the desire to be comprehensive dominated in the end. *Opera omnia* editions (even lower-quality ones) were thus privileged, though the mass of the material was difficult to reconcile with careful philological editing. Further, the editors attempted to include every writer, at any cost, even those who had been published in patently inaccurate editions. Moreover, the *Patrologia* simultaneously presented, in a single series, works from a span of many centuries originating in different places and composed by different people. This resulted in the removal of much needed historical and geographical depth from its editions, masking the historical context of each text's production as well as its original aims. Often, the citations supplied by Migne to indicate the sources used are even less clear. Still today, many works from the Latin Middle Ages are cited—even in an academic context—from "Migne," a format that makes one think of a text published in the middle of the 1800s and therefore in a philologically attentive era. However, these texts were rarely "Migne editions" at all; instead, they were vulgates of varying qualities from rather less philological eras. Likewise, in many bibliographical indices—like the *Clavis patrum Latinorum*, the *Clavis auctorum Latinorum medii aevi*, and the *Clavis scriptorum Latinorum medii aevi, Auctores Galliae*—the *Patrologia Latina* edition often represents a kind of "historical" point of reference, and no indication is given of the edition—or the other earlier ones—that was actually republished in the *Patrologia*. Though justifiable in part for the sake of synthesis, this nonetheless perpetuates the distortion that it is possible to speak of the *Patrologia* as a unitary collection. Only an accurate analysis of a given text published in the *Patrologia* and of its source—an analysis that a reader is rarely willing to undertake—would enable a more thorough appraisal of the situation.

Not least among the defects of the collection was the fact that it thereby reinforced a series of doubtful—or outright false—attributions, including some that had already been shown to be incorrect (as is sometimes indicated, somewhat oddly and not without embarrassment, in the introduction to several volumes). A few examples might be instructive. For the works of Hugh of Saint Victor (published in volumes 175–77 of the *Patrologia Latina*), Abbot Migne had recourse to an edition published by the Victorine fathers at Rouen in 1648, which in its turn had employed a previous publication from 1526. Having been produced by the religious order to which its author belonged, this edition, however serious, was not lacking in desire to celebrate a worthy member. Thus, in the case of doubts regarding the authenticity of a work, it tended to pronounce in favor of an attribution to Hugh. As a result, a good twenty-eight of his works available for reading in the *Patrologia Latina* were in fact spurious, as was already partly known by the middle of the 1800s. (Substantial progress in the reordering of the canon of the works of Hugh is due to Hauréau 1886 and to Wilmart 1933.) For the works of Boethius, Migne and his collaborators had used several previous editions—the best of the editions in circulation—that are summarized in a list at the beginning of volume 63 of the *Patrologia*. At least eight of the works contained in their edition, however, are not authentic: rather, they are for the most part Latin translations of Aristotelian works effected during the twelfth and thirteenth centuries. The presence of these falsely attributed texts contributed to a prolonged overestimation of Boethius as a translator.

Perhaps the most sensational case is that of Hildebert of Lavardin. The works of this writer, which are today considered among the most interesting of the Middle Ages, were neglected during the age of the humanists and there was no known edition until 1624, when Hildebert's short poem on the martyrdom of Saint Agnes was first published. From that moment on, several other works were brought to light and interest in the author increased. The principal problem was that these works did not circulate in a standard and reliable *corpus*; the question of attribution thus had to be discussed composition by composition, above all in the case of his sermons and poems. Several of the best scholars of the 1600s (for instance Marguerin de la Bigne, Luc D'Achery, Philippe Labbe, and Étienne Baluze) strove, at times not only with shrewdness but also with good results, to distinguish that which was authentic from that which was not. But all their efforts—which represent a remarkable moment both in the history of seventeenth-century French scholarship and in the development of seventeenth-century attribution methods—were wasted with the publication, in 1708, of the edition of Hildebert's *Opera omnia*, together with those of Marbod of Rennes, that was edited by the Maurist monk Antoine Beaugendre (Hildebert of Lavardin 1708). In his edition, Beaugendre acritically regarded as authentic all those works that either presented a vague indication of Hildebertian paternity in medieval manuscripts or appeared in collections where texts by Hildebert could also be found. Thus was an entirely unmerited and unjustified Hildebertian *corpus* formed, more than half of which is considered spurious today. (In this case, too, noteworthy and decisive advancements regarding the constitution of the canon are owed to Hauréau 1882 and Wilmart 1935.) The Beaugendre edition was soon criticized, and before the end of the eighteenth century several of his attributions were rejected, but a restructured edition that included all (but only) the authenticated works was never published. As a result, when Abbot Migne included Hildebert in the *Patrologia*, the choice fell once again on the Beaugendre edition. Since its weakness was noted by everyone, however, a revision was attempted. Entrusted to the canon Jean-Jacques Bourassé, this revision made the situation even worse (if that were possible) because it did not take relevant explanatory documents into account that were already widely available, instead adding fresh errors to the ones already present. We might read the tale of these editions of Hildebert—both the Beaugendre edition and, even more, the reprinting of it in the *Patrologia Latina*—as a history of our attempts to liberate ourselves from errors committed in the past. Even before confronting the problem of textual variants, later editors of the works of this illustrious writer have first had to do battle with their less perspicacious predecessors.

The large number of works still attributed to Alcuin today—either entirely undeservedly or in a manner not yet sufficiently substantiated—is dependent on the fact that the edition of Alcuin edited by Frobenius Forster (Alcuin 1777), afterwards republished in the *Patrologia Latina* (vols. 100–101), assigned these works to the author by absorbing various medieval pseudo-attributions, in part from earlier editions. (For a reworking of Alcuin's canon, see Gorman 2002.) The entire group of texts forming volumes 116–18 of the *Patrologia* commits an error of paternity: the exegetical works contained therein are not by Haimo of Halberstadt, as is stated on the basis of the previous editions employed, but by Haimo of Auxerre. An error originating in the distant past (dating to the *Catalogus scriptorum ecclesiasticorum* by Giovanni Tritemio, published in 1494), it was uniformly shared by the scholars of the seventeenth and eighteenth centuries, but became more grave because of the *Patrologia*, which reunited, in a single *corpus*, works that until then had been published separately, thus attributing an entire *opus* to the wrong author (Guglielmetti 2008, 187–91).

Despite these limitations, the advantage of having *all the texts* (or the vast majority of them) available at a reasonable cost and in a uniform typographic format has been undeniable. Today the *Patrologia* is present in all medium-sized research libraries and often, in the case of Catholic institutions, in minor libraries as well. The series has therefore come to constitute a new vulgate or, more precisely, to grant legitimacy once more to an earlier vulgate—one that was on the point of being discredited—and give it new life.

Abbot Migne's re-presentation of old editions in reprinted form provoked perplexity in the philologists of the mid-1800s, who had by then definitively begun to tread the path of historical philology. The texts published in the *Patrologia* were considered suspect from the beginning, and when there were better ones available— for instance the historical texts published in the *Monumenta*, but not only these— the latter were preferred. The *Patrologia*, however, continued for the most part to be considered authoritative in the Catholic world that had produced it and was most reluctant to abandon the editions of the Tridentine era and follow the method of critical philology. Nonetheless, within only a few years (1866) it was precisely in a country of Catholic tradition that the *Corpus scriptorum ecclesiasticorum Latinorum* was born. Launched by the Austrian Academy of Sciences, which proposed to replace the vulgates with a revised set of empirical editions, the activity of this series still continues—albeit with a certain slowness—to the present day. In 1952, Palémon Glorieux published a somewhat apologetic booklet (*Pour revaloriser Migne*), in which he attempted an empirical reevaluation of the *Patrologia*; his reason for doing so was to correct the numerous false attributions present in the collection, which Glorieux summarized in a list of disconcerting length. Although corrections and clarifications could be made with respect to attribution, no true reassessment was possible at the level of the text itself. It was at this time that new, systematic editions of works by ancient and medieval writers were begun, a task undertaken by two series that were both launched in 1954: the *Sources chrétiennes*, founded at Paris by Jean Daniélou and Henri de Lubac with the intention of wide distribution (the text, which appears primarily in a simplified critical edition, is accompanied by a French translation), and the *Corpus Christianorum*, founded by Eligius Dekker at Steenbrugge (Belgium), which sought to publish in its various series (the *Series Latina*, *Series Graeca*, and *Continuatio Mediaevalis*, to which other minor series have been added more recently) critical editions to replace the works collected by the *Patrologia*. The *Sources chrétiennes* and *Corpus Christianorum*, which can be considered major, systematic series, are complemented by other, minor series specializing in editions of texts from specific contexts (for example, geographical, chronological, thematic).

It could thus be said that the problems posed by the enduring presence of the vulgates—and by the poor textual quality stemming from them—were heading towards a final resolution by way of the empirical methodology that was developing around the middle of the twentieth century and that has by now been consolidated. Instead, the same problems have now reappeared, unexpectedly, in a different context—namely that of the communication revolution brought about by the information age. As is well known, the *Patrologia Latina* is currently available on the web, along with a simple and efficient search system. The collection of texts included in its database is more substantial than that of other, similar systems (like the Brepols *Library of Latin Texts*, which archives numerous medieval Latin texts, beginning with those appearing in the *Corpus Christianorum*). In this regard, the business policy of the publishing house that edits the *Patrologia* appears more liberal than that of other publishers. It is possible, for instance, to download entire texts from the online *Patrologia* with ease, something not permitted by digital archives like the *Library of Latin Texts* or the *Monumenta Germaniae Historica*. Thus the texts of the *Patrologia*, which until several years ago had been declared obsolete by the academic community, may yet come to enjoy a certain popularity, regardless either of their scant textual value or the possibility, which one would often have, of acquiring better ones.

This problem is in fact connected to the more general issue of the quality of ancient and medieval texts that are accessible online and to the need for developing systems to evaluate documents or at least to direct readers to more dependable resources. Speed and convenience can be very serious temptations, and it will be quite a task for the academic community to find an antidote to prevent us going astray. The re-publication of past editorial endeavors in a new format must be accompanied by the knowledge that their value is commensurate with the time in which they were created. Virtual communications—such as those on the Internet—facilitate anachronisms by leveling temporal planes. On a broader scale, however, the real problem is that of philological control over the information revolution: to avoid translating speed and easy access into superficial analysis and to ensure that the limitations inherent in an electronic medium do not become a shortcut to no longer making the necessary choices.

SUGGESTIONS FOR FURTHER READINGS

On the introduction of printing, with the technical innovations it entailed and the profound changes that resulted in the cultural sphere, studies now considered classic are Carter 1969, Clair 1976, and Hirsch 1967. Eisenstein 1979 spoke in terms of a veritable "revolution," although today scholars are more inclined to emphasize the various continuities with the manuscript tradition; compare also Tyson and

Wagenheim 1986 and Hindman 1991. On the humanists' reactions to the introduction of these new technologies, see De Frede 1985; on the methods and limits of humanist philology, see Kenney 1971 and Fera 1990 (with partly opposing viewpoints), and above all Rizzo 1973, who examines the philological terminology of the era, comparing both its continuities and innovations in a study that thus constitutes the best starting point for forming one's own opinion. For incunables we have a good census that is gradually being expanded (*Gesamtkataloge* 1925-; for the portions not completed Hain-Copinger 1926 is still useful). On the medieval Latin works that were published in the fifteenth century and in the first decades of the sixteenth century the only study is that of Goldschmidt 1943; information on individual authors of the high Middle Ages can be found in Chiesa-Castaldi 2004–8. On the history of philological method in the modern period, the classical study is Wilamowitz-Moellendorf 1927, continued and developed by Timpanaro 1985; see also Reynolds and Wilson 1991 (first edition 1968) and Kenney 1974. On the *Patrologia Latina* and the work of Jacques-Paul Migne, see Bloch 1994; on the problems created by the "new vulgates" now in wide circulation thanks to recently introduced textual databases, see Chiesa 2010.

BIBLIOGRAPHY

Primary sources

Alcuin. 1777. *Beati Flacci Albini seu Alcuini Opera*. Regensburg.
Dante Alighieri. 1965. *Monarchia*, edited by Pier Giorgio Ricci. Dante Alighieri, 1265–1321.
      Opere. Edizione nazionale a cura della Società dantesca italiana 5. Milano: Mondadori.
Hildebert of Lavardin. 1708. *Venerabilis Hildeberti, primo Cenomanensis episcopi, deinde Turonensis archiepiscopi, Opera tam edita quam inedita. Accesserunt Marbodi, Redonensis episcopi, Opuscula*, edited by Antoine Beaugendre. Paris: Le Conte.

Secondary sources

Berschin, Walter. 2004. "Notker Balbulus." In *La trasmissione dei testi latini del Medioevo. Mediaeval Latin Texts and their Transmission (Te.Tra.)*, edited by Paolo Chiesa and Lucia Castaldi, 1: 306–16. Millennio medievale 50. Strumenti e studi, n.s., 8. Florence: Impruneta.
Bloch, R. Howard. 1994. *God's Plagiarist: Being an Account of the Fabulous Industry and Irregular Commerce of the Abbé Migne*. Chicago: University of Chicago Press.
Braida, Lodovica. 2000. *Stampa e cultura in Europa tra XV e XVI secolo*. Biblioteca essenziale Laterza 32. Bari: Laterza.
Brown, Cynthia Jane. 1995. *Poets, Patrons and Printers: Crisis of Authority in Late Medieval France*. Ithaca, NY: Cornell University Press.
Carter, Harry. 1969. *A View of Early Typography up to about 1600*. Oxford: Clarendon Press.
Chiesa, Paolo. 2004. "Liutprandus Cremonensis ep." In *La trasmissione dei testi latini del Medioevo. Mediaeval Latin Texts and their Transmission (Te.Tra.)*, edited by Paolo Chiesa and Lucia Castaldi, 1: 268–75. Millennio medievale 50. Strumenti e studi, n.s., 8. Florence: Impruneta.

———. 2010. "Sul controllo filologico delle edizioni critiche digitali." *Filologia mediolatina* 17: 325–346.

Chiesa, Paolo and Lucia Castaldi, eds. 2004-8. *La trasmissione dei testi latini del Medioevo. Mediaeval Latin Texts and their Transmission (Te.Tra.).* 3 vols. Millennio Medievale 50, 57, 75. Strumenti e studi, n. s., 8, 10, 18. Florence: Impruneta.

Clair, Colin. 1976. *A History of European Printing* London, New York, San Francisco: Academic Press.

De Frede, Carlo. 1985. "Entusiasmi umanistici e allarmi ecclesiastico-politici per l'invenzione della stampa," in De Frede, Carlo, ed., *Ricerche per la storia della stampa e la diffusione delle idee riformate nell'Italia del Cinquecento*. Napoli: De Simone. Pp. 7–53.

Eisenstein, Elizabeth L. 1979. *The Printing Press as an Agent of Change. Communications and Cultural Transformations in Early-Modern Europe*. Cambridge: Cambridge University Press.

Fera, Vincenzo. 1990. *Problemi e percorsi della ricezione umanistica*, in *Lo spazio letterario di Roma antica*, vol. III: *La ricezione del testo*, ed. G. Cavallo, P. Fedeli, A. Giardina. Roma: Salerno Editrice.

Gesamtkatalog der Wiegendrucke. 1925–. Leipzig: Anton Hiersemann. http://www.gesamtkatalogderwiegendrucke.de/. Available to letter H in print and in complete revised form online.

Glorieux, Palémon. 1952. *Pour revaloriser Migne: Table rectificatives*. Lille: Facultés catholiques.

Goldschmidt, Ernst Philip. 1943. *Medieval Texts and Their First Appearance in Print*. London: London Bibliographical Society.

Gorman, Michael. 2002. "Alcuin before Migne." *Revue Bénédictine* 102: 101–30.

Guglielmetti, Rossana E. 2008. "Haimo Autissiodorensis mon." In *La trasmissione dei testi latini del Medioevo. Mediaeval Latin Texts and their Transmission (Te.Tra.)*, edited by Paolo Chiesa and Lucia Castaldi, 3: 187–255. Millennio medievale 75. Strumenti e studi, n.s., 18. Florence: Impruneta.

Hain, Ludwig and Walter A. Copinger. 1926. *Supplement to Hain's Repertorium bibliographicum, or collections towards a new edition of that work*. Berlin: J. Altmann.

Hauréau, Jean-Bartélemy. 1882. *Les mélanges poetiques d'Hildebert de Lavardin*. Paris: Le Mans.

———. 1886. *Les oeuvres de Hugues de Saint-Victor: essai critique*. Paris: Hachette.

Hindman, Sandra L., ed. 1991. *Printing the Written Word. The Social History of Books, circa 1450-1520*. Ithaca and London: Cornell University Press.

Hirsch, Rudolf. 1967. *Printing, Selling and Reading (1450–1550)*. Wiesbaden: Harrassowitz.

Kenney, E. J. 1971. "The Character of Humanist Philology," in R.R. Bolgar, ed. *Classical Influences on European Culture A.D. 1500–1700*. Cambridge: Cambridge University Press. Pp. 119–128.

———. 1974. *The Classical Text: Aspects of Editing in the Age of the Printed Book*. Berkeley, CA: University of California Press.

Lowry, Martin. 1979. *The World of Aldus Manutius*. Oxford: Blackwell.

Mellado Rodríguez, Joaquín. 2004. "Eulogius Cordubensis presb." In *La trasmissione dei testi latini del Medioevo. Mediaeval Latin Texts and their Transmission (Te.Tra.)*, edited by Paolo Chiesa and Lucia Castaldi, 1: 118–26. Millennio medievale 50. Strumenti e studi, n.s., 8. Florence: Impruneta.

Mercati, Giovanni. 1925. *Per la cronologia della vita e degli scritti di Niccolò Perotti arcivescovo di Siponto*. Roma: Biblioteca Apostolica Vaticana.

Reynolds, Leighton D. and Wilson, Nigel G. 1991. *Scribes and Scholars. A Guide to the Transmission of Greek and Latin Literature*. 3rd ed. Oxford: Clarendon Press.

Rizzo, Silvia. 1973. *Il lessico filologico degli umanisti*. Rome: Edizioni di Storia e Letteratura.

Timpanaro, Sebastiano. 1985. *La genesi del metodo del Lachmann*, 2nd ed. Padova: Liviana.

Tyson, G.P and Wagonheim, S.S., eds. 1986. *Print and Culture in the Renaissance. Essays on the Advent of Printing in Europe*. London and Toronto: University of Delaware Press.

Venier, Matteo. 2001. *Per una storia del testo di Virgilio nella prima età del libro a stampa*. Udine: Forum.

Wilamowitz-Moellendorff, Ulrich von. 1927. *Geschichte der Philologie*, in A. Gercke and E. Norden, eds., *Einleitung in die Altertumswissenschaften*, II, 1, 3rd ed. Leipzig: Teubner. [Engl. trans.: *History of Classical Scholarship*. London: Duckworth, 1982].

Wilmart, André. 1933. "Opuscules choisis de Hugues de Saint-Victor." *Revue Bénédictine* 45: 242–48.

———. 1935. "Les sermons d'Hildebert." *Revue Bénédictine* 47: 12–51.

———. 1936. "Le florilège de Saint-Gatien. Contribution à l'étude des poèmes d'Hildebert et de Marbode." *Revue Bénédictine* 38: 3–40, 147–81.

CHAPTER 28

MEDIEVAL LATIN IN MODERN ENGLISH: TRANSLATIONS FROM THE NINETEENTH CENTURY TO THE PRESENT DAY

JAN M. ZIOLKOWSKI

Professional and Academic Translation

Whereas translation studies have generally burgeoned as a field of scholarly investigation in recent decades, the translation of Medieval Latin into English has received only very short shrift. Medieval Latin philologists have long sought to reconstruct the manuscript tradition of Medieval Latin works and to establish their texts. They have examined far less systematically the first appearance of Medieval Latin texts in print, although they have hardly ignored the topic (see Chiesa in this volume). Yet Medieval Latinists have attempted no such study for translation.

Written translation of literary texts was not institutionalized as a profession, in the sense of becoming a full-time occupation, until the twentieth century. Translations produced at least partly for profit or patronage were made well before then, of course, but those who translated did not endeavor to—and could not—support themselves solely by translating. Even once such work became professionalized, Medieval Latin played only a marginal role in the process: professionalization presupposes a profit motive that is rarely imaginable where Medieval Latin texts or translations are at stake. In the second half of the twentieth century a few prolific translators who earned their livings through their craft became well known among readers of high-cultural literature.

In the diminutive group of those who have put Medieval Latin into English, only two come even close to qualifying as professionals. Both have been women. The first and more prominent was Helen Waddell (1889–1965), a Japanese-born Irish author who made her name mainly as a medievalist. She began to have an impact with English translations of Medieval Latin poetry in her monograph on *The Wandering Scholars* in 1927, which she extended with a full-blown and free-standing anthology of *Mediaeval Latin Lyrics* in 1929. Later came Betty Radice (1912–85), an Oxford-educated Classicist who played a central role as an editor and translator of Latin and Greek in the Penguin Classics. Radice's translation of the letters of Abelard and Heloise displaced the only serious earlier one by C. K. Scott Moncrieff (1889–1930), a minor figure of the decades around World War I who was associated with the poets Wilfred Owen (1893–1918) and Robert Graves (1895–1985). Hers has remained a staple since its first printing in 1974, still a strong seller after revision and expansion of its accompanying materials by the historian Michael Clanchy in 2003. But Waddell and Radice differed fundamentally in their positions in society, the first a belletrist and independent scholar, the second an editor in a large publishing house.

The dearth of professional translators of Medieval Latin results partly from the fragile status of translating within our larger culture and especially within academic culture, but it also reflects the marginality of Medieval Latin literature. In the nineteenth and first half of the twentieth century amateurs with a sufficient command of Latin tried their hands at translating, and sometimes they published the results. A small fraction from among them might be emboldened to publish such experiments commercially. In the second half of the twentieth century translations became commodities—but Latin had little hope of being commodified.

Quite apart from the professionals, the language-and-literature departments of universities have supported since the second half of the twentieth century a small class of professors whose oeuvre has consisted mainly of literary translations from classical or medieval vernacular languages. Examples include Allen Mandelbaum (1926–), with versions of Homer, Virgil's *Aeneid*, Ovid's *Metamorphoses*, Dante's *Divine Comedy*, and modern Italian poets; Robert Fagles (1933–2008), with translations of Bacchylides, Aeschylus, Sophocles, Homer, and Virgil's *Aeneid*; and Norman R. Shapiro, who has translated French literature on a spectrum that ranges from medieval through twentieth century. No close equivalent can be found for Medieval Latin. Some professors translate Medieval Latin, but they include few whose translations would receive (or who seek) esteem among professional poets and none whose publications would be reviewed as prominently as the poets just mentioned.

Far from poetry in either Medieval Latin or English, the name of the Romance philologist and medievalist Lewis Thorpe (1913–77) became familiar to a reasonably large audience after he translated for the Penguin Classics four volumes containing major Medieval Latin texts that could be qualified as primarily historical or of historical interest: Geoffrey of Monmouth, *The History of the Kings of Britain* (1966); Einhard and Notker the Stammerer, *Two Lives of Charlemagne* (1969—but now as translated by David Ganz in 2008); Gregory of Tours, *The History of the Franks* (1974); and Gerald of Wales, *The Journey Through Wales* and *The Description of Wales* (1978). Most of these texts had been translated at least once before. In the case of Geoffrey, Thorpe's translation sounded the death knell for the revision by Charles W. Dunn of the Sebastian Evans translation, which had appeared first in 1903. A comparison of the two translations will show why the passing of the Evans/Dunn translation was a mercy:

> Unto whom spake Merlin: "Since ye know not what it is that doth hinder the foundation being laid of this tower, ye have given counsel that the mortar thereof should be slacked of my blood, that so the tower should stand forthwith. Now tell me, what is it that lieth hid beneath the foundation, for somewhat is there that doth not allow it to stand?" (Geoffrey of Monmouth 1958, 135)

> "Just because you do not know what is obstructing the foundations of the tower which these men have begun," said Merlin to the magicians, "you have recommended that my blood should be sprinkled on the mortar to make the building stand firm. Tell me, then, what lies hidden under the foundation. There is certainly something there which is preventing it from holding firm." (Geoffrey of Monmouth 1966, 169)

The complete disappearance of the archaizing, "ye olde" style from translations of Medieval Latin can come none too soon.

Obviously less widely known to general audiences than Penguin books have been scholarly series with translations that have enjoyed *succès d'estime* or at least strong name recognition among the small guild of medievalists or even just of Medieval Latinists, for example, the Oxford Medieval Texts (1967–), which, like its predecessor series Nelson's Medieval Texts (1953–65), follows a facing text-and-translation format. The series has emphasized medieval English authors and those related to English history. To date, because of their prohibitive cost, the Oxford Medieval Texts have been sold mainly to research libraries and so cannot readily be used in teaching—but digitization opens the possibility for different models of distribution that may help the material in such series to reach larger audiences, as they deserve.

The best-seller in the Oxford Medieval Texts has been Bede's *Ecclesiastical History*, as edited by Bertram Colgrave (1889–1968) and Roger A. B. Mynors (1903–89). The English seems intended to cleave more closely to the Latin than seems to be the case with the Penguin translation by Leo Sherley-Price, as revised by R. E. Latham. Compare the very first paragraphs:

> Brittania Oceani insula, cui quondam Albion nomen fuit, inter septentrionem et occidentem locata est, Germaniae Galliae Hispaniae, maximis Europae partibus, multo interuallo aduersa. Quae per milia passuum DCCC in boream longa, latitudinis habet milia CC, exceptis dumtaxat prolixioribus diuersorum promontiorum tractibus, quibus efficitur ut circuitus eius quadrigies octies LXXV milia conpleat.

> Britain, once called Albion, is an island of the ocean and lies to the north-west, being opposite Germany, Gaul, and Spain, which form the greater part of Europe, though at a considerable distance from them. It extends 800 miles to the north, and is 200 miles broad, save only where several promontories stretch out further and, counting these, the whole circuit of the coast line covers 4,875 miles. (Bede the Venerable 1969, 15)

> Britain, formerly known as Albion, is an island in the ocean, lying towards the northwest at a considerable distance from the coasts of Germany, Gaul, and Spain, which together form the greater part of Europe. It extends 800 miles northwards, and is 200 in breadth, except where a number of promontories stretch further, so that the total coastline extends to 3600 miles. (Bede the Venerable 1968, 37, based on Bede the Venerable 1896)

Sherley-Price aspires to what could be called the transparency that is a hallmark of Penguin translations, which is to say, the illusion that it mediates with the minimum possible of interference between the medieval language and the modern English. In the note that precedes his translation, he comments simply: "My purpose is to offer an accurate and readable version in modern English" (Bede the Venerable 1968, 31). Colgrave articulates a very different ambition, saying: "To make Bede's *History* read in translation like any modern history book is not impossible, but it is only done at the cost of losing most of his overtones and producing a result which may be highly readable but is emphatically not Bede" (Bede the Venerable 1969, xxxvii). In keeping with his creed as a translator, Colgrave accepts loss of simplicity and even of naturalness in return for greater exactitude ("an island of the ocean" rather than "an island in the ocean," "save only where several promontories stretch out further and, counting these, the whole circuit of the coast line covers 4,875 miles" versus "except where a number of promontories stretch further, so that the total coastline extends to 3600 miles" [ibid., 15]).

Alongside the Oxford Medieval Texts stand other series, less known but often not a whit less distinguished, such as the Scriptores Latini Hiberniae (1955–), which is regularly bilingual, or the Auctores Britannici Medii Aevi (1968–), and the publications of the Henry Bradshaw Society (1891–), which sometimes purvey translations as companion volumes. Even roughly comparable translation-only series of any extent are few. One example would be the Translated Texts for Historians (1985–) published by Liverpool University Press, more than fifty volumes designed as working instruments to aid historians. Translated Texts for Historians makes available scholarly translations, sometimes heavily annotated, of sources not only in Latin but also in Greek, Syriac, Coptic, Arabic, Georgian, and Armenian.

The Fathers of the Church: Mediaeval Continuation is a relatively new series brought out by the Catholic University of America Press, with a focus on prose relating to religion and theology. Older series rise and fall in proportion to the driving force of their editors. Records of Civilization: Sources and Studies, edited under the auspices of the Department of History at Columbia University and published by the Columbia University Press, was very productive for a time. The Mediaeval Sources in Translation series of the Pontifical Institute of Mediaeval

Studies in Toronto has lately been revitalized. Some specialized series such as the Cistercian Fathers Series contain volumes invaluable to scholars and potentially appealing even to a larger audience if they could be produced and marketed for such readers.

The Cultural Impact of Medieval Latin in Translation

The catalogue of translations from Medieval Latin into English by significant literary figures is very short. The only anthology of such literary translations is *Latin Poetry in Verse Translation* (1957), now more than a half century old. It assembles translations into English from ancient, Medieval, and Renaissance Latin poems made by poets from Andrew Marvell (1621–78) through the compiler, Levi Robert Lind (1906–2008), and his contemporaries. Lind's anthology illustrates how in the nineteenth and twentieth century some poets of note tried their hands at translating Medieval Latin. A few examples would be Thomas Holley Chivers (1809–58), eccentric friend of Edgar Allan Poe, with an adaptation of a poem by Hildebert of Lavardin; Gerard Manley Hopkins (1844–89), a Roman Catholic convert who became a Jesuit priest, with hymns attributed to Bernard of Clairvaux and Thomas Aquinas, respectively; Kenneth Rexroth (1905–82), often mentioned for his ties to the Beat Poets, with a translation of the lyric with the opening words "Rumor letalis"; and J. V. Cunningham (1911–85), with his partial version of the Archpoet's so-called Confession. The two opening stanzas of the Latin will provide us a measure by which to judge Cunningham's version—and by which to compare it with other translations:

> Estuans intrinsecus ira vehementi
> in amaritudine loquor mee menti:
> factus de materia levis elementi
> folio sum similis de quo ludunt venti.
>
> Cum sit enim proprium viro sapienti
> Supra petram ponere sedem fundamenti,
> Stultus ego comparor fluvio labenti
> sub eodem aere nunquam permanenti.
>
> [Inwardly fired with vehement wrath,
> In bitterness I will speak my mind:
> Made of material light as lath,
> I am like a leaf tossed by the wind.
> Though it were just for the wise and brave
> To place their seat on the rock of will,

>   Fool, I am like the flowing wave
>   That under one sky is ever unstill.]
>   (Lind 1957, 372)

Cunningham hews reasonably close to the original, apart from adding a few words and phrases that mar the delicacy of the Archpoet's brilliant economy. Examples would be "as lath," "and brave," and "of will," which are nowhere to be found in the Latin.

Lind's anthology could of course be expanded, especially by adding translations of Medieval Latin hymns. To explore only one example, when Hugh Thomas Henry (1862–1946) wrote an entry on the *Dies irae* in the original *Catholic Encyclopedia* (1913), the English translations of the poem numbered at least 234. The translators and adapters from the seventeenth through the early nineteenth century included some famous writers, such as Richard Crashaw (1613–49), a member of the Metaphysical School; John Dryden (1631–1700), the great writer and literary critic; Walter Scott (1771–1832), the historical novelist and poet; and Thomas Babbington Macaulay (1800–1859), the poet, historian, and politician. Yet none of these poets put his hand regularly to the translation of Medieval Latin: their versions of the *Dies irae* stand mainly as isolated experiments within the context of their whole oeuvres.

Also significant are collections of hymns translated into English by single translators or collected by single compilers. Among the Englishmen are notable concentrations of clergymen, both Anglican and Catholic. Thus the Anglican priest John Mason Neale (1818–66), an English hymn writer most famous for "Good King Wenceslas" and other hymns and carols for Christmastide, published a collection of more than fifty *Mediaeval Hymns and Sequences*, four dozen of them never before translated into English, covering a gamut from Venantius Fortunatus through anonymous works of the fifteenth or sixteenth century. As a rule he made a practice of adopting the measure of the Latin original he followed. For instance, his translation of the trochaic *septenarii* (catalectic tetrameters) in which Venantius Fortunatus composed his famous hymn to the Holy Cross "Pange lingua gloriosi proelium certaminis" (to be distinguished from the hymn by Thomas Aquinas modeled upon it, "Pange lingua gloriosi corporis mysterium") begins:

>   Pange, lingua, gloriosi proelium certaminis
>   et super crucis trophaeo dic triumphum nobilem,
>   qualiter redemptor orbis immolatus vicerit.
>
>   [Sing, my tongue, the glorious battle,
>   With completed victory rife:
>   And above the Cross's trophy
>   Tell the triumph of the strife,
>   How the world's Redeemer conquer'd
>   By surrendering of His Life.]
>   (Neale 1867, 1)

For all the apparent simplicity of these lines, they are in their way a tour de force. Neale's translations bear witness not merely to his thorough command of Latinity but also to his flair for capturing the flavor of the originals as poems in both form and content. It has been a great loss to the appreciation of Medieval Latin that the twentieth century produced no successor to Neale in keeping alive the medieval tradition of hymnody. Neale also produced a highly popular translation of a large swatch of the *De contemptu mundi* by the twelfth-century poet Bernard of Cluny, which later attracted the attentions of Algernon Charles Swinburne (1837–1909) but was not translated in toto until 1991. The Anglican Reverend Sir Henry Williams Baker (1821–77), a composer and lyricist, deserves a place alongside Neale for his compilation of hymns.

Not long after Neale's death, Philip Schaff (1819–93), a Swiss-born, German-educated Protestant theologian who eventually lived and taught in the United States, published English versions of hymns, some of them originally Latin, by diverse hands. He offers a translation of Venantius's "Pange lingua gloriosi" by the Englishman Edward Caswall (1814–78), an Anglican clergyman and hymn writer who converted to Catholicism, which opens:

> Sing, my tongue, the Saviour's battle;
> > Tell His triumphs far and wide;
> Tell aloud the wondrous story
> > Of his body crucified,
> How upon the cross a victim,
> > Vanquishing in death, He died.
> (1849, 111)

Schaff's large anthology, which appeared in New York in 1868 and in London in 1869, is but one example of many to come out in the 1860s and 1870s on both sides of the Atlantic. Note should be taken of collections of hymns, many of them translations from Medieval Latin, that were produced by Englishmen. Examples include books published in 1868 by John Henry Newman (1801–90), perhaps the most famous convert of his day from Anglicanism—and the one responsible for Caswall's conversion—who rose within the Catholic church to become a cardinal; in 1873 (first edition in 1849) by Caswall himself; and in 1864 (first edition in 1849) by the Anglican archbishop and poet, the Englishman Richard Chenevix Trench (1807–86).

In the United States anthologies appeared in 1866 (published anonymously) by Judge Charles Cooper Nott, Sr. (1827–1916); in 1871 by William Henry Odenheimer (1817–79), Episcopal bishop of New Jersey; in 1867 by the lawyer and politician of New York, Erastus C. Benedict (1800–1880); and in 1867 by Abraham Coles (1813–91). Other translations had been printed before this dense spate, and more would follow it, but the congestion of publications in this stretch is noteworthy, all the more since the cultural contexts that inspired them differed starkly: in the United States it would seem reasonable to assume that the interest in hymns related to the trauma of the Civil War, whereas in Britain a major motivating factor may have been the strengthening of Catholicism that took place in conjunction with the Gothic Revival (of which the leading architect was the Catholic Augustus Pugin), the reestablishment of the Catholic hierarchy in 1850, and the prominence of converts such as Newman. In neither country did the efflorescence in English versions of medieval hymns connect with a broader turn to the translation of Medieval Latin literature.

The first—and sad to say, still the only—collection of English verse translated from Medieval Latin to achieve a major cultural impact was *Wine, Women, and Song: Mediaeval Latin Students' Songs* by John Addington Symonds (1840–93), published in London in 1884. Although its dedication to the writer Robert Louis Stevenson (1850–94) signals an orientation less toward universities than to broader high culture, *Wine, Women, and Song* looks amazingly learned by today's standards for a book the title of which has become a byword in mass culture. Not only does it open with a fifty-page essay, but in addition it concludes with an appendix, bibliography (with books in German, French, and Italian), and a table of correspondences to two scholarly editions. The lion's share of the lyrics—45 of 60—put into English in Symonds's anthology comes from the *Carmina Burana*.

Symonds's strengths and weaknesses as a translator are both evident in his handling of the opening to the so-called *Archpoet's Confession*, of which the Latin has already been quoted:

> Boiling in my spirit's veins
>   With fierce indignation,
> From my bitterness of soul
>   Springs self-revelation:
> Framed am I of flimsy stuff,
>   Fit for levitation,
> Like a thin leaf which the wind
>   Scatters from its station.
> While it is the wise man's part
>   With deliberation
> On a rock to base his heart's
>   Permanent foundation,
> With a running river I
>   Find my just equation
> Which beneath the self-same sky
>   Hath no habitation.
> (Symonds 1884, 55)

In brief introductory remarks, Symonds reveals his assumption that poet and persona are identical, and that to capture the spirit of this naively candid medieval bohemian he will resort to a vocabulary and syntax in alternation fey and archaizing: "This important composition lays bare the inner nature of a Wandering Student, describing his vagrant habits, his volatile and indiscriminate amours, his passion for the dice-box, his devotion to wine, and the poetic inspiration he was wont to draw from it" (ibid., 64).

Far more than a century later the 254 *Carmina Burana* remain untranslated in their entirety into English. Some forty were put into poetry by George F. Whicher (1889–1954), forming the largest section in a dual-language anthology of mainly twelfth-century Latin songs and satires that was dedicated to the American poet Robert Frost (1874–1963). Whicher's image of the poets he translated adhered closely to Symonds's. Of the Archpoet he wrote: "This nameless ecclesiastical jester, outwardly resembling the Clerk of Oxford but harboring inwardly the lusts of a Falstaff, was the greatest of all the vagabond poets" (Whicher 1949, 102). His translation of what he entitles *The Confession of Golias* opens:

> Indignation's fiery flood
> > Scalds my inmost being:
> I must chew a bitter cud,
> > One conclusion seeing:
> Light of substance is my blood,
> > Restlessness decreeing,
> So that down the wind I scud
> > Like a dead leaf fleeing.
>
> Let the wise man place his seat
> > On the firm rock founded.
> Hither, thither, I must beat
> > By my follies hounded.
> With the flowing stream I fleet,
> > So my doom is sounded;
> 'Neath the arch of heaven my feet
> > Nowhere yet have grounded.
> (ibid., 1949, 107)

Whicher's rendering contains much that is not in the Latin. In so doing it makes ham-fisted what was striking and yet delicate in the original, as when the seething of *estuans* is compounded as both "fiery flood" and "scalds." Bitterness becomes "bitter cud," blood is added in English where none had been in Latin, and the deadness of the leaf is unnecessarily spelled out. Furthermore, the translation achieves its qualities as poetry by techniques that do not correspond in any way to the Archpoet's, as for instance the foreshortening of "beneath" to "'neath" or the archaism of "hither, thither."

Not quite three dozen of the *Carmina Burana* were versified by the Germanist Edwin H. Zeydel (1893–1973), who perpetuated a profound misreading of what he called "Medieval Latin vagabond poetry" by mischaracterizing it as "the most uninhibited and individualistic expression of the medieval mind" (Zeydel 1966, 12). True to the German scholarship and culture that shaped him professionally, he does not

Anglicize the Archipoeta as the Archpoet, and he labels the poet's most famous poem *The Vagabond's Confession*:

> Boiling in my very soul,
> Wild with indignation,
> I in bitterness of heart
> Speak my declaration:
> I am of an element
> Volatile in matter,
> Like a frail and withered leaf
> Which the winds may scatter.
>
> Since it is the wise man's task
> With consideration
> Firm to set upon a rock
> Home and its foundation,
> I, a fool, may be compared
> To a flowing river,
> Always in the self-same bed,
> Transient yet forever.
> (ibid., 1966, 59)

The adjective "self-same" hints at the anxiety of influence that Zeydel, whose English is more a trot than a work of literature in its own right, felt toward Symonds as a translator, as revealed in the second paragraph of the preface to *Vagabond Verse*.

Such translations contrast unfavorably with the output of the poet Fleur Adcock (1934–), who was born in New Zealand but who has spent most of her life in Britain. In *The Virgin and the Nightingale* (1983) she presented in the original Latin and English translation a selection of lyrics from medieval anthologies such as the Cambridge Songs, the *Carmina Burana*, and the Arundel Lyrics, and from the oeuvre of Peter of Blois. Later she put into English *in toto* the poems of Hugh Primas and the Archpoet. The first two stanzas from *The Archpoet's Confession* will serve once again as our touchstone in evaluating translations:

> Deep inside me I'm ablaze with an angry passion;
> in my bitterness of mind, this is my confession:
> I'm constructed out of some light and weightless matter
> like a leaf, an idle toy for the winds to flutter.
>
> After all, a man of sense, one with penetration,
> builds his house upon a rock with a sure foundation.
> I, however (what a fool!) wander like a river
> never staying anywhere, on the move for ever.
> (Hugo Primas 1994, 115)

Adcock's is a genuinely poetic translation. Although the AABB end rhyme fails to correspond exactly to the long runs known in German as *Tiradenreim*, it conveys loosely the effect of the Latin. The length of the lines in English allows ample scope to translate all words and phrases, with the drawback that to fill out the verses it requires a bit of padding every few lines, which Adcock accomplishes through reduplication ("light and weightless," "a man of sense, one with penetration," "never staying anywhere, on the move for ever").

Anglophone Exceptionalism?

Sixty of the *Carmina Burana*, the love lyrics, were translated with precision by the noted Latinist Patrick G. Walsh, who coupled them with the Latin texts and commentary. But the circumstance that the famous songs remain to this day untranslated into English in their entirety is astonishing and dismaying—and all the more so when we consider the ubiquity in mass culture of a few lyrics from the collection in their original Latin set to the music of the composer Carl Orff (1895–1982), since in this form they are to be heard in the soundtracks of countless movies and television commercials and even sampled in rap music. The Anglophone world contrasts strikingly with the German-speaking one, where the entire collection has been translated repeatedly.

The different fates of the *Carmina Burana* and the *Carmina Cantabrigiensia* (Cambridge Songs), to cite an earlier Medieval Latin anthology that is roughly comparable in its range and beauty, is telling. The *Carmina Burana* are preserved in a manuscript that came from a Bavarian monastery to reside ultimately in a library in Munich, while the *Carmina Cantabrigiensia* are extant in a codex that was produced in a cloister in Canterbury but that now sits in Cambridge. The *Carmina Burana* are recognized to be a national treasure, a key component in the literary patrimony of medieval Germany, in spite of being in Latin. In contradistinction, the *Carmina Cantabrigiensia*, however admired by scholars, remain a footnote to broader culture.

Habent sua fata libelli. The *Carmina Cantabrigiensia* owes its relative neglect in part to the cultural distance that opened in the first half of the twentieth century as a consequence of the two World Wars. A fifth of households in the United States were German-speaking on the eve of World War I, but by the end of World War II, study of the language was in a decline that has only deepened subsequently. The mission statement that announced the Loeb Classical Library, which was founded by an American who was also a fluent German-speaker, ends with two sentences of untranslated German quoted from Goethe to affirm the value of studying French, English, and above all ancient Greek. The same prospectus proclaimed the goal, which turned out to be impossibly unwieldy, of including in the series "all that is of value and of interest in Greek and Latin literature, from the time of Homer to the Fall of Constantinople" (Loeb 1912).

The two realities—the centrality of German in Anglo-American culture and the willingness to conceive of Greek and Latin literature from the earliest times through 1453 as a continuum—were related to each other. The rapid displacement of German contributed at least a little to the marginalization of Medieval Latin, which not only had been institutionalized in the German academic system but had also earned a small but healthy niche in German literary history as a supplement to medieval literature in the German language. A Romantic formula that justified the appreciation of Medieval Latin texts such as the epyllion *Waltharius*, the beast poems *Ecbasis captivi* and *Ysengrimus*, and the lyrics of the *Carmina Burana* ultimately on the basis of the supposed proto-Germanness or Germanicity of the content or spirit they purveyed was counterbalanced later by the approach of Ernst Robert Curtius, which placed the accent upon the roots of Medieval Latin in an abiding grammatical and rhetorical culture built upon the Classics and shared by Germany and the Romance-speaking countries. In the rivalry between the French and the Germans that played a major role in coloring the various philologies that were established in the nineteenth century, Medieval Latin literature was essential for supplementing the rather sparse remains of Old High German and for countering any argument that Middle High German literature was largely derivative from its Old French counterpart. In England there was less reason for defensiveness, thanks to the richness of Old English literature and to the reality that post-Conquest Britain had its own "native" French literature in the form of Anglo-Norman.

The first commercial venture of the English-language publishing trade to encompass translations from Medieval Latin was a modest series of translations known as Bohn's Antiquarian Library, published and reprinted between 1847 and 1925. The "antiquarian" component of the name elicited unfavorable comment already in 1890, for stamping the series as being rarefied. The possessive that precedes the offending adjective designated the intrepid publisher, Henry George Bohn (1796–1884), who founded his library a decade before the Rolls Series began (1857). The Medieval Latin component of the library, which came into print between 1847 and 1863, drew upon the talents of many prominent medieval historians, especially those who edited for the Rolls Series and Camden Society, for translating texts relevant to British history.

The first half of the twentieth century saw a succession of series devoted broadly to classics of world literature, such as World's Classics (1901–78). A few incorporated translations from Medieval Latin, although in extremely meager numbers in proportion to the overall number of titles offered. For instance, the initial 505 volumes of Everyman's Library (1906–) included English translations of texts relating to Francis of Assisi and Thomas à Kempis.

No real concentration of Medieval Latin offerings was found in any major series before the Penguin Classics (1946–). The Penguin Classics had a component that was truly classic, as borne out by the fact that the series was inaugurated by a translation of *The Odyssey* by E. V. Rieu (1887–1972), who would become general editor of the series. Rieu aspired for the series to be characterized by what has been called a transparent style, without the deliberately archaic and foreign qualities he detected in other translations. The series has featured prose translations of some important texts written originally in Medieval Latin, particularly (but not exclusively) ones that bear on the history and culture of Britain in the Middle Ages. In 1969 the series included, among other books, Helen Waddell's *Mediaeval Latin Lyrics*, Bede's *History of the English People*, Geoffrey of Monmouth, and Einhard's and Notker's *Lives of Charlemagne*. Since then it has grown to encompass Gregory of Tours, Asser, Gerald of Wales, and the letters of Abelard and Heloise. Most of these translations dominated the market nearly exclusively until recently, when competitors have arrived. For example, Betty Radice's translation of Abelard and Heloise held sway unchallenged until 2007 and 2009, when two new English versions appeared by William Levitan and Mary McLaughlin, respectively. A short sample passage brings home the differences among the three:

> Maxime vero clerici ac praecipue scholares nostri intolerabilibus me lamentis et eiulatibus cruciabant ut multo amplius ex eorum compassione quam ex vulneris laederer passione, et plus erubescentiam quam plagam sentirem, et pudore magis quam dolore affligerer.

> In particular, the clerks and, most of all, my pupils tormented me with their unbearable weeping and wailing until I suffered more from their sympathy than from the pain of my wound, and felt the misery of my mutilation less than my shame and humiliation. (Abelard and Heloise 1974, 75; 2003, 17)

> The clerics were the worst and my students worst among them,
> Crucifying me with their screams and laments
> until I suffered more from their pity than my pain,
> more from chagrin than the injury itself, and more from the scandal than the scar. (Abelard and Heloise 2007, 19)

> It was chiefly the students, and particularly my own pupils, who tortured me with unbearable moaning and wailing, so that I suffered more from their pity than from the aching of my wound. I felt the embarrassment more than the injury, and my shame made me more wretched than my pain. (Abelard and Heloise 2009, 29)

Levitan attempts to convey literary qualities in the original Latin, among other things by setting the translation as if it were verse or at least something other than prose (Abelard and Heloise 2007, xxxiv). McLaughlin specifies that her goal is "to clear away the fictions and read the actual (if tightly controlled) historical record and to render the complex Latin expressions of the correspondents accurately and fluently, so that readers might be reminded of the depth and pleasure of the original Latin in which they were produced" (Abelard and Heloise 2009, 29).

Considerable, even perhaps disproportionate, space was devoted to Medieval Latin in Frederick Brittain's (1893–1969) *The Penguin Book of Latin Verse*, which was not one of the Penguin Classics more favorably received by classicists. Brittain's resolve to furnish a sampling from across the whole chronological gamut of Latin poetry, from Naevius in the third century BCE to Allen Beville Ramsey (1872–1955) in the mid-twentieth CE, put him on a collision course with reviewers who could not be persuaded that strictly classical Latin warranted less than fifty pages out of a total that verged on 400. The English, presented at the feet of the pages in a small pitch, is intended, according to J. M. Cohen (1903–89), the general editor, to simplify the task of those readers in need of linguistic guidance: "all the reader's problems can be solved by a glance at the bottom of the page" (Brittain 1962, unpaginated General Editor's Foreword). (It is charming that in 1962 such optimism existed about what could and would help a reader.) Brittain's taut version of the Archpoet's poem hardly clears up all uncertainties a reader might have, but it makes an honest effort to convey in prose what the Latin says:

> Roiling inwardly with violent indignation, I speak to my own heart in bitterness.
> Made as if from the unsubstantial element, I am like a leaf with which the winds play.
>
> While it is proper for a wise man to place the seat of his foundation on a rock,
> I am a fool and am like a running river, never standing still under the same sky.
> (ibid., 1962, 206)

Brittain was candid about his aims: "In order to help those readers who have only a limited knowledge of Latin, I have tried to make the translations as nearly literal as I could. They consequently have no literary pretensions" (ibid., 1962, lxv).

Why have the Penguin Classics not included more Medieval Latin works? In England Latin texts have not been integrated on any routine basis into either curricula for the study of English literature or series of "classic" texts of medieval literature in translation. Old English literature provides enough works such as *Beowulf* and the Old English riddles to make unnecessary recourse to early Medieval Latin literature. Notably, the small corpus of Medieval Latin from Britain that has been incorporated into the Penguin Classics has comprised historical and not literary works. Those raised in the United States may be predisposed to pay less heed to history and more to *belles lettres*, out of a perhaps mistaken sense that literature is easier to understand without a cultural background. Another explanation could be that Medieval Latin philology has never set down roots as deeply or extensively in Britain and France, except as a handmaiden to history, in comparison with its strong institutionalization in (to cite only two nations) Germany and Italy.

Facing Languages

The *en face* format has been used in English for the presentation of classical Latin texts at least since Alexander Pope's *Imitations of Horace* (1734–37), which put the Latin originals and English literary translations on facing pages. Probably because Latin from the Middle Ages has had a much lower standing than classical Latin, this format was not deployed for Medieval Latin texts even in the nineteenth century. Training in the Latin language rested largely on the translating and imitation of classical texts. Even today the legacy of this imitation sometimes remains embedded in college endowments, in the form of prizes that require translation into English from the Latin of specific ancient authors or into Latin in their style. At the other end of the translational spectrum Medieval Latin has no equivalents to the editions of classical Latin texts that were published in the early twentieth century with interlinear word-for-word glosses to help pupils as they prepared for highly literal translation in the classroom.

In the late twentieth century two series were mounted in the facing-language format. The first was the Garland Library of Medieval Literature. This initiative, which encompassed both a translation-only series and a dual-language series, arose thanks to the entrepreneurship of Gary Kuris, Vice-President of Garland Publishing from 1982 through 1986. Kuris focused on low print runs (200 to 400) in cloth of books offset from camera-ready copy. The press provided no copyediting, and the printing resulted in pages that looked typed or word-processed rather than composited and printed, but it enabled the publication in uniform bindings of translations and texts that might otherwise not have seen the light of day. Most of the Medieval Latin works chosen for the *en face* series were, in the grand scheme of things, obscure. The obscurity would have been a disadvantage if the series had been designed for marketing to a large audience, but it had the benefit of making available to medievalists hitherto underappreciated texts: *Medieval Latin Poems of Male Love and Friendship*; Gerald of Wales, *The Life of St. Hugh of Avalon*; *The Rise of Gawain, Nephew of Arthur*; and *The Story of Meriadoc, King of Cambridge*. The last two texts, although probably scarcely known outside a small coterie of specialists, might have at least some potential for appealing to a somewhat larger audience by virtue of belonging to Arthurian literature, but they have been made available subsequently only in even more expensive editions. Only the *Carmina Cantabrigiensia* stood a fighting chance of becoming standard fare within Medieval Latin studies. It was later reprinted in the Medieval and Renaissance Texts and Studies series. The English-only series had stronger offerings in terms of name recognition: *Three Lives of the Last Englishmen, Seven Medieval Latin Comedies, The Love Songs of the Carmina Burana, The Romances of Alexander,* and *The Plays of Hrotsvit of Gandersheim*.

A small cottage industry of translators has long existed around Hrotsvit, although far later in English than in German or French. An English version of the play *Dulcitius*, by Arthur Fillingham McCann (1893–1929), was privately printed in 1916, the year McCann graduated from Cornell University. *Callimachus*, translated by Richard S. Lambert (1894–1981), was also published in a very limited run in 1923, by a short-lived press (Stanton Press, 1921–24) that Lambert ran with his wife Elinor. In 1935 John Heard (1889) published in a poetry journal versions of *Callimachus* and of *Gallicanus*. But the plays did not achieve much impact except as published in 1923 in translation by the British author and political activist Christabel Gertrude Marshall (1871–1960), under the name (Christopher Marie St. James) that she took upon her conversion to Catholicism in 1912. This translation was reprinted in 1966 and 1989. It may be indicative of the declining knowledge of Latin outside the academy, but since the final quarter of the twentieth century Hrotsvit has belonged ever more to professors/translators. A complete translation of the plays, the work of the American classicist Larissa Bonfante, came out in 1979 and was reprinted in 1986. In 1985 the comparatist Katharina Wilson of the University of Georgia released the first in a series of translations and retranslations of Hrotsvit that she would bring out from different presses, including the one in 1989 published by Garland and another by D. S. Brewer in 1998.

The *en face* Cambridge Medieval Classics was conceived by Peter Dronke, who inaugurated it with *Nine Medieval Latin Plays*. The series, which produced only nine titles published over a five-year period (1994–99), put the accent upon translations and made an effort to do justice to the aesthetic dimensions of the original Latin. The original-language texts were most often largely unaltered reprints of earlier editions. On the whole the books received justifiably favorable notice from scholarly reviewers, with some discontent over the cursory annotation, but they were priced high, especially in view of their relative slimness. The works chosen offered intriguing cross-sections of Byzantine Greek and Medieval Latin literature, and most of them avoided retranslation of works that had been put into English already. Less advantageously, they presented texts not likely to figure among the few handfuls of medieval authors and works known to a general audience. Thus among lyricists, Hugh Primas and the Archpoet cannot compare with the *Carmina Burana* because of the name recognition that Orff's oratorio has bestowed upon the anthology, while among women writers Dhuoda is far less well known than even Hrotsvit, whose name is itself hardly a household word. Similarly, the *Architrenius* by Johannes de Hauvilla (Hauville) was a success in its day, but it has never enjoyed the currency of the *De planctu Naturae* or *Anticlaudianus* by Alan of Lille and will never do so, especially not so long as its author goes by such a portentously Latinate name. The last-mentioned circumstances would not have posed problems if the series had grown to encompass enough titles so that the less familiar books could have had companion or at least related volumes, to help build critical mass by genres and to ensure that first-time readers who developed a liking for one kind of text could come back later and find something at least loosely related to it. But such hopes were dashed when Cambridge University Press cut short the series.

Many translations and facing-language versions of Medieval Latin texts have been orphaned by publication as isolated volumes. Such volumes have sometimes offered excellent scholarship and production values but have not attracted the audiences they might have, had they been published in a fuller series. Cases in point include the edition and translation of Geoffrey of Monmouth's *The History of the Kings of Britain*, edited by Michael D. Reeve and translated by Neil Wright; Geoffrey's *Vita Merlini*, translated first by John Jay Parry (1889–1954), later by Basil Fulford Lowther Clarke (1907–78), and still later by Robert John Stewart; and Joseph of Exeter's Troy poem (based on the late antique prose of Dares the Phrygian), put into English twice, once in its entirety by Gildas Owen Roberts and once partially by Alan K. Bate. In what may be a sign of changes to come, the best translation by far is now what is available for free downloading on the web, by

A. G. Rigg. The Edwin Mellen Press has printed many editions, translations, and editions-and-translations of Medieval Latin works, but the books vary extraordinarily in quality.

At the moment the market for books is changing with an unnerving velocity, owing to developments not only in technology (of which we are all witnesses) but also in the international economic and cultural relations among languages. As English has strengthened its hold as a global language, the prominence of translations from other languages within the total of Anglophone book production has slipped. In recent decades translations from all foreign languages have occupied between two and four percent of the annual total of book production by the American publishing industry. Although on the face of it these figures would seem to be reassuringly stable, the reality is an ever-intensifying imbalance of trade that favors works first published in English. Medieval Latin has scant chance to benefit from such a context, in which anything truly medieval will be a comparative rarity.

The consequences of the trend toward monolingualism have been compounded by those of presentism. Precious little room has been left for the exploration of the past, especially where literature is concerned, when even the historical backdrop to present-day crises largely eludes investigation. Even foundational texts of classical antiquity do not possess the almost automatically high status that was once accorded to them. When the Middle Ages do enter the limelight, they appear frequently to be valued for the differences that set them apart from present-day life.

Despite the cultural significance that may still be accorded to books, the decision of which texts to translate and publish is governed largely by purely commercial factors, which are designated sometimes as "publication strategies." The market may be counterbalanced by cultural institutions, such as major foundations or national cultural entities. Latin has suffered from lacking such institutional backing.

The Loeb Classical Library and Its Younger Sisters

In the United States a solution to the lack of support for Medieval Latin by national or religious affiliation may be emerging from the tradition of philanthropy associated with universities. In particular, it is possible to point to text-and-translation series such as the Loeb Classical Library, founded in the early twentieth century (1911–) to advance the translation of ancient Greek and Latin; the I Tatti Renaissance Library, launched at the turn of the twenty-first century (2001–) to make available Latin works from the Renaissance; and, most recently, the Dumbarton Oaks Medieval Library (2010–), which is devoted at least initially to present texts and

English translations of Byzantine Greek, Medieval Latin, and Old English. These series, all made possible directly or indirectly through the generosity of specific Harvard alumni and all now published by Harvard University Press, provide an essential counterbalance to the market-driven choice of "greats" and constitute an interesting expression of the esteem for libraries and printed books that has been a feature of Harvard College since it took its name from a benefactor who bequeathed to it half his estate and all his books.

These series (which exemplify others published by commercial houses in both America and Europe) can exert a modest cultural influence. Primarily, they can reach audiences that would never come into contact with books published in purely philological series by university or commercial presses. Volumes from the Loeb Classical Library are found in many libraries where Latin-only or Greek-only texts have no place. In an academic context in which translation is treated as a poor relation in comparison with the production of monographs or articles, the existence of well-produced and solid volumes helps to validate the whole enterprise of translation. Secondarily, the competitive pricing of volumes in these series can contribute to more affordable books for everyone by motivating niche publishers of philological editions to make their texts available at lower prices in separate, less elaborate paperbacks or in their own translation series. The result is that original-language texts, translations, or both stand a better chance of reaching students and not merely research libraries, book reviewers who receive gratis copies, and a few motivated (and monied) individual purchasers.

Although the struggle to project past cultures before large audiences has long been challenging, there are translators and publishers willing to take the risk of standing behind translation series. Now the gamble is more important than ever and the stakes are higher, since from this point onward translations into English are likely to be the sole entrance for most people—even scholars—into many Medieval Latin texts. It is imperative that we do the job right, in both quantity and quality.

SUGGESTIONS FOR FURTHER READING

For a broad view of translation into English in Britain from the earliest days down to the present, see Ellis and Oakley-Brown (2009). Its complement is Venuti (2009), on the American tradition (with considerable attention to recent commercial factors). The little that has been written on translation of Medieval Latin into English will be found in Ailes (2000) and Ziolkowski (2000), with some excellent incidental material in Lapidge (1998). An exemplary bibliographic study of one series, Bohn's antiquarian library, appears in Tyas (1997). On inadequacies in translation (which manifest themselves often in archaic vocabulary and constructions in English versions of Medieval Latin), see Champe (2000) and Levi (2000).

BIBLIOGRAPHY

Primary sources

Abelard, Peter, and Heloise. 1925. *The Letters of Abelard and Heloise*, translated by C. K. Scott Moncrieff. London: G. Chapman.

———. 1974, 2003 (rev. by Clanchy). *The Letters of Abelard and Heloise*, translated by Betty Radice. Penguin Classics. Harmondsworth: Penguin Books.

———. 2007. *Abelard and Heloise. The Letters and Other Writings*, translated by William Levitan, Stanley Lombardo, and Barbara Thorburn. Indianapolis, IN: Hackett.

———. 2009. *The Letters of Heloise and Abelard: A Translation of Their Collected Correspondence and Related Writings*, edited by Mary Martin McLaughlin with Bonnie Wheeler. New Middle Ages. New York: Palgrave Macmillan.

Adcock, Fleur, ed. and trans. 1983. *The Virgin and the Nightingale: Medieval Latin Poems*. Newcastle upon Tyne: Bloodaxe Books.

Anderson, Graham, ed. and trans. 2007. *The Earliest Arthurian Texts: Greek and Latin Sources of the Medieval Tradition. Texts, Translations, and Commentary with a foreword by Alfred P. Smyth*. Lewiston, NY: Edwin Mellen Press.

Bede the Venerable. 1896. *Venerabilis Baedae Historiam ecclesiasticam gentis Anglorum: Historiam abbatum, Epistolam ad Ecgberctum, una cum Historia abbatum auctore anonymo*, edited by Charles Plummer. 2 vols. Oxford: Clarendon.

———. 1955. 1968 (rev. by Latham). *A History of the English Church and People*, edited by Leo Sherley Price. Penguin Classics. Harmondsworth: Penguin.

———. 1969. *Bede's Ecclesiastical History of the English People*, edited by Bertram Colgrave and Roger A. B. Mynors. Oxford Medieval Texts. Oxford: Clarendon Press.

Benedict, Erastus C., trans. 1869. *The Hymn of Hildebert and other Mediaeval Hymns, with translations*. New York: A. D. F. Randolph & Co.

Bernhard of Cluny. 1858. *Jerusalem Hymns: The Rhythm of Bernard de Morlaix, Monk of Cluny, on the Celestial Country*, edited by John M. Neale. London: J. T. Hayes.

———. 1991. *Scorn for the World: Bernard of Cluny's De Contemptu Mundi*, edited and translated by Ronald Pepin. Medieval Texts and Studies 8. East Lansing, MI: Colleagues Press.

Brittain, Frederick, ed. 1962. *The Penguin Book of Latin Verse*. The Penguin Poets. Harmondsworth: Penguin Books.

Carmina Burana. 1987. *The Love Songs of the Carmina Burana*, translated by E. D. Blodgett and Roy Arthur Swanson. Garland Library of Medieval Literature 49. New York: Garland Publishing.

———. 1993. *Love Lyrics from the Carmina Burana*, edited and translated by Patrick G. Walsh. Chapel Hill, NC: University of North Carolina Press.

Carmina Cantabrigiensia. 1994. *The Cambridge Songs (Carmina Cantabrigiensis)*, edited by Jan M. Ziolkowski. Garland Library of Medieval Literature 66. New York: Garland Publishing.

Caswall, Edward, trans. 1849. *Lyra Catholica. Containing all the Breviary and Missal Hymns together with some other hymns*. London: James Burns.

Coles, Abraham, trans. 1859, 1868 (rev.) *Latin Hymns, with Original Translations*. New York: D. Appleton and Company.

Day, Mildred Leake, ed. and trans. 1975. *The Rise of Gawain, Nephew of Arthur = De ortu Waluuanii nepotis Arturi*. Garland Library of Medieval Literature 15. New York: Garland Publishing.

Johannes de Hauvilla. 2006. *Architrenius*, edited and translated by Winthrop Wetherbee. Cambridge Medieval Classics 3. Cambridge: Cambridge University Press.

Dronke, Peter, trans. 1994. *Nine Medieval Latin Plays*. Cambridge Medieval Classics 1. Cambridge: Cambridge University Press.

Einhard and Notker the Stammerer. 1969. *Two Lives of Charlemagne*, translated by Lewis G. M. Thorpe. Penguin Classics. Harmondsworth, Baltimore: Penguin Books.

———. 2008. *Two Lives of Charlemagne*, translated by David Ganz. Penguin Classics. London, New York: Penguin Books.

Elliot, Allison Goddard, trans.1984. *Seven Medieval Latin Comedies*. Garland Library of Medieval Literature 20. New York: Garland Publishing.

Geoffrey of Monmouth. 1958. *History of the Kings of Britain*, translated by Sebastian Evans, revised by Charles W. Dunn. Dutton Paperbacks 14. New York: E. P. Dutton.

———. 1964, 1966 (rev.) *The History of the Kings of Britain*, translated by Lewis G. M. Thorpe. Penguin Classics. Harmondsworth: Penguin Books.

———. 1973. *Life of Merlin = Vita Merlini*, edited and translated by Basil Clarke. Cardiff: University of Wales Press.

———. 1986. *The Mystic Life of Merlin*, translated by R. J. Stewart. London, New York: Arkana.

Gerald of Wales. 1985. *The Life of St. Hugh of Avalon*, edited and translated by Richard M. Loomis. Garland Library of Medieval Literature 31. New York: Garland Publishing.

———. 1978. *The Journey through Wales and The Description of Wales*, translated by Lewis G. M. Thorpe. Penguin Classics. Harmondsworth, New York: Penguin Books.

Gregory of Tours. 1974. *The History of the Franks*. Penguin Classics. Harmondsworth, Baltimore: Penguin Books.

Hrotsvit of Gandersheim. 1923a. *Callimachus: a play by Roswitha the Nun of Gandersheim*, translated by Richard S. Lambert. Wembley Hill: The Stanton Press.

———. 1923b. *The Plays of Roswitha*, translated by Christopher St. John. London: Chatto & Windus.

———. 1935a. "Abraham," translated by John Heard. *Poet Lore* 42: 299–313.

———. 1935b. "Gallicanus," translated By John Heard. *Poet Lore* 42: 314–28.

———. 1979. *The Plays of Hrotswitha of Gandersheim*, translated by Larissa Bonfante with Alexandra Bonfante-Warren. New York: New York University Press.

———. 1985. *The Dramas of Hrotsvit of Gandersheim*, translated by Katharina M. Wilson. Saskatoon, SK: Peregrina.

———. 1989. *The Plays of Hrotsvit of Gandersheim*, translated by Katharina M. Wilson. Garland Library of Medieval Literature 62. New York: Garland Publishing.

Hugo Primas Aurelianensis. 1994. *Hugh Primas and the Archpoet*, edited and translated by Fleur Adcock. Cambridge Medieval Classics 2. Cambridge, New York: Cambridge University Press.

Joseph of Exeter. 1970. *The Iliad of Dares Phrygius*, edited by Gildas Owen Roberts. Cape Town: A. A. Balkema.

———. 1986. *Trojan War I–III*, edited by Alan K. Bate. Warminster: Bolchazy-Carducci, Aris & Phillips.

———. 2005. *Daretis Phrygii Ilias*, translated by A.G. Rigg. Toronto: Centre for Medieval Studies, University of Toronto.

Kratz, Dennis M., trans. 1991. *The Romances of Alexander*. Garland Library of Medieval Literature 64. New York: Garland Publishing.

Lind, Levi R., ed. 1957. *Latin Poetry in Verse Translation, from the beginnings to the Renaissance*. Boston: Houghton Mifflin.

Loomis, Richard M., ed. and trans. 1936. *The Story of Meriadoc, King of Cambridge*. London: Cambridge University Press.

Neale, John M., ed. 1866. *Stabat Mater Speciosa, Full of Beauty Stood the Mother*. London: J. T. Hayes.

———. 1867. *Mediæval Hymns and Sequences*. 3rd ed. London: J. Masters.

Newman, John Henry. 1868, 1912 (rev.). *Verses on Various Occasions*. London: Burns Oates and Washbourne.

Nott, Charles C., trans. 1866, 1883 (rev.) *The Seven Great Hymns of the Mediaeval Church*. New York: E. S. Gorham.

Odenheimer, William H. and Frederic M. Bird, trans. 1871. *Songs of the Spirit*. New York: A. D. F. Randolph & Co.

Schaff, Philip, trans. 1868, 1869. *Christ in Song: Hymns of Immanual, selected from all ages, with notes*. New York: S. Low, Marston, Searle, & Rivington.

Stehling, Thomas, trans. 1984. *Medieval Latin Poems of Male Love and Friendship*. Garland Library of Medieval Literature 7. New York: Garland Publishing.

Swanton, Michael, ed. and trans. 1984. *Three Lives of the Last Englishmen*. Garland Library of Medieval Literature 10. New York: Garland Publishing.

Symonds, John Addington, trans. 1884. *Wine, women, and song; mediaeval Latin students' songs now first translated into English verse with an essay*. London: Chatto & Windus.

Tyas, Shaun. 1997. *A Bibliographical Guide to Bohn's Antiquarian Library*. 2nd ed. Stamford: Paul Watkins Publishing.

Waddell, Helen. 1927. *The Wandering Scholars*. London: Constable & Co.

———, trans. 1933. *Mediaeval Latin lyrics*. London: Constable & Co.

Whicher, George Frisbie, ed. and trans. 1949. *The Goliard Poets: Medieval Latin Songs and Satires with verse translation*. Norfolk, CT: New Directions.

Zeydel, Edwin Hermann, ed. and trans. 1966. *Vagabond Verse. Secular Latin Poems of the Middle Ages*. Detroit: Wayne State University Press.

Secondary sources

Ailes, Marianne J. 2000. "Medieval Epic: Latin." In *Encyclopedia of Literary Translation into English*, edited by Olive Classe, 2: 936–37. 2 vols. London, Chicago: Fitzroy Dearborn Publishers.

Champe, Gertrud Graubart. 2000. "Translationese." In *Encyclopedia of Literary Translation into English*, edited by Olive Classe, 2: 1421–22. 2 vols. London, Chicago: Fitzroy Dearborn Publishers.

Ellis, Roger and Liz Oakley-Brown. 2009. "British Tradition." In *Routledge Encyclopedia of Translation Studies*, eds. Mona Baker and Gabriela Saldanha, 344–54. 2nd ed. London and New York: Routledge.

Lapidge, Michael. 1998. "The Edition of Medieval Latin Texts in the English-speaking World." *Sacris Eruditi* 38: 199–220.

Levi, Anthony. 2000. "Church Latin in English Translation." In *Encyclopedia of Literary Translation into English*, edited by Olive Classe, 1: 285–86. 2 vols. London, Chicago: Fitzroy Dearborn Publishers.

Radice, Betty. 1969. "The Penguin Classics: A Reply." *Arion* 8: 130–38.

Venuti, Lawrence. 2009. "American Tradition." In *Routledge Encyclopedia of Translation Studies*, eds. Mona Baker and Gabriela Saldanha, 320–28. 2nd ed. London, New York: Routledge.

Ziolkowski, Jan M. 2000. "Post-Classical Latin Writing." In *Oxford Guide to Literature in English Translation*, ed. Peter France. Oxford: Oxford University Press, 544–50.

Chronology of Medieval Authors

Note: The following is a chronological listing of all the medieval authors contributors mention in the form they have most commonly chosen. As editors we have not imposed an artificial consistency of nomenclature such as might be expected and would be easily achievable in an account of ancient Greek or Roman authors: we are content to have Jerome be known simply as "Jerome" rather than "Eusebius Sophronius Hieronymus," correct but unrecognizable to all but a few. We err on the side of expansiveness in permitting, for the purpose of this list, "medieval" to stretch from the early fourth-century Biblical epic poet Juvencus to the sixteenth-century French humanist Michel de Montaigne. In many cases exact birth and death dates are unknown; when there is no scholarly consensus on an even approximate lifespan we have recourse to the traditional *floruit* (abbreviated "fl.") to give the best estimate of the central period of the author's activity. Names in quotation marks indicate an authorial attribution that scholars regard as fictitious or at the least with great skepticism.

Juvencus (fl. early 4th c.)
Gaius Marius Victorinus (fl. 4th c.)
Julius Obsequens (fl. ca. 4th c.)
Hilary of Poitiers (ca. 300 – ca. 368)
Zeno of Verona (ca. 300 – 371/ 380)
Ausonius (ca. 310 – 395)
Eutropius (ca. 320 – ca. 387)
Ammianus Marcellinus (325/30 – ca. 390)
Solinus (fl. mid 4th c.)
Ambrose (ca. 338 – 397)
Quintus Aurelius Symmachus (ca. 345 – 402)
Jerome (ca. 347 – 420)
Aurelius Prudentius (348 – ca. 405)
Aelius Donatus (fl. 350)
"Lactantius Placidus" (fl. 4th century or late 5th/6th century)
Augustine of Hippo (354 – 430)
Sulpicius Severus (ca. 360 – 420/25)
John Cassian (ca. 360 – 435)
Vegetius (fl. 385 – 400)
Julius Paris (fl. late 4th c.)

Servius Honoratus (fl. 390)
Macrobius (395 – 423)
Cyprianus Gallus (fl. 397 – 430)
Tiberius Claudius Donatus (fl. ca. 400)
Rutilius Claudius Namatianus (fl. 5th c.)
Palladius (fl. 408 – 431)
Marcellus Empiricus (fl. 410)
Martianus Capella (fl. 410 – 439)
Claudius Victor (fl. 425 – 450)
Coelius Sedulius (fl. 430 – 450)
Quodvultdeus (d. ca. 450)
Sidonius Apollinaris (ca. 430 – 489)
Ammonius (of Hermias) (fl. ca. 485)
Dracontius (ca. 455 – ca. 505)
Avitus of Vienne (ca. 470 – 523)
Caesarius of Arles (ca. 470 – 542)
Ennodius (474 – 521)
Luxurius (ca. late 5th or early 6th c.)
Priscian (5th – 6th c.)
Boethius (ca. 480 – 524/5)
Benedict of Nursia (480 – 547)
Cassiodorus (ca. 485 – ca. 585)
Arator Subdiaconus (fl. 513 – 544)
Venantius Fortunatus (ca. 530 – ca.600/09)
Fulgentius (d. 532/3)
Gregory of Tours (ca. 538 – 594)
Gregory the Great (540 – 604)
Isidore of Seville (ca. 560 – 636)
Corippus (fl. 565)
Maximus the Confessor (ca. 580 – 662)
Columcille (d. 597)
Baudonivia (fl. 600 – 602)
Virgilius Maro Grammaticus (fl. 7th c.)
Aldhelm of Malmesbury (ca. 639 – 709)
Pseudo-Dionysius the Areopagite (fl. ca. 650 – ca. 725)
Augustine Eriugena (fl. 655)
Martin of Laon (ca. 660 – 680)
Bede (672/3 – 735)
John of Damascus (ca. 676 – 749)
Paul the Deacon (720 – 799)
Alcuin (730/40 – 804)
Tatwine (d. 734)
Ecgbert (d. 766)
Theodulf of Orléans (ca. 750/60 – 821)

Einhard (ca. 775 – 840)
Rabanus Maurus (ca. 780 – 856)
Gæraldus (fl. 9th c. ?)
Dunchad of Laon (fl. 9th c.)
Nithard (ca. 800 – 844)
Walahfrid Strabo (ca. 808 – 849)
Claudius of Turin (fl. 810 – 827)
Anastasius Bibliothecarius (ca. 810 – ca. 878)
Photios (ca. 810 – ca. 893)
Angilbert (d. 814)
Dhuoda of Septimania (fl. ca. 820 – 843)
Notker Balbulus, or Notker the Stammerer (ca. 840 – 912)
Abbo of St-Germain (ca. 840 – 923)
Hucbald of St-Amand (840 – 930/2)
Remigius of Auxerre (ca. 841 – 908)
Eriugena, John Scotus (fl. 847 – 877)
Alvarus, Paul (fl. ca. 850)
Sedulius Scottus (fl. ca. 850)
Haimo of Halberstadt (d. ca. 853)
Haimo of Auxerre (d. ca. 855)
Hrabanus Maurus (d. 856)
Eulogius of Córdoba (d. 859)
Otfrid of Weissenburg (d. after 870)
Eugenius Vulgarius (fl. ca. 887 – 928)
Rather of Verona (890 – 974)
"Theodolus" (fl. ca. 10th c.)
Ratpert (d. ca. 900)
Æthelwold (904/9 – 984)
Asser (d. 908/9)
Dunstan (909 – 988)
John the Deacon (d. after 910)
Liutprand of Cremona (ca. 922 – 972)
Atto of Vercelli (924/5 – 960 /61)
Widukind of Corvey (925 – 973)
Hrotsvit of Gandersheim (ca. 935 – ca. 1002)
Frithegod (fl. ca. 950 – ca. 958)
Notker III of St. Gall, or Notker Labeo (ca. 950 – 1022)
Buchard of Worms (ca. 950 – 1025)
Ælfric of Eynsham (ca. 955 – ca. 1010)
Wulfstan the Cantor (ca. 960 – early 11th century)
Walter of Speyer (967 – 1027)
Byrhtferth of Ramsey (ca. 970 – ca. 1020)
Lantfred of Fleury/Winchester (fl. 970s)
Ebracher of Liège (d. 971)

Ekkehard I (d. 973)
Avicenna, or Ibn Sīnā (ca. 980 – 1037)
Ekkehard IV, Ekkehard IV of St. Gall (ca. 980 – ca. 1056)
Oswald of Worcester (d. 992)
Ibn al-Nadīm (d. 995/8)
Æthelweard (d. ca. 998)
Berengar of Tours (ca. 999 – 1088)
Foulcoie of Beauvais (fl. 11th c.)
Ælfric Bata (fl. 1005)
Anselm of Liège (1008 – ca. 1056)
Williram of Ebersberg (ca. 1020 – 1085)
Constantine the African (ca. 1020 – 1087)
Goscelin of Canterbury (1023/35 – ca. 1107)
Fulbert of Chartres (d. 1028)
Marbod of Rennes (ca. 1035 – 1123)
Bruno of Asti (ca. 1049 – 1123)
Adam of Bremen (1050 – 1081/85)
Osbern of Canterbury (ca.1050 – ca. 1090)
Guibert of Nogent (ca. 1055/60 – 1124/5)
Hildebert of Lavardin (1056 – 1133)
Metellus of Tegernsee (fl. ca. 1060)
Eadmer (ca. 1060 – ca. 1126)
Baudri of Bourgeuil (1060 – 1130)
Tortarius, Rudolfus (b. 1063)
William of Champeaux (ca. 1070 – 1121)
Moses Ibn 'Ezra' (ca. 1070 – ca. 1138)
William of St. Thierry (1070 – 1148)
Conrad of Hirsau (ca. 1070 – ca. 1150)
Gilbert of Poitiers (1070 – 1154)
Peter Damian (d. 1073)
Godfrey of Rheims (d. 1095)
Rupert of Deutz (ca. 1075 – 1129)
Peter Abelard (1079 – 1142)
Adelard of Bath (ca. 1080 – ca. 1152)
Ælnoth of Canterbury (d. 1086)
Abraham Ibn Ezra (1089 – 1164)
Bernard of Clairvaux (1090 – 1153)
William of Conches (ca. 1090 – ca. 1154)
Peter the Venerable (ca. 1092 – 1156)
Hugh of Orléans (1094 – 1160)
William of Malmesbury (ca. 1095/96 – ca. 1143)
Christina of Markyate (ca. 1095/1100 – 1155)
Hugh of Saint Victor (ca. 1096 – 1141)
Hildegard of Bingen (1098 – 1179)

Lambert of St. Omer (fl. 1100)
Burleo, Gualtiero (fl. 12th c.)
Geoffrey of Vitry (fl. 12th c.)
Stephen of Antioch (fl. 12th c.)
Geoffrey of Monmouth (ca. 1100 – ca. 1155)
Peter Lombard (ca. 1100 – 1160)
Peter Helias (ca. 1100 – 1166)
Héloïse (ca. 1101 – 1164)
Serlo of Wilton (ca. 1105 – 1181)
Robert of Ketton (ca. 1110 – ca. 1160)
Ælred of Rievaulx (1110 – 1167)
Andrew of Saint Victor (ca.1110 – 1175)
Reginald of Canterbury (fl. 1112)
Otto von Freising (ca. 1114 – 1158)
Gerard of Cremona (1114 – 1187)
John of Salisbury (ca. 1115 – 76/80)
Hilary of Orléans (fl. 1125)
Elisabeth of Schönau (1125 – 1165)
Ibn Rushd (1126 – 1198)
Gilbert the Universal (fl. 1128 – 34)
Alan of Lille (ca. 1128–1202)
Bernard of Chartres (d. 1130)
Hildebert of Le Mans (d. 1133)
Peter of Blois (ca. 1135 – ca. 1203)
Guigo I (d. 1136)
Bernardus Silvestris (fl. 1136)
Hugh Primas (fl. 1130)
The Archpoet (ca. 1130 – ca. 1165)
Plato of Tivoli (fl. 1132 – 46)
Ralph of Laon (d. 1133)
Ogier of Locedio (1136 – 1214)
Robert of Chester (fl. 1140 – 50)
Herman of Carinthia (fl. ca. 1140 – 1150)
Walter Map (1140 – ca. 1208/10)
Daniel of Morley (ca. 1140 – ca. 1210)
Adam of Saint Victor (d. 1146)
Gerald of Wales (ca. 1146 – ca. 1223)
Thierry of Chartres (d. 1150/55)
Bernard of Cluny (fl. 1150)
Nivard of Ghent (fl. ca. 1150)
Saxo Grammaticus (ca. 1150 – 1220)
Samuel Ibn Tibbon (ca. 1150 – ca. 1230)
Leonius of Paris (fl. 1150s)
Stephen Langton (ca. 1150/9 – 1228)

Honorius of Autun, or Honorius Augustodunensis (d. ca. 1151)
Lawrence of Durham (d. 1154)
Marie de France (fl. 1155 – 1190)
Henry of Huntingdon (d. 1156/64)
Arnulf of Orléans (fl. 1156)
Neckam, Alexander (of) (1157 – 1217)
Burchard of Bellevaux (d. 1164)
Gottfried of Admont (d. 1165)
Peter Riga (fl. ca. 1165 – 1209)
John Sarracenus (fl. ca. 1167)
Archbishop Andrew Suneson, or Andreas Sunonis (ca. 1167 – 1228)
Hugh of Pisa (fl. ca. 1170 – ca. 1190)
Hartmann von Aue (ca. 1170 – 1210)
Rodrigo Jiménez (or Ximénez) de Rada (ca. 1170 – 1247)
Guigo II the Carthusian (d. ca. 1173)
Richard of Saint Victor (d. 1173)
Alexander of Villedieu (ca. 1175 – 1240/50)
Chrétien de Troyes (fl. 1170)
Walter of Châtillon (fl. 1170 – 1180)
Matthew of Vendôme (fl. ca. 1175)
Robert Grosseteste (ca. 1175 – 1253)
Peter Comestor (d. ca. 1178)
Snorri Sturluson (1179 – 1241)
Walter of St. Victor (d. ca. 1180)
Andreas Cappellanus (fl. 1180s)
Caesarius of Heisterbach (ca. 1180 – ca. 1240)
Sven Aggeson (fl. 1181/82)
John of Hauville (fl. ca. 1184)
Odo of Cheriton (ca. 1185 – 1246/7)
Joseph of Exeter (fl. ca. 1190)
Azzo (fl. 1190 – 1220)
Vincent of Beauvais (ca. 1190 – ca. 1264)
William Peraldus (ca. 1190 – 1271)
Mark of Toledo (fl. 1193 – 1216)
Enrico of Settimello (fl. ca. 1194)
Peter the Chanter (d. 1197)
Alfred of Shareshill (fl. ca. 1197 – ca. 1222)
Bovetino Bovetini (fl. 13th c.)
Eberhard the German (fl. 13th c.)
Geoffrey of Vinsauf (fl. 1200)
Alberic of London (fl. ca. 1200)
Thomas Gallus of Vercelli (ca. 1200 – 1246)
Rudolf von Ems (ca. 1200 – 1254)
Matthew Paris (ca. 1200 – 1259)

Bartholomeus Anglicus (1203 – 1272)
John of Garland (fl. ca. 1205)
Alexander of Ashby (d. 1208/14)
Guillaume de Lorris (ca. 1210 – ca. 1237)
Berthold of Regensburg (ca. 1210 – 72)
Arnold of Lübeck (d. 1211 – 1214)
Eberhard of Béthune (d. ca. 1212)
Gervase of Melkey (fl. 1212)
Roger Bacon (ca. 1214 – 1294)
Adam of Barking (fl. ca. 1217)
Henri D'Andeli (fl. first half of 13th c.)
Petrus Episcopus (d. 1219)
James of Vitry (fl. ca. 1220)
Bonaventure (1221 – 1274)
Salimbene de Adam (1221 – ca. 1288)
Urso of Genoa (fl. 1225 – 1245)
Thomas Aquinas (1225 – 1274)
Albertano of Brescia (fl. 1226 – 53)
Jacobus de Voragine (ca. 1230 – 1290)
Jacob van Maerlant (1230/1240 – 1288/1300)
William Durandus (ca. 1230 – 1296)
Ramon Llull (1232 – 1315)
Boethius of Dacia (ca. 1240 – ca. 1280)
Lovato Lovati (ca. 1240 – 1309)
Bene of Florence (d. ca. 1242)
Michael of Cornwall (fl. 1243 – 1255)
Giles of Rome (ca. 1243/7 – 1316)
Lucas de Tuy (d. 1249)
Julian of Speyer (d. 1250)
Jean de Meun (ca. 1250 – ca. 1305)
Jacopo da Cessole (1250 – 1322)
Geremia da Montagnone (1250/60 – 1320/22)
Riccobaldo of Ferrara (1251 – 1318)
Giordano da Pisa (ca. 1255 – 1311)
Gertrude of Helfta (1256 – ca. 1302)
Henry of Avranches (d. ca. 1261)
Walter of Wimborne (fl. 1261 – 1266)
Albertino Mussato (1261 – 1329)
Albert of Stade (d. ca. 1264)
Dante Alighieri (1265 – 1321)
Geri d'Arezzo (ca. 1270 – ca. 1337)
Nicholas of Lyra (ca. 1270 – 1349)
Richard Ledrede (ca. 1275 – 1360)
Joseph Ibn Caspi (1279 – 1340)

Ranulf Higdon (ca. 1280 – 1364)
Raymond Martini (d. after 1284)
Richard de Bury (1287 – 1345)
William of Ockham (ca. 1288 – ca. 1348)
Richard Rolle (1290 – 1349)
Pierre Bersuire (ca. 1290 – 1362)
Ferreto Ferreti (1294 – 1337)
Johannes Balbus (d. 1298)
Thomas of Erfurt (fl. ca. 1300)
Giambono di Andreae (fl. 13th/14th c.)
Ugo Mezzabati (fl. 13th/14th c.)
Pace da Ferrara (fl. early 14th c.)
Anonymous of Calais (fl. 14th c.)
Matthias of Linköping (ca. 1300 – 1350)
Richard FitzRalph (ca. 1300 – 1360)
Ludolphus of Saxony (ca. 1300 – 1378)
Birgitta of Sweden (ca. 1303 – 73)
Francesco Petrarch (1304 – 1374)
Benzo da Alessandria (fl. 1311 – 1329)
Bartolus de Saxoferrato (1313 – 1357)
Giovanni Boccaccio (1313 – 1375)
Giovanni del Virgilio (fl. 1319)
Anna von Munzingen (fl. 1327)
Alphonsus Bonihominis (d. 1353)
John Wycliffe (ca. 1328 – 1384)
Baldus de Ubaldis (1327 – 1400)
Katherina von Gebersweiler (d. ca. 1330)
John Ridevall (fl. 1330)
John Gower (ca. 1330 – 1408)
Guido Vicentinus (d. 1332)
William Langland (ca. 1332 – ca. 1386)
Ibn Khaldūn (1332 – 1406)
Giovanni de Matociis (d. 1337)
Giovanni da Cremenate (d. ca. 1344)
Johannes de Caulibus (fl. ca. 1340 – 60)
John of Trevisa (ca. 1342 – 1402)
Geoffrey Chaucer (1343 – 1400)
Florentius Radewijns (1350 – 1400)
Pierre d'Ailly (1351 – 1420)
Henry of Kirkestede (fl. 1360 – 1380)
Christine de Pizan (1363 – ca. 1430)
Thomas Elmham (1364 – ca. 1427)
Paolo Veneto (1369 – 1429)
John Lydgate of Bury (ca. 1370 – ca. 1451)

Theodoricus Monachus (fl. 1371)
Margery Kempe (ca. 1373 – 1438)
Bernardino of Siena (1380 – 1444)
Thomas à Kempis (ca. 1380 – 1471)
Juan de Torquemada (1388 – 1468)
Enea Silvio Piccolomini (1405 – 1464)
Hans Folz (ca. 1435 – 1513)
Antonio de Nebrija (1441 – 1522)
Angelo Poliziano (1454 – 1494)
Solomon ben Reuben Bonafed (d. after 1445)
Juan of Segovia (d. ca. 1458)
William Dunbar (ca. 1460 – ca. 1520)
Desiderius Erasmus (1466 – 1536)
Herolt, Johannes (fl. 1468)
Theodore Bibliander (1506 – 1564)
Guillaume Postel (1510 – 1581)
Michel de Montaigne (1533 – 1592)

Index of Personal Names and Titles

Note: While the "Index of Names and Titles" does not aim for utter completeness, it includes, in addition to medieval Latin authors, the names of classical Latin authors that appear in the *Handbook*; Greek authors (classical, patristic and Byzantine); Arabic and Hebrew authors; vernacular authors; select modern scholars (but none living); and other significant historical figures (e.g., popes, secular rulers). With names from so many traditions and times, absolute consistency is elusive; we have tried to list individuals under the names we anticipate our readers will look for, providing cross-references when appropriate. Variant forms of names, especially if they appear above, are listed (e.g, Ibn-Rushd and Averroes, Vergil and Virgil). Names of figures not or not certainly historical (e.g., Biblical, mythological, legendary) are generally excluded. All dates are CE unless otherwise noted.

In addition, the titles of anonymous works and anthologies are included;[1] works belonging to a named author are not listed separately under the author's name. Scriptures (of various traditions), however, are indexed in the "Index of Topics," as are names of places (e.g., cities, monasteries).

Abbo of St-Germain (ca. 840 – 923) 10
Abraham Ibn Ezra (1089 – 1164) 77
Adam of Barking (fl. ca. 1217) 269
Adam of Bremen (1050 – 1081/85) 109
Adam of Saint Victor (d. 1146) 244–45, 251, 390
Adela of Blois (ca. 1067 – 1137) 245, 347
Adelard of Bath (ca. 1080 – ca. 1152) 78, 97
Admonitio generalis 131
Æethelwold (904/9 – 984) 10
Ælfric Bata (fl. 1005) 414
Ælfric of Eynsham (ca. 955 – ca. 1010) 15, 125–27
Aelius Donatus (fl. 350); see Donatus
Ælnoth of Canterbury (d. 1086) 107
Ælred of Rievaulx (1110 – 1167) 470, 477
Aesop 576
Æthelweard (d. ca. 998) 15
Aethicus Ister; see also Virgil of Salzburg 207
Alan of Lille (ca. 1128 – 1202) xvi, 6, 27, 78, 125, 251, 260–61, 335, 346, 417, 455, 576, 608
Alberic of London (fl. ca. 1200) 341
Albert of Stade (d. ca. 1264) 442
Albertano of Brescia (fl. 1226 – 1253) 556, 564–65, 576

Albertino Mussato; see Mussato, Albertino
Alcuin (730/40 – 804) 17–18, 51–52, 60, 70, 130, 197, 200, 252, 256, 289, 315, 318, 539, 587
Aldhelm of Malmesbury (ca. 639 – 709) 11, 15, 17–18, 33, 53, 58, 130, 200, 221, 229, 242, 442
Alexander of Ashby (d. 1208/14) 359, 363
Alexander of Villedieu (ca. 1175 – 1240/50) 240, 576
al-Fārābī (d. 950) 93
Alfonso X, King, The Wise 72–73, 80
Alfred of Shareshill (fl. ca. 1197 – ca. 1222) 100
Alphonsus Bonihominis (Buenhombre) (d. 1353) 79
Altercatio Phyllidis et Florae 345
Alvarus, Paul (fl. ca. 850) 73–74, 241
Ambrose (ca. 338 – 397) 27, 128, 130, 154, 195, 243, 382, 517, 522
Ammianus Marcellinus (325/30 – ca. 390) 521–22
Ammonius (of Hermias) (fl. ca. 485) 311, 313
Anastasius Bibliothecarius (ca. 810 – ca. 878) 206
Ancrene Wisse 16, 134
Andreas Cappellanus (fl. 1180s) 575

---

[1] Since medieval and modern attributions often vary, there are some potential inconsistencies. The title of *Ecloga Theoduli* or *Theodoli* contains within it the name of its author as medieval readers thought – "Theodulus" or "Theodolos" – although modern scholars are uncertain who the author is (or even which Gottschalk, if that is the German name hidden behind the Latin Greek). Meanwhile, medieval scholars, asked who the author of the *Ilias Latina* was, might have answered either "Homer" or "Pindarus Thebanus"; they would not have known of the recent attribution to Baebius Italicus, so in our index, it remains under its Latin title.

Andrew of Saint Victor (ca. 1110 – 1175) 66, 89
Andrew Suneson/Andreas Sunonis, Archbishop (ca. 1167 – 1228) 111–15
Angilbert (d. 814) 200
Anna von Munzingen (fl. 1327) 476
Anonymous of Calais (fl. 14th c.) 278
Anselm of Canterbury (1033 – 1109) 14, 268
Anselm of Laon (d. 1117) 132, 157–59, 495–96
Anselm of Liège (1008 – ca. 1056) 414
Antonio de Nebrija (1441 – 1522) 71, 75
Apollonius of Tyre/Historia Apollonii regis Tyrii 16, 576
Apuleius (b. ca. 125) 36, 198–99, 208, 218, 570
Arator Subdiaconus (fl. 513 – 544) 27, 251, 289, 363, 519
Archpoet/Archipoeta (ca. 1130 – ca. 1165) 251, 259, 261, 277, 597–98, 600–602, 606, 608
Ari (Thorgilsson) the Learnèd (ca. 1067 – 1148) 109
Aristotle 55, 87–88, 90–93, 97–98, 100, 102, 115–16, 133, 138, 178, 198, 205, 207, 274, 277, 416, 418, 537, 576
Arnold of Lübeck (d. 1211 – 1214) 107, 108, 299,
Arnulf of Orléans (fl. 1156) 179–80, 207, 259, 349–50, 352–3,
Arthur (king) 33, 269, 270, 607
Arundel Lyrics 602
Asclepius 345
Asser (d. 908/9) 11–12
Atto of Vercelli (924/5 – 960 /61) 227–29
Augustine Eriugena (fl. 655) 67
Augustine of Hippo (354 – 430) 27, 36, 59, 63–66, 89–91, 128–29, 132, 140, 154, 161, 196–97, 199, 200, 202–3, 218–19, 224, 233, 241, 243, 257, 290, 311, 313, 315, 448, 450, 460, 473, 486, 488–501, 511, 513, 516–17, 526
Auraicept na n-Éces 285
Aurelius Prudentius (348 – ca. 405) 27, 205, 251–52, 275, 289, 363–64, 511, 516
Ausonius (ca. 310 – 395) xvi, 199, 201, 513–14, 516, 522–24, 567
Auspicius of Toul (late 5th c.) 243
Austen, Jane (1775–1817) 35
Averroes; see Ibn Rushd
Avicenna; see Ibn Sīnā
Avitus of Vienne (ca. 470 – 523) 199, 218, 251, 363, 437–38, 519
Azzo (fl. 1190 – 1220) 557

Baldus de Ubaldis (1327 – 1400) 576
Bartholomeus Anglicus (1203 – 1272) 164, 515
Bartolus de Saxoferrato (1313 – 1357) 576
Battle of Brunanburgh 273
Baudonivia (fl. 600 – 602) 33
Baudri of Bourgeuil (1060 – 1130) 6, 67, 133, 202, 245, 249–250, 252–53, 255, 258, 347–48, 424, 429, 436–37, 443, 546–48
Bede (672/3 – 735) 12, 15, 17, 52, 59–60, 66, 130, 200, 206, 224–27, 240, 290–91, 515, 575, 595–96, 605
Bédier, Joseph (1964 – 1938) 4, 203
Bene of Florence (d. ca. 1242) 240, 577
Benedict of Nursia (480 – 547) 7, 10, 58, 130, 140, 155, 162, 208, 377–81, 406–9, 415, 424, 428, 433–34, 437, 466–68, 470–71, 473, 475–77, 482, 491, 577
Benzo da Alessandria (fl. 1311 – 1329) 411, 567–68
Berengar of Tours (ca. 999 – 1088) 577
Bernard of Chartres (d. 1130) 156, 319, 404
Bernard of Clairvaux (1090 – 1153) 6, 36, 132–33, 451–55, 459, 460, 462, 479, 544, 577, 597
Bernard of Cluny (fl. 1150) 245–46, 599
Bernardino of Siena (1380 – 1444) 36
Bernardus Silvestris (fl. 1136) 183, 185, 319, 335, 339, 341–47
Bersuire, Pierre (ca. 1290 – 1362) 352
Berthold of Regensburg (ca. 1210 – 72) 288
Birgitta of Sweden (ca. 1303 – 73) 116–20, 478
Boccaccio, Giovanni (1313 – 1375) 353
Boethius (ca. 480 – 524/5) 90, 125, 133, 163, 175, 197, 286, 308, 311–13, 317, 320–21, 335–36, 339, 341, 425, 513, 517, 586
Boethius of Dacia (ca. 1240 – ca. 1280) 115, 120
Bolland, Jean 584
Bonaventure (1221 – 1274) 162, 208, 478, 577
Borges, Jorge Luis 250, 307, 432, 511–12
Bovetino Bovetini (fl. 13th c.) 562
Bruno of Asti (ca. 1049 – 1123) 554
Buchard of Worms (ca. 950 – 1025) 404, 456, 458
Burchard of Bellevaux (d. 1164) 270, 280, 404–5, 456, 458–59
Burckhardt, Jacob (1818–1897) 536, 549
Burleo, Gualtiero (fl. 12th c.) 576
Bussi, Giovanni 582–83
Byrhtferth of Ramsey (ca. 970 – ca. 1020) 10

Caelius Aurelianus (fl. 5th c.) 204
Caesar (Julius) (100–44 BCE) 194, 218, 564, 566–67
Caesarius of Arles (ca. 470 – 542) 199

Caesarius of Heisterbach (ca. 1180 – ca. 1240) 287
Calcidius (4th c.) 156, 336, 339
Cantilène de saint Eulalie 131
Carmen de gestis Frederici I Imperatoris in Lombardia 554
Carmina Burana 34, 244, 295–96, 337, 341, 396, 600–4, 607–8
Carmina Cantabrigiensia/Cambridge Songs 252, 280, 293, 602–3, 607
Carmina Einsidlensia 204
Cassiodorus (ca. 485 – ca. 585) 52, 66, 197–99, 203, 219, 308, 311, 313–14, 466, 511, 513–14, 519, 575
Catullus (ca. 84 – ca. 54 BCE) 36, 204–5, 567
Celsus (fl. 175) 204
Censorinus (3rd c.) 198, 207
Chanson de Roland 156
Chrétien de Troyes (fl. 1170) 352
Christina of Markyate (ca. 1095/1100 – 1155) 154
Christine de Pizan (1363 – ca. 1430) 30
Cicero (106 – 43 BCE) 26–27, 90, 129, 194–95, 198, 203–4, 218, 411, 416, 554, 556, 577
Claudius of Turin (fl. 810 – 827) 577
Claudius Victor (fl. 425 – 450) 519
Clement (of Alexandria) (2nd c.) 38
Coelius Sedulius (fl. 430 – 450) 17, 27, 251, 286, 290, 318, 363, 389, 519
Columcille (d. 597) 290
Conrad of Hirsau (ca. 1070 – ca. 1150) 240
Constantine I ("the Great") (272/3 – 337) 128, 131, 567
Constantine the African (ca. 1020 – 1087) 90
Corippus (fl. 565) 199, 252
Curtius, Ernst Robert (1866–1956) xv, 4, 125, 256, 299, 519, 538, 540, 604
Curtius Rufus, Quintus (1st – early 2nd c.) 111, 249
Cyprianus Gallus (fl. 397 – 430) 519

d'Ailly, Pierre (1351 – 1420) 576
Daniel of Morley (ca. 1140 – ca. 1210) 87
Dante Alighieri (1265 – 1321) 34, 68–70, 72, 136–38, 140–41, 247, 260, 350, 352–53, 497–98, 510, 568–70, 578, 594
Dares ("the Phrygian"; the text ascribed to him dates to the 5th – 6th c.) 35, 250, 259, 608
De Heinrico 293–94
Delusor Terentii 542–43
Descriptio Northfolchie 277
Dhuoda of Septimania (fl. ca. 820 – 843) 608

Dictys ("of Crete"; the text ascribed to him goes back at least to the 2nd – 3rd c.) 35
Diocletian (ca. 240 – 284) 128
Disticha Catonis 26, 318, 576
Donatus, Aelius (fl. 350) 26–27, 30, 49, 53–56, 59, 64, 90, 108, 179, 204, 280, 285, 419, 517–18
Donatus, Tiberius Claudius (fl. ca. 400) 204, 517–18
Dracontius (ca. 455 – ca. 505) 199
Dryden, John (1631 – 1700) 598
Dunchad of Laon (fl. 9th c.) 314, 316
Dunstan (909 – 988) 10–11, 14–15

Eadmer (ca. 1060 – ca. 1126) 14
Eberhard of Béthune (d. ca. 1212) 27, 240, 256, 576
Eberhard the German (fl. 13th c.) 418–19
Ebracher of Liège (d. 971) 413–14
Ecgbert (d. 766) 130, 200
Ecloga Theoduli 27, 39, 347, 363, 365, 543, 576
Edict of Rothar 284
Einhard (ca. 775 – 840) 70, 204, 291, 304, 575, 595, 605
Ekkehard IV of St. Gall (ca. 980 – ca. 1056) 206–7, 406–11, 413, 416
Elisabeth of Schönau (1125 – 1165) 475–78, 482
Ennius (239 – 169 BCE) 203
Ennodius (474 – 521) 218, 241, 513, 522
Enrico of Settimello (fl. ca. 1194) 558, 561–62
Epiphanius (315 – 403) 196
Erasmus, Desiderius (1466 – 1536) 140–41
Eriugena; see John Scotus Eriugena
Eugenius Vulgarius (fl. ca. 887 – 928) 209–11
Eulogius of Córdoba (d. 859) 578
Eusebius (ca. 260 – 339) 219, 225
Eutropius (ca. 320 – ca. 387) 522, 525

Ferreto Ferreti (1294 – 1337) 566–68
Florilegium Gallicum 208
Florilegium Thuaneum 205
Florus (epitomator of Livy) (2nd c.) 194, 546
Folz, Hans (ca. 1435 – 1513) 298
Foucault, Michel (1926 – 1984) xv, 5, 8, 33, 449, 458, 462, 486–87, 512
Foulcoie of Beauvais (fl. 11th c.) 396, 544–45
Frithegod (fl. ca. 950 – ca. 958) 10
Fulbert of Chartres (d. 1028) 379
Fulgentius (d. 532/3) 183

Gall, St. (d. 646/650) 287–88, 291, 299
Gæraldus (fl. 9th century?) 293
Gaius Cornelius Gallus (ca. 70 – 26 BCE) 487
Gaius Marius Victorinus (fl. 4th c.) 177–78, 198, 517
Geoffrey Chaucer (1343 – 1400) 15, 116, 138–40, 194
Geoffrey of Monmouth (ca. 1100 – ca. 1155) 15, 269, 595, 605, 608
Geoffrey of Vinsauf (fl. 1200) 116, 251, 253, 245, 250–51, 253, 260
Geoffrey of Vitry (fl. 12th c.) 180, 287
Gerald of Wales (ca. 1146 – ca. 1223) 281, 287, 605, 607
Gerard of Cremona (1114 – 1187) 91, 100, 556
Geremia da Montagnone (1250/60 – 1320/22) 562–63, 568
Geri d'Arezzo (ca. 1270 – ca. 1337) 568, 570
Gertrude of Helfta (1256 – ca. 1302) 478, 607
Gervase of Melkley (fl. 1212) 254
Gesta Romanorum 287, 299
Giambono di Andreae (fl. 13th/14th c.) 562
Gilbert of Poitiers (1070 – 1154) 157
Gilbert the Universal (fl. 1128 – 34) 157
Giles of Rome (ca. 1243/7 – 1316) 134–37, 178
Giordano da Pisa (ca. 1255 – 1311) 288
Giovanni da Cremenate (d. ca. 1344) 568–69
Giovanni de Matociis (d. 1337) 567–68
Giovanni del Virgilio (fl. 1319) 352–53, 568–69
Glossa Ordinaria 28, 113, 157–59, 175, 290, 359
Godfrey (of Rheims) (d. 1095) 438
Goscelin of Canterbury (1023/35 – ca. 1107) 6
Gottfried of Admont (d. 1165) 358–62
Gower, John (ca. 1330 – 1408) 16, 139–40, 296
Graves, Robert (1895 – 1985) 594
Gregory of Tours (ca. 538 – 594) 28, 575, 595, 605
Gregory the Great (540 – 604) 12, 27, 36, 87, 90–91, 129, 132, 160, 200, 202–3, 219, 257, 290, 358, 380, 466
Gregory VII, pope (ca. 1015 – 1085) 209
Guibert of Nogent (ca. 1055/60 – 1124/5) 70, 415, 486, 493–95, 498, 500, 502
Guido Vicentinus (d. 1332) 363
Guigo I (d. 1136) 486, 492, 498, 501
Guigo II the Carthusian (d. ca. 1173) 481–82
Guillaume Durand; see William Durandus
Guillaume de Lorris (ca. 1210 – ca. 1237) 30, 350
Guillaume Postel (1510 – 1581) 94–95

Haimo of Auxerre (d. ca. 855) 286, 588
Haimo of Halberstadt (d. ca. 853) 588
Hartmann von Aue (ca. 1170 – 1210) 299

Héloïse (ca. 1101 – 1164) 34, 392, 496, 594, 604–5
Henri d'Andeli (fl. first half of 13th c.) 349
Henry I, king of England (1068/1069 – 1135) 11
Henry II, king of England (1133 – 1189) 270
Henry II, duke of Bavaria (951 – 995) 294
Henry VII, king of Germany and emperor (1275 – 1313) 564–65, 568
Henry of Avranches (d. ca. 1261) 249, 257–58, 261, 266, 281
Henry of Huntingdon (d. 1156/64) 268–69, 273
Henry of Kirkestede (fl. 1360 – 1380) 160
Herman of Carinthia (fl. ca. 1140 – 1150) 100
Herolt, Johannes (fl. 1468) 287
Hilary of Orléans (fl. 1125) 180
Hilary of Poitiers (ca. 300 – ca. 368) 65
Hildebert of Lavardin (1056 – 1133) 245, 255, 258, 442, 541, 545–46, 575, 587, 597
Hildebert of Le Mans (d. 1133) 269, 271, 288, 363–64
Hildegard of Bingen (1098 – 1179) 6, 162, 229–31, 378, 391–92, 395, 397, 476, 515
Hisperica Famina 200, 229
Historia Augusta 522. 564–65, 567
Historia Norwegie 106, 108–110
Homer 34, 87, 205, 251, 336, 353, 417, 518, 524, 566, 594, 603
Honorius of Autun, or Honorius Augustodunensis (d. ca. 1151) 109, 134, 515, 619
Hopkins, Gerard Manley (1844 – 1889) 597
Horace (65 – 8 BCE) 27, 69, 110, 116, 128, 181, 184–85, 205, 228–29, 248–52, 276, 325, 559–62, 606
Hrabanus Maurus (d. 856) 200, 204, 359, 515, 525
Hrotsvit of Gandersheim (ca. 935 – ca. 1002) 6–7, 12–14, 73, 242, 250, 424–29, 441–42, 543, 607–8
Hucbald of St-Amand (840 – 930/2) 246
Hugh of Orléans; also Hugh Primas (ca. 1086 – 1160) 258–59, 266, 602, 608
Hugh of Pisa (fl. ca. 1170 – ca. 1190) 173
Hugh of Saint Victor (ca. 1096 – 1141) 89, 133, 157–58, 160, 162, 164, 208, 318, 321, 515, 586
Huysmans, Joris-Karl (1848 – 1907) 33

Ibn al-Nadīm (d. 995/8) 76, 78
Ibn Habīb (d. 852) 76
Ibn Hazm (d. 1064) 71
Ibn Khaldūn (1332 – 1406) 78

Ibn Rushd, or Averroes (1126 – 1198) 88, 91, 93, 100, 116
Ibn Sīnā, or Avicenna (ca. 980 – 1037) 100
Ilias Latina 35
Isidore of Seville (ca. 560 – 636) xvi, 56–57, 59, 171–72, 174, 199–200, 202, 220, 233, 240, 260, 308, 311, 313–14, 318–19, 358–59, 361, 364–67, 514–15, 517–18
Íslendingabók; see Ari the Learnèd

Jacob van Maerlant (1230/1240 – 1288/1300) 291
Jacobus de Voragine/James of Varazzo (ca. 1230 – 1290) 287, 576
Jacopo da Cessole (1250 – 1322) 575
James of Varazzo; see Jacobus de Voragine
James of Vitry (fl. ca. 1220) 287
Jauss, Hans Robert (1921 – 1997) 6, 34
Jean de Meun (ca. 1250 – ca. 1305) 30, 349–50
Jerome (ca. 347 – 420) 29, 31, 36, 63, 66, 86, 88–90, 102, 128–30, 141, 196, 202, 219, 240, 433, 435–37, 448, 460, 511, 517, 519–20, 522, 615
John the Archcantor (7th c.) 52
Johannes Balbus (d. 1298) 576
Johannes de Caulibus (fl. ca. 1340 – 60) 162–63
John Cassian (ca. 360 – 435) 426, 457, 468
John Chrysostom (ca. 347 – 407) 196
John Gower; see Gower, John
John Lydgate of Bury; see Lydgate, John
John of Damascus (ca. 676 – 749) 87, 91, 97, 100
John of Garland (fl. ca. 1205) 180, 218, 349, 350, 352–53, 407, 437, 576
John of Hauville/Johannes de Hauvilla (fl. ca. 1184) 254, 608
John of Salisbury (ca. 1115 – 76/80) 156, 240, 403–5, 416–17, 462, 538, 575
John of Trevisa (ca. 1342 – 1402) 138, 288, 404
John Ridevall (fl. 1330) 350–52
John Sarracenus (fl. ca. 1167) 206
John Scotus Eriugena (ca. 800 – ca. 877) 78, 90, 95, 100–1, 133, 206, 233, 314–22, 338, 340, 343–45
John the Deacon (d. after 910) 370–71
Jordanes (fl. ca. 550) 194
Joseph Ibn Caspi (1279 – 1340) 68
Joseph of Exeter (fl. ca. 1190) 250, 269
Josephus (35 – ca. 100) 35, 219, 357
Juan de Torquemada (1388 – 1468) 118
Juan of Segovia (d. ca. 1458) 78
Julian of Speyer (d. 1250) 381
Julius Obsequens (fl. ca. 4th c.) 522
Julius Paris (fl. late 4th c.) 207

Justinian (482 – 565) 112, 557
Juvenal (fl. ca. 96 – 125) 177, 179, 228–29, 242, 248
Juvencus (fl. early 4th c.) 615

Kafka, Franz (1883 – 1924) 37–40
Karolus Magnus et Leo papa; see *Paderborn epos*
Katherina von Gebersweiler (d. ca. 1330) 478

Lachmann, Karl (1795 – 1851) 203
"Lactantius Placidus" (fl. 4th century or late 5th/6th c.) 180–83, 185
Lambert of St. Omer (fl. 1100) 515
Langland, William (ca. 1332 – ca. 1386) 139
Lantfred of Fleury/Winchester (fl. 970s) 10
Laudes regiae 131
Lawrence of Durham (d. 1154) 267, 281, 364
Leabhar Breac 288
Leonius of Paris (fl. 1150s) 363, 365–67
Liutprand of Cremona (ca. 922 – 972) 575, 578, 617
Livy (59 BCE – 17 CE) 36, 194, 203, 218, 559, 563, 565, 568
Lovato Lovati/Lovato di Rolando di Lovato (ca. 1240 – 1309) 210, 558–565, 567, 570–71
Lucan (39 – 69) 179, 205, 245, 249, 251, 253, 349, 519, 537
Lucas de Tuy (d. 1249), 66
Lucretius (ca. 97 – ca. 55 BCE) 205
Ludolphus of Saxony (ca. 1300 – 1378) 478
Luxurius (ca. late 5th or early 6th c.) 524
Lydgate, John (ca. 1370 – ca. 1451) 140

Macaulay, Thomas (1800 – 1859) 598
Macer Floridus; see Odo of Meun
Macrobius (395 – 423) 35, 64, 194, 259, 336–37, 517, 525
Maimonides (ca. 1135 – 1204) 74, 90
Manegold of Lautenbach (ca. 1030 – ca. 1103) 348
Manutius, Aldus (1449 – 1515) 583
Marbod of Rennes (ca. 1035 – 1123) 245, 253, 258, 434, 442, 575, 597
Marcellus Empiricus (fl. 410) 516, 525–26
Marcus Valerius (6th century? 12th century?) 242
Margery Kempe (ca. 1373 – 1438) 120
Marie de France (fl. 1155 – 1190) 348
Mark of Toledo (fl. 1193 – 1216) 74, 92–95, 98–100

Martial (ca. 40 – ca. 102) 67, 268, 559–61
Martianus Capella (fl. 410 – 439) xvii, 35, 125, 183, 197–98, 204, 218, 232–34, 267–68, 286, 307–11, 313, 315–16, 318–19, 321–26, 328, 335–42, 345–47, 389, 513, 515
Martin of Laon (ca. 660 – 680) 314, 318, 328
Marvell, Andrew (1621 – 1678) 597
Matthew of Vendôme (fl. ca. 1175) 27, 218, 246–47, 253–55, 260, 414
Matthew Paris (ca. 1200 – 1259) 281
Matthias of Linköping (ca. 1300 – 1350) 115
Maximus the Confessor (ca. 580 – 662) 87, 100, 319
Meditationes vit(a)e Christi 136, 163, 478–80, 482
Metamorphosis Goliae Episcopi 341–46
Metellus of Tegernsee (fl. ca. 1060) 250
Michael of Cornwall (fl. 1243 – 1255) 275
Migne, Jacques-Paul (1800 – 1875) 584–88, 590
Milton, John (1608 – 1674) 34, 519
Minucius Felix (fl. 200 – 240) 36, 38
Montaigne, Michel de (1533 – 1592) 501, 615
Mosè del Brolo (first half 12th c.) 554
Moses Ibn 'Ezra' (ca. 1070 – ca. 1138) 71
Muḥammad, prophet (570 – 632) 75–76, 87
Muratori, Ludovico Antonio (1672 – 1750) 584
Mussato, Albertino (1261 – 1329) 210–11, 562–70

Neckam, Alexander (of) (1157 – 1217) 175, 232–34, 265–67, 281, 319–20, 322, 324, 328
Newman, John Henry (1801 – 1890) 599
Nicholas of Lyra (ca. 1270 – 1349) 89–90, 158, 576
Nicomachus of Gerasa (fl. ca. 100) 312
Nithard (ca. 800 – 844) 131
Nivard of Ghent (fl. ca. 1150) 292
Notker Balbulus, or Notker the Stammerer (ca. 840 – 912) 240, 388, 394, 578, 595, 605
Notker III of St. Gall, or Notker Labeo (ca. 950 – 1022) 125–27, 285–86, 289, 407–8, 410, 412

O admirabile Veneris idolum 554
Odo of Cheriton (ca. 1185 – 1246/7) 287
Odo of Meun (11th c.) 268
Otfrid of Weissenburg (d. after 870) 285, 288, 290
Ogier of Locedio (1136 – 1214) 478
Olav Haraldson (995 – 1030) 108
Orff, Carl (1895 – 1982) 34, 603, 608

Origen (ca. 184 – ca. 254) 133, 196, 313, 451–52
Orosius (5th c.) 203, 219
Osbern of Canterbury (ca. 1050 – ca. 1090) 12, 14–15
Oswald of Worcester (d. 992) 10, 17, 249
Otto of Freising (ca. 1114 – 1158) 219
Ovid (P. Ovidius Naso) (43 BCE – 17 CE) 6, 27, 34, 110, 128, 178–80, 186, 202, 205, 207–8, 246, 248–50, 252–53, 258–59, 267, 270, 273, 337, 344–53, 406, 437, 443, 455, 486–88, 495–96, 498–99, 501, 519, 537, 541, 544–46, 548, 559–62, 594
Ovide moralisé 351–52
Owen, Wilfred (1893 – 1918) 594

Pace da Ferrara (fl. early 14th c.) 565
Paderborn epos 247, 252, 536
Palladius (fl. 408 – 431) 515–16
Pamphilus 576, 582
Panegyrici latini 520–21, 528
Pannartz, Arnold (d. ca. 1476) 582
Paolo Veneto (1369 – 1429) 576, 622
Paul the Deacon (720 – 799) 132, 204, 370, 575
Perotti, Niccolò (1429 – 1480) 582
Persius (34 – 62) 228–29, 248
Peter Abelard (1079 – 1142) 34, 156, 182, 219, 240, 342, 368–69, 392, 416, 486, 495–96, 498, 502, 575, 577, 594, 605
Peter Comestor (d. ca. 1178) 65, 291, 357
Peter Damian/Pietro Damiani (d. 1073) 132, 416, 554
Peter Helias (ca. 1100 – 1166) 179
Peter Lombard (ca. 1100 – 1160) 97, 113, 158–59, 200, 416, 576
Peter of Blois (ca. 1135 – ca. 1203) 28, 251, 270, 281, 416, 602
Peter Riga (fl. ca. 1165 – 1209) 251, 254, 357, 363, 365, 367–68, 524
Peter the Chanter (d. 1197) 460
Peter the Venerable (ca. 1092 – 1156) 154
Petrarch, Francesco (1304 – 1374) xvi, 140, 352, 486, 497–501, 570
Petronius (d. 66) 203, 207
Petrus Episcopus (d. 1219) 365–66, 373
Photios/Photius (ca. 810 – ca. 893) 87
Piccolomini, Enea Silvio (1405 – 1464) 581
Pictor in Carmine 363–65
Plato (ca. 429 – 347 BCE) vi, 87, 90, 95, 156, 181, 183, 185, 193, 196, 205, 207, 311, 313, 335–36, 450
Plato of Tivoli (fl. 1132 – 46) 100

Plautus (ca. 250 – 184 BCE) 229
Pliny (the Elder) (ca. 23 – 79) 194–95, 512–13, 567, 570
Pliny (the Younger) (ca. 61 – ca .112) 567, 570
Poliziano, Angelo (1454 – 1494) 501, 527
Pompeius (Sextus Pompeius Festus, grammarian) (late 2nd c.) 54
Pompeius Trogus (3rd c.) 194, 218
Pomponius Mela (1st c.) 207,
Pope, Alexander (1688 – 1744) 606
Porphyry (234 – ca. 305) 90, 310, 313
Praefatio de poenitentia Gildae 456–57
Priscian (5th – 6th c.) 26–27, 49, 64, 78, 90, 172–73, 178–79, 319, 325
Propertius (ca. 50 – ca. 15 BCE) 36, 205, 487, 559–61
Pseudo-Dionysius the Areopagite (fl. ca. 650 – ca. 725) 36, 87, 90–91, 95, 100–1, 206, 208
Pseudo-Plautus; see *Querolus*
Ptolemy (mathematician and geographer) (2nd c.) 553

Querolus 207
Quintilian (ca. 35 – ca. 100) 198, 218, 405
Quintus Curtius; see Curtius Rufus
Quodvultdeus (d. ca. 450) 395

Rabanus Maurus (ca. 780 – 856) 66, 200, 204, 359, 515, 525, 575
Radewijns, Florentius (Florens) (1350 – 1400) 492, 497
Radice, Betty (1912 – 1985) 594, 605
Ralph of Laon (d. 1133) 157
Ramon Llull (1232 – 1315) 77, 125
Ranulf Higdon (ca. 1280 – 1364) 137
Rather of Verona (890 – 974) 205, 219, 309
Ratpert (d. ca. 900) 291, 299
Raymond Martini (d. after 1284) 77, 78
Reginald of Canterbury (fl. 1112) 269, 266, 281, 424, 433–38, 440–42
Regula monachorum 466
Remigius of Auxerre (ca. 841 – 908) 233, 308, 314–19
Riccobaldo of Ferrara (1251 – 1318) 563, 565, 567
Richard de Bury (1287 – 1345) 152, 160
Richard FitzRalph (ca. 1300 – 1360) 288
Richard Ledrede (ca. 1275 – 1360) 280
Richard of Saint Victor (d. 1173) 208
Richard Rolle (1290 – 1349) 274
Ridevall, John; see John Ridevall

Robert Grosseteste (ca. 1175 – 1253) 86–87, 90, 92, 95–98, 100–1, 159
Robert of Chester (fl. 1140 – 50) 93–95, 100
Robert of Ketton (ca. 1110 – ca. 1160) 74–75, 94–96, 100
Rodrigo Jiménez (or Ximénez) de Rada (ca. 1170 – 1247) 66, 98–99
Roger Bacon (ca. 1214 – 1294) 71, 77
Roman d'Eneas 344–45
Rudolf von Ems (ca. 1200 – 1254) 291
Rupert of Deutz (ca. 1075 – 1129) 66
Rutilius Claudius Namatianus (fl. 5th c.) 199, 522

Salimbene de Adam (1221 – ca. 1288) 69–70
Sallust (86 – 35 BCE) 27, 111, 194, 218
Samuel Ibn Tibbon (ca. 1150 – ca. 1230) 74
Saxo Grammaticus (ca. 1150 – 1220) 28, 107–8, 110–11, 120
Scott, Walter (1771 – 1832) 598
Securus Melior Felix (fl. 534) 204, 308
Sedulius Scottus (fl. ca. 850) 17, 27, 55–56, 178, 246, 250–51, 286, 290, 318, 363, 389, 519
Sén Dé 294
Seneca (the Younger) (ca. 4 BCE – 65) 203, 205, 208–11, 218, 486–89, 492, 497–98, 501, 556, 559, 563–64
Serlo of Wilton (ca. 1105 – 1181) 275
Servius Honoratus (fl. 390) 64, 175, 177–78, 180–81, 233, 242, 336–37, 339, 517–18
Shakespeare, William (1564 – 1616) 35
Shepherd of Hermas 230
Sidonius Apollinaris (ca. 430 – 489) 199, 218, 513, 522
Snorri Sturluson (1179 – 1241) 110
Solinus (fl. mid 4th c.) 35, 194–95
Solomon ben Reuben Bonafed (d. after 1445) 78
Song of Roland, The; see *Chanson de Roland*
Sophronius (ca. 560 – 638) 88, 91
Soranus of Ephesus (98 – 138) 204
Statius (ca. 45 – 96) 27, 35, 179, 180–86, 205, 245, 249, 252–53, 298, 519, 559–61
Stephen Langton (ca. 1150/9 – 1228) 113–15, 121
Stephen of Antioch (fl. 12th c.) 90, 206
Stephen VI, pope (d. 897) 209
Stevenson, Robert Louis (1850 – 1894) 600
Suavissima nonna 293–94
Suetonius (ca. 70 – ca. 130) 203, 498–99
Sulpicius Severus (ca. 360 – 420/25) 219, 522
Sven Aggeson (fl. 1181/82) 110

Sweynheym, Konrad (d. ca. 1477) 582
Swinburne, Charles Algernon (1837 – 1909) 33
Symmachus, Quintus Aurelius
(ca. 345 – 402) 522
Symonds, John Addington (1840 – 1893)
33–34, 600–1

Tacitus (ca. 56 – ca. 118) 36, 208, 218–19
Tatwine (d. 734) 33
Terence (d. 159 BCE) 31, 27, 202, 204–5, 248, 250, 252, 425, 517, 537, 542–43
Tertullian (ca. 160 – ca. 230) 38, 195
"Theodolus" (fl. ca. 10th century?); see *Ecloga Theoduli*
Theodore Bibliander (1506 – 1564) 74
Theodoric (the Great) (493 – 526) 197
Theodoricus Monachus (fl. 1371) 109
Theodulf of Orléans (ca. 750/60 – 821) 337
Thierry of Chartres (d. 1150/55) 178, 319–320
Thomas à Kempis (ca. 1380 – 1471) 493
Thomas Aquinas (1225 – 1274) 66, 87, 91, 134, 138, 141, 157, 178, 525, 576, 597–98
Thomas Elmham (1364 – ca. 1427) 278
Thomas Gallus of Vercelli (ca. 1200 – 1246) 208
Thomas of Erfurt (fl. ca. 1300) 125
Tiberius Claudius Donatus; see Donatus, Tiberius Claudius
Tibullus (d. 19 BCE) 208, 487, 559–61
Tortarius, Rudolfus (b. 1063) 442
Traube, Ludwig (1861 – 1907) 234, 537
Travels of Sir John Mandeville 90–91, 97
Tyndale, William (1494 – 1536) 140–41

Ugo Mezzabati (fl. 13th/14th c.) 562
Urso of Genoa (fl. 1225 – 1245) 558

Valerius Maximus (1st c.) 35, 111, 207, 218
Varro (116 – 27 BCE) 208, 310
Vegetius (fl. 385 – 400) 218, 515, 522, 525
Venantius Fortunatus (ca. 530 – ca.600/09) xvi, 199, 218, 248, 252, 280, 291, 511, 522, 598–99
Vergil/Virgil (70 – 19 BCE) 27, 34, 90, 110, 128, 175, 177, 179–81, 183–85, 196, 202, 205, 220, 245, 247–52, 292, 336–37, 339–41, 344–46, 389, 395, 406, 411, 431–441, 510, 517–19, 523–24, 537, 542, 560–61, 566, 568–69, 583, 594
Vibius Sequester (4th – 5th c.) 207
Vincent of Beauvais (ca. 1190 – ca. 1264) 291, 515, 525, 563, 567
Virgil of Salzburg, bishop (d. 784) 207
Virgilius Maro Grammaticus (fl. 7th c.) 56, 200, 229
Vita Adae et Evae 296–97, 299, 605
Vulgate Bible; see Index of Topics.

Waddell, Helen (1889 – 1965) 594, 605
Walahfrid Strabo (ca. 808 – 849) 33, 240
Walter Map (1140 – ca. 1208/10) 269–73, 281
Walter of Châtillon (fl. 1170 – 1180) 6, 27, 243, 247, 249–51, 442, 575
Walter of Speyer (967 – 1027) 239, 242, 262, 411–13
Walter of St. Victor (d. ca. 1180) 208, 416
Walter of Wimborne (fl. 1261 – 1266) 274–76, 280
Waltharius 28, 252, 292–93, 299, 424, 429–30, 435, 441–42, 604
Widukind of Corvey (925 – 973) 15
Wilfrid of Ripon (d. 709 or 710) 225
William Dunbar (ca. 1460 – ca. 1520) 295
William Durandus, or Guillaume Durand (ca. 1230 – 1296) 65
William Langland; see Langland, William
William of Champeaux (ca. 1070 – 1121) 156, 178, 208
William of Conches (ca. 1090 – ca. 1154) 156, 172–73, 175–76, 178–79, 183, 185, 319, 321, 323, 338–39, 344, 349–50, 405
William of Malmesbury (ca. 1095/96 – ca. 1143) 11–12, 15, 58, 291, 546
William of Ockham (ca. 1288 – ca. 1348) 577
William of St. Thierry (1070 – 1148) 491
William Peraldus (ca. 1190 – 1271) 458–61
Williram of Ebersberg (ca. 1020 – 1085) 286
Wulfstan the Cantor (ca. 960 – early 11th c.) 10
Wycliffe, John (ca. 1328 – 1384) 74

Zeno of Verona (ca. 300 – 371/ 380) 197, 222–24, 226, 234

Index of Selected Topics and Places

abbreviation/abbreviating 37, 156, 194, 198, 287–88, 292, 297–98, 351, 615
Adam 66, 69, 75, 128, 137, 140–41
Adam and Eve, vernacular lives of 296–8, 360–61, 396, 409, 467
Adamic language 296–8, 360–62, 369, 371, 396, 409, 467
aetas Horatiana 248, 537
aetas Ovidiana 248, 335, 347–53, 437, 537, 546
aetas Virgiliana 248, 537
Africa 30, 66, 73, 92, 196–99, 203, 218, 241, 352
al-Andalus 74, 80, 92–93, 100; see also Spain
anima mundi 181, 340, 345, 348
Anglo-Saxons 51–53, 130
anthologies/anthologizing 32, 87, 194, 255, 261, 420, 462, 580, 599
antiphon 296, 377–82, 394–95, 493
anti-Semitism 481
Arabic xii, xiv, xvi, 36, 64, 69, 70–80, 87–88, 90, 92–94, 98–99, 133, 174, 206–7, 211, 274, 596
– as language of revelation 67, 74–76, 78
– culture 76, 93
– -Latin translation 72–74, 77, 79, 90–91, 93–94, 98–102, 133
– literature 88, 93
– , translation into 71, 73–74, 87, 92, 102
ars dictaminis 218, 240, 554, 556–57, 564, 586, 570
artes liberales vi, xv, 90, 101, 108, 171, 185, 197, 207, 232, 307–11, 313, 315, 317–18, 320–22, 324, 329, 337–38, 347, 405, 408, 411, 418, 426, 513, 536, 589, see also *trivium*, *quadrivium*
artes mechanicae 317–18, 320
artes poeticae 253, 259, 344, 420
attribution 115, 174, 311, 314, 370, 382, 578, 580, 586–88, 615
auctor 26–27, 29, 32, 35, 39–40, 63–64, 66–67, 71, 152–53, 192, 222–23, 232–33, 240–42, 252, 258, 269, 295, 336, 468, 586, 596
auctoritas/authority xiv, xv, 9, 12–13, 16, 28–29, 31, 54, 57–58, 63–64, 66–68, 72–80, 100, 127, 131, 138–40, 152–53, 157–58, 174, 181, 186, 198, 206, 220, 227–28, 231, 248, 295, 308, 319–20,

367, 414, 423, 426, 447–48, 450, 452, 455–56, 460, 466–67, 477, 482, 580, 585
autobiography xvi, 44, 411, 485, 501, 522

Beneventan script(s) 201, 208
Bobbio 203–4
Bologna 207, 352, 499, 556–57, 568–69
Bible xv, 64, 86, 88–89, 91, 99, 102, 109, 117–18, 129–30, 138–41, 156–59, 164, 206, 218–19, 257, 280, 288, 290–91, 300, 351, 356–58, 362, 367–68, 373, 376, 490, 516, 518, 524, 542, 581
biblical poetry, vernacular 138, 220, 257, 290–91, 295, 335, 357, 368, 373, 519, 527, 555, 558, 569
Byzantium; see Constantinople

canon (literary) v, xiv, 8, 12, 16, 25–39, 40–41, 48, 65, 75, 86–88, 92, 108, 112–14, 116–18, 125, 128, 130, 132, 156–58, 161, 163–64, 174, 180, 186, 205, 208, 218–19, 233, 243, 247, 250–51, 255, 279, 295, 319, 363, 406, 408, 410, 413, 415, 428, 430, 434, 437, 441–43, 455–58, 462, 468, 510–11, 520, 542–43, 554, 557, 575–77, 584, 586–87
canon law 26, 29, 65, 108, 112–13, 233, 363, 455–56, 462, 557, 576
Canterbury 6, 12, 14, 52–53, 107, 114, 163, 200, 266, 269, 281, 293, 424, 433, 603–4
Carolingian minuscule 201
cento 249, 251, 434, 510, 519, 524, 580
Chartres 156, 178, 183, 187, 207, 259, 319–20, 334, 338, 379, 385–86, 404, 538
Chartres, cathedral school of 156, 183, 259, 338–39, 404, 538
communes, civic 555–56
Constantinople 95–96, 197, 199, 203, 206, 603
compilator 47, 164, 192–193, 305, 597–98
cross-referencing 18, 159

Devotio Moderna 492
diglossia 51, 70, 76
divisions of knowledge 175, 308, 311–14, 318–21, 312–13, 320
drama, liturgical 26, 32, 65, 130, 222, 243–44, 376, 379, 393–97, 555

Einsiedeln 222
Epicureanism 205
epistolography, Latin 554
epitome/epitomizing 78, 194, 207, 218, 357, 522, 524–26, 528, 559
etymology 56–57, 233, 317, 338

fictionality 432, 512, 542, 545–48
frontispiece 579–80
Fourth Lateran Council 456, 458, 492

gender vii, xvi, 6, 7, 30–31, 69–70, 119, 153, 231, 285, 359, 423–35, 437–39, 440–43, 452, 454–55, 465, 480
Genius 36, 184, 339, 345–47, 350, 561
Goliards/goliardic poetry 28, 33–34, 250, 258–59, 266, 276, 396
grammars 8, 12, 26, 47–49, 50, 53–59, 64, 70, 72, 75–76, 90, 94, 108–9, 117, 125, 130–31, 141, 161–62, 173, 178–80, 185, 218, 224–25, 234, 240, 242, 251, 254, 256, 265, 277, 280–81, 285, 310, 313, 318, 320, 363, 367, 397, 403–5, 410, 419, 513–14, 517–18, 520–21, 523, 526, 554, 556–58, 565, 576, 583
Greek xii, xvi, 16, 27, 29–30, 36, 39, 49, 52–53, 56, 64–65, 67, 69–70, 72, 76, 80, 86–92, 95–98, 100–2, 128–31, 133, 138, 140, 171, 184, 193, 195–96, 198, 200, 204–7, 211, 220, 229, 233, 242, 296–97, 308, 316–17, 337–38, 412, 448, 452, 485, 514, 518, 520, 524, 553–54, 584, 594, 596, 603, 609–10
– -Arabic translation 73, 87–88, 90, 102
– as sacred language xiv, 64–65, 67, 75–76, 128
– Bible 63–64, 86–87, 128; see also Septuagint
– -Latin translation 36, 77, 87–91, 95–98, 100–1, 128, 133, 138, 195–96, 248, 448, 556
– literature xii, 38, 196, 603–4, 608
–, translation into 86–87, 206
Gregorius-legends 296–99

Hadith 87–88
Hebrew language/learning xii, xvi, 29, 36, 63, 65–72, 74–75, 77–78, 80, 87–89, 127–29, 133, 137, 206, 296–97

– as language of revelation or holy language xiv, 64–69, 74–77, 128
– Bible 64, 87–89, 99, 102, 196, 351, 518–19
– -Latin translation 29, 77, 88–89, 133
– literature xii, 40
historiography 6, 30, 108, 110, 225, 416, 528, 535–36, 568, 584–85
holy languages xiv, 64–68, 73–76, 79, 94–95, 128, 134, 202
humanism, Italian vii, xvi, 79, 140–41, 281, 536, 538–39, 553, 555–57, 564, 568, 570
humanism, medieval 140–41, 255, 349–50, 545, 553–55, 557, 568, 570
hymn 17, 28, 34, 92, 206, 243, 258, 275–76, 280–81, 290–91, 296, 369, 380–85, 388, 396–97, 404, 408, 436, 516, 521–22, 527, 597–600

incunabula 297, 575–77, 580
indexing: see cross-referencing
Index of Prohibited Books 577–78
information xii, 50, 54, 109, 117, 151, 155, 157, 181, 192–93, 195, 203, 221, 261, 269, 357, 379, 579–80, 584, 589, 590
ingenium 338, 340, 352, 496
integumentum 183, 259, 338, 340, 349–50
involucrum 340, 404
Ireland 52–53, 67, 129–31, 200, 203, 296, 456

Judeo-Latin 68

Koran: see Qu'ran

language acquisition 10, 47, 48, 51–52, 95, 100, 124, 135, 321, 404, 489, 584
Latinitas 12, 72, 79, 124, 127, 129, 424
lectio: see reading, monastic
leonine hexameters 258, 275, 280, 289, 292, 394
liberal arts: see *artes liberales*
linguistic binarism (see diglossia) 128
literacy 9, 49–50, 106–7, 129, 456, 465–66, 475, 539–40, 556
literary history xiv, 4–6, 11, 25–28, 30, 33–41, 131, 202, 281, 487, 511, 525, 604; see also reception/reception history
literature, Provençal 131, 295, 557–59, 562
Lobbes 205
Lorsch 201, 204

macaronics 293–96
marginalia 92, 177, 180,

mass, liturgy of 34, 113, 138, 174, 193, 228, 280, 296, 376, 385–92, 395, 475–76, 509, 511, 518, 541, 586, 600, 603, 608
mathematics 311–13, 320
Mischsprache 286
mnemonics 157, 164
monasteries/monasticism 11, 117, 131–32, 134, 201, 204, 224, 287, 406, 416, 433–34, 436–38, 448, 453, 455, 457–58, 466–70, 472–73, 475, 477–78, 481–82, 491, 495, 555
    monastic schools 53, 73, 154–55, 158, 162, 164, 418–19, 424, 429, 434, 441, 557
    monastic scriptoria 200–2, 204, 257, 286, 324, 424, 426, 429, 436, 438, 441; see also scriptorium
Montecassino 204, 208–210

Naples 53, 60, 206
Natura, as personification 6, 76, 125, 137, 312, 316, 336, 345–47, 350, 360–61, 448, 450, 455, 457, 459–61, 469, 512, 575
Neoplatonism/Neoplatonists 87, 90, 95, 101, 206, 208, 309–13, 316, 318, 321, 335–37, 340, 349, 426, 517

office 377
ordinatio 159, 164
Orléans 163, 179, 200, 204, 207–208, 258–59, 337, 349, 393
Oxford 30, 97, 114–15, 129, 134, 138–39, 152, 156, 159, 201–2, 232, 314, 317, 594, 596, 601

Padua 210–11, 499, 558–66, 568, 570
paganism 106, 108, 526, 541
Paris 10, 74, 89, 94–96, 99, 101, 107–8, 113–16, 156, 158, 161, 175, 177, 183, 201, 208, 218, 232, 281, 285, 287, 297, 314, 316, 319, 363, 365–67, 373, 390–91, 407, 588
parody 28, 244, 250, 270, 280, 296, 370–73, 432, 542–43, 548
Pavia 200, 207, 241
periodization xvi, 235, 248, 511, 535–41, 553–56, 566–70, 575
philology/philological method xi, 3–4, 6, 8, 94, 98–99, 179–81, 203, 211, 519, 538, 553, 559, 567, 570, 578, 582–90, 593–94, 604, 606
phrasebooks 285–86
poetics 115–16, 218, 246, 251, 253–55, 260–61, 414, 435, 437, 441–42, 546
prosimetrum 219–20, 345, 455, 513
Provençal poetry/literature 295, 557–59, 562

quadrivium 100, 307, 310, 312–13, 317, 320–21, 324, 328
Qur'an 71, 74–76, 87–88, 93–95, 99, 102
    Latin translations of the Qur'an 71, 75, 78, 94–96, 98–99, 102

Ravenna 199, 207, 568
reading, clerical 64, 97, 126, 151, 155, 158, 161–62, 265, 280, 288–89, 396, 448, 455
reading, monastic 154, 158, 162, 164, 241, 289, 419, 448, 457
reading, silent 152, 154–155, 164, 516
reception of literature/reception history 6–7, 11, 33–36, 153, 178, 206, 210–11, 248, 308, 310, 315, 370, 428, 501, 511, 537, 541–42, 549
Renaissance, Carolingian 314, 535–36, 538–39, 549
Renaissance, Twelfth-Century 100, 338, 535–38, 545, 549
Roman law 112–13, 554, 556–57
romance vernaculars xvi, 26, 48, 50–52, 70–72, 74–76, 79, 109, 130–132, 138, 285, 295, 594, 604
Rome 12–13, 52, 64, 68, 78, 87, 116, 120, 129, 134–35, 137–38, 195–98, 200, 204, 206, 208–9, 247, 249, 252, 289, 380, 451, 517, 520–22, 525, 535–36, 545–46, 548, 568, 582

Salerno 207, 209
Sardinia 207
scribe/*scriptor*/copyist 56, 120, 158–61, 163, 173, 192–93, 201–2, 258, 269, 308, 497, 578, 581, 583
scriptorium 158, 200–2, 204, 208, 211, 324; see also monastic scriptoria under monasteries
Septuagint 63, 196
Scholasticism 73, 68, 111, 115, 133–34, 140, 419
schools and schooling vi, xvi, 18, 26, 27, 31, 34–35, 39, 41, 49, 52–53, 64, 73, 91, 107, 111, 113, 114, 116, 130, 132, 151, 156–57, 161–62, 175, 178, 183, 185–86, 195–96, 200, 208, 218, 241, 247, 252–53, 256, 258–60, 277, 307, 309, 314, 337, 338, 341–42, 344, 349, 358, 363, 367, 373, 390, 403–8, 411, 413–20, 424–25, 427–28, 438, 441–42, 448, 519, 538, 540, 542–43, 546, 553, 556–58, 566, 598; see also cathedral schools, monastic schools
sermons, vernacular 140, 286–88
sequence 6, 13, 240, 244, 256, 275, 376, 381, 387–92, 394, 397, 555
Sicily 69, 92, 133, 206, 211
solitary life 470–72

Spain 71–72, 92–96, 98–100, 131–33, 199–200, 556, 596; see also al-Andalus
St. Gall (monastery) 205, 291–92, 407–8, 410, 578
St. Victor (abbey) 156–58, 164, 208, 367, 373, 390
style vi, xv, 11, 13–14, 18, 26, 29, 32–33, 36
– , classical and biblical 227, 229–31, 234–35, 249–51, 253, 255–57, 260, 281, 288, 290, 337, 345, 352, 376–77, 382, 387, 391, 410, 413, 424, 448, 465, 490–91, 499, 510, 514, 517–19, 523, 525, 527, 539, 543, 545, 555, 557, 559, 563–68, 570, 595, 604, 607
– , "hermeneutic" 220, 235, 556, 564
– , lowly (*sermo humilis*) 48, 57–58, 75, 93–94, 109–10, 119, 124, 155, 181, 201, 215, 217–20, 222, 226

technical (e.g., legal, grammatical) terminology 49, 56, 70, 72, 88, 112, 115, 171, 174, 252, 285, 313, 410, 537, 554, 556–57, 576, 608
Tegernsee 250, 262, 348–49
Toledo 74, 92–93, 99–100, 133, 207
trivium 258, 307, 310, 317, 320–21, 324
trope xv, 13, 79, 230, 254, 296, 376, 385–88, 404, 496
Turin 99, 208

vernacular (language and literature) vii, 4, 9, 15, 17, 64, 97, 107, 116, 127, 131, 134, 138–39, 141, 211, 250, 256, 265, 291, 295, 298–99, 335, 344, 351, 396, 478, 480, 497, 501, 548, 558–59, 562, 569, 585
Verona 203, 205, 211, 222, 224, 563, 567, 570
Vetus Latina 448
visions and visionary literature xii, 89, 97, 117–18, 120, 153, 162, 181, 229–31, 249, 260, 337, 340, 392, 415, 417, 461, 466, 469–70, 475–78, 481–82, 486, 497
voice, poetic 226, 295, 546–548, 558–60
Vulgate 16, 36, 86, 88–91, 109, 129–30, 284, 286, 290, 296, 448, 453
vulgate editions 97, 580, 583–85, 588–90

women's education 30–31, 38, 117, 119–20, 161–62, 231, 268, 428, 465, 471–72, 475, 477–78, 480, 594, 608
women's reception of Classical literature 428, 465, 537, 541–49

York 120, 200

CPSIA information can be obtained
at www.ICGtesting.com
Printed in the USA
FFOW03n0605230516
24260FF